CLARENCE BYRD
Athabasca University

IDA CHEN
Clarence Byrd Inc.

Byrd & Chen's
Canadian
Tax
Principles

2007-2008
Edition

Please see the last page of this text for information
about the Pearson Education Canada license
agreement. Do not open either of the CD-ROM
packages until you have read this license.

PEARSON

Prentice
Hall

Toronto

Library and Archives Canada Cataloguing in Publication

Byrd, Clarence E.
    Byrd & Chen's Canadian tax principles/Clarence Byrd, Ida Chen.

Annual.
2003/2004 ed.–
Accompanied by a CD-ROM in pocket and a separately published v. called Study guide.
Issued in 2 v.
Continues: Canadian tax principles, ISSN 1204-9174.
ISSN 1707-5130
ISBN 978-0-13-206294-7 (2007/2008 edition)

1. Income tax—Canada. I. Chen, Ida II. Title. III. Title: Canadian tax principles.
IV. Title: Byrd and Chen's Canadian tax principles.

HJ4661.B84   343.7105'2   C2003-903517-4

Copyright © 2008, 2007, 2006, 2005, 2004, 2003, 2002, 2001, 2000, 1997, 1995, 1989 Clarence
Byrd Inc.

Pearson Prentice Hall. All rights reserved. This publication is protected by copyright, and
permission should be obtained from the publisher prior to any prohibited reproduction, storage in
a retrieval system, or transmission in any form or by any means, electronic, mechanical,
photocopying, recording, or likewise. For information regarding permission, write to the
Permissions Department.

ISBN-13: 978-0-13-206294-7
ISBN-10: 0-13-206294-1

Vice President, Editorial Director: Gary Bennett
Executive Editor: Samantha Scully
Executive Marketing Manager: Cas Shields
Developmental Editor: Jose Sevilla
Production Editor: Marisa D'Andrea
Production Coordinator: Deborah Starks
Cover Design: Anthony Leung

1 2 3 4 5   11 10 09 08 07

Printed and bound in Canada.

PREFACE

Web Site

The web site for this book can be found at:

www.pearsoned.ca/byrdchen/ctp2008/

Here you will find

- Glossary Flashcards and Key Terms Self-Tests
- Updates and corrections to the textbook and Study Guide
- Links to other relevant websites
- PowerPoint slides for Chapters 15 to 19 (PowerPoint slides for Chapters 1 to 14 are on the Canadian Tax Principles Student CD-ROM)
- A short on-line survey ($100 cash prize available)
- A "Guide to Using Your Student CD-ROM"
- Instructions on how to install the 2007 ProFile program and download updated sample tax returns and Cases when the updated ProFile software is available in January, 2008

This web site contains updates and corrections to the text that are available to all users. It also contains an "Instructor's Resource" area that can only be accessed with a user name and password (available from your Pearson Education Canada representative if you are a registered instructor using the book). Please check the web site for additions or corrections to the textbook and Study Guide before using this book.

Objectives

This book is designed to be used as a text in a comprehensive university or college course in taxation, usually of two semesters duration. The first 14 Chapters are largely concerned with personal taxation, Chapters 15 through 19 deal with corporate taxation, and Chapters 20, 21, and 22 deal respectively with partnerships, trusts, and international taxation.

In terms of dividing the material for use in two one semester courses, the traditional split would be to cover Chapters 1 through 14 in a first course, followed by Chapters 15 through 22 in a second course. However, this approach does create a significant imbalance, with the first course covering far more material than the second. Given this, there is a sound case for moving Chapter 14 into the second course, particularly in situations where the second course is normally taken immediately after the first. Whichever approach is used, you should note that the material in Chapters 15 through 22 requires a thorough understanding of most of the material in Chapters 1 through 14.

In terms of style, we have attempted to strike a medium ground between the kind of complete documentation that can render material on taxation incomprehensible to anyone other than a dedicated tax professional, as opposed to the total elimination of references that would make it impossible for readers to expand their understanding of particular points. In those situations where we feel the issue is sufficiently complex that further investigation may be required, at the end of each Chapter we have provided a list of references to the relevant Sections of the *Income Tax Act* or other related materials. In contrast, no direction has been provided when the material is either very straightforward, or where the relevant parts of the

Act would be obvious.

This book can be used with or without additional source material. Some instructors require students to acquire a copy of the *Income Tax Act* and permit its use as a reference during examinations. For instructors wishing to take this approach, frequent references to the *Act* have been included. In addition, there are two electronic versions of the *Income Tax Act* on the accompanying CD-ROMs.

For instructors not wishing to require the use of the *Income Tax Act*, we have designed the problem material so that students should be able to solve all of the included problems relying solely on the text as a reference.

CD #1 — Canadian Tax Principles Student CD-ROM
Content
Through our affiliation with the Canadian Institute Of Chartered Accountants (CICA), we are able to provide you with a Student CD-ROM that contains the following:

- Chapters 1 through 19 and the Glossary of *Canadian Tax Principles*, presented in Folio Views software. In addition to providing you with a highly portable version of the text, the fact that it is presented in Folio Views means that this software's powerful search engine can be utilized. In addition, this electronic version of the text has jump links to other parts of the research library (e.g., if there is a reference to a Section of the *Income Tax Act* in the text, you can "jump" from the text to that Section by clicking on the reference). Note that this electronic version of the text does not contain any problem material.

- Glossary Flashcards and Key Terms Self-Tests.

- Sample and Self Study Case tax return files in ProFile and PDF format.

- The first 14 chapters of the separate (paper) Study Guide to *Canadian Tax Principles*. This material is presented in PDF format.

- PowerPoint slide presentations for each of the first 14 chapters of the text.

- The CICA's Federal Income Tax Collection (FITAC ^{Lite}). This includes the complete *Income Tax Act* and *Regulations*, Interpretation Bulletins, Information Circulars, Guides, and Forms. These materials are presented in Folio Views software, which provides for hypertext links for all references in the electronic version of *Canadian Tax Principles*.

The availability of this group of materials should provide a setting that reflects the manner in which tax work is carried on in real world situations.

Using Folio Views
As noted in the preceding list, some of the material on the Student CD-ROM is presented in Folio Views. This is an extremely powerful software program that is being used by all Canadian publishers of electronic accounting and tax materials. It provides for sophisticated searching throughout the infobases, with hyperlinks between the various documents contained in the infobases. If you intend to do any work in the tax area, we strongly recommend that you learn to use this software.

Many of the features of the Folio Views program are intuitive and can be used with little additional assistance. However, if help is needed, it is available under the Help tab that opens with all of the infobases included on the CD-ROM.

PowerPoint Slides
As we have noted, the Student CD-ROM contains a PowerPoint slide presentation for each of the first 14 chapters of the text. Equivalent slide presentations for Chapters 15 through 19 are available on the web site. We suggest that you use these after you have completed your work on the Chapter as the basis for a quick review of the concepts and procedures that were covered in the Chapter. If you do not have access to the Microsoft PowerPoint program, the PowerPoint Viewer program can be installed from the Student CD-ROM.

CD #2 — ProFile Tax Suite CD-ROM

Through the generous co-operation of Intuit Canada, we are able to provide you with a second CD-ROM which contains the ProFile Tax Suite and InTRA. This includes:

- Intuit Canada's T1 ProFile software for preparing 2006 personal tax returns (software for 2007 is not available at the time this book is published).

- Intuit Canada's T2 ProFile software for preparing corporate tax returns.

- The Intuit Tax Research Assistant (InTRA). This extensive tax research tool contains an electronic version of the *Income Tax Act*, as well as a complete library of other tax research materials. It also includes a significant amount of commentary related to various Sections of the *Income Tax Act*.

Using The Book, The Study Guide, And The Two CD-ROMs

The Book

We have made every effort to enhance the usefulness of this book. At the beginning of the book, following this preface, you will find a summary of tax rates and other data, including relevant web sites, that will be convenient and useful references when using the book. This summary is followed by a detailed table of contents that will direct you to the subject matter in each Chapter. In addition, to facilitate easy access to any subject being researched, there is a comprehensive topical index at the end of the book.

Five types of problem material are included in the book. They can be described as follows:

Exercises   These are short problems that are generally focused on a single issue. This type of problem was first introduced several years ago and has been very favourably received by users of this text. For your convenience, each Exercise is presented in the text directly following the material that is relevant to its solution. Solutions to these Exercises can be found in the Study Guide.

Self Study Problems   These problems are more complex than the Exercises and often deal with more than one subject. As was the case with the Exercises, solutions to the Self Study Problems are included in the Study Guide.

Assignment Problems   These problems vary in difficulty and include the most difficult non-case problems contained in the text. They are often adapted from professional examinations and some problems involve a number of different issues. Solutions to these problems are available in a separate solutions manual provided only to instructors. We do not make this solutions manual available to students.

Assignment Cases (Comprehensive)   These comprehensive cases are the most challenging type of problem material in the text. They are cumulative in that they incorporate issues from previous chapters. There are two comprehensive cases per Chapter in Chapters 8 through 13.

Assignment and Self Study Cases (Tax Returns)   These cases are designed to be solved using the ProFile software provided on the ProFile Tax Suite CD-ROM. There is a Self Study Case in both Chapters 6 and 14. Solutions to these two Self Study Cases are included in the Study Guide and on the Student CD-ROM.

Assignment Cases dealing with personal tax returns, including a Progressive Running Case, are found in Chapters 6 through 14. An additional Assignment Case, involving a corporate tax return, is included in Chapter 16. Solutions to Assignment Cases are available only in a separate solutions manual that is provided to instructors.

We would note that the problem material in this text provides coverage of all of the issues that are specified in the Syllabuses of the CA, CGA, and CMA programs.

Glossary And Key Terms

A unique feature of this text is a comprehensive Glossary of terms that are used in tax work. This resource is likely to be extremely useful to both students and tax practitioners, in that it carefully defines more than 500 terms that are used throughout the text. This provides an easy solution to the problem of finding the meaning of the term that was introduced and defined in Chapter 2, but is being referred to again in Chapter 12 (e.g., Resident). The complete Glossary, including the definition for each term, is found at the back of the separate paper Study Guide, as well as on the Student CD-ROM.

Tied to this important resource, at the end of each chapter, you will find a list of the Key Terms that were used in that chapter. This provides an additional resource for reviewing the text material in that, by reviewing this list, you can ensure that you are familiar with all of the concepts that are presented in the chapter. These Key Terms are listed at the end of the chapter without definitions. Glossary Flashcards and Key Terms Self-Tests for each Chapter can be found in two places, on the Student CD-ROM and on the web site.

The Study Guide

The basic textbook is accompanied by a separate Study Guide. As noted in our discussion of the problem material, solutions to Exercises, Self Study Problems, and Cases will be found in this Study Guide. For each Chapter, there is detailed guidance on how to work through the Chapter, as well as a list of objectives for each Chapter. You may find these lists to be useful, both in working your way through the Chapter (the How To Work Through The Chapter lists) and in verifying your understanding of the concepts and procedures that were covered in the Chapter (the Objectives lists).

The sample tax returns and the complete Glossary are included in this Study Guide. For your convenience, the first 14 chapters of the Study Guide material are also available on the Student CD-ROM.

The Federal Budget

The Process

One of the great difficulties in preparing material on Canadian taxation is the fact that changes in the relevant legislation are made each year. This is complicated by the fact that the arrival date for each year's budget is no longer very predictable. Between 2002 and 2007, the arrival date ranged from December 10th of the preceding year (the 2002 budget) to May 2nd of the budget year (the 2006 budget). The 2007 budget was presented on March 19, 2007.

This situation is further complicated by the fact that budgets generally do not contain the draft legislation that is required for the implementation of their proposals. This means that, in most years, we have to complete this book without having a complete set of draft legislation for the various proposals presented in the budget.

In support of the budget presented on March 19, 2007, the government issued draft legislation for some of the proposed changes on March 27, 2007. Additional draft legislation for other 2007 budget proposals was presented on June 13, 2007. This text reflects the content of the March 19, 2007 budget, as well as the draft legislation that was presented on March 27 and June 13, 2007.

Proposed Changes From The March, 2007 Budget

A brief summary of the more important proposals included in the March, 2007 budget is as follows:

- The introduction of a new tax credit for each child under the age of 18 at the end of the year. For 2007 the credit is 15.5 percent of $2,000.
- An increase in the spousal and wholly dependant persons tax credits to the same amount as the basic personal credit. For 2007 this is 15.5 percent of $8,929.

- A working income tax benefit for low income tax payers, accompanied by a supplemental amount for disabled individuals.
- An increase in the age limit for maintaining an RRSP from age 69 to age 71.
- A provision which allows qualifying pension income to be split between spouses (this was actually announced prior to the issuance of the 2007 budget).
- A registered disability savings plan to allow funds to be put aside for the future care of disabled individuals. The government will supplement these amounts with Canada Disability Savings Grants (CDSGs) and Canada Disability Savings Bonds (CDSBs).
- An increase in the overall limit on contributions to Registered Education Savings Plans from $42,000 to $50,000. In addition, the annual limit on contributions is eliminated.
- The elimination of all taxation on elementary and secondary school scholarships. The 2006 budget eliminated all taxation on university and college scholarships.
- Improvements in the public transit pass tax credit.
- An increase in the limit on the lifetime capital gains deduction from $500,000 to $750,000.
- Increases in the deductible meal expenses of truck drivers.
- A number of fairly complex changes related to international taxation. The most important of these was the proposal to limit the deductibility of interest on amounts borrowed to make foreign investments.
- An investment tax credit for the costs incurred in creating new child care spaces.
- A increase in the instalment threshold figure for individuals from $2,000 to $3,000.
- An increase in the instalment exemption level for corporations from $1,000 to $3,000.
- A provision which will allow CCPCs to pay instalments quarterly rather than monthly under some circumstances.

Acknowledgments

We would like to thank the many students who have used this book, the instructors who have adopted it at colleges and universities throughout Canada, as well as the assistants and tutors who have been involved in these courses.

In terms of the content of the book, we would like to give special thanks to the following individuals:

Gary Donell, senior advanced tax trainer with CRA, did a technical review of significant portions of the text and problems. He made many valuable suggestions that have contributed greatly to the accuracy and clarity of the material. In addition, he was responsible for writing much of the Chapter 20 material on partnerships and the Chapter 22 material on international taxation. Mr. Donell has undertaken this work independently of his employment with the CRA. The views that are contained in this publication do not, in any way, reflect the policies of that organization.

Victor Waese, a Professor at the British Columbia Institute Of Technology has made a number of useful suggestions over several editions of this book. This year, his comments on the content and organization of Chapter 17 result in significant improvements in this material on corporate taxation and management decisions.

Larry Goldsman, a Professor at McGill University suggested that we add comprehensive assignment problems to the other problem material in Chapters 8 through 13. These problems are significantly more challenging than our other problem material. It appears that many instructors are finding them to be particularly useful in teaching this material.

In the production of the book, we were greatly assisted by the staff at Pearson Education Canada. In particular:

- Samantha Scully - Executive Editor
- Jose Gabriel C. Sevilla - Media Developmental Editor
- Laura Canning - e-Learning Resource Group Supervisor
- Dalton Miller - e-Learning Resource Group Developer
- Marisa D'Andrea - Editorial Coordinator

Also with respect to the production of the book, one other individual was particularly helpful. **Margaret Tardiff** spent long hours reviewing both the text and the problem material. In the process, she corrected numerous errors that were included in the initial draft of the material. In addition, she is responsible for much of the work on the How To Work Through The Chapter lists, and the Objectives lists.

As always, we have made every effort to accurately reflect appropriate tax rules. Every word in the text, problems, and solutions has been read by at least two and, in most cases three, individuals. However, it is virtually certain that errors remain. These errors are solely the responsibility of the authors and we apologize for any confusion that they may cause you.

We welcome any corrections or suggestions for additions or improvements. These can be sent to us at:

Clarence Byrd Inc.
139 Musie Loop Road, Chelsea, Quebec   J9B 1Y6
e-mail address: idachen@sympatico.ca

August, 2007

Clarence Byrd, Athabasca University
Ida Chen, Clarence Byrd Inc.

2007 Rates And Other Data (Including Web Sites)

Information Applicable To Individuals

Federal Tax Rates For Individuals

Taxable Income In Excess Of	Federal Tax	Marginal Rate On Excess
$ -0-	$ -0-	15.5%
37,178	5,763	22.0%
74,357	13,942	26.0%
120,887	26,040	29.0%

Federal Tax Credits For Individuals

Personal Credits [ITA 118]

Married Persons This basic personal credit is equal to 15.5% of $8,929 ($1,384).

Spousal The spousal credit is equal to 15.5% of $8,929 ($1,384), less 15.5% of the spouse's Net Income For Tax Purposes. Not available when spouse's income is more than $8,929.

> **Note** The 2007 federal budget increased this credit to the same amount as the basic personal credit. It also requires the base for the credit to be reduced by 100 percent of Net Income For Tax Purposes, not just the amount in excess of a threshold value.

Eligible Dependant This credit is the same as the one that is available for a spouse.

Child (New) 15.5% of $2,000 for each child who is under the age of 18 years at the end of the year. This produces a maximum credit of $310 [(15.5%)($2,000)] per child.

Single Persons   This basic personal credit is equal to 15.5% of $8,929 ($1,384).

Caregiver 15.5% of $4,019 ($623), less 15.5% of the dependant's Net Income in excess of $13,726. Not available when dependant's income is more than $17,745.

Infirm Dependants Over 17 15.5% of $4,019 ($623), less 15.5% of the dependant's Net Income in excess of $5,702. Not available when dependant's income is more than $9,721.

Age 15.5% of $5,177 ($802). The base for this credit is reduced by the lesser of $5,177 and 15% of the individual's net income in excess of $30,936. Not available when income is more than $65,449. If the individual cannot use this credit, it can be transferred to a spouse or common-law partner.

Pension 15.5% of the first $2,000 of eligible pension income. This produces a maximum credit of $310 [(15.5%)($2,000)]. If the individual cannot use the credit, it can be transferred to a spouse or common-law partner.

Canada Employment Credit 15.5% of $1,000. This produces a maximum credit of $155.

Other Credits (Various ITA)

Adoption Expenses 15.5% of eligible expenses, up to a maximum of $1,619 [(15.5%)($10,445)]. The eligible amount is reduced by reimbursements.

Public Transit Passes Credit 15.5% of the cost of monthly or longer transit passes.

Child Fitness Credit A maximum of 15.5% of $500 ($78) per year for eligible fees paid for each child who is under 16 at any time during the year.

Charitable Donations The general limit on amounts for this credit is 75% of Net Income. There is an addition to this general limit equal to 25% of any taxable capital gains and 25% of any recapture of CCA resulting from a gift of capital property. In addition, the income inclusion on capital gains arising from a gift of some publicly traded shares is reduced from one-half to one-quarter. For individuals, the credit is 15.5% of the first $200 and 29% of the remainder. For corporations, charitable donations are a deduction from Net Income.

Medical Expenses The medical expense tax credit is determined by the following formula:

$$[15.5\%]\ [(B - C) + D], \text{ where:}$$

B is the total of an individual's medical expenses for himself, his spouse or common-law partner, and any of his children who have not reached 18 years of age at the end of the year.

C is the lesser of 3 percent of the individual's Net Income For Tax Purposes and $1,926 (2007 figure).

D is the total of all amounts each of which is, in respect of a dependant of the individual (other than a child of the individual who has not attained the age of 18 years before the end of the taxation year), the lesser of $10,000 and the amount determined by the formula:

$$E - F, \text{ where:}$$

E is the total of the dependant's medical expenses

F is the lesser of 3 percent of the dependant's Net Income For Tax Purposes and $1,926 (2007 figure).

Refundable Medical Expense Supplement The individual claiming this amount must be over 17 and have earned income of $2,984. The amount is equal to the lesser of $1,022 and 25/15.5 of the medical expense tax credit (25 percent of allowable medical expenses). The refundable amount is then reduced by 5 percent of family Net Income in excess of $22,627.

Disability - All Ages 15.5% of $6,890 ($1,068). If not used by the disabled individual, can be transferred to a person claiming that individual as a dependant.

Disability Supplement - Under 18 And Qualifies For The Disability Tax Credit 15.5% of $4,019 ($623), reduced by child care and attendant care expenses in excess of $2,354.

Tuition Fees 15.5% of qualifying tuition fees.

Education 15.5% of $400 ($62) per month of full time attendance. 15.5% of $120 ($19) per month of part time attendance.

Textbook 15.5% of $65 ($10) per month of full time attendance. 15.5% of $20 ($3) per month of part time attendance.

Interest On Student Loans 15.5% of interest paid on qualifying student loans.

Transfer Of Tuition, Education, And Textbook If the individual cannot use these credits, is not claimed as a dependant by his spouse, and does not transfer the unused credits to a spouse, then a parent or grandparent of the individual can claim up to $775 [(15.5%)($5,000)] of any unused tuition, education, or textbook credits. The amount that can be transferred is reduced by any amounts of these credits claimed by the student for the year.

Employment Insurance 15.5% of amounts paid by employees up to the maximum Employment Insurance premium of $720 (1.8% of $40,000). This produces a maximum tax credit of $112 [(15.5%)($720)].

Canada Pension Plan 15.5% of amounts paid by employees up to the maximum Canada Pension Plan contribution of $1,990 [4.95% of ($43,700 less $3,500)]. This produces a maximum tax credit of $308 [(15.5%)($1,990)].

Political Donations Three-quarters of the first $400, one-half of the next $350, one-third of the next $525, to a maximum credit of $650.

Apprenticeship Job Creation Credit 10% of salaries and wages paid to qualifying apprentices to a maximum credit of $2,000 per year per apprentice.

Dividend Tax Credit

Eligible Dividends are grossed up by 45 percent. The federal dividend tax credit is equal to 11/18 of the gross up. The credit can also be calculated as 18.9655 percent of the grossed up dividends, or 27.5 percent of the actual dividends received.

Non-Eligible Dividends are grossed up by 25 percent. The federal dividend tax credit is equal to 2/3 of the gross up. The credit can also be calculated as 13-1/3 percent of the grossed up dividends, or 16-2/3 percent of the actual dividends received.

Other Data For Individuals

Dividend Gross Up

Eligible Dividends the gross up is 45 percent of dividends received.

Non-Eligible Dividends the gross up is 25 percent of dividends received.

Capital Gain Inclusion Rates

Period	Inclusion Rate
1972 through 1987	1/2
1988 and 1989 and February 28, 2000 through October 17, 2000	2/3
1990 through February 27, 2000	3/4
October 18, 2000 to present	1/2

Clawback Limits   The tax (clawback) on Old Age Security (OAS) benefits is based on the lesser of 100 percent of such benefits and 15 percent of the amount of the 2007 "threshold income" in excess of $63,511. For this purpose, "threshold income" is equal to Net Income For Tax Purposes, calculated without the ITA 60(w) deduction for the tax on OAS benefits.

Under the *Employment Insurance Act*, there is a similar clawback requirement with respect to Employment Insurance (EI) benefits. In this case, EI benefits must be repaid to the extent of the lesser of 30 percent of the EI benefits received, and 30 percent of the amount by which "threshold income" exceeds $50,000 (this amount is 1.25 times the maximum insurable earnings for EI purposes). For this purpose, "threshold income" is defined as Net Income For Tax Purposes, calculated without the deduction for either the ITA 60(w) deduction for tax paid on OAS benefits or the ITA 60(v.1) deduction for repayment of EI benefits received.

Provincial Tax Rates And Provincial Credits For Individuals   Provincial taxes are based on Taxable Income, with provinces adopting multiple rates. The number of brackets range from three (e.g., Ontario uses 6.05%, 9.15%, and 11.16%) to five (e.g., British Columbia uses 6.05%, 9.15%, 11.7%, 13.7%, and 14.7%). The exception to this is Alberta, which uses a single flat rate of 10.0 percent on all Taxable Income. Provincial tax credits are generally based on the minimum provincial rate applied to a credit base that is similar to that used for federal credits. In addition to regular rates, several provinces use surtaxes.

RRSP Deduction Room   For 2007, the addition to RRSP deduction room is equal to the lesser of $19,000 and 18 percent of 2006 Earned Income, reduced by the 2006 Pension Adjustment and the 2007 Past Service Pension Adjustment, and increased by the 2007 Pension Adjustment Reversal.

Information Applicable To Individuals And Corporations

Quick Method Rates (GST)

	Percentage On GST Included Sales	
	First $30,000	On Excess
Retailers And Wholesalers	1.2%	2.2%
Service Providers And Manufacturers	3.3%	4.3%

CCA Rates   See Appendix for Chapter 7.

Automobile Deduction Limits

- CCA is limited to the first $30,000 of the automobiles cost, plus applicable GST and PST (not including amounts that will be refunded through input tax credits).

- Interest on financing of automobiles is limited to $10 per day.

- Deductible leasing costs are limited to $800 per month (other constraints apply).

Prescribed Rate (ITR 4301)   The following figures show the base rate that would be used in calculations such as imputed interest on loans. It also shows the rates applicable on amounts owing to and from the CRA.   For recent quarters, the interest rates were as follows:

Year	Quarter	Base Rate	Owing From	Owing To
2006	**First**	3%	5%	7%
2006	Second	4%	6%	8%
2006	Third	4%	6%	8%
2006	Fourth	5%	7%	9%
2007	**First**	5%	7%	9%
2007	Second	5%	7%	9%
2007	Third	5%	7%	9%

Information Applicable To Corporations

Corporate Tax Rates   The federal corporate tax rates for 2007 are as follows (federal tax abatement removed):

General Business (Before General Rate Reduction)	28%
General Business (After General Rate Reduction)	21%
Income Eligible For M&P Deduction	21%
Income Eligible For Small Business Deduction	12%
Part IV Refundable Tax	33-1/3%
Part I Refundable Tax On Investment Income Of CCPC (ART)	6-2/3%

Provincial tax rates on corporations vary from a low of 3% on amounts eligible for the small business deduction in Alberta and Manitoba, to a high of 16% on general corporate income in Nova Scotia and Prince Edward Island.

Corporate Surtax   The corporate surtax rate is 4% for 2007.

Small Business Deduction Formula   For 2007, the small business deduction is equal to 16 percent of the lesser of:

  A. Net Canadian active business income.

  B. Taxable Income, less:

      1. 10/3 times the ITA 126(1) credit for taxes paid on foreign non-business income, calculated without consideration of the additional refundable tax under ITA 123.3 or the general rate reduction under ITA 123.4; and

      2. 3 times the ITA 126(2) credit for taxes paid on foreign business income, calculated without consideration of the general rate reduction under ITA 123.4.

  C. The annual business limit of $400,000, less any portion allocated to associated corporations.

Aggregate Investment Income   Aggregate Investment Income is defined in ITA 129(4) as the sum of:

  • net taxable capital gains for the year, reduced by any net capital loss carry overs deducted during the year; and

  • income from property including interest, rents, and royalties, but excluding dividends that are deductible in computing Taxable Income. Since foreign dividends are generally not deductible, they would be included in aggregate investment income.

Manufacturing And Processing Deduction Formula   For 2007, the Manufacturing And Processing Deduction is equal to 7 percent of the lesser of:

  A. Manufacturing and processing profits, less amounts eligible for the small business deduction; and

  B. Taxable Income, less the sum of:

      1. the amount eligible for the small business deduction;

      2. 3 times the foreign tax credit for business income calculated without consideration of the ITA 123.4 general rate reduction); and

      3. where the corporation is a Canadian controlled private corporation throughout the year, aggregate investment income as defined in ITA 129(4).

Foreign Tax Credits For Corporations The Foreign Non-Business Income Tax Credit is the lesser of:

  • The tax paid to the foreign government (for corporations, there is no 15 percent limit on the foreign non-business taxes paid); and

  • An amount determined by the following formula:

$$\left[\frac{\text{Foreign Non} - \text{Business Income}}{\text{Adjusted Division B Income}} \right] [\text{Tax Otherwise Payable}]$$

The Foreign Business Income Tax Credit is equal to the least of:

  • The tax paid to the foreign government;

  • An amount determined by the following formula:

$$\left[\frac{\text{Foreign Business Income}}{\text{Adjusted Division B Income}} \right] [\text{Tax Otherwise Payable}] ; \text{and}$$

  • Tax Otherwise Payable for the year, less any foreign tax credit taken on non-business income under ITA 126(1).

Additional Refundable Tax On Investment Income (ART)   ART is equal to 6-2/3 percent of the lesser of:

- the corporation's "aggregate investment income" for the year [as defined in ITA 129(4)]; and

- the amount, if any, by which the corporation's Taxable Income for the year exceeds the amount that is eligible for the small business deduction.

Refundable Portion Of Part I Tax Payable   The Refundable Portion Of Part I Tax Payable is defined as the least of three items:

Item 1   the amount determined by the formula

$$A - B, \text{ where}$$

A   is 26-2/3 percent of the corporation's aggregate investment income for the year, and

B   is the amount, if any, by which the foreign non-business income tax credit exceeds 9-1/3 percent of its foreign investment income for the year.

Item 2   26-2/3 percent of the amount, if any, by which the corporation's taxable income for the year exceeds the total of:

- the amount eligible for the small business deduction;
- 25/9 of the tax credit for foreign non-business income; and
- 3 times the tax credit for foreign business income.

Item 3   the corporation's tax for the year payable under this Part [Part I] determined without reference to Section 123.2 [the 4 percent corporate surtax].

Part IV Tax   Part IV tax is assessed at a rate of 33-1/3 percent of portfolio dividends, plus dividends received from a connected company that gave rise to a dividend refund for the connected company as a result of the payment.

Refundable Dividend Tax On Hand (RDTOH)   The RDTOH is defined in ITA 129(3) as:

- The Refundable Portion Of Part I tax for the year; plus
- The total of the taxes under Part IV for the year; plus
- The corporation's RDTOH at the end of the preceding year; less
- The corporation's dividend refund for its preceding taxation year.

General Rate Income Pool   A CCPC's General Rate Income Pool (GRIP) is defined as follows:

- The GRIP balance at the end of the preceding year; plus
- 68 percent of the the CCPC's Taxable Income after it has been reduced by amounts eligible for the small business deduction and aggregate investment income; plus
- eligible dividends received during the year; plus
- adjustments related to amalgamations and wind-ups; less
- eligible dividends paid during the preceding year

Low Rate Income Pool   A non-CCPC's Low Rate Income Pool (LRIP) is defined as follows:

- The LRIP balance at the end of the preceding year; plus
- non-eligible dividends received during the year; plus
- adjustments for reorganizations; plus
- adjustments for non-CCPCs that were a CCPC, a credit union, or an investment company, in a previous year; less
- non-eligible dividends paid during the year; less
- any Excessive Eligible Dividend Designations during the year.

Tax Related Web Sites

GOVERNMENT

CRA   www.cra.gc.ca
Department of Finance Canada   www.fin.gc.ca

CHARTERED ACCOUNTING FIRMS

BDO Dunwoody   www.bdo.ca/library/publications/tax/index.cfm
Ernst & Young   www.ey.com/global/content.nsf/Canada/Home
KPMG   www.kpmg.ca/english/services/tax
PricewaterhouseCoopers   www.ca.taxnews.com

OTHER

Canadian Institute of Chartered Accountants   www.cica.ca
Canadian Tax Foundation   www.ctf.ca
ProFile Tax Suite   www.accountant.intuit.ca/en/support/support_profile.shtm

CONTENTS

CHAPTER 5

Income Or Loss From An Office Or Employment

CHAPTER 5, continued

CHAPTER 6
Income And Tax Payable For Individuals

CHAPTER 6, continued

CHAPTER 7
Capital Cost Allowances And Cumulative Eligible Capital

(continued)

CHAPTER 7, continued

CHAPTER 8

Income Or Loss From A Business

CHAPTER 8, continued

(continued)

CHAPTER 10, continued

CHAPTER 11
Other Income And
Other Deductions

CHAPTER 12

Non-Arm's Length Transactions, Income Attribution And Deemed Dispositions At Emigration And Death

CHAPTER 13

Retirement Savings And Other Special Income Arrangements

CHAPTER 14

Taxable Income And Tax Payable For Individuals Revisited

CHAPTER 15

Taxable Income And Tax Payable For Corporations

(continued)

CHAPTER 17

Corporate Taxation And Management Decisions

CHAPTER 18

Rollovers Under Section 85

(continued)

CHAPTER 20
Partnerships

CHAPTER 21
Trusts And Estate Planning

CHAPTER 21, continued

CHAPTER 22

International Taxation

CHAPTER 22, continued

INDEX

GLOSSARY

The Glossary can be found at the back of the separate paper Study Guide and on the Student CD-ROM within the Folio Version of Canadian Tax Principles.

CHAPTER 1

Introduction To Federal Taxation In Canada

The Canadian Tax System

Alternative Tax Bases

1-1.   There are a variety of ways in which taxes can be classified. One possible basis of classification would be the economic feature or event that is to be taxed. Such features or events are referred to as the base for taxation and a large number of different bases are used in different tax systems throughout the world. Some of the more common tax bases are as follows:

Income Tax   A tax on the income of certain defined entities.

Property Tax   A tax on the ownership of some particular set of goods.

Consumption Tax   A tax levied on the consumption or use of a good or service. Also referred to as sales tax or commodity tax.

Value Added Tax   A tax levied on the increase in value of a good or service that has been created by the taxpayer's stage of the production or distribution cycle.

Tariffs or Customs Duties   A tax imposed on the importation or exportation of certain goods or services.

Transfer Tax   A tax on the transfer of property from one owner to another.

User Tax   A tax levied on the user of some facility such as a road or airport.

Capital Tax   A tax on the invested capital of a corporation.

Head Tax   A tax on the very existence of some classified group of individuals.

1-2.   At one time or another, some level of government has used, or is still using, all of these bases for taxation. For example, the Canadian federal government currently has, in addition to income taxes on corporations, individuals, and trusts, such taxes as the Goods and Services Tax (GST), an alcoholic beverages tax, special transaction taxes, a gasoline tax, as well as others. However, the dominant form of Canadian taxation at the federal level is the income taxes levied on both corporations and individuals. This fact is reflected in Figure 1-1 (following page) which provides a percentage distribution of the $236.7 billion in tax revenues that the federal government expects to collect during fiscal 2007-2008.

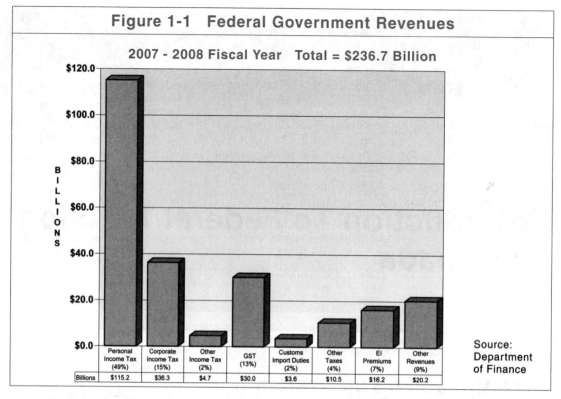

Figure 1-1   Federal Government Revenues

2007 - 2008 Fiscal Year   Total = $236.7 Billion

	Personal Income Tax (49%)	Corporate Income Tax (15%)	Other Income Tax (2%)	GST (13%)	Customs Import Duties (2%)	Other Taxes (4%)	EI Premiums (7%)	Other Revenues (9%)
Billions	$115.2	$36.3	$4.7	$30.0	$3.6	$10.5	$16.2	$20.2

Source: Department of Finance

1-3.   Figure 1-1 makes it clear that personal income taxes constitute, by far, the most important source of federal government revenues. Unfortunately, its importance seems to be growing. The share of federal government revenues provided by personal income taxes was about 46.5 percent in the 2004-2005 fiscal year and is projected to be 49.6 percent in 2008-2009.

1-4.   Corporate income taxes have also increased as a percentage of total revenues. They have grown from 14.2 percent of the total in 2004-2005, to an estimated 15.3 percent of the total in 2007-2008. However, this percentage will decline in coming years if proposed corporate tax cuts are left in place

1-5.   The increased percentage of revenues coming from personal and corporate income taxes has been offset by a decline in the percentage of total revenues provided by Employment Insurance premiums. These contributions made up over 8 percent of revenues in 2004-2005 and are estimated to fall to 6.8 percent of the total in 2007-2008.

1-6.   Although the GST is still an important source of federal government revenues, the drop in the basic rate from 7 percent to 6 percent in 2006 has resulted in a decrease in its share of the revenues. It has gone from 14.0 percent of the total in 2004-2005 to an estimated 12.7 percent of the total in 2007-2008.

Taxable Entities In Canada

Income Taxes

1-7.   Three types of entities are subject to federal income taxation. The most obvious of these taxable entities is individuals (human beings). Besides individuals, corporations and trusts are also defined by the *Income Tax Act* as separate taxable entities. You should note that the *Income Tax Act* uses the term "person" to refer to all three types of taxable entities. In contrast to the dictionary definition that defines person as a human being, the *Act* uses this term to refer to corporations and trusts as well as individuals.

1-8.   For income tax purposes, unincorporated businesses such as partnerships and proprietorships are not viewed as taxable entities. Rather, income earned by an unincorporated business organization is taxed in the hands of the individual who is a proprietor or partner. Note that members of a partnership may be individuals, trusts, or corporations.

1-9.   As discussed in Chapter 2, all three types of taxable entities are required to file income tax returns. The return for an individual is referred to as a T1, for a corporation, a T2, and for a trust, a T3. Proprietorships and partnerships are not required to file income tax returns.

GST

1-10.   The requirement to register to collect and remit GST generally extends to any person engaged in commercial activity in Canada. You should note that the definition of a person for GST purposes is different than that used in the *Income Tax Act*. For income tax purposes, a "person" is generally restricted to an individual, a corporation, or a trust. Unincorporated businesses do not file separate income tax returns.

1-11.   Under GST legislation, the concept of a person is broader, including individuals, partnerships, corporations, estates of deceased individuals, trusts, charities, societies, unions, clubs, associations, commissions, and other organizations. Chapter 4 includes detailed coverage of the GST.

Exercise One-1

Subject: Taxable Entities

Which of the following entities would be required to file an income tax return?

- Max Jordan (an individual)
- Jordan's Hardware Store (an unincorporated business)
- Jordan & Jordan (a partnership)
- The Jordan family trust (a trust)
- Jordan Enterprises Ltd. (a corporation)
- The Jordan Foundation (an unincorporated charity)

End of Exercise. Solution available in Study Guide.

Federal Taxation And The Provinces

Personal Income Taxes

1-12.   Under the Constitution Act, the federal, provincial, and territorial governments have the power to impose taxes. The provinces and territories are limited to direct taxation as delegated in the Act, a constraint that leaves all residual taxation powers to the federal government. The provinces are further limited to the taxation of income earned in the particular province and the income of persons resident in that province. Within these limitations, all of the provinces and territories impose both personal and corporate income taxes.

1-13.   Under the current federal/provincial tax collection agreement, provincial taxes are calculated by multiplying a provincial tax rate to a Taxable Income figure. With the exception of Quebec, all of the provinces use the same Taxable Income figure that is used at the federal level.

1-14.   Despite the use of the federal Taxable Income figure, the provinces have retained considerable flexibility in their individual tax systems. This flexibility is achieved in two ways:

- Each province can apply different rates and surtaxes to as many tax brackets as it wishes.

- More importantly, each province is able to set different provincial credits to apply against provincial Tax Payable. While most provinces currently have provincial credits that are similar to credits that are established at the federal level, the value of these credits varies considerably at the provincial level and many provinces have additional types of credits.

1-15.   The provincial differences complicate the preparation of tax returns. The level of complication varies from province to province, depending on the degree to which provincial tax brackets and provincial tax credits resemble those applicable at the federal level.

1-16.   Because of these complications, the problem material in this text will, in general, not require the calculation of provincial taxes for individuals. However, because the combined federal/provincial rate is important in many tax-based decisions (e.g., selecting between alternative investments), we will continue to refer to overall combined rates, despite the fact that such figures are very specific to the province in which the income is taxed, as well as the characteristics associated with the individual filing the return.

Exercise One-2

Subject: Federal And Provincial Taxes Payable

John Forsyth has Taxable Income of $27,000. For 2007, his federal tax rate is 15.5 percent, while the corresponding provincial rate is 7.5 percent. Determine Mr. Forsyth's combined federal and provincial tax, before consideration of any available credits against Tax Payable.

End of Exercise. Solution available in Study Guide.

Corporate Income Taxes

1-17.   The system used to calculate individual income tax payable is similar to the system that is applicable to corporations. Provincial corporate income tax is levied on Taxable Income. All provinces except Alberta, Ontario, and Quebec use the federal *Income Tax Act* to compute Taxable Income. Even in Alberta, Ontario, and Quebec, the respective provincial Tax Acts have many of the same features as the federal *Act*.

1-18.   With respect to the collection of corporate income taxes, only Alberta, Ontario, and Quebec collect their own corporate income taxes. In all other cases, corporate income taxes are collected by the federal government on behalf of the provinces.

GST And HST

1-19.   In making its 1987 proposals for sales tax reform, the federal government suggested a joint federal/provincial sales tax. Lack of interest by provincial governments meant the proposal was not implemented at that time. Instead, the GST was introduced at the federal level and provincial sales taxes were left in place without significant alteration. With the exception of Alberta, where no provincial sales tax has ever been levied, there were two different sales taxes collected, accounted for, and remitted.

1-20.   This situation was very costly and time consuming for businesses. Not only were they faced with the costs of filing sales tax returns in multiple jurisdictions, but each jurisdiction had its own rules for the goods or services on which the tax was applicable. This was clearly an inefficient approach to generating tax revenues and, not surprisingly, considerable pressure developed for the harmonization of the separate federal and provincial sales taxes.

1-21.   Despite the obvious efficiencies that would result from harmonization, progress has been slow. In 1992, Quebec began to operate under a harmonized system, with both the federal and provincial sales tax being collected by Quebec. Note, however, that while the Quebec and federal sales tax systems lay claim to being harmonized, there are a number of differences between the two sets of tax rules.

1-22.   In 1997, New Brunswick, Nova Scotia, and Newfoundland harmonized their sales tax regimes with the GST. The resulting harmonized system is referred to as the Harmonized Sales Tax or HST. This leaves Prince Edward Island and all provinces west of Quebec outside of the system. From the point of view of business, this is an unfortunate situation, resulting in millions of dollars being wasted in dealing with the inefficiencies of a dual system.

Taxation And Economic Objectives

1-23.   The traditional economic objective of taxation policies has been to generate revenues for the relevant taxing authority. However, it is clear that today's approach to taxation objectives is multi-faceted. We use taxation policy to effect resource allocation, to redistribute income and wealth among taxpayers with different economic resources and needs, to assist in keeping the economy stable, and to provide intergovernmental transfers. A brief description of how taxation deals with these economic objectives is as follows:

Resource Allocation   Tax revenues are used to provide public goods and services. Pure public goods such as the cost of our national defense system are thought to benefit all taxpayers. As it is not possible to allocate costs to individuals on the basis of benefits received, such costs must be supported with general tax revenues. Similar allocations occur with such widely used public goods as education, health care, and pollution control. In some cases, the tax system also has an influence on the allocation of private goods. For example, excise taxes are used to discourage the consumption of alcohol and tobacco products.

Distribution Effects   Our tax system is used to redistribute income and wealth among taxpayers. Such provisions as the federal GST tax credit and provincial sales tax exemptions on food and low priced clothing have the effect of taking taxes paid by higher income taxpayers and distributing them to lower income wage earners or taxpayers with higher basic living costs in proportion to their income.

Stabilization Effects   Taxes may also be used to achieve macro economic objectives. At various times, tax policy has been used to encourage economic expansion, increase employment, and to assist in holding inflation in check. An example of this is the emphasis placed on deficit reduction in recent federal budgets.

Fiscal Federalism   This term refers to the various procedures that are used to allocate resources among different levels of government. For 2007-2008, it is estimated that transfers to other levels of government will amount to $43.5 billion, as compared to transfers to persons of $58.5 billion, and direct program spending of $91.5 billion. In the next step in the chain, a portion of provincial tax revenue is transferred to municipal governments.

Taxation And Income Levels

General Approaches

1-24.   Policy makers are concerned about the relationship between income levels and rates of taxation. Taxes can be proportional, in that a constant rate is applied at all levels of income. In theory, this is our approach to taxing the income of corporations. For public companies, the system is based on a flat rate that is applicable to all income earned by the company. However, a wide variety of provisions act to modify the application of this rate, resulting in a situation where many Canadian companies are not subject to this notional flat rate.

1-25.   As an alternative, taxation can be regressive, resulting in lower effective rates of taxation as higher income levels are reached. Sales taxes generally fall into this regressive category as lower income individuals spend a larger portion of their total income and, as a consequence, pay a greater portion of their total income as sales taxes levied on their expenditures.

Example Consider the Werner sisters:

Gertrude Werner has income of $200,000 and spends $40,000 of this amount. She lives in a province with an 8 percent sales tax on all expenditures, resulting in the payment of $3,200 in provincial sales tax. This represents a 1.6 percent effective tax rate on her $200,000 income.

Ingrid Werner has income of $40,000 and spends all of this amount. She lives in the same province as her sister, resulting in the payment of $3,200 in provincial sales tax. This represents an 8 percent effective tax rate on her $40,000 income.

Exercise One-3

Subject: Regressive Taxes

Margie Jones has Taxable Income for the current year of $895,000, of which $172,000 is spent on goods and services that are subject to GST at 6 percent and a provincial sales tax of 8 percent. Her sister, Jane Jones, is a part-time student living in the same province and has Taxable Income of only $18,000. During the current year, as a result of using some of her savings, she spends $27,500 on goods and services that are all subject to GST at 6 percent and the provincial sales tax. Determine the effective sales tax rate as a percentage of the income of the two sisters.

End of Exercise. Solution available in Study Guide.

1-26.   In contrast to the regressive nature of sales taxes, the present system of personal income taxation is designed to be progressive, since higher rates are applied to higher levels of income. For 2007, the federal rates range from a low of 15.5 percent on the first $37,178 of Taxable Income to a high of 29 percent on Taxable Income in excess of $120,887.

Progressive Vs. Regressive

1-27.   As personal income taxes are the major source of federal tax revenues under current Canadian legislation, the system can be described as predominantly progressive. The major arguments in favour of this approach can be described as follows:

Equity   Higher income individuals have a greater ability to pay taxes. As their income is above their basic consumption needs, the relative cost to the individual of having a portion of this income taxed away is less than the relative cost to lower income individuals, where additional taxation removes funds required for such essentials as food and housing.

Stability   Progressive tax rates help maintain after-tax income stability by shifting people to lower tax brackets in times of economic downturn and to higher brackets when there is economic expansion. The resulting decreases or increases in income taxes serve to cushion the economic swings.

1-28.   There are, however, a number of problems that can be associated with progressive rates. These can be briefly described as follows:

Complexity   With progressive rates in place, efforts will be made to divide income among as many individuals (usually family members) as possible. These efforts to make maximum use of the lower tax brackets necessitate the use of complex anti-avoidance rules by taxation authorities.

Income Fluctuations   In the absence of relieving provisions, progressive rates discriminate against individuals with highly variable income streams. That is, under a progressive system, an individual with $400,000 in income in one year and no income for the next three years will pay substantially more in taxes than an individual with the same $400,000 total earned over four years at a rate of $100,000 per year.

Family Unit Problems   Progressive tax rates discriminate against single income family units. A family unit in which one spouse makes $100,000 and the other has no Taxable Income would pay significantly more in taxes than would be the case if each spouse earned $50,000.

Economic Growth   It is clear that the high tax brackets that can be associated with a progressive system can discourage both employment and investment efforts. This could serve to limit economic growth and, as will be discussed later, it is possible for rates to reach a level that will actually result in less aggregate taxes being collected.

Tax Concessions   The high brackets associated with progressive systems lead to pressure for various types of tax concessions to be made available. Because high income individuals have a greater ability to effectively take advantage of favourable provisions in the income tax legislation, they may actually wind up paying taxes at lower effective rates. In response to the possibility that, in extreme cases, some high income individuals pay no income taxes at all, there is an alternative minimum income tax that is imposed on certain taxpayers.

Tax Evasion   Progressive rates discourage income reporting and encourage the creation of various devices to evade taxation. Evasion strategies range from simple bartering, to cash only transactions, and finally to organized crime activities.

Flat Tax Systems

1-29.   While progressive tax systems continue to be pervasive, there has been a worldwide trend towards flattening rate schedules. One of the reasons for this trend is the fact that effective tax rates are not as progressive as the rate schedules indicate. High bracket taxpayers tend to have better access to various types of tax concessions, a fact that can significantly reduce the effective rates for these individuals.

1-30.   Given this situation, it has been suggested that we could achieve results similar to those which, in fact, prevail under the current system by applying a flat rate of tax to a broadened taxation base. In this context, the term base broadening refers to the elimination of tax concessions, resulting in tax rates that are applied to a larger income figure.

1-31.   In a 1988 study by Roger S. Smith of the University of Alberta, a flat 20 percent rate of tax was applied to a broadened base. This broadened base included the non-taxable component of capital gains and did not permit deductions for such items as Registered Retirement Savings Plan contributions, the interest and dividend deduction (since repealed), or the pension income deduction. (This deduction is now a credit against taxes payable.) For those individuals with incomes below $4,500, a zero tax bracket was assumed. The results of this study indicated that, for the majority of taxpayers (i.e., those with incomes between $10,000 and $100,000), the application of a flat tax to a broadened base produces a tax liability that is only marginally different from the net tax liability under the present system of progressive rates accompanied by various tax concessions.

1-32.   Starting in 2001, Canada's first flat tax system for individuals was implemented. Not surprisingly, it is in place in Alberta. Under this system, the provincial tax rate on all of the income of individuals is a flat rate of 10 percent.

1-33.   Another important factor that has encouraged the trend towards reduced progressivity is the fact that total tax revenues may actually decline if marginal tax rates are too high. This idea was developed by Professor Arthur Laffer and is often expressed in the Laffer Curve shown in Figure 1-2. As can be seen in Figure 1-2, there is an optimal tax rate beyond which total tax revenues begin to decline. Major reasons for this would be that high tax rates reduce the willingness to work and, at the same time, increase the willingness to evade taxes. While no hard evidence supports a particular rate as being the optimal rate, many experts believe that the maximum should be about 40 percent.

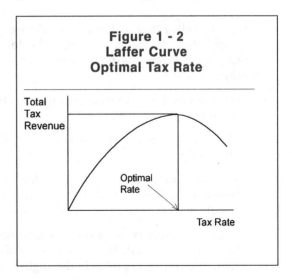

**Figure 1 - 2
Laffer Curve
Optimal Tax Rate**

Tax Incidence

1-34.   Tax incidence refers to the issue of who really pays a particular tax. While statutory incidence refers to the initial legal liability for tax payment, the actual economic burden may be passed on to a different group. For example, certain taxes on production might be the legal liability of the producer.   However, they may be partly or entirely shifted to consumers through price increases on the goods produced.

1-35.   Policy makers must be concerned with this to ensure that the system is working as intended. It is generally assumed that the incidence of personal income tax falls on individuals. In addition, in their role as consumers, individuals also assume the responsibility for a large portion of the various sales taxes that are levied in Canada. The incidence of corporate taxes is more open to speculation. Shareholders may bear the burden of corporate taxes in the short run. However, most authorities believe that, in the long run, this burden is shared by employees and consumers.

Tax Expenditures

1-36.   In contrast to government funding programs that provide payments to various entities in the economy, tax expenditures reflect revenues that have been given up by the government through the use of tax preferences, concessions, and other tax breaks. These expenditures may favour selected individuals or groups (senior citizens), certain kinds of income (capital gains), or certain characteristics of some taxpayers (the disabled).

1-37.   In an effort to quantify the importance of these expenditures, the Department of Finance produces the publication, "Tax Expenditures And Evaluations" each year. The 2006 edition contains estimates for 2001 to 2003 and projections for 2004 to 2008, of the costs of various income tax and GST expenditures. Examples of the 2003 estimates and 2008 projections of the cost of some of these expenditures include:

- The basic personal tax credit - $21.7 billion in 2003, $26.3 billion in 2008.

- The favourable treatment of capital gains - $2.0 billion in 2003, $3.4 billion in 2008.

- Small business deduction for private companies - $3.4 billion in 2003, $4.4 billion in 2008.

- The deduction for RRSP contributions - $6.0 billion in 2003, $8.6 billion in 2008.

- The GST exemption for basic groceries - $3.7 billion in 2003, $4.1 billion in 2008.

1-38.   It is clear that such tax expenditures are of considerable significance in the management of federal finances. It is equally clear that the provision of this type of government benefit has become entrenched in our tax system. This situation can be explained by a number of factors:

- It is less costly to administer tax expenditures than it is to administer government funding programs.

- More decisions are left to the private sector so that funds may be allocated more efficiently.

- Tax expenditures reduce the visibility of certain government actions. This is particularly beneficial if some social stigma is attached to the programs. For example, a child tax benefit system is more acceptable than increasing social assistance payments.

- Tax expenditures reduce the progressivity of the tax system. As many of the tax expenditures, such as tax shelters, are more available to higher income taxpayers, they serve to reduce effective tax rates in the higher rate brackets.

1-39.   Tax expenditures are not only very substantial, they are also difficult to control. This was noted by Auditor General Kenneth Dye in his 1985 Annual Report as follows:

A cost conscious Parliament is in the position of a team of engineers trying to design a more fuel efficient automobile. They think they have succeeded, but the engine seems to go on consuming as much gas as it did before. They cannot understand the problem until they notice that, hidden from view, a myriad of small holes have been punched through the bottom of the gas tank. This is too often the way of tax expenditures. Revenue leaks away, and MPs do not know about it until it is too late.

1-40. Reflecting this long-standing concern, the 1998 Auditor General's report recommended that the Department of Finance identify clear objectives for each tax expenditure in terms of its contribution to economic, social, or other objectives. It also recommended that these objectives be included in the Department's annual report on tax expenditures. The 2001 Auditor General's report noted that there has been significant progress in implementing these recommendations.

Qualitative Characteristics Of Tax Systems
General Concepts
1-41. In recent years, accounting standard setting bodies have established such concepts as relevance and reliability as being desirable qualitative characteristics of accounting information. While not established with the same degree of formality, it is clear that there are similar concepts that can be used to evaluate tax systems. Some of these desirable qualitative characteristics can be described as follows:

Equity Or Fairness Horizontal equity entails assessing similar levels of taxation for people in similar economic circumstances. If two individuals each have Taxable Income of $50,000, horizontal equity would require that they each pay the same amount of taxes.

In contrast, vertical equity means dissimilar tax treatment of people in different circumstances. If an individual has Taxable Income of $100,000, he should pay more taxes than an individual with Taxable Income of $50,000.

An interesting example of an equity problem was reported in the U.S. media. For 2003, U.S. President Bush reported income of $822,126 and paid taxes of $227,490, an effective rate of 28 percent. In contrast, U.S. Vice-President Cheney reported income of $1,900,339, but paid only $241,392 in taxes, an effective rate of 13 percent. While Mr. Cheney paid slightly more taxes than Mr. Bush, his effective rate was less than half that of Mr. Bush.

Neutrality The concept of neutrality calls for a tax system that interferes as little as possible with decision making. An overriding economic assumption is that decisions are always made to maximize the use of resources. This may not be achieved when tax factors affect how taxpayers save, invest, or consume. Taxes, by influencing economic decisions, may cause a less than optimal allocation of resources.

Adequacy A good tax system should meet the funding requirements of the taxing authority. It is also desirable that these revenues be produced in a fashion that is dependable and relatively predictable from year to year.

Elasticity Tax revenues should be capable of being adjusted to meet changes in economic conditions, without necessitating tax rate changes.

Flexibility This refers to the ease with which the tax system can be adjusted to meet changing economic or social conditions.

Simplicity And Ease Of Compliance A good tax system is easy to comply with and does not present significant administrative problems for the people enforcing the system.

Certainty Individual taxpayers should know how much tax they have to pay, the basis for payments, and the due date. Such certainty also helps taxing authorities estimate tax revenues and facilitates forecasting of budgetary expenditures.

Balance Between Sectors   A good tax system should not be overly reliant on either corporate or individual taxation. Attention should also be given to balance within these sectors, insuring that no type of business or type of individual is asked to assume a disproportionate share of the tax burden.

International Competitiveness   If a country's tax system has rates that are out of line with those that prevail in comparable countries, the result will be an outflow of both business and skilled individuals to those countries that have more favourable tax rates.

Conflicts Among Characteristics

1-42.   In designing a tax system, many compromises are required. Examples include the fact that flexibility is often in conflict with certainty, equity requires trade-offs in simplicity and neutrality, and some taxes with very positive objectives are very non-neutral in nature. An example of this last conflict is that the rates available to small businesses are very favourable because the government believes that this attracts investment to this sector, thereby encouraging employment and the development of active business efforts. However, this may not result in the optimal allocation of resources to the business sector as a whole.

Evaluation Of The Canadian System

1-43.   Canadian policy makers often refer to the preceding qualitative characteristics in discussions involving taxation policies. This would make it appropriate to consider how the current system of federal taxation stacks up against these criteria. While any comprehensive evaluation of this question goes well beyond the objectives of this text, we offer the following brief comments:

- With respect to equity, Canada continues to have situations in which high income individuals pay little or no tax and relatively low income individuals are subjected to fairly high effective rates. While the alternative minimum tax was instituted to correct this problem, inequity is unlikely to be eliminated in a tax system that attempts to accomplish as many diverse objectives as does the current Canadian system.

- As noted previously, the Canadian system has a very heavy reliance on the taxation of personal income and receives a very low portion of its revenues from the corporate sector.

- The Canadian system has had problems with stability and dependability of revenues.

- The Canadian tax system is very complex, making compliance difficult for many taxpayers. In addition, administration of the legislation is made more difficult by the large number of provisions and the lack of clarity in their content. The GST has clearly made this situation even worse for those individuals and businesses required to comply with its many complex requirements, particularly in those provinces where there is a non-harmonized provincial sales tax levied on a different group of items.

- While international competitiveness is often cited as a problem for Canada, particularly with respect to comparisons with the U.S., the situation has improved significantly in recent years. With respect to individuals, Canadian tax rates are still higher than those in the U.S. However, the impact of this is difficult to assess because of large differences between the social benefits provided in the two countries (e.g., Canada's government funded health care system vs. the private system which is in place in the U.S.).

- For corporations, the situation is clearly more favourable for Canada. In 2004, Canada's average corporate tax rate was 2.3 percent lower than the average federal rate in the U.S. Proposed tax cuts in the U.S. would reduce, but not eliminate, Canada's advantage in this area. However, with the additional rate cuts announced in the 2005, 2006, and 2007 federal budgets, Canada will see its current advantage restored by 2010, providing further cuts are not initiated in the U.S.

Also of importance to business is the fact that the top Canadian rate on capital gains is below the top rate in the U.S. In addition, Canada provides a $750,000 lifetime capital gains exemption on the sale of shares of a qualified small business corporation. There is no equivalent provision in the U.S.

Canadian Federal Income Tax Legislation

History Of The Federal Income Tax Act

1-44   The first Canadian income tax was imposed in 1917. This was the *Income War Tax Act* and it was needed as the more traditional custom and excise taxes were not capable of producing the revenues required by Canada's involvement in World War I. This Act persisted, with a large number of amendments, until 1949.

1-45.   In 1948, the *Income War Tax Act* was merged into new legislation called the *Income Tax Act*. This *Act* was largely a rewording and codification of the *Income War Tax Act* with very few actual changes in policy. This new *Income Tax Act* was applicable to 1949 and subsequent years. In 1952, the 1949 version of the *Income Tax Act* was revised. However, except for transitional provisions and a complete renumbering of sections, the revision made few real changes and, as a consequence, legal decisions based on the provisions of the 1948 Act continued to be applicable.

1-46.   In 1962, a major reform of federal income tax legislation began with the creation of a Royal Commission On Taxation under the chairmanship of Kenneth Carter. This Commission, subsequently designated the Carter Commission, presented its seven volume report in 1967. This report led to the November, 1969 White Paper On Tax Reform, followed on June 18, 1971 by Bill C-259. Bill C-259 was given Royal Assent on December 23, 1971 and became law on January 1, 1972.

1-47.   Since January 1, 1972, every budget has presented a considerable number of amendments to fine tune existing legislation, or to introduce new policies. For example, the amendments first presented in the November 12, 1981 budget appeared to many as another major reform of income tax legislation. The May 23, 1985 budget, with its introduction of the lifetime capital gains deduction, could be viewed as a major change in the approach to the taxation of individuals. The changes introduced in 1988 as the result of the June 18, 1987 White Paper On Tax Reform have also resulted in a significant overhaul of the taxation system. Despite all of these changes, the general approach to the taxation of income in Canada is still based on the reforms that were made effective beginning in 1972.

Structure Of The Federal Income Tax Act

1-48.   The fundamental source of federal income tax legislation is the federal *Income Tax Act*. The *Act* itself is an enormous document, with most paper editions approaching 2,500 pages. While we will not attempt to provide comprehensive coverage of the complete *Act*, frequent references will be made to various components of the document.

1-49.   Further, the basic organization of the material in this text tends to follow the structure of the *Income Tax Act*. As a consequence, it is desirable that you have some knowledge of the *Act's* basic structure. Figure 1-3 diagrams the basic structure of the *Act*.

1-50.   The major divisions of the *Income Tax Act* are referred to as Parts. Some, but not all of

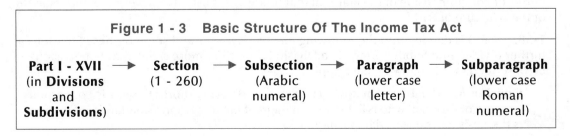

Figure 1 - 3 Basic Structure Of The Income Tax Act				
Part I - XVII → (in **Divisions** and **Subdivisions**)	**Section** (1 - 260) →	**Subsection** → (Arabic numeral)	**Paragraph** → (lower case letter)	**Subparagraph** (lower case Roman numeral)

these Parts, contain two or more Divisions (e.g., Part I of the *Act* contains Divisions A through J). Some Divisions, but again not all of them, contain Subdivisions. For example, Division B of Part I contains Subdivisions a through k.

1-51.   All of the Parts contain at least one Section. However, there is considerable variance in the size of the Parts. Part I.2, "Tax On Old Age Security Benefits", contains only one Section. In contrast, Part I, the largest and most important Part of the *Act*, contains Sections 2 to 180.

1-52.   While the Sections of the *Act* are numbered 1 through 260, there are actually more than 260 Sections. This reflects the fact that when a new Section is added, it has been more convenient to attach a decimal designation to the immediately preceding Section, as opposed to renumbering all of the Sections that follow the new Section. For example, if the Department of Finance wished to add a new Section after an existing Section 12, it would be designated as Section 12.1, rather than Section 13.

1-53.   Sections may be further subdivided into Subsections [designated with Arabic numerals as in Subsection 84(1)]. This is followed by Paragraphs [designated with lower case letters as in Paragraph 84(1)(b)], and by Subparagraphs [designated with lower case Roman numerals as in Subparagraph 84(1)(b)(i)]. In some cases, the outlining process goes even further with Clauses (designated with upper case letters) and Subclauses (designated with upper case roman numerals). Putting all of this together means that the reference:

ITA 115(1)(a)(i)(A)(I)

would be read as *Income Tax Act* Section 115, Subsection (1), Paragraph (a), Subparagraph (i), Clause A, Subclause I. Normally the relevant Part of the *Act* is not indicated in such references.

Parts Of The Act

1-54.   The Parts of the *Income Tax Act* are numbered I through XVII. As was the case with Sections of the *Act*, there are more than 17 Parts because of the use of designations within a single Roman numeral. The most extreme example of this would be the existence of Parts XII.1, XII.2, XII.3, XII.4, XII.5, and XII.6.

1-55.   About 70 percent of the Sections of the *Income Tax Act* are found in Part I, which is titled "Income Tax". This Part contains Sections 2 through 180 of the *Act* and, because of its importance, we will provide a more detailed description of this Part in the following material.

1-56.   Parts I.1 through XVII cover a variety of special taxes as well as rules related to matters of administration, enforcement, and interpretation. For example, Part V is titled "Tax In Respect Of Registered Charities" and Part XII.3 is titled "Tax On Investment Income Of Life Insurers". As the great bulk of our attention in this text will be focused on Part I of the *Act*, there is little point in providing a list of these Parts for you to read. However, if you have further interest in their content, we would refer you to the complete copies of the *Income Tax Act* that are included on the CD-ROMs that accompany the text.

Part I Of The Act

1-57.   As was previously noted, Part I is the largest and most important Part of the *Income Tax Act*. As a result, it will receive most of our attention in this text. In fact, the organization of the first 14 Chapters of this text is largely consistent with the structure of Part I of the *Act*. To facilitate your comprehension of the material that follows, it is useful to have some understanding of the structure of Part I.

1-58.   Part I is divided into the following eleven Divisions and some of these Divisions are further divided into Subdivisions. The Divisions and their more significant Subdivisions will be described in the following paragraphs:

Division A: "Liability For Tax" (ITA Section 2)   This short Division is concerned with the question of who is liable for payment of income tax in Canada. This Division is the basis for the material in Chapter 3.

Division B: "Computation Of Income" (ITA Sections 3 through 108)   This is the longest Division in Part I and concerns itself with the determination of Net Income For Tax Purposes. Its first five Subdivisions describe the major sources of income and deductions and are as follows:

- **Subdivision a** - "Income Or Loss From An Office Or Employment"   This Subdivision deals with the ordinary wages and salaries that are earned by individuals while an employee of a business entity. The material in this Subdivision provides the basis for Chapter 5.

- **Subdivision b** - "Income Or Loss From A Business Or Property"   This Subdivision deals with business income earned by corporations, trusts, and by individuals through proprietorship or partnership arrangements. Also covered in this Subdivision is property income which includes rents, interest, dividends, and royalties. The material in this Subdivision provides the basis for Chapters 7, 8, and 9.

- **Subdivision c** - "Taxable Capital Gains And Allowable Capital Losses"   This Subdivision deals with gains and losses resulting from the disposal of capital property. The material in this Subdivision is dealt with in Chapter 10.

- **Subdivision d** - "Other Sources Of Income"   Covered here are miscellaneous income sources, such as alimony received and various types of pension income, that do not fit into any of the major categories dealt with in Subdivisions a, b, and c. This material is covered in Chapter 11.

- **Subdivision e** - "Deductions In Computing Income"   Covered here are miscellaneous deductions such as moving expenses, child care costs, and alimony paid. These are deductions that do not fit into any of the categories in Subdivisions a, b, and c. This material is covered in Chapter 11.

Subdivisions a, b, and c each provide for both inclusions and deductions and, as a consequence, require the calculation of a net income figure. The deductions that are specified in Subdivisions a, b and c can only be deducted from inclusions in that same Subdivision. That is, deductions related to business income (Subdivision b) cannot be deducted from the inclusions for employment income (Subdivision a). This becomes a very important point when the inclusions in a particular Subdivision are not sufficient to support all of the available deductions in that Subdivision.

The remaining six Subdivisions of Division B do not provide new sources of income but, rather, provide additional rules related to the determination of Net Income. These remaining Subdivisions are as follows:

- **Subdivision f** - "Rules Relating To Computation Of Income"   This Subdivision contains a variety of rules related to the deductibility of expenses, income attribution, and the death of a taxpayer. These rules are covered in Chapters 8 and 12.

- **Subdivision g** - "Amounts Not Included In Computing Income"   This is a very specialized Subdivision, dealing with certain types of exempt income. It is not given significant coverage in this text.

- **Subdivision h** - "Corporations Resident In Canada And Their Shareholders"   This Subdivision presents a number of rules related to the taxation of Canadian resident corporations. This material is covered in Chapters 15 and 16.

- **Subdivision i** - "Shareholders Of Corporations Not Resident In Canada"   This is a specialized Subdivision. Limited coverage is available in Chapter 22.

- **Subdivision j** - "Partnerships And Their Members"   This Subdivision, dealing with rules related to partnerships, is given detailed coverage in Chapter 20.

- **Subdivision k** - "Trusts And Their Beneficiaries"   This Subdivision, dealing with the taxation of trusts, is given detailed consideration in Chapter 21.

Division C: "Computation Of Taxable Income" (ITA Sections 109 through 114.2) This Division covers the conversion of Division B income (commonly referred to as Net Income For Tax Purposes, or simply Net Income) into Taxable Income for residents. It is given initial coverage in Chapter 6, followed by more detailed coverage in Chapters 14 (individuals) and 15 (corporations).

Division D: "Taxable Income Earned In Canada By Non-Residents" (ITA Sections 115 through 116) No significant coverage is given to this material in this text.

Division E: "Computation Of Tax" (Sections 117 through 127.41) This Division is concerned with determining the taxes that are payable on the Taxable Income determined in Divisions C and D. It has four Subdivisions as follows:

- Subdivision a - Rules applicable to individuals
- Subdivision a.1 - Child tax benefit
- Subdivision b - Rules applicable to corporations
- Subdivision c - Rules applicable to all taxpayers

The computation of tax for individuals is largely covered in Chapter 6, with some additional coverage in Chapter 14. The corresponding material for corporations is found in Chapters 15 and 16.

Division E.1: "Minimum Tax" (Sections 127.5 through 127.55) This Division is concerned with the obligation of individuals to pay a minimum amount of tax, as well as the computation of this alternative minimum tax. This material is covered in Chapter 14.

Division F: "Special Rules Applicable In Certain Circumstances" (Sections 128 through 143.3) Much of this Division is devoted to very specialized situations (bankruptcies) or organizations (cooperative corporations). While these situations are not given coverage in this text, the Division covers two subjects that are of more general importance. These are immigration to and emigration from Canada which are covered in Chapter 12, and refundable dividends for private corporations which is covered in Chapter 16.

Division G: "Deferred And Other Special Income Arrangements" (Sections 144 through 148.1) This important Division covers the rules related to Registered Retirement Savings Plans, Registered Pension Plans, Deferred Profit Sharing Plans, as well as other deferred income arrangements. Detailed attention is given to this material in Chapter 13.

Division H: "Exemptions" (Sections 149 and 149.1) Covered here are exemptions for individuals and organizations such as certain employees of foreign countries, pension trusts, and charitable organizations. These topics are not given coverage in this text.

Divisions I And J: "Returns, Assessments, Payments And Appeals" and "Appeals To The Tax Court Of Canada And The Federal Court" (Sections 150 through 180) These Divisions deal with the resolution of disputes between taxpayers and the Canada Revenue Agency (CRA). Coverage of this material is found in Chapter 2.

1-59. As this book progresses, references to the Divisions of Part I as well as many of its Subdivisions will become very familiar. However, you may find it helpful in subsequent Chapters, to periodically review the preceding general outline as an aid to keeping some perspective on how the material you are reading fits into the larger picture of income taxation in Canada.

Other Income Tax Legislation

1-60. While the *Income Tax Act* constitutes the major source of legislation relevant to the study of the federal income tax, there are four other sources of legislative materials that are relevant. These are the Income Tax Application Rules, 1971, the Income Tax Regulations, a group of International Tax Agreements between Canada and other countries, and draft legislation. A general description of these legislative materials follows.

Income Tax Application Rules, 1971

1-61. When the *Income Tax Act* was heavily revised at the end of 1971, a large number of transitional rules were required, primarily to ensure that the effects of the new legislation were not retroactive. These transitional rules are called the Income Tax Application Rules, 1971, and they continue to be of some significance in matters such as valuation day rules and the determination of tax-free zones in calculating capital gains and losses. However, the significance of these rules declines with each passing year and, as a consequence, they will be given little attention in this text.

Income Tax Regulations

1-62. Section 221 of the *Income Tax Act* allows the Governor In Council to make Regulations concerning the administration and enforcement of the *Income Tax Act*. Some of the items listed in this Section include:

- prescribing the evidence required to establish facts relevant to assessments under this *Act*;

- requiring any class of persons to make information returns respecting any class of information required in connection with assessments under this *Act*;

- prescribing anything that, by this *Act*, is to be prescribed or is to be determined or regulated by regulation; and

- defining the classes of persons who may be regarded as dependent for the purposes of this *Act*.

1-63. While these Regulations cannot extend the limits of the law, they can serve to fill in details and, to some extent, modify the statutes. For example, most of the rules for determining the amount of Capital Cost Allowance that can be deducted are established in the Regulations. Such Regulations provide an essential element of flexibility in the administration of the *Act* in that they can be issued without going through a more formal legislative process.

1-64. You should also note that references to material in the Regulations are often referred to in the *Income Tax Act* as "prescribed". For example, the rate the CRA charges on late tax payments, a "prescribed" rate of interest, is determined by a procedure that is described in Regulation 4301.

International Tax Agreements

1-65. Canada currently has tax agreements (also known as tax treaties or tax conventions) with about 90 countries. The most important of these are the Tax Conventions with the United States and the United Kingdom. While there is considerable variation in the agreements, most of them are based on the model convention developed by the Organization For Economic Co-operation And Development (OECD).

1-66. The purpose of these agreements is twofold. First, they attempt to avoid double taxation of taxpayers who may have reason to pay taxes in more than one jurisdiction and, second, they try to prevent international evasion of taxes. In situations where there is a conflict between the Canadian *Income Tax Act* and an international agreement, the terms of the international agreement prevail.

Draft Legislation

1-67. It is traditional for the federal government to issue a budget in the first half of each year. At one point in time, this occurred with regularity in the month of February. However, in recent years there has been more variability:

- The 2004 budget was issued on March 23 of that year.
- The 2005 budget was issued on February 23 of that year.

- The 2006 budget was issued on May 2 of that year.
- The 2007 budget was issued on March 19 of this year.

1-68.   Regardless of their date, budgets are presented as a Notice Of Ways And Means Motion. As such, its content is of a general nature and does not contain the actual legislative provisions that are required to implement the proposals that are being put forward. The preparation of this legislation sometimes takes as much as a year and, when it is presented, it is referred to as draft legislation. Additional time is required for this draft legislation to be passed by parliament.

1-69.   Note, however, returns must be filed on the basis of each year's budget, without regard to when the legislation for the budget is actually implemented. That is, the content of the March 2007 budget is applicable to 2007 tax returns, even if the legislation is not passed prior to the filing date for those returns.

Other Sources Of Income Tax Information

Electronic Library Resources

1-70.   Included with this book are two electronic libraries that contain the complete *Income Tax Act* and *Regulations*, as well as the publications from the CRA that are described in Paragraph 1-72. Access to these libraries is available as follows:

- The Student CD-ROM has the CICA's Federal Income Tax Collection (FITAC ^{Lite}). These materials are presented in Folio Views software, which provides for hypertext links for all references in the electronic version of *Canadian Tax Principles*.

- The ProFile Tax Suite CD-ROM has the Intuit Tax Research Assistant (InTRA). This includes a complete library of tax research materials as well as a significant amount of commentary related to various Sections of the *Income Tax Act*.

CRA Web Site

1-71.   The CRA has an extensive web site at **www.cra.gc.ca**. Almost all of the forms, Guides, Interpretation Bulletins and other documents provided by the CRA that are described in Paragraph 1-72 are available on the web site. The forms and publications can be viewed and printed online or downloaded to a computer in one or more formats. There is also an online request service available to have printed forms or publications mailed out. The web site is constantly being expanded to provide more forms and publications and more information on electronic services (such as EFILE, NETFILE, and TELEFILE).

CRA Publications

1-72.   The CRA provides several publications to the public which, while they do not have the force of law, can be extremely helpful and influential in making decisions related to income taxes. These can be described as follows:

Interpretation Bulletins   To date, over 530 Interpretation Bulletins have been issued by the CRA. Note, however, that many of these are no longer in force. The objective of these Bulletins is to give the CRA's interpretation of particular sections of the law that it administers and to announce significant changes in departmental interpretation along with the effective dates of any such changes. Examples of important Interpretation Bulletins include IT-63R5 dealing with an employee's personal use of an automobile supplied by an employer, and IT-221R3 which provides guidance on the determination of an individual's residence status. Note that the R5 and R3 in these Bulletin numbers refer to fifth and third revisions, respectively, of the Bulletins.

Information Circulars   Of the more than 300 Information Circulars that have been issued, over 70 are currently in effect. The objective of these publications is to provide information regarding procedural matters that relate to both the *Income Tax Act* and the provisions of the Canada Pension Plan, and to announce changes in organization, personnel, operating programs, and other administrative developments.

Income Tax Technical News   The Income Tax Rulings Directorate of the CRA periodically issues a newsletter titled *Income Tax Technical News*. This newsletter provides up-to-date information on current tax issues and is considered by the CRA to have the same weight as Interpretation Bulletins. To date (May, 2007), only one Technical News was published in 2007. It dealt with a single subject, the determination of residence for the purpose of applying the provisions of an international tax treaty.

CRA News Releases, Tax Tips, And Fact Sheets   The CRA publishes News Releases on a variety of subjects, such as prescribed interest rates, corporate EFILE, deferral of taxation on employee stock options and the taxation of gifts from employers. They also provide information on when monthly payments will be released under the Child Tax Benefit System and when quarterly payments will be released under the GST tax credit program. Some of the News Releases take the form of questions and answers, while others deal with the subject in some depth. They are usually issued in advance of the relevant legislation or coverage in an Interpretation Bulletin or Information Circular.

Guides And Pamphlets   The CRA publishes a large number of non-technical Pamphlets and Guides that provide information on particular topics of interest to taxpayers. Examples of Pamphlets are "Canadian Residents Going Down South" (P151) and "Tax Information For People With Disabilities" (P149). Examples of Guides are "Business And Professional Income" (T4002), "Preparing Returns For Deceased Persons" (T4011), and "RRSPs And Other Registered Plans For Retirement" (T4040).

Advance Income Tax Rulings And Technical Interpretations   In recognition of the considerable complexity involved in the interpretation of many portions of the *Income Tax Act*, the Income Tax Rulings Directorate of the CRA will, for a fee, provide an Advance Income Tax Ruling on how it will tax a proposed transaction, subject to certain limitations and qualifications. Advance Income Tax Rulings are available to the public, but only in severed format with much of the relevant information that may permit identification of the parties deleted. The result is that such publications are of questionable value.

The Income Tax Rulings Directorate of the CRA also provides both written and telephone Technical Interpretations to the public (other than for proposed transactions where an Advance Income Tax Ruling is required) free of charge. Such interpretations however are not considered binding on the CRA.

Internal Documents

1-73.   As we have seen, the formal income tax legislation includes the *Income Tax Act*, Income Tax Application Rules, 1971, Income Tax Regulations, International Tax Agreements, as well as draft legislation. In addition, the Canada Revenue Agency (CRA) issues directives to its tax services offices in which interpretations and suggested procedures are set forth. However, these directives are not available to the public and their nature can only be determined by inference and experiences with assessments and court cases.

Court Decisions

1-74.   Despite the huge volume of information available for dealing with income tax matters, disputes between taxpayers and the CRA regularly find their way into the Canadian court system. Of the hundreds of tax cases that are reported each year, the great majority do not involve tax evasion or other criminal offences. Rather, they involve an honest difference of opinion between the taxpayer and the CRA. Common areas of litigation include:

- the deductibility of both business and employment related expenses;
- establishing a property's fair market value;
- the question of whether a transaction took place at arm's length;
- the deductibility of alimony and maintenance payments;
- distinguishing between profits that are capital in nature and those that are ordinary business income; and
- the deductibility of farm losses against other sources of income.

1-75.   With the large number of court cases and the fact that they cover the great majority of issues that might arise in the application of income tax legislation, attention must be given to the precedents that have been established in the court decisions. Given the volume and complexity of court cases on income tax, we will cite only very important cases in our coverage of the various subjects in this text. However, a careful review of all relevant case material would be essential in researching any complex tax issue.

Abbreviations To Be Used

1-76.   In our writing, we try to avoid using abbreviations because we believe that there is a tendency in accounting and tax writing to use so many of them that the material can become unreadable. However, in the tax area, some sources are so commonly cited that it is clearly inefficient to continue using their full description. As a result, in the remainder of this text, we will use the following abbreviations on a regular basis:

- **CRA** - Canada Revenue Agency
- **ITA** - Federal *Income Tax Act*
- **ITR** - Federal Income Tax Regulations, 1971
- **IT** - Interpretation Bulletins
- **IC** - Information Circulars
- **GST** - Goods and Services Tax

Key Terms Used In This Chapter

1-77.   The following is a list of the key terms used in this Chapter. These terms, and their meanings, are compiled in the Glossary Of Key Terms located at the back of the separate paper Study Guide and on the Student CD-ROM.

Advance Tax Ruling	Information Circulars
Allowable Capital Loss	Interpretation Bulletins
Business Income	Net Income For Tax Purposes
Capital Asset	Person
Capital Gain/Loss	Progressive Tax System
Capital Tax	Property Income
Consumption Tax	Property Tax
Customs Duties	Qualitative Characteristics
Employment Income	Regressive Tax System
Flat Tax System	Tariffs
Goods And Services Tax	Tax Base
GST	Tax Expenditure
Harmonized Sales Tax	Tax Incidence
Head Tax	Taxable Capital Gain
Income Tax	Taxable Entity
Income Tax Application Rules	Taxable Income
Income Tax Regulations	Transfer Tax
Income Tax Technical News	Value Added Tax

References

1-78.   The material in this Introduction has been very general in nature. As a consequence, we have not included a listing of specific references to other sources. Subsequent Chapters will include a list of references for additional study.

Assignment Problems

(The solutions to these problem are only available in
the solutions manual that has been provided to your instructor.)

Assignment Problem One - 1

The principal source of Canadian income tax information is the *Income Tax Act*. There are, however, other sources that are of considerable significance in the application of these rules.

Required: List and briefly describe these other sources of information on Canadian income tax matters.

Assignment Problem One - 2

At a recent cocktail party, Mr. Right was heard complaining vehemently about the lack of progress towards tax simplification. He was tired of spending half of his time filling out various CRA forms and, if the matter were left to him, he could solve the problem in 10 minutes. "It is simply a matter of having one tax rate and applying that rate to 100 percent of income."

Required: Discuss Mr. Right's proposed flat rate tax system.

Assignment Problem One - 3

Many of the provisions of the *Income Tax Act* are written in very general terms. For example, ITA 18 lists a number of general characteristics that must apply before a particular expense can be deducted in the computation of business income.

Required: Indicate the situations in which such generally worded provisions of the *Income Tax Act* will be overridden.

Assignment Problem One - 4

A regressive tax can be described as one which is assessed at a lower rate as income levels increase. Despite the fact that the Goods and Services Tax (GST) and provincial sales taxes are based on a single rate, they are referred to as regressive forms of taxation.

Required: Explain how a tax system with a single rate can be viewed as regressive.

Assignment Problem One - 5

The tax systems of various countries are designed to meet a variety of objectives. In addition to raising revenues, we call on our tax systems to provide fairness, to have the characteristic of simplicity, to meet social or economic goals, to balance regional disparities, and to be competitive on an international basis. While it would be a fairly simple matter to design a system that would meet any single one of these objectives, we frequently encounter conflicts when we attempt to create a system that meets several of these objectives.

Required: Discuss the possible conflicts that can arise when a tax system is designed to meet more than a single objective.

Assignment Problem One - 6

Discuss whether the following situations meet the objectives and match the characteristics of a good tax system. Identify any conflicts that exist and the probable economic incidence of the tax or tax expenditure.

A. Diamonds are South Africa's major export. Assume that a tax is levied on diamond production of Par Excellence Inc., which has a monopoly in the country. Movements of diamonds are closely monitored and accounted for.

B. Chimeree Inc. owns the largest diamond mine in Sierra Leone. A tax is levied on diamond production. Movements of diamonds are not closely controlled, and helicopters pick up shipments under the cover of darkness.

C. Gains on dispositions of principal residences are exempt from income tax in Canada.

D. A rule stipulates that only 50 percent of the cost of business meals can be deducted in calculating Canadian business income for personal and corporate Taxable Income.

E. A newly created country levies a head tax which requires every resident adult to pay an annual tax.

Assignment Problem One - 7

Concerned with her inability to control the deficit, the Minister of Finance has indicated that she is considering the introduction of a head tax. This would be a tax of $200 per year, assessed on every living Canadian resident who, on December 31 of each year, has a head. In order to enforce the tax, all Canadian residents would be required to have a Head Administration Tax identification number (HAT, for short) tattooed in an inconspicuous location on their scalp. A newly formed special division of the RCMP, the Head Enforcement Administration Division (HEAD, for short), would run spot checks throughout the country in order to ensure that everyone has registered and received their HAT.

The Minister is very enthusiastic about the plan, anticipating that it will produce additional revenues of $5 billion per year. It is also expected to spur economic growth though increased sales of Canadian made toques.

As the Minister's senior policy advisor, you have been asked to prepare a memorandum evaluating this proposed new head tax.

Required: Prepare the memorandum.

Assignment Problem One - 8

With the growing importance of free trade and e-commerce, Canada is contemplating increased harmonization of the Canadian tax system with other major tax regimes in the world. Harmonization with the United States is the first priority, with harmonization with other major economic groups being secondary. Assume the following changes are proposed:

A. Taxing all e-commerce transactions based on where the goods and services are delivered.

B. Full deduction of mortgage interest related to principal residences, combined with taxation of capital gains arising on dispositions of these residences. Currently in Canada, the capital gains on the disposition of principal residences are not taxed and mortgage interest related to principal residences is not deductible.

C. Requiring corporations that are under common control to file a single consolidated tax return for all of the corporations in the group.

D. Conversion of the GST system into a national sales tax to be applied to the sale of goods and services at the retail level.

E. Elimination of the gross up and tax credit system for dividends received from taxable Canadian corporations by individuals. The dividends would be taxed as ordinary income. For corporations, dividends would be deductible as a business expense, and corporate dividend recipients would be taxed as if dividends are ordinary property income.

Required: Indicate a significant tax advantage, other than the benefits associated with international harmonization, that would result from introducing each of the proposed changes. In addition, analyze each proposed change using two of the qualitative characteristics of tax systems that are listed in your text.

CHAPTER 2

Procedures And Administration

Introduction

2-1. This Chapter begins with a brief overview of the administration of the Canada Revenue Agency (CRA). This is followed by a description of filing and tax payment procedures applicable to individuals, corporations, and trusts.

2-2. This material on filing and tax payment procedures will be followed by a description of the assessment and reassessment process, including the various avenues that can be followed in appealing unfavourable assessments. Attention will also be given to the collection procedures that are available to the CRA in enforcing its claims against taxpayers. This Chapter concludes with a brief discussion of the general anti-avoidance rule (GAAR).

Administration Of The Department

2-3. The CRA has the responsibility for carrying out the tax policies that are enacted by Parliament. In carrying out these policies, the chief executive officer of the CRA is the Minister of National Revenue. The duties of the Minister of National Revenue, as well as those of the Commissioner of Customs and Revenue, are described in the *Act* as follows:

> **ITA 220(1)** The Minister shall administer and enforce this Act and the Commissioner of Revenue may exercise all the powers and perform the duties of the Minister under this Act.

2-4. The Minister of National Revenue is responsible for the CRA and is accountable to Parliament for all of its activities, including the administration and enforcement of program legislation such as the *Income Tax Act* and the *Excise Tax Act*. The Minister has the authority to ensure that the CRA operates within the overall government framework and treats its clients with fairness, integrity, and consistency.

2-5. The CRA has a Board of Management consisting of 15 members appointed by the Governor in Council, 11 of whom have been nominated by the provinces and territories. The Board has the responsibility of overseeing the management of the CRA, including the development of the Corporate Business Plan, and the management of policies related to resources, services, property, personnel, and contracts. The Commissioner of the CRA, who is a member of the CRA Board, is responsible for the CRA's day-to-day operations.

2-6. Unlike the boards of Crown corporations, the CRA Board is not involved in all the activities of the CRA. In particular, the CRA Board has no authority in the administration and enforcement of legislation, which includes the *Income Tax Act* and the *Excise Tax Act*, for which the CRA remains fully accountable to the Minister of National Revenue. In addition, the CRA Board is denied access to confidential client information.

2-7.   Following the ministerial mandate found in ITA 220(1), ITA 221(1) provides that the Governor in Council has the power to make Income Tax Regulations for various specific purposes or for the purpose of carrying out other provisions of the *Income Tax Act*. Unlike the provisions of the *Income Tax Act*, these Regulations may be passed by Order-In-Council without ratification by Parliament. They generally become effective when they are published in the Canada Gazette.

Source Deductions

Withholdings

Salaries And Wages

2-8.   A large portion of the income taxes paid by individuals employed in Canada is collected through source deductions. Under ITA 153, any individual who earns employment income will have the estimated taxes on this income withheld from gross pay through payroll deductions made by their employer. The tax withheld is related to the amount of the individual's income, with the required withholdings intended to cover the tax payable on this income. However, it would be unusual for such withholding to be exactly equal to the taxes payable for the year. As a consequence, most individuals will either owe taxes and be required to file a tax return or, alternatively, be entitled to a refund that can only be obtained by filing a tax return.

2-9.   The amount withheld by an employer is based on a form that is filled out by each employee, Form TD1, "Personal Tax Credits Return". This form lists personal and other credits that are available to an individual and asks the employee to indicate which of these he will be claiming.

2-10.   Also on Form TD1, an individual can ask to have the amount withheld increased beyond the required amount. An individual might choose to do this if his employment income withholding is based on rates in a low tax rate province, but his residence is in a high tax rate province (e.g., an individual who works in Alberta, but lives in Saskatchewan). Another example where additional withholding might be useful could be an individual with large amounts of investment income that are not subject to withholding. In either of these cases, requesting additional withholding would allow the individual to avoid a large tax liability when his tax return is filed.

2-11.   A different type of problem can arise when an employed individual who is subject to source deductions has significant losses or other deductions that can be used to offset employment income.

> **Example**   Monica Kinney has 2007 employment income of $74,357. Assume that she lives in a province with a 10.5 percent provincial tax rate applied to all taxable income. Her employer would normally withhold based on the assumption that she will owe income taxes totalling $21,749 ($13,942 federal, plus $7,807 provincial, ignoring all tax credits). However, if Ms. Kinney has annual deductible spousal support payments of $20,000, her income will be reduced to $54,357 and her actual 2007 federal and provincial taxes payable will only be $15,249 ($9,542 + $5,707). As will be explained later, the government will not pay interest on the extra $6,500 in taxes withheld.

2-12.   Under ITA 153(1.1), Monica can request a reduction in the amount of source deductions withheld by her employer. As long as the losses or deductions can be documented in a reasonable fashion and they are expected to recur, the CRA will normally authorize the employer to reduce the amounts withheld from the employee's remuneration. Form T1213, "Request To Reduce Tax Deductions At Source" is used to make this request.

Other Payers

2-13.   In addition to requiring employers to withhold specified amounts from the salaries and wages of employees, ITA 153 contains a fairly long list of other types of payments from which the payer must withhold prescribed amounts. These include:

- retiring allowances
- death benefits
- payments from Registered Retirement Savings Plans
- payments from Registered Education Savings Plans
- distributions under retirement compensation arrangements

2-14.   In addition to payments listed in ITA 153, withholding is required on certain payments to non-residents. While the general rate of tax on the Canadian source income of non-residents is established in ITA 212 as 25 percent, the amount that will actually be withheld is usually modified by international tax treaties. For a more complete discussion of this type of withholding, see Chapter 22, International Taxation.

Employer's Remittance Of Source Deductions

2-15.   While a variety of items may be withheld by employers from the income of their employees, the ones that are required by the federal government are for:

- estimated income taxes;
- Canada or Quebec Pension Plan (CPP or QPP) contributions; and
- Employment Insurance (EI) premiums.

2-16.   These amounts are remitted to the CRA through a Tax Services Office, a Taxation Centre, a financial institution belonging to the Canadian Payments Association, or on-line. The amounts must be remitted by the employer by a specified due date in order to avoid a penalty. Postmarks do not count as a remittance date.

Due Dates

2-17.   The schedule for remitting these source deductions is based on the amounts involved. As described in the *Employers' Guide: Payroll Deductions And Remittances*, four classes of employers are identified. These classes, along with the related remittance requirements, are as follows:

Quarterly Remitters   Only businesses with small payrolls can qualify as quarterly remitters.   They have to remit withholdings on or before the 15th day of the month immediately following the end of each calendar quarter. To qualify for quarterly remitting, an employer has to:

- have an average monthly withholding amount of less than $1,000 in either the first or the second preceding calendar year;
- have a perfect compliance history in the previous 12 months; and
- have no outstanding GST/HST returns or T4 information returns for the previous 12 months.

Regular Remitters   These employers are new employers and those employers with average monthly withholdings of less than $15,000 in the preceding calendar year, who do not qualify as quarterly remitters. Their remittances are due monthly on the 15th day of the month following the month in which the amounts were withheld.

Accelerated Remitters - Threshold 1   These employers have average monthly withholdings of $15,000 to $49,999.99 for the second preceding calendar year. They are required to remit on a twice monthly basis. Payments are due on the 25th day of the month for remuneration paid during the first 15 days of the month, while payments due on the 10th day of the following month would be for remuneration paid during the remainder of the month.

Accelerated Remitters - Threshold 2   This class of employer has average monthly withholdings of $50,000 or more for the second preceding calendar year. For these employers, remittances are required four times per month. The schedule requires payments to be made within three working days (holidays and weekends are excluded) of the 7th, 14th, 21st, and last days of each month. The payments would be for withholdings on remuneration paid during the periods ending on those dates.

2-18.   For employers with twice monthly pay periods ($15,000 to $49,999.99 in withholdings), it would be advantageous to establish pay dates on the 1st and 16th days of the month. This would provide for maximum deferral of source deduction remittances for semi-monthly pay periods. Even more tax advantageous would be the establishment of monthly pay periods, which would reduce the frequency of the required remittances.

Penalties And Interest - Source Deductions

2-19.   If an employer withholds and fails to remit by the due date, there is a penalty on the amount that should have been remitted which exceeds $500. This $500 threshold does not apply if the delay in remitting is attributable to gross negligence. As specified in a June, 2003 CRA News Release, the penalties are 3 percent of remittances that are late 3 days or less, 5 percent if 4 or 5 days late, 7 percent if 6 or 7 days late, and 10 percent if 8 or more days late.

2-20.   There are also penalties for failures to withhold the required amounts of income taxes, CPP, or EI. The basic penalty is 10 percent on the amount that exceeds $500, applicable from the first day that remittance would be late. For a second offence within the same calendar year, the penalty can double to 20 percent if the failure was made knowingly or through gross negligence.

2-21.   Whether amounts have been withheld and not remitted on time, or there has been a failure to withhold, late payments are assessed interest calculated at what is referred to as the prescribed rate. (Prescribed rates are described later in this Chapter).

2-22.   Amounts withheld must be reported by the employer on an annual information return, the T4 slip and the T4 Summary. The T4 Summary must be filed with the CRA and the T4 slips mailed to employees by the last day of February of the following taxation year. If an employer fails to do this, the penalty for each failure is $25 per day, with a minimum penalty of $100 and a maximum of $2,500.

2-23.   When a business is experiencing financial difficulties, it is not uncommon for management to stop remitting source deductions. Unlike a failure to pay a supplier, non-payment of these amounts does not have immediate consequences on the operation of the business.

2-24.   In situations where a corporation has failed to remit source deductions, the CRA has often been successful in holding corporate directors responsible for this failure, resulting in the directors having to pay these amounts from their personal assets. This can be a particularly severe problem in small private companies where directors are often individuals with deep pockets and little or no financial expertise.

Returns And Payments - Individuals

Requirement To File

2-25.   ITA 150(1) is a general rule that requires all individuals to file a T1 tax return. However, ITA 150(1.1)(b) exempts individuals from filing tax returns except when certain conditions are met. In a somewhat indirect manner, the combination of these two provisions means that an individual must file a tax return if:

- they owe taxes for the year;
- they have a taxable capital gain for the year;
- they have disposed of a capital property during the year; or
- they have an outstanding balance under the home buyers plan or lifelong learning plan legislation (see Chapter 13 for an explanation of these RRSP related balances).

2-26.   While there is no requirement for other individuals to file a tax return, if they are entitled to a refund, it will only be available if a return is filed. In addition, it is beneficial for others to file, especially low income taxpayers, in order to be eligible for income-based benefits such as the child tax benefit, the GST credit and the Guaranteed Income Supplement. If they fail to file, they will not receive these amounts, even if they qualify.

2-27.   Individuals can either file a paper form or, alternatively, use an electronic filing method. The advantage of electronic filing for the taxpayer, particularly if he is entitled to a refund, is that the return will be processed more quickly. For the CRA, electronic filing eliminates the possibility of errors in the process of transferring information from paper forms to their computerized records. While supporting documents (e.g., a receipt for a charitable donation) cannot be included with an electronic filing, the CRA retains the right to request that such receipts be provided.

2-28.   Taxpayers have three alternatives for electronic filing. They can be described as follows:

EFILE   EFILE On-Line For Tax Professionals allows registered EFILE service providers to transmit returns to the CRA using the Internet. The system can be used by virtually all taxpayers, but returns must be transmitted through an electronic filer registered with the CRA.

NETFILE   This transmission service allows taxpayers to file their own personal income tax returns directly to the CRA using an approved software program and the Internet. This system can be used by almost all individuals, including those with complex returns. The only requirement is that the individual have an access code. This code is included in an individual's tax return package, or can be obtained on-line or through a request to the CRA.

TELEFILE   Under the TELEFILE system, returns are filed via a touch tone telephone. This system has information constraints that make it useful only for individuals with relatively simple returns. To use the system, an access code is required. This code is available in an individual's tax return package, or can be requested from the CRA.

2-29.   For 2005, the most recent complete statistics available, over 23 million individual tax returns were filed. Of these, 12.7 million were filed electronically, with EFILE being the most popular format (8.2 million returns).

Due Date For Individual Returns

General Rule

2-30.   As is discussed in more detail in Chapter 3, individuals must use the calendar year as their taxation year. This means that for every individual, the taxation year ends on December 31. Given this, ITA 150(1)(d)(i) indicates that, in general, individuals must file their tax return for a particular year on or before April 30 of the following year. Although the filing due date is extended to the next business day if the due date falls on a weekend, we will use April 30 (or June 15 if applicable as explained in the following material) as the due date in our examples and problems.

Individuals Who Are Partners Or Proprietors

2-31.   Recognizing that individuals who are involved in an unincorporated business may need more time to determine their income for a taxation year, the *Income Tax Act* provides a deferral of the filing deadline. If an individual, or his cohabiting spouse or common-law partner, carried on a business during the year, ITA 150(1)(d)(ii) extends the due date for filing to June 15 of the calendar year following the relevant taxation year.

2-32.   An interesting feature of this provision is that, while the return does not have to be filed until June 15, payment of all taxes owing is required by the usual date of April 30. Any amounts that are not paid by April 30 will be assessed interest at the prescribed rate until such time as the outstanding balance is paid.

Exercise Two-1

Subject: Individual Tax Payment Date

Mr. Brandon Katarski's 2007 Net Income includes business income. When is his 2007 tax return due? By what date must his 2007 tax liability be paid in order to avoid the assessment of interest on amounts due?

End of Exercise. Solution available in Study Guide.

Deceased Taxpayers

2-33.   As is discussed in detail in Chapter 12, there are many tax related complications that arise when an individual dies. In order to provide the deceased individual's representatives with sufficient time to deal with these complications, the *Act* indicates the following:

ITA 150(1)(b)   In the case of an individual who dies after October of the year and before the day that would be the individual's filing due date for the year if the individual had not died, (a return must be filed) by the individual's legal representatives on or before the day that is the later of the day on or before which the return would otherwise be required to be filed and the day that is 6 months after the day of death.

2-34.   For an individual whose filing due date is April 30, this provision means that if death occurs between November 1 of the previous year and April 30 of the current year, the return for the previous year does not have to be filed until six months after the date of death.

Example   An individual who is not involved in an unincorporated business dies on March 1, 2008 without having filed a 2007 return.

Analysis   The due date for the 2007 return is September 1, 2008, six months after the individual's death.   The due date for the 2008 final return is April 30, 2009.

2-35.   The provision works somewhat differently for an individual with business income and a June 15 filing due date. If such an individual dies between November 1 and December 15 of a taxation year, the later of six months after the date of death and the normal filing due date, will be the normal filing date of June 15. This means that for decedents with business income and a June 15 filing due date, the six month extension is available if they die between December 16 of a taxation year and June 15 of the following year.

Example   An individual who owns an unincorporated business dies on May 2, 2008 without having filed a 2007 tax return.

Analysis   The due date for the 2007 return is November 2, 2008, six months after the individual's death. The due date for the 2008 final return is June 15, 2009.

Exercise Two-2

Subject: Deceased Taxpayer Filing Date

Ms. Sally Cheung dies on February 15, 2008. Her 2007 and 2008 Net Income included income from an unincorporated business. Her representatives must file her 2007 and 2008 tax returns by what dates?

End of Exercise. Solution available in Study Guide.

Instalment Payments For Individuals

Basis For Requiring Instalments

2-36.   As we have noted, for many individuals the withholding of taxes constitutes the major form of tax payment in any taxation year. However, in situations where an individual has large amounts of income that are not subject to withholding (e.g., self-employment income or investment income), quarterly instalment payments may have to be made towards the current year's tax liability.

2-37.   In the *Income Tax Act*, the requirement for paying instalments is stated in terms of when instalments are not required. Specifically, no instalments are required if:

ITA 156.1(2)(b)   The individual's net tax owing for the particular year, or for each of the 2 preceding taxation years, does not exceed the individual's instalment threshold for that year.

2-38.   In provinces other than Quebec, "net tax owing" is the amount, if any, by which the total federal and provincial tax owing for a particular year, exceeds all tax withheld for that year. An "individual's instalment threshold" is defined in ITA 156.1(1) as $3,000. In Quebec, net tax owing only includes federal taxes and the instalment threshold is $1,800.

2-39.   While the legislation is based on when instalments are not required, it is usually more useful to give guidance in terms of when instalments are required. On this basis, the rule is that an individual will be required to make instalment payments if his "net tax owing" is greater than $3,000 in:

- the current year; and
- either of the two preceding years.

Due Dates For Individuals

2-40.   For individuals required to pay instalments, the quarterly payments are due on March 15, June 15, September 15, and December 15.

Determining Amounts Of Instalments

2-41.   In simple terms, the required instalments will be based on the net tax owing divided by four. The *Canada Pension Plan Act* provides for instalments identical to that of the *Income Tax Act*. Since the CRA administers the Canada Pension Plan (CPP), where an individual has CPP contributions payable on self-employed income, the instalments are based on the total of net tax owing and CPP contributions payable.

2-42.   In determining the amount to be paid as instalments, individuals have a choice of three alternatives, which can be described as follows:

Alternative 1   One-quarter of the estimated net tax owing for the current taxation year [ITA 156(1)(a)(i)].

Alternative 2   One-quarter of the net tax owing for the immediately preceding taxation year [ITA 156(1)(a)(ii)].

Alternative 3   The March 15 and June 15 instalments based on one-quarter of the net tax owing for the second preceding taxation year. The instalments for September 15 and December 15 based on one-half of the excess of the net tax owing for the preceding year over one-half of the net tax owing for the second preceding year [ITA 156(1)(b)]. Note that one-half of the net tax owing for the second preceding year is the amount that should have been paid in the first two instalments under this approach.

CRA's Instalment Reminder

2-43.   It is likely that the majority of individual taxpayers are not capable of calculating their required instalments. To assist such individuals, the CRA sends out quarterly Instalment Reminders. Taxpayers are assured that, if they pay the amounts specified in these reminders on the required dates, no interest will be assessed for late instalments.

2-44.   The amounts specified in these Instalment Reminders are based on Alternative 3. The CRA uses this alternative because it is the only choice for which it can be assured of having the required information by the date on which the instalments are due for the following reasons:

- As tax returns do not have to be filed until either April 30 or June 15 of the year following the current taxation year, the CRA could not be assured of having a taxpayer's net tax owing information for either the current or the preceding year on the March 15 and June 15 instalment due dates.

- Similarly, they would not have the information required to calculate instalments based on the current year's net tax owing on the September 15 and December 15 instalment due dates.

2-45.   Given this situation, Alternative 3 is the only approach that could be used by the CRA to provide taxpayers with instalment information that would unequivocally avoid any assessment of interest.

2-46.   While using the amounts specified in the Instalment Reminder is a risk free solution to remitting instalments, it may not be the best answer for an individual taxpayer. If, for example, the individual's net tax owing has declined over the last three years, Alternative 1 or Alternative 2 would be better choices in terms of deferring the payment of taxes.

2-47.   However, in choosing these alternatives, the taxpayer is basing some or all of his payments on estimates. If his estimates are too low, he will be assessed interest. Alternatively, if they are too high, he is making an interest free loan to the government.

2-48.   As a final point, you should note that Alternatives 2 and 3 will usually result in the same total amount of instalment payments. However, one of the two methods will be preferable in terms of deferral of payments. The choice will depend on whether net tax owing in the second preceding taxation year is higher than net tax owing in the preceding year (Alternative 2 will be better) or lower (Alternative 3 will be better).

Example Of Instalments For Individuals

2-49.   A simple example will serve to illustrate the alternative approaches to calculating instalments.

> **Example** Mr. Hruba is not subject to any withholding and has the following amounts of net tax owing:
>
> | | |
> |---|---:|
> | 2005 | $20,000 |
> | 2006 | 32,000 |
> | 2007 (Estimated) | 24,000 |
>
> **Analysis** The use of alternative 1 based on the 2007 estimate of $24,000 would result in quarterly instalments of $6,000 ($24,000 ÷ 4). The total instalments would be $24,000.
>
> Alternative 2, based on the 2006 figure of $32,000 is clearly the worst alternative. The quarterly instalments would be $8,000 ($32,000 ÷ 4), totaling $32,000 for the year.
>
> Under alternative 3 (used in the CRA's Instalment Reminders), instalments 1 and 2 would each be $5,000 ($20,000 ÷ 4). However, instalments 3 and 4 would each be $11,000 [($32,000 - $10,000) ÷ 2], resulting in a total of $32,000.
>
> This analysis would suggest that alternative 1 provides the best solution. While the first two payments under alternative 3 are somewhat lower ($5,000 vs. $6,000), the total amount under alternative 1 is significantly lower ($24,000 vs. $32,000).

2-50.   As a final point here we would note that, once a particular alternative is selected, it must be applied consistently. While there are situations where it could be to the taxpayer's advantage to change alternatives for the third and fourth instalment payments, this is not acceptable to the CRA.

Exercise Two-3

Subject: Individual Instalments

Mrs. Carter, a resident of Ontario, had net tax owing for 2005 of $3,500, net tax owing for 2006 of $4,000, and expects to have net tax owing for 2007 of $1,500. Is she required to make instalment payments for 2007? If so, what would be the minimum quarterly payment?

Exercise Two-4

Subject: Individual Instalments

Mr. John Lee, a resident of Newfoundland, had net tax owing for 2005 of $3,500, net tax owing for 2006 of $1,500, and expects to have net tax owing for 2007 of $4,500. Is he required to make instalment payments for 2007? If so, what would be the minimum quarterly payment?

Exercise Two-5

Subject: Individual Instalments

Mr. Farnsworth had net tax owing for 2005 of $25,000, net tax owing for 2006 of $37,000, and expects to have net tax owing for 2007 of $32,000. What would be his minimum instalments for 2007 and when would they be due?

End of Exercises. Solutions available in Study Guide.

Interest

When Interest Is Charged

2-51.   Interest is assessed on any amounts that are not paid when they are due. This would include:

- Any balance owing for a taxation year on April 30th of the following year. We would remind you that the amount owing is due on April 30th, without regard to whether the taxpayer's filing due date is April 30 or June 15.
- Any portion of a required instalment payment that is not remitted on the required due date.

2-52.   Interest is calculated on a daily basis on these amounts. In the case of amounts owing on April 30th, the start date for interest is May 1, with the accrual continuing until the amounts are paid. For deficient instalment amounts, the interest clock starts ticking on the date the instalment is due. This accrual would continue until an offset occurs (see next paragraph) or the due date for the return. At this latter date, further interest would be based on the amount owing at that date.

2-53.   A further important point here is that interest accrued on late or deficient instalments can be offset by making instalment payments prior to their due date, or by paying an amount in excess of the amount required (creating contra interest). Note, however, if early or excess payments are made when there is no accrual of interest owed on late or deficient instalments, the government will not pay interest to the taxpayer on the excess.

Prescribed Rate Of Interest

2-54.   There are a number of provisions in the *Income Tax Act* which require the use of an assumed rate of interest. In order to implement these provisions, ITR 4301 specifies a prescribed rate of interest. As defined in this Regulation, the regular prescribed rate is determined as a quarterly rate that is based on the effective yield on three month Government of Canada treasury bills during the first month of the preceding quarter.

2-55.   At one point in time, there was a single prescribed rate. However, the government found that this rate was sufficiently low that it was commonly advantageous for taxpayers not to make required tax payments. To solve this problem, they added 4 percent to the basic rate as described in the preceding paragraph. At the same time, they established a third rate to be used when amounts were owed to taxpayers. As a result, there are, in effect, three prescribed rates:

Regular Rate   This rate, described in Paragraph 2-54, is applicable for all purposes except amounts owing to and from the CRA (e.g., the determination of the taxable benefit for an employee who receives an interest free loan from an employer). For the first quarter of 2007, this rate was 5 percent.

Regular Rate Plus 2 Percent   This rate is applicable when calculating interest on refunds to the taxpayer. For the first quarter of 2007, this rate was 7 percent.

Regular Rate Plus 4 Percent   This rate is applicable when calculating interest on late or deficient instalments, unpaid source deductions, and other amounts owing to the CRA. For the first quarter of 2007, this rate was 9 percent. Note that amounts paid to the CRA under this provision are not deductible for any taxpayer.

2-56.   Recent rates applicable to amounts owing to the Minister, including the extra 4 percentage points, are as follows:

Quarter	2005	2006	2007
First (**Rates include extra 4 percent**)	7%	7%	9%
Second	7%	8%	9%
Third	7%	8%	N/A
Fourth	7%	9%	N/A

2-57.   Since the beginning of 2005, this rate has been 7 percent or higher. This rate is higher than rates on some types of consumer debt (e.g., home mortgages), thereby reducing the incentive to use funds to pay off this type of debt in lieu of making instalment payments.

2-58.   In other cases, where taxpayers are subject to high interest rates on other balances, making instalment payments will be less attractive. For example, interest charged on outstanding balances on some credit cards is calculated using annual rates that are higher than 20 percent. In this type of situation, it would clearly be advantageous to pay off the credit card debt in lieu of paying instalments.

Penalties

Late Filing Penalty

2-59.   If the deadline for filing an income tax return is not met, a penalty is assessed under ITA 162(1). For a first offence, this penalty amounts to 5 percent of the tax that was unpaid at the filing due date, plus 1 percent for each complete month the unpaid tax is outstanding up to a maximum of 12 months. This penalty would be in addition to interest on the amounts due. If there are no taxes owed on the due date, or if the taxpayer is entitled to a refund, the late filing penalty would be nil.

2-60.   If the taxpayer has been charged a late filing penalty in any of the three preceding taxation years, ITA 162(2) can double the penalty on the second offence to 10 percent of the tax owing, plus 2 percent per month up to a maximum of 20 months.

2-61.   In terms of tax planning, the penalty for late filing is sufficiently severe that individuals should make every effort to file their income tax returns no later than the deadline (April 30 or

June 15), even if all of the taxes owing cannot be paid at that time. This is of particular importance if they have filed late in one of the three preceding years.

2-62.   This point is sometimes forgotten when the previous offence resulted in a negligible penalty. The penalty for a second offence will double, even if the amount involved in the first penalty was very small.

Late Or Deficient Instalments Penalty

2-63.   There is no penalty for late payment of income taxes or on moderate amounts of late or deficient instalments. However, there is a penalty when large amounts of late or deficient instalments are involved. This penalty is specified in ITA 163.1 and is equal to 50 percent of the amount by which the interest owing on the late or deficient instalments exceeds the greater of $1,000 and 25 percent of the interest that would be owing if no instalments were made. As this penalty does not kick in unless the amount of interest exceeds $1,000, it would only apply to fairly large amounts of late or deficient instalments.

Exercise Two-6

Subject: Individual Instalments Penalty

Despite the fact that her net tax owing has been between $3,000 and $4,000 in the two previous years, and is expected to be a similar amount during 2007, Mary Carlos has made no instalment payments for 2007. In addition, she is two months late in filing her 2007 tax return. What penalties will be assessed for the 2007 taxation year?

End of Exercise.   Solution available in Study Guide.

Due Date For Balance Owing - Individuals

General Rule

2-64.   If the combination of amounts withheld and instalments paid falls short of the total taxes payable for the taxation year, there will be a balance owing. As we have previously noted, for a living individual this balance is due on April 30 of the following year, regardless of whether the taxpayer qualifies for the June 15 filing due date.

Deceased Taxpayer

2-65.   For a deceased taxpayer, the due date for the amount owing generally coincides with the due date for the return of the year of death and the preceding year. As with living individuals, the due date for the amount owing is not extended for deceased individuals with business income for whom the June 15 filing due date is relevant.

> **Example** Before filing her 2007 tax return, Joanne Rivers dies on March 31, 2008. For 2007 and 2008, all of her income was from employment. While she was not required to make instalment payments in either year, it is likely that there will be a small net tax owing for both years. What are the due dates for these amounts?
>
> **Analysis** Her 2007 return will be due on September 30, 2008, six months after her death. Any balance owing for 2007 will be due at that time. Her final return for 2008 will be due on April 30, 2009. Any balance owing for 2008 will be due at that time.

Returns And Payments - Corporations

Due Date For Corporate Returns

2-66.   Unlike the case with individuals, the taxation year of a corporation can end on any day of the calendar year. This makes it impossible to have a uniform filing date and, as a consequence, the filing deadline for corporations is specified as six months after the fiscal year end of the company.

2-67.   Corporations (other than corporations that are registered charities) that are resident in Canada at any time in the year, carry on business in Canada, have a taxable capital gain, dispose of Taxable Canadian Property, or would be subject to Canadian tax if not for an international tax treaty, are required to file Form T2 within this specified period. Information from the financial statements must accompany this form, along with other required schedules and information.

Instalment Payments For Corporations

2-68.   Corporations are generally required to make monthly instalment payments throughout their taxation year. However, this requirement is eliminated if either the estimated taxes payable for the current year or the taxes paid for the preceding taxation year do not exceed $3,000. When instalments are required, they must be paid on or before the last day of each month, with the amount being calculated on the basis of one of three alternatives. As laid out in ITA 157(1)(a), these alternatives are as follows:

1.   Twelve instalments, each based on 1/12 of the estimated tax payable for the current year.

2.   Twelve instalments, each based on 1/12 of the tax that was payable in the immediately preceding year.

3.   Two instalments, each based on 1/12 of the tax that was payable in the second preceding year, followed by 10 instalments based on 1/10 of the amount by which the taxes paid in the immediately preceding year exceeds the sum of the first two instalments.

2-69.   Choosing between these alternatives is usually a relatively simple matter. The instalment base that provides the minimum cash outflow and the greatest amount of deferral should be the one selected. For businesses that are experiencing year to year increases in their taxes payable, the third alternative will generally meet this objective.

Example The Marshall Company estimates that its 2007 taxes payable will be $153,000. In 2006, the Company paid taxes of $126,000. The corresponding figure for 2005 was $96,000.

Analysis Given the preceding information, the choices for instalment payments would be:

1.   Twelve instalments of $12,750 each ($153,000 ÷ 12).
2.   Twelve instalments of $10,500 each ($126,000 ÷ 12).
3.   Two instalments of $8,000 each ($96,000 ÷ 12) and 10 instalments of $11,000 each [($126,000 - $16,000) ÷ 10]

While the cash outflows under alternative 3 total the same amount as those under alternative 2, alternative 3 would be selected because it permits a somewhat larger deferral of the payments.

2-70.   There is a technical point involving situations where the approach that has the lowest interest cost does not provide the lowest amount of payments. Consider the following:

Example   Nordell Ltd. estimates that its 2007 tax payable will be $99,000. In 2006, the Company paid taxes of $100,000. The corresponding figure for 2005 was nil.

Analysis   In terms of the time value of money, the best approach here would be to pay nothing for the first two instalments, followed by 10 payments of $10,000 ($100,000 ÷ 10). While the total payments would be slightly greater than the $99,000 that would be paid using the current year's base, this could still be attractive because of the large amount of deferral resulting from making no payments in the first two months. Unfortunately, ITA 161(4.1) indicates that, unless payments are based on the approach that produces minimum instalments for the year, interest could be assessed. As this approach would require the use of the current year as the instalment base, interest could be assessed with respect to the $8,250 ($99,000 ÷ 12) that should have been paid in each of the first two months of the taxation year.

Exercise Two-7

Subject: Corporate Instalments

Madco Ltd. has a December 31 year end. For 2005, its tax payable was $52,000, while for 2006, the amount was $89,000. For 2007, its estimated tax payable is $104,000. What would be the minimum instalments for 2007 and when would they be due?

Exercise Two-8

Subject: Corporate Instalments

Fadco Inc. has a December 31 year end. For 2005, its tax payable was $152,000, while for 2006, the amount was $104,000. For 2007, its estimated tax payable is $67,000. What would be the minimum instalments for 2007 and when would they be due?

End of Exercises. Solutions available in Study Guide.

Due Date For Balance Owing - Corporations

2-71.   Regardless of the instalment base selected, any remaining taxes are due within two months of the corporation's fiscal year end. An exception is made in the case of companies that claim the small business deduction and are a Canadian controlled private corporation throughout the year. For these corporations, the due date is three months after their fiscal year end. Note that the final due date for payment is earlier than the due date for filing returns. For example, a company with a March 31 year end that is not eligible for the small business deduction would not have to file its tax return until September 30. However, all of its taxes would be due on May 31. This means that this final payment will often have to be based on an estimate of the total amount of taxes payable.

Exercise Two-9

Subject: Corporate Due Date

The taxation year end for Radco Inc. is January 31, 2007. Indicate the date on which the corporate tax return must be filed, as well as the date on which any final payment of taxes is due.

End of Exercise. Solution available in Study Guide.

Interest And Penalties For Corporations

2-72.   The rules for calculating and paying interest on late payments of corporate income taxes are the same as those that apply to individuals, including the fact that such interest payments are not deductible. These rules were covered previously beginning in Paragraph 2-51. Note, however, that it is especially important that corporations avoid interest on late tax or instalment payments. Since corporations can usually deduct the interest expense that they incur, the payment of non-deductible interest on late tax payments represents an extremely high cost source of financing. For example, if a corporation is paying taxes at a rate of 35 percent, interest at a non-deductible rate of 9 percent is the equivalent of a deductible interest rate of 13.8 percent [9% ÷ (1 - .35)].

2-73.   The previously covered penalties applicable to individuals for late filing of returns and for large amounts of late instalments (see Paragraph 2-59) are equally applicable to corporations. In addition to the penalties applicable to individuals, ITA 235 contains a further penalty applicable to large corporations. It calls for a penalty equal to .0005 percent per month of a corporation's Taxable Capital Employed In Canada. (This is a technical definition that will be discussed in Chapter 15.) This will be assessed for a maximum period of 40 months.

2-74.   This is a fairly harsh penalty in that, unlike the usual penalties that are based on any additional tax payable at the time the return should have been filed, this penalty is based on the capital of the enterprise, without regard to earnings or tax payable for the year. For example, CNR has Shareholders' Equity (roughly the equivalent of Taxable Capital Employed In Canada) of $4.857 billion. If the .0005 percent penalty was applied to this balance for 40 months, the total penalty would exceed $97 million.

2-75. This additional penalty was introduced in 1991 to deal with what the CRA considered to be an excessive number of large corporations failing to file their returns by their due date. Given the harsh nature of this penalty, it is likely that most corporations will take steps to avoid its assessment.

Returns And Payments - Trusts

Testamentary Trusts

2-76.   ITA 108 defines a testamentary trust as one that arises on the death of an individual. Such trusts can have a fiscal year other than a calendar year and, as a consequence, their filing dates will vary. The basic rule is that the T3 return must be filed within 90 days of the end of the trust's taxation year.

2-77.   With respect to instalments, testamentary trusts are not required to make these payments. If the trust has a Tax Payable balance, this amount is due when the return is filed. If a return is not filed by the filing due date, or if payment of any Tax Payable is not made at this time, testamentary trusts are subject to the same interest and penalty provisions that are applicable to individuals.

Inter Vivos Trusts

2-78.   As defined in ITA 108, an inter vivos trust is any trust other than a testamentary trust. In general, such trusts are those that are established by a living individual. This type of trust is required to use the calendar year as its taxation year and, as a consequence, all such trusts will have a common filing date. In this case, the date is 90 days after December 31 of the relevant taxation year, on March 31.

2-79.   From a technical point of view, inter vivos trusts should make instalment payments. However, this requirement has been waived on an administrative basis. This means that the full amount of Tax Payable for an inter vivos trust is due when the trust's tax return is filed. If the return is not filed by the filing due date, or if payment of any Tax Payable is not made at this time, inter vivos trusts are subject to the same interest and penalty provisions that are applicable to individuals.

Income Tax Information Returns

2-80.   ITA 221(1)(d) gives the CRA the right to require certain taxpayers to file information returns in addition to the returns in which they report their taxable income. These information returns are detailed in Part II of the Income Tax Regulations and must be filed using a prescribed form. Common examples of these returns and the related prescribed form would be as follows:

T3   This form is used by trustees (which includes trustees of some mutual funds) and executors to report the allocation of the trust's income.

T4   This form is used by employers to report remuneration and taxable benefits paid to employees and the various amounts withheld for source deductions.

T5 This form is used by organizations to report interest, dividend, and royalty payments.

T4RSP This form is used by trustees to report payments out of Registered Retirement Savings Plans.

Foreign Reporting Requirements

2-81. As is explained in Chapter 3, residents of Canada are liable for income taxes on their worldwide income. This means, for example, that if a Canadian resident has a bank account in the United Kingdom, any interest earned on that account should be reported in the appropriate Canadian tax return.

2-82. In an attempt to ensure that all foreign income is reported by Canadian residents, an information return for foreign income must be filed by certain taxpayers. The filing requirement for the form is as follows:

T1135 Canadian resident individuals, corporations, and trusts, as well as partnerships, who held certain property outside Canada with a total cost amount of more than $100,000 at any time in the tax year, have to file Form T1135, "Foreign Income Verification Statement".

2-83. The reporting requirement is for specified foreign property that includes the following:

- Funds in foreign bank accounts.
- Shares of non-resident corporations (even if held by a Canadian stockbroker).
- Land and buildings located outside Canada (other than personal use property).
- Interests in mutual funds that are organized in a foreign jurisdiction.
- Debts owed to residents by non-residents.
- An interest in a partnership where non-resident members are entitled to 90 percent or more of the share of partnership income, and the partnership holds specified foreign property.
- Patents, copyrights, or trademarks held outside Canada.

2-84. The following items are not included in the definition of specified foreign property:

- Property used exclusively to carry on an active business.
- Personal use property, such as a cottage.
- Shares or debt of a non-resident corporation or trust that is a foreign affiliate.
- An interest in a U.S. Individual Retirement Account (IRA).
- An interest in a non-resident trust that provides pension or other employee benefits, but that does not pay income tax in the jurisdiction where it is resident.

2-85. While there was much weeping and gnashing of teeth when this requirement was introduced, it has likely resulted in a significant increase in the reporting of income on foreign property. This is particularly true in view of the harsh penalties associated with the requirement. A penalty of $500 per month for up to 24 months can be assessed for a failure to file this form. This will double if a demand to file is served. A further penalty of 5 percent of the cost of any unreported property, less other penalties assessed, may be applicable.

Refunds

2-86. When tax has been withheld from income and/or instalments have been paid, the CRA's assessment may show that there has been an overpayment of income tax. In this situation, the taxpayer is entitled to a refund of any excess payments and, in the great majority of cases, such refunds are sent without any further action being taken. If, for some reason, the refund is not made, the taxpayer can apply for it in writing within the normal reassessment period (see later material in this Chapter). However, if there are other tax liabilities outstanding, such as amounts owing from prior years, the Minister has the right to apply the refund against these liabilities.

2-87.   A further point here is that refunds will not generally be made if the return is filed more than three years after the end of the relevant taxation year (e.g., a refund on a 2003 tax return that is filed in 2007 will not be paid).

2-88.   Interest is paid on overpayments of income tax at the rate prescribed in ITR 4301 (the regular rate, plus two percentage points). For individuals, the interest begins to accrue on the later of two dates:

- 30 days after the balance due date (generally, April 30); or
- 30 days after the return is filed.

2-89.   For an individual with business or professional income, the normal filing date would be June 15. If such an individual was entitled to a refund and waited until this date to file, interest would not begin to accrue until July 15.

2-90.   For corporations, interest on refunds also begins to accrue at the later of two dates. These are:

- 120 days after the corporate year end; or
- 30 days after the corporation's tax return is filed (unless it is not filed prior to the due date, in which case the due date is applicable).

2-91.   An option available to corporations that is not available to individuals, is the ability to request on the corporate return that the refund be transferred to the corporation's tax instalment account. The transfer would normally be done more quickly than the issuance of a refund cheque. This could be advantageous if the corporation was required to pay instalments, as there would be less delay in the corporation's making use of the refund.

Books And Records

2-92.   For income tax purposes, every person carrying on a business, as well as every person who is required to pay or collect taxes, must keep adequate books and records. This requirement is found in ITA 230. Such records must be maintained at the taxpayer's place of business or at the individual's residence in Canada.

2-93.   As specified in ITA 230(4), the general retention period is 6 years. However, ITR 5800 provides prescribed periods for certain specific types of situations (e.g., corporations that have been dissolved). Guidance on the application of these rules can be found in IC 78-10R4, "Books And Records Retention/Destruction".

Assessments

Initial Assessments

2-94.   ITA 152(1) requires that the Minister shall, with all due dispatch, examine each return of income and assess the tax as well as the interest and penalties payable. After examining the return, the Minister is required to send a notice of assessment to the person who filed the income tax return. In the case of individuals, this notice of assessment is usually received within one or two months of filing, especially if the return was filed electronically. A somewhat longer period is normally required for corporate income tax assessments.

Reassessments

2-95.   The first notice of assessment is based on a quick pass through the data in the return to check for completeness and arithmetic accuracy. If no obvious errors are found, it will simply indicate that the Minister accepts the information that was included in the taxpayer's return. It does not, however, free the taxpayer from additional scrutiny of the return.

2-96.   For individuals, most trusts, and Canadian controlled private corporations, reassessment must normally occur within three years of the day of mailing of an original assessment. This period is extended to four years for other corporations because of the greater complexity that may be involved in the review process.

2-97.   As set out in ITA 152(4), the general time limits can be ignored and the Minister may reassess:

- At any time, if the taxpayer or person filing the return has made any misrepresentation that is attributable to neglect, carelessness or willful default, or has committed any fraud in filing the return or in supplying information under the *Income Tax Act*.

- At any time, if the taxpayer has filed a waiver of the three year time limit. A taxpayer can revoke such a waiver at any time. The waiver remains in effect for six months after revocation.

- ITA 152(4.2) allows for reassessment outside the normal reassessment period if an individual or testamentary trust has requested a reduction in taxes, interest, or penalties.

- ITA 152(4.3) indicates that reassessment can occur beyond the normal reassessment period when reassessment within the normal period affects a balance outside of this period. An example of this type of situation could involve a loss being carried back in order to claim a refund of taxes paid. For example, if a loss incurred by an individual in 2006 was being carried back to 2003, this addition of three years means that the 2003 taxation year of that individual can be reassessed until 2010 (2010 is six years after 2004, the year in which the 2003 tax return was filed).

- ITA 152(6) allows reassessment outside the normal reassessment period in situations where the taxpayer is claiming certain specified deductions for that year (e.g, a deduction for the carry over of a foreign tax credit).

Adjustments To Income Tax Returns

2-98.   There is no general provision in the *Income Tax Act* for filing a complete and detailed amended return and, in fact, such returns are generally not filed. However, this does not mean that amounts included in the returns of previous years cannot be altered. It simply means that, in most cases, the adjustment process takes place through the use of a letter, a prescribed form or through the CRA web site, rather than through the filing of a completely revised tax return for the year in question.

2-99.   Statutory authority for certain adjustments is found in ITA 152(6) which requires the Minister of National Revenue to reassess certain specific changes in the returns of previous years. This provision requires reassessment for a previous year when a current year loss is carried back to that year. This carry back is implemented for individuals through Form T1A, "Request For Loss Carryback", and for corporations through Schedule 4, "Corporation Loss Continuity And Application". These forms are included in the income tax return for the year in which the loss was incurred.

2-100.   IC 75-7R3, "Reassessment of a Return of Income", provides an administrative solution to the problem of adjustments to returns. It permits such adjustments if the following conditions are met:

- the CRA is satisfied that the previous assessment was incorrect;
- the reassessment can be made within the normal reassessment period (or the taxpayer has filed a waiver);
- the requested decrease in taxable income does not solely depend on an increase in a permissive deduction such as capital cost allowance;
- the change is not based solely on a successful appeal to the courts by another taxpayer; and

• the taxpayer's return has been filed within three years of the end of the year to which it relates.

2-101.   For individuals, changes can be requested through the Internet, by using the password protected My Account service, or by mailing Form T1-ADJ, "T1 Adjustment Request", or by sending a letter detailing the adjustment requested. The calculations required to issue a reassessment are taken care of by the CRA. This informal procedure can be used any time within the normal reassessment period, provided the return has been filed within three years of the end of the year to which it relates.

2-102.   IC 84-1 describes administrative provisions for situations where a business wishes to alter a permissive deduction. This could happen, for example, when an enterprise has a loss that it cannot carry back in full. This results in a carry forward that can be lost if the business does not produce sufficient taxable income to absorb it in the relevant carry forward period.

2-103.   In such a situation, the enterprise may wish to minimize the loss carry forward amount by revising the capital cost allowance taken in the previous year. Such revisions are only permitted when they do not change the taxes payable for the previous year. In general, this will only happen when the downward revision in capital cost allowance is accompanied by an equivalent increase in the amount of loss being carried back to that year.

Appeals

Consent Form

2-104.   At the initial stages of any dispute, a taxpayer may wish to represent himself. However, if complex issues are involved, or if the dispute progresses to a later stage where procedures require more formal representation, a taxpayer may wish to authorize some other party to act as their representative.

2-105.   In order to provide this authorization, the taxpayer must file Form T1013, "Authorizing Or Canceling A Representative" with the CRA. If a signed Consent Form is not on file, the CRA will not discuss the issue under dispute with anyone other than the involved taxpayer.

Informal Request For Adjustments

2-106.   If a taxpayer disagrees with an assessment or reassessment, the usual first step in the process of disputing the assessment is to contact the CRA immediately. In some cases the proposed change or error can be corrected or resolved through telephone contact or by letter.

Notice Of Objection

General Rules

2-107.   If the informal contact does not resolve the issue in question, ITA 165(1) gives the taxpayer the right to file a notice of objection. While its use is not required, Form T400A, "Objection", can be used for this purpose. This form simply requires a statement of the relevant facts along with the reasons for the objection. It is addressed to the Chief of Appeals in the Tax Services Office, or to any Taxation Centre.

2-108.   For corporations and inter vivos trusts, a notice of objection must be filed within 90 days of the date on which the notice of assessment was mailed. For individuals and testamentary trusts, the rules are more generous. For these taxpayers, the notice of objection must be filed before the later of:

• 90 days from the date of mailing of the notice of assessment or reassessment; or
• one year from the filing due date for the return under assessment or reassessment.

Example   An individual required to file on April 30, 2007, files on March 26, 2007. A notice of assessment was mailed on May 14, 2007.

Analysis   For this individual, a notice of objection could be filed up to the later of August 12, 2007 (90 days after the mailing) and April 30, 2008 (one year after the filing due date). In this case, the relevant date would be April 30, 2008, without regard for the fact that the return was actually filed on March 26, 2007.

2-109. When an individual dies after October of the assessment year and before May of the following year, you will recall that the filing date for the return is extended to six months after the date of death, thereby extending the date for filing a notice of objection by the same number of months.

2-110. Under ITA 166.1(1), a taxpayer can request an extension of the filing deadline for the notice of objection. However, under ITA 166.1(7) the application or request will not be granted unless:

(a) the application is made within one year after the expiration of the time otherwise limited by this Act for serving a notice of objection or making a request, as the case may be; and

(b) the taxpayer demonstrates that

(i) within the time otherwise limited by this Act for serving such a notice or making such a request, as the case may be, the taxpayer
(1) was unable to act or to instruct another to act in the taxpayer's name, or
(2) had a bona fide intention to object to the assessment or make the request,

(ii) given the reasons set out in the application and the circumstances of the case, it would be just and equitable to grant the application, and

(iii) the application was made as soon as circumstances permitted.

2-111. If the request is denied by the Minister, the taxpayer can appeal for a time extension to the Tax Court of Canada. This is provided for under ITA 166.2.

2-112. Once the notice of objection is filed, the Minister is required to reply to the taxpayer:

- vacating the assessment,
- confirming it (i.e., refusing to change it),
- varying the amount, or
- reassessing.

2-113. Unresolved objections are subject to review by the Chief of Appeals in each Tax Services Office. These appeals sections are instructed to operate independently of the assessing divisions and should provide an unbiased second opinion. If the matter remains unresolved after this review, the taxpayer must either accept the Minister's assessment or, alternatively, continue to pursue the matter to a higher level of appeal.

2-114. In the November, 2004 Auditor General's report, it was noted that in 2003-2004, over 59,000 income tax and GST objections were filed. Of these, 57,600 were resolved by appeals officers.

Rules For Large Corporations
2-115. The Department of Finance appears to believe that it has been the practice of certain corporate taxpayers to delay the dispute process by filing vague objections in the first instance, and subsequently bringing in fresh issues as the appeal process goes forward.

2-116. To prevent this perceived abuse, the Department has issued ITA 165(1.11). This legislation requires that, in filing a notice of objection, a corporation must specify each issue to be decided, the dollar amount of relief sought for each particular issue, and the facts and reasons relied on by the corporation in respect of each issue.

2-117. If the corporation objects to a reassessment or additional assessment made by the CRA, or appeals to the Tax Court of Canada, the objection or appeal can be only with respect to issues and dollar amounts properly dealt with in the original notice of objection. There is an exception to this general rule for new issues that are raised by the CRA on assessment or reassessment. These limitations are only applicable to "large corporations", defined in terms of a liability to pay the Part I.3 tax on large corporations (see Chapter 15).

Exercise Two-10

Subject: Notice Of Objection

Mr. Jerry Fall filed his 2007 tax return as required on April 30, 2008. He receives his notice of assessment during June, 2008. However, on June 1, 2009, he receives a reassessment indicating that he owes additional taxes, as well as interest on the unpaid amounts. The reassessment was mailed on May 15, 2009. What is the due date for filing a notice of objection to this reassessment?

End of Exercise. Solution available in Study Guide.

Tax Court Of Canada
Deadline For Appeal
2-118.   A taxpayer who does not find satisfaction through the notice of objection procedure may then proceed to the next level of the appeal procedure, the Tax Court of Canada. Appeals to the Tax Court of Canada can be made within 90 days of the mailing date of the Minister's response to the notice of objection which would confirm the assessment or reassessment, or 90 days after the notice of objection has been filed if the Minister has not replied. It is not possible to bypass the Tax Court of Canada and appeal directly to the Federal Court level, except in very limited circumstances [see ITA 172(3)].

Informal Procedure
2-119.   On appeal to the Tax Court of Canada, the general procedure will automatically apply unless the taxpayer elects to have his case heard under the informal procedure. The informal procedure can be elected for appeals in which the total amount of federal tax and penalty involved for a given year is less than $12,000, or where the loss in question is less than $24,000. Cases involving larger amounts can use this informal procedure, provided the taxpayer restricts the appeal to these limits.

2-120.   Advantages of the informal procedure include:

• The rules of evidence remain fairly informal, allowing the taxpayer to represent himself, or be represented by an agent other than a lawyer.
• Under the informal procedure, even if the taxpayer is unsuccessful, he cannot be asked to pay court costs.
• The informal procedure is designed as a fast-track procedure that is usually completed within 6 or 7 months whereas the general procedure may take many years.

2-121. The major disadvantage of the informal procedure is that the taxpayer generally gives up all rights to further appeals if the Court decision is unfavourable.

General Procedure
2-122.   If the general procedure applies, formal rules of evidence must be used, resulting in a situation where the taxpayer has to be represented by either himself, or legal counsel. In practical terms, this means that for cases involving substantial amounts, lawyers will usually be involved.

2-123.   Under the general procedure, if the taxpayer is unsuccessful, the Court may require that costs be paid to the Minister. Under either procedure, if the taxpayer is more than 50 percent successful (e.g., if he is claiming $10,000 and is awarded more than $5,000), the judge can order the Minister to pay all or part of the taxpayer's costs.

Appeals By The Minister
2-124.   There are situations in which the Minister may pursue a matter because of its general implications for broad groups of taxpayers. The individual taxpayer is given protection from

the costs associated with this type of appeal by the requirement that the Minister be responsible for the taxpayer's reasonable legal fees when the amount of taxes payable in question does not exceed $12,000 or the loss in dispute does not exceed $24,000. This is without regard to whether the appeal is successful.

Resolution

2-125.   Prior to the hearing by the Tax Court of Canada, discussions between the taxpayer and the Department are likely to continue. It would appear that, in the majority of cases, the dispute will be resolved prior to the actual hearing. However, if a hearing proceeds, the Court may dispose of an appeal by:

- dismissing it; or
- allowing it and
  - vacating the assessment,
  - varying the assessment, or
  - referring the assessment back to the Minister for reconsideration and reassessment.

Federal Court And The Supreme Court Of Canada

2-126.   Either the Minister or the taxpayer can appeal a general procedure decision of the Tax Court of Canada to the Federal Court of Appeal. The appeal must be made within 30 days of the date on which the Tax Court of Canada makes its decision.

2-127.   It is possible to pursue a matter beyond the Federal Court to the Supreme Court of Canada. This can be done if the Federal Court of Appeal refers the issue to the higher Court, or if the Supreme Court authorizes the appeal. These actions will not usually happen unless there are new issues or legal precedents to be dealt with and, as a result, such appeals are not common. However, when tax cases do reach the Supreme Court, they often attract a great deal of public attention.

Tax Evasion, Avoidance And Planning

Tax Evasion

2-128.   The concept of tax evasion is not difficult to understand. It was described in the now archived IC 73-10R3 as follows:

> **Paragraph 8**   Tax evasion is the **commission** or **omission** of an act knowingly, the conspiracy to commit such an act or involvement in the accommodation of such an act, which can result in a charge being laid in the Criminal Court under subsection 239(1) of the *Income Tax Act*.

2-129.   There is little ambiguity in this description as it involves deliberate attempts to deceive the taxation authorities. The most common of the offenses that fall under this description of tax evasion is probably unreported revenues of various types.

Avoidance And Planning

2-130.   When it comes to defining tax avoidance, the issue becomes more difficult. The *Income Tax Act* contains a number of specific anti-avoidance provisions. For example, ITA 69 has rules that deal with transfers of property between individuals who are not dealing at arm's length. This rule would deal with such situations as a mother transferring property to a son at an artificially low price in order to put a potential gain in the hands of the child. ITA 69 deems such transfers to be made at fair market value to the transferor, thereby preventing this type of tax avoidance from being effective.

2-131.   Since a major goal of tax planning is to avoid taxes, it would be our view that it is not possible to make a meaningful distinction between tax planning and tax avoidance. However, the government has persisted in trying to make this distinction. It appears to be their view that some tax planning arrangements, while not contravening any particular provision in the *Income Tax Act*, are so offensive that they should not be permitted. Based on this view, there have been continued attempts to find a basis for dealing with such arrangements.

2-132.   Prior to 1984, this issue was approached by applying a business purpose test. The Department assessed on the basis that a transaction which had no business purpose other than the avoidance or reduction of taxes was a sham and should not be considered acceptable for tax purposes. However, this approach was struck down by the Supreme Court in the Stubart Investments Ltd. case (84 DTC 6305).

2-133.   The case involved a transfer of the assets of a profitable subsidiary to the books of a sister subsidiary which had large accumulated losses. There was no reason for the transaction other than the desire to have the losses of the latter subsidiary absorbed before their carry forward period expired. The Supreme Court upheld the right of Stubart Investments to undertake this transaction, thereby eliminating the judicial basis for a business purpose test.

General Anti-Avoidance Rule (GAAR)

2-134.   With the Supreme Court decision in the Stubart Investments case removing the CRA's ability to assess general tax avoidance arrangements, the Department began to call for a new general anti-avoidance rule (GAAR). This was provided in the 1988 tax reform legislation in Section 245. The basic provision here is as follows:

> **Paragraph 245(2)** Where a transaction is an avoidance transaction, the tax consequences to a person shall be determined as is reasonable in the circumstances in order to deny a tax benefit that, but for this section, would result, directly or indirectly, from that transaction or from a series of transactions that includes that transaction.

2-135. The Section goes on to describe an avoidance transaction as follows:

> **ITA 245(3)**   An avoidance transaction means any transaction
>
> (a) that, but for this section, would result, directly or indirectly, in a tax benefit, unless the transaction may reasonably be considered to have been undertaken or arranged primarily for bona fide purposes other than to obtain the tax benefit; or
>
> (b) that is part of a series of transactions, which series, but for this section, would result, directly or indirectly, in a tax benefit, unless the transaction may reasonably be considered to have been undertaken or arranged primarily for bona fide purposes other than to obtain the tax benefit.

2-136.   Note that the preceding provisions provide a basic defense against the GAAR in that it does not apply to transactions which have a bona fide non-tax purpose. An additional line of defense is found in ITA 245(4) as follows:

> **ITA 245(4)**   Subsection (2) applies to a transaction only if it may reasonably be considered that the transaction
>
> (a) would, if this Act were read without reference to this section, result directly or indirectly in a misuse of the provisions of any one or more of
>   (i)   this Act,
>   (ii) the Income Tax Regulations,
>   (iii) the Income Tax Application Rules,
>   (iv) a tax treaty, or
>   (v)   any other enactment that is relevant in computing tax or any other amount payable by or refundable to a person under this Act or in determining any amount that is relevant for the purposes of that computation; or
>
> (b) would result directly or indirectly in an abuse having regard to those provisions, other than this section, read as a whole.

2-137.   Taken together, these provisions mean that the GAAR will apply to any transaction other than those where there is a bona fide non-tax purpose, or where there is no misuse or abuse of the *Act*. If a transaction is judged to be an avoidance transaction, the Section goes on to indicate that the determination of the tax consequences will be as follows:

ITA 245(5) Without restricting the generality of subsection (2), and notwithstanding any other enactment,

(a) any deduction, exemption or exclusion in computing income, taxable income, taxable income earned in Canada or tax payable or any part thereof may be allowed or disallowed in whole or in part,

(b) any such deduction, exemption or exclusion, any income, loss or other amount or part thereof may be allocated to any person,

(c) the nature of any payment or other amount may be recharacterized, and

(d) the tax effects that would otherwise result from the application of other provisions of this Act may be ignored,

in determining the tax consequences to a person as is reasonable in the circumstances in order to deny a tax benefit that would, but for this section, result, directly or indirectly, from an avoidance transaction.

2-138.   The GAAR has been heavily criticized for creating considerable uncertainty in many tax planning arrangements. Some relief from this uncertainty was provided by the issuance of IC 88-2. This Information Circular was issued in 1988, with Supplement 1 issued in 1990. These publications provide fairly detailed guidance with respect to the application of ITA 245. For example, they indicate that the following would not be considered avoidance transactions:

- the use of flow through shares
- gifts to adult children, except where the related income is given back to the parent
- most types of estate freezes (these transactions will be discussed in Chapter 21)

2-139.   In contrast, the following transactions would fall under the provisions of ITA 245:

- transitory arrangements (i.e., issuance and redemption of shares) not carried out for bona fide non-tax purposes
- a sale to an intermediary company to create a reserve, followed by a sale to a third party
- conversion of salary to capital gains by issuing preferred stock to employees entitled to profits, followed by a sale of the preferred stock

2-140.   The CRA has a GAAR Committee that reviews potential GAAR actions. As noted in a 2006 issue of Income Tax Technical News, as of June 30, 2005, 628 cases have been referred to this committee. The GAAR was approved for application in 417 of these cases. GAAR issues that were noted by the Committee include:

- International financing arrangements used to create interest expense.
- Avoidance related to the disposition of foreign affiliate shares.
- The use of stock dividends to create losses.
- Barbados spousal trust arrangements.
- Estate freezes where the future growth is shifted to offshore trusts.
- Leveraged cash donation arrangements.
- Domestic and non-resident surplus stripping.
- Abuses of retirement compensation arrangements.

2-141.   Most of these situations involve complexities that extend beyond the scope of this text.

Reasonable Expectation Of Profit (REOP)

Current Situation

2-142.   In addition to the use of GAAR, the CRA has attempted to replace the old business purpose test with a test for reasonable expectation of profit (commonly referred to as REOP). In particular, they have attempted to disallow the deduction of losses on arrangements that do not have a reasonable expectation of profit. However, under existing legislation, this approach has been rejected at the Supreme Court level. In both the Stewart case (2002 DTC

6969) and the Walls case (2002 DTC 6960), the Supreme Court indicated that, under existing legislation, expenses and losses could not be generally disallowed because there was no reasonable expectation of a profit.

2-143.   However, a note of caution is appropriate with respect to these decisions. If the undertaking involves a personal benefit or hobby element (e.g., losses incurred by a riding stable that is used extensively by the taxpayer or his family), the taxpayer will still have to show that the activities that generated the losses were undertaken in pursuit of profit.

Proposed Change

2-144.   The CRA is not a good loser. Having the administrative application of the REOP criteria shot down by the Supreme Court, the government concluded that they would solve the problem with legislation. In a release dated October 31, 2003, a new ITA 3.1(1) was proposed to apply to taxation years beginning after 2004. Its content is as follows:

> **ITA 3.1(1) (Proposed)   Limit on loss** — A taxpayer has a loss for a taxation year from a source that is a business or property only if, in the year, it is reasonable to expect that the taxpayer will realize a cumulative profit from that business or property for the period in which the taxpayer has carried on, and can reasonably be expected to carry on, that business or has held, and can reasonably be expected to hold, that property.

2-145.   This is a very important change with wide ranging implications. The accompanying technical notes make it clear that this provision must be applied on an annual basis, using objective information. Perhaps most importantly, in making the determination, a proposed ITA 3.1(2) makes it clear that capital gains and losses are not to be considered:

> **ITA 3.1(2) (Proposed)   Determination of profit** — For the purpose of subsection (1), profit is determined without reference to capital gains or capital losses.

2-146.   This inability to include capital gains will mean that many real estate and common stock investments, particularly if they are heavily financed, will not be able to meet this REOP test. The result will be an inability to deduct any losses that may arise during the period in which such investments are held.

2-147.   This proposal has been subject to significant criticism and, at this point in time (May, 2007), has not become legislation. However, like the proverbial sword of Damocles, this provision still hangs over taxpayers with an effective date extending back to 2004. This, of course, adds a significant amount of uncertainty to many tax planning arrangements.

Collection And Enforcement

Taxpayer Property

2-148.   The CRA has enforcement powers under the provisions of ITA 231.1, "Inspections" and ITA 231.2, "Requirement To Provide Documents Or Information".

2-149.   Tax officials or other persons authorized by the Minister of National Revenue have the right to enter a taxpayer's place of business, locations where anything is done in connection with the business, or any place where records related to the business are kept. Tax officials may also examine any document of another taxpayer that relates, or may relate to, the information that is, or should be, in the books and records of the taxpayer who is being audited. However, in those cases where the place of business is also a dwelling, the officials must either obtain the permission of the occupant or have a court issued warrant. In this process, the officials may audit the books and records, examine all property, and require that the taxpayer answer questions and provide assistance.

2-150.   Seizure of books and records requires a court issued warrant. If this occurs, a taxpayer may apply to have the records returned. Also requiring judicial authorization is demands for information or documents from third parties. This could include information from the files of the taxpayer's lawyer or accountant. There are additional confidentiality rules in this area that protect solicitor/client communications. However, accountant/client privilege is not protected unless they are part of the solicitor/client privilege. This usually occurs when a lawyer directs the activities of the accountant.

Collections

2-151.　As noted earlier in the Chapter, the due date for the payment of personal income taxes for a taxation year is April 30 of the following year. The due date for corporate income taxes is two months after the corporate year end (three months for Canadian controlled private corporations). Additional taxes may become payable as a result of an assessment or reassessment. If this is the case, these taxes are due at the time the notice of assessment is mailed.

2-152.　Initial collection procedures will not normally extend beyond communicating with the taxpayer about his liability and the related interest that will be charged. In the case of taxes resulting from an assessment or reassessment, the CRA cannot exercise its collection powers until:

- 90 days after the assessment or reassessment date when no objection is filed;
- 90 days from the date of the notice from the CRA appeals division confirming or varying the assessment or reassessment where an objection has been filed and no further appeal has been made; or
- 90 days after a court decision has been made and there are no further appeals.

2-153.　If informal procedures fail to result in payment of the tax owing by the defaulter, ITA 224 allows the CRA to order a taxpayer owing money to the defaulter to make payments to the Receiver General in settlement of the defaulter's liability. A common example of this would be garnishment of a defaulter's wages to pay income taxes owed. ITA 223 goes even further, allowing the CRA to obtain a judgment against a tax defaulter that can be enforced by seizure and sale of the taxpayer's property.

Other Penalties

Examples

2-154.　We have previously discussed the penalties associated with the late payment of taxes and the late filing of tax returns. There are a number of other penalties that are specified in tax legislation. Examples of such penalties would be as follows:

Failure To File An Information Return　As discussed in Paragraph 2-22, if an employer fails to file the T4 information returns by the last day of February, the penalty for each failure is $25 per day, with a minimum penalty of $100 and a maximum of $2,500.

Failure To File A Partnership Information Return　If a partnership information return is filed late, the partnership is liable for a penalty of $25 per day, with a minimum penalty of $100 and a maximum of $2,500 in each case.

False Statements Or Omissions　This penalty applies in cases of gross negligence where there is an intention to disregard the *Income Tax Act*. The penalty is the greater of $100 and 50 percent of the understated tax.

Failure To Withhold At Source Or Remit Amounts Withheld　The penalty is 10 percent of the amounts not withheld or remitted. This increases to 20 percent for a second or subsequent offence in any calendar year where gross negligence is a factor.

Evasion　Penalties here range from 50 percent to 200 percent of the relevant tax and, in addition, imprisonment for a period not exceeding two years.

Tax Advisers And Tax Return Preparers

2-155.　Civil penalties for tax advisers and tax return preparers who encourage or assist clients with tax evasive practices are found in ITA 163.2. The penalty of most concern to accountants is found in ITA 163.2(4). The penalty for participating in a misrepresentation in the preparation of a return is the greater of $1,000 and the penalty assessed on the tax return preparer's client under ITA 163(2) for making the false statement or omission. The penalty on the client is equal to 50 percent of the amount of tax avoided as a result of the misrepresentation. The total amount of the penalty is capped at $100,000, plus the gross compensation to which the tax return preparer is entitled to receive.

2-156.   IC 01-1, "Third-Party Civil Penalties", is an extensive Information Circular that contains 18 examples of the application of third-party penalties. While the examples cited in the IC and the technical notes to ITA 163.2 illustrate clear cut abuses, there are many situations in which it is to the taxpayer's advantage to pursue a more aggressive stance in claiming deductions. It is believed that these penalties discourage tax return preparers from suggesting or condoning this type of approach, out of fear that they may be liable for the third party penalties if the returns are audited. In addition, there is evidence that an increasing number of tax return preparers are refusing to service certain types of high risk clients.

Promoters Of Tax Planning Arrangements

2-157.   A penalty for misrepresentations in tax planning arrangements is specified under ITA 163.2(2). It is applicable when a person makes a statement that they either know to be false or could be reasonably expected to know to be false unless they are involved in "culpable conduct". Culpable conduct is defined in the Section as follows:

Culpable Conduct means conduct, whether an act or a failure to act, that

(a) is tantamount to intentional conduct;
(b) shows an indifference as to whether the Act is complied with; or
(c) shows a wilful, reckless or wanton disregard of the law.

2-158.   The Section makes it clear that "culpable conduct" does not generally arise when a tax adviser has relied in good faith, on information provided by the taxpayer. However, this "good faith" defense does not apply to false statements made in the course of an excluded activity. These excluded activities are described as follows:

Excluded Activity in respect of a false statement means, generally, the activity of

(a) promoting or selling (whether as principal or agent or directly or indirectly) an arrangement where it can reasonably be considered that the arrangement concerns a flow-through share or a tax shelter or is an arrangement one of the main purposes for a person's participation in which is to obtain a tax benefit; or
(b) accepting (whether as principal or agent or directly or indirectly) consideration in respect of the sale of, or participation in, such an arrangement.

2-159.   When ITA 163.2(2) is applicable, the penalty is specified under ITA 163.2(3) as the greater of $1,000 and the total of the adviser's "gross entitlements" as determined at the time the notice of assessment of the penalty is sent to that person. Gross entitlements are defined as follows:

Gross Entitlements of a person from a planning activity or a valuation activity, means all amounts to which the person is entitled, either absolutely or contingently, to receive or obtain.

Fairness Package

Basic Rules

2-160.   There is a widespread perception that the application of some of the CRA's rules on interest and penalties, as well as certain other rules, can result in individuals and other taxpayers being treated in an unfair manner. Reflecting this concern, a "fairness package" was introduced in 1991. While the implementation of this package required a number of changes in the *Income Tax Act*, specifically the addition of ITA 220(3.1) and (3.2), the guidelines for applying the rules were issued in three Information Circulars, IC 92-1, IC 92-2, and IC 92-3.

2-161.   When this legislation was introduced, requests could be made with respect to any previous taxation year. However, subsequent amendments to the legislation restricts requests to the previous 10 calendar years.

2-162.   The content of these guidelines can be briefly described as follows:

IC 92-1 - *Guidelines For Accepting Late, Amended, Or Revoked Elections* While the *Act* contains numerous elections, there is rarely any provision for revoking, amending, or making them after the specified time period has passed. This IC, which was issued in 1992, listed 14 elections that could be revoked, amended, or filed late for taxation years after 1984. Since 1992, ITR 600, "Elections", has expanded this list to over 30 items. A request would not be approved if the taxpayer had been negligent or if the request is retroactive tax planning.

IC 92-2 - *Guidelines For The Cancellation And Waiver Of Interest And Penalties* This Guideline indicates that, in certain circumstances, interest and penalties related to taxation years after 1984 can be waived. This can happen when they resulted from extraordinary circumstances beyond the taxpayer's control. Examples of this type of situation include:

- natural or human made disasters such as flood or fire;
- disruptions in civil services, such as a postal strike;
- a serious illness or accident; or
- serious emotional or mental distress, such as a death in the immediate family.

Interest and penalties may also be waived if they arose primarily because of the actions of the CRA. Examples of this would include:

- processing delays that result in the taxpayer not being informed within a reasonable time that an amount was owing;
- material available to the public contains errors that leads the taxpayer to file returns or make payments based on incorrect information;
- errors in processing;
- delays in providing information; or
- the taxpayer receives incorrect advice, for example where the CRA incorrectly advises that no instalment payments will be required for the current year.

IC 92-3 - *Guidelines For Refunds Beyond The Normal Three Year Period* This Guideline eliminates, in most cases, the normal three year limit on applying for a refund of taxes previously paid. Note, however, it does not apply if the refund relates to a permissive deduction such as capital cost allowance.

2-163.   The first two Guidelines are applicable to all taxpayers. In contrast, IC 92-3 is only applicable to individuals and testamentary trusts.

Application

2-164.   Very little has been written about the application of these fairness provisions. However, the April 16, 2002 report of the Auditor General of Canada notes that the CRA waived or cancelled an estimated $185 million in interest and penalties during the year ended March 31, 2001. It is pointed out that the CRA keeps no record of the amount of interest and penalties waived, or of the basis for the waiver or cancellation. In addition, it does not submit the underlying circumstances to systematic review at the national level to monitor for, or confirm, the consistency of decisions.

2-165.   It has become commonplace for decisions made under the authority of the fairness legislation to be challenged in court through an application for judicial review. This may result in the decision being returned to the CRA for reconsideration (see *Robertson vs. MNR* 2003 DTC 5068).

2-166.   To improve administration of the fairness provisions, the Auditor General recommends that the CRA improve the information contained in its national fairness registry, record its reasons for waiving interest and penalties, and keep records of the actual amounts waived. In addition, it suggests that the approval process be strengthened.

Key Terms Used In This Chapter

2-167.   The following is a list of the key terms used in this Chapter. These terms, and their meanings, are compiled in the Glossary Of Key Terms located at the back of the separate paper Study Guide and on the Student CD-ROM.

Assessment	Notice Of Objection
Consent Form	Penalties
EFILE	Prescribed Rate
Fairness Package	Reasonable Expectation Of Profit (REOP)
GAAR	Reassessment
Information Return	Source Deductions
Instalment Threshold	Tax Avoidance
Instalments	Tax Court Of Canada
Net Tax Owing	Tax Evasion
NETFILE	Tax Planning
Notice Of Assessment	TELEFILE

References

2-168.   For more detailed study of the material in this Chapter, we would refer you to the following:

ITA 150	Filing Returns Of Income - General Rule
ITA 151	Estimate Of Tax
ITA 152	Assessment
ITA 153(1)	Withholding
ITA 161	Interest (General)
ITA 162-163.1	Penalties
ITA 163.2	Misrepresentation Of A Tax Matter By A Third Party
ITA 164(1)	Refunds
ITA 165	Objections To Assessment
ITA 169-180	Appeals To The Tax Court Of Canada And The Federal Court Of Appeal
ITA 220-244	Administration And Enforcement
ITA 245-246	Tax Avoidance
ITR Part II	Information Returns
ITR 4301	Prescribed Rate of Interest
ITR 5800	Retention Of Books And Records
IC 71-14R3	The Tax Audit
IC 75-6R2	Required Withholding From Amounts Paid To Non-Resident Persons Providing Services In Canada
IC 75-7R3	Reassessment Of A Return Of Income
IC 78-10R4	Books And Records Retention/Destruction
IC 84-1	Revision Of CCA Claims And Other Permissive Deductions
IC 88-2	General Anti-Avoidance Rule: Section 245 Of The Income Tax Act
IC 92-1	Guidelines For Accepting Late, Amended, Or Revoked Elections
IC 92-2	Guidelines For The Cancellation And Waiver Of Interest And Penalties
IC 92-3	Guidelines For Refunds Beyond The Normal Three Year Period
IC 00-1R	Voluntary Disclosures Program
IC-01-1	Third-Party Civil Penalties
P148	Resolving Your Dispute: Objection And Appeal Rights Under The Income Tax Act
RC4163	Employer's Guide: Remitting Payroll Deductions

Problems For Self Study

(The solutions for these problems can be found in the separate Study Guide.)

Self Study Problem Two - 1

In January, 2007, you are asked to provide tax advice to Mr. Lester Gore. He has provided you with the following information about his combined federal and provincial taxes payable and the income taxes withheld by his employer for the 2005 and 2006 taxation years:

Year	Taxes Payable	Taxes Withheld
2005	$15,000	$11,500
2006	10,800	11,750

For 2007, he estimates that his combined federal and provincial taxes payable will be $17,000 and that his employer will withhold a total of $13,000 in income taxes.

He has asked you whether it will be necessary for him to pay instalments in 2007 and, if so, what the minimum amounts that should be paid are and when they should be paid.

Required: Provide the information requested by Mr. Gore.

Self Study Problem Two - 2

For its fiscal year ending December 31, 2005, Amalmor Inc. had Taxable Income of $250,000 and paid taxes of $62,500. In 2006, the corresponding figures were $320,000 and $80,000. It is estimated that for the current year ending December 31, 2007, the Company will have Taxable Income of $380,000 and taxes payable of $95,000.

Required: Determine the amount of the minimum instalments that must be made by Amalmor Inc. during 2007 and when they would be due.

Self Study Problem Two - 3

For the three years ending December 31, 2007, the taxpayer's combined federal and provincial taxes payable were as follows:

Year Ending December 31	Taxes Payable
2005	$23,540
2006	11,466
2007 (Estimated)	25,718

Case One   The taxpayer is an individual whose employer withholds combined federal and provincial taxes of $18,234 in 2005, $7,850 in 2006, and $27,346 in 2007.

Case Two   The taxpayer is an individual whose employer withholds combined federal and provincial taxes of $21,720 in 2005, $6,250 in 2006, and $21,833 in 2007.

Case Three   The taxpayer is a corporation with a taxation year that ends on December 31.

Case Four   The taxpayer is a corporation with a taxation year that ends on December 31. Assume that its combined federal and provincial taxes payable for the year ending December 31, 2006 were $32,560, instead of the $11,466 given in the problem.

Required: For each of the preceding independent Cases:

A. Determine whether the taxpayer is required to make instalment payments for the year ending December 31, 2007 and explain your conclusion.

B. Indicate the minimum instalment payments that would be required and the due date for each instalment.

Self Study Problem Two - 4

List the three types of entities that are subject to federal income taxation in Canada and, for each, state:

    A. the taxation year covered;
    B. the filing deadlines for their respective income tax returns; and
    C. how frequently income tax instalments must be made.

Self Study Problem Two - 5

Mr. Coffee is one of your major clients. He is extremely wealthy and has paid his very sizable tax payable over the years without complaint.

On August 15th of the current year, Mr. Coffee receives a notice from the CRA indicating that he is being reassessed for the preceding taxation year. The additional amount of taxes involved is $5,000, and he feels that the position of the CRA is completely unjustified.

Mr. Coffee has approached you for advice on dealing with the matter.

Required: Indicate the procedures that may be used in dealing with this dispute between the CRA and Mr. Coffee.

Assignment Problems

(The solutions for these problems are only available in
the solutions manual that has been provided to your instructor.)

Assignment Problem Two - 1

In January, 2007, you are asked to provide tax advice to Ms. Leslie Garond. She has provided
you with the following information about her combined federal and provincial taxes payable
and the income taxes withheld by her employer for the 2005 and 2006 taxation years:

Year	Taxes Payable	Taxes Withheld
2005	$22,000	$9,500
2006	18,000	9,700

For 2007, she estimates that her combined federal and provincial taxes payable will be
$14,000 and that her employer will withhold a total of $9,850 in income taxes.

She has asked you whether it will be necessary for her to pay instalments in 2007 and, if so,
what the minimum amounts that should be paid are, and when they are due.

Required: Provide the information requested by Ms. Garond.

Assignment Problem Two - 2

Because the majority of individual taxpayers have income taxes withheld at the source, not
everyone is required to make income tax instalment payments.

Required: Describe the circumstances under which an individual must make income tax
instalment payments. In addition, describe the alternative methods that can be used to determine the amount of the instalment payments.

Assignment Problem Two - 3

The fiscal year of the Sloan Company ends on October 31. During the year ending October
31, 2005, its federal taxes payable amounted to $168,000, while for the year ending October
31, 2006, the federal taxes payable were $153,000. It is estimated that federal taxes payable
for the year ending October 31, 2007 will be $144,000.

Required:

A. Calculate the instalment payments that are required for the year ending October 31, 2007
under the alternative methods available. Indicate which of the alternatives would be
preferable.

B. If the Company did not make any instalment payments towards its 2007 taxes payable,
indicate how the interest and penalty amounts assessed against it would be determined (a
detailed calculation is not required).

Assignment Problem Two - 4

For the year ending December 31, 2005, the taxpayer's combined federal and provincial taxes payable amounted to $18,000, while for the year ending December 31, 2006, the amount payable was $14,400. It is estimated that federal and provincial taxes payable for the year ending December 31, 2007 is $13,500.

Required: For each of the following independent Cases, calculate the minimum instalment payments that are required to be made towards the settlement of the taxes payable for the year ending December 31, 2007. Included in your answer should be the date that each instalment is due to be paid.

A. The taxpayer is an individual whose employer withholds combined federal and provincial taxes of $12,000 in 2005, $10,000 in 2006, and $10,000 in 2007.

B. The taxpayer is an individual whose employer withholds combined federal and provincial taxes of $7,000 in 2005, $15,000 in 2006, and $9,000 in 2007.

C. The taxpayer is a corporation with a December 31 year end.

D. The taxpayer is a corporation with a December 31 year end. Assume that its combined federal and provincial taxes payable for the year ending December 31, 2007 are estimated to be $16,000, instead of the $13,500 given in the problem.

Assignment Problem Two - 5

For the three years ending December 31, 2007, the taxpayer's combined federal and provincial taxes payable were as follows:

Year Ending December 31	Taxes Payable
2005	$56,742
2006	22,785
2007 (Estimated)	64,457

Case One   The taxpayer is a corporation with a December 31 year end.

Case Two   The taxpayer is an individual whose employer withholds combined federal and provincial taxes of $53,426 in 2005, $23,486 in 2006, and $59,426 in 2007.

Case Three   The taxpayer is an individual whose employer withholds combined federal and provincial taxes of $57,101 in 2005, $19,483 in 2006, and $58,048 in 2007.

Case Four   The taxpayer is an individual whose employer withholds combined federal and provincial taxes of $51,060 in 2005, $16,165 in 2006, and $60,472 in 2007.

Case Five   The taxpayer is a corporation with a taxation year that ends on December 31. Assume that its combined federal and provincial taxes payable for the year ending December 31, 2006 were $71,560, instead of the $22,785 given in the problem.

Required: For each of the preceding independent Cases:

A. Determine whether the taxpayer is required to make instalment payments for the year ending December 31, 2007 and explain your conclusion.

B. Indicate the minimum instalment payments that would be required and the due date for each instalment.

Assignment Problem Two - 6

In addition to interest charges on any late payment of taxes, penalties may be assessed for failure to file a return within the prescribed deadlines. These deadlines vary depending on the taxpayer.

Required: Indicate when income tax returns must be filed for each of the following types of taxpayers:

    A. Trusts.
    B. Corporations.
    C. Living individuals.
    D. Deceased individuals.

Assignment Problem Two - 7

Mr. James Simon has asked for your services with respect to dealing with a reassessment notice requesting additional tax for the 2003 taxation year which he says he has just received. Your first interview takes place on March 15, 2007, and Mr. Simon informs you that he has had considerable difficulty with the CRA in past years and, on two occasions in the past five years, he has been required to pay penalties as well as interest. With respect to the current reassessment, he assures you that he has complied with the law and that there is a misunderstanding on the part of the assessor. After listening to him describe the situation, you decide it is likely that his analysis of the situation is correct.

Required: Indicate what additional information should be obtained during the interview with Mr. Simon and what steps should be taken if you decide to accept him as a client.

Assignment Problem Two - 8

For each of the following independent cases, indicate whether you believe a penalty would be assessed against the tax return preparer under ITA 163.2. Explain your conclusion.

A. Accountant X is asked by Client A to prepare a tax return including a business financial statement to be used in the return. In response to a request by Accountant X for business related documents, Client A supplies information to Accountant X, which includes a travel expense receipt. Accountant X relies on this information provided by Client A and prepares the business statement that is filed with the return. The CRA conducts a compliance audit and determines that Client A's travel expense was a non-deductible personal expense.

B. Accountant X has several clients that have been reassessed in respect of a tax shelter. Accountant X knows that the CRA is challenging the tax effects claimed in respect of the tax shelter on the basis that the shelter is not a business, is based on a significant overvaluation of the related property and is technically deficient in its structure. The Tax Court of Canada, in a test case (general procedures), denies deductions claimed in respect of the tax shelter in a previous year by Client B (a client of Accountant X). Client B's appeal is dismissed. The case is not appealed and Accountant X is aware of the Court's decision. Accountant X prepares and files a tax return on behalf of Client C that includes a claim in respect of the same tax shelter that the Tax Court denied deductions for.

C. Taxpayer Z approaches Tax-preparer X to prepare and EFILE Z's tax return. Taxpayer Z provides X with a T4 slip indicating that Z has $32,000 of employment income. Taxpayer Z advises X that he made a charitable donation of $24,000 but forgot the receipt at home. Z asks that X prepare and EFILE the tax return. In fact, Z never donated anything to a charity. X prepares Z's tax return without obtaining the receipt.

CHAPTER 3

Liability For Tax

Liability For Tax - Residence Issues

Charging Provisions

3-1. The portion of any tax legislation that specifies who is liable to pay tax is called a charging provision. Section 2 of the *Income Tax Act* contains two Subsections dealing with this subject. ITA 2(1), the more important of these Subsections, establishes that, in general, Canadian income taxation is based on residence. This Subsection states the following:

> **ITA 2(1)** An income tax shall be paid, as required by this *Act*, on the taxable income for each taxation year of every person resident in Canada at any time in the year.

3-2. There are several terms used in this charging provision that require further explanation:

Person As used in the *Income Tax Act*, the term person refers not only to individuals, but to corporations and trusts as well. When a provision of the *Act* is directed at human taxpayers, the term "individual" is generally used.

Resident While the concept of residence would seem to be self-evident, at least for individuals, there are a number of difficulties associated with this term that are covered in detail in this Chapter.

Residence Vs. Citizenship As is the case in the United Kingdom, Canadian taxation is based on the concept of residence. This differs from the situation in the United States where U.S. citizens are subject to taxation regardless of their place of residence.

Taxation Year - Corporations ITA 249(1)(a) indicates that for a corporation, the taxation year is a "fiscal period". ITA 249.1 defines the fiscal period of a corporation as a period for which accounts are made up that does not exceed 53 weeks.

Taxation Year - Individuals And Trusts For most tax purposes, trusts are treated as individuals. In this context, ITA 249(1)(b) indicates that, for individuals other than a testamentary trust (a trust that arises as the result of the death of an individual), the taxation year is the calendar year. This means that an inter vivos trust (a trust other than a testamentary trust) must use a calendar year as its taxation year. In contrast, ITA 249(1)(c) allows a testamentary trust to use a taxation year other than a calendar year.

Taxable Income   Taxable income is defined in Section 2 of the *Act* as follows:

ITA 2(2)   The taxable income of a taxpayer for a taxation year is the taxpayer's income for the year plus the additions and minus the deductions permitted by Division C.

While the definition refers to additions under Division C, almost all of the items in the calculation of Taxable Income are deductions. Examples of these deductions would include loss carry overs for all taxpayers, the lifetime capital gains deduction for individuals, and taxable dividends received by corporations. The calculation of Taxable Income is introduced in Chapter 6. However, detailed consideration of most of the Division C deductions is found in Chapters 14 (for individuals) and 15 (for corporations).

3-3.   The second charging provision in the *Income Tax Act* deals with the taxation of non-residents. It is as follows:

ITA 2(3)   Where a person who is not taxable under subsection (1) for a taxation year

(a) was employed in Canada,
(b) carried on a business in Canada, or
(c) disposed of a taxable Canadian property,

at any time in the year or a previous year, an income tax shall be paid, as required by this *Act*, on the person's taxable income earned in Canada for the year determined in accordance with Division D.

3-4.   This charging provision identifies those situations in which non-residents are subject to Canadian income taxes. More detailed attention will be given to these three situations beginning in Paragraph 3-32.

Residence Of Individuals
General Concept

3-5.   For the average Canadian individual whose job, family, dwelling place, and other personal property are all located in Canada, the concept of residence is not at all ambiguous. Such individuals would clearly be Canadian residents and, as a result, they would be liable for Canadian taxation on their worldwide income. Short departures from the country for holidays or business activities would not have any effect on this conclusion.

3-6.   However, for a growing number of individuals, the question of residence is more complex. It is also an important question. Tax rates in different countries vary tremendously, with Canada generally being at the high end of the range. Given this, being assessed as a Canadian resident can result in a significantly higher tax liability than being taxed as a resident of another country.

3-7.   While the term resident is not specifically defined in the *Income Tax Act*, IT-221R3 provides extensive guidance in this area. The most generally applicable statement in this Bulletin is as follows:

Paragraph 4   The most important factor to be considered in determining whether or not an individual leaving Canada remains resident in Canada for tax purposes is whether or not the individual maintains residential ties with Canada while he or she is abroad. While the residence status of an individual can only be determined on a case by case basis after taking into consideration all of the relevant facts, generally, unless an individual severs all significant residential ties with Canada upon leaving Canada, the individual will continue to be a factual resident of Canada and subject to Canadian tax on his or her worldwide income.

3-8.   The IT Bulletin goes on to point out that the ties that will almost always be considered significant are:

Dwelling   If an individual maintains a dwelling place in Canada, it will generally result in the individual being considered a resident. One exception to this rule would be when an individual who leaves Canada rents out a former dwelling place to an arm's length party.

Spouse Or Common-Law Partner   If an individual has a spouse or common-law partner who remains in Canada, it will generally result in the individual being considered a Canadian resident. An exception here would be when the individual was living separate or apart from the spouse or common-law partner prior to their departure from Canada.

Dependants   If an individual has dependants, such as minor children, who remain in Canada, it will generally result in the individual being considered a Canadian resident.

3-9.   The Bulletin also implies that, even in the absence of one of the preceding ties, an individual may still be considered to be a resident of Canada on the basis of secondary residential ties. Examples of such secondary ties include:

(a) personal property in Canada (such as furniture, clothing, automobiles and recreational vehicles),
(b) social ties with Canada (such as memberships in Canadian recreational and religious organizations),
(c) economic ties with Canada (such as employment with a Canadian employer, active involvement in a Canadian business, or owning Canadian bank accounts, retirement savings plans, credit cards, and securities accounts),
(d) landed immigrant status or appropriate work permits in Canada,
(e) hospitalization and medical insurance coverage from a province or territory of Canada,
(f) a driver's license from a province or territory of Canada,
(g) a vehicle registered in a province or territory of Canada,
(h) a seasonal dwelling place in Canada or a leased dwelling place,
(i) a Canadian passport, and
(j) memberships in Canadian unions or professional organizations.

3-10.   The IT Bulletin notes that these secondary ties must be looked at collectively and that it would be unusual for a single secondary tie to be sufficient for an individual to be classified as a Canadian resident.

Exercise Three-1

Subject: Residential Ties

At the end of the current year, Simon Farr departed from Canada. He was accompanied by his wife and children, as well as all of his personal property. Due to depressed real estate prices in his region, he was unable to sell his residence at a satisfactory price. However, he was able to rent it for a period of two years. He also retained his membership in the Ontario Institute Of Chartered Accountants. After his departure, would he still be considered a Canadian resident for tax purposes? Explain your conclusion.

End of Exercise. Solution available in Study Guide.

Temporary Absences

3-11.   Many of the problems associated with establishing residency involve situations where an individual leaves Canada for a temporary period of time. The issue here is, under what circumstances should an individual be viewed as having retained their Canadian residency status during the period of their absence from Canada? It is an important issue in that, if they are viewed as having retained their Canadian residency status, they will be subject to Canadian taxation on their worldwide income during the period of absence from Canada. While credits against Canadian income tax payable would usually be available for any income taxes paid in the foreign jurisdiction, the foreign taxes paid will often be insufficient to cover the full Canadian tax liability.

3-12.   IT-221R3 makes it clear that the period of time the individual is absent from Canada is not a determining factor with respect to residency. If an individual severs all primary and secondary residential ties, it appears that he will cease to be a Canadian resident without regard to the period of his absence.

3-13.   If some residential ties are retained during a temporary absence, other factors will be considered. As described in IT-221R3, these are as follows:

Intent   The issue here is whether the individual intended to permanently sever residential ties with Canada. If, for example, the individual has a contract for employment, if and when he returns to Canada, this could be viewed as evidence that he did not intend to permanently depart. Another factor would be whether the individual complied with the rules related to permanent departures (i.e., there is a deemed disposition of much of an individual's property at the time of departure from Canada, usually resulting in the need to pay taxes on any resulting gains).

Frequency Of Visits   If the individual continues to visit Canada on a regular and continuing basis, particularly if other secondary residential ties are present, this would suggest that he did not intend to permanently depart from Canada.

Residential Ties Outside Of Canada   A further consideration is whether or not the individual establishes residential ties in another country. If someone leaves Canada and travels for an extensive period of time without settling in any one location, it will be considered as evidence that he has not permanently departed from Canada.

3-14.   It is clear that there is considerable room for differences of opinion as to whether an individual has ceased to be a Canadian resident during a temporary absence from Canada. It is equally clear that the issue should be given careful attention by taxpayers who find themselves in this situation. The potential tax consequences of failing to deal properly with residency issues can be significant.

Exercise Three-2

Subject: Temporary Absences

Jane is a Canadian citizen who is employed by a multi-national corporation. While she has worked for many years in the Canadian office of this organization, she agreed to transfer to the corporation's office in Florida. Before leaving, she disposed of her residence and other personal property that she did not wish to move. She canceled her Alberta driver's licence and health care card, and closed all of her Canadian banking and brokerage accounts.

Because her boyfriend remained in Edmonton, she flew back to Canada at least once a month. After 26 months, she decided that between the excessive heat and humidity in Florida and the travel required to maintain the relationship with her boyfriend, she would return to Canada. Would Jane be considered a Canadian resident during the 26 months that she was absent from Canada? Explain your conclusion.

End of Exercise.   Solution available in Study Guide.

Part Year Residence

3-15.   In a year in which a person clearly terminates or establishes residency in Canada, they will be taxed in Canada on their worldwide income for the part of the year in which they are resident in Canada. While the date for the establishment of residency in Canada is based on the date of entry under immigration rules, the date on which an individual becomes a non-resident is the latest of:

- the date the individual leaves Canada,
- the date the spouse or common-law partner and/or other dependants of the individual leave Canada, and
- the date the individual becomes a resident of the country to which they are immigrating.

3-16.   Situations involving part year residency require a fairly complex prorating of income, deductions, and personal tax credits. For example, an individual who is a resident of Canada for only part of the year will not be entitled to a full personal tax credit (see Chapter 6). The process for prorating such deductions and credits is specified in ITA 114 and ITA 118.91.

Exercise Three-3

Subject: Part Year Residence

Mark is a Canadian citizen and, since graduating from university, has been employed in Vancouver. He has accepted a new position in the United States and, as of February 1 of the current year flies to Los Angeles to assume his responsibilities. (He has been granted a green card to enable him to work in the U.S.) His wife remains behind with the children until June 15, the end of their school year. On that date, they fly to Los Angeles to join Mark. Their residence is sold on August 1 of the current year, at which time a moving company picks up their furniture and other personal possessions. The moving company delivers these possessions to their new house in Los Angeles on August 15. Explain how Mark will be taxed in Canada during the current year.

End of Exercise. Solution available in Study Guide.

Sojourners And Other Deemed Residents

3-17.   Individuals who are considered Canadian residents on the basis of the residential ties that we have discussed are generally referred to as factual residents. ITA 250(1) extends the meaning of resident to include certain other individuals who are considered deemed residents. As we shall see, an individual can be a deemed resident even if they do not set foot in Canada in the relevant taxation years.

3-18.   There are two important tax consequences associated with deemed residents:

- Deemed residents are taxed on their worldwide income for the entire taxation year. This is in contrast to part year residents who are only subject to Canadian taxation during that portion of the taxation year that they are present in Canada.

- Deemed residents are not deemed to reside in a specific province and, as a consequence, they are not subject to provincial taxes. In order to maintain fairness with other Canadian taxpayers, deemed residents are required to pay an additional federal tax equal to 48 percent of the basic federal tax that is otherwise payable. This may result in an overall tax liability that is lower than it would be for residents in some provinces.

3-19.   Included on the list of deemed residents of Canada are the following:

1. Sojourners in Canada for 183 days or more.
2. Members, at any time during the year, of the Canadian armed forces when stationed outside of Canada.
3. Ambassadors, ministers, high commissioners, officers or servants of Canada, as well as agents general, officers, or servants of a province, provided they were Canadian residents immediately prior to their appointment.

4. An individual performing services, at any time in the year, in a country other than Canada under a prescribed international development assistance program of the Government of Canada, provided they were resident in Canada at any time in the 3 month period preceding the day on which those services commenced.
5. A child of a deemed resident, provided they are also a dependant whose net income for the year was less than the base for the basic personal tax credit ($8,929 for 2007).
6. An individual who was at any time in the year, under an agreement or a convention with one or more other countries, entitled to an exemption from an income tax otherwise payable in any of those countries, because at that time the person was related to, or a member of the family of, an individual who was resident in Canada.

3-20.   Of these items, numbers 1 and 6 require further explanation. With respect to item 1, a sojourner is an individual who is temporarily present in Canada for a period of 183 days or more during any one calendar year. Because of ITA 250(1), this person is deemed to be a Canadian resident for the entire year.

3-21.   For this sojourner rule to apply, the individual must be a resident of another country during the 183 days in question. This means that an individual who gives up his residence in another country and moves to Canada early in a taxation year will be considered a part year resident, not a sojourner. Correspondingly, a Canadian resident who leaves Canada to take up residence in another country on September 1 will not be a sojourner, despite the fact that he is in Canada for more than 183 days in the year. As noted, this is an important distinction because the sojourner is liable for Canadian tax on his worldwide income for the entire year.

3-22.   IT-221R3 indicates that sojourning means establishing a temporary residence and would include days spent in Canada on vacation trips. However, the Bulletin makes it clear that individuals who, for employment purposes, commute to Canada on a daily basis, are not considered to be sojourning.

3-23.   Item 6 refers to situations where someone is exempt from tax in a foreign country because they are related to an individual who is a Canadian resident. For example, the spouse of a Canadian diplomat working in the U.S. would be exempt from U.S. income taxes under the governing international tax treaty because she is the spouse of the diplomat. As the diplomat would be a deemed resident of Canada under item 3, the spouse would be a deemed resident of Canada under item 6.

Exercise Three-4

Subject: Part Year Residence

Mr. Jonathan Kirsh was born in Kansas and, until the current year, had lived in various parts of the United States. On September 1 of the current year he moves to Lethbridge, Alberta to begin work at a new job. He brings his family and all of his personal property with him. However, he continues to have both a chequing and a savings account in a U. S. financial institution. Explain how Mr. Kirsh will be taxed in Canada during the current taxation year.

Exercise Three-5

Subject: Individual Residency

Ms. Suzanne Blakey was born 24 years ago in Paris, France. She is the daughter of a Canadian High Commissioner serving in that country. Her father still holds this position. However, Ms. Blakey is now working in London. The only income that she earns in the year is from her London marketing job and is subject to taxes in England. She has never visited Canada. Determine the residency status of Suzanne Blakey.

End of Exercises. Solutions available in Study Guide.

Residence Of Corporations

3-24.   Being an artificial legal entity, a corporation does not reside anywhere in the same physical sense that the term applies to an individual. To some extent, the jurisdiction of incorporation can assist in finding an answer to the residency question. More specifically, ITA 250(4)(a) indicates that corporations which are incorporated in Canada after April 26, 1965 are deemed to be resident in Canada.

3-25.   For corporations chartered in Canada prior to April 27, 1965, ITA 250(4)(c) indicates that these organizations would also be treated as residents if they were resident in Canada (under the common law concept discussed in Paragraphs 3-26 through 3-28) or carried on business in Canada in any taxation year ending after April 26, 1965.

3-26.   What jurisdiction a company was incorporated in is not, however, the end of the story. If this were the case, it would be possible to escape Canadian taxation by the simple act of incorporating outside of the country. Beyond the rules described in the preceding Paragraph, a well established common law principle applies.

3-27.   This is the idea that a corporation is resident in the jurisdiction in which the mind and management of the company are located. Such factors as the location of the board of directors meetings and where day-to-day decisions are made, are used to determine the location of the mind and management of the corporation. If the conclusion is that the mind and management is in Canada, then a corporation that is not incorporated in Canada will be considered a resident for Canadian tax purposes.

3-28.   This "mind and management" criteria would also apply to a corporation that was incorporated in Canada prior to April 27, 1965. Such a corporation would become a resident if, after April 26, 1965, its operations were controlled within Canada. Unlike the foreign jurisdiction corporation, which would be considered to be a Canadian resident only as long as the mind and management remained in Canada, a pre-April 27, 1965 Canadian corporation that became a resident because of the mind and management criteria would remain a Canadian resident, even if the mind and management were moved to a different jurisdiction.

3-29.   International tax treaties may also be influential in the determination of the residence of corporations. As noted in Chapter 1, if there is a conflict between domestic legislation and the provisions of an international tax treaty, the treaty rules override the domestic legislation.

3-30.   For example, a situation might arise where a particular corporation is considered to be a resident of Canada under Canadian legislation and a resident of a foreign country under the legislation that prevails in that country. This is a situation that could result in the corporation being taxed in both jurisdictions. If Canada has a tax treaty with the foreign country, the treaty would prevent double taxation by providing provisions that would be used to determine which of the two countries would claim the corporation as a resident.

Exercise Three-6

Subject: Corporate Residency

Roswell Ltd. was incorporated in the state of New York in 2002. It carries on business in both the United States and Canada. However, all of the directors of the Company live in Kemptville, Ontario and, as a consequence, all of the directors meetings are held in Kemptville. Determine the residency status of Roswell Ltd.   (Ignore any tax treaty implications.)

End of Exercise. Solution available in Study Guide.

Exercise Three-7

Subject: Corporate Residency

Sateen Inc. was incorporated as a Manitoba corporation in 2001. However, since 2004, all of the Company's business has been carried on outside of Canada. Determine the residency status of Sateen Inc.

End of Exercise.   Solution available in Study Guide.

Residence Of Trusts

3-31.   As with any other question of residence, establishing the residence of a trust is something that can only be determined by examining the circumstances involved in each case. In general, however, IT-447 indicates that a trust is considered to reside where the trustee, executor, administrator, heir, or other legal representative who manages the trust or controls the trust assets resides. If this location is not clear, the same IT Bulletin indicates that the authorities will look at the location where the legal rights with respect to the trust assets are enforceable, and the location of the trust assets.

Taxation Of Non-Residents

Employment Income

3-32.   As noted in Paragraph 3-4, ITA 2(3) specifies three situations in which non-residents will have Canadian Tax Payable. The first of these situations is specified under ITA 2(3)(a) which indicates that non-residents are subject to taxation on Canadian employment income. As the term is used in ITA 2(3)(a), Canadian employment income refers to income earned by a non-resident while working as an employee in Canada, generally without regard to the location of the employer. An example of this would be a U.S. citizen who is a resident of Detroit, Michigan, but is employed at an automobile plant in Windsor, Ontario. Such an individual would be subject to Canadian taxes on his employment income. However, as the individual is a non-resident, his other sources of income would not be taxed in Canada.

Business Income

3-33.   The second situation in which non-residents are subject to Canadian taxes is specified in ITA 2(3)(b). This paragraph indicates that persons who carried on business in Canada during a taxation year are subject to Canadian taxes on that income. Many of the difficulties associated with implementing this provision are related to determining what constitutes "carrying on business in Canada". Under ITA 253, an extended meaning is given to this concept which provides for a very broad interpretation of this expression. More specifically, under ITA 253, carrying on business in Canada would apply not only to persons who produce or manufacture products in Canada, but also to persons who offer things for sale in Canada through an agent or employee.

3-34.   This broad interpretation is, however, mitigated in those circumstances where the non-resident is a resident of a country with which Canada has a tax treaty. For example, if a U.S. corporation had sales staff selling products in Canada, ITA 253 would suggest that it should be taxed as a non-resident carrying on business in Canada. However, the Canada-U.S. tax treaty overrides ITA 253 in that this agreement exempts a U.S. enterprise from Canadian taxation unless it is carrying on business through permanent establishments in Canada.

3-35.   It is also important to distinguish between those situations in which a non-resident is offering something for sale in Canada through an employee and those situations in which a non-resident is selling to an independent contractor who resells the item in Canada. In the former case, the non-resident person is carrying on business in Canada, while in the latter case the non-resident is not.

Dispositions Of Taxable Canadian Property

3-36.   ITA 2(3)(c) specifies the third situation in which non-residents are subject to Canadian taxation. This provision indicates that non-residents are subject to Canadian taxation on gains resulting from the disposition of "taxable Canadian property".

3-37.   The concept of taxable Canadian property is discussed more completely in Chapters 12 and 22. However, you should note at this point that the major items included in taxable Canadian property are: real estate situated in Canada, capital property used to carry on a business in Canada, shares of Canadian private companies, and partnership interests in situations where more than 50 percent of the partnership's property is made up of taxable Canadian property. This provision means that, if a resident of the state of Washington disposes of a vacation property that he owns in Whistler, British Columbia, any gain on that sale will be subject to Canadian taxation.

Property Income

3-38.   The charging provisions in ITA 2 do not cover Canadian source property income of non-residents (e. g., rents, interest, or royalties). However, this type of income is covered in Part XIII of the *Act*. While the rate is usually reduced for payments to non-residents in countries where Canada has a tax treaty, Part XIII requires a flat 25 percent tax on Canadian property income paid to non-residents.

3-39.   This tax is withheld at the source of income, is based on the gross amount of such income, and no provision is made for any expenses related to acquiring the income. Since this inability to deduct expenses could result in serious inequities, there are provisions that allow a non-resident to elect to file a Canadian tax return for certain types of property income under Part I of the *Act*. These Part XIII tax provisions are discussed more thoroughly in Chapter 22 which deals with international taxation.

Exercise Three-8

Subject: Non-Resident Liability For Tax

Ms. Laurie Lacombe, a U.S. citizen, has Canadian employment income of $22,000. She lives in Blaine, Washington and is a resident of the United States for the entire year. Ms. Lacombe does not believe that she is subject to taxation in Canada. Is she correct? Explain your conclusion.

End of Exercise. Solution available in Study Guide.

Additional Material On Residency

3-40.   The residency related material that is included in this Chapter is sufficient for dealing with this issue in the remaining chapters of this text. However, additional and more detailed material on this subject can be found in Chapter 22, International Taxation. There is, however, no need to review the additional material at this point unless this area is of particular interest.

The Concept Of Income

The Economist's View

3-41.   In the past, economists have viewed income as being limited to rents, profits, and wages. In general, capital gains, gratuitous receipts, and other such increases in net worth were not included. In this context, most economists perceived income to be a net concept. That is, income is equal to revenues, less any related expenses.

3-42.   In more recent times, the economist's concept of income has moved in the direction of including measures of net worth or capital maintenance. The oft cited quotation "Income is the amount that can be spent during the period and still be as well off at the end of the period as at the beginning." is perhaps as good a description of the current concept as any available.

3-43.   This broader concept of income is based on the idea that income should include all increases in net economic power that occur during the relevant measurement period.

The Accountant's View

3-44.   What we currently view as Net Income from an accounting point of view is the result of applying a fairly flexible group of rules that are referred to as generally accepted accounting principles (GAAP). In general, Net Income is determined by establishing the amount of revenue on the basis of point of sale revenue recognition. Then, by using a variety of cash flows, accruals, and allocations, the cost of assets used up in producing these revenues is matched against these revenues, with this total deducted to produce the accounting Net Income for the period.

3-45.   If this same process is viewed from the perspective of the Balance Sheet, Net Income is measured as the increase in net assets for the period under consideration, plus any distributions that were made to the owners of the business during that period.

3-46.   The current accounting model generally values assets at historical cost and records changes in value only when supported by an arm's length transaction. This means that many of the increases in wealth that would be included in the economist's concept of income would not be included in accounting Net Income.

3-47.   However, the gap between the two approaches is gradually being narrowed as accounting standard setters show an increased willingness to incorporate fair value measurement into their pronouncements, both with respect to Balance Sheet values and with respect to inclusions in Net Income.

The Income Tax Act View

General Approach

3-48.   The *Income Tax Act* view of income, like that described under the accounting view, is the result of the application of a complex set of rules. The first thing to note is that, in accounting, the term Net Income is used largely in the context of the various types of income earned by a business. In contrast, Net Income For Tax Purposes includes all types of income, including business income, property income, taxable capital gains, and employment income.

3-49.   With respect to the business income that is included in Net Income For Tax Purposes, it is similar to the accounting concept of Net Income. Many of the inclusions and deductions that are used in determining the tax figure are identical to the revenues and expenses that go into the determination of Net Income under GAAP. For example, the amount of wages and salaries that are deducted under GAAP would usually be the same as the amounts deducted in the determination of business income for tax purposes.

3-50.   There are, however, differences. Some of these differences are simply alternative approaches to allocating a given total to different time periods. An example of this would be the relationship between the write-off of capital assets for tax purposes (capital cost allowance) and the amortization of capital assets for accounting purposes (amortization expense).

3-51.   In the accounting Balance Sheet, such allocation differences result in what accountants refer to as temporary differences. As you are probably aware, these temporary differences are multiplied by an appropriate tax rate to arrive at Future Income Tax Assets or, alternatively, Future Income Tax Liabilities.

3-52.   Other differences are more permanent in nature. While 100 percent of capital gains are included in accounting Net Income, one-half of these gains will never be included in Net Income For Tax Purposes. Another example of this type of difference would be the fact that dividends received by a corporation from another corporation are included in accounting Net Income, but will never be included in Taxable Income.

3-53.   Differences between accounting Net Income and the business income component of Net Income For Tax Purposes are discussed in detail in Chapter 8.

ITA Division B - Computation Of Income

3-54.   Division B of Part I of the *Income Tax Act* is devoted to the computation of what is normally called Net Income For Tax Purposes. Note that, while this amount is sometimes referred to simply as Net Income, we will not use this designation in this Chapter in order to avoid confusion with the bottom line in the accounting Income Statement prepared using GAAP.

3-55.   As is described in Chapter 1, Division B identifies and provides rules for the computation of three basic types of income:

- Income Or Loss From An Office Or Employment (Division B, Subdivision a)
- Income Or Loss From Business And Property (Division B, Subdivision b)
- Taxable Capital Gains And Allowable Capital Losses (Division B, Subdivision c)

3-56.   Each of these Subdivisions specifies inclusions and deductions applicable to the particular type of income under consideration. In later Chapters, detailed attention will be given to each of these types of income (e.g., Chapter 5 covers employment income). However, at this point we would note that each of these types of income is calculated on a net basis (i.e., inclusions, less deductions).

3-57.   In addition to these three basic components, two other Subdivisions often affect the calculation of Net Income For Tax Purposes. Division B, Subdivision d deals with miscellaneous inclusions in income. Examples of such miscellaneous inclusions would be spousal support received and pension income. Division B, Subdivision e deals with miscellaneous deductions. Examples here would include Registered Retirement Savings Plan (RRSP) contributions, moving expenses, spousal support paid, and child care costs.

3-58.   In somewhat simplified terms, Net Income For Tax Purposes (Division B Income) is calculated by adding net employment income, net business income, net property income, other sources of income as provided for in Subdivision d, and the net of taxable capital gains less allowable capital losses. From this total we subtract the other deductions listed in Subdivision e. While this description provides a general overview of the determination of Net Income For Tax Purposes, the actual calculation of this amount is subject to specific rules that are found in ITA 3. These rules will be covered in the following material.

Computing Net Income For Tax Purposes

ITA Section 3

Ordering Rules

3-59.   As previously noted, ITA 3 provides a set of rules for combining various types of income in order to calculate Net Income For Tax Purposes. Such rules are generally referred to as ordering rules in that they specify the order in which the various components of a calculation must be added or deducted.

3-60.   While some of the ideas involved in applying this formula will not be fully explained until later in the text, it is useful at this stage to provide the basic structure of this formula in order to enhance your understanding of how the material which follows is organized. The ITA 3 rules are presented graphically in Figure 3-1 (following page).

ITA 3(a) Sources Of Income

3-61.   The ordering process begins in ITA 3(a) with the addition of all positive sources of income other than taxable capital gains. This includes positive amounts of employment income, business income, property income, and other miscellaneous inclusions from Subdivision d of Division B.

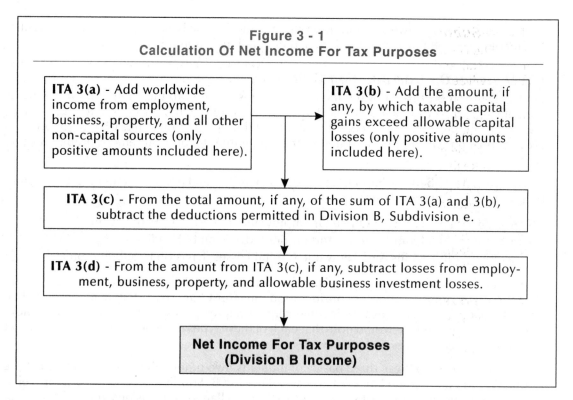

Figure 3 - 1
Calculation Of Net Income For Tax Purposes

ITA 3(a) - Add worldwide income from employment, business, property, and all other non-capital sources (only positive amounts included here).

ITA 3(b) - Add the amount, if any, by which taxable capital gains exceed allowable capital losses (only positive amounts included here).

ITA 3(c) - From the total amount, if any, of the sum of ITA 3(a) and 3(b), subtract the deductions permitted in Division B, Subdivision e.

ITA 3(d) - From the amount from ITA 3(c), if any, subtract losses from employment, business, property, and allowable business investment losses.

Net Income For Tax Purposes (Division B Income)

3-62.   Note that, while the individual components of this total are net amounts (e.g., employment income is made up of inclusions, net of deductions), the total is not a net calculation.   For example, a business loss would not be deducted against a positive employment income under ITA 3(a). Rather, such losses would be deducted at a later point in the calculation of Net Income For Tax Purposes.

ITA 3(b) Net Taxable Capital Gains

3-63.   Before discussing ITA 3(b), a point should be made here concerning capital gains terminology.   The term "taxable capital gain" refers to the portion of the gain that must be included in income (one-half since 2000). Correspondingly, the term "allowable capital loss" refers to the portion of the loss that can be deducted (one-half since 2000). If the term used is capital gain or capital loss, it means the full amount (100%) of the gain or loss, before the removal of the non-taxable or non-deductible portion (50%).

3-64.   To the total determined in ITA 3(a), ITA 3(b) requires that you "determine the amount, if any, by which" taxable capital gains exceed allowable capital losses. The phrase "if any" is commonly used in tax legislation to indicate that negative amounts are ignored.

3-65.   It is of particular importance here, since the fact that ITA 3(b) cannot be negative establishes the very important rule that the current year's allowable capital losses can only be deducted to the extent of taxable capital gains that have been recognized in the current year in the calculation of Net Income For Tax Purposes for the current year.

3-66.   Note, however, the excess allowable capital losses do not disappear. As is explained in detail in Chapter 14, current year allowable capital losses that cannot be deducted in the calculation of current year Net Income For Tax Purposes, can be deducted in the calculation of Taxable Income in past or future years.

3-67.   More specifically, such losses can be carried back to the preceding three taxation years, and forward to any future taxation year, resulting in either a refund of taxes paid (carry back situations) or a reduction in future taxes payable (carry forward situations). Note that these carry over deductions can only be made to the extent of net taxable capital gains that are recognized in that past or future year.

ITA 3(c) Subdivision e Deductions

3-68.   The ITA 3(c) component of the calculation starts with the amount, if any, of the total from ITA 3(a) and ITA 3(b). Here again, the phrase "if any" indicates that only positive amounts will be used. If the total from ITA 3(a) and ITA 3(b) is nil, Net Income For Tax Purposes is nil and the calculation is complete.

3-69.   Alternatively, if the total is positive, it is reduced by any Division B, Subdivision e deductions that are available. These deductions, which are covered in detail in Chapters 11 and 13, include payments for spousal support, moving expenses, child care costs, and contributions to Registered Retirement Savings Plans.

3-70.   Note the importance of order here. ITA 3(c) requires that subdivision e amounts be deducted prior to business and property losses. This is important because subdivision e deductions are only deductible in the year to which they relate as long as there is sufficient income to apply them against (e.g., if you cannot deduct spousal support in the current year, you cannot deduct it in a past or future year). In contrast, if you cannot use a business or property loss in the current year, it can be carried over to a past year or a future year.

ITA 3(d) Losses

3-71.   The ITA 3(d) component of the calculation begins with the amount, if any, carried forward from ITA 3(c). If this amount is nil, Net Income For Tax Purposes is nil and the calculation is complete.

3-72.   If the ITA 3(c) amount is positive, the taxpayer can deduct any current year losses other than allowable capital losses. This would include the deduction of any current year business losses, property losses, employment losses, and allowable business investment losses (allowable business investment losses are a special type of allowable capital loss that can be deducted against any type of income). Current period farm losses are also deductible here, subject to certain restrictions that are described in Chapter 8 (see the section on Income For Farmers).

Loss Carry Overs

3-73.   If the total of business losses, property losses, employment losses and allowable business investment losses for the current year exceed the amount determined under ITA 3(c), then Net Income For Tax Purposes is nil. Any excess will be eligible for carry over to other taxation years as a non-capital loss.

3-74.   In somewhat simplified form, the carry over provisions are as follows:

Carry Back Provisions   All types of unused losses, including capital losses, can be carried back to the three previous taxation years. This will result in a refund of all or part of the taxes that have been paid in those years.

Carry Forward Of Non-Capital Losses Unused non-capital losses can be carried forward to the next 20 taxation years. When applied in the determination of Taxable Income for those years, the result will be reduced Tax Payable.

Carry Forward Of Allowable Capital Losses   Unused allowable capital losses can be carried forward and applied in the determination of Taxable Income in any future taxation year, but may only be deducted to the extent of the net taxable capital gains in those other years.

3-75.   The detailed rules for this carry forward process are fairly complex, involving a number of rules that are not described in this summary. These rules are given detailed consideration in Chapter 14.

Net Income For Tax Purposes - Example

3-76.   The following example provides an illustration of how the ITA 3 rules are applied.

Example Jonathan Morley has the following income and loss components for the year:

Employment Income	$17,000
Business Loss (From Restaurant)	(21,000)
Property Income	9,000
Taxable Capital Gains	14,000
Allowable Capital Losses	(19,000)
Subdivision e Deductions (Spousal Support Paid)	(9,000)

Analysis Mr. Morley's Net Income For Tax Purposes would be calculated as follows:

Income Under ITA 3(a):		
Employment Income	$17,000	
Business Loss (See ITA 3(d) below)	Nil	
Property Income	9,000	$26,000
Income Under ITA 3(b):		
Taxable Capital Gains	$14,000	
Allowable Capital Losses	(19,000)	Nil
Balance From ITA 3(a) And (b)		$26,000
Subdivision e Deductions		(9,000)
Balance Under ITA 3(c)		$17,000
Deduction Under ITA 3(d):		
Business Loss		(21,000)
Net Income For Tax Purposes (Division B Income)		Nil

3-77.   Mr. Morley's Business Loss exceeds the amount carried forward from ITA 3(c), resulting in a Net Income For Tax Purposes of nil. However, there would be a carry over of the unused business loss equal to $4,000, and of the unused allowable capital loss in the amount of $5,000 ($14,000 - $19,000).

3-78.   As is explained in detail in Chapter 14, capital loss carry overs can only be deducted to the extent that there are capital gains in the carry over period. As a consequence, this type of loss carry over has to be segregated from other types of losses which can generally be deducted against any type of income in the carry over year (as will be explained in Chapter 8, there are also restrictions on carry over deductions of certain types of farm losses).

3-79.   If this is your first exposure to income taxation, you should not expect to have a complete understanding of ITA 3 at this point. You should review this material and make an attempt to solve the relatively simple problems and exercises that are included in this Chapter. A periodic review of this set of rules as you proceed through Chapters 5 through 14 will enhance your understanding of the organization of that material as it is being covered.

Exercise Three-9

Subject: Net Income For Tax Purposes

For the current year, Mr. Norris Blanton has net employment income of $42,000, a business loss of $15,000, taxable capital gains of $24,000, and Subdivision e deductions of $13,000. What is the amount of Mr. Blanton's Net Income For Tax Purposes for the current year?

End of Exercise. Solution available in Study Guide.

Exercise Three-10

Subject: Net Income For Tax Purposes

For the current year, Ms. Cheryl Stodard has interest income of $33,240, taxable capital gains of $24,750, allowable capital losses of $19,500, and a net rental loss of $48,970. What is the amount of Ms. Stodard's Net Income For Tax Purposes for the current year? Indicate the amount and type of any loss carry overs that would be available at the end of the current year.

Exercise Three-11

Subject: Net Income For Tax Purposes

For the current year, Mrs. Marie Bergeron has net employment income of $42,680, taxable capital gains of $27,400, allowable capital losses of $33,280, Subdivision e deductions of $8,460, and a business loss of $26,326. What is the amount of Mrs. Bergeron's Net Income For Tax Purposes for the current year? Indicate the amount and type of any loss carry overs that would be available at the end of the current year.

End of Exercises. Solutions available in Study Guide.

Principles Of Tax Planning

Introduction

3-80.   Throughout this text, there will be a great deal of emphasis on tax planning and, while many of the specific techniques that are involved can only be fully explained after the more detailed provisions of tax legislation have been covered, there are some basic tax planning principles that can be described at this point.

3-81.   Our objective here is simply to provide a general understanding of the results that can be achieved through tax planning so that you will be able to recognize the goal of more specific tax planning techniques when they are examined. In addition, this general understanding should enable you to identify other opportunities for tax planning as you become more familiar with this material.

3-82.   The basic goals of tax planning can be summarized as follows:

- tax avoidance or reduction
- tax deferral
- income splitting

3-83.   While these classifications can be used to describe the goals of all tax planning arrangements, such arrangements seldom involve a clear cut attempt to achieve only one of these goals. For example, the principal reason for making contributions to a Registered Retirement Savings Plan is to defer taxes until later taxation years. However, such a deferral can result in the taxpayer avoiding some amount of taxes if he is taxed at a lower rate in those later years.

Tax Avoidance Or Reduction

3-84.   The most desirable result of tax planning is to permanently avoid the payment of some amount of tax. This very desirability is probably the most important explanation for the scarcity of such arrangements and, while the number of possibilities in this area is limited, they do exist.

3-85.   An outstanding example of tax avoidance is the capital gains deduction that is available on the disposition of qualified farm property and qualified small business corporation shares. The first $750,000 of capital gains on such dispositions can be received by the taxpayer on a tax free basis. For individuals in a position to enjoy the benefits of this provision, it is one of the best tax avoidance mechanisms available (see Chapter 14 for a detailed discussion of this provision).

3-86.   Other forms of complete tax avoidance can be found in the employee benefits area, in that some types of benefits can be given to employees without being considered taxable. These would include an employer's contributions to disability and private health care insurance, and the provision of discounts to employees on products or services normally sold by the employer (see Chapter 5).

3-87.   Additional opportunities in this area require more complex arrangements. Such arrangements involve the use of trusts and private corporations and cannot be described in a meaningful manner at this stage of the material. We would also note that some forms of tax avoidance can be viewed as abusive. This could make them subject to attack under the General Anti-Avoidance Rule which was discussed in Chapter 2.

Tax Deferral

3-88.   The basic concept behind tax planning arrangements involving the deferral of tax payments is the very simple idea that it is better to pay taxes later than it is to pay them now. This is related to the time value of money and also involves the possibility that some permanent avoidance of taxes may result from the taxpayer being taxed at a lower marginal income tax rate at the time the deferred amounts are brought into taxable income.

3-89.   Such deferral arrangements may involve either the delayed recognition of certain types of income or, alternatively, accelerated recognition of deductions. As an example of delayed recognition, an employer can make deductible contributions to a registered pension plan on behalf of its employees without creating any taxable income for them until they actually receive retirement benefits. In other words, this arrangement allows employees to defer some of their compensation both in terms of cash flows and in terms of taxable income.

3-90.   As an example of expense acceleration, the ownership of a rental property may allow the owner to deduct its capital cost at a rate that is usually in excess of any decline in the physical condition or economic worth of the building. While this excess will normally be added back to the taxpayer's income when the building is sold, the payment of taxes on some part of the rental income from the property has been deferred.

3-91.   Deferral arrangements are available in a number of different situations and currently represent one of the more prevalent forms of tax planning.

Income Splitting

General Idea

3-92.   Progressive rates are built into Canadian federal income tax legislation. This means that the taxes payable on a given amount of taxable income will be greater if that amount accrues to one taxpayer, than would be the case if that same amount of taxable income is split between two or more people.

3-93.   This does not mean that it would be advantageous to give part of your income away to perfect strangers. What it does mean is that, within a family or other related group, it is desirable to have the group's aggregate taxable income allocated as evenly as possible among the members of the group.

Example

3-94.   The tax savings that can be achieved through income splitting are among the most dramatic examples of the effectiveness of tax planning. For example, if Mr. Jordan had taxable income of $483,548 (this is four times $120,887, the bottom threshold of the highest federal tax bracket in 2007 of 29 percent), his basic federal tax payable in 2007 would be $131,212 (this simplified calculation does not take into consideration the various tax credits that would be available to Mr. Jordan).

3-95. Alternatively, if Mr. Jordan was married and the $483,548 could be split on the basis of $241,774 to him and $241,774 to his wife, the federal taxes payable would total $122,194 [(2)($61,097)], a savings of $9,017.

3-96. If we carry this one step further and assume that Mr. Jordan is married and has two children, and that the $483,548 in taxable income can be allocated on the basis of $120,887 to each individual, the total federal taxes payable will be reduced to $104,160 [(4)($26,040)]. This represents a savings at the federal level of $27,052 when compared to the amount of taxes that would have been paid if Mr. Jordan had been taxed on the entire $483,548.

3-97. When we add provincial effects, the potential savings could be around $40,000, a substantial reduction on income of $483,548. Making this savings even more impressive is the fact that it is not a one shot phenomena but, rather, a savings that could occur in each year that the income splitting plan is in effect.

Problems With Income Splitting

3-98. While income splitting can be one of the most powerful planning tools available to taxpayers, there are several problems associated with implementing such schemes:

- There are only a limited number of simple approaches to implementation. Most of the really effective income splitting arrangements are complex and expensive to implement, limiting their use largely to wealthy individuals.

- Splitting income with children usually involves losing control over assets, a process that is emotionally difficult for some individuals.

- Splitting income involves decisions as to which individual family members are the most worthy of receiving benefits.

- The effect of the "kiddy tax", a high rate tax assessed on certain types of income received by minors, has made income splitting much more difficult. This tax is described in detail in Chapter 14.

Exercise Three-12

Subject: Tax Planning

Mr. Stephen Chung has decided to make contributions to an RRSP in the name of his spouse, rather than making contributions to his own plan. What type of tax planning is involved in this decision? Explain your conclusion.

Exercise Three-13

Subject: Tax Planning

Mr. Green's employer pays all of the premiums on a private dental plan that covers Mr. Green and his family. What type of tax planning is illustrated by this employee benefit? Explain your conclusion.

End of Exercises. Solutions available in Study Guide.

Key Terms Used In This Chapter

3-99.   The following is a list of the key terms used in this Chapter. These terms, and their meanings, are compiled in the Glossary Of Key Terms located at the back of the separate paper Study Guide and on the Student CD-ROM.

Business Income	Person
Deemed Resident	Resident
Division B Income	Residential Ties
Employment Income	Sojourner
Fiscal Period	Tax Deferral
Income	Tax Planning
Income Splitting	Taxation Year
Net Income For Tax Purposes	Taxable Canadian Property
Ordering Rule	Taxable Income
Part Year Resident	

References

3-100.   For more detailed study of the material in this Chapter, we would refer you to the following:

ITA 2(1)	Tax Payable By Persons Resident In Canada
ITA 3	Income For Taxation Year
ITA 114	Individual Resident In Canada For Only Part Of Year
ITA 118.91	Part-Year Residents
ITA 248(1)	Definitions (Taxable Canadian Property)
ITA 249	Definition Of "Taxation Year"
ITA 250(1)	Person Deemed Resident
ITA 253	Extended Meaning Of "Carrying On Business"
IT-168R3	Athletes And Players Employed By Football, Hockey And Similar Clubs
IT-221R3	Determination Of An Individual's Residence Status
IT-262R2	Losses Of Non-Residents And Part-Year Residents
IT-270R3	Foreign Tax Credit
IT-420R3	Non-Residents - Income Earned In Canada
IT-447	Residence Of A Trust Or Estate
IT-451R	Deemed Disposition And Acquisition On Ceasing To Be Or Becoming Resident In Canada
IT-465R	Non-Resident Beneficiaries Of Trusts
IT-497R4	Overseas Employment Tax Credit

Problems For Self Study

(The solutions for these problems can be found in the separate Study Guide.)

Self Study Problem Three - 1
Determine whether the following persons are Canadian residents for the current year. Explain the basis for your conclusion.

A. Jane Smith was born in Washington, D.C., where her father has been a Canadian ambassador for 15 years. She is 12 years old and has never been to Canada.

B. Marvin Black lives in Detroit, Michigan. He works on a full time basis in Windsor, Ontario.

C. John Leather was born in Canada and, until September 12 of the current year, he has never been outside of the country. On this date, he departed from Canada and established a home in Sante Fe, New Mexico.

D. Francine Donaire is a citizen of France and is married to a member of the Canadian armed forces stationed in France. She has been in Canada only on brief visits since she and her husband have been married, and had never visited the country prior to that time. She is exempt from French taxation because she is the spouse of a member of the Canadian armed forces.

E. Robert Green lived most of his life in Texas. Early in the current year, he moved to Edmonton to take a job with a local oil exploration company. As he did not enjoy Edmonton, he resigned during the fall and returned to Texas.

F. Susan Allen is a Canadian citizen who has lived in New York City for the past 7 years.

Self Study Problem Three - 2
Determine whether the following corporations are Canadian residents for the current year. Explain the basis for your conclusion.

A. AMT Ltd. was incorporated in New Brunswick in 1964. Until 1982, all of the directors' meetings were held in that province. However, since that time, the directors have met on a regular basis in Portland, Maine.

B. UIF Inc. was incorporated in the state of Montana in 1968. However, until four years ago all of the directors' meetings were held in Vancouver, British Columbia. Four years ago, the president of the Company moved to Helena, Montana and since that time all of the directors' meetings have been held in that city.

C. BDT Ltd. was incorporated in Alberta in 1984. However, it is managed in Mexico, where all directors' and shareholders' meetings have been held since incorporation.

D. QRS Inc. was incorporated in New York state. However, all of the directors are residents of Ontario and all meetings of the Board of Directors have been held in that province since incorporation.

Self Study Problem Three - 3
Determine whether the following persons are Canadian residents for the current year. Explain the basis for your conclusion.

A. Molly London was born in Salmon Arm, British Columbia. On October 31, after a very serious dispute with her fiancé, she left Salmon Arm and moved her belongings to San Diego, California. She has vowed to never set foot in Canada again.

B. Daryl Bennett is a Canadian citizen living in Sault Ste. Marie, Michigan. He has a summer cottage in Sault Ste. Marie, Ontario, where he spent July and August. As his only sister lives in Sault Ste. Marie, Ontario, he spent a total of 27 days during the year staying with her in her home.

C. Tweeks Inc. was incorporated in Vermont in 1980 by two U.S. citizens who were residents of Quebec. All of the directors are residents of Quebec and all meetings of the Board of Directors have been held in Montreal since incorporation.

D. Bordot Industries Ltd. was incorporated in British Columbia on September 29, 1973. However, the directors of the corporation have always lived in Blaine, Washington. All of their meetings have been held at a large waterfront property just south of Blaine.

Self Study Problem Three - 4

The following facts relate to three individuals who spent a part of the current year in Canada:

Mr. Aiken   Mr. Aiken is a businessman and a U.S. citizen who moved to Canada and established residence in the middle of June. After the move, he spent the remaining 192 days of the year in Canada.

Mr. Baker   Mr. Baker is a businessman and a Canadian citizen who moved out of Canada in the middle of July and established residence in the U.S. Prior to his move, he spent the preceding 192 days of the year in Canada.

Mr. Chase   Mr. Chase is a professional athlete and a U.S. citizen. His residence is located in Nashville, Tennessee, and during most of the year his wife and children live in that city. Mr. Chase plays for a Canadian team and, during the current year, his work required him to be in Canada for a total of 192 days.

Required   All of the preceding individuals were in Canada for a total of 192 days. Explain their residence status for income tax purposes in the current year and their liability for Canadian income taxes.

Self Study Problem Three - 5

The following two Cases make different assumptions with respect to the amounts of income and deductions of Miss Nora Bain for the current taxation year:

	Case A	Case B
Employment Income	$34,000	$18,500
Income (Loss) From Business	(36,000)	(28,200)
Income From Property	21,000	12,000
Taxable Capital Gains	42,000	9,000
Allowable Capital Losses	(57,000)	(12,000)
Subdivision e Deductions (Spousal Support)	(5,500)	(10,500)

Required   For both Cases, calculate Miss Bain's Net Income For Tax Purposes (Division B income). Indicate the amount and type of any loss carry overs that would be available at the end of the current year.

Self Study Problem Three - 6

The following four Cases make different assumptions with respect to the amounts of income and deductions of Mr. Knowlton Haynes for the current year:

	Case A	Case B	Case C	Case D
Employment Income	$45,000	17,000	$24,000	$18,000
Income (Loss) From Business	(20,000)	(42,000)	(48,000)	(20,000)
Income From Property	15,000	12,000	47,000	7,000
Taxable Capital Gains	25,000	22,000	22,000	13,000
Allowable Capital Losses	(10,000)	(8,000)	(73,000)	(18,000)
Subdivision e Deductions	(5,000)	(6,000)	(4,000)	(12,000)

Required For each Case, calculate Mr. Haynes' Net Income For Tax Purposes (Division B income). Indicate the amount and type of any loss carry overs that would be available at the end of the current year.

Assignment Problems

(The solutions for these problems are only available in
the solutions manual that has been provided to your instructor.)

Assignment Problem Three - 1

What are the general rules that determine whether a person is liable for the payment of taxes under Part I of the *Income Tax Act*?

Assignment Problem Three - 2

Explain the terms Net Income For Tax Purposes and Taxable Income.

Assignment Problem Three - 3

Distinguish between the accountant's, the economist's, and the *Income Tax Act* views of income.

Assignment Problem Three - 4

In most situations, residency is the factor that determines whether or not a person will be subject to Canadian income tax. As the term resident is not defined in the *Income Tax Act*, it becomes a question of fact as to whether certain individuals and corporations are considered residents subject to taxation.

Required:

A. What guidelines have been developed to determine Canadian residency in situations where an individual is present in Canada for only part of the year?

B. What approach is taken in determining the Canadian residency of corporations?

Assignment Problem Three - 5

Mr. Leduc is a U.S. citizen who has spent most of his working life in the employ of a Canadian subsidiary of a U.S. company. While he has been located in several Canadian cities where the subsidiary has offices, he has spent the last several years working in Vancouver.

Early in the current year, Mr. Leduc is offered an opportunity for advancement within the organization of the U.S. parent company. However, the opportunity is conditional on his moving to Chicago by no later than February 15. While moving on such short notice presents a considerable inconvenience to him, he concludes that the opportunity is too good to pass up and, as a consequence, he completes his move to Chicago by February 12.

Because of the short notice involved, Mr. Leduc's wife and children decide to remain in Vancouver until the end of the school term. Mr. Leduc also feels that this will provide a greater opportunity to sell the family residence at a reasonable price.

The family residence is not sold until June 20, at which time Mr. Leduc's wife and children depart from Canada and establish residency in Chicago.

Required   For purposes of assessing Canadian income taxes, determine when Mr. Leduc ceased to be a Canadian resident and the portion of his annual income which would be assessed for Canadian taxes. Explain your conclusions.

Assignment Problem Three - 6

Mr. Desmond Morris has spent his entire working life with his current employer, the Alcorn Manufacturing Company. In his first years with the Company, he was located in Winnipeg, Manitoba as a production supervisor. More recently, he was transferred to the Company's Calgary based subsidiary, where he has served as a manufacturing vice president until the current year.

Early in the current year, Mr. Morris was asked to move to the United States by April 1 to oversee the construction of a new manufacturing operation in Sarasota, Florida. It is expected that when the facility is completed, Mr. Morris will remain as the senior vice president in charge of all of the Florida operations. He does not have any intention of returning to live in Canada during the foreseeable future.

On April 1, Mr. Morris left Canada. In preparation for his departure, he had taken care to sell his residence, dispose of most of his personal property, and resign from all memberships in social and professional clubs. However, because Mr. Morris and his wife had three school age dependent children, it was decided that they would remain in Canada until the end of the current school year. As a consequence, Mrs. Morris and the children did not leave Canada until June 30. Until their departure, they resided in a small furnished apartment, rented on a month to month basis.

Required   For purposes of assessing Canadian income taxes, determine when Mr. Morris ceased to be a Canadian resident and the portion of his annual income which would be assessed for Canadian taxes. Explain your conclusions.

Assignment Problem Three - 7

For each of the following persons, indicate how they would be taxed in Canada for the year ending December 31, 2007. Your answer should explain whether the person is a Canadian resident, what parts of their income would be subject to Canadian taxation, and the basis for your conclusions (including references to the *Income Tax Act*, when relevant to your conclusion). Ignore any possible implications related to tax treaties.

A. Kole Ltd. was incorporated in Alberta in 1962 and, until December 31, 2002, carried on most of its business in that province. However, on January 1, 2003 the head office of the corporation moved to Oregon and the Company ceased doing business in Canada in all subsequent years.

B. Forman Inc. was incorporated in Syracuse, New York during 2005. However, the head office of the corporation is in Smith Falls, Ontario and all meetings of the Board of Directors are held in that city.

C. Martin Judge was born in Kamloops, British Columbia in 1977. In 1979, Martin's family moved to southern California and, until October 1, 2007, Martin did not return to Canada. On October 1, 2007, Martin accepted a position with an accounting firm in London, Ontario. He returned to Canada and began working at his new job on this date.

D. Ms. Gloria Salinas is a Canadian citizen who, on November 1, 2007, is appointed as Canada's new ambassador to Mexico. While Ms. Salinas was born in, and grew up in, Nova Scotia, she has resided in Mexico for the last 15 years. She anticipates that she will continue to live in Mexico subsequent to her appointment as the Canadian ambassador.

E. Roberto Salinas is the 12 year old son of Ms. Gloria Salinas (see item D). Roberto has lived with his mother in Mexico since his birth.

Assignment Problem Three - 8

For Canadian income tax purposes, determine the residency of each of the following persons and briefly explain your conclusions. Ignore any possible implications related to tax treaties.

A. Mr. Samuel Salazar lives in Detroit, Michigan and is a full time employee of a business in Windsor, Ontario. His responsibilities with the business in Windsor require him to be present for about eight hours per day, five days per week. He has no other source of income.

B. Mercer Ltd. was incorporated in British Columbia in 1963 and all of its directors' meetings were held in Vancouver until 1984. In 1984, all of the directors moved to Portland, Oregon and all subsequent directors' meetings were held in Portland.

C. Joan Brothers was born in Livonia, Michigan. She is seven years old and has never visited Canada. Her father has been consul in the Canadian Consulate in Livonia for the past 15 years. He was a resident of Canada immediately prior to his appointment as consul.

D. Brogan Inc. was incorporated in Montana in 1980, but until five years ago, all of the directors' meetings were held in Calgary, Alberta. Last year, the president of the Company moved to Butte, Montana and since that time all of the directors meetings have been held in Butte.

E. Mr. John Wills is a Canadian citizen who, until September 1 of the current year, had spent his entire life living in Regina. On September 1 of the current year, after disposing of all of his Canadian property, Mr. Wills moved his entire family to Bismark, North Dakota.

F. The Booker Manufacturing Company was incorporated in 1963 in Minnesota. All of the directors of the Company are residents of Winnipeg and, as a consequence, all meetings of the Board of Directors have been held in Winnipeg since the Company was first incorporated.

Assignment Problem Three - 9

The following independent Cases describe situations in which income has been earned by an individual or a corporation.

Required: In each of the Cases, indicate whether the income amounts described would be subject to Canadian taxation. Explain the basis for your conclusions.

Case A Martin Downs is a U.S. citizen who lives in Detroit, Michigan. He is employed two days each week in Windsor, Ontario and, during the current year, he is paid $15,000 (Canadian) for this work. In addition, he maintains a savings account at a bank in Windsor. This account earned interest of $1,500 during the current year.

Case B Sarah Mennan is a Canadian citizen who lives in Syracuse, New York. She works as an accountant in that city, and has professional income of $72,000. Ten years ago, she left her husband at the end of the second period of the final game of the Stanley Cup Playoffs. She departed from Canada the following day, and has vowed to never set foot in Canada again. She is divorced from her husband and has no assets in Canada, other than a small savings account on which she earned interest of $150 during the current year.

Case C Donald Plesser is a U.K. citizen who immigrated to Canada on July 1 of the current year. He immediately began employment as a retail clerk and, during the period July 1 through December 31, his employment income totaled $11,000. In addition, he has retained a large savings account in the U.K. Interest on this account, which was earned uniformly over the current year, totaled £11,000.

Case D Uta Jurgens is the spouse of Colin Jurgens, a member of the Canadian armed forces stationed in Germany. Mrs. Jurgens is a German citizen and has never visited Canada. During the current year, she has employment income of €28,000. She is exempt from German taxation because she is the spouse of a member of the Canadian armed forces.

Assignment Problem Three - 10

The following two Cases make different assumptions with respect to the amounts of income and deductions of Mr. Morris Dorne for the current taxation year:

Case A Mr. Dorne had employment income of $50,000 and interest income of $12,000. His unincorporated business lost $23,000 during this period. As the result of dispositions of capital property, he had taxable capital gains of $95,000 and allowable capital losses of $73,000. His Subdivision e deductions for the year totalled $8,000. He also experienced a loss of $5,000 on a rental property that he has owned for several years.

Case B Mr. Dorne had employment income of $45,000, net rental income of $23,000, and a loss from his unincorporated business of $51,000. As the result of dispositions of capital property, he had taxable capital gains of $25,000 and allowable capital losses of $46,000. His Subdivision e deductions for the year amounted to $10,500. Fortunately for Mr. Dorne, he won $560,000 in a lottery on February 24.

Required: For both Cases, calculate Mr. Dorne's Net Income For Tax Purposes (Division B income). Indicate the amount and type of any loss carry overs that would be available at the end of the current year.

Assignment Problem Three - 11

The following four Cases make different assumptions with respect to the amounts of income and deductions of Ms. Sharon Barnes for the current year:

	Case A	Case B	Case C	Case D
Employment Income	$35,000	$33,000	$16,000	$28,000
Income (Loss) From Business	(10,000)	(39,000)	(21,000)	(36,000)
Income From Property	12,000	14,000	22,000	15,000
Taxable Capital Gains	42,000	36,000	32,000	21,000
Allowable Capital Losses	(18,000)	(42,000)	(69,000)	(27,000)
Subdivision e Deductions (RRSP)	(4,000)	(7,000)	(5,000)	(11,000)

Required For each Case, calculate Ms. Barnes' Net Income For Tax Purposes (Division B income). Indicate the amount and type of any loss carry overs that would be available at the end of the current year.

Assignment Problem Three - 12

Ms. Norah Houston is employed by a large, publicly-traded Canadian company. She is a Canadian citizen and, for all of her life, she has been living and working in Canada. She does not have a spouse, common-law partner, or dependants. During 2007, her employer asks her if she would be willing to transfer to their Australian operation. As she believes that she will have more challenging work in that location, she agrees to the move. Both Ms. Houston and the company expect this move to be permanent.

On August 1, 2007 she departs from Canada. However, because she has taken no time off in several years, she spends the month of August visiting various cities in southeast Asia. She arrives in Australia and establishes residence in Sydney on September 1, 2007.

On July 31, 2007 she closes all of her Canadian bank accounts. This includes a savings account on which she has received interest of $3,500 during 2007 prior to her departure.

On August 1, 2007, she opens bank accounts in Sydney. Interest on her Australian savings account during the rest of 2007 was earned at a rate of $500 per month. (All amounts given in this problem are in Canadian dollars.)

Ms. Houston's annual salary for 2007 is $144,000, with monthly payments of $12,000. Because she had accumulated vacation credits, her payments were not altered by the time she spent traveling in August.

Ms. Houston lived in a rented condominium and was able to cancel the lease prior to her departure on August 1, 2007. No cancellation payment was required.

At the beginning of 2007, Ms. Houston owned shares in three Canadian public companies. All of these shares were sold prior to her departure, resulting in the following capital gains and losses:

- The sale of Cando Ltd. resulted in a capital gain of $27,300.
- The sale of Darcy Inc. resulted in a capital loss of $14,500.
- The sale of Marganto Ltd. resulted in a capital loss of $6,800.

Prior to her departure, Ms. Houston was operating a mail order business out of her condominium. On July 31, 2007, she closes down this business. For the period January 1 through July 31, 2007, the business had a loss of $27,000.

During 2007, Ms. Houston made support payments to her former spouse of $2,000 on the first day of each month until his death in a mysterious boating accident on August 28, 2007. She made a deductible contribution to her Canadian RRSP in the amount of $8,800 on May 1, 2007. The RRSP was not collapsed on Ms. Houston's departure from Canada.

Required:

A. Determine Ms. Houston's residency status for 2007 and explain your conclusion.

B. Calculate Ms. Houston's Net Income For Tax Purposes that will be included in her 2007 Canadian tax return and any loss carry overs that will be available to her at the end of 2007. Ignore any possible implications related to the Canada/Australia tax treaty.

CHAPTER 4

Goods And Services Tax

Note On May, 2006 Budget

4-0.   As most of you are probably aware, the May, 2006 Budget included a 1 percentage point reduction in the GST rate, from 7 percent, to a new level of 6 percent. While this rate change did not come into effect until July 1, 2006, in preparing the previous edition of this text, we assumed that it was in effect for the entire calendar year. This avoided the problem of dealing with some fairly complex transitional rules for that year.

While there was some discussion of a further rate reduction in 2007, this did not come to pass. The GST rate for all of 2007 is 6 percent. The text and all of the problem material in this edition of *Canadian Tax Principles* has been prepared using the 6 percent rate.

Introduction

4-1.   After significant controversy, a goods and services tax (GST, hereafter) was introduced in Canada on January 1, 1991. This broadly based, multi-stage transaction tax replaced the more narrowly focused federal sales tax on manufactured goods, a widely criticized tax that had been in place for a number of years.

4-2.   This Chapter will focus on the basic operations of the GST. In subsequent Chapters, we have integrated coverage of the GST with the related income tax provisions. A summary of how the GST applies to employee benefits is included in Chapter 5. The application of the GST to capital acquisitions and dispositions is covered in Chapter 10. Some attention will also be given to the GST implications associated with the purchase and sale of a business in Chapter 19.

4-3.   We begin this Chapter with a brief consideration of some of the basic concepts that are involved in transaction taxes. The remainder of the Chapter is devoted to the specific provisions of the GST. We view this as an extremely important subject, despite the fact that coverage of this subject is not required by the education programs of some of Canada's professional accounting organizations.

4-4.   The great majority of businesses in Canada file GST returns. In addition, many organizations, such as charities and unincorporated businesses, that are not required to file income tax returns must file GST returns. Given the pervasiveness of this tax and the amounts that can be involved, it is our view that some understanding of its application is an essential component of the knowledge base of every professional accountant and businessperson.

Transaction Tax Concepts

General

4-5.   While taxes like the GST are often referred to as commodity taxes, the title is not appropriate as the term commodity does not include services. When both goods and services are subject to a tax, what we are really concerned with is the taxation of transactions as opposed to the taxation of income.

4-6.   In both Canada and the U.S., the bulk of federal tax revenues has been generated by taxes on personal and corporate income. However, transaction taxes are widely used in both countries at the provincial or state level. In addition, there has been a worldwide trend towards increased use of transaction taxes, with many industrialized countries now relying heavily on this type of taxation.

4-7.   In Canada, transaction taxes are used both at the federal and provincial levels of government. Given this, one would expect some harmonization in the application of such taxes by these two levels of government. To a limited extent this has happened. Somewhat surprisingly, the first instance of such harmonization took place with Quebec as the participant. On July 1, 1992, the Quebec government harmonized (although not completely) its provincial sales tax with the federal GST.

4-8.   A further move towards harmonization took place on April 1, 1997, when three of the Atlantic provinces fully harmonized their provincial sales taxes with the federal GST. As a result, New Brunswick, Nova Scotia, and Newfoundland have what is referred to as a harmonized sales tax (HST). There has been no significant progress since that time. This means that in provinces such as Ontario and British Columbia, businesses have to deal with both the GST and a separate and distinct provincial sales tax regime.

4-9.   Some of the factors that support the increased use of transaction taxes are as follows:

• **Simplicity**   Transaction taxes are easy to administer and collect. No forms are required from individuals paying the tax and, if the individual wishes to acquire a particular good or service, it is difficult to evade payment.

• **Incentives To Work**   An often cited disadvantage of income taxes is that they can discourage individual initiative to work and invest. Transaction taxes do not have this characteristic.

• **Consistency**   Transaction taxes avoid the fluctuating income and family unit problems that are associated with progressive income tax systems (see Chapter 1).

4-10.   Given these advantages for transaction taxes, why is income taxation still used? The answer to this question largely involves the question of fairness. In general, transaction taxes relate to consumption. When this is combined with the fact that lower income individuals usually spend a larger portion of their total income on consumption, transaction taxes are assessed at higher effective rates on individuals with lower incomes. That is, transaction taxes are usually regressive. This is in conflict with the widely held belief that fairness requires that individuals with higher incomes should have their income taxed at higher average rates. This goal is best accomplished through the continued use of a progressive income tax system.

4-11.   The government has compensated for the regressive nature of the GST by providing a GST tax credit that is available to low income individuals who file income tax returns. Whether this is sufficient to offset the negative impact of the GST on the relative position of low income individuals is a matter that has been subject to debate.

Example

Basic Data

4-12.   In discussing the various approaches that can be used in the application of transaction taxes, a simple example is useful. Such an example is diagramed in Figure 4-1. As can be seen in Figure 4-1, our example involves a manufacturer who produces 1,000 units of product at a cost of $4 per unit, a total cost of $4,000. All of the 1,000 units are sold to a wholesaler for $10 per unit. The wholesaler then sells 800 of the units to a retailer for $25 per unit. The retailer, in turn, sells 500 of the units to a consumer for $50 per unit.

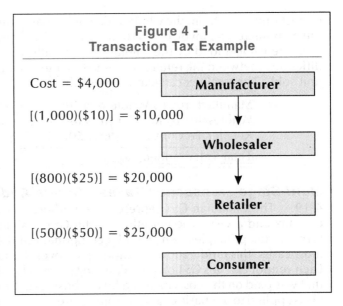

Figure 4 - 1
Transaction Tax Example

Cost = $4,000 → **Manufacturer**

[(1,000)($10)] = $10,000 → **Wholesaler**

[(800)($25)] = $20,000 → **Retailer**

[(500)($50)] = $25,000 → **Consumer**

Single Stage Transaction Taxes - Retail Sales Tax

4-13. A single stage transaction tax could be applied at any level in this example. The most common type of single stage tax is applied at the consumer level. This would be the familiar retail sales tax that is collected in several Canadian provinces. For example, if the transactions depicted in Figure 4-1 took place in Ontario, an 8 percent retail sales tax would be assessed on the $25,000 price that the retailer charged the consumer, resulting in a provincial sales tax of $2,000 being paid by the consumer.

4-14. The consumer level is probably the most appropriate level to apply a single stage transaction tax. The tax is visible and its incidence is relatively clear. In contrast, when a wholesale or manufacturer's tax is used, complications can arise when business relationships are formed that blur the lines between the manufacturing, wholesale, and retail levels. This can occur with vertical integration, and necessitates estimates or notional values for transfers between the manufacturing, wholesale, or retail levels of an organization.

Multi-Stage Transaction Taxes - Turnover Tax

4-15. Again referring to Figure 4-1, it would be possible to impose a multi-stage transaction tax at any combination of the various levels depicted. For example, the tax could be applied at the wholesale and retail levels, without application at the manufacturing level. Alternatively, the manufacturing and wholesale levels could be taxed without application at the retail level. An extension of this taxation to all levels is sometimes referred to as a turnover tax, with transactions being taxed at all levels in the distribution chain.

4-16. The problem with such a turnover tax is that it involves the pyramiding of taxes when there is no credit for taxes paid earlier in the chain. For example, if there was a 6 percent turnover tax in place, the manufacturer in Figure 4-1 would charge the wholesaler $10.60 per unit. When the wholesaler applies his normal markup of 250 percent of cost ($25 ÷ $10), the price would be $26.50 per unit [($10.60)(2.5)]. Of this $26.50, $0.034 [($0.60)(6%)] would represent a tax on the tax that was charged to the wholesaler by the manufacturer. If the 6 percent tax was also applied to the transfers to the retailer and to the ultimate consumer, there would be further applications of tax on previously assessed amounts of tax. Given this pyramiding problem, turnover taxes are not widely used.

Multi-Stage Transaction Taxes - Value Added Tax

4-17. Internationally, the most common type of multi-stage transaction tax is the value added tax (VAT, hereafter). With a VAT, transactions are taxed at each level in the distribution chain. Using whatever rate is established, the VAT is applied to the value added by the business to goods and services, rather than to the gross sales of the business.

4-18. If we assume a 6 percent rate of tax and continue to use the example presented in Figure 4-1, a VAT would require the manufacturer to charge tax on the difference between the sales price of $10 per unit sold and the related input costs of $4 per unit sold. In corresponding fashion, the wholesaler would charge the 6 percent on the difference between the manufacturer's invoice of $10 per unit sold and the wholesale price of $25 per unit sold (i.e., the value added by the wholesaler). Finally, the retailer would charge the VAT on the difference between the retail price of $50 per unit sold and the wholesaler's price of $25 per unit sold. The total tax calculation is as follows:

Manufacturer To Wholesaler [(6%)(1,000)($10 - $4)]	$ 360
Wholesaler To Retailer [(6%)(800)($25 - $10)]	720
Retailer To Consumer [(6%)(500)($50 - $25)]	750
Total Value Added Tax	$1,830

Multi-Stage Transaction Taxes - Goods And Services Tax

4-19.   The Canadian GST represents something of a compromise between a straight turn-over tax and a VAT. The net effect of the GST is similar to a VAT, but the calculations use turnover tax principles. An essential component of the GST is the input tax credit (ITC). In most cases, this credit allows vendors to recover the GST paid on their business purchases. Each vendor charges GST on the full selling price. This tax is then offset by a credit for the GST that was paid on the costs incurred by the business. Continuing to assume a 6 percent rate of tax is applied to our basic example from Figure 4-1, the GST calculations would be as follows:

Manufacturer

GST Collected [(6%)(1,000)($10)]	$600
Input Tax Credits [(6%)(1,000)($4)]	(240)
Net GST Payable	$360

Wholesaler

GST Collected [(6%)(800)($25)]	$1,200
Input Tax Credits [(6%)(1,000)($10)]	(600)
Net GST Payable	$ 600

Retailer

GST Collected [(6%)(500)($50)]	$1,500
Input Tax Credits [(6%)(800)($25)]	(1,200)
Net GST Payable	$ 300

4-20.   The total GST that was paid at all levels is $1,260 ($360 + $600 + $300), significantly less than the $1,830 that was paid using the VAT approach. The reason for this is that, when the GST approach is used, the enterprise receives ITCs for all purchases, without regard to whether or not the goods are sold. In this example, at both the wholesale and retail levels, purchases exceed sales. As ITCs are earned and received from the government on units purchased, while GST is collected and paid to the government on units sold, these enterprises benefit from having their purchases exceed their sales. In contrast, under a VAT system, the tax to be paid is based on units sold and no benefit is received for taxes paid on units that are still on hand.

4-21.   In general, if purchases and sales are equal, the tax that is assessed under a VAT system is similar to that assessed under a GST system. This can be seen at the manufacturer level in our example. In the case of the manufacturer, the units purchased and sold were equal. For this enterprise, the VAT approach resulted in exactly the same net tax as the GST approach.

4-22.   Given that the VAT approach is more commonly used on a worldwide basis, there is some question as to why Canada chose to use the alternative GST approach. While background documents on the GST do not provide a direct answer to this question, it would appear that the major advantage of the GST approach is that it does not rely on an accounting determination of value added. The tax is charged on all taxable goods sold, with input tax credits available for GST paid on all expenditures for inputs used in commercial activities.

The fact that there is no matching requirement avoids the controversies that can arise when various types of cost matching and allocation procedures are required.

4-23. It can also be argued that the GST approach is more equitable as it is more closely associated with actual cash flows than would be the case with a VAT system. The cash required to pay transaction taxes is based on purchases, without regard to when these inputs result in sales. As the GST approach provides for credits based on purchases, it can be argued that this approach is fairer to the enterprises that are involved in the production/distribution chain.

4-24. There is a further question of why the government chose to use a multi-stage tax, rather than implementing a less complex, single stage, federal sales tax at the retail level. An often cited reason is related to tighter administration and control. With the GST, a vendor does not have to determine whether or not customers of particular goods and services are exempt because they are one or more steps away from the retail or final consumption level.

4-25. An additional reason for using a multi-stage tax is that it is applied further up the distribution chain. This, of course, means that the tax revenues accrue to the government at an earlier point in time.

Exercise Four-1

Subject: GST vs. VAT

During a taxation period, Darvin Wholesalers purchased merchandise for $233,000. Merchandise sales during this period totalled $416,000 and the cost of the merchandise sold was $264,000. Ignoring all other costs incurred by Darvin and assuming a rate of 5 percent, how much tax would be paid by Darvin under a VAT system and, alternatively, under a GST system?

End of Exercise. Solution available in Study Guide.

Liability For GST

Basic Charging Provision

4-26. The basic charging provision for GST is found in the *Excise Tax Act* (ETA). The *Excise Tax Act* is available on the ProFile CD-ROM as part of the InTRA Tax Research Assistant. The GST charging provision is as follows:

> **ETA 165(1)** **Imposition of goods and services tax** — Subject to this Part, every recipient of a taxable supply made in Canada shall pay to Her Majesty in right of Canada tax in respect of the supply calculated at the rate of 6% on the value of the consideration for the supply.

4-27. In order to understand this charging provision, it will be necessary to give attention to the concept of supply. We will cover this in the next section of this chapter.

4-28. Note that the tax is assessed on the recipient of, rather than the provider of, taxable supplies. As we shall find in a later section of this Chapter, responsibility for collection of the tax is with the provider of the taxable supplies (the GST registrant).

The Concept Of Supply

Basic Definition

4-29. The *Excise Tax Act* defines supply as follows:

> **ETA 123** **Supply** means the provision of property or a service in any manner, including sale, transfer, barter, exchange, licence, rental, lease, gift or disposition.

4-30.   While this definition includes most of the items that we would consider to be revenues under GAAP, it is actually a much broader term. It would include all of the following:

- the sale, rental, or transfer of goods,
- the rendering of services,
- licensing arrangements for copyrights or patents,
- the lease, sale, or other transfer of real property, and
- barter transactions or gifts.

Supply Categories
Taxable Supplies - General Rules
4-31.   The *Excise Tax Act* defines taxable supplies as follows:

ETA 123   Taxable supply means a supply that is made in the course of a commercial activity.

4-32.   Expanding on this definition, commercial activity is defined in the *Excise Tax Act* as follows:

ETA 123   Commercial Activity of a person means

(a) a business carried on by the person (other than a business carried on without a reasonable expectation of profit by an individual, a personal trust or a partnership, all of the members of which are individuals), except to the extent to which the business involves the making of exempt supplies by the person,

(b) an adventure or concern of the person in the nature of trade (other than an adventure or concern engaged in without a reasonable expectation of profit by an individual, a personal trust or a partnership, all of the members of which are individuals), except to the extent to which the adventure or concern involves the making of exempt supplies by the person, (**Byrd/Chen Note** In somewhat simplified terms, this is a one-shot business venture, as opposed to an ongoing activity.) and

(c) the making of a supply (other than an exempt supply) by the person of real property of the person, including anything done by the person in the course of or in connection with the making of the supply

4-33.   As used here, the term business has the following meaning:

ETA 123   Business includes a profession, calling, trade, manufacture or undertaking of any kind whatever, whether the activity or undertaking is engaged in for profit, and any activity engaged in on a regular or continuous basis that involves the supply of property by way of lease, licence or similar arrangement, but does not include an office or employment;

4-34.   Stated in practical, every-day language, this says that if you are providing goods or services, including real property, in the course of a business activity, you are providing taxable supplies unless:

- the business does not have a reasonable expectation of profit;
- the supplies are exempt supplies; or
- the services are employment services.

4-35.   Taxable supplies fall into two categories. The first category is supplies that we will refer to as fully taxable supplies. The second category is supplies that are zero-rated.

Fully Taxable Supplies
4-36.   Fully taxable supplies are those that are taxed at the 6 percent federal rate. Examples of fully taxable supplies include:

- transportation in Canada,
- restaurant meals and beverages,

- clothing and footwear,
- furniture,
- admissions to concerts, athletic and other events
- contractors' services,
- legal and accounting fees,
- haircuts, and
- cleaning services.

Zero-Rated Supplies

4-37. The *Excise Tax Act* provides a list of taxable supplies that are designated as zero-rated. While these supplies are said to be taxable, they are taxed at zero percent, rather than the regular 6 percent rate.

4-38. At first glance, this concept seems a bit senseless in that there is no tax charged on either zero-rated supplies or exempt supplies. However, an important difference exists. Because zero-rated supplies are considered to be taxable supplies, the providers of such supplies can recover the GST paid on business purchases as input tax credits. In contrast, providers of exempt supplies are not eligible for input tax credits (see Paragraph 4-80).

4-39. In addition, as zero-rated supplies are considered taxable at a rate of zero percent, they are included in the threshold amounts for determining the filing frequency of a registrant's GST returns. This is covered beginning in Paragraph 4-109.

4-40. Common items that are included in the category of zero-rated supplies are as follows:

- prescription drugs,
- medical devices such as wheelchairs, eye glasses, canes, hospital beds, and artificial limbs,
- basic groceries,
- most agricultural and fishing products,
- goods and services exported from Canada, and
- foreign travel and transportation services (see following Paragraph).

4-41. Some elaboration is required for the meaning of foreign travel. Surface travel by ship, bus, or train is zero-rated when the origin or termination point is outside Canada. Other surface travel is fully taxable at the 6 percent rate.

4-42. In the case of air travel, the GST net is spread somewhat wider. Air travel is zero-rated only when the origin, stopover or termination point is outside North America. This broader definition makes transborder flights between Canada and the United States fully taxable at the 6 percent rate.

Exempt Supplies

4-43. As was the case with zero-rated supplies, the *Excise Tax Act* provides a list of supplies that are exempt from GST. Persons supplying exempt items do not collect GST and are not eligible for input tax credits for GST paid on the related purchases. As we shall see when we discuss input tax credits, this means that suppliers of exempt supplies pay GST that is not refundable to them on goods and services required to operate their business. As a consequence, the non-recoverable GST paid is a cost of doing business that is likely to be passed on to customers in the form of higher prices.

4-44. Some common items that are included in the category of exempt supplies are as follows:

- most health care and dental services,
- financial services provided to Canadian residents,
- sales of used residential housing and long-term residential rents (e.g., rentals for more than 30 days),
- most land sold by individuals where the land was not used in a business,
- educational courses leading to certificates or diplomas, tutoring for credit courses, and music lessons,

- child or personal care services, and
- a wide variety of services provided by charities, not-for-profit, and government organizations (see discussion under Specific Applications at Paragraph 4-133).

Applying the GST Rate

Basic Approach

4-45. To determine the amount of GST to be charged, the rate is applied to the amount of consideration received in return for the delivery of taxable supplies. In most cases, the consideration will be monetary and the amount to be recorded is obvious. If the consideration is non-monetary (e.g., a barter transaction), GST is still applicable. In this case, however, an estimate will have to be made of the fair market value of the consideration received.

4-46. The consideration for a supply for purposes of calculating the GST includes all non-refundable federal taxes, provincial taxes other than retail sales taxes, and duties and fees that are imposed on either the supplier or recipient in respect of the property or services supplied. While the general retail sales taxes of the provinces are excluded from the GST base, in calculating provincial sales taxes, some provinces include the GST. Specifically, Quebec and Prince Edward Island include GST in their sales tax base. In contrast, except for Alberta which does not have a provincial sales tax, all of the provinces west of Quebec exclude the GST from their sales tax base.

Effect Of Trade-Ins

4-47. Where a good is traded in by a non-registrant towards the supply of a new good, GST is only required to be levied on the net amount after the trade-in. These types of transactions are most often seen in the automotive business, where used cars are traded in when purchasing a newer automobile.

Example John Bailey, a resident of Alberta, is acquiring a new Volvo at a cost of $52,000. He is given a trade-in allowance of $21,000 on his old vehicle.

Analysis The applicable GST would be $1,860 [(6%)($52,000 - $21,000)].

4-48. If John had lived in a province that levied a sales tax, the provincial tax would be assessed using the same approach to trade-ins.

Collection And Remittance Of GST

Basic Approach

4-49. As you are aware, income taxes are collected from the same person on which the tax is assessed. An individual will calculate his Tax Payable by applying the appropriate rates to his Taxable Income. This same individual is also responsible for the payment of this tax.

4-50. The situation is different with GST. We noted previously that the basic GST charging provision assesses the tax on the recipient of the taxable supply. However, this recipient is not responsible for collecting or remitting the GST. Rather, responsibility for the collection and remittance of the GST falls on the provider of the taxable supply.

4-51. For example, if a business sells merchandise to an individual and does not collect the GST, the individual is not responsible for the payment. The business will be responsible for remitting the appropriate amount of GST, despite the fact that they did not collect this amount.

Example An Alberta store advertises a GST holiday, indicating that merchandise can be purchased without paying the GST. A customer pays $2,500 for a new freezer and no GST is paid.

Analysis In the direct sense, the customer has not paid the GST. However, the store will have to treat the $2,500 as a GST inclusive amount. It will be required to remit GST of $141.51 as a result of this sale [$2,500 - ($2,500 ÷ 1.06)].

4-52. This approach is implemented by requiring providers of taxable supplies to become GST registrants. This is discussed in the section which follows.

Registration

Meaning Of Person For GST

4-53. For GST purposes, the *Excise Tax Act* defines a person as follows:

> **ETA 123 Person** means an individual, a partnership, a corporation, the estate of a deceased individual, a trust, or a body that is a society, union, club, association, commission or other organization of any kind;

4-54. Note that this definition is broader than the one that is included in the *Income Tax Act*. For income tax purposes, the term persons includes only individuals, corporations, and trusts. Unlike that definition, the ETA 123 definition includes unincorporated businesses and partnerships.

Who Must Register

Basic Requirement

4-55. As we have previously indicated, the collection of GST is administered through a registration requirement for providers of taxable supplies. This requirement is as follows:

> **ETA 240(1)** Every person who makes a taxable supply in Canada in the course of a commercial activity engaged in by the person in Canada is required to be registered for the purposes of this Part, except where
>
> (a) the person is a small supplier;
>
> (b) the only commercial activity of the person is the making of supplies of real property by way of sale otherwise than in the course of a business; or
>
> (c) the person is a non-resident person who does not carry on any business in Canada.

4-56. This requirement contains several terms and concepts that require further elaboration. We will deal with these items in the section which follows.

Commercial Activity - Inclusions

4-57. ETA 240(1) requires registration only when "taxable supplies" are delivered in the course of "commercial activity". We have previously covered both of these definitions in our discussion of taxable supplies beginning in Paragraph 4-31.

4-58. In simple terms, any person who provides non-exempt goods or services, in the course of a business activity, is required to register for the GST unless that person is covered by one of the exceptions listed in ETA 240(1).

Commercial Activity - Exclusions

4-59. There are several items that might be considered commercial activity that are excluded in the preceding definitions:

Reasonable Expectation Of Profit Business activity that is carried on without a reasonable expectation of profit is not considered to be commercial activity.

Provision Of Exempt Supplies When a person is providing exempt supplies (e.g., financial services), there is no requirement to register.

Employment Services The provision of employment services is not considered to be commercial activity.

4-60. When a person is involved in one of these excluded activities, there is no requirement to register for the GST for that activity.

Exemption For Non-Residents

4-61.   The ETA 240(1) requirement to register, in general excludes non-residents. The major exception to this would be when a non-resident person has a permanent establishment in Canada and carries on business through that establishment. An additional exception could arise in situations where a non-resident has registered for GST on a voluntary basis

4-62.   In general, resident is defined for GST purposes in the same manner that it is defined for income tax purposes. We would refer you to Chapter 3 for a discussion of the issues associated with residence determination.

Exemption For Small Suppliers

Last Four Calendar Quarters Test

4-63.   The ETA 240(1) registration requirement indicates that it is not applicable to "small suppliers". The basic idea here is that a small supplier is a person whose delivery of taxable supplies, including those of associated businesses, is less than $30,000 per year. This provision is intended to provide compliance relief for the operators of small businesses.

4-64.   The basic test for qualification as a small supplier is based on calendar year quarters. Under this test, an entity qualifies as a small supplier in the current year if, during the four quarters preceding the current quarter, the entity and any associated entities did not have cumulative taxable supplies exceeding $30,000.

4-65.   If taxable supplies accumulate to $30,000 in any period consisting of two to four quarters (they do not have to be in the same calendar year), the entity will have to begin collecting GST on the first day of the second month following the quarter in which the $30,000 level is reached. Note that there is a 30 day grace period for registration, subsequent to the date on which the supplier begins to collect GST.

Example   Supplier A opened for business on January 1, 2007, and earned the following revenues from taxable supplies during the year:

Quarter	Months	Taxable Supplies
One	January to March	$ 7,000
Two	April to June	8,000
Three	July to September	9,000
Four	October to December	20,000
Total		$44,000

Analysis   The small supplier threshold was not exceeded in any one of the calendar quarters for 2007, and Supplier A was eligible for the small supplier exemption in each quarter. However, the total taxable supplies accumulated to $44,000 during the fourth quarter of 2007. This means that Supplier A is required to collect the GST starting on February 1, 2008, which is the first day of the second month after the quarter during which the $30,000 level is reached. Formal registration will be required within 30 days of that date.

Calendar Quarter Test

4-66.   An exception to the last four calendar quarters test exists where a person's total revenues from taxable supplies exceed $30,000 in a single calendar quarter. When the $30,000 threshold is exceeded in a single quarter, the person ceases to qualify as a small supplier and must register for, and collect, GST. The person is deemed to be a registrant beginning with the supply (sale) that caused the threshold to be exceeded. This test is referred to as the "calendar quarter test".

Example   Supplier B also started in business on January 1, 2007. The business is an art gallery and Supplier B had only two sales in 2007, one on May 15 and the other on August 28.

Quarter	Months	Taxable Supplies
One	January to March	Nil
Two	April to June	$39,000
Three	July to September	5,000
Four	October to December	Nil
Total		$44,000

Analysis   Supplier B would become a registrant as of the May 15 sale, reflecting the fact that this single sale pushes the sales for that quarter past the $30,000 threshold amount. From that point, GST should have been collected on all taxable supplies made. While collection of tax revenue is required starting on the deemed registration day, Supplier B has 30 days in which to formally register.

4-67.   In reviewing the two preceding examples, note that Supplier A and Supplier B each earned taxable revenue of $44,000 in the four calendar quarters for 2007. Supplier B, however, exceeded the $30,000 threshold in Quarter Two. This results in Supplier B being deemed to be registered starting with the May 15 transaction. In contrast, Supplier A will not have to start collecting GST until February 1, 2008 using the last four calendar quarters test.

Exercise Four-2

Subject: Requirement To Register

Ms. Sharon Salome and Mr. Rock Laughton begin separate businesses on April 1, 2007. The quarterly sales of taxable items for both businesses are as follows:

Calendar Quarter	Sharon Salome	Rock Laughton
April To June, 2007	$10,000	$ 8,000
July To September, 2007	4,000	13,000
October To December, 2007	35,000	4,000
January To March, 2008	40,000	17,000

At what point in time will Ms. Salome and Mr. Laughton have to begin collecting GST? At what point will they be required to register?

End of Exercise. Solution available in Study Guide.

Voluntary Registration

4-68.   The small supplier exemption can represent an advantage to persons with limited commercial activity whose clients are consumers and not businesses that can claim input tax credits. With some advance planning, the exemption can be extended within a family group, provided members are not considered associated. For example, it may be desirable for family members to undertake commercial activities on an individual basis rather than on a group basis to maximize any potential benefit from the small supplier exemption. In this scenario, however, the entities cannot be controlled by the same individual or group of individuals.

4-69.   There is, however, a disadvantage to this exemption. If a person does not register, they cannot receive input tax credits for GST paid. They are effectively treated as the final consumer. This means that the business must either absorb the GST or, alternatively, pass the GST paid on purchases and expenses on to its customers in the form of higher prices.

4-70.   Given this problem, voluntary registration is an alternative. Any person engaged in commercial activity in Canada can apply to be registered, even if taxable sales are less than the $30,000 small supplier threshold. It is likely that the main reasons for voluntary registrations is to claim input tax credits for the GST paid on purchases.

Registrants Ineligible For The Small Suppliers Exemption

4-71.   ETA 240 contains two other subsections which effectively prohibit the use of the small suppliers exemption for certain type of suppliers. ETA 240(1.1) indicates that suppliers of taxi and limousine services must register, even if their revenues are less than $30,000 per year. In a similar fashion, ETA 240(2) requires registration of non-registrants who enter Canada for the purpose of making taxable supplies of admissions in respect of a place of amusement, a seminar, an activity or an event.

Input Tax Credits

Vendors Of Fully Taxable And Zero-Rated Supplies

Current Expenditures

4-72.   The Canadian GST system provides vendors of taxable supplies with credits for the GST incurred on their purchases of non-capital items (e.g., inventories). Input tax credits (i.e., recovery of GST paid) can be offset against the GST that such vendors have invoiced on their taxable revenues in a particular reporting period. If, in a given reporting period, the credits exceed the amount of GST collected or collectible by the vendor, a refund of the excess can be claimed.

4-73.   To be eligible for treatment as an input tax credit, the expenditure must relate to goods or services that will be used in commercial activities. However, there is no matching of input tax credits with GST collected. For example, input tax credits on inventory purchases become available at the time the invoice for the inventory is issued, not when the goods are paid for, or when they are sold and charged to expense. Consistent with this approach, the supplier of the inventory becomes liable for payment of the GST when the invoice is issued.

4-74.   If all, or substantially all (generally understood to mean 90 percent or more), of a current expenditure is to be used for a commercial activity, then all of the GST can be claimed as an input tax credit. In contrast, if 10 percent or less of an expenditure is related to commercial activity, then no input tax credit can be claimed. If the percentage of the current expenditure used for commercial activities is between 10 and 90 percent, the input tax credit available is calculated by multiplying the total GST paid by the percentage of commercial activity usage.

Capital Expenditures

4-75.   In line with the basic idea that input tax credits are not matched against amounts of GST collected on sales, the full amount of GST paid on purchases of all capital assets used in commercial activities becomes eligible for treatment as an input tax credit at the time of purchase, regardless of when they are paid for or how they are amortized.

4-76.   In situations where a capital asset is used only partially for commercial activity, the approach used to calculate the available input tax credits will depend on the type of capital asset involved:

Real Property (Land And Buildings)   For this type of property, the input tax credit available is in proportion to the extent to which the property is used in commercial activities. That is, if the building is used 35 percent for commercial activities, the input tax credit will be equal to 35 percent of the GST paid on its acquisition. In other words, input tax credits on real property are available on a pro rata basis, with the available portion based on usage in commercial activities.

As was the case with current expenditures, if commercial usage is 10 percent or less, the purchaser cannot claim any input tax credit. Alternatively, if the usage is 90 percent or more, 100 percent of the GST paid can be claimed as an input tax credit.

Personal Capital Property (Capital Property Other Than Real Property)   In order for the input tax credits to be available on personal capital property, the assets must be used "primarily" in commercial activities. In tax work, "primarily" is generally understood to be more than 50 percent. If commercial usage is 50 percent or less, none of

	Figure 4 - 2	
	Maximum Input Tax Credits	
Taxable Purchase	**Percentage Used In Commercial Activities = X%**	**Input Tax Credit**
Current Expenditures and Real Property	X% ≤ 10%	Nil
	10% < X% < 90%	X%
	X% ≥ 90%	100%
Personal Capital Property (Except Passenger Vehicles*)	X% ≤ 50%	Nil
	X% > 50%	100%
*Special rules apply to passenger vehicles. See Chapter 8, "Income From A Business" in the section titled Restrictions On Claiming Input Tax Credits.		

the GST paid on the personal capital property's acquisition can be claimed as an input tax credit. If commercial usage is more than 50 percent, the registrant is eligible for an input tax credit equal to 100 percent of the GST paid.

Restrictions On Claiming Input Tax Credits

4-77.   As we will discover in later Chapters of this text, income tax legislation restricts the deductibility of certain types of business costs. For example, we will find that no deductions are allowed for the costs of membership fees or dues to recreational or sporting facilities, personal or living expenses, 50 percent of business meals and entertainment, and the portion of the cost of a passenger vehicle that exceeds $30,000 (excluding GST and PST). As is discussed more completely in Chapter 8, "Income From A Business", in those cases where the *Income Tax Act* does not permit the deduction of a particular cost, the *Excise Tax Act* generally provides a similar restriction on the availability of input tax credits.

4-78.   Restrictions apply to the time allowed for claiming input tax credits. For large businesses, whose sales are less than 90 percent taxable but in excess of $6 million, and listed financial institutions, the time limit is generally two years from the date the input tax credit was first available. For all other registrants the time limit is four years.

Summary Of Rules

4-79.   The rules for apportioning the maximum available input tax credits on purchases are summarized in Figure 4-2.

Vendors Of Exempt Supplies

4-80.   Vendors of exempt supplies cannot claim any GST paid on purchases that relate to exempt supplies. In some situations, vendors are involved in making taxable or zero-rated supplies, as well as exempt supplies. Since these businesses can only recover GST paid on their fully taxable or zero-rated activities, they must apportion their input tax credits on a "reasonable" basis. This applies to both current and capital expenditures that cannot be directly identified with particular exempt or taxable activities.

Accounting And The GST

Differences

4-81.   The concept of matching is integral to the determination of business income for both accounting and income tax purposes. For GST purposes, the matching concept is not relevant. GST is collected when taxable supplies are provided and input tax credits are refunded when the inputs for such provisions are purchased. No attempt is made to match credits on inputs used to make these provisions with the point in time when the provisions are made.

4-82.   Other significant differences between accounting and GST procedures are as follows:

- Most interperiod allocations, such as depreciation, amortization and CCA, are irrelevant for GST purposes. GST paid on capital expenditures that are eligible for input tax credits can generally be claimed in the period in which the expenditure is made.

- Many deductible expenses for income tax purposes do not affect the GST payable or receivable. For example, GST does not apply to employee wages, interest, property taxes, and educational services. While such costs are usually fully deductible in the calculation of Net Income For Tax Purposes, they do not require the payment of GST and, as a consequence, do not generate input tax credits.

Similarities

4-83.   In contrast to these differences, there are some features that are common to GST and income tax calculations. For example, GST is normally collected and revenue is recognized for income tax purposes when an invoice is issued for the provision of goods or services. Similarly, if an account receivable becomes uncollectible, an adjustment is required for both income tax and GST purposes.

4-84.   For current expenses, input tax credits can be claimed in the period in which the expense is recognized for income tax purposes, regardless of when the account payable is paid. As well, some of the restrictions that apply in the deductibility of certain expenses for income tax purposes (e.g., 50 percent of business meals and entertainment and certain costs of owning or leasing automobiles) are also contained in the GST legislation.

Financial Statement Presentation

4-85.   With respect to dealing with GST collected and paid in the financial statements of enterprises that must comply with GAAP, the relevant issues are dealt with in the *CICA Handbook* in Emerging Issues Committee Abstract No. 18, "Accounting For The Goods And Services Tax". This Abstract suggests that revenues should be reported net of GST collected.

4-86.   With respect to expenses, these amounts should also be reported net of GST to the extent that the amounts paid are recoverable. Note, however, that even though the revenues and expenses are reported net of GST, the amounts due to and recoverable from the government must be included in the receivables and payables of the enterprise.

Example

4-87.   The following simple example illustrates the application of the GST provisions and compares the difference between the treatment of input tax credits for vendors of zero-rated and exempt supplies.

> **Example**   In the following Income Statement of Marson Ltd. for the year ending December 31, 2007, all of the items are recorded net of any GST collected or paid.

Sales	$9,500,000
Expenses:	
Cost Of Goods Sold	$6,500,000
Amortization Expense	900,000
Salaries And Wages	1,500,000
Other Expenses	200,000
Total Expenses Excluding GST And Income Taxes	$9,100,000
Net Income Before GST And Income Taxes	$ 400,000

Other Information:

1. Of the total Sales, $6,800,000 were fully taxable supplies.

2. Purchases of merchandise exceeded the Cost Of Goods Sold by $2,200,000, net of GST. All of the merchandise purchased will be sold as fully taxable supplies. GST was paid on all of the Other Expenses as well as on the merchandise acquired during the period. Eighty percent of the Other Expenses relate to the sale of fully taxable supplies. The remaining 20 percent relate to zero-rated supplies in Case A, and to exempt supplies in Case B.

3. During 2007, capital expenditures totaled $7,500,000, net of GST, and the amounts have not been paid. These consisted of $5,000,000 for an office building that will be used 60 percent for activities related to fully taxable supplies. The remaining 40 percent is used for zero-rated supplies in Case A, and for exempt supplies in Case B.

   The other $2,500,000 in capital expenditures is for furniture and fixtures that will be used 55 percent for functions related to fully taxable supplies. The other 45 percent is used for zero-rated supplies in Case A, and for exempt supplies in Case B.

4. Marson Ltd. operates solely in Alberta and has paid no provincial sales tax on its purchases.

4-88.   To compare the difference between the treatment of input tax credits for vendors of zero-rated and exempt supplies, the GST refund is calculated for two different cases. Case A assumes that Marson Ltd. sells fully taxable and zero-rated supplies. Case B assumes that Marson Ltd. sells fully taxable and exempt supplies.

4-89.   The GST refund for the year for Marson Ltd. in both cases is calculated as follows:

	Case A Zero-Rated	Adjust-ment	Case B Exempt
GST Collected [(6%)($6,800,000)]	$408,000	Nil	$408,000
Input Tax Credits:			
Purchases [(6%)($6,500,000 + $2,200,000)]	(522,000)	Nil	(522,000)
Amortization Expense	Nil	Nil	Nil
Salaries And Wages	Nil	Nil	Nil
Other Expenses [(6%)($200,000)]	(12,000)	80% (	9,600)
Building [(6%)($5,000,000)]	(300,000)	60% (	180,000)
Furniture And Fixtures [(6%)($2,500,000)]	(150,000)	Nil (	150,000)
GST Payable (Refund)	($576,000)		($453,600)

4-90.   You will note that, while Marson Ltd. is showing a positive Net Income for accounting purposes, the Company is eligible for a GST refund. This example clearly illustrates the fact that GST reporting is not based on the matching principle. The input tax credits are available on the entire eligible amount of capital expenditures, without regard to whether they have been paid for or amortized for accounting purposes. In addition, credits are available on all of the inventory purchases, without regard to whether the merchandise has been sold.

4-91.   In Case B, as the furniture and fixtures were personal capital property and used primarily (more than 50 percent) for commercial activity, the full amount of the GST paid is eligible for an input tax credit. In contrast, the real property GST paid must be allocated on the basis of the expected use to produce taxable sales (60 percent). With respect to Other Expenses, only the 80 percent related to taxable supplies is eligible for an input tax credit.

Exercise Four-3

Subject: GST Calculation

During the current quarter, March Ltd. has taxable sales of $1,223,000 before GST. Its cost of sales for the period was $843,000 before GST and its merchandise inventories increased by $126,000, again before GST. Salaries and wages for the period totalled $87,000, interest expense was $16,000, and amortization expense was $93,000. No capital expenditures were made during the period. Determine the net GST payable or refund for the quarter.

Exercise Four-4

Subject: GST Calculation

Ms. Marsha Stone, an accountant, delivers services that are billed at $124,000 during the current year. Rent for this period on her office premises totals $25,800 and she pays a clerical assistant an annual salary of $18,500. Her capital expenditures during the period are for new office furniture with a cost of $36,000 and computer hardware and software for $20,000. All amounts are before the addition of GST or PST. She files her GST return on an annual basis. Determine the net GST payable or refund for the year.

Exercise Four-5

Subject: Input Tax Credits

During its current quarter, Modam Ltd. purchases an office building and land for a total of $1,200,000 before GST. The Company spends an additional $226,000 (before GST) on office equipment. The building will be used 40 percent for taxable supplies and 60 percent for exempt supplies. The office equipment is to be allocated in the same ratio. For accounting purposes, the building will be amortized over 40 years, while the office equipment will be written off over 4 years. Determine the input tax credits that Modam Ltd. can claim as a result of these capital expenditures.

End of Exercises. Solutions available in Study Guide.

Relief For Small Businesses

Small Suppliers Exemption

4-92.   This provision is covered in detail beginning at Paragraph 4-63 and will not be repeated here.

Quick Method Of Accounting

General Rules

4-93.   Eligible businesses, defined as businesses with annual GST included taxable sales, including those of associated businesses, of $200,000 or less during the year, can elect to use the Quick Method of determining the net GST remittance. Both fully taxable and zero-rated supplies are included in calculating the $200,000 threshold, while exempt supplies, supplies made outside of Canada, sales of real and personal capital property, and provincial sales taxes are excluded. In addition, businesses involved in legal, accounting and financial consulting services are not eligible for the Quick Method.

Figure 4 - 3
2007 Quick Method Percentages For Business Sectors

Business Sectors	Percentage on GST Included Sales	
	On First $30,000	On Excess
Retailers, Wholesalers and Manufacturers (Note 1)	1.2%	2.2%
Service Providers (Note 2)	3.3%	4.3%

Note 1 - In order to use these rates, the cost of purchased goods in the previous year must be equal to at least 40 percent of taxable supplies for that year. Examples of types of businesses eligible for this low rate include grocery and convenience stores, book stores, gas service stations, antique dealers, and boutiques.

Note 2 - Applies to service businesses such as consultants (other than financial), hair salons, restaurants, dry cleaners, travel agents, and taxi drivers. However, legal, accounting, and financial consulting businesses are not eligible.

4-94.   If the Quick Method election is filed, the registrant charges GST at the normal 6 percent rate on taxable sales. The major advantage of this method is that the business is not required to keep detailed records of current expenditures that are eligible for input tax credits. Note, however, that when this method is used for current expenditures, the registrant can still claim input tax credits on capital expenditures. This means that there will still be a need to track the input tax credits on specific capital expenditures.

4-95.   In the absence of detailed records on current expenditures eligible for input tax credits, a specified percentage is applied to the GST inclusive total of fully taxable sales to determine the amount of GST to be remitted.

4-96.   Note that the specified percentage is not an alternative GST rate. It is based on the estimated GST that would be remitted by a particular type of business, net of input tax credits on non-capital expenditures that would be claimed. For example, if the specified quick method rate for a particular business is 4.3 percent of sales, this is based on the assumption that its available input tax credits on non-capital expenditures, if they were tracked, would be equal to 1.44 percent of taxable sales [6% - (4.3%)(1.06)].

Rates

4-97.   Rates have been established for two different types of businesses. The lower rates are available to retailers, wholesalers, and manufacturers, while the higher Quick Method rates are applicable to service providers. This difference likely reflects a belief that taxable expenses are a larger percentage of sales in retail, wholesale, and manufacturing activity than is the case for services.

4-98.   In the application of each of the two rates, there is a 1 percentage point credit that is applicable to the first $30,000 of GST inclusive annual sales. The relevant rates are shown in Figure 4-3.

Example Of Quick Method

4-99.   As an example of the application of the Quick Method, consider a quarterly filing office supply store with annual taxable sales of less than $200,000. Its first quarter taxable sales were $40,000, resulting in GST included sales of $42,400 [(106%)($40,000)]. Purchases of inventory totalled $26,600 before GST. Qualifying capital expenditures during the first quarter were $3,000 before GST. Under the regular method, the first quarter GST remittance would be $624 [(6%)($40,000 - $26,600 - $3,000)].

4-100.   The required first quarter GST remittance, as determined by the Quick Method, is calculated as follows:

First $30,000 (GST Inclusive) At 1.2%	$360
Remaining $12,400 [(106%)($40,000) - $30,000] At 2.2%	273
Subtotal	$633
Input Tax Credit On Current Expenditures	Nil
Input Tax Credits On Capital Expenditures [(6%)($3,000)]	(180)
First Quarter GST Remittance	$453

4-101.   The Quick Method can be preferable, even if adequate data is available to make the calculations under the regular method. For example, a freelance writer, operating out of his principal residence, is not likely to have significant expenditures that qualify for input tax credits. In this case, the Quick Method may result in a smaller net GST payment than the regular calculation of actual GST collected, less input tax credits. It will certainly be less time consuming to file his GST return since input tax credit information on non-capital expenditures will not be needed.

Exercise Four-6

Subject: Quick Method

During the first quarter of the year, Robbins Hardware has taxable sales of $42,500, before the inclusion of GST. They have taxable purchases totalling $21,000 before GST and PST. They do not make any capital expenditures during the quarter. Using the Quick Method, determine the GST that is payable for the quarter.

Exercise Four-7

Subject: Quick Method

During the first quarter of the year, Guy's Books has taxable sales of $56,100, before the inclusion of GST. Current expenses on which GST was paid total $23,400. Due to a major renovation of the store, Guy's Books has capital expenditures of $42,000. The store is used exclusively for the sale of taxable merchandise. Compare the use of the Quick Method and the regular method for this quarter.

End of Exercises. Solutions available in Study Guide.

Simplified Input Tax Credit Method

4-102.   A simplified method for claiming input tax credits and rebates is available to registrants with annual GST taxable sales, including those of associated businesses, of less than $500,000 in their preceding year and annual GST taxable purchases of less than $2,000,000. Rather than tracking GST paid on each purchase, the simplified method bases input tax credits on GST inclusive amounts of fully taxable purchases. This total is multiplied by 6/106 to arrive at an input tax credit for the GST return. The base to which the 6/106 is applied includes any non-refundable provincial sales taxes such as Ontario's 8 percent sales tax. It also includes expenditures for capital assets other than real property. Note that the input tax credit on real property is not lost. While it cannot be included in the simplified method base, it can still be tracked separately to claim an input tax credit.

4-103.   The following items are excluded from the base to which the 6/106 is applied:

• Capital expenditures for real property.
• Purchases of exempt and zero-rated supplies, such as salaries and interest payments.
• Purchases made outside Canada, which are not subject to GST.
• Purchases from non-registrants.

- Refundable provincial sales taxes (e.g., refundable Quebec sales tax).
- Expenses not eligible for input tax credits (e.g., 50 percent of the cost of meals and entertainment).

4-104.   There is no election required to use this method and it does not affect the calculation of the GST payable on sales. The following example illustrates the use of the simplified input tax credit method.

> **Example** The activities of Garth Steel Ltd. involve the provision of fully taxable supplies. During the current year, it has current expenditures of $75,000 and expenditures for capital property other than real property of $25,000. Both of these figures are before GST or provincial sales tax. These expenditures are subject to a provincial sales tax of 8 percent. In addition, the Company has real property expenditures of $145,000 that are subject to GST, but not subject to the 8 percent provincial sales tax.

> **Analysis** The Company's input tax credit for the current year would be calculated as follows:

> | GST And PST Included Amounts For Expenditures | |
> | --- | --- |
> | Other Than Real Property [(114%)($75,000 + $25,000)] | $114,000 |
> | Factor | 6/106 |
> | Input Tax Credit On Purchases | $ 6,453 |
> | Input Tax Credit On Real Property Expenditure [(6%)($145,000)] | 8,700 |
> | Input Tax Credit For The Current Year | $ 15,153 |

4-105.   As noted, the simplified method base only includes purchases of fully taxable goods. A further restriction on the amounts claimed is that credits can be claimed only to the extent that the purchases included in the simplified method base are used to provide fully taxable or zero-rated goods and services. Where a supply is used to provide both taxable and exempt goods and services, the input tax credit claim must be pro-rated so that only the portion that applies to taxable goods and services is claimed.

Exercise Four-8

Subject: Simplified Input Tax Credits

For the current year, Simplicity Inc. has GST inclusive sales of $318,000. It has GST inclusive purchases of merchandise and other current expenditures of $190,800. Capital expenditures consist of real property (land and a building) costing $150,000 and personal capital property totalling $50,000. These amounts are before the inclusion of GST. Simplicity operates exclusively in Alberta, where there is no provincial sales tax. Using the simplified method of accounting for input tax credits, determine Simplicity's GST payable or refund for the current year.

End of Exercise. Solution available in Study Guide.

Procedures And Administration

Returns And Payments

Timing Of Liability

4-106.   In general, the supplier becomes responsible for the tax at the earliest of when the invoice for goods or services is issued, when payment is received, and when payment is due under a written agreement. Following this rule, a registrant usually becomes responsible for remitting GST in the reporting period in which a customer is invoiced, even if this is not the same period in which the cash is actually received.

4-107.   Similarly, input tax credits for GST payable to suppliers can be claimed in the reporting period invoices are issued, even if the supplier is paid in a later period. As discussed earlier in the Chapter, registrants have an extended period of time in which to claim input tax credits for GST paid on qualifying purchases. For a particular business, these requirements may create a cash flow advantage or disadvantage, depending on how quickly receivables are collected and payables are settled.

Taxation Year For GST Registrants

4-108.   Every registrant is required to have a "fiscal year" for GST purposes. Normally, this fiscal year corresponds to the taxation year for income tax purposes. However, if registrants are using a non-calendar year for income tax purposes they have the option of using the calendar year or, alternatively, using their fiscal year for income tax purposes. For example, a company with a fiscal year ending on January 31, 2007 and subject to quarterly filing requirements could choose a three month reporting period ending January 31, 2007, or a three month reporting period ending March 31, 2007. The GST fiscal year determines the reporting periods and filing deadlines for GST returns.

Filing

4-109.   All businesses and organizations that are registered to collect GST are required to file a GST Return on a periodic basis, even if there is no activity during the relevant period. Filing frequencies for the remittance of GST are determined by the total annual worldwide taxable supplies made by the registrant and its associated entities. If the annual taxable sales exceed $6,000,000, monthly filing and remittances are required. If annual taxable sales are less than $6,000,000, but greater than $1,500,000, quarterly filing is required. Annual filing applies if taxable sales are less than $1,500,000.

4-110.   A registrant may elect to have quarterly filing periods even if sales are less than $1,500,000. Similarly, a registrant with annual taxable supplies that are less than $6,000,000 may elect to file GST returns on a monthly basis. This may be advantageous for registrants who normally receive a GST refund, such as businesses with significant exports or zero-rated sales (e.g., pharmacies and grocery stores).

4-111.   For monthly and quarterly filers, returns are due one month after the end of the filing period. In general, for annual filers, the return is due three months after the end of the reporting period.

Payments And Instalments

4-112.   In general, payment of amounts owing are due when the GST returns are due. This is one month after the end of the reporting period for monthly and quarterly filers, and three months after the year end for annual filers (with the exception described in the preceding Paragraph). However, annual filers are required to make quarterly instalments if the net GST remitted for the previous fiscal year was more than $3,000.

4-113.   The instalments are based on the lesser of the previous year's remittances or an estimate of the current year's GST. These instalments are due one month after the end of each quarter. For example, calendar year filers are required to make instalments by April 30, July 31, October 31, and January 31. Annual filers below the $3,000 threshold can pay the net tax due when they file their GST return within three months of the end of their fiscal year, or by April 30 if the June 15 filing due date is applicable.

Interest

4-114.   If the GST return shows an amount owing and it is not paid by the due date, interest is assessed. Until 2007, interest rates applicable to GST balances were different than those applicable to income balances owing. The May, 2006 budget served to change this situation. For GST returns filed after April 1, 2007, the rates for the two types of taxes have been harmonized. You will recall from Chapter that:

- the rate applicable to taxes owed to the government is the prescribed rate plus 4 percent; and
- the rate applicable to amounts owed to the taxpayer is the prescribed rate plus 2 percent.

4-115.   A further change relates to the deductibility of the interest paid on late GST payments. Prior to the May, 2006 budget, interest on late GST payments was deductible. This is no longer the case. As is the case with interest on late income tax instalments, interest on late GST payments is not longer deductible.

Penalties

4-116.   Prior to the May, 2006 budget, there was a penalty of 6 percent for late payment of GST balances. In a further effort to harmonize income tax and GST procedures, this tax has been repealed and replaced with a penalty for late filing. The GST late filing penalty is equal to one percent of the unpaid amount, plus one-quarter of one percent per month for a maximum of 12 months. Unlike the income tax situation, there is no doubling of this penalty for a second offense.

Associated Persons

4-117.   You may have noticed that there are a number of GST rules that are related to the amount of supplies delivered during the period. In order to prevent the avoidance of these rules (e.g., splitting a business into two parts so that each would qualify for the Quick Method), GST legislation has rules for associated persons.

4-118.   Two or more persons are associated for GST purposes where there is substantial common ownership. For example, where one corporation controls another, the two corporations are associated. An association may exist between two or more corporations, between an individual and a corporation, and among an individual, partnership, trust and corporation.

4-119.   While associated persons file separate GST returns, they must combine their total taxable sales of goods and services in certain situations, such as when determining:

- whether they qualify for the small supplier's exemption,
- whether they are eligible for the quick method of accounting,
- whether they are eligible for the simplified method of calculating input tax credits,
- the required filing frequency of their returns (i.e., monthly, quarterly or annual).

Refunds And Rebates

4-120.   In a period during which input tax credits exceed GST collections, a refund may be claimed in the GST return for that period. Provided all required returns have been filed and are up to date, interest on unpaid refunds starts accruing 30 days after the later of the last day of the reporting period and the day after the registrant's return is filed.

4-121.   The *Excise Tax Act* also provides for a number of rebates of the GST paid by consumers under certain circumstances. For example, if a GST amount is paid in error, or by a foreign diplomat, a rebate of the GST may be claimed on a General Rebate Application Form. Also, visitors to Canada can recover most of the GST they pay on goods that are acquired for use outside of Canada by completing a Visitors' Rebate Application Form.

Books And Records

4-122.   For GST purposes, every registrant must keep adequate books and records. This requirement is found under Subsection 286(1) of the *Excise Tax Act*. Such records must be maintained at the registrant's place of business or at the individual's residence in Canada.

4-123.   All books and records, along with the accounts and vouchers necessary to verify them, must be kept for a period of six years from the end of the last taxation year to which they relate. This is the same record retention limit that is applicable for income tax purposes.

Appeals
Informal Procedures
4-124.   As is the case with income tax disputes, the usual first step in disputing an assessment or reassessment is to contact the CRA. In many cases the proposed change or error can be corrected or resolved through telephone contact or by letter. In order to authorize a person or firm to represent a GST registrant in such disputes, a consent form must be signed and filed with the CRA.

Notice Of Objection
4-125.   If the informal contact with the CRA does not resolve the issue in question, the taxpayer should file a notice of objection. For GST purposes, a formal notice of objection procedure is required.

4-126.   For GST disputes, the notice of objection must be filed within 90 days of the date on the notice of assessment. Unlike the situation with income tax objections, there is no general extension of this time period for GST registrants who are individuals, nor is there any extension for individual GST registrants in the year of their death. Failure to meet the 90 day deadline may result in the taxpayer losing all rights to pursue the matter in question.

4-127.   On receiving the notice of objection, the Minister is required to reply to the GST registrant:

* vacating the assessment;
* confirming the assessment (refusing to change);
* varying the amount of the assessment; or
* reassessing.

4-128.   Unresolved objections will be subject to review by the Assistant Director of Appeals in each Tax Services Office. These reviewers are instructed to operate independently of the assessing divisions and should provide an unbiased second opinion. If the matter remains unresolved after this review, the taxpayer must either accept the Minister's assessment or, alternatively, continue to pursue the matter to a higher level of appeal. The taxpayer has the right to bypass this notice of objection procedure and appeal directly to a higher level.

4-129.   As noted in Chapter 2, in income tax disputes, the Minister cannot institute collection procedures until after the notice of objection period has expired. When dealing with GST disputes, collection procedures are not delayed by the objection process. This more aggressive approach is allowed by GST legislation and probably reflects the fact that the government considers GST balances assessed as amounts collected in trust by the registrant on behalf of the government.

Tax Court Of Canada, Federal Court Of Appeal, And Supreme Court Of Canada
4-130.   Procedures for handling GST disputes in these courts are basically the same as the procedures for handling income tax disputes. These procedures are described in Chapter 2 and will not be repeated in this Chapter.

General Anti-Avoidance Rule
4-131.   The GST legislation includes a general anti-avoidance rule (GAAR). This rule is found under Section 274 of the *Excise Tax Act* and is very similar to the GAAR found in the *Income Tax Act*.

4-132.   While the GST GAAR is intended to prevent abusive tax avoidance transactions, it is not intended to interfere with legitimate commercial transactions. If a transaction is considered by the CRA to be an avoidance transaction, the tax consequences of the transaction may be adjusted. This could involve denying an input tax credit, allocating an input tax credit to another person, or recharacterizing a payment. But, as with the application of the income tax

GAAR, it does not apply if a transaction is undertaken primarily for bona fide purposes other than to obtain a GST benefit.

Specific Applications

4-133.   There are many GST procedures that are specific to certain types of transactions or organizations (e.g., import transactions or charitable organizations). Detailed coverage of such procedures clearly goes beyond the scope of a text which focuses on income taxation. However, we do believe that it is useful to provide you with some general information on some of these specific areas:

- **Imports**   In general, imports are subject to GST.

- **Exports**   In general, exports of goods and services from Canada are zero-rated. This means that while no GST is charged on exports, input tax credits can be claimed by the exporter.

- **Charities**   In general, the revenues of registered charities are exempt from GST. However, revenues from commercial activities (e.g., museum gift shop revenues) are fully taxable subject to the small suppliers threshold of $30,000. A special provision provides for a 50 percent rebate of GST paid on purchases related to exempt activities.

- **Not-For-Profit Organizations**   In general, the revenues of not-for-profit organizations are fully taxable (in contrast to the situation with registered charities). However, exemptions are provided for such services as subsidized home care and meals on wheels. As was the case with registered charities, qualifying not-for-profit organizations receive a 50 percent rebate of GST paid on purchases related to their exempt activities. To be classified as a qualifying not-for-profit organization, the organization must receive significant government funding. Such funding is regarded as significant when at least 40 percent of total revenues come from this source.

- **Government Bodies**   All federal government departments receive a full rebate of the GST paid on purchases by means of a tax remission order. Each provincial and territorial government is registered as a separate entity for the GST, and uses "certificates" to receive point of purchase relief from the GST.

- **Crown Corporations**   Crown corporations are not GST exempt and are registered as separate persons for purposes of the GST.

- **Municipalities, Universities, Schools And Hospitals (MUSH)**   These organizations are classified as "Public Institutions" in the GST legislation and, except where there are specific exemptions, their revenues are fully taxable. Examples of exemptions include property taxes for municipalities, course fees for universities, and medical services for hospitals. Rebates for GST paid on purchases related to exempt activities are available, with the rates varying from 67 percent for universities to 83 percent for hospitals to 100 percent for municipalities.

- **Financial Institutions**   The GST legislation defines financial institutions to include "listed" financial institutions, such as banks and insurance companies, as well as deemed financial institutions (e.g., businesses with financial revenues exceeding specified threshold levels). Revenues from providing financial services are designated as exempt. This means that, for an institution where the bulk of its revenues is from the provision of financial services, only limited input tax credits will be available.

4-134.   These brief comments serve only to give a very general view of the approach taken to these specific types of transactions and organizations. If you are dealing with any of these applications you will, of course, have to consult a more specialized source of information.

Harmonized Sales Tax (HST)

4-135.   On April 1, 1997, the retail sales taxes in Nova Scotia, New Brunswick, Newfoundland and Labrador, and the GST in those provinces (a.k.a., the participating provinces) were replaced by a single harmonized tax, the Harmonized Sales Tax (HST). The HST is governed by the *Excise Tax Act* and operates in the same manner as the GST. The HST and GST are effectively the same tax system except that two different rates are used. The HST rate is 14 percent, which applies to the same base of goods and services as the GST, and is made up of a 6 percent federal and an 8 percent provincial component.

4-136.   The HST represents a step towards the goal of a fully harmonized sales tax system in Canada. In the meantime, in addition to the GST which is assessed in all provinces, we have to deal with HST in the participating provinces, the Quebec sales tax in Quebec, and separate retail sales taxes for all the other provinces, except Alberta, which has no sales tax.

4-137.   While the HST only applies in the participating provinces, it affects any GST registrant doing business there. The *Excise Tax Act* outlines the related rules. Issues may arise relating to the "place of supply" of a particular good or service. Whenever a taxable supply is deemed to take place in a participating province, the HST applies. Conversely, if a taxable supply is deemed to occur outside of a participating province, the GST applies.

4-138.   Any GST registrant providing taxable goods or services in a participating province must collect HST at 14 percent rather than GST at 6 percent. For example, a furniture retail outlet operating in Halifax should collect only HST on its sales and no separate provincial sales tax. A clothing manufacturer with its head office in Ontario should charge HST on all goods it sells and ships to New Brunswick. Registrants anywhere in Canada who purchase goods and services in the participating provinces are eligible to recover the 14 percent HST as an input tax credit.

4-139.   The reporting requirements contained in the *Excise Tax Act* apply to both the GST and the HST and the same registration number is used to report both taxes. Registrants do not have to differentiate between the tax collected at 6 percent versus 14 percent. Similarly, no need exists to separately identify input tax credits claimed at 6 percent versus 14 percent.

Key Terms Used In This Chapter

4-140.   The following is a list of the key terms used in this Chapter. These terms, and their meanings, are compiled in the Glossary Of Key Terms located at the back of the separate paper Study Guide and on the Student CD-ROM.

Commercial Activity	Quick Method
Commodity Tax	Registrant
Exempt Goods And Services	Simplified ITC Accounting
Fully Taxable Goods And Services	Small Suppliers Exemption
Goods And Services Tax (GST)	Supply
Harmonized Sales Tax (HST)	Transaction Tax
Input Tax Credit (ITC)	Value Added Tax (VAT)
MUSH	Zero-Rated Goods And Services

Problems For Self Study

(The solutions for these problems can be found in the separate Study Guide.)

Self Study Problem Four - 1

The government is considering introducing a pure turnover tax, so that businesses will only have to account for and remit tax collected on transactions.

Assume goods normally move from the manufacturer, to the wholesaler, to the distributor, to the retailer, and finally to the consumer. There is a mark-up of 50 percent at each turnover and the tax applies to the selling price at each turnover. Assume a cost of $100 to manufacture a particular good.

Required: Calculate the transaction tax rate required to raise the same amount of tax revenue as a 6 percent GST on consumer goods.

Self Study Problem Four - 2

Chantelle Chance is a hairdresser who started in business on October 1, 2006 and has not registered to collect the GST. Revenues from her business for her first year of operation were as follows:

First Quarter	$ 4,000
Second Quarter	6,500
Third Quarter	9,000
Fourth Quarter	9,500
Total Ending September 30, 2007	$29,000

For the quarter ending December 31, 2007, business revenues were $11,500.

Required: Advise Chantelle if she needs to register her business for the GST, and if so, state when collection should start.

Self Study Problem Four - 3

Bombardeaux provides commuter train plumbing services in Canada and France. The firm has offices in each country. Bombardeaux is registered for GST purposes and files annually. The firm has elected to use the Quick Method for its GST remittances. It paid no GST install-ments for the current year as none were required. The following transactions occurred in the current year:

	Amount	GST At 6%	Total
Operating Revenue			
Canada	$70,000	$4,200	$74,200
France	43,000	Nil	43,000
Operating Expenses			
Canada - Taxable	22,000	1,320	23,320
Canada - Non-Taxable	15,000	Nil	15,000
France	21,000	Nil	21,000
Capital Purchases			
Canada	20,000	1,200	21,200
France	88,000	Nil	88,000

Required: Calculate the GST remittance (refund) for the current year.

Self Study Problem Four - 4

The Income Statement of Lassen Ltd., an Alberta corporation, for the current fiscal year ending December 31 is as follows (all amounts are shown without the inclusion of applicable GST):

Sales		$5,700,000
Less Expenses:		
Cost Of Goods Sold	$2,600,000	
Amortization	720,000	
Salaries And Wages	640,000	
Other Operating Expenses	370,000	
Accrued Interest	120,000	4,450,000
Income Before Taxes		$1,250,000
Less: Federal And Provincial Income Taxes		(340,000)
Net Income		$ 910,000

Other Information:

1. Sales included $1,200,000 in exempt supplies and $2,400,000 in zero-rated supplies. The remaining sales were fully taxable for GST purposes.

2. All of the goods sold involved the provision of either fully taxable or zero-rated supplies. During the year, inventories of these goods decreased by $200,000. GST was paid on all goods that were purchased for resale during the year.

3. Capital expenditures for the year amounted to $4,000,000, with GST being paid on all amounts. Of this total, $3,000,000 was for an office building that will be used 40 percent for the provision of fully taxable or zero-rated supplies. The remaining $1,000,000 was for equipment that will be used 70 percent in the provision of exempt supplies. GST was paid on the acquisition of all assets on which amortization is being taken during the year.

4. All of the Other Operating Expenses involved the acquisition of fully taxable supplies and were acquired to assist in the provision of fully taxable supplies.

5. Of the Salaries And Wages, 40 percent were paid to employees involved in providing exempt supplies.

Required: Calculate the net GST payable or refund that Lassen will remit or receive for the current year.

Self Study Problem Four - 5

Kapit Ltd. is a corporation that sells goods and services in Canada. Its Income Statement for the current fiscal year ending December 31 is as follows:

Sales		$2,300,000
Expenses:		
Cost Of Goods Sold	($1,356,000)	
Amortization Expense	(248,000)	
Salaries And Wages	(362,000)	
Interest Expense	(47,000)	
Other Operating Expenses	(162,000)	(2,175,000)
Income Before Taxes		$ 125,000
Less: Income Taxes		(46,000)
Net Income		$ 79,000

The above amounts do not include any applicable GST amounts. Kapit is an annual filer for GST purposes.

Other Information:

1. Of the total Sales, $1,955,000 were for supplies that are fully taxable for GST purposes at 6 percent.

2. GST was paid on all merchandise purchased. During the year, inventories of these goods decreased by $212,000, net of GST.

3. Capital expenditures for the year amounted to $2,175,000, with GST being paid on all amounts. Of this total, $725,000 was for equipment that will be used 48 percent in the provision of fully taxable supplies. The remaining $1,450,000 was for a building that will be used 73 percent for providing fully taxable supplies.

4. GST was paid on all of the Other Operating Expenses. These expenses related to the provision of fully taxable supplies.

5. Of the Salaries And Wages, 61 percent were paid to employees involved in providing fully taxable supplies.

Required: Calculate the net GST payable or refund that Kapit will remit or receive for the current year assuming:

A. that Kapit's sales, other than the $1,955,000 in fully taxable supplies, were of zero-rated supplies.

B. that Kapit's sales, other than the $1,955,000 in fully taxable supplies, were of exempt supplies.

Assignment Problems

(The solutions for these problems are only available in
the solutions manual that has been provided to your instructor.)

Assignment Problem Four - 1

Each of the following companies owns the same model lawn tractor:

X Ltd. This company is a GST registrant and owns both commercial and residential rental properties. The lawn tractor is used exclusively at the residential rental properties.

Y Ltd. This company is a GST registrant and is in the business of taking care of homeowners' lawns.

Z Ltd. This company is also in the business of taking care of homeowners' lawns. It is not a GST registrant because its annual sales are less than $30,000.

Required: Indicate the GST consequences for each company if it sold its lawn tractor to a non-registrant for $25,000.

Assignment Problem Four - 2

The following is a summary of the financial statement information for December for Bestomer's Best Balloons. The entity is a proprietorship registered to file a GST tax return on a monthly basis. GST was paid on purchases of balloons and operating costs. There were no capital purchases or dispositions in the month. All amounts are presented without the inclusion of applicable GST.

Sales	$69,000
Expenses:	
Cost Of Balloons Sold (Note)	$12,000
Salaries And Wages	19,000
Operating Costs	14,500
Amortization Expense	10,000
Total Expenses	$55,500
Income Before Income Taxes	$13,500
Less: Federal And Provincial Income Taxes	4,500
Net Income	$ 9,000

Note   The inventory of balloons at the end of the month was $4,000. The corresponding figure at the beginning of the month was $3,000.

Required: Outline the GST treatment of each of the items presented and calculate the GST remittance for December.

Assignment Problem Four - 3

Rhapsody Music Supplies is a GST registrant, and reported the following sales and expenditures in October. All sales were cash sales, and all expenditures were invoiced for and paid in the month. An 8 percent provincial sales tax (PST) applied to all sales and some purchases.

	Amount	GST	PST	Total
Sales	$2,400	$144	$192	$2,736
Expenditures				
Capital Equipment	$ 400	$ 24	$ 32	$ 456
Interest	100	-0-	-0-	100
Purchases Of Inventory	600	36	-0-	636
Rent	400	24	-0-	424
Salaries	400	-0-	-0-	400
Supplies	200	12	16	228
Total Expenditures	$2,100	$ 96	$ 48	$2,244

Required: Using the simplified input tax credit calculation, determine the total input tax credit that can be claimed for the month and the required net GST remittance.

Assignment Problem Four - 4

Quarterhorse Saddles started operations on April 1, 2007, and has selected a September 30th year end. Calendar quarters are selected for GST reporting. The business specializes in the custom manufacture of saddles for quarter horses. All billings for a given month are billed on the last day of the month.

During the first year of operations, Quarterhorse Saddles provided the following services:

Month	Value Of Services
April, 2007	$12,000
May	16,000
June	9,000
July	9,000
October	5,000
November	7,000
February, 2008	4,000
March	10,000
April	in progress

Required:

A. Identify when Quarterhorse Saddles was required to register for and collect the GST.

B. Assume the GST is only applied to services after the $30,000 threshold is passed. Calculate the GST collectible for each quarter and specify the due date.

Assignment Problem Four - 5

Come-By-Chance operates white-water rafting trips along the Fraser River in British Columbia and is not registered for the GST. The business is seasonal, with the following trip fees received in 2006:

June	$ 5,200
July	13,400
August	9,500
Total 2006 Revenue	**$28,100**

To date, revenue received in 2007 is as follows:

May	$ 1,300
June	$ 6,200

Required: Come-By-Chance would like to know if, and when, the business needs to register for, and collect, GST.

Assignment Problem Four - 6

Claire, Nicole, Barbara, and Elizabeth Sperry are sisters and each runs a separate unincorporated business. They provide you with the following annual information for their businesses. All amounts are reported inclusive of GST. None of the sales or purchases were zero-rated or exempt.

	Type Of Business	Sales	Purchases
Claire	Lawn Maintenance	$150,000	$ 35,000
Barbara	Tennis Supplies	150,000	100,000
Nicole	Pro Golf Instruction	120,000	35,000
Elizabeth	Golf Watch Sales	120,000	75,000

Required: Recommend whether any of the businesses should use the Quick Method to calculate net GST remittances.

Assignment Problem Four - 7

The Income Statement of Montagne Inc. for the current fiscal year ending December 31 is as follows (applicable GST has been excluded from all amounts):

Sales And Other Revenues		$823,000
Less Expenses:		
Cost Of Goods Sold	$478,000	
Amortization Expense	132,000	
Salaries And Wages	57,000	
Other Operating Expenses	32,000	
Accrued Interest	16,000	715,000
Income Before Taxes		$108,000
Less: Federal And Provincial Income Taxes		(23,000)
Net Income		$ 85,000

Other Information:

1. Sales And Other Revenues included $120,000 in exempt supplies and $116,000 in zero-rated supplies. The remaining sales were fully taxable for GST purposes.

2. All of the goods sold involved the provision of either fully taxable or zero-rated supplies. During the year, inventories of these goods decreased by $74,000. GST was paid on all goods that were purchased for resale during the year.

3. Capital expenditures for the year amounted to $1,200,000, with GST being paid on all amounts. Of this total, $800,000 was for an office building that will be used 85 percent for the provision of fully taxable or zero-rated supplies. The remaining $400,000 was for equipment that will be used 27 percent in the provision of exempt supplies. GST was paid on the acquisition of all assets on which amortization is being taken during the year.

4. All of the Other Operating Expenses involved the acquisition of fully taxable supplies and were acquired to assist in the provision of fully taxable supplies.

5. Of the Salaries And Wages, 32 percent were paid to employees involved in providing exempt supplies.

6. Ignore provincial sales taxes.

Required: Calculate the net GST payable or refund that Montagne Inc. will remit or receive for the current year.

Assignment Problem Four - 8

Norton's Variety is an unincorporated business owned by Sheila Norton. The business is a GST registrant that sells both fully taxable and zero-rated goods. In addition, Norton's Variety provides exempt services. The Income Statement for the current year is as follows (all amounts are before the addition of applicable GST):

Revenues:		
Fully Taxable Goods	$250,000	
Zero-Rated Goods	100,000	
Exempt Services	150,000	$500,000
Less Expenses:		
Cost Of Fully Taxable Goods Sold	$175,000	
Cost Of Zero-Rated Goods Sold	60,000	
Amortization	40,000	
Salaries And Wages	20,000	
Other Operating Expenses	10,000	
Accrued Interest	5,000	310,000
Income Before Taxes		$190,000
Less: Federal And Provincial Income Taxes		82,000
Net Income		$108,000

Other Information:

1. Inventories of fully taxable goods increased by $10,000 during this period, while inventories of zero-rated goods declined by $7,000. The zero-rated sales were generated by purchasing and selling zero-rated supplies.

2. Capital expenditures for this period amounted to $600,000, with GST being paid on all amounts. Of this total, $480,000 was for a building that will be used 40 percent for the provision of fully taxable or zero-rated supplies. The remaining $120,000 was for equipment that will be used 70 percent in the provision of exempt supplies. GST was paid on the acquisition of all assets on which amortization is being taken during this period.

3. Of the Other Operating Expenses, 91 percent were related to the provision of either fully taxable or zero-rated supplies.

4. Of the Salaries And Wages, 40 percent were paid to employees involved in providing exempt supplies.

5. Ignore provincial sales tax.

Required: Calculate the net GST payable or refund that Norton's Variety will remit or receive for the current year.

Assignment Problem Four - 9

Kole Ltd. is a retail business situated in southern Manitoba. It has no associated businesses. Its Income Statement for the current year is as follows (all amounts are without the inclusion of applicable GST):

Revenues:		
Fully Taxable Goods	$175,000	
Exempt Services	50,000	$225,000
Less Expenses:		
Cost Of Goods Sold	$ 95,000	
Amortization Expense	15,000	
Salaries And Wages	12,000	
Other Operating Expenses	35,000	
Accrued Interest	10,000	167,000
Income Before Taxes		$ 58,000
Less: Federal And Provincial Income Taxes		(18,000)
Net Income		$ 40,000

Other Information:

1. Inventories of taxable goods decreased by $10,000 during the year.

2. A capital expenditure was made during the year at a GST inclusive cost of $53,000. The expenditure was for equipment that will be used 60 percent for the provision of fully taxable goods. GST was paid on the acquisition of all assets on which amortization is being taken during this period.

3. All of the Other Operating Expenses involved the acquisition of fully taxable supplies and were acquired to assist in the provision of fully taxable supplies.

4. Of the Salaries And Wages, 40 percent were paid to employees involved in providing exempt services.

5. Ignore provincial sales taxes.

Required:

A. Calculate the net GST payable or refund that Kole Ltd. will remit or receive for the current year using regular GST calculations.

B. Determine if Kole is eligible to use the Quick Method.

C. Assume that Kole is eligible to use the Quick Method. Calculate the net GST payable or refund that Kole Ltd. will remit or receive for the current year using the Quick Method.

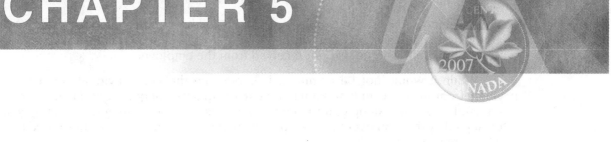

CHAPTER 5

Income Or Loss From An Office Or Employment

Employment Income Defined

General Rules

5-1. Income or loss from an office or employment (employment income, hereafter) is covered in Part I, Division B, Subdivision a of the *Income Tax Act*. This relatively short Subdivision is made up of Sections 5 through 8, the general contents of which can be described as follows:

Section 5 contains a definition of employment income.

Section 6 provides detailed information on what amounts must be included in the determination of employment income.

Section 7 is a more specialized Section that provides the tax rules related to the issuance of stock options to employees.

Section 8 provides detailed information on what amounts can be deducted in the determination of employment income.

5-2. The basic description of employment income is as follows:

ITA 5(1) Subject to this Part, a taxpayer's income for a taxation year from an office or employment is the salary, wages and other remuneration, including gratuities, received by the taxpayer in the year.

5-3. While ITA 5(2) contemplates the possibility of a loss from an office or employment, the limited amount of deductions that can be made against employment income inclusions would make such an event unusual.

5-4. Employment is generally defined in ITA 248(1) as the position of an individual in the service of some other person. Similarly, office is defined as the position of an individual entitling him to a fixed or ascertainable stipend or remuneration. As will be discussed later, determining whether an individual is, or is not, an employee can be a contentious issue.

5-5. As to what is included in employment income, the terms salary and wages generally refer to monetary amounts provided in return for employment services. However, the term remuneration is somewhat broader, bringing in any type of reward or benefit associated with employment services. With the specific inclusion of gratuities, it is clear that employment income includes not only payments from an employer but, in addition, includes any other payments that result from a taxpayer's position as an employee.

5-6.   As the preceding suggests, any benefit received by an employee that is related to the quantity, or quality, of services performed by the employee would constitute employment income, even if the amount was not received from the employer.

5-7.   While it would not be common, it is possible that an individual could receive a payment from an employer that is not related to the quantity or quality of services performed as an employee. For example, if the employee made a personal loan to the employer, any interest paid by the employer to the employee on the loan would not be considered employment income.

Cash Basis And The Use Of Bonus Arrangements

Amounts Received

5-8.   As presented in Paragraph 5-2, the definition of an employee's income states that it is made up of amounts "received by the taxpayer in the year". This serves to establish that employment income must be reported on a cash basis, not on an accrual basis.

Tax Planning Opportunity

5-9.   This fact, when combined with the fact that business income for tax purposes is calculated on an accrual basis (see Chapter 8), provides a tax planning opportunity. A business can declare a bonus to one of its employees and, because it is on an accrual basis, deduct it for tax purposes by simply recognizing a firm obligation to pay the amount. In contrast, the employee who has earned the bonus will not have to include it in employment income until it is actually received.

> **Example**   A business with a December 31 year end declares a bonus to one of its employees in December, 2007, but stipulates that it will not be paid until January, 2008.

> **Analysis**   While the business would get the deduction in 2007, the employee would not have to include the amount in income until the 2008 taxation year. If the bonus had been paid in December, 2007, the employee would have had to include it in income in 2007. In effect, this arrangement defers the taxation applicable to the employee by one taxation year.

Limits On Deferral

5-10.   There are, however, limits to this procedure. ITA 78(4) indicates that, where such a bonus is not paid within 180 days of the employer's year end (note that this is not always December 31), the employer will not be able to deduct the amount until it is paid.

> **Example**   An employer with a June 30 year end declares a bonus for an employee on June 30, 2007 that is payable on January 1, 2008.

> **Analysis**   As January 1, 2008 is more than 180 days after the employer's year end, the employer will not be able to deduct the bonus in the fiscal year ending June 30, 2007. It will have to be deducted in the fiscal year ending June 30, 2008.

5-11.   A further problem arises when a "bonus" will not be paid until more than three years after the end of the calendar year in which the employee's services were rendered. In this case, the "bonus" may become a "salary deferral arrangement", resulting in the employee being taxed on the relevant amounts in the year in which the services were rendered. This type of arrangement is discussed in more detail in Chapter 13.

5-12. The tax consequences associated with the three types of bonus arrangements are summarized in the following Figure 5-1:

Figure 5 - 1 Bonus Arrangements	
Type Of Bonus Arrangement	**Tax Consequences**
Standard Bonus (Paid within 180 days of business year end.)	The employer deducts when declared. The employee includes when received.
Other Bonus (Paid more than 180 days after the employer's year end, but prior to three years after the end of the year in which the bonus was earned.)	The employer deducts when paid. The employee includes when received.
Salary Deferral Arrangement (Paid more than three years after the end of the year in which it was earned.)	The employer deducts when earned. The employee includes when earned. (See Chapter 13)

Exercise Five-1

Subject: Bonus

Neelson Inc. has a September 30 year end. On September 30, 2007, it declares a bonus of $100,000 payable to Mr. Sam Neelson, an executive of the Company. The bonus is payable on May 1, 2008. Describe the tax consequences of this bonus to both Neelson Inc. and Mr. Neelson.

End of Exercise. Solution available in Study Guide.

Net Concept

5-13. Employment income is a net income concept. That is, it is made up of both inclusions (e.g., salaries and wages) and deductions (e.g., registered pension plan contributions and union dues). In conjunction with this, we would point out that the deductions that are described in ITA 8 can only be deducted against employment income inclusions. Given the limited deductions available in the determination of employment income, it would be very rare for these deductions to exceed the inclusions.

5-14. If this unusual result were to occur, the Section 8 deductions could not be applied against any other source of income. However, if other sources of income are available, the same result will be accomplished by deducting the net employment loss under ITA 3(d) as per the calculation of Net Income For Tax Purposes that is described in Chapter 3.

Employee Versus Self-Employed

Introduction

5-15. An individual doing work for an organization will be undertaking this activity in one of two possible roles. He may be working as an employee. If this is the case, he is earning employment income and is subject to the rules discussed in this Chapter.

5-16. In contrast, he may be working as a self-employed individual, often referred to as an independent contractor (from the point of view of the organization using the individual's services, this is often referred to as contracting out). The payments made to such self-employed individuals are classified as business income and are subject to the rules that are covered in Chapter 8.

5-17. This distinction is of considerable importance, both to the individual worker and to the organization using his services. Further, individuals and organizations can structure their arrangements in a manner that will provide the desired classification of the income that will be received by the individual. As a consequence, the following material outlines the tax features of these alternatives from the point of view of the worker and from the point of view of the organization using his services.

Employee Perspective

Deductions Available

5-18.   As will be discussed later in this Chapter, an individual's ability to deduct expenses from employment income is quite limited. This is in comparison to self-employed individuals. If an individual is self-employed, any income that he earns is classified as business income, making it eligible for the wider range of deductions that is available under Subdivision b of the *Income Tax Act*.

Tax Deferral - Withholdings Vs. Instalments

5-19.   A further advantage of being self employed is that, unlike the situation where employee status is involved, the organization that the individual is working for is not required to make any source deductions for income tax, Canada Pension Plan contributions, or Employment Insurance premiums. While this may offer some deferral of tax, this is not a clear cut conclusion.

5-20.   In the absence of withholdings, self-employed individuals should, in most situations, be making instalment payments. However, there can be some deferral involved here in that instalments are only required each calendar quarter. This is in contrast to the withholdings against employment income that must be made in each pay period.

5-21.   Also a possible advantage for the self-employed individual is that, as long as he is willing to be assessed interest, there is no legal requirement to make instalment payments. As was discussed in Chapter 2, for an individual owing large amounts of high interest debt (e.g., credit card balances being assessed interest at an annual rate of 20 percent or more), it may be more advantageous to pay down such debt rather than make instalment payments.

CPP And EI Contributions

5-22.   The self-employed individual has no liability for Employment Insurance (EI) premiums. For 2007, the employee's share of these contributions amounts to 1.8 percent of the first $40,000 in gross wages, with a maximum annual value of $720 (the employee's employer is assessed 1.4 times this amount, an effective rate of 2.52 percent). While a self-employed individual is spared having to pay EI premiums, this may not be a completely desirable situation. The offsetting disadvantage is that self-employed individuals are not eligible for the EI benefits that are provided by this program.

5-23.   With respect to Canada Pension Plan (CPP) contributions, for 2007 both the employee and the employer are required to contribute 4.95 percent of gross wages in excess of a basic exemption of $3,500, up to a maximum of $43,700. This results in maximum contributions by both the employee and employer of $1,990, or a total of $3,980.

5-24.   While nothing is withheld from their revenues, self-employed individuals are required to contribute to this program. In fact, self-employed individuals have to make a double contribution, reflecting both the employee's share as well as what would have been the employer's share. The eventual pension benefits received by the self-employed individual will be the same as those received by an employed individual with the same earnings. Clearly, the self-employed individual is worse off with respect to making contributions to the Canada Pension Plan.

Fringe Benefits

5-25.   A significant disadvantage of being classified as an independent contractor rather than an employee is the fact that independent contractors do not receive fringe benefits. An employee may receive a wide variety of benefits such as dental and drug plans, membership in a registered pension plan, vacation pay, or life insurance coverage. These benefits may, in some cases, add as much as 20 percent to an employee's remuneration. The fact that such benefits are not available to a self-employed individual means that he will have to receive significantly higher basic remuneration to be in the same economic position as an individual working as an employee who has generous benefits.

Opportunity For Tax Evasion

5-26.   While we certainly do not condone this, as a practical matter, being self-employed can offer significantly larger opportunities for tax evasion. When employment income is received from a business, there are stringent reporting requirements that make it difficult for an employee not to report employment income.

5-27.   In contrast, self-employment income is sometimes received partially or wholly in cash, depending on the clients. Usually when cash is received, the work is being done for an individual who cannot deduct the cost of the work and does not require a receipt to be issued (e.g., the owner of a residence hiring a self-employed contractor to do renovations). If the self-employed individual is willing to evade taxes by not reporting these revenues, then the lack of withholding on self-employment earnings becomes a permanent reduction in taxes. Although it is a clearly illegal form of behavior, for some individuals, not reporting earnings received in cash is one of the main motivations behind being self-employed.

Conclusion

5-28.   As the preceding indicates, the desirability of self-employed status is not clear cut. For an individual with limited deductible expenses, self-employment may not be advantageous from an economic point of view. Alternatively, if the individual's work is such that large amounts of business expenses are generated, it is probably desirable to be taxed as a self-employed contractor.

5-29.   Other possible advantages could include the ability to set work schedules and the freedom to choose the amount and type of work accepted. The added cost of accounting for the business and the implications of the GST would also have to be considered. As noted in Chapter 4, in most cases, a self-employed individual would have to register for the GST if he is not a small supplier.

Employer Perspective

5-30.   There are several advantages to a business from using the services of self-employed individuals as opposed to employees. One of the major advantages associated with the hiring of these independent contractors (a.k.a. contracting out) is that the employer avoids payments for Canada Pension Plan (CPP), Employment Insurance (EI), Workers' Compensation, and Provincial Health Care (where applicable). The amounts involved here are consequential. CPP and EI payments alone can add over 7 percent to the wage costs. Provincial payroll taxes can push the total of these costs above 10 percent of wage costs. Further savings result from the fact that the employer will avoid the administrative costs associated with having to withhold and remit income taxes and the employee's share of CPP and EI payments.

5-31.   Also in favour of using independent contractors is the fact that the business will avoid the costs of any fringe benefits that it normally extends to its employees. A less measurable benefit is that employers are freed from ongoing commitments to individuals because there is generally no long-term contract with self-employed workers. Given these advantages, it is not surprising to find more businesses are contracting out in order to control labour costs.

Making The Distinction

5-32.   The general approach to distinguishing between an employee and an independent contractor is the question of whether an employer/employee relationship exists. As there is no clear definition of employer/employee relationships, disputes between taxpayers and the CRA are not uncommon. To avoid such disputes, and to assist taxpayers in determining whether or not an individual is an employee, the CRA provides a pamphlet titled "Employee

Or Self-Employed" (RC4110). As described in this pamphlet, the major factors to be considered in this determination are as follows:

Control   In an employer/employee relationship, the employer usually controls, directly or indirectly, the way the work is done and the work methods used. The employer assigns specific tasks that define the real framework within which the work is to be done.

Ownership Of Tools   In an employer/employee relationship, the employer usually supplies the equipment and tools required by the employee. In addition, the employer covers the following costs related to their use: repairs, insurance, transport, rental, and operations (e.g., fuel).

In some trades, however, it is customary for employees to supply their own tools. This is generally the case for garage mechanics, painters, and carpenters. Similarly, employed computer scientists, architects, and surveyors sometimes supply their own software and instruments.

Chance Of Profit/Risk Of Loss   In an employer/employee relationship, the employer alone normally assumes the risk of loss. The employer also usually covers operating costs, which may include office expenses, employee wages and benefits, insurance premiums, and delivery and shipping costs. The employee does not assume any financial risk, and is entitled to his full salary or wages regardless of the financial health of the business.

The income of an employee paid by the piece, or on commission, does not depend on the profits or losses of the employer's business. The employee is paid the same per unit amount no matter how many pieces the employer requires him to produce or sell.

Ability To Subcontract Or Hire Assistants   If the individual must personally perform the services, he is likely to be considered an employee. Alternatively, if the individual can hire assistants, with the payer having no control over the identity of the assistants, the individual is likely to be considered self-employed.

Responsibility For Investment And Management   If the individual has no capital investment in the business and no presence in management, he is likely to be considered an employee. Alternatively, if the individual has made an investment and is active in managing the business, he should be considered self-employed.

5-33.   The CRA pamphlet includes a long list of questions that can be asked in making this determination (e.g., Who is responsible for planning the work to be done?). This pamphlet can be quite helpful if more detailed information in this area is required.

5-34.   We would point out that it is extremely important for a business to be sure that any individual who is being treated as a self-employed contractor qualifies for that status. Actions that can be taken to ensure self-employed status for the individual include:

- Having the individual register for the GST.
- Having the individual work for other businesses.
- Having the individual advertise his services.
- To the extent possible, having the individual cover his own overhead, including phone service, letterhead, equipment, and supplies.
- Having the individual prepare periodic invoices, preferably on an irregular basis.
- Having a lawyer prepare an independent contractor agreement.
- If feasible, having the individual incorporate.

5-35.   A failure to take these steps could prove to be very costly to a business using the services of that individual. It is possible that, if the CRA judges the individual to be an employee, the business could be held liable for CPP and EI amounts that should have been withheld from the individual's earnings, as well as the employer's share of these amounts.

Inclusions - Salaries And Wages

5-36.   We have noted that ITA 5 specifies that employment income includes salaries, wages, and other remuneration. When only salaries or wages are involved, there is little need to elaborate on this point. Such amounts clearly must be included in the determination of employment income. However, for a variety of reasons, employers make use of many benefits other than salaries or wages. These alternative forms of compensation are commonly referred to as fringe benefits and they create additional complexity in the determination of employment income for income tax purposes.

Inclusions - Fringe Benefits

ITA 6(1) - Amounts To Be Included In Income

5-37.   ITA 6 contains a number of Subsections dealing with inclusions in employment income. The first of these, ITA 6(1), contains a number of Paragraphs that either list specific items to be included in employment income (e.g., standby charge for automobiles), or describe a type of item that must be incorporated into this determination (e.g., personal or living expenses).

5-38.   The first of these Paragraphs, ITA 6(1)(a), contains a general provision which states that all benefits received or enjoyed by an individual by virtue of an office or employment must be included in income. However, this same Paragraph also notes a number of important items that can be excluded. These include:

- employer's contributions to:
    - registered pension plans;
    - group sickness or accident insurance plans;
    - private health services plans;
    - supplementary unemployment benefit plans;
    - deferred profit sharing plans;

- counseling services related to the mental or physical health of the employee or a related party, or related to re-employment or retirement of the employee; and,

- benefits under a retirement compensation arrangement, employee benefit plans (e.g. death benefit plans), and employee trusts. However actual payments or allocations from such plans or arrangements are taxable elsewhere.

5-39.   Other Paragraphs under ITA 6(1) provide additional guidance in the form of specific items that must be included in employment income. These are:

- 6(1)**(b)**   amounts received as personal or living expenses or as an allowance for any other purpose;
- 6(1)**(c)**   director's or other fees;
- 6(1)**(d)**   allocations under profit sharing plans;
- 6(1)**(e)**   standby charge for automobiles;
- 6(1)**(f)**   employment insurance benefits (e.g. disability insurance benefits);
- 6(1)**(g)**   employee benefit plan benefits;
- 6(1)**(h)**   allocations under employee trusts;
- 6(1)**(i)**   salary deferral arrangement payments;
- 6(1)**(j)**   reimbursements and awards; and
- 6(1)**(k)**   automobile operating expense benefit.

CRA Administrative Practice On Fringe Benefits (IT-470R)

5-40.   At a less formal level, an important Interpretation Bulletin provides guidance with respect to fringe benefits. This Bulletin, IT-470R, indicates that the following benefits should be considered as part of employment income:

- board and lodging that is provided free or at an unreasonably low rate
- rent free and low rent housing
- personal use of an automobile furnished by an employer
- premiums that are allocated to specific employees under provincial hospitalization and medical care insurance plans, and certain Government of Canada plans
- travel expenses of the employee's spouse if there is no business reason for the travel
- travel benefits for the employee or the employee's family
- holiday trips, other prizes and incentive awards
- points used for personal travel that were earned in frequent flyer programs while traveling on employer paid business trips
- employer reimbursement for the cost of tools required to perform work
- amounts related to interest free or low interest loans
- financial counseling and income tax preparation
- tuition fees paid for, or reimbursed by, the employer (see Paragraph 5-41)
- gifts (see Paragraph 5-43)

Tuition Fees

5-41.   The basic idea here is that employer-paid educational costs are not a taxable benefit if the learning experience is primarily for the benefit of the employer. If it is primarily for the benefit of the employee, it will be considered a taxable benefit. To assist in making this distinction, IT-470R describes three different situations:

- **Specific Employer-Related Training**   Courses that are taken for maintenance or upgrading of employer-related skills will generally be considered to primarily benefit the employer and therefore be non-taxable.

- **General Employment-Related Training**   Other business-related courses, even if not directly related to the employer's business, will generally be considered non-taxable. Examples of non-taxable general training would include stress management, employment equity, first-aid, and language skills.

- **Personal Interest Training**   Employer-paid courses for personal interest or technical skills that are not related to the employer's business are considered of primary benefit to the employee and thus taxable. For example, fees paid for a self-interest music course would result in a taxable benefit.

5-42.   Note that the employer will be able to deduct these costs, without regard to whether they create a taxable benefit for the employee. The Bulletin also indicates that the relevant costs could include meals, travel, and accommodation as required by the educational program, again without regard to whether the employee is receiving a taxable benefit.

Gifts

5-43.   IT-470R has not been updated to reflect the CRA News Release titled "Gifts And Awards Given By Employers To Their Employees" that was issued in December, 2001. This News Release indicates that:

- Employers are able to give two non-cash gifts per year, on a tax-free basis, to employees for special occasions such as Christmas, Hanukkah, birthday, marriage or a similar event where the aggregate cost of the gifts to the employer is $500 or less, including taxes, per employee, per year.

- Similarly, employers are able to give employees two non-cash awards per year, on a tax-free basis, in recognition of special achievements such as reaching a set number of years of service, meeting or exceeding safety standards, or reaching similar milestones where the total cost of the awards to the employer is $500 or less, including taxes, per employee, per year.

- The cost of the gifts and awards are deductible to the employer, even for those gifts and awards that are received tax free by the employee.

5-44.   Note that, while the two "gifts" cannot have a total value greater than $500 and the two "awards" cannot have a total value greater than $500, a combination of awards and gifts could be given with a total value of up to $1,000. Other points to be made here are as follows:

- Near-cash gifts or awards (e.g., a gift certificate) are not eligible for this tax free treatment.

- If there are more than two awards or two gifts, or if the total awards or total gifts have a value in excess of $500, the employer can choose the gift(s) or award(s) that will be considered tax free in complying with these limits.

- If a single gift or award has a value in excess of $500, the full fair market value of the item must be included in the employee's income.

Non-Taxable Benefits (IT-470R)

5-45.   Also found in IT-470R is a list of non-taxable benefits that are not included in employ-ment income. These include:

- discounts on merchandise and the waiving of commissions on sales of merchandise or insurance for the personal use of the employee
- subsidized meals provided in employer facilities
- uniforms and special clothing
- subsidized school services in remote areas
- transportation to the job in employer vehicles in specific circumstances
- use of employer recreational facilities and membership fees, where it is an advantage to the employer for the employee to belong to a social or athletic club
- reimbursement of certain moving expenses (See Chapter 11 for a detailed discussion of moving costs.)
- premiums under private health services plans
- employer's required contributions under certain provincial hospitalization and medical care insurance plans where remittances are based on some percentage of total payroll .
- transportation passes for employees of bus or rail companies, and certain passes for employees of airline companies
- the costs of establishing, maintaining, or dismantling a blind trust when required by a public office holder
- the costs of providing counseling services related to the mental or physical health of the employee, his re-employment, or his retirement [as previously noted, this item is explicitly excluded from employment income under ITA 6(1)(a)]
- the cost of an employee's professional membership fees where the professional asso-ciation is related to an employee's duties and membership is a requirement of employment

Other ITA 6 Inclusions

5-46.   ITA 6(1) is the most broadly based Subsection in ITA 6. There are, however, a number of other Subsections that deal with individual items. These Subsections and where their coverage begins are as follows:

- ITA 6(2) and (2.1) **"Reasonable Standby Charges"** - Paragraph 5-70.
- ITA 6(3) and (3.1) **"Payments By Employer To Employee"**, which requires the inclusion of amounts paid either immediately before employment begins, or subsequent to the period of employment - Paragraph 5-173.
- ITA 6(4) **"Group Term Life Insurance"** - Paragraph 5-122.
- ITA 6(6) **"Employment At Special Work Site Or Remote Location"** - Paragraph 5-61.
- ITA 6(7) **"Cost Of Property Or Service"**, which requires the addition of applicable GST and provincial sales taxes to the amount of some taxable benefits - Paragraph 5-58.

- ITA 6(9) **"Amount In Respect Of Interest On Employee Debt"** - Paragraph 5-131.
- ITA 6(11) **"Salary Deferral Arrangements"** are covered in Chapter 13, Retirement Savings And Other Special Income Arrangements.
- ITA 6(15) and (15.1) **"Forgiveness Of Employee Debt And Forgiven Amount"**, which require that employee debt forgiven by an employer must be included in employment income - Paragraph 5-174.
- ITA 6(19) through (22) **"Housing Loss And Eligible Housing Loss"** limit the amount that can be reimbursed on a tax free basis to an employee who has suffered a housing loss as the result of a required move. These Subsections are covered in this Chapter beginning in Paragraph 5-175, as well as in Chapter 11 as part of our discussion of moving expenses.

Exercise Five-2

Subject: Employee Benefits

John Nilson is an employee. During the current year, John receives the following benefits from his employer:

- A 35 percent discount on merchandise with a total value of $10,000.
- Reimbursement of $2,000 in tuition fees for a course in creative writing.
- Business clothing with a value of $8,500 to be worn during working hours. (John's employer felt he needed a better image in dealing with clients.)
- A set of china on the occasion of John's wedding anniversary costing $450, including taxes.
- A private health care plan for John and his family. The employer pays an annual premium of $780 for this plan.

Describe the tax consequences for John that result from receiving these benefits.

End of Exercise. Solution available in Study Guide.

Tax Planning Considerations

Salary The Benchmark

5-47.   As previously discussed, some of the benefits provided to employees are fully taxable while other benefits can be extended without creating a taxable benefit. This has important implications in planning employee compensation.

5-48.   As the bulk of compensation for most employees is in the form of wages or salaries, such payments provide the benchmark against which other types of compensation must be evaluated. From an income tax point of view, these benchmark payments are fully deductible to the employer in the year in which they are accrued and fully taxable to the employee in the year in which they are received. There is no valid tax reason for using a type of fringe benefit that has these same characteristics.

5-49.   For example, if an employer rewards a valued employee with a holiday trip, the cost of the trip will be fully deductible to the employer. Further, the trip's cost will be fully taxable to the employee on the same basis as if the amount had been paid in the form of additional salary. This means that, while there may be a motivational reason for using a holiday trip as a form of compensation, there is no significant income tax advantage in doing so.

Tax Avoidance

5-50.   The most attractive form of non-salary compensation involves benefits that are deductible to the employer, but are received tax free by the employee. Since IT-470R indicates that private health care benefits are not taxable, an employer can provide employees with, for example, a dental plan without creating any additional tax liability. From a tax point of view, this type of compensation should be used whenever practical, provided it is desirable from the point of view of the employee.

Tax Deferral

5-51.   Also attractive are those benefits that allow the employer to deduct the cost currently, with taxation of the employee deferred until a later period. An important example of this would be contributions to a registered pension plan. The employer can deduct the contributions in the period in which they are made, while the employee will not be taxed until the benefits are received in the form of pension income. This will usually involve a significant deferral of taxation for the employee.

Club Dues And Recreational Facilities

5-52.   In the preceding cases, the tax planning considerations are very clear. There are no tax advantages associated with benefits that are fully and currently taxable to the employee. In contrast, advantages clearly arise when there is no taxation of the benefit, or when the taxation is deferred until a later point in time.

5-53.   There is, however, a complicating factor in the case of certain employer provided recreational facilities or employer payment of club dues. While IT-470R indicates that such benefits are not taxable to the employee, the employer is not allowed to deduct the cost of providing such benefits (see Chapter 8 for a more detailed description of these rules). This means that the advantage of no taxes on the employee benefit is offset by the employer's loss of deductibility.

5-54.   Whether this type of benefit is advantageous has to be evaluated on the basis of whether the tax savings to the employee are sufficient to offset the extra tax cost to the employer of providing a non-deductible benefit. The decision will generally be based on the relative tax rates applicable to the employee and the employer. If the employee's tax rate is higher than the employer's, this form of compensation may be advantageous from a tax point of view.

Two Problem Benefits - Automobiles and Loans

5-55.   Before leaving this general discussion of tax planning considerations related to employee benefits, we would note that two important types of benefit present significant difficulties with respect to determining their desirability. These two benefits are employer provided automobiles and loans to employees and they are discussed in detail in this Chapter.

5-56.   The basic problem in both cases is that the benefit to the employee is not based on the cost to the employer. In the case of the employee benefit associated with having the use of an employer supplied car, it is partially based on an arbitrary formula, under which the assessed benefit can exceed the cost of the car. In the case of employee loans, the benefit is assessed using the prescribed rate of interest, not the cost of the funds to the employer.

5-57.   Because of this inequality, a case-by-case analysis is required. In each situation, it must be determined whether the cost to the employer is greater than, or less than, the benefit to the employee. If the cost is greater, the employer may wish to consider some alternative, and more tax effective, form of compensation. This makes these benefits considerably more difficult to administer.

Exercise Five-3

Subject: Planning Employee Benefits

As part of her compensation package, Jill Tyler is offered the choice of: a dental plan for her family, an annual vacation trip for her family, or an annual birthday gift of season's tickets to the ballet for her and her spouse. The alternative benefits are each worth about $4,000 per year. Indicate which benefit would be best for Jill from a tax point of view and explain your conclusion.

End of Exercise.   Solution available in Study Guide.

Inclusions - GST On Taxable Benefits

5-58.   Many benefits included in employment income are taxable supplies on which an employee would have to pay GST if he personally acquired the item. For example, if an employer provides a free domestic airline ticket to reward an employee for outstanding service, this is an item on which the employee would have to pay GST if he purchased the ticket on his own. This means that the benefit calculated should also include a GST component as the employee has received a benefit with a real value that includes both the price of the ticket and the related GST amount.

5-59.   Given this situation, ITA 6(7) requires the calculation of employee benefits on a basis that includes any provincial sales tax (PST), harmonized sales tax (HST), or GST that was paid by the employer on goods or services that are included in the benefit. In situations where the employer is exempt from GST or PST, a notional amount is added to the benefit on the basis of the amounts that would have been paid had the employer not been exempt. Employers who are registered for the GST must remit the GST that is deemed to be included in the benefits allocated to their employees.

Exercise Five-4

Subject: GST On Taxable Benefits

Ms. Vicki Correli, as the result of an outstanding sales achievement within her organization, is awarded a two week vacation in the Bahamas. Her employer pays a travel agent $4,500, plus 6 percent GST for the trip. What is the amount of Ms. Correli's taxable benefit?

End of Exercise. Solution available in Study Guide.

Inclusions - Board And Lodging

5-60.   Two aspects of this fringe benefit require further explanation. The first relates to valuation. Under IT-470R, any board and/or lodging benefit received is valued at fair market value, less any amounts recovered from the employee. Also of note is that subsidized meals do not have to be included as long as the employee is required to pay a reasonable charge. This puts subsidized meals provided in conjunction with free or subsidized lodging on a similar tax footing as subsidized meals in general. There is a difference, however, in that any benefit associated with lodging is based on fair market value, while any benefit related to meals is valued at the cost to the employer.

5-61.   As an exception to this general approach to employer provided meals and housing, ITA 6(6) indicates that under certain circumstances, these benefits will not be considered employment income. If an employee is required to work at a remote location some distance away from the employee's ordinary residence, the work is of a temporary nature such that establishment of a new residence would not be practical, and the benefits are provided for not less than 36 hours, then such benefits will not be considered taxable.

5-62.   In general, if an amount has to be included in income for board and/or lodging, the value of the benefit should be computed on a GST included basis. However, long-term residential rents are GST exempt. As a result, the supply of a house, apartment, or similar accommodation to an employee is not subject to GST if the employee occupies it for at least one month, and no GST amount would be associated with this type of employee benefit. For GST purposes, provision of lodging at remote work sites is deemed not to be a supply and therefore not subject to GST.

Inclusions - Automobile Benefits

Employees And Automobiles

Employer Provided Automobiles

5-63.   Automobiles have an influence on the determination of an individual's employment income in three different situations. The first situation arises when an employee is provided with an automobile by the employer. Under ITA 6, the benefits associated with any non-business use of that vehicle must be included in the individual's employment income.

5-64.   The two types of taxable benefits associated with such personal use are referred to as a standby charge [ITA 6(1)(e)] and an operating cost benefit [ITA 6(1)(k)]. The calculation of both these taxable benefits is covered in detail in the following material.

Allowances And Travel Costs

5-65.   The other two situations in which automobiles influence employment income are discussed later in this Chapter. While we are deferring the discussion of these situations, they are briefly described here in order to avoid possible confusion:

Allowances   As an alternative to providing an employee with an automobile, some employers pay an allowance to the employee for business use of his personally owned automobile. This allowance may be included in employment income and, when this is the case, the employee will be able to deduct some portion of the automobile's costs against such inclusions.

Deductible Travel Costs   Under certain circumstances, employees can deduct various travel costs. If the employee uses his personally owned automobile for travel related to his employment, a portion of the costs associated with this vehicle can be deducted in the determination of employment income.

5-66.   Both allowances and deductible travel costs involve the determination of amounts that can be deducted by an employee who owns or leases his own automobile. As you may be aware, tax legislation places limits on the amounts that can be deducted for automobile costs (e.g., for 2007, lease payments in excess of $800 per month before taxes are not deductible and tax depreciation (capital cost allowance or CCA) cannot be deducted on capital costs in excess of $30,000 before taxes). As these limits are the same for an employee who owns or leases a vehicle that is used in employment activities, and for a business that owns or leases a vehicle that is used in business activities, they are given detailed coverage in Chapter 8 on business income.

5-67.   However, it is important to note here that the limits that are placed on the deductibility of automobile costs have no influence on the amount of the taxable benefit that will be assessed to an employee who is provided with a vehicle by his employer. The taxable benefit to the employee will be the same, without regard to whether the employer can deduct the full costs of owning or leasing the vehicle. This means that if an employer provides an employee with an automobile that costs $150,000, the employee's benefits will be based on the full $150,000, despite the fact that the employer will only be able to deduct capital cost allowance on $30,000.

General Approach

5-68.   Two types of benefits will be added to employment income when an employee makes any personal use of an employer supplied automobile. These benefits will be covered in detail in this Chapter, but they can be described briefly here as follows:

Standby Charge   This benefit could be thought of as relating to the fixed costs of having an automobile. If the employee owned the automobile, he would have to absorb the cost associated with depreciation on the vehicle. Within a broad range, this cost does not vary with the number of kilometers driven and, by having a car supplied by an employer, the employee avoids this cost. As a consequence, it would seem fair that some type of fixed cost benefit be allocated to the employee for those

Inclusions - Automobile Benefits

periods of time during which the automobile is available to him.

Operating Cost Benefit   Operating costs are other types of costs, most of which have a direct relationship to the number of kilometers the automobile is driven. Such costs as gasoline, oil, and maintenance costs are roughly proportional to usage of the vehicle. It would follow that, when an employer pays these costs and others such as license fees and insurance for an automobile that is available for an employee's personal use, a taxable benefit should be assessed to that employee. Given the nature of these costs, it would seem logical that the amount of this benefit should be calculated with reference to the amount of personal use that the employee has made of the automobile.

5-69.   As discussed in Paragraph 5-58, a GST component must be included when taxable benefits provided to employees involve goods or services that would normally be subject to GST. Personal use of an automobile falls into this category. Both the standby charge benefit and the operating cost benefit that are discussed in the following material are calculated in a manner that includes a GST component.

Standby Charge
Employer Owned Vehicles
5-70.   While ITA 6(1)(e) requires the inclusion of a standby charge in income, ITA 6(2) provides the formulas for calculating this amount. If the employer owns the automobile, the basic standby charge is determined by the following formula:

$$[(2\%)(\text{Cost Of Car})(\text{Periods Of Availability})]$$

5-71.   The components of this formula required some additional explanation:

Cost Of Car   The cost of the car is the amount paid, without regard to the list price of the car. It includes all GST and PST amounts that were included.

Periods Of Availability   Periods of availability is roughly equal to months of availability. However, it is determined by dividing the number of days the automobile is "made available" by 30 and rounding to the nearest whole number. Oddly, a ".5" amount is rounded down rather than up.

Made Available   The CRA considers an employer to have made an automobile available to an employee if the employee has access and control of the automobile. In the view of the CRA, the employee has access and control as long as he is in possession of the keys to the vehicle. This means that, if an employee who normally uses his employer's car is confined to a hospital for two months, he will be assessed a standby charge during that period unless the keys are returned to the employer.

5-72.   If we assume that a vehicle was available throughout the year and cost $34,200, including $1,800 in GST and $2,400 in PST, the standby charge would be $8,208 [(2%)($34,200)(12)]. If the vehicle continues to be available to the employee throughout the year, for subsequent years, the benefit would be the same each year, without regard to the age of the car.

5-73. You should note that the application of this formula can result in a situation where the cumulative standby charge will exceed the cost of the automobile. For example, if the employee was to have the use of the automobile for 60 months, the taxable benefit resulting from the standby charge calculation would be $41,040 [(2%)($34,200)(60)]or 120 percent ($41,040 ÷ $34,200) of the cost of the car.

Employer Leased Vehicles
5-74.   In those cases where the employer leases the automobile, the basic standby charge is determined by the following formula:

[(2/3)(Lease Payments For The Year Excluding Insurance)(Availability Factor)]

5-75.   As was the case with the formula for employer owned vehicles, the components of this formula require additional explanation:

Lease Payments   The amount to be included here is the total lease payments for the year, including any GST and PST that is included in the payments. This total would be reduced by any amounts that have been included for insuring the vehicle. The insurance costs are excluded as the CRA considers them to be part of the operating cost benefit.

Availability Factor   This is a fraction in which the numerator is the number of days during the year the vehicle is available to the employee and the denominator is the number of days during the year for which lease payments were made. If the employee had the use of the vehicle throughout the lease period, the value of this fraction would be 1.

5-76.   An example will illustrate these procedures:

Example   A vehicle is leased for 3 months at a rate of $750 per month, including GST and PST. The $750 includes a monthly insurance payment of $75 per month. An employee has use of the vehicle for 85 of the 92 days in the lease term.

Analysis   The standby charge would be $1,247 [(2/3)(3)($750 - $75)(85 ÷ 92)].

5-77.   Unlike the situation with an employer owned vehicle, it is unlikely that the taxable benefit associated with a leased vehicle will exceed the value of the automobile. While we have seen no comprehensive analysis to support this view, it seems clear to us that, in most normal leasing situations, the taxable benefit on a leased vehicle will be significantly less than would be the case if the employer purchased the same vehicle.

5-78.   In the real world, a $55,000 (GST and PST inclusive) vehicle could be leased for 48 months with a lease payment of $800 per month (GST and PST inclusive). If the car is purchased, the standby charge will be $13,200 per year [(2%)($55,000)(12)]. Alternatively, the standby charge on the leased vehicle will be $6,400 per year [(2/3)(12)($800)(365/365)]. It is our belief that this general conclusion would only be altered if the lease was for a very short period (e.g., less than one year).

Reduced Standby Charge

5-79.   When an employer provides an automobile to an employee, it is usually used by that employee for a combination of personal activities and employment related activities. Among different employees, there are significant variations in the mix of these activities. Employees of some organizations may use the car almost exclusively in carrying out employment related activities. In other situations, particularly when the employer and the employee are not at arm's length (e.g., the employee is the owner of the business), the car may be used almost exclusively for personal travel.

5-80.   This would suggest that there should be some modification of the basic standby charge in situations where there is only limited personal use of the automobile. This, in fact, is the case. The ITA 6(2) standby charge formula provides for a reduction based on the amount of personal usage of the vehicle.

5-81.   The reduction involves multiplying the regular standby charge for either an employer owned or an employer leased vehicle by the following fraction:

Non - Employment Kilometers (Cannot Exceed Denominator)

1,667 Kilometers Per Month Of Availability *

*The number of months of availability is calculated by dividing the number of days that the employee is in possession of the keys to the vehicle by 30, and rounding to the nearest whole number.

5-82.   In applying this formula, the numerator is based on the number of kilometers driven for personal or non-employment activities. To prevent the fraction from having a value in excess of one, the numerator is limited to the value in the denominator. The denominator is based on the idea that, if the employee uses the automobile for as much as 1,667 kilometers of personal activities in a month (20,004 kilometers per year), the vehicle has fully replaced the need for a personally owned vehicle.

5-83.   This fraction can be used to reduce the basic standby charge provided three conditions are met:

  • The employee is required by the employer to use the automobile in his employment duties.

  • The use of the automobile is "primarily" employment related. In general, "primarily" is interpreted by the CRA to mean more than 50 percent. Note that this standby charge reduction formula is not completely fair to everyone, in that it fails to distinguish between an employee who uses the employer's automobile 49 percent for employment related activity from an employee who uses the automobile exclusively for personal travel.

  • The total non-employment use of the automobile is less than 1,667 kilometers per month (20,004 kilometers for the year).

Operating Cost Benefit
Basic Calculation
5-84.   In those cases where the employer pays the operating costs for an automobile that is available to an employee, that employee is clearly receiving a benefit related to the portion of these costs that are associated with his personal use of the automobile. An obvious approach to assessing an operating cost benefit would be to simply pro rate operating costs paid by the employer between personal and employment related usage.

5-85.   The problem with this, however, is that the employer would be required to keep detailed cost and milage records for each employee. This approach is further complicated by the fact that some operating costs incur GST (e.g., gasoline), while other operating costs are exempt from GST (e.g., insurance and licenses).

5-86.   Given these problems, ITA 6(1)(k) has provided an administratively simple solution. The operating cost benefit is determined by multiplying a prescribed amount by the number of personal kilometers driven. For 2006 and 2007, this prescribed amount is $0.22 per kilometer. This amount includes a notional GST component and, as a consequence, no further GST benefit has to be added to this amount.

5-87.   Note that this amount is applicable without regard to the level of the actual operating costs, resulting in favourable treatment for employees driving cars with high operating costs and unfavourable treatment for employees using vehicles with low operating costs.

Alternative Calculation
5-88.   There is an alternative calculation of the operating cost benefit. Employees who use an employer provided automobile "primarily" (i.e., more than 50 percent) in the performance of the taxpayer's office or employment can elect to have the operating cost benefit calculated as one-half of the standby charge. Employees wishing to use this method must notify the employer in writing before the end of the relevant year. This alternative calculation does not have to be used and, in many situations, it will not be a desirable alternative as it will produce a higher figure for the operating cost benefit.

5-89.   It should be noted that ITA 6(1.1) specifically excludes any benefit related to employer provided parking from the automobile benefit. This does not mean that employer provided parking is not a taxable benefit. While it is not considered to be a component of the automobile benefit calculation, it would still have to be included in the employee's income under ITA 6(1)(a). The logic of this is that parking may be provided to employees who are not provided with an automobile and, as a consequence, it should be accounted for separately in the employee benefit calculation.

Payments By Employee For Automobile Use

5-90.   Under ITA 6(1)(e), the standby charge benefit can be reduced by payments made by the employee to the employer for the use of the automobile. In corresponding fashion under ITA 6(1)(k), the operating cost benefit can be reduced by such payments.

5-91.   Note, however, that if the employee pays any part of the operating costs directly (e.g., the employee personally pays for gasoline), it does not reduce the basic $0.22 per kilometer benefit. This is not a desirable result and, if the employee is going to be required to pay a portion of the operating expenses, the employer should pay for all of the costs and have the employee reimburse the employer for the appropriate portion. Under this approach, the payments will reduce the operating cost benefit.

Example - Employer Owned Automobile

5-92.   The following data will be used to illustrate the calculation of the taxable benefit where an employee is provided with a vehicle owned by an employer in 2007.

Cost Of The Automobile ($30,000 + $1,800 GST + $2,400 PST)	$34,200
Months Available For Use (310 Days Rounded)	10
Months Owned By The Employer	12
Total Kilometers Driven	30,000
Personal Kilometers Driven	16,000

5-93.   The basic standby charge benefit to be included in employment income would be calculated as follows:

Standby Charge = [(2%)($34,200)(10)] = **$6,840**

5-94.   As less than 50 percent [(30,000 - 16,000) ÷ 30,000 = 46.7%] of the driving was related to the employer's business, no reduction in the basic standby charge is available. Also note that the cost figure used in the preceding calculation includes both PST and GST.

5-95.   The operating cost benefit to be included in employment income is as follows:

Operating Cost Benefit = [($0.22)(16,000)] = **$3,520**

5-96.   As the employment related use of the car was less than 50 percent, there is no alternative calculation of the operating cost benefit.

5-97.   As the employee does not make any payments to the employer for personal use of the automobile, the total taxable benefit to be included in employment income is as follows:

Total Taxable Benefit = ($6,840 + $3,520) = **$10,360**

Exercise Five-5

Subject: Taxable Benefits - Employer Owned Automobile

Mrs. Tanya Lee is provided with an automobile by her employer. The employer acquired the automobile in 2006 for $25,000, plus $1,500 GST and $2,000 PST. During 2007, she drives the automobile a total of 28,000 kilometers, 16,000 of which were related to employment duties. The automobile is available to Mrs. Lee throughout the year. Calculate Mrs. Lee's minimum 2007 taxable benefit for the use of the automobile.

End of Exercise. Solution available in Study Guide.

Example - Employer Leased Vehicle

5-98.   To provide a direct comparison between the employer owned and employer leased cases, this example will be based on the same general facts that were used in the ownership example. If the employer was to lease a $30,000 car with a 36 month lease term, the lease payment, calculated using normal lease terms, would be approximately $822 per month, including PST and GST (this cannot be calculated with the information given).   With the exception of the fact that the car is leased rather than purchased by the employer, all of the other facts are the same as in the Paragraph 5-92 example. The standby charge benefit would be calculated as follows:

$$\text{Standby Charge} = [(2/3)(12)(\$822)(10/12)] = \underline{\$5,480}$$

Note   When the car is owned by the employer, the *Act* clearly requires the availability period to be based on the days of availability, rounded to the nearest number of 30 day periods. In contrast, when the car is leased, a strict reading of the *Act* requires the availability period to be based on the days available as a fraction of the days in the lease period. However, the Employers' Guide: Taxable Benefits (T4130), uses the 30 day rounding rule for both purchase and lease situations. We will be using this latter approach in our examples and problems. If the *Act* was strictly followed, the 10/12 in the preceding calculation would be replaced by 310/365, resulting in a benefit of $5,585.

5-99.   As was the case when the car was owned by the employer, there is no reduction for actual business kilometers driven because the car was driven less than 50 percent for employment related purposes. Also note that the benefit is based on the lease payment including both PST and GST.

5-100.   The operating cost benefit is the same as the employer owned case and is as follows:

$$\text{Operating Cost Benefit} = [(\$0.22)(16,000)] = \underline{\$3,520}$$

5-101.   As in the case where the employer owned the car, with the employment related use of the car at less than 50 percent, there is no alternative calculation of the operating cost benefit.

5-102.   As the employee does not make any payments to the employer for the personal use of the automobile, the total taxable benefit is as follows:

$$\text{Total Taxable Benefit} = (\$5,480 + \$3,520) = \underline{\$9,000}$$

5-103.   Note that, as was discussed previously, the total benefit is significantly less ($9,000 as compared with $10,360) when the employer leases the car as opposed to purchasing it.

Exercise Five-6

Subject: Taxable Benefits - Employer Leased Automobile

Mr. Michael Forthwith is provided with a car that is leased by his employer. The lease payments for 2007 are $6,300, plus $378 GST and $504 PST. During 2007, Mr. Forthwith drives the automobile a total of 40,000 kilometers, of which 37,000 kilometers are employment related. The automobile is available to him for 325 days during the year. Calculate Mr. Forthwith's minimum 2007 taxable benefit for the use of the automobile.

End of Exercise. Solution available in Study Guide.

Employer Provided Cars And Tax Planning

5-104.   Providing employees with company cars is not a clearly desirable course of action. As is discussed in Chapter 8, there are limits on the ability of the company to deduct the costs of owning or leasing the vehicle (e.g., they cannot deduct leasing costs in excess of $800 per month before taxes). Further, the taxable benefit calculations are such that they may produce a taxable benefit that exceeds the value to the employee of having the car.

5-105.   This means that a decision to provide employees with a company car requires a careful analysis of all of the relevant factors. While a complete analysis of all of these issues goes beyond the scope of this material on employment income, some general tax planning points can be made.

Return The Keys   As the car will be considered to be available for the employee's use unless the keys are returned to the employer, the vehicle and its keys should be left with the employer during significant periods when the employee is not using it. This procedure can substantially reduce the taxable benefit to the employee and, in general, will not have any effect on the amounts that can be deducted for the car by the employer.

Record Keeping   In the absence of detailed records, an employee can be charged with the full standby charge and 100 percent personal usage. To avoid this, it is essential that records be kept of both employment related and personal kilometers driven and of the actual number of days that the car was available for the employee's personal use.

Leasing Vs. Buying   As was demonstrated in our leased car example, in most cases, a lower taxable benefit will result when the employer leases the car rather than purchases it. If employees are already using cars that have been purchased, it could be beneficial for the employer to sell the cars to a leasing company and reacquire them through a lease. One adverse aspect of leasing arrangements should be noted. Lease payments are made up of a combination of both interest and principal payments on the car. As the taxable benefit is based on the total lease payment, the interest portion becomes, in effect, a part of the taxable benefit.

Minimizing The Standby Charge   This can be accomplished in a variety of ways including longer lease terms, lower trade-in values for old vehicles in purchase situations, larger deposits on leases, and the use of higher residual values in leasing arrangements. However, this minimization process is not without limits. As is explained in Chapter 8, refundable deposits in excess of $1,000 on leases can reduce the deductible portion of lease costs.

Cars Costing More Than $30,000   With the taxable benefit to the employee based on the full cost of the car and any portion of the cost in excess of $30,000 not being deductible to the employer (this limit on the deductibility of automobile expenses is discussed more completely in Chapter 8), it is difficult to imagine situations in which it would make economic sense for a profit oriented employer to provide any employee with a luxury car. As the taxable benefit to the employee is based on the actual cost of the car, while the deductible amount is limited to $30,000, a situation is created in which the employee is paying taxes on an amount which is larger than the amount that is deductible to the employer. For example, the standby charge on a $150,000 Mercedes-Benz is $36,000 per year [(2%)($150,000)(12)], an amount that may be fully taxable to the employee. In contrast, the employer's deduction for capital cost allowance in the first year of ownership is only $4,500 [($30,000)(30%)(1/2)]. The only winner in this type of situation is the CRA.

Consider The Alternative   The alternative to the employer provided automobile is to have the employer compensate the employee for using his own automobile. In many cases this may be preferable to providing an automobile. For example, in those situations where business use is less than 50 percent, the provision of an automobile to an employee will result in a benefit assessment for the full standby charge. If business use was 45 percent, for example, it is almost certain that the amount assessed will exceed the actual benefit associated with 55 percent personal use of the vehicle. If, alternatively, the employee is reasonably compensated for using his own personal vehicle, there is no taxable benefit.

Inclusions - Allowances

Allowance Vs. Reimbursement

5-106.   A reimbursement is an amount paid to an employee to compensate that individual for amounts that he has disbursed in carrying out his employment duties. An example of this would be an employee who purchases an airline ticket for travel on behalf of his employer. The employee will present the receipt to the employer who reimburses the employee for the amount shown on the receipt. In such cases the employee will have no net cost and will have neither an income inclusion nor a deduction. The employer will, of course, be able to deduct the amount reimbursed.

5-107.   The situation is more complex with allowances. These are amounts that are paid, usually to provide a general level of compensation, for costs that an employee incurs as part of his employment activities. However, as there is no direct, dollar-for-dollar relationship with the actual costs incurred, the tax treatment of these items is more complicated. These complexities are dealt with in the material that follows.

General Rules

5-108.   The term allowance is used to refer to amounts received by employees from an employer other than salaries, wages, benefits, and reimbursements. In practice, allowances generally involve payments to employees as compensation for travel costs, use of their own automobile, or other costs that have been incurred by employees as part of their efforts on behalf of the employer. A milage allowance for a traveling salesperson or a technician who does service calls would be typical examples of such an allowance.

5-109.   ITA 6(1)(b) provides a general rule which requires that allowances for personal or living expenses must be included in an employee's income. However, many of the items for which employees receive allowances are costs that an employee can deduct against employment income under ITA 8. (See the discussion of deductions later in this Chapter for a full explanation of these amounts.) Examples of such deductible items are as follows:

- ITA 8(1)(**f**) - salesperson's expenses
- ITA 8(1)(**h**) - traveling expenses other than motor vehicle expenses
- ITA 8(1)(**h.1**) - motor vehicle traveling expenses
- ITA 8(1)(**i**) - professional dues, office rent, salaries, and supply costs
- ITA 8(1)(**j**) - motor vehicle capital costs (interest and capital cost allowance)

5-110.   If allowances for these items are included in the employee's income, a circular process is involved in which they are added under ITA 6(1)(b) and then subtracted under ITA 8. In view of this, ITA 6(1)(b) indicates that there are exceptions to the rule that allowances must be included in income. While there is a fairly long list of such items, the most important of these exceptions involve allowances paid for the types of costs that would be deductible under ITA 8. Specifically, the following allowances are among those that do not have to be included in an employee's income:

- ITA 6(1)(b)(**v**) - Reasonable allowances for traveling expenses paid during a period in which the employee was a salesperson (includes payment for use of a motor vehicle).

- ITA 6(1)(b)(**vii**) - Reasonable allowances for traveling expenses for employees other than salespersons, not including payments for use of a motor vehicle.

- ITA 6(1)(b)(**vii.1**) - Reasonable allowances for use of a motor vehicle for employees other than salespersons.

Taxable Vs. Non-Taxable Allowances

5-111.   The preceding general rules mean that there are two possible treatments of allow-ances paid to employees for travel and motor vehicle costs.

Non-Taxable Allowances   If a reasonable allowance is paid to an employee, it will not be included in the employee's income records (Information Return T4). However, when such allowances are not included in income, the employee will not be able to deduct his actual costs. For example, if an individual received $150 per day of travel to cover hotel costs, this would probably be considered reasonable and not included in his income. If the employee chose to stay at a luxury hotel for $400 per day, he would not be able to deduct the additional cost associated with this choice. Alternatively, if he chose to stay at a hostel for $50 per day, he would pocket the excess allowance on a tax free basis.

Taxable Allowances   If an allowance is not considered to be reasonable, it will be included in the employee's T4 Information Return for the period. To the extent the employee can qualify for the deduction of business travel or commission salespersons expenses, related expenses incurred by the employee can be deducted in the deter-mination of his net employment income. If the employee's actual costs exceed the allowance, having the allowance included in his income will be advantageous. Conversely, if his actual costs are less than the allowance, the result will be a net inclu-sion in employment income.

5-112.   It is not clear what constitutes a reasonable amount in the case of the general costs of travel. It appears that, as long as an allowance appears to be in line with actual costs for food, lodging, and miscellaneous costs, any allowance that is provided is likely to be viewed as reasonable. However, if a junior employee was given $30,000 a month for food and lodging and he was known to be staying at budget motels and eating fast food, it is likely that the allow-ance would have to be included in income and reduced, to the extent possible, by actual costs incurred (while this example sounds unrealistic, it might be attempted in an owner-managed business where the employee was not dealing at arm's length with the employer). Although it may be more difficult to administer, reimbursement of actual costs is less likely to cause this type of tax problem than providing an arbitrarily determined general allowance to cover all possible costs.

Reasonable Allowances For Motor Vehicles

5-113.   In Paragraph 5-110, we noted that ITA 6(1)(b)(v) and 6(1)(b)(vii.1) indicate that "reasonable allowances" for an employee's use of a motor vehicle do not have to be included in the employee's income. While the *Act* is not specific as to what constitutes a reasonable allowance for the use of a motor vehicle, it does point out that an allowance will be deemed not to be reasonable:

- if it is not based solely on the number of kilometers for which the vehicle is used in employment duties [ITA 6(1)(b)(x)]; or
- if the employee, in addition to the allowance, is reimbursed for all or part of the expenses of using the vehicle [(ITA 6(1)(b)(xi)].

5-114.   With respect to the first of these conditions, it is clear that an allowance of $200 per month would have to be included in the employee's income. Any allowance that is not specif-ically based on kilometers is deemed to be unreasonable. This, however, does not answer the question as to what constitutes a reasonable allowance.

5-115.   On the upper end, the CRA has indicated that if a per kilometer allowance exceeds the prescribed amount that is deductible for a business, it will be considered unreasonable, resulting in its inclusion in the employee's income. As we shall see in Chapter 8, for 2007, these amounts are $0.50 for the first 5,000 kilometers driven by each employee, and $0.44 for each additional kilometer.

5-116.   If the per kilometer allowance is less than this prescribed amount, it appears that the administrative practice of the CRA is to view the allowance as reasonable. This means that, unless an employee is willing to pursue the matter, he does not have the option of including a non-taxable allowance in income and deducting his actual costs. While there has been one case (Brunet Vs. H.M.Q.) where an employee was allowed to include a $0.15 per kilometer allowance and deduct actual costs, there have been other cases where this was not allowed.

Exercise Five-7

Subject: Deductible Automobile Costs

Ms. Lauren Giacomo is required by her employer to use her own automobile in her work. To compensate her, she is paid an annual allowance of $3,600. During the current year, she drove her automobile a total of 24,000 kilometers, of which 6,500 kilometers were employment related. Her total automobile costs for the year, including lease costs, are $7,150. What amounts should Ms. Giacomo include and deduct in determining net employment income for the current year?

Exercise Five - 8

Subject: Automobile Allowances

During the current year, Jacob Lorenz leases an automobile for $450 per month, a total for the year of $5,400. He drives a total of 60,000 kilometers, of which 35,000 are employment related. His total operating costs for the year are $15,000. His employer pays him $0.10 for each employment related kilometer driven, a total of $3,500. What amounts should Mr. Lorenz include and deduct in determining net employment income for the current year?

End of Exercises. Solutions available in Study Guide.

Employer's Perspective Of Allowances

5-117.   From the point of view of the employer, paying taxable allowances is the easiest solution. All amounts paid will be included in the income of the employees and, as a consequence, there is no necessity for the employer to maintain detailed records of actual costs. It is up to the employee to keep these records and to claim the relevant deductible costs against the allowances included in their T4 Information Return.

5-118.   Somewhat more onerous is an approach which uses direct reimbursements of the employee's actual costs. Some efficiencies are available here in that the CRA will generally accept a modest per diem for food without requiring detailed documentation from either the employer or the employee. However, for more substantial costs, the reimbursement approach involves more detailed record keeping than is the case with the use of taxable allowances.

5-119.   In the case of employee owned automobile costs, the use of non-taxable allowances is particularly complex. As we have noted, the 2007 amounts that can be deducted by an employer for automobile costs are generally limited to $0.50 per kilometer for the first 5,000 kilometers of use by a given employee, and $0.44 per kilometer for subsequent kilometers. If a non-taxable allowance is given to an employee (i.e., one that is based on kilometers driven), the employer will have to keep detailed employee-by-employee milage records in order to support any deduction of automobile costs.

Employee's Perspective Of Allowances

5-120.   From the employee's point of view, the receipt of a non-taxable allowance represents a very simple solution to the problem. While records may have to be kept for the information needs of the employer, the employee has the advantage of simply ignoring the allowance and the related costs when it comes time to file a tax return.

5-121. In real terms, however, the non-taxable allowance approach may or may not be advantageous. If the employee's actual deductible costs exceed the allowance, a failure to include the allowance in income eliminates the deductibility of the additional costs. Alternatively, if the actual costs are less than the allowance, the employee has, in effect, received a tax free benefit.

Exercise Five-9

Subject: Travel Allowances

Sandra Ohm travels extensively for her employer. Her employer provides an allowance of $200 per day to cover hotel costs. In addition, she is paid $0.39 per kilometer when she is required to use her automobile for travel. For her work, during the current year, she traveled a total of 82 days and drove 9,400 kilometers. Her employer paid her $16,400 for lodging [(82)($200)], as well as $3,666 dollars for milage [(9,400)($0.39)]. Her actual lodging costs were $18,300, while her total automobile costs were $7,200, including monthly lease payments. Her total milage on the car during the year was 23,500 kilometers. What amounts should Ms. Ohm include and deduct in determining net employment income for the current year?

End of Exercise. Solution available in Study Guide.

Inclusions - Employee Insurance Benefits

Life Insurance

5-122. The cost of providing life insurance benefits to employees is a taxable benefit under ITA 6(4). This means that any premiums paid on a life insurance policy by the employer must be included in employment income. In the event of the employee's death, the benefit payment received by his estate would not be taxable. As insurance services are exempt from GST, no GST amount would be included in this benefit.

Disability Insurance
(a.k.a. Group Sickness Or Accident Insurance Plan)

5-123. The normal situation here is one in which an employer pays all or part of the premiums on a group sickness or accident insurance plan. The contributions made by the employer to such group plans are not treated as a taxable benefit to the employee at the time that they are made. This exclusion from treatment as a taxable benefit is found in ITA 6(1)(a)(i) and is only applicable to group plans. If the plan is not a group plan, contributions by the employer must be treated as a taxable benefit to the employee.

5-124. Any contributions made by the employee towards the premiums on the sickness or accident insurance plan are not deductible by the employee at the time they are made. This would be the case regardless of whether the employee was sharing the cost of the premiums with an employer, or paying the entire cost of the premiums.

5-125. The tax status of benefits received from a disability plan will depend on whether or not the employer has contributed to the plan. If the employer has made any contributions to the plan, even if the contributions were treated as a taxable benefit when they were made, benefits received by an employee must be included in employment income under ITA 6(1)(f). However, in this case, the cumulative contributions made by the employee to the particular plan that is paying the benefits can be used to reduce the amount of this inclusion. This, of course, compensates for the fact that such employee contributions were not deductible at the time they were made.

5-126.   If the employer has not made any contributions to the plan, it is an employee pay all plan. As the employee's contributions to such plans were not deductible when they were made, it is appropriate that the benefits received are not treated as taxable income. Note, however, if the employer makes any contribution to the plan, it will taint the plan in the sense that all of the benefits received, reduced by the total of the employee's contributions, will become taxable.

> **Example**   During the current year, the premiums on Jane Forthy's disability insurance plan totalled $1,600. The plan is a group plan sponsored by Jane's employer who pays one-half of the annual cost of premiums. Jane pays the remaining one-half. As the result of a car accident during the current year, Jane received disability benefits of $16,000. In previous years, Jane has contributed a total of $3,600 towards the disability insurance premiums.
>
> **Analysis**   Jane's income inclusion for the current year would be $11,600 [$16,000 - (1/2)($1,600) - $3,600].

5-127.   As noted previously, insurance services are exempt from GST, and no GST amount is associated with taxable benefits related to disability insurance.

Exercise Five-10

Subject: Disability Insurance Benefits

Mr. Lance Bardwell is a member of a group disability plan sponsored by his employer. During 2007, his employer's share of the annual premium was $1,800. Beginning in 2006, Mr. Bardwell was required to contribute $300 per year to this plan. The 2006 and 2007 contributions were withheld from his wages by his employer. During 2007, Mr. Bardwell was incapacitated for a period of six weeks and received $5,250 in benefits under the plan. What amount will Mr. Bardwell include in his 2007 employment income?

End of Exercise. Solution available in Study Guide.

Health Care Insurance

5-128.   Where an employer pays the individual premiums on provincial (e.g., Alberta and British Columbia) or Government of Canada health care plans, the amounts are considered taxable benefits of the employees. Where provincial health care is funded by an employer payroll tax or other general levy (e.g., Manitoba and Quebec) and there are no individual premiums, these payments are not allocated to employees as a taxable benefit.

5-129.   Payments made for private health services plans, for instance a dental plan, are specifically excluded from treatment as a taxable benefit under guidelines provided in ITA 6(1)(a)(i). The benefits received under such plans are not taxable and, in addition, any contributions made by the employee to such private health care plans can be treated as a medical expense eligible for a credit against taxes payable. (See Chapter 6.)

5-130.   As was the case with other types of insurance benefits, there is no GST amount associated with taxable health care benefits.

Loans To Employees

General Rules

5-131.   If an employer extends a loan to an employee and the interest rate is below the going market rate, the employee is clearly receiving a benefit that should be taxed. This view is reflected in ITA 6(9), which requires the assessment of a taxable benefit on all interest free or low interest loans to employees. This provision applies whether the loan is made as a consequence of prior, current, or future employment.

5-132. As specified in ITA 80.4(1), the taxable benefit would be the imputed interest calculated at the prescribed rate specified in ITR 4301, (see Chapter 2 for a discussion of the term, prescribed rate) less any interest paid on the loan by the employee during the year or within 30 days of the end of the year.

> **Example** On January 1 of the current year, Ms. Brooks Arden borrows $50,000 from her employer at an annual rate of 1 percent. During this year, the prescribed rate is 3 percent during the first two quarters, and 4 percent during the last two quarters. Ms. Arden pays the required 1 percent interest on December 31.

> **Analysis** The taxable benefit to be included in Ms. Arden's net employment income would be calculated as follows:

Imputed Interest:	
Quarters I and II [(3%)($50,000)(2/4)]	$ 750
Quarters III and IV [(4%)($50,000)(2/4)]	1,000
Total Imputed Interest	$1,750
Interest Paid [(1%)($50,000)]	(500)
Taxable Benefit	**$1,250**

In calculating the imputed interest, the example illustrates the approach used in IT-421R2 and treats each calendar quarter as one-quarter of the year. This is acceptable as long as the loan is outstanding for the entire year. For shorter periods, a calculation based on the number of relevant days is required.

5-133. Several additional points should be made with respect to these loans:

- In this application of the prescribed rate, it does not include the extra 2 percent applicable to amounts that are due from the CRA, or the extra 4 percent on amounts owed to the CRA.

- If the rate negotiated with the employer is at least equal to (or greater than) the rate that the employee could have negotiated himself with a bank, then under ITA 80.4(3), no benefit will be assessed to the employee regardless of subsequent changes to the prescribed rate.

- ITA 80.4(2) contains a different set of rules that is applicable to loans made to certain shareholders of a company. The different rules that are applicable to shareholders are described in Chapter 9, "Income from Property".

- Proceeds from a loan to an employee could be used to invest in assets that produce business or property income. In general, interest paid on loans to finance investments is deductible against the income produced. ITA 80.5 clearly states that an imputed interest benefit assessed under ITA 80.4(1) or 80.4(2) is deemed to be interest paid for the purposes of determining net business or property income. Referring to the example in Paragraph 5-132, if Ms. Arden had invested the $50,000 loan proceeds in income producing assets, her deductible interest would total $1,750, the $500 that she paid, plus the assessed $1,250 taxable benefit.

- When the purpose of the loan is to assist an employee with a home purchase or home relocation (see Paragraph 5-134), ITA 80.4(4) indicates that the annual amount of interest used in the benefit calculations cannot exceed the annual amount determined using the prescribed rate in effect when the loan was extended. Note that this rule is applied on a quarter by quarter basis, rather than an annual one.

- This provides a ceiling for the benefit and, at the same time, allows the taxpayer to benefit if the prescribed rate becomes lower. This ceiling on the benefit is only available for the first five years such loans are outstanding. ITA 80.4(6) indicates that, after this period of time, the loan will be deemed to be a new loan, making the calculation of the benefit subject to the prescribed rate in effect at this point in time. This new rate will again serve as a ceiling for the amount of the benefit for the next five years.

Home Relocation Loans

5-134.   If an employer provides a home purchase loan when an employee moves to a new work location, it is referred to as a home relocation loan if certain conditions are met. If this is an interest free or low interest loan, the ITA 80.4(1) rules apply as outlined in the preceding section. However, in the case of a home relocation loan, there is an offsetting deduction.

5-135.   This deduction is equal to the benefit associated with an interest free home relocation loan of up to $25,000. Note, however, the deduction is applied in the calculation of Taxable Income. This being the case, the usual ITA 80.4(1) imputed interest benefit will be included in net employment income, a figure that will not be changed by the home relocation loan deduction. The deduction will be applied after net employment income has been added to other sources in the determination of Net Income For Tax Purposes. The details of this deduction from Taxable Income are covered in Chapter 6.

No GST Benefit

5-136.   There is no GST benefit on imputed interest on a low or no interest loan as it is considered an exempt supply of a financial service.

Exercise Five-11

Subject: Housing Loan

On January 1, 2007, Mrs. Caldwell receives a $100,000 loan from her employer to assist her in purchasing a home. The loan requires annual interest at a rate of 2 percent, which she pays on December 31, 2007. Assume that the relevant prescribed rate is 4 percent during the first quarter of 2007, 5 percent during the second quarter, and 3 percent during the remainder of the year. Calculate Mrs. Caldwell's taxable benefit on this loan for the year (1) assuming that the loan qualifies as a home relocation loan and (2) assuming that it does not qualify.

End of Exercise. Solution available in Study Guide.

Tax Planning For Interest Free Loans

5-137.   Tax rules result in a taxable benefit to the employee if the interest rate on the loan is lower than the prescribed rate. Given this, the question arises as to whether the use of employee loans is a tax effective form of providing employee benefits. As with other types of benefits, the question is whether it is better that the employer supplies the benefit or, alternatively, provides sufficient additional salary to allow the employee to acquire the benefit directly. In the case of loans, this additional salary would have to be sufficient to allow the employee to carry a similar loan at commercial rates.

5-138.   The answer to the question of whether or not employee loans are a tax effective form of compensation depends on several factors:

- the employer's rate of return on alternative uses for the funds
- the employer's tax rate
- the employee's tax rate
- the prescribed rate
- the rate available to the employee on a similar arm's length loan

5-139.   In analyzing the use of loans to employees, we begin with the assumption that we would like to provide a requested benefit to one or more employees and we are looking for the most cost effective way of providing the benefit. As noted, the alternative to providing an employee with a loan is to provide that employee with sufficient after tax income to carry an equivalent loan at commercial rates of interest.

5-140.   It then becomes a question of comparing the cash flows associated with the employer providing the loan (this would have to include sufficient additional income to pay the taxes on any loan benefit that will be assessed), with the cash flows required for the employer to provide the employee with sufficient income to carry an equivalent loan acquired from a commercial lender.

Example In 2006, a key executive asks for a $100,000 interest free housing loan. The loan does not qualify as a home relocation loan. At this time, the employer has an investment opportunity that is expected to provide a rate of return of 12 percent before taxes. The prescribed rate is 3 percent, while the rate for home mortgages is 5 percent. The employee is subject to a marginal tax rate of 48 percent, while the employer pays corporate taxes at a marginal rate of 40 percent.

Alternative 1 - Provide Additional Salary   In the absence of the interest free loan, the employee would borrow $100,000 at 5 percent, requiring an annual interest payment of $5,000. In determining the amount of salary required to carry this loan, consideration has to be given to the fact that additional salary will be taxed at 48 percent. In terms of the algebra that is involved, we are trying to solve the following equation:

$$\$5,000 = [(X)(1 - 0.48)]$$

You will recall that this type of equation will be solved by dividing both sides by (1 - 0.48), resulting in a required salary of $9,615:

$$X = [\$5,000 \div (1 - 0.48)] = \$9,615$$

Using this figure, the required after tax cash flow resulting from providing sufficient additional salary for the employee to carry a conventional $100,000 mortgage would be calculated as follows:

Required Salary [$5,000 ÷ (1 - 0.48)]	$9,615
Tax Savings From Deducting Salary [($9,615)(40%)]	(3,846)
Employer's After Tax Cash Flow - Additional Salary	$5,769

Alternative 2 - Provide The Loan   If the loan is provided, the employee will have a taxable benefit of $3,000 [(3% - Nil)($100,000)], resulting in additional taxes payable of $1,440 [(48%)($3,000)]. To make this situation comparable to the straight salary alternative, the employer will have to provide the executive with both the loan amount and sufficient additional salary to pay the $1,440 taxes on the taxable benefit that will be assessed. The required amount would be $2,769 [$1,440 ÷ (1 - 0.48)].

The employer's after tax cash flow associated with the after tax cost of providing the additional salary as well as the after tax lost earnings on the $100,000 loan amount would be calculated as follows:

Required Salary [$1,440 ÷ (1 - 0.48)]	$2,769
Tax Savings From Deducting Salary [($2,769)(40%)]	(1,108)
After Tax Cost Of Salary	$1,661
Employer's Lost Earnings [(12%)(1 - 0.40)($100,000)]	7,200
Employer's After Tax Cash Flow - Loan	$8,861

Conclusion   Given these results, payment of additional salary appears to be the better alternative. However, the preceding simple example is not a complete analysis of the situation. Other factors, such as the employee's ability to borrow at going rates and the employer's ability to grant this salary increase in the context of salary policies, would also have to be considered.

Exercise Five-12

Subject: Loans To Employees

In 2007, a key executive asks for a $125,000 interest free housing loan that does not qualify as a home relocation loan. At this time, the employer has investment opportunities involving a rate of return of 7 percent before taxes. Assume the relevant prescribed rate is 2 percent, while the market rate for home mortgages is 6 percent. The employee is subject to a marginal tax rate of 42 percent, while the employer pays corporate taxes at a marginal rate of 35 percent. Determine whether the employer should grant the loan or, alternatively, provide sufficient salary to carry an equivalent loan from a commercial lender.

End of Exercise.   Solution available in Study Guide.

Inclusions - Stock Option Benefits

The Economics Of Stock Option Arrangements

5-141.   Stock options allow, but do not require, the holder to purchase a specified number of shares for a specified period of time at a specified acquisition price. Because of tax considerations, at the time of issue the option price is usually at or above the market price of the shares. For example, options might be issued to acquire shares at a price of $10 at a time when the shares are trading at that same $10 value.

5-142.   At first glance, such an option would appear to have no value as it simply allows the holder to acquire a share for $10, at a time when that share is only worth that amount. In reality, however, this option could have significant value, in that it allows the holder to participate in any upward price movement in the shares without any obligation to exercise the option if the price stays at, or falls below, $10. Stated alternatively, the option provides full participation in gains on the option shares, with no downside risk. Further, for an employee receiving such options, they provide this participation with no real investment cost until such time as the options are exercised.

5-143.   Stock options are granted to employees in the belief that, by giving the employee an interest in the stock of the company, he has an incentive to make a greater effort on behalf of the enterprise. In some companies, use of this form of compensation is restricted to senior executives. In contrast, other corporations makes options available to larger groups of employees.

5-144.   Prior to 2004, a significant advantage to the use of stock options was that the cost of issuing such options was not recorded in the financial statements of the issuing corporation. Because of an inability of accountants to agree on the appropriate value for options that are not "in-the-money" (options are referred to as in-the-money if the market price of the shares exceeds the option price), corporations were generally able to issue huge quantities of stock options without recording any compensation expense.

5-145.   This situation, however, has changed. Section 3870 of the *CICA Handbook* now requires the recognition of an expense when stock options are issued, even if these options are not in-the-money. This requirement is effective for fiscal years beginning on or after January 1, 2004.

5-146.   For tax purposes, the issuance of these derivative securities has no current consequences, either for the issuer or the recipient. The issuer cannot deduct any amount to reflect the economic value of the issued options. Further, the recipient does not have any income inclusion at this point in time.

5-147. As a final point, we would note that some options may not be vested when they are issued. Non-vested stock options cannot currently be exercised because the employee has not yet satisfied the vesting requirements (e.g., a minimum period of employment is necessary in order to earn the right to the options). In other words, an option is vested only when the employee has an irrevocable right to exercise it.

Overview Of The Tax Rules

5-148. This is a difficult subject to present in that it involves several different areas of tax legislation. In addition to issues related to employment income, stock options influence the determination of Taxable Income and the calculation of taxable capital gains. While it would be possible to present this material on a piecemeal basis, we have found this to be confusing to our readers. An alternative would be to defer any discussion of this issue until all of the relevant material has been covered.

5-149. However, this fails to reflect the fact that stock option issues relate most directly to employment income. As a consequence, most of our material on stock options will be presented in this Chapter. As this involves some material that will not be covered until later Chapters, an overview of the stock option material that will be presented in this Chapter is useful. The basic points here are as follows:

Value At Issue As noted previously, the tax rules give no recognition to the fact that stock options have a positive value at the time of issue. The issuer can make no deduction and the recipient employee has no income inclusion.

Employment Income Inclusion - Measurement The employment income inclusion will be measured on the date that the options are exercised. The amount will be equal to the excess of the fair market value on the exercise date, less the option price, with the difference multiplied by the number of shares issued. This amount will never be negative as the employee would only exercise the options in situations where the value of the shares are equal to, or exceed, the option price.

Employment Income Inclusion - Recognition While the employment income inclusion will always be measured at the time the options are exercised, it may not be recognized until the shares are sold. Whether the inclusion will be recognized at the time of exercise or at the time of sale will depend on the type of corporation involved and whether an available election is made.

Taxable Income Deduction As many of you are aware, gains on securities are considered to be capital gains, subject to taxation on only one-half of their total amount. In the absence of some mitigating provision, the full amount of the employment income inclusion would be subject to tax. As this would not be an equitable situation, tax legislation permits a deduction in the calculation of Taxable Income equal to the non-taxable one-half of the employment income inclusion. While general coverage of Taxable Income is found in Chapters 6 and 14, this deduction will be covered here as part of our discussion of stock options. Note, however, this deduction does not influence the calculation of Net Employment Income. This means, that if you are solving a problem that requires the calculation of Net Employment Income, you will NOT include this deduction in your calculation.

Capital Gains With the difference between fair market value at the exercise date and the option price being treated as an employment income inclusion, fairness requires that the adjusted cost base of the acquired shares be increased to reflect the fact that this amount has already been subject to tax. This means that, when the shares are eventually sold, there will be a capital gain or loss based on the difference between the sale price and the fair market value of the shares at the time of exercise. As is discussed more fully in Chapter 10, only one-half of capital gains are subject to tax (referred to as the "taxable capital gain"). One-half of capital losses are deductible (referred to as the "allowable capital loss"), but only to the extent that there are taxable capital gains in the year.

5-150.   A simple example will serve to illustrate the relevant calculations:

Example An executive receives options to acquire 1,000 of his employer's common shares at an option price of $25 per share. At this time, the common shares are trading at $25 per share. He exercises the options when the shares are trading at $40 per share. In the following year, he sells the shares for $50 per share.

Analysis Assuming that the employment income inclusion must be recognized when the options are exercised, the tax consequences for the year of exercise would be as follows:

Employment Income [(1,000)($40 - $25)]	$15,000
Taxable Income Deduction (One-Half)	(7,500)
Taxable Income In Year Of Exercise	**$ 7,500**

When the shares are sold, the additional tax consequences to the employee would be as follows:

Proceeds Of Disposition [(1,000)($50)]	$50,000
Adjusted Cost Base [(1,000)($40)]	(40,000)
Capital Gain	$10,000
Inclusion Rate	1/2
Taxable Capital Gain In Year Of Sale	**$ 5,000**

5-151.   Several points should be made with respect to this example:

• The employment income inclusion will always be measured at the time the options are exercised. However, its recognition for tax purposes may be deferred until the acquired shares are sold. This will be discussed in more detail in the material that follows.

• The $7,500 deduction is from Net Income For Tax Purposes in the calculation of Taxable Income, not from employment income. The net employment income that will be included in the executive's current or future Net Income For Tax Purposes, as well as his Earned Income for RRSP purposes (see Chapter 13), is $15,000.

• The availability of the $7,500 deduction requires that certain conditions be met. These conditions will be discussed in detail in the material that follows.

• As we have noted, when the employment income benefit is included in income, ITA 53(1)(j) indicates that this amount will be added to the adjusted cost base of the shares.

Private Vs. Public Companies

5-152.   As is discussed more fully in Chapter 15, a Canadian controlled private corporation (CCPC) is a corporation that is controlled by Canadian residents and does not have its shares traded on a prescribed stock exchange. Tax legislation makes a distinction between these companies and public companies in its approach to recognizing the employment income resulting from stock options.

5-153.   In very simplified terms, with respect to options issued by public companies, the employment income inclusion is generally taxed when the options are exercised. In contrast, for options issued by Canadian controlled private corporations, the employment income inclusion is measured when the options are exercised. However, the measured benefit is not taxed until the acquired shares are sold.

5-154.   This approach was viewed as problematical in that, for public companies, taxation at the time of exercise often forced the employee to sell a portion of the shares in order to pay the taxes due on the employment income inclusion. As the result of considerable lobbying by the business community, the legislation was changed.

5-155.   The changes did not alter the basic rules for public companies. The employment income inclusion is still measured and, in general, included in employment income as at the exercise date. However, the current legislation provides for an election that allows an individual who has exercised stock options to defer recognition of all or part of the employment income inclusion until such time as the acquired shares are sold.

5-156.   Again, in somewhat simplified terms, the election provides the individual with an annual deferral of the employment income inclusion on public company options that are exercised during the year, for up to $100,000 of the "specified value" of the shares. As will be discussed in more detail in Paragraph 5-169, the specified value is the market value of the option shares at the time the options are granted.

5-157.   Note carefully that the general approach (i.e., taxation at time of exercise) applies unless the individual files an election. Further, the general approach is also applicable to amounts in excess of the $100,000 deferral amount. This means that it will provide only limited benefits to those high-level executives who receive millions of dollars worth of options. However, significant benefits will be provided to lower and middle management recipients of options.

General Rules For Public Companies

5-158.   Under ITA 7(1)(a), when options to acquire the shares of a publicly traded company are exercised, there is an employment income inclusion equal to the excess of the fair market value of shares acquired over the price paid to acquire them. A deduction, equal to one-half of the employment income that is included under ITA 7(1)(a), can be taken under ITA 110(1)(d).

5-159.   Note, however, this ITA 110(1)(d) deduction in the calculation of Taxable Income is only available if, at the time the options are issued, the option price was equal to, or greater than, the fair market value of the shares at the option grant date. If the option price is less than the fair market value of the shares at the time of issue (i.e., in-the-money), the deduction will not be available and the individual will be subject to tax on the full amount of the employment income inclusion.

> **Example** On December 31, 2005, John Due receives options to buy 10,000 shares of his employer's common stock at a price of $25 per share. The employer is a publicly traded company and the options are vested and exercisable as of their issue date. At this time, the shares are trading at $25 per share.
>
> On July 31, 2007, Mr. Due exercises all of these options. At this time, the shares are trading at $43 per share. Mr. Due does not make an election to defer the employment income inclusion. On September 30, 2008, Mr. Due sells the shares that he acquired with his options. The proceeds from the sale are $45 per share.
>
> **Analysis** The tax consequences of the preceding events and transactions are as follows:
>
> - **Issue Date** (December 31, 2005)   Despite the fact that the options clearly have a positive value at this point in time, there are no tax consequences resulting from the issuance of the options.
>
> - **Exercise Date** (July 31, 2007)   As the option price was equal to the fair market value of the shares at the option grant date, Mr. Due can use the ITA 110(1)(d) deduction in calculating his Taxable Income. The tax consequences resulting from the exercise of the options, if no deferral election is made, would be as follows:

| Fair Market Value Of Shares Acquired [(10,000)($43)] | $430,000 |
| Cost Of Shares [(10,000)($25)] | (250,000) |

ITA 7(1)(a) Employment Income Inclusion	
= Increase In Net Income For Tax Purposes	$180,000
ITA 110(1)(d) Deduction [(1/2)($180,000)]	(90,000)
Increase In Taxable Income	$ 90,000

- **Disposition Date** (September 30, 2008)   The tax consequences resulting from the sale of the shares would be as follows:

Proceeds Of Disposition [(10,000)($45)]	$450,000
Adjusted Cost Base [(10,000)($43)]	(430,000)
Capital Gain	$ 20,000
Inclusion Rate	1/2
Taxable Capital Gain	$ 10,000

Note that, in the 2008 calculation, the adjusted cost base of the shares has been bumped up to the value of the shares at the time of exercise, reflecting the fact that the difference between the $43 per share value on that date and the $25 option price has already been included in the taxpayer's Net Income For Tax Purposes.

Also note that, if the taxpayer had sold the shares for less than the bumped up value of $43, he would have an allowable capital loss. If this were the case, the taxpayer would not be able to deduct the loss in 2008, unless he had taxable capital gains from some other source. This creates a situation that some would view as being unfair in that the taxpayer has had to include gains up to the $43 value, but might not be able to deduct the loss resulting from a subsequent decline in value.

Exercise Five-13

Subject: Stock Options - Public Company

During 2005, Mr. Gordon Guise was granted options to buy 2,500 of his employer's shares at a price of $23.00 per share. At this time, the shares are trading at $20.00 per share. His employer is a large publicly traded company. During July, 2007, he exercises all of the options at a point in time when the shares are trading at $31.50 per share. In September, 2007, the shares are sold for $28.00 per share. What is the effect of the exercise of the options and the sale of the shares on Mr. Guise's 2007 Net Income For Tax Purposes and Taxable Income?

End of Exercise. Solution available in Study Guide.

General Rules For Canadian Controlled Private Corporations (CCPCs)

5-160.   The basic public company rules that we have just described require the recognition of a taxable benefit when the options are exercised, prior to the realization in cash of any benefit from the options granted. This may not be an insurmountable problem for employees of publicly traded companies, in that they can sell some of the shares or use them as loan collateral if they need to raise the cash to pay the taxes on the benefit.

5-161.   However, for employees of a CCPC, a requirement to pay taxes at the time an option is exercised could create severe cash flow problems. As a consequence, a different treatment is permitted for stock options issued by CCPCs. The employment income inclusion is still measured at the time the options are exercised, but it is not taxed until the shares are sold.

5-162.   For CCPCs, the employment income inclusion is determined under ITA 7(1)(a) and 7(1.1). The ITA 110(1)(d) deduction from Taxable Income is also available to CCPCs provided the option price was equal to, or more than, the fair market value of the shares at the option grant date.   However, if this condition is not met, an additional provision under ITA 110(1)(d.1) allows the taxpayer to deduct one-half of the employment income inclusion, provided the shares are held for at least two years after their acquisition.

5-163.   Using the same information that is contained in the example in Paragraph 5-159, altered only so that the employer is a CCPC, the tax consequences would be as follows:

Analysis For CCPC Example

- **Issue Date** (December 31, 2005)   Despite the fact that the options clearly have a positive value at this point in time, there are no tax consequences resulting from the issuance of the options.

- **Exercise Date** (July 31, 2007)   While the amount of the employment income inclusion would be measured on this date, it would not be included in income at this point. Based on the increase in share value from $25 to $43 per share, the benefit would be measured as $180,000 [($43 - $25)(10,000 Shares)].   This benefit, along with the related $90,000 Taxable Income deduction, would be deferred until such time as the shares are sold.

- **Disposition Date** (September 30, 2008)   The tax consequences resulting from the sale of the shares would be as follows:

Deferred Employment Income		$180,000
Proceeds Of Disposition [(10,000)($45)]	$450,000	
Adjusted Cost Base [(10,000)($43)]	(430,000)	
Capital Gain	$ 20,000	
Inclusion Rate	1/2	10,000
Increase In Net Income For Tax Purposes		$190,000
ITA 110(1)(d) Deduction [(1/2)($180,000)]		(90,000)
Increase In Taxable Income		$100,000

5-164.   Note that this is the total increase in Taxable Income that would have resulted from simply purchasing the shares at $25 and later selling them for $45 [(10,000)(1/2)($45 - $25) = $100,000]. The structuring of this increase is different and, in some circumstances, the difference could be significant. For example, the fact that the $180,000 increase in value has been classified as employment income rather than capital gains means that it is not eligible for the lifetime capital gains deduction (see Chapter 14), but it will increase Earned Income for RRSP purposes (see Chapter 13). Although the timing is different, the $100,000 total increase in Taxable Income is the same as in the public company example in Paragraph 5-159.

Exercise Five-14

Subject: Stock Options - Private Company

In 2003, Ms. Milli Van was granted options to buy 1,800 of her employer's shares at a price of $42.50 per share. At this time, the shares have a fair market value of $45.00 per share. Her employer is a Canadian controlled private corporation. In June, 2007, at a time when the shares have a fair market value of $75.00 per share, she exercises all of her options. In September, 2007, Ms. Van sells her shares for $88,200 ($49.00 per share). What is the effect of the exercise of the options and the sale of the shares on Ms. Van's 2007 Net Income For Tax Purposes and Taxable Income?

End of Exercise.   Solution available in Study Guide.

Charitable Donation Of Employee Stock Option Shares

5-165.   In those situations where options are used to acquire public company shares, and the shares are subsequently donated to an organization that can issue a charitable donation tax receipt, a further deduction is available against the stock option benefit employment income inclusion. Further coverage of this subject is provided in Chapter 14, "Taxable Income And Tax Payable For Individuals Revisited".

Deferral On Publicly Traded Shares

Qualifying Acquisitions

5-166.   As noted earlier, when options are exercised to acquire the shares of a publicly traded company, there is a general requirement to include the difference between the share's fair market value on the exercise date and the option price in employment income. Also as described previously, there is a limited deferral of this employment income inclusion. This deferral is available under ITA 7(8) provided two general conditions are met:

1. The acquisition must be a "qualifying acquisition".

2. The taxpayer must make an election under ITA 7(10) in order to have Subsection ITA 7(8) apply.

5-167.   "Qualifying acquisition" is defined in ITA 7(9). This Subsection indicates that the exercise of options involves a qualifying acquisition if:

- The acquired shares are listed on a prescribed stock exchange.
- The employee is entitled to a deduction under ITA 110(1)(d). This requires that the option price be greater than, or equal to, the fair market value of the common shares at the time the options were granted.
- The employee is not a specified shareholder of the employer. A specified shareholder is an individual who owns at least 10 percent of the shares of a corporation.

Making The Election

5-168.   The election to have the deferral provision apply must be made no later than January 15th of the year following the year in which the securities are acquired. In general, the election will be filed with the employer. The employer then has the responsibility for reporting the information to the Minister of National Revenue, and including the amount deferred as a special item on the employee's T4. The election can only be filed by an individual who is a resident of Canada when the relevant securities are acquired.

Specified Value

5-169.   While the election will be filed in the taxation year in which the shares are acquired through the exercise of options, the limit on the amount that can be elected is based on a value that is determined at the time the options are granted. This limiting amount is referred to as the "specified value", defined in ITA 7(11) as the fair market value of the acquired securities at the time the options are granted. As the definition is in terms of a single security, there is a mechanism for adjusting this value for stock splits, stock dividends, and exchanges of shares.

5-170.   The annual limit for the election is $100,000 in specified value. While specified value is measured when the options are granted, it only counts towards the $100,000 limit in the year in which the options become vested. (For an explanation of the term, "vested", see Paragraph 5-147.) For example, assume that in 2006, an individual was granted vested options for which the specified value of the shares was $200,000. If he exercised the options in 2009, he could only elect on one-half of this amount or $100,000. Alternatively, if one-half of the options vested in 2006, with the remaining one-half vesting in 2007, he could elect on the full $200,000 of specified value if he exercised the options in 2009. Note that the $100,000 annual limit is not altered by either the granting of non-vested options or the exercise of options.

5-171. The following relatively simple example serves to illustrate these rules. A more complex illustration is provided in Paragraph 5-172.

> **Example** In January, 2007, Suzanne's corporate employer grants her options to acquire 16,000 of the company's publicly traded shares. The exercise price is $10 per share, which is the fair market value of the shares at the time the options are granted. Half of the options vest in 2007, the other half in 2008. Suzanne exercises all of the options in 2010, at which time the shares have a fair market value of $100 each. Suzanne wishes to take maximum advantage of the deferral that is available under ITA 7(8).

> **Analysis - Total Deferral** As the annual $100,000 limit on the deferral is based on the year in which the options vest, the total number of options granted in 2007 can be divided into two blocks of 8,000 shares each. Both of these blocks have a specified value of $80,000 [(8,000)($10)], which is less than $100,000. As a consequence, all of the employment income measured in 2010 can be deferred.

> The total amount of employment income measured on the exercise date is $1,440,000 [(16,000)($100 - $10)]. While Suzanne's employer will have to report this deferred employment income amount as a special item on her 2010 T4, it will not become taxable until Suzanne disposes of the shares. Note that the related ITA 110(1)(d) deduction will also be deferred until this later point in time.

> **Analysis - Partial Deferral** If all 16,000 of the options had vested in the same year, the total specified value would have been $160,000 [(16,000)($10)]. In this case, the employment income deferral would have been reduced by the $100,000 limit to the gain applicable to 10,000 shares ($100,000 ÷ $10). This would result in a $900,000 deferral [(10,000)($100 - $10)]. The remaining $540,000 [(16,000 - 10,000)($100 - $10)] would have to be taken into income in 2010. An ITA 110(1)(d) deduction of $270,000 [(1/2)($540,000)] would be available in 2010 to reduce Taxable Income.

Exercise Five-15

Subject: Stock Option Deferral - Public Company

Ms. Meridee Masterson is employed by a large public company. In 2005, she was granted options to acquire 1,000 shares of her employer's common stock at a price of $23 per share. The options vest at the time of granting and, at this time, the shares were trading at $20 per share. In 2007, when the shares are trading at $45 per share, she exercises her options and acquires 1,000 shares. At the end of 2007, she makes an election to defer the maximum amount of any employment income benefit. In 2008, she sells these shares for $42 per share. What is the effect of these transactions on Ms. Masterson's 2007 and 2008 Net Income For Tax Purposes and Taxable Income?

Exercise Five-16

Subject: Stock Option Deferral - Private Company

How would your answer to Exercise Five - 15 differ if Ms. Masterson's employer was a Canadian controlled private corporation?

End Of Exercises. Solutions available in Study Guide.

5-172. This additional example illustrates the deferral rules in a more complex situation in which the specified value of the shares that vest is in excess of the $100,000 limit.

Example On January 1, 2007, Mario's corporate employer grants him options to acquire 10,000 of the company's publicly traded shares. The exercise price is $10 per share, which is the fair market value of the shares at the time the options are granted. The options vest on January 1, 2009.

On July 1, 2008, his employer grants him options on another 10,000 shares. The exercise price is $5 per share, which is the fair market value of the shares at that time. These options vest on July 1, 2009.

Mario exercises all of the $10 options on January 1, 2009, when the shares have a fair market value of $100. He exercises all of the $5 options on July 1, 2009, when the shares have a fair market value of $150.

Analysis The specified value of the options that vested in January, 2009 is $100,000 [(10,000)($10)]. The specified value of the options that vested in July, 2009 is $50,000 [(10,000)($5)]. As this total exceeds the $100,000 annual limit, he cannot defer the total employment income generated by the exercise of all the options. His goal is to defer on the options that will maximize his employment income deferral.

The per share benefit on the options exercised in January, 2009 is $90 per share ($100 - $10). The corresponding benefit on the options exercised in July, 2009 is $145 per share ($150 - $5). Given this, Mario elects to defer on all of the options exercised in July, 2009. The specified value of these shares is $50,000 [(10,000)($5)] and the deferred employment income is $1,450,000 [(10,000)($150 - $5)].

As $50,000 of the $100,000 annual limit remains, he can also elect to defer on 5,000 ($50,000 ÷ $10) of the options exercised in January, 2009. This election provides an employment income deferral of $450,000 [(5,000)($100 - $10)]. The remaining $450,000 of employment income on the options for the other 5,000 shares exercised in January, 2009 cannot be deferred.

On Mario's T4 for 2009, his employer will report deferred employment income of $1,900,000 ($1,450,000 + $450,000), as well as an employment income inclusion of $450,000. An ITA 110(1)(d) deduction of $225,000 [(1/2)($450,000)] will be available in 2009 to reduce Taxable Income.

Exercise Five-17

Subject: Stock Option Deferral - Public Company

In March, 2006, John Traverse is granted options to acquire 25,000 shares of his employer's publicly traded common stock at a price of $12 per share. At this time, the shares were trading at $12 per share. The option arrangement is such that options for 10,000 shares vest in 2007, with the remaining options vesting in 2008. All of the options are exercised during 2009, at which time the shares are trading at $32 per share. Mr. Traverse makes the election required to defer the maximum amount of employment income in 2009. How will these transactions be reflected on Mr. Traverse's 2009 T4 slip?

End of Exercise. Solution available in Study Guide.

Other Inclusions

Payments By Employer To Employee

5-173. As previously noted, ITA 6(3) deals with employment related payments made prior to, or subsequent to, the employment period. This includes payments for accepting employment, as well as payments for work to be completed subsequent to the termination of employment. ITA 6(3) requires that all such amounts be included in employment income.

Forgiveness Of Employee Loans

5-174.   There may be circumstances in which an employer decides to forgive a loan that has been extended to an employee. As noted previously, ITA 6(15) requires that the forgiven amount be included in the income of the employee in the year in which the forgiveness occurs. The forgiven amount is simply the amount due, less any payments that have been made by the employee.

Housing Loss Reimbursement

5-175.   When an employee is required to move, employers often provide various types of financial assistance. As is discussed in Chapter 11, an employer can pay for the usual costs of moving (e.g., shipping company costs) without tax consequence to the employee. In recent years, particularly when an employee is moved from an area with a weak housing market, it has become more common for employers to reimburse individuals for losses incurred in the disposition of their principal residence.

5-176.   Initially this type of reimbursement was allowed, with no limits on the amount that could be received by the employee on a tax free basis. However, the current rules limit the amount of housing loss that can be reimbursed without tax consequences. This is accomplished in ITA 6(19) by indicating that amounts paid to employees for housing losses, except for amounts related to "eligible housing losses", must be included in income.

5-177.   ITA 6(22) defines an "eligible housing loss" as a loss that is related to a move that qualifies for the deduction of moving expenses. While this issue is discussed in more detail in Chapter 11, we would note here that an employee is generally allowed to deduct moving expenses when he moves at least 40 kilometers closer to a new work location.

5-178.   ITA 6(20) limits the amount of housing loss reimbursement that can be received by indicating that one-half of any amount received in excess of $15,000 as an eligible housing loss must be included in the employee's income as a taxable benefit. Stated alternatively, the tax free amount of housing loss reimbursement is limited to the first $15,000, plus one-half of any amount paid in excess of $15,000.

Discounts On Employer's Merchandise

5-179.   When an employee is allowed to purchase merchandise which is ordinarily sold by an employer, any discount given to the employee is not generally considered to be a taxable benefit. If discounts are extended by a group of employers, or if an employer only extends the discounts to a particular group of employees, a taxable benefit may arise. In addition, this administrative position is not intended to apply to big-ticket items (e.g., a contractor giving an employee a discount on a new home).

5-180.   A further interesting note is that the CRA has indicated that, in the case of airline employees, a benefit is assessed if the employee travels on a space confirmed basis and pays less than 50 percent of the economy fare. The benefit is the difference between 50 percent of the economy fare and the amount paid.

5-181.   When a benefit must be included in income as the result of merchandise discounts, it will include any GST that is applicable to these amounts.

Club Dues And Recreational Facilities

5-182.   With respect to employer provided recreational facilities, IT-470R notes that they are not considered a taxable benefit to the employee. In the case of employers paying membership fees in social or recreational clubs, the IT Bulletin indicates that as long as the facilities are used to the advantage of the employer, they would not be considered a taxable benefit to the employee.

5-183.   While this would seem to indicate that such fees do become a taxable benefit unless they are used primarily to further the business interests of the employer, the CRA has not pursued this approach with any rigour. As a consequence, employer payments for social or recreational club memberships generally do not result in a taxable benefit to the employee. As noted previously, the attractiveness of this type of employee benefit is reduced by the fact that, in general, employers cannot deduct the cost of club dues or recreational facilities in the determination of business income.

Specific Deductions

Overview

5-184.   All of the material on deductions that can be made against employment income are found in ITA 8. In addition, ITA 8(2) contains a general limitation statement that makes it clear that unless an item is listed in ITA 8, it cannot be deducted in the calculation of employment income.

5-185.   We have noted previously that the ITA 8 list of deductions is very limited, particularly in comparison with the list of deductions available to self-employed individuals earning business income. Despite the shortness of its list, the application of ITA 8 is fairly complex. This results from the fact that there are restrictions on the type of employee that can deduct certain items, restrictions on the items that can be deducted, and additional restrictions against simultaneous usage of some of the statutory provisions. Given this complexity, a listing and brief description of the more significant deductions available is a useful introduction to this material.

ITA 8(1)(b) Legal Expenses This Paragraph allows an employee to deduct any legal costs incurred to collect or establish the right to salary or wages owed by an employer or former employer. Also deductible are legal costs incurred to recover benefits, such as health insurance, that are not paid by an employer or former employer, but that are required to be included in employment income when received.

ITA 8(1)(f) Sales Expenses This Paragraph covers the deductions available to individuals who earn commission income. It covers travel expenses, motor vehicle expenses, and other types of expenses associated with earning commissions (e.g., licenses required by real estate salespersons).

ITA 8(1)(h) Travel Expenses This Paragraph covers deductions available to all employees for travel expenses, other than motor vehicle expenses. An employee earning commissions can deduct travel costs under ITA 8(1)(f) or ITA 8(1)(h), but cannot use both provisions simultaneously.

ITA 8(1)(h.1) Motor Vehicle Travel Expenses This Paragraph covers deductions available to all employees for motor vehicle expenses. An employee earning commissions can deduct motor vehicle costs under ITA 8(1)(f) or ITA 8(1)(h.1), but cannot use both provisions simultaneously.

ITA 8(1)(i) Dues And Other Expenses Of Performing Duties This Paragraph covers a variety of items, the most important of which are:

- Dues paid to professional organizations or unions.
- Office rent paid.
- Salaries to an assistant who assists with employment duties. The employer's CPP contributions or EI premiums that were made on behalf of the assistant can be deducted under ITA 8(1)(l.1).
- The cost of supplies used in employment related activities.

ITA 8(1)(j) Motor Vehicle And Aircraft Costs In general, employees cannot deduct capital costs. This includes tax depreciation (capital cost allowance or CCA) and interest on funds borrowed to acquire a motor vehicle or aircraft. This Paragraph creates an exception for motor vehicles and aircraft.

While less important, we would note that ITA 8(1)(p) allows the deduction of capital cost allowance on musical instruments required by employment activities. Note, however, this provision does not include the deduction of interest related to the financing of such instruments.

ITA 8(1)(m) Employee's Registered Pension Plan (RPP) Contributions As was noted previously, ITA 6(1)(a) excludes employer's contributions to an RPP from treatment as a taxable benefit. Adding to the attractiveness of these arrangements is the fact that ITA 8(1)(m) provides for the employee's contributions to be treated as a deduction. This deduction is given detailed attention in Chapter 13 which provides comprehensive coverage of the various retirement savings arrangements that are available to Canadian taxpayers.

ITA 8(1)(s) Tradespeople's Tool Expenses This deduction, which was introduced in the May, 2006 budget, provides for the deduction of up to $500 for tools that are required by a tradesperson. Only costs in excess of $1,000 can be deducted.

ITA 8(4) Meals Both ITA 8(1)(f) and ITA 8(1)(h) refer to travel costs. As such costs could include meals, ITA 8(4) specifies when meals can be considered a part of travel costs. This Subsection notes that, for meals to be deductible as travel costs under ITA 8(1)(f) or ITA 8(1)(h), the meal must be consumed when the taxpayer is required, by his employment duties, to be away from the municipality or metropolitan area where his employer's establishment is located for at least 12 hours.

We would also note here that ITA 67.1(1) limits the deductibility of food and entertainment costs to 50 percent of the amount paid. This limitation applies without regard to whether the individual is working as an employee, or as a self-employed individual earnings business income.

ITA 8(13) Work Space In Home This Subsection provides rules for an employee deducting the costs of a work space in his home.

5-186.   Most of these provisions will be given more detailed attention in the material which follows. Other, less commonly used Paragraphs such as ITA 8(1)(e) which allows the deduction of certain expenses of railway employees and ITA 8(1)(r) which allows apprentice mechanics to deduct the full cost of their tools, will not be given further coverage.

Salesperson's Expenses Under ITA 8(1)(f)

5-187.   Individual employees who are involved with the selling of property or the negotiating of contracts are permitted to deduct all expenses that can be considered necessary to the performance of their duties. Items that can be deducted under this provision include:

- advertising and promotion
- meals and entertainment (subject to the previously noted 50 percent limit)
- lodging
- motor vehicle costs (other than CCA and interest)
- parking (which is not considered a motor vehicle expense)
- work space in home (maintenance, property taxes, and insurance — no mortgage interest or amortization)
- supplies (including long distance telephone calls and cellular phone airtime, but not the basic monthly charge for a telephone or amounts paid to connect or licence a cellular phone)
- licences (e.g., for real estate sales)
- bonding and liability insurance premiums
- medical fees (life insurance sales)
- salary to assistant or substitute
- office rent

- training costs
- transportation costs
- computers and office equipment (leased only - see following Paragraph)

5-188.   Except in the case of an automobile or aircraft, an employee who is a salesperson cannot deduct capital cost allowance. This means that if a salesperson purchases a computer to maintain customer records, he will not be able to deduct capital cost allowance on it. Alternatively, if the computer is leased, the lease payments can be deducted.

5-189.   In order to deduct 50 percent of the cost of meals, the salesperson must be away from the municipality or metropolitan area where the employer's establishment is located for at least 12 hours. As is the case in the determination of business income, no deduction is permitted for membership fees for clubs or recreational facilities. A salesperson is permitted to deduct motor vehicle costs and the cost of maintaining an office in his home. However, these costs can also be deducted by other types of employees and, as a consequence, will be dealt with later in this Chapter.

5-190.   As stated in ITA 8(1)(f), to be eligible to deduct salesperson's expenses, all of the following conditions must be met:

1. The salesperson must be required to pay his own expenses. The employer must sign Form T2200 certifying that this is the case. While the form does not have to be filed, it must be available if requested by the CRA.

2. The salesperson must be ordinarily required to carry on his duties away from the employer's place of business.

3. The salesperson must not be in receipt of an expense allowance that was not included in income.

4. The salesperson must receive at least part of his remuneration in the form of commissions or by reference to the volume of sales.

5-191.   The amount of qualifying expenses that can be deducted under ITA 8(1)(f) is limited to the commissions or other sales related revenues earned for the year. This limitation does not, however, apply to capital cost allowance or interest on a motor vehicle or aircraft. These costs are deductible under ITA 8(1)(j) (see Paragraph 5-202). The deduction under ITA 8(1)(j) is not limited to commission income and, because it can be used in conjunction with ITA 8(1)(f), the salesperson's total deductions can exceed commission income.

Travel Expenses And Motor Vehicle Costs
Under ITA 8(1)(h) and 8(1)(h.1)

5-192.   ITA 8(1)(h) provides for the deduction of travel costs such as accommodation, airline or rail tickets, taxi fares, and meals. As was the case with salespersons' expenses, only 50 percent of the cost of meals is deductible. Here again, the deductibility of meals is conditional on being away from the municipality or metropolitan area in which the employer's establishment is located for at least 12 hours.

5-193.   ITA 8(1)(h.1) provides for the deduction of motor vehicle costs, other than capital cost allowance and financing costs, when an employee uses his own vehicle to carry out employment duties. Note that these are the same costs that could be deducted by a salesperson under ITA 8(1)(f).

5-194.   These deductions can be claimed by any employee who meets specified criteria. Further, they are effectively not limited by employment income. They can be used to create a net employment loss which, if not usable against other types of income in the current year, is subject to the carry over provisions that are discussed in Chapter 14.

5-195.   The conditions for deducting expenses under ITA 8(1)(h) and (h.1) are similar to those for deductions under ITA 8(1)(f), except that there is no requirement that some part of the employee's remuneration be in the form of commissions. The conditions are as follows:

1. The person must be required to pay his own travel and motor vehicle costs. As was the case with commission salespersons, the employee must have Form T2200, signed by the employer, certifying that this is the case.

2. The person must be ordinarily required to carry on his duties away from the employer's place of business.

3. The person must not be in receipt of an allowance for travel costs that was not included in income.

5-196. There is one further condition that will be discussed more fully in the next section. Both ITA 8(1)(h) and (h.1) state that, if a deduction is made under ITA 8(1)(f), no deduction can be made under these Paragraphs.

The Salesperson's Dilemma

5-197. All of the travel and motor vehicle costs that a salesperson could deduct under ITA 8(1)(h) and (h.1), could also be deducted using ITA 8(1)(f). However, the use of ITA 8(1)(f) involves both good news and bad news:

- **Good News** The good news is that, if the salesperson uses ITA 8(1)(f), he can deduct expenses related to sales activity that are not deductible under any other provision (e.g., advertising and promotion).

- **Bad News** The bad news is that, if a salesperson uses ITA 8(1)(f), the amount that he can deduct is limited to the amount of commission income.

5-198. At first glance, the logical course of action here would be to use ITA 8(1)(h) and (h.1) for the travel and motor vehicle costs (this deduction would not be limited by commission income), and to then use ITA 8(1)(f) to deduct the maximum amount of other items that are available under this latter Paragraph (subject to the commission income limitation). However, this cannot be done — ITA 8(1)(h) and (h.1) cannot be used if a deduction is made under ITA 8(1)(f).

5-199. The result is, in situations where potential deductions under ITA 8(1)(f) exceed commission income, the salesperson must undertake an additional calculation to determine whether the total travel costs under ITA 8(1)(h) and (h.1) would be greater than the commission limited amount of deductions under ITA 8(1)(f). Should this be the case, the salesperson would deduct the larger amount that is available under ITA 8(1)(h) and (h.1). It is difficult to understand the tax policy goal that is achieved through this complexity.

5-200. Note that this choice does not influence the amount of other deductions available to the salesperson. The amounts deducted under other ITA 8(1) Paragraphs will be unchanged by whether the salesperson uses ITA 8(1)(f) or the combination of ITA 8(1)(h) and (h.1).

Exercise Five-18

Subject: Commission Salesperson Expenses

Mr. Morton McMaster is a commission salesperson. During 2007, his gross salary was $82,000 and he earned $12,200 in commissions. During the year he had advertising costs of $8,000 and expenditures for entertainment of clients of $12,000. His travel costs for the year totaled $13,100. He is required to pay his own expenses and does not receive any allowance from his employer. What is Mr. McMaster's maximum expense deduction for 2007?

End of Exercise. Solution available in Study Guide.

Other Expenses Of Performing Duties Under ITA 8(1)(i)

5-201.   ITA 8(1)(i) contains a list of other items that can be deducted in the determination of employment income. The major items included here are as follows:

- Annual professional membership dues, if their payment was necessary to maintain a professional status recognized by statute.

- Union dues that are paid pursuant to the provisions of a collective agreement.

- Office rent and salary paid to an assistant or a substitute. In order to deduct these amounts, the employee must be required to incur the costs under a contract of employment. This must be supported by Form T2200, signed by the employer and certifying that the requirement exists. Also deductible here would be the costs of maintaining a home office (see Paragraph 5-205).

- The cost of supplies consumed in the performance of employment duties. Here again, the employee must be required to provide these supplies under his employment contract and this contract must be supported by a signed Form T2200.

Automobile And Aircraft Expenses Under ITA 8(1)(j)

5-202.   Under either ITA 8(1)(f) or ITA 8(1)(h.1) an employee can deduct the operating costs of an automobile used in employment duties. With respect to operating costs, this would include an appropriate share (based on the proportion the employment related kilometers are of the total kilometers driven) of such costs as fuel, maintenance, normal repair costs, insurance, and licensing fees.

5-203.   In addition, under ITA 8(1)(j), an employee can deduct capital cost allowance and interest costs on an automobile or an aircraft that is used in employment related activities. The deductible amounts are calculated in the same manner as they would be for a business. Capital cost allowance would be calculated on a 30 percent declining balance basis on automobiles and a 25 percent declining balance basis on aircraft, while deductible interest would be based on actual amounts paid or payable (see Chapter 7 for a more complete discussion of capital cost allowance calculations).

5-204.   However, there are limits on the amounts that can be deducted here for business purposes, and these limits are equally applicable to the calculation of employment income deductions. While these limits are discussed more completely in Chapter 8 on Business Income, we would note that for 2007 there is no deduction for capital cost allowance on the cost of an automobile in excess of $30,000 (before GST and PST), that deductible interest is limited to $300 per month, and that deductible lease payments are limited to $800 per month (before GST and PST). With respect to employees, their deduction would be based on the fraction of these costs, subject to the preceding limits, that reflects the portion of employment related kilometers included in the total kilometers driven.

Home Office Costs For Employees

5-205.   We have noted that salespersons can deduct the costs associated with an office in their home under ITA 8(1)(f), and that any employee who is required by his employment contract to maintain an office can make a similar deduction under ITA 8(1)(i). Because of the obvious potential for abuse in this area, ITA 8(13) establishes fairly restrictive conditions with respect to the availability of this deduction. Under the provisions of this Subsection, costs of a home office are only deductible when the work space is either:

- the place where the individual principally performs the duties of the office or employment, or

- used exclusively during the period in respect of which the amount relates for the purpose of earning income from the office or employment and used on a regular and continuous basis for meeting customers or other persons in the ordinary course of performing the duties of the office or employment.

5-206.   Once it is established that home office costs are deductible, it becomes necessary to determine what kind of costs can be deducted. We have noted previously that, for employees, the only assets on which capital cost allowance and interest can be deducted are automobiles, aircraft, and musical instruments. This means that no employee can deduct capital cost allowance or mortgage interest related to an office that is maintained in their residence.

5-207.   With respect to other costs, IT-352R2 indicates that an employee making a deduction under ITA 8(1)(i) can deduct an appropriate portion (based on floor space used for the office) of maintenance costs such as fuel and electricity, light bulbs, cleaning materials, and minor repairs.

5-208.   For salespersons making a deduction for a home office under ITA 8(1)(f), IT-352R2 indicates that they can deduct the items listed in the preceding paragraph, plus an appropriate portion of property taxes and house insurance premiums.

5-209.   If the home office is in rented property, the percentage of rent and any maintenance costs paid related to the home office are deductible.

5-210.   The amount deductible for home office costs is limited to employment income after the deduction of all other employment expenses. Stated alternatively, home office costs cannot be used to create or increase an employment loss. Only the income related to the use of the home office can be included in this calculation. Any home office costs that are not deductible in a year can be carried forward to the following year. They become part of the home office costs for that year and, to the extent that this total cannot be deducted in that year, the balance can be carried forward to the following year. This, in effect, provides an indefinite carry over of these costs.

Employee And Partner GST Rebate

General Concept

5-211.   Many of the expenses employees can deduct against employment income include a GST component. If the individual was a GST registrant earning business income, these GST payments would generate input tax credits. However, employment is not considered to be a commercial activity and, as a consequence, employees who have no separate commercial activity cannot be registrants. This means that they will not be able to use the usual input tax credit procedure to obtain a refund of GST amounts paid with respect to their employment expenses. A similar analysis applies to partners who have partnership related expenses that are not included in partnership net income or loss.

5-212.   The Employee and Partner GST Rebate allows employees and partners to recover the GST paid on their employment or partnership related expenditures, including vehicles and musical instruments, in a way that is similar to the input tax credits that they would have received if they were GST registrants. Form GST370 is used to claim the GST rebate and is filed with the employee or partner's tax return.

5-213.   To qualify for this rebate, the individual must be either an employee of a GST registrant, or a member of a partnership that is a GST registrant. Employees of financial institutions are not eligible for the rebate. However, employees of charities, not-for-profit organizations, universities, school boards, and municipalities are eligible as long as the organizations that they work for are registered. In addition, employees of provincial governments, Crown corporations, and the federal government qualify for the rebate. To claim the rebate, the individual must have unreimbursed expenses that are eligible for income tax deductions against employment or partnership income.

Calculating The Amount

5-214.   As explained in the preceding section, the rebate is based on the GST amounts included in those costs that can be deducted in the determination of employment income. In terms of calculations, this is accomplished by multiplying the GST included cost by a fraction in which the GST rate is the numerator and one plus the GST rate is the denominator

> **Example** Marcia Valentino has deductible cell phone expenses during 2007 of $2,000. She paid $120 in GST (6%) and deducted $2,120 in her calculation of 2007 employment income.
>
> **Analysis** Ms. Valentino's rebate would be $120 [($2,120)(6/106)], the GST she paid.

Example

5-215.   The following simple example illustrates the calculation of the GST rebate for an employee:

> **Example** Tanya Kucharik, a very successful sales manager, used her car 93 percent for employment related purposes during 2007. She claimed the following expenses on Form T777, Statement of Employment Expenses, for 2007 (all amounts include applicable GST):
>
> | | |
> |---|---:|
> | Cellular phone charges | $ 1,200 |
> | Gas, maintenance and car repairs (93%) | 17,500 |
> | Insurance on car (93%) | 1,023 |
> | Capital cost allowance (CCA) on car (93%) | 3,100 |
>
> The car on which the CCA was deducted was purchased during 2007.
>
> **Analysis** On Form GST370, her GST rebate would be as follows:
>
> | | Eligible Expenses | GST Rebate (6/106) |
> |---|---:|---:|
> | Eligible Expenses Other Than CCA | $18,700 | $1,058 |
> | Eligible CCA On Which GST Was Paid | 3,100 | 175 |
> | Totals | $21,800 | $1,233 |

5-216.   Eligible expenses exclude expenses for which a non-taxable allowance was received, zero-rated and exempt supplies, supplies acquired outside of Canada, supplies acquired from non-registrants, and expenses incurred when the employer was a non-registrant. In this example, the car insurance is excluded as it is an exempt supply on which no GST was charged.

5-217.   The employment related expenses that are listed in this calculation will be deducted in Ms. Kucharik's income tax return for 2007. Under normal circumstances, the GST rebate for 2007 expenses will be claimed in Ms. Kucharik's 2007 tax return. As a result, this amount will be received in 2008, either as part of the 2007 refund or as a decrease in the amount owed for 2007.

5-218.   As the rebate constitutes a reduction in the incurred costs that were deducted by the employee, an adjustment of the deduction is required for amounts that are received. This is accomplished by including the $1,058 GST rebate on expenses other than capital cost allowance in Net Income For Tax Purposes in the year in which it is received (2008 in Ms. Kucharik's case). In similar fashion, the amount of any rebates received that related to capital cost allowance ($175) will be deducted from the capital cost of the relevant asset in the year in which it is received (again 2008, in the case of Ms. Kucharik).

5-219.   While the rebate is normally claimed in the return in which the expenses are deducted, it can be claimed in any income tax return submitted within four years of the year in which the expenses are claimed.

Key Terms Used In This Chapter

5-220. The following is a list of the key terms used in this Chapter. These terms, and their meanings, are compiled in the Glossary Of Key Terms located at the back of the separate paper Study Guide and on the Student CD-ROM.

Allowance	Prescribed Rate
Bonus Arrangement	Public Corporation
Canadian Controlled Private Corporation	Qualifying Acquisition
Employee	Salary
Employer/Employee Relationship	Self-Employed Individual
Employment Income	Specified Shareholder
Fringe Benefits	Standby Charge
Home Relocation Loan	Stock Option
Imputed Interest	Taxable Allowance
Operating Cost Benefit	Taxable Benefit
	Vested Benefit

References

5-221. For more detailed study of the material in this Chapter, we would refer you to the following:

ITA 5	Income From Office Or Employment
ITA 6	Amounts To Be Included As Income From Office Or Employment
ITA 7	Agreement To Issue Securities To Employees
ITA 8	Deductions Allowed
ITA 80.4	Loans
ITA 80.5	Deemed Interest
ITR 4301	Interest Rates [Prescribed Rate Of Interest]
IC 73-21R9	Claims for Meals and Lodging Expenses of Transport Employees
IT-63R5	Benefits, Including Standby Charge For An Automobile, From The Personal Use Of A Motor Vehicle Supplied By An Employer - After 1992
IT-85R2	Health And Welfare Trusts For Employees
IT-91R4	Employment At Special Or Remote Work Locations
IT-99R5	Legal And Accounting Fees
IT-103R	Dues Paid To A Union Or To A Parity Or Advisory Committee
IT-113R4	Benefits To Employees - Stock Options
IT-158R2	Employees' Professional Membership Dues
IT-196R2	Payments By Employer To Employee
IT-202R2	Employees' Or Workers' Compensation
IT-352R2	Employee's Expenses, Including Work Space in Home Expenses
IT-389R	Vacation Pay Trusts Established Under Collective Agreements
IT-421R2	Benefits To Individuals, Corporations And Shareholders From Loans Or Debt
IT-428	Wage Loss Replacement Plans
IT-470R	Employees' Fringe Benefits
IT-504R2	Visual Artists And Writers
IT-514	Work Space In Home Expenses
IT-518R	Food, Beverages And Entertainment Expenses
IT-522R	Vehicle, Travel and Sales Expenses of Employees
IT-525R	Performing Artists

Problems For Self Study

(The solutions for these problems can be found in the separate Study Guide.)

Self Study Problem Five - 1

Ms. Tamira Vines is a salesperson for Compudata Ltd., a Regina based software company that is a GST registrant. As her work requires her to travel extensively throughout southern and central Saskatchewan, the Company provides her with an automobile. The provincial sales tax rate for Saskatchewan is 7 percent.

From January 1, 2007 through May 31, 2007, the Company provided her with an Acura TL. This car was purchased by the Company on January 1, 2007 at a cost of $39,000, plus $2,730 in provincial sales tax and $2,340 in GST. During the period January 1, 2007 through May 31, 2007, the car was driven 38,800 kilometers for employment related purposes and 3,400 kilometers for personal use. The Company paid all operating costs during the period, an amount of $3,656, including applicable provincial sales tax and GST.

On June 1, 2007, following a late evening sales conference at the Shangri La Hotel in Moose Jaw, Ms. Vines was involved in an accident in which the Acura was destroyed. Ms. Vines was hospitalized and was not able to return to work until July 1, 2007. Compudata's insurance company paid $27,500 to the Company for the loss of the car.

When she returned to work on July 1, 2007, the Company provided Ms. Vines with a Ford Crown Victoria. The Company leased this vehicle at a monthly cost of $699 per month, including applicable provincial sales tax and GST. This monthly payment also includes a $100 per month charge for insurance. For the period July 1, 2007 through December 31, 2007, operating costs, other than insurance, totaled $3,456, including applicable provincial sales tax and GST. These were paid for by the Company. During this period, Ms. Vines drove the car 15,600 kilometers for business and 14,600 kilometers for personal use.

Ms. Vines paid to the Company $0.10 per kilometer for the personal use of the cars owned or leased by the Company for the year.

Required: Calculate the minimum taxable car benefit, including GST effects, that will be included in Ms. Vines' employment income for the year ending December 31, 2007.

Self Study Problem Five - 2

During the current year, the Carstair Manufacturing Company provides automobiles for four of its senior executives, with the value of the cars being in proportion to the salaries which they receive. While each of the individuals uses their car for employment related travel, they also have the vehicles available to them for personal use. The portion of personal use varies considerably among the four individuals. The details related to each of these cars, including the amount of personal and business travel recorded by the executives, are as follows:

Mr. Sam Stern Mr. Stern is the president of the Company and is provided with a Mercedes which has been purchased by the Company at a cost of $78,000. The car was new last year and, during the current year, it was driven a total of 38,000 kilometers. Of this total, only 6,000 kilometers were for employment related purposes, while the remaining 32,000 were for personal travel. Operating costs totaled $.50 per kilometer and, because Mr. Stern made an extended trip outside of North America, the car was only available to Mr. Stern for eight months during the current year. The car and its keys were left with the Company during the duration of Mr. Stern's trip.

Ms. Sarah Blue Ms. Blue is the vice president in charge of marketing and has been provided with a Corvette. The Company leases this vehicle at a cost of $900 per month. During the current year, the car was driven a total of 60,000 kilometers, with all but 5,000 of these kilometers being for employment related purposes. The car was available to Ms. Blue throughout the current year, and total annual operating costs amount to $18,000.

Mr. John Stack   Mr. Stack is the vice president in charge of finance and he has been provided with an Acura that was purchased by the Company in the preceding year at a cost of $48,000. During the current year, Mr. Stack drove the car 42,000 kilometers for employment related purposes and 10,000 kilometers for personal travel. Operating costs for the year were $20,800, and the car was available to Mr. Stack throughout the current year. In order to reduce his taxable benefit, Mr. Stack made a payment of $7,000 to the Company for the use of this car.

Mr. Alex Decker   Mr. Decker, the vice president in charge of industrial relations, chose to drive a Lexus. This car was leased by the Company at a cost of $500 per month. The lease payment was significantly reduced by the fact that the Company made a refundable deposit of $10,000 to the leasing Company at the inception of the lease. During the current year, Mr. Decker drove the car 90,000 kilometers for employment related purposes and 8,500 kilometers for personal use. The operating costs were $0.35 per kilometer and, because of an extended illness, he was only able to use the car for the first ten months of the year. He left the car and its keys with his employer during his illness.

Required: Calculate the minimum amount of the taxable benefit for the current year that will accrue to each of these executives as the result of having the cars supplied by the Company. In making these calculations, ignore GST and PST considerations. From the point of view of tax planning for management compensation, provide any suggestions for the Carstair Manufacturing Company with respect to these cars.

Self Study Problem Five - 3

Mr. Thomas Malone is employed by Technocratic Ltd. in a management position. Because of an outstanding performance in his division of the Company, he is about to receive a promotion accompanied by a large increase in compensation. He is discussing various possible ways in which his compensation might be increased without incurring the same amount of taxation as would be assessed on an increase in his salary. As he is currently in the process of acquiring a large new residence in a prestigious neighbourhood, he has suggested that it might be advantageous for the Company to provide him with a five year interest free loan in the amount of $200,000 as part of any increase in compensation. Other relevant information is as follows:

- Given Mr. Malone's present salary, any additional income will be taxed at 45 percent.
- Technocratic Ltd. is able to invest funds at a before tax rate of 18 percent. It is subject to taxation at a 40 percent rate.
- The loan would not qualify as a home relocation loan.
- Assume the current rate for five year mortgages on residential properties is 5 percent.
- Assume the current Regulation 4301 rate for imputing interest on various tax related balances is 5 percent.

Required: Evaluate Mr. Malone's suggestion of providing him with an interest free loan in lieu of salary from the point of view of the cost to the Company.

Self Study Problem Five - 4

During 2006, Ms. Sara Wu's employer, Imports Ltd., granted her stock options that allowed her to acquire 12,000 shares of the Company's common stock at a price of $22 per share. At this time, the shares have a fair market value of $20 per share.

On June, 1, 2007, Ms. Wu exercises all of these options. At this time, Imports Ltd. shares have a fair market value of $31 per share. Ms. Wu makes any available elections to defer any employment income inclusion.

On January 31, 2008, Ms. Wu sells the 12,000 Imports Ltd. shares at a price of $28 per share.

Required   For each of the following Cases, calculate the tax consequences of the transactions that took place during 2006, 2007, and 2008 on Ms. Wu's Net Income For Tax Purposes and Taxable Income.

> **Case A**   Imports Ltd. is a public company and Ms. Wu is a specified shareholder (i.e., she owns more than 10 percent of the outstanding shares of the corporation).

> **Case B**   Imports Ltd. is a public company and Ms. Wu is not a specified shareholder.

> **Case C**   Imports Ltd. is a Canadian controlled private corporation that is not a small business corporation.

Self Study Problem Five - 5

For the last three years, Sam Jurgens has been employed in Halifax as a loan supervisor for Maritime Trust Inc. Maritime Trust is a large public company and, as a consequence, Mr. Jurgens felt that he did not have the opportunity to exhibit the full range of his abilities. To correct this situation, Sam decided to accept employment in Toronto effective July 1, 2007 as the general manager of Bolten Financial Services, a Canadian controlled private corporation specializing in providing financial advice to retired executives.

In January, 2007, prior to leaving Maritime Trust, Mr. Jurgens exercised options to purchase 5,000 shares of the public company's stock at a price of $15 per share. At the time that he exercised these options, the shares were trading at $16 per share. He did not make an election to defer the income inclusion. On February 10, 2008, he sold these shares at a price of $8 per share.

Mr. Jurgens had an annual salary at Maritime Trust of $65,000, while in his new position in Toronto, the salary is $50,000 per year. However, he has the option of acquiring 1,000 shares per year of Bolten stock at a price of $20 per share. On July 1, when he was granted the option, Bolten stock had a fair market value of $14 per share. On December 1, 2007, when the Bolten stock has a fair market value of $22 per share, Mr. Jurgens exercises these options and acquires 1,000 shares. It is his intent to hold these shares for an indefinite period of time.

Because there is extensive travel involved in the position with Bolten Financial Services, the Company has provided Mr. Jurgens with a $25,000 company car. Between July 1 and December 31, 2007, Mr. Jurgens drove this car a total of 25,000 kilometers, of which 15,000 kilometers were clearly related to his work with Bolten Financial Services. The operating costs associated with the car for this period, all of which were paid for by the Company, amount to $5,000. Because of extensive repairs resulting from a manufacturer's recall, the car was not available to Mr. Jurgens during October and November of 2007.

At the time of his move to Toronto, Bolten Financial Services provided Mr. Jurgens with a $200,000 home relocation loan to purchase a personal residence near the center of town. No interest was charged on this loan.

During the year, Mr. Jurgens earned $15,000 in interest and received $45,000 in dividends from taxable Canadian corporations.

Assume that the relevant prescribed rate through all of 2007 is 5 percent (not including the extra 2 or 4 percent applicable to payments that are due from or owing to the CRA).

Required: Compute Sam Jurgens' minimum net employment income for the year ending December 31, 2007.

Self Study Problem Five - 6

This problem is continued in Self Study Problem Six-2.

Mr. John Barth has been employed for many years as a graphic illustrator in Kamloops, British Columbia. His employer is a large publicly traded Canadian company. During 2007, his gross salary was $82,500. In addition, he was awarded a $20,000 bonus to reflect his outstanding performance during the year. As he was in no immediate need of additional income, he arranged with his employer that none of this bonus would be paid until 2012, the year of his expected retirement.

Other Information:
For the 2007 taxation year, the following items were relevant.

1. Mr. Barth's employer withheld the following amounts from his income:

Federal Income Tax	$16,000
Employment Insurance Premiums	720
Canada Pension Plan Contributions	1,990
United Way Donations	2,000
Registered Pension Plan Contributions	3,200
Payments For Personal Use Of Company Car	3,600

2. During the year, Mr. Barth is provided with an automobile owned by his employer. The cost of the automobile was $27,500. Mr. Barth drove the car a total of 10,000 kilometers during the year, of which only 4,000 kilometers were related to the business of his employer. The automobile was available to Mr. Barth for ten months of the year. During the other two months, he was out of the country and left the automobile with one of the other employees of the corporation.

3. During the year, the corporation paid Mega Financial Planners a total of $1,500 for providing counseling services to Mr. Barth with respect to his personal financial situation.

4. In order to assist Mr. Barth in purchasing a ski chalet, the corporation provided him with a five year loan of $150,000. The loan was granted on October 1 at an interest rate of 3 percent. Mr. Barth paid the corporation a total of $1,125 in interest for the year on January 20, 2008. Assume that, at the time the loan was granted, the relevant prescribed rate was 5 percent.

5. Mr. Barth was required to pay professional dues of $1,800 during the year.

6. In 2006, when Mr. Barth exercised his stock options to buy 1,000 shares of his employer's common stock at a price of $15 per share, the shares were trading at $18 per share. When the options were issued, the shares were trading at $12 per share. At the time of exercise, he elected to defer the income inclusion on the stock options. During 2007, the shares were sold at $18 per share.

Required: Calculate Mr. Barth's minimum net employment income for the year ending December 31, 2007. Provide reasons for omitting items that you have not included in your calculations. Ignore GST and PST considerations.

Self Study Problem Five - 7

Ms. Sandra Firth is a commission salesperson who has been working for Hadley Enterprises, a Canadian public corporation, for three years. During the year ending December 31, 2007, her gross salary, not including commissions or allowances, was $72,000. Her commissions for the year totalled $14,000. The following amounts were withheld by Hadley Enterprises from Ms. Firth's gross salary:

Federal and provincial income taxes	$22,000
Registered pension plan contributions (Note One)	3,200
Payments for group disability insurance (Note Two)	250
Payments for personal use of company car (Note Three)	2,400
Payments for group term life insurance (Note Four)	450
Interest on home purchase loan (Note Five)	3,000
Purchase of Canada Savings Bonds	2,060

Note One   Hadley Enterprises made a matching $3,200 contribution to Ms. Firth's registered pension plan.

Note Two   Ms. Firth is covered by a comprehensive disability plan which provides income benefits during any period of disability. Prior to 2007, Hadley Enterprises paid all of the $500 per year premium on this plan. However, as of 2007, Ms. Firth is required to pay one-half of this premium, the $250 amount withheld from her gross salary. During 2007, Ms. Firth was hospitalized for the month of March. For this period, the disability plan paid her $500 per week, for a total of $2,000.

Note Three   Hadley Enterprises provides Ms. Firth with a Lexus that was purchased in 2006 for $58,000. During 2007, she drove the car 92,000 kilometers, 7,000 of which were personal in nature. Ms. Firth paid all of the operating costs of the car, a total of $6,200 for the year ending December 31, 2007. However, the Company provides her with an allowance of $600 per month ($7,200 for the year) to compensate her for these costs. While Ms. Firth was hospitalized during the month of March (see Note Two), another unrelated employee of Hadley Enterprises had the use of the car.

Note Four   Ms. Firth is covered by a group term life insurance policy that pays her beneficiary $160,000 in the event of her death. The 2007 premium on the policy is $1,350, two-thirds of which is paid by her employer.

Note Five   On January 1, 2007, the Company provided Ms. Firth with a $400,000 loan to assist with the purchase of a new residence. The loan must be repaid by December 31, 2008. All of the interest that is due on the loan for 2007 is withheld from Ms. Firth's 2007 salary. This loan does not qualify as a home relocation loan.

Other Information:

1. At Christmas, the Company gives all of its employees a Palm Pilot (a hand-held personal digital assistant). Each Palm Pilot costs the Company $350, including all applicable taxes. The Company deducts this amount in full in its corporate tax return.

2. During 2006, Ms. Firth received stock options from Hadley to acquire 1,000 shares of its common stock. The option price is $5.00 per share and, at the time the options are issued, the shares are trading at $4.50 per share. In June, 2007, the shares have increased in value to $7.00 per share and Ms. Firth exercises her options to acquire 1,000 shares. She is still holding them at the end of the year and has no intention of selling them. Due to an extended vacation in the Galapagos Islands, Ms. Firth neglects to file the election with her employer to defer the employment income benefit on the exercise of the options.

3. The Company provides Ms. Firth with a membership in the Mountain Tennis Club. The cost of this membership for the year is $2,500. During the year, Ms. Firth spends $6,500 entertaining clients at this club. The Company does not reimburse her for these entertainment costs.

4. Ms. Firth had travel costs related to her employment activities as follows:

Meals	$1,300
Lodging	3,500
Total	**$4,800**

Her employer provides her with a travel allowance of $300 per month ($3,600 for the year) which is included on her T4 for the year.

5. Assume that the relevant prescribed rate for the entire year is 5 percent (not including the extra 2 or 4 percent applicable to payments that are due from, or to, the CRA).

Required: Calculate Ms. Firth's minimum net employment income for the year ending December 31, 2007. Ignore any GST or PST implications.

Self Study Problem Five - 8

Mr. Worthy is a commissioned salesman and has asked for your assistance in preparing his 2007 income tax return. He has provided you with the following information:

Employment Income		
Salary		$65,000
Commissions		$11,000
Telephone Charges		
Monthly Charge For Residential Line	$ 250	
Long Distance To Clients From Home Office	400	
Cellular Phone Airtime To Clients	800	$ 1,450
Office Supplies And Postage At Home Office		$ 295
Cost of Tickets To Basketball Games With Clients		$ 2,550
Travel Expenses		
Car Operating Costs	$2,700	
Meals	900	
Hotels	2,850	$ 6,450
Capital Cost Allowance On Car (100%)		$ 2,450
Cost Of Maintaining Home Office		
(Based On A Proportion Of Space Used)		
House Utilities	$485	
House Insurance	70	
House Maintenance	255	
Capital Cost Allowance - House	750	
Capital Cost Allowance - Office Furniture	475	
Mortgage Interest	940	
Property Taxes	265	$ 3,240
Interest		
On Loan To Buy Office Furniture	$1,700	
On Loan To Buy Car	2,300	$ 4,000

Mr. Worthy's car was purchased, used, several years ago for $28,000. Twenty percent of the milage on the car is for personal matters. He is required by his employer to maintain an office in his home and is eligible to deduct home office costs. Mr. Worthy has received no reimbursement from his employer for any of the amounts listed.

Required: Ignore GST and PST implications in your solutions.

A. Calculate Mr. Worthy's minimum net employment income for 2007.

B. Assume Mr. Worthy had only $4,000 in commission income in addition to his $65,000 salary. Calculate Mr. Worthy's minimum net employment income for 2007.

Assignment Problems

(The solutions for these problems are only available in
the solutions manual that has been provided to your instructor.)

Assignment Problem Five - 1

The Jareau Manufacturing Company owns a car with an original cost of $30,000. The car has been owned by the Company for two years. During the year, the car has been at the disposal of the Company's sales manager, Mr. Robert Stickler. During the year, Mr. Stickler drove the car 36,000 kilometers, with all of the expenses being paid for by the Company. The operating costs paid for by the Company total $3,920. In addition, the Company deducted capital cost allowance of $5,610 related to this car for the current year.

Required: Ignore all GST and PST implications. Indicate the minimum taxable benefit that would be allocated to Mr. Stickler in each of the following Cases:

Case A Mr. Stickler has the car available to him for the entire year and drives it a total of 7,200 kilometers for personal purposes.

Case B Mr. Stickler has the car available to him for 10 months of the year and drives it a total of 15,000 kilometers for personal purposes.

Case C Mr. Stickler has the car available to him for 6 months of the year and drives it a total of 25,200 kilometers for personal purposes.

Assignment Problem Five - 2

Mark DiSalvo is an employee of Noble Ltd., a GST registrant involved exclusively in making taxable supplies. The Company provides Mr. DiSalvo with an automobile which was acquired in 2006 at a cost of $39,900 (including $2,800 in provincial sales tax and $2,100 in GST). During 2007, Mr. DiSalvo drives the automobile a total of 50,000 kilometers, 35,000 of which were employment related.

During 2007, the Company paid for all of the costs of operating the automobile. These amounts were as follows:

Gas, Oil, And Maintenance	
(Includes $400 In Provincial Sales Tax and $300 In GST)	$5,700
Insurance And Licence Fees (No Provincial Sales Tax Or GST)	2,000
Total	$7,700

The Company also provides Mr. DiSalvo with group life insurance coverage in the amount of $250,000. The 2007 premium on this policy is $4,000.

As the result of winning a sales contest, the Company gives Mr. DiSalvo a large screen, high definition television set. The television set cost the Company $9,120, including $640 in provincial sales tax and $480 in GST.

Required: Determine the taxable benefits including GST effects that will be included in Mr. DiSalvo's 2007 income as a result of his employment by Noble Ltd.

Assignment Problem Five - 3

Three employees of the Cancar Company were given the use of company cars on January 1 of the current year. The three cars are identical. Each car was driven 16,000 kilometers during the year and the operating costs were $2,400 for each car during the year, all of which were paid by the company.

Required: Ignore all GST and PST implications. For each of the following cars, calculate the minimum taxable benefit to the employees for the current year ending December 31.

Car A is purchased for $30,000. It is available to Aaron Abbott for the whole year. He drives it for personal purposes for a total of 9,000 kilometers.

Car B is leased for $635 per month. It is available to Babs Bentley for 11 months of the year. She drives it for personal purposes for a total of 6,000 kilometers and pays Cancar Company $500 for the use of the car.

Car C is purchased for $30,000. It is available to Carole Cantin for 10 months of the year. She drives it for personal purposes for a total of 7,000 kilometers.

Assignment Problem Five - 4

The Martin Distributing Company provides cars for four of its senior executives. While the cars are used for employment related travel, the executives also use them for personal matters. The personal use varies considerably among the four individuals. The details related to each of these cars, including the amount of personal and employment related travel recorded by the executives, are as follows:

Mr. Joseph Martin Mr. Martin is the president of the Company and is provided with a Mercedes that has been leased by the Company for $2,100 per month. During the current year, the car was driven a total of 42,000 kilometers, of which 19,000 could be considered employment related travel. Operating costs averaged $0.80 per kilometer. Because of an extended illness which required hospitalization, the car was only available to Mr. Martin for the first seven months of the year.

Mrs. Grace Martin Mrs. Martin, the vice president in charge of marketing, is provided with a Lexus that the Company has purchased for $78,000. During the current year, this car was driven a total of 15,000 kilometers, of which all but 2,000 kilometers were employment related. Operating costs for the year amounted to $3,500 and the car was available to Mrs. Martin throughout the year.

Mr. William Martin William Martin, the vice president in charge of finance, is provided with a Ford Five Hundred that the Company leases for $600 per month. The total milage during the current year amounted to 38,000 kilometers, of which 32,000 kilometers related to personal matters. Operating costs for the year were $7,400 and the car was available to Mr. Martin throughout the year. William Martin paid the Company $400 per month for the use of the car.

Mrs. Sharon Martin-Jones Mrs. Martin-Jones, the vice president in charge of industrial relations, is provided with a Nissan Maxima that the Company purchased for $39,000. During the current year, the car was driven 24,000 kilometers on employment related matters and 9,500 kilometers on personal matters. The operating costs average $0.40 per kilometer and, as the result of considerable travel outside of North America, the car was only available to Mrs. Martin-Jones for nine months of the year.

Required: Calculate the minimum taxable benefit that will accrue to each of these executives as the result of having the cars supplied by the Company. Ignore all GST and PST implications.

Assignment Problem Five - 5

Eileen Lee is an extremely successful computer salesperson living and working in Hearst, Ontario, who is unhappy with her current employer. She is discussing a compensation package with her future employer, HER Ltd., a Canadian controlled private corporation. As

Ms. Lee's current and anticipated investment income place her in the 45 percent income tax bracket, she is very interested in finding ways in which she can be compensated without incurring the same amount of taxation as would be assessed on an equivalent amount of salary.

Ms. Lee is contemplating a major cash outlay. She plans to completely renovate a commercial property that she owns. She had been planning to obtain a loan of $100,000 at a 9 percent rate in order to finance the renovations. She has suggested that it might be advantageous for the Company to provide her with an interest free loan of $100,000 as part of her compensation.

HER Ltd. is able to invest funds at a before tax rate of 20 percent. It is subject to taxation at a 28 percent rate. Assume that the relevant prescribed rate is 5 percent.

Required: Evaluate Ms. Lee's suggestion of providing her with an interest free loan in lieu of sufficient salary to carry a commercial loan at the rate of 9 percent.

Assignment Problem Five - 6

On February 24, 2005, during her first year as an employee of Hardin Weaving Ltd., Ms. Jones was granted options to purchase 5,000 shares of the Company's stock at a price of $20 per share.

When Ms. Jones paid the Company $100,000 in order to exercise the options and acquire the 5,000 shares, the shares had a fair market value of $28 per share. Ms. Jones makes any available elections to defer employment income.

On October 3, 2007, Ms. Jones sells all of her 5,000 Hardin Weaving Ltd. shares at a price of $32 per share.

Required: For each of the following Cases, calculate the tax consequences of the transactions that took place during 2005, 2006, and 2007 on the Net Income For Tax Purposes and Taxable Income of Ms. Jones.

A. Hardin Weaving Ltd. is a Canadian controlled private corporation. At the time the options were granted, the Company's shares had a fair market value of $18 per share. The options were exercised on December 1, 2006.

B. Hardin Weaving Ltd. is a Canadian public company. At the time the options were granted, the shares were trading at $18 per share. The options were exercised on December 1, 2006.

C. Hardin Weaving Ltd. is a Canadian public company. At the time the options were granted, the shares were trading at $22 per share. The options were exercised on December 1, 2006.

D. Hardin Weaving Ltd. is a Canadian controlled private corporation. At the time the options were granted, the Company's shares had a fair market value of $22 per share. The options were exercised on October 1, 2005.

Assignment Problem Five - 7

Ms. Forest is employed by Noface Cosmetics to demonstrate a line of beauty products for women. While Ms. Forest lives in Burnaby, British Columbia, her employment contract requires her to travel extensively in all of the western provinces. Ms. Forest is paid a generous salary but must pay for all of her own travel costs. As a consequence, she keeps very careful records of her expenses.

Required: Do you believe that Ms. Forest is entitled to deduct her travel expenses against her salary as an employee? Explain your position on this issue.

Assignment Problem Five - 8

Mr. Carlos Segovia is a very successful salesperson and is employed by a large Canadian public company. For 2007, his base salary is $252,000. In addition, he earns commissions of $18,500. Other information relevant to Mr. Segovia's 2007 employment income is as follows:

1. Mr. Segovia is required by his employer to pay all of his own employment related expenses. He is also required to provide his own office space. Mr. Segovia has a Form T2200 signed by his employer that certifies this.

2. His travel costs for 2007, largely airline tickets, food, and lodging, total $29,000. This includes $9,500 spent on business meals and entertainment.

3. His annual dues to the Salesperson's Association (a trade union) were $450.

4. He is a member of his employer's registered pension plan. During 2007, his employer contributed $5,500 to this plan on his behalf. In addition, $5,500 was withheld from his salary and contributed to the plan.

5. During 2007, Mr. Segovia was billed a total of $13,500 by his golf club. Of this amount, $3,300 was the annual membership fee, with the remainder being charges for meals and drinks with clients.

6. During 2007, Mr. Segovia used 35 percent of his personal residence as an office. The designated space is where he principally performs his employment duties. Interest payments on his mortgage totalled $11,500 for the year and property taxes were $4,800. Utilities paid for the house totalled $2,600 and house insurance paid for the year was $1,250. Other maintenance costs associated with the property amounted to $1,450. Mr. Segovia does not intend to deduct CCA on the home office portion of the house.

7. For business travel, Mr. Segovia drives a car that he purchased in 2006 for $49,000. He financed the purchase of the car through his local bank and, for 2007, the interest on the loan was $2,250. During 2007, he drives the car a total 60,000 kilometres, 45,000 of these being for employment related travel. His accountant has advised him that, if the car were used 100 percent for employment related activities, the CCA (tax depreciation) for 2007 would be $7,650. The costs of operating the car during the year totaled $7,500.

8. As rewards for winning various sales contests during the year he received three non-cash awards. The first, a spa weekend at a local hotel, had a fair market value of $300. The second was a $400 gift-certificate at a men's clothing store. The third award, a bottle of 1995 Haut Brion, had a fair market value of $450.

9. In 2006, his employer granted him options to buy 1,000 shares of the company's stock at $20 per share. At the time of the grant, the shares were trading at $19 per share. On June 1, 2007, all of these options are exercised. At this time the shares are trading at $31 per share. He does not sell the shares in 2007.

10. Assume that Mr. Segovia makes any elections that are available to reduce his income inclusions or increase his deductions.

Required: Calculate Mr. Segovia's minimum net employment income for the 2007 taxation year. Ignore GST and PST considerations.

Assignment Problem Five - 9

Mr. Jones is a salesman handling a line of computer software throughout Western Canada. During 2007, he is paid a salary of $25,800 and receives sales commissions of $47,700. He does not receive an allowance from his employer for any of his expenses. During the year, Mr. Jones made the following employment related expenditures:

Airline Tickets	$ 2,350
Office Supplies And Postage	415
Purchase Of Laptop Computer	2,075
Client Entertainment	1,750
Cost Of New Car	24,000
Operating Costs Of Car	7,200

The new car was purchased on January 5, 2007, and replaced a car which Mr. Jones had leased for several years. During 2007, Mr. Jones drove the car a total of 50,000 kilometers, of which 35,000 kilometers were for employment related purposes. The capital cost allowance for the car (100 percent) is $3,600.

In addition to expenditures to earn employment income, Mr. Jones has the following additional disbursements:

Alberta Blue Cross Medical Insurance Premiums	$435
Group Life Insurance Premiums	665

Mr. Jones indicates that he regularly receives discounts on his employer's merchandise and, during the current year, he estimates that the value of these discounts was $1,300.

One of the suppliers of his employer paid $2,450 to provide Mr. Jones with a one week vacation at a northern fishing lodge.

Required: Determine Mr. Jones' net employment income for the 2007 taxation year. Ignore all GST and PST implications.

Assignment Problem Five - 10

Ms. Marsh has been employed by the Ace Distributing Company for the past three years. During 2007, the following amounts were credited to Ms. Marsh's payroll account:

- Salary of $40,500 as per her employment contract.

- Reimbursement of business travel costs as per invoices supplied by Ms. Marsh totalling $4,250.

- Reimbursement of $1,100 in tuition fees for a work related course.

- A $1,560 dividend on Ace Distributing Company shares acquired through the employee purchase program.

- Fees of $1,200 for serving as the employee's representative on the Company's board of directors.

From the preceding credits to Ms. Marsh's payroll account, the following amounts were withheld by the Company:

Income taxes	$6,423
Premiums on group medical insurance	342
Contributions to registered pension plan	1,400

With respect to the registered pension plan, the Company also made a $1,400 contribution on behalf of Ms. Marsh. In addition to the preceding, Ms. Marsh made the following payments during the year:

Dental expenses	$1,250
Charitable contributions	275
Costs of moving to a larger apartment	2,800
Tuition fees for work related course (reimbursed)	1,100
Life insurance premiums	850
Cost of travel to and from place of employment	620
Cost of business travel (reimbursed)	4,250

The dental expenses were not covered by her medical insurance.

Required: Determine Ms. Marsh's net employment income for the 2007 taxation year. Provide reasons for omitting items that you have not included in your calculations. Ignore all GST implications.

Assignment Problem Five - 11

Ms. Sarah Kline is a copy editor for a major Canadian publisher. Her gross salary for the year ending December 31, 2007 is $73,500. For the 2007 taxation year, Ms. Kline's employer withheld the following amounts from her income:

Federal And Provincial Income Taxes	$26,000
Registered Pension Plan Contributions	2,400
Contributions To Group Disability Plan	200

Ms. Kline's employer made a $2,400 matching contribution to her registered pension plan and a $200 matching contribution for the group disability insurance.

Other Information:

1. During 2007, Ms. Kline is provided with an automobile that has been leased by her employer. The lease payments are $700 per month, an amount which includes a $50 monthly payment for insurance. The car is available to her for 11 months of the year and she drives it a total of 40,000 kilometers. Of this total, 37,000 kilometers were for travel required in pursuing the business of her employer, and the remainder was for personal use. The operating costs of the car totalled $5,200 for the year and were paid by her employer. She reimbursed her employer $.30 per kilometer for her personal use of the automobile.

2. During 2007, Ms. Kline was hospitalized for a period of three weeks. The disability plan provided her with benefits of $1,800 during this period. Ms. Kline began making contributions to this plan in 2006 at the rate of $200 per year.

3. Ms. Kline paid dues to her professional association in the amount of $1,650 for the year.

4. In 2005, Ms. Kline was given options to buy 200 shares of her employer's publicly traded stock at a price of $50 per share. At the time the options were issued, the shares were trading at $50 per share. On June 6, 2007, Ms. Kline exercises the options. At the time of exercise, the shares are trading at $70 per share. She is still holding the shares on December 31, 2007. As she expects to have a much higher Taxable Income in 2008, when she plans to sell the shares, she does not file the election to defer the employment income inclusion.

Required: Calculate Ms. Kline's minimum net employment income for the year ending December 31, 2007. Ignore all GST and PST considerations.

Assignment Problem Five - 12

This problem is continued in Assignment Problem Six-4.

For the past five years, Mr. Brooks has been employed as a financial analyst by a large Canadian public firm located in Winnipeg. During 2007, his basic gross salary amounts to $53,000. In addition, he was awarded an $11,000 bonus based on the performance of his division. Of the total bonus, $6,500 was paid in 2007 and the remainder is to be paid on January 15, 2008.

During 2007, Mr. Brooks' employer withheld the following amounts from his gross wages:

Federal Income Tax	$8,000
Employment Insurance Premiums	720
Canada Pension Plan Contributions	1,990
Registered Pension Plan Contributions	2,800
Donations To The United Way	480
Union Dues	240
Payments For Personal Use Of Company Car	1,000

Other Information:

1. Due to an airplane accident while flying back from Thunder Bay on business, Mr. Brooks was seriously injured and confined to a hospital for two full months during 2007. As his employer provides complete group disability insurance coverage, he received a total of $4,200 in payments during this period. All of the premiums for this insurance plan are paid by the employer.

2. Mr. Brooks is provided with a car that the company leases at a rate of $684 per month, including both GST and PST. The company also assumes all of the operating costs of the car and these amounted to $3,500 during 2007. Mr. Brooks drove the car a total of 35,000 kilometers during 2007, 30,000 kilometers of which were carefully documented as employment related travel. While he was in the hospital (see Item 1), the car and its keys were left with his employer.

3. On January 15, 2006, Mr. Brooks received options to buy 200 shares of his employer's common stock at a price of $23 per share. At this time, the shares were trading at $20 per share. Mr. Brooks exercised these options on July 6, 2007, when the shares were trading at $28 per share. He does not plan to sell the shares for at least a year. He was not aware that there is an election to defer the income inclusion on stock options, and did not file the required election.

4. In order to assist Mr. Brooks in acquiring a new personal residence in Winnipeg, his employer granted him a five year loan of $125,000 at an annual interest rate of 4 percent. The loan qualifies as a home relocation loan. The loan was granted on October 1, 2007 and, at this point in time, the interest rate on open five year mortgages was 9 percent. Assume the relevant ITR 4301 rate was 5 percent on this date. Mr. Brooks pays the interest on the loan on January 15, 2008.

5. Other disbursements made by Mr. Brooks include the following:

Advanced financial accounting course tuition fees	$1,200
Music history course tuition fees	
(University of Manitoba night course)	600
Fees paid to financial planner	300
Payment of premiums on life insurance	642

Mr. Brooks' employer reimbursed him for the tuition fees for the accounting course, but not the music course.

Required: Calculate Mr. Brooks' net employment income for the taxation year ending December 31, 2007. Provide reasons for omitting items that you have not included in your calculations.

CHAPTER 6

Taxable Income And Tax Payable For Individuals

Introduction

6-1.   As discussed in Chapter 3, Taxable Income is Net Income For Tax Purposes, less a group of deductions that are specified in Division C of Part I of the *Income Tax Act*. Also noted in the Chapter 3 material was the fact that Net Income For Tax Purposes is made up of several different income components. The more important of these components are employment income, business and property income, taxable capital gains, other sources, and other deductions.

6-2.   Most tax texts have deferred any coverage of Taxable Income until all of the income components that make up Net Income For Tax Purposes have been given detailed consideration. Despite the fact that the only component of Taxable Income that we have covered to this point is employment income, we have decided to introduce material on Taxable Income and Tax Payable for individuals at this point in the text.

6-3.   The major reason for this approach is that it allows us to introduce the tax credits that go into the calculation of Tax Payable at an earlier stage in the text. We believe that this will enhance the presentation of the material in subsequent Chapters on business income, property income, and taxable capital gains. For example, in our discussion of property income, we can deal with after tax rates of return, as well as provide a meaningful discussion of the economics of the dividend gross up/tax credit procedures.

6-4.   Other reasons for this organization of the material are more pedagogical in nature. One factor here is the fact that leaving the coverage of tax credits until after the completion of the material on all of the components of Taxable Income places this complex subject in the last week of most one semester tax courses. This appears to create significant difficulties for students. A further consideration is the fact that, by introducing Taxable Income and Tax Payable at this earlier stage in the text, instructors who wish to do so can make more extensive use of the tax software programs provided with the text.

6-5.   Since a significant portion of the material on Taxable Income can be best understood after covering the other types of income that make up Net Income For Tax Purposes, we require a second Chapter dealing with the subject of Taxable Income and Tax Payable. In addition, a few of the credits that are available in the calculation of Tax Payable require an understanding of additional aspects of business income, property income, and taxable capital gains. Given this, Chapter 14 is devoted to completing the necessary coverage of Taxable Income and Tax Payable for individuals. For corporations, these subjects are covered in Chapters 15 and 16.

Taxable Income Of Individuals

Available Deductions

6-6.   The deductions that are available in calculating the Taxable Income of an individual can be found in Division C of Part I of the *Income Tax Act*. As indicated in the introduction to this Chapter, some of these deductions will be dealt with in this Chapter. However, coverage of the more complex items is deferred until Chapter 14. The available deductions, along with a description of their coverage in this text, are as follows:

ITA 110(1)(d), (d.01), and (d.1) - Employee Stock Options   Our basic coverage of stock options and stock option deductions is included in Chapter 5. This coverage will not be repeated here. There are, however, some additional and more complex issues related to stock options. These include revoked elections, application of the identical property rules on dispositions, and stock options held at the time of emigration. These subjects are dealt with in Chapter 14.

ITA 110(1)(f) - Deductions For Payments   This deduction, which is available for social assistance and workers' compensation received, is covered beginning in Paragraph 6-8.

ITA 110(1)(j) - Home Relocation Loan   We refer to this deduction in Chapter 5 as it is related to a taxable benefit that is included in employment income. However, more detailed coverage is found beginning in Paragraph 6-11.

ITA 110.2 - Lump Sum Payments   This Section provides a deduction for certain lump-sum payments (e.g., an amount received as a court-ordered termination benefit and included in employment income). It provides the basis for taxing this amount as though it were received over several periods (i.e., income averaging). Because of its limited applicability, no additional coverage is given to this provision.

ITA 110.6 - Lifetime Capital Gains Deduction   The provisions related to this deduction are very complex and require a fairly complete understanding of capital gains. As a consequence, this deduction is covered in Chapter 14.

ITA 110.7 - Residing In Prescribed Zone (Northern Residents Deductions)   These deductions, which are limited to individuals living in prescribed regions of northern Canada, are covered in Paragraph 6-15.

ITA 111 - Losses Deductible   This is a group of deductions that is available for carrying over various types of losses from preceding or subsequent taxation years. The application of these provisions can be complex and requires a fairly complete understanding of business income, property income, and capital gains. Coverage of this material is deferred until Chapter 14.

Ordering Of Deductions

6-7.   ITA 111.1 specifies, to some degree, the order in which individuals must subtract the various deductions that may be available in the calculation of Taxable Income. With respect to the deductions covered in this Chapter, the deductions for payments and home relocation loans can be made in any order. However, both of these deductions must be made prior to deducting the northern residents deductions. We will provide more complete coverage of the ordering of deductions in Chapter 14, after we have presented material on the other deductions available in calculating the Taxable Income of an individual.

Deductions For Payments - ITA 110(1)(f)

6-8.   ITA 110(1)(f) provides for the deduction of certain amounts that have been included in the calculation of Net Income For Tax Purposes. The items listed here are amounts that are exempt from tax in Canada by virtue of a provision in a tax convention or agreement with another country, workers' compensation payments received as a result of injury or death, income from employment with a prescribed international organization, and social assistance payments made on the basis of a means, needs, or income test and included in the taxpayer's income.

6-9.   At first glance, this seems to be a fairly inefficient way of not taxing these items. For example, if the government does not intend to tax social assistance payments, why go to the trouble of including them in Net Income For Tax Purposes, then deducting an equivalent amount in the calculation of Taxable Income?

6-10.   There is, however, a reason for this. There are a number of items that influence an individual's tax obligation that are altered on the basis of the individual's Net Income For Tax Purposes. For example, we will find later in this Chapter that the amount of the age tax credit is reduced by the individual's Net Income For Tax Purposes in excess of a specified level. In order to ensure that income tests of this type are applied on an equitable basis, amounts are left in Net Income For Tax Purposes even in situations where the ultimate intent is not to assess tax on these amounts.

Home Relocation Loan - ITA 110(1)(j)

6-11.   As discussed in Chapter 5, if an employer provides an employee with a loan on which interest is payable at a rate that is less than the prescribed rate, a taxable benefit must be included in the employee's income. Under ITA 80.4(1), the benefit will be measured as the difference between the interest that would have been paid on the loan at the prescribed rate and the amount of interest that was actually paid. This taxable benefit must be included in income, even in situations where the loan qualifies as a "home relocation loan".

6-12.   A home relocation loan is defined in ITA 248(1) as a loan made by an employer to an employee in order to assist him in acquiring a dwelling. This acquisition must be related to employment at a new work location, and the new dwelling must be at least 40 kilometers closer to the new work location. As is discussed more completely in Chapter 11, the distance is the same 40 kilometer test that is used in determining whether or not an individual can deduct moving expenses.

6-13.   ITA 110(1)(j) provides a deduction in the calculation of the individual's Taxable Income for home relocation loans equal to the lesser of:

- The taxable benefit that would be assessed under ITA 80.4(1). As covered in Chapter 5, in general, this benefit is calculated by applying the prescribed rate that is applicable to each quarter that the loan is outstanding [ITA 80.4(1)(a)]. However, in the case of the first five years of a housing loan, this amount cannot exceed the amount that results from applying the prescribed rate that was in effect when the loan was granted, to the loan for the entire period that it was outstanding during the year [ITA 80.4(4)]. The amount of the benefit is reduced by any payments made by the employee during the year or within 30 days of the end of the year [ITA 80.4(1)(c)] for the home relocation loan.

- The amount of interest, calculated at the prescribed rate, that would be applicable to a $25,000 home relocation loan. As is the case with the loan benefit, the rate used is the lesser of the rate that was in effect when the loan was granted and the current prescribed rate. This amount is not reduced for payments made by the employee.

6-14.   This deduction is available for a period of up to five years. However, as the deduction is designed to offset a benefit that is included in employment income, the deduction will not be available after the loan has been paid off and there is no longer an employment income inclusion. While the calculation of the benefit and the deduction can be based on the number of days in each quarter, an example in IT-421R2 makes it clear that treating each calendar quarter as one-quarter of a year is an acceptable procedure.

Exercise Six-1

Subject: Home Relocation Loan

On January 1 of the current year, in order to facilitate an employee's relocation, Lee Ltd. provides her with a five year, $82,000 loan. The employee pays 2 percent annual interest on the loan on December 31 of each year. Assume that at the time the loan is granted the prescribed rate is 4 percent. However, the rate is increased to 5 percent for the third and fourth quarters of the current year. What is the effect of this loan on the employee's Taxable Income for the current year?

End of Exercise.   Solution available in Study Guide.

Northern Residents Deductions - ITA 110.7

6-15.   Residents of Labrador, the Territories, as well as parts of some of the provinces, are eligible for deductions under ITA 110.7. To qualify for these deductions, the taxpayer must be resident in these prescribed regions for a continuous period of six months beginning or ending in the taxation year. The amount of the deductions involve fairly complex calculations that go beyond the scope of this text. The purpose of these deductions is to compensate individuals for the high costs that are associated with living in such prescribed northern zones.

Calculation Of Tax Payable

Federal Tax Payable Before Credits

6-16.   The calculation of federal Tax Payable for individuals requires the application of a group of progressive rates to marginal amounts of Taxable Income. The rates are progressive, starting at a low rate of 15.5 percent and increasing to rates of 22 percent, 26 percent, and 29 percent as the individual's Taxable Income increases. In order to maintain fairness, the brackets (i.e., income segments) to which these rates apply are indexed to reflect changes in the Consumer Price Index. Without such indexation, taxpayers could find themselves subject to higher rates without having an increased level of real, inflation adjusted income.

6-17.   For 2007, the brackets to which these four rates apply are as follows:

Taxable Income In Excess Of	Federal Tax	Marginal Rate On Excess
$ -0-	$ -0-	15.5%
37,178	5,763	22.0%
74,357	13,942	26.0%
120,887	26,040	29.0%

6-18.   Note that the average rate for someone just entering the highest 29 percent bracket is 21.5 percent ($26,040 ÷ $120,887). This illustrates the importance of keeping an annual income level below this bracket. To this point, the average rate is 21.5 percent. For all income that exceeds this level, the federal rate goes to 29 percent.

6-19.   There is a common misconception that once Taxable Income reaches the next tax bracket, all income is taxed at a higher rate. This is not the case as the tax rate is a marginal rate. For example, if Taxable Income is $120,888, only $1 is taxed at 29 percent.

6-20.   The preceding table suggests that individuals are taxed on their first dollar of income. While the 15.5 percent rate is, in fact, applied to all of the first $37,178 of Taxable Income, a portion of this amount is not really subject to taxes. As will be discussed later in this Chapter, every individual resident in Canada is entitled to a personal tax credit. For 2007, this tax credit is $1,384 [(15.5%)($8,929)]. In effect, this means that no taxes will be paid on at least the first $8,929 of an individual's Taxable Income. The amount that could be earned tax free would be even higher for individuals with additional tax credits (e.g., the age credit).

6-21.   As an example of the calculation of federal Tax Payable before credits, consider an individual with Taxable Income of $82,300. The calculation would be as follows:

Tax On First $74,357	$13,942
Tax On Next $7,943 ($82,300 - $74,357) At 26%	2,065
Federal Tax Payable Before Credits	$16,007

6-22.   Until 2001, there was a federal surtax. A surtax is an additional tax calculated on the basis of the regular Tax Payable calculation. In our opinion, this type of additional taxation is used as a politically expedient way of raising taxes, without raising stated tax rates. Fortunately, this practice has ended at the federal level for individuals. However, surtaxes are still used in several provinces, most notably in Ontario. For 2007, Ontario has a surtax of 56 percent on amounts of Ontario Tax Payable in excess of $5,172. This significantly increases the highest rate in Ontario from the stated 11.16 percent to 17.41 percent.

Provincial Tax Payable Before Credits

6-23.   As is the case at the federal level, provincial Tax Payable is calculated by multiplying Taxable Income by either a single tax rate or a group of progressive rates. In general, the provinces other than Quebec use the same Taxable Income figure that is used at the federal level.

6-24.   With respect to rates, Alberta uses a single flat rate of 10 percent applied to all levels of income. All of the other provinces use either 3, 4, or 5 different rates which are applied in tax brackets that are similar to those established at the federal level. In addition, four of the provinces apply surtaxes when the provincial Tax Payable figure reaches a certain level (Ontario, Nova Scotia, P.E.I., and Newfoundland).

6-25.   To give you some idea of the range of provincial rates, the 2007 minimum and maximum rates, along with applicable surtaxes, are as found in the following table:

Province	Minimum Tax Rate	Maximum Tax Rate	Applicable Surtax
Alberta	10.00%	10.00%	N/A
British Columbia	6.05%	14.70%	N/A
Manitoba	10.90%	17.40%	N/A
New Brunswick	9.68%	17.84%	N/A
Newfoundland	10.57%	18.02%	9%
Nova Scotia	8.79%	17.50%	10%
Ontario	6.05%	11.16%	20% and 56%
Prince Edward Island	9.80%	16.70%	10%
Quebec*	16.00%	24.00%	N/A
Saskatchewan	11.00%	15.00%	N/A

*Quebec's system is sufficiently different that the rates given here are not directly comparable to the rates provided for the other provinces.

6-26.   You should note the significant differences in rates between the provinces. The maximum rate in Newfoundland is nearly double the corresponding rate in Alberta. This amounts to extra taxes of nearly $10,000 per year on each additional $100,000 of income. This can make provincial tax differences a major consideration when an individual decides where he should establish provincial residency.

6-27.   When these provincial rates are combined with the federal rate schedule, the minimum combined rate varies from a low of 21.55 percent in British Columbia and Ontario (15.5 percent federal, plus 6.05 percent provincial), to a high of 26.5 percent in Saskatchewan (15.5 percent federal, plus 11 percent provincial).

6-28.   Maximum combined rates are lowest in Alberta where the rate is 39 percent (29 percent federal, plus 10 percent provincial). They are highest in Newfoundland where the combined rate is 48.64 percent (29 percent federal, plus 19.64 percent provincial, including the surtax).

Exercise Six-2

Subject: Calculation Of Tax Payable Before Credits

During 2007, Joan Matel is a resident of Ontario and has calculated her Taxable Income to be $46,700. Ontario's rates are 6.05 percent on Taxable Income up to $35,488, 9.15 percent on the next $35,488, and 11.16 percent on the excess. Calculate her 2007 federal and provincial Tax Payable before consideration of credits.

End of Exercise. Solution available in Study Guide.

6-29.   Given the significant differences in provincial tax rates on individuals, it is somewhat surprising that the rules related to where an individual will pay provincial taxes are fairly simple. With respect to an individual's income other than business income, it is deemed to have been earned in the province in which he resides on the last day of the taxation year. This means that, if an individual moves to Ontario from Nova Scotia on December 30 of the current year, any income for the year, other than business income, will be deemed to have been earned in Ontario.

Types Of Income

6-30.   In terms of the effective tax rates, the income accruing to Canadian individuals can be divided into three categories:

Ordinary Income   This would include employment income, business income, property income other than dividends, and other sources of income. In general, the effective tax rates on this category are those presented in the preceding tables. For example, the marginal rate for an individual living in Alberta and earning more than $120,887, would be 39 percent (29 percent federal, plus 10 percent provincial).

Capital Gains   As will be discussed in detail in Chapter 10, capital gains arise on the disposition of capital assets. Only one-half of such gains are included in Net Income For Tax Purposes and Taxable Income. This means that the effective tax rate on this category of income is only one-half of the rates presented in the preceding tables. Returning to our Alberta resident who is earning more than $120,887, his effective rate on capital gains would be 19.5 percent [(1/2)(29% + 10%)].

Dividends   As will be explained in Chapter 9, dividends from taxable Canadian companies are subject to a gross up and tax credit procedure which reduces the effective tax rate on this type of income. Prior to the May, 2006 budget, for individuals in the maximum tax bracket, the rate reduction was about one-third. For example, in Ontario, the combined federal/provincial rate on dividends was about 31 percent. This compared to around 46 percent on ordinary income. However, this was not nearly as favourable as the 23 percent [(1/2)(46%)] rate applicable to capital gains.

The May, 2006 budget introduced the concept of eligible dividends. These dividends, which include most dividends paid by Canadian public companies, are provided with an enhanced dividend gross up and tax credit procedure which reduces the effective rate on these eligible dividends to a level that is comparable to that applicable to capital gains. For example, in Ontario, the 2006 rate on eligible dividends was about 25 percent.

6-31.   A more complete discussion of the different effective tax rates mentioned here is provided in Chapter 9 (dividends) and Chapter 10 (capital gains).

Taxes On Income Not Earned In A Province

6-32.   As we have noted, it is possible for an individual to be considered a resident of Canada for tax purposes, without being a resident of a particular province or territory. This would be the case, for example, for members of the Canadian Armed Forces who are stationed outside of Canada. It is also possible for non-residents to earn income in Canada that is not taxed in a particular province.

6-33.   Income that is not subject to provincial or territorial tax is subject to additional taxation at the federal level. In addition to the regular federal Tax Payable, there is also a federal surtax equal to 48 percent of basic federal Tax Payable under ITA 120(1). This is paid instead of a provincial or territorial tax.

Calculating Tax Credits

Federal Amounts

6-34.   The most direct way of applying a tax credit system is to simply specify the amount of each tax credit available. In 2007, for example, the basic personal tax credit could have been specified to be $1,384. However, the Canadian tax system is based on a less direct approach. Rather than specifying the amount of each credit, a base amount is provided, to which the minimum federal tax rate (15.5 percent for 2007) is applied. This means that, for 2007, the basic personal tax credit is calculated by taking 15.5 percent of $8,929 (we will refer to this number as the tax credit base), resulting in a credit against Tax Payable in the amount of $1,384.

6-35.   Note that the legislation is such that, when the minimum federal tax rate of 15.5 percent is changed, the new rate will be used in determining individual tax credits. In our tax credit examples and problems, we will generally use the tax credit base in our calculations and apply the 15.5 percent rate to the subtotals and totals. This approach makes the relationships between the various credits easier to see and reduces calculation errors.

6-36.   As was the case with the tax rate brackets, in order to avoid having these credits decline in value in terms of real dollars, the base for the tax credits needs to be adjusted for changing prices. While most of the credit bases are adjusted using the same CPI rate that is applied to the tax brackets, there are exceptions. An example of this is the pension income credit. The base for this credit, after being at $1,000 for many years, was increased to $2,000 by the May, 2006 budget, a change that has nothing to do with the rate of inflation.

6-37.   A technical problem in calculating credits will arise in the year a person becomes a Canadian resident, or ceases to be a Canadian resident. As discussed in Chapter 3, such individuals will only be subject to Canadian taxation for a part of the year. Given this, it would not be appropriate for them to receive the same credits as an individual who is subject to Canadian taxation for the full year. This view is reflected in ITA 118.91, which requires a pro rata calculation for personal tax credits, the disability tax credit and tax credits transferred from a spouse or a person supported by the taxpayer. Other tax credits, for example the tax credits for charitable donations and adoption expenses, are not reduced because of part year residence.

Provincial Amounts

6-38.   In determining provincial tax credits, the provinces use the same approach as that used at the federal level. That is, the minimum provincial rate is applied to a base that is indexed each year. In most cases, the base used is different from the base used at the federal level. For example, the 2007 base for the federal basic personal tax credit is $8,929. Provincially, the base varies from a low of $7,410 in Newfoundland, to a high of $15,435 in Alberta. Applying the provincial minimum rates to these bases gives a provincial basic personal tax credit in Newfoundland of $783 [(10.57%)($7,410)] and a provincial basic personal tax credit in Alberta of $1,544 [(10%)($15,435)].

Personal Tax Credits - ITA 118(1)

Individuals With A Spouse Or Common-Law Partner - ITA 118(1)(a)

Married Persons

6-39.   For individuals with a spouse or common-law partner filing tax returns in 2007, ITA 118(1)(a) provides for two tax credits — one for the individual (sometimes referred to as the basic personal credit) and one for his or her spouse or common-law partner (sometimes referred to as the spousal credit).

6-40.   Prior to 2007, these two credits had a different base for their calculation. This, however, was changed by the 2007 federal budget. Both credits now have the same base. For 2007, the basic personal tax credit is calculated as follows:

$$[(15.5\%(\$8,929)] = \$1,384$$

Spousal Amount

6-41.   While the spousal credit uses the same base, this base must be reduced by the spouse or common-law partner's Net Income For Tax Purposes. The calculation is as follows:

$$[(15.5\%)(\$8,929 - \text{Spouse Or Common-Law Partner's Net Income})]$$

6-42.   As an example, if an individual had a spouse with Net Income For Tax Purposes of $5,200, the total personal credits under ITA 118(1)(a) would be equal to:

$$[15.5\%][\$8,929 + (\$8,929 - \$5,200)] = \underline{\$1,962}$$

6-43.   There are several other points to be made with respect to the credits for an individual with a spouse or common-law partner:

Spouse Or Common-Law Partner's Income   The income figure that is used for limiting the spousal amount is Net Income For Tax Purposes, with no adjustments of any sort. We would also note that, prior to 2007, only Net Income in excess of a threshold amount was used in this calculation. In conjunction with the change in the base for the spousal credit, the 2007 budget eliminated this threshold.

Applicability To Either Spouse Or Common-Law Partner   The ITA 118(1)(a) provision is applicable to both spouses and, while each is eligible to claim the basic amount of $8,929, IT-513R specifies that only one spouse or common-law partner may claim the additional spousal amount. IT-513R indicates that the spouse making the claim should be the one that supports the other, a fairly vague concept.

Eligibility   The additional credit can be claimed for either a spouse or a common-law partner. There is no definition of spouse in the *Income Tax Act*, so it would appear that the usual dictionary definition would apply. That is, a spouse is one of a pair of persons who are legally married. With respect to common-law partner, ITA 248(1) defines such an individual as a person who cohabits with the taxpayer in a conjugal relationship for a continuous period of at least one year, or is the parent of a child of whom the taxpayer is also a parent. There is no requirement in the income tax legislation that either a spouse or a common-law partner be a person of the opposite sex.

Multiple Relationships   Based on these definitions, it would be possible for an individual to have both a spouse and a common-law partner. ITA 118(4)(a) makes it clear that, if this is the case, a credit can only be claimed for one of these individuals.

Year Of Separation Or Divorce   In general, ITA 118(5) does not allow a tax credit based on the spousal amount in situations where the individual is making a deduction for the support of a spouse or common-law partner (spousal support is covered in

Chapter 11). However, IT-513R indicates that, in the year of separation or divorce, an individual can either deduct amounts paid for spousal support, or claim the additional tax credit for a spouse.

Exercise Six-3

Subject: Spousal Tax Credit

Mr. Johan Sprinkle is married and has 2007 Net Income For Tax Purposes of $35,450. His spouse has 2007 Net Income For Tax Purposes of $2,600. Determine Mr. Sprinkle's personal tax credits for 2007.

End of Exercise. Solution available in Study Guide.

Individuals Supporting An Eligible Dependant - ITA 118(1)(b)
Eligibility And Amount
6-44.   For individuals who are not married, but are supporting an eligible dependant, ITA 118(1)(b) provides the same two credits as those provided under ITA 118(1)(a) for individuals with a spouse or common-law partner. Such individuals will be eligible for the $1,384 credit that ITA 118(1)(a) provides for married individuals.

6-45.   In addition, if the individual is supporting a dependant in a self-contained domestic establishment, he will be eligible for the same $1,384 credit that ITA 118(1)(a) provided for a spouse. As was the case with the spousal credit, the base for the credit is reduced by Net Income For Tax Purposes. In this case, it is the Net Income For Tax Purpose of the eligible dependant.

Dependant Defined
6-46.   For purposes of this credit, as well as the credit for an infirm dependant over 17 [ITA 118(1)(d)], the *Income Tax Act* defines dependant as follows:

> **ITA 118(6)**   Definition of "dependant" — ..."dependant" of an individual for a taxation year means a person who at any time in the year is dependent on the individual for support and is
>
> (a) the child or grandchild of the individual or of the individual's spouse or common-law partner; or
> (b) the parent, grandparent, brother, sister, uncle, aunt, niece or nephew, if resident in Canada at any time in the year, of the individual or of the individual's spouse or common-law partner.

6-47.   In view of today's less stable family arrangements, the question of exactly who is considered a child for tax purposes requires some elaboration. As explained in IT-513R, the credit may be taken for natural children, children who have been formally adopted, as well as for natural and adopted children of a spouse or common-law partner.

Application
6-48.   This credit is most commonly claimed by single parents who are supporting a minor child. More generally, this credit is available to individuals who are single, widowed, divorced, or separated, and supporting a dependant who is:

- related to the individual by blood, marriage, adoption or common-law relationship;
- under 18 at any time during the year, or the individual's parent or grandparent, or mentally or physically infirm;
- living with the individual in a home that the individual maintains (this would not disqualify a child who moves away during the school year to attend an educational institution as long as the home remains the child's home); and
- residing in Canada.

6-49.   The residence requirement is not applicable to the individual's children. However, the child must still be living with the individual. This would be applicable, for example, to an individual who is a deemed resident (e.g., a member of the Canadian Armed Forces) and living with their child outside of Canada.

6-50.   In terms of limitations on this credit, the eligible dependant credit cannot be claimed by an individual:

- for more than one person;
- if the dependant's Net Income exceeds $8,929;
- if the individual is claiming the spousal credit;
- if the individual is living with, supporting, or being supported by a spouse (the claim is only available for individuals who are either single, or living separately from their spouse);
- if someone other than the individual is making this claim for the same individual; or
- for the individual's child, if the individual is making child support payments to another individual, for that child. As is noted in Chapter 11, when child support is being paid, only the recipient of such payments can claim this tax credit. This is the case without regard to whether or not the individual making the child support payments is able to deduct the payments in determining Net Income For Tax Purposes.

Child Tax Credit - ITA 118(1)(b.1)

6-51.   The March 2007 budget introduced a new child tax credit. It is available for each child who is under 18 years of age at the end of the taxation year. The credit has a value of $310 per child [(15.5%)($2,000)]. Somewhat surprisingly, it is not reduced by the child's income or family income. Also surprising is the fact that this credit can be claimed for a particular child, even when the ITA 118(1)(b) eligible dependant credit is being claimed for that same child. Other relevant points are as follows:

- Provided the child resides with both parents throughout the year, it can be claimed by either parent. The phrase "throughout the year" applies to the fraction of the year subsequent to the birth or adoption of the child and the fraction of the year prior to the death of a child.

- If the parents are living separately, this credit can only be claimed by the parent who claims the ITA 118(1)(b) eligible dependant credit for the child. However, unlike the ITA 118(1)(b) credit, the ITA 118(1)(b.1) can be claimed for more than one child.

Single Persons - ITA 118(1)(c)

6-52.   Individuals living with a spouse or common-law partner receive a credit for themselves under ITA 118(1)(a), and individuals living with an eligible dependant receive a corresponding credit under ITA 118(1)(b). For individuals who do not have a spouse, a common-law partner, or an eligible dependant, this same credit is received under ITA 118(1)(c). As noted previously, for 2007, this credit is equal to $1,384 [(15.5%)($8,929)].

Caregiver Tax Credit - ITA 118(1)(c.1)

6-53.   ITA 118(1)(c.1) allows for a caregiver tax credit to an individual who provides in home care for a related adult (18 years or older). To be eligible for this credit, the individual has to maintain a dwelling in which the individual and the relative ordinarily reside, and the relative has to be the child, grandchild, parent, grandparent, brother, sister, aunt, uncle, nephew, or niece of the individual, the individual's spouse, or the individual's common-law partner.

6-54.   Except where the relative is the individual's child or grandchild, the relative must be resident in Canada. Also, except where the relative is the individual's parent or grandparent who is 65 years old or over, the relative must be dependent on the individual because of the relative's mental or physical infirmity. A credit may be claimed for each individual who qualifies.

6-55.   For 2007, the credit has a value of $623 [(15.5%)($4,019)]. The base for the credit is reduced by the amount of the dependant's Net Income in excess of $13,726. This means that this tax credit is not available once the dependant's Net Income is more than $17,745 ($13,726 + $4,019).

Exercise Six-4

Subject: Caregiver Tax Credit

Joan Barton lives with her husband. Two years ago her father, who is 69 years old and very active, moved in with her. His Net Income For Tax Purposes for 2007 is $15,600. Determine the amount of Joan's caregiver tax credit, if any, for 2007.

End of Exercise. Solution available in Study Guide.

Infirm Dependant Over 17 Tax Credit - ITA 118(1)(d)

6-56.   ITA 118(1)(d) specifies a credit for dependants who are age 18 or older prior to the end of the year, provided they are dependent by reason of mental or physical infirmity. For 2007, the credit has a value of $623 [(15.5%)($4,019)]. The base for the credit is reduced by the amount of the dependant's Net Income in excess of $5,702. This means that this tax credit is not available once the dependant's Net Income is more than $9,721 ($5,720 + $4,019).

6-57.   The ITA 118(1)(d) infirm dependant over 17 credit should not be confused with the mental and physical impairment credit (a.k.a., disability tax credit) that is available to individuals under ITA 118.3 (see Paragraph 6-110). The credit under ITA 118(1)(d) is for an individual with sufficient infirmity that they cannot be self-supporting and, as a result, that individual is dependent on the supporting person who is eligible to claim the credit.

6-58.   For example, a supporting mother would be eligible for this credit if her adult son suffered from a physical handicap severe enough to prevent him from working at a full time job. A doctor's certification of this type of mental or physical infirmity is not required.

6-59.   In contrast, the disability tax credit under ITA 118.3 requires a doctor to certify that there is a prolonged impairment that severely restricts basic living activities. Note, however, because this latter credit can be transferred to a supporting person, one individual may be able to claim both of these credits for the same dependant.

Exercise Six-5

Subject: Infirm Dependant Over 17 Tax Credit

Harold Reed is married and has a 25 year old daughter who lives in a group home. The daughter is dependent on Harold because of a physical infirmity. Her Net Income For Tax Purposes for 2007 is $7,600. Determine the amount of Harold's infirm dependant over 17 tax credit for 2007.

End of Exercise. Solution available in Study Guide.

Interaction: Eligible Dependant Vs. Caregiver Or Infirm Dependant Over 17

6-60.   In reading through the material related to these three tax credits, it may have occurred to you that a taxpayer could have a dependant who was eligible for both the ITA 118(1)(b) eligible dependant credit and either the caregiver credit or infirm dependant over 17 credit. This did not happen in either Exercise Six-4 or Six-5 because both Joan Barton and Harold Reed were living with their spouses, making them ineligible to take the eligible dependant credit.

6-61.   In contrast, assume a single individual has a disabled child over 17 years of age. In the absence of some restriction, this individual could claim both the eligible dependant credit and the infirm dependant over 17 credit. ITA 118(4)(c) provides such a restriction. This paragraph indicates that, if an individual is eligible for the ITA 118(1)(b) eligible dependant credit, they cannot claim either the caregiver credit or the infirm dependant over 17 credit. Note that ITA 118(4)(c) refers to "entitled to", without regard to whether the credit is actually taken.

6-62.   Because the eligible dependant credit has no income threshold and is not available if the dependant's Net Income For Tax Purposes is greater than $8,929, the ITA 118(4)(c) restriction could result in a lower, or no tax credit. To avoid this, ITA 118(1)(e) allows an additional credit to be taken based on the difference between the amount of the caregiver or infirm dependant over 17 credits, and the amount available under the eligible dependant credit.

Exercise Six-6

Subject: Eligible Dependant Vs. Caregiver Tax Credits

Barry Litvak is a single individual with a 67 year old mother. While his mother is not mentally or physically infirm, she lives with Barry. She has Net Income For Tax Purposes for 2007 of $7,500. Calculate the tax credits that will be available to Barry as a result of his mother living with him.

End of Exercise. Solution available in Study Guide.

Interaction: Caregiver Vs. Infirm Dependant Over 17

6-63.   It is likely that you have also noted that a single individual may qualify for both the caregiver and infirm dependant over 17 tax credits. In terms of qualifying individuals, there are two differences:

- In general, both credits require the qualifying individual to be mentally or physically infirm. However, the caregiver credit makes an exception for parents and grandparents who are over 65. These individuals qualify for the caregiver credit, but not the infirm dependant over 17 credit.

- The caregiver credit requires that the qualifying individual live with the taxpayer. The infirm dependant over 17 credit does not have this requirement.

6-64.   Despite these differences, it is clear that in many cases, an individual who qualifies for the caregiver credit would also qualify for the infirm dependant over 17 credit. In this situation, ITA 118(4)(d) indicates that, if a taxpayer is entitled to the caregiver credit for a particular individual, that individual is deemed not to be a dependant for purposes of the infirm dependant over 17 credit.

6-65.   As both credits have a 2007 maximum value of $623, the choice between the two credits does not affect the ultimate Tax Payable. There is, however, a difference in the income thresholds, with the caregiver amount being significantly higher, $13,726 vs. $5,702. Because of this, the caregiver credit will be more desirable. This means that, in effect, ITA 118(4)(d) forces the taxpayer to make the correct decision on this issue.

Exercise Six-7

Subject: Caregiver Vs. Infirm Dependant Over 17 Tax Credits

Suki Leonard is married and has a 28 year old son. He lives with her and is dependant because of a physical infirmity. For 2007, he has investment income of $8,250. Suki would like to know whether she should take the caregiver tax credit for her son or, alternatively, the infirm dependant over 17 tax credit.

End of Exercise. Solution available in Study Guide.

Exercise Six-8

Subject: Multiple Credits For Dependants

Ms. Jane Forest is 48 years old and divorced from her husband. Her Net Income For Tax Purposes for 2007 is $43,000. She has retained the family home and both of the children of the marriage live with her. Her son is 20 years old and suffers from Down Syndrome. He does not qualify for the disability tax credit. Her daughter is 16 years old and in good health. Her son has no income during 2007, while her daughter has Net Income For Tax Purposes of $1,800. Determine Ms. Forest's maximum tax credits for 2007.

End of Exercise. Solution available in Study Guide.

Other Tax Credits For Individuals

Age Tax Credit - ITA 118(2)

6-66.   For individuals who attain the age of 65 prior to the end of the year, ITA 118(2) provides an additional tax credit of $802 [(15.5%)($5,177)]. However, the base for this credit is reduced by 15 percent of the individual's Net Income For Tax Purposes in excess of $30,936. This means that, at an income level of $65,449 [($5,177 ÷ 15%) + $30,936], the reduction will be equal to $5,177 and the individual will not receive an age credit.   As an example, a 67 year old individual with 2007 Net Income of $35,000 will have an age credit of $708 {[15.5%][$5,177 - (15%)($35,000 - $30,936)]}.

6-67.   As we shall see when we consider the transfer of credits to a spouse, if an individual does not have sufficient Tax Payable to use this credit, it can be transferred to a spouse.

Exercise Six-9

Subject: Age Tax Credit

Joshua Smythe is 72 years old and has 2007 Net Income For Tax Purposes of $51,500. Determine Mr. Smythe's age credit for 2007.

End Of Exercise. Solution available in Study Guide.

Pension Income Tax Credit - ITA 118(3)

6-68.   For many years, ITA 118(3) provided a credit based on the first $1,000 of eligible pension income. As we noted earlier, this $1,000 base has not been indexed, resulting in a situation where the real value of this credit has declined each year. In something of a surprise move, the May, 2006 budget increased the base for this credit from $1,000 of eligible pension income to $2,000 of eligible pension income resulting in a maximum pension income credit of $310 [(15.5%)($2,000)].

6-69.   Not all types of pension income are eligible for this credit. ITA 118(8) specifically excludes payments under the Old Age Security Act, the Canada Pension Plan, certain provincial pension plans, a salary deferral arrangement, a retirement compensation arrangement, an employee benefit plan, and death benefits.

6-70.   For individuals who have reached age 65 before the end of the year, this credit is available on "pension income" as defined in ITA 118(7). This includes pension payments that are:

- a life annuity out of, or under, a pension plan;
- an annuity payment out of a Registered Retirement Savings Plan (RRSP);

- a payment out of a Registered Retirement Income Fund (RRIF);
- an annuity payment from a Deferred Profit Sharing Plan (DPSP); and
- the interest component of other annuities.

6-71.   Like the age credit, if an individual does not have sufficient Tax Payable to use this credit, it can be transferred to a spouse.

6-72.   For an individual who has not reached age 65 before the end of the year, the credit is based on "qualified pension income", also defined in ITA 118(7). This includes the life annuities out of, or under, a pension plan and, in situations where such amounts are received as a consequence of the death of a spouse or common-law partner, the other types of pension income described in Paragraph 6-70. However, this means that, in ordinary circumstances, individuals who have not reached age 65 will only be eligible for the pension income tax credit to the extent that their pension income is made up of life annuity payments.

Canada Employment Tax Credit - ITA 118(10)

6-73.   This credit, which was introduced in the May, 2006 budget, is available to all individuals who have Canadian employment income. From a conceptual point of view, it is designed to provide limited recognition of the fact that there are costs associated with earning employment income. As only limited deductions are available against employment income, this would appear to be an appropriate form of relief.

6-74.   For 2007, the amount of the credit is equal to 15.5 percent of the lesser of:

- $1,000; and

- the individual's Net Employment Income, calculated without any employment income deductions.

6-75.   For most employed individuals, this will produce a credit of $155 [(15.5%)($1,000)].

Adoption Expenses Credit - ITA 118.01

6-76.   The adoption expenses tax credit is available to a taxpayer who adopts an eligible child, defined in ITA 118.01(1) as follows:

"eligible child" of an individual, means a child who has not attained the age of 18 years at the time that an adoption order is issued or recognized by a government in Canada in respect of the adoption of that child by that individual.

6-77.   The 2007 credit is based on up to $10,445 in eligible adoption expenses, resulting in a maximum of $1,619 [(15.5%)($10,445)]. The expenses can only be claimed in the year in which the adoption is finalized. In addition, the amount of these expenses is reduced by any reimbursement that is received by the taxpayer.

6-78.   Eligible adoption expenses are defined as follows:

"eligible adoption expense", in respect of an eligible child of an individual, means an amount paid for expenses incurred during the adoption period in respect of the adoption of that child, including

(a) fees paid to an adoption agency licensed by a provincial government;
(b) court costs and legal and administrative expenses related to an adoption order in respect of that child;
(c) reasonable and necessary travel and living expenses of the child and the adoptive parents;
(d) document translation fees;
(e) mandatory fees paid to a foreign institution; and
(f) any other reasonable expenses related to the adoption required by a provincial government or an adoption agency licensed by a provincial government.

6-79.   The preceding definition makes reference to the adoption period. This period is defined in ITA 118.01(1) as follows:

"adoption period", in respect of an eligible child of an individual, means the period that

(a) begins at the earlier of the time that the eligible child's adoption file is opened with a provincial ministry responsible for adoption (or with an adoption agency licensed by a provincial government) and the time, if any, that an application related to the adoption is made to a Canadian court; and

(b) ends at the later of the time an adoption order is issued by, or recognized by, a government in Canada in respect of that child, and the time that the child first begins to reside permanently with the individual.

6-80.   In the usual situation, a child will be adopted by a couple, either legally married or co-habiting on a common-law basis. The legislation points out that, while both parties are eligible for this credit, the eligible expenses and the $10,445 limit must be shared. The claim can be made by either party or shared. If the individuals cannot agree as to what portion of the amount each can deduct, the Minister may fix the portions.

Exercise Six-10

Subject: Adoption Expenses Tax Credit

Ary Kapit and his spouse have adopted an infant Chinese orphan. The adoption process began in June, 2006 when they traveled to China to discuss the adoption and view available children. The cost of this trip was $4,250. Their provincial government opens the adoption file on February 13, 2007, and the adoption order is issued on August 27, 2007. In September, the couple returns to China to pick up their new daughter. The happy family returns to Canada on September 18, 2007. The cost of this trip is $6,420.

Additional expenses paid during the first week of September, 2007 were $1,600 paid to the Chinese orphanage and $3,200 paid to a Canadian adoption agency. Legal fees incurred during the adoption period were $2,700. After arrival in Canada, an additional $2,500 in medical expenses were incurred for the child prior to the end of 2007. Mr. Kapit's employer has a policy of providing reimbursement for up to $5,000 in adoption expenses eligible for the adoption expenses tax credit. This amount is received in September, 2007. What is the maximum adoption expenses tax credit that can be claimed by Mr. Kapit or his spouse?

End of Exercise. Solution available in Study Guide.

Public Transit Pass Credit - ITA 118.02

6-81.   This credit was also introduced in the May, 2006 budget. It provides for a credit equal to 15.5 percent of the cost of eligible public transit passes paid for by an individual, his spouse or common-law partner, and his children who have not attained the age of 19 during the year.

6-82.   In the original legislation, eligible public transit passes had to provide for unlimited travel for a period of at least 28 days. In effect, this meant that the credit was only available when an individual acquired monthly passes. The March, 2007 budget will expand the definition of eligible passes in two ways:

The definition will now include electronic payment cards that provide at least 32 one-way trips during an uninterrupted period of not more than 31 days.

• It will also include the cost of weekly passes where an individual purchases at least four consecutive weekly passes.

6-83.   The following definition is provided for "public commuter transit services":

ITA 118.02(1)   Public commuter transit services means services offered to the general public, ordinarily for a period of at least five days per week, of transporting individuals, from a place in Canada to another place in Canada, by means of bus, ferry, subway, train or tram, and in respect of which it can reasonably be expected that those individuals would return daily to the place of their departure.

6-84.   The cost that is eligible for the credit must be reduced by any amounts that are reimbursed (e.g., an employer pays one-half of the cost of the pass). If the pass can be used by more than one individual, for purposes of this tax credit, the cost must be apportioned between them.

Child Fitness Tax Credit - ITA 118.03

6-85.   Another credit introduced in the May, 2006 budget was for expenses related to the costs of providing fitness programs for an individual's children. For 2007, it is equal to 15.5 percent of up to $500 of such costs or a maximum of $78 [(15.5%)($500)]. The eligible costs must be reduced by any amounts that have been reimbursed.

6-86.   A qualifying child is defined as a child of the individual who had not, prior to the beginning of the taxation year, attained the age of 16 years. The Section defines an eligible fitness expense as follows:

ITA 118.03(1)   "eligible fitness expense" in respect of a qualifying child of an individual for a taxation year means the amount of a fee paid to a qualifying entity (other than an amount paid to a qualifying entity that is, at the time the amount is paid, the individual's spouse or common-law partner or another individual who is under 18 years of age) to the extent that the fee is attributable to the cost of registration or membership of the qualifying child in a program of prescribed physical activity and, for the purposes of this section, that cost

(a) includes the cost to the qualifying entity of the program in respect of its administration, instruction, rental of required facilities, and uniforms and equipment that are not available to be acquired by a participant in the program for an amount less than their fair market value at the time, if any, they are so acquired; and

(b) does not include

(i) the cost of accommodation, travel, food or beverages, or

(ii) any amount deductible under section 63 (i.e., child care expenses) in computing any person's income for any taxation year.

Charitable Donations Credit - ITA 118.1

Extent Of Coverage In This Chapter

6-87.   For tax purposes, donations, even in the form of cash, are segregated into categories, each with a different set of rules. Additional complications arise when non-cash donations are made. To be able to deal with gifts of depreciable capital property, a full understanding of capital gains and CCA procedures is required. Given these complications, a comprehensive treatment of charitable gifts is deferred until we revisit Taxable Income and Tax Payable in Chapter 14. However, limited coverage of charitable donations is included in this Chapter.

Eligible Gifts

6-88.   In our coverage of donations in this Chapter, we will deal only with gifts of cash or monetary assets. Donations of other types of property are covered in Chapter 14.

6-89.   In this Chapter, our coverage will be limited to what is referred to in ITA 118.1 as total charitable gifts. These include all amounts donated by an individual to a registered charity, a registered Canadian amateur athletic association, a housing corporation resident in Canada that is exempt from tax under ITA 149(1)(i), a Canadian municipality, the United Nations or an agency thereof, a university outside of Canada which normally enrolls Canadian students, and a charitable organization outside of Canada to which Her Majesty in right of Canada has made a gift.

Limits On Amount Claimed

6-90.   It is the policy of the government to limit charitable donations that are eligible for the tax credit to a portion of a taxpayer's Net Income For Tax Purposes. Note that, while corporations deduct their donations from Taxable Income as opposed to receiving a credit against Tax Payable, the limits on the amount of eligible donations are the same for corporations as they are for individuals.

6-91.   The general limit on eligible amounts of charitable gifts is 75 percent of Net Income For Tax Purposes. For individuals, this limit is increased to 100 percent of Net Income For Tax Purposes in the year of death and the preceding year.

Carry-Forward Of Charitable Donations

6-92.   With the limit set at 75 percent of Net Income, individuals will normally be able to claim all of the donations that they make in a year. However, if their donations exceed the 75 percent limit, or they choose not to claim all of the donations that year, any unused amounts can be carried forward and used in the subsequent five year period.

6-93.   A further point here is that this limit is based on Net Income For Tax Purposes. This means that an individual could have eligible donations in excess of Taxable Income. This could occur, for example, if the individual deducted a large loss carry forward from a previous year. In situations such as this, it is important to recognize that the charitable donations tax credit is non-refundable. Given this, only the amount of donations required to reduce Tax Payable to nil should be claimed. Any additional amounts should be carried forward to future periods.

Calculating The Credit

6-94.   Once the contribution base is established, the credit is equal to 15.5 percent of the first $200, and 29 percent of any additional donations. The charitable donations credit is the only credit that features two rates for determining the allowable credit. The reason for this approach was concern that, because charitable donations are voluntary, an overall credit at the lowest bracket rate of 15.5 percent would have resulted in a decline in donations. The 29 percent credit on larger donations was added in order to mitigate this result.

6-95.   While the same level of total giving could probably have been achieved with a compromise rate somewhere between 15.5 and 29 percent, this would have changed the composition of sources for donations. Such a compromise rate would have been an incentive for low income donors and would have increased donations to organizations such as churches that rely on this sector of the population. In contrast, high income donors would have less incentive to contribute, and this would have reduced donations to such beneficiaries as educational institutions. The government did not view this as a desirable result and, as a consequence, we have a two rate system for charitable donations.

6-96.   The following example illustrates the calculation of the charitable donations tax credit, including the determination of eligible amounts:

Example   Nancy Hart has 2007 Net Income For Tax Purposes of $100,000 and Taxable Income of $40,000. On the receipt of a large inheritance, she makes a charitable donation of $15,000. She chooses to claim only $2,000 in donations in 2007.

Analysis   The total for all eligible gifts is limited to 75 percent of her Net Income For Tax Purposes, or $75,000. As her gift is less than $75,000, she could have claimed all of it. However, since she has chosen to claim $2,000, $13,000 ($15,000 - $2,000) in donations are carried forward and her tax credit would be calculated as follows:

15.5 Percent Of $200	$ 31
29 Percent Of $1,800 ($2,000 - $200)	522
Total Credit	$553

6-97.   For couples, the CRA's administrative practices permit either spouse or common-law partner to claim all of the donations made by both spouses or common-law partners. Given the dual rates on the credit, there is a small advantage in combining the donations. In addition, this may be an important consideration when one spouse has a sufficiently low income that it is limiting the use of his or her donations.

Exercise Six-11

Subject: Charitable Donations Tax Credit

Marion Scalpal has 2007 Net Income For Tax Purposes of $65,000. Although she is not a compulsive gambler, she enjoys the ambiance of casino environments and usually spends at least one evening per week at the blackjack tables. While over the years she has generally experienced small losses, an improvement in her luck resulted in 2007 winnings of over $200,000. As she had promised in her prayers, at the end of 2007 she donates $100,000 of these winnings to her church. She chooses to claim $10,000 of her donations in 2007. In 2008, her income remains at $65,000 and she makes no further donations. Determine her charitable donations tax credit for 2007, as well as the base for the maximum allowable charitable donations tax credit for 2008. Until what year can she claim any unused portions of her 2007 donation?

End of Exercise.   Solution available in Study Guide.

Medical Expense Credit - ITA 118.2
Qualifying Medical Expenses
6-98.   Medical expenses which qualify for the credit are described in ITA 118.2(2) and IT-519R2. They include amounts paid to doctors and dentists, to full time home attendants, for full time nursing home care, to institutions for the disabled, for ambulance transportation, for reasonable travel expenses for medical care, for artificial limbs, for prescription eyeglasses or contact lenses, for oxygen, for seeing eye dogs, for any device prescribed by a medical practitioner, for drugs or medicine, for laboratory work, and for premiums paid for private health services plans.

6-99.   This definition has been repeatedly extended in various budgets. Additions in the last few years include:

- the costs of arranging a bone marrow or organ transplant,
- the costs of home modifications for those with severe mobility restrictions, and to allow individuals confined to a wheelchair to be mobile within their home,
- costs of up to $10,000 in a year for a part time attendant to help a person with a severe and prolonged mental or physical impairment,
- the costs for a specially trained animal to help persons with restricted use of arms and legs,
- products for the incontinent,
- the cost of rehabilitative therapy to adjust for speech or hearing loss,
- real-time captioning for individuals with a speech or hearing impairment,
- note-taking services for individuals with a physical or mental impairment,
- voice recognition software for individuals with a physical impairment, and
- the incremental cost of acquiring gluten-free foods for individuals with celiac disease.

Determining The Credit
6-100.   The amount of the medical expense tax credit is determined by the following formula:

$$A [(B - C) + D]$$

Where:

A is the appropriate percentage for the taxation year (15.5 percent).

B is the total of an individual's medical expenses for himself, his spouse or common-law partner, and any of his children who have not reached 18 years of age at the end of the year.

C is the lesser of 3 percent of the individual's Net Income For Tax Purposes and $1,926 (2007 figure).

D is the total of all amounts each of which is, in respect of a dependant of the individual (other than a child of the individual who has not attained the age of 18 years before the end of the taxation year), the lesser of $10,000 and the amount determined by the formula:

$$E - F$$

Where:

E is the total of the dependant's medical expenses

F is the lesser of 3 percent of the dependant's Net Income For Tax Purposes and $1,926 (2007 figure).

6-101. If the taxpayer has no dependants who are 18 years of age or older, components D, E and F in the formula are not relevant. In this case, the credit base is equal to the total of the qualifying medical expenses of the individual taxpayer, his spouse or common-law partner, and his minor children. This balance is reduced by the lesser of 3 percent of the taxpayer's income and an indexed figure which for 2007 is equal to $1,926. This latter figure will be the limiting factor once an individual's 2007 Net Income For Tax Purposes reaches $64,200 ($1,926 ÷ 3%).

6-102. If the taxpayer has dependants who are 18 years of age or older, a separate credit base calculation is required for each of the dependants who are not minors. This credit base is equal to the dependant's qualifying medical expenses, reduced by the lesser of 3 percent of the dependant's Net Income For Tax Purposes and $1,926 (E and F in the formula). The maximum credit base that can be claimed by the taxpayer for each dependant is subject to a limit of $10,000. The taxpayer adds the total of these credit bases (to a maximum of $10,000 per dependant) to the credit base calculated for the taxpayer, his spouse or common-law partner and his minor children.

6-103. A further point here relates to who actually pays for medical expenses. The credit is only available to the individual who actually pays the eligible amounts. For an individual to claim the medical expenses of a child or other dependant, he must pay for them. When the individual does make the actual payments, the child or dependant cannot make the claim for the credit.

Twelve Month Period

6-104. Medical expenses can be claimed for any 12 month period ending in the year and must be documented by receipts. The ability to claim expenses for a 12 month period ending in the year is advantageous for individuals with large expenses in a 12 month period other than a calendar year.

Example An individual has Net Income For Tax Purposes of $60,000 in both 2006 and 2007. In the period July to December, 2006, he has $10,000 in medical expenses. He has a further $12,000 in the period January to June, 2007.

Analysis The 2006 claim could be deferred and the $22,000 total could be claimed in full in the 2007 taxation year. The advantage of doing this is that the threshold amount reduction would be applied only once in 2007. If medical expenses had to be claimed in the year in which they were incurred, this individual would have to apply the threshold reduction of $1,800 [(3%)($60,000)] in both years. If the full amount is claimed in 2007, federal tax savings at the 2006 minimum rate of 15.25 percent would total $275 [(15.25%)($1,800)]. Note that the rate for credits in 2006, the year in which the tax savings occurs, was 15.25 percent.

Example Of Medical Expense Tax Credit Calculation

6-105.   The following example will serve to illustrate the application of the medical expense tax credit formula:

Example Sam Jonas and his dependent family members had the following Net Income For Tax Purposes and medical expenses for 2007:

Individual	Net Income	Medical Expenses
Sam Jonas	$100,000	$ 5,000
Kelly Jonas (Sam's Wife)	12,000	4,400
Sue Jonas (Sam's 16 Year Old Daughter)	8,500	4,100
Sharon Jonas (Sam's 69 Year Old Mother)	6,000	16,500
Martin Jonas		
(Sam's 70 Year Old Blind Father)	12,000	4,000
Total Medical Expenses		$34,000

Analysis Sam's 2007 medical expense tax credit, using the formula in Paragraph 6-100, would be calculated as follows:

Amount B Qualifying Expenses ($5,000 + $4,400 +$4,100) $13,500

Amount C
Lesser of:
- $[(3\%)(\$100,000)] = \$3,000$
- 2007 Threshold Amount = $1,926   (1,926)

Subtotal	$11,574

Amount D
Sharon - Lesser Of:
- $[\$16,500 - (3\%)(\$6,000)] =$ $16,320
- Absolute limit = $10,000 $10,000
Martin - Lesser Of:
- $[\$4,000 - (3\%)(\$12,000)] = \$3,640$
- Absolute Limit = $10,000   3,640   13,640

Allowable Amount Of Medical Expenses	$25,214
Amount A The Appropriate Rate	15.5%
Medical Expense Tax Credit	$ 3,908

Exercise Six-12

Subject: Medical Expense Tax Credit

Ms. Maxine Davies and her spouse, Lance Davies, have 2007 medical expenses which total $4,330. While Ms. Davies has 2007 Net Income For Tax Purposes in excess of $150,000, Lance has no income during the year. They have two children. Their 12 year old daughter, Mandy, has 2007 medical expenses of $4,600 and no Net Income For Tax Purposes. Their 21 year old son, Max, has 2007 medical expenses of $8,425 and Net Income For Tax Purposes of $8,250. Ms. Davies pays the medical expenses for both children. Determine Ms. Davies' medical expense tax credit for 2007.

End of Exercise. Solution available in Study Guide.

Refundable Medical Expense Supplement - ITA 122.51

6-106.   The tax credits that we have discussed to this point are referred to as non-refundable. This means that, if the individual does not have sufficient Tax Payable to use the credit, it is of no benefit to the taxpayer. In contrast, there are a limited number of refundable credits. In the case of these credits, if the individual does not have sufficient Tax Payable to use the credit, the government will issue a cheque for the unused amount. The ITA 122.51 refundable medical expense credit is of this type.

6-107.   To be eligible for the 2007 medical expense supplement, the individual must be 18 or over at the end of the year, and must have earned income (employment or business) of at least $2,984. The credit is the lesser of $1,022 and 25/15.5 of the medical expense tax credit that can be claimed for the year. This can also be described as 25 percent of the expenses eligible for the medical expense tax credit.

6-108.   The lesser amount is reduced by 5 percent of family Net Income For Tax Purposes in excess of an indexed threshold amount. For 2007, the amount is $22,627. The credit is completely eliminated when family Net Income For Tax Purposes reaches $43,067. A simple example will serve to illustrate this provision:

> **Example**   For 2007, Mr. Larry Futon and his spouse have medical expenses that total $4,650. His Net Income For Tax Purposes is $26,900, all of which qualifies as earned income. His spouse has Net Income For Tax Purposes of $500. Mr. Futon is also eligible for the full caregiver tax credit for his mother.
>
> **Analysis**   Mr. Futon's allowable medical expenses for tax credit purposes would be $3,843 [$4,650 - (3%)($26,900)], resulting in a tax credit of $596 [(15.5%)($3,843)]. Given this, 25/15.5 of the credit, or alternatively, 25 percent of the allowable medical expenses, would equal $961. His refundable credit would be based on the lesser of this $961 and the maximum of $1,022, less a reduction of $239 [(5%)($26,900 + $500 - $22,627)], leaving a balance of $722 ($961 - $239).

6-109.   The receipt of this refundable credit does not affect an individual's ability to claim a tax credit for the same medical expenses that are used to calculate the refundable credit. Assuming he has no tax credits other than the basic personal, spousal, caregiver, and medical expense, his federal Tax Payable would be reduced to $260 [(15.5%)($26,900 - $8,929 - $8,429 - $4,019 - $3,843)]. When this result is combined with the refundable credit of $722, Mr. Futon winds up with a refund of $462 ($722 - $260) for the year.

Exercise Six-13

Subject: Refundable Medical Expense Supplement

During 2007, Ms. Lara Brunt and her common-law partner, Sara, have medical expenses that total $6,250. Her Net Income For Tax Purposes is $25,400, all of which qualifies as earned income. Sara has no income of her own. Determine Lara's minimum Tax Payable for 2007.

End of Exercise.   Solution available in Study Guide.

Disability Credit - ITA 118.3

Calculation

6-110.   The disability credit is available under ITA 118.3 and, for 2007, it is equal to $1,068 [(15.5%)($6,890)]. In addition, there is a supplement to this amount for a disabled child who is under the age of 18 at the end of the year. For 2007, the base for the supplement is $4,019, providing a total credit for a disabled minor of $1,691 [(15.5%)($6,890 + $4,019)]. Note, however, that the supplement amount of $4,019 is reduced by child care and attendant care costs in excess of $2,354. This means that once such costs reach $6,373 for the year, the supplement is completely eliminated.

6-111. To qualify for this credit, the requirement has been that the impairment must be such that there is a "marked" restriction of the activities of daily living. In addition, it must have lasted, or be expected to last, for at least 12 months. This has been amended to include situations where there is a "significant" restriction in more than one activity (while both terms are undefined, it appears that significant is less severe than marked).

6-112. In general, a medical doctor, or optometrist, must certify on Form T2201 that a severe physical or mental impairment exists. In the case of restrictions on the ability to walk, recent amendments allow a physiotherapist to make the required certification.

6-113. ITA 118.4(1) tries to make the conditions for qualifying for this credit as clear as possible. This Subsection points out that an individual clearly qualifies if they are blind. They also qualify if 90 percent of the time they cannot perform, or take an inordinate amount of time to perform, a basic activity of daily living. The following are listed as basic activities:

- mental functions necessary for everyday life;
- feeding oneself or dressing oneself;
- speaking such that the individual can be understood in a quiet setting by someone familiar with the individual;
- hearing such that the individual can, in a quiet setting, understand someone familiar with the individual;
- bowel or bladder functions; or
- walking.

6-114. There have been several attempts to provide improved guidance in this area. The 2006 budget incorporates the recommendations contained in the December 2004 report of the Technical Advisory Committee On Tax Measures For Persons With Disabilities. It is hoped that this will improve a situation where reassessments appear to be common. Many practitioners feel that the CRA is, perhaps, overly aggressive in its interpretation of the terms "markedly restricted" and an "inordinate amount of time" (e.g., the credit was denied for an individual with cerebral palsy because he was able to walk with braces).

Disability Credit Transfer To A Supporting Person

6-115. In many cases, an individual who is sufficiently infirm to qualify for the disability credit will not have sufficient Tax Payable to use it. In these situations, all or part of the credit may be transferred to a spouse or a supporting person who claimed the disabled individual as a dependant under the eligible dependant provision, or as a disabled dependant over 17. The list of potential transferees includes parents, grandparents, children, grandchildren, brothers, sisters, aunts, uncles, nieces, and nephews.

6-116. In order to make the disability credit transfer available in most situations where a disabled child, parent, or grandparent is dependent on a taxpayer for support, the transfer is extended by a somewhat awkward measure to situations in which the supporting person:

- could have claimed the eligible dependant credit, if neither the supporting person nor the disabled dependant were married; and
- could have claimed the disabled dependant over 17, or the caregiver credit, if the dependant had been 18 years of age or older and had no income.

6-117. The amount that can be transferred is the same $1,068 (or $1,691 if the under 18 supplement is available) that could be claimed by the disabled individual. However, if the disabled individual has Tax Payable in excess of his ITA 118 (see preceding items) and 118.7 (CPP and EI credits), the credit must first be applied to reduce the disabled individual's Tax Payable to nil. If a balance remains after all Tax Payable has been eliminated, it can be transferred to the supporting person.

Other Credits and Deductions Related To Disabilities

6-118. Disabled individuals, or a supporting person, may have medical expenses that are eligible for tax credits, including attendant care and nursing home care. For disabled individuals who are able to work or who are attending a designated educational institution or secondary school, the disability supports deduction provides tax relief for a number of medical expenses, including attendant care, that would assist a disabled person to work or go to school. (See Chapter 11 for a detailed discussion of this deduction from Net Income For Tax Purposes.) Finally, a supporting person may be in a position to deduct child care costs for a disabled individual. There is a fairly complex interplay among these provisions with respect to which of them can be used for a given individual. While a full discussion of this point goes beyond the scope of this material, the following points are relevant:

- Neither the individual, nor a supporting person, can claim the disability credit if a medical expense credit is claimed for a full time attendant, or for full time care in a nursing home. However, the individual or supporting person can claim either of the two amounts.

- The disability credit can be claimed if a medical expense credit is claimed for a part time attendant. Part time is defined as expenses of less than $10,000 for the year ($20,000 in the year of death). Note that part-time attendant care can only be claimed as a medical expense credit if no part of that care is claimed as child care costs or for attendant care required to produce income.

2007 Budget Proposals

6-119.   The March 19, 2007 budget contained two proposals that are designed to provide assistance to individuals who are eligible for this credit:

Registered Disability Savings Plans   The budget provides for a new registered savings plan for the benefit of individuals who qualify for the disability tax credit. These plans, which operate along the same lines as registered education savings plans, are discussed in Chapter 11.

Working Income Tax Benefit Supplement   The budget introduces a new refundable tax credit for low income individuals. This proposal adds an additional amount for individuals who qualify for the disability tax credit. The working income tax benefit, including the supplement provision, will be covered later in this Chapter.

Exercise Six-14

Subject: Disability Tax Credit

John Leslie lives with his wife and 21 year old blind son, Keith, who qualifies for the disability tax credit. Keith has no income of his own. During 2007, John paid medical expenses of $16,240 for Keith. None of these expenses involve attendant care. John has medical expenses of his own of more than $3,000. His Taxable Income for 2007 was $100,000. Determine the total amount of tax credits related to Keith that will be available to John.

End of Exercise. Solution available in Study Guide.

Education Related Credits

Tuition Credit - ITA 118.5

6-120.   Under ITA 118.5, individuals receive a credit against Tax Payable equal to 15.5 percent of qualifying tuition fees paid with respect to the calendar year, regardless of the year in which they are actually paid. There is no upper limit on this credit. To qualify, the fees must be paid to:

- a university, college, or other institution for post-secondary courses;
- an institution certified by the Minister of Human Resources and Skills Development for a course that developed or improved skills in an occupation (the individual must be 16 or

older);
- a university outside Canada, if enrolled full time in a course that was at least 13 consecutive weeks long; or
- for individuals who live near the U.S. border and commute, a U.S. college or university for part-time studies.

6-121.   It has been noted that universities are relying more heavily on ancillary fees for such items as health services, athletics, and various other services. As a reflection of this situation, ITA 118.5(3) extends the tuition tax credit to cover all mandatory ancillary fees that are imposed by universities on all of their full time, or all of their part-time students. In addition, ITA 118.5(3)(d) allows up to $250 in such ancillary fees to be added to the total, even if they do not meet the condition of being required for all full or part-time students.

Education Credit - ITA 118.6
6-122.   Under ITA 118.6(2), there is a credit for 2007 equal to $62 [(15.5%)($400)] per month of full time attendance at a designated educational institution or enrollment in a qualifying educational program. For this purpose, designated educational institutions include universities, colleges, and institutions certified by the Minister of Human Resource Development for a course that develops or improves skills in an occupation.

6-123.   Enrollment in a qualifying educational program is described in IT-515R2 as a program that must run for at least three consecutive weeks, and must require instruction or work in the program of at least 10 hours a week throughout its duration. Both of these descriptions can be thought of as full time pursuit of educational activities.

6-124.   An alternative education credit of $19 [(15.5%)($120)] per month is available for attendance in a specified educational program. In general terms, this is defined as a program that, were it not for the requirement that at least 10 hours per week be devoted to its requirements, would be a qualifying educational program. In somewhat simplified terms, this credit is available to individuals pursuing part-time studies, defined in terms of a minimum of 12 hours per month of course work.

6-125.   A further modification of the general rules for the education credit is available to individuals who either qualify for the disability tax credit or, because of a mental or physical disability, cannot pursue educational activities on a full time basis. The full education credit of $62 per month is available to such individuals, without regard to whether their attendance is full or part-time.

Textbook Credit - ITA 118.6(2.1)
6-126.   An additional education related credit was introduced in the May, 2006 budget. While it is described as a "textbook" tax credit, it is not based on an actual purchase of such books. Rather, it is simply an addition to the education credit. This "textbook" credit is equal to $10 [(15.5%)($65)] for each month in which the student is entitled to claim the education credit as a full-time student, or $3 [(15.5%)($20)] for each month in which the student is entitled to claim the education credit as a part-time student.

6-127.   This new credit can be added to the tuition and education credits as part of the amount that is eligible for a carry forward by the student (see Paragraph 6-129). It will also be added to these credits in determining the amount that can be transferred to a spouse, parent or grandparent (see Paragraph 6-133). The education credit rule for disabled students will also apply to this credit (see Paragraph 6-125).

Interest On Student Loans Credit - ITA 118.62
6-128.   If a student or a related person has paid interest on student loans, ITA 118.62 permits the deduction of 15.5 percent of amounts paid in the year, or in any of the five preceding years. The interest paid must be on a loan under the *Canada Student Loans Act*, the *Canada Student Financial Assistance Act*, or a provincial statute governing the granting of financial assistance to students at the post-secondary school level.

Exercise Six-15

Subject: Education Related Tax Credits

During 2007, Sarah Bright attends university for four months of full time study and two months of part-time study. Her total tuition for the year, including all ancillary fees, is $3,200 of which she paid $1,000 in 2006. The amount paid in 2007 includes $400 in fees that are only charged to students in her geology program. Interest for the year on her student loan was $325. Determine the total amount of education related tax credits that would be available for Ms. Bright for 2007.

End of Exercise. Solution available in Study Guide.

Carry Forward Of Tuition, Education, And Textbook Credits - ITA 118.61

6-129.   There are situations in which a student does not have sufficient Tax Payable to use their tuition, education, and textbook credits and, in addition, has not transferred them to a spouse, parent, or grandparent (see Paragraph 6-133). To deal with this type of situation, ITA 118.61 allows a carry forward of unused tuition, education, and textbook credits. In addition, ITA 118.62 provides for a five year carry forward of unused interest on student loans.

6-130.   Unfortunately, the calculation of the amount that is carried forward can be complex. Although the *Income Tax Act* uses Tax Payable and credit amounts to calculate carry forwards and transfers, Schedule 11 in the personal tax return uses Taxable Income and credit base amounts in its calculations. We will explain the *Income Tax Act* approach in the text, but illustrate both approaches in the example in Paragraph 6-137.

6-131.   To carry amounts forward, the total available credits must be reduced by the student's Tax Payable, calculated using only the credits available under ITA 118 (various personal), 118.01 (adoption expenses), 118.02 (public transit pass), 118.03 (child fitness), 118.3 (disability), and 118.7 (CPP and EI). Of the credits we have previously covered in this chapter, the excluded credits include ITA 118.1 (charitable donations), 118.2 (medical expenses) and 122.51 (refundable medical expense supplement). The carry forward amount is further reduced by any transfer to another individual.

6-132.   The resulting balance can be carried forward and is available for the student's personal use in any subsequent year. However, once it is carried forward, it cannot be transferred to another individual.

Exercise Six-16

Subject: Carry Forward Of Education Related Credits

At the beginning of 2007, Kerri Holmes has an education credit carry forward from 2006 of $305 [(15.25%)($2,000)]. During 2007, she is in full time attendance at a Canadian university for 8 months of the year. Her tuition fees total $4,800 for the year. Her Taxable Income for 2007 is $22,000. Other than education related tax credits, her only tax credit is her personal credit of $1,384 [(15.5%)($8,929)]. Determine Kerri's total education related tax credits for 2007 and any available carry forward.

End of Exercise. Solution available in Study Guide.

Transfer Of Tuition, Education, And Textbook Credits - ITA 118.81

6-133.   ITA 118.9 provides for a transfer of these tax credits to a parent or grandparent. ITA 118.8 provides for a transfer of these credits (plus several others), to a spouse or common-law partner. ITA 118.81 limits the total amount of tuition, education, and textbook credits that can be transferred under either of these provisions. The transfer is at the discretion of the student and the legislation states that he must indicate in writing the amount that he is willing to transfer.

6-134.   For 2006 and subsequent years, the maximum transfer for an individual student is the lesser of the available credits and $5,000 multiplied by the tax rate for the minimum tax bracket (referred to as the "appropriate percentage"). For 2007, this amount will be $775 [(15.5%)($5,000)].

6-135.   This $775 maximum amount must be reduced by the student's Tax Payable calculated after the same credits used to calculate the carry forward of education related credits. As described in Paragraph 6-131, these are the credits available under ITA 118, 118.01, 118.02, 118.03, 118.3 and 118.7. Added to the list for this purpose are any education related credits carried forward from a previous year under ITA 118.61. If these credits reduce the student's Tax Payable to nil, the full $775 is available for transfer.

6-136.   The $775 limit is on a per student basis. A parent or grandparent could have $775 transfers from any number of children or grandchildren. For obvious reasons, transfers from more than one spouse would not be acceptable for tax purposes (tax considerations might be the least of such an individual's problems). If the student is married, the supporting parent or grandparent can make the claim only if the student's spouse did not claim the spousal credit, or any unused credits transferred by the student.

Transfer To A Parent Or Grandparent - ITA 118.9

6-137.   As we have indicated, ITA 118.9 provides for a transfer to a parent or grandparent. An example will serve to illustrate this provision.

Example   Megan Doxy has 2007 Taxable Income of $11,000 (none of this is employment income). She attends university full time for 8 months of the year, paying a total amount for tuition of $8,000. This gives her a tuition amount of $8,000, an education amount of $3,200 [(8)($400)], and a textbook amount of $520 [(8)($65)], a total of $11,720. Her only other tax credit is her personal amount of $1,384 [(15.5%)($8,929)]. She would like to transfer the maximum credits to her father.

Analysis   Megan's education related credits total $1,817 [(15.5%)($11,720)], well in excess of the maximum transfer of $775. However, this maximum of $775 would have to be reduced by Megan's Tax Payable after the deduction of her personal amount. This amount would be $321 [(15.5%)($11,000 - $8,929)], leaving a maximum transfer of $454 ($775 - $321). This would leave Megan with remaining unused credits of $1,042 ($1,817 - $321 - $454) which can be carried forward to future years, for her own use. These calculations are the result of using the approach presented in the *Income Tax Act*.

The alternative calculation approach that is used in the tax return would begin with the total education related amount of $11,720. The maximum transfer amount in this approach is $5,000. This would be reduced by $2,071 ($11,000 - $8,929), the excess of Megan's Taxable Income over her basic personal amount. This results in a maximum transfer of $2,929 ($5,000 - $2,071). Megan's carry forward amount is $6,720 ($11,720 - $2,071 - $2,929). Multiplying these amounts by the 15.5 percent minimum rate will give you the same $1,042 of unused credits as the calculations using the preceding *Income Tax Act* approach.

Exercise Six-17

Subject: Transfer And Carry Forward Of Education Related Credits

Jerry Fall has 2007 Taxable Income of $11,250, none of which is employment income. He attends an American university on a full time basis for 11 months of the year, paying a total amount for tuition of $23,500 (Canadian dollars). His only tax credits, other than education related credits, are his basic personal amount and a medical expense credit of $240 [(15.5%)($1,550)]. Determine Jerry's education related credit amounts and indicate how much of this total could be transferred to a parent and how much would be carried forward.

End of Exercise. Solution available in Study Guide

Employment Insurance (EI) And
Canada Pension Plan (CPP) Credits - ITA 118.7

6-138.   ITA 118.7 provides a tax credit equal to 15.5 percent of the Employment Insurance (EI) premiums paid by an individual, all of the Canada Pension Plan (CPP) contributions paid on employment income, and half of the CPP contributions paid on self-employed income.

6-139.   For 2007, EI premiums are based on maximum insurable earnings of $40,000. The employee's rate is 1.8 percent, resulting in a maximum annual premium of $720. This results in a maximum credit against federal Tax Payable of $112 [(15.5%)($720)].

6-140.   Employers are also required to pay EI premiums, the amount being 1.4 times the premiums paid by the employee. However, these premiums do not provide the employee with a tax credit. Further, self-employed individuals are not eligible to participate in the EI program and, as a consequence, since they do not pay EI premiums, they will not be eligible for any EI tax credit.

6-141.   For 2007, an employee's CPP contributions are based on maximum pensionable earnings of $43,700, less a basic exemption of $3,500. The rate for 2007 is 4.95 percent, resulting in a maximum contribution of $1,990 [(4.95%)($43,700 - $3,500)]. This provides for a maximum 2007 credit against federal Tax Payable of $308 [(15.5%)($1,990)]. The employer matches the contributions made by the employee. However, this matching payment has no tax consequences for the employee.

6-142.   A self-employed individual earning business income must make a matching CPP contribution for himself, effectively paying twice the amount he would as an employee. As discussed in Chapter 11, the matching contribution is a deduction from Net Income For Tax Purposes under ITA 60(e) (a Division B, Subdivision e deduction). This treatment for the matching CPP contribution as a deduction is analogous to the treatment used by employers. This means that a self-employed individual will have a tax credit equal to one-half of his CPP contributions for self-employed income, and a deduction for the remaining one-half.

Overpayment Of EI Premiums And CPP Contributions

6-143.   It is not uncommon for employers to withhold EI and CPP amounts that are in excess of the amounts required. This can happen through an error on the part of the employer's payroll system. Even in the absence of errors, overpayments can arise when an individual changes employers.

6-144.   A refund of these excess amounts is available on an individual's tax return. While any CPP or EI overpayment is not part of the base for the tax credit, it will increase the refund available or decrease the tax liability that is calculated in the return.

Example   Jerry Weist changed employers during 2007 and, as a consequence, the total amount of EI premiums withheld during the year was $885. In a similar fashion, the total amount of CPP contributions withheld by the two employers was $2,099. His employment income was well in excess of the maximum insurable and pensionable earnings.

Analysis   In filing his 2007 tax return, Jerry will claim a refund of $274, calculated as follows:

EI Premiums Withheld	$ 885	
2007 Maximum	(720)	$165
CPP Contributions Withheld	$2,099	
2007 Maximum	(1,990)	109
Refund		$274

Transfers To A Spouse Or Common-Law Partner - ITA 118.8

6-145.   ITA 118.8 permits the transfer of six specific tax credits to a spouse or common-law partner. The credits that are eligible for transfer are:

- the age credit (see Paragraph 6-66),
- the pension income credit (see Paragraph 6-68),
- the disability credit (see Paragraph 6-110), and
- the current year tuition, education, and textbook credits to a maximum of $775 (see material beginning in Paragraph 6-133).

6-146.   The maximum amount that can be transferred is based on the sum of these credits, reduced by a modified calculation of the spouse or common-law partner's Tax Payable.   While the legislation is based on Tax Payable, the T1 tax return uses a simplified approach based on Taxable Income. This approach starts with the sum of the base for all of the preceding credits. From this amount is subtracted the spouse's taxable income, reduced by the bases of the basic personal credit, the CPP and EI credits, the tuition credits, the education credits, and the textbook credits. The resulting remainder is the amount that can be transferred to a spouse or common-law partner.

Exercise Six-18

Subject: Transfer Of Credits From A Spouse

Mr. Martin Levee is 68 years old and has Net Income For Tax Purposes of $42,000. Of this total, $24,000 was from a life annuity that he purchased with RRSP funds. His spouse is 66 years old, has no income of her own (she is ineligible for OAS), and is attending university on a full time basis. Her tuition fees for the year were $2,200 and she was in full time attendance for 4 months of the year. Determine Mr. Levee's maximum federal tax credits for 2007.

End of Exercise. Solution available in Study Guide.

Dividend Tax Credit

6-147.   The dividend tax credit is covered in Chapter 9 as part of our discussion of property income.

Foreign Tax Credits

6-148.   The credits that are available for taxes paid in foreign jurisdictions are covered in Chapters 9 and 14.

Investment Tax Credits

6-149.   When taxpayers make certain types of expenditures, they become eligible for investment tax credits. These credits reduce federal Tax Payable. While these credits can be claimed by individuals as well as corporations, they are much more commonly used by corporations and, as a consequence, we cover investment tax credits in Chapter 15.

Political Contributions Tax Credits - ITA 127(3)

Federal Elections Act

6-150.   While no changes have been made in the *Income Tax Act*, the introduction of the *Federal Accountability Act* placed new limits on the ability of persons to make contributions. More specifically, this *Act* contains the following provisions:

- The amount that can be contributed annually by an individual to a registered party is reduced to $1,100.
- The amount that can be contributed annually to a candidate or a leadership contestant is reduced to $1,100.
- The amount that can be contributed annually to a nomination contestant is reduced to $1,100.
- There is a total ban on contributions by corporations, trade unions and unincorporated associations.

Income Tax Rules

6-151.   A federal tax credit is available on political contributions made to a registered federal political party, or to candidates at the time of a federal general election or by-election. The maximum value is $650 and it is available to both individuals and corporations. However, as discussed in the preceding Paragraph, the *Federal Elections Act* totally bans contributions by corporations. The credit is calculated as follows:

	Contributions	Credit Rate	Tax Credit
First	$ 400	3/4	$300
Next	350	1/2	175
Next	525	1/3	175
Maximum Credit	$1,275		$650

6-152.   The $650 credit is achieved when contributions total $1,275. Contributions in excess of this amount do not generate additional credits. Also note that most provinces have a similar credit against provincial Tax Payable. There is a difference, however, in that the eligible contributions must be made to a registered provincial political party.

6-153.   The proposed Subsections ITA 248(30) and ITA 248(31), (July 18, 2005), would require the amount of charitable and political contributions that are eligible for tax credits to be reduced by the amount of any advantage received by the taxpayer. While recent events, (such as the sponsorship scandal), make it clear that individuals do receive benefits related to their political contributions, it is unlikely that this would occur in the form of a documented transaction that could be used as a basis for assessing the contributing taxpayer. This suggests that these proposed Subsections will have greater applicability in the area of charitable contributions. Given this, we will defer discussion of these proposals until Chapter 14 where we provide our more comprehensive discussion of donations to charitable organizations.

Exercise Six-19

Subject: Political Contributions Tax Credit

Ms. Vivacia Unger contributes $785 to the Liberal New Conservative Democratic Party, a registered federal political party. Determine the amount of her federal political contributions tax credit.

End of Exercise. Solution available in Study Guide.

Labour Sponsored Funds Tax Credit - ITA 127.4

6-154.   The government wishes to encourage investment in small and medium sized enterprises. To that end, ITA 127.4 provides a credit for individuals investing in the shares of prescribed labour sponsored venture capital corporations.

6-155.   For purposes of this Section, these corporations must be set up under provincial legislation and managed by a labour organization. The assets of the corporation must be invested in small and medium sized businesses. Proposed legislation will make the credit unavailable if the province or territory where the company is registered does not provide a similar credit. The credit is based on the cost of the shares purchased by the individual.

6-156.   The federal credit is equal to 15 percent of the net cost of the labour sponsored venture capital corporation (LSVCC) shares. To be eligible for the credit, the investor must be the first registered holder of the LSVCC shares. In addition, the maximum credit for a year is $750. This limits the net cost of investments eligible for the credit to $5,000.

Exercise Six-20

Subject: Labour Sponsored Funds Credit

On June 30, 2007, Mr. Brad Clintor purchases newly issued shares in a prescribed labour sponsored venture capital corporation at a cost of $3,000. The province in which Mr. Clintor lives provides a provincial tax credit for this investment. Determine the amount of the federal tax credit that will result from this purchase.

End of Exercise. Solution available in Study Guide.

Refundable Credits

Introduction

6-157.   With the exception of the refundable medical expense supplement, the credits that we have encountered to this point can be described as non-refundable. This means that, unless the taxpayer has Tax Payable for the current taxation year, there is no current benefit from the credit. Further, with the exception of the charitable donations credit and education related credits, there is no carry over of these non-refundable credits to subsequent taxation years.

6-158.   In this section we will describe three refundable credits. The first two, the refundable GST credit and the child tax benefit, have been around for a number of years. The third, the refundable working income tax benefit was introduced in the March, 2007 budget.

6-159.   Our coverage of these refundable credits will be limited. This reflects the fact that, unlike non-refundable credits, taxpayers do not calculate the eligible amount in the tax returns that they submit to the CRA. Rather, the CRA calculates the credits from the tax returns that the taxpayer has filed in previous years. These amounts are then sent to the eligible taxpayers on a prepaid basis. Given this, there is no need to provide coverage of the detailed calculation of these credits.

Refundable GST Credit

6-160.   One of the major problems with the goods and services tax (GST) is the fact that it is a regressive tax. In order to provide some relief from the impact of the GST on low income families, there is a refundable GST credit available under ITA 122.5. Features that make this credit different from other types of credits are that the CRA calculates it for the individual, and it cannot be used as a credit against Tax Payable. Unlike other tax credits, where the relevant calculations are included in the individual's tax return, the GST credit is determined by the

CRA on the basis of eligibility information supplied in the individual's tax return. It is only paid if tax returns have been filed.

6-161. For 2007, the system provides for a total credit that is calculated as follows:

- $237 for the "eligible individual". An eligible individual includes a Canadian resident who is 19 years of age or over during the current taxation year, or is married or living common-law, or is a parent who resides with their child. In the case of a married couple, only one spouse can be an eligible individual.

- $237 for a "qualified relation". A qualified relation is defined as a cohabiting spouse or common-law partner. If the eligible individual does not have a qualified relation, he is entitled to an additional credit that is the lesser of $125 and 2 percent of the individual's Net Income For Tax Purposes in excess of $7,705.

- $237 for a dependant eligible for the eligible dependant tax credit.

- $125 for each "qualified dependant". A "qualified dependant" is defined as a person who is the individual's child or is dependent on the individual or the individual's cohabiting spouse or common-law partner for support. In addition, the child or dependent person must be under 19 years of age, reside with the individual, have never had a spouse or common-law partner, and have never been a parent of a child he has resided with. Further, this credit cannot be claimed for a dependant if the $237 was claimed for that dependant because he or she was eligible for the eligible dependant tax credit.

6-162. The total of these amounts must be reduced by 5 percent of the excess of the individual's "adjusted income" over an indexed threshold amount. For 2007, this threshold amount is $30,936. "Adjusted Income" is defined as total income of the individual and his qualified relation, if any.

6-163. The refundable GST credit is available to all eligible individuals, without regard to whether they have Tax Payable. The amount of the credit is calculated by the CRA on the basis of information included in the individual's tax return for a particular year, and the amounts are automatically paid to the taxpayer in subsequent years.

Refundable Child Tax Benefit

Regular Amount

6-164. The Child Tax Benefit is in the form of a non-taxable monthly payment. As is the case with the refundable GST credit, the amount of this benefit is calculated by the CRA. The benefits are subject to indexation. For the period July, 2006 through June, 2007, the benefits are as follows:

- $1,283 per year (paid monthly) for each qualified dependant, basically a child who is under 18; and

- an additional $90 per year (paid monthly) for each dependant in excess of two.

6-165. This basic benefit is reduced when family Net Income reaches $37,178. For a family with one child, the phase out is at the rate of 2 percent of the excess income. For a family with two or more children, the reduction is based on 4 percent of the excess income.

National Child Benefit Supplement

6-166. In addition to the regular Child Tax Benefit, there is also a National Child Benefit supplement. The amount of the supplement is $1,988 per year for the first child, $1,758 per year for the second, and $1,673 per year for the third and subsequent child. All of these benefits are paid monthly.

6-167. The benefit is reduced when family Net Income reaches $20,883. The phase out rate is 12.2 percent for a one child family, 22.8 percent for a two child family, and 32.9 percent for families with more than two children.

Universal Child Care Benefit

6-168.   While this is not part of the child tax benefit system, we would note here that the May, 2006 budget provided for a universal child care benefit. The benefit consists of a payment of $100 per month for each child under the age of 6 years. It will be paid to the lower income spouse or common-law partner and will be included in their Net Income For Tax Purposes.

Refundable Working Income Tax Benefit

The Welfare Wall

6-169.   Despite the rantings of ostensibly virtuous individuals of a right-wing persuasion, many individuals who are receiving various types of social assistance are not necessarily lazy or lacking in motivation. The simple fact is that, given the types of wages such individuals receive, they are often better off economically if they do not work. The types of work that such individuals can earn is typically at the legal "minimum" (currently $7.00 per hour in the very wealthy province of Alberta). The amounts earned at this wage are typically offset by reductions in social assistance payments. Additional negative effects flow from loss of subsidized housing, prescription drug assistance, and other benefits that flow to individuals with little or no income.

6-170.   It has been demonstrated that, if such individuals find employment, the result can be a reduction in their real income. Instead of rewarding their efforts, our current system can actually punish individuals who make an effort to improve their economic status. This is commonly referred to as the welfare wall.

Proposed Solution

6-171.   The March 2007 budget includes a Working Income Tax Benefit (WITB) that is designed to alleviate this problem. This provision can be described as follows:

- The WITB will provide a refundable credit equal to 20 percent of each dollar of earned income in excess of $3,000. For an individual, the maximum credit is $500 which will be available when his earned income reaches $5,500. For couples and single parents, the maximum benefit will be $1,000. This will be available when the family income reaches $8,000.

- In order to restrict the WITB to low income individuals, it will be phased out at higher income levels. For single individuals, the benefit will be reduced by 15 percent of earned income in excess of $9,500. It will disappear at an earned income level of $12,833 ($9,500 + $3,333). For couples and single parents, the 15 percent reduction begins at an earned income level of $14,500. In this case it will disappear at an earned income level of $21,167 ($14,500 + $6,667).

Supplement For Disabled Persons

6-172.   For individuals qualifying for the disability tax credit, an additional benefit is proposed. In this case, the 20 percent benefit begins at an earned income level of $1,750. It reaches a maximum benefit level of $250 when earned income reaches $3,000. For a single individual, it will be reduced by 15 percent of earned income in excess of $12,833. For couples and single parents, the reduction begins at a family income level of $21,167.

Social Benefits Repayment (OAS And EI)

Basic Concepts

6-173.   While at one time Canada applied its social assistance programs on a universal basis, this has not been the case for some time. Both Old Age Security (OAS) and Employment Insurance (EI) benefits are reduced or eliminated for high income individuals.

6-174.   With respect to OAS payments, the government assesses a Part I.2 tax on OAS benefits received by individuals with an adjusted Net Income above a threshold amount. While the legislation is in the form of a tax on OAS benefits, this tax is often referred to as a repayment or clawback of OAS benefits.

6-175.   In similar fashion, the *Employment Insurance Act* requires that individuals with an adjusted Net Income above a specified threshold amount repay a portion of any Employment Insurance (EI) benefits received. While the source of this requirement is a different legislative Act, both the OAS tax and the EI benefits repayment create a deduction in calculating an individual's Net Income For Tax Purposes. In the T1 tax return, the total of these deductions is referred to as the "Social Benefits Repayment".

6-176.   These deductions are based on income tests and, because the amounts determined in these tests are deductions in the calculation of Net Income For Tax Purposes, there is a potentially circular calculation process. As will be explained in the material which follows, this problem is avoided by basing the income tests on an income figure which does not include these deductions.

Employment Insurance (EI) Benefits Clawback

6-177.   The *Employment Insurance Act* requires the partial repayment of benefits received if the recipient's threshold income is greater than $50,000 (1.25 times the 2007 maximum insurable earnings of $40,000). For the purposes of this test, the individual's threshold income is equal to Net Income For Tax Purposes computed without consideration of the deduction for repayment of EI benefits [ITA 60(v.1)] or the deduction for the tax on OAS benefits [ITA 60(w)]. As the EI clawback is deducted from the threshold income used for determining the OAS clawback, the EI clawback must be determined prior to calculating the amount of the OAS clawback.

6-178.   Once the amount of threshold income over $50,000 is determined, it must be compared to the EI benefits included in the current year's Net Income For Tax Purposes. The lesser of these two amounts is multiplied by 30 percent and this becomes the amount that must be repaid for the year as a social benefits repayment. This amount can then be deducted under ITA 60(v.1) in the determination of Net Income For Tax Purposes for the year.

Old Age Security (OAS) Benefits Clawback

6-179.   ITA 180.2 assesses a tax on OAS benefits in an amount equal to 15 percent of the taxpayer's threshold income in excess of $63,511. For this purpose, the threshold income is equal to Net Income For Tax Purposes computed after any EI clawback, but without consideration of the ITA 60(w) deduction for the tax on OAS benefits.

6-180.   For some individuals, all or part of the OAS benefits are taxed away on a recurring basis. Because of this, the government estimates what the taxpayer will have to repay and withholds this amount at the time the payments are made. Estimates are made on the basis of the income for the "base taxation year". For OAS payments made during the first six months of a year, the base taxation year is the second preceding year and for OAS payments made during the last six months of the year, the base taxation year is the immediately preceding year.

6-181.   For individuals with consistently high levels of income, this withholding procedure results in the full amount of the OAS benefits being withheld. For the first quarter of 2007, OAS benefits are $491.93 per month (they are adjusted on a quarterly basis). If this rate does not change, the 2007 benefit will be $5,903. This means that the benefit will be completely withheld or repaid at an income level of about $102,864. Note that, even in cases where no OAS payments are made because the total has been withheld, the individual will receive an information slip [T4A(OAS)] indicating that they were entitled to the amount of the benefit, with the same amount being shown as taxes withheld from the payment.

Exercise Six-21

Subject: EI and OAS Clawbacks

For 2007, Ms. Marilyn Jacobi has net employment income of $60,000, receives EI payments of $10,000, and receives $5,900 in Old Age Security (OAS) payments. No amount was withheld from the OAS payments because she had very low income in the previous two years due to large rental losses. Determine Ms. Jacobi's Net Income For Tax Purposes for 2007.

End of Exercise. Solution available in Study Guide.

Comprehensive Example

6-182.   While this Chapter has provided a reasonably detailed description of the determination of Tax Payable for individuals, including small examples of some of the issues that arise in this process, a more comprehensive example is appropriate at this point. To simplify calculations, we have ignored provincial income taxes. In the separate paper Study Guide, there is an additional example containing a completed tax return which includes provincial income taxes.

Taxpayer Information

Mr. Thomas Baxter is 66 years of age and his 2007 income is made up of net employment income of $73,800 and Old Age Security benefits of $5,900 (because of large business losses during the previous two years, no amount was withheld from these payments). For 2007, Mr. Baxter's employer withheld maximum CPP and EI contributions and a total of $20,000 in income tax. Other information pertaining to 2007 is as follows:

1.   Mr. Baxter's spouse is 49 years old and is physically disabled. Her only income for the year is $5,000 in Canadian source interest. The investment funds were inherited from her father at the time of his death.

2.   Mr. and Mrs. Baxter have two daughters and, at the end of the year, their ages were 14 and 17. Kim, the younger daughter, has income of $2,700, none of which was employment income. Lori, the older daughter, had net income of $2,000, none of which was employment income. In September, 2007, Lori began full time attendance at a Canadian university. Mr. Baxter paid her tuition fees of $5,000, of which $2,500 was for the fall semester.

3.   The family medical expenses for the year, all of which were paid by Mr. Baxter, totalled $2,843. Of this amount, $900 was paid for Lori.

4.   During the year, Mr. Baxter made cash donations to registered Canadian charities in the amount of $3,000.

5.   During the year, Mr. Baxter made contributions to federal political parties totalling $800.

6.   During the year, Mr. Baxter paid $960 for monthly public transit passes.

7.   Because of an ongoing problem with her weight, Mr. Baxter enrolled his daughter, Kim, in an eligible fitness program. The annual cost of this program is $1,800.

Net And Taxable Income

Mr. Baxter's Net and Taxable Income would be calculated as follows:

Net Employment Income	$73,800
OAS Benefits	5,900
Net Income Before Clawback	$79,700
OAS Clawback (Note One)	(2,428)
Net Income For Tax Purposes And Taxable Income	**$77,272**

Note One   The required repayment of OAS is the lesser of the actual OAS payments of $5,900 and $2,428 [(15%)($79,700 - $63,511)].

Federal Tax Payable

Using the preceding Taxable Income, the balance owing (refund) would be as follows:

Federal Tax On First $74,357		$13,942
Federal Tax On Next $2,915 ($77,272 - $74,357) At 26 Percent		758
Gross Tax		$14,700
Tax Credits:		
Basic Personal Amount	($ 8,929)	
Spousal ($8,929 - $5,000)	(3,929)	
Child - Kim	(2,000)	
Child - Lori	(2,000)	
Mr. Baxter's Age (Note Two)	Nil	
Mr. Baxter's Canada Employment	(1,000)	
Public Transit Passes	(960)	
Kim's Fitness Program (Note Three)	(500)	
Medical Expenses (Note Four)		
($2,843 - $1,926)	(917)	
Mrs. Baxter's Disability Transferred	(6,890)	
Lori's Tuition, Education, And Textbook		
Transferred (Note Five)	(4,360)	
EI Premiums (Maximum)	(720)	
CPP Contributions (Maximum)	(1,990)	
Total	($34,195)	
Rate	15.5%	(5,300)
Charitable Donations		
{[(15.5%)($200)] + [(29%)($3,000 - $200)]}		(843)
Political Contributions Tax Credit - Lesser Of:		
• $650 (Maximum)		
• [($400)(3/4) + ($350)(1/2) + ($50)(1/3)] = $492		(492)
Federal Tax Payable		$ 8,065
Social Benefits Repayment (Note One)		2,428
Total Payable		$10,493
Income Tax Withheld		(20,000)
Balance Owing (Refund) Before Provincial Income Taxes		**($ 9,507)**

Note Two   Mr. Baxter's age credit would be calculated as follows:

Full Base Amount		$5,177
Reduction - Lesser Of:		
• [(15%)($77,272 - $30,936)] = $6,950		
• Full Base Amount = $5,177		(5,177)
Age Credit		**Nil**

Note Three   While Mr. Baxter paid $1,800 for this program, the maximum credit base is $500.

Note Four   Medical expenses eligible for the credit are the actual expenditures of $2,843, less the maximum of $1,926 as this limit is less than 3 percent of Mr. Baxter's Net Income. Since both daughters are under 18 at the end of the year, their expenses can be aggregated with those of Mr. Baxter for the purposes of this calculation.

Note Five   Lori's total education related amount is calculated as follows:

Tuition For 2007 Semester ($5,000 - $2,500)	$2,500
Education (Four Months At $400)	1,600
Textbook (Four Months At $65)	260
Total Amount Available For Transfer Or Carry Forward	$4,360

Since Lori has no Tax Payable before consideration of her education related credits, the solution assumes that they are all transferred to her supporting parent as they total less than the $5,000 transfer limit. Alternatively, she could choose to carry forward these credits to apply against her own Tax Payable in a subsequent year.

Key Terms Used In This Chapter

6-183.   The following is a list of the key terms used in this Chapter. These terms, and their meanings, are compiled in the Glossary Of Key Terms located at the back of the separate paper Study Guide and on the Companion CD-ROM.

Adoption Expenses Tax Credit	Labour Sponsored Funds Tax Credit
Age Tax Credit	Medical Expense Tax Credit
Canada Employment Credit	Non-Refundable Tax Credit
Canada Pension Plan (CPP)	Northern Residents Deductions
Canada Pension Plan Tax Credit	OAS Clawback
Caregiver Tax Credit	Old Age Security (OAS) Benefits
Charitable Donations Tax Credit	Pension Income Tax Credit
Charitable Gifts	Personal Tax Credits
Child Tax Benefit	Political Contributions Tax Credit
Child Tax Credit	Progressive Tax System
Child Fitness Tax Credit	Public Transit Pass Tax Credit
Clawback	Refundable Medical Expense Supplement
Common-Law Partner	Refundable Tax Credit
Dependant	Regressive Tax System
Disability Tax Credit	Social Benefits Repayment
Disability Tax Credit Supplement	Spouse
Education Tax Credit	Tax Credit
Eligible Dependant Tax Credit	Taxable Income
Employment Insurance (EI)	Textbook Tax Credit
Employment Insurance Tax Credit	Tuition Tax Credit
GST Tax Credit	Universal Child Care Benefit
Home Relocation Loan	Wholly Dependant Person
Indexation	Working Income Tax Benefit

References

6-184.   For more detailed study of the material in this Chapter, we would refer you to the following:

ITA 110	Deductions Permitted
ITA 111.1	Order Of Applying Provisions
ITA 117	Tax Payable Under This Part
ITA 117.1	Annual Adjustment
ITA 118(1)	Personal Credits
ITA 118(2)	Age Credit
ITA 118(3)	Pension Credit
ITA 118(10)	Canada Employment Credit
ITA 118.01	Adoption Expense Credit
ITA 118.02	Public Transit Pass Credit
ITA 118.03	Child Fitness Credit
ITA 118.1	Definitions (Charitable Gifts)
ITA 118.2	Medical Expense Credit
ITA 118.3	Credit For Mental Or Physical Impairment
ITA 118.5	Tuition Credit
ITA 118.6	Education Credit And Textbook Credit
ITA 118.61	Unused Tuition And Education Tax Credits
ITA 118.7	Credit for EI and QPIP premiums and CPP contributions
ITA 118.8	Transfer Of Unused Credits To Spouse Or Common-Law Partner
ITA 118.9	Transfer To Parent Or Grandparent
ITA 122.5	Definitions (GST Credit)
ITA 122.6	
To 122.64	Canada Child Tax Benefit
ITA 127(3)	Monetary Contributions - Canada Elections Act (Political Contributions Credit)
ITA 127.4	Labour Sponsored Funds Tax Credit
IC 75-2R7	Contributions To A Registered Political Party Or To A Candidate At A Federal Election
IC 75-23	Tuition Fees And Charitable Donations Paid To Privately Supported Secular and Religious Schools
IC 84-3R5	Gifts To Certain Organizations Outside Canada
IC 92-3	Guidelines For Refunds Beyond The Normal Three Year Period
IT-110R3	Gifts And Official Donation Receipts
IT-113R4	Benefits To Employees — Stock Options
IT-226R	Gift To A Charity Of A Residual Interest In Real Property Or An Equitable Interest In A Trust
IT-244R3	Gifts By Individuals Of Life Insurance Policies As Charitable Donations
IT-407R4	Dispositions Of Cultural Property To Designated Canadian Institutions
IT-513R	Personal Tax Credits
IT-515R2	Education Tax Credit
IT-516R2	Tuition Tax Credit
IT-519R2	Medical Expense And Disability Tax Credits And Attendant Care Expense Deduction
IT-523	Order Of Provisions Applicable In Computing An Individual's Taxable Income And Tax Payable

Problems For Self Study

(The solutions for these problems can be found in the separate Study Guide.)

Self Study Problem Six - 1

The following five independent Cases make varying assumptions with respect to Mr. Stanley Murphy and his 2007 tax status. In all Cases, where Mr. Murphy earned employment income, his employer withheld the maximum EI premiums and CPP contributions.

Case A   Mr. Murphy is 48 years of age and has employment income of $50,000. During the year, Stanley makes contributions to federal political parties in the amount of $1,000. Mr. Murphy is not married and has no dependants.

Case B   Mr. Murphy is 48 years of age and has income from employment of $50,000. His wife, Helen Murphy, is 43 years of age and has Net Income For Tax Purposes of $4,650. They have one child, Eileen, who is 11 years of age. During the year, the family had eligible medical expenses of $1,050 for Stanley, $1,800 for Helen, and $300 for Eileen. Eileen has no income in 2007.

Case C   Mr. Murphy is 48 years of age and his wife, Helen, is 43. Mr. Murphy has income from employment of $50,000. Helen has Net Income For Tax Purposes of $5,050. They have a son, Albert, who is 19 years old and lives at home. He attends university on a full time basis during 8 months of the year. Stanley pays $5,400 for Albert's tuition for two semesters during the 2007 calendar year and $525 for required textbooks. Albert had employment income of $3,000 that he earned during the summer. He will transfer any unused credits to his father.

Case D   Mr. Murphy is 67 and his wife Helen is 68. Helen has been completely disabled for a number of years. The components of Stanley and Helen's income are as follows:

	Stanley	Helen
Interest	$ 300	$ 50
Canada Pension Plan Benefits	4,400	200
Old Age Security Benefits	5,900	5,900
Income From Registered Pension Plan	31,150	450
Total Net Income	$41,750	$6,600

Case E   Mr. Murphy is 48 years of age and his wife, Helen, is 43. Her 68 year old father, Ahmed, and her 70 year old aunt, Jaleh, live with them. Ahmed's 2007 Net Income For Tax Purposes is $9,200 and Jaleh's Net Income For Tax Purposes is $11,000. In June of last year, Stanley graduated from a Canadian university with a degree in mathematics. In January, 2007, Stanley began to repay his student loan of $25,000 in monthly installments of $325. Stanley paid $375 in interest related to his student loan in 2007. His only income is $50,000 in net employment income. Helen has employment income of $10,000.

Required: In each Case, calculate Mr. Murphy's Taxable Income and minimum federal Tax Payable.   Ignore any amounts Mr. Murphy might have had withheld or paid in instalments. Indicate any carry forwards available to him and his dependants and the carry forward provisions.

Self Study Problem Six - 2

This is an extension of Self Study Problem Five-6.

Mr. John Barth has been employed for many years as a graphic illustrator in Kamloops, British Columbia. His employer is a large publicly traded Canadian company. During 2007, his gross salary was $82,500. In addition, he was awarded a $20,000 bonus to reflect his outstanding performance during the year. As he was in no immediate need of additional income, he arranged with his employer that none of this bonus would be paid until 2012, the year of his expected retirement.

Other Information:
For the 2007 taxation year, the following items were relevant.

1. Mr. Barth's employer withheld the following amounts from his income:

Federal Income Tax	$16,000
Employment Insurance Premiums	720
Canada Pension Plan Contributions	1,990
United Way Donations	2,000
Registered Pension Plan Contributions	3,200
Payments For Personal Use Of Company Car	3,600

2. During the year, Mr. Barth is provided with an automobile owned by his employer. The cost of the automobile was $27,500. Mr. Barth drove the car a total of 10,000 kilometers during the year, of which only 4,000 kilometers were related to the business of his employer. The automobile was available to Mr. Barth for ten months of the year. During the other two months, he was out of the country and left the automobile with one of the other employees of the corporation.

3. During the year, the corporation paid Mega Financial Planners a total of $1,500 for providing counseling services to Mr. Barth with respect to his personal financial situation.

4. In order to assist Mr. Barth in purchasing a ski chalet, the corporation provided him with a five year loan of $150,000. The loan was granted on October 1 at an interest rate of 3 percent. Mr. Barth paid the corporation a total of $1125 in interest for the year on January 20, 2008. Assume that, at the time the loan was granted, the relevant prescribed rate was 5 percent.

5. Mr. Barth was required to pay professional dues of $1,800 during the year.

6. In 2006, when Mr. Barth exercised his stock options to buy 1,000 shares of his employer's common stock at a price of $15 per share, the shares were trading at $18 per share. When the options were issued, the shares were trading at $12 per share. At the time of exercise, he elected to defer the income inclusion on the stock options. During 2007, the shares were sold at $18 per share.

7. Mr. Barth lives with his wife, Lynda. Lynda is blind and qualifies for the disability tax credit. She has Net Income For Tax Purposes of $1,250.

8. His 22 year old dependent daughter, Marg, is a full time student at the University of British Columbia for 8 months of the year. She lives in Vancouver and has Net Income For Tax Purposes and Taxable Income of $12,400. She had withheld from her employment income EI premiums of $223 [(1.8%)($12,400)] and CPP contributions of $441 [(4.95%)($12,400 - $3,500)]. Mr. Barth paid Marg's tuition for 2007 of $6,300. She has agreed to transfer the maximum credit available to her father.

9. Mr. Barth paid the following medical costs:

For Himself	$ 200
For His Wife	3,550
For Marg	720
Total	$4,470

Required: Calculate, for the 2007 taxation year:

A. Marg's minimum federal Tax Payable and any carry forward amounts available to her at the end of the year.

B. Mr. Barth's minimum Taxable Income and federal Tax Payable (Refund).

Self Study Problem Six - 3

This is an extension of Self Study Case Six-1. It has been updated for 2007 rates.

Ms. Eleanor Trubey's husband died two years ago. After her husband died, she moved from her house in Prince George, B.C., to a rented house in Victoria, B.C.

Ms. Trubey's widowed mother, Marjorie Takarabe, had extremely bad luck the last time she was in Las Vegas. She lost all of her life savings and her house. As a result, she has moved in with Ms. Trubey and takes care of the house, Ms. Trubey's younger daughter, Amy, and all of the household cooking. Marjorie has never filed a tax return and has no Social Insurance Number.

Diane Trubey, Eleanor's older daughter, is studying psychology at McGill University in Montreal. Her field is addiction research with a special emphasis on gambling. She does volunteer work at a gambling addiction treatment centre in Montreal in the summers. As Eleanor has paid for her tuition and living costs, Diane has agreed that any credits available should be transferred to her mother.

Diane has decided not to file a tax return this year as she is too busy with her studies and volunteer work. Her income was earned driving for a client of the addiction treatment centre who had lost his licence after being charged with driving under the influence.

Other information concerning Ms. Trubey for 2007 is as follows:

1. Eleanor was born on May 15, 1959. She lives in Victoria, B.C.

2. She paid instalments of $2,528 for 2007.

3. The birth dates and income for the year of her dependants are as follows:

	Birth Date (Y/M/D)	Annual Income
Diane	1987-05-14	$2,300
Amy	1995-10-11	Nil
Marjorie	1926-05-21	$5,900 (OAS)

4. Eleanor's T4 for 2007 showed the following:

Employment Income	$60,202
Employee's EI Premiums	720
Employee's CPP Contributions	1,990
RPP Contributions	2,406
Pension Adjustment	7,829
Income Tax Deducted	19,408
Union Dues	749
Charitable Donations	175

5. Eleanor and her family had the following medical expenses for 2007:

Patient	Medical Expenses	Description	Amount
Eleanor	Grace Hospital	Ambulance Charge	$ 392
Eleanor	Paramed Home Health	Nursing Care	1,350
Marjorie	Dr. Zhang	Acupuncture	50
Marjorie	Pharmacy	Prescription	75
Diane	Dr. Glassman	Physiotherapist	100
Amy	Walk Right Foot Clinic	Orthotics	450
Amy	Dr. Tamo	Dental	1,120
Total			$3,537

6. In addition to the $175 in charitable contributions withheld by Eleanor's employer, Eleanor and Diane had the following charitable donations for 2007:

Donor	Charitable Donation Receipts	Amount
Eleanor	Heart And Stroke	$ 375
Eleanor	Terry Fox Foundation	50
Diane	Addiction Research Council Of Canada	100

7. Diane's T2202A showed tuition fees of $7,000, full-time attendance for 8 months, and part-time attendance for 2 months.

8. Assume that Eleanor's provincial Tax Payable has been calculated correctly as $2,312.

Required: Calculate Ms. Trubey's minimum balance owing to (refund from) the CRA for 2007.   List any assumptions you have made, and any notes and tax planning issues you feel should be placed in the file.

Self Study Case

Self Study Case Six - 1   (Using ProFile T1 Software For 2006 Tax Returns)

This is extended in Self Study Problem Six-3 to use 2007 rates.   This Case is continued in Chapter 14.

Ms. Eleanor Trubey's husband died two years ago. After her husband died, she moved from her house in Prince George, B.C., to a rented house in Victoria, B.C.

Ms. Trubey's widowed mother, Marjorie Takarabe, had extremely bad luck the last time she was in Las Vegas. She lost all of her life savings and her house. As a result, she has moved in with Ms. Trubey and takes care of the house, Ms. Trubey's younger daughter, Amy, and all of the household cooking. Marjorie has never filed a tax return and has no Social Insurance Number.

Diane Trubey, Eleanor's older daughter, is studying psychology at McGill University in Montreal. Her field is addiction research with a special emphasis on gambling. She does volunteer work at a gambling addiction treatment centre in Montreal in the summers. As Eleanor has paid for her tuition and living costs, Diane has agreed that any credits available should be transferred to her mother.

Diane has decided not to file a tax return this year as she is too busy with her studies and volunteer work. Her income was earned driving for a client of the addiction treatment centre who had lost his licence after being charged with impaired driving.

Information concerning Ms. Trubey for 2006 is given on the following pages.

Required: With the objective of minimizing Ms. Trubey's Tax Payable, prepare the 2006 income tax return of Eleanor Trubey using the ProFile tax software program. List any assumptions you have made, and any notes and tax planning issues you feel should be placed in the file.

Personal Information	
Title	Ms.
First Name	Eleanor
Last Name	Trubey
SIN	527-000-087
Date of birth (Y/M/D)	1958-05-15
Marital Status	Widowed
Provide information to Elections Canada?	Yes
Own foreign property of more than $100,000 Canadian?	No
Instalments paid on March 15 and June 15 of $1,264	$2,528 total for 2006

Taxpayer's Address

1415 Vancouver Street, Victoria, B.C. V8V 3W4
Phone number (250) 363-0120

Dependants	Child 1	Child 2	Mother
First Name	Diane	Amy	Marjorie
Last Name	Trubey	Trubey	Takarabe
SIN	527-000-293	None	None
Date of birth (Y/M/D)	1986-05-14	1994-10-11	1925-05-21
Net income	$2,300	Nil	$5,800

T4	Box	Amount
Issuer - 1750 Canada Inc.		
Employment income	14	60,201.80
Employee's CPP contributions	16	1,910.70
Employee's EI premiums	18	729.30
RPP contributions	20	2,406.16
Pension adjustment	52	7,829.00
Income tax deducted	22	19,408.00
Union dues	44	748.59
Charitable donations	46	175.00

T2202A - (Diane)	Box	Amount
Tuition fees - for Diane Trubey (daughter)	A	7,000
Number of months in school - part-time	B	2
Number of months in school - full-time	C	8

Patient	(Y/M/D)	Medical Expenses	Description	Am't
Eleanor	2006-08-15	Grace Hospital	Ambulance charge	392
Eleanor	2006-08-18	Paramed Home Health	Nursing care	1,350
Marjorie	2006-05-20	Dr. Zhang	Acupuncture	50
Marjorie	2006-07-06	Pharmacy	Prescription	75
Diane	2006-09-01	Dr. Glassman	Physiotherapist	100
Amy	2006-05-11	Walk Right Foot Clinic	Orthotics	450
Amy	2006-01-23	Dr. Tamo	Dental	1,120

Donor	Charitable Donation Receipts	Am't
Eleanor	Heart and Stroke	375
Eleanor	Terry Fox Foundation	50
Diane	Addiction Research Council of Canada	100

Assignment Problems

(The solutions for these problems are only available in
the solutions manual that has been provided to your instructor.)

Assignment Problem Six - 1

All of the following Cases are independent and involve the determination of personal tax credits for the 2007 taxation year. Assume that in all Cases, unless stated differently, the Net Income For Tax Purposes does not include employment income.

1. Ms. Smith is married and has Net Income For Tax Purposes of $123,000, none of which is employment income. Her husband is currently unemployed, but has interest income from investments of $3,750. Her 20 year old dependent son attends university and lives at home. Her son has Net Income For Tax Purposes of $4,800 and does not wish to transfer his tuition, education or textbook credits to her.

2. Ms. Finkly is 66 years old and has Net Income For Tax Purposes of $24,050, . This total is made up of OAS of $5,900, plus pension income of $18,150. Her husband is 51 years old and blind. He has no income of his own.

3. Mr. Saladin has Net Income For Tax Purposes of $72,350, none of which is employment income. He provides full support for his common-law partner and her three children from a previous relationship. The children are aged 13, 15, and 20. The 20 year child is dependent because of a physical disability. However, the disability is not sufficiently severe to qualify for the disability tax credit. Neither the common-law partner nor any of the children have any source of income.

4. Mr. Renaud was divorced two years ago and maintains a residence separate from his former spouse. He has custody of the three children of the marriage, aged 8, 9, and 10 and receives $2,500 per month in child support payments. Mr. Renaud has Net Income For Tax Purposes of $62,300, none of which is employment income. None of the children have any income of their own.

5. Ms. Hill has Net Income For Tax Purposes of $175,000, all of which is employment income. Her employer has withheld and remitted the required EI and CPP amounts. She was married on December 1, 2007. Her new husband is an accounting student with a large firm. His salary for the period January 1 through November 30, 2007 was $33,000. For the month of December, 2007, his salary was $3,000.

6. Mr. Rajit has 2007 Net Income For Tax Purposes of $85,000, none of which is employment income. He lives in a residence that he has owned for many years. He does not currently have a spouse or common-law partner. However, he has custody of his ten year old son who lives with him. Also living with him is his 68 year old, widowed mother. His son had no income during 2007. His mother had OAS benefits and pension income which totaled $14,500 during 2007.

Required: In each of the preceding independent Cases, determine the maximum amount of 2007 personal tax credits, including transfers from a spouse or dependant, that can be applied against federal Tax Payable by the taxpayer.

Assignment Problem Six - 2

Mr. William Norris is 45 years old. The following five independent Cases make varying assumptions for the 2007 taxation year with respect to Mr. Norris' marital status and number of dependants. In all Cases, Mr. Norris earned employment income of $46,000 and his employer withheld the required EI premiums and CPP contributions.

Case A   Mr. Norris is married and his wife, Susan, has employment income of $8,800. Susan's 73 year old mother, Bernice, lives with them. Bernice, an avid skier, had Net Income For Tax Purposes of $14,000 for the year.

Case B   Mr. Norris is married and his wife, Susan, has employment income of $4,410. They have one child, Martha, who is 10 years of age. Martha had no income during the year. During the year, the family had medical expenses as follows:

William	$1,200
Susan	1,600
Martha	350
Total	$3,150

Case C   Mr. Norris is married and his wife, Susan, has employment income of $4,500. They have a son, Allen, who is 19 years old and lives at home. He attends university on a full time basis during 8 months of the year. Mr. Norris pays $4,000 for Allen's tuition and $900 for required textbooks. Allen had employment income during the summer months of $2,200. He will transfer any unused credits to his father.

Case D   Mr. Norris is not married and has no dependants. On receipt of a $300,000 inheritance in December, he donates $50,000 to his local hospital, a registered charity. He chooses to claim $15,000 in 2007. In addition, he makes contributions to federal political parties in the amount of $1,000.

Case E   Mr. Norris is a single father. He has a daughter, Mary, who is 8 years old and lives with him. Mary had no income for the year. Two years ago, Mr. Norris graduated from a Canadian university. He currently has a Canada Student Loan outstanding.

Mr. Norris pays back this loan in monthly instalments of $300. During the year, he paid $450 in interest on this loan.

Required: In each Case, calculate Mr. Norris' minimum federal Tax Payable. In making this calculation, ignore any tax amounts that Mr. Norris might have had withheld or paid in instalments. Indicate any carry forwards available to him and his dependants and the carry forward provisions.

Assignment Problem Six - 3

Mr. Dennis Lane has been a widower for several years. For 2007, both his Net Income For Tax Purposes and Taxable Income were equal to his net employment income of $65,000. Mr. Lane's employer withheld $10,100 in income taxes, $720 for Employment Insurance premiums and $2,025 in Canada Pension Plan contributions. Because of an error by his employer, an overcontribution of $35 was made for the Canada Pension Plan.

Other Information:

1. Mr. Lane made political contributions to federal political parties in the amount of $450.

2. Due to an extensive business trip, Mr. Lane did not file his 2007 return until June 1, 2008.

3. Mr. Lane has three children, aged 10, 12, and 15. They all live with him in his principal residence and, other than his 15 year old son, have no income of their own. Mr. Lane paid no medical expenses other than $4,400 for hospital care for his 15 year old son. His son had 2007 Net Income For Tax Purposes of $8,200. His son did not use the medical expense credit as he had no Tax Payable.

4. His two younger children are enrolled in an eligible fitness program. The annual cost for each child is $425.

5. Mr. Lane's provincial Tax Payable, net of all applicable credits, has been correctly calculated to be $4,250.

6. Assume that the prescribed interest rate for all relevant periods, including the extra 4 percent on amounts owing to the Minister, is 9 percent compounded on an annual basis.

Required: Calculate Mr. Lane's amount owing (refund) for 2007. Include in your solution any penalties and interest that will result from the late filing.

Assignment Problem Six - 4

This is an extension of Assignment Problem Five-12.

For the past five years, Mr. Brooks has been employed as a financial analyst by a large Canadian public firm located in Winnipeg. During 2007, his basic gross salary amounts to $53,000. In addition, he was awarded an $11,000 bonus based on the performance of his division. Of the total bonus, $6,500 was paid in 2007 and the remainder is to be paid on January 15, 2008.

During 2007, Mr. Brooks' employer withheld the following amounts from his gross wages:

Federal Income Tax	$8,000
Canada Pension Plan Contributions	1,990
Employment Insurance Premiums	720
Registered Pension Plan Contributions	2,800
Donations To The United Way	480
Union Dues	240
Payments For Personal Use Of Company Car	1,000

Other Information:

1. Due to an airplane accident while flying back from Thunder Bay on business, Mr. Brooks was seriously injured and confined to a hospital for two full months during 2007. As his employer provides complete group disability insurance coverage, he received a total of $4,200 in payments during this period. All of the premiums for this insurance plan are paid by the employer.

2. Mr. Brooks is provided with a car that the company leases at a rate of $684 per month, including both GST and PST. The company also assumes all of the operating costs of the car and these amounted to $3,500 during 2007. Mr. Brooks drove the car a total of 35,000 kilometers during 2007, 30,000 kilometers of which were carefully documented as employment related travel. While he was in the hospital (see Item 1), the car and its keys were left with his employer.

3. On January 15, 2006, Mr. Brooks received options to buy 200 shares of his employer's common stock at a price of $23 per share. At this time, the shares were trading at $20 per share. Mr. Brooks exercised these options on July 6, 2007, when the shares were trading at $28 per share. He does not plan to sell the shares for at least a year. He was not aware that there is an election to defer the income inclusion on stock options, and did not file the required election.

4. In order to assist Mr. Brooks in acquiring a new personal residence in Winnipeg, his employer granted him a five year loan of $125,000 at an annual interest rate of 4 percent. The loan qualifies as a home relocation loan. The loan was granted on October 1, 2007 and, at this point in time, the interest rate on open five year mortgages was 9 percent. Assume the relevant ITR 4301 rate was 5 percent on this date. Mr. Brooks pays the interest on the loan on January 15, 2008.

5. Other disbursements made by Mr. Brooks include the following:

Advanced financial accounting course tuition fees	$1,200
Music history course tuition fees (University of Manitoba night course)	600
Fees paid to financial planner	300
Payment of premiums on life insurance	642
Payment for eligible public transit passes	860

Mr. Brooks' employer reimbursed him for the tuition fees for the accounting course, but not the music course.

6. Mr. Brooks is a widower. His wife was killed in a car accident in 2005 that injured his 8 year old son, Harold, so badly that he qualifies for the disability tax credit. Mr. Brooks' mother, Grace, lives with Mr. Brooks and cares for Harold. Harold has no Net Income For Tax Purposes. Grace is 67 years old and her only income is OAS payments of $5,900. Grace refused to take any payments for caring for Harold. As a result, Mr. Brooks did not pay any child care or attendant costs for Harold.

7. Mr. Brooks paid the following medical costs:

For Himself	$ 7,300
For Harold	4,450
For Grace	1,220
Total	$ 12,970

The medical expenses for himself included $5,700 for acupuncture treatments for pain from a licenced practitioner while he was confined to the hospital.

Required: Calculate, for the 2007 taxation year, Mr. Brooks' minimum Taxable Income and federal Tax Payable (Refund).

Assignment Problem Six - 5

This is an extension of Assignment Case Six-3. It has been updated for 2007 rates.

Seymour Gravel and Mary Walford have been married for more than 10 years. Mary has progressed quickly in the firm she is working for due to her strong tax and accounting background and has been rewarded with a large bonus in 2007.

Other information concerning Seymour and Mary for 2007 is as follows:

1. Seymour was born on January 29, 1948. Mary was born on December 8, 1969. Their son, William, was born on February 24, 2000. He has no income for 2007. They live in Saint John, New Brunswick.

2. Mary's T4 showed employment income of $152,866. Her withholdings included CPP contributions of $1,990, EI premiums of $720, and charitable donations of $1,000.

3. Seymour has no income for 2007.

4. In addition to the charitable donations withheld by Mary's employer, Seymour donated $500 to the Canadian Cancer Foundation and $250 to the Salvation Army.

5. To help deal with his son, who has been refusing to go to school and is displaying hostile tendencies, Seymour enrolled in a three month course on child psychology at Dalhousie University. His T2202A showed tuition fees of $2,200 and full-time attendance for 3 months.

Required: Calculate Ms. Walford's minimum federal Tax Payable for 2007, without consideration of any income tax withheld.

Assignment Problem Six - 6

This is an extension of Assignment Case Six-2. It has been updated for 2007 rates.

George Hall is a pharmaceutical salesman who has been very successful at his job in the last few years. Unfortunately, his family life has not been very happy. Three years ago, his only child, Anna, was driving a car that was hit by a drunk driver. She and her husband were killed and their 13 year old son, Kevin, was blinded in the accident. He also suffered extensive injuries to his jaw that have required major and prolonged dental work.

George and his wife, Valerie, adopted Kevin. Valerie quit her part-time job to care for him. She also cares for her mother, Joan Parker. Joan suffers from diabetes and severe depression and lives with George and Valerie. Valerie's parents separated two years ago in Scotland after her father, David Parker, suffered enormous losses in the stock market. They were forced to sell their home and David moved to South America. David phones periodically to request that money be deposited in his on-line bank account. Valerie does not meet the residency requirements necessary to qualify for Canadian Old Age Security payments.

George's brother, Martin, completed an alcohol rehabilitation program after being fired for drinking on the job. He is also living with George and Valerie while he is enrolled as a full-time student at the Northern Alberta Institute of Technology. George is paying his tuition and Martin has agreed to transfer the maximum education related credits to George. Although Martin plans to file his 2007 tax return, he has not done so yet.

In addition to George's salary, he also earns commissions. His employer requires him to have an office in his home and has signed Form T2200 each year to this effect.

Other information concerning George for 2007 is as follows:

1. George was born on July 2, 1943 and lives in Edmonton, Alberta.

2. The birthdates and income for the year of his family members are as follows:

	Birth Date (Y/M/D)	Annual Income
Valerie (income from CPP)	1942-12-30	$5,800
Kevin	1991-10-17	Nil
Joan Parker	1922-02-24	500
David Parker	1923-01-12	Nil
Martin	1960-06-02	8,300

3. George's T4 showed employment income of $378,000, which includes employment commissions of $82,000. His withholdings consisted of income tax of $125,000, CPP contributions of $1,990, EI premiums of $720, and charitable donations of $400.

4. Martin's T2202A showed tuition fees of $6,000 and full-time attendance for 8 months.

5. During the year, Valerie donated $1,000 to Mothers Against Drunk Drivers (MADD). George donated $3,000 to the Canadian National Institute For The Blind (CNIB).

6. George and his family had the following medical expenses for 2007:

Patient	Medical Expenses	Description	Amount
George	Johnson Inc.	Out Of Canada Insurance	$ 731
George	Dr. Smith	Dental Fees	155
George	Optician	Prescription Glasses	109
Valerie	Pharmacy	Prescription	67
Joan	Dr. Wong	Psychiatric Counseling	2,050
David	Tropical Disease Centre	Prescription	390
Martin	Dr. Walker	Group Therapy	6,000
Kevin	Dr. Takarabe	Orthodontics and Dental	30,000
Total			$39,502

7. George paid $800 for the care and feeding of Kevin's seeing eye dog, Isis, during 2007.

8. George's home has a total area of 5,000 square feet. The area of the home used as a home office is 650 square feet. Other costs for the home are as follows:

Telephone Line (including high speed internet connection)	$ 620
Hydro	3,200
Insurance - House	4,000
Maintenance And Repairs	3,800
Mortgage Interest	6,200
Mortgage Life Insurance Premiums	400
Property Taxes	6,700
Total	$24,920

9. George purchased a new computer and software that will be used solely in his home office for employment related uses. The computer cost $3,600 and the various software programs cost $1,250.

Required: Calculate Mr. Hall's minimum federal Tax Payable for 2007, without consideration of any income tax withheld. List any assumptions you have made, and any notes and tax planning issues you feel should be placed in the file. Assume that George does not qualify for the GST rebate for employees.

Assignment Cases

Assignment Case Six - 1 (Using ProFile T1 Software For 2006 Tax Returns)

This Case is continued in Chapter 14.

Mr. Buddy Cole (SIN 527-000-061) was born on August 28, 1939. He has spent most of his working life as a pianist and song writer. He and his family live at 1166 West Pender Street, Vancouver, B.C. V6E 3H8, phone (604) 669-7815.

Mr. Cole's wife, Natasha (SIN 527-000-129), was born on June 6, 1981. She and Mr. Cole have four children. Each child was born on April 1 of the following years, Linda; 2001, Larry; 2002, Donna; 2003, and Donald; 2004. Natasha had Net Income For Tax Purposes of $4,800 for 2006. This consisted of $2,400 [(4)($100)(6)] in universal child care benefits and $2,400 in interest income.

Buddy and Natasha Cole have two adopted children. Richard (SIN 527-000-285) was born on March 15, 1989 and has income of $2,800 for the year. Due to his accelerated schooling, he started full time attendance at university in September of 2006 at the age of 17. His first semester tuition fee is $3,000 and he requires books with a total cost of $375. These amounts are paid by Mr. Cole.

The other adopted child, Sarah, was born on September 2, 1986, and is in full time attendance at university for all of 2006 (including a four month summer session). Her tuition is $9,600 and she requires textbooks which cost $750. These amounts are also paid by Mr. Cole. Sarah has no income during the year.

Neither Richard nor Sarah will have any income in the next three years. Any unused credits of either child are available to be transferred to their father.

Mr. Cole's mother, Eunice, was born on April 10, 1919 and his father, Earl, was born on November 16, 1917. They both live with Mr. Cole and his wife. While his father is still physically active, his mother is blind. Eunice Cole had income of $9,500 for the year, while Earl Cole had income of $7,500.

Other information concerning Mr. Cole and his family for 2006 is as follows:

1. Mr. Cole earned $16,500 for work as the house pianist at the Loose Moose Pub. His T4 showed that his employer withheld $4,200 for income taxes and $349 for EI. Due to an error on the part of the payroll accountant, he overpaid his EI by $40. No CPP was withheld.

2. During the year, Mr. Cole made $3,000 in donations to Planned Parenthood Of Canada, a registered Canadian charity.

3. Mr. Cole has been married before to Lori Cole (SIN 527-000-319). Lori is 52 years old and lives in Fort Erie, Ontario.

4. Mr. Cole has two additional children who live with their mother, Ms. Dolly Holt (SIN 527-000-582), in Burnaby, British Columbia. The children are Megan Holt, aged 15 and Andrew Holt, aged 16. Neither child has any income during 2006. While Ms. Holt and Mr. Cole were never married, Mr. Cole acknowledges that he is the father of both children. Although Buddy has provided limited financial aid, the children are not dependent on Buddy for support.

5. Mr. Cole wishes to claim all his medical expenses on a calendar year basis. On December 2, 2006, Mr. Cole paid dental expenses to Canada Wide Dental Clinics for the following individuals:

Himself	$1,200
Natasha (wife)	700
Richard (adopted son)	800
Sarah (adopted daughter)	300
Linda (daughter)	100
Earl (father)	1,050
Lori (ex-wife)	300
Dolly Holt (mother of two of his children)	675
Megan Holt (daughter of Dolly Holt)	550
Total	$5,675

6. Mr. Cole has not applied to receive either OAS or CPP benefits.

Required: With the objective of minimizing Mr. Cole's Tax Payable, prepare his 2006 income tax return using the ProFile tax software program. List any assumptions you have made, and any notes and tax planning issues you feel should be placed in the file.

Assignment Case Six - 2 *(Using ProFile T1 Software For 2006 Tax Returns)*

This is extended in Assignment Problem Six-6 to use 2007 rates. This Case is continued in Chapter 14.

George Hall is a pharmaceutical salesman who has been very successful at his job in the last few years. Unfortunately, his family life has not been very happy. Three years ago, his only child, Anna, was driving a car that was hit by a drunk driver. She and her husband were killed and their 13 year old son, Kevin, was blinded in the accident. He also suffered extensive injuries to his jaw that have required major and prolonged dental work.

George and his wife, Valerie, adopted Kevin. Valerie quit her part-time job to care for him. She also cares for her mother, Joan Parker. Joan suffers from diabetes and severe depression and lives with George and Valerie. Valerie's parents separated two years ago in Scotland after her father, David Parker, suffered enormous losses in the stock market. They were forced to sell their home and David moved to South America. David phones periodically to request that money be deposited in his on-line bank account. Valerie does not meet the residency requirements necessary to qualify for Canadian Old Age Security payments.

George's brother, Martin, completed an alcohol rehabilitation program after being fired for drinking on the job. He is also living with George and Valerie while he is enrolled as a full time student at the Northern Alberta Institute of Technology. George is paying his tuition and Martin has agreed to transfer the maximum tuition and education amounts to George. Although Martin plans to file his 2006 tax return, he has not done so yet.

In addition to George's salary, he also earns commissions. His employer requires him to have an office in his home and has signed the form T2200 each year to this effect.

Other information concerning George for 2006 is given on the following pages.

Required: Prepare the 2006 income tax return of George Hall using the ProFile tax software program. List any assumptions you have made, and any notes and tax planning issues you feel should be placed in the file. Assume that George does not qualify for the GST rebate.

Personal Information	Taxpayer
Title	Mr.
First Name	George
Last Name	Hall
SIN	527-000-509
Date of birth (Y/M/D)	1942-07-02
Marital Status	Married
Provide information to Elections Canada?	Yes
Own foreign property of more than $100,000 Cdn?	No

Taxpayer's Address
97 Jasper Avenue, Apt 10, Edmonton, Alberta   T5J 4C8
Phone number (780) 495-3500

Family Members	Spouse	Child	Mother-In-Law
First Name	Valerie	Kevin	Joan
Last Name	Hall	Hall	Parker
SIN	527-000-483	527-000-517	None
Date of birth (Y/M/D)	1941-12-30	1990-10-17	1921-02-24
Net income	$5,800 in CPP	Nil	$500

Family Members	Father-In-Law	Brother
First Name	David	Martin
Last Name	Parker	Hall
SIN	None	527-000-533
Date of birth (Y/M/D)	1922-01-12	1959-06-02
Net income	Nil	$8,300

T2202A - (Martin)	Box	Amount
Tuition fees - for Martin Hall (brother)	A	6,000
Number of months in school - part-time	B	0
Number of months in school - full-time	C	8

Assignment Cases

T4	Box	Amount
Issuer - Mega Pharma Inc.		
Employment income	14	378,000.00
Employee's CPP contributions	16	1,910.70
Employee's EI premiums	18	729.30
Income tax deducted	22	125,000.00
Employment commissions	42	82,000.00
Charitable donations	46	400.00

Donor	Charitable Donation Receipts	Am't
Valerie	Mothers Against Drunk Drivers (MADD)	1,000
George	Canadian Institute For The Blind (CNIB)	3,000

(Y/M/D)	Patient	Medical Expenses	Description	Am't
2006-12-31	George	Johnson Inc.	Out of Canada insurance	731.30
2006-08-31	George	Dr. Smith	Dental fees	155.40
2006-09-19	George	Optician	Prescription glasses	109.00
2006-11-07	Valerie	Pharmacy	Prescription	66.84
2006-06-07	Joan	Dr. Wong	Psychiatric counseling	2,050.00
2006-03-22	David	Tropical Disease Centre	Prescription	390.00
2006-12-20	Martin	Dr. Walker	Group therapy	6,000.00
2006-10-01	Kevin	Dr. Takarabe	Orthodontics and Dental	30,000.00

George paid $800 for the care and feeding of Kevin's seeing eye dog, Isis, during 2006.

House Costs	
Area of home used for home office (square feet)	650
Total area of home (square feet)	5,000
Telephone line including high speed internet connection	620
Hydro	3,200
Insurance - House	4,000
Maintenance and repairs	3,800
Mortgage interest	6,200
Mortgage life insurance premiums	400
Property taxes	6,700

George purchased a new computer and software that will be used solely in his home office for employment related uses. The computer cost $3,600 and the various software programs cost $1,250.

Assignment Case Six - 3 (Progressive Running Case - Chapter 6 Version Using ProFile T1 Software For 2006 Tax Returns)

This version of the Progessive Running Case is extended in Assignment Problem Six-5 to use 2007 rates.

This Progressive Running Case requires the use of the ProFile tax software program. We have referred to this as a Progressive Running Case (PRC) because more complex versions will be provided in subsequent Chapters.

It is introduced in this Chapter and is continued in Chapters 8 through 14. Each version must be completed in sequence. The information in each version is applicable to all subsequent versions.

Seymour Gravel and Mary Walford are your tax clients. They have been married for two years. In late December, 2006, Mary comes to your office with the tax information for 2006 which she has managed to obtain before the end of the year.

Mary has progressed quickly in MoreCorp, the large, publicly traded firm she is working for due to her strong tax and accounting background. She has been rewarded with a large bonus in 2006. Her firm has an excellent health and dental plan that reimburses 100 percent of all medical expenses.

Although Seymour has been working, his increasing ill health makes it likely that he will not be able to continue to work in 2007. He is contemplating a return to university as a student of music.

In order to estimate her possible financial position in 2007, she would like you to prepare her 2006 tax return assuming that Seymour has no income for 2006. She would also like you to compare her 2006 tax liability in the different provinces assuming Seymour has no income for 2006.

Personal Information	Taxpayer	Spouse
Title	Ms.	Mr.
First Name	Mary	Seymour
Last Name	Walford	Gravel
SIN	527-000-129	527-000-079
Date of Birth (Y/M/D)	1968-12-08	1947-01-29
Marital Status	Married	Married
Provide Information To Elections Canada?	Yes	Yes
Own Foreign Property of More Than $100,000 Cdn?	No	No

Taxpayer's Address
126 Prince William Street, Saint John, N.B.   E2L 4H9
Phone number (506) 636-5997
Spouse's address same as taxpayer? Yes

Assignment Cases

Dependant	Child
First Name	William
Last Name	Gravel
SIN	527-000-319
Date of Birth (Y/M/D)	1998-02-24
Net Income	Nil

T4 - Mary	Box	Amount
Issuer - MoreCorp		
Employment Income	14	152,866.08
Employee's CPP Contributions	16	1,910.70
Employee's EI Premiums	18	729.30
RPP Contributions	20	Nil
Income Tax Deducted	22	48,665.11
Charitable Donations	46	1,000.00

Donor	Charitable Donation Receipts	Amount
Seymour	Canadian Cancer Foundation	500
Seymour	Salvation Army	250

Required:

A. With the objective of minimizing Mary's Tax Payable, prepare, but do not print, her 2006 income tax return using the ProFile tax software program. Assume that Seymour has no income in 2006. **Hint:** On her "Info" page, answer "Yes" to the question in the spousal information box "Is spouse's net income zero?". List any other assumptions you have made and provide any explanatory notes and tax planning issues you feel should be placed in the files.

B. Access and print Mary's summary (Summary on the Form Explorer, not the T1Summary). This form is a two column summary of the couple's tax information. In this version, the second column is blank.

C. Create and print a schedule that compares the total federal and provincial Tax Payable (Refund) for Mary for all the territories and provinces other than Quebec. **Hint:** On the "Info" screen, you can change the province of residence. (You must press the "Enter" key for the change to take effect.) The data monitor at the bottom of the screen should show the new balance/refund. The difference can also be seen on the "Summary" form. To see a detailed analysis of the effect of various changes such as province of residence, use the "Snapshot/Variance" feature (information on this feature is available from the Help menu) to create a separate snapshot of the finished return for Mary. Then open the Auditor <Ctrl+F9> and select the Variance tab.

CHAPTER 7

Capital Cost Allowances And Cumulative Eligible Capital

Capital Cost Allowance System

General Rules

7-1. In Chapter 8, we will give consideration to the calculation of business income as described in Subdivision b of the *Income Tax Act*. As was the case with employment income, business income is based on a group of inclusions and deductions that are combined to arrive at a net income or loss for the taxation year.

7-2. In Subdivision b, ITA 18(1) lays out a group of general limitations with respect to what can be deducted in the determination of net business income. In Paragraph 18(1)(b), it is noted that a taxpayer cannot deduct capital outlays except as expressly permitted in the *Act*. In this same Subdivision, ITA 20(1) provides a list of specific items that can be deducted in the determination of net business income. Paragraph 20(1)(a) notes that taxpayers can deduct such part of the capital cost of property "as is allowed by regulation". Taken together, these two Paragraphs provide the basis for the deduction of the tax equivalent of what financial accountants refer to as amortization. This tax "amortization" is referred to as capital cost allowance (CCA).

7-3. While ITA 20(1)(a) provides the legislative basis for deducting CCA, all of the detailed rules for determining the amounts to be deducted are found in the *Income Tax Regulations* (ITR). More specifically, ITR Part XI lists the items to be included in the various CCA classes, while ITR Schedules II through VI provide the rates for each of these classes.

Tax And Accounting Procedures Compared

Introduction

7-4. There are many similarities between the capital cost allowance system that is used for tax purposes and the amortization procedures that are used by financial accountants. In fact, the general goal of both sets of procedures is to allocate the cost of a depreciable asset to the expenses (deductions) of periods subsequent to its acquisition. However, there are a number of differences that are described in the material which follows.

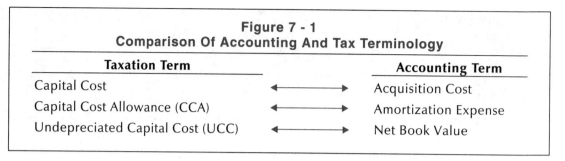

Figure 7 - 1
Comparison Of Accounting And Tax Terminology

Taxation Term		Accounting Term
Capital Cost	←——→	Acquisition Cost
Capital Cost Allowance (CCA)	←——→	Amortization Expense
Undepreciated Capital Cost (UCC)	←——→	Net Book Value

Terminology

7-5.   The two sets of procedures use different terms to describe items that are analogous. While the amounts involved will be different, the underlying concepts are the same. For example, both Undepreciated Capital Cost (UCC) and Net Book Value refer to the original cost of a depreciable asset, less amounts that have been deducted in the calculation of income.

7-6.   However, one difference in the use of the terms is that where Net Book Value at the end of the year is reduced by the amortization expense for the year, UCC is reduced by CCA deducted in preceding years only.   In other words, the December 31, 2007 UCC is not reduced by the 2007 CCA. The 2007 CCA is deducted in the calculation of the January 1, 2008 UCC. A general comparison of these analogous terms is found in Figure 7-1.

7-7.   With respect to dispositions of depreciable assets, the accounting and tax procedures are very different and, as a result, the related terminology cannot be directly compared. For accounting purposes, a disposition will simply result in a gain or loss. For tax purposes, this transaction could result in a capital gain, recapture of CCA, a terminal loss, or no tax effect. There is no real equivalency between these two sets of terminology.

Acquisitions

7-8.   The accounting and tax procedures for acquisitions can be described as follows:

Accounting   In general, accountants record an acquisition cost for each material asset acquired. The acquisition cost that will be recorded in individual asset records is the amount of consideration given up to acquire the asset. This would include all costs directly attributable to the acquisition, including installing it at the relevant location and in the condition necessary for its intended use.

Tax   In general, the capital cost of acquired assets will be allocated to what is referred to as a class. These classes are, in most cases, broadly defined (e.g., Class 10 contains most types of vehicles acquired by an enterprise). The capital cost to be recorded is, with a limited number of exceptions, the same number that would be recorded as the acquisition cost in the accounting records.

Dispositions

7-9.   The accounting and tax procedures for dispositions can be described as follows:

Accounting   For accounting purposes, the Net Book Value of the asset being disposed of is subtracted from the proceeds resulting from that disposition. If the result is positive, a gain is recorded. Alternatively, if the result is negative, a loss is recorded. It would be extremely unusual for a disposition to have no effect on accounting Net Income.

Tax   Tax procedures require that the lesser of the proceeds of disposition and the capital cost of the specific asset be deducted from the UCC balance of its class. While in the majority of cases this procedure will have no current tax consequences, there are several other possibilities. There may be a capital gain, recapture of CCA, or a terminal loss. These more complex concepts will be explained in detail at a later point in this Chapter.   Note that, while CCA is based on classes of assets, for the purpose of dealing with dispositions, records must be kept of the capital cost of each individual asset.

Amortization And Capital Cost Allowance

7-10.   The accounting and tax procedures for allocating the cost of depreciable assets can be described as follows:

Accounting   Accounting amortization is based on the consistent application of generally accepted accounting principles (GAAP). While these principles would encompass a wide variety of methods, including those used for calculating the maximum CCA for tax purposes, the straight-line method is by far the most widely used method for accounting purposes.

Once a method is chosen, it is generally applied to individual assets. The adopted method must be applied consistently, with the full amount that results from its application being charged as an expense in the determination of accounting Net Income for the current period.

Tax   The *Income Tax Regulations* specify the method that must be applied to each class. Two methods are used for this purpose — the straight-line method and the declining balance method. The required method will be applied to the balance in the class to calculate a maximum deduction for the taxation year.

While taxpayers will generally wish to deduct this maximum amount, they are not required to do so. They can deduct all of it, none of it, or any value in between. While the regulations specify consistency in the calculation method used, there is no requirement for year-to-year consistency in the portion of the maximum amount deducted.

7-11.   We have noted that, for accounting purposes, most companies use straight-line amortization. In contrast, the *Income Tax Regulations* require the use of declining balance procedures on the majority of important CCA classes. This results in a situation where the amount of CCA deducted is usually larger than the amount of accounting amortization charged to expense. Because of this, most companies will have accounting values for their depreciable assets that are significantly larger than the corresponding tax values. These differences are referred to as temporary differences and, as many of you are aware, GAAP requires the recording of Future Income Tax Liabilities to reflect these differences.

Additions To Capital Cost

Determination Of Amounts

General Rules

7-12.   To be added to a CCA class, an asset must be owned by the taxpayer and, in addition, it must be used for the purpose of producing income from business, property, and in certain limited circumstances, employment. To qualify for inclusion in a CCA class, the asset must be a capital asset rather than inventory. This means that whether an asset should be added to a CCA class depends on the nature of the business. A drill press is a capital asset for a taxpayer using it in a manufacturing process. However, it would be treated as inventory by a taxpayer in the business of selling that type of equipment.

7-13.   Capital cost means the full cost to the taxpayer of acquiring the property and would include all freight, installation costs, duties, non-refundable provincial sales taxes, legal, accounting, appraisal, engineering, or other fees incurred to acquire the property. Note that, neither GST nor refundable provincial sales taxes (e.g., the Quebec sales tax) would be added to the Capital Cost.

7-14.   In the case of property constructed by the taxpayer for use in producing income, it would include material, labour, and an appropriate allocation of overhead. If the property is paid for in a foreign currency, the Canadian dollar capital cost would be determined using the exchange rate on the date of acquisition.

Capitalization Of Interest

7-15.   In addition to the direct costs described in the two preceding Paragraphs, ITA 21(1) allows a taxpayer to elect to add the cost of money borrowed to acquire depreciable property to its capital cost. This election is in lieu of deducting the interest in the current taxation year and will usually be an undesirable choice.

7-16.   However, if the deduction of the interest in the current year would result in a non-capital loss, this election may be desirable. By adding the interest to the capital cost of the asset, the amount can be deducted as part of the CCA on the asset's class for an unlimited number of future years. Alternatively, if it serves to increase the non-capital loss for the year, it will become part of the loss carry over for the year and would be subject to the time limits that are applicable to business and property loss carry forwards. The carry forward period for such losses is currently 20 years.

Government Assistance

7-17.   Another consideration in determining the capital cost of an addition to a CCA class is government assistance. Under ITA 13(7.1), any amounts received or receivable from any level of government for the purpose of acquiring depreciable assets must be deducted from the capital cost of those assets. This would include grants, subsidies, forgivable loans, tax deductions, and investment tax credits.

7-18.   This tax requirement is consistent with the requirements of Sections 3800 and 3805 of the *CICA Handbook* which, in general, require government assistance, including investment tax credits, to be deducted from the cost of assets for accounting purposes (under Section 3800, an alternative treatment using a deferred charge is also permitted, but not widely used).

Non-Arm's Length Acquisitions

7-19.   If transfers of depreciable property between persons not dealing at arm's length are not made at fair market value, they are subject to very unfavourable tax treatment. This may result in the capital cost of the asset not being equal to the amount of consideration given for the asset. This point is discussed in more detail in Chapter 12 under the heading "Inadequate Considerations".

GST And PST Considerations

7-20.   GST, PST (Provincial Sales Tax), or HST (Harmonized Sales Tax) is usually paid on the acquisition of depreciable assets. Whether or not these amounts will be included in the Capital Cost of depreciable assets will generally depend on whether or not these amounts will be refunded as input tax credits. If they are refunded, they will not be added to the base for calculating CCA deductions. Alternatively, it they are permanent outflows of enterprise resources, they will become deductible as part of the cost of depreciable assets.

7-21.   You may recall from Chapter 4 that only GST, the Quebec sales tax, and the Harmonized Sales Tax (applicable to all of the maritime provinces except Prince Edward Island) are eligible for input tax credits. The sales tax assessed in other provinces are never eligible for input tax credits and, as a consequence, will always be included in Capital Cost.

7-22.   For GST and eligible provincial sales taxes, input tax credits are available on real property in a pro rata amount based on their use in commercial activity. For other types of capital property other than automobiles, input tax credits are 100 percent available when at least 50 percent of their usage is for commercial activity. If the usage is less than 50 percent, no input tax credits are available. To the extent that GST and eligible provincial sales taxes cannot be recovered via input tax credits, they will be included in the Capital Cost of the acquired assets.

7-23.   The treatment of GST and PST for automobiles is complicated by special rules. For passenger vehicles that are included in Class 10.1 (i.e., vehicles with a 2007 cost in excess of $30,000), none of the GST or PST paid on amounts in excess of $30,000 will be eligible for input tax credits. Despite this, these ineligible amounts will not be included in the Capital

Cost of these assets.

7-24. A further complication involves employees, proprietors, and some partners who own a vehicle that is used, at least in part, for employment or business related purposes. As discussed in Chapter 5, these individuals can claim a GST/PST rebate on the automobile CCA deducted as an employment expense for the year. Such individuals will include eligible GST/PST amounts in the Capital Cost of the vehicle. Then, when the rebate is received, usually in the year following the year in which the expenses are deducted and the rebate claimed, it will be deducted from the UCC of the automobile on which the CCA was taken.

Summary

7-25. In reviewing the detailed tax rules applicable to depreciable asset acquisitions, it is clear that these rules will produce capital costs for depreciable assets that are almost always identical to the acquisition costs produced when GAAP is applied. While differences between amortization amounts and the corresponding CCA deductions will cause these values to diverge significantly as the assets are used, the initial amounts recorded for depreciable assets will normally be the same for both accounting and tax purposes.

Available For Use Rules

7-26. For many types of assets, the available for use rules do not present a problem. Most acquired assets are put into use immediately and the acquirer is allowed to deduct CCA in the year of acquisition. For other assets, the rules can make CCA calculations quite complicated. Real estate assets, especially those that require several years to develop, can be particularly hard hit by the fact that there can be a deferral of the right to deduct CCA for two years, or until the structure is considered available for its income producing use.

7-27. The basic rules are found in ITA 13(26) through 13(32). In simplified terms, properties are considered to be available for use, and thereby eligible for CCA deductions, at the earliest of the following times:

- For properties other than buildings, when the property is first used by the taxpayer for the purpose of earning income.
- For buildings, including rental buildings, when substantially all (usually 90% or more) of the building is used for the purpose for which it was acquired.
- The second taxation year after the year in which the property is acquired. This maximum two year deferral rule is also referred to as the rolling start rule.
- For public companies, the year in which amortization is first recorded on the property under generally accepted accounting principles.
- In the case of motor vehicles and other transport equipment that require certificates or licences, when such certificates or licences are obtained.

7-28. The preceding is a very incomplete description of the available for use rules. There are other special rules for particular assets, as well as significant complications in the area of rental properties. Detailed coverage of these rules goes beyond the scope of this text.

Segregation Into Classes
General Rules

7-29. Part XI and Schedules II through VI of the *Income Tax Regulations* provide a detailed listing of classes and rates for the determination of CCA. There are over 40 classes that vary from extremely narrow (Class 26 which contains only property that is a catalyst or deuterium enriched water) to extremely broad (Class 8 contains all property that is a tangible capital asset that is not included in another class). As the applicable rates vary from a low of 4 percent to a high of 100 percent, the appropriate classification can have a significant impact on the amount of CCA that can be taken in future years. This, in turn, has an impact on Taxable Income and Tax Payable.

7-30. Assets do not belong in a class unless they are specifically included in the ITR description of that class. However, there are a large number of classes and, in addition, Class 8 contains a provision for tangible property not listed elsewhere. This means that all tangible assets that have a limited life and are normally considered as capital assets, would have an appropriate classification.

7-31.   For your convenience in working with CCA problems, the Appendix to this Chapter provides an alphabetical list of common assets, indicating the appropriate CCA class as well as the rate applicable to that class.

Separate Classes

7-32.   The general rule is that all of the assets that belong in a particular class are allocated to that class, resulting in a single class containing all of the assets of a particular type. There are, however, a number of exceptions to this general rule that are specified in ITR 1101. Some of these exceptions, for instance the requirement of a separate Class 30 for each telecommunication spacecraft, are not of general importance. However, some of the other exceptions are applicable to a large number of taxpayers. These important exceptions are as follows:

Separate Businesses An individual may be involved in more than one unincorporated business. While the income of all of these businesses will be reported in the tax return of the individual, separate CCA classes will have to be maintained for each business. For example, an individual might own both an accounting practice and a coin laundry. Both of these unincorporated businesses would likely have Class 8 assets. However, a separate Class 8 would have to be maintained for each business.

Rental Properties Of particular significance in the tax planning process is the requirement that each rental property acquired after 1971 at a cost of $50,000 or more be placed in a separate CCA class. When the property is sold, the lesser of the proceeds of disposition and the cost of the asset will be removed from the particular class. This will commonly result in a negative balance in the class and this amount will have to be taken into income by the taxpayer (see later discussion of recapture of CCA). If it were not for the separate class requirement, this result could be avoided by adding other properties to a single rental property class.

Luxury Cars The separate class rules apply to passenger vehicles that have a cost in excess of a prescribed amount. While this prescribed amount is changed periodically, it has been $30,000 from 2001 through 2007.

Elections For the assets described in the preceding three paragraphs, separate classes must be used. The taxpayer has no choice in the matter. There are, however, certain other types of assets (e.g., photocopiers with a cost in excess of $1,000) where the taxpayer has the choice of either allocating each acquired asset to a separate class or, alternatively, grouping all such assets into a single class.

To understand the reasons for making such elections, an understanding of the tax consequences of depreciable asset dispositions is required. Given this, we will defer our discussion of these separate class elections until Paragraph 7-71, which is after we have covered our material on dispositions.

Exercise Seven - 1

Subject: Segregation Into CCA Classes

For each of the following depreciable assets, indicate the appropriate CCA Class. (The Appendix to this Chapter contains a listing of CCA classes.)

- Taxicab
- Manufacturing and processing equipment acquired in 2006
- Franchise with a limited life
- Passenger vehicle with a cost of $120,000
- Water storage tank
- Photocopy machine

- Leasehold improvements
- Rental property acquired in 2002 for $150,000 (Value of land equals $50,000)

End of Exercise. Solution available in Study Guide,

Capital Cost Allowances

General Overview

Methods

7-33.   Once capital assets have been allocated to appropriate classes, these amounts form the base for the calculation of CCA. The maximum CCA is determined by applying a rate that is specified in the Regulations to either the original capital cost of the assets in the class (straight-line classes) or, more commonly, to the end of the period UCC for the class (declining balance classes). The following example will illustrate this difference:

> **Example**   A particular CCA class contains assets with a capital cost of $780,000 and an end of the period UCC balance of $460,000. There have been no additions to the class during the year. The rate for the class is 10 percent.

> **Declining Balance Class**   If we assume that this is a declining balance class, the rate would be applied to the $460,000 end of the period UCC balance. This would result in a maximum CCA for this class of $46,000 [(10%)($460,000)].

> **Straight-Line Class**   If we assume that this is a straight-line class, the rate would be applied to the $780,000 cost of the assets. This would result in a maximum CCA for this class of $78,000 [(10%)($780,000)].

7-34.   This relatively simple process is complicated by the following:

> **Half-Year (a.k.a. First Year) Rules**   For most classes, one-half of any excess of additions for acquisitions over deductions for dispositions to a class for the year must be subtracted prior to the application of the appropriate CCA rate.

> **Class Changes**   When the government wishes to change the rate applicable to certain types of assets, they normally implement this decision by allocating such assets to a new or different class. This means that the same type of asset may be found in more than one class, depending on the year in which it was acquired (e.g., computer hardware acquired before March 23, 2004 is in Class 10 with a 30 percent CCA rate, while computer hardware acquired after March 22, 2004 is in Class 45 with a 45 percent CCA rate).

> **Rental Property CCA Restriction**   In general, taxpayers are not permitted to create or increase a net rental loss by claiming CCA on rental properties. This topic is covered in detail in Chapter 9, Property Income.

March, 2007 Budget Proposals

7-35.   The government appears to believe that CCA rates should reflect the useful lives of the various assets to which they apply. In working towards this objective, the March, 2007 budget proposes several changes. The most important of these are as follows:

> **Buildings Used For Manufacturing And Processing**   These buildings will remain in Class 1 where the applicable rate is 4 percent. However, if they are used 90 percent or more for manufacturing and processing, they will receive an additional allowance of 6 percent, bringing the total rate to 10 percent. This allowance is available on buildings acquired after March 19, 2007. To qualify, each eligible building must be allocated to a separate Class 1.

> **Other Non-Residential Buildings**   These buildings will also remain in Class 1. If they do not meet the 90 percent manufacturing and processing use test, they will

qualify for a special allowance of 2 percent, bringing the total rate to 6 percent. As was the case with buildings used in manufacturing and processing, this allowance is available on buildings acquired after March 19, 2007. Each building must be allocated to a separate Class 1.

Computer Equipment   Computer equipment is currently in Class 45, where it is subject to a 45 percent rate applied to a declining balance. The budget proposes increasing the rate to 55 percent by allocating such assets to a different class. As there is no existing class with a 55 percent rate, this will require the creation of a new class

Manufacturing And Processing Machinery And Equipment   These assets are currently in Class 43, where they are subject to a 30 percent rate applied to a declining balance. For assets acquired after March 19, 2007 and before 2009, the budget proposes increasing this to a 50 percent straight line class. While the Department Of Finance staff could not confirm this, it is likely that this will be implemented by allocating these assets to Class 29. For those of us who have been involved in tax for a number of years, this is "deja vu all over again". Class 29 was used for this equipment prior to 1992.

Rates For Major Classes

7-36.   The following is a brief description of the more commonly used CCA classes, including the items to be added, the applicable rates, and the method to be used:

Class 1 - Buildings (4%)   Class 1 is a 4 percent declining balance class. Most buildings acquired after 1987 are added to this class. If a rental building with a cost of $50,000 or more is involved, it must be allocated to a separate Class 1. This class also includes bridges, canals, culverts, subways, tunnels, and certain railway roadbeds.

As described in Paragraph 7-35, there are additional allowances here for manufacturing and processing buildings and other non-residential buildings.

Class 3 - Buildings Pre-1988 (5%)   Class 3 is a 5 percent declining balance class. It contains most buildings acquired before 1988. As is the case for Class 1 rental properties, separate classes were required for each rental building with a cost of $50,000 or more. This class also includes breakwaters, docks, trestles, windmills, wharfs, jetties, and telephone poles.

The fact that there are two major classes for buildings provides a good example of the government's approach to changing CCA rates. Prior to 1988, most buildings were included in Class 3 where they were subject to a 5 percent declining balance rate. The government concluded that this rate was too high and that it should be lowered to 4 percent. Rather than change the rate on Class 3, they dealt with this problem by indicating that buildings acquired after 1987 should be allocated to Class 1, an existing class which had a rate of 4 percent. The advantage of this approach is that it avoided having to apply the new rate of 4 percent on a retroactive basis to buildings that were acquired before the change took place.

Class 8 - Various Machinery, Equipment, and Furniture (20%)   Class 8 is a 20 percent declining balance class. It includes most machinery, equipment, structures such as kilns, tanks and vats, electrical generating equipment, advertising posters, bulletin boards, and furniture not specifically included in another class. As will be discussed at a later point in the Chapter, individual photocopiers, fax machines, and pieces of telephone equipment purchased for $1,000 or more can be allocated to a separate Class 8 at the election of the taxpayer.

Class 10 - Vehicles (30%)   Class 10 is a 30 percent declining balance class. It includes most vehicles (excluding certain passenger vehicles that are allocated to Class 10.1), automotive equipment, trailers, wagons, contractors' movable equipment, mine railway equipment, various mining and logging equipment, and TV channel converters and decoders acquired by a cable distribution system. Prior to March 23, 2004, computer hardware and systems software were included in this Class. However, these items are now allocated to Class 45 where they are eligible for a higher CCA rate of 45 percent.

Class 10.1 - Luxury Cars (30%)   Class 10.1 is a class established for passenger vehicles with a cost in excess of an amount prescribed in ITR 7307(1)(b). For cars acquired in 2001 through 2007, the prescribed amount is $30,000. Like Class 10, where most other vehicles remain, it is a 30 percent declining balance class. However, each vehicle must be allocated to a separate Class 10.1. Also important is that the amount of the addition is limited to the prescribed amount, thereby restricting the amount of CCA that can be deducted on the vehicle to this same amount. In the year in which the vehicle is retired, one-half of the normal CCA for the year can be deducted, despite the fact that there will be no balance in the class at the end of the year. A further difference is that, in the year of retirement, neither recapture nor terminal losses are recognized for tax purposes.

Class 12 - Computer Software and Small Assets (100%)   Class 12 includes computer software that is not systems software, books in a lending library, dishes, cutlery, jigs, dies, patterns, uniforms and costumes, linen, motion picture films, and videotapes. Dental and medical instruments, kitchen utensils, and tools are included, provided they cost less than $500. This class is subject to a 100 percent write-off in the year of acquisition. As will be noted when we discuss this issue, the half-year rule must be applied to some, but not all, Class 12 assets. When this rule is applicable, the relevant Class 12 assets are effectively subject to a two year write off at 50 percent per year.

Class 13 - Leasehold Improvements (Straight-Line)   In general, only assets that are owned by the taxpayer are eligible for CCA deductions. However, an exception to this is leasehold improvements which are allocated to Class 13. For Class 13, the Regulations specify that CCA must be calculated on a straight-line basis for each capital expenditure incurred. The maximum deduction will be the lesser of:

- one-fifth of the capital cost of the improvement; and
- the capital cost of the lease improvement, divided by the lease term (including the first renewal option, if any).

The lease term is calculated by taking the number of full 12 month periods from the beginning of the taxation year in which the particular leasehold improvement is made until the termination of the lease. For purposes of this calculation, the lease term is limited to 40 years. Note that, in the case of such straight-line classes, the application of the half-year rules (see later discussion) will mean that the maximum CCA in the first and last years will be based on one-half of the straight-line rate.

Class 14 - Limited Life Intangibles (Straight-Line, No Half-Year Rules Apply) Class 14 covers the cost of intangible assets with a limited life. These assets are subject to straight-line amortization over their legal life. IT-477 indicates that CCA should be calculated on a pro rata per diem basis in the year of acquisition and the year of disposition. Because of this pro rata approach, the half-year rules are not applicable to this class. Unless the taxpayer elects to include them in this class, patents are not included (see discussion of Class 44).

Class 43 - Manufacturing and Processing Assets (30%)   Assets acquired before March 20, 2007 were included in Class 43 where the rate is 30 percent applied to a declining balance. As will be discussed in Paragraph 7-77, certain individual manufacturing and processing assets purchased for $1,000 or more can be allocated to a separate Class 43.

As noted in Paragraph 7-35, for manufacturing and processing assets acquired after March 19, 2007 and before 2009, the March, 2007 budget proposes to allocate these assets to a class with a 50 percent straight line rate.

Class 44 - Patents (25%)   At one point in time, patents were allocated to Class 14 where they were amortized over their legal life of 20 years. This approach failed to recognize that the economic life of this type of asset was usually a much shorter period. To correct this problem, patents are now allocated to Class 44, where they are subject to write-off at a 25 percent declining balance rate. Note, however, that a taxpayer can elect to have these assets allocated to Class 14. This would be a useful alternative if a patent was acquired near the end of its legal life.

Class 45 - Computer Hardware And Systems Software (45%)   As noted in the coverage of Class 10, computer hardware and systems software acquired after March 22, 2004 has been moved from Class 10 to Class 45. The rate for this class is 45 percent, applied to a declining balance.

As noted in Paragraph 7-35, the March, 2007 budget proposes to allocate these assets to a new class with a 55 percent declining balance rate.

Half-Year Rules (a.k.a. First Year Rules)
General Rules
7-37.   At one time, a taxpayer was permitted to take a full year's CCA on any asset acquired during a taxation year. This was true even if the asset was acquired on the last day of the year. This was not an equitable situation and the most obvious solution would have been to base CCA calculations on the proportion of a taxation year that the asset was used. Despite the fact that this pro rata approach is widely used for accounting purposes, the government decided that this would be too difficult to implement and an alternative approach was chosen.

7-38.   The approach adopted is based on the arbitrary assumption that assets acquired during a particular taxation year were in use for one-half of that year. Stated simply, in determining the end of period UCC for the calculation of maximum CCA, one-half of the excess, if any, of the additions to UCC for acquisitions over the deductions from UCC for dispositions is removed. This adjustment is only made when the net amount is positive.

7-39.   The following example is a simple illustration of the half-year adjustment for additions to most CCA classes. It has not been complicated by the presence of capital gains, recapture of CCA, or terminal losses.

Example   Radmore Ltd., with a taxation year that ends on December 31, has a Class 10 (30 percent) UCC balance on January 1, 2007 of $950,000. During 2007, it acquires 15 cars at a cost of $20,000 each, for a total addition of $300,000, and disposes of 18 cars for total proceeds of $144,000. In no case did the proceeds of disposition exceed the capital cost of the vehicle being retired. The maximum CCA for 2007 and the January 1, 2008 UCC balance are calculated as follows:

January 1, 2007 UCC Balance		$ 950,000
Add: Acquisitions During The Year	$300,000	
Deduct: Dispositions During The Year	(144,000)	156,000
Deduct: One-Half Net Additions [(1/2)($156,000)]		(78,000)
Base Amount For CCA Claim		$1,028,000
Deduct: 2007 CCA [(30%)($1,028,000)]		(308,400)
Add: One-Half Net Additions		78,000
January 1, 2008 UCC Balance		$ 797,600

Exceptions

7-40. There are some classes, or parts of classes, to which the half-year rules do not apply. For the classes that we have described in this Chapter, the exceptions are as follows:

- All assets included in Class 14 (limited life intangibles).

- Some Class 12 assets such as medical or dental tools costing less than $500, uniforms, and chinaware. Other Class 12 assets such as certified Canadian films, computer software, and rental video cassettes, are subject to the half-year rules.

7-41. A further exception is available for some property transferred in non-arm's length transactions. Specifically, depreciable property acquired in non-arm's length transactions is generally exempt from the half-year rule if, prior to the transfer, the property was depreciable property that was owned for at least one year. The property remains in the CCA class that it was in prior to its transfer. This prevents the double application of this rule in situations where there is no real change in the ownership of the property (e.g., the transfer of a depreciable asset from an unincorporated business to a corporation controlled by the owner of the unincorporated business).

Exercise Seven-2

Subject: CCA Error

During 2007, your company acquired a depreciable asset for $326,000 and your accountant included this asset in Class 1 at the end of the year. Early in 2008, you discover that the asset should have been allocated to Class 10. What was the impact of this error on your 2007 deductions from business income?

Exercise Seven-3

Subject: Class 13 And Half Year Rule

Vachon Ltd. leases its office space under a lease that was signed on January 1, 2002. The lease term is 10 years, with an option to renew at an increased rent for an additional five years. In 2002, the Company spends $52,000 renovating the premises. In 2007, changing needs require the Company to spend $31,000 renovating the space. Determine the maximum amount of Class 13 CCA that the Company can deduct for 2007.

Exercise Seven-4

Subject: Class 8 And Half Year Rule

Justin Enterprises, an unincorporated business, has a Class 8 UCC balance on January 1, 2007 of $212,000. During 2007, it acquires additional Class 8 assets at a cost of $37,400. Also during 2007, it deducts $18,300 from the UCC balance for dispositions. Determine the maximum CCA for 2007 and the January 1, 2008 UCC balance.

End of Exercises. Solutions available in Study Guide.

Short Fiscal Periods

7-42. The previous material noted that a half-year assumption has been built into the capital cost allowance system to deal with assets that are acquired or disposed of during a given taxation year. In contrast to this somewhat arbitrary provision for dealing with part year ownership, a more precise rule has been included in the Regulations for dealing with short fiscal periods.

7-43.   In the first or last years of operation of a business, or in certain other types of situations that will be covered in later chapters, a taxation year with less than 365 days may occur. Under these circumstances, the maximum CCA deduction for most classes must be calculated using a proration based on the relationship between the days in the actual fiscal year and 365 days.

7-44.   For example, assume that a business with a taxation year that ends on December 31 begins operations on November 1. On December 1, $100,000 of Class 8 assets (20 percent declining balance) are purchased.   There are no further additions or dispositions in December. The CCA for the first fiscal year, taking into consideration the half-year rules, would be calculated as follows:

$$[(1/2)(20\%)(\$100,000)(61/365)] = \underline{\$1,671}$$

7-45.   As is illustrated in the preceding calculation, the half-year rules also apply in these short fiscal period situations. Note it is the length of the taxation year for the business, not the period of ownership of the asset, which determines the proration.

7-46.   Two additional points are relevant here:

- As noted previously, Class 14 assets are subject to pro rata CCA calculations, based on the number of days of ownership in the year. This obviates the application of the short fiscal period rules.

- When an individual uses assets to produce property income (e.g., rental income), the full calendar year is considered to be the taxation year of the individual. This means that the short fiscal period rules are not applicable in these situations.

Exercise Seven-5

Subject: Short Fiscal Periods

Olander Inc. is incorporated on August 1, 2007. On September 15, 2007, the Company acquires $115,000 in Class 8 assets. The Company has a December 31 year end and no other depreciable assets are acquired before December 31, 2007. Determine the maximum CCA for the year ending December 31, 2007.

End of Exercise. Solution available in Study Guide.

Tax Planning Considerations

7-47.   As previously noted, the tax rules on capital cost allowances are expressed in terms of maximum amounts that can be deducted. There is, however, no minimum amount that must be deducted, and this leaves considerable discretion as to the amount of CCA to be taken in a particular year. In fact, under certain circumstances, a taxpayer is even allowed to revise the CCA for the previous taxation year. This can, in effect, create a "negative" CCA for the current year. The guidelines for this type of amendment are found in IC 84-1. Note, however, that a revision of CCA for a previous year is only permitted if there is no change in the Tax Payable of any year.

7-48.   If the taxpayer has Taxable Income and does not anticipate a significant change in tax rates in future years, tax planning for CCA is very straightforward. The optimum strategy is to simply take the maximum CCA allowed in order to minimize Taxable Income and Tax Payable.

7-49.   The situation becomes more complex in a loss year. If a taxpayer wishes to minimize a loss for tax purposes, one approach is to reduce the amount of CCA taken for the year (whether or not the taxpayer will wish to minimize a loss is affected by the loss carry over provisions that are discussed in Chapter 14). In these circumstances, it is necessary to decide on which class or classes the CCA reduction should be applied.

7-50.   The general rule is that CCA reductions should be allocated to the classes with the highest rates, while taking full CCA on those classes with the lowest rates.

Example   A taxpayer wishes to reduce CCA by $100,000 in order to eliminate a loss and has the choice of reducing Class 1 CCA (4 percent) or Class 10 CCA (30 percent) by the required $100,000.

Analysis   If the full CCA is taken on Class 1, the following year's maximum CCA will be reduced by only $4,000 (4 percent of $100,000). In contrast, taking the full $100,000 CCA on Class 10 would reduce the following year's maximum CCA by $30,000 (30 percent of $100,000). It would clearly be preferable to take the full CCA on Class 1 and take $100,000 less CCA on Class 10, so that the following year's CCA can be maximized, if needed.

7-51.   Similar opportunities arise when current tax rates are below those expected in the future. For example, some provinces institute periodic tax holidays for certain types of businesses. As taxes will be applied in future years, it may be advantageous to stop taking CCA in order to maximize Taxable Income during the years of tax exemption.

Exercise Seven-6

Subject: CCA And Tax Planning

Monlin Ltd. has determined that, for the current year, it has Taxable Income before the deduction of CCA of $45,000. It is the policy of the Company to limit CCA deductions to an amount that would reduce Taxable Income to nil. At the end of the year, before the deduction of CCA, the following UCC balances are present:

Class 1	$426,000
Class 8	126,000
Class 10	89,000
Class 10.1	21,000

There have been no additions to these classes during the year. Which class(es) should be charged for the $45,000 of CCA that will be required to reduce Taxable Income to nil? Explain your conclusion.

End of Exercise. Solution available in Study Guide.

Dispositions Of Depreciable Assets

General Rules

7-52.   Prior to this point in the Chapter we have used terms such as recapture of CCA, capital gains, and terminal losses without providing a full explanation of their meaning. As these terms relate to the disposition of capital assets, a discussion of their meaning has been deferred until we deal here with the procedures related to dispositions.

7-53.   In most cases, when an enterprise disposes of a depreciable asset, the proceeds of disposition will be less than the original cost of the asset, and less than the UCC balance in the class. Further, there will often be other assets left in the class. In such situations, the rules related to dispositions can be simply stated:

Simple Dispositions   The proceeds of disposition will be subtracted from the UCC of the class, resulting in a reduction in this balance. There will be no immediate tax consequences resulting from this transaction. However, the reduced UCC balance will result in a reduced maximum CCA in current and future years.

7-54.   This is in contrast to the accounting procedures where the net book value of the individual asset is subtracted from the proceeds of disposition, a process which will almost invariably result in an accounting gain or loss.

7-55.   There are situations, however, where the disposition of a depreciable asset will have immediate tax consequences. In terms of the resulting tax consequences, these situations can be described as follows:

Capital Gain   A capital gain will arise on the disposition of a depreciable asset if the proceeds of disposition exceed the capital cost of the asset. Note that a capital loss cannot occur, under any circumstances, on the disposition of a depreciable asset.

Recapture Of CCA   Subtraction of the proceeds of disposition from the UCC may result in the creation of a negative balance in the class. This can occur whether or not there are any assets left in the class. If this negative balance is not eliminated by new acquisitions prior to the end of the taxation year, this negative amount must be included in income as recapture of CCA. The amount will also be added to the UCC for the class, thereby restoring the balance to nil for the beginning of the next year.

Terminal Loss   This occurs only when there are no assets left in the class at the end of the year. If, when the proceeds from the disposition of the last asset(s) are deducted from the UCC for the class, a positive balance remains, this balance can be deducted as a terminal loss. Note that it is not a capital loss. A terminal loss is 100 percent deductible against any other income. The amount of the terminal loss will also be deducted from the UCC for the class, thereby leaving the balance at nil.

7-56.   These situations will be described in more detail in the material that follows.

Capital Gains

7-57.   The tax rules related to capital gains are fairly complex and will be covered in detail in Chapter 10. However, in order to fully understand the tax procedures related to dispositions of depreciable assets, some understanding of this component of Net Income For Tax Purposes is required. The basic idea is that, if a capital asset is sold for more than its capital cost, the excess of the proceeds of disposition over the capital cost of the asset is a capital gain. As many of you are aware, only one-half of this gain will be included in the taxpayer's Net Income For Tax Purposes.

7-58.   The more important point to remember when calculating CCA is that this excess amount will not be deducted from the UCC. When the proceeds of disposition exceed the capital cost of the asset, the amount deducted from the UCC on the disposition is limited to its capital cost. This leads to a more general statement on the procedure to be used when there is a disposition of a depreciable asset:

General Rule For Dispositions   When there is a disposition of a depreciable asset, the amount to be deducted from the UCC is the lesser of:

- the proceeds of disposition; and
- the capital cost of the individual asset.

7-59.   As an example of this type of situation, consider the disposition of a Class 8 asset with an original cost of $20,000. If it was sold for $25,000, only $20,000 would be deducted from the Class 8 UCC. The $5,000 excess would be treated as a capital gain. In the usual situation, there would be additional assets in Class 8 and the class would continue to have a positive balance. This would mean that there would not be recapture of CCA, or a terminal loss.

7-60.   You should note that, while CCA and UCC amounts are based on class amounts rather than values for individual assets, it is still necessary to track the cost of individual assets so that the appropriate amount can be deducted from the UCC when there is a disposition.

Recapture Of Capital Cost Allowance

7-61.   Recapture of capital cost allowance refers to situations in which a particular class contains a negative, or credit, balance at the end of the taxation year. As previously described, the UCC ending balance for a particular class is calculated by starting with the opening balance of the class, adding the cost of acquisitions, and subtracting the lesser of the proceeds of disposition and the capital cost of any assets sold (CCA is subtracted at the beginning of the following taxation year). If the disposal subtraction exceeds the balance in the class, a negative balance will arise.

7-62.   Note, however, that a disposition that creates a temporary negative balance at some point during the year does not create recapture. If additions to the class that are made later in the year eliminate this negative balance prior to year end, no recapture will have to be included in income.

7-63.   It is important to note that acquiring additional assets of a particular class will not eliminate negative balances in those situations where each individual asset has to be allocated to a separate class (e.g., rental buildings costing $50,000 or more). As was intended by policy makers, when individual assets must be allocated to separate classes, a disposition that creates a negative balance at any time during the taxation year will result in recapture.

7-64.   Recapture of CCA arises when deductions from the class exceed additions and this generally means that the proceeds of the dispositions, when combined with the CCA taken, exceed the cost of the assets added to the class. In effect, recapture is an indication that CCA has been deducted in excess of the real economic burden of using the assets (cost minus proceeds of disposition). As a reflection of this situation, ITA 13(1) requires that the recaptured CCA be added back to income. The recapture amount is also added to the UCC balance, leaving a balance of nil at the beginning of the next taxation year.

Exercise Seven-7

Subject: Recapture of CCA

At the beginning of 2007, Codlin Inc. has two assets in Class 8. The cost of each asset was $27,000 and the Class 8 UCC balance was $24,883. On June 30, 2007, one of the assets was sold for $28,500. There are no other additions or dispositions prior to the Company's December 31, 2007 year end. What is the effect of the disposition on the Company's 2007 net business income? In addition, determine the January 1, 2008 UCC balance.

End of Exercise. Solution available in Study Guide.

Terminal Losses

7-65.   When the last asset in a class is sold, the proceeds are deducted from the class in the usual manner. If the resulting UCC balance is negative, the negative amount will be recapture. However, it is also possible for this final asset retirement to leave a positive balance in the class. Such a balance creates a terminal loss.

7-66.   The presence of a positive balance subsequent to the sale of the last asset in the class is an indication that the taxpayer has deducted less than the full cost of using the assets in this class. Under these circumstances, ITA 20(16) allows this terminal loss to be deducted in full. The terminal loss is also deducted from the UCC balance, leaving a balance of nil at the beginning of the next taxation year. Note that this is not a capital loss. While it is possible to have capital gains on assets that are subject to CCA, it is not possible to have a capital loss on the disposition of a depreciable asset.

7-67.   A terminal loss occurs only when there are no assets in the class at the end of the period. If there is a positive balance in the class at some point during the year, but no assets in the class, there is no terminal loss if additional assets are acquired prior to the end of the year.

7-68.   An additional point here relates to employment income. While employees can deduct CCA on automobiles and aircraft and are subject to the usual rules with respect to recapture, IT-478R2 indicates that terminal losses cannot be deducted on such assets. The reason for this position is that ITA 8(2) indicates that employees can only deduct items that are listed in ITA 8. As terminal losses are not covered by this Section, no deduction is available.

Exercise Seven-8

Subject: Terminal Losses

At the beginning of 2007, Codlin Inc. has two assets in Class 8. The cost of each asset was $27,000 and the Class 8 UCC balance was $24,883. On June 30, 2007, both of these assets are sold for a total of $18,000. There are no other additions or dispositions prior to the Company's December 31, 2007 year end. What is the effect of the disposition on the Company's 2007 net business income? In addition, determine the January 1, 2008 UCC balance.

Exercise Seven-9

Subject: Depreciable Asset Dispositions

Norky Ltd. disposes of a Class 8 asset for proceeds of $126,000. The capital cost of this asset was $97,000 and it had a net book value of $43,500. The Company's Class 8 contains a number of other assets and the balance for the Class prior to this disposition was $2,462,000.   Describe briefly the accounting and tax treatments of this disposition.

End of Exercises. Solutions available in Study Guide.

CCA Schedule

7-69.   At this point, it is useful to summarize the CCA calculations in a schedule. A commonly used format is illustrated in the following example.

Example   The fiscal year end of Blue Sky Rentals Ltd. is December 31. On January 1, 2007, the UCC balance for Class 8 is $155,000. During the year ending December 31, 2007, $27,000 was spent to acquire Class 8 assets. During the same period, used Class 8 assets were sold for $35,000. The capital cost of these assets was $22,000.

UCC Of The Class At The Beginning Of The Year		$155,000
Add: Acquisitions During The Year	$27,000	
Deduct: Dispositions During The Year - Lesser Of:		
• Capital Cost = $22,000		
• Proceeds Of Disposition = $35,000	(22,000)	5,000
Deduct: One-Half Net Additions [(1/2)($5,000)] (Note)		(2,500)
Base Amount For CCA Claim		$157,500
Deduct: CCA For The Year [(20%)($157,500)]		(31,500)
Add: One-Half Net Additions		2,500
UCC Of The Class At The Beginning Of The Subsequent Year		$128,500

Note   This adjustment for one-half of the excess of additions over disposal deductions is only made when the net amount is positive.

CCA Determination - Special Situations

Separate Class Election

The Problem

7-70.   In our discussion of CCA procedures we noted that, in general, all assets of a particular type must be allocated to a single CCA class. However, we also noted that there were a number of exceptions to this general approach. For certain specified assets, for example, rental properties with a cost in excess of $50,000, the *Income Tax Regulations* require that a separate class be used for each individual asset.

7-71.   As a further point, we noted that for certain other types of assets, the taxpayer could elect to use a separate CCA class for each individual asset. Now that you have an understanding of the procedures associated with dispositions of depreciable assets, we can meaningfully discuss the reasons for making such an election.

7-72.   Consider a $25,000 colour photocopier that would normally be allocated to Class 8. Over the first two years of the asset's life, CCA would be calculated as follows:

Year One [(20%)(1/2)($25,000)]	$2,500
Year Two [(20%)($25,000 - $2,500)]	4,500
Total CCA	$7,000

7-73.   Given the rate of technological change in this area, it is possible that this photocopier would be replaced after two years. Further, the value of the old photocopier would likely be relatively small. If this was the only Class 8 asset owned by the taxpayer, the balance in this class would be $18,000 ($25,000 - $7,000). If the photocopier was disposed of for proceeds of $5,000, there would be a terminal loss equal to $13,000 ($18,000 - $5,000).

7-74.   There are two problems with this analysis:

• Most businesses will own more than one asset that is allocated to Class 8. The disposition will leave other assets in the class and no terminal loss can be recognized.

• Even if the photocopier is the only Class 8 asset, if the photocopier is replaced, the replacement will likely be acquired within the same taxation year, again resulting in a situation where no terminal loss can be recognized because there are remaining assets in the class.

7-75.   The election to allocate this photocopier to a separate Class 8 balance alleviates these problems. When the photocopier is retired, a terminal loss can be recognized, even if the business replaces it prior to year end or has other Class 8 assets.

Eligible Assets

7-76.   There are a number of high tech or electronic products that are normally included in Class 8 (20 percent declining balance) or Class 10 (30 percent declining balance) that have actual service lives that are significantly shorter than the rates applicable to those classes would imply. Under ITR 1101(5p), some of these assets are eligible for separate class treatment. The following assets are eligible, provided they have a capital cost of $1,000 or more:

• computer equipment and software (Classes 10 and 12, but not Class 45)
• photocopiers (Class 8)
• electronic communications equipment, such as a facsimile transmission device or telephone equipment (Class 8)

7-77.   In recognition of the fact that certain types of manufacturing equipment have unusually short economic lives, ITR 1101(5s) allows taxpayers to allocate individual Class 43 assets to separate classes, provided they have a cost in excess of $1,000. While there is no specification of the Class 43 assets that are eligible for this treatment, it would be assumed that the election would only be made for manufacturing assets with relatively short lives.

7-78.   As noted in our earlier discussion, the purpose of this separate class election is to provide for the recognition of terminal losses on the disposition of certain short-lived assets. Under the usual single class procedures, such recognition is not usually possible, either because there are assets remaining in the particular CCA class, or because the retired assets are being replaced on a regular and ongoing basis.

Exercise Seven-10

Subject: Separate Class Election

In January, 2007, Edverness Inc. acquires 10 photocopiers at a cost of $20,000 each. In December, 2007, two of these photocopiers are traded in on faster machines with more features. The new photocopiers cost $22,000 each, and the Company receives a trade-in allowance for each old machine of $3,000. Indicate the amount(s) that would be deducted from 2007 business income if no election is made to put each photocopier in a separate class. Contrast this with the deduction(s) that would be available if the separate class election is used.

End of Exercise.   Solution available in Study Guide.

Special Rule For Buildings

7-79.   For dispositions of buildings, a special rule applies. If a building is the last asset in its class, its disposal will commonly result in a terminal loss on the building, combined with a capital gain on the land. There is concern with respect to the possibility that the total proceeds will be allocated in a manner that maximizes the terminal loss on the building (100 percent deductible), while minimizing the capital gain on the land (one-half taxable).

Example   Martin Ltd. has only one Class 1 building. During 2007, the Company disposes of the building and replaces it with a leased property. The following information relates to this disposition:

Proceeds Of Disposition (Fair Market Value):	
Land	$300,000
Building	110,000
Total Proceeds Of Disposition	**$410,000**
Adjusted Cost Base Of Land	$200,000
Original Cost Of Building	175,000
UCC Class 1	150,000

Analysis - No Special Rule   In the absence of the special rules, there would be a $50,000 taxable capital gain on the land [(1/2)($300,000 - $200,000)]. There would also be a $40,000 ($150,000 - $110,000) terminal loss on the building. The inclusion in Net Income For Tax Purposes would be $10,000 ($50,000 - $40,000).

Analysis - Special Rule   ITA 13(21.1)(a) modifies these results in situations where the proceeds of disposition for a building are less than the UCC for its class. The goal of this provision is to prevent the recognition of a terminal loss on the building that could be used to offset a capital gain on the land.

In such situations, ITA 13(21.1)(a) requires deemed proceeds of disposition for the building to be determined as follows:

The Lesser Of:

- The FMV of the land and building $410,000
  Reduced By The Lesser Of:
  - The ACB of the land = $200,000
  - The FMV of the land = $300,000   (200,000) $210,000

- The Greater Of:
  - The FMV of the building = $110,000
  - The Lesser Of:
    The cost of the building = $175,000
    The UCC of the building = $150,000 $150,000

7-80.   In this case, the proceeds that would be allocated to the building would be $150,000, leaving $260,000 ($410,000 - $150,000) to be allocated to the land. The net result is that the $40,000 terminal loss is completely eliminated and the capital gain is reduced by a corresponding amount to $60,000 ($260,000 - $200,000). The taxable amount of $30,000 [($60,000)(1/2)] would be included in the taxpayer's income instead of $10,000.

7-81.   If the potential capital gain had been less than the potential terminal loss, the terminal loss would have been reduced by the amount of the potential capital gain and the capital gain would have been eliminated.

Exercise Seven-11

Subject: Building Dispositions

On February 24, 2007, Drucker Ltd. disposed of a piece of real estate for total proceeds of $1,250,000. Relevant information with respect to this property is as follows:

Original cost of building	$930,000
UCC Class 1 (Building - only asset in class)	615,000
Fair market value of building on February 24, 2007	500,000
Adjusted cost base of land	425,000
Fair market value of land on February 24, 2007	750,000

Determine the tax consequences of this disposition.

End of Exercise.   Solution available in Study Guide.

Deferral Provisions On Replacement Property
The Problem
7-82.   The disposition of a capital property can give rise to capital gains and, in the case of depreciable capital property, recapture of CCA. In certain situations, such dispositions are unavoidable, with the related income inclusions creating significant financial problems for the taxpayer.

7-83.   For example, if an enterprise has its major plant building destroyed in a fire, the building will commonly be insured for its replacement cost. As this replacement cost will usually be higher than the original capital cost of the building, the disposition will often result in both capital gains and recapture of CCA. Payment of taxes on these amounts can significantly erode the insurance proceeds, to the point where it may be difficult for the taxpayer to replace the destroyed property.

7-84.   Given this situation, the government has concluded that it is appropriate to provide tax relief when such events occur. In simple terms, any capital gain or recapture resulting from these dispositions can be, within certain limits, removed from income, provided the assets are replaced within a specified period of time. The removal of these items from income is accompanied by a corresponding reduction in the capital cost and UCC of the replacement assets. This, in effect, defers these income inclusions until the replacement assets are sold or used.

7-85.   With respect to recapture of CCA, the relevant provisions are contained in ITA 13(4). These provisions will be discussed in this Chapter. With respect to capital gains, the corresponding provisions are found in ITA 44. This material will be discussed in Chapter 10, after our more general discussion of taxable capital gains and allowable capital losses.

7-86.   When the replacement of the assets takes place in the same taxation year as the disposition, the application of the provisions relating to recapture of CCA is relatively simple. As the cost of the replacement assets will be added to the UCC of the class before the end of the year in which the disposition took place, there will usually be a positive balance in the class at this time and dealing with recapture is not an issue. In this type of situation, no special provision is required.

7-87.   However, when the replacement takes place in a subsequent taxation year, any recapture resulting from the disposition will have to be included in income in the year of disposition. However, if the replacement takes place within a specified period of time, ITA 13(4) provides for a reversal of this income inclusion through an amended return for the year of disposition. This amended return will normally result in a refund of taxes applicable to the year of disposition.

7-88.   As a final point, it should be noted that ITA 13(4) is applicable only if an election is filed. It does not apply automatically and, if the taxpayer fails to make the election, the result can be a significant increase in Tax Payable in the year of disposition.

Voluntary And Involuntary Dispositions

7-89.   There are two types of situations for which ITA 13(4) provides relief. They can be described as follows:

Involuntary Dispositions   This description is used to describe dispositions of depreciable property resulting from theft, destruction, or expropriation under statutory authority. In the case of this type of disposition, the relieving provisions cover all types of depreciable property. In addition, these provisions are available as long as the replacement occurs within 24 months after the end of the year in which the disposition took place.

Voluntary Dispositions   As the name implies, these are voluntary dispositions, usually involving the relocation of a business. As a relocation may involve a disposition, taxpayers undergoing a move may encounter problems similar to those experienced when there is an involuntary disposition. In these voluntary dispositions, the applicability of ITA 13(4) is more limited.

Specifically, this provision only applies to "former business property", a term that is defined in ITA 248 to consist, in general, of real property. Also included in some circumstances would be a franchise, concession or license for a limited period that is wholly attributable to the carrying on of a business. This means that assets other than those specified in the ITA 248 definition (e.g., equipment, furniture and fixtures) will not benefit from this provision. A further difference here is that the replacement must occur within 12 months after the year in which the disposition took place for the relieving provision to be available.

7-90.   For dispositions meeting the conditions described above, an election under ITA 13(4) provides for a reversal of the unfavourable tax consequences that occurred in the year of disposition.

Example

7-91.   A simple example will serve to illustrate the application of ITA 13(4). Since the insurance proceeds are less than the original cost of the building, no capital gain arises on this disposition. As a result, the ITA 44 provisions that allow a deferral of a capital gain are not relevant in this situation.

Example A company's only building is destroyed in a fire in February, 2006. The original cost of the building was $2,500,000, the fair market value is $2,225,000, and it is an older building with a UCC of only $275,000. The insurance proceeds, all of which are received in 2006 prior to the December 31 year end, equal the fair market value of $2,225,000. The replacement building is completed in July, 2007 at a cost of $3,000,000.

Analysis Deducting $2,225,000, the lesser of the proceeds of disposition and the capital cost of the building, from the UCC of $275,000 will leave a negative balance of $1,950,000. As there is no replacement of the asset during 2006, this negative balance will remain at the end of this year, resulting in recapture of CCA. This amount will have to be included in income for the 2006 taxation year and will be added back to the UCC, reducing the class balance to nil.

In 2007, the year in which the replacement occurs, the ITA 13(4) election provides for an alternative calculation of the 2006 recapture as follows:

January 1, 2006 UCC Balance		$275,000
Deduction:		
Lesser Of:		
• Proceeds Of Disposition = $2,225,000		
• Capital Cost = $2,500,000	$2,225,000	
Reduced By The Lesser Of:		
• Normal Recapture = $1,950,000		
• Replacement Cost = $3,000,000	(1,950,000)	(275,000)
Recapture Of 2006 CCA (Amended)		**Nil**

7-92. IT-259R4 indicates that the election, including the relevant calculations, should be made in the form of a letter attached to the tax return in 2007, the year of replacement. In this example, the election would result in a $1,950,000 reduction in the company's 2006 Net Income For Tax Purposes and would provide the basis for a tax refund.

7-93. The $1,950,000 reduction of the deduction in the preceding calculation will have to be subtracted from the UCC of the replacement asset, as deemed proceeds of disposition, leaving a balance of $1,050,000 ($3,000,000 - $1,950,000). This $1,050,000 balance reflects the economic substance of the events in that it is made up of the original UCC of $275,000, plus the $3,000,000 cost of the new building, less the $2,225,000 received from the company's insurer.

7-94. Note that the reversal of recapture is limited to the cost of the replacement property. In our example, if the cost of the replacement property had only been $1,800,000, this amount would have been the limit on the recapture reversal and the remaining $150,000 [$275,000 - ($2,225,000 - $1,800,000)] would have remained in 2006 income. In this case, the UCC of the replacement building would be nil ($1,800,000 - $1,800,000).

Exercise Seven-12

Subject: Involuntary Disposition

During 2006, the only building owned by Foran Inc. is destroyed by a meteorite. Its original cost was $1,500,000, its fair market value was $1,400,000, and the Class 1 UCC was $650,000. The Company receives $1,400,000 in insurance proceeds during 2006 and replaces the building at a cost of $2,350,000 in 2007. The Company makes the ITA 13(4) election to defer any recaptured CCA. What is the UCC of the new building?

End of Exercise. Solution available in Study Guide.

Damaged Property

7-95.   If compensation is received for damages to depreciable property, ITA 12(1)(f) requires that the amount be included in income to the extent that it is expended to repair the damages. This will, of course, be offset by the deduction for the repairs. If the amount of damages received exceeds the expenditures for the repairs, ITA 13(21) defines "proceeds of disposition" to include the excess. This means that this amount will be deducted from the UCC for the class.

Change In Use

General Rules

7-96.   The basic idea here is that when a property used to produce income is converted to some other purpose or, alternatively, when a property that was acquired for some other purpose becomes an income producing property, ITA 13(7) requires that the change be treated as a deemed disposition combined with a simultaneous deemed reacquisition.

Business To Personal Use

7-97.   This situation is straightforward. If the conversion is from business to personal use, the deemed proceeds will be equal to fair market value, with the transferor recognizing a capital gain, recapture, or terminal loss in the usual manner. The fair market value will also be used as the acquisition cost of the personal use asset.

Personal To Business Use

7-98.   If a personal use asset is converted to an income producing asset, the deemed proceeds will be equal to fair market value. With respect to the capital cost of the business use of the asset, the acquisition will be deemed to occur at fair market value. In those cases where the fair market value of the property is less than its cost, this will also be the figure used for the UCC of the asset and subsequent CCA calculations.

7-99.   As will be discussed in Chapter 10, Capital Gains And Capital Losses, when a personal use property is disposed of, any loss is not deductible, but any gain on the disposition will be treated as a capital gain, with one-half of this amount being included in the taxpayer's Net Income For Tax Purposes. As a result, there is a problem when the transferor has experienced a capital gain on a change in use.

> **Example** Shirley Malone owns a pleasure boat which cost $100,000. She is changing its use to a charter boat and, at the time of the change, the fair market value of the boat is $150,000.

> **Analysis** Shirley's deemed proceeds of disposition will be $150,000, resulting in a capital gain of $50,000. This will increase her Net Income For Tax Purposes by one-half of this amount or $25,000.

> The deemed Capital Cost of the boat to the charter operation will also be $150,000. This value will be used in the determination of any future capital gains.

> If the $150,000 was also used as the basis for CCA, Shirley would be able to deduct 100 percent of the $50,000 increase in value that occurred while she owned the boat for personal use. This would not be an equitable result as Shirley only paid taxes on $25,000 of this increase. Given this, in situations where there is a gain on the change in use, the UCC addition will be limited to the cost of the asset, plus one-half of the gain (the taxable portion of the capital gain). This means that for the purpose of determining CCA or recapture, Shirley's UCC balance will be $125,000 [$100,000 + (1/2)($150,000 - $100,000)].

Example - Change In Use

7-100.   The following example will serve to illustrate some of the concepts discussed in the preceding Paragraphs:

Example On January 1, 2006, Ms. Barker, a professional accountant, acquires a building at a cost of $500,000, with $400,000 allocated to the building and $100,000 allocated to the land. During the entire year, 20 percent of the floor space was used for her accounting practice, while the remainder was used as her principal residence.

On January 1, 2007, an additional 30 percent of the total floor space was converted to business use. On this date, the fair market value of the real property had increased to $620,000, with $480,000 allocated to the building and $140,000 allocated to the land.

On January 1, 2008, the entire building was converted to residential use as Ms. Barker's accounting practice had grown to the point where it had to move to more extensive facilities. On this date, the fair market value had increased to $700,000, with $550,000 allocated to the building and $150,000 allocated to the land.

2006 CCA Calculation The calculation of CCA for 2006 would be as follows:

January 1, 2006 UCC	Nil
Add: Cost Of Acquiring Business Portion [(20%)($500,000 - $100,000)]	$80,000
Deduct: One-Half Net Additions [(1/2)($80,000)]	(40,000)
Base Amount For CCA Claim	$40,000
Deduct: CCA For The Year [(4%)($40,000)]	(1,600)
Add: One-Half Net Additions	40,000
January 1, 2007 UCC	**$78,400**

2007 CCA Calculation The calculation of CCA for 2007 would be as follows:

January 1, 2007 UCC		$ 78,400
Add: Deemed Cost Of Increase In Business Usage:		
Cost [(30%)($400,000)]	$120,000	
Bump Up [(30%)(1/2)($480,000 - $400,000)]	12,000	132,000
Deduct: One-Half Net Additions* [(1/2)($132,000)]		(66,000)
Base Amount For CCA Claim		$144,400
Deduct: CCA For The Year [(4%)($144,400)]		(5,776)
Add: One-Half Net Additions		66,000
January 1, 2008 UCC		**$204,624**

*Non-arm's length transfers are exempt from the half-year rule, provided the transferor used the property as a depreciable property prior to the transfer. The portion of the property being transferred was not previously used as a depreciable property and, as a consequence, the half-year rule is applicable.

7-101. As the asset is no longer being used for business purposes in 2008, there would be no 2008 CCA. With respect to the deemed disposition on the conversion of 50 percent of the property back to personal use, the deemed proceeds of the conversion are $275,000 [($550,000)(50%)]. The capital cost of the 50 percent of the building that was converted would be calculated as follows:

Cost Of 2006 Acquisition [(20%)($400,000)]	$ 80,000
Cost Of 2007 Acquisition [(30%)($480,000)]	144,000
Total Capital Cost Of Business Portion	**$224,000**

7-102. Based on these figures, the 2008 deemed disposition would result in a capital gain of $51,000 ($275,000 - $224,000). In addition to the capital gain, there would be recapture, calculated as follows:

January 1, 2008 UCC	$204,624
Lesser Of:	
• Cost For CCA Purposes ($80,000 + $132,000) = $212,000	
• Proceeds Of Deemed Disposition = $275,000	(212,000)
Recapture Of CCA	($ 7,376)

7-103.   Note that the amount of this recapture of CCA is equal to the sum of the CCA ($1,600 + $5,776) that was taken in the two years during which some of the asset was used for business purposes.

Exercise Seven-13

Subject: Change In Use

For a number of years, Ms. Mellisa Cornglow has owned a large sailboat that has been used for her personal enjoyment. The boat cost $111,000 in 2001 and, on May 1, 2007, it has a fair market value of $183,000. On this date, she opens a chartering business with a December 31 year end in order to rent out her boat for the rest of the year. What is the maximum amount of CCA that she can deduct on the sailboat for 2007? The appropriate CCA rate for sailboats is 15 percent of the declining balance (Class 7).

End of Exercise. Solution available in Study Guide.

Special Rules For Automobiles

7-104.   As was illustrated in the Example in Paragraph 7-100, the change in use rules generally apply when there is a change in use involving only a part of an asset. While this is usually not a serious problem with high value assets where changes in use are infrequent, it could be a significant problem in the case of automobiles that are used partially for employment or business, and partially for personal travel.

7-105.   For example, consider an individual who acquires a car for $29,000 and, in the first year of ownership, uses it two-thirds for business and one-third for personal purposes. It is likely that, in each subsequent year, the portions of personal and business use will vary. If the changes in use rules were strictly applied to this situation, the fair market value for the vehicle would have to be determined each year, with these values being used in an annual deemed disposition/re-acquisition of a portion of the vehicle.

7-106.   Fortunately, an alternative approach appears to be acceptable to the CRA. CCA is calculated each year on 100 percent of the value of the car. Using this figure, the deductible amount is determined by multiplying the 100 percent figure by the portion of the use that was business related during the current year. This procedure avoids the complications associated with determining market values and recording annual deemed dispositions/re-acquisitions.

Cumulative Eligible Capital (CEC)

Eligible Capital Expenditures Defined

7-107.   IT-123R6, "Transactions Involving Eligible Capital Property", describes eligible capital property as "intangible capital property, such as goodwill and other 'nothings', the cost of which neither qualifies for capital cost allowance nor is deductible in the year of its acquisition as a current expense". IT-143R3, "Meaning Of Eligible Capital Expenditures", lists the following items to be included in eligible capital expenditures:

• Goodwill purchased as one of the assets of a business.
• Customer lists purchased and not otherwise deductible.
• The cost of trademarks, patents, licences, and franchises with unlimited lives. (In general,

if these expenditures have limited lives they are Class 14 or Class 44 assets.)
- Expenses of incorporation, reorganization, or amalgamation.
- Appraisal costs associated with valuing eligible capital property. Also appraisal costs on an anticipated property purchase that does not take place.
- The costs of government rights.
- Initiation or admission fees to professional or other organizations for which the annual maintenance fees are deductible.
- Some payments made under non-competition agreements.
- Fines or penalties paid or incurred in the acquisition of an eligible capital property. While the IT Bulletin has not been revised to remove this item, it would appear that ITA 67.6, which eliminates the deductibility of fines and penalties incurred after March 22, 2004, would override this inclusion.

7-108. To clarify the matter further, IT-143R3 specifically excludes the following from the definition:

- The cost of non-depreciable tangible assets (land).
- The cost of depreciable intangibles (such as Class 14 patents).
- Payments made to produce exempt income.
- Payments made to creditors for redemption or cancellation of bonds or other debt instruments.
- Payments by a corporation to a person as a shareholder of the corporation (dividends, payments to redeem shares, or for appropriations of property).
- The cost of acquiring or issuing shares, bonds, mortgages, notes, or an interest in a trust or partnership.

Terminology

7-109. While eligible capital expenditures are treated in much the same manner as expenditures for depreciable assets, the terminology is sufficiently different that some explanation would be useful. The term, "eligible capital expenditure", is the equivalent of capital cost for depreciable capital assets. When these expenditures are made, three-quarters of the cost is added to a cumulative balance designated "cumulative eligible capital" (CEC). This CEC balance is the equivalent of the UCC balance for a particular class of depreciable capital assets. As such, it is reduced by amounts deducted, as well as by three-quarters of the proceeds of any dispositions.

7-110. For tax purposes, amortization of depreciable capital assets is called capital cost allowance (CCA) and is deducted under ITA 20(1)(a) at a variety of rates that are prescribed in the *Income Tax Regulations*. Amortization of CEC is deducted under ITA 20(1)(b) at the 7 percent rate specified in that Paragraph. The term "CEC amount" is usually applied to this deduction.

7-111. The terminology for dispositions is more complex. We will find that there will be results that are similar to capital gains, recapture of CCA, and terminal losses on depreciable capital assets.

Additions, Amortization, And Dispositions

General Procedures

7-112. All acquisitions and dispositions of eligible capital expenditures are accounted for in a single cumulative eligible capital account for each business. The ending balance in this account is used to calculate the deductible amortization. The rules for dealing with eligible capital expenditures are similar to the procedures used for depreciable capital assets. There are, however, important differences that will be described in the following material.

Applicability

7-113. The depreciable property rules are applicable to business income, property income, and, in somewhat more limited circumstances, employment income (see Chapter 8 for an explanation of the difference between business income and property income). In contrast, the rules for dealing with eligible capital expenditures are only applicable to business income calculations. The ITA 20(1)(b) deduction of CEC cannot be made against either property income or employment income.

Additions

7-114.   When an eligible capital expenditure is acquired, three-quarters of its cost is added to the CEC account. The probable reason for limiting the inclusion to three-quarters of the cost is because the other party to the expenditure will often record a capital gain on the disposition. For example, when an individual sells a business including its goodwill, the goodwill will usually not have a tax value. This means that the total amount allocated to goodwill will be treated as a capital gain and, as you are aware, only a portion of such gains are subject to tax.

7-115.   Based on the preceding analysis, it would logical to expect that the inclusion rate for CEC additions would be adjusted when the inclusion rate for capital gains is changed. This, in fact, happened in 1990. In that year, when the capital gains inclusion rate was changed from one-half to three-quarters, the inclusion rate for CEC additions was also increased from one-half to three-quarters.

7-116.   For reasons that have not been clearly explained by the Department of Finance, a similar adjustment did not accompany the changes in the capital gains inclusion rate that occurred in 2000. When the capital gains inclusion rate was reduced from three-quarters to one-half in 2000, the inclusion rate for CEC additions was left at three-quarters.

Amortization

7-117.   Amortization is deducted under ITA 20(1)(b). The write-off procedures for the cumulative eligible capital account are similar to those used for declining balance UCC classes. As noted previously, the rate is specified in ITA 20(1)(b) as 7 percent. This rate is applied to the end of the period balance in the cumulative eligible capital account.

7-118.   As with CCA, any amount up to the maximum can be claimed and deducted from the account. For CEC, there is no equivalent of the half-year rules that can apply to CCA calculations. However, ITA 20(1)(b) indicates that, in situations where there is a short fiscal period, the amount deducted must be prorated on the basis of the number of days in the short fiscal period.

Dispositions

7-119.   When there is a disposition of cumulative eligible capital, three-quarters of the proceeds of disposition are deducted from the CEC account. There are two things of note here. First, as was the case with the inclusion rate for additions to CEC, the amount to be deducted on a disposition was not changed by the 2000 budget. It remains at three-quarters of the proceeds of disposition, as opposed to the one-half inclusion rate for capital gains.

7-120.   Also note that, unlike the situation with depreciable asset dispositions, three-quarters of the proceeds will be deducted even in cases where this amount exceeds three-quarters of the original cost of the asset. For cumulative eligible capital dispositions, the deduction is always based on the proceeds of disposition. This is in contrast to the situation with depreciable capital assets where we deduct the lesser of the proceeds of disposition and the capital cost. This difference eliminates the need to track the cost of individual eligible capital expenditures. However, as will be discussed beginning in Paragraph 7-127, there is an election available that may make this cost information useful.

7-121.   If a positive CEC balance remains after making the deduction for the disposition, the business continues to deduct a CEC amount at the rate of 7 percent applied to the remaining balance.

7-122.   Alternatively, if the deduction creates a negative balance, we have a situation that is analogous to recapture. Prior to the 2000 budget, this negative balance was taken into income as an inclusion under ITA 14(1), and added back to the CEC balance to begin the next taxation year with a nil balance. As there was no need to limit the deduction from the CEC balance on the basis of the cost of the eligible capital expenditure, this ITA 14(1) income inclusion was made up of a combination of previously deducted CEC (the equivalent of recapture), as well as possible capital gains.

7-123. As long as the capital gains inclusion rate was at three-quarters, the same rate that was used for CEC additions, this was an equitable situation. As additions to, and deductions from, the CEC balance were also based on this fraction, any capital gain that was included in the negative balance was, in effect, included in income at the same three-quarters rate that was applicable to capital gains in general.

7-124. However, we now have a situation where the CEC amounts have remained at the three-quarters level, while capital gains are being included at a lower one-half rate. As part of a negative CEC balance may reflect amounts that are similar to capital gains, following the pre-2000 budget procedures would result in these amounts being taxed on a three-quarters basis. To deal with this problem, ITA 14(1) has been modified to require that any negative balance be divided into two components. These components, along with their tax treatment, are as follows:

- To the extent that there have been CEC deductions in the past, the negative amount will be added to income under ITA 14(1). This is the equivalent of recapture for depreciable assets.

- Any excess of the negative amount over past CEC deductions will be viewed as similar to a capital gain. To give this excess amount treatment analogous to that given to capital gains, it will be multiplied by two-thirds prior to its inclusion in the taxpayer's income. This factor reduces the amount from a three-quarters inclusion to a one-half inclusion [(3/4)(2/3) = 1/2].

Example - Cumulative Eligible Capital

7-125. The example that follows will clarify the procedures used to deal with CEC:

Example A corporation begins operations on March 1, 2006 and acquires goodwill for $40,000 on May 24, 2006. In July, 2008, the goodwill is sold for $46,000. The company's fiscal year ends on December 31.

Analysis The analysis of the cumulative eligible capital account would be as follows:

	CEC Balance	CEC Deductions
Addition, May 24, 2006 [(3/4)($40,000)]	$30,000	
2006 CEC Amount [($30,000)(7%)(306/365)]	(1,761)	$1,761
Balance, January 1, 2007	$28,239	
2007 CEC Amount [($28,239)(7%)]	(1,977)	1,977
Balance, January 1, 2008	$26,262	
Proceeds Of 2008 Sale [(3/4)($46,000)]	(34,500)	
Balance After Sale	($ 8,238)	$3,738

An amount of $3,738 ($1,761 + $1,977) would be added to income that represents recapture of previous CEC deductions. It will be taxed on the same three-quarters basis on which these amounts were deducted.

The $4,500 excess ($8,238 - $3,738) would be multiplied by two-thirds to arrive at an income inclusion of $3,000. The logic behind this approach becomes clear when you recognize that $3,000 is one-half of the $6,000 ($46,000 - $40,000) gain on the sale of the goodwill, demonstrating that these procedures give capital gains treatment to gains on the disposition of CEC balances.

7-126. As a final point on dispositions, an income inclusion under ITA 14(1) only occurs when the CEC balance is negative at the end of the year. As was the case with recapture, the income inclusion can be avoided if there are additions to the balance that eliminate the negative amount prior to the end of the taxation year.

Exercise Seven-14

Subject: CEC

On January 1, 2005, Keddy Inc. purchases another business and pays $85,600 for goodwill. At this time, the cumulative eligible capital of the Company is nil. There are no additions to this balance in 2006 or 2007. On June 30, 2007, the business acquired in 2005 was sold and the sale price included a payment for goodwill of $93,400. The Company has a December 31 year end and takes the maximum deduction for cumulative eligible capital in both 2005 and 2006. What amount, if any, will be included in the Company's 2007 income as a result of this sale?

End of Exercise. Solution available in Study Guide.

CEC Disposal Election

7-127. Prior to the 2000 budget, three-quarters of the entire proceeds from any disposition had to be deducted from the CEC balance. For companies with large CEC balances containing a number of different items, this was unlikely to result in a negative balance. Further, as this deduction was not limited to the cost of the inclusion, this requirement had the effect of deducting amounts which were, in effect, capital gains from the CEC balance. For companies that wished to recognize capital gains (e.g., companies with capital losses), this was not a totally equitable situation.

7-128. To correct this situation, ITA 14(1.01) provides for an election that effectively allows for separate treatment of individual dispositions. Under this election, the amount deducted from the CEC balance is limited to three-quarters of the cost of the individual item being disposed of. The excess is then treated as an ordinary capital gain.

Example On January 1, 2007, Marq Ltd.'s CEC balance was nil. During 2007, Marq Ltd. acquires two eligible capital expenditures, one for $80,000 and the other for $140,000. For the taxation year ending December 31, 2007, the Company deducts the maximum CEC amount. In early 2008, the $80,000 asset is sold for $120,000.

Analysis The following table compares the balance in the CEC account assuming the election is not made with the balance assuming the election is made:

	No Election	With Election
2007 Addition [(3/4)($80,000 + $140,000)]	$165,000	$165,000
2007 CEC Amount [($165,000)(7%)]	(11,550)	(11,550)
January 1, 2008 CEC Balance	$153,450	$153,450
Proceeds Of Sale [(3/4)($120,000)]	(90,000)	Nil
Deemed Proceeds Of Sale [(3/4)($80,000)]	Nil	(60,000)
Balance After Sale	$ 63,450	$ 93,450

If no election is made in 2008, there will be no income inclusion and the only tax consequence of the disposition is a reduction in the 2008 and future CEC amounts.

If an election is made under ITA 14(1.01), Marq Ltd. is deemed to have disposed of a capital property with an adjusted cost base equal to the cost of $80,000 for proceeds of disposition equal to the actual proceeds of $120,000. This results in a capital gain of $40,000 ($120,000 - $80,000), with a taxable amount of $20,000 [(1/2)($40,000)].

7-129. This election can only be used for eligible capital expenditures that have a cost that can be determined. The election cannot be used to recognize a loss and ITA 14(1.03)(a) does not allow the use of the ITA 14(1.01) election with respect to goodwill, regardless of whether it has been purchased or generated internally.

Exercise Seven-15

Subject: CEC Election

On January 1, 2006, Que Industries Ltd. has no CEC balance. During the taxation year ending December 31, 2006, it has made the following eligible capital expenditures:

Government License	$156,000
Payment For Non-Competition Agreement	85,000
Customer List	223,000
Purchased Goodwill	50,000
Total	$514,000

The Company deducts the maximum amount of CEC for 2006. In November, 2007, the customer list is sold for $296,000. Compare the tax consequences associated with the sale of the customer list (1) assuming an election is made under ITA 14(1.01) to treat the disposition of the customer list separately and (2) assuming no election is made.

End of Exercise. Solution available in Study Guide.

Special Situations
Business Terminations

7-130. When a business is terminated, a positive balance may remain in the CEC account. If this is the case, the situation is similar to that involving terminal losses on depreciable capital assets. With respect to terminal losses, the balance remaining can be deducted in the computation of Net Income For Tax Purposes. In similar fashion, any CEC balance that is left when a business terminates can also be deducted.

7-131. However, an important difference from the terminal loss situation on depreciable assets is that the deductible amount of any loss on CEC is only three-quarters of the actual amount of the real economic loss. As is the case with terminal losses, any amount deducted from income is also deducted from the CEC balance in order to leave a balance of nil.

7-132. A limitation on this involves situations where a taxpayer ceases doing business and the business is continued by the taxpayer's spouse, common-law partner, or a corporation controlled by the taxpayer. Under these circumstances, ITA 24(2) prohibits the deduction of a loss, requiring that the balance must be transferred to the opening CEC balance of the continuing business.

Death Of A Taxpayer

7-133. ITA 70(5.1) provides that when a taxpayer dies, and the taxpayer's eligible capital property is acquired by some other person who continues to carry on the business, he is deemed to have disposed of it immediately before death at proceeds that are equal to the cumulative eligible capital balance. This would mean that no income inclusion or terminal loss occurs at this time.

Replacement Properties

7-134. As is the case with depreciable capital property, there are provisions that defer any ultimate tax liability associated with involuntary dispositions or certain voluntary dispositions, provided replacement occurs within a relatively short period of time. These rules, contained in ITA 14(6) and 14(7), indicate that, if replacement occurs within 12 months of the end of the taxation year in which the disposition took place, any income inclusion related to the disposition can be deferred.

Key Terms Used In This Chapter

7-135.   The following is a list of the key terms used in this Chapter. These terms, and their meanings, are compiled in the Glossary Of Key Terms located at the back of the separate paper Study Guide and on the Companion CD-ROM.

Capital Cost	Former Business Property
Capital Cost Allowance (CCA)	Half-Year Rules (a.k.a. First Year Rules)
Capital Gain	Involuntary Disposition
Class	Non-Depreciable Capital Property
Cumulative Eligible Capital (CEC)	Recapture Of CCA
Declining Balance Method	Replacement Property Rules
Deemed Disposition	Separate Class Rules
Depreciable Capital Property	Straight-Line Method
Disposition	Taxable Capital Gain
Eligible Capital Expenditure	Terminal Loss
First Year Rules	Undepreciated Capital Cost (UCC)

References

7-136. For more detailed study of the material in this Chapter, we would refer you to the following:

ITA 13(1)	Recaptured Depreciation
ITA 14(1)	Eligible Capital Property - Inclusion In Income From Business
ITA 20(1)(a)	Capital Cost Of Property
ITA 20(1)(b)	Cumulative Eligible Capital Amount
ITA 20(16)	Terminal Loss
ITR Part XI	Capital Cost Allowances
ITR II-VI (Schedules)	Capital Cost Allowances
IC-84-1	Revision Of Capital Cost Allowance Claims And Other Permissive Deductions
IT-79R3	Capital Cost Allowance - Buildings Or Other Structures
IT-123R6	Transactions Involving Eligible Capital Property
IT-128R	Capital Cost Allowance - Depreciable Property
IT-143R3	Meaning Of Eligible Capital Expenditure
IT-147R3	Capital Cost Allowance - Accelerated Write Off Of Manufacturing And Processing Machinery And Equipment
IT-190R2	Capital Cost Allowance - Transferred And Misclassified Property
IT-195R4	Rental Property - Capital Cost Allowance Restrictions
IT-206R	Separate Businesses
IT-220R2	Capital Cost Allowance - Proceeds Of Disposition Of Depreciable Property
IT-259R4	Exchanges Of Property
IT-267R2	Capital Cost Allowance - Vessels
IT-285R2	Capital Cost Allowance - General Comments
IT-304R2	Condominiums
IT-306R2	Capital Cost Allowance - Contractor's Movable Equipment
IT-313R2	Eligible Capital Property - Rules Where A Taxpayer Has Ceased Carrying On A Business Or Has Died
IT-386R	Eligible Capital Amounts
IT-418	Capital Cost Allowance - Partial Dispositions Of Property
IT-469R	Capital Cost Allowance - Earth-Moving Equipment
IT-472	Capital Cost Allowance - Class 8 Property
IT-476	Capital Cost Allowance - Gas and Oil Exploration and Production Equipment
IT-477	Capital Cost Allowance - Patents, Franchises, Concessions, And Licenses
IT-478R2	Capital Cost Allowance - Recapture And Terminal Loss
IT-482R	Capital Cost Allowance - Pipelines
IT-492	Capital Cost Allowance - Industrial Mineral Mines
IT-501	Capital Cost Allowance - Logging Assets

Appendix - CCA Rates For Selected Assets

This Appendix lists the CCA Class and rate for assets commonly used in business. Restrictions and transitional rules may apply in certain situations. ITR Part XI contains detailed descriptions of the CCA Classes.

Asset	Class	Rate
Aircraft (including components)	9	25%
Airplane runways	17	8%
Automobiles, passenger		
• Cost < or = Prescribed amount ($30,000 in 2007)	10	30%
• Cost > Prescribed amount	10.1	30%
Automotive equipment	10	30%
Bar code scanners	8	20%
Billboards	8	20%
Boats, canoes and other vessels	7	15%
Bridges, canals, culverts and dams	1	4%
Buildings		
• acquired after 1987 (Most)	1	4%
• acquired before 1988 (see Paragraph 7-36 of text)	3	5%
Buses	10	30%
Calculators	8	20%
Cash registers	8	20%
China, cutlery and tableware	12	100%
Computer hardware		
• acquired after March 22, 2004	45	45%
• acquired before March 23, 2004	10	30%
Computer software (systems)		
• acquired after March, 19, 2007	??	55%
• acquired after March 22, 2004, before March 20, 2007	45	45%
• acquired before March 23, 2004	10	30%
Computer software (applications)	12	100%
Copyrights	14	Straight-line
Data network infrastructure equipment	46	30%
Dies, jigs, patterns, and molds	12	100%
Docks, breakwaters and trestles	3	5%
Electrical advertising billboards	8	20%
Electronic point-of-sale equipment	8	20%
Equipment (not specifically listed elsewhere)	8	20%
Fences	6	10%
Films	10	30%
Franchises (limited life)	14	Straight-line
Franchises (unlimited life)	CEC	N/A
Furniture and fixtures (not specifically listed elsewhere)	8	20%
Goodwill	CEC	N/A
Instruments, dental or medical (See Tools)		
Kitchen utensils (See Tools)		

Asset	Class	Rate
Land	**N/A**	**N/A**
Landscaping	N/A	Deductible
Leasehold improvements	13	Straight-line
Licences (limited life)	14	Straight-line
Licences (unlimited life)	CEC	N/A
Linen	12	100%
Machinery and equipment		
(not specifically listed elsewhere)	**8**	**20%**
Manufacturing and processing equipment		
• acquired after March 19, 2007 and before 2009	??	Straight-line
• acquired before March 20, 2007	43	30%
Office equipment (not specifically listed elsewhere)	**8**	**20%**
Outdoor advertising billboards	8	20%
Parking area and similar surfaces	**17**	**8%**
Patents (limited life)	44	25%
Patents (unlimited life)	CEC	N/A
Photocopy machines	8	20%
Portable buildings and equipment	10	30%
Power operated movable equipment	38	30%
Radio communication equipment	**8**	**20%**
Railway cars		
• acquired after February 27, 2000	7	15%
• acquired before February 28, 2000	35	7%
Roads	17	8%
Sidewalks	**17**	**8%**
Software (applications)	12	100%
Software (systems)	10	30%
Storage area	17	8%
Storage tanks, oil or water	6	10%
Tangible Capital Assets		
(not specifically listed elsewhere)	**8**	**20%**
Taxicabs	16	40%
Telephone systems	8	20%
Television commercials	12	100%
Tools		
• acquired before May 2, 2006 (under $200)	12	100%
• acquired before May 2, 2006 ($200 or over)	8	20%
• acquired after May 1, 2006 (under $500)	12	100%
• acquired after May 1, 2006 ($500 or over)	8	20%
Trailers	10	30%
Trucks and tractors for hauling freight	16	40%
Trucks (automotive), tractors and vans	10	30%
Uniforms	**12**	**100%**
Video games (coin operated)	**16**	**40%**
Video tapes	10	30%
Video tapes for renting	12	100%
Wagons	**10**	**30%**

Problems For Self Study

(The solutions for these problems can be found in the separate Study Guide.)

Self Study Problem Seven - 1

Mr. Marker has been the sole proprietor of Marker Enterprises since its establishment in 1994. This business closes its books on December 31 and, on January 1, 2007, the following information on its assets was contained in the records of the business:

Type Of Asset	Undepreciated Capital Cost	Original Capital Cost	CCA Rate
Equipment (Class 8)	$ 96,000	$130,000	20 Percent
Vehicles (Class 10)	$ 6,700	$ 30,000	30 Percent
Building (Class 1)	$115,000	$190,000	4 Percent

Other Information:

1. During the year ending December 31, 2007, Mr. Marker's business acquired additional Class 8 equipment at a total cost of $52,000. This new equipment replaced equipment that had an original cost of $75,000, which was sold during the year for total proceeds of $35,000.

2. During the year ending December 31, 2007, Mr. Marker acquired a used automobile to be used in his business for a total cost of $8,000. Also during this year, Mr. Marker sold one of the trucks that was used in his business for proceeds of $25,000. This truck, which had an original capital cost of $20,000, had achieved a high value as the result of its extra features, which were no longer available on later models.

3. As the result of a decision to lease its premises in future years, Mr. Marker sold his building for total proceeds of $110,000. Mr. Marker's business did not own any other buildings, and this building was located on land that Mr. Marker had leased for a number of years. The lease terminated with the sale of the building.

Required: Calculate the effects of all of the preceding information on Mr. Marker's Net Income For Tax Purposes for the year ending December 31, 2007. Your answer should include the maximum CCA that can be deducted by Mr. Marker for this year. In addition, calculate the January 1, 2008 balance for the UCC of each of the three classes of depreciable assets.

Self Study Problem Seven - 2

Golden Dragon Ltd. begins operations in Vancouver on September 1, 2002. These operations include an elegant sit down restaurant specializing in northern Chinese cuisine, as well as a take out operation that provides home delivery throughout the city. To facilitate this latter operation, on October 12, 2002, the Company acquires 20 small cars to be used as delivery vehicles. The cost of these cars is $12,000 each and, for purposes of calculating CCA, they are classified as Class 10 assets.

During the first year of operations, the Company establishes a fiscal year ending on December 31. In the fiscal periods 2003 through 2007, the following transactions take place with respect to the Company's fleet of delivery cars:

2003   The Company acquires five more cars at a cost of $12,500 each. In addition, three of the older cars are sold for total proceeds of $27,500.

2004   There are no new acquisitions of cars during this year. However, four cars are sold for total proceeds of $38,000.

2005   In December, 2005, 16 of the remaining 18 cars are sold for $128,000. It was the intent of the Company to replace these cars. However, because of a delay in delivery by the car dealer, the replacement did not occur until January, 2006.

2006 In January of 2006, the Company takes delivery of 25 new delivery cars at a cost of $16,000 each. No cars are disposed of during 2006.

2007 In March, 2007, there is a change in management at Golden Dragon Ltd. They conclude that the Company's take out operation is not in keeping with the more elegant image that the sit down restaurant is trying to maintain. As a consequence, the take out operation is closed, and the 27 remaining delivery cars are sold. Because of the large number of cars being sold, the total proceeds are only $268,000.

Golden Dragon Ltd. takes maximum CCA in each of the years under consideration.

Required: For each of the fiscal years 2002 through 2007, calculate CCA, recapture, or terminal loss and the UCC with respect to the fleet of delivery cars owned by Golden Dragon Ltd.

Self Study Problem Seven - 3

For its taxation year ending December 31, 2007, Marion Enterprises has determined that its operating Net Income For Tax Purposes before any deduction for CCA amounts to $53,000. The Company does not have any Division C deductions, so whatever amount is determined as Net Income For Tax Purposes will also be the amount of Taxable Income for the taxation year.

On January 1, 2007, the Company has the following UCC balances:

Class 1	$876,000
Class 8	220,000
Class 10	163,000

During 2007, the cost of additions to Class 10 amounted to $122,000, while the proceeds from dispositions in this class totalled $87,000. In no case did the proceeds of disposition exceed the capital cost of the assets retired, and there were still assets in Class 10 on December 31, 2007.

There were no acquisitions or dispositions in either Class 1 or Class 8 during 2007. During the preceding three taxation years, the Company reported Taxable Income totalling $46,000 for the three years.

Required:

A. Calculate the maximum CCA that could be taken by Marion Enterprises for the taxation year ending December 31, 2007.

B. As Marion Enterprises' tax advisor, indicate how much CCA you would advise the Company to take for the 2007 taxation year, and the specific classes from which it should be deducted. Provide a brief explanation of the reasons for your recommendation. In determining your solution, ignore the possibility that 2007 losses can be carried forward to subsequent taxation years.

Self Study Problem Seven - 4

Trail Resources Ltd. has a taxation year that ends on December 31. During 2006, its storage building was destroyed in a flash flood. This building was purchased in 1993 at a cost of $500,000 and, on January 1, 2006, its UCC was $368,000. After negotiations with adjustors from the insurance company, a settlement of $490,000 was agreed upon and paid during 2006.

A replacement building was contracted for, and started in, September, 2006. It was completed in January, 2007 for a cost of $650,000. Trail Resources Ltd. does not own any other buildings and always takes maximum CCA. The appropriate election is made by the Company to defer any recapture under ITA 13(4).

Required: Explain how the preceding transactions will affect the balance in the Company's UCC during the period January 1, 2006 through January 1, 2008.

Self Study Problem Seven - 5

Miss Coos purchased a building to be used as her personal residence in 2003 at a cost of $120,000. Of this total, it is estimated that the value of the land is $30,000 and the value of the building is $90,000. On January 1, 2005, a portion of this residence was converted to an office and rented to a local accountant for $400 per month. At the time of the conversion, the fair market value of the building was $120,000. The market value of the land is unchanged. Based on the amount of floor space allocated to the office, Miss Coos indicates that 30 percent of the building was converted into office space at this time.

On January 1, 2007, the office was rented by a new tenant who did not require the same amount of floor space as the previous tenant. As a result, one room was converted back to personal use. This room contained 10 percent of the total floor space, and the fair market value of the building was $140,000 at this time. The market value of the land remains at $30,000.

Required: What is the maximum CCA that can be deducted in 2005, 2006, and 2007? Ignore land values in calculating your solution.

Self Study Problem Seven - 6

The fiscal year of the Atlantic Manufacturing Company, a Canadian public company, ends on December 31. On January 1, 2007, the UCC balances for the various classes of assets owned by the Company are as follows:

Class 1 - Building	$625,000
Class 8 - Office Furniture And Equipment	155,000
Class 10 - Vehicles	118,000
Class 13 - Leasehold Improvements	61,750
Class 43 - Manufacturing Equipment	217,000
Class 45 - Computer Hardware	10,000

During the year ending December 31, 2007, the following acquisitions of assets were made:

Class 8 - Office Furniture And Equipment	$ 27,000
Class 10 - Vehicles (Delivery Truck)	33,000
Class 12 - Tools	34,000
Class 13 - Leasehold Improvements	45,000
Class 45 - Computer Hardware*	28,000

*Acquired before March 20, 2007

During this same period, the following dispositions occurred:

Class 8 - Used office furniture and equipment was sold for cash proceeds in the amount of $35,000. The original cost of these assets was $22,000.

Class 10 - A delivery truck with an original cost of $23,000 was sold for $8,500.

Class 43 - Since the manufacturing operations will be done by subcontractors in the future, all of the manufacturing equipment was sold for total proceeds of $188,000.

Other Information:

1. The Company leases a building for $27,000 per year that houses a portion of its manufacturing operations. The lease was negotiated on January 1, 2004 and has an original term

of eight years. There are two renewal options on the lease. The term for each of these options is four years. The Company made $78,000 of leasehold improvements immediately after signing the lease. No further improvements were made until the current year.

2. On February 24, 2007, one of the Company's cars was totally destroyed in an accident. At the time of the accident, the fair market value of the car was $12,300. The proceeds from the Company's insurance policy amounted to only $8,000. The original cost of the car was $17,000.

3. The Class 12 tools purchased are not subject to the half-year rule.

4. The Atlantic Manufacturing Company was organized in 2002 and has no balance in its cumulative eligible capital account on January 1, 2007. During March, 2007, the Company granted a manufacturing licence for one of its products to a company in southern Ontario. This licensee paid $87,000 for the right to manufacture this product.

5. It is the policy of the Company to deduct maximum CCA in all years.

Required: Calculate the maximum 2007 CCA that can be taken on each class of assets, the January 1, 2008 UCC balance for each class, and any other 2007 income inclusions or deductions resulting from the information provided in the problem.

Self Study Problem Seven - 7

On January 1, 2004, Miss Nash acquires an unincorporated business operation for a total price of $2,500,000. While most of this amount can be allocated to specific identifiable assets, an amount of $500,000 is left and must be allocated to goodwill.

Miss Nash operates the business until October 15, 2007. At that point, she receives an offer of $3,800,000 for the business and decides to sell it. Of the total sales price, an amount of $780,000 is allocated to goodwill.

Required: Prepare a schedule showing the cumulative eligible capital amount that can be deducted in each year of business and the tax effect related to the sale of goodwill by Miss Nash.

Assignment Problems

(The solutions for these problems are only available in
the solutions manual that has been provided to your instructor.)

Assignment Problem Seven - 1

Global Manufacturing Ltd. has a taxation year that ends on December 31. On May 1, 2006, Global purchased equipment to be used in manufacturing and processing for $500,000. For 2006, it claimed $50,000 in CCA on this equipment. There are no other assets in this CCA class.

During 2007, the Company received a government grant of $40,000, specifically for the equipment purchased in the previous year. In addition, one-half of the equipment was sold for $275,000.

Required: Calculate the maximum amount of CCA that Global can deduct for 2007 and the January 1, 2008 UCC balance. In addition, describe the tax effects of the equipment sale.

Assignment Problem Seven - 2

Mr. Taylor bought a large triplex on January 1, 2005 for a total cost of $345,000. Of this amount, it is estimated that $255,000 should be allocated to the building and $90,000 to the land on which it is located. The three rental units in the triplex are identical in size and features and, for purposes of allocation to a CCA class, the property is considered to be a single unit. At a bankruptcy sale in January, Mr. Taylor purchases furniture and appliances for one of the units at a total cost of $2,800.

Early in 2005, all three units are rented. Mr. Taylor's net rental income for 2005, before the deduction of any CCA, amounts to $10,200.

In November, 2006, the tenants in the furnished unit move out and purchase all the furniture and appliances from Mr. Taylor for $3,200. Mr. Taylor's net rental income for 2006, before consideration of CCA, is $12,600.

Early in 2007, Mr. Taylor decides to move into the empty unit. At this time, Mr. Taylor has no other personal residence, and the market value of the triplex is estimated to be $315,000 for the building and $120,000 for the land. In March of 2007, one of the other tenants moves out. Because he cannot find another tenant, Mr. Taylor's net rental income for 2007, before consideration of CCA, is only $5,300. Mr. Taylor does not own any other rental properties.

Required:

A. Calculate the maximum CCA that can be deducted by Mr. Taylor in each of the years 2005, 2006, and 2007. Also, determine his UCC balance on January 1, 2006, 2007, and 2008. In addition, indicate the amount of any recapture or terminal loss that occurs in any of the three years.

B. (This part requires an understanding of capital gains and losses which are covered in detail in Chapter 10.) Indicate any tax consequences that may arise as a result of Mr. Taylor's decision to move into the building.

Assignment Problem Seven - 3

Opening Balances   The taxation year of Burton Steel Ltd. ends on December 31. On January 1, 2007, the UCC balances for the various classes of assets owned by the Company are as follows:

Class 3 - Building	$1,562,000
Class 8 - Office Furniture And Equipment	278,000
Class 10 - Vehicles	204,000
Class 13 - Leasehold Improvements	106,250
Class 43 - Manufacturing Equipment	126,000
Class 45 - Computer Hardware	11,000

Acquisitions   During the year ending December 31, 2007, the following acquisitions of assets were made. All of these acquisitions occurred prior to the March 19, 2007 budget.

Class 1 - Building	$258,000
Class 8 - Office Furniture And Equipment	72,000
Class 10 - Vehicles	63,000
Class 13 - Leasehold Improvements	58,000
Class 45 - Computer Hardware	17,000

The addition to Class 10 was made up of three passenger vehicles, with a cost of $21,000 each.

Dispositions   During this same period, the following dispositions occurred:

Class 8 - Office furniture and equipment were sold for cash proceeds of $42,000. The original cost of these assets totalled $38,000.

Class 10 - A delivery truck with an original cost of $37,000 was sold for $12,000.

Class 43 - Since Burton Steel Ltd. will only be involved in retail operations in the future, all of the manufacturing equipment was sold for total proceeds of $89,000.

Other Information:

1. The Company leases its main office building for $47,000 per year. The lease was negotiated on January 1, 2005 and had an original term of eight years. There are two renewal options on the lease, each for a period of two years. The Company made $125,000 of leasehold improvements immediately after signing the lease. No further improvements were made until the current year.

2. During the year ending December 31, 2007, some of the Company's office furniture and equipment was destroyed in a small fire. At the time of the accident, the fair market value of the destroyed property was $19,000. However, proceeds from the Company's insurance policy amounted to only $11,000. The original cost of the destroyed property was $18,000.

3. Maximum CCA has always been taken by Burton Steel.

Required: Calculate the maximum CCA that can be taken by Burton Steel Ltd. on each class of assets for the year ending December 31, 2007, and calculate the UCC for each class of assets on January 1, 2008. Indicate any other inclusions or deductions from Taxable Income resulting from the preceding information.

Assignment Problem Seven - 4

Sorrento Pizza begins operations in Ottawa on June 30, 2002. These operations include a formal dining room specializing in the cuisine of northern Italy, as well as a take out operation that provides home delivery throughout the city. To facilitate this latter operation, on July 1, 2002, the Company acquires ten small cars to be used as delivery vehicles. The cost of these cars is $10,000 each and, for purposes of calculating CCA, they are allocated to Class 10 (30 percent declining balance CCA). Sorrento Pizza takes maximum CCA in each year of operation.

During the first year of operations, the Company establishes a fiscal year ending on December 31. In 2003 through 2007, the following transactions take place with respect to the Company's fleet of delivery cars:

2003 The Company acquires ten more cars at a cost of $10,500 each. In addition, three of the older cars are sold for total proceeds of $21,500.

2004 There are no new acquisitions of cars during this year. However, four cars are sold for total proceeds of $30,000.

2005 Near the end of 2005, 12 of the remaining 13 cars are sold for $84,000. It was the intent of the Company to replace these cars. However, because of a delay in delivery by the car dealer, the replacement did not occur until early 2006.

2006 In January of 2006, the Company receives 20 new delivery cars at a cost of $14,000 each. No cars are disposed of during the year.

2007 Early in this year, the management of Sorrento Pizza concludes that the take out operation is not profitable and is causing severe employee discipline problems. As a consequence, the take out operation is closed and the 21 remaining delivery cars are sold. Because of the large number of cars being sold, the total proceeds are only $174,000.

Required: For each of the fiscal years 2002 through 2007, calculate CCA, recapture, or terminal loss and the UCC with respect to the fleet of delivery cars owned by Sorrento Pizza.

Assignment Problem Seven - 5

For its taxation year ending December 31, 2007, Brownlee Inc. has determined that its Net Income For Tax Purposes, before any deductions for CCA, amounts to $23,500. The Company does not have any Division C deductions, so whatever amount is determined as Net Income For Tax Purposes will also be the amount of Taxable Income for the 2007 taxation year.

On January 1, 2007 the Company has the following UCC balances:

Class 3	$263,000
Class 8	72,000
Class 10	52,000

During 2007, the cost of additions to Class 10 amounted to $38,000, while the proceeds from dispositions in this class totalled $23,000. In no case did the proceeds of disposition exceed the capital cost of the assets retired, and there were still assets in the class as of December 31, 2007. There were no acquisitions or dispositions in either Class 3 or Class 8 during 2007.

Required:

A. Calculate the maximum CCA that could be taken by Brownlee Company for the taxation year ending December 31, 2007.

B. As Brownlee's tax advisor, indicate how much CCA you would advise them to take for the 2007 taxation year and the specific classes from which it should be deducted. Provide a brief explanation of the reason for your recommendation. In providing this advice, do not take into consideration the possibility that losses can be carried either back or forward.

Assignment Problem Seven - 6

Farnham Inc. has a taxation year that ends on December 31. The Company carries on its operations in a single building. This building has a capital cost of $850,000 and, on January 1, 2006, its UCC was $113,000. The building's furniture and fixtures (all Class 8) have a capital cost of $220,000 and a January 1, 2006 UCC of $152,000. The Company has no other Class 8 assets.

On February 12, 2006, the building and its contents were completely destroyed in a fire. The building was insured for its capital cost of $850,000 and the furniture and fixtures were insured for $180,000. As the fire completely destroyed all of these assets, on June 18, 2006, the Company received a payment from its insurer for $1,030,000 ($850,000 + $180,000).

In February, 2007, Farnham Inc. acquires a replacement building for $925,000. During the following month, furniture and fixtures are installed in this new building at a cost of $235,000. The Company files an election under ITA 13(4).

Required:

A. Indicate the 2006 tax consequences that would result from the destruction of the building and its contents.

B. Indicate the maximum amendments that could be made to the results described in Part A. Assuming that these amendments have been made, determine the maximum CCA on the new building and the new Class 8 assets for the year ending December 31, 2007. In addition, calculate the January 1, 2008 UCC balance for each Class.

C. Assume that, instead of having the building and contents destroyed by fire, the Company had sold the building and its contents for $1,030,000 in 2006 in order to voluntarily move to the new location in 2007. How would the results in Part B differ?

D. Assume that the replacement building for the burned building had cost $700,000 instead of $925,000. How would the results in Part B differ?

Assignment Problem Seven - 7

On January 1, 2006, Mr. Jean Lessard acquires a real property that he will use to operate his appliance repair business. The cost of this property is $425,000, with $125,000 of this total being the estimated value of the land. During 2006, his business occupies all of the property.

As during 2006 he did not achieve the volume of business that he anticipated, on January 1, 2007, Mr. Lessard converts 40 percent of the property's floor space into an apartment which he will occupy. At this time, due to the strong possibility that a crematorium would be built next door, the estimated fair market value of the property has fallen to $375,000, with $100,000 of this total attributable to the land.

During 2007, his volume of business increases significantly, resulting in the need to convert his apartment back to business usage. This conversion occurs on January 1, 2008, with the entire building being used for business throughout the following year. On January 1, 2008, the fair market value of the building has increased to $450,000, due to the bankruptcy of the owner of the proposed crematorium, with $135,000 of this total attributable to the land.

Required: Determine the maximum CCA that can be deducted by Mr. Lessard in 2006, 2007, and 2008.

Assignment Problem Seven - 8

McLean Stores is a group of unincorporated retail stores, owned and operated by George McLean, specializing in the sale of bulk foods in Vancouver. In 2005, in order to expand his operations to Vancouver Island, he purchased five similar stores that were being operated as a group in the city of Victoria. The purchase price of these stores included a payment of $90,000 for the goodwill of the operation. The availability of this goodwill was insured by a long-term no competition agreement signed by the former owner of the stores. The agreement covers all of Vancouver Island and is transferable.

In 2007, Mr. McLean sells McLean Stores at a price that includes a payment for goodwill of $300,000. It is estimated that $200,000 of this goodwill should be allocated to the Vancouver operations, while the remaining $100,000 relates to the Victoria stores that were purchased in 2005.

The Company's year end is December 31. Mr. McLean has taken the maximum cumulative eligible capital deductions in all years.

Required:

A. What is the maximum deduction that Mr. McLean can claim for amortization of cumulative eligible capital in 2005 and 2006?

B. What amounts will be included in Mr. McLean's 2007 Net Income For Tax Purposes as a result of the sale of McLean Stores?

Assignment Problem Seven - 9

The following information relates to Bartel Ltd. for its fiscal year that ends on December 31, 2007:

1. The Company has UCC balances on January 1, 2007 for its tangible assets as follows:

Class 1	$590,000
Class 8	570,000
Class 10	61,000

2. During 2007, the Company purchased office furniture for $14,000.

3. During 2007, the Company purchased a truck from its majority shareholder for $22,000. The truck was four years old, had a fair market value of $36,000, and a UCC of $26,000.

4. On January 1, 2005, the Company expanded its operations by purchasing another business. The purchase price for this business included a payment of $92,000 for goodwill, $120,000 for a franchise with a six year life, and $28,000 for a franchise with an unlimited life.

5. During 2005, one of the Company's buildings was destroyed in a flood. The building was acquired at a cost of $475,000 and had a fair market value of $440,000 at the time of the flood. The Company received $440,000 from its insurance company in 2005, signed a construction contract for replacement of the building on January 1, 2006, and saw the replacement building completed in January, 2007. The replacement cost was $350,000. As the insurance proceeds did not create recapture for the class, no election was made under ITA 13(4).

6. During 2006, the Company sold part of its original operations. The proceeds of disposition included a payment for goodwill of $59,000.

7. Bartel Ltd. has always deducted the maximum CCA and the maximum write-off of cumulative eligible capital allowable in each year of operation.

Required: Calculate the maximum CCA and the maximum write-off of cumulative eligible capital that can be deducted for 2007.

Assignment Problem Seven - 10

Ms. Georgia Valentine is an employee of Peach Ltd., a public corporation and GST registrant. She is required to travel as part of her job. She uses a car that she owns for this travel and pays all other costs out of her own funds. She does not receive any reimbursement or allowance from her employer.

The car is used 100 percent for employment related purposes. The car was purchased in December, 2006 for a total of $22,800, which includes $1,600 (8%) in provincial sales tax and GST of $1,200 (6%). During 2006, she claimed $3,420 of CCA on the car and claimed a GST rebate on the CCA of $209.

Her Notice of Assessment, received in June, 2007, indicated that her 2006 return was accepted as filed.

In her 2007 tax return, she deducts the following amounts in the calculation of employment income:

Accommodation (Includes Provincial Sales Tax Of $240 And GST Of $180)	$ 3,420
Deductible Portion Of Meals And Entertainment	
(Includes Provincial Sales Tax Of $160 And GST Of $120)	2,280
Automobile Costs:	
Gas And Maintenance	
(Includes Provincial Sales Tax Of $400 And GST Of $300)	5,700
Interest On Automobile Loan	1,800
Insurance	800
Total Deductions Excluding CCA	$14,000

Ms. Valentine intends to claim the maximum CCA on her car.

Required: Calculate the maximum CCA that Ms. Valentine can claim on her car for 2007. In addition, calculate the 2007 GST rebate that Ms. Valentine will claim as a result of her deductible expenses.

CHAPTER 8

Income Or Loss From A Business

Defining Business Income

The Nature Of Business Activity

Defined

8-1. The subject of income or loss from a business is given coverage in ITA Division B, Subdivision b, Sections 9 through 37.3. Because of the many similarities in the procedures used to compute income from property, these ITA Sections also deal with property income. There are differences, however, in the treatment of these two types of income (e.g., a loss cannot be created through the deduction of CCA on property that is producing rental income). Given these differences, the provisions associated with property income are given separate coverage in Chapter 9.

8-2. In very general terms, business activity involves organizations offering for sale, merchandise they have purchased, products they have manufactured, or services they have the ability to provide. A definition that is consistent with this view is as follows:

> **ITA 248(1)** Business includes a profession, calling, trade, manufacture or undertaking of any kind whatever and, … , an adventure or concern in the nature of trade but does not include an office or employment.

Controversial Areas

8-3. While this definition is fairly general in nature, its application in many situations is fairly straightforward (e.g., a retail store with all of its revenues from sales of merchandise is clearly earning business income). However, there are three areas in which distinguishing business income from other types of income is an important and sometimes controversial problem. Briefly described, these areas are as follows:

Business Income Vs. Employment Income This distinction is important in that an individual earning business income is able to deduct more items than an individual earning employment income. This issue is discussed in Chapter 5.

Business Income Vs. Property Income This distinction is important in that a corporation earning business income can be eligible for the small business deduction. The availability of this deduction, along with a similar rate reduction at the provincial level, can reduce the corporation's combined federal/provincial tax rate by over 20 percentage points. This distinction is discussed in Chapter 15.

Business Income Vs. Capital Gains   On dispositions of property, it is sometimes difficult to establish whether the resulting gain is business income or, alternatively, a capital gain. This distinction is important due to the tax treatment of capital gains. When losses are involved, further importance attaches to this distinction in that capital losses can only be deducted against capital gains. The distinction between business income and capital gains is discussed in this Chapter.

Adventure Or Concern In The Nature Of Trade

8-4.   A final point here relates to what is referred to in the ITA 248(1) definition of business as an "adventure or concern in the nature of trade". There are situations in which a taxpayer engages in a single purchase and sale transaction, as opposed to carrying on a regular and continuous business activity. This, in effect, creates a third class of property in addition to business property and capital property.

8-5.   An example of this would be land purchased by an individual, who is not in the land development business, with the intent of subdividing it into smaller lots and selling them at a profit. Property such as this is treated in part like business income, in that profits or losses on the property are recognized in the income account and, in part like capital property, in that the profits or losses are recognized only on disposition.

Business Income Vs. Capital Gains

Importance Of The Distinction

8-6.   When an asset is disposed of, there may be a question as to whether any resulting gain or loss should either be included in the income account (i.e., treated as business or property income) or included in the capital account (i.e., treated as a capital gain or loss). This distinction is important for two reasons:

- Only one-half of a capital gain is taxed and only one-half of a capital loss is deductible. If a gain transaction can be classified as capital in nature, the savings to the taxpayer is very significant.

- Allowable capital losses (i.e., the deductible one-half) can only be deducted against taxable capital gains (i.e., the taxable one-half). This can be of great importance, particularly to individual taxpayers and smaller business enterprises. It may be years before such taxpayers realize taxable capital gains, resulting in a situation where there is significant deferral of the tax benefits associated with allowable capital losses.

8-7.   This distinction is a source of much litigation. Those taxpayers experiencing gains will, of course, wish to have them classified as capital. Alternatively, those taxpayers who have incurred losses will wish to have them classified as on the income account. This makes it extremely important to understand the distinction between a capital asset and an asset whose disposition results in business income.

Capital Assets Defined

8-8.   The basic concept is a simple one — capital assets are held to produce income through their use, as opposed to producing income through being sold. Take, for example, the assets of a retail store. These will include inventories of purchased merchandise that are being held for resale. Such assets are not part of the capital assets of the business, and any income related to their sale would be classified as business income. However, the building in which the merchandise is being offered for sale, as well as the furniture and fixtures necessary to the operation of the business, are capital assets. This would mean that if the operation were to sell these assets, any resulting gain would be capital in nature.

8-9.   In general, capital assets are somewhat analogous to the accounting classification of non-current assets. An additional analogy, sometimes applied in court cases, is with a fruit bearing tree. The tree itself is a capital asset and its sale would result in a capital gain or loss. In contrast, the sale of the fruit from the tree would generate business income.

8-10. In general, it is the use of the asset that determines the appropriate classification. A particular type of asset can be classified as capital by one business and as inventory by another. Consider a piece of equipment such as a backhoe. For a construction company using this asset for excavating construction sites, it would clearly be a capital asset. Alternatively, if it were held for sale by a dealer in construction equipment, it would be classified as inventory, with any gain on its sale being taxed as business income.

Criteria For Identifying Capital Gains

8-11. While in many situations the preceding distinction is clear, problems often arise, particularly with respect to investments in real estate and securities. In general, the courts have taken the position that for an investment to qualify as a capital asset, it must be capable of earning income in the form of interest, dividends, royalties, or rents. Further, it must be the intent of the investor to hold the asset for its income producing capabilities, not simply for quick resale at a profit. Various criteria have been used in making this distinction, the most common of which are as follows:

Intent And Course Of Conduct   This involves attempting to determine whether the investor intended to hold the investment as an income producing asset, or to merely profit from a quick resale of the asset. In many cases, this intent will be judged by the length of time the investment was held. The question of secondary intent would also apply here. If the investor made some effort to earn a return on the investment, but was clearly aware of an ability to sell at a profit if the investment return was inadequate, the investment might not qualify for capital gains treatment.

Number And Frequency Of Transactions   A large number of closely spaced transactions would be an indication that the investor was in the business of dealing in this type of asset, not holding it to produce income.

Relationship To The Taxpayer's Business   If the transaction is related to the taxpayer's business, this may be sufficient to disqualify any gain or loss from capital gains treatment. For example, a gain on a mortgage transaction might be considered business income to a real estate broker.

Supplemental Work On The Property   Additional work on the property, directed at enhancing its value or marketability, would indicate an adventure in the nature of trade resulting in business income.

Nature Of The Assets   The conventional accounting distinction between fixed assets and working capital has been used in some cases to determine whether income was business or capital in nature. Note, however, the discussion in Paragraph 8-10 concerning this issue.

Objectives Declared In Articles Of Incorporation   Gains and losses on transactions that fall within the corporation's declared objectives may be considered business income. However, as most corporations state their objectives in a very broad manner, this criteria is not frequently used.

8-12. For more specific guidance with respect to the classification of real estate transactions, IT-218R, "Profit, Capital Gains And Losses From The Sale of Real Estate, Including Farmland And Inherited Land And Conversion Of Real Estate From Capital Property To Inventory And Vice Versa", provides a check list of factors that the courts have considered in making the capital gains/business income distinction. A similar list for transactions in securities can be found in IT-479R, "Transactions In Securities".

Exercise Eight-1

Subject: Business Vs. Capital Gain

During 2007, Sandra Von Arb acquired a four unit apartment building for $230,000. While it was her intention to operate the building as a rental property, one month after her purchase she received an unsolicited offer to purchase the building for $280,000. She accepts the offer. Should the $50,000 be treated as a capital gain or as business income? Justify your conclusion.

End of Exercise.   Solution available in Study Guide.

Business Income And GAAP

8-13.   Financial statements requiring audit opinions must be prepared in accordance with generally accepted accounting principles, or GAAP. These principles have had a significant influence on the development of the tax concept of business income. This is reflected in the fact that, for tax purposes, business income is usually an accrual, rather than a cash based calculation and it is a net, rather than a gross concept. In addition, GAAP continues to be influential in that income as computed under these principles is usually required for tax purposes, unless a particular provision of the *Act* specifies alternative requirements.

8-14.   This means that business income under the *Income Tax Act* will not be totally unfamiliar to anyone who has had experience in the application of GAAP. However, there are a number of differences between GAAP based Net Income and net business income for tax purposes. While many of these will become apparent as we proceed through the discussion of the specific provisions of the *Act*, it is useful to note some of the more important differences at this point. They are as follows:

Amortization (Depreciation)   As was noted in Chapter 7, the *Income Tax Regulations* provide the methods and rates to be used in determining the maximum CCA that can be deducted in a given taxation year. However, there is no requirement that this maximum amount be deducted, nor is there any requirement that a consistent policy be followed as long as the annual amount involved is no greater than the maximum amount specified in the *Act*. In contrast, GAAP allows management to choose from a variety of amortization methods. Further, once a method is adopted, it must be used consistently to deduct the full amount as calculated by that method.

Because of these different approaches, CCA deducted will be different and usually larger, than the corresponding amortization expense under GAAP. This is the most common and, for most enterprises, the largest difference between accounting Net Income and Net Income For Tax Purposes.

Other Allocations   There are other items, similar to amortization charges, where the total cost to be deducted will be the same for tax and accounting purposes. However, they will be deducted using different allocation patterns. Examples would be pension costs (funding payments are deducted for tax purposes), warranty costs (cash payments are deducted for tax purposes), and scientific research and experimental development expenditures (some capital costs are fully deductible for tax purposes in the year of acquisition).

Permanent Differences   There are some differences between tax and accounting income that are permanent in nature. For example, 100 percent of capital gains are included in accounting Net Income, while only one-half of this income is included in Net Income For Tax Purposes. Other examples of this type of difference would be the non-deductible 50 percent of business meals and entertainment and the non-deductible portion of automobile lease payments (see discussion later in this Chapter).

Unreasonable Expenses In applying GAAP, accountants are generally not required to distinguish between expenses that are reasonable and those that are not. If assets were used up in the production of revenues of the period, they are expenses of that period. This is not the case for tax purposes. ITA 67 indicates that only those expenditures that may be considered reasonable in the circumstances may be deducted in the computation of Net Income For Tax Purposes. If, for example, a large salary was paid to a spouse or to a child that could not be justified on the basis of the services provided, the deduction of the amount involved could be disallowed under ITA 67. The fact that this salary could be deducted in the determination of accounting income would not alter this conclusion.

Non-Arm's Length Transactions ITA 69 deals with situations involving transactions between related parties and provides special rules when such non-arm's length transactions take place at values other than fair market value (see Chapter 12 for a complete discussion of these rules). For example, if a taxpayer acquired an asset with a fair market value of $2,000 from a parent for $2,500 (a value in excess of its fair market value), the transferee is deemed to have acquired it at its fair market value of $2,000, while the parent is taxed on the basis of the $2,500 consideration received. If the transferee was a business, no similar adjustment would be required under GAAP. Note, however, there are requirements under GAAP for disclosing related party transactions.

8-15. As many of you are aware, the financial reporting rules applicable to accounting for taxes focus on temporary differences. Section 3465 of the *CICA Handbook* defines these differences with reference to Balance Sheet items. However, in determining business income (for tax purposes), the normal approach is to reconcile accounting Net Income with Net Income For Tax Purposes. As a consequence, individuals working in the tax area will focus on Income Statement differences, as opposed to Balance Sheet differences.

Business Income - Inclusions (Revenues)

Inclusions In The *Income Tax Act*

8-16. In subdivision b of the *Income Tax Act*, inclusions in business and property income are covered in Sections 12 through 17. The focus in this Chapter will be on Section 12 where we find the tax treatment of most of the items that we commonly think of as operating revenues for a business.

8-17. We would note, however, that ITA 12(1)(c) deals with interest income and ITA 12(1)(j) and (k) deal with dividends received. As these inclusions most commonly relate to property income, they will be discussed in Chapter 9, Income From Property.

8-18. In addition, ITA 12(1)(l) requires the inclusion of partnership income and ITA 12(1)(m) requires the inclusion of benefits from trusts. These inclusions will be dealt with in Chapters 20 and 21 which deal, respectively, with partnerships and trusts.

8-19. Sections 13 and 14, which deal with recapture of CCA and CEC inclusions, were covered in Chapter 7. Section 15, which deals with benefits conferred on shareholders of corporations, will be covered in Chapter 9, Income From Property. Sections 16 and 17 deal with specialized issues that will not be covered in this text.

Amounts Received And Receivable

8-20. The most important inclusion in business income is found in ITA 12(1)(b) which requires the inclusion of amounts that have become receivable during the year for goods and services that have been, or will be, delivered during the year. It also notes that amounts are deemed to be receivable on the day on which the services were rendered. You will note that this is consistent with the accountant's point of sale approach to revenue recognition.

8-21.   The wording of ITA 12(1)(b) makes it clear that, in general, business income is on an accrual basis. However, the inclusion varies from the usual GAAP definition of a revenue in that it includes amounts received for goods and services that have not yet been delivered or rendered. Under GAAP, advances from customers are treated as a liability, rather than as a revenue. We will find that the tax treatment is, in fact, reconciled with GAAP through the use of a reserve.

8-22.   In the following material we will examine how reserves are used to modify the amount of revenues recorded under ITA 12(1)(b). While, at first glance, these procedures appear to be somewhat different than those used under GAAP, they will generally result in a final inclusion that is identical to the amount of revenue that is recognized under GAAP.

Reserves

The General System

8-23.   In tax work, the term reserve is used to refer to a group of specific items that can be deducted in the determination of net business income. Unlike most deductions that relate either to cash outflows or the incurrence of liabilities, these items are modifications of amounts received (reserve for undelivered goods) or amounts receivable (reserve for bad debts and reserve for uncollected amounts).

8-24.   With respect to the use of such reserves, the basic rules are as follows:

Deductible Reserves   ITA 18(1)(e) indicates that a particular reserve cannot be deducted unless it is specifically provided for in the *Act*. This means that, for example, when estimated warranty costs are deducted as an accounting expense in the year in which the related product is sold, no reserve can be deducted for tax purposes, as a reserve for estimated warranty costs is not specified in the *Act*. Note that while ITA 20(1)(m.1) does refer to a manufacturer's warranty reserve, careful reading shows that amounts can only be deducted under this provision when they are for an extended warranty covered by an insurance contract.

Addition To Income   When a reserve is deducted in a particular taxation year, it must be added back to income in the immediately following year. These additions are required under various Paragraphs in ITA 12 (e.g., ITA 12(1)(d) requires the addition of reserves deducted for bad debts in the preceding year).

8-25.   The most common reserves deducted from business income are as follows:

- ITA 20(1)(l) - **Reserve For Doubtful Accounts**
- ITA 20(1)(m) - **Reserve For Undelivered Goods And Services**
- ITA 20(1)(n) - **Reserve For Unpaid Amounts**

8-26.   The more specific details of these reserves will be covered in the following material.

Bad Debts Reserve - ITA 20(1)(l)

8-27.   While specific tax procedures for dealing with bad debts differ from those used under GAAP, the alternative procedures will normally produce identical results. Specifically, under ITA 20(1)(l), a year end deduction is permitted for anticipated bad debts. During the subsequent year, actual bad debts may be deducted under ITA 20(1)(p). Then, at the end of this subsequent year, the old reserve is included in business income under ITA 12(1)(d), and a new reserve is established under ITA 20(1)(l).

Example   On December 31, 2006, at the end of its first year of operations, Ken's Print Shop estimates that $5,500 of its ending Accounts Receivable will be uncollectible. For 2006, an Allowance For Bad Debts is established for this amount for accounting purposes and a reserve is deducted under ITA 20(1)(l). During the year ending December 31, 2007, $6,800 in accounts receivable are written off. At December 31, 2007, estimated uncollectible accounts total $4,800.

8-28. For accounting purposes, the 2006 estimate of bad debts would be charged to expense and credited to an Allowance For Bad Debts (a contra account to Accounts Receivable). For tax purposes, the same amount would be deducted from net business income as a reserve.

8-29. During 2007, the accountant for Ken's Print Shop would credit Accounts Receivable and debit Allowance For Bad Debts for the actual write offs of $6,800. This would leave a debit (negative) balance in this account of $1,300 ($5,500 - $6,800), indicating that last year's estimate was too low. This error would be corrected by adding this amount to the Bad Debt Expense for 2007. The total expense for 2007 would be as follows:

Estimated Future Bad Debts	$4,800
Correction To Eliminate The Debit Balance In The Allowance	1,300
2007 Bad Debt Expense For Accounting Purposes	$6,100

8-30. For tax purposes, the total Bad Debt Expense would be the same $6,100. However, the calculation follows a different pattern:

Add: 2006 Reserve		$ 5,500
Deduct:		
2007 Write-Offs	($6,800)	
2007 Reserve	(4,800)	(11,600)
2007 Net Deduction For Tax Purposes		($ 6,100)

Exercise Eight-2

Subject: Reserve For Doubtful Accounts

On December 31, 2006, Norman's Flowers estimates that $16,000 of its ending Accounts Receivable will be uncollectible. An Allowance For Bad Debts is established for this amount and a reserve is deducted under ITA 20(1)(l). During the year ending December 31, 2007, $17,200 in bad accounts are written off. At December 31, 2007, estimated uncollectible accounts total $18,400. By what amount will the 2007 net business income of Norman's Flowers be increased or decreased by the preceding information with respect to bad debts?

End of Exercise. Solution available in Study Guide.

Reserve For Undelivered Goods And Services - ITA 20(1)(m)

8-31. It was previously noted that, unlike the situation under GAAP, amounts received for goods or services to be delivered in the future must be included in the calculation of revenues for tax purposes. However, this difference is offset by the ability to deduct, under ITA 20(1)(m), a reserve for goods and services to be delivered in the future. This means that, while the procedures are somewhat different, the treatment of amounts received for undelivered goods and services is the same under both the *Income Tax Act* and GAAP.

Example During the taxation year ending December 31, 2007, Donna's Auto Parts has receipts of $275,000. Of this amount, $25,000 is a prepayment for goods that will not be delivered until 2008.

Analysis While the $275,000 will be considered an inclusion in 2007 net business income, Donna will be able to deduct a reserve of $25,000 under ITA 20(1)(m). This $25,000 amount will have to be added back to her 2008 net business income, reflecting the fact that the goods have been delivered and the revenue realized.

Exercise Eight-3

Subject: Reserve For Undelivered Services

As an unincorporated business, Barbra's Graphic Design keeps its records on a cash basis. During 2007, its first year of operation, the business has cash sales of $53,400. At the end of the year, an additional $26,300 of revenues was receivable. Of the amounts received, $5,600 was for services to be delivered during 2008. Barbra estimates that $425 of the end of year receivable amounts will be uncollectible. What amount will be included for sales in the 2007 net business income of Barbra's Graphic Design?

End of Exercise. Solution available in Study Guide.

Reserve For Unpaid Amounts - ITA 20(1)(n)

8-32.   When a business sells goods with the amount being receivable over an extended period (i.e., instalment sales), ITA 20(1)(n) permits the deduction of a reasonable reserve based on the profit on the sale. Note that this type of reserve should not be confused with capital gains reserves which are covered in Chapter 10.

8-33.   While this is analogous to the use of the cash basis of revenue recognition for instalment sales, its applicability in tax work is more restricted than it is in accounting. Generally, a reserve can only be deducted under ITA 20(1)(n), if some of the proceeds are not receivable until two years after the property is sold (this two year requirement does not apply to sales of real property inventory).

8-34.   ITA 20(8) further limits the applicability by specifying that no reserve can be deducted in a year, for any type of property, if the sale took place more than 36 months before the end of that year. In addition, the reserve is not available if the purchaser is a corporation controlled by the seller, or a partnership in which the seller has a majority interest.

Exercise Eight-4

Subject: Reserve For Unpaid Amounts

During November, 2007, Martine's Jewels Ltd. sells a necklace for $120,000. The cost of this necklace was $55,000, resulting in a gross profit of $65,000. The $120,000 sales price is to be paid in four equal annual instalments on December 31 in each of the years 2008 through 2011. Martine's Jewels Ltd. has a December 31 year end. Indicate the amount of the reserve that can be deducted in each of the years 2007 through 2011.

End of Exercise. Solution available in Study Guide.

Other Inclusions

8-35.   There are a number of other inclusions in business income. While some are of limited interest in a text such as this (e.g., ITA 12(1)(z.4) requires the inclusion of eligible funeral arrangements), several of these inclusions warrant additional comment:

Damage Payments Received Damages are generally received as the result of non-performance of a contractual arrangement. As they will generally serve to offset deductible costs, they are included in income.

Profits From Betting Or Gambling Generally speaking, these items are not included in net business income. As lotteries are a form of gambling, lottery winnings would be received on a tax free basis.

However, if a taxpayer's gambling activities were so extensive as to constitute a business, such income could become taxable (e.g., a full time bookmaker). This would also suggest that losses would be fully deductible.

Profits From An Illegal Business   Many people are aware that the famous American gangster Al Capone was sent to jail, not for his illegal activities involving alleged robbery and murder, but rather for his failure to pay taxes on the resulting profits. As illegal revenues must be included in business income, related expenses are generally deductible. This can lead to interesting conclusions as evidenced by a 1999 publication of the New Zealand Inland Revenue Department. This publication provided a detailed list of items that could be deducted by what was referred to as "sex workers". Without going into detail, we would note that see-through garments and whips were on the list, provided they were used in delivering services to a client.

Debt Forgiveness   Situations arise in which outstanding debt is forgiven, often by a related taxpayer. When this happens, ITA 80 contains a complex set of rules that apply when the debtor has been able to deduct the interest expense on the forgiven debt. These rules may require the amount of debt forgiven to be applied to reduce loss carry over balances and, in some situations, to be included in income in the year of forgiveness. The details of these rules are beyond the scope of this text.

Government Assistance   Whether or not government assistance will be included in current income depends on the nature of the assistance. The tax rules here largely reflect the accounting rules that are found in Section 3805 of the *CICA Handbook*. That is, assistance related to current revenues and expenses will be included in current income while, in contrast, assistance related to the acquisition of capital assets will be deducted from the cost of these assets.

Inducement Receipts   Businesses may receive payments that induce them to undertake some activity. An example of this would be a payment received by a lessor to induce him to undertake leasehold improvements. The taxpayer has several alternatives here. The amount received can be included in current income, used to reduce the cost of any related assets, or used to reduce any required expenses. These are the same alternatives that are available under GAAP.

Restrictive Covenant Receipts   A restrictive covenant is an agreement entered into, an undertaking made, or a waiver of an advantage or right by a taxpayer. A proposed ITA 56.4 would, in general, require that these payments be included in income. There are a limited number of exceptions, one of which would allow the receipt to be allocated to Cumulative Eligible Capital.

Restrictions On Deductions From Business And Property Income

General Approach

8-36.   It would be extremely difficult to provide a detailed list of all of the items that might possibly be considered a business expense. While ITA 20 spells out many such items, it is often necessary to have more general guidance when new types of items arise. ITA 18 through ITA 19.1 gives this guidance in a somewhat backwards fashion by providing guidelines on what should not be deducted in computing business income. However, this negative guidance frequently provides assistance in determining what should be deducted in computing business income.

8-37.   Note, however, that if an item is specifically listed in the *Act* as a deduction, the specific listing overrides the general limitation. For example, Section 18 prohibits the deduction of capital costs, thereby preventing the immediate write-off of a capital asset. The fact that ITA 20(1)(aa) permits the deduction of landscaping costs, some of which would be capital expenditures, overrides the general prohibition found in Section 18.

8-38.   The restrictions contained in ITA 18 apply only to deductions from business and property income.   There are other restrictions, for example the cost of business meals and entertainment, that apply to deductions from either business and property income or employment income.   Most of these more general restrictions are found in Subdivision f, "Rules Relating To Computation Of Income", and are discussed later in this Chapter.   The more important of the ITA 18 through 19.1 limiting provisions are discussed here.

General Limitations
Incurred To Produce Income
8-39.   One of the most important of the limiting provisions is as follows:

> **ITA 18(1)(a)**   No deduction shall be made in respect of an outlay or expense except to the extent that it was made or incurred by the taxpayer for the purpose of gaining or producing income from the business or property.

8-40.   When there is a question as to the deductibility of an item not covered by a particular provision of the *Act*, it is usually this general limitation provision that provides the basis for an answer.   As a consequence, there are many Interpretation Bulletins dealing with such matters as legal and accounting fees (IT-99R5) and motor vehicle expenses (IT-521R).   In addition, there have been hundreds of court cases dealing with particular items.   For example, with respect to insurance costs, there have been cases in the following areas:

- Damage insurance on business assets (deductible)
- Life insurance when required by creditor (deductible, if interest on loan is deductible)
- Life insurance in general (not deductible)
- Partnership insurance on partners' lives (not deductible)
- Insurance against competition (deductible)

8-41.   As can be seen from the preceding list, this is a complex area of tax.   If there is doubt about a particular item's deductibility, it will sometimes be necessary to do considerable research to establish whether it is dealt with in an Interpretation Bulletin or a court case.

8-42.   In applying this provision, it is not necessary to demonstrate that the expenditure actually produced income.   It is generally sufficient to demonstrate that it was incurred as part of an income earning process or activity.

Reasonable Expectation Of Profit
8-43.   A second general consideration which may restrict the deductibility of certain items is the proposed legislation on reasonable expectation of profit.   This was discussed in Chapter 2.   In addition, as these rules often relate to the deductibility of interest costs, this material will be discussed in more detail in Chapter 9, Income From Property.

Restrictions On Specific Business And Property Income Deductions
Capital Expenditures
8-44.   ITA 18(1)(b) prohibits the deduction of any expenditures that are designated as capital expenditures.   However, deductions are permitted under ITA 20(1)(a) for capital cost allowances.   The limitations on this deduction were discussed in detail in Chapter 7.

Appraisal Costs
8-45.   The treatment of appraisal costs on capital property will depend on the reason for their incurrence:

- If they are incurred on a capital property for the purpose of its acquisition or disposition, they are generally added to the adjusted cost base of the property.
- If they are incurred incurred with respect to a proposed acquisition that does not take place, they should be treated as eligible capital expenditures (see Chapter 7).
- If they are incurred for the purpose of gaining or producing income from a business

(e.g., the cost of an appraisal required for insurance purposes), they are deductible in computing income for the year.

Exempt Income Expenditures

8-46. ITA 18(1)(c) prohibits the deduction of any expenditures that were incurred to produce income that is exempt from taxation. For a business, this would have limited applicability as few sources of business income are tax exempt.

Fines And Penalties

8-47. It is not uncommon for fines and penalties to be incurred in the process of carrying on business activity (e.g., the driver for a courier company receives a parking ticket while making a delivery). While some uncertainty existed with respect to the deductibility of these amounts in the past, the issuance of ITA 67.6 eliminated this uncertainty. This Section states that no deduction can be made for any fine or penalty imposed under a law of a country or of a political subdivision of a country.

Illegal Payments

8-48. Payments made to government officials that constitute an offence under either the *Corruption of Foreign Officials Act* or Canada's *Criminal Code* are not deductible. This would be the case, even if the related income was taxable.

Personal And Living Expenses

8-49. ITA 18(1)(h) prohibits the deduction of an expenditure that is a personal or living expense of the taxpayer. An example of this would be a situation where a business pays for the travel costs of one of its employees or owners. If the travel is business related, the costs would be deductible. Alternatively, if no business purpose was involved, the travel would be classified as a non-deductible personal or living expense.

8-50. This can create a very unfortunate tax situation in that, not only will the costs of such travel be non-deductible to the business, the beneficiary of the trip may have to include the value of the trip in their income as a shareholder or employee benefit. Clearly, it would be preferable to simply pay additional salary equal to the value of the trip. Using this alternative, the tax consequences to the employee or owner would be the same. However, the business would benefit from being able to deduct the amount paid.

8-51. Somewhat indirectly, ITA 18(1)(h) introduces an additional rule with respect to the deductibility of costs. The ITA 248(1) definition of "personal or living expenses" indicates that the expenses of properties maintained for the use of an individual or persons related to that individual are personal unless the properties maintained are connected to a business that is either profitable or has a reasonable expectation of being profitable.

Recreational Facilities And Club Dues

8-52. ITA 18(1)(l) prohibits the deduction of amounts that have been incurred to maintain a yacht, camp, lodge, golf course or facility, unless the taxpayer is in the business of providing such property for hire. Because of the fairly specific wording of this provision, it would appear that the costs of providing other types of recreational benefits would be deductible. For example, a corporation could deduct the costs of providing a general fitness center for their employees, provided it was made available to all employees.

8-53. A similar prohibition is made against the deduction of membership fees or dues to dining, sporting, or recreational facilities. Note, however, that there is no prohibition against deducting the cost of legitimate entertainment expenses incurred in such facilities, subject to the 50 percent limitation that will be described shortly.

Deferred Income Plans

8-54. ITA 18(1)(i) restricts the deductibility of contributions under supplementary unemployment benefit plans to the amount specified in ITA 145. ITA 18(1)(j) and 18(1)(k) provide similar limitations for contributions to deferred profit sharing plans and profit sharing plans. ITA 18(1)(o) prohibits the deduction of contributions to an employee benefit plan. Finally, under ITA 18(1)(o.1) and (o.2), limits are placed on the deductibility of amounts paid to salary deferral arrangements and retirement compensation arrangements. These amounts are only deductible as specified under ITA 20(1)(r) and (oo). All of these provisions are discussed in detail in Chapter 13, Retirement Savings And Other Special Income Arrangements.

Expenses Of A Personal Services Business

8-55.   A personal services business is a corporation that has been set up by an individual to provide personal services that are, in effect, employment services. ITA 18(1)(p) restricts the deductible expenses of such a corporation to those that would normally be deductible against employment income. Chapter 15, Taxable Income And Tax Payable For Corporations, provides coverage of this subject.

Automobile Mileage Payments

8-56.   As is discussed in Chapter 5, a business may pay its employees or shareholders a per kilometer fee for having them use their own automobile on behalf of the business. The amount of such payments that can be deducted by a business is limited by ITA 18(1)(r) to an amount prescribed in ITR 7306. For 2006 and 2007, this amount is 50 cents for the first 5,000 kilometers and 44 cents for additional kilometers driven by an employee.

8-57.   Amounts paid in excess of these limits will not be deductible to the business. However, provided they are reasonable, such larger amounts will still not be considered a taxable benefit to the employee. As was noted in Chapter 5, if the reimbursement is paid on a tax free basis and not included on the employee's T4 (i.e., an amount based on actual kilometers), it will be necessary for the employer to keep detailed records of each employee's mileage for the year.

Interest And Property Taxes On Land

8-58.   Many businesses pay interest and property taxes on land. To the extent that the primary purpose of holding this land is to produce income, these payments clearly represent amounts that can be deducted as part of the costs of carrying the land while it is producing income.

8-59.   In contrast, when land is vacant or generating insignificant amounts of income, ITA 18(2) restricts the deduction for property taxes and interest to the amount of net revenues produced by the land. For example, if a parcel of land that is being held as a future plant site is producing some revenues by being rented for storage, interest and property taxes on the land can only be deducted to the extent of the net revenues from the rent. ITA 53(1)(h) allows the non-deductible interest and property taxes to be added to the adjusted cost base of the property, thereby reducing any future capital gain resulting from the disposition of the property.

8-60.   In the case of land that is being held as inventory, ITA 10(1.1) permits the non-deductible interest and property taxes to be added to the cost of the land.

8-61.   The preceding general rules could be viewed as too restrictive for those companies whose "principal business is the leasing, rental or sale, or the development for lease, rental or sale, of real property". As a consequence, these real estate companies are allowed to deduct interest and property tax payments to the extent of net revenues from the property, plus a "base level deduction".

8-62.   This base level deduction is defined in ITA 18(2.2) as the amount that would be the amount of interest, computed at the prescribed rate, for the year, in respect of a loan of $1,000,000 outstanding throughout the year. This means that, if the prescribed rate for the year was 5 percent, real estate companies could deduct interest and property taxes on the land that they are carrying to the extent of net revenues from the land, plus an additional $50,000 [(5%)($1,000,000)].

Soft Costs

8-63.   Costs that are attributable to the period of construction, renovation, or alteration of a building, or in respect of the ownership of the related land, are referred to as soft costs. These costs could include interest, legal and accounting fees, insurance, and property taxes. In general, ITA 18(3.1) indicates that such costs are not deductible and must be added to the cost of the property.

Interest In Thin Capitalization Situations

8-64.   In general, interest paid on debt is deductible to a business, whereas dividends paid on outstanding shares are not. Given this, there is an incentive for a non-resident owner of a Canadian resident corporation to take back debt rather than equity, for the financing that he provides to the corporation. This could result in a situation where the interest on the debt reduces the profits of the Canadian corporation and the non-resident investor is not subject to Part I tax, or is subject to only a low withholding rate under Part XIII.

8-65.   To prevent this from happening, ITA 18(4) through 18(6) limit the deductibility of interest paid in such situations. Interest paid or payable to a non-resident specified shareholder is disallowed if it is paid on amounts of debt in excess of two times the sum of the individual's share of contributed capital (average for the year) plus 100 percent of the corporation's Retained Earnings at the beginning of the year. For this purpose, a specified shareholder is defined in ITA 18(5) as a person who holds shares that give him 25 percent or more of the votes, or 25 percent or more of the fair market value of all issued and outstanding shares. A simple example will serve to clarify these rules:

> **Example**   Mr. Lane, a resident of the U.S., owns 45 percent of the shares and holds $3,000,000 of the long-term debt securities of Thinly Ltd. The capital structure of Thinly Ltd. throughout the year is as follows:
>
> | | |
> |---|---:|
> | Long-Term Debt (11% Rate) | $5,000,000 |
> | Common Stock | 200,000 |
> | Retained Earnings | 300,000 |
> | Total Capital | $5,500,000 |
>
> **Analysis** Mr. Lane is clearly a specified shareholder as he holds 45 percent of the corporation's shares. His relevant equity balance is $390,000 [(45%)($200,000) + (100%)($300,000)]. His debt holding is clearly greater than two times this relevant equity balance. As a consequence, there would be disallowed interest of $244,200 calculated as follows:
>
> | | |
> |---|---:|
> | Total Interest Paid To Mr. Lane [(11%)($3,000,000)] | $330,000 |
> | Maximum Deductible Interest [(11%)(2)($390,000)] | (85,800) |
> | Disallowed Interest | $244,200 |

Exercise Eight-5

Subject: Interest In Thin Capitalizations

On January 1, 2006, a new Canadian corporation is formed with the issuance of $8,600,000 in debt securities and $2,400,000 in common shares. On this date, Ms. Sally Johnson, who is a resident of Mexico, acquires $4,500,000 of the debt securities and 30 percent of the common shares. The debt securities pay interest at 9 percent. The company has a December 31 year end. On January 1, 2007, the Retained Earnings balance of the company is $900,000. How much, if any, of the interest paid on Ms. Johnson's holding of debt securities during 2007 would be disallowed under ITA 18(4)?

End of Exercise.   Solution available in Study Guide.

Restrictions On Deductions From Business And Property Income

Prepaid Expenses

8-66.   ITA 18(9) prevents the deduction of amounts that have been paid for goods or services that will be delivered after the end of the taxation year. As a result, the tax treatment of these items is the same as their treatment under GAAP.

8-67.   With respect to interest, the normal calculation of interest involves multiplying a principal amount by an interest rate, and then adjusting the result for the period of time that the principal amount is outstanding. Given this calculation, any payments over and above the calculated interest must be viewed as a reduction in the principal amount. Despite the clarity of this concept, we continue to see references to so-called "prepaid interest".

8-68.   The most recent resurrection of this concept has been in a form that attempts to avoid the payment of taxes. This scheme involves designing a debt arrangement so that future interest payments are "prepaid", in order to create a larger current deduction in the calculation of Taxable Income for the payor. Consider the following example:

Example   The Martian Company issues $1,000,000 in debt securities on January 1, 2007. The face amount of the securities must be repaid after five years, on December 31, 2011. The securities pay interest at 10 percent with the $100,000 payments for 2007 and 2008 being made on December 31, 2007 and December 31, 2008. However, the discounted value of the 2009, 2010, and 2011 interest payments is also paid on December 31, 2007. The payment, equal to the present value of the three $100,000 payments discounted at 10 percent, is $226,077. The Company's year ends on December 31.

Analysis   In the absence of a special provision, the full $226,077 would be deductible as interest expense for the year ending December 31, 2007. However, this deduction is affected by Sections ITA 18(9.2) through ITA 18(9.8), which require this "prepaid interest" to be treated as a reduction in the principal amount of the debt. Although the interest deducted over the life of the debt will still total $426,077 [($100,000)(2) + $226,077], the deductions will be allocated over the life of the debt. Given this, the deductible interest for the years 2007 through 2011 would be as follows:

Year		Deductible Interest
2007	[(10%)($1,000,000)]	$100,000
2008	[(10%)($1,000,000 - $226,077)]	77,392
2009	[(10%)($773,923 - $100,000 + $77,392)]	75,132
2010	[(10%)($751,315 + $75,132)]	82,644
2011	[(10%)($826,447 + $82,644)]	90,909
Total		$426,077

Home Office Costs

8-69.   Many self-employed individuals maintain an office in their personal residence. Under certain circumstances, some of the costs associated with owning and maintaining this residence are deductible. More specifically, ITA 18(12) restricts the deductibility of home office costs to those situations where:

• the work space is the individual's principal place of business; or

• the space is used exclusively for the purpose of earning income from business and is used on a regular and continuous basis for meeting clients, customers, or patients of the individual.

8-70.   If an individual qualifies for this deduction because it is his principal place of business, the space does not have to be used exclusively for business purposes. If, for example, a dining room table is used to run a mail order business and that room qualifies as the principal place of business for the operation, home office costs can be deducted for the dining room space. Note, however, that in determining the appropriate amount of costs, consideration would have to be given to any personal use of that space.

8-71.   If the work space is not the principal place of business, it must be used exclusively for the purpose of earning income. This requires that some part of the home must be designated as the home office and not used for any other purpose.

8-72.   In addition, this second provision requires that the space be used on a regular and continuous basis for meeting clients, customers, or patients. IT-514, "Work Space In Home Expenses", indicates that a work space for a business that normally requires infrequent meetings, or frequent meetings at irregular intervals, would not meet this requirement.

8-73.   When the conditions for deductibility are met, expenses must be apportioned between business and non-business use in a reasonable manner, usually on the basis of floor space used. Pro rata deductions can be made for rent, mortgage interest, property taxes, property insurance, utilities, and various operating costs.

8-74.   You will recall from Chapter 5 that there is a similar deduction available to employees under ITA 8(13). As an employee, an individual cannot deduct the mortgage interest or CCA on the property. However, as we are dealing with business income here, these deductions are available.

8-75.   While the interest deduction should be used, individuals are generally advised not to deduct CCA, as this is likely to cause the business portion of the residence to lose its principal residence status (as explained in Chapter 10, capital gains on the disposition of a property that qualifies as a principal residence will usually be eligible for treatment that exempts it from taxation).

8-76.   Regardless of the types of costs deducted, home office costs cannot create or increase a business loss. As a result, the total deduction will be limited to the amount of net business income calculated without reference to the home office costs (IT-514). Any expenses that are not deductible in a given year because they exceed the business income in that year, can be carried forward and deducted in a subsequent year against income generated from the same business. In effect, there is an indefinite carry forward of unused home office costs. This carry forward is conditional on the work space continuing to meet the test for deductibility in future years.

Foreign Media Advertising

8-77.   In order to provide some protection to Canadian media, the *Act* places limitations on the deductibility of advertising expenditures in foreign media. For print media, this limitation is found in ITA 19, with ITA 19.1 containing a corresponding provision for broadcast media. In general, these provisions deny a deduction for expenditures made in foreign print or foreign broadcast media in those cases where the advertising message is directed primarily at the Canadian market. It does not apply where such foreign media expenditures are focused on non-Canadian markets.

8-78.   A modification of this general rule was made with the addition of ITA 19.01 to the *Income Tax Act*. ITA 19.01 modifies ITA 19 in a manner that exempts certain foreign periodicals from the general non-deductibility rule. Canadian businesses will be able to deduct 100 percent of advertising costs in the publications, without regard to whether it is directed at the Canadian market, provided 80 percent or more of its non-advertising content is "original editorial content". Original editorial content is defined as non-advertising content:

- the author of which is a Canadian citizen or a permanent resident of Canada and, for this purpose, "author" includes a writer, a journalist, an illustrator and a photographer; or

- that is created for the Canadian market and has not been published in any other edition of that issue of the periodical published outside Canada.

8-79.   If the periodical cannot meet the 80 percent criteria, only 50 percent of such advertising costs will be deductible. Note that ITA 19.01 applies to periodicals only, and not to other foreign media.

Provincial Capital And Payroll Taxes

8-80.   In the late 1980s and early 1990s, several provinces switched from having individual premiums for health care to a payroll tax applicable to all wages and salaries. This change had significant implications for the federal government because, as you may recall from Chapter 5, when an employer pays for individual provincial health care premiums, it is considered a taxable benefit to the employee. Given that many employers did, in fact, pay the individual provincial health care premiums, the switch to a non-individualized payroll tax resulted in a significant loss of revenues for the federal government.

8-81.   In response to such changes, the 1991 federal budget proposed limiting the deduction of provincial capital and payroll taxes to an annual amount of $10,000. This proposal proved to be very controversial and, as a consequence, is still pending. While the government has indicated that, as an interim measure, it will deny deductibility to any increases in provincial payroll or capital taxes, at present these amounts continue to be fully deductible.

Restrictions On Specific Deductions From Business Income

Introduction

8-82.   The restrictions that are found in ITA 18 through ITA 19.1 are applicable only to business and property income. For the most part, they involve expenses that would only be deductible against this type of income and so the restriction has no influence on the determination of other types of income. The exception to this is home office costs, which can be deducted in the calculation of either employment income or business and property income. Note, however, that in this case, a separate ITA Section is applicable to each type of income.

8-83.   Other types of expenses, for example business meals and entertainment, can generally be deducted against either employment or business income. The restrictions on deductions of these more general types of expenses are applicable to business, property, or employment income and, as a consequence, they are found in other Sections of the *Act*. More specifically, Division B's Subdivision f, "Deductions In Computing Income", covers these restrictions.

Reasonableness

8-84.   Subdivision f begins with a broad, general rule which limits deductible expenses to those that are "reasonable in the circumstances". This general limitation, which is applicable to the determination of business, property, or employment income, is as follows:

> **ITA 67**   In computing income, no deduction shall be made in respect of an outlay or expense in respect of which any amount is otherwise deductible under this Act, except to the extent that the outlay or expense was reasonable in the circumstances.

8-85.   This general rule is most commonly applied in non-arm's length situations. For example, it is not uncommon for the sole owner of a small private company to attempt income splitting through salary payments to a spouse or children. While there is a considerable amount of latitude for making such arrangements, the owner should be able to demonstrate that the individual who received the payment provided services that had a value that could reasonably be associated with the amount received.

Meals And Entertainment

General Rules

8-86.   It can be argued that business expenditures for food, beverages, or entertainment involve an element of personal living costs and, to the extent that this is true, such amounts should not be deductible in calculating Net Income For Tax Purposes. This idea is embodied in ITA 67.1(1) which restricts the amount that can be deducted for the human consumption of food or beverages, or the enjoyment of entertainment. The amount of these costs that can be deducted is equal to 50 percent. The Subsection makes it clear that this limit does not apply to meals related to moving costs, child care costs, or amounts eligible for the medical expense tax credit.

8-87. The March, 2007 budget contains a proposal which would alter this provision with respect to the food and beverage costs of long-haul truck drivers. For costs incurred in 2007 after March, 19, 2007, the deductible percentage of these costs will be increased to 60 percent. This will be increased to 65 percent in 2008, 70 percent in 2009, 75 percent in 2010, and 80 percent for years after 2010. These increases do not apply to any "entertainment" costs that long-haul drivers might incur.

Exceptions

8-88. ITA 67.1(2) provides for a number of exceptions to the general 50 percent limitation. These exceptions include:

- Hotels, restaurants, and airlines provide food, beverages, and entertainment in return for compensation from their customers. The costs incurred by these organizations in providing these goods and services continue to be deductible. However, when the employees of these organizations travel or entertain clients, their costs are subject to the 50 percent limitation.

- Meals and entertainment expenses relating to a fund raising event for a registered charity are fully deductible.

- Where the taxpayer is compensated by someone else for the cost of food, beverages, or entertainment, the amounts will be fully deductible against this compensation. For example, if Mr. Spinner was a management consultant, whose client reimbursed all his travel costs, there would be no 50 percent limitation on meals and entertainment for Mr. Spinner. However, his client would only be able to deduct 50 percent of any reimbursements for meals and entertainment that are paid to Mr. Spinner.

- When amounts are paid for meals or entertainment for employees and, either the payments create a taxable benefit for the employee, or the amounts do not create a taxable benefit because they are being provided at a remote work location, the amounts are fully deductible to the employer.

- When amounts are incurred by an employer for food, beverages, or entertainment that is generally available to all individuals employed by the taxpayer, the amounts are fully deductible. Note, however, this exception applies to no more than six special events held by an employer during a calendar year.

8-89. In addition to the preceding exceptions, ITA 67.1(3) provides a special rule for meals that are included in conference or convention fees. When the amount included in the fee for meals and entertainment is not specified, the Subsection deems the amount to be $50 per day. In these circumstances, it is this $50 per day that is subject to the 50 percent limitation.

8-90. Airline, bus, and rail tickets often include meals in their price. It appears that the government views the value of such meals as being fairly immaterial. This is reflected in the fact that ITA 67.1(4) deems the food component of the ticket cost to be nil. Individuals who have been subjected to these "meals" are likely to agree with this assessment!

Costs Of Automobile Ownership And Leasing

Basic Concept

8-91. When a business provides an automobile to an employee or shareholder, it is clear that these individuals have received a taxable benefit to the extent that they make any personal use of the vehicle. This fact, along with the methods used to calculate the benefit, were covered in detail in Chapter 5. As you will recall, the amount of the benefit is based on the cost of cars purchased or, alternatively, the lease payments made on cars that are leased.

8-92.   A different issue relates to the costs that can be deducted by a business in the determination of its net business income, or by any employee in the determination of net employment income. For a number of years, it has been the policy of the government to discourage the deduction of costs related to the use of what is perceived to be luxury automobiles. This has been accomplished by limiting the amounts that can be deducted for CCA, leasing costs and interest on automobiles that are used for business or employment activities.

8-93.   Before describing these limitations, we would again remind you that the taxable benefit resulting from a business providing an automobile to an employee or shareholder is calculated without regard to restrictions on deductibility. For example, if an employee has the use of a $150,000 passenger vehicle that is owned by his employer, his taxable benefit will not be affected by the fact that the employer's deduction for CCA on this automobile is limited to $30,000.

CCA And Interest

8-94.   With respect to cars that are owned by the business, ITA 13(7)(g) limits the deductibility of capital costs to a prescribed amount. From 2001 through 2007, this prescribed amount has been unchanged at $30,000, plus GST/HST and PST. This amount would be reduced by any GST/HST and PST that was recoverable as input tax credits.

8-95.   When the automobile is owned by the business, there may be interest costs associated with related financing. If this is the case, ITA 67.2 restricts the amount of interest that can be deducted on a loan to acquire an automobile to a prescribed amount. From 2001 through 2007, this prescribed amount has remained at $10 per day. Note that this amount is often expressed as $300 per month. While this is accurate for months with 30 days, the actual legislation is expressed as $300 ÷ 30, or $10 per day.

Exercise Eight-6

Subject: Deductible Automobile Costs (Business Owns Automobile)

On September 15, 2007, Ms. Vanessa Lord purchased an automobile to be used exclusively in her newly formed unincorporated business that commenced operations on September 15, 2007. The cost of the automobile was $45,000, before GST and PST. She finances a part of the purchase price and, as a consequence, has financing charges for the year of $1,200. In calculating her net business income for 2007, how much can Ms. Lord deduct for CCA and interest? Ignore GST and PST considerations.

End of Exercise. Solution available in Study Guide.

Lease Costs

8-96.   When a business leases a passenger vehicle, ITA 67.3 restricts the deductibility of the lease payments to a prescribed amount. The basic formula that is used to implement this limitation is as follows:

$$\left[A \ X \ \frac{B}{30} \right] - C - D - E, \text{ where}$$

A   is a prescribed amount ($800 for 2001 through 2007);
B   is the number of days from the beginning of the term of the lease to the end of the taxation year (or end of the lease if that occurs during the current year);
C   is the total of all amounts deducted in previous years for leasing the vehicle;
D   is a notional amount of interest since the inception of the lease, calculated at the prescribed rate on refundable amounts paid by the lessee in excess of $1,000;
E   is the total of all reimbursements that became receivable before the end of the year by the taxpayer in respect of the lease.

8-97.   In simplified language, this Section restricts the deductibility of lease payments to $800 (Item A), plus non-recoverable GST/HST and PST, per 30 day period for leases entered into in 2001 through 2007. Note that the prescribed amount applicable to the year in which the lease is signed is applicable throughout the lease term. That is, if the $800 limit was increased after 2007, the change would have no effect on the leasing cost limit calculations for years subsequent to 2007. The formula also contains components that:

- remove lease payments that were deducted in previous taxation years (Item C);
- require the deduction of imputed interest on refundable deposits that could be used by the lessee to reduce the basic lease payments (Item D);
- require the removal of reimbursements that are receivable by the taxpayer during the year (Item E).

8-98.   In applying this formula, it is important to note that all of the components are cumulative from the inception of the lease.

8-99.   While the basic concept of limiting the deductible amount to a prescribed figure is fairly straightforward, it would be very easy to avoid the intended purpose of the preceding formula. Almost any vehicle can be leased for less than $800 per 30 day period through such measures as extending the lease term, or including a required purchase by the lessee at the end of the lease term at an inflated value.

8-100.   Because of this, a second formula is required. This second formula is based on the manufacturer's suggested list price for the vehicle. The deductible amount is the lesser of the figures produced by the two formulas. This second formula is as follows:

$$\left[A \ X \ \frac{B}{.85 \ C} \right] - D - E, \text{ where}$$

A   is the total of the actual lease charges paid or payable in the year;

B   is a prescribed amount ($30,000 for vehicles leased in 2001 through 2007);

C   is the greater of a prescribed amount ($35,294 for vehicles leased in 2001 through 2007) and the manufacturer's list price for the vehicle (note that this is the original value, even when a used vehicle is leased);

D   is a notional amount of interest for the current year, calculated at the prescribed rate on refundable amounts paid by the lessee in excess of $1,000;

E   is the total of all reimbursements that became receivable during the year by the taxpayer in respect of the lease.

8-101.   Note that, unlike the calculations in the basic cumulative formula, the components of this formula are for the current year only. Also note that the .85 in the denominator is based on the assumption of a standard 15 percent discount off the manufacturers' list price. When the list price is $35,294, 85 percent of this amount is $30,000, leaving the (B ÷ .85C) component equal to one. This means that this component only kicks in when the list price exceeds $35,294, a vehicle that the formula assumes has been acquired for $30,000.

Example   A car with a manufacturer's list price of $60,000 is leased on December 1, 2006 by a company for $1,612 per month, payable on the first day of each month. The term of the lease is 24 months and a refundable deposit of $10,000 is made at the inception of the lease. In addition, the employee who drives the car pays the company $200 per month for personal use. Assume that the prescribed rate is 5 percent per annum for all periods under consideration. Ignoring GST and PST implications, determine the maximum deductible lease payments for 2006 and 2007.

2006 Solution   For 2006, the D component in the ITA 67.3 cumulative formula is $38 [(5%)($10,000 - $1,000)(31/365)] and the E component is $200 [($200)(1)]. The maximum deduction for the lease payment of $1,612 paid for 2006 is the lesser of:

- $\left[\$800 \times \dfrac{31}{30}\right] - \$0 - \$38 - \$200 = \underline{\underline{\$589}}$

- $\left[\$1,\!612 \times \dfrac{\$30,\!000}{(85\%)(\$60,\!000)}\right] - \$38 - \$200 = \underline{\underline{\$710}}$

The lesser of these figures is $589 and that is the maximum deduction for lease payments for 2006.

2007 Solution   Because the lease was entered into during 2006, the 2006 limit of $800 applies for the life of the lease. For 2007, the D components in the ITA 67.3 formula are $488 [(5%)($10,000 - $1,000)(396/365)] in the cumulative formula and $450 [(5%)($10,000 - $1,000)(365/365)] in the non-cumulative formula.

The 2007 E components are $2,600 [($200)(13)] in the cumulative formula, and $2,400 [($200)(12)] in the non-cumulative formula.

Given these calculations, the maximum deduction for the lease payments of $19,344 paid for 2007 is the lesser of:

- $\left[\$800 \times \dfrac{396}{30}\right] - \$589 - \$488 - \$2,\!600 = \underline{\underline{\$6,\!883}}$

- $\left[\$19,\!344 \times \dfrac{\$30,\!000}{(85\%)(\$60,\!000)}\right] - \$450 - \$2,\!400 = \underline{\underline{\$8,\!529}}$

The lesser of these figures is $6,883 and that is the maximum deduction for lease payments for 2007.

Exercise Eight-7

Subject: Deductible Automobile Costs (Business Leases Automobile)

On August 1, 2007, Mr. Sadim Humiz leases an automobile to be used 100 percent of the time in his unincorporated business. The lease cost is $985 per month. The manufacturer's suggested list price for the automobile is $78,000. Mr. Humiz makes no down payment and no refundable deposits. Determine his maximum deduction for lease payments for 2007. Ignore GST and PST considerations.

End of Exercise.   Solution available in Study Guide.

Leasing Property

8-102.   While from a legal perspective, leasing a property is a distinctly different transaction than purchasing the same property, the economic substance of many long-term leases is that they are arrangements to finance the acquisition of assets. From the perspective of the CRA, the problem with such long-term leases is that they may be structured to provide the enterprise with accelerated deductions in comparison with the CCA schedule that would have been applicable had the assets in question been purchased.

8-103.   Until 2001, IT-233R provided rules that looked through the legal form of some leases, requiring that they be treated as a purchase (lessee perspective) or sale (lessor perspective). For example, this Interpretation Bulletin indicated that leases, under which title passed to the lessee at the end of the lease term, should be treated as a purchase and sale by the parties to the transaction.

8-104.   However, in Shell Canada Limited vs. The Queen (99 DTC 5669), the Supreme Court of Canada indicated that, in general, it was not appropriate for the CRA to re-characterize a legal arrangement on the basis of its economic substance. This effectively overruled the content of IT-233R and, in light of this situation, the CRA canceled this Bulletin. This means that leases must now be accounted for as leases, without regard to whether the lease terms suggest that they are, essentially, instalment purchases.

8-105. This creates a significant difference between the accounting and tax rules for dealing with leasing arrangements. As many of you are aware, Section 3065 of the *CICA Handbook* requires the capitalization of long-term leases that meet certain criteria. These accounting rules focus on economic substance and, if the usual risks and rewards of ownership are transferred to the lessee, the lease must be treated as a sale and purchase. In contrast, the tax rules focus on legal form, requiring an actual transfer of title before the sale/purchase treatment is applied.

Exercise Eight-8

Subject: Leases: Tax vs. GAAP Treatment

Markit Ltd. signs a 10 year lease for an asset with an economic life of 11 years. The lease payments are $23,000 per year. Compare the tax treatment of the lease with its treatment under GAAP.

End of Exercise. Solution available in Study Guide.

Restrictions On Claiming Input Tax Credits

8-106. We have previously noted a number of restrictions related to the ability of a business to deduct certain types of costs in the calculation of income tax payable. For many of these items, there is a corresponding restriction on the ability of the business to claim input tax credits for GST purposes. Some of the more common restrictions are as follows:

Club Memberships   No input tax credit is allowed for GST paid on membership fees or dues in any club whose main purpose is to provide dining, recreational, or sporting facilities. Likewise, no credits are available for the GST costs of providing certain types of recreational facilities to employees, owners, or related parties.

Business Meals And Entertainment   The recovery of GST on meals and entertainment expenses is limited to 50 percent.

Passenger Vehicles   No input tax credits are available for GST paid on the portion of the cost or lease payment of a passenger vehicle that is in excess of the deduction limits ($30,000 cost for cars acquired in 2001 through 2007 and $800 monthly lease payments for leases entered into in 2001 through 2007). Also, if the vehicle is owned by a registrant who is an individual or a partnership and the vehicle is used partly for business (less than 90 percent) and partly for personal use, the input tax credit is prorated based on the annual CCA claimed.

Personal Or Living Expenses   Input tax credits cannot be claimed on costs associated with the personal or living expenses of any employee, owner, or related individual. An exception is available when GST is collected on the provision of the item to the employee, owner, or related individual.

Reasonableness   Both the nature and value of a purchase must be reasonable in relation to the commercial activities of the registrant before an input tax credit can be claimed. This is similar to the test of reasonableness that is found in the *Act*.

Business Income - Specific Deductions

Inventory Valuation (Cost Of Sales)

General Procedures

8-107.   IT-473R points out that ITA 10 and ITR 1801 allow two alternative methods of inventory valuation. They are:

- valuation at lower of cost or fair market value for each item (or class of items if specific items are not readily distinguishable) in the inventory;
- valuation of the entire inventory at fair market value.

8-108.   The selected method must be applied consistently from year to year, and cannot normally be changed. IT-473R indicates that, in exceptional circumstances, the CRA will allow a change, provided it can be shown that the new method is more appropriate and the taxpayer uses the new method for financial statement purposes.

8-109.   In determining market value, the usual accounting definitions are acceptable. This means that market refers to either replacement cost or net realizable value. Cost can be determined through specific identification, an average cost assumption, a First In, First Out (FIFO) assumption, or through the use of the retail method. In IT-473R, the CRA indicates that the use of a Last In, First Out (LIFO) assumption is not allowed and, while Interpretation Bulletins do not have the force of law, the prohibition against using LIFO has been upheld in the courts (M.N.R. v. Anaconda American Brass, 55 DTC 1120) and it is unlikely that this decision will be reversed.

8-110.   Most of you will recognize that, with the exception of the CRA's prohibition against LIFO, the tax rules for the valuation of inventory coincide with GAAP. This means that, unless LIFO is being used for accounting purposes, no adjustment will be required in converting accounting Net Income into Net Income for Tax Purposes.

Overhead Absorption

8-111.   While not discussed in ITA 10, IT-473R indicates that, in the case of the work in process and finished goods inventories of manufacturing enterprises, an applicable share of overhead should be included. The CRA will accept either direct costing, in which only variable overhead is allocated to inventories, or absorption costing, in which both variable and fixed overhead is added to inventories.

8-112.   However, the Bulletin indicates that, if the method followed for financial statement purposes is one of these acceptable methods, the same method must be used for tax purposes. IT-473R also indicates that the Department will not accept prime costing, a method in which no overhead is allocated to inventories.

8-113.   Under absorption costing, amortization will generally be a component of the overhead included in beginning and ending inventories. In calculating net business income, the amounts recorded as accounting amortization will be replaced by amounts available as CCA deductions. This process will require adjustments reflecting any amounts of amortization included in beginning and ending inventories. While these adjustments go beyond the scope of this text, interested readers will find that they are illustrated in an Appendix to IT-473R.

CICA Handbook Changes

8-114.   The preceding comments on the accounting requirements reflect the content of the *CICA Handbook* as per Release No. 44 (April, 2007). An Exposure Draft is outstanding that contains important changes in GAAP for inventories. The more important of these changes can be described as follows:

Inventory Valuation   The Exposure Draft requires that inventories must be carried at lower of cost and net realizable value. While fair market value can be used for tax purposes, it will no longer be acceptable for accounting purposes.

Cost Determination   The Exposure Draft prohibits the use of LIFO for cost determination. This is consistent with current tax policy in this area.

Overhead Allocation   The Exposure Draft does not permit direct costing. As IT-473R requires that the overhead allocation approach used for accounting also be used for tax purposes, this would appear to eliminate the use of direct costing for tax purposes.

Special Rule For Artists

8-115.   When artists are required to apply normal inventory valuation procedures, it prevents them from writing off the cost of their various works until they are sold. Given the periods of time that such works are sometimes available for sale, this can result in hardship for some artists. As a consequence, ITA 10(6) allows artists to value their ending inventories at nil, thereby writing off the costs of producing a work prior to its actual sale.

Exercise Eight-9

Subject: LIFO vs. FIFO

Maxim Inc. uses LIFO to measure the costs of its merchandise inventories. On January 1, 2007, the LIFO value was $13,500 less than the FIFO value. On December 31, 2007, the LIFO figure was $11,200 less than the FIFO figure. Determine, for Maxim's 2007 taxation year, the amount of the adjustment required to convert accounting Net Income to net business income with respect to cost of sales.

End of Exercise.   Solution available in Study Guide.

Other Deductions

8-116.   The preceding material has described some of the many restrictions that the *Income Tax Act* places on the deduction of items in the determination of net business income. In considering these restrictions, it becomes clear that they also serve to provide general guidance on the items that are deductible.

8-117.   In addition to this general guidance, ITA 20 contains a detailed list of specific items that can be deducted in computing net business income. If an item falls clearly into one of ITA 20's deduction categories, it is not subject to the restrictions listed in ITA 18. Some of the more important deductions described in ITA 20 are as follows:

- 20(1)(a) - **Capital Cost Of Property**   This Paragraph provides for the deduction of a portion of the cost of capital assets as capital cost allowances. The detailed provisions related to this deduction are covered in Chapter 7.

- 20(1)(b) - **Cumulative Eligible Capital Amount**   This relates to the write-off of certain long-lived assets, including goodwill and other intangibles as discussed in Chapter 7.

- 20(1)(c) and (d) - **Interest**   These two Paragraphs cover both current and accrued interest, provided the borrowed money was used to earn business or property income. Chapter 9 contains a detailed discussion of some of the problems that arise in this area.

- 20(1)(e) - **Expenses Re Financing**   In general, costs related to the issuance of shares or incurred on the borrowing of funds must be deducted on a straight-line basis over five years. Any undeducted financing costs can be written off when the loan is repaid.

- 20(1)(f) - **Discount On Certain Obligations**   For tax purposes, bond discounts cannot be amortized over the life of the bonds, the normal accounting treatment. If the bonds are issued for not less than 97 percent of their maturity amount and, if the effective yield is not more than 4/3 of the coupon rate, the full amount of the discount can be deducted when the bonds are retired. If these conditions are not met, the payment of the discount at maturity is treated as a capital loss, only one-half of which can be deducted. Note that the tax treatment of bond premiums also differs from the normal accounting treatment. We would note here that, for tax purposes, bond premiums will not normally be amortized over the life of the bond. This issue is discussed in more detail in Chapter 9 which deals with property income.

- 20(1)(j) - **Repayment Of Loan By Shareholder**   As is explained in Chapter 9, if a loan to a shareholder is carried on the Balance Sheet of a corporation for two consecutive year ends, the principal amount must be added to the income of the borrower. This Paragraph provides for a deduction when such loans are repaid.

- 20(1)(l) - **Reserves For Doubtful Debts**

- 20(1)(m) - **Reserves For Goods And Services To Be Delivered In Future Taxation Years**

- 20(1)(m.1) - **Reserves For Warranties**   This provision only applies to amounts paid to third parties to provide warranty services. It does not apply to so-called "self warranty" situations where the business that sold the warrantied item assumes the risk of providing warranty services.

- 20(1)(n) - **Reserve For Unpaid Amounts**   This reserve provides for limited use of cash based revenue recognition in computing net business income.

- 20(1)(p) - **Actual Write Offs Of Bad Debts**

- 20(1)(q) - **Employer's Contributions To Registered Pension Plans**   This deduction is subject to the limitations described in Chapter 13. In addition, only amounts paid during the year can be deducted.

- 20(1)(y) - **Employer's Contributions Under A Deferred Profit Sharing Plan**   Only amounts that are paid during the year can be deducted.

- 20(1)(z) and (z.1) - **Costs Of Cancellation Of A Lease**   This deduction, in effect, requires amounts paid by a lessor to cancel a lease to be treated as a prepaid expense. Such amounts can be deducted on a pro rata per diem basis over the original term of the lease. If the property is sold subsequent to the cancellation, the remaining balance can be deducted at that time. If the property is a capital property, only one-half of the remaining balance can be deducted.

- 20(1)(aa) - **Costs For Landscaping Of Grounds**   In the absence of this provision, landscaping costs would have to be treated as a capital expenditure. While this provision allows for an immediate deduction, it is based on amounts paid in the year. Costs accrued at the end of the taxation year cannot be deducted.

- 20(1)(cc) - **Expenses Of Representation**

- 20(1)(dd) - **Costs Of Investigation Of A Site To Be Used In The Business**

- 20(1)(oo) - **Amounts Deferred Under A Salary Deferral Arrangement**

- 20(1)(qq) and (rr) - **Disability Related Costs**   These two paragraphs allow the costs of disability related building modifications and acquisitions of disability related equipment to be treated as current deductions, rather than as capital assets. Like the similar provision for landscaping costs, the deduction is only available for amounts paid during the year.

- 20(4) - **Uncollectible Portion Of Proceeds From Disposition Of A Depreciable Property**

- 20(10) - **Convention Expenses**   This allows the taxpayer to deduct the costs of attending no more than two conventions held during the year, provided they are in a location that is consistent with the territorial scope of the organization.

- 20(11) - **Foreign Taxes On Income From Property Exceeding 15 Percent**   This provision is only applicable to individuals and reflects the fact that an individual's credit for foreign taxes paid is limited to 15 percent. This matter is discussed in Chapters 9 and 22.

- 20(16) - **Terminal Losses**   This deduction was explained in Chapter 7.

Reconciliation Schedule

8-118.   While it would be possible to calculate net business income starting with a blank page, adding inclusions, and subtracting deductions, this approach is rarely used. Since most businesses have an accounting system that produces an accounting Net Income figure, the normal approach to determining net business income is to start with accounting Net Income, then add and deduct various items that are different for tax purposes. Note, however, that some smaller businesses that do not require audited financial statements base their regular accounting system on tax rules. In such cases, no reconciliation is needed.

8-119.   For those businesses that base their accounting system in whole or part on GAAP, a reconciliation between accounting Net Income and net business income is required. While there are many other items that could require adjustment, the items shown in the reconciliation schedule in Figure 8-1 (following page) are the common items for most taxpayers.

8-120.   We have tried to list the deduction beside the related addition where possible. While most of these adjustments related to the determination of Net Business Income, some relate to the determination of Net Taxable Capital Gains. We would also note that these adjustments are the same, without regard to whether the business is an unincorporated proprietorship or partnership or, alternatively, an incorporated business (a corporation).

8-121.   In working with this schedule, several general points are relevant:

- Accounting Net Income is an after tax concept. This means that the Tax Expense that is recorded in the accounting records must be added back in this reconciliation schedule. This addition would include both the current tax expense and any future tax expense recorded under GAAP.

- The amounts deducted in the accounting records for amortization, scientific research, and resource amounts will generally be different from the amounts deducted for tax purposes. While it would be possible to simply deduct the net difference (the tax amount is normally larger than the accounting amount), the traditional practice here is to add back the accounting amount and subtract the tax amount (e.g., we add back accounting amortization and subtract CCA).

- Accounting gains on the disposition of capital assets will be deducted and losses added in this schedule. With these amounts removed, they will be replaced by the relevant tax amounts. As explained in Chapter 7, the disposition of capital assets can result in capital gains, recapture, or terminal losses. These amounts are listed in the Figure 8-1 schedule.

- As was noted in Chapter 3, allowable capital losses can only be deducted against taxable capital gains. As a consequence, only the excess of taxable capital gains over allowable capital losses is included in this schedule. If there is an excess of allowable capital losses over taxable capital gains in the current year, the excess can be carried forward or carried back, but it cannot be deducted in the current year. As a consequence, such amounts are not included in this reconciliation schedule.

- Two major items in the GAAP based financial statements rarely require adjustments. These are Sales and Cost Of Goods Sold. As noted previously in this Chapter, the various reserves that are associated with the sales figure (e.g., bad debts), generally produce tax results that are identical to those in the accounting records. Similarly, the inventory valuation methods that are available for tax purposes are, with the exception of the CRA's refusal to accept LIFO, identical to those used in the GAAP based financial statements.

```
┌─────────────────────────────────────────────────────────────────────────┐
│                           Figure 8 - 1                                     │
│         Conversion Of Accounting Net Income To Net Income For Tax Purposes  │
├─────────────────────────────────────────────────────────────────────────┤
```

Additions To Accounting Income:

- Amortization, depreciation, and depletion of tangible and intangible assets (Accounting amounts)
- Recapture of CCA
- Tax reserves deducted in the prior year
- Losses on the disposition of capital assets (Accounting amounts)
- Scientific research expenditures (Accounting amounts)
- Warranty expense (Accounting amounts)
- Amortization of discount on long-term debt issued (see discussion in Chapter 9)
- Foreign tax paid (Accounting amounts)
- Excess of taxable capital gains over allowable capital losses
- Income tax expense
- Interest and penalties on income tax assessments
- Non-deductible automobile costs
- Fifty percent of business meals and entertainment expenses
- Club dues and cost of recreational facilities
- Non-deductible reserves in current year (Accounting amounts)
- Political contributions
- Charitable donations
- Asset write-downs including impairment losses on intangibles

Deductions From Accounting Income:

- Capital cost allowances (CCA)
- Amortization of cumulative eligible capital (CEC)
- Terminal losses
- Tax reserves claimed for the current year
- Gains on the disposition of capital assets (Accounting amounts)
- Deductible scientific research expenditures
- Deductible warranty expenditures
- Amortization of premium on long-term debt issued
- Foreign non-business tax deduction [ITA 20 (12)]
- Allowable business investment losses

- Political contributions are added back in this schedule as they cannot be deducted for tax purposes. However, the *Income Tax Act* provides for a tax credit with respect to limited amounts of such contributions. As covered in Chapter 6, despite the availability of this credit in the *Income Tax Act*, the new *Federal Accountability Act* includes a ban on contributions by corporations, trade unions and unincorporated associations. This legislation is effective January 1, 2007 and, given the ban that it contains, there will generally be no deductions for political contributions in the determination of accounting Net Income for corporations. Consequently, there will be no need for this reconciliation item. We have retained it in the schedule for this year as you may encounter it in other similar schedules.

Business Income - Example

Example Data

8-122.   The Markee Company has a December 31 accounting and taxation year end and, for the year ending December 31, 2007, its GAAP determined income before taxes amounted to $1,263,000. You have been asked to calculate the Company's 2007 Net Income For Tax Purposes, and have been provided with the following additional information concerning the 2007 fiscal year:

1. Accounting amortization expense totalled $240,000. For tax purposes, the Company intends to deduct CCA of $280,000.

2. Accounting income includes a gain on the sale of land in the amount of $20,000. For tax purposes, one-half of this amount will be treated as a taxable capital gain.

3. During December, the Company spent $35,000 on landscaping costs. These costs were capitalized in the Company's accounting records. As the expenditure was near the end of the year, no amortization was recorded.

4. The Company's Interest Expense includes $5,000 in bond discount amortization.

5. Financing costs, incurred on January 1, to issue new common stock during the year totaled $60,000. All of these costs were charged to expense in the accounting records.

6. Accounting expenses include $48,000 in business meals and entertainment.

7. During the year, the Company begins selling a product on which it provides a five year warranty. At the end of the year, it recognizes a warranty liability of $20,000.

8. In the accounting records, the Company recognized a Pension Expense of $167,000. Contributions to the pension fund totaled $150,000.

9. The Company leased a car beginning on June 1, 2006 that is used by the sales manager. The lease payments are $750 per month on a car with a manufacturer's suggested list price of $33,000. No refundable deposit was paid.

10. For accounting purposes, the Company uses the LIFO approach to inventory cost determination. The opening Inventories would have been $22,000 higher using a FIFO approach, while the closing Inventories would have been $18,000 higher using FIFO.

Example Analysis

8-123.   The following points are relevant to the Net Income calculation:

- Item 3 - Despite the fact that landscaping costs are usually capital costs, ITA 20(1)(aa) specifically permits their immediate deduction.

- Item 5 - Financing costs must be amortized over five years on a straight-line basis. As a result, only $12,000 is deductible in the current year and $48,000 must be added back to income.

- Item 6 - Only 50 percent of business meals and entertainment can be deducted.

- Item 7 - Warranty costs can only be deducted as incurred.

- Item 8 - Pension costs can only be deducted when they are funded.

- Item 9 - The lease payments are not limited by the restrictions described beginning in Paragraph 8-96. As a result, the payments are fully deductible and no adjustment is needed.

- Item 10 - As LIFO cannot be used for tax purposes, an adjustment to Cost Of Goods Sold is required. The LIFO adjustment to the opening inventories would increase Cost Of Goods Sold by $22,000, while the corresponding adjustment to the closing inventories would reduce Cost Of Goods Sold by $18,000. The net effect is an increase in Cost Of Goods Sold of $4,000 and a reduction in Net Income For Tax Purposes in the same amount.

8-124.   Taking into consideration the preceding points, the calculation of 2007 Net Income For Tax Purposes would be as follows:

Accounting Income Before Taxes		$1,263,000
Additions (Identified By Item Number):		
1- Accounting amortization	$240,000	
2 - Taxable capital gain on land sale [(1/2)($20,000)]	10,000	
4 - Bond discount amortization	5,000	
5 - Financing costs [(80%)($60,000)]	48,000	
6 - Meals and entertainment [(50%)($48,000)]	24,000	
7 - Warranty liability	20,000	
8 - Unfunded pension expense ($167,000 - $150,000)	17,000	364,000
Deductions (Identified By Item Number):		
1 - Capital Cost Allowance (CCA)	($280,000)	
2 - Accounting gain on sale of land	(20,000)	
3 - Landscaping costs	(35,000)	
10 - LIFO adjustment	(4,000)	(339,000)
Net Income For Tax Purposes		$1,288,000

Taxation Year

General Rules

8-125.   The *Act* defines a taxation year as follows:

ITA 249(1)   For the purpose of this Act, a "taxation year" is

(a) in the case of a corporation, a fiscal period, and
(b) in the case of an individual, a calendar year,

and when a taxation year is referred to by reference to a calendar year, the reference is to the taxation year or years coinciding with, or ending in, that year.

8-126.   For corporations, ITA 249.1(1) defines a fiscal period as a period that does not exceed 53 weeks. The 53 week designation provides for situations where a corporation wishes to have a fiscal period that ends in a specified week within a month. For example, if the corporate year end is the last Friday in January, the fiscal year will, in some years, include 53 weeks.

8-127.   A new corporation can select any fiscal year end. However, subsequent changes require the approval of the Minister. In most situations, corporations will have a fiscal year for tax purposes that coincides with the fiscal period used in their financial statements.

Unincorporated Businesses - Non-Calendar Fiscal Year

8-128.   Unincorporated businesses such as proprietorships and partnerships are not, for income tax purposes, separate taxable entities. The income of such businesses is included in the tax return of the individual proprietor or partner. As noted, the general rule applicable to individuals is that their taxation year is the calendar year.

8-129.   While unincorporated businesses are not required to file an income tax return, they are required to calculate an annual business income figure to be included in the tax returns of their owners. Given that the individuals who are the owners of proprietorships and partnerships must use a taxation year based on the calendar year, it would seem logical to require that these unincorporated businesses also base their taxation year on a calendar year.

8-130.   This logic is overridden, however, by the fact that there can be important reasons, unrelated to income tax, for the use of a non-calendar fiscal year (e.g., having the year end at a low point in the activity of the business). As a consequence, under ITA 249.1(4), a proprietorship or partnership can elect to have a fiscal year that does not end on December 31.

8-131.   This election is available to any new unincorporated business. However, it must be made on or before the filing date for the individual proprietor or partner. This would be June

15 of the year following the year in which the business commences. The election cannot be made in a subsequent year.

8-132.   If the election is made, ITA 34.1(1) requires taxpayers to include an amount of income for the period between the end of their normal fiscal year and December 31 of that year. This income is referred to as "additional business income" and, in simple terms, it is a pro rata extrapolation of the income earned during the non-calendar fiscal period that ends in the year. It is used to create an estimate of the income that will be earned from the end of the non-calendar fiscal period to the end of the calendar year. A simple example will illustrate this process.

> **Example**   Jack Bartowski forms a new business on November 1, 2006. It has a fiscal year end of January 31 and, for the period November 1 through January 31, 2007, it has income of $25,000. The "additional business income" that must be added for 2007 is calculated as follows:
>
> $$[(\$25,000)(334 \text{ Days} \div 92 \text{ Days})] = \$90,761$$
>
> The 334 days is for the period February 1, 2007 through December 31, 2007. The 92 days is for the period November 1, 2006 through January 31, 2007. The income that will be reported by Mr. Bartowski in his 2007 personal tax return is $115,761 ($25,000 + $90,761). Note that he will be taxed on his estimated income for 14 months. There is an election available that would alleviate this situation by allowing him to report the November and December 2006 income in 2006, and not 2007.
>
> In 2008, Mr. Bartowski's tax return will include his actual business income for the period February 1, 2007 through January 31, 2008, plus an "additional business income" amount similar to the preceding calculation, but based on the income for the fiscal period ending on January 31, 2008. This total is reduced by the "additional business income" of $90,761 included in his 2007 tax return, to provide an estimate of the income that will be earned in calendar 2008.

Exercise Eight-10

Subject: Additional Business Income - Non-Calendar Fiscal Year

Mr. Morgan Gelato starts a business on February 1, 2007. Because it will be a slow time of year for him, he intends to have a fiscal year that ends on June 30. During the period February 1, 2007, through June 30, 2007, his business has income of $12,300. What amount of business income will Mr. Gelato report in his personal tax return for the year ending December 31, 2007?

End of Exercise.   Solution available in Study Guide.

Special Business Income Situations

Income For Farmers

Farm Losses

8-133.   For an individual who looks to farming as his chief source of activity and income, farm losses are fully deductible against other types of income. The difficulty with farm losses is that there are various levels of interest in farming activity, ranging from a full time endeavour to produce profits from farming, through situations where an individual acquires a luxury home in a rural setting, allows three chickens to run loose in the backyard, and then tries to deduct all the costs of owning and operating the property as a "farm loss". In the latter case, the ownership of a "farm" is nothing more than a hobby or a means to enhance the individual's lifestyle.

8-134.   For such hobby farmers, engaged in farming activity as merely an attractive addition to a lifestyle and with no serious intent to produce a profit from this type of activity, the costs of farming must be viewed as personal living expenses. This means that no portion of farm losses should be considered deductible by hobby farmers.

Restricted Farm Losses

8-135.   The more complex situation is an individual who expects to make a profit from farming, but for whom farming is not his chief source of income. This individual is described in IT-322R, "Farm Losses", as:

> **Paragraph 1(b)**   A taxpayer whose chief source of income is not farming or a combination of farming and some other source of income, but who still carries on a farming business. Such a taxpayer must operate the farm with a reasonable expectation of profit but devotes the major part of his or her time and effort to other business or employment.

8-136.   In this situation, ITA 31 comes into effect. This Section limits the amount of farm losses that can be deducted against other sources of income to the first $2,500 of such losses, plus one-half of the next $12,500, for a total deduction of $8,750 on the first $15,000 of farm losses.

8-137.   Any amount that is not deductible in the current year is commonly referred to as a "restricted farm loss" and is subject to carry over provisions. These carry over provisions are given detailed consideration in Chapter 14.

8-138.   While the preceding distinctions between various types of farming activity may appear to be reasonably clear, this is not the case in actual practice. It is rare that a month goes by without a case involving these distinctions being heard at some stage of the assessment appeals process. In order to provide some clarification of the distinctions between hobby farmers, farmers eligible for the deduction of all farm losses, and farmers whose losses are restricted under ITA 31, the CRA issued Income Tax Technical News #30 in May, 2004.

Exercise Eight-11

Subject: Farm Losses

Ms. Suzanne Morph is a high school teacher. In her spare time she grows vegetables for sale in the local farmers' market. While in most years she has shown a profit, she incurred a loss in 2007 of $18,700. How much of this loss is deductible in her 2007 tax return?   Calculate any farm loss carry over available to her.

End of Exercise. Solution available in Study Guide.

Losses And Cash Basis Accounting

8-139.   As previously noted in this Chapter, business income is generally computed on the basis of accrual accounting. A major exception to this applies to taxpayers engaged in a farming or fishing business. ITA 28 permits an election for a farming or fishing business to determine income on a cash basis. This is in contrast to the required use of accrual accounting in the computation of other types of business income.

8-140.   As most farmers will have receivables and inventories in excess of their payables, the ability to calculate income on a cash basis has a general tendency to defer the payment of tax. While it is clear that the original intent of ITA 28 was to provide this form of relief to the farming industry, the government has become concerned that taxpayers were using even bona fide farms, in contrast to those described previously as hobby farms, as tax shelters, particularly in years when losses were incurred.

8-141.   The remedy to this problem that has evolved is to require an inventory adjustment in those cases where the use of the cash basis produces a loss. This requires the lesser of the amount of the cash basis loss and the value of purchased inventories to be added back to the cash basis income.

8-142.   Although the procedures involved are complicated by a number of factors such as transitional rules and the treatment of the preceding year's mandatory inventory adjustment, a simple example will illustrate some of the procedures:

> **Example**   Garfield Farms begins operations on January 1, 2007. At this time, it has no Accounts Receivable, Accounts Payable, or Inventories. The Loss on a cash basis for the year ending December 31, 2007 amounted to $600,000. On December 31, 2007, Garfield Farms has the following:
>
> - Accounts Receivable of $2,000,000
> - Inventories that total $1,400,000
> - Accounts Payable of $750,000
>
> **Accrual Basis Income**   Accrual basis income for the year ending December 31, 2007 would amount to $2,050,000 (-$600,000 + $2,000,000 + $1,400,000 - $750,000).
>
> **Inventory Adjustment**   A mandatory inventory adjustment of $600,000 (lesser of the $600,000 loss and $1,400,000 in inventories) would be added to the loss of $600,000, resulting in a final income figure of nil.

Capital Gains Deduction

8-143.   One of the most important tax benefits available to Canadian residents is the life-time capital gains deduction. This deduction essentially provides for a significant amount of capital gains on dispositions of farm property and shares of a qualified small business corporation to be received tax free. Until the March, 2007 budget, this amount was $500,000. For dispositions on or after March 19, 2007, the maximum deduction has been increased to $750,000. This provision is discussed in detail in Chapter 14.

Income For Professionals

8-144.   When a business involves the delivery of professional services, clients are billed on a periodic basis, normally after a block of work has been completed. This block of work may be task defined (e.g., billing when a client's tax return is finished), time defined (e.g., billing on a monthly basis), or on some other basis. However, in the majority of professional income situations, billing does not occur until after the work has been completed.

8-145.   If the normal accrual approach was applied to this type of business income, the inclusion in net business income would be recorded at the time work is being done. This would require the inclusion of work in progress (i.e., unbilled receivables) in net business income. However, ITA 34 contains a special rule that is applicable to accountants, dentists, lawyers, medical doctors, veterinarians, and chiropractors. These professionals can elect not to include unbilled work in progress in their income. This so-called "billed basis of income recognition" is not available to other professionals such as architects, engineers, and management consultants.

> **Example**   Ms. Shelly Hart begins her new accounting practice on January 1, 2007. During her first year of operation, she records 2,050 billable hours. Her regular billing rate is $100 per hour and, at the end of her first year, she has billed 1,750 hours, or a total of $175,000. Of this amount, $32,300 is uncollected at the end of the year.
>
> **Analysis**   As Ms. Hart is an accountant, she can elect the use of the billed basis. If she does so, her inclusion in Net Income For Tax Purposes will be $175,000. Alternatively, if she used the normal accrual approach, the inclusion would be $205,000 [($100)(2,050)]. It would clearly be to her advantage to use the billed basis.

Exercise Eight-12

Subject: Income Of Professionals

Jack Winters is a lawyer and, at the beginning of the current year, he had unbilled work in process of $35,000, as well as uncollected billings of $57,000. During the year, he bills the remaining work in process and collects all of these new receivables, as well as the uncollected amounts that were present at the beginning of the year. His work during the year totals potential billings of $245,000. Of this amount, $185,000 has been billed and $160,000 of these billings have been collected. Calculate his inclusion in net business income for the year using:

- the cash basis;
- the billed basis; and
- accrual accounting.

End of Exercise.   Solution available in Study Guide.

Scientific Research And Experimental Development
General Rules

8-146.   In an effort to encourage expenditures in this area of business activity, special provisions for scientific research and experimental development (SR&ED) expenditures are provided in ITA 37 as well as other Sections of the *Income Tax Act*. SR&ED is defined in ITA 248(1), with further guidance provided by IC 86-4R3, "Scientific Research And Experimental Development", and IT-151R5, "Scientific Research And Experimental Development Expenditures".

8-147.   The concepts that are involved here are very technical in nature and, as a reflection of the value of the tax incentives associated with these expenditures, often the subject of dispute between taxpayers and the CRA. Because of this, taxpayers intending to make claims in this area are well advised to seek specialized professional assistance.

8-148.   One of the advantages of SR&ED expenditures is that they, in effect, have an unlimited carry forward. Any expenditures that are not deducted in the current year are added to a pool and may be deducted in any future year.

8-149.   A second advantage associated with SR&ED expenditures is that, to the extent they involve capital assets other than buildings, the full cost of acquisition can be deducted in the year of acquisition. Even in the case of buildings, this immediate write-off is available for those acquisitions that have a special SR&ED purpose (e.g., a wind tunnel). This provides for a much faster write-off than the application of normal CCA rules.

8-150.   A further advantage associated with SR&ED expenditures is the fact that they generate some of the most generous investment tax credits that are available under today's tax legislation. As is discussed in Chapter 15, if a Canadian controlled private corporation spends $2 million on qualified SR&ED, under certain circumstances, the government may write that company a cheque for $700,000.

Ceasing To Carry On A Business
General Rules

8-151.   ITA 22 through 25 contain a group of provisions that deal with situations where a person ceases to carry on business. Of particular importance are ITA 22, "Sale Of Accounts Receivable", and ITA 23, "Sale Of Inventory". These provisions apply to both incorporated and unincorporated businesses.

8-152.   When a business ceases to operate, its assets are likely to be sold in their entirety. As a business in its entirety is considered to be a capital asset, any resulting gains and losses would normally be considered to be capital in nature. While this may be appropriate with respect to many of the assets of a business, inventories and accounts receivable would generally not be viewed as capital assets if they were sold separately by a business that was continuing to operate. Because of this anomaly, there are special provisions with respect to gains and losses on the disposition of inventories and accounts receivable that are sold as part of a business liquidation.

Inventories

8-153.   ITA 23 provides that when inventories are included in the sale of a business, the sale will be viewed as being in the ordinary course of carrying on the business. This means that any gain or loss resulting from a sale of inventory will be treated as business income or loss. No election is required to produce this result.

Accounts Receivable - ITA 22 Election

8-154.   In dealing with the sale of accounts receivable as part of the disposition of a business, there are two basic problems. The first is that, if the receivables are worth less than their carrying value, the difference will be considered to be a capital loss. This means that only one-half of the amount of the loss will be deductible, and that the deduction can only be made against taxable capital gains.

8-155.   The second problem is that bad debts cannot be deducted, or a reserve established, unless the receivables have been previously included in income. In the case of the sale of a business, this would create a problem for the purchaser in that the purchased receivables would not have been included in income.

8-156.   To deal with these two problems, ITA 22 provides for a joint election by the vendor and purchaser of the accounts receivable. The following example illustrates the application of this election.

> **Example**   Mr. Whitney agrees to buy Mr. Blackmore's business. As part of the transaction, Mr. Whitney acquires Mr. Blackmore's trade receivables for $25,000. These receivables have a face value of $30,000 and Mr. Blackmore has deducted a $4,000 reserve for bad debts with respect to these receivables.

> **Analysis - Vendor**   Whether or not the election is made under ITA 22, Mr. Blackmore will have to include the $4,000 reserve in income. If no election is made, he will then record an allowable capital loss of $2,500 [(1/2)($30,000 - $25,000)]. Assuming Mr. Blackmore has taxable capital gains against which the $2,500 loss can be deducted, the transaction will result in a net inclusion in income of $1,500 ($4,000 - $2,500).

> In contrast, if the ITA 22 election is made, Mr. Blackmore would still have to include the $4,000 reserve in income. However, it will be offset by a business loss of $5,000 on the sale of the receivables, a distinct improvement over the results with no election. Under this approach, there will be a net deduction from income of $1,000.

> **Analysis - Purchaser**   From the point of view of Mr. Whitney, if no election is made he will record the receivables as a $25,000 capital asset. If more or less than $25,000 is actually collected, the difference will be a capital gain or a capital loss.

> If, however, the ITA 22 election is made, he will have to include the $5,000 difference between the face value and the price paid in income, in the year the receivables are acquired. Subsequent to the sale, any difference between the $30,000 face value of the receivables and amounts actually collected will be fully deductible in the calculation of net business income. Mr. Whitney could establish a new reserve for doubtful accounts related to the purchased receivables that are still outstanding at the year end. If the amount collected is equal to $25,000, Mr. Whitney will be in exactly the same position, whether or not the election is made. If more than $25,000 is collected, he will be worse off with the election because 100 percent rather than one-half of the excess will be taxable. Correspondingly, if less than $25,000 is collected, he will be better off with the election as the shortfall will be fully deductible.

Exercise Eight-13

Subject: Sale Of Receivables

Mr. Donato Nero is selling his unincorporated business during 2007. Included in his assets are accounts receivable with a face value of $53,450. He and the purchaser of the business, Mr. Labelle, have agreed that the net realizable value of these receivables is $48,200. In 2006, he deducted a reserve for bad debts of $3,800. Determine the tax consequences of the sale of these receivables for Mr. Nero and Mr. Labelle, provided that they jointly elect under ITA 22.

End of Exercise.   Solution available in Study Guide.

Key Terms Used In This Chapter

8-157.   The following is a list of the key terms used in this Chapter. These terms, and their meanings, are compiled in the Glossary Of Key Terms located at the back of the separate paper Study Guide and on the Companion CD-ROM.

Accrual Basis	Net Income
Allowable Capital Loss	Net Property Income
Billed Basis	Property Income
Business Income	Reserve
Capital Asset	Restricted Farm Loss
Capital Gain/Loss	Specified Non-Resident Shareholder
Cash Basis	Specified Shareholder
Fiscal Period	Taxable Capital Gain
GAAP	Taxation Year
Hobby Farmer	Thin Capitalization
Net Business Income	

References

8-158.   For more detailed study of the material in this Chapter, we would refer you to the following:

ITA 10	Valuation Of Inventory
ITA 12	Income Inclusions
ITA 18	General Limitations [On Deductions]
ITA 20	Deductions Permitted In Computing Income From Business Or Property
ITA 22	Sale Of Accounts Receivable
ITA 23	Sale Of Inventory
ITA 24	Ceasing To Carry On Business
ITA 28	Farming Or Fishing Business
ITA 31	Loss From Farming Where Chief Source Of Income Not Farming
ITA 34	Professional Business
ITA 37	Scientific Research And Experimental Development
IC 86-4R3	Scientific Research And Experimental Development (Draft For R4)
IT-51R2	Supplies On Hand At The End Of A Fiscal Period
IT-99R5	Legal And Accounting Fees (Consolidated)
IT-104R3	Deductibility Of Fines Or Penalties
IT-148R3	Recreational Properties and Club Dues
IT-151R5	Scientific Research And Experimental Development Expenditures
IT-154R	Special Reserves
IT-185R	Losses From Theft, Defalcation, Or Embezzlement
IT-188R	Sale Of Accounts Receivable
IT-218R	Profit, Capital Gains And Losses From The Sale Of Real Estate, Including Farmland And Inherited Land And Conversion Of Real Estate From Capital Property To Inventory And Vice Versa
IT-256R	Gains From Theft, Defalcation Or Embezzlement
IT-287R2	Sale Of Inventory
IT-322R	Farm Losses
IT-357R2	Expenses Of Training
IT-359R2	Premiums And Other Amounts With Respect To Leases
IT-364	Commencement Of Business Operations
IT-417R2	Prepaid Expenses And Deferred Charges
IT-433R	Farming Or Fishing - Use Of Cash Method
IT-442R	Bad Debts And Reserves For Doubtful Debts
IT-457R	Election By Professionals To Exclude Work In Progress From Income
IT-473R	Inventory Valuation
IT-475	Expenditures On Research And For Business Expansion
IT-479R	Transactions In Securities
IT-487	General Limitation On Deduction of Outlays or Expenses
IT-514	Work Space In Home Expenses
IT-518R	Food, Beverages And Entertainment Expenses
IT-521R	Motor Vehicle Expenses Claimed By Self-Employed Individuals
IT-525R	Performing Artists (Consolidated)

Income Tax Technical News #30 (contains restricted farm loss guidance)

Appendix - Taxable Income And Tax Payable For Corporations

Introduction

8A-1.   It is not really possible to teach corporate tax without a fairly complete understanding of the material in Chapters 5 through 14 of this text. Comprehension of the issues involved in calculating Taxable Income and Tax Payable for a corporation requires familiarity, not only with the rules associated with net business income, but also with the rules associated with net property income, net taxable capital gains, and the calculation of Taxable Income and Tax Payable for individuals. Because of this need, this text, as well as all of the other widely used Canadian tax texts, place the coverage of corporate tax subsequent to the chapters dealing with the various components of Net Income For Tax Purposes.

8A-2.   In terms of normal university and college course loads, coverage of the material in the first 14 Chapters of this text (or the corresponding chapters in other Canadian tax texts), provides the basis for a full one semester course in tax. In fact, in comparison with other university and college business courses, the coverage of this material in a single course would be viewed as constituting a very heavy course load. As a reflection of this, most universities and colleges in eastern Canada offer two one semester courses in tax. The first course would cover Chapters 1 through 14 of this text (or the corresponding chapters in other texts), with the second course, dealing largely with corporate tax, covering all or part of Chapters 15 through 22 of this text (or the corresponding chapters in other texts).

8A-3.   In contrast to the situation in eastern Canada, a number of universities and colleges in western Canada offer only a single course in tax and include some corporate tax in that course. The reason for this difference is likely the fact that the CA School Of Business, which manages the professional education of CA students in the western provinces, requires only a single tax course for admission to their program. However, the requirement specifically requires coverage of corporate tax as part of the qualifying course.

8A-4.   As none of the leading Canadian tax texts are designed to be used in a one semester course which includes corporate tax, universities and colleges have dealt with this situation in a variety of ways. One approach that we have seen is to try to cover all of the material in a text-book designed for two courses in the context of a one semester course. In other cases, the single tax course has been designed to skip some earlier chapters and include some of the material on corporate tax. This latter approach creates difficulties in that the text and problem material in the chapters on corporate tax have been prepared on the assumption that students will have a good understanding of all of the preceding material in the text.

8A-5.   While we continue to believe that corporate tax can only be effectively taught in a second tax course, after students have acquired a solid background in how to deal with the components of Net Income For Tax Purposes, we are aware that this book is being used in courses which include corporate tax issues in the context of a single tax course. In order to facilitate such courses, we are including this Appendix which provides a general overview of the basic rules involved in the determination of Net Income For Tax Purposes, Taxable Income, and Tax Payable for corporations. We would note that this material does not serve as a substitute for the material on corporate tax in Chapters 15 through 19. Individuals wishing to have a useful working knowledge of corporate tax should refer to those chapters.

Net Income For Tax Purposes For Corporations

8A-6.   For individuals, we have learned that Net Income For Tax Purposes is made up of net employment income, net business income, net property income, net taxable capital gains, income from other sources, and other deductions from income. For many individuals, net employment income is the most important of these components. Once these amounts are determined, they are combined as per the rules in ITA 3.

8A-7.   In terms of the components of Net Income For Tax Purposes, the most important difference between individuals and corporations is that corporations cannot earn employment income. While less important in most situations, none of the other sources of income listed in Subdivision d, nor the other deductions listed in Subdivision e, are applicable to corporations. This means that the Net Income For Tax Purposes of a corporation is made up of net business income, net property income, and net taxable capital gains.

8A-8.   With respect to net business income, we noted in this Chapter that this amount is usually determined through a reconciliation with accounting Net Income as determined under GAAP. We provided a fairly detailed list of the items that are commonly found in the reconciliation schedule in Figure 8-1 and indicated that these items would be the same without regard to whether you are dealing with an unincorporated partnership or proprietorship or, alternatively, an incorporated business (a corporation).   This means that in determining net business income, the material in this chapter is complete and requires no modification when we are required to deal with corporate taxpayers.

8A-9.   We have not, at this point in the text, dealt with either net property income (Chapter 9) or net taxable capital gains (Chapter 10). However, when we get to this material we will find that the rules and procedures that are applicable to individuals are equally applicable to other types of taxpayers, including corporations and trusts.

8A-10.   Putting all of this together, we find that, while the components of Net Income For Tax Purposes are different for individuals and corporations, the calculation of the amounts to be included for the specific components is the same. This means that this is a subject that needs no additional coverage in corporate tax material.

Taxable Income For Corporations
Deductions Available To Individuals And/Or Corporations
8A-11.   In Chapter 6 we indicated that, in the calculation of Taxable Income, individuals could deduct the following items:

- Employee stock option deduction.
- Deduction for worker's compensation and social assistance payments received.
- Home relocation loan deduction.
- Deduction for lump sum payments.
- Lifetime capital gains deduction.
- Northern residents deductions.
- Deductions for loss carry overs.

8A-12.   Only one of these deductions is available to corporations. This is the deduction that is available for various types of loss carry backs and loss carry forwards. When an individual or a corporation experiences a loss in the current period, there are provisions that allow such losses to be carried back and applied against the income of preceding taxation years and, if there is not sufficient income in those preceding years to absorb all of the current period loss, any excess can be carried forward and applied against Taxable Income in subsequent years.

8A-13.   As was noted in Chapter 6, the application of these provisions is very complex and, because of this, coverage of this subject for individuals was deferred to Chapter 14. Also, there are some additional rules applicable to the use of loss carry overs by corporations (e.g., acquisition of control rules). This means that we will have to return to this subject in Chapter 15 where we provide detailed coverage of corporate Taxable Income. It should be noted, however, that the general provisions related to the application of loss carry overs are the same for corporations and individuals.

Deductions Available Only To Corporations
8A-14.   In addition to loss carry over amounts, the deduction of which is available to both individuals and corporations, corporations can deduct two other items in the determination of their Taxable Income. These items are charitable donations and dividends received from taxable Canadian corporations.

Appendix - Taxable Income And Tax Payable For Corporations

8A-15.   In Chapter 6, we learned that donations made to registered charities and certain other eligible organizations could be used as the base for a credit against Tax Payable. More specifically, individuals receive a credit against federal Tax Payable that is equal to 15.5 percent of the first $200 of such deductions, plus 29 percent of any excess. For corporations, the amount of eligible donations is generally determined in the same way that it is for individuals. However, for corporations, this amount does not form the base for a credit against Tax Payable. Rather, this amount is deducted in the determination of corporate Taxable Income.

8A-16.   Two points should be noted here. First, under GAAP, charitable donations will be deducted in the calculation of accounting Net Income. However, for tax purposes they are not deducted in the calculation of Net Income For Tax Purposes, they are deducted in the calculation of Taxable Income. This means that in the reconciliation of accounting Net Income with a corporation's Net Income For Tax Purposes, charitable donations must be added back. They will subsequently be deducted when Net Income For Tax Purposes is converted to Taxable Income.

8A-17.   The other point is that the rules that limit the amount of eligible donations and that provide a carry forward of unused amounts of charitable donations are generally the same for both individuals and corporations. That is, the amount of eligible donations that can be used, either as the base for a credit by individuals, or as a deduction from Net Income For Tax Purposes by corporations, is limited to 75 percent of the Net Income For Tax Purposes of the taxpayer. If the amount of donations that can be used in the current year is less than the total eligible amounts, either because of the 75 percent income limit, or because the taxpayer does not have sufficient Tax Payable to make effective use of the credit or deduction, any unused amount can be carried forward and used during the following five years.

8A-18.   When a corporation declares dividends, the declared amounts are not deductible for tax purposes. This means that, for a taxable Canadian corporation, dividends have to be declared and paid out of after tax income. If dividends are paid to an affiliated corporation, they become an inclusion in the Net Income For Tax Purposes of that corporation. In the absence of some offsetting provision, these amounts would be taxed again in the hands of this second corporation. Given today's complex intercorporate relationships, taxation of intercompany dividends could lead to double, triple, or even more excessive levels of taxation applied to the same income stream.

8A-19.   To provide relief in this situation, dividends received from taxable Canadian corporations can be deducted in the calculation of corporate Taxable Income. Note, however, they remain in both accounting Net Income and Net Income For Tax Purposes. This means that there is no adjustment for dividends received from taxable Canadian corporations in the reconciliation of accounting Net Income with Net Income For Tax Purposes. These amounts are only deducted in the conversion of corporate Net Income For Tax Purposes to corporate Taxable Income.

Tax Payable For Corporations
Basic Federal Rate
8A-20.   The basic amount of federal tax for a corporation is determined by applying a rate specified in ITA 123 to the Taxable Income of the corporation. The rate that is found in ITA 123 is 38 percent, a rate that has not been changed in many years.

General Rate Reduction
8A-21.   In the 2000 budget, the government announced its intention to gradually reduce the basic federal tax rate by 7 percentage points. While the easy way to do this would have been through reductions in the rate specified in ITA 123, it was decided to accomplish this goal through a separate ITA 123.4(2). This Subsection provides a deduction from the amount determined using the basic rate, starting with a 1 percentage point deduction in 2001, and increasing to the full 7 percentage point deduction for 2004. Income that is eligible for the small business deduction (see discussion of this deduction beginning in Paragraph 8A-24) is not eligible for this general rate reduction.

Federal Tax Abatement

8A-22.   In some cases, a corporation may earn all of its income in Canada. To the extent that income is earned in Canada, it will be allocated to one or more provinces where it will be subject to provincial corporate income taxes. To the extent that it is allocated to a province, federal legislation provides for a 10 percentage point reduction in the federal tax rate. The reduction is found in ITA 124(1) and is referred to as the federal tax abatement. Income that is earned outside of Canada and not allocated to a province is not eligible for this abatement.

Corporate Surtax

8A-23.   For 2007, there is a corporate surtax equal to 4 percent of tax otherwise payable. This surtax has been repealed for 2008 and subsequent years.

Small Business Deduction

8A-24.   To be eligible for this important deduction, a corporation must be a Canadian Controlled Private Corporation (CCPC). To qualify as a CCPC, the shares of the company must not be traded publicly and it must be controlled by resident Canadian persons.

8A-25.   For 2007 and subsequent years, the deduction is available on the first $400,000 of active business income. In simplified terms, the deduction is equal to 16 percentage points times the CCPC's active business income. Active business income is income that results from carrying on a business and, in general, does not include property income (e.g., interest and rents) or taxable capital gains.

8A-26.   As noted previously, income that is eligible for this deduction is not eligible for the general rate reduction.

Manufacturing And Processing Deduction

8A-27.   This deduction is available to corporations that have profits from manufacturing and processing activities. Manufacturing and processing profits are calculated using a formula that is prescribed in the *Income Tax Regulations*. The formula reflects the portion of the corporation's labour costs and capital assets that are devoted to this type of activity.

8A-28.   In simplified terms, this deduction is equal to 7 percent of the manufacturing and processing profits. It is not available on income that is eligible for the small business deduction. More importantly, income that is eligible for the manufacturing and processing deduction is not eligible for the general rate reduction. Given that, as of 2004, the general rate reduction and the manufacturing and processing deduction are both equal to 7 percent, this deduction no longer has value at the federal level.

Provincial Corporate Income Taxes

8A-29.   A corporation's income is allocated to the various provinces in which it has permanent establishments. The amount to be allocated is calculated using a formula which takes into consideration the corporation's wages and salaries in the province, as well as the revenues that have been recognized in the province.

8A-30.   Once the income is allocated to one or more provinces, the provincial corporate income tax is calculated by multiplying Taxable Income by an applicable rate for that province. All of the provinces use at least two corporate tax rates. Each province has a low rate that is applicable to income eligible for the small business deduction. There will also be a high rate that is the general rate applicable to other types of income. In some provinces, there are additional rates that are applicable to other specified types of income.

Example

Example Data

8A-31.　The following example will serve to illustrate the material covered in this Appendix. This simplified example contains a calculation of Net Income For Tax Purposes, Taxable Income, and the combined federal and provincial Tax Payable for a corporation.

Rattan Ltd. has a December 31 accounting and taxation year end and, for the year ending December 31, 2007, its GAAP determined income before consideration of income taxes amounted to $175,000. Other information related to 2007 is as follows:

1. The Company deducted amortization expense for the year of $54,000. It intends to claim maximum CCA for the year, an amount of $62,000.

2. The accounting expenses include $30,000 in business meals and entertainment.

3. The Company deducted $5,000 in charitable donations in determining its accounting Net Income.

4. The accounting revenues include $15,000 in dividends received from taxable Canadian corporations.

5. The Company has a non-capital (business) loss from the previous year of $3,500. It intends to carry forward this loss and apply it against this year's Taxable Income.

6. All of the Company's income is allocated to a province that has an 8 percent rate on income eligible for the small business deduction and a 15 percent rate on income that is not eligible for this deduction. These rates are applied to Taxable Income as determined under federal tax legislation.

7. All of the Company's income is the result of active business activities.

Net Income For Tax Purposes

8A-32.　Rattan's Net Income For Tax Purposes would be calculated as follows:

Accounting Income Before Taxes		$175,000
Additions:		
Amortization Expense	$54,000	
Meals And Entertainment (50%)	15,000	
Charitable Donations	5,000	74,000
Deductions:		
CCA		(62,000)
Net Income For Tax Purposes		$187,000

Taxable Income

8A-33.　Rattan's Taxable Income would be calculated as follows:

Net Income For Tax Purposes	$187,000
Charitable Donations	(5,000)
Dividends Received	(15,000)
Non-Capital (Business) Loss Carry Forward	(3,500)
Taxable Income	$163,500

Tax Payable (Public Company)

8A-34.　If we assume that Rattan Ltd. is a public company, its Tax Payable for the year ending December 31, 2007 would be calculated as follows:

Basic Federal Tax [(38%)($163,500)]	$62,130
Federal Tax Abatement [(10%)($163,500)]	(16,350)
Corporate Surtax [(4%)(38% - 10%)($163,500)]	1,831
General Rate Reduction [(7%)($163,500)]	(11,445)
Federal Tax Payable	$36,166
Provincial Tax Payable [(15%)($163,500)]	24,525
Total Tax Payable	$60,691

Tax Payable (CCPC)

8A-35.   If we assume that Rattan Ltd. is a Canadian Controlled Private Corporate (CCPC), its Tax Payable for the year ending December 31, 2007 would calculated as follows:

Basic Federal Tax [(38%)($163,500)]	$62,130
Federal Tax Abatement [(10%)($163,500)]	(16,350)
Corporate Surtax [(4%)(38% - 10%)($163,500)]	1,831
Small Business Deduction [(16%)($163,500)]	(26,160)
Federal Tax Payable	$21,451
Provincial Tax Payable [(8%)($163,500)]	13,080
Total Tax Payable	$34,531

8A-36.   As can be seen in this example, the availability of the small business deduction results in a significant reduction in Tax Payable. Rattan's Tax Payable is reduced by $26,160 when we assume that it is a CCPC and can use both the federal small business deduction, as well as the more favourable provincial rate.

A Word Of Caution

8A-37.   As was indicated in the introduction to this Appendix, it is our view that corporate tax cannot be understood in any meaningful way until an individual has a thorough understanding of all of the components of Net Income For Tax Purposes, as well as some understanding of Taxable Income and Tax Payable for individuals. While we have added this Appendix on corporate tax in order to accommodate the need to include corporate tax in a single tax course, this material is very basic. Given this, it should not be relied on as a serious reference source on corporate tax. If you need to have a real understanding of this material, you should refer to the material in Chapters 15 and 16 where you will find a much more in-depth treatment of the subject matter contained in this Appendix.

Problems For Self Study

(The solutions for these problems can be found in the separate Study Guide.)

Self Study Problem Eight - 1

Ms. Wise is a very successful salesperson. She pays all of her own business expenses and provides the following information related to her taxation year ending December 31, 2007.

1. Travel costs, largely airline tickets, food, and lodging on trips outside the area in which she resides, totaled $23,000. Included in this amount is $8,000 of business meals.

2. During the year, she used 40 percent of her personal residence as an office. She has owned the property for two years. It is her principal place of business and it is used exclusively for meeting clients on a regular basis throughout the year. Interest payments on the mortgage on this property totalled $13,500 and property taxes for the year were $4,700. Utilities paid for the house totalled $3,550 and house insurance paid for the year was $950. Other maintenance costs associated with the property amounted to $1,500. The January 1, 2007 UCC of the 40 percent portion of the residence that is used for business is $48,000.

3. For business travel, Ms. Wise drove a car that she purchased for $53,000 on October 15, 2006. During 2007, she drove a total of 50,000 kilometers, 35,000 of these being for business purposes. The business usage of her car varies from 60 to 80 percent each year. The total operating costs for the year were $6,000. In addition, there were financing costs of $2,500 on a bank loan used to purchase the car. She has always taken maximum CCA on her car.

4. She paid dues to the Salesperson's Association (a trade union) of $600.

5. She was billed a total of $12,000 by a local country club. Of this amount, $2,500 was a payment for membership dues and the remaining $9,500 was for meals and drinks with clients.

Required:

A. Calculate the maximum amount of expenses that would be deductible by Ms. Wise for 2007 assuming:

    i. She is an employee of a manufacturing company. Her employment income of $137,000 includes $15,000 in commissions.

    ii. She represents a group of manufacturers with a diversified product line. During 2007, she earned total commissions of $137,000.

In making these calculations, ignore GST and PST considerations.

B. Comment on the desirability of taking CCA on Ms. Wise's personal residence.

Self Study Problem Eight - 2

You have been engaged to calculate Net Income For Tax Purposes for Lawson Tools Ltd. for the year ending October 31, 2007. The president and founder of the Company is Mr. William Green. However, he is no longer a shareholder of the Company.

The accounting records of the Company show a Net Income After Taxes for this period of $298,000. An examination of the Company's records discloses the following information relative to this calculation:

1. The opening inventory for tax purposes amounts to $202,000. In the financial statements, the closing inventory was determined to be $271,000 under a Last In, First Out (LIFO) cost flow assumption. The First In, First Out (FIFO) cost of this ending inventory would have been $296,000.

2. The increase in the Company's reserve for warranties during the year was $14,500. This amount is based on a self-insurance warranty program.

3. The Company's income tax expense amounted to $158,000, of which $112,000 had been paid.

4. During the year, the Company spent $15,600 landscaping the premises of its office building. This amount was deducted as an expense in the determination of accounting Net Income.

5. Depreciation was deducted in the financial statements in the amount of $53,750.

6. Because of a failure to pay its municipal property taxes on their due date, the Company was charged interest of $975.

7. A contribution of $4,300 was made to a registered charity during the year.

8. Included in revenues was a payment of $31,200 from an insurance company to compensate for loss of profits when the Company was closed for two weeks because of a fire.

9. The Company follows a policy of providing various types of volume discounts to its regular customers. During the year, such discounts amounted to $21,250.

10. A life insurance premium in the amount of $3,100 was paid on the life of Mr. Green. The Company is the beneficiary of the policy, and the policy was not part of a group life insurance plan for the employees of the Company.

11. During the fiscal year, the Company amortized $5,900 in premiums on its outstanding bonds payable, which decreased its interest expense.

12. The Company paid $1,400 for membership in a local golf and country club. The total of all meals charged at the club by Mr. Green and paid by the Company during the fiscal year was $3,400. These meals were all business related and his guests were always important clients or suppliers.

13. The Company paid $14,300 to amend its articles of incorporation prior to a reorganization of the Company's capital structure.

14. The Company incurred and expensed appraisal costs of $7,400 in order to determine the current market value of certain capital assets that it intends to sell.

15. The Company paid legal and accounting fees of $15,600 in relation to a new issue of common shares during the year.

Required: Calculate Lawson Tools Ltd.'s Net Income For Tax Purposes for the year ending October 31, 2007. Ignore any deductions that might be made with respect to depreciable property or eligible capital property. Indicate why you have not included any of the preceding items in your calculations.

Self Study Problem Eight - 3

Barnes Industries Ltd. is a Canadian private company located in Nova Scotia. Mike Barnes, the majority shareholder of the Company, devotes all of his time to managing the operations of this enterprise. Over the years, the business has consistently shown a profit and, for the taxation year ending December 31, 2007, Mike has determined that the Company's Net Income Before Income Taxes is $426,000. In determining this income figure, Mike has used generally accepted accounting principles as specified in the *CICA Handbook*. (Mike is a Certified Management General Accountant who received his professional designation in 1983.) Other information with respect to the determination of accounting income before taxes for 2007 is as follows:

1. It is Mike's estimate that the income tax expense for Barnes Industries Ltd. for the year will be $186,000, including $23,000 in future income taxes.

2. During the year, the Company has deducted contributions to various registered charities in the amount of $3,500.

3. For accounting purposes, the Company uses LIFO to determine the cost of its inventory balances. The opening and closing figures under this method, as well as the corresponding figures using FIFO are as follows:

	January 1, 2007	December 31, 2007
LIFO	$346,000	$423,000
FIFO	366,000	447,000

4. The Company recorded amortization expense for the year of $241,000.

5. After attending a seminar on the tax advantages of income splitting among family members, Mike hires his unemployed cousin to do filing in the office. She proves to be totally incapable of doing the job and is asked to leave after only one day. In the interests of family harmony, he pays her $10,000, which is deducted in the accounting records of the Company.

6. The maximum CCA for the year has been correctly determined to be $389,000.

7. The Company has deducted $23,000 for advertising in newspapers in the New England states. The advertising is directed towards selling the Company's products in that region.

8. The Company provides warranties on several of the products that it sells. For its accounting records, it estimates the cost of providing these warranties and records a liability on the basis of these estimates. The liability at the beginning of the year was $18,000 and the corresponding figure at the end of the fiscal year was $27,000.

9. At the end of 2006, the Company estimated that its bad debts on ending accounts receivable would total $31,000. Actual write-offs during 2007 amounted to $35,000. At the end of 2007, the estimate of bad debts on ending accounts receivable was $33,000. The accounting estimates are considered appropriate for tax purposes.

10. On December 31, 2007, the Company issued new common shares. The legal and accounting fees related to this issue of shares were $8,000. For accounting purposes, these costs were added to the intangible asset, organization costs. As the issue of shares was on December 31, there was no 2007 amortization of this amount for accounting purposes.

11. In January, 2007, the Company paid landscaping costs of $11,000 that were expected to have a useful life of 10 years. These costs were capitalized for accounting purposes and are being amortized on a straight line basis over a period of ten years. (This amortization is included in the amortization expense of $241,000 listed in Part 4.)

12. As a result of Mike's business travel, the Company incurred costs for meals and entertainment in the amount of $13,500. All of these costs were deducted in the determination of accounting income before taxes.

13. Amortization of bond discount for the year was $1,800.

14. On January 1, 2007, the Company leases a Mercedes for five years for Mike to use in his business travels. The total 2007 lease payments amount to $18,000 and, in addition, the Company pays all of the operating costs. These operating costs total $6,200 for the year. There are no refundable deposits associated with the lease and the lease payments do not include any amounts for insurance or licensing. All of these amounts are expensed in the determination of the Company's accounting income. The manufacturer's suggested list price for the car is $128,000. Mike has use of the car throughout the year. He drives it a total of 92,000 kilometers, of which 38,000 kilometers were employment related.

Required: For Barnes Industries Ltd.'s 2007 taxation year, determine Net Income For Tax Purposes. Indicate why you have not included any of the preceding items in your calculations. Ignore any GST or PST implications.

Self Study Problem Eight - 4

Darby Inc. has just completed its fiscal year ended December 31, 2007. The accountant has determined that, for financial statement purposes, the Company has experienced a Net Loss Before Taxes for the year of $113,000. The accountant provides the following information that was used in the determination of the Net Loss for accounting purposes:

1. The Company was forced to pay damages of $12,300 for failure to perform a service contract. The amount was paid when the client threatened to bring action for breach of contract. The $12,300 was expensed in the current year.

2. The Company's property tax expense of $19,500 includes an amount of $1,100 that was paid to a regional municipality in which the Company maintains a recreational facility for its employees.

3. The Company's expenses include contributions to registered charities of $13,700.

4. The Company's expenses include costs of new landscaping at their administration building in the amount of $9,800.

5. The Company deducted a loss of $10,100 resulting from a theft by one of its clerical employees.

6. Effective December 31, 2007, as the result of a change in its distribution system, the Company was forced to cancel a tenant's lease that would have been in force until January 1, 2015. During the 2007 taxation year, the Company agreed to pay, and deducted, damages in the amount of $17,000. On December 31, 2007, $5,000 of this amount had not been paid.

7. The current salary expense included a bonus payable to the Company's president in the amount $14,500. It will be paid on February 1, 2008.

8. The insurance expense included the premium on a whole life policy on the life of the president's wife in the amount of $9,500. This was not a group life policy and the proceeds were payable to the Company.

9. During the year, the Company switched from a FIFO basis of inventory valuation to a LIFO basis. The opening inventories, valued on a FIFO basis, were recorded at $182,360. The ending inventories, valued on a LIFO basis, were $193,400, an amount that was $37,200 less than would have been recorded had the Company continued to use FIFO. In its accounting records, the Company did not make a retroactive adjustment for this change.

10. As the Company changed property and casualty insurers during the year, all of its assets had to be appraised. The cost of this appraisal was $4,150, with the entire amount being expensed in the year.

11. The Company's wage expense included $51,000 in management bonuses (other than that of the president described in item 7) that will not be paid until May 1, 2008. In addition, $34,000 in unpaid bonuses, which were deducted for both tax and accounting purposes in 2006, were forfeited in 2007 as the result of various employees terminating their employment with the Company. These forfeited amounts were included in the determination of the Net Loss for the year.

12. Bad debt expense amounted to $11,000.

13. Renovation costs in the amount of $153,000 were charged to expense during the year. This amount resulted from the need to completely renovate one of the Company's offices and involved the installation of plumbing and air conditioning systems, as well as rewiring and installation of new concrete foundations.

14. The president and his wife attended a convention that resulted in $5,200 in travel expenses for the Company. Of this amount, $1,900 related to the fact that the president's wife chose to accompany him on this trip.

15. The Company's interest expense included bond discount amortization of $950.

16. The Company's legal expenses for the year amount to $10,500 and were related to the following transactions:

Defense of breach of contract (see item 1)	$2,450
Cost of amending articles of incorporation	3,600
Defense costs related to income tax reassessment	4,450

17. The Company's expenses included a total amount of $12,500 for business meals and entertainment.

Required: Compute the Company's Net Income For Tax Purposes for the year ending December 31, 2007. Ignore any tax deductions associated with depreciable assets or eligible capital property. Indicate why you have not included any of the preceding items in your calculations.

Self Study Problem Eight - 5

Darlington Inc. has a fiscal year ending December 31. For the year ending December 31, 2007, the Company's accounting Net Income, determined in accordance with generally accepted accounting principles, was $596,000. Other information related to the preparation of its 2007 tax return is as follows:

1. The income tax expense was $55,000, including $7,000 in future income tax expense.

2. The Company uses a LIFO assumption for inventory valuation purposes. The January 1, 2007 LIFO inventory was $15,000 less than it would have been under a FIFO assumption, while the December 31, 2007 LIFO inventory was $20,000 less than the corresponding FIFO value.

3. The Company spent $95,000 on landscaping for its main office building. This amount was recorded as an asset in the accounting records and, because the work has an unlimited life, no amortization was recorded on this asset.

4. The Company spent $17,000 on advertisements in *Fortune* Magazine, a U.S. based publication. Approximately 90 percent of its non-advertising content is original editorial content. The advertisements were designed to promote sales in Canadian cities located on the U.S. border.

5. The amortization expense was $623,000. At the beginning of 2007, the Company has a balance in Class 1 of $1,000,000, representing the UCC of its headquarters buildings. In general, other buildings are leased. However, in February, 2007, a policy change results in the acquisition of a new store building at a cost of $650,000, of which $125,000 is allocated to land.

    The January 1, 2007 balance in Class 8 was $4,200,000. During 2007, there were additions to this class in the total amount of $700,000. In addition, Class 8 assets with a cost of $400,000 were sold for proceeds of $550,000. The net book value of these assets in the accounting records was $325,000, and the resulting gain of $225,000 was included in the accounting income for the year. There are numerous assets remaining in the class at the end of the 2007 taxation year.

    At the beginning of 2007, the UCC in Class 10 was $800,000, reflecting the Company's fleet of cars. As the Company is changing to a policy of leasing its cars, all of these cars were sold during the year for $687,000. The capital cost of the cars was $1,200,000, and their net book value in the accounting records was equal to the sale proceeds of $687,000.

6. Included in travel costs deducted in 2007 for accounting purposes was $12,000 for airline tickets and $41,400 for business meals and entertainment.

7. The Company paid, and deducted, for accounting purposes, a $2,500 initiation fee for a corporate membership in the Highland Golf And Country Club.

8. The Company paid, and deducted, property taxes of $15,000 on vacant land that was being held for possible future expansion of its headquarters site.

Required: Calculate Darlington Inc.'s minimum Net Income For Tax Purposes for the 2007 taxation year. In addition, calculate the January 1, 2008 UCC balances for each CCA class.

Self Study Problem Eight - 6

Christine Powell is a visual designer. Until May, 2007, she worked as an employee for a printing supply firm. In June, she became self-employed when she started up "Design Power". Through this business, Christine works with several advertising agencies in the design and desktop publishing of promotional materials.

In January, 2008, she comes to you for tax advice. Being vaguely aware of the complexity of the tax laws, she has kept meticulous track of all business related costs for the period from June 1 to December 31, 2007.

Christine works out of her home. Her studio occupies 20 percent of the useable space in the house. The total operating costs related to the house during the period June 1, 2007 through December 31, 2007 are:

Utilities	$1,500
Home Insurance	700
Mortgage Interest	1,600
Property Taxes	2,600
Total Home Operating Costs	$6,400

Christine does not intend to claim any CCA on the house.

On June 1, 2007, Christine bought a used car for business and personal use. The total purchase price of the car was $18,000, financed with a $3,000 cash down-payment and a $15,000 term loan. Her detailed records show that she uses the car 70 percent for business. The automobile costs include:

Down Payment On Car Purchase	$3,000
Gasoline And Oil	1,100
Licence And Registration	200
Insurance	800
Interest On Car Loan	700
Total Automobile Costs	$5,800

On July 15, 2007, Christine purchased computer equipment for $5,000 and various applications software for $1,200. On August 1, she purchased several pieces of office furniture for $2,000. All of these assets were acquired solely for business use.

Christine's fiscal year end for the business is December 31. Her revenues and other costs for the period June 1, 2007 to December 31, 2007 were as follows:

Revenues

Collected	$22,000
Billed, but not collected	4,000
Unbilled work-in-progress	1,500

Costs

Legal fees	$1,000
Meals and entertainment with clients	500
Office and computer supplies	650
Printing sub-contract fees	1,800

Required: Calculate the minimum net business income Christine would include in her 2007 personal income tax return. In preparing your solution, ignore PST and GST implications.

Assignment Problems

(The solutions for these problems are only available in
the solutions manual that has been provided to your instructor.)

Assignment Problem Eight - 1

Dr. Allworth is a dentist with an office in one of the less prosperous sections of Vancouver. While he has very large gross billings, his patients are such that he often has trouble collecting the amounts that are due to him. As a consequence, he takes great care in keeping track of outstanding balances in accounts receivable and in making estimates of the amounts that he expects will not be collectible.

At the end of the previous taxation year, his accounts receivable balance was $104,000 and he established an allowance for bad debts of $11,500. The corresponding balances at the end of the current year were $208,000 in total receivables, with an allowance for bad debts of $15,900. Both of the bad debt estimates were established on the basis of a detailed aging schedule, applied on a receivable by receivable basis.

During the previous taxation year, there were recoveries of amounts written off as uncollectible in the amount of $190.

During the current taxation year, $8,800 in accounts were written off as bad. However, $700 of this amount related to a patient where there was some hope of collecting the amount due. As the patient was a personal friend of Dr. Allworth, no real effort had been made to collect the amount and further dental services had been extended on a credit basis. In addition, accounts totalling $1,500 that had been previously written off were recovered during the current taxation year.

Required: How would the preceding information affect the calculation of Dr. Allworth's business income for the current taxation year?

Assignment Problem Eight - 2

Jasper Retailers Inc. began business on January 1 of the current year. Purchases during the year are as follows:

Date	Quantity	Price	Total Cost
January 1	15,000	$10.00	$ 150,000
March 1	·35,000	$11.00	385,000
June 15	42,000	$11.50	483,000
September 1	27,000	$12.00	324,000
October 1	17,000	$12.50	212,500
Totals	136,000		$1,554,500

On December 31, the end of the Company's taxation year, the inventory on hand amounts to 22,000 units. It is estimated that these units have a net realizable value of $11.75 per unit.

Required: For purposes of calculating business income, what values would the CRA accept for the value of the December 31 inventory?

Assignment Problem Eight - 3

Borris Industries is a Canadian controlled private corporation with a taxation year that ends on December 31. Mr. John Borris is the president of the Company and its only shareholder. He is also considered to be an employee of the Company.

On December 1, 2006, Borris Industries leases a new Mercedes to be used by Mr. Borris. The lease calls for monthly payments of $1,800 per month, payable on the first day of each month for a period of three years. At the time the lease is signed, the Company is required to make a refundable deposit of $10,000. The manufacturer's suggested list price for the car is $85,000. Mr. Borris will pay the Company $500 per month for his personal use of the car. This is the only automobile that is leased by Borris Industries.

During December, 2006, Mr. Borris drives the car a total of 2,500 kilometers, none of which are related to his Company's business activities. Operating costs for this period, all of which are paid by the Company, totaled $1,100.

During 2007, Mr. Borris drives the car 45,000 kilometers, of which 23,000 were related to his Company's business. Operating costs for this period, all of which are paid by the Company, totaled $10,200.

During the period December 1, 2006 through December 31, 2007, the automobile was always available to Mr. Borris.

Assume that the prescribed rate is 6 percent (not including the extra 4 percent that is applicable for amounts owing to the Minister) for the period December 1, 2006 through December 31, 2007.

Required: Determine the following:

A. The maximum deduction for automobile lease payments that Borris Industries can take in each of the two years 2006 and 2007.

B. The minimum amount of the taxable benefit that Mr. Borris will have to include in his Net Income For Tax Purposes for each of the two years 2006 and 2007 as a result of having the Mercedes available for his personal use.

C. (The solution to this Part C requires knowledge of shareholder benefits which is covered in Chapter 9.) Would there be any difference for Borris Industries if the automobile benefit is considered an employee benefit or a shareholder benefit? Explain your conclusion.

Ignore GST and PST considerations in all parts of this question.

Assignment Problem Eight - 4

The Vernon Manufacturing Company, a Canadian controlled private corporation, has just ended its first fiscal year. During that year, a number of outlays were made for which the Company is uncertain as to the appropriate tax treatment. You have been asked to advise them in this matter and, to that end, you have been provided with the list of outlays and expenditures that follows:

1. A part of the Company's raw materials had to be imported from Brazil. In order to obtain local financing for these inventories, the Company paid a $1,200 fee to a Brazilian financial consultant for assistance in locating the required financing.

2. Donations totalling $12,000 were given to various registered Canadian charities.

3. The Company paid $2,500 to the owner of a tract of land in return for an option to purchase the land for $950,000 for a period of 2 years. The land is adjacent to the Company's main factory and management believes it may be required for future expansion of the Company's manufacturing facilities.

4. Direct costs of $7,500, related to incorporating the Company, were incurred during the

year.

5. An amount of $10,000 was paid for a franchise giving the Company the right to manufacture a Brazilian consumer product for a period of ten years.

6. Because of its rapid growth, the Company was forced to move into a building that they had originally leased to another company. In order to cancel the lease, it paid $8,000 to the tenant. In addition, $9,500 was spent to landscape the facilities and another $13,000 was spent to provide a parking lot for employees.

7. As some of its employees use public transportation, a pedestrian bridge over an adjacent highway was required to allow these employees to reach the plant from the public transportation terminal. The cost of this bridge was $12,000.

Required: Indicate which of the preceding expenditures you feel that the Vernon Manufacturing Company will be able to deduct in the calculation of business income for the current year, and the tax treatment of the non-deductible expenditures. Explain your conclusions.

Assignment Problem Eight - 5

Dr. Sweet is a dentist with a well established practice in Smith Falls, Ontario. She has sought your advice regarding the deductibility of the following expenditures made during the current taxation year:

1. Insurance payments included a $680 premium for coverage of her office and contents, $1,800 for malpractice coverage, and $1,700 in life insurance premiums.

2. Payments were made to a collection agency in the amount of $1,250 for assistance in collecting past due amounts from patients.

3. Contributions of $600 were made to various registered charities.

4. Dr. Sweet paid a total of $18,000 to her husband for his services as a full time bookkeeper and receptionist.

5. Dr. Sweet paid $5,000 for a painting by a Canadian artist that has been hung in her waiting room.

6. A total of $4,600 was spent to attend a dental convention in Phoenix, Arizona. Dr. Sweet was accompanied by her husband and $1,500 of the total cost of the trip relates directly to him.

7. An amount of $1,000 was paid for membership in a racquets club. In addition, $1,300 was spent for court time, approximately 40 percent of which was for time spent playing with patients.

8. Dr. Sweet paid $1,200 in legal and accounting fees. These fees related to fighting a personal income tax reassessment for a previous tax year. The fight was not successful and, as a consequence, Dr. Sweet was required to pay additional taxes of $13,000, plus $1,600 in interest on the late payments.

9. During the year, Dr. Sweet spent $3,200 purchasing provincial lottery tickets.

Required: Advise Dr. Sweet with respect to the deductibility of the preceding expenditures in the calculation of Net Income For Tax Purposes. Explain your position on each expenditure.

Assignment Problem Eight - 6

The fiscal year for Morton Forms Ltd. has just ended and the accounting staff have prepared the following before tax Income Statement from information that will be included in its published financial statements:

Sales Revenue	$8,726,000
Cost Of Goods Sold	$4,253,000
Operating Expenses	1,785,000
Other Expenses (Not Including Income Taxes)	756,000
Total Expenses (Not Including Income Taxes)	$6,794,000
Income Before Taxes	$1,932,000

Other Information:

1. During the year, the Company spent $18,900 for landscaping the grounds around its Vancouver office. In accordance with generally accepted accounting principles, this amount was treated as a capital expenditure. As the work was done late in the year, no amortization was deducted for the current year.

2. Operating Expenses included the following amounts:

Amortization expense	$693,000
Cost of sponsoring local baseball teams	7,200
Reserve for inventory obsolescence	15,000
Advertising on a foreign television station (Directed at Canadian market)	9,600
Advertising circulars (Only one-quarter distributed)	12,400
Business meals and entertainment	22,000

3. Maximum CCA has been determined to be $942,000 for the fiscal year just ended.

4. Other Expenses (Not Including Income Taxes) contains the following amounts:

Charitable contributions	$31,900
Interest on late income tax instalments	2,000
Loss from theft	16,200
Interest paid on bonds issued	34,200
Amortization of bond discount	2,600
Appraisal costs on land to be sold	4,200
Damages resulting from breach of contract	3,800

Required: Calculate the minimum Net Income For Tax Purposes for the current year for Morton Forms Ltd.

Assignment Problem Eight - 7

Fairway Distribution Inc. is a Canadian controlled private corporation that provides for the distribution to retailers of a wide variety of health aid products. All of the shares of the Company are owned by Mr. John Fairway. His wife, Jane Fairway, is an avid golfer with no interest or experience in business matters.

During the taxation year ended December 31, 2007, the Company's financial statements, as prepared for the exclusive use of Mr. Fairway, reported a Net Income of $573,000. In preparing these statements, Mr. Fairway's accountant relied on generally accepted accounting principles except for the fact that no provision is made at the end of the year for anticipated bad debts. This variance from generally accepted accounting principles resulted from the accountant's belief that Mr. Fairway is a much more reasonable and pleasant person when he is presented with a higher Net Income figure.

Other Information   Other information related to the 2007 taxation year is as follows:

1. The reported Net Income was after the deduction of $143,000 in federal and provincial income taxes.

2. In the previous year, a reserve for bad debts was deducted for tax purposes in the amount of $15,000. Actual bad debt write-offs during 2007 amounted to $17,500 and the

accountant felt that an appropriate reserve to be deducted for tax purposes at the end of 2007 would be $19,200.

3. Accounting income included a deduction for amortization in the amount of $78,500. The accountant has determined that the maximum CCA for 2007 would be $123,600.

4. Mr. Fairway's accountant uses inventory valuation based on LIFO cost for accounting purposes. As this method is not allowed for tax purposes, he also calculates information based on FIFO cost. On December 31, 2006, the LIFO cost of inventories was $326,000, while the corresponding FIFO figure was $345,000. On December 31, 2007, the LIFO figure was $297,000, while the FIFO amount was $312,000.

5. The following items were included in the accounting expenses:

Cost of advertising in a foreign newspaper that is distributed in Canada	$ 3,500
Contributions to registered charities	1,260
Cost of appraisal on real estate to be sold	1,470
Costs of landscaping work done on the	
grounds of Mr. Fairway's personal estate	5,260
Management fee to Mrs. Jane Fairway	123,000

Required: Calculate the minimum 2007 Net Income For Tax Purposes for Fairway Distribution Inc.

Assignment Problem Eight - 8

Astrolab Industries has a taxation year that ends on December 31. For the year ending December 31, 2007, the Company's accounting statements prepared in accordance with generally accepted accounting principles showed a Net Income of $278,000. The accountant has provided the following other information that was used in the preparation of this Net Income figure:

1. A total of $123,000 was deducted as income tax expense. This amount included $16,000 in future income taxes.

2. As the Company was late in making its required income tax instalments, it was required to pay interest of $400.

3. The Company uses LIFO for the determination of cost of goods sold. Using this approach, the January 1, 2007 inventories totaled $127,000 and the December 31, 2007 inventories totaled $135,000. On a FIFO basis, the corresponding opening and closing inventories were $112,000 and $122,000, respectively.

4. For the year ending December 31, 2007, the Company recorded $83,000 in amortization expense. Maximum available CCA deductions for this period were $97,000.

5. The Company's accounting expenses included a payment of dues in a local golf club of $2,500. The cost of entertaining clients at this club during the year ending December 31, 2007 was $9,600.

6. For accounting purposes, no allowance for bad debts was established at either the beginning or the end of 2007. The $5,200 bad debt expense that was included in the accounting records reflected only the amounts that were written off during the year. For tax purposes, the Company deducted a reserve of $3,400 for the taxation year ending December 31, 2006. An appropriate reserve for the year ending December 31, 2007 would be $4,200.

7. The 2007 accounting expenses include $1,500 for the premiums on a life insurance policy on the life of the Company's president. The Company is the beneficiary of this policy. One of the Company's major creditors requires that this policy be in force during all periods in which there are loan balances outstanding.

8. The 2007 accounting expenses included $37,000 in bonuses that were declared in favour

of Company executives. Only $12,000 of these bonuses were paid in 2007, with the balance being payable in February, 2008.

9. The bond interest expense that is included in the accounting records includes $3,200 in discount amortization.

10. On December 31, 2007, the Company paid landscaping costs of $27,000. These costs were treated as capital expenditures for accounting purposes and, as the expenditure was made at the end of the year, no depreciation was recorded in the 2007 financial statements.

Required: For each of the preceding items, indicate the appropriate treatment in the tax records of Astrolab Industries Ltd. for the year ending December 31, 2007. For those items that require adjustments of accounting Net Income in order to arrive at Net Income For Tax Purposes, indicate the specific adjustment that would be required. The calculation of Net Income For Tax Purposes is not required.

Assignment Problem Eight - 9

The Montpetit Fashion Group is a partnership that custom designs and retails high-fashion clothing in Calgary. The partnership commenced operations on February 1, 2007.

Part I The three partners have sought your advice on a number of issues related to the tax procedures to be used by their business. Provide the requested advice on each of the following issues:

A. Explain to the partners how business income from partnerships is taxed in Canada.

B. The partners have not picked a partnership year end and would like to know what options they have.

C. The partnership has not made any income tax instalments. Will the partnership be penalized for this apparent oversight? To avoid the possibility in the future, how should instalments be calculated and when should they be paid?

D. Designer gowns, for which there are no production economies of scale, are designed and made by private seamstresses who work in their own homes. Montpetit supplies the fabric and accessories, and pays a previously agreed fixed amount upon satisfactory completion of each gown. The partners are uncertain as to the need for source deductions (income tax, EI and CPP contributions) on these amounts.

Part II The partners would like you to review the following transactions that occurred during their first fiscal year of business ending on December 31, 2007. Advise the partners on the taxability of income amounts in the calculation of net business income for the year. Similarly, for expenditures, provide advice on the specific deductions (with amounts) that can be claimed.

A. Legal fees of $800 were paid for the drafting of a partnership agreement.

B. Five industrial sewing machines were acquired at the beginning of the year at a cost of $1,100 each. Sewing accessories (thread, needles, scissors, etc.) were also acquired for a total of $850.

C. Each partner contributed $10,000 to get the business off the ground. On July 1, 2007, each partner loaned the partnership $15,000. Interest of 4 percent per year on the loans were paid by the partnership for the last six months of the year. In addition, the partners are planning to deduct the $10,000 payments on their personal income tax returns for the current year.

D. At year-end, designer clothes with a retail price of $26,000 are held on consignment by boutiques throughout the city. The cost of making these clothes was $5,000 labour and $4,500 fabric. The partners consider that overhead is approximately 30 percent of the direct labour cost of making designer clothes.

E. Montpetit paid $15,000 for the exclusive right to distribute Dali sweaters for five years.

F. During 2007, payments totalling $3,250 were made to the Champs Elysee Club. Of this amount, $1,100 was for the annual membership fee and the remaining $2,150 was for charges in the Crepe Suzette Diner. Of the dining charges, $1,500 was spent for entertaining clients and the remainder was for the personal use of the three partners.

Assignment Problem Eight - 10

For the taxation year ending December 31, 2007, Voxit Inc. recorded Net Income of $565,000. This amount was determined under generally accepted accounting principles.

Other Information:

1. The following items were deducted (added) during the year

Current Income Tax Expense	$210,000
Future Income Tax Benefit	(23,000)
Interest Expense (Includes $3,500 In Discount Amortization)	22,000
Interest On Deficient Corporate Tax Instalments	1,250
Reserve For Inventory Declines	12,600
Amortization Expense	51,500
Charitable Donations	14,500
Cost Of Sponsoring Local Soccer Team	4,600
Loss From Employee Theft	5,200
Loss On The Sale Of Vehicles	36,200
Cost Of Appraisal Of Property To Be Sold	2,600

2. On January 1, 2007, the Company has the following UCC Balances:

Class 1	$325,236
Class 8	226,964
Class 10	87,468
Class 13	29,322

During the year ending December 31, 2007, the Company acquired furniture and fixtures at a cost of $262,000. Furniture and fixtures with a cost of $275,000 and a fair market value of $189,000 were traded in on the new assets.

The balance in Class 10 reflects the Company's fleet of delivery vehicles. In the accounting records, their net book value was $92,700. During the year ending December 31, 2007, all of these vehicles were sold and replaced with leased vehicles. The sale proceeds amounted to $56,500, with the amount received for each vehicle being less than its cost.

The Class 13 assets relate to a lease that was signed on January 1, 2003. At that time, the cost of the improvements on the leased property was $36,400. The basic term of the lease is 10 years and there are two 4 year renewal options.

3. On January 1, 2007, the Company had no CEC balance. On that date, the Company sold one of its divisions. The sale proceeds included a payment for internally generated goodwill of $43,000.

On December 31, 2007, the Company acquired an unincorporated business. The purchase price included a $55,000 payment for goodwill. As the acquisition was late in the year, none of the acquired assets were amortized for accounting purposes.

4. During the current year, the Company collected $211,000 in GST and claimed input tax credits of $256,000, for a net refund of $45,000.

Required: Using the preceding information, calculate Voxit Inc.'s minimum Net Income For Tax Purposes for the year ending December 31, 2007.

Assignment Problem Eight - 11

Beckett Enterprises is an unincorporated business that has operated successfully for a number of years under the direction of its owner, Ms. Joan Close. However, in early 2007, she decides to dispose of the business and retire. She will sell all of the assets of the business to an unrelated party, Mr. John Phar.

The date of the disposition is February 1, 2007 and, on that date, the business has accounts receivable with a face value of $120,000. Because of anticipated bad debts, the realizable value of these receivables is estimated to be $107,000. During the previous year, Ms. Close deducted a reserve for bad debts in the amount of $8,000.

Beckett Enterprises has a December 31 year end. Mr. Phar will continue the business on an unincorporated basis and will also have a December 31 year end.

During the year ending December 31, 2007, $100,000 of the accounts receivable are collected, with the remainder being written off as non-recoverable.

Both Ms. Close and Mr. Phar have heard of an election under ITA 22 that may have some influence on the tax treatment of the transfer of accounts receivable. They would like to have your advice on this matter. They will both have significant capital gains in 2007.

Required: Indicate the tax effects, for both Ms. Close and Mr. Phar, of the disposition of the accounts receivable and the subsequent 2007 collections and write-offs, assuming:

A. that no election is made under ITA 22.

B. that they make an election under ITA 22.

Assignment Problem Eight - 12

Billy Jow is a music instructor at a local high school in your area. He is employed by the school board and earns approximately $50,000 annually. To supplement his income, Billy started to teach music on April 1, 2007, to a number of children in the neighbourhood in the evenings and on weekends.

Billy comes to you for advice on how he should report this supplementary teaching income and what expenses are deductible. Billy does not mind paying his fair share of income taxes, but he wants to pay no more than he has to. From discussions with friends, he understands that he may be entitled to claim a portion of the costs of his home.

Since he was not using the den in his home, he decided to use it for this supplementary teaching. He purchased his home a few years ago for about $250,000. The home is approximately 2,000 square feet in size. The den is approximately 200 square feet.

From April 1, 2007 to December 31, 2007, Billy earned $3,700 in music fees. He has chosen December 31 as his year end and has incurred the following costs since April 1:

Purchase Of Music Books	$ 250
Supplies (Paper, Pens, Etc.)	1,000
Tuxedo For Students' Performances	350
Snacks For Students (Pizza, Milk, Etc.)	250
Utilities For Home (Heat, Light, And Water)	3,500
Mortgage Interest Paid	11,000
Repairs And Maintenance For Home	2,600
Chair	500
Piano And Bench	5,000
Total	$24,450

Required:

A. When are expenses for work space in the home deductible? Explain.

B. Compute the minimum net business income or loss that Billy should report in his 2007 personal income tax return.

C. Briefly describe any issues that should be discussed with Billy concerning his home office costs.

Assignment Cases

Assignment Case Eight - 1 (Comprehensive Case Covering Chapters 5 to 8)

Mr. Allen Archer is employed by Global Inc., a Canadian controlled public company. For 2007, his salary is $56,000. In addition, his commissions for the year total $48,000. For the year ending December 31, 2007, his employer withholds the following amounts from his income.

RPP Contributions*	$4,200
EI Premiums	720
CPP Contributions	1,990
Parking Fees At Employer's Lot	600

*Mr. Archer's employer makes a matching contribution of $4,200 to his RPP.

Mr. Archer's employer requires him to use his own car for traveling to clients. The car that Mr. Archer is currently using was acquired on January 1, 2007 at a cost of $28,500. During 2007, Mr. Archer drove the car a total of 21,000 kilometers, of which 18,500 were employment related. The other 2,500 kilometers involved personal use. His total operating costs for the year were $3,750. Global Inc. provided an allowance of $500 per month to reimburse him for the use of the car.

His employment related travel did not require overnight stays and, as a consequence, he has no hotel expenses. However, he spent $7,200 during 2007 on meals and entertainment for clients. These amounts were fully reimbursed by his employer.

In 2005, Mr. Archer's employer granted him options to acquire 1,000 shares of the Global Inc. stock for $12 per share. At the time the options were granted, the Global Inc. shares were trading at $10 per share. During 2007, Mr. Archer exercises the options. At the time of exercise, the Global Inc. shares were trading at $18.25 per share. He does not elect to defer the employment income inclusion related to the stock options.

Mr. Archer has a spouse and two children. During 2007, his spouse, Jan, had Net Income For Tax Purposes of $7,500. His 22 year old son, Ron, is dependent on Mr. Archer because he is disabled. However, the disability is not severe enough to create a marked restriction in his daily activities. Ron has no income during 2007. His 18 year old daughter, Mona, was in full time attendance at a Canadian university for 8 months during 2007. While she has 2007 Net Income For Tax Purposes of $4,750, Mr. Archer paid her tuition fees of $4,800. Mona has agreed to transfer her education related tax credits to Mr. Archer.

During 2007, Mr. Archer paid medical expenses as follows:

Allen	$ 3,780
Jan	2,000
Ron	6,400
Mona	1,500
Total	$13,680

Because of his interest in antiques, Mr. Archer opened a retail operation to sell antiques on January 1, 2007. Mr. Archer invests $239,000 of his savings in this unincorporated business. Of this amount $183,000 was used to purchase a store location, with the remaining $56,000 invested in fixtures for the store. He estimates that $42,000 of the $183,000 paid for the store represents the value of the land. The business is called Allen's Oldies and, as the retail operation is only a few blocks from his residence, Mr. Archer makes no use of his car in this business.

As Mr. Archer has had no formal training as an accountant, he keeps the records for Allen's Oldies on a cash basis. As at December 31, 2007, the business had accumulated total cash of $32,800. Mr. Archer's informal records indicate that at December 31, 2007, the business had receivables from customers of $2,600, inventories with a cost of $12,600, and obligations to suppliers of $5,750. The business had no other debt obligations on this date.

Required: Calculate Mr. Allen's 2007 Net Income For Tax Purposes, his 2007 Taxable Income, and his minimum 2007 federal Tax Payable without consideration of any income tax withheld by his employer. Ignore GST and PST considerations.

Assignment Case Eight - 2 (Comprehensive Case Covering Chapters 5 to 8)

Ms. Lacy Compton is a 45 year old widow with two children:

John Compton Her son John is 22 years old and, because he has been blind since birth, he lives with her in a residence that she owns. He qualifies for the disability tax credit and has no income of his own during 2007.

Allison Compton Her 17 year old daughter Allison has just started university and, during 2007, she attended on a full time basis for 4 months. Her tuition fees that were paid during 2007 were $2,850. Because she has no income of her own, she intends to transfer all of her education related credits to her mother. As she is attending a local university, Allison lives in her mother's home throughout 2007. She will not reach 18 years of age prior to the end of 2007.

During 2007, her family's qualifying medical expenses are as follows:

Lacy	$ 4,220
John	11,500
Allison	2,180
Total	$17,900

The entire family purchases monthly passes to use public transit. During 2007, the cost of the pass is $60 per month for Ms. Compton and $25 per month ($50 in total) for John and Allison, payable on the first day of each month.

During 2007, Ms. Compton makes donations to registered charities of $1,250, as well as contributions to registered federal political parties in the amount of $350.

Ms. Compton is employed as a salesperson by a large Canadian public company. For 2007, her salary is $68,000. In addition, she earns $13,500 in commissions during the year. For the year ending December 31, 2007, her employer withholds the following amounts from her income:

Federal And Provincial Income Tax	$18,500
RPP Contributions*	2,800
EI Premiums	720
CPP Contributions	1,990
Professional Association Dues	250
Payments For Personal Use Of Employer's Car	1,800

*Ms. Compton's employer makes a matching contribution of $2,800 to her RPP.

The car that she used during 2007 cost her employer $32,000. During 2007, it was available to her for 11 months of the year. It was driven a total of 27,000 kilometres, of which 22,500 was for employment related activities.

She is required by her employer to maintain an office in her home. During 2007, this office occupied 15 percent of the floor space in her home. The cost of the home is $335,000. Her 2007 operating costs for 100 percent of the floor space were as follows:

Mortgage Interest	$5,800
Property Taxes	2,450
Utilities And Maintenance	1,100
Insurance	425
Total	$9,775

In conjunction with her sales activities, she incurred costs for meals and entertainment of $4,350. These were not reimbursed by her employer.

In addition to her employment activities, Ms. Compton owns and manages an unincorporated retail business. The fiscal year of the business ends on December 31 and, for 2007, the business had accounting Net Income of $53,500. Other information related to the business is as follows:

1. As the business is unincorporated, no taxes were deducted in calculating Net Income.

2. During 2007, the business spent $8,600 landscaping its premises. For accounting purposes, this amount is being amortized over 10 years on a straight line basis.

3. At the beginning of 2007, Ms. Compton owned depreciable assets used in the business with the following UCC balances:

	Class 1	Class 8	Class 10
January 1, 2007 UCC	$233,000	$41,500	$27,000

In March, 2007, Class 8 assets with a cost of $12,000 were sold for $8,600. They were replaced by Class 8 assets with a cost of $13,400.

4. The Net Income figure is after the deduction of Amortization Expense of $12,600 and $6,000 in meals and entertainment with clients of the business.

Required: Calculate Ms. Compton's 2007 Net Income For Tax Purposes, her 2007 Taxable Income, and her minimum 2007 federal Tax Payable without consideration of any income tax withheld by her employer. Ignore GST and PST considerations.

Assignment Case Eight - 3 (Progressive Running Case - Chapter 8 Version Using ProFile T1 Software For 2006 Tax Returns)

This Progressive Running Case requires the use of the ProFile tax software program. It was introduced in Chapter 6 and is continued in Chapters 8 through 14. Each version must be completed in sequence. While it is not repeated in this version of the Case, the information in the previous version (e.g., Mary's T4 content) is applicable to this version of the Case.

If you have not prepared a tax file incorporating the previous version, please do so before continuing with this version.

On December 27, 2006, Seymour Gravel, at the urging of his wife, Mary Walford, has brought you his preliminary figures for his business. Seymour carries on a business writing and editing instruction manuals on a contract basis. He has six different clients and operates under the business name Crystal Clear Communications from an office in their home.

He knows from past experience that one of his clients will issue him a T4A for the work that he has done for them and has included this information, though he does not yet have the T4A. He is currently missing the information on interest he has paid during the year, except for interest related to his house and his car. He anticipates receiving this shortly.

During the year, Seymour is a full time student at Dalhousie University for three months. He is attending courses in child psychology in order to help deal with Mary's son, William, who has been refusing to go to school and is displaying hostile tendencies.

T2202A - Seymour	Box	Amount
Tuition fees	A	2,200
Number of months in school - part-time	B	0
Number of months in school - full-time	C	3

T4A - Seymour	Box	Amount
Issuer - 3065 Canada Inc.		
Contract payment	28	20,000.00
Income tax deducted	22	Nil

Business or Professional Income - Seymour	
Revenues without T4A	41,603.17
T4A's issued (see T4A information)	20,000.00
Membership dues - Business Writers Association	231.00
Business insurance	126.16
Bank service charges	156.20
Cell phone air time	485.27
Postage and courier charges	110.00
Supplies	2,982.17
Separate business phone line charge and long distance charges	577.86
Fees for accounting and tax advice	500.00
Air fare (business travel)	526.97
Hotels (business travel)	1,240.91
Meals when traveling on business	607.14
Meals and drinks when entertaining clients	887.12
UCC of furniture- beginning of year	2,254.94
UCC of software - beginning of year	219.15
UCC of computer hardware - beginning of year	1,101.58
Software for desktop publishing purchased May 12, 2006	525.00
Laptop computer purchased May 12, 2006	2,048.00

House Costs	
Area of home used for business (square feet)	160
Total area of home (square feet)	1,500
Gas for heating	1,712.86
Hydro	1,641.18
Insurance - house	757.55
Snow plowing contract	440.00
Installation of new gas furnace	3,675.00
Painting of house interior	2,548.05
Mortgage interest	8,456.22
Mortgage life insurance premiums	375.00
Mortgage principal paid	1,279.58
Property taxes	2,533.01
Interest on late property taxes	122.52

Car Costs - Seymour	
Description - Subaru, cost = $35,000, bought 2003-02-15	
January 1 odometer	89,726
December 31 odometer	124,701
Business kilometers driven	8,412
Parking	321.71
Gas	2,582.12
Maintenance and repairs	458.63
Insurance	779.00
Licence and registration fees	49.87
Interest on car loan	597.89
UCC of Class 10.1 - beginning of year	15,470.00

Required:

A. Open the file that you created for the Chapter 6 version of the Case and save a copy under a different name. This will enable you to check the changes between different versions of the Case.

B. Create a return for Seymour that is coupled to Mary's. (Use the F5 key with Mary's return open to create Seymour's return.) Prepare and print in the following order:

   i.   the motor vehicle expenses worksheet for Seymour.
   ii. the CCA worksheet for Crystal Clear Communications.
   iii. the Statement of Professional Activities (T2032) for Crystal Clear Communications.

   Ignore any GST implications.

C. Access and print Mary's summary (Summary on the Form Explorer, not the T1Summary). This form is a two column summary of the couple's tax information. By opening this form from Mary's return, the order of the columns is the same as the one in the previous chapter. For both returns, list the changes on this Summary form from the previous version of this Case. Exclude totals calculated by the program, such as federal tax, the total for non-refundable tax credits and provincial tax from the list, but include the final Balance Owing (Refund) amount.

CHAPTER 9

Income From Property

Introduction

9-1.   Subdivision b of Division B of the *Income Tax Act* provides simultaneous coverage of both income from business and income from property. The parts of these Sections relating to business income are covered in Chapter 8, and many of these provisions are equally applicable to income from property. However, there are sufficient features that are unique to income from property that separate coverage of this subject is warranted and is provided in this Chapter. We have also included coverage of some of the basic issues related to interest deductibility in this Chapter.

Property Income: General Concept

9-2.   Income from property is thought of as the return on invested capital in situations where little or no effort is required by the investor to produce the return. Falling into this category would be rents, interest, dividends, and royalties paid for the use of purchased property. In terms of tax legislation, capital gains are not treated as a component of property income, even in cases where they arise on investments being held to produce property income (e.g., capital gains on dividend paying shares).

9-3.   In cases where a great deal of time and effort is directed at producing interest or rents, such returns can be considered business income. For example, the rents earned by a large property management company would be treated as a component of business income. As explained in Chapter 15, this is an important distinction for corporations since business income qualifies for the small business deduction, while property income generally does not.

9-4.   The primary characteristic that distinguishes property income from business income is the lack of effort directed towards its production. However, in some circumstances, other factors must also be considered. Some examples of why the correct classification is important are as follows:

- When property income is being earned, the deduction of capital cost allowance (CCA) cannot be used to create or increase a net loss for the period.

- When property income is being earned by individuals, there is no requirement for a pro rata CCA reduction to reflect a short fiscal period.

- When property income is being earned, the income attribution rules (see Chapter 12) are applicable. This is not the case when business income is being earned.

- Certain expenses can be deducted against business income, but not property income. These include write-offs of cumulative eligible capital and convention expenses. In contrast, for individuals, there is a deduction for foreign taxes on property income in excess of 15 percent that is not available against foreign business income.

Interest As A Deduction

The Problem

9-5.   There are differing views on the extent to which interest costs should be considered a deductible item for various classes of taxpayers. At one extreme we have the situation that, at one time, existed in the U.S. In that country it was once possible for individuals to deduct all interest costs, without regard to the purpose of the borrowing. In contrast, there are other tax regimes where the deductibility of interest is restricted to certain, very specific types of transactions.

9-6.   From a conceptual point of view, it can be argued that interest should only be deductible to the extent it is paid on funds that are borrowed to produce income that is fully taxable in the period in which the interest is paid. The application of this concept would clearly disallow the current deduction of interest when it relates to:

- the acquisition of items for personal consumption;
- the acquisition of assets which produce income that is only partially taxed (e.g., capital gains); or
- the acquisition of assets which produce income that will not be taxed until a subsequent taxation year (e.g., gains on investments in land).

9-7.   To some extent, the preceding view is incorporated into the current legislation. The real problem, however, is that there are such a multitude of provisions related to the special treatment of certain types of income and to the deferral of income, that the application of these fairly straightforward principles becomes very complex.

9-8.   As is noted in Chapter 8, the general provision for the deduction of interest is found in ITA 20(1)(c). This provision provides for the deduction of interest only if it relates to the production of business or property income. This means that, in general, interest cannot be deducted if it relates only to such other sources of income as employment income or capital gains. Note, however, that the deduction is available to all types of taxpayers, including corporations, individuals, and trusts.

9-9.   As a final general point here, you will recall that when an employee receives an interest free or low interest loan from an employer, imputed interest on the loan will be included in employment income as a taxable benefit. Under ITA 80.5, this imputed interest is deemed to be interest paid and, if the loan is used to produce business or property income, the amount that was included in the employee's income will be deductible under ITA 20(1)(c).

The Government Response

1991 Draft Legislation

9-10.   In response to the problems related to the deductibility of interest, in 1991, the government issued draft legislation which was intended to deal with a number of issues. The issues dealt with in this draft legislation, along with the conclusions reached, can be described as follows:

Employee And Shareholder Loans   The issue here is whether interest paid on money borrowed to make loans to employees and shareholders should be deductible to the business. A proposed ITA 20(1)(c)(v) indicates that all such interest is deductible with respect to amounts borrowed to make loans to employees. When the borrowing is to make loans to shareholders, a proposed ITA 20(1)(c)(vi) would limit deductible interest to the amount of interest income received or receivable by the corporation on the loan.

Acquisition Of Preferred Shares The problem here is that the interest on the loan may exceed the taxable dividends on the preferred shares. A proposed ITA 20(1)(qq) would limit the deduction of interest in this situation to the amount of taxable dividends on the preferred shares. Any excess interest could be carried over and deducted in the following year, subject to the same taxable dividends limitation. Note that this proposed rule does not apply to common shares since their right to dividends is generally considered limitless.

Investment In Business If the proceeds of the borrowing are used to make an interest free or low interest loan to a business in which the borrower has an interest, then there is no reasonable expectation of a profit on the loan. However, a proposed ITA 20(3.1) and 20(3.2) deem the borrowing to have been made for the purpose of producing income, provided two conditions are met:

- The proceeds of the loan must be used by the business to produce Canadian source income.
- There must be an indication that the business could not have borrowed the funds on comparable terms.

Funds Borrowed For Distributions Under a proposed ITA 20.1 and 20.2, such borrowings will be deemed to have been made for the purpose of producing income. However, the applicable amount will be limited to the equity (assets, less liabilities as specifically defined for this purpose) of the business. Interest on amounts borrowed within this limit will be deductible.

9-11. To date (May, 2007), nothing further has happened with this legislation. It has not been passed nor has there been any formal notice that it has been canceled. This is somewhat puzzling in that other proposals were put forward on October 31, 2003 that have the effect of making this legislation largely irrelevant. Subsequent to a brief discussion of two important cases which may have influenced decisions related to this legislation, we will give detailed consideration to these more recent draft proposals.

The Singleton And Ludco Court Cases

9-12. Two cases that wound their way through the court system in the late 1990s probably had some influence on the willingness of the government to proceed with the 1991 draft legislation, as well as on the proposals that were put forward on October 31, 2003. While any thorough analysis of these cases goes well beyond the scope of this text, your understanding of this material on interest deductibility will be enhanced by some awareness of the conclusions reached in these two cases.

9-13. The facts in the Singleton case (The Queen vs. Singleton; 2001 DTC 5533) involved a lawyer who made a withdrawal of funds from his capital account in the law firm where he worked. These funds were used to purchase a residence for his personal use. Immediately after, he borrowed sufficient funds to replace the capital balance that he had withdrawn from his firm and then proceeded to deduct the interest on these borrowings.

9-14. The CRA denied this deduction on the basis that the real purpose of the borrowings was to finance the purchase of his residence, a view that was supported by the Tax Court of Canada. However, both the Federal Court of Appeals and the Supreme Court of Canada disagreed. In making this decision, the Supreme Court noted that, in the absence of a sham or a specific provision in the *Act* to the contrary, the economic realities of a transaction cannot be used to recharacterize a clearly established legal relationship.

9-15. The facts in the Ludco case (Ludco Enterprises Ltd. vs. The Queen; 2001 DTC 5505) involved the Company borrowing $7.5 million which was used to finance investments in two offshore companies. During the period that these investments were held, Ludco paid $6 million in interest on the borrowings and received $600,000 in dividends on the shares held. When the shares were ultimately redeemed, Ludco realized a $9.2 million capital gain.

9-16. The CRA denied the deduction of the interest on the grounds that the shares were acquired for the purpose of earning a capital gain, not for the purpose of earning property income. While the Federal Court of Appeal agreed with the CRA, the Supreme Court of Canada did not. They concluded that an investment can have multiple purposes and, as long as one of these was the earning of property income, the condition that borrowing must be for the purpose of earning income was satisfied. That provision does not require either a quantitative determination of income or a judicial assessment of the sufficiency of income in order to satisfy its requirements.

October, 2003 Draft Proposals

9-17.   On October 31, 2003, the Department of Finance released an unusual document which consisted of a combination of draft legislation, along with a new Interpretation Bulletin, IT-533, "Interest Deductibility And Related Issues". The draft legislation deals with the issue of reasonable expectation of profit and is discussed in Chapter 2. We would note, however, that it also has implications for interest deductibility.

9-18.   Interest related issues in real estate investments can be particularly problematical. Such investments are often highly leveraged, sometimes to the point where interest expense is so large that there is no "reasonable expectation" of a positive amount of net rental income. While such investments may be profitable overall, this profitability is usually dependent on realizing a capital gain at the time of sale. As the proposed legislation makes clear, in determining whether there is a reasonable expectation of profit, capital gains cannot be considered.

9-19.   In an indirect manner, this has the effect of limiting the deductibility of interest expense. While CCA deductions cannot be used to create or increase a loss on real estate investments, interest expense can be used for this purpose. If such losses are denied by the reasonable expectation of profit legislation, the indirect result is to limit the deductibility of some interest payments on highly leveraged real estate investments.

9-20.   The other component of the 2003 material, IT-533, is much more direct in dealing with the deductibility of interest. We will give detailed consideration to the content of this Interpretation Bulletin in the following material.

March, 2007 Budget

9-21.   The March 19, 2007 budget contains a proposal which would significantly limit the deductibility of interest related to investments in foreign affiliates. We would note, however, that this proposal has unleashed a storm of criticism. It appears unlikely that this proposal will be adopted in its present form.

IT-533 - "Interest Deductibility And Related Issues"

What Is Interest?

9-22.   In order to be considered interest for tax purposes, IT-533 indicates that the amount has to satisfy three criteria:

- It must accrue on a continuous basis (note that it may be compounded using a different basis).
- It must be calculated on a principal sum.
- It must be compensation for the use of that principal sum.

9-23.   IT-533 notes that participating payments meet this definition and will be deductible, provided there is an upper limit on the applicable rate and that upper limit reflects prevailing market conditions. However, payments that are contingent on some future event are not deductible until that event occurs. Further, if the event occurs in a future year, the payment would not be deductible in that year as the payment is not in respect of that year.

9-24.   It is also noted that when a contract does not explicitly identify any amount as interest, deductible interest may still be present if any of the payments under the contract can reasonably be regarded as interest. An example of this would be some of the prescribed debt obligations that are discussed beginning in Paragraph 9-56.

Direct Or Indirect Use

9-25. In order for the interest to be deductible, it must be paid on money that has been borrowed to produce income from business or property. This raises the question of whether it is the direct use, or the indirect use that is relevant. This was the issue in the Singleton court case where the direct use of the borrowings was to invest capital in the partnership, but the indirect use was to purchase a personal residence. This case, along with others, seems to make clear that it is the direct use that must be considered. The fact that Singleton was, in economic reality, financing the purchase of his home, cannot override the fact that the direct use of the borrowed money was to invest in an income producing partnership.

9-26. IT-533 does indicate, however, that there are exceptions to the direct use rule. Several exceptions are described as follows:

Filling The Hole The Bulletin uses the term "filling the hole" to describe situations where money is borrowed to pay dividends, to redeem shares, or to return capital of a corporation or partnership. The basic idea here is that the new debt replaces other forms of capital that were invested in income producing assets. In the case of dividends, this seems to be a bit of a stretch. However, the argument is that the borrowings replace the retained earnings that are being distributed in the form of dividends.

Interest-Free Loans In general, money borrowed to make interest-free loans would not be deductible as the purpose of the borrowing is not to produce income. However, it can be argued that an interest-free loan to a wholly owned subsidiary has been made with a view to helping the subsidiary produce income which can ultimately be used to pay dividends. The Bulletin indicates that the interest on borrowings to make interest-free loans of this type would be deductible.

A further exception is when money is borrowed to make interest-free loans to employees. The argument here is that the interest-free loan is a form of employee compensation, the purpose of which is to encourage the employees to help the employer produce income.

Linking Interest To Current Use

9-27. Several court decisions have made it clear that it is the current use of the borrowed money that establishes deductibility. To illustrate this point, consider the following example:

Example An individual borrows $100,000 and invests it in an income producing property. This income producing property is subsequently sold and the proceeds invested in personal use property.

Analysis Subsequent to the sale of the income producing investment, interest on the borrowings is no long deductible as the current use of the property is no longer income producing.

If, alternatively, the proceeds of the sale of the income producing property had been invested in another income producing property, the interest would continue to be deductible.

Looking at this from the other direction, if the original borrowings had been to finance personal use property, the interest would not have been deductible at the time of the borrowing. However, if the personal use property were sold and the proceeds invested in an income producing property, the interest would commence being deductible at that point in time.

9-28. A widely used technique for facilitating the linking process is referred to as "cash damming". This involves establishing two separate bank accounts, with one account receiving only deposits of borrowed funds and the other account receiving all other deposits. Management then takes steps to ensure that only expenditures which qualify for interest deductibility are made from the account that receives the borrowed funds.

9-29.   A further problem with linking can arise when there is a reinvestment of proceeds that involved a gain or loss on the sale of the original investment.

Example   An individual borrows $100,000 and invests it in an income producing property. This property is subsequently sold and the proceeds invested in other income producing properties.

Analysis   If we assume that the original property is sold for $150,000 and invested in property A which costs $110,000 and property B which costs $40,000, the borrowed money can be allocated in any way the investor wishes. He could allocate the full $100,000 to property A or, alternatively, $40,000 to property B, with the remaining $60,000 to property A. The decision will probably be based on which property he plans to dispose of first, particularly if he does not anticipate re-investing the funds in income producing assets.

In contrast, if we assume that the original asset is sold for $90,000, with the proceeds used to acquire property A for $60,000 and property B for $30,000, IT-533 suggests that the borrowing must be allocated to the two investments on a pro rata basis. This would result in $66,667 [($60,000 ÷ $90,000)($100,000)] being allocated to property A, and $33,333 [($30,000 ÷ $90,000)($100,000)] being allocated to property B. Note that the debt allocated to each property is more than its cost. This is permitted by the disappearing source rules that are described in the following Paragraph.

Disappearing Source Rules

9-30.   A problem can arise if an investment, which has been financed with debt, is sold for proceeds that are less than the debt. As a result, the investor does not have sufficient funds to pay off all the related debt.

9-31.   ITA 20.1 deals with the obvious inequity that could arise in disappearing source situations such as that illustrated in the following example:

Example   An investor buys shares at a cost of $75,000, using borrowed funds to finance the purchase. At a later point in time, the investment is sold for $40,000, with the proceeds used to pay off $40,000 of the debt. The remaining $35,000 of the debt remains unpaid.

Analysis   If the current use approach is used, the interest on the remaining debt would no longer be deductible as it is not currently in use to finance income producing property. However, in situations such as this, the remaining debt would be deemed under ITA 20.1 to be used in producing income and the interest would continue to be deductible.

Investments In Common Shares

9-32.   IT-533 deals with a number of other issues associated with interest deductibility. Its guidance on dealing with premium and discount on the issuance of debt is discussed later in this Chapter. Most of the other issues covered are sufficiently specialized that they go beyond the scope of this text. There is, however, one other issue here of general importance.

9-33.   This is the question of whether interest on funds used to invest in common shares should be considered deductible. The problem is that common shares generally do not carry a stated interest or dividend rate and, in some cases, simply do not pay dividends, either currently or for the foreseeable future. While capital gains may ultimately make such investments profitable, there are many cases where investments in common shares could be viewed as not producing property income.

9-34.   Fortunately, IT-533 indicates that in most circumstances the CRA will consider interest on funds borrowed to invest in common shares to be deductible. This is on the basis of a reasonable expectation, at the time the shares are acquired, that the holder will at some time in the future receive dividends. They do, however, give an example of a situation where this expectation is not viable:

Example   R Corp. is an investment vehicle designed to provide only a capital return to the investors in its common shares. The corporate policy with respect to R Corp. is that dividends will not be paid, that corporate earnings will be reinvested to increase the value of the shares, and that shareholders are required to sell their shares to a third-party purchaser in a fixed number of years in order to realize their value.

9-35.   In this situation, it is not reasonable to expect income from such shareholdings and any interest expense on money borrowed to acquire R Corp. shares would not be deductible.

Discount And Premium On Long-Term Issued Debt

Economic Background

9-36.   When a debt security is issued with an interest rate below the current rate, investors will react by offering a price that is less than the maturity value of the security. Such securities are said to sell at a discount and, in economic terms, this discount generally represents an additional interest charge to be recognized over the life of the security.

9-37.   For example, a 10 year bond with a maturity value of $100,000 and a 10 percent stated interest rate, would sell for $88,700 to investors expecting a 12 percent interest rate. The discount of $11,300 would then be added to interest expense at the rate of $1,130 per year for the ten year period (to simplify the presentation, we are using the straight-line amortization of discount and premium, an approach that is no longer acceptable under GAAP).

9-38.   In a corresponding fashion, a debt security that offered an interest rate above that currently expected by investors would command a premium. Such a premium would then be treated as a reduction in interest expense over the remaining life of the debt security.

9-39.   The procedures described in the preceding Paragraph are, of course, well known to anyone familiar with generally accepted accounting principles. Surprisingly, the tax rules for dealing with bond premium and discount do not reflect these well established principles.

9-40.   The required tax procedures are completely different from the accounting procedures, are inconsistent in the treatment of premium and discount, and have no conceptual basis of support. Despite this, IT-533, "Interest Deductibility And Related Issues" (previously discussed beginning in Paragraph 9-22), makes it clear that these strange procedures reflect the intent of the government.

Tax Procedures - Issuers Of Discount Bonds

9-41.   From the point of view of the issuer of a discount bond, the deductible amount of interest will be based on the stated, or coupon, rate without consideration of the difference between the proceeds received from the sale of the bonds and the larger amount that must be paid when the bonds mature. This excess will be treated as a loss on the retirement of the debt (i.e., a liability is being extinguished by paying more than its carrying value for tax purposes). You may recall from Chapter 8 that, under ITA 20(1)(f), this loss will be considered a fully deductible amount, provided:

- the bonds are issued for not less than 97 percent of their maturity value; and
- the effective yield on the bonds is not more than 4/3 of the stated, or coupon, rate.

9-42.   If these conditions are not met, only one-half of the loss will be deductible. This, in effect, treats the loss as a capital loss. It would appear that the goal here is to prevent the use of deep discount bonds which, because of the failure of tax legislation to deal appropriately with bond discount, results in the investor having a part of his interest income being converted to a capital gain. A more logical solution to this problem would be to revise the relevant tax legislation to better reflect the economic substance of bond discount.

Exercise Nine-1

Subject: Discount Bonds

On January 1, 2007, Moreau Ltd. issues bonds with a maturity value of $1,000,000 and a maturity date of December 31, 2009. The bonds pay interest on December 31 of each year at an annual coupon rate of 4 percent. They are sold for proceeds of $985,000 for an effective yield of 4.6 percent. The maturity amount is paid on December 31, 2009. Moreau uses the straight-line method to amortize the discount on the bonds. What are the tax consequences related to this bond issue for Moreau Ltd. in each of the years 2007, 2008, and 2009? How would these tax consequences differ from the information included in Moreau's GAAP based financial statements? In order to simplify your solution, assume that the straight-line amortization of discount is acceptable under GAAP (it is not).

End of Exercise. Solution available in Study Guide.

Tax Procedures - Issuers Of Premium Bonds

9-43.   IT-533 makes it clear that premium situations are not treated in a manner that is analogous with the treatment of discounts. This Bulletin indicates that, depending on the situation, three different possible approaches may be used by debt issuers for dealing with bond premium. These alternatives can be described as follows:

Money Lenders   The Bulletin indicates that, in situations where the borrowed money constitutes stock-in-trade for a taxpayer that is in the financing business, premium on the debt must be taken into income immediately. The Bulletin also makes it clear that this amount would not be given capital gains treatment and, as a consequence, would be 100 percent taxable. Given this treatment of the premium, the deductible amount of interest would be equal to the stated, or coupon, rate.

Other Taxpayers   In what constitutes something of a windfall for taxpayers issuing debt at a premium, the Bulletin indicates that the amount of premium received at the time of issue would be considered a non-taxable capital receipt. While IT-533 is not clear on this issue, it appears that there will be no further tax consequences related to the premium when the bonds are retired. Unlike the case with bond discount, where there is a specific ITA Paragraph which provides for the deduction of this amount at the maturity of the bonds, there is no corresponding provision that requires the premium to be treated as a gain when the bonds are retired.

Deliberate Creation Of A Premium   IT-533 introduces a third approach based on the very fuzzy concept of a "premium which arises because the debt was deliberately priced to give rise to a premium". There appears to be concern here that an enterprise might create additional tax deductions by setting an unrealistically high rate of interest on the issuance of debt. While it is not clear how "unrealistically high" will be measured, the tax consequence is that the contractual amount of interest paid will be viewed as unreasonable and will be reduced to a reasonable amount over the life of the debt. As this appears to be consistent with the premium amortization approach used in accounting, it seems the CRA's position is that only in unreasonable circumstances is it appropriate to use a reasonable approach to dealing with bond premium.

9-44.   With most conventional debt issuances, the second approach would be applicable. It is interesting to note that, in comparison with the applicable accounting procedures, this approach produces a larger interest deduction and this enhanced deduction is not offset by a gain when the bonds are retired. This permanent difference between accounting and tax income should make taxpayers who issue premium bonds very happy.

Exercise Nine-2

Subject: Premium Bonds

On January 1 of the current year, Cannon Inc. issues 10 year bonds payable with a maturity value of $1,000,000. The bonds have a coupon rate of 18 percent, pay interest on January 1 of each year, and are sold for $1,400,000. The Company has a December 31 year end. Determine the current year tax consequences under each of the following assumptions:

- Cannon is in the business of lending money.
- Cannon is not in the business of lending money and did not make a deliberate effort to create a premium on the issuance of the bonds.
- Cannon is not in the business of lending money and made a deliberate effort to create a premium on the issuance of the bonds.

End of Exercise. Solution available in Study Guide.

Interest Income

General Provision

9-45.   ITA 12(1) lists inclusions in business and property income. Paragraph (c) of this Subsection is as follows:

> **Interest**   ... any amount received or receivable by the taxpayer in the year (depending on the method regularly followed by the taxpayer in computing the taxpayer's income) as, on account of, in lieu of payment of or in satisfaction of, interest to the extent that the interest was not included in computing the taxpayer's income for a preceding taxation year.

9-46.   The wording of ITA 12(1)(c) suggests that taxpayers can use the cash basis to recognize interest income (amounts received or receivable). This is not the case. ITA 12(3) and 12(4) require the use of an accrual approach by all taxpayers. As is discussed in the following material, the accrual approach used by individuals differs from that used by corporations and partnerships.

Corporations And Partnerships

9-47.   ITA 12(3) requires that corporations, partnerships, and some trusts use accrual accounting. The concept of accrual accounting that is applied to these taxpayers is the conventional one in which interest income is recorded as a direct function of the passage of time.

9-48.   For these organizations, interest income for tax purposes is, generally speaking, identical to that required under the application of generally accepted accounting principles. However, as will be explained later in this Chapter, an exception to this is interest income on bonds that have been purchased at a premium or a discount.

Individuals

9-49.   While ITA 12(3) requires conventional accrual accounting for corporations and partnerships, ITA 12(4) provides for a less familiar version of this concept for individuals. Under this modified version of accrual accounting, interest is not accrued on a continuous basis. Rather, ITA 12(4) requires the accrual of interest on each anniversary date of an investment contract.

9-50.   ITA 12(11) defines "investment contracts" to include most debt securities and "anniversary date" to be that date that is one year after the day before the date of issue of the security, and every successive one year interval. This would mean that, for a five year contract issued on July 1, 2007, the anniversary dates would be June 30 of each of the five years 2008 through 2012. If the holder of the investment contract disposes of it prior to its maturity, the disposal date is also considered to be an anniversary date from the point of view of that particular taxpayer.

9-51.   To the extent that the income accrued on the anniversary date has not been previously included in income, it must then be included in the individual's income, regardless of whether the amount has been received or is receivable.

9-52.   The following example is an illustration of the annual accrual rule.

Example An investment contract with a maturity value of $100,000 and an annual interest rate of 10 percent is issued on July 1, 2007. The $100,000 maturity amount is due on June 30, 2012. An interest payment for the first 2.5 years of interest ($25,000) is due on December 31, 2009. The remaining interest ($25,000) is due with the principal payment on June 30, 2012. The contract is purchased by an individual at the time that it is issued.

Analysis As no interest has been received in 2007 and no anniversary date has occurred during the year, no interest would have to be included in the individual's tax return for that year. As compared to the use of the full accrual method, this provides a one year deferral of $5,000 of interest.

Annual interest of $10,000 would have to be accrued on the first two anniversary dates of the contract, June 30, 2008 and June 30, 2009. This means that $10,000 would be included in Net Income For Tax Purposes for each of these two years. When the $25,000 payment is received on December 31, 2009, an additional $5,000 would be subject to taxation for that year because it has been received, and not previously accrued. This results in taxation of $15,000 in 2009. At this point, the cumulative results are identical to those that would result from the application of the full accrual approach.

For 2010, the June 30, 2010 anniversary date would require the accrual of $10,000. However, as $5,000 of this amount was already included in income during 2009, only $5,000 of this amount would be subject to taxation in 2010. There would be a further accrual of $10,000 on each of the anniversary dates in the years 2011 and 2012.

9-53.   Note that the anniversary date is established by the date on which the investment contract is issued. It is not influenced by the date on which the individual investor acquires the contract.

Exercise Nine-3

Subject: Annual Accrual Rules

On October 1, 2007, Ms. Diane Dumont acquires an investment contract with a maturity value of $60,000. It matures on September 30, 2013 and pays interest at an annual rate of 8 percent. Payment for the first three and one-quarter years of interest is due on December 31, 2010, with interest for the remaining two and three-quarters years payable on the maturity date. What amount of interest will Ms. Dumont have to include in her tax returns for each of the years 2007 through 2013?

End of Exercise. Solution available in Study Guide.

Discount And Premium On Long-Term Debt Holdings

9-54.   Tax legislation takes the view that the taxable amount of interest is based on the accrual of the stated, or coupon, rate, without consideration of the fact that, in the case of bonds sold at a discount or premium, the investor will receive an amount at maturity that is larger or smaller than the amount that was paid for the bonds. Because tax procedures do not provide for the usual amortization of this discount or premium, it will be treated as a gain or loss at maturity by the investor.

9-55.   If the bonds are acquired at a discount, the additional amount that will be received at maturity (the discount) will be treated as a capital gain, only one-half of which will be taxable. In similar fashion, if the bonds are acquired at a premium, the receipt of just the face value at maturity will result in the premium being treated as a capital loss, only one-half of which will be deductible.

Prescribed Debt Obligations

9-56.   Over the last two or three decades, a large number of financial instruments have been developed that provide a return to investors in a less conventional manner. For example, debt obligations were developed that specified low interest payments during the early years of issue, followed by compensation in the form of higher rates during the later years. Other instruments, such as the principal component of strip bonds and zero coupon bonds, provided for no payment of interest. Investors were compensated for this lack of "interest" by maturity payments in excess of the initial issue price of the securities.

9-57.   The government responded to this situation with the issuance of more sophisticated regulations. Specifically, ITR 7000(1) identifies four types of prescribed debt obligations and indicates their required tax treatment as follows:

ITR 7000(1)(a) describes obligations that only pay a specified sum at maturity, with no interim interest payments. In the case of these obligations, referred to as zero coupon bonds, interest must be accrued by the effective rate method at the rate which will equate the original cost of the obligation to the present value of its maturity value.

ITR 7000(1)(b) describes stripped bonds in which the maturity value and the interest payments are sold separately. Interest on the maturity value component will be determined as per ITR 7000(1)(a). The interest to be recognized on the interest payment component will be based on the yield that equates the cost of that component with the present value of all future payments.

ITR 7000(1)(c) describes debt obligations that contain variable interest rate provisions. Here the interest to be accrued will be based on the greater of the maximum interest rate stipulated for the year, or the accrued interest based on the yield that equates the principal amount of the debt to the present value of the maximum future payments.

ITR 7000(1)(d) describes debt obligations in which the interest rate to be paid is contingent on a future event. In this case, the interest to be recognized must be based on the maximum rate potentially payable. For example, if an extra 1 percent interest was added to the investment's return if the obligation is held to maturity, the annual accrual would have to include this extra 1 percent.

9-58.   A comprehensive treatment of these obligations goes beyond the scope of this material. However, an example of the types of calculations that are involved would be as follows:

Example   On January 1, 2007, Albert Litton purchases a zero coupon bond with a maturity value of $10,000. The bond is issued on this date and the maturity value is due on December 31, 2009. The price paid by Mr. Litton is $7,312, providing an effective annual yield of 11 percent.

Analysis   The total interest income of $2,688 ($10,000 - $7,312) would have to be reported by Mr. Litton as follows:

Year	Opening Balance	Interest At 11%	Closing Balance
2007	$7,312	$804	$ 8,116
2008	8,116	893	9,009
2009	9,009	991	10,000
Total Interest		$2,688	

Exercise Nine-4

Subject: Prescribed Debt Obligations

On January 1, 2007, a debt obligation is issued with a coupon interest rate of 7 percent, a maturity value of $250,000, and a maturity date of December 31, 2009. Annual interest of $17,500 is paid on December 31. The interest coupons and the maturity amount are sold separately at prices that provide an effective yield of 7 percent. The price of the maturity payment is $204,075, while the price of the interest coupons is $45,925. Calculate the amount of interest that the purchasers of these two financial instruments will have to include in their tax returns in each of the three years.

End of Exercise.   Solution available in Study Guide.

Indexed Debt Obligations

9-59.   Debt obligations are sometimes issued with the amount of interest and principal to be paid determined by reference to a change in the purchasing power of money. ITR 7001 requires that changes resulting from indexing the principal amount be included in income at the time such adjustments are required. An example will serve to illustrate this provision:

Example   On November 1, 2007, an individual acquires, at par, a $1,000 bond issued on that date. The bond is indexed to the Consumer Price Index (CPI) and on maturity, will be redeemed for $1,000 plus an amount that reflects the increase in the CPI while the bond was outstanding. The bond also pays interest each November 1 of 4 percent of the indexed principal, measured as of each payment date. Assume that from November 1, 2007 to October 31, 2008, the CPI increases by 5 percent and from November 1, 2008 to October 31, 2009 it increases a further 3 percent.

Analysis   Given the preceding, the amounts that would be included in the taxpayer's income for 2007, 2008, and 2009 would be calculated as follows:

Year		Amount
2007		Nil
2008:		
Interest [($1,000)(1.05)(4%)]	$42.00	
Inflation Adjustment [($1,000)(5%)]	50.00	$ 92.00
2009:		
Interest [($1,000)(1.05)(1.03)(4%)]	$43.26	
Inflation Adjustment [($1,050)(3%)]	31.50	74.76
Three Year Total		$166.76

9-60.   While the inflation adjustment amounts will have to be included in the taxpayer's income in the years indicated in the preceding table, these amounts will not be received until the bond matures. However, as they have already been included in the taxpayer's income, they will not be taxed again at that time. Also note that, under the provisions of this Regulation, the amounts that have to be included in the income of the purchaser of the bond would also be deductible to the issuer.

Accrued Interest At Transfer

9-61.   Publicly traded debt securities are bought and sold on a day-to-day basis, without regard to the specific date on which interest payments are due. To accommodate this situation, accrued interest from the date of the last interest payment date will be added to the purchase price of the security.

9-62.   Consider, for example, a 10 percent coupon, $1,000 face value bond, with semi-annual interest payments of $50 on June 30 and December 31 of each year. If we assume that the market value of the bond is equal to its face value and it is purchased on October 1, 2007, the price would be $1,025, including $25 of interest for the three month period from June 30, 2007 through October 1, 2007.

9-63.   In the absence of a special provision dealing with this situation, the $25 would have to be included in the income of the purchaser when it is received as part of the $50 December 31, 2007 interest payment. Further, the extra $25 received by the seller would receive favourable treatment as a capital gain. To prevent this result, ITA 20(14) indicates that the seller must include the accrued interest in income and the purchaser can deduct a corresponding amount from the interest received on the bonds.

Exercise Nine-5

Subject: Accrued Interest At Transfer

On May 1, 2007, Mr. Milford Lay purchases bonds with a face value of $50,000 at par. These bonds pay semi-annual interest of $3,000 on June 30 and December 31 of each year. He purchases the bonds for $52,000, including interest accrued to the purchase date. He holds the bonds for the remainder of the year, receiving both the June 30 and December 31 interest payments. What amount of interest will be included in Mr. Lay's 2007 tax return?

End of Exercise. Solution available in Study Guide.

Payments Based On Production Or Use (Royalties)

9-64.   The relevant *Income Tax Act* Paragraph here reads as follows:

ITA 12(1)(g) Payments based on production or use — any amount received by the taxpayer in the year that was dependent on the use of or production from property whether or not that amount was an instalment of the sale price of the property, except that an instalment of the sale price of agricultural land is not included by virtue of this paragraph.

9-65.   While ITA 12(1)(g), by referring only to amounts received, suggests the use of cash basis revenue recognition, this has limited application. ITA 12(2.01) indicates that ITA 12(1)(g) cannot be used to defer the inclusion of any item that would normally be included in the determination of business income.

9-66.   The provision also requires that, except in the case of agricultural land, payments that represent instalments on the sale price of the property must also be included if their payment is related to production or use. An example will serve to illustrate this provision:

Example   The owner of a mineral deposit sells the asset with the proceeds to be paid on the basis of $2 per ton of ore removed. The total amount to be paid is not fixed by the sales agreement.

9-67.   In this situation, the original owner of the property would have to include in income the full amount received in subsequent years, even though a portion of the payment may be of a capital nature.

Rental Income

General Rules

9-68.   Rental income is not specifically mentioned in the ITA Sections that deal with income from property. There is some merit in the view that rental receipts fall into the category of payments for production or use. However, rents are generally payable without regard to whether or not the property is used and, as a consequence, this view may not be appropriate. In any case, it is clear that rental receipts must be included in income and, given this fact, income from property would appear to be the most logical classification.

9-69.   While there is no specific guidance in the *Income Tax Act*, it would appear that rental income is to be recorded on an accrual basis. Referring to the CRA's Guide on Rental Income (T4036), this source indicates that, in most cases, rental income should be determined on an accrual basis.

9-70.   However, the Guide goes on to note that "if you have practically no amounts receivable and no expenses outstanding at the end of the year", you are allowed to use a cash basis for recognizing rental expenses and revenues. This leads to the conclusion that, unless the cash basis produces results that are nearly identical to those that would be determined on an accrual basis, the accrual basis must be used.

9-71.   Once the rental revenues are included in income, a variety of expenses become deductible against them. These would include utilities (heat, electricity, water), repairs, maintenance, interest, insurance, property taxes, management fees, and fees to rental agents for locating tenants.

Capital Cost Allowances

General Rules

9-72.   In addition to other expenses, CCA on rental properties can be claimed. In the year of acquisition, the half-year rule is applied when calculating the maximum available amount. For individuals, the calendar year is considered the fiscal year for property income purposes. As a consequence, there is no adjustment for a short fiscal period in the year of acquisition.

9-73.   Rental properties acquired after 1987 will generally fall into Class 1, where they are eligible for CCA calculated on a declining balance basis at a rate of 4 percent. As mentioned in Chapter 7, rental properties acquired prior to 1988 were allocated to Class 3, where the rate was 5 percent. This rate is still available on properties that were allocated to Class 3 prior to 1988. Note, however, that in both classes the rate is applied to the UCC of the building only. Some part of the value of the total cost of the property must be allocated to land, and this amount is not subject to CCA.

9-74.   You may recall from Chapter 7 (CCA) that the 2007 Budget proposes additional allowances for CCA on buildings used for manufacturing and processing and buildings used for other non-residential purposes. While it is likely that these additional allowances would be available on rental properties that are used for these purposes, in this Chapter and the related problem material, we will assume that rental properties are used exclusively for residential purposes.

Special Rules

9-75.   There are two special rules that apply to CCA calculations on rental properties. These rules, along with a brief explanation of the reason that each was introduced, are as follows:

Separate CCA Classes   Each rental building that is acquired after 1971 at a cost of $50,000 or more must be placed in a separate class for calculating CCA, recapture, and terminal losses. In most real world situations, the amount of CCA that can be deducted on a rental property exceeds any decline in the value of the building. In fact, it is not uncommon for the value of such properties to increase over time. This means that, if an investor is required to account for each rental property as a separate item, a disposition is likely to result in recapture of CCA and an increase in Tax Payable.

In the absence of this special rule, all rental properties would be allocated to a single class. This would mean that the investor could avoid recapture for long periods of time by simply adding new properties to the class. This separate class rule prevents this from happening.

Rental Property CCA Restriction   In general, taxpayers are not permitted to create or increase a net rental loss by claiming CCA on rental properties. For this purpose, rental income is the total rental income or loss from all properties owned by the taxpayer. This amount includes any recapture, as well as any terminal losses. The reason for this restriction is a desire to limit the use of rental losses for purposes of sheltering other types of income (e.g., applying rental losses against employment income).

The fact that CCA is the only restricted deduction is probably based on the fact that, unlike most depreciable assets, the value of many rental properties does not usually decline over time. This restriction does not apply to a corporation or a corporate partnership whose principal business throughout the year is the rental or sale of real property. Also note that this restriction, unlike the separate class restriction, applies to any property that is leased or rented, not just real estate.

9-76.   Without question, these special rules make real estate less attractive as an investment. However, a number of advantages remain:

- taxation on a positive cash flow can be eliminated through the use of CCA;
- some part of the capital cost of an asset can be deducted despite the fact that real estate assets are generally not decreasing in value;
- increases in the value of the property are not taxed until the property is sold; and
- any gain resulting from a sale is taxed as a capital gain, only one-half of which is taxable.

9-77.   These factors continue to make the tax features of investments in rental properties attractive to many individuals.

Rental Income Example

9-78.   An example will serve to illustrate the basic features involved in determining net rental income.

Example   On January 1, 2007, Mr. Bratton owns the following two rental properties:

- Property A was acquired in 1987 at a cost of $120,000, of which $20,000 was allocated to land. It has a UCC of $68,000.
- Property B was acquired in 2000 at a cost of $90,000. It has a UCC of $74,200 and is situated on land that Mr. Bratton leases. On August 28, 2007, Property B is sold for $125,000.

On December 1, 2007, Mr. Bratton acquires Property C at a cost of $200,000, of which $50,000 is allocated to land. Rents on all of the properties totaled $35,000 during 2007 and the cost of maintenance, property taxes, and mortgage interest totaled $45,400.

Net Rental Income Calculation   The maximum available CCA on the three properties would be as follows:

- Property A (Class 3) = $3,400 [(5%)($68,000)]
- Property B (Class 1) = Nil (The property was sold during the year.)
- Property C (Class 1) = $3,000 [($150,000)(1/2)(4%)]

Since a rental loss cannot be created by claiming CCA, the net rental income would be calculated as follows:

Gross Rents	$35,000
Recapture Of CCA On Property B ($90,000 - $74,200)	15,800
Expenses Other Than CCA	(45,400)
Income Before CCA	$ 5,400
CCA Class 1 (Maximum)	(3,000)
CCA Class 3 (Limited)	(2,400)
Net Rental Income	Nil

9-79.   Note that the maximum CCA was taken on Class 1, the 4 percent class, leaving the limited CCA deduction for Class 3 which has the higher rate of 5 percent. This follows the general tax planning rule that suggests that, when less than the maximum allowable CCA is taken, the CCA that is deducted should be taken from the classes with the lowest rates. Also note that there would be a taxable capital gain of $17,500 [(1/2)($125,000 - $90,000)] on the sale of Property B. The taxable capital gain is not part of the rental income or loss calculation.

Exercise Nine-6

Subject: Rental Income

Ms. Sheela Horne acquires a rental property in September, 2007 at a total cost of $185,000. Of this total, $42,000 can be allocated to the value of the land. She immediately spends $35,000 to make major improvements to the property. Rents for the year total $7,200, while rental expenses other than CCA total $5,100. This is the only rental property owned by Ms. Horne. Determine the maximum CCA that Ms. Horne can deduct in calculating her 2007 net rental income.

End of Exercise. Solution available in Study Guide.

Cash Dividends From Taxable Canadian Corporations

The Concept Of Integration

9-80.   While this concept will be given much more detailed attention in the Chapters dealing with corporate taxation, it is virtually impossible to understand the tax procedures associated with dividends received from taxable Canadian corporations without some elementary understanding of the concept of integration. It is fundamental, both to the procedures associated with the taxation of dividends, as well as to many other provisions related to the taxation of corporations.

9-81.   An individual who owns an unincorporated business or, alternatively, holds investments that earn property income, can choose to transfer these assets to a corporation. The various reasons for doing this will be given detailed consideration in Chapter 17. At this point, however, our concern is with the fact that, in making such a transfer, the taxpayer creates an additional taxable entity. As depicted in Figure 9-1, if the individual incorporates his source of business or property income, the corporation will be taxed on the resulting income. In addition, the individual will pay taxes on the dividends which the corporation will distribute from the corporation's after tax income.

9-82.   As is also depicted in Figure 9-1, the goal of integration is to ensure that the use of a corporation does not alter the total amount of taxes that will be paid on a given stream of business or property income. Stated alternatively, the procedures associated with integration are directed at equating the amount of taxes paid by an individual who does not incorporate an income source and pays taxes only at the individual level, with the amount of taxes that would be paid if the relevant assets were transferred to a corporation and taxed at both the corporate level and at the individual level on distribution of the after tax corporate income.

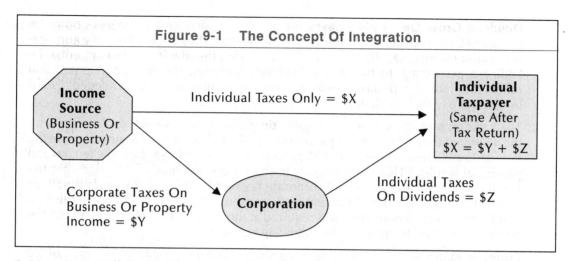

Figure 9-1   The Concept Of Integration

9-83.   As we will find in Chapters 15 through 17, there are a number of procedures associated with achieving this goal. However, from the point of view of individual taxpayers, the dividend gross up and tax credit procedures are the primary tools in the quest for integration of corporate and individual tax amounts.

Eligible Vs. Non-Eligible Dividends
The Problem
9-84.   Prior to 2006, the dividend gross up and tax credit procedures were based on the notional assumption that all corporations were taxed at a combined federal/provincial rate of 20 percent. While this rate was appropriate for Canadian Controlled Private Corporations (CCPCs) that were eligible for the small business deduction, it was significantly lower than the rate applicable to most large public companies. These companies are subject to tax rates that are typically in excess of 35 percent.

9-85.   The fact that these larger corporations were taxed at rates well above 20 percent meant that, for a given income stream, the combined taxes paid by a corporation and its shareholders were much greater than the taxes on the same stream when received directly by an individual. In these situations, the goal of integration was clearly not being achieved.

The Solution
9-86.   The May, 2006 budget dealt with this problem by introducing an enhanced dividend gross up and tax credit procedure for what it refers to as eligible dividends. In somewhat simplified terms, eligible dividends are dividends paid after 2005 by publicly traded companies. This provision makes an effort to restore integration in situations where corporations are taxed at rates in excess of 20 percent.

9-87.   Given the richness of the enhanced dividend gross up and tax credit system, it is not surprising to find that there are many complications in the determination of which dividends are eligible and which are non-eligible. These complications will be dealt with in Chapter 16 of this text.

9-88.   In this Chapter, we will focus on the procedures for determining the calculation of Tax Payable for individuals receiving eligible and non-eligible dividends. We will begin with a discussion of the dividend gross up and tax credit mechanism as it applies to non-eligible dividends. This will be followed by consideration of the modifications to this system that are required when it is applied to eligible dividends.

Gross Up And Tax Credit Procedures - Non-Eligible Dividends
The Dividend Gross Up Procedure
9-89.   For non-eligible dividends, the concepts and procedures associated with the dividend gross up can be described as follows:

Dividend Gross Up Unlike payments of interest, dividend payments cannot be deducted by the paying corporation. This means that they are paid out of a corporation's after tax income. The concept that underlies the dividend gross up is that, by adding a percentage to the actual dividends received, the resulting amount will reflect the amount of pretax income that the corporation would have needed to earn in order to pay that dividend.

The gross up mechanism for non-eligible dividends requires individuals to gross up the dividends they receive by 25 percent (as all of the provinces have agreed to use the federal Taxable Income figure, the 25 percent gross up applies at both the federal and provincial levels). This percentage is based on the notional assumption that the combined federal and provincial corporate tax rate is 20 percent and, in situations where this is the case, the 25 percent gross up adjusts the taxable amount of the dividend to the pretax amount that was required at the corporate level in order to pay the dividend. This is illustrated in the following example.

Example Marin Ltd. is subject to a combined federal/provincial tax rate of 20 percent. During the current year, the company has Taxable Income of $100,000. All of the Company's after tax income is paid to Mr. Marin, its only shareholder, as a dividend.

Analysis The results at the corporate and individual levels are as follows:

Taxable Income	$100,000
Corporate Income Taxes (At 20 Percent)	(20,000)
Corporate After Tax Income And Dividends Paid	$ 80,000
25 Percent Gross Up [($80,000)(25%)]	20,000
Mr. Marin's Taxable Dividends	$100,000

9-90. As demonstrated in the preceding table, the 25 percent gross up has resulted in a taxable dividend that is equal to the pretax corporate income that is required to pay the dividend. This is also the amount of income that Mr. Marin would have received directly had he chosen not to incorporate his source of income.

9-91. You should note that, for non-eligible dividends, this procedure only works if the corporate tax rate is exactly 20 percent. If it was higher, Mr. Marin's Taxable Dividends would be less than the corporation's Taxable Income. If it was lower, the Taxable Dividends would be greater than the corporation's Taxable Income.

The Dividend Tax Credit Procedure

9-92. Provided the corporate tax rate is 20 percent, the gross up procedure has served to increase the dividend recipient's Taxable Income to the $100,000 amount of corporate Taxable Income on which the non-eligible dividend payment was based. What is now required is a credit against Mr. Marin's Tax Payable to make up for the $20,000 in taxes that were paid at the corporate level. The required tax credit procedure can be described as follows:

Dividend Tax Credit Since the amount of the gross up is designed to reflect the amount of taxes paid at the corporate level, it would seem logical to base the dividend recipient's credit on this figure. This, in fact, is the approach taken in the *Income Tax Act*. Under ITA 121, the individual will receive a credit against federal Tax Payable that is equal to two-thirds of the gross up on non-eligible dividends. This credit can also be expressed as 13-1/3 percent of taxable (i.e., grossed up) dividends or as 16-2/3 percent of dividends received. In our example, this amount would be $13,333 [(2/3)(25%)($80,000), or (13-1/3%)($100,000), or (16-2/3%)($80,000)].

9-93. You will note that the $13,333 dividend tax credit that we have calculated is less than the $20,000 in corporate taxes paid and, in the absence of additional credits towards this total, integration would not be working properly. The remedy to this problem lies in the fact that all of the provinces have some type of dividend gross up and credit procedure. If we assume a provincial dividend tax credit that is equal to one-third of the gross up, the combined federal/provincial dividend tax credit is equal to $20,000 [($20,000)(2/3 + 1/3)], the amount of corporate taxes paid. Provincial dividend tax credits on non-eligible dividends vary from a low of 18.5 percent of the gross up to a high of 38.5 percent of the gross up.

Example Of Non-Eligible Dividends

9-94.   In the preceding section we have explained how, in situations where the combined federal/provincial tax rate on corporations is 20 percent and the provincial dividend tax credit is equal to one-third of the gross up, the dividend gross up and tax credit procedures will provide for integration. This is the case, without regard to the marginal tax rate that is applicable to the individual. The example which follows illustrates the mechanics of this process.

Example   During 2007, Mr. Plummer and Ms. Black each have a business that produces $10,000 in Taxable Income. While they both live in the same province, Mr. Plummer's income is subject to a 15.5 percent federal tax rate and an 8 percent provincial tax rate. In contrast, Ms. Black's income is subject to a 29 percent federal tax rate and a 14.5 percent provincial tax rate. The provincial dividend tax credit is equal to one-third of the gross up and the combined federal/provincial tax rate on corporations is 20 percent.

Analysis - Direct Receipt Of Income   If Mr. Plummer and Ms. Black received the business income directly, the taxes paid and the after tax retention of the income would be as follows:

	Mr. Plummer	Ms. Black
Taxable Income	$10,000	$10,000
Total Individual Tax Payable:		
At 23.5 Percent (15.5% + 8.0%)	(2,350)	
At 43.5 Percent (29.0% + 14.5%)		(4,350)
After Tax Retention - Direct Receipt	$ 7,650	$ 5,650

Analysis - Incorporation Of Income   If the businesses were incorporated, the taxes paid and the after tax retention of the income would be as follows:

	Mr. Plummer	Ms. Black
Corporate Taxable Income	$10,000	$10,000
Corporate Taxes At 20 Percent	(2,000)	(2,000)
Available For Dividends	$ 8,000	$ 8,000
Dividends Received	$ 8,000	$ 8,000
Gross Up At 25 Percent [(25%)($8,000)]	2,000	2,000
Taxable Dividends	$10,000	$10,000

	Mr. Plummer	Ms. Black
Individual Federal Tax:		
At 23.5 Percent (15.5% + 8.0%)	$2,350	
At 43.5 Percent (29.0% + 14.5%)		$4,350
Dividend Tax Credit [(2/3 + 1/3)($2,000)]	(2,000)	(2,000)
Total Tax Payable	$ 350	$2,350
Dividends Received	$8,000	$8,000
Total Tax Payable	(350)	(2,350)
After Tax Retention - Use Of Corporation	$7,650	$5,650

9-95.   As you would expect in this example, the after tax retention for both Mr. Plummer and Ms. Black is exactly the same, without regard to whether the $10,000 of business income was received directly or channeled through a corporation. Note also that this conclusion is not altered by the fact that Ms. Black is in a much higher tax bracket than Mr. Plummer.

Exercise Nine-7

Subject: Dividend Income - Non-Eligible Dividends

Mr. John Johns receives $17,000 in non-eligible dividends from a taxable Canadian corporation. His income is such that all additional amounts will be taxed at a 29 percent federal rate and a 12 percent provincial rate. His provincial dividend tax credit is equal to 30 percent of the gross up. Determine the total federal and provincial tax that will be payable on these dividends and his after tax cash retention.

End of Exercise. Solution available in Study Guide.

Gross Up And Tax Credit Procedures - Eligible Dividends
The Problem Illustrated

9-96.   As was noted in our discussion of non-eligible dividends, the assumption of a 20 percent tax rate that is inherent in the treatment of these dividends is not appropriate for publicly traded companies. These corporations are typically subject to combined federal/provincial tax rates in excess of 35 percent. The problem that this creates is illustrated in the following example which applies the non-eligible dividend procedures in a situation where the corporation is taxed at 35 percent.

Example Suzanne Mills has a business with Taxable Income of $100,000. Her combined federal/provincial tax rate is 43.5 percent. In her province, the combined federal/provincial tax rate on corporations is 35 percent and the provincial dividend tax credit is equal to one-third of the gross up.

Analysis - Direct Receipt Of Income   If Ms. Mills receives the income directly, she will pay taxes of $43,500 [(43.5%)($100,000)] and retain income of $56,500 ($100,000 - $43,500).

Analysis - Use Of Corporation If Ms. Mills incorporates her business and has the corporation pay out all of its after tax income in dividends, the results are as follows:

Corporate Taxable Income	$100,000
Corporate Taxes At 35 Percent	(35,000)
Available For Dividends	$ 65,000
Dividends Received	$65,000
Gross Up At 25 Percent	16,250
Taxable Dividends	$81,250
Individual Federal Tax At 43.5 Percent	$35,344
Dividend Tax Credit [(2/3 + 1/3)($16,250)]	(16,250)
Total Tax Payable	$19,094
Dividends Received	$65,000
Total Tax Payable	(19,094)
After Tax Retention - Use Of Corporation	$45,906

9-97.   As you can see, when a typical public corporation tax rate is used, integration does not work. In this example, there is a $10,594 ($56,500 - $45,906) advantage for the direct receipt of income.

9-98.   This problem has existed for many years and, until recently, it did not attract a great deal of attention. However, the rise of income trusts as an overwhelmingly popular investment medium has focused attention on this issue. As will be discussed later in this Chapter, income trust units are a publicly traded investment vehicle that allows an active business to avoid corporate taxes by flowing through its income directly to investors. Because of the ability of income trusts to avoid corporate taxes, more and more corporations were transferring their assets to income trusts, resulting in a significant reduction in taxes collected on corporate income.

9-99.   While various solutions were proposed for this problem, it was clear to anyone who understood the issues that the real problem was the fact that, for large public companies, the existing dividend gross up and tax credit procedures were based on totally unrealistic tax rates. This situation was corrected in the May, 2006 budget.

9-100.   Before proceeding to our discussion of the enhanced dividend gross up and tax credit procedures for eligible dividends, we would note that the 25 percent gross up and tax credit procedures did not disappear. As previously explained, these procedures continue to apply to dividends paid out of income that has received some form of favourable tax treatment, most commonly the application of the small business deduction. These non-eligible dividends are subject to a 25 percent gross up, with a federal dividend tax credit equal to two-thirds of the 25 percent gross up.

Definition Of Eligible Dividends

9-101.   ITA 89(1) defines "eligible dividends" as a taxable dividend that has been designated as such by the paying corporation. To make this designation, the paying corporation simply notifies the recipient that the dividend is eligible for the enhanced gross up and tax credit procedures.

9-102.   With respect to the types of dividends that can be designated as eligible dividends, this issue will be discussed in detail in Chapter 16. However, in simplified terms, eligible dividends will be made up of dividends paid after 2005 by:

- public corporations that are subject to the general corporate tax rate,
- Canadian controlled private corporations (CCPCs), out of active business income that has been taxed at the general corporate tax rate, and
- CCPCs, out of eligible dividends that it has received.

Gross Up And Tax Credit Procedures For Eligible Dividends

9-103.   For eligible dividends, gross up and tax credit amounts are as follows:

- **Dividend Gross Up**   The gross up of dividends received is 45 percent. As noted previously, since the provinces use the federal Taxable Income figure, this 45 percent gross up applies to eligible dividends at both the federal and provincial levels.

- **Dividend Tax Credit**   The federal dividend tax credit is equal to 11/18ths of the dividend gross up. This could also be expressed as 18.9655 percent of the grossed up dividends or 27.5 percent of dividends received. Provincial dividend tax credits on eligible dividends vary from a low of 21.5 percent of the gross up to a high of 38.5 percent of the gross up.

9-104.   For integration to work, the corporate tax rate has to be such that the 45 percent gross up will increase an individual's Taxable Income to the corporation's level of income before the application of that rate. As shown in the following calculation, the assumed corporate rate that is inherent in the 45 percent gross up is 31.034483 percent.

Pretax Corporate Income	$100,000.00
Corporate Tax At 31.034483 Percent*	(31,034.48)
Available For Dividends	$ 68,965.52
Gross Up At 45 Percent	31,034.48
Taxable Dividends	$100,000.00

* In subsequent examples, we will round this to 31.03 percent.

9-105.   The other requirement for integration to be effective is that the combined federal/provincial dividend tax credit be equal to the corporate taxes paid. This means that this combined credit must be equal to the gross up. With the federal credit at 11/18ths of the gross up (or 27.5 percent of dividends received), the provincial credit must be set equal to 7/18ths of the gross up (or 17.5 percent of dividends received) for this condition to be met.

9-106.   The final point that should be made here is that the assumed 31.03 corporate rate is higher than the combined federal/provincial tax rate on low income individuals. A typical combined rate would be 23.5 percent (15.5 percent federal and 8 percent provincial). In this situation, integration will not work because, at this rate, the credit cannot compensate for the corporate taxes paid. This is illustrated in the following example.

Example Of Eligible Dividends

9-107.   This example illustrates how integration works when the dividend gross up is 45 percent and the federal dividend tax credit is equal to 11/18ths of the gross up. It uses the same situation as the example in Paragraph 9-94 and can be used for comparison purposes.

Example   During 2007, Mr. Plummer and Ms. Black each have a business that produces $10,000 in Taxable Income. While they both live in the same province, Mr. Plummer's income is subject to a 15.5 percent federal tax rate and an 8 percent provincial tax rate. In contrast, Ms. Black's income is subject to a 29 percent federal tax rate and a 14.5 percent provincial tax rate. The provincial dividend tax credit is equal to 7/18th of the gross up and the combined federal/provincial tax rate on corporations is 31.03 percent.

Analysis - Direct Receipt Of Income   If Mr. Plummer and Ms. Black received the business income directly, the taxes paid and the after tax retention of the income would be as follows:

	Mr. Plummer	Ms. Black
Taxable Income	$10,000	$10,000
Total Individual Tax Payable:		
At 23.5 Percent (15.5% + 8.0%)	(2,350)	
At 43.5 Percent (29.0% + 14.5%)		(4,350)
After Tax Retention - Direct Receipt	$ 7,650	$ 5,650

Analysis - Incorporation Of Income   If the businesses were incorporated, the taxes paid and the after tax retention of the income would be as follows:

	Mr. Plummer	Ms. Black
Corporate Taxable Income	$10,000	$10,000
Corporate Taxes At 31.03 Percent	(3,103)	(3,103)
Available For Dividends	$ 6,897	$ 6,897
Dividends Received	$ 6,897	$ 6,897
Gross Up At 45 Percent	3,103	3,103
Taxable Dividends ($1 rounding error)	$10,000	$10,000

Cash Dividends From Taxable Canadian Corporations

	Mr. Plummer	Ms. Black
Individual Federal Tax:		
At 23.5% (15.5% + 8.0%)	$2,350	
At 43.5% (29.0% + 14.5%)		$4,350
Dividend Tax Credit		
[(11/18 + 7/18)($3,103)]	(3,103)	(3,103)
Total Tax Payable	$ Nil	$1,247
Dividends Received	$6,897	$6,897
Total Tax Payable	(Nil)	(1,247)
After Tax Retention - Use Of Corporation	$6,897	$5,650

9-108.   You will note that Mr. Plummer's after tax dividends are $6,897, $753 less than the $7,650 that he would have retained on the direct receipt of the business income. This reflects the fact that the assumed corporate tax rate of 31.03 percent is higher than his personal tax rate of 23.5 percent, a situation that cannot be corrected by a non-refundable credit against his tax payable.

Exercise Nine-8

Subject: Dividend Income - Eligible Dividends

Ms. Ellen Holt receives $15,000 in eligible dividends from taxable Canadian corporations. Her income is such that all additional amounts will be taxed at a 29 percent federal rate and a 14.5 percent provincial rate. Her provincial dividend tax credit is equal to 30 percent of the gross up. Determine the total federal and provincial tax that will be payable on these dividends, as well as her after tax retention.

End of Exercise. Solution available in Study Guide.

Comparison Of Investment Returns

9-109.   For an individual in the maximum federal tax bracket of 29 percent, living in a province with a maximum individual rate of 14 percent, the tax rates for interest income, capital gains, non-eligible dividends, and eligible dividends are as follows:

	Interest Income	Capital Gains	Non-Eligible Dividends	Eligible Dividends
Tax Rate (In Maximum Bracket)	43.0%	21.5%	28.8%	23.6%

Note As will be discussed in Chapter 10, only one-half of capital gains is included in Taxable Income, resulting in an effective tax rate on these gains of 21.5 percent [(1/2)(43%)]. For non-eligible dividends we have assumed a provincial dividend tax credit equal to one-third of the gross up. For eligible dividends, we have assumed a provincial dividend tax credit of 25 percent of the gross up (this is roughly the average for the provinces).

9-110.   While the individual rates would change, depending on the provincial tax rate on individuals and the provincial dividend tax credit, the preceding table provides a general overview of the attractiveness of various types of investment income.

9-111.   Both capital gains and dividends have always received favourable tax treatment. However, until the introduction of eligible dividends in the May, 2006 budget, the rates applicable to capital gains were significantly lower than the rates applicable to dividends (21.5 percent vs. 28.8 percent in our example). This has clearly changed. In general, the rate on capital gains will continue to be a bit lower than the rate on eligible dividends. However, in provinces that have adopted more generous dividend tax credits, the rate on dividends will actually be lower than the rate on capital gains.

Other Dividends

Stock Dividends

9-112. A stock dividend involves a pro rata distribution of additional shares to the existing shareholders of a company. For example, if the XYZ Company had 1,000,000 shares outstanding and it declared a 10 percent stock dividend, the Company would be distributing 100,000 new shares to its present shareholders on the basis of one new share for each ten of the old shares held.

9-113. While there is no real change in anyone's financial position as a result of this transaction, in the accounting records it is accompanied by a transfer from the Company's Retained Earnings to contributed capital or paid up capital. The amount of this transfer is normally the fair market value of the shares to be issued, determined on the date of the dividend declaration.

9-114. For tax purposes, stock dividends are dealt with in the same manner as cash dividends. The value of the dividend is based on the amount of the increase in the paid up capital of the payor, usually the fair market value of the shares issued. This amount is subject to the usual gross up and tax credit procedures and is added to the adjusted cost base of all of the shares owned by the investor.

9-115. However, this approach places the investor in the position of having to pay taxes on an amount of dividends that has not been received in cash, an unfavourable situation with respect to the investor's cash flows. As a consequence, the use of stock dividends is much less common than the use of cash dividends.

Capital Dividends

9-116. Most dividends paid by corporations will be taxable in the hands of individuals. However, ITA 83(2) provides an exception to this when the dividend is a capital dividend. The tax free portion (one-half) of capital gains realized by a private corporation is allocated to a special "capital dividend account". (As is explained in Chapter 16, other amounts are allocated to this account as well.) When the corporation elects to have amounts that are paid out to shareholders from this account treated as capital dividends under ITA 83(2), they will be received by investors on a totally tax free basis. Also to be noted here is that, for Canadian residents, such capital dividends do not have to be deducted from the adjusted cost base of the investor's shares. The procedures associated with these dividends are covered in Chapter 16.

Mutual Funds

Objective

9-117. Mutual funds are organized to provide investment management, largely for individual taxpayers. The basic idea is that investors provide funds to these organizations which they, in turn, use to make direct investments in stocks, bonds, and other types of investment property. As will be discussed in the following material, mutual funds can be organized as either trusts or as corporations.

Organization

Mutual Fund Trusts

9-118. In Canada, most mutual funds are organized as trusts. While the taxation of trusts is given detailed coverage in Chapter 21, the important point to understand here is that, from a tax perspective, trusts can be a flow-through entity. As we noted in Chapter 1, trusts are a taxable entity for income tax purposes. However, taxes are only assessed on income that is retained in the trust. This means that, in any taxation year in which all of the income earned in the trust is distributed (flowed through) to the beneficiaries of the trust (referred to as unit holders in the case of mutual fund trusts), no taxes will be paid by the trust.

9-119. Mutual fund trusts are generally structured to make use of this flow-through feature. In most cases, the by-laws will require that the trust distribute all of the income it earns during a taxation year to the unit holders of the trust. This will free the mutual fund trust from any obligation to pay taxes on income earned during the year.

Mutual Fund Corporations

9-120. Mutual fund corporations are less common than mutual fund trusts. In this case, the mutual fund will be taxed at regular corporate tax rates on the investment income that it earns. As the investors will be shareholders rather than trust unit holders, they will receive dividends and, as these dividends are paid from after tax corporate funds, they are eligible for the usual gross up and tax credit procedures. As is the case with mutual fund trusts, mutual fund corporations are usually committed to distributing all of the income earned during a taxation year to their shareholders.

9-121. There are other complications here involving capital dividends and refundable taxes on investment income that go beyond the scope of this material.

Distributions

Mutual Fund Trusts

9-122. An important feature of the trust form of organization is that various types of income retain their tax characteristics as they flow through the trust. That is, if the mutual fund has a capital gain, the distribution of that gain will be a capital gain to the investor in the mutual fund. This means that, when a mutual fund provides an investor with an information return (a T3, if the fund is organized as a trust), it will indicate the various types of income that are included in its distributions. These types will commonly include:

- **Capital Gains** As with capital gains earned directly by the individual, only one-half of these amounts will be subject to taxes (this type of income is discussed in Chapter 10).

- **Dividends From Taxable Canadian Corporations** These amounts will be subject to the gross up and tax credit procedures that were previously discussed in this Chapter. Eligible dividends received by the trust will be distributed as eligible dividends to the trust unit holders.

- **Canadian Net Interest Income** These amounts will be taxed as ordinary interest income. On the T3 they are included in the box titled "Other Income".

- **Foreign Non-Business (Interest And Dividend) Income** These amounts are taxable on the same basis as Canadian interest income. As will be discussed in a later section of this Chapter, the gross amount of this income will be included in income, with amounts withheld at the foreign source being eligible for tax credit treatment.

- **Capital Distributions** A fund can make distributions that exceed its income for the year. These are identified as returns of capital and are received tax free. They do, however, reduce the adjusted cost base of the investment.

Mutual Fund Corporations

9-123. Shareholders in mutual fund corporations receive dividends from the after tax income earned by the corporation's investments. Unlike the situation with mutual fund trusts, the investment income earned by the mutual fund corporation does not retain its tax features when distributed to shareholders. Without regard to whether the income of the mutual fund corporation was interest, dividends, or capital gains, it is paid out as taxable dividends.

9-124. As we have noted, these dividends will be eligible for the usual gross up and tax credit procedures and, as was discussed earlier in this Chapter, this provides the recipient with a reduced rate of taxation. Dividends paid by mutual fund corporations will, in general, be considered to be eligible dividends with respect to the enhanced gross up and tax credit procedures.

Adjusted Cost Base

Units Held By Individuals

9-125.   Whether you are dealing with a mutual fund trust or a mutual fund corporation, most distributions to investors are taxed in the hands of the investor. If the distributions are actually paid in cash to investors, the adjusted cost base of the trust units or shares is not altered. However, this is not the common practice in the industry. Most mutual funds have a reinvestment option and investors are encouraged to authorize the mutual fund to reinvest their earnings in more units of the mutual fund, rather than receive the earnings in cash.

9-126.   This reinvestment process complicates the adjusted cost base calculation for mutual fund units held directly by individuals. In this case, the amount of reinvested income must be added to the adjusted cost base of the group of units held. In addition, for determining per unit adjusted cost base values, the number of additional units must be added to the total number of units held. A simple example will illustrate the calculations:

> **Example**   On October 15, 2007, Martin Diaz purchases 1,000 units of CIC Growth Fund for $7.30 per unit. On December 1, 2007, the fund has a distribution of $.50 per unit. At this time, the fund has a purchase price of $6 per unit. If Mr. Diaz chooses not to reinvest the distribution, he will receive $500 [(1,000 units)($0.50)] in cash. He would then have 1,000 units with his original adjusted cost base of $7.30 per unit. Alternatively, if the distribution is reinvested, he will receive 83.33 ($500 ÷ $6) additional units. This will leave him with a holding of 1,083.33 units with an adjusted cost base of $7,800 ($7,300 + $500), or $7.20 ($7,800 ÷ 1,083.33) per unit.

9-127.   Without regard to whether the distribution is received in cash or reinvested, Mr. Diaz will have to include the distribution in his income. The amount of the income inclusion would depend on the type of income included in the distribution. If the distribution was interest, the increase in income would be $500. In contrast, if the distribution was dividends from taxable Canadian corporations, it would be subject to the same gross up and tax credit procedures as other dividends. It is likely that most of these dividends would be eligible dividends that qualify for the 45 percent gross up. Finally, if the distribution was capital gains, the taxable capital gain would be $250 [(1/2)($500)].

Units Held In RRSPs

9-128.   As will be discussed more completely in Chapter 13, when mutual funds are held in a Registered Retirement Savings Plan (RRSP), distributions are not taxed when they are paid into an RRSP. Amounts withdrawn from an RRSP are taxed as regular income, regardless of the type of income that was paid into the RRSP. As a consequence, there is no requirement to track the adjusted cost base of mutual funds that are held in these registered plans.

Exercise Nine-9

Subject: Mutual Fund Distributions

Ms. Marissa Tiompkins owns 3,500 units of the RB Small Cap Fund. These units were purchased at a price of $11.25 per unit, for a total value of $39,375. There have been no changes in her adjusted cost base prior to the current year. On September 1 of the current year, the Fund has a distribution of $0.30 per unit, resulting in a reinvestment of $1,050 in Ms. Tiompkins' account. At this time, the purchase price per unit is $13. What will be her adjusted cost base per unit after the reinvestment?

End of Exercise.   Solution available in Study Guide.

Income Trusts

How Do Trusts Work?

9-129. While this subject is covered in detail in Chapter 21, it is impossible to discuss the taxation of income trusts without an understanding of the basic nature of trusts. Trusts are essentially flow-through entities. What this means is that, if the income earned by a trust is distributed immediately to its beneficiaries, the trust will pay no taxes. Further, the beneficiaries of the trusts will pay taxes on that income as though they had received it directly from its source. If a trust earns $100,000 in interest and distributes the full amount to the beneficiaries, these beneficiaries will be taxed on $100,000 of interest income.

9-130. The other important characteristic of trusts, including publicly traded income trusts, is that, for tax purposes, various types of income retain their character as they flow through. For example, if a capital gain is earned in a trust, it will be distributed as a capital gain to the trust beneficiaries. The various types of income that can flow through a trust are listed in Paragraph 9-122 in our coverage of mutual fund trusts.

New Uses For Trusts

9-131. The use of trusts has been common for many years for both estate planning (e.g., a deceased parent leaves his assets in a trust for his children) and for retirement savings (e.g., RRSPs are trusts). What is new here is that trusts have been created to raise financing through the public sale of their units, with the funds being used to acquire various types of businesses.

> **Example** The Zorin Energy Income Trust sells 1,000,000 units at a price of $50 per unit. The $50 million that was raised is used to acquire the assets and operations of Zorin Ltd., a Canadian public company. The trust is committed to distributing 100 percent of the Taxable Income from the Zorin operations to its unitholders.

Tax Consequences

9-132. What are the tax consequences associated with this transaction?

- Prior to the existence of the trust, the income from the Zorin operations was subject to corporate taxes at a rate of 30 to 35 percent. The after tax income could then be distributed to shareholders as dividends. Assuming they are eligible dividends and the shareholders are in the maximum tax bracket, they would be taxed at a rate of around 20 percent.

- The Zorin Trust will pay no taxes if it distributes all of its income. However, the distributions to its unitholders will be taxed as ordinary (business) income, subject to maximum personal rates of over 40 percent. Unlike the situation when the income from the Zorin operations was subject to corporate taxes, there will be no dividend gross up and tax credit benefits.

9-133. Without going through additional detailed examples, you should recognize that, if integration is working properly, this change from a corporate structure to a trust structure should not be a big deal. When the trust structure is used, the taxation is analogous to that which would apply to direct receipt of income. As we demonstrated in our examples, with the introduction of the enhanced tax credits for eligible dividends, taxes paid on direct receipt of income are roughly the same as the combined corporate and personal taxes paid when an income source is channeled through a corporation. A similar comparison could be made between income that has flowed tax free through an income trust and income that has been subject to both corporate and personal taxes.

Basis For Popularity

Individual Canadian Investors

9-134. In the 1990's, most investors had never heard of income trusts, much less considered investing substantial amounts of their savings in such organizations. This has changed dramatically, with billions of Canadian investment dollars flowing into the rapidly growing number of such investment entities.

9-135.   Given the analysis in the preceding section, what is the basis for this popularity? For individual Canadian investors, there are probably two reasons for this:

- In order to avoid taxes, the trust must distribute all of its earnings to unitholders. In contrast, corporations generally retain a significant part of their income.

- Most income trusts were committed to paying out 100 percent of the cash flows from the acquired operations. As these cash flows would typically exceed both accounting and tax income, a part of the distribution was received as a tax free return of capital.

9-136.   These factors combined to provide very high rates of returns to investors in income trusts. Rates in excess of 10 percent were not uncommon. The attractiveness of these rates was enhanced by the fact that rates on most types of fixed income securities were mired in the 4 to 5 percent range.

Non-Resident And RRSP Investors

9-137.   In our discussion of tax consequences associated with income trusts, we pointed out that integration should act to neutralize the choice between using a corporation and using an income trust. There is, however, a major flaw in this argument.

9-138.   Integration assumes that direct receipts of income will be taxed at full federal and provincial rates at the time that it is received. If an income trust unit is held by a resident Canadian individual, this individual will, in fact, be taxed at full federal and provincial rates on distributions from the trust. In this case, the use of an income trust is analogous to the direct receipt of income.

9-139.   This argument breaks down in two types of situations:

Non-Resident Investors   If the income trust units are held by a non-resident investor, they may not be subject to any Canadian taxes. At most, the taxes will be at the low Part XIII rates. (See Chapter 22, International Income.)

RRSP Investors   If the income trust units are held inside an RRSP, they will not be subject to tax at the time of the distribution. While they will eventually be subject to tax when they are withdrawn from the registered plan, this taxation could be deferred for 30 to 40 years.

9-140.   When trust units are held by either of these types of investors, there is a clear tax advantage to the use of an income trust. The use of this investment structure results in:

- little or no payment of taxes when the units are held by non-resident investors; and
- major tax deferral when the units are held in RRSPs.

October 31, 2006 Changes

The Problem

9-141.   In the preceding sections we have described the situation that existed prior to October 31, 2006.   When income trust units were held by resident Canadian individuals, integration procedures served to level the playing field between corporate investment structures and income trust structures. However, when the units were held by non-residents or inside RRSPs, integration broke down, resulting in a significant loss in aggregate tax revenues.

The Solution

9-142.   Despite campaign promises to the contrary, on October 31, 2006, the Harper government announced that it was going to begin taxing income trusts. Further, the solution that was adopted did not focus on the problem areas involving holdings by non-residents and RRSPs. Rather it was a broad based approach which altered the taxation of all income trusts, without regard to their ownership. Needless to say, a great cry of anguish could be heard from Canadian investors. This was particularly the case with older Canadians who watched while a substantial portion of their retirement savings wafted into the vapors.

9-143.   The proposed legislation defines a Specified Investment Flow-Through Trust (SIFT) as a trust in which the units are publicly traded and which holds non-portfolio property. Non-portfolio properties include resource property and property used to carry on business in Canada. This definition would cover most of the income trusts that were popular with Canadian investors.

9-144.   In simplified terms, the proposed legislation assesses taxes on distributions by SIFTS at roughly the combined federal/provincial rate applicable to public corporations. This will result in smaller distributions by the trusts. However, this is offset by the fact that these after tax distributions will be treated as deemed dividends. This means that they will be subject to the lower individual tax rates on income that is eligible for the enhanced gross up and tax credit procedures.

9-145.   The proposed legislation is fairly complex. However it will not be applied to existing SIFTs until 2011. While it is also applicable to new SIFTs, the nature of the proposals is such that it is unlikely that there will be any new SIFTs. Given this, we will not provide a discussion of the details of this legislation in this edition of *Canadian Tax Principles*.

Market Reaction

9-146.   As is often the case, the market overreacted to these proposed changes. Billions of dollars evaporated overnight, with some trusts losing as much as 50 percent of their pre-October 31 market values. There was a focus on the fact that the after tax distributions of income trusts would be smaller, without any recognition of the fact that application of the dividend gross up and tax credit procedures would lower the taxes paid on these distributions.

9-147.   Fortunately, there appears to be a recognition that, while non-resident investors and beneficiaries of RRSPs will be hurt by the proposed legislation, it will not significantly change the after tax amounts retained by most individual investors. Since October 31, 2006, many income trusts have experienced a significant recovery. Some, in fact, are approaching their pre-announcement values.

Adjusted Cost Base

9-148.   The adjusted cost base of income trust units is determined in the same manner as the adjusted cost base of mutual fund trust units, a process that was discussed beginning at Paragraph 9-125. Distributions of income that are paid directly to the unit holder do not alter the adjusted cost base. However, as was the case with mutual fund trusts, it is common for income trust investors to elect to have the earnings reinvested in additional trust units when the income trust makes that option available.

9-149.   While mutual fund trusts sometimes return capital to unit holders, it is much less common than is the case with income trusts. Many, perhaps even the majority, of income trusts regularly include a return of capital in their distributions. In fact in some cases, it is a major component of the distribution.

9-150.   In our discussion of mutual fund trusts we noted that, while returns of capital (i.e., capital distributions) can be received tax free, they reduce the adjusted cost base of the trust units. An example will serve to illustrate this process.

> **Example**   On January 1, 2007, Joan Arden acquires 1,000 units of the Newcor Income Trust at a total cost of $100,000 or $100 per unit. During 2007, the trust distributes $6 per unit, $2 of which is a return of capital and $4 of which is a distribution of income earned in the trust. The $4,000 income component of the distribution [($4)(1,000 units)] is reinvested in additional trust units at a cost of $110 per unit (36.36 units).
>
> **Analysis**   Ms. Arden will include $4,000 in her 2007 Net Income For Tax Purposes. The adjusted cost base of the shares at the end of the year will be $102,000 ($100,000

- $2,000 + $4,000). Taking into consideration the additional reinvestment units, the per unit adjusted cost base will be $98.42 ($102,000 ÷ 1,036.36).

Exercise Nine-10

Subject: Income Trust Distributions

On January 1, 2007, John Dore acquires 2,000 units of Xeron Income Trust at $55 per unit, a total cost of $110,000. During 2007, the trust distributes $5.00 per unit, $1.50 of which is a return of capital and $3.50 of which is an income distribution. John has asked the trust to reinvest all distributions. The $5.00 per unit distribution was reinvested at a cost of $57 per additional unit. What are the tax consequences to John of the 2007 distribution and its reinvestment? What will be his adjusted cost base per unit after the reinvestment?

End of Exercise. Solution available in Study Guide.

Foreign Source Income

General Rules

9-151.   As Canadian taxation is based on residency, income that has a foreign source must be included in full in the calculation of Net Income For Tax Purposes of any Canadian resident. This is complicated by the fact that most foreign jurisdictions levy some form of withholding tax on such income. The general approach is to require Canadian residents to include 100 percent of any foreign income earned in their Net Income For Tax Purposes and to provide a credit against Tax Payable for taxes withheld in the foreign jurisdiction.

9-152.   The basic idea behind this approach is to have the combined foreign and Canadian tax on this income be the same as that which would be levied on the same amount of income earned in Canada.

> **Example**   An individual earned $1,000 in a foreign jurisdiction. As the authorities in that jurisdiction withhold $100, his net receipt is $900.

> **Analysis**   The gross or pre-withholding amount of $1,000 would be included in the taxpayer's Canadian Taxable Income. If we assume that this individual is taxed at a combined federal/provincial rate of 45 percent, his taxes on this $1,000 would $450. This would be reduced by a $100 credit for the foreign taxes paid. The balance of $350 in Canadian taxes, when combined with the $100 paid in the foreign jurisdiction, would be equal to the $450 that would be paid on the receipt of $1,000 in Canadian source income.

Foreign Non-Business (Property) Income

9-153.   Following the general rule, 100 percent of foreign source non-business income is included in Net Income For Tax Purposes. However, for individuals, the credit against Tax Payable that is provided under ITA 126(1) is limited to a maximum of 15 percent of the foreign source non-business income. If the withheld amounts exceed 15 percent, the excess can be deducted under ITA 20(11). The following example illustrates this calculation:

> **Example**   Mr. Grant earns foreign source non-business income of $1,000.   The foreign government withholds 40 percent ($400) and he receives $600.

> **Analysis**   The gross income of $1,000 will be included in Net Income For Tax Purposes. The $150 of withholding that is within the 15 percent limit will be used to calculate a credit against Tax Payable.   The $250 of withholding in excess of 15 percent will be a deduction against the foreign source income. Note that the $250 deduction will only reduce Mr. Grant's Tax Payable by this amount, multiplied by his

marginal tax rate. This will not fully compensate him for the $250 in tax withheld.

Foreign Business Income

9-154. In the case of foreign source business income, there is no direct limitation on the use of the amounts withheld as a credit against Tax Payable and, correspondingly, no deduction in the calculation of Net Income For Tax Purposes for any part of the amount withheld by the foreign jurisdiction. The following example can be compared to the preceding example to illustrate the difference in the treatment of tax withheld on foreign business income.

> **Example** Mr. Grant earns foreign source business income of $1,000. The foreign government withholds 40 percent ($400) and he receives $600.

> **Analysis** The gross income of $1,000 will be included in Net Income For Tax Purposes. The full $400 of withholding will be used to calculate a credit against Tax Payable.

Exercise Nine-11

Subject: Foreign Source Income

Norah Johns has foreign source income of $30,000 during the current year. As the foreign jurisdiction withholds 25 percent of such income, she only receives $22,500. She has other income such that this foreign source income will be taxed at the maximum federal rate of 29 percent. Determine the amount by which this foreign income would increase Norah's Taxable Income and federal Tax Payable, assuming that the foreign source income (1) is non-business income and (2) is business income.

End of Exercise. Solution available in Study Guide.

Shareholder Benefits

Benefits Other Than Loans

9-155. ITA 15(1) deals with situations where a corporation has made payments to a shareholder, where corporate property has been appropriated for the benefit of a shareholder, or where a corporation has conferred a benefit on a shareholder. Examples of this type of situation would include:

- a corporation providing a shareholder with a jet for personal use;
- a corporation building a swimming pool at a shareholder's personal residence; or
- a corporation selling assets to a shareholder at prices that are substantially below fair market value.

9-156. When any of these events occur, the shareholder is required to include the value of these benefits or appropriations in his income. Such amounts will not be considered dividends and, as a consequence, they will not be eligible for the dividend tax credit.

9-157. A further point here is that, when an amount is included in a shareholder's income under ITA 15(1), IT-432R2 indicates that the corporation is not allowed to deduct the amount that has been included in the shareholder's income.

> **Example** A corporation provides a shareholder with a $10,000 holiday trip to Italy.

> **Analysis** ITA 15(1) requires the inclusion of the $10,000 cost of the trip in the income of the shareholder. Despite the fact that this amount is being taxed in the hands of the shareholder, the corporation would not be able to deduct the cost of the trip.

9-158.   It would seem clear, given this non-deductibility, that corporations should avoid providing benefits that will be assessed to shareholders under ITA 15(1).

Shareholder Loans
General Rule
9-159.   ITA 15(2) is applicable when a corporation makes a loan to a shareholder or an individual connected to a shareholder. Under ITA 15(2.1), persons are connected for this purpose if they do not deal with each other at arm's length. When such loans are made, this general rule requires that the full principal amount of the loan be included in the Net Income For Tax Purposes of the recipient of the loan (the shareholder or the person connected to the shareholder) in the taxation year in which the loan is made.

9-160.   This general rule applies without regard to the amount of interest paid on the loan. Note, however, in periods subsequent to the inclusion of the principal amount of the loan in the income of the shareholder, there is no imputed interest benefit, even in cases where the loan is on an interest free basis.

9-161.   Under this general rule, the granting of the loan to a shareholder has the same tax consequences as the payment of an equivalent amount of salary to the shareholder. However, there is an important difference. Taxes paid on salary cannot normally be recovered by repaying the salary. In contrast, when all or part of a shareholder loan that has been included in the taxpayer's income under ITA 15(2) is repaid, the amount of the repayment can be deducted from Net Income For Tax Purposes under ITA 20(1)(j).

Exceptions To The General Rule
9-162.   There are three exceptions to this general rule that are available to shareholders, without regard to whether or not they are also employees of the corporation. They can be described as follows:

Non-Resident Persons   ITA 15(2.2) indicates that the general rule does not apply to indebtedness between non-resident persons. This means that, if both the corporation and the shareholder receiving the loan were non-residents, the principal amount of any loan would not have to be included in income.

Loans In Ordinary Course Of Business   ITA 15(2.3) indicates that the general rule does not apply when the loan is in the ordinary course of the corporation's business. This would cover such situations as a customer, who is also a shareholder, taking advantage of an on-going promotion by a furniture store that provides interest free loans to purchase furniture. In addition, ITA 15(2.3) notes that this would apply to loans made by a corporation that is in the business of making loans. This covers situations where, for example, an individual happens to be a shareholder of the bank that provides him with a personal loan.

Repayment Within One Year   ITA 15(2.6) indicates that the general rule does not apply when the loan is repaid within one year after the end of the taxation year of the lender or creditor in which the loan was made or the indebtedness arose. If, for example, a corporation with a June 30 year end extended a $100,000 loan to a shareholder on January 1, 2007, the $100,000 would not have to be included in income if it is repaid by June 30, 2008.

A further point with respect to this exception is that IT-119R4 indicates that this exception is not available when the repayment is part of a series of loans and repayments. The primary evidence of this type of situation would be a repayment near the end of a corporate taxation year, followed by a loan for a similar amount early in the following corporate taxation year.

9-163. Additional exceptions to the general rule requiring the principal of shareholder loans to be included in income involve situations where the shareholder is also an employee of the corporation making the loan. These exceptions are found in ITA 15(2.4) and can be described as follows:

Not Specified Employee ITA 15(2.4)(a) indicates that loans made to a shareholder, who is an employee, are not subject to the general rule if the shareholder is not a specified employee. A specified employee is one who, at any time of the year, owns 10 percent or more of the shares of the corporation, or who does not deal at arm's length with the corporation. This exception applies without regard to the purpose of the loan.

Dwelling Loans ITA 15(2.4)(b) indicates that loans made to a shareholder, who is an employee, to acquire a dwelling are not subject to the general rule. This would also apply to loans made to the spouse or common-law partner of the employee.

Stock Acquisition Loans ITA 15(2.4)(c) indicates that loans made to a shareholder, who is an employee, to acquire shares in the lending corporation or a corporation related to the lending corporation, are not subject to the general rule.

Motor Vehicle Loans ITA 15(2.4)(d) indicates that loans made to a shareholder, who is an employee, to acquire a motor vehicle to be used in employment duties, are not subject to the general rule.

9-164. In order for these exceptions to apply, the following conditions must be met:

- the loan must be made to the individual because he is an employee, not because he is a shareholder; and

- at the time the loan is made, bona fide arrangements must be made to repay the loan within a reasonable period of time [ITA 15(2.4)(f)].

9-165. The first of these conditions can create significant problems for owner-managers of private corporations wishing to give themselves loans. In order to avoid having the principal amount of the loan included in Net Income For Tax Purposes, the owner-manager must demonstrate that he received the loan because of his role as an employee.

9-166. In order to demonstrate that he has received the loan in his role as an employee, the owner-manager will likely have to make similar loans available to all employees with duties similar to those of the owner-manager. That is, if the company gives the owner-manager a $100,000, low interest loan to purchase a residence, such loans would have to be made available to all employees with duties similar to those of the owner-manager. If this is not the case, the CRA is likely to conclude that the owner-manager received the loan because of his role as a shareholder.

9-167. A further problem would arise if, as would not be uncommon in owner-managed situations, there are no other employees of the business. It is not clear in this case whether the owner-manager would be able to demonstrate that he received a loan in his capacity as an employee. However, there is some evidence to suggest that the CRA will look at the loan practices of other similar corporations as an approach to making this determination.

Imputed Interest Benefit

9-168. It was previously noted that, if the principal amount of a shareholder loan is included in the taxpayer's income, there is no imputed interest benefit related to a low rate or interest free loan. However, if the loan is exempted from the general inclusion in income rule by one of the exceptions described in Paragraphs 9-162 and 9-163, ITA 80.4(2) is applicable and a benefit may be assessed. (The analogous benefit for employees is assessed under ITA 80.4(1).)

Example   On July 1, 2007, Andros Ltd. extends a $100,000 loan to its only share-holder, George Andros. The loan bears interest at 2 percent and, because it will be repaid in January, 2008, the $100,000 principal amount does not have to be included in his income. Assume the prescribed rate throughout 2007 is 5 percent.

Analysis   For 2007, Mr. Andros will be assessed a taxable benefit under ITA 80.4(2) equal to $1,500 [(5% - 2%)($100,000)(6/12)]. In the examples in IT-421R2, "Benefits To Individuals, Corporations, And Shareholders From Loans Or Debt", interest is calculated on the basis of the number of months the loan is outstanding. While not illustrated, calculations could also be based on the number of days the loan is outstanding. We would remind you that, if the loan proceeds are invested in income producing assets, the imputed interest will be deductible.

9-169.   In the fairly common situation where the shareholder also works as an employee of the business, the benefit may be assessed under either ITA 80.4(1) or 80.4(2). As far as the calculation of the benefit is concerned, this distinction makes no difference. However, if the purpose of the loan is to acquire a home, there is a significant difference.

9-170.   In the case of a benefit assessed to an employee under ITA 80.4(1), for the first five years of the loan, the benefit calculation will use a rate no higher than the prescribed rate that prevailed when the loan was made. Should the rate go down, the employee is entitled to use the lower prescribed rate for the benefit calculation. Alternatively, in the case of a home purchase loan to a shareholder, the ITA 80.4(2) benefit must be calculated using the actual quarterly prescribed rates that prevail over the term of the loan.

9-171.   A further difference between home purchase loans to employees and home purchase loans to shareholders relates home relocation loan deduction. As discussed in Chapters 5 and 6, if a loan qualifies as a home relocation loan, an employee will get a deduction in the calculation of Taxable Income equal to the benefit on a $25,000 interest free home purchase loan from the calculated benefit on the loan. This deduction is not available to shareholders.

Exercise Nine-12

Subject: Shareholder Loans

Ms. Martha Rourke is an employee of Rourke Inc., a large private company in which her husband owns 70 percent of the outstanding shares. Ms. Rourke owns the remaining 30 percent of the shares. On July 1 of the current year, she receives a $50,000 interest free loan that will be used to purchase an automobile to be used in her employment duties. The loan is to be repaid in four annual instalments to be made on June 30 of each year. Assume the prescribed rate for the current year is 4 percent. What are the current year tax implications of this loan for Ms. Rourke?

Exercise Nine-13

Subject: Shareholder Loans

On June 1, 2007, Generic Inc. loans $162,000 to its principal shareholder, Ms. Jan Fisk, in order to finance her gambling debts. Generic Inc. has a taxation year that ends on June 30. The loan bears interest at 2 percent. Assume that, during all periods, the relevant prescribed rate is 5 percent. What are the tax consequences to Ms. Fisk if the loan is repaid (1) on January 1, 2008 and (2) on December 31, 2008?

End of Exercises. Solutions available in Study Guide.

Exercise Nine-14

Subject: Shareholder Loans

On November, 1, 2007, Hasid Ltd. loans Mr. Aaron Hasid, the CEO and principal shareholder of the Company, $123,000 in order to assist in his purchase of a principal residence. The Company has a taxation year that ends on December 31. The loan does not bear interest and, during all periods, assume that the relevant prescribed rate is 5 percent. The loan is repaid on January 1, 2009. What are the tax consequences of this loan to Mr. Hasid? State any assumptions that you have made in providing your answer.

End of Exercise. Solution available in Study Guide.

Tax Credits Revisited

Dividend Tax Credits

9-172.   Most of the credits that are available to individuals in determining their Tax Payable are discussed in Chapter 6. However, because an understanding of some amount of additional material was required, it was appropriate to defer coverage of a few of these credits to later Chapters. Given the content of this Chapter, we have added two additional credits.

9-173.   The first of these was the dividend tax credit and there are two different versions of this credit:

Eligible Dividends   For eligible dividends from taxable Canadian corporations, the federal dividend tax credit is equal to 11/18ths of a 45 percent gross up. It can also be calculated as 19 percent (18.9655 percent to be exact) of the grossed up amount of dividends or, alternatively, as 27.5 percent of dividends received.

Non-Eligible Dividends   For non-eligible dividends from taxable Canadian corporations, the credit is equal to two-thirds of a 25 percent gross up. It can also be calculated as 13-1/3 percent of the grossed up amount of dividends or, alternatively, as 16-2/3 percent of dividends received.

Foreign Income Tax Credits

9-174.   The other tax credit that was introduced in this Chapter was the credit for foreign taxes paid on foreign source income. For the purposes of this Chapter, we have indicated that this credit is equal to the amount of foreign taxes withheld, subject to the limitation that, in the case of foreign source non-business income earned by individuals, the credit is limited to 15 percent of the foreign source income.

9-175.   This, however, is not the end of the story. For both foreign source non-business income and foreign source business income, the amount of the credit may be limited by the total amount of taxes paid by the individual. This limit is based on an equation that requires an understanding of loss carry overs. As this material has not been covered at this point, we will have to return to coverage of the credits for foreign taxes paid when we revisit Taxable Income and Tax Payable in Chapter 14.

Key Terms Used In This Chapter

9-175.   The following is a list of the key terms used in this Chapter. These terms, and their meanings, are compiled in the Glossary Of Key Terms located at the back of the separate paper Study Guide and on the Companion CD-ROM.

Accrual Basis	Eligible Dividends
Business Income	Foreign Taxes Paid Credit
Capital Dividend	Indexed Debt Obligations
Capital Dividend Account	Interest Income
Cash Basis	Net Business Income
Cash Damming	Net Property Income
Disappearing Source Rules	Prescribed Debt Obligations
Dividend Gross Up	Property Income
Dividend Tax Credit	Specified Employee
Dividends	Stock Dividend

References

9-176.   For more detailed study of the material in this Chapter, we refer you to the following:

ITA 12	Income Inclusions
ITA 15(1)	Benefit Conferred On Shareholder
ITA 15(2)	Shareholder Debt
ITA 80.4	Loans - Imputed Interest
ITA 80.5	Deemed Interest
IT-67R3	Taxable Dividends From Corporations Resident In Canada
IT-119R4	Debts of Shareholders And Certain Persons Connected With Shareholders
IT-195R4	Rental Property - Capital Cost Allowance Restrictions
IT-373R2	Woodlots
IT-396R	Interest Income
IT-421R2	Benefits To Individuals, Corporations, And Shareholders From Loans Or Debt
IT-432R2	Benefits Conferred On Shareholders
IT-434R	Rental Of Real Property By Individual
IT-443	Leasing Property - Capital Cost Allowance Restrictions
IT-462	Payments Based On Production Or Use
IT-506	Foreign Income Taxes As A Deduction from Income
IT-533	Interest Deductibility And Related Issues

Problems For Self Study

(The solutions for these problems can be found in the separate Study Guide.)

Self Study Problem Nine - 1

On January 1 of the current year, Mr. Drake owns a total of four rental properties. All of the properties were acquired in 1990 and are of brick construction. The cost and UCC for the properties as at January 1 of the current year are as follows:

	Original Cost	UCC
Property A	$36,000	$21,500
Property B	48,000	43,000
Property C	63,000	46,000
Property D	90,000	64,000

During the year, rental revenues and cash expenses on the four properties are as follows:

	Rental Revenue	Property Taxes	Interest	Other Expenses
Property A	$ 5,200	$ 1,200	$ 1,750	$ 500
Property B	6,700	1,550	Nil	1,800
Property C	12,200	2,750	7,800	1,700
Property D	15,300	3,750	13,500	3,900

Other transactions that occurred during the year are as follows:

1. Property A was sold for cash proceeds of $72,000 on July 20.

2. Property C was sold for $61,000 in cash on August 24.

3. A new residential rental property, Property E, was acquired on February 1 at a cost of $192,000. It was not rented until late in the year and, as a result, rents for the year total only $2,000, interest charges $2,300, property taxes $275, and other expenses $325.

Mr. Drake wants to take the maximum CCA permitted on all of his properties and he owns no other properties.

Required: Calculate Mr. Drake's income from property, net taxable capital gains, and recapture for the current taxation year.

Self Study Problem Nine - 2

Mr. James Loyt is in the middle of the 26 percent federal tax bracket and the 12 percent provincial tax bracket. The province in which he lives provides a dividend tax credit equal to 30 percent of the gross up. He has $20,000 in cash to invest for a period of one year and is considering the following two investments:

• Bonds issued by Faxtext Ltd., a Canadian public corporation. These bonds are selling at their maturity value and pay interest at an annual rate of 7.75 percent.

• Preferred shares issued by the same corporation. These shares pay an annual eligible dividend of 5 percent on all amounts invested.

Required: Based on your calculations, advise Mr. Loyt as to which investment he should make.

Self Study Problem Nine - 3

On January 1, 2007, Ms. Joan Bagley has $650,000 in a bank account at ING DIRECT. While this account has great flexibility in terms of deposits and withdrawals, it pays interest at an annual rate of only 2 percent. She would like to retain $50,000 of this balance as a contingency fund, while investing the $600,000 balance for a year. After consulting with her financial advisor, she is considering the following investment alternatives:

- A $600,000 guaranteed investment certificate that will mature on December 31, 2007. The certificate will pay annual interest at a rate of 4.5 percent on December 31.

- Preferred shares of a Canadian public company with a stated value of $600,000. These shares pay an annual eligible dividend of 5.25 percent on December 15. Ms. Bagley anticipates selling these shares on December 31, 2007 for their stated value.

- Shares of a public high tech company at a cost of $600,000. While these shares do not pay dividends, Ms. Bagley anticipates selling these shares on December 31, 2007 for $675,000.

Ms. Bagley will have over $200,000 of employment income in 2007. Her provincial tax rate on any additional income is 12 percent, while the provincial dividend tax credit is equal to 31 percent of the gross up.

The preferred and common shares are sold at the anticipated values on December 31, 2007.

Required: For each of the three investment alternatives, calculate Ms. Bagley's after tax return for the year ending December 31, 2007.

Self Study Problem Nine - 4

During December, 2006, Ms. Holmes reaches a settlement with her former husband that requires him to make a lump sum payment to her of $100,000 on January 1, 2007. While Ms. Holmes has no immediate need for the funds, she will require them on January 1, 2008 in order to finance a new business venture that she plans to launch. As a consequence, she would like to invest the funds for the year ending December 31, 2007. She is considering the following alternatives:

- Investment of the full $100,000 in a one year, guaranteed investment certificate that pays annual interest of 5.5 percent.

- Investment of the full $100,000 in a rental property with a cost of $165,000. The property currently has a tenant whose lease calls for rental payments during 2007 of $13,200. Cash expenses for the year (interest, taxes, and condominium fees) are expected to be $9,600. Of the total cost of $165,000, an amount of $15,000 can be allocated to the land on which the building is situated. Ms. Holmes believes that the property can be sold on December 31, 2007, to net her $175,000.

- Investment of the full $100,000 in the shares of Norton Ltd., a publicly traded Canadian company. Ms. Holmes expects that the Company will pay eligible dividends on these shares during 2007 of $5,000. She anticipates that by the end of 2007, the shares will be worth at least $106,000.

Ms. Holmes expects to have employment income in excess of $225,000 during 2007. Her provincial tax rate on any additional income is 15 percent, while the provincial dividend tax credit is equal to 35 percent of the gross up.

Required: Write a brief memorandum providing investment advice to Ms. Holmes on the three alternatives.

Self Study Problem Nine - 5

Mr. Arthur Blaine is president and sole shareholder of Blaine Enterprises, a Canadian controlled private corporation with 10 employees. He is also employed by the Company at a salary of $57,000 per year. Since arriving at his office this morning by bicycle, two things have come to Mr. Blaine's attention. They are as follows:

1. Mr. Blaine's accountant has submitted financial statements indicating that his Company has income before taxes of $195,000 for the current year. As the Company is eligible for the small business deduction, this income is taxed at a rate of about 20 percent, leaving an after tax profit in excess of $150,000.

2. Mr. Blaine's neighbour has just informed him he is planning to put his house on the market. Mr. Blaine has coveted that house for many years. To purchase it, Mr. Blaine would need a $125,000 mortgage immediately.

Putting these two items of information together, Mr. Blaine concludes that it would make sense for his corporation to lend him the required $125,000 on an interest free basis for a period of ten years. He believes that there should be no problem with this action in that he is the sole shareholder of the Company, and the Company has sufficient extra cash to make the loan without interfering with its basic business operations.

Required: As Mr. Blaine's personal and corporate tax advisor, give your advice on Mr. Blaine's solution to his mortgage problem.

Assignment Problems

(The solutions for these problems are only available in
the solutions manual that has been provided to your instructor.)

Assignment Problem Nine - 1

Each of the following independent Cases involves the payment of interest and the issue of whether the interest will be deductible for tax purposes.

Case A John Artho owns 1,000 shares of Bee Ltd., a publicly traded company. He also owns a personal use condominium that was financed with borrowed money. Mr. Artho sells the 1,000 shares of Bee Ltd. and uses the proceeds to pay down the mortgage on the condominium. He subsequently borrows money to acquire another 1,000 shares of Bee Ltd. Would the interest on the new loan be deductible? Explain your conclusion.

Case B Meridee Burns acquired an income producing property for $100,000. She subsequently sells the property for $150,000 and, without repaying the funds borrowed to acquire the first property, uses the proceeds to acquire two other properties. The cost of property A is $40,000, while the cost of property B is $110,000. How will the $100,000 in borrowing be linked to the two new properties?

Case C Meridee Burns acquired an income producing property for $100,000. She subsequently sells the property for $80,000 and, without repaying the funds borrowed to acquire the first property, uses the proceeds to acquire two other properties. The cost of property A is $60,000, while the cost of property B is $20,000. How will the $100,000 in borrowing be linked to the two new properties?

Case D Jason Bridges invests $100,000 in the shares of Loser Inc. Six months later, he sells these shares for $40,000. The proceeds of the sale are used to pay off $40,000 of the loan, leaving an ongoing balance of $60,000. Can he continue to deduct the interest payments on this $60,000 balance? Explain your conclusion.

Assignment Problem Nine - 2

Bill Martin, Dave Martin, and Charles Martin are three brothers living in the same province. They each have $20,000 that they wish to invest. Because of differences in their current employment situations, they are in different tax brackets. These brackets are as follows:

	Federal Tax Bracket	Provincial Tax Bracket
Bill Martin	15.5 Percent	6.5 Percent
Dave Martin	22 Percent	9 Percent
Charles Martin	29 Percent	14 Percent

The provincial dividend tax credit is equal to one-third of the dividend gross up.

For a number of years, they have been interested in the securities of Moland Industries, a Canadian public corporation, and, at the present time, they are considering two securities of the Company that are currently outstanding. These securities and their investment characteristics are as follows:

Bonds   The Company has a large issue of debenture bonds that has a coupon interest rate of 6 percent. They are selling at par value and mature in 18 years.

Preferred Stock The Company has an issue of preferred shares that is offering an eligible dividend of 4 percent based on the current market price. The dividend is cumulative, but not participating.

The income from these investments would not move Bill or Dave Martin to a higher tax bracket. Each brother has sufficient income to use all of his available tax credits.

Required:

A. Calculate the after tax income that would be generated for each of the three brothers, assuming that they invested their $20,000 in the Moland Industries Bonds.

B. Calculate the after tax income that would be generated for each of the three brothers, assuming that they invested their $20,000 in the Moland Industries Preferred Stock.

Assignment Problem Nine - 3

For a number of years, Mr. Stanton has invested his excess funds in various rental properties in Hearst, Ontario. At the beginning of 2007, he owned four properties, as well as some furnishings used in one of the older buildings. The relevant information on these rental properties for 2007 is as follows:

Furniture   The furniture was used in the building at 18 Prince Street. It had a capital cost of $15,000, a UCC of $8,000 at the beginning of the year, and was sold during the year for $5,000.

18 Prince Street   This is a Class 3 building that had a capital cost of $42,000. It was sold on August 1. For CCA purposes, it was included in the same Class 3 pool as 4 McManus Street. Of the sale proceeds, $60,000 was allocated to the building. From January 1 to July 31, the building generated rents of $6,000 and incurred property taxes of $1,200, interest charges of $1,750, and other expenses (excluding CCA) of $1,000.

4 McManus Street   This is a Class 3 building that has a capital cost of $45,000. At the beginning of the year, the UCC of the Class 3 pool, which included both 4 McManus Street and 18 Prince Street, was $50,000. During the year, it generated rents of $5,000 and incurred property taxes of $1,550, interest charges of $650, and other expenses (excluding CCA) of $2,500.

94 George Street   This is a Class 3 building that has a capital cost of $850,000. Its UCC at the beginning of the year was $550,000. During the year, it generated rents of $42,000 and incurred property taxes of $5,200, interest charges of $7,800, and other expenses (excluding CCA) of $8,500.

125 West Street   This Class 1 building has a capital cost of $102,000. Its UCC at the beginning of the year was $98,000. During the year, the unit generated rents of $10,000 and incurred property taxes of $1,750, interest charges of $5,000, and other expenses (excluding CCA) of $4,000.

Required: Calculate Mr. Stanton's net rental income for 2007. Specify how much CCA should be taken for each building.

Assignment Problem Nine - 4

For the last 12 years, Miss Stone has been the president and only shareholder of Stone Enterprises, a Canadian controlled private corporation. She handles all marketing and oversees the day-to-day operations of the business. Her annual salary is $80,000.

The Company has a December 31 year end. During the four year period, January 1, 2004 through December 31, 2007, there were a number of transactions between Miss Stone and her Company. They can be described as follows:

2004   Stone Enterprises loaned $28,000, on an interest free basis, to Miss Stone for various personal expenditures.

2005   The Company loaned an amount of $40,000 to Miss Stone in her capacity as an employee to assist her with the acquisition of a new car. The loan calls for payments of $10,000 per year for the next four years, but does not require the payment of any interest. Payments have been made in 2006 and 2007. The car is to be used solely for Company business. Stone Enterprises makes car loans available to all employees with at least five years of service with the Company.

2006   The Company provided Miss Stone with a $90,000 loan to assist her in purchasing a new home. The loan is to be paid off at the rate of $6,000 per year with interest at 2 percent per annum. Stone Enterprises makes housing loans available to all employees with at least five years of service with the Company.

Also in 2006, the Company accrued a bonus to Miss Stone in the amount of $32,000 to be paid in 2007.

2007   Miss Stone receives her 2006 bonus in March, 2007. The bonus is redeposited in the Company on March 31, 2007 and is used by the Company for purchasing inventories. The Company considered $28,000 of these redeposited funds a repayment of the 2004 loan to Miss Stone.

During 2007 the Company declared and paid non-eligible dividends of $22,000.

Miss Stone has only one competitor in her region and, in order to diminish the effectiveness of this company, Miss Stone purchases 40 percent of its outstanding shares for $72,000. Stone Enterprises loans her the entire $72,000 in 2007 on an interest free basis and Miss Stone anticipates that she will repay the loan in 2010.

Required: Discuss, without showing any numerical calculations, the tax effects of the transactions described in the preceding paragraphs.

Assignment Problem Nine - 5

On January 1, 2007, Miss Heather Plant receives a $50,000 cheque from an attorney representing the estate of her recently deceased aunt, Mildred. The money was bequeathed by Miss Plant's aunt without any conditions and is not subject to any form of taxes at the time that it is received.

In anticipation of this bequest, Miss Plant has purchased a condominium that will be available for occupancy on January 1, 2008. As she has no need for the $50,000 until the condominium becomes available, she would like to invest the funds for the year ending December 31, 2007. She is considering the following two alternatives:

- Investment of the full $50,000 in a guaranteed investment certificate that will pay annual interest at the rate of 6 percent for the year ending December 31, 2007.

- Investment of the full $50,000 in 1,000 shares of a common stock of a Canadian public company that is selling for $50 per share on January 1, 2007. For a number of years, this stock has paid an annual eligible dividend of $1 per share. In addition, Miss Plant is advised that the unit price of the shares is likely to increase to at least $55 by December 31, 2007.

Miss Plant has sufficient employment income that she is in the 29 percent federal tax bracket and the 14 percent provincial tax bracket. The provincial dividend tax credit is equal to 25 percent of the gross up.

Required: Write a brief memorandum providing investment advice to Miss Plant.

Assignment Problem Nine - 6

Mrs. Norton is a lawyer with a well established practice located in Regina. During the taxation year ending December 31, 2007, she had professional fees of $169,500 and operating expenses associated with running her practice of $42,800. In addition to these operating expenses, Mrs. Norton spent $1,500 for accommodations and seminar fees attending a convention in Saskatoon, and $5,400 in travel costs (air fare, accommodations, and 50 percent of meals) attending a convention in Singapore on doing business in Asia.

In addition to her professional income, Mrs. Norton received $1,000 in eligible dividends from a Canadian public company and $1,250 in interest on Canada Savings Bonds. Mrs. Norton also owns a rental property that generated revenues of $6,000 and incurred cash expenses of $4,000. The UCC of this property at the beginning of the current year was $55,000 and it is subject to CCA at a rate of 4 percent.

Required: Determine Mrs. Norton's minimum Net Income For Tax Purposes for the year ending December 31, 2007.

Assignment Cases

Assignment Case Nine - 1 (Comprehensive Case Covering Chapters 5 to 9)

Ms. Shelly Spring is a 48 year old widow. While her deceased husband left her financially secure, she continues to work as a course assistant at a local college. Her 2007 salary is $64,000, from which her employer withheld the following amounts:

RPP Contributions	$2,960
EI Contributions	720
CPP Contributions	1,990
Disability Insurance Premium	250

Ms. Spring pays one-half of the total disability insurance premium to the group plan, with her employer paying the balance. She started making payments in 2005 and made payments of $180 in that year, $225 in 2006, and $250 in 2007. During 2007, during an extended illness, she received benefits of $5,600.

In addition to her salary, her employer provides her with an allowance of $400 per month for maintaining an office in her home. This office is her principal work location. The office occupies 15 percent of her home and, for the year 2007, the costs of operating the home were as follows:

Interest On Mortgage	$4,200
Property Taxes	2,750
Electricity And Water Costs	1,340
Maintenance And Repairs	1,800
Insurance	820

Ms. Spring has two children and they both live with her. Her daughter, Amy, is 18 years old and, during 2007, she was in full time attendance at the local university for eight months of the year. Her tuition fees of $5,200 were paid by Ms. Spring. Amy has Taxable Income of $7,300 for the year. She has agreed to to transfer the maximum education related tax credits to her mother.

Her son, Mark, is 23 years old and is dependent because of a physical disability. The disability is not severe enough, however, to qualify for the ITA 118.3 disability tax credit. Mark had no income during 2007.

The family's medical expenses, all of which have been paid by Ms. Spring, were as follows:

Ms. Spring	$ 962
Amy	2,450
Mark	8,600
Total	$12,012

At the beginning of 2007, Ms. Spring owns two residential rental properties, both acquired in 1995. On January 1, 2007, the UCC of property A was $156,000. The cost of this property was $205,000. Property B had a cost of $326,000 and a January 1, 2007 UCC of $276,000. On June 1, 2007, property A was sold for $161,000. On that same date, a new residential rental property was acquired at a cost of $247,000. During 2007, Ms. Spring received rents of $42,000 and had rental expenses, other than CCA, of $32,500. All three rental properties are part of the same condominium development and are located on leased land.

On December 31, 2006, Ms. Spring purchased a zero coupon bond with a maturity value of $100,000. The bond was issued on that date and matures on December 30, 2011. She paid $68,058 for the bond, a price which provides an 8 percent effective yield.

Ms. Spring owns shares of Canadian public companies which paid eligible dividends of $9,300 during 2007. She also owns shares in a foreign company which paid dividends of $5,600 (Canadian). The government in the foreign country withheld taxes of $840, giving Ms. Spring a net receipt of $4,760.

Required: Calculate Ms. Spring's 2007 minimum Net Income For Tax Purposes, her 2007 minimum Taxable Income, and her 2007 minimum federal Tax Payable without consideration of any income tax withheld by her employer. Ignore GST and PST considerations.

Assignment Case Nine - 2 (Comprehensive Case Covering Chapters 5 to 9)

Mr. Jean Benoit is 67 years of age, is married, and has two children. His spouse, Suzie is 65 years of age and her Net Income For Tax Purposes for the year is $6,250. This is made up of OAS benefits of $2,000 and $4,250 in pension income. During 2007, Suzie attends university on a full time basis for 10 months of the year. Jean paid her tuition fees of $7,800.

Jean's daughter, Sylvie, is 29 years of age and has a disability that qualifies her for the disability tax credit. For 2007, her Net Income For Tax Purposes is nil. She lives with Jean and is totally dependent on him.

Jean's son, Pierre, is 26 years of age. Because of difficulties with substance abuse, he has been unemployed for the last three years. During 2007, his Net Income For Tax Purposes is nil and he remains dependent on his father. Until January, 2007, Pierre had lived in an apartment in a building that Jean owns and uses to operate his business. At this time, Jean concluded that it would be best if Pierre moved back into the family residence. This reflected both the fact that Jean needed the additional space for his business and a desire to exercise more control over his son's attempt at substance abuse recovery.

The family's medical expenses, all of which have been paid by Jean, are as follows:

Jean	$ 3,240
Suzie	1,850
Sylvie	10,550
Pierre	4,320
Total	$19,960

During 2007, Jean and Suzie make contributions to registered charities of $4,450 and contributions to the federal Conservative Party in the amount of $870.

For many years Jean was employed as an engineer by a large Canadian public company. He retired in 2003 and, during 2007, receives income from this employer's pension plan of $37,000. In addition, he has retained options to acquire 5,000 of his employer's shares at a price of $12 per share. When the options were granted the shares were trading at $12 per share.

On July 1, 2007, Jean exercises all of these options. At this time the shares are trading at $21 per share and Jean immediately sells the shares for that price. The employer did not deduct EI premiums or CPP contributions on behalf of Jean.

Jean received CPP benefits of $10,000 in 2007. Since Jean has had income of over $150,000 for the last five years and anticipates income at this level for the rest of his life, he has not applied to receive OAS benefits.

During 2007, Jean received the following dividends (all amounts in Canadian dollars):

Eligible Dividends From Taxable Canadian Corporations	$ 9,250
Non-Eligible Dividends On Shares In His Brother's CCPC	4,670
Dividends On Foreign Shares - Net Of 10 Percent Withholding	7,785
Total Dividends	$21,705

In addition to dividends, Jean had 2007 interest income of $8,742.

Because of the continuing financial needs of his family, after his retirement from his employer, Jean started an engineering services business. In 2004 he acquired a duplex for $320,000 of which $80,000 was the estimated value of the land. He used one unit of the duplex as an office for his business and, until January 1, 2007, allowed Pierre to live rent free in the other half. Jean did not deduct any of the expenses on the half of the duplex that was occupied by Pierre.

On January 1, 2007, the UCC of the business half of the duplex was $108,380 and the UCC for the furniture and fixtures in the business half of the duplex was $22,579 (their capital cost was $25,000). On this date, Jean takes over both units for his business operations. He is advised that the market value of the building has not changed since its acquisition in 2004. He spends $28,000 on improving the building. In addition, he sells the old furniture and fixtures for $12,500 and acquires replacement furniture and fixtures for $42,100.

As Jean has no reason to keep detailed accounting records, he records business income on a cash basis. For 2007, his net cash flow from operations was $67,500. Relevant figures for the beginning and end of 2007 are as follows:

	January 1	December 31
Billed Receivables	$12,800	$15,400
Unbilled Work In Process	15,600	17,800
Accounts Payable	4,500	5,250

Until 2007, Jean has used his personal vehicle for business purposes. However, as of January 1, 2007, he leases an automobile with a manufacturer's list price of $47,000. The lease payment, which does not include any payment for insurance, is $810 per month. No down payment or security deposit is required on the lease and he is not required to purchase the car at the end of the lease term. The lease payments were deducted in the determination of his net cash flow from operations. The car is used 100 percent for business activity.

Required: Calculate Mr. Benoit's 2007 minimum Net Income For Tax Purposes, his 2007 minimum Taxable Income, and his 2007 minimum federal Tax Payable. Ignore GST and PST considerations.

Assignment Case Nine - 3 (Progressive Running Case - Chapter 9 Version Using ProFile T1 Software For 2006 Tax Returns)

This Progressive Running Case requires the use of the ProFile tax software program. It was introduced in Chapter 6 and is continued in Chapters 8 through 14. Each version must be completed in sequence. While it is not repeated in this version of the Case, all of the information in each of the previous versions (e.g., Mary's T4 content) is applicable to this version of the Case.

If you have not prepared a tax file incorporating the previous versions, please do so before continuing with this version.

Seymour was previously married and has a 19 year old daughter from the previous marriage. As part of the property settlement, he received the house that he and his family had lived in. Since Mary already owned a much nicer home, he moved in with her when they were married in 2004 and rented out the property.

On December 28, 2006, Seymour Gravel drops off information about his rental property and additional interest he has paid during the year. (You already have the interest related to his car and principal residence.) Mary has received data that will be on her T3 and T5 information slips from her stockbroker and bank and this is also included in the package you receive. The interest from the TD Bank is from a joint chequing account in the name of both Mary and Seymour.

Seymour believed that in June he had paid an instalment of $2,400 for 2006, but could find no record of it. You call the CRA and find that the June payment was towards his 2005 tax liability. Seymour had tax owing of more than $10,000 for 2005 and has not completely paid off the liability yet. He has paid no instalments for 2006.

Mary also paid no instalments for 2006. She has received tax refunds in the last two years.

Mary has invested in the stock market over the years and has done well. Seymour holds no securities outside of his RRSP during 2006.

During 2004, one of his clients convinced Seymour to take out a demand loan to purchase shares in the public company, XXX Art Films Ltd. for $37,000. Later that year, the company's president was indicted for fraud. In 2005, Seymour sold his shares for $2,000 and used the proceeds to pay down his demand loan. During 2006, Seymour did not have sufficient funds to pay off the demand loan, but managed to reduce the principal by $10,000.

The interest and penalties paid by Seymour during 2006 were as follows:

Interest on credit cards for business expenses	$ 527.27
Interest on loan to make 2005 RRSP contribution	162.15
Interest on loan to purchase XXX Art Films securities	1,372.52
Interest on late payment of 2005 income tax	233.72
Interest on insufficient tax instalments for 2005	52.81
Interest on late GST payments	204.24
Penalty for late filing of 2005 tax return	303.92
Total	$2,856.63

T5	Box	Slip 1	Slip 2
Issuer		Power Corp.	TD Bank
Recipient (Input both on Mary's return)		Mary	Joint 50% each
Actual amount of eligible dividends	24	950.00	
Taxable amount of eligible dividends	25	1,377.50	
Interest from Canadian sources	13		236.11

T3	Box	Amount
Issuer - TD Asset Management		
Recipient - Mary Walford		
Foreign country - United States		
Foreign non-business income	25	1,553.10
Other income - interest	26	214.50
Actual amount of eligible dividends	49	346.00
Taxable amount of eligible dividends	50	501.70
Foreign income tax paid - investment	34	37.00

Real Estate Rental - Seymour	Amount
Address - 50 King Street, Moncton, NB, E1C 4M2	
Gross rents	12,000.00
Property taxes	3,610.00
Insurance	650.00
Interest on mortgage	4,207.25
Payment on principal	1,511.92
Wiring and furnace repairs	2,282.71
Snow removal and landscaping annual contract	1,070.00
Building purchased May 1, 1993 for $150,000 - UCC beginning of year	150,000.00
Appliances purchased June 6, 2003 for $1,700 - UCC beginning of year	1,350.00

Required:

A. Open the file that you created for the Chapter 8 version of the Case and save a copy under a different name. This will enable you to check the changes between different versions of the Case.

B. Revise and print Seymour's Statement of Professional Activities (T2032) for Crystal Clear Communications after incorporating the information on interest paid.

C. Prepare and print Seymour's Statement of Real Estate Rentals and the related CCA worksheet.

D. Input the T3 and T5 information. (Note that by inputting the joint T5 on Mary's return, the T5 information will appear on Seymour's Statement Of Investment Income (Schedule 4), but not on his T5 slip screen.) Prepare and print Schedule 4 for both Mary and Seymour.

E. Review both returns with the objective of minimizing the tax liability for the family and make any changes required.

F. Access and print Mary's summary (Summary on the Form Explorer, not the T1Summary). This form is a two column summary of the couple's tax information. By opening this form from Mary's return, the order of the columns is the same as the one in the previous chapter. For both returns, list the changes on this Summary form from the previous version of this Case. Exclude totals calculated by the program, but include the final Balance Owing (Refund) amount.

CHAPTER 10

Capital Gains And Capital Losses

Economic Background

Capital Assets And Income Taxation Policy

10-1. The discussion of business income in Chapter 8 stated that capital gains and losses arise on the disposition of assets that are earning business or property income. In general, the income from the sale of such assets will be incidental to the ongoing activities that produce business income and, as a consequence, a case can be made for exempting any resulting capital gains and losses from income taxation.

10-2. This case is reinforced during periods of high inflation. If a business is going to continue operating as a going concern, it will usually have to replace any capital assets that are sold. As gains on the sale of capital assets often reflect nothing more than inflationary price increases, such gains cannot be distributed to the owners of the business as they must be used to finance the replacement of the assets sold.

10-3. Until 1972, Canadian tax legislation did not levy any income tax on capital gains. This left Canada as one of the few industrialized nations that imposed no tax on these gains. Further, there was some feeling that, despite the arguments against taxing capital gains, the ability to completely escape taxation on this type of income was creating severe inequities in the taxation system. As a result, one of the more significant changes in the 1972 tax reform legislation was the introduction of taxation on capital gains.

10-4. The capital gains taxation that became effective January 1, 1972, represented a compromise between the view that capital gains should be exempt from tax and the position that such freedom from taxation creates serious inequities among various classes of taxpayers. Taxation of capital gains was introduced, but on a basis that was very favourable to the taxpayer.

10-5. In simple terms, the 1972 rules indicated that one-half of a capital gain would be treated as a taxable capital gain and, similarly, one-half of a capital loss would be deductible against capital gains as an allowable capital loss. This meant that for a taxpayer in the 50 percent tax bracket, the effective tax rate on capital gains was an attractive 25 percent.

Lifetime Capital Gains Deduction

10-6. In 1985, the government introduced one of the most complex and controversial provisions ever added to the *Income Tax Act*. In simple terms, this legislation provided that every Canadian resident could enjoy up to $500,000 in capital gains on a tax free basis over their lifetime. This provision was heavily criticized as a gift to higher income Canadians, particularly in view of the fact that it was available on any type of capital gain. It was difficult for many analysts to see the economic justification for providing favourable tax treatment of gains on the sale of a wealthy Canadian's Florida condominium.

10-7.   As a result of such criticism, this deduction is no longer available on a general basis. However, a $500,000 "super " deduction continued to be available on gains resulting from the disposition of shares of a qualified small business corporation, or the disposition of a qualified farm property. The May, 2006 budget extend this deduction to fishing properties. In addition, for dispositions after March 19, 2007, the March, 2007 budget increases the available deduction to $750,000.

10-8.   It should be noted here that the provisions related to the lifetime capital gains deduction do not affect any of the material in this Chapter. The lifetime capital gains legislation did not alter the determination of the amount of taxable capital gains to be included in Net Income For Tax Purposes. Rather, the legislation provided for a deduction in the determination of Taxable Income for all or part of the taxable capital gains included in Net Income For Tax Purposes. This material is covered in Chapter 14, Taxable Income And Tax Payable For Individuals Revisited.

Changes In The Inclusion Rate

10-9.   For gains and losses on capital assets disposed of subsequent to October 17, 2000, the inclusion rate has been one-half. As the focus of this text is on the 2007 taxation year, the only relevance of alternative inclusion rates is for allowable loss carry forwards resulting from dispositions that occurred prior to October 18, 2000. This relevance results from the fact that such losses can be carried forward indefinitely.

10-10.   Given this situation, we will give only limited attention to examples involving alternative inclusion rates. For reference purposes in dealing with alternative inclusion rates when they occur, inclusion rates for the period 1972 to the present are as follows:

Period	Inclusion Rate
1972 Through 1987	1/2
1988 And 1989	2/3
1990 Through February 27, 2000	3/4
February 28, 2000 through October 17, 2000	2/3
October 18, 2000 To Present	1/2

General Rules

Capital Gains In The Income Tax Act

10-11.   The material in this Chapter is a continuation of our discussion of the calculation of Net Income For Tax Purposes. In Chapter 5, detailed attention was given to employment income. In terms of the *Income Tax Act*, this discussion was based on Subdivision a of Division B. Chapters 7, 8, and 9 dealt with Subdivision b of Division B and provided a comprehensive consideration of business and property income. This included detailed consideration of the calculations related to capital cost allowance (CCA), an important deduction in the determination of both business and property income.

10-12.   Capital gains and losses are the third major component of Net Income For Tax Purposes. This subject is covered in Subdivision c of Division B, Sections 38 through 55. Sections 38 and 39 define capital gains, capital losses, and other items that relate to the calculation of these amounts. Section 40 provides the general tax rules for computing these amounts. The remaining Sections 41 through 55 deal with more specific matters, such as identical properties (Section 47), adjustments to the cost base (Section 53), and various additional definitions (Section 54).

Capital Gains Defined

Capital Assets

10-13. In general, capital gains can occur when a taxpayer disposes of a capital asset. You will recall that capital assets were described in Chapter 8 as being those assets which are capable of earning income in the form of business profits, interest, dividends, royalties, or rents. Further, the assets must be held for this income producing purpose, rather than for a quick resale at a profit.

10-14. It was also noted in Chapter 8 that, in making the determination as to whether a particular amount of income was capital in nature, the courts would take into consideration the intent and course of the taxpayer's conduct, the number and frequency of transactions involving the type of asset under consideration, the nature of the asset, the relationship of the asset to the business of the taxpayer, and the objectives set out in the articles of incorporation.

Capital Gains Election On Canadian Securities

10-15. Despite these guidelines, the fact that capital gains receive favourable income tax treatment has led to much controversy and litigation with respect to the distinction between capital and other assets. In the case of equity securities, it is often difficult to distinguish between those situations where a taxpayer is holding the securities in order to earn dividend income or, alternatively, holding the securities in order to generate a capital gain on their ultimate disposition. Fortunately, the *Income Tax Act* provides an election which keeps this issue out of the courts.

10-16. ITA 39(4) allows taxpayers, including corporations and trusts, to elect to have all Canadian securities that they own deemed to be capital property, and all sales of such securities deemed to be dispositions of capital property. Once this election is made, it applies to all future dispositions of Canadian securities by the taxpayer, thus assuring the taxpayer that all gains and losses will be treated as capital.

10-17. ITA 39(5) indicates that this election is not available to traders or dealers in securities, banks, trustees, credit unions, insurance companies, or non-residents. This election is obviously advantageous in the case of gains since only one-half is taxable. However, in the case of losses, this means only one-half is deductible and only against taxable capital gains.

Dispositions

10-18. As defined in ITA 248(1), a disposition is any transaction or event that entitles the taxpayer to proceeds of disposition of property. This would include:

- sales of property;
- redemptions;
- cancellations;
- expirations;
- expropriations; and
- conversions.

10-19. In addition, transfers are considered to be dispositions, provided there is a change in beneficial ownership. For example, a transfer of property between two trusts with identical beneficiaries would not be considered a change in beneficial ownership and, as a result, no disposition would occur. Transfers of property to an RRSP, and other similar trusts, regardless of whether the beneficiary is the contributor or a spouse are an exception to the general beneficial ownership rule and will result in a disposition.

10-20. In addition to actual dispositions of capital property, there are a number of situations in which a disposition is deemed to have occurred. These would include changes in use as discussed in Chapter 7. Other deemed disposition situations such as the death of a taxpayer, the taxpayer ceasing to be a resident of Canada, and the gifting of capital property in certain situations are given consideration in Chapter 12.

Proceeds Of Disposition

10-21.   The term, "proceeds of disposition", is defined in ITA 54 and ITA 13(21). Included in both of these definitions are the following:

- The sale price of property sold.
- Compensation for property unlawfully taken or for property destroyed, including related proceeds from insurance policies.
- Compensation for property that has been appropriated or injuriously affected whether lawfully or unlawfully.
- Compensation for damaged property, including amounts payable under insurance policies.

10-22.   In addition to actual proceeds of disposition, there are a number of situations for which an amount is deemed to be the proceeds of disposition. We encountered this with the change in use rules introduced in Chapter 7. Under these rules a change in use is a deemed disposition. In such situations, the proceeds are, in general, deemed to be the fair market value of the asset whose use is being changed.

Adjusted Cost Base

Definition

10-23.   The adjusted cost base of an asset is defined in ITA 54 as follows:

   (i) where the property is depreciable property of the taxpayer, the capital cost to him of the property as of that time, and

  (ii) in any other case, the cost to the taxpayer of the property adjusted, as of that time, in accordance with Section 53.

10-24.   This definition means that, in general, the adjusted cost base of a capital asset is analogous to the accounting concept of historical cost. As with the GAAP approach to historical cost, it includes the invoice cost, delivery and setup charges, non-refundable provincial sales taxes, and any other costs associated with acquiring the asset, or putting it into use.

10-25.   As indicated in the definition, ITA 53 specifies a number of adjustments to the cost base. Some of the more important of these adjustments can be described as follows:

    Government Grants And Assistance   When a taxpayer receives government grants or other types of assistance, these amounts are deducted from the adjusted cost base of the related asset. This is consistent with the accounting treatment of government grants specified in Section 3800 of the *CICA Handbook*.

    Superficial Losses   A superficial loss occurs when a taxpayer or his spouse or common-law partner disposes of a property and, within the period of 30 days before the disposition or 30 days after the disposition, one of the cited taxpayers acquires the same or identical property. The identical property is referred to as the substitute property and any loss on the disposition of the original property is called a superficial loss. Such losses cannot be deducted, but must be added to the adjusted cost base of the substitute property.

    As an example, assume that in 2003 Ms. Deffett acquires 100 shares of Norton Limited for $75 per share. On December 27, 2007 the shares are trading at $60 and, because she has realized capital gains in 2007, Ms. Deffett sells the shares on this date in order to realize a loss that can be used to offset the capital gains. One-half of the capital loss of $15 per share on the December 27, 2007 sale would be deductible, provided no Norton Limited shares are purchased between November 27, 2007 and January 26, 2008. If, however, she were to purchase 100 Norton shares on December 15, 2007 or January 15, 2008 for $65 per share, the December, 2007 loss would be disallowed. The disallowed loss would be added to the adjusted cost base of the new shares, giving these shares an adjusted cost base of $80 ($65 + $15) per share. This amount would be appropriate in that it reflects her net cash outlay per share ($75 - $60 + $65).

Other Adjustments To The Cost Base   Other important adjustments would include the addition of interest and property taxes on holdings of vacant land to the adjusted cost base, the addition of subsequent capital contributions by a shareholder to a corporation to the cost base of the shares, and the requirement that under certain circumstances, forgiveness of debts on property must be deducted from the cost base of that property. There are several other such adjustments in ITA 53. You should note, however, that in the case of depreciable property, any deductions taken for CCA do not change the adjusted cost base of the property. Capital gains are determined on the basis of the original capital cost of the asset, not the UCC.

Exercise Ten-1

Subject: Government Assistance

On January 1 of the current year, Rotan Ltd. acquires a property at a cost of $5,600,000. Of this amount, $600,000 represents the fair market value of the land. In order to encourage Rotan's move to this location, the local government has given them $1,500,000 to assist in the acquisition of the building. What is the maximum amount of CCA that Rotan can deduct on this building for the current year?

Exercise Ten-2

Subject: Superficial Loss

Ms. Nadia Kinski owns 1,000 shares of Bord Ltd. They have an adjusted cost base of $23 per share. On August 20, 2007, she sells all of these shares at $14.50 per share. On August 25, 2007, she acquires 600 shares of Bord Ltd. at a cost of $13.75 per share. What are the tax consequences of these transactions?

End of Exercises. Solutions available in Study Guide.

Negative Adjusted Cost Base

10-26.   It is possible that sufficient adjustments could be made to an adjusted cost base that its balance will become negative. When this occurs, ITA 40(3) requires that the deficiency be treated as a capital gain and the adjusted cost base of the asset be adjusted to nil. Note that, unlike the situation with recapture of CCA, this would apply even if additions to the cost base prior to the end of the taxation year were sufficient to eliminate the deficit balance.

10-27.   Also note that ITA 40(3) is not applicable to most partnership interests. That is, a negative adjusted cost base for a partnership interest does not automatically trigger a capital gain and can be carried forward indefinitely. However, this exemption from ITA 40(3) does not apply to limited partners or certain inactive partners. For more details on this point, see Chapter 20.

GST Considerations

10-28.   When capital assets are used in commercial activities, all or part of the GST paid on their acquisition can be recovered as input tax credits. When this is the case, the GST amount recovered would not be included in the adjusted cost base of the asset.

10-29.   There are, however, situations in which there will be no input tax credits available for GST paid on the acquisition of capital assets. Examples of this would be acquisitions of capital assets that will be used in providing exempt services, or that will not be used primarily for commercial activities. In these situations, all or part of the GST payment on the asset acquisition is a permanent outflow of enterprise resources and must be added to the adjusted cost base of the asset. A more complete discussion of the GST implications associated with capital assets can be found at the end of this Chapter.

Calculating The Capital Gain Or Loss

10-30.   The general formula for determining the amount of a capital gain or loss can be described very simply. The calculation, using assumed data, is as follows:

Proceeds Of Disposition		$4,750
Less - The Aggregate Of:		
Adjusted Cost Base	($3,890)	
Expenses Of Disposition	(560)	(4,450)
Capital Gain (Loss)		$ 300
Inclusion Rate		1/2
Taxable Capital Gain		$ 150

10-31.   If, as in the preceding example, there is a capital gain, one-half of the amount will be treated as a taxable capital gain. The adjective "taxable" is consistently used to indicate the portion of the total gain that will be included in income. Similarly, one-half of a negative amount (a capital loss) resulting from the application of the preceding formula would be treated as an allowable capital loss. The adjective "allowable" is consistently used to indicate the deductible portion of the total amount of the loss. As is noted in Chapter 3, allowable capital losses can only be deducted against taxable capital gains.

Detailed Application Of The Rules

Identical Properties

Basic Rules

10-32.   A taxpayer can own a group of identical properties that have been acquired over a period of time at different capital costs. This would arise most commonly with holdings of securities such as common stock in a particular corporation. If part of such a group of assets is disposed of, ITA 47 requires that the adjusted cost base for the assets being disposed of be based on the average cost of the entire group.

10-33.   The following example illustrates the application of this requirement:

Example   An individual has engaged in the following transactions involving the common stock of Gower Company, a Canadian public company:

Year	Number Of Shares Purchased (Sold)	Cost (Proceeds) Per Share	Total Cost (Proceeds)
1991	4,000	$10	$40,000
1993	3,000	12	36,000
1997	(2,000)	(10)	(20,000)
2000	2,500	11	27,500
2005	3,000	10	30,000
2007	(1,500)	(13)	(19,500)

Analysis   The average cost for the first two purchases was $10.86 [($40,000 + $36,000) ÷ (4,000 + 3,000)]. This means that the loss to be recorded on the 1997 sale would be as follows:

Proceeds Of Disposition [(2,000)($10)]	$20,000
Adjusted Cost Base [(2,000)($10.86)]	(21,720)
Capital Loss	($ 1,720)
1997 Inclusion Rate (Not 1/2)	3/4
Allowable Capital Loss	($ 1,290)

This sale would leave the remaining 5,000 shares with a total cost of $54,280 ($76,000 - $21,720). The new average cost for the 2007 sale would be $10.65 [($54,280 + $27,500

+ $30,000) ÷ (5,000 + 2,500 + 3,000)]. Given this, the gain on the 2007 sale would be calculated as follows:

Proceeds Of Disposition [(1,500)($13)]	$19,500
Adjusted Cost Base [(1,500)($10.65)]	(15,975)
Capital Gain	$ 3,525
Inclusion Rate	1/2
Taxable Capital Gain	$ 1,763

Exercise Ten-3

Subject: Identical Properties

Ms. Chantal Montrose makes frequent purchases of the common shares of Comco Inc. During 2006, she purchased 650 shares at $23.50 per share on January 15, and 345 shares at $24.25 per share on March 12. She sold 210 shares on September 15, 2006 at $25.50 per share. On February 14, 2007, she purchases an additional 875 shares at $26.75 per share and, on October 1, 2007, she sells 340 shares at $29.50 per share. Determine Ms. Montrose's taxable capital gains for 2006 and 2007.

End of Exercise. Solution available in Study Guide.

Shares Acquired With Stock Options

10-34. As we have noted, the application of the identical property rules results in any share of a particular stock that is sold being valued at the average cost of all of the shares of that stock that are owned by the taxpayer. Given this, the question of what order the shares are being sold in is not relevant. Whether the shares were the first acquired or the last acquired makes no difference in the determination of the gain or loss on the transaction.

10-35. There is a problem, however, with some shares that have been acquired through the exercise of stock options. You will recall from Chapter 5 that an employment income benefit is measured at the time shares are acquired through the exercise of stock options. In some cases, the taxation of this benefit is deferred until such time as the acquired shares are sold. More specifically, this occurs when:

- the acquired shares were issued by a Canadian controlled private corporation (CCPC); or
- the acquired shares were issued by a public company, but the acquirer has filed an election under ITA 7(8) to defer the benefit.

10-36. This creates a problem for holders of shares on which the employment income inclusion has been deferred in that, if this individual has other holdings of the same securities for which there is no deferred compensation, the question of which block of shares is being sold becomes very relevant.

10-37. If we assume that the shares with deferred compensation are sold, the deferral is terminated and the compensation must be taken into income, along with any gain or loss resulting from the sale. Alternatively, if we assume that the other shares are being sold, the deferred compensation remains deferred and the only tax consequence is the gain or loss on the disposition.

10-38. To deal with this problem, ITA 47(3), in simple terms, indicates that certain securities that have been acquired through the exercise of stock options are deemed not to be identical properties. Unfortunately, the application of this legislation is complex to a degree that extends beyond the interest of general users of this text. However, for readers with an interest in this subject, Appendix B to this Chapter provides detailed coverage of identical property rules as they apply to shares acquired with stock options.

Partial Dispositions

10-39.   In those situations where a taxpayer disposes of part of a property, ITA 43 requires that a portion of the total adjusted cost base be allocated to the disposition on a reasonable basis. For example, if a 500 hectare tract of land had an adjusted cost base of $6,000,000 and 200 hectares of the tract were sold, it would be reasonable to allocate $2,400,000, or 40 percent (200 hectares ÷ 500 hectares), of the total adjusted cost base to the land that was sold. If, however, there was some reason that the part of the tract sold had a value that was not proportionate to the total tract, some alternative basis of allocation could be used.

Warranties

10-40.   If a taxpayer disposes of capital property and the proceeds include some payment for a warranty or other contingent obligation, ITA 42 requires that the full proceeds must be used in determining the capital gain. Stated alternatively, no reserve can be established to provide for any future obligations. However, one-half of any outlays related to such contingent obligations that are made in a subsequent year can be deducted as allowable capital losses, provided the taxpayer has past or present taxable capital gains that can absorb them.

Exercise Ten-4

Subject: Warranties

During the taxation year ending December 31, 2006, Vivid Ltd. sells a capital asset with an adjusted cost base of $237,000 for proceeds of $292,000. The Company provides the purchaser with a one year warranty and the Company estimates that it will cost $4,500 to fulfill the warranty provisions. On October 1, 2007, the Company spends $4,800 to fulfill the warranty provisions. Determine the effect of these transactions on Net Income For Tax Purposes for 2006 and 2007.

End of Exercise.   Solution available in Study Guide.

Capital Gains Reserves

General Principles

10-41.   In some instances, all of the proceeds from a capital asset disposition will not be received in cash in the year of disposition. For example, assume Mr. Filoso sold a piece of land for a capital gain and collected only 10 percent of the total proceeds in the year of sale. It would seem reasonable to allow him to defer recognition of a part of the capital gain. This deferral can be accomplished through the establishment of a capital gains reserve.

10-42.   The general idea is that a reserve can be deducted from the total gain when not all of the proceeds are receivable in the year of the sale. The reserve would reflect the portion of the gain that is contained in the uncollected proceeds. As with other reserves, this amount must be added back to the following year's income, with a new reserve deducted to reflect any remaining uncollected proceeds.

10-43.   At one point in time, the deductible reserve was simply based on the portion of the proceeds of disposition that were not yet received. If a taxpayer collected only 10 percent of the proceeds, the reserve could be equal to 90 percent of the gain. It appears that this provision was being used for what the government viewed as excessive deferrals and, as a consequence, ITA 40(1)(a)(iii) limits the reserve to the lesser of:

- [(the total gain)(the proceeds not receivable until after the end of the current taxation year ÷ the total proceeds of disposition)]

- [(20% of the total gain)(4, less the number of preceding taxation years ending after the disposition)].

10-44.   This has the effect of permitting a maximum reserve of 80 percent in the year of disposition, 60 percent in the following year, 40 percent in the second year after the disposition, 20 percent in the third year, and nil in the fourth. Stated alternatively, a minimum of 20 percent of the gain must be recognized in each year. If the proceeds are collected faster than 20 percent per year, the reserve will be based on the actual uncollected proceeds and the total gain will be recognized more quickly.

10-45.   While this reserve is similar to the ITA 20(1)(n) reserve for uncollected amounts described in Chapter 8, its application is different. The ITA 20(1)(n) reserve is used when there is a sale of an inventory item and part of the proceeds are not due until at least two years after the end of the current taxation year. In contrast, this ITA 40(1)(a)(iii) reserve can be used when there is a capital asset disposition and all or part of the proceeds are not due until after the end of the current taxation year.

Example - Cash Received Is Less Than 20 Percent Of Total Proceeds

10-46.   Assume that during 2007, Mr. Filoso sells a piece of land with an adjusted cost base of $340,000, for total proceeds of $1,000,000, resulting in a capital gain of $660,000 ($1,000,000 - $340,000) and a taxable capital gain of $330,000 [(1/2)($660,000)]. He received only $100,000 of the total amount in cash in 2007 and accepted a $900,000 note payable for the balance. The note is payable at the rate of $100,000 per year beginning in 2008.

10-47.   The maximum reserve for 2007 is $528,000, the lesser of:

- $594,000 [($660,000)($900,000 ÷ $1,000,000)]
- $528,000 [($660,000)(20%)(4 - 0)]

10-48.   This means that $132,000 ($660,000 - $528,000) of the capital gain would be recognized in 2007 even though only $66,000 [($100,000 ÷ $1,000,000)($660,000)] of the total capital gain was realized in terms of cash collected. The taxable amount of the 2007 gain would be $66,000 [(1/2)($132,000)].

10-49.   In 2008, the $528,000 reserve would have to be added back to income. The new reserve for 2008 would be $396,000, the lesser of:

- $528,000 [($660,000)($800,000 ÷ $1,000,000)]
- $396,000 [($660,000)(20%)(4 - 1)]

10-50.   Adding back the previous year's reserve of $528,000, and deducting the new maximum reserve of $396,000, gives a 2008 capital gain of $132,000. This would result in a net addition to 2008 income of $66,000 [(1/2)($528,000 - $396,000)], or 20 percent of the $330,000 taxable capital gain.

10-51.   Based on similar calculations, the maximum reserve in 2009 would be $264,000. This would decline to $132,000 in 2010 and, at the end of 2011, no reserve would be available. This would result in $66,000 [(1/2)($132,000)] being added to income each year. The entire $330,000 of the taxable capital gain will have been included in income by the end of 2011. This is despite the fact that, at the end of this five year period, $500,000 of the initial proceeds remains uncollected.

Example - Cash Received Exceeds Minimum Reserve Levels

10-52.   In the preceding example, collections of cash were less than 20 percent in all years under consideration. As a result, the use of the maximum reserve resulted in the recognition of the minimum 20 percent per year of the gain.

10-53.   Situations in which the proportion of the proceeds of disposition received in cash exceeds minimum recognition requirements would result in more than 20 percent of the gain being taxed in a year. As an illustration of this possibility, assume that in the Paragraph 10-46 example, Mr. Filoso collected $250,000 in the year of the disposition, and that the required payments were $75,000 per year for the following ten years.

10-54.   Based on this information, the maximum reserve for 2007 would be the lesser of:

- $495,000 [($660,000)($750,000 ÷ $1,000,000)]
- $528,000 [($660,000)(20%)(4 - 0)]

10-55.   This means that a taxable capital gain of $82,500 [(1/2)($660,000 - $495,000)] would be recognized in 2007.

10-56.   In 2008, the $495,000 reserve would be added back to income. The new reserve for 2008 would be $396,000, the lesser of:

- $445,500 [($660,000)($675,000 ÷ $1,000,000)]
- $396,000 [($660,000)(20%)(4 - 1)]

10-57.   This results in the recognition of a $49,500 [(1/2)($495,000 - $396,000)] taxable capital gain in 2008. At this point, the minimum 20 percent per year recognition requirement has become the determining factor in calculating the capital gain to be included in income. As a consequence, the amount to be included in income in the years 2009, 2010, and 2011 would be as presented in Paragraph 10-51.

Exercise Ten-5

Subject: Capital Gains Reserves

During December 2006, Mr. Gerry Goodson sells a capital property with an adjusted cost base of $293,000 for proceeds of disposition of $382,000. Selling costs total $17,200. In the year of sale, he receives $82,000 in cash, along with the purchaser's note for the balance of the proceeds. The note is to be repaid at the rate of $60,000 per year beginning in 2007. He receives the 2007 payment in full. Determine the maximum capital gains reserve that Mr. Goodson can deduct in 2006 and in 2007.

End of Exercise. Solution available in Study Guide.

Bad Debts On Sales Of Capital Property

10-58.   When an amount receivable results from the disposition of a capital property, the possibility arises that some of the proceeds of disposition will have to be written off as a bad debt. When this occurs, ITA 50(1) allows the seller to elect to have disposed of the receivable and immediately reacquired it at a proceeds and cost of nil. Consider the following:

Example   During 2007, a capital property with a cost of $500,000 is sold for $510,000. The proceeds are made up of $360,000 in cash, plus the purchaser's note for $150,000.

10-59.   If the vendor of the capital property does not choose to deduct a capital gains reserve for the uncollected amount, a capital gain of $10,000 would be recognized in 2007. If, during 2007, the note received from the purchaser turns out to be uncollectible, the deemed disposition and reacquisition would result in a capital loss of $150,000, more than offsetting the $10,000 capital gain on the disposition. If, at a later point in time, some amount of debt was recovered, any excess over the deemed nil proceeds would be considered a capital gain.

Exercise Ten-6

Subject: Bad Debts (Capital Property)

During 2006, a capital property with an adjusted cost base of $125,000 is sold for $110,000. The proceeds of disposition are made up of $75,000 in cash, plus the purchaser's one-year note for $35,000. In 2007, the note proves to be uncollectible. What are the tax consequences of these events in 2006 and in 2007?

End of Exercise. Solution available in Study Guide.

Deferral Provisions On Replacement Property

Basic Rules

10-60.   As indicated in Chapter 7, the ITA 13(4) and ITA 44 replacement property rules can apply when there are certain types of dispositions. The special rules apply to involuntary dispositions where capital property is lost, stolen, destroyed, or expropriated. In this case, the rules apply to all types of capital property. When the disposition is voluntary, the rules are only applicable to real (capital) property (i.e., land and buildings), a limited life franchise, a concession or a license that is a former business property.

10-61.   The applicability of the rules is also limited by the timing of the replacement. For involuntary dispositions, the replacement must occur within 24 months after the end of the year in which the disposition takes place. This period is reduced to 12 months for voluntary dispositions.

10-62.   Note that, from a technical point of view, the disposition does not take place until the proceeds become receivable. In the case of voluntary dispositions, the proceeds will become receivable at the time of sale. However, in the case of involuntary dispositions, the receipt of insurance or expropriation proceeds may occur in a taxation year subsequent to the theft, destruction, or expropriation of the property. For purposes of determining the 24 month replacement period, the clock will begin ticking in this later year.

10-63.   The ITA 13(4) rules related to recapture of CCA were discussed and illustrated in Chapter 7. Our concern here is with the ITA 44 rules related to capital gains. If a qualifying property is disposed of and replaced within the required time frame, ITA 44 allows a taxpayer to elect to reduce the capital gain on the disposition to the lesser of:

- an amount calculated by the usual approach (proceeds of disposition, less adjusted cost base); and
- the excess, if any, of the proceeds of disposition of the old property over the cost of the replacement property.

10-64.   In somewhat simplified terms, if the cost of the replacement property is greater than the proceeds of disposition for the replaced property, no capital gain will be recorded if the appropriate election is made. We would remind you that, in those cases where the replacement occurs in a period subsequent to the disposition, this election will have to be applied as an adjustment to the return for the year of disposition.

Example - Replacement Cost Greater Than Proceeds Of Disposition

10-65.   The following example illustrates the election under both ITA 13(4) and ITA 44:

Example   During its 2007 taxation year, the Martin Company decides to change the location of its operations. Its current property consists of land with an adjusted cost base of $500,000, as well as a building with a capital cost of $1,500,000 and a UCC of $340,000. These assets are sold for a total price of $2,400,000, of which $600,000 is allocated to the land and $1,800,000 is allocated to the building. During January, 2008, a replacement property is acquired at a new location at a cost of $2,800,000, of which $700,000 is allocated to the land and $2,100,000 is allocated to the building.

Analysis - Capital Gain   As a result of the disposition, the Martin Company will include the following amounts in its 2007 Net Income For Tax Purposes:

	Land	Building
Proceeds Of Disposition	$600,000	$1,800,000
Adjusted Cost Base	(500,000)	(1,500,000)
Capital Gain	$100,000	$ 300,000
Inclusion Rate	1/2	1/2
Taxable Capital Gain	$ 50,000	$ 150,000
Recapture Of CCA ($340,000 - $1,500,000)	N/A	$1,160,000

When the replacement occurs in 2008, the cost allocated to land and building exceeds the proceeds of disposition from these assets. As a consequence, the revised capital gain for 2007 will be nil, a fact that would be reflected in an amended 2007 tax return. However, the capital cost of the replacement assets would be reduced as follows:

	Land	Building
Actual Capital Cost	$700,000	$2,100,000
Capital Gain Deferred By Election	(100,000)	(300,000)
Adjusted Capital Cost	$600,000	$1,800,000

10-66.   The economic basis for this result can be seen by noting that the combined adjusted capital cost of the new land and building is $2,400,000 ($600,000 + $1,800,000). This is equal to the combined adjusted capital cost of the old land and building of $2,000,000 ($500,000 + $1,500,000), plus the additional $400,000 in cash ($2,800,000 - $2,400,000) required to finance the acquisition of the new land and building.

10-67.   Using the ITA 13(4) formula, the amended 2006 recapture of CCA would be calculated as follows:

UCC Balance		$340,000
Deduction:		
Lesser Of:		
• Proceeds Of Disposition = $1,800,000		
• Capital Cost = $1,500,000	$1,500,000	
Reduced By The Lesser Of:		
• Normal Recapture = $1,160,000		
• Replacement Cost = $2,100,000	(1,160,000)	(340,000)
Recapture Of CCA (Amended)		Nil

10-68.   As would be expected when the replacement cost of the new building exceeds the normal recapture of CCA, the amended recapture of CCA is nil. The reduction in the 2006 recapture of CCA will be reflected in the UCC of the new building as follows:

Adjusted Capital Cost Of Building	$1,800,000
Recapture Deferred By Election	(1,160,000)
Adjusted UCC	$ 640,000

10-69.   As was the case with the capital cost of the new building, the economic basis for this result can also be explained. The new UCC of $640,000 is equal to the old UCC of $340,000, plus the $300,000 in cash ($2,100,000 - $1,800,000) required to finance the acquisition of the new building.

Example - Replacement Cost Less Than Proceeds Of Disposition

10-70.   In the preceding example, we are able to remove 100 percent of the capital gain through the application of the ITA 44 election. This resulted from the fact that the cost of the replacement property exceeded the proceeds of disposition for the old property. If this is not the case, some of the capital gain will have to remain in income. This point can be illustrated by making a small change in our previous example:

Example   During its 2007 taxation year, the Martin Company decides to change the location of its operations. Its current property consists of land with an adjusted cost base of $500,000, as well as a building with a capital cost of $1,500,000 and a UCC of $340,000. These assets are sold for a total price of $2,400,000, of which $600,000 is allocated to the land and $1,800,000 is allocated to the building. During January, 2008, a replacement property is acquired at a new location at a cost of $2,650,000, of which $550,000 is allocated to the land and $2,100,000 is allocated to the building.

10-71.   The capital gains and recapture on the disposition will be as presented in Paragraph 10-65. However, in the 2007 amended return, a taxable capital gain equal to one-half of the excess of the proceeds of disposition of the old land, over the cost of the replacement land will remain in 2007 income. This amount is $25,000 [(1/2)($600,000 - $550,000)]. The relevant tax values for the replacement assets are as follows:

	Land	Building
Actual Capital Cost	$550,000	$2,100,000
Capital Gain Deferred By Election	(50,000)	(300,000)
Adjusted Capital Cost	$500,000	$1,800,000
Recapture Deferred By Election	N/A	(1,160,000)
Adjusted UCC	N/A	$ 640,000

Election To Reallocate Proceeds Of Disposition

10-72.   In the preceding example, the fact that the replacement cost of the land was less than the proceeds of disposition of the previously owned land, resulted in a situation where a portion of the capital gain on this disposition had to remain in the 2007 tax return. Fortunately, a further election contained in ITA 44 provides, in many cases, a solution to this problem.

10-73.   Under ITA 44(6), the taxpayer is allowed to reallocate the total proceeds of disposition on the sale of a former business property, without regard to the respective market values of the land and building. If, in the example presented in Paragraph 10-70 , the total proceeds of $2,400,000 are allocated on the basis of $550,000 (originally $600,000) to the land and $1,850,000 (originally $1,800,000) to the building, the 2006 taxable capital gains will be as follows:

	Land	Building
Proceeds Of Disposition	$550,000	$1,850,000
Adjusted Cost Base	(500,000)	(1,500,000)
Capital Gain	$ 50,000	$ 350,000
Inclusion Rate	1/2	1/2
Taxable Capital Gain	$ 25,000	$ 175,000

10-74.   While the total taxable capital gain remains the same, this reallocation of the total proceeds of disposition results in a situation where the replacement cost of both the land and building are equal to, or exceed, the proceeds of disposition. This, in turn, means that all of the capital gains on both of these capital assets will be removed from the 2007 amended tax return. Under this scenario, the tax values for the replacement assets would be as follows:

	Land	Building
Allocated Cost	$550,000	$2,100,000
Capital Gain Deferred By Election	(50,000)	(350,000)
Adjusted Capital Cost	$500,000	$1,750,000
Recapture Deferred By Election	N/A	(1,160,000)
Adjusted UCC	N/A	$ 590,000

10-75.   Note that this election is not made without a cost. Had the $50,000 been left as a capital gain, tax would have applied on only one-half of the total. While we have eliminated this $25,000 in income, we have given up future CCA for the full amount of $50,000. In other words, we have given up $50,000 in future deductions in return for eliminating $25,000 of income in 2006. As explained in our Chapters 15 and 16 on corporate taxation, for some corporations, capital gains are initially taxed at higher rates than business income, which could be a factor in this decision. In addition, anticipated future tax rates could be a consideration.

10-76. In situations where the reallocation process shifts proceeds from the building to the land, the results can be reversed. However, as the preceding examples illustrate, the combination of ITA 13(4) and ITA 44 elections can provide significant tax relief in situations where a business is relocating. Similar advantages are available for involuntary dispositions.

Exercise Ten-7

Subject: Involuntary Dispositions

Hadfeld Ltd., a company with a December 31 year end, operates out of a single building that cost $725,000 in 2000. At the beginning of 2006, the UCC for its Class 1 was $623,150. On June 30, 2006, the building was completely destroyed in a fire. The building was insured for its fair market value of $950,000 and this amount was received in September, 2006. The building is replaced in 2007 at a cost of $980,000. Describe the 2006 and 2007 tax consequences of these events, including the capital cost and UCC for the new building, assuming Hadfeld Ltd. wishes to minimize taxes.

End of Exercise. Solution available in Study Guide.

Deferral Provisions On Small Business Investments

Basic Provision

10-77. ITA 44.1 was introduced to provide small businesses, especially start-up companies, with greater access to risk capital. It provides for the deferral of capital gains resulting from the disposition of "eligible small business corporation shares" when sold by an individual. The deferral is conditional on reinvestment of some or all of the proceeds of disposition in other small business corporation shares (replacement shares). As you would expect, the adjusted cost base of these replacement shares will be reduced by the capital gain that is eliminated in the current year. In effect, this defers the gain until such time as the new investment is sold and not reinvested in replacement shares.

Definitions

10-78. As it stands, ITA 44.1 is a very technical Section of the *Act* and, as such, requires a number of definitions. Some of the more important definitions are as follows:

Eligible Small Business Corporation To be eligible for the deferral, the corporations must comply with the definition of an eligible small business corporation. This is a Canadian controlled private corporation that has substantially all (meaning more than 90 percent) of the fair market value of its assets devoted principally to an active business carried on primarily (meaning more than 50 percent) in Canada. The corporation's qualifying assets include its holdings of shares or debt in other eligible small business corporations. To be eligible for the ITA 44.1 provisions, the small business corporation and corporations related to it cannot have assets with a carrying value in excess of $50 million. Shares or debt of related corporations are not counted when determining the $50 million limit on assets.

Qualifying Disposition To qualify for the deferral, the gain must result from the sale of common shares in an eligible small business corporation that was owned by the investor throughout the 185 day period that preceded the disposition.

Replacement Shares These are shares of an eligible small business corporation that are acquired within 120 days after the end of the year in which the qualifying disposition took place. They must be designated as replacement shares in the individual's tax return.

Permitted Deferral   The deferral is limited to a fraction of the capital gain resulting from the qualifying disposition. The fraction is based on the ratio of the lesser of the cost of the replacement shares and proceeds of disposition, divided by the proceeds of disposition (the value cannot exceed one). As an example of this calculation, assume that the common shares of an eligible small business corporation with an adjusted cost base of $2,000,000, are sold for $2,500,000. Within 30 days, $1,800,000 of the proceeds are used to purchase replacement shares. With the total gain at $500,000 ($2,500,000 - $2,000,000), the permitted deferral would be $360,000 [($500,000)($1,800,000 ÷ $2,500,000)].

Adjusted Cost Base Reduction   The permitted deferral will be subtracted from the adjusted cost base of the replacement shares. Using the preceding example, the adjusted cost base of the replacement shares would be $1,440,000 ($1,800,000 - $360,000). If there is more than one block of replacement shares, this reduction will be allocated in proportion to their qualifying costs.

Example
10-79.   The following example illustrates the application of the ITA 44.1 deferral:

Example   During the current year, an individual makes a qualifying disposition of shares of Corporation A with an adjusted cost base of $3,000,000, for proceeds of disposition of $4,500,000.

Within 120 days of the qualifying disposition, the individual purchases replacement shares in Corporation B with a cost of $2,200,000 and in Corporation C with a cost of $2,300,000. Corporations A, B, and C are unrelated.

Analysis   As the $4,500,000 proceeds of disposition is equal to the $4,500,000 ($2,200,000 + $2,300,000) cost of the replacement shares, the permitted deferral is equal to $1,500,000 [($1,500,000)($4,500,000 ÷ $4,500,000)], which is the total capital gain on the disposition.

In terms of the adjusted cost base of the new shares, the reduction would be allocated $733,333 [($1,500,000)($2,200,000 ÷ $4,500,000)] to the B shares, and $766,667 [($1,500,000)($2,300,000 ÷ $4,500,000)] to the C shares. The resulting adjusted cost bases would be $1,466,667 ($2,200,000 - $733,333) for the B shares and $1,533,333 ($2,300,000 - $766,667) for the C shares. The total adjusted cost base is $3,000,000 ($1,466,667 + $1,533,333), which was the adjusted cost base of The Corporation A shares.

Exercise Ten-8

Subject: Deferral Of Small Business Gains

On January 15, 2007, Jerri Hamilton sells all of her shares of Hamilton Ltd., an eligible small business corporation. The adjusted cost base of these shares is $750,000 and they are sold for $1,350,000. On February 15, 2007, $1,200,000 of these proceeds are invested in the common shares of JH Inc., a new eligible small business corporation. How much of the capital gain arising on the sale of the Hamilton Ltd. shares can be deferred by the investment in JH Inc.? If the maximum deferral is elected, what will be the adjusted cost base of the JH Inc. shares?

End of Exercise. Solution available in Study Guide.

Changes In Use
10-80.   In Chapter 7, we noted that when an asset's use is changed from personal to business, or from business to personal, it is considered to be a deemed disposition and reacquisition of the asset. In general, the proceeds of disposition are equal to the fair market

value of the asset, and the capital cost of the reacquisition is equal to the same value. An exception occurs when:

- the change is from personal use to business use; and
- the fair market value of the asset exceeds its original capital cost.

10-81. In this case, the cost for CCA purposes of the reacquired asset is deemed to be equal to the original capital cost, plus one-half of the excess of the current fair market value over the original capital cost. This procedure reflects the fact that the gain on the deemed disposition will be a capital gain, only one-half of which will be taxed. In order to prevent a partially taxed capital gain from being converted to a fully deductible UCC balance, the addition to this balance is limited to one-half of the excess of fair market value over the original capital cost.

10-82. There is no similar limit on the capital cost of the reacquired asset. In all cases, the capital cost of the reacquisition will be equal to the fair market value of the asset.

Example On September 1, 2007, Mr. Reid converts his summer cottage to a rental property. The cost of the building was $100,000, its fair market value is $130,000, and it has not been designated as his principal residence.

Analysis The deemed reacquisition value for capital gains purposes is the fair market value of $130,000, resulting in a taxable capital gain of $15,000 [(1/2)($130,000 - $100,000)].

In contrast, as the change is from personal to business use and the fair market value exceeds the cost, the deemed reacquisition value for the purposes of calculating CCA or recapture would be $115,000 [$100,000 + (1/2)($130,000 - $100,000)]. This is equal to the original cost of $100,000, plus one-half of the difference between this value and the current fair market value of $130,000. Given this value, the maximum CCA for 2007 is $2,300 [($115,000)(4%)(1/2)].

Note that, because the asset had not previously been used for income producing purposes, the first year rule is applicable, even though the transfer is not at arm's length.

If the cottage was later sold for $150,000, there would be a capital gain of $20,000 ($150,000 - $130,000). However, only $115,000 would be subtracted from the UCC, thereby limiting recapture to the amount of CCA taken since the change in use.

10-83. As a final point, when the change is from personal to business use, ITA 45(2) allows the taxpayer to elect not to have the deemed disposition rules from ITA 13(7) and ITA 45(1) apply. This would eliminate the recognition of capital gains and possible recapture at the time of the change.

10-84. However, the election requires the taxpayer to assume that he has not started to use the property for business purposes. This means that no deduction for CCA will be available on the property. This provision is of particular importance when a principal residence is converted to a rental property and, as a consequence, it will be given further attention in the next section of this Chapter.

Exercise Ten-9

Subject: Change In Use

During July, 2007, Ms. Lynn Larson decides to use her summer cottage as a rental property. It has an original cost of $23,000 and its current fair market value is $111,000. It has never been designated as her principal residence. Describe the 2007 tax consequences of this change in use, including the capital cost and UCC that will be applicable to the rental property. In addition, indicate the maximum amount of CCA that would be available for 2007.

End of Exercise. Solution available in Study Guide.

Provisions For Special Assets

Principal Residence

Principal Residence Defined

10-85.   For many individuals resident in Canada, one of the most attractive features of our tax system is the fact that, in general, capital gains arising on the disposition of a principal residence can be received free of tax. Since 1982, only one taxpayer in a family unit can designate a property as a principal residence for a particular year. For these purposes, a family unit includes a spouse, as well as children unless they are married or over 18 during the year.

10-86.   ITA 54 defines a principal residence as any accommodation owned by the taxpayer that was ordinarily inhabited in the year by the taxpayer, his spouse, a former spouse, or a dependent child, and is designated by the taxpayer as a principal residence. The definition notes that this would include land up to a limit of one-half hectare as well as a building. If the property includes additional land, it will be subject to capital gains taxation unless the taxpayer can demonstrate that the additional land was necessary for the enjoyment of the property.

10-87.   If a taxpayer owns more than one property that might qualify as a residence, only one property can be designated as a principal residence in any given year. From an administrative point of view, however, the CRA does not require that such a designation be made from year to year. Rather, the filing of form T2091, *Designation Of A Principal Residence*, is only required when a property is disposed of, and a taxable capital gain remains after applying the reduction formula described in the following material. From an administrative point of view, this requirement is often ignored, reflecting its irrelevance in situations where the family has only one property that could be designated as a principal residence.

Gain Reduction Formula

10-88.   Technically speaking, capital gains on a principal residence are taxable. However, ITA 40(2)(b) provides a formula for reducing such gains. The formula calculates the taxable portion, which is based on the relationship between the number of years since 1971 that the property has been designated a principal residence and the number of years since 1971 that the taxpayer has owned the property. It is as follows:

$$A - \left[A \times \frac{B}{C} \right] - D, \text{ where}$$

    A   is the total capital gain on the disposition of the principal residence;
    B   is one plus the number of years the property is designated as the taxpayer's principal residence;
    C   is the number of years since 1971 that the taxpayer has owned the property;
    D   relates to the 1994 capital gains election (not of general interest to users of this text).

10-89.   The formula in Paragraph 10-88 is applied to any capital gain resulting from the disposition of a principal residence in order to determine the amount that will be subject to taxation. For example, assume a property was purchased in 1999 and was sold in 2007 for an amount that resulted in a capital gain of $100,000. If it was designated as a principal residence for six of the nine years of ownership, the calculation of the taxable portion of the capital gain would be as follows:

$$\left[\$100,000 - (\$100,000)\left(\frac{1+6}{9} \right) \right]\left[\frac{1}{2} \right] = \$11,111$$

10-90.   If a taxpayer has only a single property that could qualify as a principal residence, that property can be designated as the principal residence for all years owned. In such situations, the use of this formula will then completely eliminate any capital gains on the disposition of that property.

10-91.   When only one residence is involved in each year, the plus one in the B component of the formula is not relevant. However, if a taxpayer sells one home and acquires another in a single year, the plus one becomes important. This point can be illustrated with the following example:

Example   During 2002, Mr. Fodor acquires a principal residence at a cost of $130,000. The residence is sold in 2005 for $150,000. A replacement residence is acquired in 2005 at a cost of $170,000. In 2007, the second residence is sold for $200,000, with Mr. Fodor moving to an apartment.

Analysis   During 2005, Mr. Fodor owns two properties, only one of which can be designated as a principal residence for that year. If there was no extra year in the numerator of the reduction formula (component B), Mr. Fodor would be taxed on a portion of one of the gains. For example, assume Mr. Fodor allocates the three years 2002 through 2004 to the first property and the three years 2005 through 2007 to the second. All of the $30,000 gain on the second property would be eliminated. Since the first property was sold in 2005, the denominator in the reduction formula (component C) is 4 (2002 to 2005).   If the plus one was not in the numerator, only three-quarters of the $20,000 gain would be eliminated, leaving a capital gain of $5,000 [$20,000 - ($20,000)(3 ÷ 4)]. However, with the addition of the plus one to the years in the numerator of the reduction formula, the fraction on the first property becomes four-fourths, and there is no taxable capital gain.

Exercise Ten-10

Subject: Sale Of Principal Residence

Mr. Norm Craft purchases his first home in 1998 at a cost of $89,000. In 2003, this home is sold for $109,500 and a second home is purchased for $152,000. In 2007, this second home is sold for $178,000 and Mr. Craft moves to a rental property. Determine the minimum tax consequences of the two property sales.

Exercise Ten-11

Subject: Sale Of Principal Residence

Ms. Jan Sadat owns a house in Ottawa, as well as a cottage in Westport. She purchased the house in 1996 for $126,000. The cottage was gifted to her in 1999 by her parents. At the time of the gift, the fair market value of the cottage was $85,000. During June, 2007, both properties are sold, the house for $198,000 and the cottage for $143,500. She has lived in the Ottawa house during the year, but has spent her summers in the Westport cottage. Determine the minimum capital gain that she can report on the 2007 sale of the two properties.

End of Exercises. Solutions available in Study Guide.

Change In Use - Principal Residence To Rental

10-92.   We have previously noted that when the use of a property is changed from personal to business, ITA 45(1) requires that this change be treated as a deemed disposition and reacquisition at fair market value. The conversion of a principal residence to a rental property is a common example of this type of situation and, in the absence of any election, the fair market value at the time of the change will become the adjusted cost base of the rental property. As was previously discussed, if the fair market value exceeds the cost, a different value will be used for the calculation of CCA.

10-93.   An alternative to this treatment is provided under ITA 45(2). Under this Subsection, the taxpayer can make an election under which he will be deemed not to have commenced using the property for producing income. If this election is made, the taxpayer will still have to include the rents from the property as rental income. The taxpayer will be able to deduct all of the expenses associated with the property other than CCA. However, use of the ITA 45(2) election prevents the taxpayer from deducting any amounts for CCA on this property.

10-94.   While this inability to deduct CCA can be viewed as a disadvantage associated with the election, the election does, in fact, have an offsetting advantage. Based on the ITA 54 definition of a principal residence, the property can continue to be designated as a principal residence for up to four years while the election is in effect. This would appear to be the case even in situations where the individual does not return to live in the property.

10-95.   In practical terms, the preceding means that an individual who moves out of a principal residence can retain principal residence treatment for the property, for up to four years. This allows the individual to enjoy any capital gains that accrue on that property on a tax free basis.

10-96.   This would be of particular importance to an individual who moves to a rental property and does not have an alternative principal residence during this period. Even if the individual purchases an alternative residential property, the election can be helpful as it allows a choice as to which property will be designated as the principal residence during the relevant years. If one of the properties experiences a substantially larger capital gain during this period, the use of this election could produce a significant savings in taxes.

10-97.   Also of interest is the fact that the four year election period can be extended. ITA 54.1 specifies that if the following conditions are met either by the taxpayer or the taxpayer's spouse or common-law partner, the election can be extended without limit:

* you leave the residence because your employer requires you to relocate;
* you return to the original residence while still with the same employer, or before the end of the year following the year you leave that employer, or you die before such employment terminates; and
* the original residence is at least 40 kilometers further from your new place of employment than your temporary residence.

Exercise Ten-12

Subject: ITA 45(2) Election - Principal Residence To Rental

During 2002, Jan Wheatley acquired a new home at a cost of $220,000. On December 31, 2007, she moves from this home into an apartment. At this time, the home is appraised for $210,000. Because she believes that real estate in her area is temporarily undervalued, she decides to rent the property for a period of time and sell it at a later date. During 2008, she receives rents of $21,600 and has expenses, other than CCA, of $12,600. On January 1, 2009, she sells the home to the current tenant for $345,000. Indicate the 2008 and 2009 tax consequences to Ms. Wheatley assuming that, in 2008, she does not elect under ITA 45(2). How would these results differ if she made the ITA 45(2) election? In providing your answers, ignore the cost of the land on which the home is located.

End of Exercise. Solution available in Study Guide.

Change In Use - Rental To Principal Residence

10-98.   Here again, unless an election is made, this change in use will be treated as a deemed disposition at fair market value, with possible results including capital gains, recapture, or terminal loss. When this type of change occurs, ITA 45(3) allows an individual to elect out of the deemed disposition for capital gains purposes as long as no CCA has been taken on the property. The election must be made by the taxpayer's filing deadline for the year following the disposition (April 30 or June 15). Also note that this is an election that can be late filed under the provisions of the fairness package, provided the relevant criteria are met.

10-99.   When the ITA 45(3) election is used, it is possible to designate the property as a principal residence for up to four years prior to the time it stopped being used as a rental property. This can be beneficial both to individuals who did not own another residential property during this four year period, and to individuals with an alternative residential property that experiences a capital gain at a lower annual rate, or a loss.

Exercise Ten - 13

Subject: ITA 45(3) Election - Rental To Principal Residence

On January 2, 2006, Lance Ho acquires a small condominium in downtown Toronto for $375,000. When his mother threatens to commit suicide if he moves out, he rents the unit to a friend until December 31, 2006. Net rental income, before any deduction for CCA, is $9,800. Mr. Ho's mother dies on December 26, 2006 and Mr. Ho moves into the unit on January 1, 2007. At this time, the appraised value of the property is $450,000.

After moving in, he finds that living in the downtown area is far too hectic and, on December 31, 2007, he sells the unit for $510,000. Indicate the 2006 and 2007 tax consequences to Mr. Ho, assuming that he deducts CCA in 2006 and does not elect under ITA 45(3). How would these results differ had he not taken CCA and made the ITA 45(3) election? In providing your answers, ignore the cost of the land on which the condominium is located.

End of Exercise. Solution available in Study Guide.

Non-Residential Usage

10-100.   A complication arises when a taxpayer either begins to rent a part of his principal residence, or begins to use it for non-residential purposes (e.g., a self-employed individual who maintains an office at home). Under the general rules for capital assets, this would be a partial disposition of the property, potentially resulting in a capital gain.

10-101.   However, the CRA has indicated that it will not apply the partial disposition rules so long as the income use is ancillary to the main use as a principal residence, there is no structural change to the property, and no capital cost allowance is claimed. Given this, the standard tax planning advice to taxpayers who use a portion of their principal residence for business purposes is not to deduct CCA on this property.

Farm Properties

10-102.   Many farmers have a principal residence that is a part of their farm property. This means that when the farm is sold, the farmer's principal residence will generally be included in the package that is sold. In this situation, ITA 40(2)(c) identifies two approaches that can be used in this situation.

10-103.   The first approach requires that the land be divided into two components — the portion used for farming and the portion used for the enjoyment of the principal residence. Separate capital gains are calculated for each, with the gain on the principal residence portion being eligible for the principal residence reduction. Note that the ITA 54 definition of principal residence indicates that, as a general guideline, the land required for the enjoyment of the principal residence is limited to one-half hectare.

10-104.   As an alternative, a farmer can elect to be taxed on the capital gain from the sale of the entire property, reduced by $1,000, plus an additional $1,000 per year for every year for which the property was a principal residence.

Personal Use Property
Definition
10-105.   ITA 54 defines personal use property as any property that is owned by the taxpayer and used primarily for his enjoyment, or for the enjoyment of one or more individuals related to the taxpayer. In non-technical terms, we are talking about any significant asset owned by a taxpayer that is not used for earning business or property income. This would include personal use automobiles, principal residences, vacation homes, boats, furniture, and many other items.

Capital Gains And Losses
10-106.   In general, gains on the disposition of personal use property are taxed in the same manner as gains on other capital assets. However, there is an important difference with respect to losses. In general, losses on such property are not deductible. The reason for this is that most types of personal use property depreciate over time and to allow capital losses or CCA on the property to be deductible would, in effect, permit a write-off of the cost of normal wear and tear. As explained later, beginning in Paragraph 10-110, the exception to this is losses on listed personal property that can be deducted on a restricted basis.

10-107.   To simplify the enforcement of capital gains taxation on personal use property, ITA 46(1) provides a $1,000 floor rule. In using this rule to calculate capital gains on personal use property, the proceeds are deemed to be the greater of $1,000 and the actual proceeds. In a similar fashion, the adjusted cost base is deemed to be the greater of $1,000 and the actual cost base. This rule is illustrated in the following example involving dispositions of personal use property in four different cases:

Capital Gains (Losses) On Personal Use Property

	Case A	Case B	Case C	Case D
Proceeds Of Disposition (POD)	$300	$850	$ 500	$1,500
Adjusted Cost Base (ACB)	800	400	1,300	900
Using the $1,000 floor rule results in the following capital gain or loss:				
Greater Of Actual POD Or $1,000	$1,000	$1,000	$1,000	$1,500
Greater Of ACB Or $1,000	(1,000)	(1,000)	(1,300)	(1,000)
Gain (Non-Deductible Loss)	Nil	Nil	($ 300)	$ 500

10-108.   In situations where a taxpayer disposes of a part of an item of personal use property while retaining the remainder, the taxpayer must establish the ratio of the adjusted cost base of the part disposed of, to the total adjusted cost base of the property. Then, in applying the $1,000 floor rule, the adjusted cost base is deemed to be the greater of the portion of the adjusted cost base associated with the part disposed of, or the same portion of $1,000. In the same fashion, the proceeds would be deemed to be the greater of the actual proceeds and the appropriate portion of $1,000.

10-109.   The government perceived an abuse of this $1,000 floor rule in art donation schemes where individuals would acquire art in bulk for nominal amounts ($10 each) and would then donate them immediately to various educational institutions at values apparently determined by questionable appraisers ($1,000 or less). The capital gains would be exempt because of the $1,000 floor rule, but the individuals would receive charitable donation receipts of $1,000. As a result, ITA 46(5) excludes certain property from the $1,000 deemed adjusted cost base rule when it is donated as part of a scheme to receive donation receipts of artificially high value.

Listed Personal Property
10-110.   Listed personal property consists of certain specified items of personal use property. The specified items are found in ITA 54 as follows:

(i) print, etching, drawing, painting, sculpture, or other similar work of art,
(ii) jewelry,
(iii) rare folio, rare manuscript, or rare book,
(iv) stamp, or
(v) coin.

10-111. In general, listed personal property is subject to the same capital gains rules as would apply to other personal use property. This would include the applicability of the $1,000 floor rule. However, there is a very important difference. While any losses on personal use property cannot be deducted, allowable capital losses on listed personal property can be deducted subject to a significant restriction.

10-112. The restriction is that allowable capital losses on listed personal property can only be deducted against taxable capital gains on listed personal property. In the absence of such taxable capital gains, the listed personal property losses cannot be deducted. However, any undeducted losses are subject to the carry over provisions described in Chapter 14.

Exercise Ten-14

Subject: Personal Use Property

During the current year, Martha Steward disposes of several items. The proceeds of disposition and the adjusted cost base of the various items are as follows:

	Adjusted Cost Base	Proceeds Of Disposition
Sailboat	$43,000	$68,000
Oil Painting	200	25,000
Personal Automobile	33,000	18,000
Diamond Necklace	46,000	23,000

What is the net tax consequence of these dispositions?

End of Exercise. Solution available in Study Guide.

Gains And Losses On Foreign Currency
Introduction

10-113. As foreign currency exchange rates are constantly fluctuating, any taxpayer that engages in foreign currency transactions is certain to experience gains and losses that relate to these fluctuations. With respect to dealing with the tax aspects of foreign currency transactions, there are two basic issues:

Income Vs. Capital Transactions If a foreign exchange gain or loss arises as the result of an income transaction (i.e., buying or selling goods or services with the amounts denominated in foreign currency), the full amount will be taxable or deductible. In contrast, if a foreign exchange gain or loss arises as the result of a capital transaction (i.e., purchase of, sale of, or financing of, a capital asset), only one-half of the amount will be taxable or deductible.

Regular Vs. Foreign Currency Capital Gains The issue here is whether the gain on a particular capital transaction is a regular capital gain as defined in ITA 39(1) or, alternatively, a "capital gain or loss in respect of foreign currencies" as described in ITA 39(2). While this is not a major issue, for individuals, the first $200 of the total gains for the year under ITA 39(2) can be excluded from income.

Foreign Currency Income Transactions

10-114.   Foreign currency income transactions usually result in exchange gains and losses. For example, if an enterprise acquires goods in the U.S. for US$5,000 at a point in time when US$1.00 = C$1.10, no gain or loss would arise if the goods were paid for immediately. However, if the goods are paid for at a later point in time when US$1.00 = C$1.07, there would be an exchange gain of C$150 [(US$5,000)(C$1.10 - C$1.07)]. The issue here is whether the gain should be recognized only when the payable is settled or, alternatively, accrued if a Balance Sheet date occurs before the payment.

10-115.   IT-95R indicates that, with respect to income transactions, the taxpayer can use any method that is in accordance with generally accepted accounting principles (GAAP). Under Section 1651 of the *CICA Handbook*, "Foreign Currency Translation", current payables and receivables must be recorded at current rates of exchange as at each Balance Sheet date.

10-116.   The resulting changes in value must be recorded as gains or losses at the time they are measured. As this is the only acceptable method under GAAP, this would appear to require that foreign exchange gains and losses on income transactions be taken into income on an accrual basis, rather than waiting until the foreign exchange balance is settled in Canadian dollars.

Capital Transactions Involving Foreign Currency Financing

10-117.   Purchases or sales of capital assets may be financed with long-term payables or receivables that are denominated in a foreign currency. In such situations, the foreign exchange gains and losses on the payables or receivables are considered to be capital gains or losses.

10-118.   The accounting rules here are consistent with those applicable to income transactions. That is, Section 1651 of the *CICA Handbook* requires that changes in the value of payables and receivables be recognized and taken into income as of each Balance Sheet date.

10-119.   It is somewhat surprising that the CRA does not permit this approach. While it does not address the issue of gains and losses on long-term receivables, Paragraph 13 of IT-95R states that:

> The Department considers that a taxpayer has "made a gain" or "sustained a loss" in a foreign currency ... resulting in the application of subsection 39(2) ...

> (c) at the time of repayment of part or all of a capital debt obligation.

10-120.   This means that, if a Canadian company has used long-term foreign currency debt to finance capital assets, no exchange gain or loss will be included in the determination of Net Income For Tax Purposes until the debt matures and is paid off in Canadian dollars. This may result in significant differences between accounting Net Income and Net Income For Tax Purposes.

Foreign Currency Purchase And Sale Of Capital Assets

10-121.   Individuals will most commonly encounter foreign exchange gains or losses when they are involved in purchasing or selling securities with settlement amounts denominated in a foreign currency. For purposes of distinguishing between ordinary capital gains and those that can be classified under ITA 39(2) as being in respect of foreign currencies, IT-95R provides the following examples of the time when the Department considers a transaction resulting in the application of ITA 39(2) to have taken place:

> (a) At the time of conversion of funds in a foreign currency into another foreign currency or into Canadian dollars.

> (b) At the time funds in a foreign currency are used to make a purchase or a payment (in such a case the gain or loss would be the difference between the value of the foreign currency expressed in Canadian dollars when it arose and its value expressed in Canadian dollars when the purchase or payment was made).

10-122. An example will serve to illustrate this approach:

Example On August 1, 2004, Mr. Conrad White uses $202,000 to open a British pound (£) account with his broker. At this time, £1 = $2.02, so that his $202,000 is converted to £100,000.

On December 31, 2004, he uses his entire British pound balance to acquire 10,000 shares in a British company, Underling Ltd. at a cost of £10 per share. At this time, £1 = $2.04. On July 1, 2007, the shares are sold for £21 per share. On this date, £1 = $2.05, and all of the proceeds from the sale are immediately converted into Canadian dollars ($430,500).

Analysis - Purchase As a result of his December 31, 2004 purchase, he will have an exchange gain of $2,000 [(£100,000)($2.04 - $2.02)]. As this qualifies as an ITA 39(2) foreign currency capital gain (see Paragraph 10-113), Mr. White will only include $900 [(1/2)($2,000 - $200)] of this in his Net Income For Tax Purposes.

Analysis - Sale When he sells the shares for £21 per share, his total capital gain is $226,500 [(£210,000)($2.05) - (£100,000)($2.04)]. This entire amount would be treated as an ITA 39(1) (regular) capital gain and would not be eligible for the $200 exclusion that is available to individuals. This result is not influenced by the conversion of the British currency into Canadian dollars. However, if the £210,000 proceeds were not converted and, at a later point in time, were converted into Canadian dollars at a rate other than £1 = $2.05, an ITA 39(2) foreign currency capital gain or loss would arise.

10-123. Without going into detail, these procedures are not consistent with GAAP or reasonable economic analysis. Under GAAP, no gain would be recognized at the time of the share purchase, resulting in a gain at the time of sale of $228,500 [(£210,000)($2.05) - (£100,000)($2.02)].

Funds On Deposit

10-124. IT-95R also notes that foreign currency funds on deposit are not considered to be disposed of until they are converted into another currency, or are used to purchase a negotiable instrument or some other asset. This means that foreign funds on deposit may be moved from one form of deposit to another, as long as such funds can continue to be viewed as "on deposit".

Exercise Ten-15

Subject: Foreign Currency Gains And Losses

On January 5, 2006, Mr. Michel Pratt purchases 35,000 Trinidad/Tobago dollars (TT$) at a rate of TT$1 = C$0.18. Using TT$30,600 of these funds, on June 5, 2006, he acquires 450 shares of a Trinidadian company, Matim Inc., at a price of TT$68 per share. At this time, TT$1 = C$0.20. During September, 2007, the shares are sold for TT$96 per share. The Trinidad/Tobago dollars are immediately converted into Canadian dollars at a rate of TT$1 = C$0.21. What amounts will be included in Mr. Pratt's 2006 and 2007 Net Income For Tax Purposes as a result of these transactions?

End of Exercise. Solution available in Study Guide.

Options

10-125. The term "option" would include stock rights, warrants, options to purchase capital assets, as well as stock options granted to executives and other employees (the special rules related options granted to employees were covered in Chapter 5). From the point of view of the taxpayer acquiring these options, they are treated as capital property. The tax consequences related to such option will vary depending on future events:

- If they are sold before their expiry date, a capital gain or loss will usually arise.
- If they are exercised, the cost of acquiring the options will be added to the adjusted cost base of the assets acquired.
- If the options expire before they are either sold or exercised, a capital loss equal to the cost of the options will be incurred.

10-126.   From the point of view of the issuer of the option, any proceeds from the sale of the option will usually be treated as a capital gain at the time the option is issued. If the holder decides to exercise the option, the sale price of the option becomes part of the proceeds of disposition to the issuer and the original gain on the sale of the option is eliminated. If the sale of the option occurs in a different taxation year than the exercise of the option, the issuer is permitted to file an amended return for the year of sale.

10-127.   An example will serve to illustrate the preceding rules.

Example   John Powers has a capital property with an adjusted cost base of $250,000. During 2007, he sells an option on this property to Sarah Myers for $18,000. This option allows her to acquire the capital property for $300,000 at any time prior to December 31, 2010.

Analysis - Option Expires   Mr. Powers, as a result of selling the option in 2007, will have to record a taxable capital gain of $9,000 [(1/2)($18,000)] in that year. If the option expires, there will be no further tax consequences to Mr. Powers as he has already recognized the $9,000 taxable capital gain in 2007. For Ms. Myers, the expiry of the option will allow her to recognize an allowable capital loss of $9,000.

Analysis - Option Is Exercised   If the option is exercised in 2010, Mr. Powers can file an amended return for 2007, removing the capital gain that was recognized in that year. However, if he does, he will have to include the $18,000 in the proceeds of disposition from the sale of the asset, thereby recording a capital gain of $68,000 ($18,000 + $300,000 - $250,000). Ms. Myers will have acquired the capital property at a cost of $318,000 ($300,000 + $18,000).

10-128.   There are two exceptions to the preceding general rules for vendors of options. The first of these is an exemption from taxation on the proceeds of any options sold on a taxpayer's principal residence.

10-129.   The second involves options sold by a corporation on its capital stock or debt securities. In this situation, the corporation will not be taxed on the proceeds at the time the options are sold. Rather, the proceeds will be treated as part of the consideration for the securities issued if the options are exercised. However, if the options expire without being exercised, the corporation will have a capital gain equal to the amount of the proceeds.

Capital Gains And Tax Planning

10-130.   The capital gains area offers many opportunities for effective tax planning since the realization of capital gains or losses is largely at the discretion of the taxpayer. If the taxpayer desires that gains or losses fall into a particular taxation year, this can often be accomplished by deferring the disposition of the relevant asset until that period. This means that gains can often be deferred until, perhaps retirement, when the taxpayer may be in a lower tax bracket.

10-131.   Other examples of tax planning would include selling securities with accrued losses in order to offset gains realized earlier in the taxation year, and deferring until after the end of the year the sale of any asset on which there is a significant capital gain.

10-132.   Tax planning for capital gains is more complex if an individual owns small business corporation shares or a farm or fishing property. This is due to the fact that such properties may be eligible for the $750,000 lifetime capital gains deduction. Additional complications result from the application of capital losses, particularly with respect to carry overs of such amounts. These issues are discussed in Chapter 14.

Capital Property And The GST

GST Definition

10-133.   Chapter 4 provided general coverage of the GST. This Chapter covers the application of the GST to capital acquisitions and dispositions. For GST purposes, capital property includes any property that is capital property for income tax purposes. This includes any property on which CCA may be claimed as well as any property that, if disposed of, would result in a capital gain or loss.

10-134.   Excluded from the definition of capital property is property included in CCA Classes 12, 14, and 44. Class 12 includes assets such as small tools, dishes, cutlery, software, and video tapes, while Class 14 includes patents, franchises, concessions and licenses with a limited life. Class 44 includes property that is a patent, or right to use patented information, for a limited or unlimited period.

10-135.   Capital property is divided into two principal groups for the purposes of the GST — capital real property and capital personal property. Different rules apply to each group of property with respect to the collection of GST by the vendor, and to the availability of input tax credits to the purchaser.

10-136.   Capital real property includes land, buildings, mobile homes, and interests therein. Capital personal property includes all other capital properties. Examples of capital personal property include the following assets, provided they are not being held for resale:

- store fixtures, display shelving, and shopping carts
- office furniture, photocopiers, laser printers, and offset presses
- refrigerators, freezers, and ovens used by restaurants and grocery stores
- computers, cash registers, telephone systems, and cellular phones
- machinery and equipment used in production processes

Input Tax Credits On Capital Personal Property

10-137.   When capital property is purchased for use in a commercial activity, input tax credits can be claimed for any GST paid on the purchase. As input tax credits are not matched against amounts of GST collected on the purchaser's revenues, the full amount of GST paid on purchases of capital assets, including real property, becomes a potential input tax credit at the time of purchase. There is no need to amortize the credit, or to wait until such time as the asset is actually paid for.

10-138.   Input tax credits on capital personal property are restricted in that the assets must be used primarily (defined as more than 50 percent) for commercial activity, including both fully taxable and zero-rated activities. If this condition is met, all of the GST paid on acquisition can be claimed as an input tax credit. If this condition is not met, no part of the GST paid on the acquisition of capital personal property can be claimed as an input tax credit. If, in a particular reporting period, the asset ceases to meet this test, there will be a deemed disposition at the fair market value to which the GST will be applied.

10-139.   If an existing asset, which did not meet the criteria of primary use for commercial activity in earlier periods, meets it in the current period, an input tax credit will be available based on the lesser of the GST paid at acquisition and the GST on the fair market value of the asset at the time of its change in use.

Input Tax Credits On Capital Real Property

10-140.   The rules governing how input tax credits can be claimed on the purchase of capital real property depend on whether the registrant is an individual, a partner, or another business. For corporations, input tax credits are available on the purchase of real property in proportion to its use for commercial activity, unless the property is used less than 10 percent, or more than 90 percent, for commercial purposes. If the commercial usage is 90 percent or more, 100 percent of the input tax credit can be claimed.

10-141.   There is a special rule that is applicable to individuals and partners. If the capital real property is used primarily (50 percent or more) for personal use and enjoyment, no input tax credit can be claimed on the property. This would be the case even if commercial usage was 49 percent. The available input tax credit would still be nil.

10-142.   Assuming the overall business use tests are met, when there is a significant (defined as 10 percent or more) increase in commercial use, an input tax credit will be available on the new portion. It will be based essentially on a pro rata share of the lesser of the GST paid at the time of acquisition, and the GST that would be paid on the asset's current fair market value. Similarly, if the proportion of use decreases by 10 percent or more, there will be a deemed disposition, with GST applicable on a pro rata share of the lesser of the asset's original cost and its value at the time of the change.

Sales Of Capital Personal Property
General Rules
10-143.   In general, the sale or resale of capital personal property is subject to GST. GST applies regardless of whether the asset is sold outright or is traded in. Sale of equipment that was used in zero-rated activities, such as in a grocery, prescription drug, or agricultural business, is also subject to GST on resale or trade-in. There are some exceptions for large equipment used in farming and fishing, which may be sold on a zero-rated basis.

10-144.   When capital property is sold that was previously used in taxable activities for less than 50 percent of the time, the vendor is not required to collect GST as the vendor would not have been entitled to an input tax credit at the time of purchase. For example, if a computer was used 30 percent of the time to provide taxable supplies and 70 percent of the time to provide tax exempt supplies, no input tax credit would be available at the time of purchase, and GST would not be collected when it is sold.

Vehicle Sales With Trade-Ins
10-145.   The GST treatment of vehicle sales requires clarification when there is a trade-in associated with the purchase of a vehicle. In most provinces, the trade-in and purchase of a vehicle are considered to be a single transaction for provincial sales tax (PST) purposes. The PST is applied to the difference between the selling price of the new vehicle and the trade-in value. Effectively, PST applies only on the net amount after the trade-in.

10-146.   For vehicles traded in by non-registrants, or registrants who are not required to charge the GST on the trade-in because they engage in a combination of taxable and exempt activities, the tax is applied in a fashion similar to PST. That is, GST is charged on the difference between the selling price of the new vehicle and the value of the trade-in.

10-147.   When a registrant, who claimed an input tax credit on the initial vehicle purchase, trades it in on the purchase of another vehicle, the trade-in and purchase are viewed as two separate transactions. In effect, the registrant sells the trade-in vehicle to the dealer, collecting the applicable GST. He then purchases a vehicle from the dealer, paying the applicable GST. The dealer will charge GST on the full price of the new vehicle and the purchaser will charge GST on the full trade-in value. Both the dealer and the purchaser will usually be able to claim input tax credits for the GST paid.

10-148.   A final point on vehicle transactions relates to trade-ins of Class 10.1 vehicles (cars costing more than a prescribed amount ($30,000 for 2001 through 2007). When such vehicles are purchased, input tax credits are not available on any portion of the cost of the vehicle that exceeds the prescribed amount. For example, if a business purchased a $100,000 passenger vehicle in 2007, $6,000 in GST would be paid. However, the input tax credit would be limited to $1,800 [(6%)($30,000)].

10-149.   When such vehicles are traded in, a special rule provides for an input tax credit for the trade-in amount in excess of the prescribed amount. Continuing our example, if the business received a trade-in allowance of $50,000 on the $100,000 vehicle, an input tax credit of $1,200 would be available [(6%)($50,000 - $30,000)].

Sale Of All Capital Assets Of A Business

10-150.   If a person is selling a business, and all or substantially all of the assets that are necessary to carry on that business are being transferred, an election can be filed to not collect the GST on the sale of the assets. The details of this election are included in our coverage of how the GST affects the sale of the assets or shares of a business in Chapter 19.

Sales Of Capital Real Property

Exemptions

10-151.   Special rules apply to the collection and remittance of GST when real property (i.e., land and buildings) is sold. The special treatment begins with a number of exemptions for particular types of transactions. These include:

- **Sale Of Used Residential Units**   These sales are exempt from GST. By contrast, the sale of new residential housing is taxable. There is, however, a partial rebate on new housing that will be explained beginning in Paragraph 10-158.

- **Sale Of Personal Use Real Property**   Included in this category are cottages and other vacation or recreational properties. The sale of personal use property is exempt from GST when it was not used in a business of the vendor.

- **Certain Sales Of Farmland**   Sales of farmland to related individuals or family farm corporations are often not taxable.

- **Sales And Rentals Of Real Property By Charities, Not-For-Profit Organizations And Other Public Service Bodies**   Usually, sales of real property by these organizations are exempt. However, if the property has been used in a commercial activity, then its resale is taxable.

Responsibility For GST Payment

10-152.   As a general rule, vendors are required to collect GST on behalf of the government. However, for certain real property transactions, the purchaser, rather than the vendor, is responsible for remitting the related GST directly to the CRA. This occurs when:

- the vendor is a non-resident of Canada or,
- the sale does not involve a residential complex being sold to an individual.

10-153.   If the above conditions are met and the purchaser is registered for GST, the purchaser is responsible for determining and remitting the net GST owing on any taxable real property transaction. For example, if a GST registered corporation purchases a warehouse from another GST registered corporation, the purchaser self-assesses the GST owing on the purchase. If the purchaser can claim an offsetting input tax credit, there will effectively be no GST outlay on the purchase as the GST charged on the purchase and the corresponding input tax credit are reflected on the same GST return.

10-154.   If the preceding conditions are not met (e.g., the purchaser is not registered for the GST), the vendor will be required to collect the GST on a taxable sale of real property, even if the vendor is not registered.

Timing Of Liability

10-155.   When there is a sale of capital real property, GST is generally payable on the earlier of the day the purchaser of the taxable property is required, under a written agreement, to pay the vendor for the property, and the date of payment.

Other Taxable Supplies

10-156.   Payments required under commercial rental or leasing agreements are dealt with as a taxable supply. In addition, the GST applies to commissions or fees charged by real estate brokers, lawyers, and appraisers for services provided when property is bought or sold.

10-157.   If the vendor is a registrant who uses the Quick Method, the assigned percentage rate does not apply to tax collected on the sale of real property. Instead, the full 6 percent GST on the sale must be remitted.

Residential Property And The New Housing Rebate

General Rules

10-158.   Residential real estate is an area of considerable importance to most Canadians. Given this, it is not surprising that residential real estate is provided special treatment under the GST legislation.

10-159.   In somewhat simplified terms, GST applies to residential property only on the first sale of a new home. If this new home is resold in substantially unaltered condition, no GST will apply on this later transaction. If the owner undertakes renovations, GST will be charged on the materials and other costs going into the renovation. By contrast, if a used home is acquired and substantial renovations are made before the home is lived in by the purchaser, the acquisition will be treated as a new home purchase and the transaction will be taxable for GST purposes.

New Housing Rebate

10-160.   While sales of new homes attract GST at the full 6 percent rate, the government provides a rebate equal to 36 percent of the GST paid for a primary place of residence.

10-161.   With its traditional aversion to providing tax incentives related to luxury expenditures, the government has limited this rebate to a maximum value of $7,560, the amount of GST at 6 percent on a $350,000 home [(36%)(6%)($350,000) = $7,560]. In addition, the rebate is phased out for houses costing more than $350,000 and completely eliminated for homes costing more than $450,000. All of these amounts are before the inclusion of GST.

10-162.   The government's policy goals are accomplished by calculating the rebate as follows:

$$[A][(\$450,000 - B) \div \$100,000]$$

Where:
A = The lesser of 36 percent of the GST paid and $7,560; and
B = The greater of $350,000 and the cost of the home.

10-163.   A simple example will illustrate the application of this formula.

Example On November 1, 2007, Gilles and Marie Gagnon acquire a new home with a cost of $420,000, paying an additional amount in GST of $25,200 [(6%)($420,000)].

Analysis As 36 percent of the GST paid is $9,072, an amount in excess of the limit of $7,560, the rebate available to Gilles and Marie will be $2,268 {[$7,560][($450,000 - $420,000) ÷ $100,000]}.

Implementation

10-164.   While the GST could be included in the price paid by the home purchaser, with that individual claiming the rebate, this is not the usual industry practice. The usual practice is for the builder to charge the purchaser an amount that is net of the rebate, with the purchaser assigning rights to the GST rebate to the builder. In the case of our example, the builder would charge Gilles and Marie $442,932 ($420,000 + $25,200 - $2,268). From the point of view of convenience for the purchaser, this appears to be an appropriate practice.

10-165.   The cost of improvements subsequent to the purchase of a new residence will generally be taxed at the full 6 percent GST rate. To be eligible for the new residence rebate, the improvements must be done by the builder and be included in the overall price of the residence.

Appendices To Chapter 10

10-166.   This Chapter contains three Appendices that cover the following specialized topics:

- Appendix A: **Application Of The Median Rule**
- Appendix B: **Disposition Of Shares Acquired With Stock Options**
- Appendix C: **Election For Pre-1982 Residences**

Key Terms Used In This Chapter

10-167.   The following is a list of the key terms used in this Chapter. These terms, and their meanings, are compiled in the Glossary Of Key Terms located at the back of the separate paper Study Guide and on the Student CD-ROM.

Adjusted Cost Base	Personal Use Property
Allowable Capital Loss	Principal Residence
Capital Asset	Proceeds Of Disposition
Capital Cost	Recapture Of CCA
Capital Gain	Replacement Property Rules
Capital Gains Reserve	Reserve
Capital Loss	Rollover
Deemed Disposition	Small Business Corporation
Disposition	Superficial Loss - ITA 54
Former Business Property	Taxable Capital Gain
Identical Property Rules	Terminal Loss
Involuntary Disposition	Undepreciated Capital Cost (UCC)
Listed Personal Property	

From Chapter 10 - Appendix A
Median Rule
Valuation Day (V-Day)

References

10-168.   For more detailed study of the material in this Chapter, we would refer you to the following:

ITA 38	Taxable Capital Gain And Allowable Capital Loss
ITA 39	Meaning Of Capital Gain And Capital Loss
ITA 40	General Rules
ITA 41	Taxable Net Gain From Disposition Of Listed Personal Property
ITA 42	Dispositions Subject To Warranties
ITA 43	General Rule For Part Dispositions
ITA 44	Exchanges Of Property
ITA 44.1	Definitions (Eligible Small Business Shares)
ITA 45	Property With More Than One Use
ITA 46	Personal Use Property
ITA 47	Identical Properties
ITA 49	Granting Of Options
ITA 53	Adjustments To Cost Base
ITA 54	Definitions (Capital Gains)
IC 88-2	General Anti-Avoidance Rule — Section 245 Of The Income Tax Act
IT-66R6	Capital Dividends
IT-88R2	Stock Dividends
IT-95R	Foreign Exchange Gains And Losses
IT-96R6	Options Granted By Corporations To Acquire Shares, Bonds Or Debentures And By Trusts To Acquire Trust Units
IT-102R2	Conversion Of Property, Other Than Real Property, From Or To Inventory
IT-104R3	Deductibility Of Fines Or Penalties
IT-120R6	Principal Residence
IT-159R3	Capital Debts Established To Be Bad Debts
IT-259R4	Exchanges Of Property
IT-262R2	Losses Of Non-Residents And Part-Year Residents
IT-264R	Part Dispositions
IT-268R4	Inter Vivos Transfer Of Farm Property To A Child
IT-297R2	Gifts In Kind To Charity And Others
IT-381R3	Trusts — Capital Gains And Losses And The Flow Through Of Taxable Capital Gains To Beneficiaries
IT-387R2	Meaning Of Identical Properties
IT-403R	Options On Real Estate
IT-418	Capital Cost Allowance — Partial Dispositions Of Property
IT-437R	Ownership Of Property (Principal Residence)
IT-456R	Capital Property — Some Adjustments To Cost Base
IT-479R	Transactions In Securities
IT-484R2	Business Investment Losses
IT-491	Former Business Property

Appendix A: Application Of The Median Rule

10A-1.   For many years after 1971, an understanding of pre-1972 transitional rules was essential for tax practitioners. However, at this point in time, pre-1972 asset dispositions are no longer common. Since they do still occur and, in some cases, have significant tax consequences, we have included this brief Appendix in the text in order to alert you to the potential problems that can arise.

Assets Acquired Before 1972

Concept Of Valuation Day (V-Day)

10A-2.   Prior to 1972 there was no taxation of capital gains. However, there was a problem with the introduction of capital gains taxation in that many taxpayers were holding assets that had already experienced accrued capital gains prior to the end of 1971.

10A-3.   As an example, assume that Mr. Munro purchased a piece of land in 1965 for $15,000 and sold it on January 1, 1972 for $25,000. As it is clear that the resulting gain of $10,000 accrued prior to the introduction of capital gains taxation, it would not be equitable to assess Mr. Munro for taxes on this $10,000 capital gain.

10A-4.   In order to avoid retroactive application of taxation on capital gains that accrued prior to 1972, the Federal Government established the concept of valuation day (V-Day). For publicly traded securities, V-Day was December 22, 1971. For other types of capital property, V-Day is specified to be December 31, 1971.

Application Of The Median Rule

10A-5.   For non-depreciable capital assets that were owned by a taxpayer on December 31, 1971, the relevant transitional legislation states that the adjusted cost base for the asset will be the median value of three amounts:

- the proceeds of disposition,
- the actual cost of the asset, and
- the valuation day value of the asset.

10A-6.   Consider an asset acquired on December 31, 1968 at a cost of $500. As of V-Day, its value has increased to $700 and, during 2007, it is sold for $2,000. The capital gain would be calculated as follows:

Proceeds Of Disposition	$2,000
Adjusted Cost Base (Median Of $500, $700, And $2,000)	(700)
Capital Gain	$1,300

10A-7.   As this simple example illustrates, the median rule limits the gain to the amount that accrued after the introduction of capital gains taxation in Canada. The pre V-Day accrual of $200 ($700 - $500) is realized on a tax free basis. Similar results will be achieved when capital losses are involved, so that only the capital loss accruing after V-Day is deductible.

Appendix B: Disposition Of Shares Acquired With Stock Options

Shares Deemed Not Identical Properties

10B-1.   In the text of this Chapter, we noted the general rule under ITA 47(1) which states that the adjusted cost base for identical properties is equal to the average cost of all such properties that have been acquired. For example, if Mark acquired 50 common shares of Quron Ltd. for $45 per share and another 75 shares of the Company for $58 per share, the adjusted cost base of each of these 125 shares would be $52.80 {[(50)($45) + (75)($58)] ÷ (75 + 50)}.

10B-2.   This is the value that would be used in determining the amount of any capital gain or loss on a subsequent disposition of all or part of the 125 shares acquired, if there are no other acquisitions of these shares. Given the use of this average cost, the question of which shares are being sold is not a relevant issue.

10B-3.   There is, however, a problem in situations where an employment income inclusion has been deferred from the time an option has been exercised until the time when the acquired shares are sold. In situations such as this, the disposition not only triggers a capital gain or loss, it also ends the deferral of the employment income inclusion. If a taxpayer is holding shares on which an employment income deferral is present, as well as other shares that are identical except for the deferral, the question of which shares are being sold can become very important.

10B-4.   To deal with this problem, ITA 47(3) deems the deferral shares not to be identical properties under ITA 47(1). This means that the cost averaging rule is not applicable and each block of deferral shares can be separately identified and will have a unique adjusted cost base. This unique adjusted cost base will be used to determine any capital gain or loss on the disposition of the shares. While there are other more technical applications, the most important deferral securities to which ITA 47(3) applies are:

- Shares of a Canadian controlled private corporation acquired through options. While the employment income inclusion on these shares is measured at the time of exercise, its inclusion in Net Income For Tax Purposes is usually deferred until the shares are sold.

- Shares of a public company acquired through options, if an election has been filed to defer the employment income inclusion. The election defers the employment income inclusion on up to $100,000 worth of publicly traded shares from the time the shares are acquired through exercising the options, until the acquired shares are actually sold.

10B-5.   ITA 7(1.3) establishes the order in which deferral and non-deferral shares are sold and specifies the following:

- When there is a disposition by a taxpayer holding both deferral and non-deferral shares, the non-deferral shares are considered to be sold first. This rule applies even in situations where the non-deferral shares were acquired after the deferral shares.

- After all non-deferral shares have been disposed of, if the taxpayer has deferral shares that were acquired at different points in time, the assumption for subsequent dispositions is that the shares will be sold in the order they were acquired (First-In, First-Out).

- In situations where the taxpayer has acquired identical deferral shares at a single point in time, but under different option arrangements, subsequent dispositions will be based on the assumption that the sales occur in the order the options were granted.

Appendix B: Disposition Of Shares Acquired With Stock Options

Example

10B-6.   The following example illustrates the preceding rules:

Example   Mark is an employee of Quron Ltd., a Canadian public company. During 2004, he purchases 50 shares of the Company for $45 per share through his discount stockbroker and in February, 2005 he acquires an additional 75 shares for $58. This provides an average cost for these shares of $52.80 {[(50)($45) + (75)($58)] ÷ (75 + 50)}.

During 2005, Mark becomes a member of his employer's stock option plan. In April, 2005, he is granted options to buy 10 shares at $50 per share. In October, 2005, he is granted additional options for 15 shares at $58 per share. In March, 2006, he is granted options to acquire a further 25 shares at $40 per share. In all cases, the option price was equal to the fair market value of the shares at the time the options were granted and the options vest immediately.

On July 1, 2007, Mark exercises the March, 2006 options. At this time, the shares are selling for $45 per share. On December 1, 2007, he exercises both the April, 2005 options and the October, 2005 options. At this time the shares are selling for $85 per share. Mark files an election with his employer to defer all of the employment income related to the exercise of the options. The total amount deferred by the election would be as follows:

Exercise Date	Grant Date	Amount Deferred
July 1, 2007	March, 2006	[(25)($45 - $40)] = $125
December 1, 2007	April, 2005	[(10)($85 - $50)] = 350
December 1, 2007	October, 2005	[(15)($85 - $58)] = 405
Total		$880

During 2008, Mark sells 100 of his Quron Ltd. shares for $110 per share. During 2009, he sells a further 35 shares for $120 per share. During 2010, he sells 25 shares for $95 per share. During 2011, he sells his remaining 15 shares for $32 per share.

2007 Tax Consequences   Other than the fact that his T4 will indicate a deferral of $880 of employment income, there are no tax consequences for Mark in 2007.

2008 Tax Consequences   As required under ITA 7(1.3), the 100 shares sold during 2008 would be from the 125 non-deferral shares that were purchased on the open market. This would result in a taxable capital gain of $2,860 [(100)($110.00 - $52.80)(1/2)].

2008 Tax Consequences   The 35 shares sold in 2008 would consist of the remaining 25 that were acquired on the open market, plus 10 of the 25 shares acquired through the use of the options granted in March, 2006. While these options were granted at a later date than those granted in 2005, they were exercised sooner and, under the ordering rules found in ITA 7(1.3), they would be considered the first sold. The tax consequences of the sale of 35 shares are as follows:

Taxable Capital Gains:	
Open Market Shares [(25)($120.00 - $52.80)(1/2)]	$ 840
March, 2006 Option Shares [(10)($120.00 - $45.00)(1/2)]	375
Employment Income [(10)($45.00 - $40.00)]	50
ITA 110(1)(d) Deduction [(1/2)($50)]	(25)
Increase In Taxable Income	$1,240

2010 Tax Consequences   The 25 shares sold in 2010 would consist of the remaining 15 shares from the March, 2006 options, plus the 10 shares from the April, 2005 options. As the April and October, 2005 options were exercised on the same date, the choice of the shares from the April options is based on the fact that they were granted at an earlier date. The tax consequences of the sale of the 25 shares would be as follows:

Taxable Capital Gains:	
March, 2006 Options [(15)($95.00 - $45.00)(1/2)]	$375.00
April, 2005 Options [(10)($95.00 - $85.00)(1/2)]	50.00
Employment Income:	
March, 2006 Options [(15)($45.00 - $40.00)]	75.00
April, 2005 Options [(10)($85.00 - $50.00)]	350.00
ITA 110(1)(d) Deduction [(1/2)($75 + $350)]	(212.50)
Increase In Taxable Income	**$637.50**

2011 Tax Consequences   When the remaining 15 shares are sold, they would all be from the October, 2005 options. The tax consequences of the sale would be as follows:

Employment Income [(15)($85.00 - $58.00)]	$405.00
ITA 110(1)(d) Deduction [(1/2)($405)]	(202.50)
Increase In Taxable Income	**$202.50**

Allowable Capital Loss [(15)($32.00 - $85.00)(1/2)]	($397.50)

Note that we have not netted these two amounts. This reflects the fact that the allowable capital loss cannot be deducted against employment income.

Exercise Ten-16

Subject: Sale Of Deferral Shares

On December 31, 2006, Jean Martine owns 500 shares of his employer's common stock. These shares were acquired through purchases on a listed stock exchange at an average cost of $23.50 per share. At this time, he is also holding options to acquire an additional 500 shares at $20 per share. These options are fully vested and were granted at a time when the market price of the shares was $20 per share. On January 15, 2007, when the shares are trading at $35 per share, he exercises options to acquire 250 shares. On October 3, 2007, when the shares are trading at $50 per share, he exercises the remaining options to acquire another 250 shares. He makes the appropriate election to defer all of the employment income arising on these two transactions. During 2008, he sells 700 shares at $55 per share. During 2009, he sells the remaining 300 shares at $30 per share. Determine the tax consequences of these transactions for each of the years 2007, 2008 and 2009.

End of Exercise. Solution available in Study Guide.

Appendix C: Election For Pre-1982 Residences

10C-1.   At this point in time, situations where the ITA 40(6) election on pre-1982 residences are relevant are no longer common. Since they can still occur and, in some cases, have significant tax consequences, we have included this brief Appendix in the text in order to alert you to the existence of this election.

10C-2.   Before 1982, both spouses were allowed to have a principal residence. This meant that a second property which was owned by a married couple could also escape capital gains taxation. It is no longer possible to have more than one principal residence per family unit.

10C-3.   When this change was introduced in 1982, it was recognized that it could have some retroactive effect on real estate purchases made in earlier years on the assumption that they would always be treated as principal residences. To mitigate this effect, ITA 40(6) contains a transitional provision. It provides an election that allows the taxpayer to calculate his gain on the actual sale of a principal residence on the assumption that there was a deemed disposition and reacquisition of the residence on December 31, 1981 at fair market value. This allows the gain to be split into two components — a pre-1982 component and a post-1981 component. Note, however, there is no plus one in the numerator of the reduction formula for the post-1981 component of the gain.

10C-4.   When a taxpayer owns more than one property that could qualify as a principal residence (e.g., a city home and a cottage), this election may help minimize the portion of capital gains on the properties that will have to be taken into income. The following example serves to illustrate this point:

Example   Ms. Jones acquired both a cottage and a city home on June 30, 1976. Both properties are sold on July 1, 2007. Relevant information is as follows:

	Cottage	City Home
Cost - June 30, 1976	$ 50,000	$110,000
Fair Market Value - December 31, 1981	80,000	120,000
Proceeds Of Disposition - July 1, 2007	120,000	240,000
Selling Costs	7,200	13,200

10C-5.   If one only considers the full 32 year period from 1976 through 2007 and applies ITA 40(2)(b), the city home experiences the larger gain and would be designated the principal residence for 31 of the 32 years. The result of this designation would be as follows:

Capital Gain Without ITA 40(6) Election

	Cottage	City Home
Proceeds Of Disposition	$120,000	$240,000
Adjusted Cost Base	(50,000)	(110,000)
Selling Costs	(7,200)	(13,200)
Total Capital Gain	$ 62,800	$116,800
Reduction:		
[$62,800][(1 + 1) ÷ 32]	(3,925)	
[$116,800][(1 + 31) ÷ 32]		(116,800)
Capital Gain After Reduction	$ 58,875	Nil

10C-6.   While the use of ITA 40(2)(b) has eliminated a significant part of the capital gains resulting from the disposition of the two properties, a better solution can be achieved using the election under ITA 40(6). This is because the cottage experienced the larger gain during the pre-1982 period and the city home experienced the larger gain after 1981. The ITA 40(6) election allows the taxpayer to take advantage of this difference. With this election, the results would be as follows:

Capital Gain With ITA 40(6) Election

1976 Through 1981	Cottage	City Home
Fair Market Value - December 31, 1981	$ 80,000	$120,000
Adjusted Cost Base	(50,000)	(110,000)
Total Capital Gain	$ 30,000	$ 10,000
Reduction:		
$30,000 [(5 + 1) ÷ 6)]	(30,000)	
$10,000 [(1 + 1) ÷ 6)]		(3,333)
Capital Gain After Reduction	Nil	$ 6,667

1982 Through 2007	Cottage	City Home
Proceeds Of Disposition - July 1, 2007	$120,000	$240,000
Adjusted Cost Base (Deemed)	(80,000)	(120,000)
Selling Costs	(7,200)	(13,200)
Total Capital Gain	$ 32,800	$106,800
Reduction = $106,800 (26 ÷ 26) (Note)	Nil	(106,800)
Capital Gain After Reduction	$ 32,800	Nil

Note When the ITA 40(6) election is used, the plus one year rule does not apply to the post-1981 period.

10C-7. Using this approach, the non-exempt portion of the capital gain is reduced from $58,875 to $39,467 ($6,667 + $32,800). For someone in a combined federal/provincial tax bracket of 45 percent, this $19,408 reduction will generate a tax savings of $4,367 [($19,408)(1/2)(45%)].

Problems For Self Study

(The solutions for these problems can be found in the separate Study Guide.)

Self Study Problem Ten - 1

Over the past few years, Mr. Hall has taken an interest in the common shares of Clarkson Industries Ltd., a Canadian public company. As he is approaching retirement age and anticipates moving to Florida, he sold his total holding of Clarkson shares on March 15, 2007, when the shares were trading at $174 per share. Over the years, Mr. Hall has had the following transactions in the shares of Clarkson Industries:

- On October 15, 2001, he purchases 5,500 shares at $40 per share.
- On November 8, 2001, he sells 1,500 shares at $52 per share.
- On December 12, 2003, he purchases 3,200 shares at $79 per share.
- On February 3, 2004, he sells 2,600 shares at $94 per share.
- On January 15, 2005, he receives a 10 percent stock dividend that has been paid by Clarkson Industries. As part of this transaction, the Company transfers retained earnings of $99 per share to contributed capital.
- On June 15, 2005, he acquires 3,800 shares at $104 per share.
- On December 23, 2006, he receives a 10 percent stock dividend that has been paid by Clarkson Industries. As part of this transaction, the Company transfers $125 per share from retained earnings to contributed capital.

Required: Determine the amount of the taxable capital gain or allowable capital loss that would arise from:

- the sale on November 8, 2001,
- the sale on February 3, 2004, and
- the sale on March15, 2007.

Ignore transaction costs in all of your calculations.

Self Study Problem Ten - 2

On November 1, 2007, Miss Stevens sells a capital property for $500,000. The adjusted cost base of the property is $230,000 and she incurs selling costs in the amount of $20,000. She receives an immediate cash payment of $200,000 on November 1, 2007, with the balance of the $500,000 to be paid on June 1, 2013.

Required: Calculate the taxable capital gain that would be included in Miss Stevens' Net Income For Tax Purposes for each of the years 2007 through 2013.

Self Study Problem Ten - 3

On January 1, 2007, a fire completely destroys Fraser Industries Ltd.'s Edmonton office building and all of its contents. An immediate settlement is negotiated with the Company's fire and casualty insurer. The insurer agrees to pay $4,800,000 for the building and an additional $1,256,000 for the contents of the building. These amounts represent the estimated fair market values of the destroyed assets and a cheque is received for these amounts on May 15, 2007.

As the City has been acquiring adjacent land for the development of a park, the Company is notified on January 15, 2007 that the land on which the building was located will be expropriated in order to expand the park area. The expropriation takes place on April 30, 2007 and Fraser Industries Ltd. receives $723,000, which is the estimated fair market value of the land.

Other information on the Edmonton property is as follows:

Land The land was acquired in 1988 at a cost of $256,000.

Building The building was constructed during 1990 at a total cost of $3,700,000. It is the only building owned by Fraser Industries Ltd. and, at the beginning of 2007, the UCC in Class 1 was $1,856,000.

Building Contents The contents of the building consisted entirely of Class 8 assets. These assets had an original cost in 1989 of $972,000 and the UCC of Class 8 was $72,000 at the beginning of 2007. Fraser Industries Ltd. does not own any other Class 8 assets.

In replacing the destroyed property, the Company decides to relocate to an area that has lower land costs. As a consequence, a replacement property is found in Hinton at a cost of $6,200,000. It is estimated that the fair market value of the land on which the building is located is $500,000. The remaining $5,700,000 is allocated to the building. The acquisition closes on November 1, 2008 and, during the following month, contents are acquired at a cost of $1,233,000. All of the contents are Class 8 assets.

Fraser Industries has a December 31 year end.

Required:

A. Determine the amounts that would be included in Fraser Industries Ltd.'s 2007 Net Income For Tax Purposes as a result of receiving the insurance and expropriation proceeds.

B. Assume that, in the year ending December 31, 2008, Fraser Industries files an amended 2007 tax return using the elections that are available under ITA 13(4) and ITA 44(1), but not the election under ITA 44(6). Determine the revised amounts that would be included in the Company's 2007 Net Income For Tax Purposes. In addition, indicate the adjusted cost base and, where appropriate, the UCC of the new items of property.

C. Indicate the maximum amount of any reduction in 2007 Net Income For Tax Purposes that could result from the use of the ITA 44(6) election, in addition to the elections under ITA 13(4) and ITA 44(1). Should the Company make the election? Explain your conclusion.

Self Study Problem Ten - 4

Mr. Larson, the president of Larson Distributing Inc., was offered $1,875,000 for the land, building, and equipment used by his business at its suburban Toronto location. As he believed that his business could be operated at a less valuable rural location, he accepts the offer and sells the business property on October 15, 2007. The details relating to this property are as follows:

Land The land was acquired in 1992 at a cost of $137,000. At the time of the sale, it was estimated that the fair market value of the land was $772,000.

Building The building was constructed in 1993 at a total cost of $605,000. At the time of the sale, its UCC was $342,000, while its estimated fair market value was $989,000.

Equipment The equipment had an original cost of $452,000. On October 15, 2007, its UCC was $127,000 and its estimated fair market value was $114,000.

On January 5, 2008 (prior to the filing date for the 2007 tax return), Mr. Larson acquires a replacement property in Barry's Bay at a total cost of $1,500,000. This cost is allocated as follows:

Land	$ 253,000
Building	1,042,000
Equipment	205,000
Total	$1,500,000

The Company would like to defer any capital gains or recapture resulting from the sale of the Toronto property. The Company's tax year ends on December 31, 2007, and it does not own any buildings or equipment on this date.

Required:

A. Indicate the 2007 tax effects related to the sale of the Toronto property, assuming maximum deferrals under ITA 44(1) and 13(4), but no use of the ITA 44(6) election to transfer proceeds between the land and the building. Indicate the adjusted cost base and, where appropriate, the UCC of the three new items of property at the time of acquisition.

B. Indicate the maximum amount of any reduction in Net Income For Tax Purposes that could result from the use of the ITA 44(6) election.

Self Study Problem Ten - 5

Mr. Blake purchased a house on June 30, 1988 at a total cost of $176,000. Mr. and Mrs. Blake and their two teenaged children moved in during the next month. On January 1, 2006, a portion of this property was converted to an apartment, and rented to a tenant at a rate of $850 per month, for a term of 18 months. At the time of this conversion, the fair market value of the total property was $253,000. The apartment was located in the back of the house, faced a busy parking lot, and occupied 32 percent of the total floor space of the property.

On June 30, 2007, at the end of the lease term, Mr. Blake and the tenant agree to reduce the size of the area rented to 21 percent of the total floor space of the property. A new lease is signed with a reduced rent of $750 per month and a new term of 30 months. On June 30, 2007, the fair market value of the property is $278,000. Two months after the new lease is signed, Mr. Blake makes improvements in the rented area of the property at a cost of $12,350.

On June 30, 1988, the fair market value of the land on which the property is situated is $83,000. By January 1, 2006, it has increased to $106,000 and on June 30, 2007, it is estimated to be $110,000.

During the year ending December 31, 2006, Mr. Blake made payments for insurance, hydro, and property taxes on his property in the amount of $5,600. The corresponding figure for the period January 1, 2007 through June 30, 2007 was $2,900. For the period July 1, 2007 through December 31, 2007, this amount was $3,200. There were no repair costs during either 2006 or 2007. Mr. Blake deducts maximum CCA in each year.

Mr. Blake does not make an election under ITA 45(2) with respect to his change in use. (This election deems that the change in use has not occurred.)

Required: For each of the two taxation years 2006 and 2007, indicate the amounts that would be included in Mr. Blake's Net Income For Tax Purposes as the result of the preceding transactions and events.

Self Study Problem Ten - 6

Mr. Stewart Simms has lived most of his life in Vancouver. In 1983, he purchased a three bedroom home near English Bay for $125,000. In 1988, he acquired a cottage in the Whistler ski area at a cost of $40,000. In all subsequent years, he has spent at least a portion of the year living in each of the two locations. When he is not residing in these properties they are left vacant.

On October 1, 2007, Mr. Simms sells the English Bay property for $515,000 and the cottage at Whistler for $320,000.

Required: Calculate the minimum capital gain that Mr. Simms would be required to report as a result of selling the two properties in 2007.

Self Study Problem Ten - 7

Tiffany Inc. is a registrant for GST purposes. In November, 2007, Tiffany Inc. plans to purchase a commercial property in Saskatoon for $10,000,000, before GST. Tiffany's business will occupy 40 percent of the floor space, and 60 percent will be leased to commercial tenants. Tiffany provides taxable and exempt supplies. For general administrative expenses, Tiffany recovers 20 percent of GST paid as input tax credits.

Required: Tiffany Inc. has asked for your advice on:

A. How the GST will apply to the proposed purchase.

B. Whether any special elections can be made to minimize the GST cash outlays to the Company.

C. Whether Tiffany will have to charge GST on the lease.

Self Study Problem Ten - 8

Vivian Driver is planning to purchase a home in September, 2007 and she is considering three properties. The prices of the homes and the costs of any improvements planned, all before GST, commissions, and transfer fees, are as follows:

Property	Purchase Price	Improvements
Shuswap Cedar A-Frame - Used	$120,000	None
Millcreek Bi-Level - New (Note 1)	90,000	$24,000
Sunset Beach Cottage - Used (Note 2)	60,000	56,000

Note 1   As the Millcreek Bi-level is under construction, $14,000 of the improvements would be made by the contractor at the same time as the house is being finished. Then, as a winter project, Vivian would finish the fireplace with a materials cost of $10,000.

Note 2   The Sunset Beach cottage needs to be winterized, requiring the replacement of electrical wiring, wall and roof insulation, and new inside walls. The improvements would be made by a home renovation firm at a GST inclusive cost of $56,000. The renovations would be done by the vendor prior to the purchase and added to the purchase price. The total purchase price would be $116,000 ($60,000 + $56,000).

Required: Before making any offer to purchase, Vivian has asked you to determine what the GST and total out-of-pocket costs of each purchase would be.

Assignment Problems

(The solutions for these problems are only available in
the solutions manual that has been provided to your instructor.)

Assignment Problem Ten - 1

Miss Wells has purchased the shares of two companies over the years. Purchases and sales of shares in the first of these companies, Memo Inc., are as follows:

February, 2003 purchase	60 @ $24
November, 2004 purchase	90 @ 28
April, 2005 purchase	45 @ 30
October, 2005 sale	(68) @ 36
September, 2007 purchase	22 @ 26
November, 2007 sale	(53) @ 40

Purchases and sales of shares in the second company, Demo Ltd., are as follows:

April, 2006 purchase	200 @ $24
December, 2006 purchase	160 @ 33
July, 2007 sale	(260) @ 36

Required:

A. Determine the cost to Miss Wells of the Memo Inc. shares that are still being held on December 31, 2007.

B. Determine the taxable capital gain resulting from the July, 2007 disposition of the Demo Ltd. shares.

Assignment Problem Ten - 2

On May 1, 2006, Mr. Rowe sold a parcel of suburban land to a developer for $2,600,000. The land had cost Mr. Rowe $1,400,000 in 1992, and no additions or improvements had been made to the land. He classifies any gain on the land sale as a capital gain. In order to convince the purchaser that he should pay the full $2,600,000 in cash, Mr. Rowe has agreed to refund a part of the purchase price if less than 100 lots are sold by December 1, 2007. The agreement calls for a refund of $26,000 for each of the 100 lots that is not sold within the specified period. At the time of the sale, Mr. Rowe estimates that he will probably have to pay $104,000 to the purchaser on December 1, 2007.

Over the next two years, a number of plants in the area are closed, substantially reducing the demand for the lots in the development. By December 1, 2007, only 60 lots have been sold and Mr. Rowe is obliged to pay the purchaser $1,040,000 [($26,000)(40 Lots)] as agreed.

Required: Describe the tax effects associated with the guarantee provided by Mr. Rowe at the time the land is sold and with the payment that he is required to make on December 1, 2007. Include the effects of this payment on the Tax Payable of other years.

Assignment Problem Ten - 3

During July, 2006, Mrs. Simpkins sold a painting to a friend for $25,000. She had purchased the painting in 1995 at a cost of $15,000. As her friend was short of cash, Mrs. Simpkins accepted a down payment of $15,000 and a note that required the friend to make a payment of $10,000 at the end of 2007. No interest payments were required on the note and, because Mrs. Simpkins had no other income during 2006, she did not establish a capital gains reserve.

Shortly before the end of 2007, Mrs. Simpkins tried to locate her friend. She was not successful and it appeared that the friend, along with the painting, had disappeared without a trace. As a reflection of this fact, Mrs. Simpkins wishes to write off the bad debt in 2007.

Required: Determine the 2006 and 2007 tax effects resulting from the preceding transactions.

Assignment Problem Ten - 4

Mr. Rhodes purchased a large tract of land on the edge of Edmonton in 1984 for $750,000. It was sold during April, 2007 to a developer for $2,500,000. He receives a down payment of $625,000 and accepts a 25 year, 8 percent mortgage for the balance of $1,875,000. The payments on this mortgage begin in the second year and require the repayment of $75,000 per year in capital.

Mr. Rhodes wishes to use reserves to defer the payment of taxes on capital gains for as long as possible. He classifies any gain on the land sale as a capital gain.

Required: Calculate the capital gains taxation effects of this sale, assuming that Mr. Rhodes deducts the maximum capital gains reserve in 2007 and subsequent years.

Assignment Problem Ten - 5

In 1984, Ms. Gerhardt purchased a substantial parcel of land in northern Ontario at a cost of $600,000. During May, 2007, she sells it for $1,350,000.

The terms of the sale call for a down payment at the time of closing, with Ms. Gerhardt accepting a 9 percent mortgage for the balance of the $1,350,000. The terms of the mortgage require annual payments beginning in the year subsequent to the sale. The payments are designed to include principal payments of 5 percent of the sales price, or $67,500, per year.

Ms. Gerhardt wishes to use reserves to defer the payment of taxes on capital gains for as long as possible.

Required: Compare the capital gains taxation effects of this sale assuming:

A. The down payment was 15 percent of the sales price.

B. The down payment was 45 percent of the sales price.

Assignment Problem Ten - 6

The following two independent Cases involve dispositions of eligible small business corporation shares, with the proceeds being invested in replacement shares.

Case A   On March 31, 2007, Harold sells his shares in Corporation A, which are eligible small business investments. His proceeds of disposition are $100,000 and his capital gain is $60,000. On July 1, 2007, Harold invests $90,000 in shares of Corporation B, which are new eligible small business investments.

Case B   On November 6, 2006, Kate disposes of shares in Corporation C, which are eligible small business investments. Her proceeds of disposition are $1,000,000 and she realizes a capital gain of $600,000. On February 1, 2007, Kate acquires shares in Corporation D, which are new eligible small business investments, at a cost of $1,000,000.

Required: For both Cases, determine the maximum permitted capital gains deferral, as well as the adjusted cost base of the replacement shares.

Assignment Problem Ten - 7

Each of the following independent Cases describes a situation with a proposed tax treatment.

1. Mr. Acker has owned a small triplex for a number of years and, throughout this period, all three of the units have been rented. In determining his income from this property, he has deducted CCA in each year. During the current year, Mr. Acker has moved into one of the three units and, as a result, will be reporting reduced rental revenues in his tax return. As he has not sold any property, he will not report any capital gains or losses during the current year.

2. Mr. Jones has sold a property with an adjusted cost base of $72,000 for total proceeds of $105,000. He is providing a warranty on the property that he estimates will cost him $6,000 to service. As a consequence, he is recognizing a capital gain of $27,000.

3. Ms. Turner sold her dining room table to her daughter for $400 and a painting to her brother for $900. These prices equalled their estimated fair market values. Several years ago, she purchased the table for $950, and the painting for $667. She does not plan to report any capital gain or loss.

4. Mrs. Brown purchased corporate bonds for $11,200, of which $800 was accrued interest and $10,400 represented the principal. The bonds were later sold for $11,600 that includes $200 for accrued interest. Mrs. Brown recognizes a taxable capital gain of $500.

5. Several years ago, Miss Lee transferred three sports cars, with a total value of $182,000, to a corporation in return for all of the shares of the company. The cars are profitably used in her personal escort business. During the current year, all of the cars are destroyed in a fire on her estate. Unfortunately, Miss Lee did not believe that people in her financial position needed insurance and, as a consequence, no compensation was available for the loss. As the corporation had no assets other than the cars, there was no reason for her to continue to hold the shares. In view of this situation, she sells the shares to a friend who requires a corporate shell for some business operations. The sale price is $500 and Miss Lee uses the allowable capital loss of $90,750 [(1/2)($182,000 - $500)] to offset taxable capital gains resulting from real estate transactions.

Required: In each of the preceding Cases, indicate whether or not you believe that the tax treatment being proposed is the correct one. Explain your conclusion.

Assignment Problem Ten - 8

On July 1, 2006, the manufacturing plant of Janchek Ltd. was expropriated by the provincial government in order to make way for a new expressway. It is the only building that Janchek Ltd. owns. The land on which the plant was situated was purchased in 1994 for $88,000. The building, a Class 1 asset, was erected in 1995 at a cost of $290,000. The Company's year end is December 31.

On November 23, 2006, after extended negotiations between Janchek and the provincial government, the Company received compensation in the amount of $130,000 for the land and $430,000 for the building. On January 1, 2006, the UCC balance in Class 1 was $248,000.

On June 20, 2007, a new manufacturing plant was purchased for a total cost of $1,050,000. Of this amount, $210,000 was allocated to the land, with the remaining $840,000 going to the building.

Janchek Ltd. will make any available elections in order to reduce the tax effects of the replacement of the expropriated property.

Required:

A. Explain the tax effects of the receipt of compensation resulting from the expropriation.

B. Calculate the adjusted cost base for the land and the building, and the UCC of the building after the 2007 replacement occurs, but before the deduction of CCA for the year.

Assignment Problem Ten - 9

On August 1, 1998, Ms. Marnie Houston acquired a residence for a total cost of $235,000. At the time of purchase, it was estimated that the value of the land on which the house was situated was $85,000. Until January 1, 2007, Marnie and her two children occupied all of the house.

Early in 2007, Marnie's two children moved out, leaving a significant portion of the house unused. Because of this, Marnie decides to move to a small apartment and retain the former residence as a rental property. On April 1, 2007, a tenant moved into the house. Marnie does not make an election under ITA 45(2). (This election deems that the change in use has not occurred.)

Marnie had the house appraised on April 1, 2007. The appraiser indicated that the total value of the property was $392,000, with $112,000 of this amount reflecting the value of the land on which the house was situated.

For the period April 1, 2007 through December 31, 2007, Marnie's expenses on the property were as follows:

Property Taxes	$4,600
Insurance	1,100
Maintenance And Operating Costs	1,850
Mortgage Interest	8,200

The monthly rent was set at $1,900 per month, payable at the beginning of each month. The tenant paid all amounts required during 2007.

Required: For the year ending December 31, 2007, determine Ms. Houston's minimum net rental income (loss). Indicate any other tax consequences that will result from the change in use.

Assignment Problem Ten - 10

At the end of 2007, Mr. Vaughn sold both his city home and his summer cottage. Relevant information on the two properties is as follows:

	City Home	Cottage
Date acquired	1991	1991
Cost	$264,000	$ 36,000
Gross proceeds from sale	528,000	330,000
Real estate commissions	32,000	16,000

Mr. Vaughn wishes to minimize any capital gains resulting from the sale of the two properties.

Required: Describe how the residences should be designated in order to accomplish Mr. Vaughan's goal. In addition, calculate the amount of the gain that would arise under the designation that you have recommended.

Assignment Problem Ten - 11

On August 1, 2007, Mrs. Vargo sold a number of personal assets, all of which she had acquired in the last five yers. The relevant information on these sales is as follows:

	Cost	Proceeds	Selling Costs
Automobile	$25,000	$27,000	$150
Coin Collection	1,600	1,300	50
Rare Manuscript	1,700	800	30
Boat	4,500	3,500	175
Painting	700	1,100	50
Antique Clock	800	1,700	50

Required: Determine the net taxable capital gain that Mrs. Vargo will have to include in her income for the current year. Indicate any amounts that may be available for carry over to other years.

Assignment Problem Ten - 12

Ms. Petra Nobel is a Canadian resident who, on occasion, purchases securities for her brokerage account in the Netherlands. In September of 2004, she acquired a large block of shares of Gardengrow for 53,000 euros (€, hereafter). She purchased these shares with euros acquired at a rate of €1.00 = $1.60.

In March, 2007, the Gardengrow shares were sold for €97,000, with the funds remaining in her euro bank account until September. In September, the €97,000 was converted into Canadian dollars and transferred to her Canadian bank account.

Assume relevant exchange rates between the euro and Canadian dollar are as follows:

September, 2004	€1.00 = $1.60
March, 2007	€1.00 = $1.35
September, 2007	€1.00 = $1.40

Required: Calculate the minimum amount that will have to be included in Ms. Nobel's Net Income For Tax Purposes for 2007 as a result of these transactions.

Assignment Problem Ten - 13

All of the following independent Cases involve the purchase of a new house for $200,000 on October 1, 2007. Varying assumptions are made with respect to what is included in the $200,000.

Case A The price includes GST.

Case B The price does not include any GST.

Case C The price includes GST, net of the new housing rebate.

Required: For each Case, determine the GST rebate that can be claimed on the purchase on the net GST paid.

Assignment Problem Ten - 14

A house renovator purchases a used house on July 20, 2007 from a private individual for upgrading and resale. The purchase price of the house is $85,000. The renovator, a GST registrant, makes substantial renovations including an addition to the house that includes a country kitchen, jacuzzi room, and art studio. The electrical wiring is replaced and a new roof is installed. As a result of the renovations, the renovator sells the house for $200,000 before consideration of commissions and transfer fees.

The costs associated with the house and its renovation are as follows:

Purchase Price		$ 85,000
Renovation Costs:		
Subcontractors - No GST Included	$10,700	
Subcontractors - GST Included	21,200	
Materials - GST Included	31,800	
Employee Wages	6,000	69,700
Total Costs		$154,700

Required: What are the GST consequences of this undertaking for the renovator and the purchaser of the renovated house? Calculate the cost of the house to the purchaser and the net profit on the sale for the renovator, ignoring the effect of commissions and transfer fees. Include a calculation of the GST remittance of the renovator in your solution.

Assignment Problem Ten - 15

A new building is purchased on August 28, 2007, for $5,000,000, before GST. The purchaser, Total Health Inc., provides all types of health care services and products, and is a GST registrant. Sixty percent of the building will be used by Total Health Inc. employees as medical and dental offices. The remaining 40 percent will be used to house a pharmacy run and managed by Total Health Inc. staff.

Required:

A. How much GST will be payable on the purchase?

B. Explain who will be responsible for payment of the GST?

C. Can an input tax credit be claimed, and if so, for how much?

Assignment Cases

Assignment Case Ten - 1 (Comprehensive Case Covering Chapters 5 to 10)

Mr. Arnold Bosch is 41 years old and earns most of his income through an unincorporated business, Bosch's Better Boats (BBB). For the taxation year ending December 31, 2007, Mr. Bosch's accountant has determined that BBB had accounting income before taxes, determined in accordance with generally accepted accounting principles, of $196,000. In determining his business income for tax purposes, the following information is relevant:

1. The accounting income figure included a deduction for amortization of $29,000.

2. On January 1, 2007, BBB had the following UCC balances:

    - Class 1 $275,000
    - Class 8   83,000
    - Class 10   28,000

    On March 1, 2007, Class 8 assets with a cost of $46,000 were sold for $28,500. On March 15, 2007, these assets were replaced with other Class 8 assets costing $63,250.

3. During 2007, BBB spent $30,000 landscaping the grounds around its building. This amount was recorded as an asset in the accounting records. It is being amortized over 10 years on a straight line basis and the amortization is included in the $29,000 amortization figure in Part 1 of this problem.

4. BBB's 2007 accounting income included a deduction for meals and entertainment of $27,600.

5. BBB's 2007 accounting income included a deduction for charitable donations of $5,500, as well as a deduction for donations to federal political parties of $700.

6. For accounting purposes, BBB charges estimated warranty costs to expense. On January 1, 2007, the liability for these warranties was $22,000. On December 31, 2007, the liability balance was $17,500.

Because of the income earned by his business, Mr. Bosch is required to make CPP contributions of $3,980 [(2)($1,990)]. He is not required to make EI contributions.

Mr. Bosch has a common-law partner, Mr. Fritz Mann. Three years ago, Mr. Bosch and his partner adopted two Chinese orphans. Chris, aged 9, has a severe and prolonged disability that qualifies him for the ITA 118.3 disability tax credit. Martin, aged 12, is in good health. Neither Chris nor Martin have any income of their own. Because Mr. Mann provides full time care for the children, he has no income during 2007.

The family's 2007 medical expenses, all paid for by Mr. Bosch, are as follows:

Arnold	$ 2,050
Fritz	1,080
Chris	16,470
Martin	1,645
Total Medical Expenses	**$21,245**

During 2007, Mr. Bosch sold a piece of vacant land for $85,000. Mr. Bosch received a payment of $35,000 during 2007, with the $50,000 balance due in 5 equal instalments in the years 2008 through 2012. The adjusted cost base of this land was $33,000.

Mr. Bosch owns a rural cottage property that he purchased at a property auction in 1999 at a cost of $25,000. As of June 30, 2007, an appraiser indicates that it has a value of $375,000, with $100,000 of that value being associated with the land. The appraiser indicates that, when Mr. Bosch purchased the cottage, the land value was probably about $5,000. As Mr. Bosch and his family have made little use of this property, he decides to begin renting it as of July 1, 2007.

During the period July 1, 2007 through December 31, 2007, rents on the cottage total $12,000. Expenses other than CCA during this period total $3,200. For 2007, he intends to take maximum CCA on the property.

Mr. Bosch purchased his city home in 2002. Prior to that, he and Mr. Mann lived in a rented apartment. As the city home has experienced a greater increase in value during the last six years, he will designate the city home as his principal residence for the years 2002 through 2007.

Over the years, Mr. Bosch has made several purchases of the common shares of Low Tech Ltd., a widely held public company. In 2005 he bought 150 shares at $55 per share. In 2006, he bought an additional 125 shares at $75 per share. In February, 2007, he bought an additional 300 shares at $95 per share. On November 11, 2007, after the company announced that most of its product claims had been falsified, Mr. Bosch sold 275 shares at $5 per share.

Required: Calculate Mr. Bosch's minimum 2007 Net Income For Tax Purposes, his 2007 minimum Taxable Income, and his minimum 2007 Balance Owing to the CRA, including any CPP contributions payable. Ignore provincial income taxes, any instalment payments he may have made during the year, and GST considerations.

Assignment Case Ten - 2 (Comprehensive Case Covering Chapters 5 to 10)

Laura Barnes is 27 years of age and lives with her 32 year old common-law partner, Julia Stinson. Julia's 2007 Net Income For Tax Purposes is $4,600.

Also living with the couple are two children that were born to Julia in two previous relationships. The daughter, Allison, is 8 years old and the son, Andrew, is 12 years old. During 2007, Laura formally adopts these two children. Due to stiff opposition from Andrew's father, she incurs legal costs of $14,200 to complete his adoption. The legal fees paid to adopt Allison total $4,000.

Laura's 52 year old mother, Alicia, also lives with her. While she does not qualify for the disability tax credit, she has a physical impairment that makes her totally dependent on Laura. She attends university on a full time basis for four months of the year and Laura pays her tuition fees of $2,400. Alicia has 2007 Net Income For Tax Purposes of $9,400.

Laura pays the following 2007 medical expenses for herself and her dependants:

Laura	$ 1,800
Julia	2,200
Alicia	4,600
Allison	800
Andrew	6,600
Total Medical Expenses	$16,000

Laura and all of her dependants use public transit. During 2007, the monthly passes are $100 for each adult and $50 per child, payable at the beginning of the month.

During 2007, Laura makes contributions to registered charities in the amount of $1,600.

During the first 6 months of 2007, Laura operated a successful retail business out of a building which she owned. She keeps her accounting records on a cash basis and, for the 6 month period ending June 30, 2007, her net cash inflow was $53,000. Information on inventories and accruals are as follows:

	January 1, 2007	June 30, 2007
Accounts Receivable	$10,000	$ 8,000
Accounts Payable	14,000	16,000
Inventories	22,000	18,000

Information on the capital assets used in the business is as follows:

	Capital Cost	January 1 2007 UCC	June 30, 2007 Fair Market Value
Building	$250,000	$211,000	$308,000
Land (Building's Location)	50,000	N/A	125,000
Furniture And Fixtures	35,000	12,900	9,800
Automobile (Used Exclusively In The Business)	29,500	25,075	18,000

On July 1, 2007, the capital assets were sold for their fair market value, with Laura incurring $17,320 in commissions on the sale of the land and building. The Accounts Receivable and Inventories were sold for their carrying values, with part of the proceeds being used to pay off the Accounts Payable.

On July 3, 2007, she is employed by a large public company as a sales consultant. Her salary for the period July 3, 2007 through December 31, 2007 is $56,000. In addition, because of her excellent performance she is awarded a $12,000 bonus. The bonus will be paid on April 30, 2008.

During 2007, her employer withholds the following amounts from her income:

RPP Contributions	$2,500
EI	720
CPP	1,990

Because her employer has withheld the maximum amount for 2007, Laura will not have to make CPP contributions on the income from her unincorporated business.

Laura's employer also contributes $2,500 to her RPP. In addition, the employer provides her with an automobile that cost $62,000. The car is available to her for the period July 3, 2007 through December 31, 2007 and, during this period she drives the car 22,000 kilometers, 18,000 of which were employment related.

Information on Laura's investments is as follows:

Dividends Eligible dividends received during 2007 total $5,600.

Interest 2007 interest on Laura's GICs is $4,275.

Income Trusts At the beginning of 2007, Laura had income trust units with an adjusted cost base of $56,000. During the year, she receives distributions of $6,800, of which $2,600 is designated as a return of capital with the remainder designated as income. On December 15, 2007, she sells all of the trust units for $63,000.

Mutual Funds In January, 2007, Laura acquires 1,000 units of the New World Equity Fund at $9.65 per unit. On June 30, 2007, the fund has a distribution of interest income of $0.50 per unit. At this time the units are trading at $9.40 and Laura chooses to have the distribution re-invested. On December 10, 2007, she sells all of the units for $9.00 per unit.

To assist with her investment decisions, during 2007, Laura pays fees to a professional investment counsellor of $875.

Required: Calculate Ms. Barnes' minimum 2007 Net Income For Tax Purposes, her 2007 minimum Taxable Income, and her minimum 2007 federal Tax Payable. Ignore provincial income taxes, any instalments she may have paid during the year, any withholdings that would be made by her employer, and GST considerations.

Assignment Case Ten - 3 (Progressive Running Case - Chapter 10 Version Using ProFile T1 Software For 2006 Tax Returns)

This Progressive Running Case requires the use of the ProFile tax software program. It was introduced in Chapter 6 and is continued in Chapters 8 through 14. Each version must be completed in sequence. While it is not repeated in this version of the Case, all of the information in each of the previous versions (e.g., Mary's T4 content) is applicable to this version of the Case.

If you have not prepared a tax file incorporating the previous versions, please do so before continuing with this version.

When Mary's grandmother died in 1998, she inherited some pieces of jewelry, as well as a dining room set and a chandelier. Since the jewelry is not suited to Mary's relaxed style of dress, she sold some pieces during the year. She replaced the dining room set and chandelier and sold them separately to two colleagues at work.

On December 28, 2006, Mary Walford faxes to you information about her sales of securities and other items. Mary has purchased Extreme Wi-Fi Technologies stock over the years. Her transactions in this stock are as follows:

Acquisition Date	Shares Purchased (Sold)	Cost Per Share	Total Cost
April 1, 2004	1,500	$ 2	$ 3,000
October 1, 2004	2,000	12	24,000
April 1, 2005	(1,000)	?	
June 1, 2005	400	25	10,000
January 6, 2006	(800)	?	
February 1, 2006	800	20	16,000
March 14, 2006	(600)	?	

Asset Dispositions	Disposition 1	Disposition 2	Disposition 3
(All owned by Mary) Description	Extreme Wi-Fi Technologies	Extreme Wi-Fi Technologies	Fidelity Small Cap Fund
Number of units	800	600	258.92
Year of acquisition	2004	2004	2001
Date of disposition	January 6	March 14	February 17
Proceeds of disposition	11,806	13,465	2,982.31
Adjusted cost base	?	?	5,300.33
Outlays and expenses	29	29	Nil

Asset Dispositions	Disposition 4	Disposition 5	Disposition 6
Description	Diamond Pendant	Gold Ring	Pearl Brooch
Year of acquisition	1998	1998	1998
Date of disposition	July 20	July 20	July 20
Proceeds of disposition	4,000	750	1,300
FMV at grandmother's death	5,800	600	850

Asset Dispositions	Disposition 7	Disposition 8
Description	Dining room set	Crystal Chandelier
Year of acquisition	1998	1998
Date of disposition	July 20	July 20
Proceeds of disposition	200	1,500
FMV at grandmother's death	3,000	800

Required:

A. Open the file that you created for the Chapter 9 version of the Case and save a copy under a different name. This will enable you to check the changes between different versions of the Case.

B. Input the asset disposition information on the form S3Details. Prepare and print the Capital Gains and Losses (Schedule 3) for Mary. As part of your solution, include any calculations and notes that were needed to complete Schedule 3.

C. Access and print Mary's summary (Summary on the Form Explorer, not the T1Summary). This form is a two column summary of the couple's tax information. By opening this form from Mary's return, the order of the columns is the same as the one in the previous chapter. For both returns, list the changes on this Summary form from the previous version of this Case. Exclude totals calculated by the program, but include the final Balance Owing (Refund) amount.

CHAPTER 11

Other Income And
Other Deductions

Content Of Chapters 11 Through 13

Coverage Of Chapters 11 and 12

11-1.   At this point we have provided detailed coverage of all of the major components of Net Income For Tax Purposes. There are, however, certain inclusions and deductions that do not fit into any of the categories that we have described. For example, the receipt of a pension benefit cannot be categorized as employment income, business or property income, or a taxable capital gain. Correspondingly, an RRSP deduction can be related to any type of earned income and, as a consequence, cannot be specifically allocated to any of the previously described income categories. These miscellaneous inclusions and deductions will be given detailed attention in this Chapter.

11-2.   In terms of the *Income Tax Act*, these miscellaneous sources and deductions are covered in two Subdivisions of Division B. Subdivision d, made up of Sections 56 through 59.1, is titled Other Sources Of Income. Subdivision e, made up of Sections 60 through 66.8, is titled Other Deductions.

11-3.   With coverage of these Subdivisions, we have largely completed our coverage of the components of Net Income For Tax Purposes. However, before moving on to additional work on the calculation of Taxable Income for individuals in Chapter 14, there are some other issues that must be dealt with. Chapter 12 provides coverage of a group of miscellaneous topics, including the income attribution rules, the tax rules associated with emigration from Canada, and the tax issues that arise when an individual dies.

Organization Of Chapters 11 And 13

The Problem

11-4.   There are several Subdivision d inclusions that do not directly relate to Subdivision e deductions or other sections of the *Income Tax Act* (e.g., death benefits). Correspondingly, there are Subdivision e deductions that do not relate to Subdivision d inclusions or other sections of the *Act* (e.g., CPP and EI contributions by self-employed individuals).

11-5.   However, many of the items in these two subdivisions either have directly related provisions in both subdivisions (e.g., deductible and taxable spousal support), or require an understanding of other sections of the *Act* (e.g., registered education savings plans). This makes it somewhat difficult to organize this material in a manner that will enhance your understanding of its content.

Our Solution

11-6.   To deal with this problem, we have organized this Chapter as follows:

- The first section of the Chapter will deal with those Subdivision d inclusions that do not involve Subdivision e or other parts of the *Income Tax Act*.
- The second section of the Chapter will deal with those Subdivision e deductions that do not involve Subdivision d inclusions or other parts of the *Income Tax Act*.
- The remaining sections of the Chapter will give individual attention to issues that either involve both Subdivision d and Subdivision e or, alternatively, involve one of these subdivisions and some other part of the *Income Tax Act*.

11-7.   Retirement savings vehicles (e.g., Registered Retirement Savings Plans) involve both Subdivision d and Subdivision e, as well as several other parts of the *Act*. As such, they would fit logically into the structure of this Chapter. However, these provisions are extremely complex. Further, in terms of tax planning for individuals, we view this material as among the most important in this text. Given this, we are providing a separate Chapter 13 to deal with this material.

Other Income - Subdivision d Inclusions

Pension Benefits - ITA 56(1)(a)(i)

11-8.   ITA 56(1)(a)(i) requires that payments received from certain types of pension plans be included in the income of individuals. For many individuals, the major item here would be amounts received under the provisions of Registered Pension Plans. Also included would be pension amounts received under the *Old Age Security Act* (OAS), as well as any similar payments received from a province. In addition, benefits received under the Canada Pension Plan or a provincial pension plan would also become part of the individual's Net Income For Tax Purposes.

11-9.   As will be discussed later in this Chapter, as of 2007, new legislation allows most types of pension income to be split between spouses or common-law partners. We would note here that this tax planning opportunity has been available with respect to Canadian Pension Plan receipts for a number of years. The amount that can be shared is based on the length of time the individuals have been living together relative to the length of the contributory period.

Retiring Allowances - ITA 56(1)(a)(ii)

11-10.   ITA 56(1)(a)(ii) requires that retiring allowances be included in an individual's Net Income For Tax Purposes. ITA 248 defines these payments as follows:

"retiring allowance" means an amount (other than a superannuation or pension benefit, an amount received as a consequence of the death of an employee or a benefit described in subparagraph 6(1)(a)(iv)) received

- (a) on or after retirement of a taxpayer from an office or employment in recognition of the taxpayer's long service, or
- (b) in respect of a loss of an office or employment of a taxpayer, whether or not received as, on account or in lieu of payment of, damages or pursuant to an order or judgment of a competent tribunal,

by the taxpayer or, after the taxpayer's death, by a dependant or a relation of the taxpayer or by the legal representative of the taxpayer.

11-11.   The term "retiring allowance" covers most payments on termination of employment. This includes rewards given for good service, payments related to early retirement (e.g., federal government buyout provisions) at either the request of the employee or the employer, as well as damages related to wrongful dismissal actions.

11-12.   Within specified limits, amounts received as a retiring allowance for service prior to 1996 can be deducted if they are transferred to either a Registered Pension Plan (RPP) or a Registered Retirement Savings Plan (RRSP) within 60 days of the end of the year in which they are received. (See Chapter 13.) This serves to defer the taxation on amounts transferred until the funds are withdrawn from the registered plan. For individuals who are retiring, this can be an important component of their tax planning. Note, however, while a deduction is available for the eligible transfer, the entire retiring allowance must be included in income.

Death Benefits - ITA 56(1)(a)(iii)

11-13.   Death benefits are included in income under ITA 56(1)(a)(iii). ITA 248 defines these death benefits as follows:

> **"death benefit"** means the total of all amounts received by a taxpayer in a taxation year on or after the death of an employee in recognition of the employee's service in an office or employment ...

11-14.   When death benefits are received by a surviving spouse or common-law partner, the definition goes on to indicate that only amounts in excess of an exclusion of $10,000 are considered to be a death benefit for purposes of ITA 56(1)(a)(iii). This $10,000 exclusion would be available, even if the benefit was payable over a period of several years. A CPP death benefit is not eligible for the $10,000 exemption as it is not a death benefit paid in recognition of an employee's service.

11-15.   The $10,000 exclusion is also available on payments to individuals other than a spouse or common-law partner, with the amount being reduced to the extent it has been used by the spouse or common-law partner. For example, if Ms. Reid dies and her employer pays a death benefit of $8,000 to her husband and an additional $8,000 to her adult son, the husband could exclude the entire $8,000 from income and the son could use the remaining $2,000 of the exclusion to reduce his income inclusion to $6,000.

11-16.   Although death benefits are normally paid to the family of the deceased, it would appear that the $10,000 exclusion is available without regard to whom the death benefit is paid. This would suggest that an employer could pay any individual, including a related party, a $10,000 tax free death benefit on the death of any employee. Further, it would seem that an employer could repeatedly make such payments on the death of each of his employees.

Income Inclusions From Deferred Income Plans -
ITA 56(1)(h), (h.1), (h.2), (i), and (t)

11-17.   Income inclusions from deferred income plans such as Registered Retirement Savings Plans (RRSPs), Registered Retirement Income Funds (RRIFs), and Deferred Profit Sharing Plans (DPSPs) do not fall into any of the major categories of income. Such amounts do not directly relate to employment efforts, business activity, ownership of property, or the disposition of capital assets. However, they clearly constitute income and, as a consequence, the *Income Tax Act* requires that payments from these various deferred income plans be included in the taxpayer's income.

11-18.   The details of these various types of plans are discussed in Chapter 13 where we provide comprehensive coverage of retirement savings arrangements. While you should not expect to understand these plans at this stage, you should note that the various income inclusions that are related to these plans are included in Net Income For Tax Purposes under the provisions of Subdivision d of Division B. Brief descriptions of the various inclusions in this area are as follows:

> **Payments From RRSPs**   All amounts that are removed from a Registered Retirement Savings Plan must be included in income under ITA 56(1)(h).

Income Inclusions From Home Buyers' And Lifelong Learning Plans   If repayments to the RRSP are not made as per the required schedule for these plans (see Chapter 13), the specified amounts must be included in income. These amounts would be included in income under ITA 56(1)(h.1) and (h.2), respectively.

Payments From DPSPs   Under ITA 56(1)(i), all amounts removed from a Deferred Profit Sharing Plan must be included in income.

RRIF Withdrawals   The required minimum withdrawal, plus any additional withdrawals from Registered Retirement Income Funds, must be included in income under ITA 56(1)(h) and (t). Note that ITA 56(1)(t) would require the inclusion of the minimum withdrawal amount in income, even if the amount was not actually withdrawn.

Education Assistance Payments - ITA 56(1)(n) and (o)
Scholarships And Bursaries
11-19.   ITA 56(1)(n) requires that all amounts received as scholarships, bursaries, grants, and prizes be included in income, to the extent that these amounts exceed the student's scholarship exemption. The scholarship exemption in ITA 56(3) is currently $500. However, recent budgets have changed the $500 exemption to fully exempt scholarships and bursaries for 2007 and subsequent taxation years.

11-20.   At one point in time, there was an additional $2,500 exemption for amounts that related to a program that qualified for the education tax credit. This appears to have been removed given the budget changes.

Research Grants
11-21.   Research grants are included in income under ITA 56(1)(o). The amount to be included is net of unreimbursed expenses related to carrying on the research work.

Social Assistance And Workers' Compensation Payments - ITA 56(1)(u) And (v)
11-22.   Payments received under various social assistance programs must be included in income under ITA 56(1)(u), while workers' compensation payments are included under ITA 56(1)(v). It is not, however, the intent of the government to tax these amounts. They are sometimes referred to as exempt income, as they have no net effect on Taxable Income. However, they are included in Net Income For Tax Purposes, a figure that is used in a variety of eligibility tests.

11-23.   For example, to get the full tax credit for an infirm dependant over 17, the dependant's income must be less than a threshold amount ($5,702 for 2007). Since the policy is to reduce this credit in proportion to the dependant's income in excess of that amount, it is important that all types of income be included in the Net Income For Tax Purposes calculation. To accomplish this goal, social assistance and workers' compensation payments are included in the calculation of Net Income For Tax Purposes and then deducted in the calculation of Taxable Income.

Universal Child Care Benefit - ITA 56(6)
11-24.   For many years, the issue of providing for child care costs has been a "hot" topic for politicians of all stripes. Various proposals have been put forward, followed by considerable rhetoric as to their merits. With the 2006 election of Stephen Harper's Conservatives, action was finally taken.

11-25.   Harper's government introduced the *Universal Child Care Benefit Act*. Under the provision of this *Act*, families receive $100 per month for each child under the age of six. The amounts received are included in the income of the lower income spouse or common-law partner under ITA 56(6). To receive the payments, a one-time application is required.

11-26.   Other relevant points are as follows:

- The amounts received under the Universal Child Care Benefit (UCCB) are not taken into account for the purposes of calculating income tested benefits delivered through the *Income Tax Act* (e.g., the GST tax credit).
- The amounts received under the UCCB do not reduce Old Age Security or Employment Insurance benefits.
- The amounts received under the UCCB do not reduce the amount of child care expenses that are deductible.

Other Deductions - Subdivision e Deductions

CPP Contributions On Self-Employed Earnings - ITA 60(e)
11-27.   As was noted in Chapter 5, individuals who are self-employed are required to contribute larger amounts to the CPP than individuals who are employees. The maximum employee CPP contribution for 2007 is $1,990. When an individual is an employee, the employer matches the amount paid by the employee, resulting in a total maximum payment of $3,980. Self-employed individuals are, in effect, required to pay double the employee amount, analogous to the combined employee plus employer shares.

11-28.   An employer deducts any CPP contributions made on behalf of employees in the determination of business income. In order to give CPP contributions by self-employed individuals the same treatment, one-half of all CPP contributions payable on self-employed income is deducted in the calculation of net business income under ITA 60(e). The remaining one-half of the CPP contributions payable on self-employed income is treated in the same manner as CPP contributions made by an employee. These payments generate a credit against Tax Payable equal to 15.5 percent of one-half of the contribution made for the year.

Moving Expenses - ITA 62
General Rules
11-29.   ITA 62(1) indicates that a taxpayer can deduct moving expenses incurred as part of an "eligible relocation". Eligible relocation is defined in ITA 248(1) to mean a relocation that occurs to enable the taxpayer:

- to carry on business or to be employed at a new work location (this includes moving from an old work location, moving from a location where the individual was unemployed, and moving from a location where the individual was in full-time attendance at a college or university); or
- to be a student in full-time attendance at a college or university.

11-30.   The definition also requires that the taxpayer's residence, both before and after the move be in Canada. In addition, it specifies that the distance between the old residence and the new work location or institution be not less than 40 kilometers greater than the distance between the new residence and the new work location or institution. This distance is measured using the routes that would normally be traveled by an individual rather than "as the crow flies" (e.g., you can take the bridge, rather than swimming directly across the river).

11-31.   Moving expenses can only be deducted against income, including research grants, received in the new work location or institution. If the moving expenses exceed the income earned at the new location during the year of the move, the *Act* provides for a one year carry over and deduction against the following year's income at the new location.

11-32.   To the extent that the moving expenses are directly reimbursed by the employer, they cannot be claimed by the taxpayer. Note, however, if the employer provides an allowance rather than an item by item reimbursement, the allowance will be included in income, thereby creating a situation in which the employee will be able to deduct the actual amount of expenses incurred.

11-33.   As described in ITA 62(3), moving expenses include:

- Traveling costs (including a reasonable amount expended for meals and lodging for the taxpayer and the taxpayer's family), in the course of moving the taxpayer and members of the household from the old residence to the new residence.

- The cost of transporting or storing household effects.

- The cost of meals and lodging for the taxpayer and the taxpayer's family near either the old or new residence for a period not exceeding 15 days. Note that, in measuring the 15 days, days spent while en route to the new location are not included.

- The cost of canceling a lease on the old residence.

- The selling costs of the old residence.

- The legal and other costs associated with the acquisition of the new residence, provided an old residence was sold in conjunction with the move. Note that this does not include any GST paid on the new residence.

- Up to $5,000 of interest, property taxes, insurance, and heating and utilities costs on the old residence, subsequent to the time when the individual has moved out and during which reasonable efforts are being made to sell the property.

- Costs of revising legal documents to reflect a new address, replacing driver's licenses and non-commercial vehicle permits, and connecting and disconnecting utilities.

11-34.   Any costs associated with decorating or improving the new residence would not be included in the definition of moving expenses, nor would any loss on the sale of the old residence. Also note that, in general, costs associated with trips to find accommodation at the new location are not included in the definition. The exception to this is meals and lodging near the new residence after it has been acquired.

Simplified Method Of Calculating Vehicle And Meal Expenses
11-35.   In an effort to simplify claiming vehicle and meal expenses, the CRA permits the optional use of pre-established flat rates. Receipts are not needed to claim these amounts. For 2006 (the 2007 rates have not been released at this time), the flat rate for meals is $17 per meal, to a daily maximum of $51, per person, per day. The flat rate for vehicle expenses depends on the province from which the move begins and ranges from $0.445 per kilometer for Saskatchewan to $0.57 per kilometer for the Yukon. The vehicle claim is calculated by multiplying the total kilometers driven during the year related to the move by the rate of the originating province.

Employer Reimbursements
11-36.   As noted in Chapter 5, an employer can reimburse an employee's moving expenses without creating a taxable benefit. It would appear that, for this purpose, the definition of moving expenses is broader than that which applies when an employee is deducting such expenses directly.

11-37.   For example, if an employee incurs costs to visit a new work location in order to find housing or evaluate local schools, he cannot deduct these costs. Despite the fact that the employee would not be able to deduct such costs, a reimbursement by the employer does not appear to create a taxable benefit.

11-38.   Another example of this situation involves employer reimbursement for a loss on the sale of a residence at the old work location. ITA 6(20) indicates that one-half of any reimbursement in excess of $15,000 will be included in the employee's income as a taxable benefit. This means, for example, if an employer provided a $40,000 reimbursement for a loss on an old residence, the employee would be assessed a taxable benefit of $12,500 [(1/2)($40,000 - $15,000)]. Note that, if the loss is not related to an eligible relocation (i.e., 40 kilometers closer to a new work location), the full amount of any loss reimbursement would be considered to be a taxable benefit.

11-39.   Employers have also attempted to compensate employees for being required to move to a new work location where housing costs are significantly higher. While there has been a considerable amount of litigation in this area, the issues now seem to be clarified:

Lump Sum Payments   In those situations where an employer provides an employee with a lump sum payment to cover the increased cost of equivalent housing at the new work location, the decision in *The Queen v. Phillips* (94 DTC 6177) has established that such an amount will be treated as a taxable benefit to the employee.

Interest Rate Relief And Other Subsidies   ITA 6(23) makes it clear that an amount paid, or assistance provided in respect of an individual's office or employment, in respect of the acquisition or use of a residence, is an employment benefit.

Tax Planning

11-40.   In those cases where the employer does not reimburse 100 percent of an employee's moving expenses, the fact that employers can reimburse certain costs that would not be deductible to the employee can be of some tax planning importance.

11-41.   In such partial reimbursement cases, it is to the advantage of the employee to have the employer's reimbursements specifically directed towards those moving costs that the employee would not be able to deduct from Net Income For Tax Purposes. This procedure costs the employer nothing and, at the same time, it permits the employee to maximize the deduction for moving expenses.

Example   An employee has total moving expenses of $22,000. This includes an $8,000 loss on his old residence as a result of the relocation. All of the costs, other than the loss on the old residence, are deductible to the employee. His employer has agreed to pay one-half of all moving costs.

Analysis   Of the $11,000 that will be paid by the employer, $8,000 should be allocated to the loss on the old residence. As this is less than the $15,000 that can be reimbursed without creating a taxable benefit, the employee will be able to deduct the full $11,000 that he must pay out of personal funds. If the employer had simply paid an allowance of $11,000, the employee would have been able to deduct only $3,000 of the amount that he paid ($14,000 in deductible expenses, less the $11,000 allowance).

Exercise Eleven-1

Subject: Moving Expenses

On December 20, 2007, at the request of her employer, Ms. Martinova Chevlak moves from Edmonton to Regina. She has always lived in a rented apartment and will continue to do so in Regina. The total cost of the actual move, including the costs of moving her personal possessions, was $6,400. In addition, she spent $1,300 on a visit to Regina in a search for appropriate accommodation, and $1,200 as a penalty for breaking her lease in Edmonton. During the year, her salary totalled $64,000, of which $2,000 can be allocated to the period after December 20, 2007. Her employer is prepared to pay $6,000 towards the cost of her move. Determine Ms. Chevlak's maximum moving expense deduction for 2007 and any amounts that can be carried over to the subsequent year.

End of Exercise. Solution available in Study Guide.

Child Care Expenses - ITA 63
Basic Definitions

11-42.   The basic idea here is that a taxpayer is permitted to deduct the costs of caring for children if the costs were incurred in order to produce Taxable Income or receive an education. However, it is the policy of the government to place limits on the amount that can be deducted and, in the process of setting these limits, the rules related to child care costs have become quite complex. In applying these rules, a number of definitions are relevant:

Eligible Child   An eligible child is defined in ITA 63(3) to include a child of the taxpayer, his spouse or common-law partner, or a child who is dependent on the taxpayer or his spouse or common-law partner and whose income does not exceed the basic personal credit amount ($8,929 for 2007). In addition, the child must be under 16 years of age at some time during the year or dependent on the taxpayer or his spouse or common-law partner by reason of physical or mental infirmity.

There are different limits for disabled children who are eligible to claim the disability tax credit and those who are not (see following material). To be defined as an eligible child in the aged 16 or over category requires only that they be dependent solely as the result of some form of mental or physical disability. IT-513R does not provide examples of this level of disability, but states that the degree of the infirmity must be such that it requires the child to be dependent for a considerable period of time.

Annual Child Care Expense Amount   There are three annual limits. For a dependent child of any age who is eligible for the disability tax credit (e.g., a blind child), the amount is $10,000. For a child under 7 years of age at the end of the year, the amount is $7,000. For a child aged 7 to 16, or a dependent child over 16 who has a mental or physical infirmity, but is not eligible for the disability tax credit, the amount is $4,000.

Periodic Child Care Expense Amount   This weekly amount is defined as being equal to 1/40 of the annual child care expense amount applicable to the particular child. Depending on the child, the value per week will be $250 [(1/40)($10,000)], $175 [(1/40)($7,000)], or $100 [(1/40)($4,000)].

Earned Income   For use in determining deductible child care expenses, earned income is defined as gross employment income (for this purpose, no deductions from employment income are taken into consideration), net business income (for this purpose, business losses are ignored), and income from scholarships, training allowances, and research grants. Note that the calculation of earned income for child care expense purposes is different than the earned income calculation used to determine RRSP deduction limits (see Chapter 13). Also note that this calculation does not include payments under the Universal Child Care Benefit Plan.

Supporting Person   A supporting person is usually the child's parent, or the spouse or common-law partner of the child's parent. However, a supporting person is also an individual who can claim the amount for an eligible dependant, an infirm dependant over 17, or the caregiver amount for the child.

11-43.   Using the definitions, we can now give attention to the rules applicable to determining the deductible amount of child care expenses.

Lower Income Spouse Or Single Parent

11-44.   There is an implicit assumption in the child care cost legislation that two parent families with a single bread winner should not be able to deduct child care costs. This assumption is implemented through the requirement that, in general, only the spouse (or "supporting person") with the lower income can deduct child care costs. In general, this means that in families that have a house parent who is earning no outside income, is not a student, and is capable of taking care of the children, child care costs cannot be deducted.

11-45.   The amount that can be deducted by the spouse with the lower Net Income For Tax Purposes in a two parent family, or by the single parent when there is no other supporting person, is the least of three amounts:

1.   The amount actually paid for child care services, plus limited amounts (see Paragraph 11-48) paid for lodging at boarding schools and overnight camps.

2.   The sum of the **Annual Child Care Expense Amounts** for the taxpayer's eligible children ($10,000, $7,000, or $4,000 per child).

3.   2/3 of the taxpayer's **Earned Income**.

11-46. Note that there is no requirement that these amounts be spent on specific children. For example, a couple with three children under the age of 7 would have an overall amount under limit 2 of $21,000 [(3)($7,000)]. This $21,000 amount would be the applicable limit even if all of it was spent on care for one child and nothing was spent for the other children.

11-47. Actual costs include amounts incurred for care for an eligible child in order that the taxpayer may earn employment income, carry on a business, or attend a secondary school (e.g. a high school) or a designated educational institution (i.e., an institution that qualifies the individual for the education tax credit). In order to be deductible, amounts paid for child care must be supported by receipts issued by the payee and, where the payee is an individual, the Social Insurance Number of the payee must be provided. Other constraints indicated in IT-495R3, "Child Care Expenses", are that payments are not deductible if they are made to:

- the mother or father of the child;

- a related party under the age of 18 (this does not include nieces, nephews, aunts, or uncles); or

- an individual for whom a supporting person can claim the amount for an eligible dependant, an infirm dependant over 17 or the caregiver amount.

Attendance At Boarding School Or Camp

11-48. A further limitation on actual costs involves situations where one or more children are attending a boarding school or an overnight camp. The federal government does not wish to provide tax assistance for the cost of facilities that provide services that go beyond child care (e.g., computer lessons). As a consequence, when the actual costs involve overnight camps or boarding school fees, the deductible costs are limited to the Periodic Child Care Expense Amount ($250, $175, or $100 per week, per child). Amounts paid to the camp or boarding school in excess of these amounts would not be deductible.

11-49. Note that this weekly limit does not apply to fees paid to day camps or sports camps that do not include overnight stays. However, for fees to day camps and day sports schools to be eligible for a child care deduction, the primary goal of the camp must be to care for the children as opposed to providing sports education.

11-50. You will recall from Chapter 6 that there is a tax credit for eligible child fitness costs. It is possible that costs associated with a boarding school or camp could qualify as both a child care cost and a child fitness expenditure. To avoid double counting of these costs, the definition of an eligible child fitness expenditure excludes any amounts that have been deducted as child care costs. As the credit is calculated using the lowest tax bracket of 15.5 percent, in those cases where the individual making the claim is in a higher tax bracket, it is preferable to deduct such amounts as child care costs, rather than using them for the child fitness credit.

Higher Income Spouse

11-51. In the preceding material, we noted the general rule that child care costs are to be deducted by the lower income spouse. There are however, a number of exceptions to this general rule. Specifically, the higher income spouse is allowed to make the deduction if:

- the lower income spouse is a student in attendance at a secondary school or a designated educational institution and enrolled in a program of the institution or school that is not less than 3 consecutive weeks duration and provides that each student in the program spend not less than:

  - 10 hours per week on courses or work in the program (i.e., full time attendance); or
  - 12 hours per month on courses or work in the program (i.e., part time attendance);

- the lower income spouse is infirm and incapable of caring for the children for at least 2 weeks (this requires a written certificate from a medical doctor supporting the fact that the individual is incapable of caring for children);

- the lower income spouse is a person confined to a prison or similar institution throughout a period of not less than 2 weeks in the year; or

- the spouses are separated for more than 90 days beginning in the year.

11-52. In situations where the higher income spouse is making the deduction, the amount of the deduction would be subject to the same limitations that are applicable when the deduction is being made by the lower income spouse. However, the higher income spouse has a further limitation. This additional limit is calculated by multiplying the sum of the Periodic Child Care Expense Amounts for all eligible children, by the number of weeks that the lower income spouse is attending an educational institution, infirm, in prison, or separated from the higher income spouse.

If A Parent Is A Student

11-53. ITA 63(2.2) allows a taxpayer who is attending a secondary school or a designated educational institution on a full or part time basis to deduct child care costs if there is no other supporting person or, alternatively, if the income of the taxpayer exceeds the income of a supporting person of the child for the year. The calculation of the deductible amount is specified under ITA 63(2.3) and generally follows the rules for deductibility by the higher income spouse. That is, the amount deductible is limited to the sum of the Periodic Child Care Expense Amounts for all eligible children. There is a difference, however, in that for this type of situation, the income limitation is based on Net Income For Tax Purposes, not just earned income as defined in ITA 63(3).

Example

11-54. The following example will serve to clarify some of the general rules for child care costs.

> **Example** Jack and Joanna Morris have three children, Bruce, Bobby, and Betty. At the end of 2007, Bruce is aged 18 and, while he is physically disabled, his disability is not severe enough that he qualifies for the disability tax credit. With respect to their other children, Bobby is aged 6 and Betty is aged 2 at the end of the year. Jack has 2007 earned income of $45,000, while Joanna has 2007 earned income of $63,000.
>
> The couple has full time help to care for their children during 49 weeks of the year. The cost of this help is $210 per week ($10,290 for the year). During July, the children are sent to music camp in a provincial park for three weeks. The camp fees total $3,500 for this period for all three children. As the result of a substance abuse conviction, Jack spends seven weeks in November and December in prison.
>
> The general limits on deductible child care costs would give the following amounts:

	Joanna	Jack
Actual child care costs plus		
maximum deductible camp fees {$10,290 +		
[(2)($175)(3 weeks)] + [(1)($100)(3 weeks)]}	$11,640	$11,640
Periodic Child Care Expense Amounts		
[(2)($175)(7 weeks) + (1)($100)(7 weeks)]	3,150	N/A
Annual Child Care Expense Amount		
[(2)($7,000) + (1)($4,000)]	18,000	18,000
2/3 of earned income	42,000	30,000

While Joanna is the higher income spouse, she will be able to deduct child care costs during the seven weeks that Jack is in prison. Her maximum deduction is $3,150. As the lower income spouse, Jack will deduct additional child care costs of $8,490 ($11,640 - $3,150). Note that, while Bruce is an eligible child because of his disability, the fact that the disability is not severe enough to qualify Bruce for the disability tax credit means that his annual limit is $4,000 rather than $10,000, and that the periodic limit for Joanna and for the camp fees is $100 rather than $250.

Exercise Eleven-2

Subject: Child Care Expenses

Mr. and Mrs. Sampras have three children. The ages of the children are 4, 9, and 14, and they are all in good mental and physical health. During the current year, Mr. Sampras has net employment income of $14,000, after the deduction of employment expenses of $5,500. Mr. Sampras also received $1,200 in universal child care benefits. Mrs. Sampras has net business income during this period of $54,000, after deducting business expenses of $21,000. The child care costs for the current year, all properly documented for tax purposes, are $10,500. Determine the maximum deduction for child care costs and indicate who should claim them.

End of Exercise. Solution available in Study Guide.

Disability Supports Deduction - ITA 64
Eligibility And Coverage
11-55.   In order to assist disabled individuals work and go to school, ITA 64 provides a disability supports deduction that is available to disabled individuals who are:

- performing duties of an office or employment,
- carrying on a business, either alone or as a partner actively engaged in the business,
- attending a designated educational institution or a secondary school, or
- carrying on research in respect of which the individual received a grant.

11-56.   The deduction is available for an extensive list of costs that can be associated with a disabled person working or going to school. The costs must be paid for by the disabled individual and include the cost of: sign-language interpretation services, a teletypewriter or similar device, a braille printer, an optical scanner, an electronic speech synthesizer, note-taking services, voice recognition software, tutoring services, and talking textbooks.

11-57.   The availability of this deduction is not limited to individuals who qualify for the disability tax credit. If the individual has a hearing impairment that requires sign language assistance, the costs of such services are deductible, without regard to whether the individual is eligible for the disability tax credit. In most cases, a medical practitioner must provide a prescription, or certify that there is a need for incurring the specific type of cost.

Limits On The Amount Deducted
11-58.   The amount of qualifying costs that can be deducted under ITA 64 is limited to the lesser of:

- An amount determined by the formula:

$$A - B, \text{ where}$$

- **A**   is equal to the qualifying disability support costs and
- **B**   is equal to any reimbursement of the amounts (such as payments from medical insurance) included in **A**.

- The total of:

1.   Employment income, business income, scholarships, and research grants.

2.   Where the individual is in attendance at a designated educational institution or secondary school, the least of:

- $15,000;
- $375 times the number of weeks of school attendance at a designated educational institution or secondary school; and
- the amount by which the individual's Net Income For Tax Purposes exceeds

the sum of his employment income, business income, scholarships, and research grants.

Disability Supports Deduction Vs. Medical Expenses Tax Credit

11-59. Since most of the costs that can be deducted under the disability supports deduction could also be claimed for the medical expenses tax credit, it may be difficult for a disabled person to determine the more advantageous way to claim the expenditures. As you would expect, amounts that are deducted under the ITA 64 disability supports deduction cannot be included in the base for the medical expense tax credit.

11-60. As a general rule, the deduction is preferable because the medical expense credit base is reduced by 3 percent of Net Income For Tax Purposes and the deduction is not. In addition, as the medical expense tax credit is based on the lowest tax bracket, the fact that ITA 64 provides a deduction in the calculation of Net Income For Tax Purposes will be an advantage to taxpayers who have sufficient income to be in a higher tax bracket.

11-61. An additional consideration is the fact that the deduction is only available to the disabled person on costs that have been paid for personally by the disabled person. If a spouse or supporting person has paid the costs, the spouse or supporting person could claim the medical expense credit with respect to these costs, but could not claim the disability supports deduction.

Complications Related To Attendant Care Costs

11-62. If an individual qualifies for the ITA 118.3 disability tax credit, he can claim attendant care costs as a medical expense. You may recall from Chapter 6 that, if the medical expense claim is for full time attendant care (defined as more than $10,000 per year), the individual loses the ability to claim the disability tax credit. This medical expense credit for attendant care is available without regard to whether the individual is working or attending a designated educational institution or secondary school.

11-63. Form T929 indicates that only individuals who qualify for the ITA 118.3 disability tax credit can claim amounts paid for part time attendant care as a disability supports deduction (part time is defined as less than $10,000 per year). In some circumstances, where the attendant care costs are over $10,000, it may be beneficial to limit the credit to $10,000 in order to have it qualify as a part time attendant care cost. This results in a very complex situation with respect to these costs. We have tried to simplify the possibilities in the following general summary:

- If an individual qualifies for, and claims, the disability tax credit, he can claim part time or full time attendant care costs (up to a $10,000 maximum) as either an addition to the base for the medical expense tax credit, or as a deduction within the limits of ITA 64.

- If an individual qualifies for, but does not claim the disability tax credit, he can claim full time attendant care costs (more than $10,000), either as an addition to the base for the medical expense tax credit, or as a disability supports deduction within the limits of ITA 64. It would also be possible to claim a portion of the full time attendant care costs as an addition to the base for the medical expense tax credit, with the remainder claimed as a disability supports deduction within the limits of ITA 64.

- If an individual is disabled, but does not qualify for the disability tax credit, he can claim full time attendant care costs (more than $10,000) under ITA 64, subject to certification by a medical practitioner. However, he cannot deduct the costs of part time attendant care (up to $10,000).

Exercise Eleven-3

Subject: Disability Supports Deduction

Jose Morph has visual, speech, and hearing disabilities. However, they are not severe enough to allow him to qualify for the ITA 118.3 disability tax credit. During 2007, he worked on a full time basis as a programmer for a large public company and his employment income totaled $78,000.

His need for full time attendant care has been certified by a medical practitioner and, during 2007, such care cost Jose $23,000. Other deductible costs required to support his ability to work as a disabled person totaled $18,000, all of which were certified by a medical practitioner. His medical insurance reimbursed him for $5,000 of these expenses.

Jose will not include any of these costs in his base for the medical expenses tax credit. Calculate Jose's disability supports deduction for 2007.

End of Exercise. Solution available in Study Guide.

Related Inclusions And Deductions

Introduction
11-64.   At the beginning of this Chapter, we noted that there were several Subdivision e deductions that were directly related to an item that was included in Subdivision d. These items will be dealt with in this Section.

Employment Insurance Benefits - ITA 56(1)(a)(iv) And 60(n)
11-65.   ITA 56(1)(a)(iv) requires that Employment Insurance (EI) benefits received be included in income, even if they are subsequently repaid. Repayment of these benefits can be required if an individual has Net Income in excess of a specified level. If EI benefits must be repaid, the repayment can be deducted under ITA 60(n).

Pension Income Splitting - ITA 56(1)(a.2) And 60(c)
11-66.   When the Harper government announced that it was going to begin taxing the distributions of income trusts, it is likely that the most affected group was senior citizens. They had invested significant portions of their retirement savings in these securities and, as a direct result of the government's change in policy, they lost billions of dollars.

11-67.   To offset the pain for senior citizens, the Harper government simultaneously announced other measures which would benefit this very vocal group of taxpayers. One of the most important of these measures was a provision which provided for reallocation of up to 50 percent of a taxpayer's pension income.

11-68.   While the ability to split CPP amounts has been available to couples for many years, this provision extends this privilege to include most other types of pension income. However, unlike the CPP situation where there is an actual split of the payments being made, this additional split is implemented entirely in the tax returns.

11-69.   The basic provision for the split is found in a ITA 60.03. This Section allows a pensioner (i.e., any resident Canadian who receives pension income) to file a joint election with a spouse or common-law partner to reallocate up to 50 percent of his pension income to a pension transferee (i.e., the spouse or common-law partner). When the election is made, the pension transferee will include the elected amount in income under ITA 56(1)(a.2). The same amount can be deducted by the pensioner under ITA 60(c).

11-70. The types of pension income that are eligible for splitting are the same as those that are eligible for the pension income tax credit. You may recall from Chapter 6 that this included most types of pension income other than OAS and CPP.

Exercise Eleven-4

Subject: Pension Income Splitting

Joanna Sparks lives with her husband of many years, John Sparks. They are both 67 years of age. During 2007, Joanna received $5,900 in OAS payments. She also receives $85,000 of pension income from a plan that was sponsored by her former employer. She has not, at this point in time, applied for CPP. John's only source of 2007 income is $5,900 in OAS payments. Neither Joanna or John have any tax credits other than the basic personal credit, the age credit, and the pension income credit.

Joanna has asked you to indicate the savings in federal tax that would result from making maximum use of pension income splitting for the 2007 taxation year.

End of Exercise. Solution available in Study Guide.

Spousal And Child Support - ITA 56(1)(b) And 60(b)

History

11-71. For many years, no tax distinction was made between payments made by an individual for child support and payments made for spousal support. These amounts were referred to in earlier legislation as alimony or maintenance and, provided they were paid to a former spouse on a periodic basis under the terms of a formal agreement, they were fully deductible to the payor and fully taxable in the hands of the recipient.

11-72. This approach was challenged in a highly publicized case that reached the Supreme Court of Canada. Ms. Thibaudeau claimed that being taxed on child support payments violated her constitutional rights. As the Supreme Court rejected her arguments, this left in place a system in which such payments were deductible to the payor and taxable to the recipient.

11-73. Provided tax considerations are included in the determination of the amounts that must be paid, that arrangement was clearly in the best interests of the family unit. The fact that the person paying child support is usually in a higher tax bracket than the recipient of such payments provides for a significant form of income splitting. There is no question that, if a specified level of after tax support is to be provided to a low income recipient, this goal can be accomplished at a lower aggregate tax cost if the amounts paid are deductible to the high income payor and taxable to the low income recipient.

11-74. Despite the income splitting benefits of the old system, Ms. Thibaudeau's arguments had widespread support, particularly among women. In short, the government was placed in a situation where it could change the tax rules in what appeared to be a response to the needs of women and, at the same time, increase aggregate tax revenues. It is hardly surprising that they took advantage of this opportunity.

11-75. Changes were introduced which, in effect, implemented the view of Ms. Thibaudeau. The terms alimony and maintenance were replaced by the more general term, support. To the extent this support is for a child, as opposed to a spouse, the payments are not deductible to the payor, or taxable to the recipient.

11-76. The current rules are applicable to agreements made after April, 1997 and, in certain circumstances, to agreements made before that time. In general, however, agreements made before May, 1997 and any amounts paid for spousal support, as opposed to child support, will continue to operate under the old rules. This dual system is reflected in ITA 56(1)(b) for inclusions and ITA 60(b) for deductions.

General Conditions For Deduction And Inclusion

11-77.   Even in the case of payments that are eligible for the deduction/inclusion treatment, certain conditions must be satisfied in order for this to occur.   As outlined in IT-530R, the specific conditions that must be met are as follows:

- the amount is paid as alimony or an allowance for the maintenance of the spouse or common-law partner, or former spouse or common-law partner;

- the spouses or common-law partners, or former spouses or common-law partners, are living apart at the time the payment is made, and were separated pursuant to a divorce, judicial separation, or written separation agreement;

- the amount is paid pursuant to a decree, order, or judgment of a competent tribunal or pursuant to a written agreement;

- the recipient has discretionary use of the amount; and

- the amount is payable on a periodic basis.

11-78.   If all of these conditions are met, eligible payments are deductible to the payor and taxed in the hands of the recipient. If one or more of these conditions is not met, the payor will not receive a deduction for the payments and the recipient will not be taxed on the receipts.

11-79.   The reasons for most of these conditions are fairly obvious. For example, without the condition that the spouses are living apart, a couple could effectively split income simply by getting a written separation agreement and having the spouse with the higher income make payments to the spouse with the lower income.

11-80.   While payments prior to the date of a court decree cannot technically be made pursuant to that decree, ITA 56.1(3) and ITA 60.1(3) deem that payments made in the year of the decree or the preceding year will be considered paid pursuant to the decree, provided that the order or agreement specifies that they are to be so considered.

11-81.   Problems often arise with respect to the requirement that payments be made on a periodic basis. Clearly, a single lump sum payment does not qualify, nor does a payment that releases the payor from future obligations. Payments that are in excess of amounts required to maintain the spouse and/or children in the manner to which they were accustomed are also likely to be disallowed. Other factors that should be considered are the interval at which the payments are made and whether the payments are for an indefinite period, or a fixed term.

11-82.   Under some circumstances, a person who receives support payments and includes the amount received in income may be required to repay some portion of these amounts. In these circumstances, ITA 60(c.2) allows the person making the repayment to deduct the amount repaid. Correspondingly, ITA 56(1)(c.2) requires the recipient to include a corresponding amount in income.

Rules For Agreements Made After April, 1997

11-83.   For agreements made after April, 1997, payments for child support are not deductible to the payor under ITA 60(b), nor taxable to the recipient under ITA 56(1)(b). The ITA definition of child support payments is such that any amount that is not clearly identified as being for the benefit of the spouse will be considered child support. This makes it extremely important for the written agreement, which describes the payments, to clearly specify any amounts that are to be designated spousal support.

11-84.   A further problem relates to situations where less than the full amount of required payments is made. If the required payments include both child support and spousal support, the formula used in ITA 56(1)(b) and 60(b) is such that only payments in excess of the required child support will be deductible/taxable. For example, consider an individual required to pay $4,000 in child support and $12,000 in spousal support. If a total of $7,000 is paid during the year, only $3,000 of that amount will be deductible/taxable.

11-85.   A number of additional points are relevant here as follows:

- In general, payments to third parties that are clearly for the benefit of the spouse are deductible to the payor and taxable to the spouse.

- Non-deductible child support payments will not reduce the payor's earned income for RRSP purposes, nor increase the recipient's earned income for RRSP purposes (see Chapter 13).

- The recipient of child support payments will continue to be eligible for the credit for an eligible dependant (see Chapter 6).

- ITA 118(5) prevents an individual from taking a tax credit for a spouse or eligible dependant and, at the same time, deducting support payments to that spouse or child.

- While it is not part of the legislation, the Government of Canada has published an extensive, province by province list of guidelines for child support. These guidelines are dependent on the number of children involved and the income of the payor.

Rules For Agreements Made Before May, 1997

11-86.   Under the revised provisions, the old rules for support payments are still in effect for agreements that were made before May, 1997, provided that they have not been altered since that date. This means that both child and spousal support payments are treated as income to the recipient under ITA 56(1)(b), and are deductible to the individual making the payments under ITA 60(b).

11-87.   Under some circumstances, the current rules with respect to child support become applicable to agreements made before May, 1997. These circumstances are as follows:

1.   Where the payor and recipient file a joint election with the CRA that, for income tax purposes, the payor will not deduct from income, and the recipient will not include in income, payments in respect of child support obligations that arise on or after a specified commencement day.

2.   Where the agreement or order is changed or varied after April, 1997 to change the amount of child support.

3.   Where a new commencement day is specified in an agreement or order.

Exercise Eleven-5

Subject: Support Payments

On July 1, 2007, Sandra and Jerry Groom sign a separation agreement that calls for Sandra to pay Jerry $1,500 per month in child support (Jerry will have custody of their five children) and $2,500 per month in spousal support. To the end of 2007, Sandra's payments total only $11,000. How will these payments be dealt with in Sandra and Jerry's 2007 tax returns?

End of Exercise. Solution available in Study Guide.

Annuity Payments Received - ITA 56(1)(d) And 60(a)

Annuities Purchased In Tax Deferred Plans

11-88.   ITA 248 defines an annuity as an amount payable on a periodic basis, without regard to whether it is payable at intervals longer or shorter than a year. As the term is usually applied, it refers to the investment contracts that are usually sold by insurance companies, either directly to individuals, or to trustees administering RPPs, RRSPs, or DPSPs.

11-89.   In simple terms, the investor pays a lump sum to the insurance company in return for the promise of a periodic payment over either a fixed term, or over the remainder of the individual's life. The payments are designed to return the purchaser's capital and to provide a rate of return on the funds held by the insurance company.

11-90.　　A common approach to receiving retirement benefits from an RRSP is to have the trustee use the funds in the plan to purchase an annuity that is payable to the beneficiary of the RRSP. As will be discussed in more detail in Chapter 13, the funds in an RRSP are a tax deferred balance (i.e., contributions to the plan were deductible when made and earnings on the funds in the RRSP accumulate on a tax free basis).

11-91.　　Given the tax deferred nature of the RRSP balance, all withdrawals from such plans are subject to tax. This means that, when an annuity is purchased inside the RRSP, the full amount of the payments to the taxpayer will be subject to tax. As noted in Paragraph 11-17, they will be included in the taxpayer's Net Income For Tax Purposes under ITA 56(1)(h). Note that a similar analysis would be applicable to payments made from an annuity purchased with funds within a RRIF, DPSP, or RPP.

Annuities Purchased With After Tax Dollars

11-92.　　A different situation exists when an annuity is purchased outside of an RRSP using after tax funds.

> **Example**　An individual purchases a five year ordinary annuity with payments of $2,309 at the end of each year. The cost of the annuity is $10,000, providing the investor with an effective yield of 5 percent.
>
> **Analysis**　The total payments on this annuity would be $11,545, of which $10,000 would represent a return of capital and the $1,545 balance would represent interest earned. As the individual used after tax funds to purchase the annuity, only $1,545 ($11,545 - $10,000) of the annuity payments will be taxed. The balance of the payments will be treated as a tax free return of capital.
>
> In contrast, if the annuity had been purchased within an RRSP, the total $11,545 in payments would be taxable.

11-93.　　The *Income Tax Act* distinguishes between these two situations in a somewhat indirect manner. ITA 56(1)(d) requires the inclusion in income of all annuity payments that are not "otherwise included in income". As payments from RRSPs, DPSPs, RRIFs, and RPPs, are "otherwise included" under other provisions of the *Income Tax Act*, this means that only annuities purchased with after tax funds would be included here.

11-94.　　Note, however, that if RRSP funds were withdrawn and the after tax funds were used to purchase an annuity outside of the plan, the annuity payments would be included under ITA 56(1)(d) and the capital portion of the payments would not be taxable. This reflects the fact that the full amount withdrawn from the RRSP was taxed at the time of withdrawal.

11-95.　　To reflect the fact that a portion of the annuity payments included in income under ITA 56(1)(d) represents a return of after tax investment funds, ITA 60(a) allows a deduction for the capital amount of payments included in income under this Paragraph. As presented in ITR 300, the formula for calculating the capital element of a fixed term annuity payment is as follows:

$$\frac{\text{Capital Outlay To Buy The Annuity}}{\text{Total Payments To Be Received Under The Contract}}$$

11-96.　　This ratio would be multiplied by the annuity payment that was included in income for the year to provide the capital element that is eligible for deduction. To illustrate this procedure, refer to the example in Paragraph 11-92. If this annuity had been purchased with $10,000 in after tax funds, the entire annual payment of $2,309 would be included in income under ITA 56(1)(d). However, this would be offset by a deduction under ITA 60(a) that is calculated as follows:

$$\left[\frac{\$10,000}{\$11,545}\right][\$2,309] = \$2,000$$

Exercise Eleven-6

Subject: Annuity Payments

On January 1 of the current year, Barry Hollock uses $55,000 of his savings to acquire a fixed term annuity. The term of the annuity is four years, the annual payments are $15,873, the payments are received on December 31 of each year, and the rate inherent in the annuity is 6 percent. How much of the $15,873 annual payment must Mr. Hollock include in his annual tax return?

End of Exercise.   Solution available in Study Guide.

Registered Savings Plans

Introduction

11-97.   From a tax perspective, a registered savings plan is one in which some type of savings is allocated to a trust that is registered with the CRA. The registration document requires that the trustee of the plan provide information returns with respect to contributions to and withdrawals from these plans.

11-98.   The *Income Tax Act* provides for a fairly large group of such plans, the most important of which are related to retirement savings. These plans include Registered Pension Plans (RPPs) and Registered Retirement Savings Plans (RRSPs) and will be dealt with in Chapter 13.

11-99.   In this Chapter we will be concerned with two registered plans that are not related to retirement savings. These are Registered Education Savings Plans (RESPs) and Registered Disability Savings Plans (RDSPs). While the RESPs have been around for several years, the RDSPs were introduced by the March, 2007 budget. However, it does not appear that the necessary administrative procedures for RDSPs will be in place until 2008.

11-100.   The basic operation of both RESPs and RDSPs is depicted in Figure 11-1 (facing page). As shown in that Figure, the contributions to these plans are non-deductible to the taxpayer. This is in contrast to both RPPs and RRSPs where the contributions can be deducted at the time they are made.

11-101.   While the contributions to the plans that we are considering are not deductible, they do have significant tax advantages. They can be described as follows:

Tax Deferral   Once contributions have been made, they will be invested in various types of income producing assets. These earnings will not be taxed until they are withdrawn from the registered plan. Further, the earnings can also be invested, resulting in tax free compounding. This provides for significant tax deferral.

Tax Reduction   Typically, contributions to these plans will be made by an individual in a tax bracket that is higher than the tax bracket of the individual who will receive the earnings from the plan. For example, contributions to an RESP are normally made by a parent or grandparent. While this individual may not be in the maximum 29 percent tax bracket, it is likely that they will have sufficient income that payment of taxes is required. This means that if they had invested the funds in their own name, the investment income would have been taxed, in some cases at maximum rates.

In contrast, the RESP earnings will typically be paid out to a student. In most cases, this individual will either be paying no taxes, or will be in a lower bracket than their parents or grandparents.

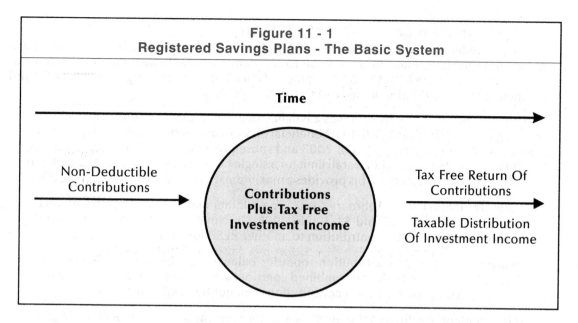

Figure 11 - 1
Registered Savings Plans - The Basic System

11-102.   While there are differences in the detailed rules associated with RESPs and RDSPs, the basic operations of both types of plans are the same. Non-deductible contributions are invested on a tax free basis for a limited period of time. When the accumulated amounts are subsequently distributed, the contributions are paid out on a tax free basis, while the earnings are paid to specified beneficiaries on a taxable basis. The arrangements provide for significant tax deferral and, in most cases a significant reduction of tax.

Registered Education Savings Plans (RESPs)

Contributions

11-103.   The contribution rules for Registered Education Savings Plans (RESPs) are found in ITA 146.1. As we have noted, unlike contributions to an RRSP, contributions to an RESP do not provide a deduction for the taxpayer. However, they do share the second major tax advantage that is available to contributors to RRSPs. This is the fact that, once contributions to these plans are invested, the earnings accrue on a tax free basis.

11-104.   As is discussed more completely in Chapter 13, over extended periods of time, there is a very large benefit associated with this tax free accumulation of earnings. Note, however, that in the case of RESPs, this tax free accumulation is limited to 25 years after the plan is established (30 years for plans with a single beneficiary who is eligible for the ITA 118.3 disability tax credit). At the end of that period, the plan is automatically deregistered.

11-105.   As of 2007, total contributions are limited to $50,000 for each beneficiary. Also as of 2007, there is no annual limit on contributions. This means that an individual could contribute the full $50,000 in the first year of the plan or, alternatively, the full $50,000 could be contributed in any subsequent year. There is completely flexibility with respect to the timing.

11-106.   There is a penalty for excess contributions. If, at the end of any month, the contributions for a particular beneficiary exceed the total limit of $50,000, the contributors to the plan are subject to a 1 percent per month tax on the excess. Note that these limits apply for each beneficiary. If several individuals are contributing to plans with the same beneficiary (e.g., Joan's father and her grandmother are both contributing to a plan on her behalf), the sum of their contributions to Joan's plan cannot exceed the specified limits. Any tax assessed on excess contributions must be shared on a pro rata basis by the contributors.

Canada Education Savings Grants (CESGs)

11-107.   Under the Canada Education Savings Grant (CESG) program, the government will make additional contributions to an RESP to supplement those being made by the contributor(s). The grants are based on a percentage of contributions made by the contributor and are subject to a contribution limit.

11-108.   Prior to 2007, this limit was a balance that accumulated at the rate of $2,000 per year, beginning in the year a potential beneficiary is born and ending in the year in which that individual attains the age of 17. For 2007 and subsequent years, this limit was increased to $2,500 per year. However, the overall limit for a single beneficiary remains at the old figure of $36,000 [(18 Years)($2,000)]. This provides a maximum CESG of $7,200 [(20%)($36,000)].

> **Example** Tom is born in February, 2007. Tom's father makes an RESP contribution of $1,300 for Tom in 2007 and $1,300 in 2008. In November of 2008, Tom's grandmother makes a $3,000 contribution to another RESP for Tom.
>
> **Analysis** Tom's 2008 contribution room for balances eligible for CESGs is $3,700 [(2)($2,500) - $1,300]. As the combined contributions of the father and grandmother total $4,300, $600 of the total contributions will not be eligible for CESGs.
>
> It is important to note that the $600 excess does not carry over and become eligible for CESGs in the following year when more contribution room accrues to Tom. If it is expected that annual contributions to Tom's RESP will be less than $2,500 in the future, this would suggest that Tom's father should limit his 2008 contribution to $700 and defer the extra $600 to the following year. In that year, it would eligible for a grant.

11-109.   Once the amount of eligible contributions for a particular year has been established, the calculation of the amount of the grant will depend on the family income in the preceding taxation year.

> **Family Income Greater Than $74,357** In this case, the grant will be equal to 20 percent of all contributions in the year that are within the beneficiary's contribution room.
>
> **Family Income Between $37,178 And $74,357** In this case there will be a 30 percent grant on the first $500 of contributions for each beneficiary, along with a 20 percent grant on any additional contributions that are within the beneficiary's contribution room.
>
> **Family Income $37,178 Or Less** In this case, the grant will be equal to 40 percent of the first $500 of contributions for a given beneficiary, along with a 20 percent grant on any additional contributions that are within the beneficiary's contribution room.

11-110.   You will probably recognize the $37,178 and $74,357 as the top of the 15.5 and 22 percent federal tax brackets for 2007. These amounts will be indexed in subsequent years.

11-111.   CESGs will not be paid for RESP beneficiaries for the year in which they turn 18 years of age, or in any subsequent year. In addition, in a year in which the beneficiary is 16 or 17, CESG payments will be made only where:

- a minimum of $2,000 of RESP contributions was made in respect of the beneficiary before the year in which the beneficiary attains 16 years of age (while the March, 2007 budget did not deal with this issue, it is likely that will be changed to $2,500 for 2007 and subsequent years); or

- a minimum of $100 in annual RESP contributions was made in respect of the beneficiary in any four years before the year in which the beneficiary attains 16 years of age.

Exercise Eleven-7

Subject: Canada Education Savings Grants

Jeanine was born in 2007. During 2007, her father establishes a RESP for her and contributes $500 to the plan, while Jeanine's grandfather contributes an additional $1,200. During 2008, her father contributes $1,500 and her grandfather adds a further $2,400. In all of the years 2006 through 2008, Jeanine's family has family income of less than $37,178. Determine the amount of the CESGs that would be added to Jeanine's RESP In 2007 and 2008.

End of Exercise.   Solution available in Study Guide.

Canada Learning Bonds (CLBs)

11-112.   A further enhancement to the RESP system was introduced in 2004. This enhancement, designated Canada Learning Bonds (CLBs), is like the CESGs in that the government makes contributions to an individual's RESP. However, unlike the CESGs, the CLB contributions are not based on contributions made to the RESP by others.

11-113.   The CLB provisions apply to children born after 2003 who have an RESP established in their names. Such children will be eligible for a CLB contribution to their RESP in each year that their family is eligible for the National Child Benefit supplement. This potential eligibility begins in the year the child is born and ends in the year that the child turns 15 years of age. As noted in Chapter 6, for 2007, this supplement begins to be phased out when family income reaches $20,883. The family income level at which it disappears varies with the number of children in the family.

11-114.   The CLB contributions to individual RESPs will be as follows:

- In the first year that the child is eligible for a CLB contribution, an amount of $500 will be provided. In addition, a one-time additional amount of $25 will be added in order to help defray the costs of establishing the RESP.

- In each subsequent year of eligibility, a CLB contribution of $100 will be made. This continues until the year in which the child turns 15 years of age.

11-115.   The child's eligibility will vary with the income of his or her family. In some families, the National Child Benefit supplement will be available every year and, correspondingly, the CLB contributions will be made each year. In situations such as this, the maximum total contribution would be $2,025 {$500 + $25 + [(15)($100)]}. In other cases, eligibility may be present in some years and not present in other years. In such cases, the total contributions will be less.

11-116.   For families who qualify for the CLB contributions, the establishment of an RESP for each child is clearly a desirable course of action. A potential problem with the CLB program is that families in the income brackets that qualify for this benefit may not be aware of the program or have access to the kind of assistance required to establish an RESP.

Types Of Plans

11-117.   RESP legislation provides for "family plans" in which each of the beneficiaries is related to the contributor by blood or adoption. Family plans, which are typically established for several siblings under age 18, are subject to the same contribution limits per beneficiary, but provide additional flexibility for the contributor because educational assistance payments need not be limited to the proportion of each child's "share" of the contributions.

11-118.   This feature is important when an individual has several children and not all of them pursue higher education. Because of the flexibility inherent in family plans, all of the plan distributions could be directed towards the children who are eligible to received such funds. To ensure that family plans do not provide unintended benefits, no beneficiaries 21 years of age or older can be added to a family plan that is submitted for registration after 1998.

11-119.   There are basically two types of RESPs available. They can be described as follows:

Scholarship Plans are available through "scholarship trust companies" such as the Canadian Scholarship Trust Plan. These plans are distinguished by the fact that all of their funds must be invested in government guaranteed investments. These companies offer group plans (earnings are allocated only to those children who attend college or university), as well as individual plans (contributors can recover their share of the investment earnings).

Self-Directed Plans allow investors to choose their own investments. The list of qualified investments is similar to that applicable to self-directed RRSPs. For example, publicly traded stocks are eligible, but income producing real estate is not. As is now the case with RRSPs, there is no foreign content limit for self-directed RESPs.

Payments To Beneficiaries

11-120.   Prior to 2007, payments could be made to a beneficiary of a plan, only when they were a full time student at an institution that would qualify the individual for the education tax credit (i.e., college or university courses, as well as other courses designated by the Minister of Human Resources Development Canada). For 2007 and subsequent years, the March, 2007 budget proposes adding part-time students to the list of eligible beneficiaries. This will be based on eligibility for the education tax credit for part-time studies.

11-121.   To the extent that these payments are made up of the contributions made to the plan, they will be received on a tax free basis. In contrast, the component of the distribution that represents the tax deferred earnings of the plan and any CESG and CLB amounts will be taxed in the hands of the student. For RESPs created after 1998, there is an initial limit of $5,000 in RESP payments to full time students, but this limit is not applicable once the student has completed 13 consecutive weeks in a qualifying educational program.

Payments To Contributors

11-122.   If the intended beneficiary is not pursuing post-secondary education by age 21, and the plan has been running for at least ten years, a contributor who is a Canadian resident will be able to withdraw both his contributions and accumulated earnings from the plan. The contributions will be received tax free. With respect to the distribution of the earnings, there are two possibilities:

- Up to $50,000 of such receipts can be transferred to an RRSP, provided the contributor has sufficient contribution room (see Chapter 13 for coverage of RRSP contribution room). The distribution that will be included in income will be offset, in this case, by the RRSP deduction. Note that this is not an addition to the RRSP contribution room. The transfer has to be within the existing RRSP contribution limit for the plan.

- Any earnings distribution that cannot be transferred to an RRSP as described in the preceding paragraph will be subject to regular tax, as well as a special 20 percent additional tax at the federal level. This additional tax is a sort of catch-up mechanism for the tax that was deferred while the funds were in the plan. It should serve to discourage the use of RESPs for tax deferral that is unrelated to funding education.

Repayment Of CESG Contributions

11-123.   Payments for non-educational purposes can be complicated by the fact that some of the assets in the plan may reflect CESG contributions. As these contributions were intended to assist with the cost of post-secondary education, they are not intended to be available for non-educational purposes. As a reflection of this, when contributions that have given rise to a CESG are withdrawn for non-educational purposes, the RESP trustee will be required to make a CESG repayment equal to 20 percent of the total withdrawal. A simple example will clarify these rules:

Example A father establishes an RESP for his six year old daughter in 2007 and contributes $1,500 a year for six years. The family's income is over $100,000 each year and no CLB contributions are received by the plan. CESGs paid to the plan total $1,800 [(6)($1,500)(20%)]. In 2022, after his daughter has turned 21 and made it clear she has no interest in attending university, her father withdraws $3,000 of contributions from the plan for non-educational purposes.

Analysis In this situation, all of the father's contributions were assisted by a 20 percent CESG. Given this, the RESP trustee is required to make a $600 [(20%)($3,000)] CESG repayment to the government.

11-124.   Where a plan also contains unassisted contributions, assisted contributions will be considered to be withdrawn before unassisted contributions. The 20 percent repayment will be applied until the assisted contributions are withdrawn. Subsequent withdrawals will not be subject to repayment.

11-125.   An RESP trustee will also be required to repay CESG contributions in certain other situations:

- when the plan is terminated or revoked;

- when a beneficiary under the plan is replaced, except where the new beneficiary is under 21 years of age and either, the new beneficiary is a brother or sister of the former beneficiary, or both beneficiaries are related to the contributor by blood or adoption; and

- when there is a transfer from the plan to another RESP involving either a change of beneficiaries, or a partial transfer of funds.

11-126.   If the RESP is a group plan in which earnings are allocated to other beneficiaries, repayment will not be required when a specific RESP beneficiary does not pursue post-secondary education.

Evaluation Of RESPs

11-127.   For families who manage their resources in a manner that permits taking full advantage of all types of tax deferred investments, there is little question that such plans should be established for children who will likely pursue post-secondary education.

11-128.   However, in the real world, many families expend all of their resources on current consumption and have few funds left for any type of tax deferred investment. For example, only a fraction of the deductible contributions that could be made to RRSPs are, in fact, actually made.

11-129.   In situations where there are sufficient resources to contribute to either an RRSP or an RESP, but not to both, there is the question of which of these two vehicles is more advantageous. A rigorous analysis of this question is dependent on a large number of assumptions and goes beyond the scope of this material. Although detailed coverage of RRSPs is found in Chapter 13, several relevant points can be made here:

- A major advantage of RESPs relative to RRSPs is the fact that RESP contributions can be eligible for a Canada Education Savings Grant.

- A further advantage of RESPs relative to RRSPs is the fact that the establishment of such plans allows contributions to be made under the Canada Learning Bonds program. Note that this program could justify establishing an RESP for children in low income families, even if no contributions were made to the plan.

- A major advantage of RRSPs relative to RESPs is the fact that RRSP contributions are deductible against current Taxable Income. Given a particular before tax amount available, this allows for larger contributions to be made in the case of RRSPs.

- Offsetting the deductibility of RRSP contributions, payments out of RRSPs to planholders are normally taxed. While some individuals may be in a lower tax bracket in the period of payment, many individuals will be taxed at the same rates as were applicable when their contributions were deductible. In contrast, a distribution of RESP earnings to a student attending university or college may be received without the recipient having to pay tax. With personal and education related tax credits available, a student can receive a significant amount of income before having to pay any taxes. Even when taxes must be paid, all amounts are likely to be taxed in the minimum tax bracket.

- Both RRSPs and RESPs offer the advantage of having earnings compound on a tax free basis. As is illustrated in detail in Chapter 13, this is a very powerful mechanism for tax deferral. In this area, an advantage for RRSPs is that the tax free compounding period is potentially longer.

11-130.   Given these offsetting advantages, the choice between contributing to an RRSP and contributing to an RESP can be a very difficult decision.

Registered Disability Savings Plans (RDSPs)
The Problem

11-131.   Parents of children who are severely disabled are usually faced with a life-long commitment for care and support of their children. Further, the needs of these disabled individuals for care and support may extend well beyond the lifetime of the parents. Parents facing this possibility would like to ensure that the needed care and support is, in fact, available as long as it is required.

11-132.   While there are a number of provisions that provide year-to-year tax assistance for disabled individuals and their parents, there is nothing currently in place that would provide for longer term care that could extend past the life of the parents. To deal with this problem, the March, 2007 budget has introduced Registered Disability Savings Plans (RDSPs).

11-133.   The mechanics of these plans are largely the same as those applicable to RESPs. Non-deductible contributions are made to a registered trust, the contributions are invested in income producing assets, the earnings accumulate and compound within the trust on a tax free basis, and taxes are assessed on these accumulated earnings when they are distributed to the beneficiary.

11-134.   Because fairly complex administrative procedures are required to implement plans of this sort, it is unlikely that any RDSPs will be established prior to 2008. At this point in time, draft legislation for these plans has not been put forward. Given this, the discussion that follows is based on the fairly basic description of these plans that is found in the budget papers.

Basic Features
Eligibility

11-135.   An individual who qualifies for the ITA 118.3 disability tax credit, that individual's parent, or that individual's legal representative, is eligible to establish an RDSP with the disabled individual as the beneficiary. The individual must qualify for the disability tax credit when the plan is established, as well as in each subsequent year. Failure to qualify will result in the distribution of all amounts in the plan.

Contributions

11-136.   For each beneficiary of an RDSP, contributions are limited to $200,000 over the individual's lifetime. There is no annual limit. However, contributions can only be made until the end of the year in which the beneficiary reaches 59 years of age.

11-137.   The contributions cannot be deducted by the person making them. Given this lack of deductibility, it is not surprising that there are no restrictions on who can make contributions.

Canada Disability Savings Grants (CDSGs)

11-138.   As was the case with RESP contributions, the government will match the RDSP contributions that are made in a particular year. The rate of the matching CDSGs will depend on the family income in the preceding year. It will be at rates of 100, 200, or 300 percent as per the following schedule:

Family Income Up To $74,357:   300 percent of the first $500, plus 200 percent of the next $1,000.

Family Income Over $74,357:   100 percent of the first $1,000.

11-139.   As is the case with Canada Education Savings Grants, $74,357, the top of the 22 percent federal tax bracket for 2007, is used as a limit in the calculations. It will be indexed in subsequent years.

11-140.   For each beneficiary, there is a lifetime CDSG maximum of $70,000. Payments are available until the end of the year in which the beneficiary attains 49 years of age. Until the beneficiary is 18, amounts distributed will be taxed in the hands of the beneficiary. After that age, distributions can be paid to the beneficiary or his spouse or common-law partner.

Canada Disability Savings Bonds (CDSBs)

11-141.   Again, following the pattern of RESPs, RDSPs will have additional payments for low income families. The CDSB payments to an RDSP will be up to $1,000 per year, with a lifetime maximum of $20,000. They will start to be phased out when family income reaches $20,883, and will disappear when it reaches $37,178. (These are the 2007 levels and they will be indexed in future years.) These payments are available until the end of the year in which the beneficiary attains 49 years of age.

RDSP Distributions

11-142.   Both contributed amounts and accumulated earnings must be paid to the beneficiary or his legal representative. Contributors will not be entitled to recover the amounts that they have provided to the plan.

11-143.   Payments have to begin by the end of the year in which the beneficiary attains 60 years of age. They will be subject to an annual maximum based on the beneficiary's life expectancy and the fair market value of the assets in the plan. Under certain circumstances, the beneficiary or his legal representative will be allowed to encroach on the capital of the plan.

11-144.   While the budget papers do not make this clear, it would appear that distributions of earnings that have accumulated in the plan will be taxable to the beneficiary. They do note, however, that distributions from an RDSP will not be taken into consideration for purposes of calculating income benefits, Old Age Security payments, or Employment Insurance Benefits.

Death Or Cessation Of Disability

11-145.   If an RDSP beneficiary dies or no longer qualifies for the disability tax credit, all of the funds in the RDSP will have to be paid to the beneficiary or his estate. To the extent that this distribution includes CDSGs or CDSBs that have been paid in the preceding 10 years, these amounts will have to be refunded to the government.

Key Terms Used In This Chapter

11-146.   The following is a list of the key terms used in this Chapter. These terms, and their meanings, are compiled in the Glossary Of Key Terms located at the back of the separate paper Study Guide and on the Student CD-ROM.

Alimony

Annual Child Care Expense Amount

Annuity

Canada Disability Savings Bonds

Canada Disability Savings Grants

Canada Education Savings Grants

Canada Learning Bonds

Child Care Expenses

Child Support

Common-Law Partner

Death Benefit

Deferred Income Plans

Disability Supports Deduction

Earned Income (Child Care Expenses)

Eligible Child

Income Splitting

Moving Expenses

Periodic Child Care Expense Amount

Registered Disability Savings Plan (RDSP)

Registered Education Savings Plan (RESP)

Retiring Allowance

Spousal Support

Spouse

Support Amount

Universal Child Care Benefit

References

11-147.   For more detailed study of the material in this Chapter, we refer you to the following:

ITA 56	Amounts To Be Included In Income For Year
ITA 56.1	Support
ITA 60	Other Deductions
ITA 60.1	Support
ITA 62	Moving Expenses
ITA 63	Child Care Expenses
ITA 64	Disability Supports Deduction
ITA 146.1	Registered Education Savings Plans
ITR 300	Capital Element Of Annuity Payments
IC 93-3R	Registered Education Savings Plans
IT-75R4	Scholarships, Fellowships, Bursaries, Prizes And Research Grants
IT-178R3	Moving Expenses (Archived)
IT-337R4	Retiring Allowances
IT-340R	Scholarships, Fellowships, Bursaries, And Research Grants - Forgivable Loans, Repayable Awards, And Repayable Employment Income
IT-495R3	Child Care Expenses
IT-499R	Superannuation Or Pension Benefits
IT-508R	Death Benefits
IT-530R	Support Payments

Problems For Self Study

(The solutions for these problems can be found in the separate Study Guide.)

Self Study Problem Eleven - 1

In May of the current year, following a dispute with her immediate superior, Ms. Elaine Fox resigned from her present job in Halifax and began to look for other employment. She was not able to find suitable work in Halifax. However, she did locate another job in Regina and was expected to report for work on October 1.

After locating the new job, Ms. Fox flew to Regina to find living quarters for herself. After two days of searching, Ms. Fox was able to locate a suitable house. Subsequent to purchasing her new home, Ms. Fox remained in Regina for an additional four days in order to purchase various furnishings for this residence. Her expenses for this trip were as follows:

Air Fare (Halifax - Regina, Return)	$ 689
Car Rental (6 Days At $35)	210
Hotel (6 Days At $110)	660
Food (6 Days At $40)	240
Total Expenses	**$1,799**

On her return to Halifax, she received the following statements from her attorneys:

Real Estate Commission - Old Home	$ 9,500
Legal Fees - Old Home	1,400
Unpaid Taxes On Old Home To Date Of Sale	800
Legal Fees - New Home	1,850
Transfer Tax On New Home	600
Total	**$14,150**

On August 31 of the current year, after supervising the final packing of her property and its removal from the old house, Ms. Fox spent three days in a Halifax hotel while she finalized arrangements for her departure. Expenses during this period were as follows:

Hotel (Three Days At $95)	$285
Food (Three Days At $45)	135
Total	**$420**

On September 3, she leaves Halifax by automobile, arriving in Regina on September 10. As her new residence is not yet available, she is forced to continue living in a Regina hotel until September 26. Her expenses for the period September 3 through September 26 are as follows:

Gasoline	$ 350
Hotel (23 Days At $95)	2,185
Food (23 Days At $45)	1,035
Total	**$3,570**

On moving into the new residence, she is required to pay the moving company a total of $3,800. This fee includes $675 for the 16 days of storage required because the new home was not available when the furnishings arrived.

Ms. Fox's only income for the current year was employment income and the net amounts to be included in her Net Income For Tax Purposes are as follows:

Problems For Self Study

Old Job (5 Months)	$15,000
New Job (3 Months)	10,500
Net Employment Income	**$25,500**

Ms. Fox's new employer did not provide any reimbursement for moving expenses.

Required: Calculate the maximum allowable moving expenses that Ms. Fox can deduct from her Net Income For Tax Purposes for the current year and any amount that can be carried over to the subsequent year. If Ms. Fox wanted to calculate her moving expenses using the simplified method for vehicle and meal expenses, what additional information does she need?

Self Study Problem Eleven - 2

Mr. and Mrs. Pleasant have three children who are 8, 10, and 15 years of age and live at home. All of the children enjoy good physical and mental health. In order to keep up with the costs of a family of this size, both Mr. Pleasant and Mrs. Pleasant are employed. However, this requires that a considerable amount be spent on care for their children.

During 2007, Mr. Pleasant had earned income of $33,000, while Mrs. Pleasant had earned income of $18,000. Payments for child care amounted to $100 per week, for a total of 48 weeks.

Also during 2007, there was a period of six weeks during which Mrs. Pleasant was hospitalized for injuries suffered in a fall while rock climbing. This period was part of the 48 weeks for which child care payments were made.

Required: Determine the amount of child care expenses that can be deducted by Mr. Pleasant and by Mrs. Pleasant for the year ending December 31, 2007.

Self Study Problem Eleven - 3

Arthur Madison, Jules Madison, and Stanley Madison are brothers and they have asked you to assist them in preparing their tax returns for the 2007 taxation year. They have provided you with the following information:

	Arthur	Jules	Stanley
Net employment income	$6,000	$18,000	$23,000
Net business income (loss)	Nil	5,000	(12,000)
Net property income (loss)	8,000	(4,000)	11,000
Capital gains	5,625	14,000	Nil
Capital losses	Nil	(17,000)	(10,000)
Employment insurance received	3,000	Nil	Nil
Pension benefits received	Nil	3,000	Nil
Charitable donations	(4,000)	(2,000)	(1,000)
Tuition fees paid	Nil	Nil	(800)
Spousal support payments made	Nil	Nil	(4,800)

Required: Determine the 2007 Net Income For Tax Purposes for each of the Madison brothers and indicate any losses that can be carried over to other years.

Assignment Problems

(The solutions for these problems are only available in
the solutions manual that has been provided to your instructor.)

Assignment Problem Eleven - 1

On January 2, 2007, Mrs. Long died in an automobile crash. Mrs. Long was 55 years old and, at the time of her death, was a full time employee of Apex Distribution Systems. During 2006, Mrs. Long earned $47,000 in employment income.

Because of her years of faithful service, Apex decides to pay a death benefit to Mrs. Long's surviving spouse in the amount of $24,000. The amount is to be paid in annual instalments of $6,000 per year, with the first instalment being paid in 2007.

Required: What effect will this death benefit have on the Net Income For Tax Purposes of Mrs. Long's spouse in 2007 and in subsequent years?

Assignment Problem Eleven - 2

Mr. Masters commenced studies on a full-time basis at the University of Manitoba on September 1, 2007. His tuition fees for the period September 1, 2007 through April 30, 2008 were $5,000 and his textbook purchases totalled $640. One-half of the tuition fees and textbook purchases were for the September to December, 2007 semester. The remainder related to the January to April, 2008 semester.

All of these amounts were paid by Mr. Masters' wife, a very successful trial lawyer.

During 2007, Mr. Masters received the following amounts:

Wages from part time employment	$ 2,400
Scholarship granted by university	3,500
Eligible dividends from Canadian public corporations	2,000
Inheritance	25,000

On December 15, 2007, Mr. Masters contributed $5,300 to his 9 year old son's Registered Education Savings Plan.

Required: Determine the minimum Net Income For Tax Purposes that Mr. Masters will have to report for his 2007 taxation year. Provide any advice you feel would assist him in planning future actions concerning his son's RESP.

Assignment Problem Eleven - 3

Mr. Tully resigned from his job in Calgary on September 30 of the current year, after completing his executive MBA. His new position at a high tech firm in Ottawa started on December 1. In October, Mr. Tully flew to Ottawa to find a new home for himself and his family. While he located a suitable house and signed the purchase agreement after four days in the city, finalizing all of the details associated with the purchase required him to remain in Ottawa for another three days. His expenses for this trip were as follows:

Air fare (Calgary - Ottawa, Return)	$ 675
Car rental (7 days at $30)	210
Hotel (7 days at $90)	630
Food (7 days at $30)	210
Total Expenses	$ 1,725

Assignment Problems

On his return to Calgary, he received the following information from his lawyer:

Real estate commission - old home	$ 9,000
Legal fees - old home	1,500
Unpaid taxes on old home to date of sale	1,200
Legal fees - new home	1,750
Transfer tax on new home	1,100
Total	**$14,550**

On November 14 of the current year, after supervising the final packing of their property and its removal from the old house, Mr. Tully and his family leave Calgary in their minivan. They arrive in Ottawa on November 20th. However, because of some delays in the completion of their new home, they are unable to move in until November 30. Their expenses during the period November 14 through November 30 are as follows:

Gasoline	$ 415
Hotel (16 days at $75)	1,200
Food (16 days at $60)	960
Total	**$2,575**

The moving company invoice totals $4,500. Included in the fee is $450 for the 9 days of storage required because the furniture could not be moved into the new home on its arrival in Ottawa.

Mr. Tully's only income for the current year was employment income and the net amounts to be included in his Net Income For Tax Purposes are as follows:

Old job (9 months)	$54,000
New job (1 month)	8,000
Net Employment Income	**$62,000**

Mr. Tully's new employer did not provide any reimbursement for moving expenses.

Required: Calculate the maximum allowable moving expenses that Mr. Tully can deduct from his Net Income For Tax Purposes for the current year and any amount that can be carried over to the subsequent year. Mr. Tully does not use the simplified method of calculating travel expenses.

Assignment Problem Eleven - 4

Mr. and Mrs. Harris have four children and, at the end of 2007, their ages are 5, 10, 12, and 15. The 15 year old child has a prolonged physical handicap, which qualifies him for the disability tax credit.

Mrs. Harris is a stock broker and had 2007 salary and commissions of $63,500. Mr. Harris is involved in a travel business and, due to some bad strategic decisions, his share of the earnings of this business for the year ending December 31, 2007 amounts to only $4,200. In addition to his business earnings, Mr. Harris has interest income for 2007 of $12,500. Mr. Harris also received $1,200 in universal child care benefits.

As both spouses must spend considerable time at work, full time child care is required. As a consequence, their payments for child care amount to $250 per week for 49 weeks of the year. With respect to the other three weeks, all of the children attend a prestigious music camp with a special program for the disabled during the month of June. The cost of this camp is $3,000 per child, or a total of $12,000 for the three weeks.

In February, 2007, Mr. Harris fell off a chair lift while skiing and was in the hospital for a period of four weeks.

In late September, 2007, Mrs. Harris is convicted of insider trading activities and sentenced to six months in prison. She immediately begins serving the sentence and spends the last 12 weeks of 2007 in jail.

Required: Determine the maximum amount that can be deducted by Mr. and Mrs. Harris for child care costs with respect to the 2007 taxation year.

Assignment Cases

Assignment Case Eleven - 1 *(Comprehensive Case Covering Chapters 5 to 11)*

Ms. Priya Saigon is 37 years old and divorced from her former spouse. She has two children from the marriage, Vera, aged 5 and Leo, aged 9. Neither of these children have any 2007 income.

The divorce decree, which was issued in 2005, requires her former spouse to pay $3,000 per month in child support and an additional $1,000 per month in spousal support. While all of the payments for previous years have been made, during 2007, her former spouse has experienced financial difficulties and has paid only $40,000 of the required amounts.

Ms. Saigon also provides care for her 85 year old grandfather who lives with her and her children. While her grandfather is not mentally or physically infirm, his 2007 income was only $7,950, leaving him as a dependant of Ms. Saigon.

Ms. Saigon is employed by Viet Foods Ltd., a large public company. For 2007, she has a base salary of $75,000 per year. During 2006, she was awarded a bonus of $19,500, all of which was paid in January, 2007. For her employment related travel, the company provides her with an automobile which the company leases for $560 per month. Ms. Saigon is required to pay all of her own operating and maintenance costs on the automobile. During 2007, these costs totaled $6,300. The automobile was available for use for 11 months during 2007 and was driven a total of 43,360 kilometers. Of these kilometers, all but 8,240 were for employment related use.

Her employer withheld the following amounts from her 2007 earnings:

RPP Contributions	$3,400
EI Contributions	720
CPP Contributions	1,990
Employee Share Of Life Insurance Premiums	250

Her employer pays her Alberta provincial health care premium of $44 per month.

During 2007, Ms. Saigon is transferred by Viet Foods Ltd. from their Edmonton office to their Calgary office. The Company has agreed to fully compensate her for any loss on the sale of her Edmonton house, but will not compensate her for the legal fees associated with the sale. The Company will provide her with a $15,000 payment when she purchases a home in order to compensate her for the higher cost of Calgary housing.

Viet Foods Ltd. is also providing her with a $200,000 interest free housing loan to help finance her new house purchase. This loan is granted on April 1, 2007 and must be repaid at the end of five years. In addition to these other amounts, the Company is providing a $10,000 allowance to cover any additional costs of the move.

On January 3, 2007, Ms. Saigon flies to Calgary at a cost of $325 to locate a new residence for her and her family. During the three days that she is there, her food and lodging costs total $575. Both the air fare and the food and lodging costs are reimbursed by Viet Foods Ltd. After considering the properties that she has seen, she makes an offer on a property on January 10. The offer is accepted that same day.

Later that month she sells her Edmonton home which she purchased for $265,000 in 2005. The house is sold for $257,800. While Ms. Saigon managed to sell the house without using a real estate agent, legal fees associated with the sale total $950.

Ms. Saigon and her family leave Edmonton on March 15 and arrive in Calgary that same day. She uses her Company's car to transport herself and her family. This milage is included in the 43,360 kilometer total and is viewed as being employment related. As the family brought a picnic lunch for the trip, she ignores food costs for the day.

Unfortunately, her new Calgary home is not available until April 3 and, as a consequence, she and her family stay in a Calgary hotel from March 15 through April 3. The room and food costs for this 19 day period averaged $600 per day, a total of $11,400.

The cost for moving her household effects and leaving them in storage until her Calgary home was ready totaled $3,500. Her legal fees associated with acquiring the Calgary home are $600.

Ms. Saigon has belonged to her employer's stock purchase plan since 2005. In that year she acquired 360 shares at $5.00 per share. In 2006, she acquired an additional 500 shares at $5.25 per share. On February 1, 2007, she acquired 400 more shares at $6.00 per share. On July 1, 2007, all of her shares paid an eligible dividend of $0.30 per share. In order to help finance some of the costs of the move, she sold 900 of these shares in December, 2007 at $6.10 per share.

On January 1, 2007, Ms. Saigon purchases an annuity for $28,733. The annuity was purchased with after-tax funds and will provide a payment of $5,000 at the end of each year for eight years. Given its price, the effective yield on the annuity is 8 percent.

Before moving to Calgary, child care costs in Edmonton were $200 per week for 11 weeks. In Calgary, the weekly cost increased to $250 per week and were paid for a total of 36 weeks. In the summer, both children spent four weeks at an exclusive summer camp for gifted children. The fees at this camp were $500 per child per week.

The 2007 medical expenses for Ms. Saigon and her dependants, which were all paid for by Ms. Saigon, are as follows:

Ms. Saigon	$ 1,465
Vera	493
Leo	1,245
Grandfather	12,473
Total Medical Expenses	$15,676

During 2007 Ms. Saigon receives payments for the Universal Child Care Benefit of $1,200.

Required: Calculate Ms. Saigon's minimum 2007 Net Income For Tax Purposes, her minimum 2007 Taxable Income, and her minimum 2007 federal Tax Payable without consideration of any income tax withheld by her employer. Ignore GST and PST considerations. Assume a prescribed rate of 3 percent during all four quarters of 2007.

Assignment Case Eleven - 2 (Comprehensive Case Covering Chapters 5 to 11)

Mr. Carlos Santini is 45 years of age and divorced from his former spouse, Gloria. Because Gloria is an extremely successful actress, she is constantly traveling. Given this, Carlos and Gloria concluded it would be best if he retained custody of their three children. None of the children had any income during 2007. They can be described as follows:

Andrew Andrew is five years old.

Lolita Lolita is 12 years old and blind.

Estelle Estelle is 18 years old and is dependent on Carlos because of a physical disability. She does not, however, qualify for the disability tax credit.

Carlos receives $1,200 in Universal Child Care Benefits during 2007.

Gloria is very well paid for her work and, as a consequence, is required to make monthly payments of $10,000 per month to Carlos. Of this amount, $3,500 is designated as spousal support, with the remaining $6,500 designated as child support. All required amounts were paid during 2007. In addition, because she experienced a large increase in her performance fees during 2007, Gloria paid an additional lump-sum amount to Carlos of $15,000.

Medical expenses for Mr. Santini and his dependants during 2007 were as follows:

Carlos	$ 850
Andrew	1,250
Lolita	8,560
Estelle	10,260
Total Medical Expenses	$20,920

Mr. Santini uses a national agency to provide full time child care. The 2007 costs for the three children total $22,500. In addition, Lolita and Estelle attend a music camp for four weeks during 2007. The cost of this camp is $500 per child per week. During the period when Lolita and Estelle are at camp, Carlos incurs additional costs for care of Andrew of $1,000.

In 2005 and previous years, Carlos worked for a large public company. During this period he received options to purchase 8,000 shares of the Company's stock for $15 per share. The shares were trading for $14 per share at this time. On June 1, 2007, he exercises these options. On this date, the shares are trading at $22.50 per share. His former employer withholds the maximum 2007 CPP contributions due to the exercise of the stock options.

On December 1, 2007, he sells all of these shares for $25.00 per share. The commission on the transaction is $2,000.

Beginning in 2002 on a part time basis and then on a full time basis beginning in 2005, Mr. Santini operated an unincorporated accounting and tax return preparation business in Toronto. On January 1, 2007, the business has the following capital assets (all computer equipment is leased):

	Capital Cost	UCC
Building (Class 1)	$200,000	$165,000
Land (Site For The Building)	100,000	N/A
Furniture And Fixtures	45,000	28,600

Mr. Santini owns a minivan that he uses for personal purposes. On January 3, 2007, he purchased an automobile for $52,000 that he will use exclusively for business purposes.

Despite the fact that he is an accountant, he keeps his business records on a cash basis. For 2007, the business has a net cash flow of $59,300, not including the January 3 payment for the automobile. Relevant balances at the beginning and end of 2007 are as follows:

	January 1	December 31
Billed Receivables	$37,000	$15,000
Unbilled Work In Process	42,000	26,000
Accounts Payable	14,000	32,000

During April, 2007, Carlos' parents and twin brother are arrested in a highly publicized raid on a counterfeit operation and he loses most of his clients. As a result, he decides to move his family and his business from Toronto, Ontario to Kamloops, British Columbia. He flies to Kamloops in June, 2007 to find a suitable home. He returns to Toronto where he learns that his offer to purchase a house has been accepted. Carlos plans to move to his new home in September, 2007 and open a new tax practice in Kamloops in January, 2008.

Mr. Santini arranges to have his business automobile stored at a Toronto garage belonging to his brother, who will drive the automobile to Kamloops in January, 2008.

The building in which his business operates in Toronto is sold for $425,000. Of this amount, it is estimated that $125,000 relates to the land. The furniture and fixtures are sold for $32,400. Carlos acquires a new building in Kamloops in November, 2007 for $520,000 of which $140,000 relates to the value of the land. New furniture and fixtures are acquired in December, 2007 at a cost of $58,000.

Mr. Santini always deducts the maximum available CCA, even if this results in a loss for the current year. Ignore the possibility that the CCA rate for non-residential buildings could be eligible for an additional 2 percent increase as proposed in the March, 2007 budget.

Since 1996, Mr. Santini has owned both a house in Toronto and a cottage near Huntsville where he and his family spent the summers. The house cost $273,900 and is sold in 2007 for $420,000. As part of the sale agreement, he replaced the heating system at a cost of $5,000. The cottage cost $156,000 and is sold in 2007 for $350,000.

A selling commission is paid on each sale in the amount of 4.5 percent of the selling price. On the advice of his accountant, Mr. Santini plans to deduct the sales commission and legal fees on the house as moving expenses and account for the sales commission and legal fees on the cottage as selling costs.

Other costs associated with the move are as follows:

Legal Fees On Sale Of Huntsville Cottage	$ 675
Legal Fees On Sale Of Toronto House	850
Legal Fees On Acquisition Of Kamloops House	940
Payments For Moving And Storage	9,800
Cost Of Kamloops Trip To Locate New Residence	1,400
Hotel, Food, And Gasoline On Drive To Kamloops (5 Days)	1,860
Costs Of Hotel And Food In Kamloops While Waiting For Completion Of Renovations On New House (12 Days)	4,675
Total	$20,200

Mr. Santini receives the following amounts of investment income during 2007:

Interest	$2,500
Eligible Dividends From Taxable Canadian Companies	3,820
Total Investment Income Received	$6,320

During 2007, Mr. Santini makes contributions to registered charities in the amount of $2,400.

Required: Calculate the following for Mr. Santini:

- his minimum 2007 Net Income For Tax Purposes,
- his minimum 2007 Taxable Income,
- his minimum 2007 Balance Owing to the CRA, including any CPP contributions payable,
- the January 1, 2008 adjusted cost base and UCC of any business assets, and
- any carry overs available to Mr. Santini and any rules applicable to claiming the carry overs.

Ignore GST and PST considerations.

Assignment Case Eleven - 3   (Progressive Running Case - Chapter 11 Version Using ProFile T1 Software For 2006 Tax Returns)

This Progressive Running Case requires the use of the ProFile tax software program. It was introduced in Chapter 6 and is continued in Chapters 8 through 14. Each version must be completed in sequence. While it is not repeated in this version of the Case, all of the information in each of the previous versions (e.g., Mary's T4 content) is applicable to this version of the Case.

If you have not prepared a tax file incorporating the previous versions, please do so before continuing with this version.

During a phone call from Mary Walford on December 28, 2006, she tells you that Seymour made all of the required payments to his ex-wife Monica Gravel (SIN 527-000-186) in 2006. In your files, you have noted that his 2002 divorce agreement requires Seymour to pay spousal support to his ex-wife of $200 per month. He also pays her child support of $250 per month for his daughter.

Mary tells you that her parents have established an RESP for William in 2006, and are the sole contributors. They have contributed $300 in lieu of Christmas and birthday presents.

Although Seymour found being a full time student at Dalhousie University for three months very difficult, he felt that he had learned a great deal. Through one of his courses on child psychology, Seymour came to the conclusion that a better knowledge of art would help William deal with his aggression and hostility. As a result, Mary registered William for private art lessons at the Da Vinci Institute on Saturdays. Mary faxes you the following receipts:

Child	Child Related Expenses (Organization or Name and SIN)	No. of weeks	Amount
William	Gaye Normandin SIN 527-000-392		3,100
	(after school and summer)		
William	Da Vinci Institute - private lessons @ $25/hour		2,750

Required:

A. What advice would you give Mary on the RESP for William?

B. Open the file that you created for the Chapter 10 version of the Case and save a copy under a different name. This will enable you to check the changes between different versions of the Case.

C. Input the information needed on Seymour's "Support Payments" form and print the form.

D. With the objective of optimizing the deduction for the family, prepare and print the T778 Child Care Expenses Deduction forms.

E. Access and print Mary's summary (Summary on the Form Explorer, not the T1Summary). This form is a two column summary of the couple's tax information. By opening this form from Mary's return, the order of the columns is the same as the one in the previous chapter. For both returns, list the changes on this Summary form from the previous version of this Case. Exclude totals calculated by the program, but include the final Balance Owing (Refund) amount.

CHAPTER 12

Non-Arm's Length Transactions, Income Attribution And Deemed Dispositions At Emigration And Death

Introduction

12-1.   As is apparent from the title, this Chapter is something of a potpourri. It contains a discussion of several aspects of Canadian income taxation that are more or less related, but do not conveniently fit under any single description. One of these subjects is non-arm's length transfers of property for inadequate consideration. This relates to Chapter 10 since there may be complications in the calculation of capital gains and losses. We will also cover transfers to spouses and minors that give rise to the application of income attribution rules. This material may involve both the Chapter 10 material on capital gains as well as Chapter 9, which deals with income from property. Attention will also be given to those deemed dispositions that arise when a taxpayer leaves Canada or dies. This will usually involve the calculation of capital gains and losses.

Non-Arm's Length Transfers Of Property

Inadequate Considerations

The Problem

12-2.   When a transfer of capital property takes place between taxpayers who are dealing with each other at arm's length, there is usually no reason to assume that the transfer took place at a value that was significantly different from the fair market value of the property transferred. In fact, fair market value is often described as the value that would be used by arm's length parties in an exchange transaction.

12-3.   Given this, the consideration given for the property would normally be used as both the proceeds of the disposition for the vendor and the adjusted cost base for the new owner. However, when a transfer takes place between taxpayers who are not dealing at arm's length, there is the possibility that the consideration can be established at a level that will allow one or both taxpayers to reduce or avoid taxes.

Example   During 2007, Martin Horst, whose marginal federal tax rate is 29 percent, sells a property with a fair market value of $200,000 to his 25 year old son for its adjusted cost base of $150,000. The son, who has no other source of income in 2007, immediately sells the property for its fair market value of $200,000.

Analysis   If Martin had sold the property for its fair market value of $200,000, he would have paid federal taxes of $7,250 [($200,000 - $150,000)(1/2)(29%)]. In contrast, if the $50,000 capital gain was taxed in the hands of his son, the federal tax would only be $2,491 {[($200,000 - $150,000)(1/2)(15.5%)] - $1,384}, a savings of $4,759 at the federal level alone.

12-4.   To prevent tax avoidance in such situations, ITA 69 provides rules for dealing with inadequate considerations (i.e., the transfer of property for consideration that is greater or less than the fair market value of that property).

Non-Arm's Length Defined

12-5.   ITA 251(1), in effect, defines the term, "arm's length", by noting that for purposes of the *Act* "related persons shall be deemed not to deal with each other at arm's length". With respect to individuals, ITA 251(2)(a) points out that they are related if they are connected by blood relationship, marriage, common-law partnership or adoption.

12-6.   With respect to the question of whether corporations are related, ITA 251(2)(b) and (c) have a fairly long list of possibilities. For example, a corporation is related to the person who controls it, and two corporations are related if they are both controlled by the same person. There are, of course, many complications in this area. However, the examples used in this Chapter involve situations in which the taxpayers are obviously related and, as a consequence, not at arm's length.

General Rules

12-7.   When there is a non-arm's length transfer of property, the tax consequences for the transferor and transferee will depend on the relationship between the amount received as proceeds of disposition and the fair market value of the asset at the time of transfer. The various possible relationships, along with the tax consequences for both the transferor and the transferee, are as shown in Figure 12-1:

Figure 12 - 1 Non-Arm's Length Transfers - ITA 69		
Transfer Price	**Proceeds Of Disposition For Transferor**	**Adjusted Cost Base For Transferee**
Fair Market Value	Fair Market Value	Fair Market Value
Above Fair Market Value	Actual Proceeds	Fair Market Value
Below Fair Market Value	Fair Market Value	Actual Proceeds
Nil (Gift)	Fair Market Value	Fair Market Value

Example

12-8.   In order to illustrate the rules presented in Figure 12-1, assume that John Brown has a capital asset with an adjusted cost base of $50,000 and a fair market value of $75,000. If the asset is sold for consideration equal to its fair market value of $75,000, the result will be a capital gain of $25,000 for John Brown and an adjusted cost base for the new owner of $75,000. This would be the result without regard to whether the purchaser was related to John Brown.

12-9.   If the asset is transferred to a non-arm's length party, and the consideration provided is not equal to its fair market value, ITA 69 becomes applicable. The following three Cases illustrate the various possible alternatives. In each Case, we will assume the transfer is to John Brown's brother, Sam Brown.

Case A - Transfer At $100,000 (Above Fair Market Value) The proceeds to John Brown will be the actual amount of $100,000 and will result in an immediate capital gain to John Brown of $50,000 ($100,000 - $50,000). The adjusted cost base to Sam Brown will be limited by ITA 69(1)(a) to the $75,000 fair market value. This means that $25,000 of the amount that he has paid is not reflected in his adjusted cost base. If, for example, he were to sell the asset for $100,000 (the amount he paid), he would have a capital gain of $25,000 ($100,000 - $75,000) and there will have been double taxation of the $25,000.

Case B - Transfer At $60,000 (Below Fair Market Value)   If the transfer took place at a price of $60,000, ITA 69(1)(b) would deem John Brown to have received the fair market value of $75,000. As there is no special rule applicable to the purchaser in this case, the adjusted cost base to Sam Brown would be the actual transfer price of $60,000. Here again, double taxation could arise, this time on the difference between the transfer price of $60,000 and the fair market value of $75,000.

Case C - Gift, Bequest, Or Inheritance   In this case, ITA 69(1)(b) would deem the proceeds of disposition to be the fair market value of $75,000, and ITA 69(1)(c) would deem Sam Brown's adjusted cost base to be the same value. Note that this is the same result that would be achieved if the asset were sold to Sam Brown at its fair market value of $75,000. However, there is no double taxation involved in this Case.

12-10.   Given the presence of ITA 69, the general rules for transferring property to related parties are very clear. Either transfer the property at a consideration that is equal to its fair market value or, alternatively, gift the property. A non-arm's length transfer, at a value that is either above or below the fair market value of the property, will result in double taxation on some part of any gain recognized when there is a later sale of the property by the transferee.

Applicability Of ITA 69

12-11.   The inadequate consideration rules in ITA 69 are prefaced by the phrase "except as expressly otherwise provided in this Act". This means that if there is a provision that deals with a particular non-arm's length transfer, that provision takes precedence over the general provisions of ITA 69. For example, in the following material, ITA 73(1) indicates that non-depreciable capital property that is gifted to a spouse or common-law partner will be transferred at its adjusted cost base. This provision overrides the general requirement under ITA 69 that gifted property be transferred at fair market value.

Exercise Twelve-1

Subject: Inadequate Consideration - Non-Depreciable Property

Mr. Carl Lipky owns a piece of land with an adjusted cost base of $100,000 and a fair market value of $75,000. He sells the land to his brother for $95,000 who immediately sells it for $75,000. Determine the amount of any capital gain or loss to be recorded by Mr. Lipky and his brother.

End of Exercise.   Solution available in Study Guide.

Inter Vivos Transfers To A Spouse Or Common-Law Partner
General Rules For Capital Property

12-12.   An inter vivos transfer is one that occurs while the transferor is still alive, rather than at the time of, or subsequent to, that individual's death. ITA 73(1.01) indicates that the ITA 73(1) rules apply to the following qualifying transfers:

- a transfer to the individual's spouse or common-law partner;

- a transfer to the individual's former spouse or former common-law partner in settlement of rights arising out of their marriage or common-law partnership; and

- a transfer to a trust for which the individual's spouse or common-law partner is the income beneficiary (this type of trust has traditionally been referred to as a spousal trust and the conditions related to this concept are discussed in Chapter 21).

12-13.   For the qualifying transfers listed in ITA 73(1.01), ITA 73(1) specifies rules that provide a tax free transfer. With respect to the proceeds of disposition for the transferor, the rules are as follows:

Non-Depreciable Capital Property   The proceeds will be deemed to be the adjusted cost base of the property transferred.

Depreciable Capital Property   The proceeds will be deemed to be the UCC of the class or, if only part of a class is transferred, an appropriate portion of the class.

12-14.   From the point of view of the transferee, ITA 73(1) indicates that he will be deemed to have acquired the property at an amount equal to the deemed proceeds to the transferor. Based on this, his values will be as follows:

Non-Depreciable Capital Property   The cost to the transferee will be deemed to be the adjusted cost base to the transferor.

Depreciable Capital Property   The UCC to the transferee will be the old UCC to the transferor. However, under ITA 73(2), the old capital cost will also be retained by the transferee, with the difference between this and his UCC being considered to be deemed CCA. This rule ensures that if the property is subsequently sold for a value in excess of its UCC, the excess will be treated as fully taxable recapture of CCA, not a capital gain, only one-half of which would be taxed.

12-15.   These rules mean that the transfer will have no tax consequences for the transferor and that the transferee will retain the same tax values that were contained in the transferor's records. This is illustrated by the following example:

Example Marg Cardiff gifts land with an adjusted cost base of $100,000 and a fair market value of $250,000 to her husband, Bernie. At the same time, three-quarters (based on fair market values) of her Class 10 assets are also given to Bernie. The specific Class 10 assets transferred have a capital cost of $225,000 and a fair market value of $310,000. The UCC for Class 10, prior to the gift, is $260,000.

Analysis Marg would be deemed to have received $100,000 for the disposition of the land and $195,000 [(3/4)($260,000)] for the Class 10 assets. Given these values, the transactions would have no tax consequences for Marg. For Bernie, the land would have an adjusted cost base of $100,000. The transferred Class 10 assets would have a UCC of $195,000, combined with a capital cost of $225,000. This means that, if Bernie sold all the transferred assets immediately for their fair market value of $560,000 ($250,000 + $310,000), there would be a capital gain of $235,000 ($560,000 - $100,000 - $225,000) and recapture of CCA of $30,000 ($195,000 - $225,000).

12-16.   Before leaving this example, we would note that tax rules such as ITA 73(1) are referred to as rollover provisions. They allow taxpayers to transfer assets to other parties without incurring any current Tax Payable. In addition, the property transferred retains the transferor's tax values (i.e., adjusted cost base or UCC) in the hands of the transferee.

12-17.   We will encounter two additional rollovers in this Chapter. These are, a provision that allows a tax free transfer of farm or fishing property to a child, and a second provision that allows for a tax free transfer of all property to a spouse or common-law partner at the time of the individual's death. Other important rollovers applicable to corporations are given attention in Chapters 18 and 19.

Electing Out Of The Spousal Rollover

12-18.   The ITA 73(1) rollover automatically applies to spousal rollovers unless the taxpayer takes positive action to remove its applicability. However, the taxpayer can elect out of this approach if he wishes to recognize capital gains or recapture at the time of the transfer. There are a variety of reasons that a taxpayer may wish to make this election. However, the most common probably involves situations where the taxpayer has unused allowable capital losses and wishes to trigger taxable capital gains in order to make use of these losses.

12-19.   With respect to the process of electing to be taxed on an inter vivos spousal transfer, ITA 73(1) uses the phrase "elects in his return of income". The use of this phrase in the *Income Tax Act* means there is no official tax form required in order to make the election. In contrast, in situations where a form is required, the usual *Income Tax Act* terminology is the phrase "elects in the prescribed manner".

12-20.   For a taxpayer wishing to elect out of ITA 73(1), the only requirement is that they include any income resulting from the spousal transfer in their tax return in the year of disposition.

> **Example Continued**   In the example from Paragraph 12-15, Marg could have elected to record the land transaction at the fair market value of $250,000, resulting in a $150,000 capital gain being recorded at the time of transfer. In this case, the adjusted cost base to Bernie would be $250,000. The election would be made by simply including the taxable portion of the $150,000 gain in Marg's tax return.

12-21.   You should note that, if the taxpayer elects out of ITA 73(1), ITA 69 becomes applicable. This means that, in such situations, if the transfer is not a gift, or is made in return for consideration that is not equal to the fair market value of the property, the ITA 69 provisions will result in double taxation as was discussed previously.

Non-Arm's Length Transfers Of Depreciable Assets

12-22.   When there is a non-arm's length transfer of depreciable property to someone other than a spouse or common-law partner, ITA 13(7)(e) contains provisions which affect the capital cost to the transferee for purposes of determining recapture and CCA. Similar rules are discussed in the coverage of changes in use in Chapter 7.

12-23.   In situations where ITA 69 is not relevant, if the transferee's cost exceeds the capital cost of the transferor, the capital cost to the transferee, for CCA and recapture purposes only, will be equal to the transferor's capital cost, plus one-half the amount by which the proceeds of disposition exceed the transferor's capital cost. If ITA 69 is relevant, the fair market value is used rather than the proceeds of disposition in the formula.

> **Example**   John Dore transfers a depreciable property with a fair market value of $120,000, a capital cost of $100,000 and a UCC of $80,000 to his son for $120,000.
>
> **Analysis**   As the son's cost of $120,000 exceeds John's capital cost of $100,000, the capital cost to the son for recapture and CCA purposes will be $110,000 [$100,000 + (1/2)($120,000 - $100,000)]. This value would remain the same even if the amount paid was greater than the fair market value, for example, $130,000, as ITA 69 would limit the cost to the son to the fair market value of $120,000.

12-24.   If the transferee's cost is less than the capital cost of the transferor, the capital cost of the transferee will be deemed to be equal to the capital cost of the transferor. The difference between the actual cost and the deemed capital cost will be deemed to be amounts deducted for CCA.

Exercise Twelve-2

Subject: Inter Vivos Transfer Of Depreciable Asset To A Spouse

During the current year, Mary Sharp transferred a depreciable property to her spouse. The property had a fair market value of $225,000, a capital cost of $175,000, and a UCC of $110,000. In return for the property, she received $300,000 in cash. Describe the tax consequences to Ms. Sharp and her spouse, assuming (1) that she does not elect out of ITA 73(1) and (2) that she elects out of the rollover provision.

Exercise Twelve-3

Subject: Inadequate Consideration - Depreciable Property

Ms. Jennifer Lee owns a depreciable asset that she has used in her unincorporated business. It has a cost of $53,000 and a fair market value of $56,600. It is the only asset in its CCA class, and the balance in the class is $37,200. Ms. Lee sells the asset to her father for $37,200 who immediately sells it for $56,600. Determine the amount of income to be recorded by Ms. Lee and her father.

End of Exercises. Solutions available in Study Guide.

Non-Arm's Length Leasing Arrangements

12-25.   In the past, it was possible to avoid the provisions of ITA 69 through the use of leasing arrangements. These arrangements involved the rental of a property to a person with whom the owner/lessor was not dealing at arm's length. The required lease payment was set at a sufficiently low level that the fair market value of the property was significantly reduced. This would allow a sale or gift to be made, with the deemed proceeds of disposition being based on this lower value.

12-26.   As an example of this type of arrangement, consider a situation where an individual has a property with a fair market value of $100,000. If this property was leased on a long-term basis to a spouse or common-law partner for an unrealistically low value, say $2,000 per year, the fair market value of the property might be reduced to about $20,000. If there were no restrictions, it could then be gifted or sold for $20,000 to a child, and there would be no double taxation under the provisions of ITA 69.

12-27.   ITA 69(1.2) is designed to make this an unattractive strategy. Under the provisions of this Subsection, the taxpayer's proceeds of disposition on the gift or sale will be the greater of the actual fair market value at the time of the disposition ($20,000) and the fair market value determined without consideration of the non-arm's length lease ($100,000). This means the transferor will be taxed on the basis of having received the full $100,000 and, under the usual provisions of ITA 69, the transferee will have an adjusted cost base of $20,000. This will result in double taxation of the difference between $100,000 and $20,000 and should serve to discourage this type of avoidance strategy.

Exercise Twelve-4

Subject: Inadequate Consideration - Leased Property

Mr. Ned Bates has land with an adjusted cost base of $33,000 and an unencumbered fair market value of $211,000. He leases this land to his wife for $3,300 per year, for a period of 35 years. Similar leases are based on 10 percent of the value of the property and, as a consequence, the fair market value of the land with the lease in place falls to $33,000. He sells the land to a corporation controlled by his wife for this reduced value. Determine the amount of capital gain or loss to be recorded by Mr. Bates as a result of this sale, as well as the adjusted cost base of the land to the corporation.

End of Exercise. Solution available in Study Guide.

Farm Or Fishing Property Rollover To A Child

Farm Property To A Child

12-28.   ITA 73(3) and (4) provide for direct inter vivos transfers of farm property through family run unincorporated farms, or indirect inter vivos transfers of farm property by transferring shares of family farm corporations or interests in family farm partnerships, to children on a tax-free basis. As was the case with ITA 73(1), the provisions of ITA 73(3) and (4) take precedence over the provisions of ITA 69.

12-29.   For the purposes of this Section, "child" refers to children and their spouses, grandchildren, great grandchildren, and any other person that, prior to their attaining the age of 19, was dependent on the taxpayer and under his custody or control. To qualify, the child must be a resident of Canada at the time of the transfer. In addition, the property must be in use in a farming business operated by the taxpayer, the taxpayer's spouse, or any of their children.

12-30.   The transfer is deemed to have taken place at the actual proceeds of disposition, restricted by floor and ceiling amounts. For depreciable property, the floor is the property's UCC, while the ceiling is its fair market value. For non-depreciable property, including shares in a farm corporation, the floor is the adjusted cost base, while the ceiling is the fair market value. If the transfer is made to a child who disposes of the property before reaching age 18, all capital gains, both those existing at transfer and those accruing subsequently, are attributed back to the transferor and taxed in the transferor's hands.

> **Example** Tim Johnson's farm consists of land with an adjusted cost base of $200,000 and a fair market value of $350,000, and depreciable assets with a UCC of $400,000, a capital cost of $550,000, and a fair market value of $675,000. It is transferred to Tim's son.
>
> **Analysis - Land**   If the transfer is for proceeds of disposition below $200,000 (this includes gifts), the deemed proceeds of disposition and adjusted cost base to the child would be $200,000. If the transfer is for an amount in excess of $350,000, the deemed proceeds of disposition and adjusted cost base to the child would be limited to $350,000. For transfers between $200,000 and $350,000, the actual proceeds of disposition would be used.
>
> **Analysis - Depreciable Property**   For transfers below the UCC of $400,000, the deemed proceeds of disposition and transfer price to the child would be $400,000. Correspondingly, for transfers above $675,000, the deemed proceeds of disposition and capital cost to the child would be $675,000. For transfers between $400,000 and $675,000, the actual proceeds of disposition would be used. Note, that when the transfer price for the child is less than the taxpayer's capital cost of $550,000, the difference is deemed to be CCA taken by the child. This means that the $550,000 value will be retained as the capital cost to the child, and that this value will be used to determine capital gains or recapture on any subsequent disposition by the child.

Fishing Property To A Child

12-31.   The May, 2006 budget extended the rollover of farm property to a child, to situations involving fishing properties. This was accomplished by simply adding references to fishing properties to the farm property rollover provisions. As a result, the rules for this rollover are identical to those applicable to the farm property transfer.

Exercise Twelve-5

Subject: Farm Property Transfer To A Child

Thomas Nobel owns farm property consisting of land with an adjusted cost base of $250,000 and a fair market value of $325,000, along with a barn with a UCC of $85,000, a capital cost of $115,000, and a fair market value of $101,000. The property is transferred to his 40 year old daughter in return for a payment of $280,000 for the land. No payment is made for the barn. Describe the tax consequences of this transfer, both for Mr. Nobel and for his daughter.

End of Exercise. Solution available in Study Guide.

Income Attribution

The Problem

12-32.   In the general discussion of tax planning in Chapter 3, it was noted that income splitting can be the most powerful tool available to individuals wishing to reduce their tax burden. The basic goal is to redistribute income from an individual in a high tax bracket to related individuals, usually a spouse or children, in lower tax brackets. As was illustrated in Chapter 3, when such redistribution can be achieved, it can produce very dramatic reductions in the aggregate tax liability of the family unit.

12-33.   It is obvious that, if there were no restrictions associated with transfers of property to related persons, there would be little standing in the way of a complete equalization of tax rates within a family unit and the achievement of maximum income splitting benefits. For many years, it has been the policy of the government to limit access to the tax benefits of income splitting and, as a consequence, we have a group of legislative provisions that are commonly referred to as the income attribution rules.

12-34.   These attribution rules could be criticized on the basis of fairness. They are very effective in preventing income splitting by low-income Canadians. For example, they prevent income splitting benefits from accruing to an individual who simply gives a term deposit to a spouse or his minor children.

12-35.   However, these rules are less effective in preventing income splitting benefits from accruing to wealthy Canadians. While the imposition of the tax on split income (see Chapter 14) has restricted the ability of high income individuals to distribute certain types of income to their minor children, it is clear that wealthy Canadians, with access to expensive tax counseling and the ability to use complex corporate structures, still benefit far more from income splitting than do those in the middle class.

12-36.   If the policy objective was to curtail income splitting, we would have hoped that the government could have dealt with this in a fashion that was more equitable to all Canadians. To a certain extent, this was accomplished with the addition of provisions that allow the splitting of pension income (see Chapter 11).

Basic Rules - ITA 74.1(1) And (2)

Applicable Individuals

12-37.   The income attribution rules are applicable to situations where an individual has transferred property to:

• a spouse or common-law partner [ITA 74.1(1)]; or
• an individual who is under the age of 18 and who does not deal with the individual at arm's length [ITA 74.1(2)].

12-38.   Note that the rules are applicable, not just to children or grandchildren under the age of 18, but to any non-arm's length individual who is under the age of 18. In addition, ITA 74.1(2) specifically notes that nieces and nephews are subject to these rules, even though they are not non-arm's length individuals as defined in the *Income Tax Act*.

12-39.   The general idea here is that, unless certain conditions are met, income associated with holding or disposing of a transferred property may be attributed back to the transferor of the property (i.e., included in the Net Income For Tax Purposes of the transferor).

Applicable To Property Income And Capital Gains

12-40.   There are two types of income that may be attributed under these rules. The first type would be property income, such as interest, dividends, rents, and royalties, that accrues while the transferee is holding the transferred assets. This type of income may be attributed back to the transferor without regard to whether the transferee is a spouse, or a related individual under the age of 18.

12-41.   The second type of income that may be subject to the attribution rules is capital gains resulting from a disposition of the transferred property. Whether or not this type of income is subject to the attribution rules will depend on the relationship of the transferee to the transferor:

Transferee Is A Spouse   When property is transferred to a spouse or common-law partner, the application of ITA 73(1) generally means that the property is transferred at the transferor's tax cost, with no taxation at the time of transfer. This means that the transferred property will be recorded at the adjusted cost base value for non-depreciable assets and at the UCC for depreciable assets. Given this, it seems logical that any capital gain or recaptured CCA from a subsequent sale by the spouse would be measured from that tax cost and attributed back to the transferor. This approach is, in fact, required under ITA 74.2(1).

Transferee Is A Related Individual Under 18   There is no general rollover provision for related minors that corresponds to ITA 73(1) for a spouse or common-law partner. This means that when property is transferred to a related minor, the transfer will normally take place at the fair market value of the property, resulting in the transferor recognizing any capital gains or recaptured CCA that have accrued to the time of transfer. Reflecting this fact, any gain on a subsequent sale by the related minor would be measured using the fair market value at the time of transfer. Further, such gains are not attributed back to the transferor, but are taxed in the hands of the related minor.

Not Applicable To Business Income

12-42.   Note that business income is not subject to the attribution rules. If the assets that are transferred to a spouse, common-law partner, or related minor, are used to produce business income, this type of income will be taxed in the hands of the transferee. The logic of this seems clear. In order to earn business income, an effort is required on the part of the transferee. This means that the resulting business income is not a simple gift, but something that has to be earned. In these circumstances, it would not seem equitable to attribute these amounts to the transferor who provided the property.

12-43.   Note, however, that if a business is transferred to a spouse or common-law partner, any capital gain on a subsequent sale of the business assets will be attributed back to the transferor, despite the fact that business income earned between the transfer and the sale will not be attributed to the transferor.

Not Applicable If Subject To Tax On Split Income

12-44.   A further exception to the income attribution rules is income that is subject to the tax on split income. While this tax is discussed in detail in Chapter 14, we would note here that this is a special tax on certain types of income that are earned by individuals under the age of 18 on property that has been transferred to them from related parties. This special tax is assessed on the minor individual at the maximum rate of 29 percent, beginning with the first dollar of such income received.

12-45.   With income subject to the tax on split income being taxed at the maximum federal rate of 29 percent, any potential income splitting advantage has been eliminated. As a consequence, there is really no point in applying the income attribution rules to income that is subject to this tax. This view is reflected in ITA 74.5(13) which indicates that the income attribution rules in ITA 74.1(2) are not applicable to income that is subject to the tax on split income.

Avoiding Income Attribution

12-46.   The basic idea behind the income attribution rules is to restrict an individual's ability to simply give a source of income to a related individual for income splitting purposes. The procedure for avoiding these rules on a transfer to a related minor is straightforward:

Transfers To A Related Minor   In this case, ITA 74.5(1)(a) indicates that the income attribution rules are not applicable if the related minor provides, from his own resources, consideration equal to the fair market value of the asset transferred. ITA 74.5(1)(b) indicates that, if such consideration includes debt payable by the related minor, it is acceptable only if it requires interest based on at least the prescribed rate at the time of the transfer.

12-47.   The avoidance of the income attribution rules on transfers to a spouse is complicated by the presence of the ITA 73(1) rollover:

Transfers To A Spouse   In the case of transfers to a spouse or common-law partner, avoiding income attribution requires that the transferor elect out of ITA 73(1). Unless this individual elects to record the transfer at fair market value and include any resulting gain or loss in income at the time of transfer, ITA 74.5(1)(c) indicates that the income attribution rules will apply without regard to the consideration provided by the transferee.

In addition to having the transferor elect out of ITA 73(1), avoidance of the income attribution rules requires that the transferee must provide, from his or her own resources, consideration equal to the fair market value of the asset transferred. As noted previously, ITA 74.5(1)(b) indicates that, if such consideration includes debt payable by the related spouse, it is acceptable only if it requires interest based on the prescribed rate at the time of the transfer.

Consider a situation in which John Doan has a capital property with an adjusted cost base of $100,000 and a fair market value of $150,000. If he sells this property to his spouse for consideration equal to the fair market value of $150,000, the income attribution rules will apply unless he elects out of ITA 73(1) by recognizing the $50,000 capital gain in his income. Note that, if he fails to elect out of ITA 73(1), the adjusted cost base to his spouse will be John's adjusted cost base of $100,000, not the price she paid of $150,000. This means that any capital gains attribution will be measured from this $100,000 value.

Alternatively, if he gifts the property to his spouse and elects out of ITA 73(1) by recording a $50,000 capital gain, the income attribution rules will apply because she did not give consideration equal to $150,000. Note that, in this case, because ITA 69 applies to spousal transfers when the transferor elects out of ITA 73(1), his spouse's adjusted cost base would be the $150,000 fair market value at the time of the transfer. Any subsequent capital gain attribution would be measured using her adjusted cost base of $150,000.

Example

12-48.   The following example will illustrate the provisions that we have just discussed.

Example   Mrs. Blaine owns a group of equity securities with an adjusted cost base of $200,000. On December 31, 2006, the fair market value of these securities is $300,000. On this date, she gives one-half of the securities to her unemployed husband Mark, and the other one-half to her 5 year old daughter Belinda.

Both Mark and Belinda hold the securities until December 31, 2007, at which point they are sold for a total of $350,000 ($175,000 each). During 2007, the securities paid $37,500 in dividends ($18,750 to both Mark and Belinda).

Transfer To Spouse   Assuming that Mrs. Blaine has not elected out of the ITA 73(1) rules, the transfer to her husband would take place at the adjusted cost base of $100,000 [(1/2)($200,000)] and she would not record a 2006 gain. However, the adjusted cost base of the shares to Mr. Blaine would be Mrs. Blaine's adjusted cost base of $100,000. This means that when Mr. Blaine sells the shares, the taxable capital gain will be $37,500 [(1/2)($175,000 - $100,000)], all of which will be attributed to Mrs. Blaine in 2007. In addition, the $18,750 in dividends received by Mr. Blaine in 2007 would also be attributed to Mrs. Blaine.

Transfer To Minor   As indicated previously, the rules for minors are somewhat different. As there is no rollover provision for minor children in this case, the gift to Belinda would be treated as a disposition at fair market value, resulting in a 2006 taxable capital gain for Mrs. Blaine of $25,000 [(1/2)(1/2)($300,000 - $200,000)]. Belinda's adjusted cost base for the shares would then be $150,000 [(1/2)($300,000)]. When the shares are sold by Belinda, the additional taxable capital gain of $12,500 [(1/2)($175,000 - $150,000)] would be taxed in Belinda's hands and would not be attributed to Mrs. Blaine. The treatment of the dividends for Belinda is the same as for Mr. Blaine, resulting in an additional $18,750 in dividends being attributed to Mrs. Blaine for 2007.

12-49.   If either Mr. Blaine or Belinda reinvests the proceeds from selling the shares, dividend or interest income resulting from the reinvestment will also be attributed back to Mrs. Blaine. Any capital gains on the new investments that are realized by Mr. Blaine will also be attributed to Mrs. Blaine. This will not be the case with capital gains realized by Belinda. Note, however, that the compound earnings resulting from the reinvestment of the dividends received from the new investment are not subject to the attribution rules.

Exercise Twelve-6

Subject: Income Attribution From A Spouse

On December 31, 2006, Mrs. Norah Moreau gives shares with an adjusted cost base of $23,000 and a fair market value of $37,000 to her husband, Nick Moreau. On February 24, 2007, the shares pay eligible dividends of $2,500 ($3,625 taxable amount) and, on August 31, 2007, Mr. Moreau sells the shares for $42,000. What are the tax consequences for Mr. and Mrs. Moreau for the 2006 and 2007 taxation years?

Exercise Twelve-7

Subject: Income Attribution From A Related Minor

On December 31, 2006, Mrs. Norah Moreau gives shares with an adjusted cost base of $23,000 and a fair market value of $37,000 to her 12 year old daughter, Nicki Moreau. On February 24, 2007, the shares pay eligible dividends of $2,500 ($3,625 taxable amount) and, on August 31, 2007, Nicki sells the shares for $42,000. What are the tax consequences for Mrs. Moreau and Nicki for the 2006 and 2007 taxation years?

End of Exercises. Solutions available in Study Guide.

Exercise Twelve-8

Subject: Income Attribution - Use Of Loans

On December 31, 2006, Mr. Nadeem Bronski gives corporate bonds to his wife in exchange for a note with a face value of $122,000. The corporate bonds have an adjusted cost base of $115,000 and a fair market value of $122,000. The note from his wife does not pay interest and has no specific maturity date. During 2007, the bonds pay interest to Mrs. Bronski in the amount of $6,100. On October 1, 2007, immediately after an interest payment, Mrs. Bronski sells the bonds for $129,000. She uses $122,000 of the proceeds to pay off the loan owing to her husband. What are the tax consequences for both Mr. and Mrs. Bronski in the 2006 and 2007 taxation years?

End of Exercise. Solution available in Study Guide.

Anti-Avoidance Provisions

12-50.   Given the attractiveness of income splitting, it is not surprising that tax planners have shown considerable ingenuity in devising procedures to avoid these attribution rules. It is equally unsurprising that the federal government has continued to come up with new rules to deal with these procedures.

12-51.   Current legislation contains a number of provisions directed at preventing the use of indirect transfers, corporations, or trusts to circumvent the attribution rules. Complete coverage of these anti-avoidance rules is beyond the scope of this material. However, some of the more important anti-avoidance rules can be described as follows:

- ITA 74.1(3) prevents the substitution of a new low rate or interest free loan for an existing commercial rate loan.

- ITA 74.5(6) prevents a loan from being made to a person who is not subject to the attribution rules, who then makes a similar loan to a person who would be subject to the attribution rules if the loan had been directly made to that individual. The use of the intermediary would be disregarded and indirect attribution would apply.

- ITA 74.5(7) prevents the use of loan guarantees to avoid the attribution rules. That is, a higher income spouse cannot get around the attribution rules by providing a guarantee on a low rate or interest free loan to a spouse that is made by a third party.

- ITA 74.3 and 74.4 contain a variety of rules designed to prevent the avoidance of the attribution rules through the use of a trust (ITA 74.3) or a corporation (ITA 74.4).

Tax Planning

12-52.   In recent years it has become increasingly difficult to avoid the income attribution rules. Further, many of the plans that are available for this purpose involve corporations and trusts and are too complex to be dealt with in detail in an introductory level text such as this. However, there are a number of relatively simple points that can be helpful:

Split Pension Income   As discussed in Chapter 11, it is now possible to transfer up to 50 percent of qualified pension income to a lower income spouse. As illustrated in that Chapter, this is an important new provision which can provide for a significant reduction in family unit taxes.

RESPs   Also as discussed in Chapter 11, Registered Education Savings Plans can be used for a limited amount of income splitting.

Spousal RRSPs   As is discussed in Chapter 13, the spousal Registered Retirement Savings Plan is a readily available device for a limited amount of income splitting.

Assets With Capital Gains Potential   As there is no attribution of capital gains on transfers to related minors, assets with capital gains potential should be given to children, rather than to a spouse.

Segregating Gifts To Spouses And Minors   If a spouse or minor child receives a gift or inheritance from a source to which attribution would not apply, the funds should be segregated for investment purposes and, if possible, should not be used for such non-deductible purposes as vacations, reducing the mortgage on the family home, or purchases of personal effects.

Detailed Records   In order to have low income family members acquire investment income, it is necessary for them to have funds to invest. Having the higher income spouse pay for non-deductible expenditures such as household expenses, clothing, vacations, and the lower income spouse's income tax liability can help provide for this. Although tuition fees can be eligible for a tax credit (see Chapter 6), they do not have to be paid by the student to be eligible for the credit. It may be desirable to maintain separate bank accounts and relatively detailed records to ensure that it is clear that the lower income family members' funds are being used for investment purposes.

Loans   The prescribed rate is currently 5 percent (3rd quarter of 2007). With the rate at this level, it is possible to find safe investments that have a higher yield. Given this, it may be useful to loan funds at this prescribed rate to a low income family member who reinvests the funds at a rate higher than 5 percent.

New Businesses   When a new business is started, low income family members should be allowed to acquire an equity position, particularly if the capital requirements are small. Note, however, if the business experiences losses in its first years of operation, this may not be the best alternative.

Salaries To Family Members   When business income is earned in the family unit, or through a related corporation, the lower income spouse and any children should be paid reasonable salaries for any activity that can be justified as business related. Examples would include bookkeeping, filing, and other administrative work.

Income Attribution - Other Related Parties

12-53.   The applicability of the income attribution rules that were previously discussed is limited to transfers and loans to spouses and related individuals under the age of 18. There is another income attribution provision that applies to a broader group of individuals. This is found in ITA 56(4.1) and indicates that, if an interest free or low rate loan is made to a related party for the purpose of producing property income, the income can be attributed back to the individual making the loan. A further condition for this attribution is that one of the main reasons for making the loan is to reduce or avoid tax.

12-54.   The most important application of this provision is to loans made by parents to their adult children. For children 18 or over, the general income attribution rules do not apply. Although there are no tax consequences associated with cash gifts to adult children, parents interested in providing some financial assistance to their children can be reluctant to completely lose control over the resources involved.

12-55.   As an example, a parent might extend an interest free loan to an adult child to assist with the purchase of a property. If the child decides to live in the property, there is no attribution related to the interest free loan used to purchase the principal residence. However, if the child uses the property to produce rental income, this income can be attributed back to the parent making the loan.

12-56.   The tax planning conclusion in this situation is obvious. If a parent wishes to provide financial assistance to an adult child to earn property income, the appropriate route is to use an outright gift. While an interest free loan can accomplish the goal of providing financial assistance to the child, ITA 56(4.1) can eliminate the potential tax savings associated with this form of income splitting.

Leaving Or Entering Canada

Taxable Canadian Property

12-57.   We have previously encountered the concept of Taxable Canadian Property in Chapter 3. In our discussion of the liability for Canadian income tax, we noted that one of the instances in which non-residents are subject to Canadian taxation is when they dispose of a Taxable Canadian Property. As a result, the tax effect of capital gains or losses arising on the disposition of Taxable Canadian Property is not changed by the taxpayer leaving or entering Canada.

12-58.   Taxable Canadian Property is defined in ITA 248. The main categories listed in that definition are as follows:

- real or immovable property situated in Canada;
- property used or held by the taxpayer in carrying on a business in Canada (including eligible capital property), or inventory of such a business;
- unlisted shares of Canadian resident corporations;
- unlisted shares of non-resident corporations if, at any time during the preceding 60 month period, the fair market value of the company's Canadian real and resource properties made up more than half the fair market value of all of its properties;
- listed shares if, at any time during the preceding 60 month period, the taxpayer owned 25 percent or more of the issued shares of any class of stock; and
- a partnership interest if, at any time in the preceding 60 month period, more than 50 percent of the partnership's value was attributable to Taxable Canadian Property.

12-59.   The actual definitions contained in ITA 248 are somewhat more complex than those presented here. However, the preceding will suffice for our purposes.

Entering Canada - Immigration

Deemed Disposition/Reacquisition

12-60.   The rules related to entering Canada are found in ITA 128.1(1). Paragraph (b) of this subsection indicates that, with certain exceptions, a taxpayer is deemed to have disposed of all of their property immediately before entering Canada for proceeds equal to fair market value. Paragraph (c) calls for a deemed reacquisition of the property at the same fair market value figure.

12-61.   This process establishes a new cost basis for the taxpayer's property, as at the time of entering Canada. The goal here is to avoid having Canadian taxation apply to gains that accrued prior to the individual's immigration.

> **Example** An individual enters Canada with securities that cost $100,000 and have a current fair market value of $150,000.

> **Analysis** In the absence of the ITA 128.1(1)(b) and (c) deeming provisions, a subsequent sale of these securities would result in the $50,000 accrued gain being taxed in Canada, despite the fact that it accrued prior to the individual becoming a Canadian resident.

12-62.   The properties that are excluded from the deemed disposition/reacquisition are listed in ITA 128.1(1)(b). These exclusions are Taxable Canadian Property, inventories and eligible capital of a business carried on in Canada, and rights to receive various types of income (e.g., income from an RRSP or RRIF). In general, these are items that were already subject to tax in Canada.

Departures From Canada - Emigration

Deemed Disposition On Leaving Canada

12-63.   When a taxpayer leaves Canada, ITA 128.1(4)(b) calls for a deemed disposition of all property owned at the time of departure. The disposition is deemed to occur at fair market value. If the taxpayer is an individual, certain types of property are exempted from this deemed disposition rule. The major categories of exempted property are as follows:

- Real property situated in Canada, Canadian resource properties, and timber resource properties.

- Property of a business carried on in Canada through a permanent establishment. This would include capital property, eligible capital property, and inventories.

- "Excluded Right or Interest" This concept is defined in ITA 128.1(10). The definition includes Registered Pension Plan balances, Registered Retirement Savings Plan balances, Deferred Profit Sharing Plan balances, stock options, death benefits, retiring allowances, as well as other rights of individuals in trusts or other similar arrangements.

12-64. This list of exemptions was once much more broadly based, simply indicating that anything that was classified as Taxable Canadian Property would be considered exempt. Without going into a detailed analysis, the major difference between the current list of exemptions, and assets designated Taxable Canadian Property, is shares of private companies. This means that a departure from Canada will now trigger taxation on gains that have accrued on the shares of Canadian controlled private corporations owned by an emigrant. Not surprisingly, this change was not greeted with enthusiasm by the business community.

Exercise Twelve-9

Subject: Emigration

Ms. Gloria Martell owns publicly traded securities with an adjusted cost base of $28,000 and a fair market value of $49,000. On April 21, 2007, she permanently departs from Canada still owning the shares. What would be the tax consequences of her departure, if any, with respect to these securities?

Exercise Twelve-10

Subject: Emigration

Mr. Harrison Chrysler owns a rental property in Nanaimo, B.C. with a capital cost of $190,000 and a fair market value of $295,000. The land values included in these figures are $45,000 and $62,000, respectively. The UCC of the building is $82,600. On December 31, 2007, Mr. Chrysler permanently departs from Canada. What are the tax consequences of his departure with respect to this rental property?

End of Exercises. Solutions available in Study Guide.

Problems With The Current System

12-65. Taxpayer emigration is a problem area for those in charge of Canadian tax policy. To begin, Canada is significantly out of line with all of its trading partners in the manner in which it deals with the accrued capital gains of emigrants.

12-66. As an illustration of this problem, consider Mr. Poutine, who departs from Canada at a time when he owns capital assets with an adjusted cost base of $80,000 and a fair market value of $120,000. On his departure from Canada, Mr. Poutine will be deemed to have disposed of these assets at their fair market value of $120,000, resulting in an assessment for a capital gain of $40,000.

12-67. In the great majority of other countries, in particular the United States, this would not occur. If Mr. Poutine was leaving the U.S., he could take the capital assets to a new country of residence, without incurring any taxation on these assets in the U.S. on departure. It would be assumed that, when the assets are ultimately disposed of, all of the gain on the assets will be taxed in the new country of residence. This situation clearly raises the possibility of double taxation for individuals emigrating from Canada.

12-68.   A further problem in this area is the ability of some taxpayers to avoid the Canadian emigration tax rules, resulting in large sums of money being removed from Canada on a tax free basis. Some types of assets can be removed tax free on the assumption that they will be subject to Canadian taxation at a later point in time. This might not happen if one of Canada's bilateral tax treaties prohibits Canadian taxation after an individual has been a non-resident for a specified period of time.

12-69.   Other leakages can occur when assets are bumped up in value for foreign tax purposes, with no corresponding change in the Canadian tax base. This is essentially what happened in the Bronfman trust case, in which several billion dollars in assets were removed from Canada without being subject to Canadian income taxes on accrued gains.

12-70.   Recent changes in legislation have dealt with some of these problems. However, as we will see later in this Chapter, potential difficulties remain in this area.

Elective Dispositions

12-71.   As noted in the preceding Paragraphs, certain types of property are exempted from the ITA 128.1(4)(b) deemed disposition rules. There may, however, be circumstances in which an individual wishes to override these exemptions and trigger capital gains at the time of departure. The most important example of this would be farm property that qualifies for the $750,000 lifetime capital gains deduction. (See Chapter 14 for details of this deduction.)

12-72.   An individual may wish to trigger capital gains on the exempted property at the time of departure for other reasons. An example of this would be an emigrant who wants to realize a loss on exempt property in order to offset a gain on non-exempt property. This situation is provided for in ITA 128.1(4)(d), which allows an individual to elect to have a deemed disposition on certain types of properties that are exempt from the general deemed disposition rule.

12-73.   The properties on which the election can be made include real property situated in Canada, Canadian resource and timber resource properties, as well as property of a business carried on in Canada through a permanent establishment. Note that, if this election results in losses, they can only be used to offset gains resulting from other deemed dispositions. They cannot be applied against other sources of income, including capital gains from actual dispositions, for the taxation year.

Exercise Twelve-11

Subject: Emigration

Ms. Gloria Lopez owns shares in a Canadian private company with an adjusted cost base of $120,000 and a fair market value of $235,000. In addition, she owns a rental property with a fair market value of $130,000 ($30,000 of this can be attributed to the land) and a capital cost of $220,000 ($60,000 of this can be attributed to the land). The UCC of the building is $142,000. During the current year, Ms. Lopez permanently departs from Canada. Calculate the minimum Net Income For Tax Purposes that will result from her departure with respect to the shares and the rental property.

End of Exercise.   Solution available in Study Guide.

Security For Departure Tax

12-74.   The preceding deemed disposition rules can be very burdensome for an emigrating individual. If the individual has substantial amounts of property on which gains have accrued, the deemed disposition rules can result in a hefty tax bill. This is further complicated by the fact that there are no real dispositions to provide funds for paying this liability.

12-75.   In recognition of this problem, ITA 220(4.5) through (4.54) allow the taxpayer to provide security in lieu of paying the tax that results from the application of ITA 128.1(4)(b). Similar provisions have been added such as ITA 220(4.6) through (4.63) for dealing with trusts distributing Taxable Canadian Property to non-residents.

12-76.   ITA 220(4.5) requires the CRA to accept "adequate security". While the exact meaning of this phrase is not entirely clear, it is understood that, in the case of a gain on shares, the CRA will not exclude the possibility of accepting some or all of the shares as security.

12-77.   If the taxpayer elects under ITA 220(4.5), interest does not accrue on the tax that has been deferred until the amount becomes unsecured. This will usually be at the time when there is an actual disposition of the property that was subject to the deemed disposition.

12-78.   A final point here is that ITA 220(4.51) creates deemed security on an amount that is the total amount of taxes under Parts I and I.1 that would be payable, at the highest tax rate that applies to individuals, on Taxable Income of $50,000. This amount is one-half of a $100,000 capital gain, and the effect of this provision is to exempt emigrants from the requirement to provide security on the first $100,000 in capital gains resulting from their departure.

Unwinding A Deemed Disposition
The Problem
12-79.   A potential problem can arise when an individual departs from Canada and, at a later point in time, returns. A simple example will serve to illustrate this difficulty:

> **Example**   John Fuller emigrates from Canada on June 1, 2006. At that time, he owns shares of a private company with a fair market value of $200,000 and an adjusted cost base of $125,000. As a result of the deemed disposition/reacquisition of these shares, he has a taxable capital gain of $37,500 [(1/2)($200,000 - $125,000)]. In 2007, he returns to Canada. At the time of immigration, he still owns the shares and their fair market value has increased to $260,000.

12-80.   In the absence of any special provision, Mr. Fuller's departure from Canada would cost him the taxes paid on the $37,500 taxable capital gain arising on the deemed disposition at emigration. While on his return, the adjusted cost base of his property has been increased to $200,000 by the deemed disposition, the fact remains that his temporary absence has resulted in an out-of-pocket tax cost on the $37,500 taxable capital gain.

The Solution
12-81.   ITA 128.1(6) provides relief in this type of situation. With respect to Taxable Canadian Property such as Mr. Fuller's, ITA 128.1(6)(a) allows a returning individual to make an election with respect to property that was Taxable Canadian Property at the time of emigration. The effect of making this election is that the deemed disposition that was required under ITA 128.1(1)(b) at the time of departure, is reversed when the individual returns to Canada. As there is no real basis for establishing whether an emigrant will eventually return as an immigrant, ITA 128.1(6) has no influence on the tax consequences arising at the time of emigration.

12-82.   Returning to our example from Paragraph 12-79, if this election is made, the addition to Taxable Income that was assessed when Mr. Fuller left Canada would be reversed through an amended return, resulting in a refund of the taxes paid.

12-83.   As the deemed disposition at departure has been reversed, there would be no need for a disposition/reacquisition when he returns to Canada. This means that after the appropriate election and amended return are filed, Mr. Fuller would wind up in the same tax position as he was in before he departed from Canada. That is, he would own securities with an adjusted cost base of $125,000 with no net taxes paid as a result of his departure and return.

12-84.   ITA 128.1 contains additional provisions for specialized situations. Coverage of the following topics goes beyond the scope of this text, but they have been listed here for your information:

- ITA 128.1(6)(b) contains a fairly complex provision related to situations in which dividends are paid on shares while the individual is absent from Canada.

- ITA 128.1(6)(c) contains a further provision dealing with property other than Taxable Canadian Property. This includes an election that allows the emigrant to partially reverse the tax effects resulting from his deemed disposition on departure.

- ITA 128.1(7) contains a provision that deals with situations where there is a loss on the property while the individual is absent from Canada.

Short-Term Residents

12-85.   With the increasing presence of multi-national firms in the Canadian business environment, it has become common for executives and other employees to find themselves resident in Canada for only a small portion of their total working lives. In the absence of some special provision, the deemed disposition rules could be a significant hardship to employees who are in this position.

12-86.   For example, if Ms. Eng was transferred from Hong Kong to work in Canada for three years, she could become liable on departure for capital gains taxation on all of her capital property owned at the time that she ceases to be a resident of Canada. The liability could put a severe drain on her available liquid assets and could result in taxation on personal items such as paintings and furniture. This would not be an equitable situation and could discourage the free movement of employees to and from Canada.

12-87.   In recognition of the preceding problem, ITA 128.1(4)(b)(iv) provides an exception to the deemed disposition rules that applies to taxpayers who, during the ten years preceding departure, have been resident in Canada for a total of 60 months or less. For such taxpayers, the deemed disposition rules do not apply to any property that was owned immediately before the taxpayer last became resident in Canada, or was acquired by inheritance or bequest during the period after he last became resident in Canada. However, the rules still apply to property acquired other than by inheritance or bequest during the period of residency.

Exercise Twelve-12

Subject: Short Term Residents

During 2004, Charles Brookings moves to Canada from the U.K. He has not previously lived in Canada. At this time his capital assets consist of shares in a U.K. company and a tract of vacant land in Canada which he had inherited. The shares have a fair market value of $250,000 and an adjusted cost base of $175,000. The land has a cost of $95,000 and a fair market value of $120,000. During 2005, he acquires shares of a Canadian public company for $75,000. During 2007, after finding Canada a tad uncivilized for his tastes, he moves back to the U.K. At this time, the shares in the U.K. company have a fair market value of $280,000, the shares of the Canadian company have a fair market value of $92,000 and the land has a fair market value of $130,000. What are the tax consequences of his emigration from Canada?

End of Exercise.   Solution available in Study Guide.

Emigration And Stock Options

12-88.   The deemed disposition at emigration on the shares of both public and private companies creates significant problems for individuals who are holding shares that were acquired through the exercise of stock options. To understand the consequences of this provision on such individuals, consider the following example:

Example Joan Martin holds options to buy 1,000 shares of Dermo Ltd., a Canadian controlled private corporation (CCPC), at a price of $50 per share. When the options were issued, the fair market value of the shares was equal to the option price of $50 per share. On May 1, 2007, Joan exercises the options and, at this time, the shares are trading at $71 per share. On December 1, 2007, when the shares are trading at $80 per share, Joan emigrates from Canada.

12-89.   As the shares were those of a CCPC, the employment income benefit is deferred from the time the options are exercised until such time as the shares are sold. However, in the absence of any special provision, the deemed disposition resulting from Joan's emigration would have the following tax consequences:

Employment Income Inclusion [($71 - $50)(1,000)]	$21,000
ITA 110(1)(d) Deduction [(1/2)($21,000)]	(10,500)
Balance	$10,500
Taxable Capital Gain [(1/2)($80 - $71)(1,000)]	4,500
Increase In Taxable Income	$15,000

12-90.   Fortunately, there are provisions that provide relief in these situations. ITA 7(1.6) indicates that, when an individual emigrates from Canada while holding shares of a CCPC acquired through a stock option arrangement, the usual deemed disposition on departure from Canada is not considered to be a disposition for the purposes of determining the employment income inclusion under ITA 7(1.1), nor the related deduction under ITA 110(1)(d) or (d.1).

12-91.   Unfortunately, this unwinding of the deemed disposition creates a different problem. ITA 53(1)(j) is written in such a fashion that the adjusted cost base of the shares is increased by the amount of the employment income inclusion only at the time this inclusion is recognized. This means that, in the absence of a further provision, the capital gain at the time of emigration would be based on a cost of $50, a situation that would ultimately result in double taxation of the difference between $71 and $50.

12-92.   A second provision, ITA 128.1(4)(d.1), deals with this situation by indicating that the taxpayer can deduct from the deemed proceeds of disposition, the amount of the benefit that would have been recognized in the absence of ITA 7(1.6). Overall, the tax consequences of Joan's emigration would be as follows:

Deemed Proceeds Of Disposition [($80)(1,000)]	$80,000
Employment Income Inclusion [($71 - $50)(1,000)]	(21,000)
Adjusted Cost Base [($50)(1,000)]	(50,000)
Capital Gain	$ 9,000
Inclusion Rate	1/2
Taxable Capital Gain	$ 4,500

12-93.   This somewhat circuitous process, while continuing to defer the employment income inclusion and related ITA 110(1) deduction, results in the same taxable capital gain that would have been recorded on an actual disposition of the shares (See Paragraph 12-89). The employment income inclusion will be subject to tax when the shares are actually sold.

12-94.   Note that these provisions apply only to the shares of a CCPC. If an individual departs Canada while holding option acquired shares of a public company, any employment income benefit that has been deferred under ITA 7(8) will have to be recognized at that time.

Death Of A Taxpayer

Representation

12-95.   The deceased do not, of course, file tax returns. However, a considerable amount of filing and other tax work may need to be done by the legal representative of the deceased. This legal representative may be an executor. This is an individual or institution appointed in the will to act as the legal representative of the deceased in handling his estate.

12-96.   In the absence of a will, or in situations where an executor is not appointed in the will, a court will generally appoint an administrator as the legal representative of the deceased. This administrator will normally be the spouse or next of kin of the deceased.

12-97.   The basic tax related responsibilities of the legal representative of an estate are as follows:

- filing all necessary tax returns;
- paying all taxes owing;
- obtaining a clearance certificate from the CRA for all tax years, before property under his control is distributed to the beneficiaries (a failure to do this can result in a personal liability for taxes owing); and
- advising beneficiaries of the amounts of income from the estate that will be taxable in their hands.

12-98.   In order to deal with the CRA in these matters, the legal representative will have to provide a copy of the deceased person's death certificate, as well as a copy of the will or other document identifying him as the legal representative of the deceased. Without this documentation, the CRA will not provide any of the deceased person's income tax information.

Deemed Disposition Of Capital Property

General Rules

12-99.   ITA 70(5) provides the following general rules for the capital property of a deceased taxpayer:

Capital Property Other Than Depreciable Property   The deceased taxpayer is deemed to have disposed of the property at fair market value immediately before his death. The person receiving the property is deemed to have acquired the property at this time, at a value equal to its fair market value.

Depreciable Property   The basic rules for this type of property are the same. That is, there is a deemed disposition of the property by the deceased taxpayer at fair market value, combined with an acquisition of the property at the same value by the beneficiary. When the capital cost of the property in the hands of the deceased exceeds its fair market value, the beneficiary is required to retain the original capital cost, with the difference being treated as deemed CCA.

12-100.   A simple example will serve to illustrate the rules for depreciable property:

Example   Eric Nadon dies, leaving a depreciable property to his son that has a capital cost of $100,000, a fair market value of $60,000, and a UCC of $50,000.

Analysis   Under ITA 70(5), the transfer will take place at the fair market value of $60,000. This means that Mr. Nadon's final tax return will include recaptured CCA of $10,000 ($60,000 - $50,000). While the son's UCC will be the $60,000 transfer price, the capital cost of the asset will remain at Mr. Nadon's original capital cost of $100,000. This means that, if the asset is later sold for a value between $60,000 and $100,000, the resulting gain will be treated as recaptured CCA, rather than as a more favourably taxed capital gain.

12-101.   The transfer of non-capital property (i.e., property not used to produce income) at the time of death usually has no income tax implications. This reflects the fact that items such as cash or personal use property (e.g., a sailboat used only by the individual) represent after tax amounts of funds that should not be taxed a second time.

Rollover To A Spouse, A Common-Law Partner, Or A Spousal Trust

12-102.   ITA 70(6) provides an exception to the general rules contained in ITA 70(5) in situations where the transfer is to a spouse, a common-law partner, a spousal or a common-law partner trust. This is a rollover provision that allows the transfer of non-depreciable property at its adjusted cost base and depreciable property at its UCC.

12-103.   This means that the transfer does not generate a capital gain or loss, recapture, or terminal loss, and that the surviving spouse or common-law partner will assume the same property values as those carried by the deceased. This has the effect of deferring any capital gains or recapture until the surviving spouse or common-law partner disposes of the property, or dies.

12-104.   It is possible for the legal representative of the deceased to elect in the final return to have one or all asset transfers take place at fair market value. This election could be used to take advantage of charitable donations, medical expenses, unused loss carry forwards, and, in the case of qualified farm property, a qualified fishing property, or the shares of a qualified small business corporation, an unused lifetime capital gains deduction. As was the case with electing out of the ITA 73 inter vivos transfer to a spouse rules, electing out of ITA 70(6) is implemented in the deceased's final tax return and does not require the filing of a form.

12-105.   To qualify as a spousal trust, ITA 70(6) indicates that the surviving spouse or common-law partner must be entitled to receive all of the income of the trust that arises before the death of the surviving spouse or common-law partner. In addition, no person other than the spouse or common-law partner may receive the use of any of the income or capital of the trust, prior to the death of this spouse or common-law partner.

12-106.   There are at least two advantages to using a spousal trust:

• This arrangement allows the deceased to determine the ultimate disposition of any property. For example, if after his death, Mr. Hall wishes his property to go only to his children, this can be specified in the trust arrangement and avoid the possibility that property could be redirected to a new husband, or any additional children that his spouse or common-law partner might have on remarrying.

• Such arrangements can provide for the administration of the assets of the deceased in those situations where the surviving spouse or common-law partner is not experienced in business or financial matters.

Exercise Twelve-13

Subject: Transfers On Death

Ms. Cheryl Lardner, who owns two trucks that were used in her business, dies in July, 2007. Her will transferred truck A to her husband, Michel, and truck B to her daughter, Melinda. Each of the trucks cost $42,000 and had a fair market value at the time of her death of $33,000. The UCC balance for the class that contains the trucks was $51,000. What are the tax consequences resulting from Ms. Lardner's death with respect to these two trucks? Your answer should include the capital cost and the UCC for the trucks in the hands of Michel and Melinda.

End of Exercise. Solution available in Study Guide.

Tax Free Transfers Other Than To A Spouse Or Common-Law Partner

12-107.   As we have seen, the most common situation in which capital property can be transferred at the time of death on a tax free basis is when the transfer is to a spouse or a spousal trust. However, ITA 70(9) provides for other tax free transfers involving specific types of farm and fishing assets. These are similar to the inter vivos transfers of farm property to a child that were previously covered. For each of the following types of transfers, the legal representatives of the deceased can elect to transfer the property at any value between its adjusted cost base and its fair market value. These elections can be used to utilize any accumulated losses of the deceased, or any unused lifetime capital gains deduction.

- **Farm Or Fishing Property**   When farm or fishing property has been used by a taxpayer or the taxpayer's family, it can be transferred on a tax free basis to a resident child, grandchild, or great grandchild at the time of the taxpayer's death. These provisions can also be used to transfer farm property from a child to a parent in situations where the child dies before the parent.

- **Shares Of A Family Farm Or Fishing Corporation**   Shares of a family farm or fishing corporation can be transferred on a tax free basis to a resident child, grandchild, or great grandchild at the time of a taxpayer's death. It is possible to have tax free transfers of farm or fishing corporation shares from a child to a parent and, in addition, the rules provide for the rollover of shares in a family farm or fishing holding company.

- **Interests In Family Farm Or Fishing Partnerships**   Rules similar to those described in the two preceding situations allow for the tax free transfer of interests in family farm or fishing partnerships to resident children at the time of the taxpayer's death.

Filing Requirements

Prior Year Returns

12-108.   As discussed in Chapter 2, if an individual dies between January 1 of the current year and the normal due date for the prior year's return (April 30 of the current year or, if the individual or his spouse or common-law partner had business income, June 15 of the current year), it is unlikely that he will have filed the return for the prior year. In this situation, the due date for the prior year's return is six months after the date of death. For example, if a taxpayer died on January 10, 2007, his representative would have until July 10, 2007 to file his 2006 tax return.

12-109.   Under ITA 111(2), a deceased taxpayer is allowed to deduct unused capital losses against other sources of income in the year of death and the immediately preceding year. Charitable donations can also be carried back to the preceding year if not needed on the final return. If either item is applied to the preceding year, the prior year's return must be amended.

Multiple Returns

12-110.   Filing the appropriate tax returns in the most advantageous manner for a deceased taxpayer can be complicated as there are a number of exceptions to the normal rules. In addition, there are special rules for final returns.

12-111.   In fact, in some situations, more than one return will be filed on behalf of a deceased individual. Some of these are required by the ordinary provisions of the *Income Tax Act*. Other can be filed on the basis of an election and may or may not be filed in particular cases. The potential returns and their deadlines can be described as follows:

- **Ordinary Return - Year Of Death**   The ordinary return for the year of death, also referred to as the final or terminal return, will be due on April 30 or June 15 of the subsequent year. However, if the death occurs between November 1 and December 31 of the current year, the deceased taxpayer's representative has until the later of the normal filing date and six months after the date of death to file the current year's return. For example, if a taxpayer died on December 1, 2007 and his normal filing date was April 30, 2008, his representative would have until June 1, 2008 to file his 2007 tax return. Alternatively, if his return contained business income, his normal filing date of June 15, 2008 would be applicable.

- **Elective Return - Rights Or Things**   Under ITA 70(2), this special return is due the later of one year from the date of death or 90 days after the mailing date of the notice of assessment of the final return. (See Paragraph 12-121, which explains rights or things.)

- **Elective Return - Non-Calendar Fiscal Year End**   If the deceased had business income from a partnership or proprietorship with a non-calendar fiscal year, his death creates a deemed year end for the business. If the death occurred after the fiscal year end, but before the end of the calendar year in which the fiscal period ended, the representative of the deceased can elect to file a separate return for the income earned by the business between the end of the fiscal year and the date of death. For example, if Mr. Samuel Rosen had a proprietorship with a June 30 year end and he died on November 23, 2007, his representative could file a separate return for the period July 1 through November 23, 2007. This would allow the representative to limit the business income in his final return to the 12 month period ending June 30, 2007. The filing deadline for this return is the same as the one applicable to the final return.

- **Elective Return - Testamentary Trust Beneficiary**   Under ITA 104(23)(d), if the deceased is an income beneficiary of a testamentary trust, the representative may elect to file a separate return for the period between the end of the trust's fiscal year and the date of the taxpayer's death. The filing deadline is the same as the one applicable to the final return.

12-112.   There are two basic reasons for filing as many tax returns as possible. The first relates to the fact that the income tax rates are progressive and income starts at nil in each return. This means that the first $37,178 in each return has the advantage of being taxed at the lowest federal rate of 15.5 percent. If multiple returns are not filed, there may be amounts taxed at the higher rates of 22, 26, or 29 percent that would have been eligible for this lower rate if multiple returns had been filed.

12-113.   The second advantage of filing multiple returns is that some personal tax credits can be deducted in each return. As will be discussed in the following material, this could save the deceased taxpayer's estate several thousand dollars for each tax return filed.

Use Of Deductions And Credits

Multiple Usage

12-114.   The full amount of applicable personal credits is claimed, regardless of when the individual died in the year. As previously noted, one of the major advantages of being able to file multiple returns is that some personal tax credits can be used in all of the returns filed. It appears that the rationale for claiming certain tax credits on multiple returns is to recognize the fact that the income reported on the different returns could have been included in a later year's tax return if the deceased had lived. In that later year, personal tax credits would have been available to reduce Tax Payable.

12-115.   The CRA's Guide, "Preparing Returns For Deceased Persons" (T4011) provides a great deal of information relevant to the returns of deceased taxpayers. In the Guide, it notes that there are three groups of amounts that can be claimed on optional returns. More specifically, the following non-refundable credits can be claimed in the final return and in each optional return filed:

- basic personal amount [$1,384 (15.5%)($8,929) for 2007]
- age [$802 (15.5%)($5,177) for 2007]
- spousal amount or amount for an eligible dependant [$1,384 (15.5%)($8,929) for 2007]
- amount for infirm dependant over 17 [$623 (15.5%)($4,019) for 2007]
- caregiver amount [$623 (15.5%)($4,019) for 2007]

12-116.   The combined value of these federal tax credits, if applicable, is $4,816. When combined with similar credits in the various provinces, the total value is over $6,000. This represents a significant tax savings that becomes available in each tax return filed. Achieving these savings is, of course, conditional on each of the individual returns having sufficient Tax Payable to make use of the credits.

Elective Usage

12-117.   Other non-refundable credits can be split between, or deducted in full, in any of the returns filed. However, the total claimed cannot exceed the amount that would be included in the ordinary return for the year of death. These credits include the following:

- adoption expenses
- disability amount for the deceased person
- disability amount for a dependant other than a spouse
- interest paid on certain student loans
- tuition, education and textbook amount for the deceased person
- tuition, education and textbook amount transferred from a child
- medical expenses (note that the total expenses must be reduced by the lesser of $1,926 and 3 percent of the total Net Income reported on all returns)
- charitable donations, including amounts gifted in the will (limited to 100 percent of Net Income)

Usage With Related Income

12-118.   With respect to the following deductions and non-refundable credits, they can only be claimed in the return in which the related income is reported:

- Canada or Quebec Pension Plan contributions credit
- Employment Insurance premiums credit
- pension income credit
- employee home relocation loan deduction
- stock option deduction
- social benefits repayment (clawback)

Usage With Ordinary Return

12-119.   Deductions and credits that cannot be claimed on elective returns are claimed on the final return. The following deductions and non-refundable credits are listed in the CRA Guide as amounts that cannot be claimed on an optional return, but that can be claimed in the deceased's ordinary final return (it is not a complete list):

- Registered Pension Plan deduction
- Registered Retirement Savings Plan deduction
- annual union or professional dues
- amounts transferred from a spouse or common-law partner
- child care expenses
- carrying charges and interest expenses
- disability supports deduction
- allowable business investment losses
- moving expenses
- support payments made
- losses from other years
- lifetime capital gains deduction
- northern residents deduction

Procedures For Specific Returns

Ordinary Return(s)

12-120.   As noted previously, the legal representative of the deceased is responsible for filing a return for the year of death (a.k.a., final return) and, if required, a return for the previous year. This return would contain the usual sources of income, including employment income, business income, property income, and net taxable capital gains. With respect to employment income, it would include salary or wages from the end of the last pay period to the date of death.

> **Example** A taxpayer dies on June 4th. His last pay period is from May 16th through May 31st, with the amount being payable on June 7th.

> **Analysis** The accrual for the period from June 1st, the first day after the end of his last pay period, through the June 4th date of his death, must be included in his ordinary return for the year of death. With respect to the amount that is accrued but unpaid at his death, this can either be included in the taxpayer's ordinary return or, alternatively, in a separate rights or things return.

Rights Or Things Return

12-121.   Rights or things are defined as unpaid amounts that would have been included in the deceased's income when they were realized or disposed of, had the taxpayer not died. Included would be:

- unpaid salaries, commissions, and vacation pay for pay periods which ended before the date of death (e.g., the salary for the period May 16th through May 31st in the example in Paragraph 12-120)
- uncashed matured bond coupons, provided they were not required to be included in a previous year's income
- harvested farm crops and livestock on hand
- inventory and accounts receivable of taxpayers using the cash method
- declared, but unpaid dividends

12-122.   While some of these amounts could be included in the ordinary return of the taxpayer, it is generally advisable, provided the amounts are material, to file this separate return as it permits a doubling up of certain tax credits and, in many cases, will result in additional amounts being taxed at the lowest federal rate.

12-123.   Interest accrued at the time of death is somewhat problematical. If, at the time of his death, a taxpayer owns a term deposit or similar investment that pays interest on a periodic basis, ITA 70(1)(a) requires that interest accrued to the date of death be included in the taxpayer's ordinary return of income. This would be the case even if the taxpayer ordinarily used the cash basis of interest recognition. Under ITA 70(2), any accrued interest that is required to be included in the final ordinary return cannot be included in the rights or things return.

12-124.   In contrast, if the debt instrument does not pay periodic interest, the accrued interest can be treated as a right or thing. As examples of this, IT-210R2, "Income Of Deceased Persons - Periodic Payments", refers to a matured treasury bill that has not been realized and to matured, but uncashed bond coupons.

12-125.   As a final point, note that rights or things can be transferred to a beneficiary, provided this is done within the time limit for filing a separate rights or things return. If this election is made, the amounts will be included in the beneficiary's income when they are realized, and should not be included in either the ordinary, or the rights or things return of the deceased.

Other Elective Returns

12-126.   None of the other elective returns warrant additional discussion in a general text such as this. We would note, however, that it is normally advisable to file these returns, both for the additional credits that can be claimed and for the additional amounts that will be allocated to the lowest federal tax bracket.

Payment Of Taxes

12-127.   Regardless of the extension of filing dates for the final and elective returns, the tax owing is due on April 30 of the year following the year of death, unless the death occurs between November 1 and December 31. If this is the case, the due date for the payment of taxes is six months after the date of death. We would also remind you that the due date for payment of taxes is unchanged by the deferral of the normal filing date to June 15 for taxpayers with business income.

12-128.   With respect to income from the value of rights or things and from deemed dispositions of capital property at death, the legal representative for the deceased individual can elect to defer the payment of taxes. Under ITA 159(5), payment can be made in ten equal annual instalments, with the first payment due on the regular payment due date of the final return. Security acceptable to the Minister must be furnished to guarantee payment of the deferred taxes. Interest will be charged on amounts outstanding and, as is the usual case, such interest is not deductible.

Allowable Capital Losses - Special Rules At Death

12-129.   One of the difficulties with allowable capital losses is that they can normally only be deducted against taxable capital gains. As there is no time limit on the carry forward of such undeducted losses, an individual can die with a substantial balance of these amounts on hand. Losses may also arise in the year of death, either through a disposition prior to death or through a deemed disposition at death.

12-130.   ITA 111(2) contains a special provision with respect to both net capital losses from years prior to death and to allowable capital losses arising in the year of death. Essentially, this provision allows these accumulated losses to be applied against any type of income in the year of death, or the immediately preceding year.

12-131.   Two points should be noted with respect to the application of this provision:

• The ability to use this provision is reduced by the previous deduction of amounts under the lifetime capital gains provision (see Chapter 14). This reduction reflects the actual amount of the lifetime capital gains deduction made, without regard to the capital gains inclusion rate that was applicable at the time.

• Unlike the usual procedure with capital loss carry overs, this carry over deduction is applied at the capital gain/loss inclusion rate that prevailed in the year in which the capital loss was realized.

12-132.   An example will illustrate these provisions

Example   Ms. Vincent has a net capital loss of $22,500 [(3/4)($30,000)], which has been carried forward from 1990. She dies in December, 2007 and, as the result of a disposition in June of that year, has a taxable capital gain of $4,500 [(1/2)($9,000)].

Analysis   The amount of the 1990 carry forward, adjusted to the 1/2 inclusion rate, is $15,000 [(2/3)($22,500) or (1/2)($30,000)]. Of this amount, $4,500 will be deducted against the 2007 taxable capital gain. This will leave a balance of $10,500 [(1/2)($30,000 - $9,000)] which, in order to use the ITA 111(2) provision, must be adjusted back to the 3/4 inclusion rate for 1990. This will leave $15,750 [(3/2)($10,500)]. This can be verified using the 100 percent figures, which give the same $15,750 [(3/4)($30,000 - $9,000)] amount. This $15,750 can be applied against any type of income in 2007. If there is not enough income to fully utilize the loss, it can be carried back to 2006 in an amended return.

12-133.   Capital losses realized by the estate on dispositions of an individual's property in the first taxation year after his death can be carried back and applied against any type of income in the final return of the deceased. Note, however, that these losses cannot be carried back to the tax return for the year preceding death.

Exercise Twelve-14

Subject: Death Of A Taxpayer

Mr. Derek Barnes has an undeducted net capital loss from 1990 of $7,500 [(3/4)($10,000)]. He dies during June, 2007 and, as the result of a deemed disposition on death, has a taxable capital gain of $2,000 [(1/2)($4,000)]. Describe the tax treatment of these two items in his final tax return.

End of Exercise.   Solution available in Study Guide.

Charitable Donations - Special Rules At Death

12-134.   Charitable donations made in the year of death, or through bequests in the will, can be claimed for tax credit purposes subject to a limit of 100 percent of Net Income, as opposed to the normal limit of 75 percent. Any charitable donations that are not claimed in the final return can be carried back to the immediately preceding year, subject to the 100 percent of Net Income limit. There are additional rules for charitable donations that are not cash. These are covered in Chapter 14.

Medical Expenses - Special Rules At Death

12-135.   Medical expenses paid can normally be claimed for any 12 month period ending in the year to the extent they exceed a threshold amount (see Chapter 6). In the year of death, the time period is extended to the 24 month period prior to death.

Deferred Income Plans At Death

12-136.   In many cases, a deceased individual will have Registered Retirement Savings Plan (RRSP) or a Registered Retirement Income Fund (RRIF) at the time of death. There are a number of special rules associated with this situation. However, it is difficult to provide a meaningful presentation of these rules until you have a more complete understanding of how these plans work. As our detailed coverage of RRSPs and RRIFs is found in Chapter 13, we will defer coverage of deferred income plans at death until that Chapter.

Key Terms Used In This Chapter

12-137.   The following is a list of the key terms used in this Chapter. These terms, and their meanings, are compiled in the Glossary Of Key Terms located at the back of the separate paper Study Guide and on the Student CD-ROM.

Anti-Avoidance Provision	Inadequate Consideration
Business Income	Income Attribution
Capital Gain	Income Splitting
Capital Loss	Inter Vivos Transfer
Deemed Disposition	Interest Income
Disposition	Net Business Income
Dividend Gross Up	Net Property Income
Dividend Tax Credit	Property Income
Election	Resident
Emigration	Rights Or Things
Final Tax Return	Rollover
Immigration	Taxable Canadian Property

References

12-138.   For more detailed study of the material in this Chapter, we would refer you to the following:

ITA 56(4.1)	Interest Free Or Low Interest Loans
ITA 69	Inadequate Considerations
ITA 70	Death Of A Taxpayer
ITA 73	Inter Vivos Transfer To Individuals (e.g., Transfers To A Spouse)
ITA 74.1(1)	Transfers And Loans To Spouse Or Common-Law Partner
ITA 74.1(2)	Transfers And Loans To Minors
ITA 74.2	Gain Or Loss Deemed That Of Lender Or Transferor
ITA 74.5	Transfers For Fair Market Consideration
ITA 128.1(1)	Immigration
ITA 128.1(4)	Emigration
IC 72-17R5	Procedures Concerning The Disposition Of Taxable Canadian Property By Non-Residents Of Canada - Section 116
IT-209R	Inter Vivos Gifts Of Capital Property To Individuals Directly or Through Trusts
IT-210R2	Income Of Deceased Persons - Periodic Payments And Investment Tax Credits
IT-212R3	Income Of Deceased Persons - Rights Or Things
IT-226R	Gift To A Charity Of A Residual Interest In Real Property Or An Equitable Interest In A Trust
IT-268R4	Inter Vivos Transfer Of Farm Property To A Child
IT-278R2	Death Of A Partner Or Of A Retired Partner
IT-295R4	Taxable Dividends Received After 1987 By A Spouse
IT-325R2	Property Transfers After Separation, Divorce And Annulment
IT-326R3	Returns Of Deceased Persons As "Another Person"
IT-349R3	Intergenerational Transfers Of Farm Property On Death
IT-385R2	Disposition Of An Income Interest In A Trust
IT-419R2	Meaning Of Arm's Length
IT-451R	Deemed Disposition And Acquisition On Ceasing To Be Or Becoming Resident In Canada
IT-490	Barter Transactions
IT-510	Transfers And Loans Of Property Made After May 22, 1985 To A Related Minor
IT-511R	Interspousal And Certain Other Transfers And Loans Of Property

Problems For Self Study

(The solutions for these problems can be found in the separate Study Guide.)

Self Study Problem Twelve - 1

John Bolton owns 5,000 shares of Marker Manufacturing Ltd., a Canadian public company. These shares were purchased three year ago, at a price of $45 per share. They are currently trading at $105 per share.

Consider the following four independent Cases with respect to an immediate transfer of these shares to Alex Bolton, John's 16 year old brother, a successful computer games consultant:

Case A   The 5,000 shares are sold to Alex Bolton at a price of $75 per share.

Case B   The 5,000 shares are sold to Alex Bolton at a price of $125 per share.

Case C   The 5,000 shares are sold to Alex Bolton at a price of $105 per share.

Case D   The 5,000 shares are given to Alex Bolton as a gift.

Required: For each of these four Cases, determine the effect on John Bolton's Net Income For Tax Purposes and the adjusted cost base that will apply for Alex Bolton on any future sale of the Marker Manufacturing Ltd. shares.

Self Study Problem Twelve - 2

During the current year, Mr. Langdon makes a non-interest bearing loan of $100,000 to his wife, who acquires a $100,000 bond with the proceeds. He also makes a non-interest bearing loan of $100,000 to both of his children:

- Pat, aged 15, who uses the funds to acquire a $100,000 bond, and

- Heather, aged 23, who uses the funds as a down payment on her principal residence. Without this loan she would have paid mortgage interest of $6,000 during the year.

During the year, the bonds acquired by Mr. Langdon's spouse pay interest of $5,000. The bonds acquired by Pat pay interest of $5,500.

Required: Determine the amount of income that will be attributed to Mr. Langdon for the current taxation year as the result of the non-interest bearing loans.

Self Study Problem Twelve - 3

Dr. Sandra Bolt is 49 years of age and an extremely successful physician in Halifax, Nova Scotia. She is married to Tod Bolt and has two children. On December 31, 2007, her son, Dirk, is 20 years old and her daughter, Dolly, is 15 years old. Each of the children earns about $10,000 per year in income from part time acting jobs. While her husband Tod qualified as a professional accountant, he did not enjoy the work and, for the last ten years, he has assumed the role of house parent. As a consequence, his only current source of income is the interest on $335,000 that he has in his personal savings account. This interest amounts to about $20,000 per year and all of the savings were accumulated from amounts that he earned while working as a professional accountant.

On December 28, 2007, Dr. Bolt is holding equity securities with an adjusted cost base of $185,000 and a fair market value of $225,000. She is considering transferring these securities to either her husband or to one of her two children. She seeks your advice as to the tax consequences, both to herself and to the transferee, that would result from such a transfer.

During your discussions, Dr. Bolt has indicated the following:

- The transfer will take place on December 31, 2007.
- Any proceeds she receives from her family on the share transfer will not be invested in income producing assets.
- She wishes you to assume that the securities would pay eligible dividends during 2008 of $18,500 ($26,825 taxable amount) and that the transferee would sell the securities on January 1, 2009 for $260,000.

Required: Each of the following independent Cases involves a transfer by Dr. Bolt to a member of her family. Indicate, with respect to the Net Income For Tax Purposes of both Dr. Bolt and the transferee, the 2007, 2008, and 2009 tax effects of:

- the transfer on December 31, 2007,
- the assumed 2008 receipt of the dividends, and
- the assumed 2009 disposition by the transferee.

Note that some of the Cases have been included to illustrate specific provisions of the relevant legislation and do not necessarily represent a reasonable course of action on the part of Dr. Bolt.

Case A   Dr. Bolt gives the securities to her husband and does not elect out of the provisions of ITA 73(1).

Case B   Dr. Bolt's husband uses money from his savings account to purchase the securities for their fair market value of $225,000. Dr. Bolt does not elect out of the provisions of ITA 73(1).

Case C   Dr. Bolt's husband uses money from his savings account to purchase the securities for their fair market value of $225,000. Dr. Bolt elects out of the provisions of ITA 73(1).

Case D   Dr. Bolt's husband uses money from his savings account to purchase the securities for $140,000. Dr. Bolt does not elect out of the provisions of ITA 73(1).

Case E   Dr. Bolt's husband uses money from his savings account to purchase the securities for $140,000. Dr. Bolt elects out of the provisions of ITA 73(1).

Case F   Dr. Bolt gives the securities to her daughter, Dolly.

Case G   Dr. Bolt gives her daughter, Dolly, a $225,000 loan. The loan requires interest to be paid at commercial rates and Dolly uses the proceeds of the loan to purchase her mother's securities at fair market value. Dr. Bolt believes that the combination of dividends on the securities and Dolly's income from part time jobs will be sufficient to pay the interest on the loan.

Case H   Dr. Bolt gives her son, Dirk, a $225,000 interest free loan. Dirk uses the proceeds to purchase his mother's securities at their fair market value of $225,000.

Self Study Problem Twelve - 4

Mrs. Sarah Long, a management consultant, is married with two children. Her son, Barry, is 27 years old and her daughter, Mary, is 13. Mrs. Long has not previously gifted or sold property to her husband or either of her children.

On April 1 of the current year, Mrs. Long owns the following properties:

Long Consulting Ltd.   Mrs. Long owns 100 percent of the voting shares of Long Consulting Ltd., a Canadian controlled private corporation. These shares have a cost of $210,000 and a current fair market value of $475,000.

Rental Property   Mrs. Long owns a rental building that is located on leased land. The building was acquired at a cost of $190,000. On April 1 of the current year, its UCC is $125,000 and its fair market value is estimated to be $275,000.

Dynamics Inc.   Mrs. Long owns 4,000 shares of Dynamics Inc., a Canadian public company. These shares have a cost of $212,000 and a current fair market value of $384,000.

Farm Land   Mrs. Long owns farm land with a cost of $80,000 and a current fair market value of $175,000. Mrs. Long's son, Barry, uses the farm land on a full time basis to grow various crops.

Mrs. Long is considering giving all or part of the properties to her spouse and/or her two children.

Required: You have been hired as a tax consultant to Mrs. Long. She would like a report that would detail, for each of the four properties, the tax consequences to her of making a gift of the item to her husband or to either of her children. Your report should include the resulting tax position of the beneficiary of the gift and some indication of the tax effects that might arise if the beneficiary later sold the gifted property for its current fair market value.

Self Study Problem Twelve - 5

Mr. Howard Caswell is 67 years of age and his spouse, Charlene, is 58. They have one son, John, who is 36 years of age. On September 1 of the current year, Mr. Howard Caswell owns the following properties:

Rental Property   Mr. Caswell owns a rental building that is located on leased land. The building was acquired at a cost of $95,000. As at September 1 of the current year, its UCC is $67,000 and its fair market value is estimated to be $133,000.

General Industries Ltd.   Mr. Caswell owns 5,000 shares of General Industries Ltd., a Canadian public company. These shares have a cost of $200,000 and a current fair market value of $350,000. Mr. Caswell has never owned more than 3 percent of the outstanding shares of this Company.

Farm Land   Mr. Caswell owns farm land with a cost of $325,000 and a current fair market value of $550,000. The land is farmed on a full time basis by Mr. Caswell's son, John.

Caswell Enterprises   Mr. Caswell owns 100 percent of the voting shares of Caswell Enterprises, a Canadian controlled private corporation. The Company was established with an investment of $275,000 and it is estimated that the current fair market value of the shares is $426,000.

Required: Explain the tax consequences that would result in each of the following Cases:

A. Mr. Caswell dies on September 1 of the current year, leaving all of his property to his spouse, Charlene.

B. Mr. Caswell dies on September 1 of the current year, leaving all of his property to his son, John.

C. Mr. Caswell departs from Canada and ceases to be a resident on September 1 of the current year.

Assignment Problems

(The solutions for these problems are only available in
the solutions manual that has been provided to your instructor.)

Assignment Problem Twelve - 1

Ms. Carmen Bryers owns 1,000 shares of Karmac Distributing Company, a Canadian public company. These shares were purchased four years ago at a price of $20 per share. On December 31 of the current year they are trading at $80 per share.

Ms. Bryers transfers these shares on December 31 to Marcello Bryers, her 35 year old brother.

Required: For each of the following four Cases, determine the effect on Carmen Bryers' Net Income For Tax Purposes for the current year and the adjusted cost base that will apply for Marcello Bryers on any future sale of the Karmac Distributing Company shares.

A. The 1,000 shares are sold to Marcello Bryers at a price of $60 per share.

B. The 1,000 shares are sold to Marcello Bryers at a price of $95 per share.

C. The 1,000 shares are sold to Marcello Bryers at a price of $80 per share.

D. The 1,000 shares are given to Marcello Bryers as a gift.

Assignment Problem Twelve - 2

Mr. Goodby, a self-employed contractor, is married and has two children. His son, Harry, is 25 years old and his daughter, Martha, is 14. Mr. Goodby has not previously gifted or sold property to his spouse or either of his children.

At the end of the current year, Mr. Goodby owns the following property:

Farm Land   Mr. Goodby owns farm land that cost $160,000 and has a current fair market value of $350,000. Mr. Goodby's son, Harry, uses the farm land on a full time basis to grow various crops.

DRC Ltd.   Mr. Goodby owns 5,000 shares of DRC Ltd., a Canadian public company. These shares have a cost of $320,000 and a current fair market value of $573,000.

Rental Property   Mr. Goodby owns an apartment building that is located on leased land. The building was acquired at a cost of $256,000. At the end of the current year, its UCC is $178,000 and its fair market value is $386,000.

Goodby Construction Company   Mr. Goodby owns 100 percent of the voting shares of Goodby Construction Company, a Canadian controlled private corporation. These shares have a cost of $227,000 and a current fair market value of $452,000.

Mr. Goodby is in poor health and is considering giving all or part of the properties to his spouse and/or his two children. He has fully utilized his lifetime capital gains deduction.

Required: You have been hired as a tax consultant to Mr. Goodby. He would like a report that would detail, for each of the four properties, the tax consequences to him of making a gift of the item to his wife or to either one of his children. Your report should include the resulting tax position of the beneficiary of the gift and some indication of the tax effects that might arise if the beneficiary sold the gifted property for its current fair market value later in the year.

Assignment Problem Twelve - 3

After an extensive period of marital counselling, Mr. and Mrs. Hadley agree to a separation in June of the current year. Mr. Hadley has owned two small rental properties for many years and these properties are still in his name at the time of the separation. On June 1 of the current year, Mr. Hadley agrees to transfer one of these properties to Mrs. Hadley. The relevant information on the property at the time of its transfer is as follows:

	Land	Building
Original Cost	$26,000	$ 85,000
Market Value - Date Of Transfer	51,000	107,000
UCC - Date Of Transfer	N/A	48,500

Prior to the end of the current year, as the result of a decision to move to another province, Mrs. Hadley sells the property for $165,000. Of this total, $55,000 is allocated to the land and the remaining $110,000 to the building. During the period that the property was in her name, the net rental income was nil and no CCA was deducted on the building'. Mr. and Mrs. Hadley were formally divorced the following year.

Required: Determine the tax effects associated with the transfer and subsequent sale of the property for both Mr. and Mrs. Hadley assuming:

A. In keeping with a verbal understanding reached in negotiating the separation, Mr. Hadley gives Mrs. Hadley the building in lieu of any support payments.

B. Mr. Hadley agrees to pay spousal support and Mrs. Hadley agrees to purchase the property at its fair market value on June 1.

Assignment Problem Twelve - 4

Mr. John Tucker is 45 years old and married to Janet Tucker. On December 31, 2007, their son, Martin, is 23 years old, while their daughter, Doreen, is 12 years old.

At the end of 2007, John is holding equity securities of a public company with an adjusted cost base of $85,000 and a fair market value of $123,000. He is considering transferring these securities to either his wife or to one of his two children. He seeks your advice as to the tax consequences, both to himself and to the transferee, that would result from such a transfer.

During your discussions, Mr. Tucker has indicated the following:

- The transfer will take place on December 31, 2007.
- Any proceeds he receives from his family on the share transfer will not be invested in income producing assets.
- He wishes you to assume that the securities would pay eligible dividends during 2008 of $6,500 ($9,425 taxable amount) and that the transferee would sell the securities on January 1, 2009 for $151,000.

Required: Each of the following independent Cases involves a transfer by Mr. Tucker to a member of his family. Indicate, with respect to the Net Income For Tax Purposes of both Mr. Tucker and the transferee, the 2007, 2008, and 2009 tax effects of:

- the transfer on December 31, 2007,
- the assumed 2008 receipt of the dividends, and
- the assumed 2009 disposition by the transferee.

Case A   Mr. Tucker gives the securities to his wife and does not elect out of the provisions of the ITA 73(1) spousal rollover.

Case B   Mr. Tucker's wife uses money from her savings account to purchase the securities for their fair market value of $123,000. Mr. Tucker does not elect out of the provisions of the ITA 73(1) spousal rollover.

Case C   Mr. Tucker's wife uses money from her savings account to purchase the securities for $95,000. Mr. Tucker elects out of the provisions of the ITA 73(1) spousal rollover.

Case D   Mr. Tucker gives the securities to his daughter, Doreen.

Case E   Mr. Tucker's son, Martin, uses funds from his stock trading account to purchase his father's securities at their fair market value of $123,000.

Assignment Problem Twelve - 5

For all of his adult life, Mr. Lange has been a resident of Canada. However, in recent years, the severity of the climate has begun to have an adverse influence on his health. As a consequence, on June 15 of the current year, he is planning to move to Sarasota, Florida. On this date, he owns the following assets:

	Adjusted Cost Base	Fair Market Value
Vacant land	$15,000	$ 46,000
Automobile	31,000	18,000
Coin collection	5,000	11,000
Inco Ltd. shares	24,000	38,000
Alcan shares	42,000	35,000
Royal Bank shares	15,000	23,000
Nal Enterprises Ltd. shares (a Canadian controlled private corporation)	26,000	153,000

Mr. Lange has come to you for advice just prior to moving to Florida.

Required:

A. What elections with respect to his assets would you recommend that he consider before leaving Canada? Explain your recommendations.

B. Assume he has made no elections regarding his assets. Determine the amount of the taxable capital gain or allowable capital loss that Mr. Lange will report in his Canadian income tax return for the current year.

Assignment Problem Twelve - 6

In 1997, Mr. Forsyth purchased a small apartment building at a cost of $350,000. Of the total cost, $100,000 was allocated to the land with the $250,000 balance going to the building. For CCA purposes, the building was included in Class 1.

During the years 1997 through 2006, the building was usually fully occupied. At the beginning of 2007, the UCC of the building was $170,000.

On October 10, 2007, Mr. Forsyth is killed in an automobile accident. At the time of his death, the fair market value of the land was $212,000 and the fair market value of the building was $325,000.

In February of 2008, the building is sold for a total price of $600,000, of which $225,000 is allocated to the land and $375,000 to the building.

Required: Indicate the tax effects to be included in Mr. Forsyth's tax return as a result of the 2007 deemed disposition at his death and calculate the tax effects associated with the 2008 sale of the building in both of the following Cases:

Case A   His will leaves the apartment building to his 23 year old daughter, Eileen. During 2007, she continues to operate the building and takes maximum CCA for that year.

Case B   His will leaves the apartment building to his wife, Christine. During 2007, she continues to operate the building and takes maximum CCA for that year.

Assignment Problem Twelve - 7

Mr. Cheever is 66 years of age and his wife, Doreen, is 56. They have one daughter, Mary, who is 32 years of age. On July 1 of the current year, Mr. Cheever owns the following properties:

Rental Property   Mr. Cheever owns a rental building that is located on leased land. The building was acquired at a cost of $45,000. On July 1 of the current year, its UCC is $27,000 and its fair market value is estimated to be $87,000.

Brazeway Dynamics   Mr. Cheever owns 2,500 shares of Brazeway Dynamics, a Canadian public company. These shares have a cost of $275,000 and a current fair market value of $425,000. Mr. Cheever has never owned more than 1 percent of the outstanding shares of this Company.

Farm Land   Mr. Cheever owns farm land with a cost of $525,000 and a current fair market value of $750,000. The land is farmed on a full time basis by Mr. Cheever's daughter, Mary.

Cheever Inc.   Mr. Cheever owns 100 percent of the voting shares of Cheever Inc., a Canadian controlled private corporation. The Company was established with an investment of $155,000 and it is estimated that the current fair market value of the shares is $227,000.

Required: Explain the tax consequences to Mr. Cheever for the current year, in each of the following Cases:

A.   Mr. Cheever dies on July 1 of the current year, leaving all of his property to his spouse, Doreen.

B.   Mr. Cheever dies on July 1 of the current year, leaving all of his property to his daughter, Mary.

C.   Mr. Cheever departs from Canada and ceases to be a resident on July 1 of the current year.

Assignment Cases

Assignment Case Twelve - 1 (Comprehensive Case Covering Chapters 5 to 12)

Mr. Wally Bronson is 67 years old and has been retired for several years. His spouse, Melissa, is 62 and has been blind for the last ten years. Mr. Bronson receives pension income of $83,000 in 2007 from his employer's registered pension plan. Due to his high income in the last few years, Mr. Bronson has not applied for OAS benefits. However, he has applied for Canada Pension Plan payments and received $10,680 in CPP benefits in 2007. He chooses not to split his pension income with his spouse.

Melissa has no income and none of the family's investments are in her name.

Wally and Melissa have two children. Their son, Jerome, is 42 years old and their daughter, Jerri, is 38 years old. Neither child is dependent on Mr. Bronson. While Jerome has no children, Jerri has a 12 year old daughter, Brenda.

In December, 2006, Mr. Bronson is diagnosed with terminal cancer, with the doctor indicating that he probably has about 12 months to live. To this point, Mr. Bronson had not dealt with the prospect of death and, beyond the preparation of a fairly simple will which left all of his assets to Melissa, had done little in the way of estate planning.

Given his current state of health, he has decided to undertake a number of transactions in order to minimize the tax consequences of his death. He is particularly concerned with the fact that, in the province in which he lives, probate fees equal 1-1/2 percent of the fair market value of all of the assets that are transferred in his will. Given this, he intends to transfer a significant amount of his assets into the hands of others prior to his death. At this time he also revises his will, leaving some property to his two children with the remainder going to his wife.

Mr. Bronson owns two tracts of vacant land. Plot A has a cost of $125,000 and a fair market value of $150,000. Plot B has a cost of $175,000 and a fair market value of $210,000. While he had intended to develop rental properties on these sites, he has decided that this is no longer feasible and the properties should be sold.

Because his younger brother, Phil, is in a low tax bracket, during 2007, he sells Plot A to him, with the only consideration being a note for $50,000 which is paid on December 1, 2007. In contrast, his older brother, Gary, is very wealthy and is in the highest tax bracket. Given Gary's substantial bank balances, during 2007, Mr. Bronson sells Plot B to him for $250,000 in cash.

On January 1, 2007, Mr. Bronson acquires units in the YP Income Trust at a cost of $300,000. These units distribute $800 per month on the 25th of each month. This distribution represents only interest income and does not include dividends, capital gains, or a return of capital. On February 1, 2007, after receiving the January payment of $800, Mr. Bronson gifts all of these units to his granddaughter, Brenda. At this time, the units have a fair market value of $310,000.

Mr. Bronson owns a large block of Baron Inc. shares. He acquired 4,000 shares of this widely held public company in 2005 at $50 per share. In 2006, he acquired an additional 8,000 shares at $65 per share. On March 1, 2007, he gifts 1,500 shares to each of his children and an additional 1,500 shares to his wife. At this time, the shares are trading at $68 per share. On July 1, 2007, Baron Inc. pays an eligible dividend of $1.50 per share.

Mr. Bronson owns three identical units in a condominium building. Each unit cost $300,000 nine years ago and, on January 1, 2007, each had a separate class UCC of $205,000. Assume that the cost of the units do not include a value for land. During 2007, these units produced net rental income, before consideration of CCA, of $93,750.

On December 31, 2007, Mr. Bronson dies peacefully in his home. On this date he has the following assets:

Baron Inc. Shares The 7,500 shares that remain in Mr. Baron's name on this date are trading at $70 per share. Mr. Bronson's will leaves all of these shares to his spouse, Melissa.

Condominium Units In his will, Mr. Baron has left one of these units to each of his two children, with the remaining unit going to his spouse. On the date of Mr. Bronson's death, each of these units has a fair market value of $420,000.

Principal Residence Mr. Bronson and his wife have lived in the same home since 1972. The house cost $145,000 and has a current market value of $562,000. The title to the property is in Mr. Bronson's name. Mr. Bronson's will leaves this property to his spouse.

GICs On April 1, 2007, Mr. Bronson purchases $500,000 in guaranteed investment certificates. These certificates pay interest at a rate of 3 percent on March 31 of each of the next five years. Mr. Bronson's will leaves this property to his spouse.

Uncashed Bond Coupons Mr. Bronson's personal effects included uncashed bond coupons with a cash value of $16,000. The bonds themselves have matured and the face value was received on December 1, 2007. They were purchased on February 1, 2007. Mr. Bronson's will does not specifically identify who these coupons should go to.

During 2007, medical expenses for Mr. Bronson totaled $45,000, while those of his spouse totaled $12,000.

In 1989, Mr. Bronson had a net capital loss of $40,000 [(2/3)($60,000)]. He has not been able to use this loss in any previous or subsequent year.

Mr. Bronson's brother, Gary, is named executor in his will. He will file any elective tax returns that will reduce Wally's 2007 Tax Payable.

Required: Calculate Mr. Bronson's minimum 2007 Net Income For Tax Purposes, his 2007 minimum Taxable Income, and his minimum 2007 federal Tax Payable without consideration of any instalment payments he may have made. Ignore GST and PST considerations.

Assignment Case Twelve - 2 *(Comprehensive Case Covering Chapters 5 to 12)*

At the beginning of 2007, Ms. Katherine O'Hara is 46 years old and married to Mick O'Hara. She dies in an automobile accident on December 31, 2007. Mick is the executor of her estate. He is a stockbroker and, during 2007, his Net Income For Tax Purposes is $153,000.

Katherine and Mick had two children. Their son Sean is 15 years old and their daughter Sylvia is 20 years old. Neither child has any income during 2007 and at the beginning of the year, they own no investments. While Sylvia lives at home throughout 2007, she attends a local university on a full time basis for 11 months during 2007. Her tuition fees for the year total $6,150 and were paid for by her father.

Medical expenses for Katherine and her family during 2007 were as follows:

Katherine	$3,700
Mick	2,420
Sean	300
Sylvia	2,360
Total	$8,780

Mick's medical plan reimburses him for 50 percent of his medical expenses, as well as those of Katherine and Sean.

Ms. O'Hara was employed by a large publicly traded company. Her salary for 2007 was $85,000. Her only employment benefit is a $150,000 interest free loan that was provided by her employer in 2006. The loan was granted to assist Katherine with the purchase of a larger home (it does not qualify as a home relocation loan) and, at the time the loan was granted, the prescribed rate was 3 percent . The loan must be repaid on January 1, 2008.

Her employer withheld the following amounts from her income during 2007:

RPP Contributions	$2,875
EI Premiums	720
CPP Contributions	1,990

Katherine's employer makes a matching contribution of $2,875 to her RPP account.

On January 1, 2007, Katherine owned two Class 1 rental properties. Information on these properties is as follows:

	Property A	Property B
Capital Cost - Building	$326,000	$347,000
UCC	297,000	311,000
Adjusted Cost Base - Land	50,000	60,000
December 31, 2007 Fair Market Value:		
Building	395,000	495,000
Land	75,000	60,000
2007 Rents	26,400	28,800
2007 Expenses Other Than CCA	23,500	23,100

The family's principal residence was also in Katherine's name. It was acquired in 2006 for $472,000. There is no other property that can be designated as a principal residence in either 2006 or 2007.

On January 1, 2007, Katherine owned the following securities:

	Original Cost	Adjusted Cost Base
10,000 Shares Of Darcy Inc.		
(A Canadian Public Company)	$120,000	$120,000
12,000 Units Of Barton Income Trust	201,000	180,000
8,000 Units of Fidel Mutual Fund	60,000	72,000

Other information related to these investments is as follows:

1. On January 2, 2007, when the Darcy Inc. shares were trading at $14 per share, Katherine gifted 2,500 shares of Darcy Inc. to each of her two children. An additional 2,500 shares were sold to her daughter Sylvia at their market value of $14 per share. Sylvia finances the acquisition with funds that she acquired with a winning lottery ticket. The remaining 2,500 shares are gifted to her husband Mick. None of these shares are resold during the year.

2. During July 2007, the Darcy Inc. shares pay eligible dividends of $0.90 per share.

3. The Barton Income Trust's annual distribution for 2007 is $1.50 per share. Of this amount, $0.50 is designated a return of capital.

4. During April, 2007, the Fidel Mutual Fund has a 2007 distribution of interest income of $1.00 per share. This amount is reinvested in additional units at $10.00, the net asset value per unit on that date.

On January 1, 2007, Katherine had a net capital loss from 1997 of $15,000 [(3/4)($20,000)].

Katherine's will contains the following provisions:

- Her son Sean will receive the family's principal residence. At December 31, 2007, it is estimated that the fair market value of this property is $510,000. In addition, Sean will receive one-half of the Barton Income Trust units. On December 31, 2007, these units are trading at $17.50 per unit.

- Her daughter Sylvia will receive rental property B. In addition, Sylvia will receive the remaining one-half of the Barton Income Trust units.

- Her husband Mick will receive rental property A. Mick will also receive the Fidel Mutual Fund units. On December 31, 2007, these units have a net asset value of $8.30 per unit.

In discussions with the family accountant in early 2008, Mick agrees that the 2007 family medical expenses and any credits or transfers related to either child will be claimed on Katherine's return. He also asks the accountant to prepare any elective tax returns that will reduce her 2007 Tax Payable.

In order to pay for the accountant's fees, Mick sells both the rental property A and all of the Fidel Mutual Fund units in January, 2008 for their December 31, 2007 fair market values.

Required:

A. Calculate Katherine O'Hara's minimum 2007 Net Income For Tax Purposes, her 2007 minimum Taxable Income, and her minimum 2007 federal Tax Payable without consideration of any withholdings her employer may have made.

B. Calculate the Net Income For Tax Purposes that will result from Mick O'Hara's sale of the rental property and fund units.

Assume the prescribed rate for the first quarter of 2007 is 3 percent, increasing to 4 percent in the second and subsequent quarters of the year. Ignore GST and PST considerations.

Assignment Case Twelve - 3 (Progressive Running Case - Chapter 12 Version Using ProFile T1 Software For 2006 Tax Returns)

This Progressive Running Case requires the use of the ProFile tax software program. It was introduced in Chapter 6 and is continued in Chapters 8 through 14. Each version must be completed in sequence. While it is not repeated in this version of the Case, all of the information in each of the previous versions (e.g., Mary's T4 content) is applicable to this version of the Case.

If you have not prepared a tax file incorporating the previous versions, please do so before continuing with this version.

On December 30, 2006, you receive a call from Mary Walford with the terrible news that Seymour has just suffered a massive heart attack and died. She has read his will and she inherits all of his assets except for the rental property and appliances in Moncton (see Chapter 9 version of this Case). He has left that house to his 19 year old daughter. Assume the transfer of the property and appliances takes place in 2006.

As Seymour was thinking of selling the property, he had it appraised in early December. The appraisal valued the land at $60,000, the building at $180,000, and the appliances at $700. Seymour had purchased the property on May 1, 1993 for $195,000 (land of $45,000 and building of $150,000) and lived in it until his marriage to Mary in 2004.

Mary has learned that Seymour's mother purchased Canada Savings Bonds in William's name in 2006. The bonds paid interest of $120 in 2006 which Seymour had spent without advising her. She expects a T5 to be issued in William's name.

You verify with the CRA that Seymour has a net capital loss carry forward of $17,500 [(1/2)($35,000)] from the sale of his XXX Art Films Ltd shares in 2005.

Required:

A. Open the file that you created for the Chapter 11 version of the Case and save a copy under a different name. This will enable you to check the changes between different versions of the Case.

B. Complete and print the T2091, Designation Of Property As A Principal Residence for Seymour's Moncton property. Print his Schedule 3 which shows the capital gain from the disposition of his house.

C. Revise Seymour's Statement of Real Estate Rentals for any changes necessary. Print the statement and the related CCA worksheet.

D. With the objective of minimizing Seymour's Tax Payable, prepare, but do not print, his final income tax return. List any assumptions you have made and provide any explanatory notes and tax planning issues you feel should be placed in the files. Ignore GST implications. *Hint:* On his "Info" page, input his date of death. On Mary's return, change her marital status to widowed and include the date of change.

E. Review both returns with the objective of minimizing the tax liability for the family and make any changes required.

F. Access and print Mary's summary (Summary on the Form Explorer, not the T1 Summary). This form is a two column summary of the couple's tax information. By opening this form from Mary's return, the order of the columns is the same as the one in the previous chapter. For both returns, list the changes on this Summary form from the previous version of this Case. Exclude totals calculated by the program, but include the final Balance Owing (Refund) amount.

CHAPTER 13

Retirement Savings And Other Special Income Arrangements

Planning For Retirement

Introduction

13-1.   Increasing life expectancies and lower birth rates are creating a situation in which the portion of the Canadian population that is of retirement age has been increasing, and will continue to do so. This, in turn, leads to the need to allocate a growing proportion of our society's resources to caring for this older segment of the population. There are enormous social and economic considerations resulting from this trend and, given the growing political clout of Canadian senior citizens, it is not a situation that the government can ignore.

Providing Consistency

13-2.   Minimal financial requirements for the retirement years are provided by Old Age Security payments and the Canada Pension Plan system. However, maximum payments under these two systems total around $16,000 per year, an income level that will not provide for the lifestyle most individuals would like to enjoy during their retirement years. In response to this situation, the Canadian income tax system contains a number of provisions that encourage the development of various private retirement savings arrangements to supplement benefits provided under the Canada Pension Plan system. These include:

- Registered Retirement Savings Plans (RRSPs)
- Registered Pension Plans (RPPs)
- Registered Retirement Income Funds (RRIFs)
- Deferred Profit Sharing Plans (DPSPs)

13-3.   The current retirement savings system was initiated in 1990. At the heart of this system is the concept that retirement savings should have an annual limit that is consistently applied. In general, this limit is defined in terms of an annual amount of contributions to a money purchase (a.k.a., defined contribution) retirement savings plan. This limit was subject to a "phase in" schedule which has been modified several times since the system was introduced. As of 2007, the "phase in" schedule will not end until 2009. The annual limit is currently scheduled to be subject to indexation after 2009, but there have been so many revisions over the years to the schedule, it is likely more changes will occur before then.

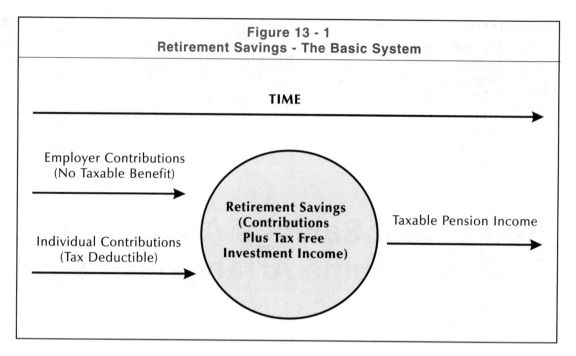

Figure 13 - 1
Retirement Savings - The Basic System

13-4.   The major problem faced by the government in designing the current system was to ensure that, despite the variety of retirement savings vehicles available, the annual contribution limit was applied in a consistent manner, without regard to the variety of retirement savings vehicles used by an individual, or the manner in which the ultimate retirement benefit was determined. In our view, an outstanding job was done in accomplishing this goal.

13-5.   The detailed provisions related to the different types of tax assisted retirement savings plans show considerable variation. For example, Registered Pension Plans and Deferred Profit Sharing Plans require employer sponsorship. In contrast, any Canadian resident can establish a Registered Retirement Savings Plan or a Registered Retirement Income Fund.

13-6.   Despite such variations, the basic idea underlying all of these plans is the same. They allow individuals to invest a considerable amount of funds into a trusteed arrangement. The amounts invested are either deductible to the taxpayer (RRSP contributions and employee RPP contributions) or can be paid by an employer without creating a taxable benefit (employer RPP and DPSP contributions). Inside the trusteed arrangement, the invested funds earn income on a tax free basis for long periods of time. While all amounts will ultimately be subject to taxation, there is a substantial amount of tax deferral. This arrangement can be seen graphically in Figure 13-1.

13-7.   You will recall that we also discussed registered savings plans in Chapter 11. The discussion in that Chapter focused on Registered Education Savings Plans (RESPs) and Registered Disability Savings Plans (RDSPs). We would remind you of a major difference between those plans and the ones that are under consideration here. The contributions made to RESPs and RDSPs were not deductible. In contrast, the retirement savings plans under consideration here provide tax advantaged contribution arrangements. As noted in Paragraph 13-6, contributions made by beneficiaries are tax deductible and contributions made by employers are not taxable benefits.

Tax Deferred Savings

Sources Of Deferral

13-8.   As shown in Figure 13-1, there are two basic sources for the investment funds going into retirement savings plans. First, for employed individuals, employers may make contributions to RPPs and DPSPs. As these contributions are not considered to be taxable until the funds are withdrawn from the plan, the employee has received a benefit on which the payment of tax has been deferred.

13-9.   The second source of investment funds is the contributions made by employed individuals to RPPs, and by all individuals to RRSPs. As the individual can deduct these contributions against all types of income, they are the equivalent of receiving income on which the tax has been deferred.

13-10.   This means that, whether an employer has made contributions on behalf of the individual, or the individual has personally made the contributions, the taxes on the amounts involved have been deferred from the year of contribution to the year of withdrawal from the plan. This period may exceed 45 years for contributions made at the beginning of an individual's working life.

Tax Free Compounding

13-11.   Also of great importance is the fact that the income earned by investments contained in these plans is not taxed until it is withdrawn. This allows earnings to accumulate at before tax rate, rather than after tax rates. Given that such plans may be in place over long periods of time, this provides for a significantly larger accumulation of assets.   As illustrated in the following example, the importance of tax free accumulation should not be underestimated.

> **Example** Mr. Kerr is a 35 year old taxpayer who pays taxes at a marginal rate of 45 percent. For the next 30 years, he has $5,000 per year of pre-tax income that he wishes to put aside for his anticipated retirement at age 65.

> **Analysis**   If Mr. Kerr contributes this amount to an RRSP, it can be deducted and no taxes will be paid on the $5,000 per year of pre-tax income. If this $5,000 per year is invested in an RRSP at a 10 percent per annum rate of return, it will accumulate to $822,470 at the end of 30 years. If the full amount is withdrawn when he reaches age 65, and he is still paying taxes at a marginal rate of 45 percent, he will be left with after tax funds of $452,359.

> If Mr. Kerr had not invested in an RRSP, taxes at 45 percent would have been paid on the $5,000, leaving only $2,750 per year to invest. If this $2,750 could be invested at an after tax rate of 10 percent outside of the RRSP, he would reach age 65 with the same after tax funds of $452,359 that were retained using the RRSP. However, the 10 percent rate used in the RRSP reflects the fact that investment income is not taxed while in the plan.

> If the before tax rate is 10 percent, the after tax rate for funds invested outside the RRSP would be 5.5 percent. (To simplify the example, we have assumed that the return on the investment is not in the form of dividends or capital gains.) At this after tax rate, the investment of $2,750 per year for 30 years would result in an accumulation of only $199,198 by the time Mr. Kerr is 65 years old, less than half of the after tax accumulation resulting from using the RRSP approach.

13-12.   In effect, the deferral of taxes on the deductible contributions, as well as the deferral of tax on the income from fund investments, has allowed for an additional accumulation of income resulting from the investment of the amounts deferred. As this fairly realistic example illustrates, the amounts involved can be very substantial.

Early Contributions

13-13.   The availability of tax free compounding in an RRSP makes it advantageous to contribute as early as possible. RRSP contributions for 2007 can be made as early as January 1, 2007, or as late as 60 days after the end of 2007. It can be demonstrated that, over a contribution period of 35 years, making contributions at the earliest date as opposed to the latest date can result in a 10 percent increase in the balance in the plan.

Advantages At Retirement

13-14.   The use of these tax deferred retirement savings plans may have additional advantages. There appears to be a trend towards lowering federal and provincial tax rates which could mean that overall tax rates will be lower in the future when the funds are paid out of the retirement savings plans.

13-15.   In addition, for some individuals, retirement may result in a sufficient reduction in income that they find themselves in a lower tax bracket. Someone who spends their working life subject to a 45 percent tax rate could find that, subsequent to retirement, they are subject to taxes at 25 percent. As this lower rate would apply to amounts withdrawn from a retirement savings plan, the deferral of taxation on contributions and investment earnings will result in an absolute reduction in taxes paid.

13-16.   Even if the individual is not paying taxes at a lower rate after retirement, there are additional advantages associated with the funds taken out of these plans. The first $2,000 of eligible pension income entitles the recipient to a credit against federal Tax Payable each year equal to 15.5 percent of amounts received. This is worth $310 and can be increased to $620 per couple through the new pension income splitting provisions. (See Chapter 11.)

Defined Benefit Vs. Money Purchase Plans

13-17.   A major problem in the design of Canada's retirement savings system is the fact that, unlike RRSPs, DPSPs, and RRIFs, RPPs may be designed to provide a specified benefit after retirement. Such plans are normally referred to as defined benefit plans, while other types of RPPs are referred to as money purchase (a.k.a. defined contribution) plans. A basic understanding of the difference between these two types of plans is essential to the comprehension of the material in this Chapter. In view of this, the following brief descriptions are provided:

Defined Benefit Plans   In defined benefit plans, the plan sponsor undertakes to provide a specified benefit, usually expressed as a percentage of earnings, for each year of qualifying service. For example, such a plan might require an employer to provide a retirement benefit equal to 2 percent of an employee's average lifetime earnings for each year of service. Thus, if an employee worked for 20 years and earned an average salary of $50,000 per year, the retirement benefit would be $20,000 per year [(2%)(20)($50,000)].

In promising this benefit, the employer has effectively agreed to make whatever amount of contributions is required to provide these benefits. The required amount of contributions will vary depending on a number of factors, including earnings rates on fund assets, employee turnover, and employee life expectancy at retirement. In this type of plan, the employer is assuming all of the risks associated with these factors.

Money Purchase Plans (a.k.a. Defined Contribution Plans)   These plans are distinguished by the fact that the employer agrees to make specified contributions for each plan participant. A typical plan might find an employer agreeing to contribute 3 percent of each employee's annual wages to a fund that would be established to provide retirement benefits. The employer would have no obligations beyond making the specified contributions and the employee would have no guarantee as to the amount of the retirement benefit that is to be received.

The actual benefit that will be received will be based on the amounts contributed and the rates of return earned on the investment of these contributions. In money purchase plans, it is the employee who is assuming the risks associated with investment of the contributed funds.

13-18.   Before leaving these descriptions we would note that, while the term is not usually applied to them, RRSPs, DPSPs, and RRIFs are essentially money purchase plans. That is, the benefits to be received from such plans are based on the amounts transferred into the plan and the earnings resulting from the investment of these amounts. Such plans do not guarantee that the individual will receive a specified benefit after retirement. The only widely used retirement savings arrangement that uses the defined benefit approach is the employer sponsored RPP. However, RPPs can take either form and, in recent years, there has been a trend towards the use of money purchase plans.

Registered Retirement Savings Plans (RRSPs)

Basic Operations

Establishment

13-19. The general rules for Registered Retirement Savings Plans (RRSPs) are contained in ITA 146. Under these rules, an RRSP is simply a trust with the individual as the beneficiary and a financial institution acting as the administrator. Financial institutions offering such plans include Canadian chartered banks, Canadian mutual funds, Canadian trust companies, Canadian credit unions, Canadian brokerage firms, and Canadian insurance companies.

13-20. Registration of the plan results in the investor being able to deduct a specified amount of contributions to the plan for income tax purposes. Further, the individual is not subject to tax on the income earned by the assets in the plan until it is withdrawn.

Withdrawals

13-21. Amounts that an individual withdraws from an RRSP must be included in income unless received under the Home Buyers' Plan or the Lifelong Learning Plan. (These programs are discussed in Paragraphs 13-117 and 13-130.) Depending on the amount withdrawn, the trustee will be required to withhold a percentage of the amount withdrawn as a partial payment towards the tax that will be assessed on the withdrawal.

13-22. Withdrawals are treated as an ordinary income inclusion under ITA 56(1)(h), even if they were earned as dividends or capital gains within the plan. This latter point is important in that dividends and capital gains are normally taxed at more favourable rates than other types of income. This favourable treatment is lost when the amounts are earned inside an RRSP.

Investment Options For An RRSP

13-23. There are two basic types of RRSPs available. The managed RRSP is managed by the financial institution that holds the fund assets. The self-administered (a.k.a. self-directed) RRSP is managed by the individual taxpayer. For individuals who prefer to make their own investment decisions with respect to the fund assets, the self-administered type of plan is the obvious choice.

13-24. An additional advantage of the self-administered type of plan is that the taxpayer can transfer securities that he already owns into the plan. As the RRSP is a separate taxable entity, such transfers are dispositions and any gains arising on the transfer will be subject to tax. Note, however, that ITA 40(2)(g)(iv) prevents the recognition of losses on such transfers.

13-25. If the taxpayer's preference is to have a financial institution manage the plan, he will be confronted with a wide variety of choices. Managed funds include those that invest entirely in equity securities, funds that hold only long-term bonds, funds with mixed portfolios, and funds that specialize in one type of asset such as Canada Savings Bonds or mortgages.

13-26. Choosing between the alternatives involves an assessment of many factors, including the investment goals of the individual taxpayer, as well as the fees charged by the various plans. With literally hundreds of choices available, the decision can be a very difficult one to make. However, considering the amount of financial resources that may eventually be invested in RRSP assets, it is not a decision that should be made without a thorough investigation of the alternatives.

13-27. Since an individual can own any number of RRSPs, it is possible to have both a self-administered and a managed plan. Further diversification could be achieved by having two or more types of managed plans. However, the extra effort and costs required to keep track of the multiple plans should be considered.

13-28. The *Act* is flexible with respect to the types of investments that can be included in either a self-administered or a managed RRSP. ITR Part XLIX provides a detailed listing of the specific investment categories and includes publicly traded shares, mutual fund units, bonds, mortgages, warrants, and rights. The only significant restrictions relate to investments in the shares of private companies and direct investments in real estate. There is no limit on foreign content (e.g., shares of U.S. public companies).

13-29.   It is interesting to note that an RRSP can provide a mortgage on Canadian real property to the registrant of the plan, provided that the mortgage is insured under the National Housing Act, or by some other company providing mortgage insurance. The extra costs associated with this insurance have served to limit the use of this option.

The Capital Gains Problem

13-30.   As noted previously, capital gains that are earned within an RRSP are treated as ordinary income when they are withdrawn from the plan. As the favourable tax treatment that this type of income normally receives is lost when earned in an RRSP, it would appear that it is better to earn capital gains outside an RRSP. This would suggest that, if an individual has investments both inside and outside an RRSP, it would be preferable to hold those investments that earn capital gains outside the plan.

13-31.   There has been some discussion of whether it makes sense to hold investments with potential capital gains inside an RRSP. The discussion is based on two considerations. First, with the inclusion rate at one-half, the tax on capital gains earned inside an RRSP is essentially double the tax that would apply to capital gains earned outside of an RRSP.

13-32.   The other factor is that, in situations where investors hold securities for long periods of time, tax free earnings accumulation effectively occurs even when investments are held outside of an RRSP. The fact that capital gains are not taxed until there is a disposition of the investment significantly reduces the importance of the tax free deferral feature of RRSP investing.

13-33.   Offsetting these factors which favour keeping capital gains outside of RRSPs is the fact that amounts invested in these retirement savings accounts are deductible. For an individual in a marginal tax bracket of 48 percent, this means that the government is, in effect, putting up half of the investment funds.

13-34.   A meaningful analysis of this issue goes beyond the scope of this text. In fact, it is unlikely that there is a unique solution to the problem. The appropriate course of action will require a complex analysis of a number of factors including how long the funds will be in the plan and the tax bracket of the investor, both when the funds are placed in the plan and when they are withdrawn. The only thing that we can state with confidence is that, for individuals who have maximized their RRSP contributions and, as a result, have investments both inside and outside their RRSP, our original suggestion that investments with capital gains potential be held outside the plan is still appropriate.

The Eligible Dividends Problem

13-35.   As was the case with capital gains, dividend income loses its favourable tax treatment when it is earned within an RRSP. When such income is withdrawn from the plan, it is taxed as ordinary income and does not qualify for the dividend tax credit procedures.

13-36.   Prior to the May, 2006 Budget, this problem with dividends was less severe than the problem with capital gains. While an individual in the 44 percent bracket would pay taxes at 22 percent on capital gains, the corresponding rate on dividends was around 30 percent. In addition, unlike capital gains where taxation could be deferred until the relevant investments were sold, dividend income earned outside of an RRSP was taxed as it was received.

13-37.   Legislation introduced in the May, 2006 Budget has altered this analysis. In some provinces, high tax bracket individuals now pay about the same tax rates on eligible dividends as they pay on capital gains. This clearly makes it less attractive to earn dividends inside an RRSP. It is not clear, however, whether this change is sufficient to warrant the exclusion of dividend paying securities from RRSPs. Here again, the only guidance that we can unequivocally provide is that, if investors have investments both inside and outside their RRSPs, there is a case for keeping those that pay dividends outside of the RRSP.

Figure 13 - 2
RRSP Deduction Limit Formula - ITA 146(1)

"RRSP deduction limit" of a taxpayer for a taxation year means the amount determined by the formula

$$A + B + R - C, \text{ where}$$

A   is the taxpayer's **unused RRSP deduction room** at the end of the preceding taxation year,

B   is the amount, if any, by which

     (a) the lesser of the **RRSP dollar limit** for the year and 18% of the taxpayer's **earned income** for the preceding taxation year,

     exceeds the total of all amounts each of which is

     (b) the taxpayer's **pension adjustment** for the preceding taxation year in respect of an employer, or

     (c) a **prescribed amount** in respect of the taxpayer for the year,

C   is the taxpayer's net **past service pension adjustment** for the year, and

R   is the taxpayer's total **pension adjustment reversal** for the year.

Non-Deductible Financing Costs

13-38. As a final point, it is important to note that interest paid on funds borrowed to finance RRSP contributions is not deductible. This suggests that it may not be desirable for an individual to borrow in order to make RRSP contributions. A complete analysis of this issue requires an estimate of how long the loan will be outstanding and a comparison of the individual's borrowing rate with his expected return on funds invested in the plan.

RRSP Deduction Limit

The Basic Formula

13-39. At the heart of this retirement savings system is the RRSP Deduction Limit. It is this amount that determines the maximum contribution to an RRSP that can be deducted in a year. While this amount is sometimes referred to as the contribution limit, this is not an accurate description. The definition of RRSP Deduction Limit is found in ITA 146(1) and is reproduced in Figure 13-2. There are several technical terms included in this definition and they are highlighted in Figure 13-2 with bold, italic type. Explanations for each term will be provided in the material which follows.

13-40. The RRSP Deduction Limit is neither a limit on contributions that can be made during the current year, nor a requirement that the contributions deducted in the current year be made in that year. A limited amount of non-deductible contributions can be made that are in excess of the RRSP Deduction Limit. Further, contributions made in earlier years that were not deducted in those years, or contributions made in the first 60 days of the following year, can be deducted under the RRSP Deduction Limit for the current year.

> **Example** Contributions made during the first 60 days of 2008 and undeducted contributions made in years prior to 2007, can be deducted against the RRSP Deduction Limit for 2007. Adding to the confusion is the fact that the RRSP Deduction Limit for 2007 is based on Earned Income for 2006, as well as a Pension Adjustment that is calculated using 2006 figures.

13-41. Note that the limit is based on the individual's Earned Income for the previous year. The advantage of this approach is that it allows the individual to determine his maximum contribution for the current year during the early part of that year. If the limit had been based on the current year's Earned Income, the individual would have to make contributions during the year based only on an estimate of his Earned Income, a situation that would commonly result in contributions that are either over or under the limit.

13-42.   To assist taxpayers in dealing with this limit, the CRA issues an RRSP Deduction Limit Statement to individuals who have filed income tax returns. It is included with the Notice of Assessment and, assuming the return is filed on time, calculates the taxpayer's maximum RRSP deduction for the year after the assessed year.

> **Example**   The RRSP Statement included with the Notice of Assessment for the 2007 return will normally be received during April or May, 2008. . This statement indicates the maximum RRSP contribution that can be deducted for 2008.

Unused RRSP Deduction Room

13-43.   As it is used in the Figure 13-2 formula, a taxpayer's Unused RRSP Deduction Room at the end of the preceding year is simply the cumulative total of all of the amounts determined under the formula for years prior to the current year, less any amounts that have been deducted in those years.

13-44.   This approach provides for a carry over of deduction room that is not time limited. As a result, a taxpayer who lacks the funds to make a deductible contribution in a particular year- does not lose the deduction room applicable to that year. The deduction room is carried forward and provides the basis for a deductible contribution in any future year.

RRSP Dollar Limit

13-45.   The RRSP Dollar Limit is defined in terms of the Money Purchase Limit that is specified in quantitative terms in ITA 147.1(1). The Money Purchase Limit is the annual ceiling applicable to contributions made to RPPs. Because of the one year lag in the data used for the RRSP Deduction Limit, the RRSP Dollar Limit is generally defined as the Money Purchase Limit for the preceding year.

13-46.   As the legislation currently stands, Money Purchase Limits and the RRSP Dollar Limits for the years 1996 through 2011 are as follows:

Year	Money Purchase Limit	RRSP Dollar Limit
1996 to 2002	$13,500	$13,500
2003	15,500	14,500
2004	16,500	15,500
2005	18,000	16,500
2006	19,000	18,000
2007	**20,000**	**19,000**
2008	21,000	20,000
2009	22,000	21,000
2010	Indexed	22,000
2011	Indexed	Indexed

Exercise Thirteen-1

Subject: Unused RRSP Deduction Room

Mr. Victor Haslich has 2005 Earned Income for RRSP purposes of $38,000. He is not a member of an RPP or a DPSP. At the end of 2005, his Unused RRSP Deduction Room was $4,800. During 2006, he contributes $6,000 to his RRSP and makes an RRSP deduction of $4,500. What is the amount of Mr. Haslich's Unused RRSP Deduction Room and undeducted RRSP contributions at the end of 2006?

End of Exercise. Solution available in Study Guide.

Earned Income

13-47.   Earned Income for RRSP purposes is defined in ITA 146(1). Note that Earned Income for child care expense purposes (see Chapter 11) is different than Earned Income for RRSP purposes. The basic idea underlying this definition is that the income to be included in this designation is earned by the individual, rather than received as the result of owning property. This means that interest, dividends, and capital gains are excluded from the definition.

13-48.   Surprisingly, however, net rental income is included, despite the fact that, for individuals, rental income is usually a form of property income. Another unusual feature of the definition is that it does not include either net or gross employment income in unaltered form. Rather, the net employment income component of Earned Income is a hybrid concept that excludes RPP contributions and is not used anywhere else in the determination of Net Income For Tax Purposes.

13-49.   As found in ITA 146(1), the basic components of Earned Income are as follows:

Additions

- Net employment income, computed without the deduction for RPP contributions
- Royalties, provided the recipient is the author, composer, or inventor of the work
- Taxable support payments received by a spouse (This does not include non-taxable child support payments. See Chapter 11 for a discussion of child support payments.)
- Supplementary unemployment benefit plan payments
- Income from carrying on a business
- Income earned as an active partner
- Net rental income from real property
- Research grants, net of certain related expenses
- Canada and Quebec Pension Plan disability benefits received

Deductions

- Deductible support payments (does not include non-deductible child support payments)
- Losses from carrying on a business
- Losses allocated to an active partner
- Losses from the rental of real property

Exercise Thirteen-2

Subject: Earned Income

Mr. Jarwhol Nacari has net employment income of $56,000 (he is not a member of an RPP), interest income of $22,000, net rental income of $2,500, and receives taxable support payments from his former spouse of $12,000 during the current year. What is Mr. Nacari's Earned Income for RRSP purposes for the current year?

Exercise Thirteen-3

Subject: Earned Income

Ms. Shelly Devine has net employment income of $82,000 (after the deduction of $3,000 in RPP contributions), a business loss of $12,500, dividend income of $4,200, and pays deductible support to her former spouse of $18,000 during the current year. What is Ms. Devine's Earned Income for RRSP purposes for the current year?

End of Exercises. Solutions available in Study Guide.

Pension Adjustments (PAs)

13-50.   If an individual participates in an RPP or a DPSP, his RRSP Deduction Limit must be reduced to reflect retirement savings that are taking place in these plans. If this did not happen, individuals belonging to RPPs and DPSPs could have access to larger amounts of tax deferred retirement savings than would be the case for other individuals.

13-51.   Pension Adjustments (PAs) are designed to reflect the benefits earned by an individual through defined benefit RPPs or contributions made to money purchase RPPs and DPSPs by an individual or his employer during a particular year. As RPPs and DPSPs are always sponsored by an employer, the CRA requires the employer to calculate an annual PA for each employee who is a member of that employer's RPP or DPSP. This amount is reported on the employee's T4.

13-52.   Employers do not issue T4s until January or February of the year following the calendar year in which contributions are made or benefits granted. Because of this, the PA that is deducted in the calculation of the taxpayer's RRSP Deduction Limit for the current year, is based on the employer's contributions or benefits granted during the preceding year. More specifically, the 2007 RRSP Deduction Limit is reduced by PAs calculated with reference to 2006 RPP benefits earned and RPP and DPSP contributions made. These PAs are reported to the CRA and the taxpayer in the T4s that are issued in January or February of 2007. These PAs are also incorporated into the 2007 RRSP Deduction Limit Statement that the CRA includes with the Notice of Assessment for the 2006 taxation year.

Exercise Thirteen-4

Subject: Retirement Savings

How does the Canadian retirement savings system prevent individuals who are a member of their employer's RPP or DPSP from being treated more favourably than individuals who can only use an RRSP for retirement savings?

End of Exercise.   Solution available in Study Guide.

13-53.   **Money Purchase RPPs And DPSPs**   The calculation of PAs for money purchase plans is relatively straightforward. As RRSPs operate in the same general format as money purchase plans (i.e., they do not promise a specific benefit), contributions to money purchase plans are directly comparable, on a dollar for dollar basis, with contributions to an RRSP.

13-54.   As a consequence, the PA for a money purchase RPP is simply the sum of all employee and employer contributions for the year. Following the same reasoning, an employee's PA for a DPSP is simply the employer's contributions for the year that are allocated to the individual (employees cannot contribute to a DPSP). A simple example will illustrate these calculations:

Example   Ms. Jones' employer sponsors a money purchase RPP and a DPSP. Ms. Jones is a member of both. During 2006, she has Earned Income of $70,000 and contributes $2,000 to the RPP. Her employer contributes $2,000 to the RPP and $1,500 to the DPSP on her behalf. She has no Unused RRSP Deduction Room at the end of 2006. Calculate Ms. Jones' maximum deductible RRSP contribution for 2007.

Analysis   Ms. Jones' 2006 PA is $5,500 ($2,000 + $2,000 + $1,500), an amount that will be reported on the 2006 T4 that she will receive in early 2007. After filing her 2006 tax return, Ms. Jones will receive her RRSP Deduction Limit Statement for 2007 from the CRA that will contain the following calculation.

As she has no Unused RRSP Deduction Room at the end of 2006, her RRSP Deduction Limit will be calculated by taking the lesser of the $19,000 RRSP Dollar Limit for 2007 and $12,600, 18 percent of Ms. Jones' 2006 Earned Income. The 2006 PA of $5,500 will be subtracted from the lesser figure of $12,600, to arrive at her maximum deductible RRSP contribution for 2007 of $7,100.

13-55. **Defined Benefit RPPs** As defined benefit plans guarantee the benefit to be provided, rather than specify the amount of contributions required, contributions made to these plans cannot be compared directly to contributions made to RRSPs, DPSPs, or money purchase RPPs. However, if retirement savings limits are to be applied equitably to all individuals, without regard to the type of arrangements available to them, it is necessary to find a basis for equating the benefits earned under these plans with the contributions made to the other types of plans.

13-56. Unfortunately, there is no simple way to convert a benefit earned into an equivalent amount of contributions. While there are a number of problems in dealing with this conversion, the most significant is the age of the employee. Because of the difference in years during which earnings will accumulate, it costs an employer much less in terms of current contributions to provide a $1 per year retirement benefit to an employee who is 25 years old and 40 years away from receiving that benefit, than it does to provide the same retirement benefit to an employee who is 60 years old and only 5 years away from receiving the benefit.

13-57. To have a completely equitable system for dealing with this problem, different values would have to be assigned to benefits that are earned by employees of different ages. Benefits earned by older employees would have to be assigned a higher value than those earned by younger employees. It appears that the government believes that the benefits of such an equitable system do not warrant the costs of associating different levels of benefits with individuals of differing ages.

13-58. Rather than a system that takes into account the different ages of participants in defined benefit RPPs, the current solution is to equate $1 of benefits earned with $9 of contributions. If, during the current year, an individual earns $1 of future benefits under the provisions of a defined benefit RPP, in the calculation of his PA for the year, this will be viewed as the equivalent of $9 in contributions to a money purchase RPP or DPSP.

13-59. The use of the multiple nine is an arbitrary solution that fails to give any consideration to the age of the employee. (There is an unconfirmed rumour that this number was selected because it was the shoe size of the Minister of Finance at the time the legislation was passed.) It is systematically unfair to younger individuals as it overstates the cost of providing their pension benefits, thereby generating an excessive PA which, in turn, creates a corresponding reduction in their ability to contribute to their RRSP.

Example Bryan is 25 years of age. In 2007, he earns a pension benefit in his employer's defined benefit RPP of $1,000 per year to be received beginning in 2047 when Bryan reaches 65 years of age. His PA for 2007 is $9,000 which decreases his RRSP deduction room by $9,000.

Analysis If, alternatively, he had deposited this same $9,000 per year in his RRSP and made investments that earned 10 percent per annum, the balance in 2047 would be over $400,000. Even at a low interest rate of 5 percent, this would purchase an annuity of over $32,000 per year for 20 years. This is far in excess of the value of a $1,000 per year benefit that would be received at age 65 under the defined benefit plan.

13-60. While it was probably essential to the implementation of this system that some type of averaging process be used, it is unfortunate that the selected alternative has such a systematic bias against younger individuals. It is unlikely that the government could have arrived at any administratively convenient solution that would not appear inequitable to some individuals. However, it would have been more equitable to have used some type of age dependent sliding scale, as opposed to the inflexible application of the factor of nine.

Exercise Thirteen-5

Subject: Pension Adjustments

Mr. Arnett's employer sponsors both a money purchase RPP and a DPSP. During the current year, his employer contributes $2,300 to the RPP and $1,800 to the DPSP on behalf of Mr. Arnett. Mr. Arnett contributes $2,300 to the RPP. Calculate the amount of the Pension Adjustment that will be included on Mr. Arnett's T4 for the current year.

End of Exercise.   Solution available in Study Guide.

Prescribed Amount - ITA 146(1)

13-61.   The Prescribed Amount (see Figure 13-2) is a deduction that may arise as the result of an individual transferring accumulated benefits from one RPP to a different RPP.

Past Service Pension Adjustments (PSPAs)

13-62.   Past Service Pension Adjustments (PSPAs) are designed to deal with benefits under defined benefit RPPs related to credit for past service. They are far less common than PAs. Some of the events giving rise to PSPAs are as follows:

- A new RPP is implemented by an employer and benefits are extended retroactively for years of service prior to the plan initiation.

- The benefit formula is changed, increasing the percentage that is applied to pensionable earnings to determine benefits earned. Again, a PSPA is created only if the increased benefits are extended retroactively to years of service prior to the plan amendment.

- An individual, either voluntarily or because of terms contained in the plan, works for a number of years without being a member of the plan. On joining the plan, the employee is credited for the post-1989 years of service prior to entry into the plan.

13-63.   If an individual were to receive such past service benefits without experiencing any reduction in his RRSP Deduction Limit, he would have effectively beaten the system. That is, he would be receiving additional pension benefits over and above the limits that are normally applicable to individual taxpayers. The role of PSPAs is to prevent this from happening.

13-64.   PSPAs are calculated on the basis of all of the PAs that would have applied in the previous years if the plan or improvement had been in effect, or if the individual had been a member in those years. From these "as if" PAs, the actual PAs reported would be deducted. The resulting difference is then reported as a PSPA for the current year.

13-65.   As with PAs, the employer is responsible for calculating and reporting PSPAs, normally within 60 days of the past service event. The amount is reported on a PSPA information form (not on a T4) that is sent to both the employee and the CRA. Note that, unlike the one year lag in deducting PAs, PSPAs are deducted from the RRSP deduction room formula in the year in which they occur.

13-66.   A simplified example will serve to illustrate the basic procedures involved in PSPA calculations:

Example   Wally Oats has been a member of his employer's defined benefit RPP since 2001. Until 2007, the benefit formula provided a retirement benefit equal to 1.5 percent of pensionable earnings for each year of service. During 2007, the benefit formula was increased to 1.75 percent of pensionable earnings for each year of service, a change that is to be applied to all prior years of service. Mr. Oats has had $48,000 in pensionable earnings in each prior year.

Analysis   The calculation of the PSPA for 2007 would be based on the six years of service prior to the current year (2001 to 2006) as follows:

New Formula PAs [(1.75%)($48,000)(9)(6 Years)]	$45,360
Previously Reported PAs [(1.50%)($48,000)(9)(6 Years)]	(38,880)
2007 PSPA	**$ 6,480**

13-67.   Note that PSPAs only occur in the context of defined benefit plans. If additional contributions for past service are made to a money purchase plan, these amounts will be included in the regular Pension Adjustment for the year in which the contributions are made. This eliminates the need for any sort of catch up adjustment.

Pension Adjustment Reversals (PARs)

13-68.   A vested pension benefit is one in which the employee has an irrevocable property right. That is, he is entitled to receive the value of the benefit, without regard to whether he remains an employee of the employer providing the benefit.

13-69.   In order to give their employees an incentive to remain with them, many employers grant pension benefits that do not become vested unless the employee remains for a specified period of time. A common arrangement would be for an employer to grant benefits that do not vest until the employee has completed five years of service. If an employee leaves before the end of this five year period, he loses the benefits that he has earned to that point in time.

13-70.   This creates a problem in that employers are required to report PAs for all benefits or contributions earned by an employee during the year, regardless of when the pension benefits become vested. This means that an employer may report PAs for benefits that will not, in fact, be received by the employee. This, in turn, means that the RRSP deduction room that was eliminated by these PAs would also be lost.

13-71.   To deal with this problem, Pension Adjustment Reversals (PARs) were added to the pension legislation. Note that this is only a problem with the employer's share of benefits or contributions earned. Provincial legislation requires that employees have a vested right to all of their own contributions.

13-72.   A PAR is calculated by the employer whenever an employee terminates membership in an RPP or DPSP and receives less from the plan than the total of the PAs and PSPAs reported for the employee. The PAR is reported to the CRA and to the employee, and will be added to the individual's RRSP deduction room in the year of termination.   The following simple example illustrates the use of a PAR:

Example   Stan Kapitany is a member of an RPP in which benefits are not vested until the fourth year of service. He leaves after three years when he is offered an opportunity to develop high performance race cars. His employer was required to report PAs for the first three years of his employment and this, in turn, reduced Mr. Kapitany's ability to make deductible contributions to an RRSP.

Analysis   Since he ceases to work for his employer prior to the benefits becoming vested, the benefits for which PAs were previously reported will not be transferred to him. This means that there will be no retirement benefits corresponding to the previously reported PAs and, as a consequence, Mr. Kapitany might have lost a portion of his entitlement to tax deferred retirement savings. This problem is solved with the addition of a PAR to Mr. Kapitany's RRSP deduction room.

Examples Of RRSP Deduction Calculations

13-73.   The following three examples illustrate the calculation of the RRSP Deduction Limit, Unused RRSP Deduction Room, and the carry over of undeducted RRSP contributions.

Example A

Miss Brown has 2006 net employment income of $15,000, 2006 net rental income of $10,000, and 2006 interest income of $5,000. She is not a member of an RPP or a DPSP. During 2007, she contributes $5,000 to her RRSP and makes an RRSP deduction of $4,000 in her 2007 tax return. At the end of 2006, her Unused RRSP Deduction Room was nil and there were no undeducted contributions in her RRSP account.

Unused Deduction Room - End Of 2006	Nil
Lesser Of:	
• 2007 RRSP Dollar Limit = $19,000	
• 18% Of 2006 Earned Income Of $25,000 = $4,500	$4,500
2007 RRSP Deduction Limit	$4,500
RRSP Deduction ($5,000 Contributed)	(4,000)
Unused Deduction Room - End Of 2007	$ 500

Although Miss Brown could have deducted $4,500, she chose not to deduct her maximum. She has an undeducted RRSP contribution of $1,000 ($5,000 - $4,000) that can be carried forward and deducted in a subsequent year. The interest income is not included in Earned Income as defined in ITA 146(1).

Example B

After deducting an RPP contribution of $2,000, Mrs. Blue has 2006 net employment income of $34,000. In February, 2007, her employer reports a PA of $4,500 on Mrs. Blue's 2006 T4. Her 2007 RRSP contributions total $5,000 and she deducts $3,200 of this amount in her 2007 tax return. At the end of 2006, her Unused RRSP Deduction Room was $2,500 and there were no undeducted contributions in her RRSP account.

Unused Deduction Room - End Of 2006	$2,500
Lesser Of:	
• 2007 RRSP Dollar Limit = $19,000	
• 18% Of 2006 Earned Income Of $36,000 = $6,480	6,480
Less 2006 PA	(4,500)
2007 RRSP Deduction Limit	$4,480
RRSP Deduction ($5,000 Contributed)	(3,200)
Unused Deduction Room - End Of 2007	$1,280

Mrs. Blue has 2006 Earned Income of $36,000 (net employment income of $34,000, plus her $2,000 RPP contribution that was deducted). She has an undeducted RRSP contribution of $1,800 ($5,000 - $3,200) that can be carried forward and deducted in a subsequent year.

Example C

Mr. Green receives taxable 2006 spousal support of $150,000 and has no other source of income during 2006. He is not a member of an RPP or DPSP. In January, 2007, he contributes $11,500 to his RRSP. This full amount is deducted in his 2007 tax return. At the end of 2006, his Unused RRSP Deduction Room was $1,200 and there were no undeducted contributions in his RRSP account.

Unused Deduction Room - End Of 2006	$ 1,200
Lesser Of:	
• 2007 RRSP Dollar Limit = $19,000	
• 18% Of 2006 Earned Income Of $150,000 = $27,000	19,000
2007 RRSP Deduction Limit	$20,200
RRSP Deduction ($11,500 Contributed)	(11,500)
Unused Deduction Room - End Of 2007	$ 8,700

Exercise Thirteen-6

Subject: Maximum RRSP Deduction

During 2006, Mr. Black has taxable capital gains of $23,650, net rental income of $6,530, pays spousal support of $18,000, and has net employment income of $75,600. Based on his RPP contributions of $2,400 and the matching contributions made by his employer, his employer reports a 2006 PA of $4,800. At the end of 2006, Mr. Black has Unused RRSP Deduction Room of $10,750. Also at this time, his RRSP contains undeducted contributions of $6,560. During 2007, he makes contributions to his RRSP of $13,200. Determine Mr. Black's maximum RRSP deduction for 2007. Assuming he deducts his maximum, determine the amount of any Unused RRSP Deduction Room that he will have available at the end of 2007, and indicate whether he has any undeducted contributions remaining at the end of 2007.

End of Exercise.   Solution available in Study Guide.

Undeducted RRSP Contributions

General Rules

13-74.   As we have previously noted, there is no requirement that contributions made to an RRSP be deducted immediately. If an individual has available funds to invest, it is usually desirable to transfer these funds into an RRSP in order to enjoy the tax deferral on investment earnings that these arrangements provide. However, in some situations, it may be desirable to defer the deduction of all or part of these contributions.

13-75.   An example of this type of situation would be a taxpayer who is currently in a low tax bracket and expects to be in a higher bracket in the future. Provided an amount was contributed after 1990, it can be deducted in any subsequent taxation year in which there is sufficient RRSP deduction room. There is no time limit applicable to this deduction and, in the event of death, it can be deducted in the taxpayer's final tax return.

Excess RRSP Contributions

13-76.   As long as an individual has a corresponding amount of available deduction room, the CRA is not concerned about undeducted contributions. However, because of the desirability of having earnings accumulate on a tax free basis inside an RRSP, it is not surprising that rules have been developed to limit the amount of contributions that are in excess of an individual's deduction room.

13-77.   The basic limiting provision is found in ITA 204.1(2.1) which imposes a tax of 1 percent per month on the "cumulative excess amount in respect of registered retirement savings plans". The "cumulative excess" is defined in ITA 204.2(1.1), as undeducted contributions in excess of the sum of the RRSP Deduction Limit, plus a $2,000 cushion. This, in effect, means that the penalty applies to undeducted contributions that are more than $2,000 greater than the individual's RRSP Deduction Limit.

13-78.   This $2,000 cushion provides for a margin of error when a taxpayer makes contributions early in the taxation year on the basis of estimates of the amount that will be deductible. Note, however, the $2,000 cushion is only available to individuals who are 18 years of age or older throughout the year. This is to prevent parents from making undeducted contributions to an RRSP in the name of their minor children.

13-79.   The following simple example illustrates the application of this rule.

Example   At the end of 2005, Mr. Woods has an RRSP Deduction Limit of nil and no undeducted contributions in his plan. During 2006, his RRSP Deduction Limit increases by $9,000. On April 1, 2006, Mr. Woods makes a contribution of $10,000 to his RRSP. No RRSP deduction is taken for 2006.

Registered Retirement Savings Plans (RRSPs)

During 2007, his RRSP Deduction Limit increases by $10,000. On July 1, 2007, $15,000 is contributed to the plan. No RRSP deduction is taken for 2007.

Analysis   There would be no penalty for 2006 as his $10,000 in undeducted contributions is only $1,000 more than his $9,000 unused deduction room for 2006. There would, however, be a penalty in 2007. It would be calculated as follows:

	January To June	July To December
Undeducted RRSP Contributions	$10,000	$25,000
RRSP Deduction Limit	(19,000)	(19,000)
Cushion	(2,000)	(2,000)
Monthly Cumulative Excess Amount	$ Nil	$ 4,000
Penalty Rate	1%	1%
Monthly Penalty	$ Nil	$ 40
Number Of Months	N/A	6
Total Penalty	$ Nil	$ 240

Exercise Thirteen-7

Subject: RRSP Excess Contributions

Ms. Lucie Brownell is not a member of an RPP or a DPSP. At the beginning of 2005, Ms. Brownell has no Unused RRSP Deduction Room. During 2005 and 2006 she has Earned Income of $120,000 each year. On July 1, 2006, she makes a $18,500 RRSP contribution, but does not make any deduction for the year. In 2007, she has Earned Income of $50,000, makes a $21,000 contribution on May 1, but still does not make a deduction for the year. Determine any penalty that will be assessed to Ms. Brownell for excess contributions during either 2006 or 2007.

End of Exercise. Solution available in Study Guide.

Tax Planning - Excess RRSP Contributions

13-80.   It would be very difficult to find an investment for which the elimination of tax effects would offset a non-deductible penalty of 1 percent per month. Clearly, excess contributions that subject the taxpayer to this penalty should be avoided.

13-81.   This still leaves the question of whether it is worthwhile to make use of the $2,000 penalty free cushion. When the $2,000 is withdrawn from the RRSP, it will generally have to be included in the taxpayer's income, whether or not it has been deducted.

13-82.   Mitigating this is the fact that, if the $2,000 is withdrawn from the RRSP prior to the end of the year, following the year in which an assessment is received for the year in which the contribution is made, an offsetting deduction is available under ITA 146(8.2). If, however, any excess is not withdrawn within this specified time frame, it will be included in income and taxed on withdrawal, even though it was never deducted from income.

13-83.   Some analysts have expressed concern that, while the excess $2,000 cannot be deducted, it will be taxed at full individual rates when it is withdrawn. Even it this were the case, the advantages of tax free compounding of earnings could offset the taxation of the original $2,000.

13-84.   More to the point, however, is the fact that undeducted contributions can be used in any subsequent year. Given this, making use of the $2,000 excess contribution cushion becomes a clearly desirable procedure for those with sufficient available funds. Whether the amount is left in the RRSP for a long or short period, it can be used as a deduction in any future year prior to the collapse of the plan. The only restriction on this procedure is that the taxpayer must have sufficient RRSP deduction room to be able to deduct the $2,000 in a future period. As this would apply to most working individuals, it is difficult to see any reason not to make use of the $2,000 cushion, if the funds are available.

RRSP And RRIF Administration Fees

13-85.   Administration fees for these plans, as well as investment counseling fees related to investments in these plans, cannot be deducted by an individual. As a consequence, such fees should be paid with funds that are in the plan. While there was some controversy associated with this issue, it has been concluded that such payments are not a withdrawal from the plan, nor do they create a taxable benefit for the taxpayer.

RRSP Withdrawals And Voluntary Conversions

13-86.   A lump sum withdrawal from an RRSP is possible at any point in time. The tax consequences of partial or complete withdrawals are very straightforward. In general, the amount withdrawn must be added to income in the year of withdrawal. Further, as a withdrawal does not result in an increase in the ability to make future contributions, such transactions result in a permanent reduction in the balances that will enjoy tax free earnings accumulation.

13-87.   Even when the individual is at or approaching retirement, a complete withdrawal of all funds would not usually be a reasonable alternative. This course of action could subject a large portion of the withdrawal to maximum tax rates at that time and, in the absence of other retirement income, would result in lost tax credits in subsequent years.

13-88.   We would also call your attention to the fact that lump sum withdrawals are subject to withholding. The trustee of the plan is required to withhold a portion of the funds withdrawn and remit them to the government. The taxpayer will, of course, be able to deduct these withholdings from the taxes that will be assessed on the amounts withdrawn. Withholding is based on the following schedule:

Amount	Rate
Less Than $5,001	10%
$5,001 To $15,000	20%
More Than $15,000	30%

13-89.   Besides lump sum withdrawals, the following options are available for converting an RRSP into an income stream:

Life Annuity   Funds from within an RRSP can be used to purchase a single life annuity or, alternatively, a joint life annuity with a spouse or common-law partner. Although the funds are no longer in the RRSP, this purchase is not considered a withdrawal of funds and, as a consequence, taxation occurs only as the annuity payments are received.

Note that a life annuity can guarantee that it is paid for a minimum number of periods. For example, a life annuity with a ten year guaranteed term would make payments for a minimum of ten years, even if the annuitant died prior to the end of the period.

A further point here is that the term annuitant is correctly used only with respect to an individual who is receiving an annuity. Unless the individual has chosen to convert his RRSP to an annuity, the appropriate description of the individual is registrant (he may or may not be the beneficiary of the plan). Unfortunately, tax publications often use the term annuitant to describe someone who is, in fact, a registrant.

Fixed Term Annuity   In a similar fashion, a fixed term annuity can be purchased. As with the life annuity, taxation would occur as the annuity payments are received.

13-90.   Note that these conversions can be made at any age, and without regard to whether the taxpayer has retired. Further, there are no tax consequences resulting from the conversion. However, the income stream from the annuity will be fully taxable as it is received (see the discussion in Chapter 12 with respect to the taxation of annuity payments).

13-91.   A final alternative for winding up an RRSP is as follows:

Registered Retirement Income Fund (RRIF) The funds can be transferred on a tax free basis to one or more Registered Retirement Income Funds (RRIFs). This arrangement will be described beginning in Paragraph 13-157.

Involuntary Termination Due To Age Limitation
Objective

13-92.   The options for termination of an RRSP that were discussed in the preceding section are available at any age and without regard to whether the individual actually retires. However, government policy in this area takes the view that the tax sheltering features of RRSPs should not continue to be available to taxpayers in periods that are substantially beyond normal retirement age. Prior to the March, 2007 budget, the government's position was that RRSPs should be terminated in the year in which the beneficiary reached age 69.

March, 2007 Budget

13-93.   This position was changed by the March, 2007 budget. This budget indicates that, as of 2007, RRSPs do not have to be terminated until the year in which the beneficiary reaches age 71. As was the case when terminations was required at age 69, if an individual does not select one of the available voluntary options by the end of the year in which they turn 71, the RRSP is automatically deregistered. For tax purposes, this deregistration is treated as if it is a lump sum withdrawal.

13-94.   For those individuals who previously transferred funds from an RRSP to a RRIF in anticipation of reaching age 69, they will be allowed to transfer funds back to an RRSP. This RRSP can then be maintained until they reach age 71. However, if they do not do so, the RRIF mandatory withdrawal requirement will be waived for 2007 and 2008 for individuals who turn 70 in 2007, and for 2007 only for individuals who turn 71 in 2007.

Post Termination

13-95.   While individuals cannot have their own RRSP after reaching the age of 71, it is still possible for such individuals to make deductible RRSP contributions. If their spouse or common-law partner has not reached the age of 71, and if the individual continues to have income that qualifies as Earned Income for RRSP purposes (pension income does not), contributions can still be made to an RRSP in the name of the spouse or common-law partner.

Departure From Canada

13-96.   ITA 128.1(4)(b) requires a deemed disposition of most capital property when an individual departs from Canada (see coverage of this subject in Chapter 12). However, most pension benefits are exempt from these rules and, as a consequence, a departure from Canada will not automatically result in the collapse of an RRSP.

13-97.   Once the taxpayer has ceased to be a resident of Canada, he may find it desirable to collapse the plan. The collapse and subsequent payment to a non-resident will result in taxation under ITA Part XIII. The Part XIII tax is a 25 percent tax on payments to a non-resident and, for those countries with which Canada has a tax treaty, the rate can be as low as 10 percent. Unlike the withholding tax that is assessed on withdrawals by Canadian residents, this is a final tax, and the individual will not be subject to further taxation in Canada.

13-98.   Whether or not the proceeds resulting from the collapse of the plan will be taxed in the new country of residence will depend on a number of factors, including which country is involved and the manner in which the RRSP income was reported prior to the individual leaving Canada. While there are significant tax planning opportunities in this area, detailed coverage of this subject goes beyond the scope of this text.

13-99.   If the plan is not collapsed and payments are made to a non-resident, such payments are also subject to Part XIII tax at a 10 percent, or greater, rate. As was the case with the proceeds resulting from collapsing the plan, how this will be taxed in the individual's new country of residence is determined by a number of factors.

Death Of The Registrant
General Rules
13-100.   As we noted in Chapter 12, when an individual dies, there are complications associated with any RRSP that he has not been collapsed through a voluntary (e.g., lump-sum withdrawal of funds) or involuntary (e.g., reaching age 71) termination. Also as indicated in that Chapter, we have deferred consideration of these complications to this point, where you should now have a better understanding of the mechanics of these plans.

13-101.   The general rules depend on whether the plan is an unmatured plan (i.e., the registrant has not converted the plan to an annuity) or a matured plan (i.e., the plan has been converted to an annuity which is producing a regular stream of income). As described in RC4177, "Death Of An RRSP Annuitant", the general rules are as follows:

> **Unmatured RRSPs** When the annuitant of an unmatured RRSP dies, he or she is considered to have received, immediately before death, an amount equal to the fair market value of all the property held in the RRSP at the time of death. This amount, and all other amounts the annuitant received in the year from the RRSP, have to be reported on the annuitant's return for the year of death.

> **Matured RRSPs** When the annuitant of a matured RRSP dies, the annuitant is considered to have received, immediately before death, an amount equal to the fair market value of all remaining annuity payments under the RRSP at the time of death. This amount, and all other amounts the annuitant received in the year from the RRSP, have to be reported on the annuitant's return for the year of death.

13-102.   If these general rules are applied, with the lump-sum or annuity amounts included in the decedent's final tax return, the assets will pass to the specified beneficiaries at fair market value, with no immediate tax consequences for that individual. However, when the RRSP assets or annuity are transferred to certain specific beneficiaries, there are important exceptions to this general rule.

13-103.   An additional point here is that there are two different ways in which RRSP assets can be transferred at death. The preferable approach is for the registrant to specify the beneficiary, or beneficiaries, in the RRSP contract. This will result in the assets being passed immediately at death. Perhaps more importantly, probate fees will be avoided.

13-104.   If this approach is not used, the RRSP assets will pass into the deceased's estate. If this happens, their distribution will be subject to probate fees. In Ontario, these fees are 1.5 percent of the value of the estate with no upper limit.

Exception - Transfers To A Spouse Or Common-Law Partner
13-105.   The various possibilities that arise when the ultimate disposition of an RRSP is to a spouse or common-law partner can be described as follows:

> **Unmatured RRSP - Spouse Is Beneficiary Of RRSP** If the spouse is the sole beneficiary and there is a direct transfer to an RRSP with the spouse as the registrant, there will be no tax consequences for either the decedent or the spouse. The assets in the decedent's RRSP simply become assets in the spouse's RRSP. This is clearly the most tax advantageous arrangement for dealing with an unmatured RRSP.

> **Matured RRSP - Spouse Is Beneficiary** If the RRSP is in the form of an annuity with the spouse as the sole beneficiary, the RRSP will continue with the spouse receiving the payments. There will be no tax consequences for the decedent and the spouse will be taxed as the annuity payments are received. For matured RRSPs, this is clearly the most tax advantageous arrangement.

Estate Is Beneficiary Whether the RRSP has or has not matured, the general rules will be applicable here. If the spouse is the beneficiary of the estate, the same rollover results can be achieved here through the use of elections. However, probate fees will be applicable and the procedures will be more complex.

Exception - Transfers To A Financially Dependent Child Or Grandchild

13-106.   Without becoming involved in the details, there are provisions that allow both matured and unmatured RRSPs to be transferred to a financially dependent child or grand-child on a basis that shifts the tax burden from the decedent to the transferee.

13-107.   While the relevant amounts could be taxed in the hands of the dependant, there are other options. If the child has a physical or mental infirmity, the dependant can avoid current taxation by transferring the amounts to an RRSP, RRIF, or an annuity. If there is no physical or mental infirmity, the only option that avoids current taxation is to purchase an annuity. In this case, the life of the annuity cannot exceed 18 years, minus the age of the child or grandchild when the annuity is purchased. As a result, if the child is over 17 years of age, this option cannot be used.

Spousal RRSP

Benefits

13-108.   Under ITA 146(5.1), a taxpayer can deduct payments that are made to a plan that will provide RRSP payments to a spouse or common-law partner. Any RRSP that is registered with the taxpayer's spouse or common-law partner as the annuitant, and to which the taxpayer has made a contribution, is considered to be a spousal RRSP. This term is still the most commonly used, despite the fact that the legislation covers both spouses and common-law partners. This means that, if an individual makes any contribution to his spouse or common-law partner's existing RRSP, that plan becomes a spousal RRSP, even if the great majority of the contributions were made by the individual's spouse or common-law partner.

13-109.   A spousal RRSP is one of the few relatively simple income splitting devices that is generally available to all couples. (The new pension income splitting provision is only avail-able to couples with eligible pension income.) In situations where one spouse or common-law partner is likely to have either no retirement income or a significantly lower amount, having the spouse or common-law partner with the higher expected retirement income make contributions to a plan in which the spouse or common-law partner is the annu-itant will generally result in the income from the plan being taxed at lower rates.

13-110.   In addition, if one spouse or common-law partner has no other source of retire-ment income, a spousal RRSP allows that individual to make use of the $310 [(15.5%)($2,000)] annual pension income credit against Tax Payable. Note, however, that the new provision for splitting pension income could accomplish this same goal.

13-111.   When an individual makes contributions to an RRSP in the name of his spouse or common-law partner, the contributions will be deductible in the contributor's tax return. However, the individual must have available deduction room and, as you would expect, contributions to a spousal plan erode this room in exactly the same manner as would contribu-tions to an RRSP in the individual's name.

13-112.   We have noted previously that an individual can continue making contributions to a spousal RRSP, even if his own plan has been collapsed because he is over 71 years of age. In addition, a deceased taxpayer's representative can make contributions to a spousal RRSP for up to 60 days after the end of the year of death.

Attribution Rules

13-113.   The objective of all of the RRSP legislation is to encourage retirement savings. In the case of spousal RRSPs, the legislation also provides for an element of income splitting. However, as the federal government does not want this element of income splitting to over-ride the basic objective of retirement savings, there is an income attribution provision that discourages the use of spousal RRSPs in a manner that provides for an immediate transfer of income to a lower income spouse.

13-114.   ITA 146(8.3) contains an income attribution provision that requires certain withdrawals from a spousal RRSP to be attributed to the spouse or common-law partner who made the contribution. Withdrawals from non-spousal RRSPs are normally taxed in the hands of the annuitant. However, if a withdrawal is made from a spousal RRSP and the annuitant's spouse or common-law partner has made a contribution to the plan, either in the current year or in the two preceding calendar years, the withdrawal will be attributed to the contributing spouse or common-law partner, not the annuitant of the plan.

13-115.   This attribution rule applies to withdrawals up to the amount of the relevant contribution, but does not apply to withdrawals in excess of this amount. It also applies whether or not the contributing spouse or common-law partner has deducted the contributions. In addition, it is applicable even when there are funds that were contributed by the annuitant of the plan prior to the spouse or common-law partner making additional contributions. However, the rule does not apply when the taxpayer and spouse or common-law partner are living apart due to a marital breakdown at the time of the withdrawal.

13-116.   When the taxpayer's spouse or common-law partner is eligible to make his or her own contributions to an RRSP, it can be useful to have these contributions made to a separate, non-spousal RRSP. If there is a need to withdraw funds, this precaution allows the withdrawal to be made from a plan that has not received spousal contributions. As a result, there would be no attribution and the withdrawal would be taxed in the hands of the individual making the withdrawal. However, if no withdrawals are anticipated in the foreseeable future, there is no tax related need to have a separate, non-spousal plan.

Exercise Thirteen-8

Subject: Spousal RRSP

During 2005, Mr. Garveau makes a $5,000 contribution to a new RRSP in which he is the annuitant. His wife, Mrs. Charron Garveau also makes a $5,000 contribution to his RRSP in 2005. In 2006, Mrs. Garveau does not make any further contribution to her husband's RRSP. However, Mr. Garveau makes a $6,500 contribution. During 2007, Mr. Garveau withdraws $9,000 from his RRSP. How will this withdrawal be taxed?

End of Exercise. Solution available in Study Guide.

Home Buyers' Plan (HBP)

Qualifying HBP Withdrawals

13-117.   The Home Buyers' Plan (HBP) permits a withdrawal of up to $20,000 of "eligible amounts" from one or more of an individual's RRSPs. This amount can be removed from the RRSP(s) without the usual tax consequences associated with withdrawals. In order to receive this withdrawal without tax consequences, the individual must meet several conditions:

- On January 1 of the year of withdrawal, all amounts related to previous HBP withdrawals must have been repaid.

- All amounts, up to the limit of $20,000 per individual, must have been received in a single year or by the end of January of the following year.

- The individual must have bought or built a "qualifying home" before October 1 of the year following the year of withdrawal(s). Extensions of the deadline are available where there is a written agreement to purchase a home, or payments have been made towards the construction of a home, by the October 1 deadline. A "qualifying home" is defined as a housing unit located in Canada, including a share of the capital stock of a cooperative housing corporation that provides an equity interest in the housing unit.

- Within one year of the acquisition of this "qualifying home", the taxpayer must begin, or intend to begin, using it as a principal place of residence. Note, however, there is no minimum holding period for the home, provided that at some point it becomes a principal residence.

- Neither the individual nor his spouse or common-law partner can have owned a home that he or she has occupied during the four calendar years preceding the withdrawal. However, there is an exception to this constraint for disabled individuals. More specifically, if the home purchase is being made by, or for the benefit of, an individual who qualifies for the disability tax credit (see Chapter 6), and the home is more accessible for the individual, or is better suited for the care of the individual, the HBP can be used even if the individual owned a home that was occupied during the specified four year period.

- The individual must complete Form T1036, Home Buyers' Plan Request To Withdraw Funds From An RRSP.

13-118.   There is nothing in these rules to prevent the use of a HBP by both an individual and his or her spouse or common-law partner. This would allow couples to make withdrawals totaling $40,000 towards the purchase of a home.

Restrictions On The Deduction Of New RRSP Contributions

13-119.   The intent of this legislation is to allow individuals, who have not recently owned a home, to use accumulated RRSP contributions to acquire a residence. The government does not want to allow individuals to abuse the HBP by making contributions that are immediately withdrawn. To prevent this from happening, a special rule denies a tax deduction for contributions to an RRSP or a spousal RRSP that are withdrawn within 90 days under the Home Buyers' Plan.

13-120.   For this purpose, contributions to an RRSP within the 90 day period will not be considered to be part of the funds withdrawn, except to the extent that the RRSP balance after the withdrawal is less than the amount of the new contributions. This means that an individual can make the maximum $20,000 withdrawal and still make deductible contributions in the preceding 90 days, provided they had at least $20,000 in the RRSP prior to making the additional contributions.

> **Example**   Mr. Garth has an accumulated RRSP balance of $15,000. In order to make the maximum $20,000 HBP withdrawal, he makes a $5,000 contribution to the RRSP. If he then withdraws the $20,000 within 90 days of making the $5,000 contribution, the resulting nil balance will be less than the amount of the contribution and no deduction will be allowed for the $5,000 contribution. If Mr. Garth withdrew only $12,000, the resulting $8,000 balance will be greater than the $5,000 contribution and the contribution will be deductible.

13-121.   As a final point you should note that this rule is applied on a plan by plan basis. If a withdrawal under the HBP serves to reduce the balance of a particular plan below the level of contributions made in the preceding 90 days, the contributions will not be deductible to the extent of this deficiency. This would be the case even if the taxpayer has balances in excess of $20,000 in other RRSPs.

Repayment Of HBP

13-122.   Eligible amounts are not taxed when they are withdrawn from the RRSP and, if there was not a requirement for these funds to be returned to the plan at some point in time, they would constitute a significant tax free leakage from the retirement savings system. As a consequence, repayment of amounts withdrawn must begin as per a specified schedule in the second calendar year following the year of withdrawal.

13-123.   Any portion of an RRSP contribution made during the year, or in the first 60 days of the following year, can be designated an HBP repayment on Schedule 7, which is filed with the T1 tax return. These repayments are not deductible in the determination of Taxable Income. Any amounts that are not returned to the plan as per the required schedule must be included in the taxpayer's income in the year in which they were scheduled to be returned.

13-124. There is no upper limit on the amounts that can be repaid in any year subsequent to withdrawal. However, repayment must be made within 16 years. This is accomplished by requiring a minimum repayment based on the following calculation:

Eligible Amounts Withdrawn	$xx,xxx
Repayments In Previous Years	(xxx)
Amounts Included In Income In Previous Years	(xxx)
Balance	**$ x,xxx**

13-125. A fraction is then applied to this balance, beginning at 1/15 for the second year following the withdrawal. In each subsequent year, the denominator of the fraction is then reduced by one, resulting in 1/14 for the third year after withdrawal, 1/13 for the fourth year after withdrawal, and so on, until the fraction reaches 1/1 in the sixteenth year following the withdrawal. These are minimum payments and, if they are made as per this schedule, there will be a 15 year, straight line repayment of the eligible amounts.

13-126. If the payments are less than these minimum amounts, any deficiency must be included in that year's Taxable Income. As any income inclusions will be deducted from the balance to which the fraction is applied in the same manner as if they were repayments, this will not alter the schedule for the remaining payments.

13-127. However, if payments are accelerated in any year, the schedule is changed. While the multiplier fractions remain the same, the excess payments will reduce the balance to which the fractions are applied. A simple example will help clarify these points:

Example Ms. Ritchie withdraws an eligible amount of $15,000 from her RRSP in July, 2005, and uses the funds for a down payment on a qualifying home. In 2007, a repayment of $2,400 is made and, in 2008, a repayment of $600 is made.

Analysis The minimum payment for 2007 is $1,000 [(1/15)($15,000)] and, since this is less then the actual payment, no income inclusion is required. The required payment for 2008 is $900 [(1/14)($15,000 - $2,400)]. As the actual payment is $600, an income inclusion of $300 will be required. This is the case, despite the fact that the $3,000 in cumulative payments for the two years exceeds the $2,000 minimum that would have been required for the two years. This illustrates the fact that making payments in excess of the required level in one year does not provide an equivalent reduction in the payment for the following year. Note that the required payment for 2008 is also $900 [(1/13)($15,000 - $2,400 - $600 - $300)].

Departures From Canada

13-128. If an individual ceases to be a resident of Canada, any unpaid balance under the HBP must be repaid before the tax return filing date for the year of departure, or 60 days after becoming a non-resident, whichever date is earlier. If this deadline is not met, the unpaid balance must be included in income.

Death Of The Annuitant

13-129. If a participant in the HBP dies prior to repaying all amounts to the RRSP, any unpaid balance will be included in income in the final tax return. However, a surviving spouse may elect with the legal representatives of the deceased to avoid the income inclusion. If this election is made, the surviving spouse assumes the position of the deceased by being treated as having received an eligible amount equal to the unpaid balance outstanding at the time of the deceased's death. This amount is added to any balance of eligible amounts received by the surviving spouse that have not been previously repaid to the RRSPs.

Exercise Thirteen-9

Subject: Home Buyers' Plan

During 2005, Ms. Farah DeBoo withdraws $18,000 from her RRSP under the provisions of the Home Buyers' Plan. Due to some unexpected income received during 2006, she repays $5,000 in that year. What is the amount of her minimum repayment during 2007?

End of Exercise. Solution available in Study Guide.

Lifelong Learning Plan (LLP)

General Format

13-130.   ITA 146.02 contains provisions that allow an individual to make tax free withdrawals from their RRSPs in order to finance the education of themselves or their spouse or common-law partner. Withdrawals under this Lifelong Learning Plan (LLP) must be repaid over a period of ten years. The repayment amounts are not deductible and, if they are not made as per the required schedule, deficiencies will be included in the individual's income.

Withdrawals

13-131.   To qualify for the tax free withdrawals, the individual or his spouse or common-law partner must be enrolled as a full-time student in a qualifying educational program at a designated educational institution. In general, a qualifying educational program is a post-secondary program that requires students to spend ten hours or more per week on courses that last three consecutive months or more. A designated educational institution is a university, college, or other educational institution that qualifies the individual for the education tax credit (see Chapter 6).

13-132.   The maximum withdrawal is $10,000 in any one calendar year, to a maximum of $20,000 over a period of up to four calendar years. While the designated person for these withdrawals can be either the individual or his spouse or common-law partner, an individual cannot have a positive LLP balance (withdrawals, less repayments) for more than one person at any point in time. However, both an individual and his spouse or common-law partner can participate at the same time, provided they use funds from their own RRSPs.

13-133.   As is the case with HBPs (see Paragraph 13-119), if an RRSP contribution is withdrawn within 90 days as a non-taxable amount under the LLP provisions, it is not deductible in the calculation of the individual's Net Income For Tax Purposes.

Repayment Of LLP

13-134.   Minimum repayments must be made on a straight line basis over a period of ten years. In a manner similar to that used for HBPs, this is accomplished by using a formula in which 1/10 is repaid the first year, 1/9 the second year, 1/8 the third year, etc. Also in a manner similar to HBPs, deficient repayments will be included in the taxpayer's income. Repayments in excess of the required minimum reduce the balance to which the fractions will be applied.

13-135.   Any RRSP contribution made during the year, or in the first 60 days of the following year, can be designated a LLP repayment. Repayments must begin no later than the fifth year after the year of the first LLP withdrawal (actually the sixth year if payments are made within 60 days of the end of the fifth year).

Example   Sarah makes LLP withdrawals from 2007 to 2010. She continues her education from 2007 to 2012, and is entitled to claim the education tax credit as a full time student for at least three months on her return every year. Since 2012 is the fifth year after the year of her first LLP withdrawal, Sarah's repayment period is from 2012 to 2021. The due date for her first repayment is no later than March 1, 2013, which is 60 days after the end of 2012, her first repayment year.

13-136.   Repayments must begin earlier if the beneficiary of the program does not qualify for the full time education tax credit (see Chapter 6) for at least three months in each of two consecutive years. Specifically, repayment must begin in the second of the two non-qualifying years (or the first 60 days of the following year).

> **Example**   Joseph makes an LLP withdrawal in 2007 for a qualifying educational program he is enrolled in during 2007. He is entitled to the education tax credit as a full time student for five months of 2007. Joseph completes the educational program in 2008, and he is entitled to the education tax credit as a full time student for five months of 2008. He is not entitled to the education tax credit for 2009 or 2010. As a result, Joseph's repayment period begins in 2010.

Other Considerations

13-137.   There is no limit on the number of times an individual can participate in the LLP. However, an individual may not participate in a new plan before the end of the year in which all repayments from any previous participation have been made.

13-138.   For a withdrawal to be eligible for tax free status, the designated person must complete the qualified educational program before April of the year following the withdrawal or, alternatively, be enrolled in a qualified educational program at the end of March of the year following the withdrawal. If this is not the case, the withdrawal will still be eligible for tax free treatment, provided less than 75 percent of the tuition paid for the program is refunded.

13-139.   Similar to the provisions under the HBP, if an individual ceases to be a resident of Canada, any unpaid balance under the LLP must be repaid before the date the tax return for the year of departure should be filed, or no later than 60 days after becoming a non-resident, whichever date is earlier. If this deadline is not met, the unpaid balance must be included in income.

13-140.   If an individual dies and has a positive LLP balance, this balance must be included in the individual's income for the year of death. As was the case with HBPs, there is an election that allows a spouse to make the repayments under the deceased's LLP terms.

Exercise Thirteen-10

Subject: Lifelong Learning Plan

Jean Paul Riopelle makes a Lifelong Learning Plan (LPP) withdrawal of $5,000 during July, 2007. This is subsequent to his acceptance in a community college art program that runs from September to November, 2007. He completes the course.

On February 28 of each year from 2010 through 2019, he makes payments of $500 per year to his RRSP. These amounts are designated as LLP repayments in his tax returns for the years 2009 through 2018. Indicate the tax consequences to Jean Paul of these transactions.

End of Exercise.   Solution available in Study Guide.

Registered Pension Plans (RPPs)

Establishing An RPP

Types Of Plans

13-141.   The most important type of Canadian pension arrangement is the Registered Pension Plan (RPP) provided by some employers for their employees. These plans have assets that are nearly double those of all other types of plans combined. Such plans are established by a contract between the employer and the employees and provide either for a pension benefit that is determined under a prescribed formula (a defined benefit or benefit based plan), or for a specified annual contribution by the employer that will provide a benefit that will be based on the funds available at the time of retirement (a money purchase or contribution based plan).

13-142.   An additional variable is the question of whether, in addition to the contributions made by the employer, the employees make contributions to the plan. If they do, it is referred to as a contributory plan. Both employer and employee contributions to the RPPs are normally deposited with a trustee who is responsible for safeguarding and managing the funds deposited.

Registration Of The Plan
13-143.   It would be possible for an employer to have a pension plan that is not registered. However, such an arrangement would make very little sense. In order to deduct contributions for tax purposes, an employer sponsored pension plan must be registered with the CRA.

13-144.   In most situations, the basic requirements for registration are not difficult to meet. The plan must provide a definite arrangement, established as a continuing policy by an employer, under which benefits are provided to employees after their retirement. The terms and conditions must be set out in writing and the amounts of benefits to be provided must be reasonable in the circumstances.

Employer Contributions To The RPP
General Rules
13-145.   As is noted in Chapter 8 on business income, ITA 20(1)(q) allows an employer to deduct contributions to an RPP in the determination of Net Income For Tax Purposes. It indicates that such amounts can be deducted to the extent that they are provided for by ITA 147.2(1).

13-146.   Turning to ITA 147.2(1), we find that contributions to money purchase plans are deductible as long as they are made in accordance with the plan as registered. For defined benefit plans there is a similar requirement. Contributions made during the year, or within 120 days after the year end, are deductible as long as they have not been deducted previously.

13-147.   Note that the reference is to contributions made, establishing the fact that the availability of deductions for pension costs is on a cash basis. As deductions under GAAP must be determined on an accrual basis, there are likely to be differences between the accounting expense for the period and the tax deduction for the period.

Restrictions
13-148.   The preceding general rules appear to provide for any level of deductions, as long as the amount is consistent with the plan as registered. As we have noted, however, the restrictions on contributions are implemented through the registration process. More specifically, ITA 147.1(8) indicates that RPPs become revocable if the PA of a member of the plan exceeds the lesser of:

- the money purchase limit for the year, and
- 18 percent of the member's compensation from the employer for the year.

13-149.   Given the fact that the RRSP Deduction Limit is also based on these same factors (with a one year lag), this restriction means that, in general, an RPP cannot provide for more retirement savings than would be available to an individual whose only retirement savings vehicle is an RRSP. To illustrate this, consider a member of a money purchase RPP who has 2007 compensation of $110,000. The RPP must be designed in such a fashion that it does not produce a combined employer/employee contribution that is in excess of the lesser of $20,000 (the money purchase limit for 2007) and $19,800 (18 percent of the compensation of $110,000).

13-150.   An individual with Earned Income equal to the same $110,000 compensation, who is not a member of an RPP or DPSP, would be subject to the same limit, with a one year lag. That is, in 2008, the maximum RRSP deduction for this individual would be the lesser of 18 percent of 2007 Earned Income of $110,000, and the 2008 RRSP Dollar Limit of $20,000. The money purchase limit is $20,000 for 2007 and increases to $21,000 in 2008. The RRSP Dollar Limit has the same increase with a one year delay, going to $20,000 in 2008 and to $21,000 in 2009.

13-151.   An RPP that provides benefits to an employee that creates a PA in excess of the money purchase limit for the year or 18 percent of the employee's compensation will have its registration revoked. Given that registration is required for RPP contributions to be deductible, this requirement should ensure that benefits are limited to the specified levels.

13-152.   Before leaving this discussion of employer contributions, you should note that this restriction on PAs would effectively restrict both employer and employee contributions to an RPP. Both types of contributions go into the PA calculation and, as a consequence, placing the limit on this measure of pension benefits ensures that the combined employee/employer contributions will be restricted to the desired maximum level.

Employee Contributions To The RPP

13-153.   As is noted in Chapter 5, the basic provision here is ITA 8(1)(m) which indicates that, in the determination of employment income, individuals can deduct contributions to an employer's RPP as specified in ITA 147.2(4). Taking the same approach that was used for employer contributions, this Subsection indicates that amounts contributed for current service are deductible if they are made in accordance with the terms of the plan. This places employee contributions under the same overall limit as employer contributions. That is, they must be made under the terms of a plan that does not produce a PA that exceeds the lesser of the money purchase limit for the year and 18 percent of the employee's compensation for the year.

Options At Retirement

13-154.   Individual RPPs generally involve rules that are applicable to the employee group in its entirety. As a consequence, the employee's options are usually limited to the receipt of the specified pension benefit. If the plan permits a lump sum payment of benefits, it would become taxable on receipt by the employee. The plan might also permit transfers to other types of plans at, or before, retirement age. Such transfers are discussed beginning in Paragraph 13-183.

Phased Retirement

The Problems

13-155.   Under current *Income Tax Regulations*, an employee cannot accrue benefits under a defined benefit RPP if he is currently receiving benefits from that plan. This prohibition also applies if the employee is receiving benefits from another defined benefit RPP sponsored by the same employer or an employer related to that employer. This means that:

- If an individual wants to phase in retirement by working on a part time basis after he has started to receive his basic pension benefits, he cannot receive any further pension benefits for this part time work.

- If an individual continues on a full time basis after beginning to receive his basic pension benefit, he cannot be rewarded with a partial pension benefit for this additional work.

March, 2007 Budget

13-156.   The March, 2007 budget proposed to change this situation. Starting in 2008, an employer will be able to offer employees up to 60 percent of their accrued defined benefit pension entitlement, while accruing additional pension benefits on a current service basis with respect to their post-pension commencement employment. This program is limited to employees who are at least 55 years of age and who are otherwise eligible to receive a pension without being subject to an early retirement reduction.

Registered Retirement Income Funds (RRIFs)

Establishment

Only Transfers From Other Plans

13-157. A RRIF is a trusteed arrangement, administered in much the same manner as an RRSP. A basic difference, however, is the fact that deductible contributions cannot be made to a RRIF. ITA 146.3(2)(f) makes it clear that the only types of property that can be accepted by the RRIF trustee are transfers from other types of retirement savings arrangements. The most common type of transfer would be the tax free rollover that can be made from an RRSP. As was indicated previously, this commonly occurs when an individual reaches age 71 and can no longer maintain an RRSP.

13-158. There is no limit on the number of RRIFs that can be owned by a taxpayer and, in addition, the taxpayer has complete flexibility as to the number of RRSPs that can be transferred to a RRIF on a tax free basis. Further, the taxpayer is free to divide any RRSP and only transfer a portion of the funds to a RRIF. This in no way limits the options available for any remaining balance from the RRSP. You should also note that a lump sum payment from an RPP can be transferred to a RRIF.

Other Considerations

13-159. A RRIF can be established by an individual of any age and without regard to whether the individual is retiring. However, RRSPs have all of the same tax advantages as RRIFs, without the requirement that there be a minimum withdrawal in each year. Given this, there is no obvious reason for establishing a RRIF prior to age 71.

13-160. Any amount transferred from an RRSP to a RRIF is not subject to taxation until such time as it is withdrawn by the taxpayer from the RRIF. As was the case with RRSPs, withdrawals are taxed as ordinary income, without regard to how they were earned inside the RRIF (e.g., capital gains realized within the RRIF are taxed in full on withdrawal from the plan).

13-161. Once inside the RRIF, the assets can be managed by the trustee of the plan according to the directions of the taxpayer. The list of qualified investments for RRIFs is similar to that for RRSPs and Deferred Profit Sharing Plans and allows for considerable latitude in investment policies. As is the case with RRSPs, fees paid by an individual for the administration of a RRIF are not deductible.

Minimum Withdrawals

13-162. We noted previously that, unlike the situation with RRSPs, an individual cannot make contributions to a RRIF. The second difference between an RRSP and a RRIF is that a minimum annual withdrawal must be made from a RRIF beginning in the year following the year it is established (as discussed earlier, because of the increase in the age at which RRSPs have to be terminated, this requirement is being partially waived for individuals who are turning 70 or 71 in 2007).

13-163. If an individual chooses to establish a RRIF prior to reaching age 71, the minimum withdrawal is determined by dividing the fair market value of the RRIF assets at the beginning of the year, by 90 minus the age of the individual at the beginning of the year. For example, if a 65 year old individual, who had established a RRIF in a previous year, had $1,000,000 in RRIF assets at the beginning of the year, he would have to withdraw a minimum of $40,000 [$1,000,000 ÷ (90 - 65)].

13-164. Once an individual is 71 or over at the beginning of the year, the rules require a different calculation. A specified percentage [ITR 7308(4)] is applied to the fair market value of the RRIF assets at the beginning of the year. The percentage increases each year, starting at 7.38 percent at age 71, rising to 8.75 percent at age 80, and 13.62 percent at age 90. However, when it hits 20 percent at age 94, it remains at that level until the annuitant dies. This, of course, means that the RRIF balance will never reach zero if minimum withdrawals are made.

13-165.   It is possible to irrevocably elect to use a spouse's age to calculate the minimum RRIF withdrawal. If the spouse is younger, the minimum amount is lower and offers an opportunity to defer the tax effect of the withdrawals.

13-166.   While legislation establishes the minimum withdrawal from a RRIF, there is no maximum withdrawal. The entire balance in the RRIF can be withdrawn at any time. However, as was noted, any amounts removed from the RRIF must be included in Net Income For Tax Purposes in the year of withdrawal.

Exercise Thirteen-11

Subject: Minimum RRIF Withdrawal

On January 1, 2007, Mr. Larry Harold transfers all of his RRSP funds into a RRIF. Mr. Harold is 65 years old on that date. The fair market value of these assets on January 1, 2007 is $625,000. The corresponding figure on January 1, 2008 is $660,000. What is the minimum withdrawal that Mr. Harold must make from the RRIF during 2007 and during 2008?

End of Exercise. Solution available in Study Guide.

Death Of The Registrant

General Rules

13-167.   As was the case with an RRSP, the general rule is that, when a taxpayer dies, the fair market value of the assets in his RRIF will be included as income in his final tax return. Also following this pattern, there are exceptions when the beneficiary who is left the RRIF is either a spouse or common-law partner, or a financially dependent child or grandchild.

Rollovers

13-168.   If an individual has a spouse or common-law partner, the most tax advantageous approach to estate planning is to name that person as the beneficiary of the RRIF. In this situation, the RRIF is simply rolled over to the surviving spouse, with no tax consequences for the decedent. Future withdrawals from the RRIF will be taxed in the hands of the spouse.

13-169.   This is even more important here than in the case of RRSPs. If an RRSP is left to the decedent's estate, it is possible to have a tax free rollover to a spouse by making appropriate elections. This does not appear to be the case with RRIFs. If a RRIF is left to an estate, it will be taxed in the final return, even if the assets are ultimately distributed to a surviving spouse.

13-170.   Rollovers are also available to a financially dependent child or grandchild. Here again, they must be beneficiaries of the RRIF, rather than beneficiaries of the decedent's estate. As was the case with RRSPs, if the dependent is physically or mentally infirm, the assets can go to an RRSP, a RRIF, or an annuity. In the absence of a physical or mental infirmity, the only option is the purchase of a limited term annuity.

Evaluation Of RRIFs

13-171.   For individuals required by age to terminate their RRSP, lump sum withdrawals are usually not a good solution. This reflects the fact that such withdrawals can often result in a large portion of the income being taxed at high rates. In addition, the pension income splitting provisions cannot be utilized. A possible exception to this view would be situations in which the taxpayer plans to give up Canadian residency.

13-172.   This leaves individuals with a choice between using a RRIF and purchasing an annuity. The fact that life annuities are only available through life insurance companies means that the rates of return implicit in these financial instruments are often not competitive with other investments.

13-173.   Further, annuities lack flexibility. Once an individual has entered into an annuity contract, there is usually no possibility of acquiring larger payments if they are required by some unforeseen event. In contrast, RRIFs offer some degree of flexibility with respect to amounts available to the taxpayer.

13-174.   As a final point, the wide range of qualifying investments that can be acquired in RRIFs provide individuals with the opportunity to achieve better rates of return than those available through the purchase of annuities. It would appear that, for most individuals, the use of a RRIF is the most desirable option when the individual's age forces the collapse of an RRSP.

Deferred Profit Sharing Plans

General Rules

13-175.   ITA 147 provides for an arrangement where an employer can deduct contributions made to a trustee of a Deferred Profit Sharing Plan (DPSP, hereafter) for the benefit of the employees. Employees cannot make contributions to an employer sponsored DPSP. However, certain direct transfers of balances from other plans belonging to the employee can be made (see Paragraph 13-183).

13-176.   Amounts placed in the plan will be invested, with investment earnings accruing on a tax free basis. As with the other retirement savings vehicles, the beneficiary of the plan is taxed only when assets are distributed from the plan.

13-177.   As was the case with RPPs, the employer's contributions to these plans are limited by a maximum PA that must be complied with to avoid having the DPSP revoked. This is found in ITA 147(5.1) and is more restrictive than the corresponding limit for RPPs. Specifically, the PA for any individual with respect to benefits under a DPSP cannot exceed the lesser of:

- one-half of the money purchase limit for the year, and
- 18 percent of the beneficiary's compensation from the employer for the year.

Tax Planning

13-178.   From the point of view of the employer, DPSPs are similar to RPPs. However, they have the advantage of providing greater flexibility in the scheduling of payments. Such plans are tied to the profits of the business and, if the business has a bad year, it will normally result in a reduction of payments into the DPSP. Further, no specific benefits are promised to the employees. This relieves the employer from any responsibility for bad investment decisions by the fund trustee or estimation errors in the actuarial valuation process, factors that can cause significant uncertainty for the sponsors of defined benefit RPPs.

13-179.   From the point of view of the employee, a DPSP operates in a manner similar to an RPP. The major difference is that employees are not permitted to contribute to DPSPs.

13-180.   DPSPs must invest in certain qualified investments and there are penalties for purchases of non-qualified investments. A final important consideration is that DPSPs cannot be registered if the employer or a member of the employer's family is a beneficiary under the plan. This would include major shareholders if the employer is a corporation, individual owners if the employer is a proprietorship or partnership, and beneficiaries when the employer is a trust.

Profit Sharing Plans

13-181.   ITA 144 provides for Profit Sharing Plans. These plans are similar to DPSPs in that the employer can deduct contributions made on behalf of employees. Unlike the DPSPs, there are no specified limits on the employer's contributions as long as they are reasonable and are paid out of profits.

13-182.   However, these plans have not achieved the popularity of DPSPs for a very simple reason. The employer's contributions to Profit Sharing Plans are taxable income to the employee in the year in which they are made. In addition, any income that accrues on the assets in the fund is allocated to the employee as it accrues. Although payments to the employees out of the fund are received on a tax free basis, this form of compensation offers no deferral of tax and requires the payment of taxes on amounts that have not been realized by the employee. Given these facts, it is not surprising that such Profit Sharing Plans have not been a popular compensation mechanism.

Transfers Between Plans

Accumulated Benefits

13-183.   As individuals may belong to several different retirement savings plans over their working lives, it is important that tax free transfers between different types of retirement savings plans can be made. For example, an individual who goes from a position where the employer provides RPP benefits, to a different position where no such benefits are provided, may wish to have his accumulated RPP benefits transferred to his RRSP. In the absence of a special provision to deal with this transfer, the benefits coming out of the RPP would have to be included in the individual's Taxable Income in the year of withdrawal. This, of course, would make such a transfer very unattractive.

13-184.   Fortunately, the *Act* allows for great flexibility in this area. Provided the transfer is made directly between the plans, the following transfers can be made on a tax free basis:

Registered Pension Plans   ITA 147.3 provides for the direct transfer of a lump sum amount from an RPP to a different RPP, to an RRSP, and to a RRIF. The Section also permits a transfer from a taxpayer's RPP to an RPP, RRSP, or RRIF of his or her spouse, former spouse, common-law partner or former common-law partner under a court order or written separation agreement in the event of a marriage or common-law partnership breakdown.

Registered Retirement Savings Plans   ITA 146(16) provides for the transfer of lump sum amounts from an RRSP to a RRIF, an RPP, or to another RRSP. The Subsection also permits a transfer from a taxpayer's RRSP to an RRSP or RRIF of his or her spouse, former spouse, common-law partner or former common-law partner under a court order or written separation agreement in the event of a marriage or common-law partnership breakdown.

Deferred Profit Sharing Plans   ITA 147(19) provides for the direct transfer of a lump sum amount from a DPSP to an RPP, an RRSP, or to a different DPSP. There are additional tax free transfers to the taxpayer's RRIF and to an RPP, RRSP, DPSP or RRIF of his or her spouse, former spouse, common-law partner or former common-law partner under a court order or written separation agreement in the event of a marriage or common-law partnership breakdown.

Retiring Allowances

13-185.   The full amount of any retiring allowance, which includes amounts received for loss of office or employment and unused sick leave, must be included in the taxpayer's income in the year received. However, a deduction is available under ITA 60(j.1) for certain amounts transferred to either an RPP or an RRSP. This, in effect, creates a tax free transfer of all, or part, of a retiring allowance into an RRSP, without affecting the available RRSP deduction room. The limit on this tax free transfer is as follows:

- $2,000 for each year, or part year, the taxpayer was employed by the employer prior to 1996. This includes non-continuous service with the same employer.

- An additional $1,500 for each year, or part year, the taxpayer was employed by the employer prior to 1989 for which the employer's contributions to an RPP or DPSP had not vested by the time the retiring allowance was paid.

13-186.   This transfer does not have to be directly from the employer to the RRSP. The deduction is available if the taxpayer receives the funds and deposits the eligible amount into his RRSP within 60 days of the end of the year it is received. However, if a direct transfer is used, the taxpayer will avoid having income tax withheld on the retiring allowance. It should also be noted that, for the individual to deduct the amount transferred to his RRSP, the trustee must issue the usual RRSP contribution receipt.

Example   Joan Marx retires at the end of 2007, receiving from her employer a retiring allowance of $150,000. She began working for this employer in 1982. The employer has never sponsored an RPP or a DPSP.

Analysis   The entire $150,000 must be included in Ms. Marx's 2007 Net Income For Tax Purposes. Provided she makes a $38,500 [($2,000)(14 Years) + ($1,500)(7 Years)] contribution to her RRSP, she will be able to deduct the $38,500 RRSP contribution, without affecting her RRSP deduction room.

Exercise Thirteen-12

Subject: Retiring Allowance

On December, 31, 2007, Mr. Giovanni Bartoli retires after 32 years of service with his present employer. In recognition of his outstanding service during these years, his employer pays him a retiring allowance of $100,000. His employer has never sponsored an RPP or a DPSP. What is the maximum tax free transfer that Mr. Bartoli can make to his RRSP as a result of receiving this retiring allowance?

End of Exercise. Solution available in Study Guide.

Retirement Compensation Arrangements

The Problem

13-187.   As we have seen throughout this Chapter, the rules related to maximum contributions by employers to RPPs and DPSPs are very specific. While these maximum limits are sufficient to provide a reasonable level of retirement income to the majority of employees, they fall short of this goal for highly paid senior executives. Such individuals are often accustomed to a lifestyle that cannot be sustained by the maximum amounts that can be produced by RPPs and DPSPs. A similar analysis can be made for owner/managers of successful private corporations.

13-188.   Given this situation, both public and private corporations use plans other than RPPs and DPSPs to provide benefits that are not limited by the rules applicable to the more conventional plans. In general, such arrangements can be classified as Retirement Compensation Arrangements (RCAs).

Arrangements Defined

13-189.   RCAs are defined in the *Income Tax Act* as follows:

> **ITA 248(1)   Retirement compensation arrangement** means a plan or arrangement under which contributions are made by an employer or former employer of a taxpayer, or by a person with whom the employer or former employer does not deal at arm's length, to another person or partnership in connection with benefits that are to be received or may be received or enjoyed by any person on, after, or in contemplation of any substantial change in the services rendered by the taxpayer, the retirement of the taxpayer or the loss of an office or employment of the taxpayer.

13-190.   The definition goes on to indicate that the term retirement compensation arrangement does not include RPPs, DPSPs, RRSPs, profit sharing plans, supplementary unemployment benefit plans, or plans established for the purpose of deferring the salary or wages of a professional athlete.

13-191.   Provided the arrangement involves a contractual obligation to ultimately make payments to the covered employees, a corporation's contributions to a RCA are fully deductible when made. However, as we shall see in the following material, both contributions and subsequent earnings on the invested contributions are subject to a special refundable tax.

Part XI.3 Refundable Tax

13-192.   Contributions made to a RCA are subject to a 50 percent refundable tax under ITA Part XI.3. In addition, earnings on the assets contained in the plan are subject to this same 50 percent refundable tax. The tax amounts are refunded at a 50 percent rate when distributions are made to the beneficiaries of the plan.

> **Example** During 2007, Borscan Ltd. contributes $50,000 to a plan established for several of its senior executives. The funds are used to purchase investments that earn interest of $4,500, and no payments are made to the executives during the year. On January 1, 2008, $20,000 is distributed to the beneficiaries of the plan.

> **Analysis** Borscan Ltd. would be able to deduct the $50,000 payment into the plan in determining its 2007 Net Income For Tax Purposes. However, the Company would be required to pay Part XI.3 tax of $27,250 [(50%)($50,000 + $4,500)]. In 2008, when the $20,000 distribution is made to the beneficiaries, the Company would receive a refund of $10,000 [(50%)($20,000)].

13-193.   In legislating this tax provision, it was clearly the intent of the government to discourage the use of RCAs. The 50 percent tax that is required at the corporate level is higher, in some provinces significantly so, than the rate that would be paid by an individual if the equivalent funds were simply distributed as salary.

13-194.   As a result, this means that more taxes will be paid initially, in situations where a RCA is used to compensate employees. Although the Part XI.3 tax is totally refundable, the corporation will not receive any refund of the tax until distributions from the RCA are made.

13-195.   Despite this analysis, the use of RCAs appears to be on the rise, particularly with respect to providing retirement benefits to the owner/managers of private corporations. The explanation for this phenomena probably lies in the not always rational preference that such owner/managers have for having taxation occur at the corporate, rather than the personal level.

Salary Deferral Arrangements

The Problem

13-196.   The fact that business income is on an accrual basis while employment income is on a cash basis has made it advantageous for employees to defer the receipt of salaries that can be accrued and deducted by employers. To the extent that these amounts are described as bonuses, ITA 78(4) has limited this deferral practice by deferring the deductibility of amounts that are not paid within 180 days of the employer's taxation year end. However, even if the employer cannot deduct the amounts until they are paid, it remains attractive for an employee to defer some part of their salary in order to postpone the payment of taxes.

The Solution

13-197.   The *Act* defines a salary deferral arrangement as follows:

> **ITA 248(1)   Salary deferral arrangement**   A plan or arrangement, whether funded or not, under which any person has a right in a taxation year to receive an amount after the year where it is reasonable to consider that one of the main purposes for the creation or existence of the right is to postpone tax payable under this Act by the taxpayer in respect of an amount that is, or is on account or in lieu of, salary or wages

of the taxpayer for services rendered by the taxpayer in the year or a preceding taxation year (including such a right that is subject to one or more conditions unless there is a substantial risk that any one of those conditions will not be satisfied).

13-198.   Converting this to everyday terms, a salary deferral arrangement involves an amount of salary that has been earned by an individual during the taxation year. However, the employee has made an arrangement with his employer to defer the actual receipt of the amount with the intent of postponing the payment of taxes.

13-199.   The definition of a salary deferral arrangement also contains a number of exclusions from its scope. These include RPPs, DPSPs, profit sharing plans, supplementary unemployment benefit plans, plans for providing education or training (sabbaticals), or plans established for the purpose of deferring the salary of a professional athlete.

13-200.   Employers can deduct amounts that fall within this definition, but employees cannot defer taxation on these amounts. They are required to include such amounts in their Net Income For Tax Purposes on an accrual basis, rather than on the cash basis that is the normal basis for employment income. In many cases, this will serve to remove any tax incentive from this type of arrangement and will discourage their continued use.

13-201.   Although the salary deferral rules do not apply to a bonus that is to be paid within three years following the end of the year in which the bonus was declared, if the bonus is not paid within 180 days of the employer's taxation year end, the employer cannot deduct the amount until it is paid.

13-202.   Despite these restrictions, certain salary deferral arrangements can be effective in that they do not fall within the ITA 248(1) definition. These include:

- self funded leave of absence arrangements (sabbaticals);
- bonus arrangements with payment deferred not more than three years, provided the employer accepts the loss of deductibility that occurs after 180 days;
- deferred compensation for professional athletes; and
- retiring allowances. (These escape the salary deferral arrangement rules and, within limits, can be transferred on a tax free basis to an RRSP as discussed in Paragraph 13-185.)

Individual Pension Plans (IPPs)

13-203.   In recent years it has become possible to establish a defined benefit plan for a single individual. Such plans are usually marketed in conjunction with insurance products and their establishment requires the use of an actuarial valuation for the specific individual covered by the plan.

13-204.   Such plans have grown in popularity in recent years, particularly for owner/managers of private companies. However, the actuarial concepts involved in these plans go beyond the scope of this text. As a consequence, we will not provide detailed coverage of these arrangements.

Key Terms Used In This Chapter

13-205.   The following is a list of the key terms used in this Chapter. These terms, and their meanings, are compiled in the Glossary Of Key Terms located before the index at the back of the book.

Annuitant	Pension Adjustment (PA)
Annuity	Pension Adjustment Reversal (PAR)
Beneficiary	Pension Income Tax Credit
Business Income	Phased Retirement
Canada Pension Plan (CPP)	Profit Sharing Plan
Capital Gain	Property Income
Deferred Income Plans	Refundable Part XI.3 Tax
Deferred Profit Sharing Plan	Registered Pension Plan (RPP)
Defined Benefit Plan	Registered Retirement Income Fund (RRIF)
Defined Contribution Plan	Registered Retirement Savings Plan (RRSP)
Earned Income (RRSP Limit)	Retirement Compensation Arrangement
Employment Income	Retiring Allowance
Fixed Term Annuity	Rollover
Home Buyer's Plan (HBP)	RRSP Deduction Limit
Income Attribution	RRSP Deduction Room
Income Splitting	RRSP Dollar Limit
Life Annuity	Salary Deferral Arrangement
Lifelong Learning Plan (LLP)	Spousal RRSP
Money Purchase Limit	Spouse
Money Purchase Plan	Tax Deferral
Net Income For Tax Purposes	Unused RRSP Deduction Room
Past Service Cost	Vested Benefit
Past Service Pension Adjustment (PSPA)	Vested Contribution

References

13-206.   For more detailed study of the material in this Chapter, we would refer you to the following:

ITA 144	Employees Profit Sharing Plans
ITA 146	Registered Retirement Savings Plans
ITA 146.01	Home Buyers' Plan
ITA 146.02	Lifelong Learning Plan
ITA 146.3	Registered Retirement Income Funds
ITA 147	Deferred Profit Sharing Plans
ITA 147.1	Definitions, Registration And Other Rules (Registered Pension Plans)
ITA 147.2	Pension Contributions Deductible – Employer Contributions
ITA 147.3	Transfer – Money Purchase To Money Purchase, RRSP Or RRIF
ITA 147.4	RPP Annuity Contract
IC 72-13R8	Employees' Pension Plans
IC 72-22R9	Registered Retirement Savings Plans
IC 77-1R4	Deferred Profit Sharing Plans
IC 78-18R6	Registered Retirement Income Funds
IT-124R6	Contributions To Registered Retirement Savings Plans
IT-167R6	Registered Pension Plans — Employees' Contributions
IT-280R	Employees Profit Sharing Plans - Payments Computed By Reference To Profits

References

IT-307R4	Spousal Or Common-Law Partner Registered Retirement Savings Plans
IT-320R3	Qualified Investments - Trusts Governed by Registered Retirement Savings Plans, Registered Education Savings Plans and Registered Retirement Income Funds
IT-337R4	Retiring Allowances
IT-379R	Employees Profit Sharing Plans — Allocations To Beneficiaries
IT-500R	Registered Retirement Savings Plans — Death of An Annuitant
IT-528	Transfer Of Funds Between Registered Plans
RC4112	Lifelong Learning Plan (Guide)
RC4135	Home Buyers' Plan (Obsolete Guide)
RC4177	Death Of An RRSP Annuitant (Pamphlet)
T4040	RRSPs And Other Registered Plans For Retirement (Guide)
T4041	Retirement Compensation Arrangements (Guide)

Problems For Self Study

(The solutions for these problems can be found in the separate Study Guide.)

Self Study Problem Thirteen - 1

During the calendar year 2006, Mr. Donald Barnes has the following income and loss data:

Gross Salary	$55,000
Taxable Benefits	1,150
Profit From Tax Advisory Service	4,150
Net Loss From Rental Property	(11,875)
Spousal Support Received From Former Wife	2,400
Taxable Dividends (Grossed Up Amount)	3,210
Interest On Government Bonds	3,640

In addition to the preceding information, Mr. Barnes paid union dues of $175, made Canada Pension Plan contributions of $1,911, and paid Employment Insurance premiums of $729.

At the end of 2006, Mr. Barnes had Unused RRSP Deduction Room of $700.

Required: For the calendar year 2007, determine Mr. Barnes' maximum allowable deduction for contributions to a Registered Retirement Savings Plan under the following assumptions:

A. During 2006, Mr. Barnes is not a member of a Registered Pension Plan or a Deferred Profit Sharing Plan.

B. Mr. Barnes is a member of a Registered Pension Plan, but not a member of a Deferred Profit Sharing Plan. His employer reports that his 2006 Pension Adjustment is $4,200.

Self Study Problem Thirteen - 2

Mr. Jonathan Beasley graduated from university in May, 2006. He immediately began work as an industrial designer, earning gross employment income of $24,000 during the calendar year ending December 31, 2006. Prior to 2006, Mr. Beasley had no Earned Income and had made no contributions to any type of retirement savings plan.

Up until May, 2006, Mr. Beasley had been supported by his spouse, Samantha. However, they were separated on June 1, 2006. On July 1, 2006, Samantha was convicted of spouse abuse and was ordered by the court to pay spousal support to Jonathan in the amount of $1,500 per month (a total of $9,000 was received during 2006). In addition, she was required to pay damages to Jonathan in the amount of $100,000. Jonathan deposited this entire amount in his savings account, resulting in 2006 interest income of $1,500.

Jonathan did not contribute to an RRSP during 2006. However, his employer sponsored an RPP to which Jonathan contributed $1,300 during 2006. This contribution was matched by a $1,300 contribution by Jonathan's employer, resulting in a 2006 Pension Adjustment of $2,600.

During 2006, Jonathan received royalties of $500 on a song written by his mother, eligible dividends from Canadian public corporations totaling $700, and a $5,000 gift from his parents. His parents also gave him a rental property in early 2006. This property experienced a net rental loss of $5,000 for the year ending December 31, 2006.

For 2006, Mr. Beasley's income places him in the lowest federal income tax bracket. Further, he anticipates that most of his 2007 income will also be taxed at this rate. However, he expects to receive a significant promotion at the end of 2007 and, as a consequence, he is likely to be in the maximum federal income tax bracket in 2008 and subsequent years.

Required:

A. Calculate Mr. Beasley's net employment income for 2006.

B. Determine Mr. Beasley's maximum deductible RRSP contribution for 2007.

C. As Mr. Beasley's personal financial consultant, what advice would you give him regarding his RRSP contribution and deduction for 2007?

Self Study Problem Thirteen - 3

Ms. Stratton has been the controller for a large publicly traded corporation for the last five years. The following information relates to the year ending December 31, 2007:

1. Ms. Stratton had a gross salary of $120,000, from which her employer made the following deductions:

Income taxes	$33,342
Registered Pension Plan contributions	2,390
Employment Insurance premiums	720
Canada Pension Plan contributions	1,990
Contributions to registered charities	1,600
Employee's portion of benefit plans (See Part 2 below)	1,436

2. It is the policy of the company to pay one-half of the cost of certain benefit plans. The following amounts were paid by the company for Ms. Stratton:

Group term life insurance	$ 96
Provincial health insurance plan	482
Dental plan	173
Major medical care (Private insurer)	396
Group income protection	289

3. Ms. Stratton's employer paid $2,300 for her annual membership in the Hot Rocks Curling Club. Ms. Stratton uses the club largely for business related entertaining.

4. Because of assistance she provided with a difficult tax matter, Ms. Stratton was rewarded with a one week trip to Bermuda by one of her employer's major clients. The fair market value of this trip was $4,500.

5. Ms. Stratton is required to travel to the offices of her employer's clients on a regular and continuing basis. As a result, her employer paid her a monthly travel allowance based on actual milage and expenses. These payments totaled $8,462 for the year.

6. During the year, Ms. Stratton paid professional dues of $225 and made contributions to a Registered Retirement Savings Plan in the amount of $15,000. At the end of 2006, Ms. Stratton's Unused RRSP Deduction Room was nil and she had no undeducted RRSP contributions. Her employer reported that she had a 2006 Pension Adjustment of $5,560. Her Earned Income for 2006 is equal to her 2007 Earned Income.

Required:

A. Calculate Ms. Stratton's net employment income for the year ending December 31, 2007 and indicate the reasons that you have not included items in your calculations. Ignore GST and PST implications.

B. Comment on the advisability of her $15,000 contribution to her Registered Retirement Savings Plan.

Self Study Problem Thirteen - 4

Mr. Colt, an employee of Jeffco Ltd., has agreed to accept early retirement in 2007, in return for a retiring allowance of $125,000. Mr. Colt began working for Jeffco Ltd. in 1977. He has been a member of the Company's Registered Pension Plan for only the last 10 years and his pension plan entitlement is vested.

At the beginning of 2006, Mr. Colt had Unused RRSP Deduction Room of $32,000. His 2006 Earned Income was $46,000 and his 2006 T4 included a Pension Adjustment of $8,000.

Jeffco will transfer $50,000 of the retiring allowance into a Registered Retirement Savings Plan (RRSP) in Mr. Colt's name, and the remainder into a spousal RRSP.

Required:

A. Determine the maximum RRSP contribution that Mr. Colt can deduct in 2007.

B. What are the tax implications of the above payments for Mr. Colt in 2007 ($50,000 payment to his RRSP and the remainder to a spousal RRSP)?

Self Study Problem Thirteen - 5

Mr. Jones is 62 years old and his wife, Mabel, is 58 years old. Mabel has no income of her own as she spends most of her waking hours maintaining her supernatural phenomena blog.

In January, 2007, he agreed to undertake a special project for the Martin Manufacturing Company, a company that produces large industrial use motors. The project is expected to take three years to complete. Mr. Jones was previously employed by the Martin Manufacturing Company for a period of 11 years. However, for the last 13 years, he has operated his own consulting organization in Vancouver.

Accepting the special project for the Martin Manufacturing Company will require that Mr. Jones discontinue his consulting operation and move to Hamilton, where the head offices of the Company are located. This does not concern Mr. Jones as he plans to retire in three years under any circumstances. It will, however, require that he sell his home in Vancouver and acquire a new residence in Hamilton. Mr. Jones anticipates that he will require a mortgage of approximately $100,000 in order to purchase a residence.

Mr. Jones and the Company have agreed to a salary of $100,000 per year for the three year period, with no additional benefits other than the required payments for Employment Insurance and the Canada Pension Plan. However, the Company has indicated that it is prepared to be flexible with respect to the type of compensation that is given to Mr. Jones, subject to the condition that the total cost of providing the compensation does not exceed $300,000 over the three year period.

The Martin Manufacturing Company is a Canadian controlled public company and is subject to a combined federal and provincial tax rate of 40 percent. It currently has a Registered Pension Plan for its employees. However, this plan was not in place during the earlier eleven year period in which Mr. Jones was employed by the Company.

Mr. Jones has other income and is concerned about the fact that his $100,000 per year salary will attract high levels of taxation. He is seeking your advice with respect to how his compensation arrangement with the Martin Manufacturing Company might be altered to provide some reduction or deferral of taxes. He indicates that, subsequent to retirement, his income is likely to be less than $60,000 per year.

Required: Advise Mr. Jones with respect to alternative forms of compensation that could reduce or defer taxes on the $300,000 that he is to receive from the Martin Manufacturing Company.

Assignment Problems

(The solutions for these problems are only available in
the solutions manual that has been provided to your instructor.)

Assignment Problem Thirteen - 1

During 2006, Mr. Robert Sparks had the following amounts of income and deductions under the various Subdivisions of Division B of the *Income Tax Act*:

Net employment income	$60,000
Income (Loss) from business	(16,000)
Income from property (Interest on term deposits)	6,000
Taxable capital gains	7,500
Allowable capital losses	(10,500)
Subdivision e deductions (Child care costs)	(3,000)

At the end of 2006, Mr. Sparks' Unused RRSP Deduction Room was nil and there were no undeducted contributions in his RRSP account.

Required:

A. Calculate his 2006 Net Income For Tax Purposes and any carry overs available to him.

B. Calculate the maximum deductible contribution Mr. Sparks can make to his RRSP for the 2007 taxation year for the following **independent** Cases:

Case 1   During 2006, he is a member of a money purchase Registered Pension Plan (RPP) in which he has contributed $1,000 and his employer has contributed $1,500.

Case 2   During 2006, he is a member of a Deferred Profit Sharing Plan (DPSP) in which his employer has contributed $1,500 per employee.

Case 3   During 2006, he is not a member of a RPP or DPSP. Assume that in addition to the preceding information, he also has net rental income of $140,000. He has contributed $1,500 to his wife's RRSP in August, 2007.

Assignment Problem Thirteen - 2

After being unemployed for two years, Donald Parker found employment with a large, publicly traded corporation in early 2006. His gross 2006 salary was $40,000 and, in addition, he earned commissions of $20,000. The corresponding figures for 2007 were $53,000 and $32,000. Deductible expenses related to the commission income were $3,000 in 2006 and $4,000 in 2007.

From his earnings, Donald's employer withheld the following:

	2007	2006
Federal And Provincial Income Taxes	$26,000	$18,000
CPP Contributions	1,990	1,911
EI Premiums	720	729
Disability Insurance Premiums	250	250
Registered Pension Plan (RPP) Contributions	1,500	1,400

The Registered Pension Plan is a money purchase plan. The employer makes RPP contributions and pays disability insurance premiums in amounts equal to those amounts withheld from employee earnings for these items. In addition, the employer provided Donald with a low interest loan. The taxable benefit on this loan was $2,750 in 2006 and $2,500 in 2007.

Other information for the years 2006 and 2007 is as follows:

	2007	**2006**
Net Rental Income (Loss)	$1,400	($2,500)
Taxable Spousal Support Received	2,600	2,400
Deductible Spousal Support Paid	(3,600)	(3,500)
Capital Gains (Losses)	(2,200)	1,750
Royalties*	875	920
Interest Income	273	496

*The royalties are on a song written by Donald's mother in 1962.

In 2004, just prior to losing his job, Donald contributed $7,500 to an RRSP. As he realized he would be in the minimum tax bracket until he found work, Donald did not deduct this RRSP contribution prior to 2007. He has Unused RRSP Deduction Room of $25,000 at the end of 2006.

In December, 2007, Donald wins $200,000 in a lottery. He would like to put as much of this amount as possible into his RRSP prior to the end of 2007.

Required:

A. Determine Donald's RRSP Deduction Limit for 2007.
B. Calculate the amount you would recommend that Donald contribute to his RRSP for 2007.

Assignment Problem Thirteen - 3

Mrs. Holly Goh is a graphic designer with two young children. Her current husband, a body builder who once held the Mr. Alberta title, takes care of the children and the household, and has no source of income. As this was also the situation with her former husband, she is required to pay him $200 per month in spousal support. In addition, she must pay $150 per month in child support for the child that is still in the custody of her former husband. These amounts were established in a December, 2005 court decree.

Mrs. Holly Goh has a self-administered RRSP. At the end of 2006, Mrs. Goh has Unused RRSP Deduction Room of $6,200. In addition, she has undeducted contributions in the plan of $5,500. As he has never earned any income, her current husband does not have an RRSP.

Mrs. Goh's 2006 salary is $98,000. Her only employment benefits are a dental plan that costs her employer $1,200 per year, $100,000 in group term life insurance for which her employer pays a premium of $850 per year, and a Registered Pension Plan (RPP). During 2006, her employer contributes $3,200 to this plan and Mrs. Goh contributes $2,500. The RPP is a money purchase (a.k.a., defined contribution) plan.

During 2006, Mrs. Goh has various types of income as follows:

- Interest on term deposits of $4,600.
- Taxable capital gains of $14,500.
- A loss on a rental property of $8,000.
- Royalties of $4,800 on a design process that was invented by her father. (The patent for the process was awarded to Mrs. Goh's father and was left to Mrs. Goh in her father's will.)

Early in 2007, Mrs. Goh has indicated to you, her tax advisor, that she would like to maximize her RRSP deduction and contribution for 2007.

Required:

A. Determine Mrs. Goh's RRSP Deduction Limit for 2007.

B. Determine the maximum RRSP contribution that can be made by Mrs. Goh during 2007 without attracting the penalty for excess contributions.

C. Briefly explain to Mrs. Goh the advantages of making her 2007 contributions to a spousal RRSP.

Assignment Problem Thirteen - 4

Mr. Frank Sabatini has been a salesman for a large, publicly traded Canadian corporation for the last fifteen years. During the year ending December 31, 2007, he earned a base salary of $58,000 and commissions of $74,000. In addition, the corporation reimbursed him for invoiced travel costs of $12,300. Included in these travel costs were $5,600 in expenditures for business meals and entertainment.

Other Information:

1. The corporation made a number of deductions from Mr. Sabatini's salary. The amounts were as follows:

Canada Pension Plan contributions	$ 1,990
Employment Insurance premiums	720
Income taxes	51,000
Registered Pension Plan contributions	3,500
Contributions to a registered charity	600
Parking fees - company garage	240
Employee share of life insurance premium	1,500
Employee share of sickness and accident insurance premium	550

2. Mr. Sabatini is covered by a group life insurance policy that pays $150,000 in the event of his death. The total annual premium on this policy is $3,000, with one-half of this amount paid by the employer.

3. Mr. Sabatini is covered by a group sickness and accident insurance plan that he joined on January 1, 2007. The premium on this plan is $100 per month, one-half of which is paid by Mr. Sabatini's employer. During 2007, Mr. Sabatini was hospitalized during all of June and received a benefit from the sickness and accident insurance plan in the amount of $4,500. Payment of the monthly premium was waived during the one month period of disability.

4. Mr. Sabatini's employer provides him with an automobile that was purchased in 2006 for $68,000. During 2007 Mr. Sabatini drives this automobile 99,000 kilometers, 92,000 of which are employment related. All operating costs, amounting to $16,200 for 2007, are paid by the employer. During the period of his hospitalization, the automobile was returned to the employer's garage and was not available to Mr. Sabatini. Mr. Sabatini pays the company $1,000 for his personal use of the automobile during 2007.

5. As a result of his extensive business travel, Mr. Sabatini has accumulated over 300,000 points in a frequent flier program. All of this travel has been paid for by Mr. Sabatini's employer. On December 30, 2007, he uses 150,000 of these points for two first class tickets to Cancun. Mr. Sabatini is accompanied on this one week trip by his secretary and, while there is some discussion of business matters, the trip is primarily for pleasure. At the same time, Mr. Sabatini uses another 30,000 of the points to provide his wife with an airline ticket to visit her mother in Leamington, Ontario. The normal cost of the Cancun tickets is $11,000, while the normal cost of the Leamington ticket is $600.

6. In 2004, Mr. Sabatini received options to purchase 1,000 shares of his employer's stock at a price of $12.50 per share. At the time the options were granted, the shares were trading at $10.00 per share. During December, 2007, Mr. Sabatini exercises these options. At the time of exercise, the stock is trading at $23.50 per share. Due to the Cancun trip and the resulting divorce proceedings, Mr. Sabatini neglects to file the election to defer the income inclusion related to the exercise of the stock options.

7. Mr. Sabatini's employer allows him to purchase merchandise at a discount of 30 percent off the normal retail prices. During 2007, Mr. Sabatini acquires such merchandise at a

cost (after the applicable discount) of $6,790.

8. In addition to reimbursing him for invoiced travel costs, Mr. Sabatini's employer pays a $5,000 annual fee for his membership in a local golf and country club. During 2007, Mr. Sabatini spends $6,800 entertaining clients at this club. None of these costs are reimbursed by Mr. Sabatini's employer.

9. Mr. Sabatini's employer contributes $2,400 to the company's Registered Pension Plan on his behalf and, in addition, contributes $2,000 in his name to the company's Deferred Profit Sharing Plan.

10. Mr. Sabatini has correctly calculated his 2006 Earned Income for RRSP purposes to be $111,000. At the end of 2006, Mr. Sabatini's Unused RRSP Deduction Room was nil and he had no undeducted RRSP contributions. His employer reports that his Pension Adjustment for 2006 was $6,800.

11. On May 18, 2007, Mr. Sabatini contributes $2,600 to his wife's RRSP. He contributed $10,000 to his own RRSP in February, 2007. This contribution was deducted in full on his 2006 tax return.

Required:

A. Determine Mr. Sabatini's minimum net employment income for the year ending December 31, 2007, and indicate the reasons that you have not included items in your calculations. Ignore GST implications.

B. Calculate Mr. Sabatini's maximum deductible RRSP contribution for the year ending December 31, 2007.

Assignment Problem Thirteen - 5

On December 1, 2006, Mary Jo Bush, on the advice of her hairdresser, deposited her inheritance of $54,000 in her RRSP. She had made no RRSP contributions prior to this. Because she had very little Taxable Income in 2006, she did not deduct any portion of her RRSP contribution in that year.

She has provided you with the following information:

- Her Unused RRSP Deduction Room is $10,000 at the end of 2006.
- She made an additional RRSP contribution of $5,000 on February 1, 2007.
- Mary Jo withdraws $35,000 from the RRSP on December 1, 2007.
- For 2007, the annual increase in Mary Jo's RRSP Deduction Limit is $9,000 (18 percent of her 2006 Earned Income of $50,000).

Required: Determine the ITA 204.1 penalty (excess RRSP contributions), if any, that would be assessed to Mary Jo for the year ending December 31, 2007.

Assignment Problem Thirteen - 6

Jerry White is married and his wife has not worked since she gave birth to triplets 8 years ago. Mr. White began working for Dynamics Inc. in 1984. The Company does not have a Registered Pension Plan or a Deferred Profit Sharing Plan.

Due to competitive pressures, Dynamics Inc. is attempting to reduce its overall work force. With this goal in mind, they have offered Mr. White a cash payment of $68,000 if he will immediately resign his position with the Company.

Required: Describe the tax consequences to Mr. White if he accepts this offer in 2007. Explain any alternatives that he might have in this regard and advise Mr. White as to an appropriate course of action.

Assignment Problem Thirteen - 7

In each of the following **independent** Cases, calculate the Pension Adjustment (PA) or Past Service Pension Adjustment (PSPA) that would be reported by the employer:

Case A   Mrs. Anderson's employer sponsors both a money purchase RPP and a DPSP. She is a member of both. During 2006, the employer contributes, on her behalf, $2,200 to the RPP and $1,500 to the DPSP. Mrs. Anderson contributes $1,800 to the RPP. Mrs. Anderson's employment earnings for 2006 are $80,000. Calculate her 2006 PA.

Case B   Mr. Block's employer sponsors a defined benefit RPP and, during 2006, contributes $2,900 on Mr. Block's behalf. Mr. Block also contributes $2,900 to the plan in 2006. The plan provides a benefit equal to 1.75 percent of pensionable earnings for each year of service. Mr. Block's pensionable earnings for 2006 are $45,000. Calculate his 2006 PA.

Case C   Miss Carr has worked for her current employer since 2005. In January, 2007, this employer institutes a defined benefit RPP, with benefits extended for all years of service prior to the inception of the plan. The benefit formula calls for a retirement benefit equal to 1.25 percent of pensionable earnings for each year of service. In both of the previous years, Miss Carr's pensionable earnings were $38,000. Calculate her 2007 PSPA.

Case D   Ms. Dexter has worked for her current employer since 2005. She has been a member of her employer's defined benefit RPP during all of this period. In January, 2007, the employer agrees to retroactively increase the benefit formula from 1.6 percent of pensionable earnings for each year of service, to 1.8 percent of pensionable earnings for each year of service. In both of the previous years, Ms. Dexter's pensionable earnings were $59,000. Calculate her 2007 PSPA.

Assignment Problem Thirteen - 8

Carla Goodman has been employed by Army Brake Products (ABP), a Canadian controlled private corporation, since 2005. The following information pertains to her income over the past two years:

	2007	2006
Salary Before Benefits	$100,000	$100,000
Employee Stock Option Benefit	8,000	5,000
Benefit On Interest Free Loan	6,000	5,000
Registered Pension Plan Contributions	(4,000)	(3,000)
Deductible Employment Expenses	(4,500)	(4,000)
Interest Income	1,800	1,600
Taxable Capital Gains	15,000	10,000
Business Income	34,000	35,000
Royalty Income	7,000	5,000
Rental Loss	(5,000)	(10,000)
Spousal Support Payments	(15,000)	(12,000)
Non-Eligible Dividends On ABP Stock	900	1,000
Totals	$144,200	$133,600

Ms. Goodman had no Earned Income for RRSP purposes prior to 2004. While in 2004 and 2005, she had sufficient Earned Income to enable her to deduct the maximum allowable RRSP contribution for 2005 and 2006, she made no RRSP contributions in either of these years.

Beginning in 2006, Ms. Goodman participates in ABP's employee money purchase Registered Pension Plan. ABP contributes twice the amount contributed by an employee to the plan. Her Pension Adjustment for 2006 is $9,000.

The royalty income listed above is 2 percent of the sales of the "Handy Shopper," a gadget Ms. Goodman invented three years ago. The business income listed above is earned from selling leather goods.

Required   Ignore all GST considerations.

A. Calculate Ms. Goodman's Earned Income for the purpose of determining her maximum 2007 RRSP contribution by listing the items and amounts that would be included in her Earned Income. List separately the items that are not included in the Earned Income calculation.

B. Based on the above information, calculate Ms. Goodman's maximum deductible RRSP contribution for 2007.

Assignment Cases

Assignment Case Thirteen - 1 (Comprehensive Case Covering Chapters 5 to 13)

Mr. Sali is 42 years of age and lives in Calgary, Alberta, a province that does not have a provincial sales tax. He has never been married and has no dependants.

During the year ending December 31, 2007, Mr. Ron Sali earned a gross salary of $76,000. In addition, he has commission income of $2,800. His employer withheld the following amounts from his salary:

Canada Pension Plan Contributions	$1,990
Employment Insurance Premiums	720
Registered Pension Plan Contributions	3,500
Parking Fees - Company Garage	480
Donations To United Way	800
Union Dues	360

Other Information:

1. Mr. Sali has accumulated a large number of Aeroplan frequent flyer miles as a result of travel that he has done for his employer. During 2007, he uses these miles to acquire two airline tickets. The first is a round trip to Miami which he uses for a short vacation. The economy fare to Miami is $625. The second ticket is a round trip to Edmonton to deal with one of his employer's clients. The economy fare to Edmonton is $575.

2. Mr. Sali is a member of his employer's money purchase RPP. His employer made a contribution on his behalf that was equal to the $3,500 contribution that was withheld from his salary.

3. Mr. Sali's employer provides him with a car that is leased for $642 per month. Mr. Sali drives the car a total of 38,000 kilometers during the year, 24,000 kilometers of which were for employment related purposes. The car was available to Mr. Sali for the entire year, with the exception of the one month that he was away from the business on sick leave. During this one month period, he left the keys to the car with his employer.

4. Mr. Sali is required to maintain an office in his home without reimbursement from his employer. Based on the portion of the house used for this office, the related costs are as follows:

Utilities And Maintenance	$ 600
Insurance	900
Property Taxes	1,200
Mortgage Interest	1,800

5. Mr. Sali is required by his employer to pay his own travel costs. During 2007, these amounted to $3,700. This amount does not include any costs incurred for meals or entertainment.

6. During 2007, in addition to his employment income, Mr. Sali had taxable capital gains from stock market trading of $6,200, a net rental loss of $3,900, and a self-employed business loss of $2,600. He also received eligible dividends of $2,500.

7. In 2006, his Net Income For Tax Purposes was $71,000. This was made up of net employment income of $77,000 (after the deduction of $3,200 in RPP contributions), grossed up dividend income of $8,000, a net rental loss of $9,000, and a business loss of $5,000.

8. At the end of 2006, Mr. Sali's Unused RRSP Deduction Room was $3,400 and he had no undeducted RRSP contributions. His employer reported that he had a 2006 Pension Adjustment of $6,400.

9. Due to his illness during his sick leave, Mr. Sali has medical expenses totalling $16,250 in 2007. His medical plan covers 80 percent of all of his medical expenses and he receives the reimbursement during 2007.

In addition to the $800 in United Way donations that were deducted by his employer, Mr. Sali makes contributions to other registered charities of $1,400.

Required: Ignore GST considerations.

A. Calculate Mr. Sali's maximum deductible RRSP contribution for 2007.

B. Assume that Mr. Sali contributes the amount calculated in Part A to his RRSP. Calculate Mr. Sali's 2007 minimum Net Income For Tax Purposes, his 2007 minimum Taxable Income, and his 2007 minimum federal Tax Payable before consideration of any amounts that would have been withheld or paid in instalments.

Assignment Case Thirteen - 2 *(Comprehensive Case Covering Chapters 5 to 13)*

Ms. Kerri Sosteric is 33 years of age. She is divorced from her former husband but has custody of the two children from that marriage. Her son Barry is 5 years old and her daughter Kim is 8 years old. During 2007, she receives $1,200 in universal child care benefit payments.

The terms of Kerri's 2005 divorce decree require that her former husband pay $1,500 per month in child support and an additional $500 per month in spousal support. During 2006 and 2007, all amounts were paid in a timely fashion.

Because she works on a full time basis, Kerri sends her children to a commercially operated day care centre. During 2007, the cost of this care was $8,600. The day care centre provides receipts for this amount.

During 2007, medical expenses for Kerri and her family are as follows:

Kerri	$ 560
Barry	240
Kim	1,820
Total	**$2,620**

Kerri is employed by a large public company. Employment related information for the years 2006 and 2007 is as follows:

	2006	**2007**
Gross Salary	$47,000	$53,000
Commissions	6,200	7,800
Canada Pension Plan Contributions	1,911	1,990
Employment Insurance Premiums	729	720
RPP Contributions (Note)	1,800	1,950

> **Note** Kerri's employer makes a matching contribution to the money purchase RPP in each of the two years.

Other than the RPP contributions, Kerri's employer provides no other benefits. In addition, she is required to maintain an office in her home with no reimbursement provided. Kerri's home had cost $420,000 on January 1, 2006, with $120,000 of this amount being the estimated value of the land. For 2006 and 2007, the total costs of owning and operating this home are as follows:

	2006	**2007**
Utilities And Maintenance	$ 1,850	$ 2,040
Insurance	625	715
Property Taxes	4,200	4,400
Mortgage Interest	12,000	11,800

Kerri's home office occupies 15 percent of the total floor space in the home.

In January 1, 2006, Kerri acquires a duplex that she uses as a rental property. The cost of the property is $340,000, with $80,000 of this amount being the estimated value for the land. For the two years 2006 and 2007 rents and expenses other than CCA are as follows:

	2006	**2007**
Rents	$ 8,400	$13,800
Expenses Other Than CCA	10,300	11,100

In January, 2006, Kerri acquired 5,000 shares of her employer's stock at its fair market value of $12.00 per share. During 2006, these shares paid eligible dividends of $0.75 per share. During 2007, she receives eligible dividends of $0.60 per share. During December, 2007, Kerri sells all of her shares at their fair market value of $14.75 per share.

At the end of 2006, Kerri has unused RRSP deduction room of $6,200. In addition, her plan contains $5,800 in undeducted contributions. Based on the undeducted contributions in the plan, along with any additional contributions required to meet this goal, Kerri would like to deduct an amount in 2007 that would reduce her unused RRSP deduction room to nil at the end of the year.

Required: Calculate Ms. Sosteric's 2007 minimum Net Income For Tax Purposes, her 2007 minimum Taxable Income, and her 2007 minimum federal Tax Payable before consideration of any amounts that would have been withheld or paid in instalments. Include in your solution the additional contribution she must make to her RRSP. Ignore GST and PST considerations.

Assignment Case Thirteen - 3 (Progressive Running Case - Chapter 13 Version Using ProFile T1 Software For 2006 Tax Returns)

This Progressive Running Case requires the use of the ProFile tax software program. It was introduced in Chapter 6 and is continued in Chapters 8 through 14. Each version must be completed in sequence. While it is not repeated in this version of the Case, all of the information in each of the previous versions (e.g., Mary's T4 content) is applicable to this version of the Case.

If you have not prepared a tax file incorporating the previous versions, please do so before continuing with this version.

On January 10, 2007, you receive a phone call from Mary Walford. She has just received a T4RSP in the mail which shows that Seymour had withdrawn virtually all the funds from his RRSP without her knowledge. She knows this could substantially increase Seymour's tax liability and is very concerned. At the moment, she cannot find any trace of the funds that were withdrawn.

She faxes you the following T4RSP as well as information related to her and Seymour's RRSP limits.

T4 RSP - Seymour	Box	Amount
Issuer of receipt - Royal Bank		
Withdrawal payments	22	126,000
Income tax deducted	30	12,600

RRSP information - Mary	(Y/M/D)	Amount
Issuer of receipt - TD Asset Management	2006-12-10	5,400
Issuer of receipt - TD Asset Management	2007-01-05	16,800
Contributions made prior to 2007/03/02 and not deducted		Nil
Unused deduction room at the end of 2005		14,091
Earned income for 2005		125,000

RRSP information - Seymour	(Y/M/D)	Amount
Issuer of receipt - TD Asset Management		Maximum ?
Contributions made prior to 2007/03/02 and not deducted		Nil
Unused deduction room at the end of 2005		19,762
Earned income for 2005		45,000

Her stockbroker has told her that a spousal contribution can be made to her RRSP to utilize Seymour's unused contribution room. She would like you to calculate the maximum RRSP contribution that can be deducted on Seymour's return. Mary will contribute that amount to her RRSP and have the RRSP receipt issued with Seymour's name as the contributor.

As Mary expects to receive a substantial life insurance benefit shortly, she hopes to have funds to contribute to her RRSP in her own name before the end of February, 2007.

Required:

A. Open the file that you created for the Chapter 12 version of the Case and save a copy under a different name. This will enable you to check the changes between different versions of the Case.

B. Calculate Seymour's maximum RRSP deduction for 2006 and assume that Mary contributes the amount you have calculated. Print the RRSP form for Seymour.

C. Revise Seymour's 2006 final income tax return to incorporate the T4RSP and RRSP contribution, but do not print the return.

D. Complete and print Mary's RRSP form. Assume she does not contribute further to her RRSP in her name in 2006. Print the RRSPLimit form for Mary which calculates her maximum RRSP deduction for 2007.

E. What advice would you give Mary regarding her RRSP contributions?

F. Access and print Mary's summary (Summary on the Form Explorer, not the T1 Summary). This form is a two column summary of the couple's tax information. By opening this form from Mary's return, the order of the columns is the same as the one in the previous chapter. For both returns, list the changes on this Summary form from the previous version of this Case. Exclude totals calculated by the program, but include the final Balance Owing (Refund) amount.

CHAPTER 14

Taxable Income And Tax Payable For Individuals Revisited

Introduction

The Problem

14-1.   The subjects of Taxable Income for individuals and Tax Payable for individuals were introduced in Chapter 6. This earlier Chapter provided a general overview of how we arrive at the Taxable Income figure and, in addition, covered in detail the majority of credits that can be applied in the determination of Tax Payable. We chose to cover this material in Chapter 6 in order to enhance your understanding of some of the material dealing with specific types of income in Chapters 7 through 11.

14-2.   The problem with this early coverage of these subjects is that there are some concepts and procedures involved in determining Taxable Income and Tax Payable for individuals that cannot be explained without some understanding of the additional components of Net Income For Tax Purposes that are covered in subsequent chapters.

14-3.   For example, it is not possible to meaningfully discuss the deduction of loss carry overs in calculating Taxable Income without knowledge of the difference between capital and non-capital losses, a subject that is not covered until Chapter 10. A similar problem arises in dealing with the transfer of dividend tax credits to a spouse. This idea is not comprehensible to an individual who does not have an understanding of the dividend gross up and tax credit procedures which are not introduced until Chapter 9.

Our Solution

14-4.   Our solution to this problem is this second chapter on Taxable Income and Tax Payable for individuals. At this point, we have provided comprehensive coverage of all of the components of Net Income For Tax Purposes. Chapters 7 and 8 dealt with CCA and business income, Chapter 9 provided coverage of property income, and Chapter 10 dealt with taxable capital gains and allowable capital losses. This coverage of income components concluded with Chapter 11's coverage of miscellaneous sources of, and deductions from, Net Income For Tax Purposes.

14-5.   With this additional background, we can now finish our coverage of Taxable Income and Tax Payable for individuals. With respect to Taxable Income, we will provide complete coverage of both loss carry overs and the lifetime capital gains deduction. In addition, we will be able to deal with the additional credits required in the determination of Tax Payable, as well as the additional procedures associated with the determination of alternative minimum tax.

Taxable Income Overview

14-6.   As was discussed in Chapter 6, Taxable Income is calculated by deducting certain specified items from Net Income For Tax Purposes. These deductions, which are found in Division C of the *Income Tax Act*, are as follows:

ITA 110(1)(d), (d.01), and (d.1) - Employee Stock Options   Our basic coverage of stock options and stock option deductions was included in Chapter 5. Additional coverage of dispositions of shares acquired through stock options was included in Chapter 10, while coverage of such shares held at the time of emigration was dealt with in Chapter 12. Gifts of stock option shares are covered in this Chapter's coverage of charitable donations. A very technical issue, revoked deferral elections, is covered in an Appendix to this chapter.

ITA 110(1)(f) - Deductions For Payments   This deduction is designed to ensure that certain amounts are not subject to tax. Included here are such amounts as social assistance received, workers' compensation received (covered in Chapter 6), and amounts exempted from Canadian tax by tax treaty (covered in Chapter 22). Also included here are deductions for employment income received from certain prescribed international organizations and employment income earned by a member of the Canadian forces serving in certain prescribed missions.

ITA 110(1)(j) - Home Relocation Loan   This deduction, which is available to employees who receive a loan from their employer to assist with moving, was covered in Chapter 6.

ITA 110.2 - Lump-Sum Payments   This Section provides a deduction for certain lump-sum payments (e.g., an amount received as a court-ordered termination benefit and included in employment income). It provides the basis for taxing this amount as though it was received over several periods (i.e., income averaging). Limited coverage of this provision can be found in the next section of this Chapter.

ITA 110.6 - Lifetime Capital Gains Deduction   The provisions related to this deduction are very complex and require a fairly complete understanding of capital gains. As a consequence, it was not covered in Chapter 6 and will be given coverage in this Chapter.

ITA 110.7 - Residing In Prescribed Zone (Northern Residents Deductions)   These deductions, which are limited to individuals living in prescribed regions of northern Canada, were covered in Chapter 6.

ITA 111 - Losses Deductible   This is a group of deductions that is available for carrying over various types of losses from preceding or subsequent taxation years. The application of these provisions can be complex and requires a fairly complete understanding of business income, property income, and capital gains. As a consequence, this group of deductions was not covered in Chapter 6 and will be covered in detail in this Chapter.

14-7.   As noted in the preceding list, the material in this Chapter will complete our coverage of Taxable Income for individuals. Of the Taxable Income deductions available to individuals, only amounts exempted by treaty under ITA 110(1)(f) and loss carry overs under ITA 111 are available to corporations. There are, however, additional deductions available to corporate taxpayers for charitable contributions and dividends received from other taxable Canadian corporations. These additional deductions are covered in Chapter 15.

Lump-Sum Payments

The Problem

14-8.   For individuals, such income receipts as wages and salaries, pension income, and spousal support are taxed on a cash basis. As a consequence, retroactive lump-sum payments are taxable when they are received, even though a significant portion of the amount may relate to prior years.

14-9.   There is an advantage in that there has been some deferral of the tax on these amounts. However, because of the presence of progressive rates in the Canadian tax system, the tax liability on such lump-sum payments may be higher than would have been the case had the payments been received and taxed in different years. This would be a particularly severe problem in situations where a very large taxable amount is involved. Because of this problem, there is tax relief available for certain lump-sum payments.

Qualifying Amounts

14-10.   The relief can be applied to payments that are referred to as "qualifying amounts". These are given a technical definition in ITA 110.2(1). In the Explanatory Notes that accompany the legislation, the following more general description is found:

> A qualifying amount is the principal portion of certain amounts included in income. Those amounts are: spousal or child support amounts, superannuation or pension benefits otherwise payable on a periodic basis, employment insurance benefits and benefits paid under wage loss replacement plans. Also included is the income received from an office or employment (or because of a termination of an office or employment) under the terms of a court order or judgment, an arbitration award or in settlement of a lawsuit.

Relief Mechanism

14-11.   ITA 110.2(2) provides a deduction for the "specified portion" of a "qualifying amount" that was received by an individual during a particular taxation year. The "specified portion" is the fraction of the qualifying amount that relates to an "eligible taxation year". An "eligible taxation year" is any prior year after 1977 in which the individual was a resident of Canada throughout the year and during which the individual did not become bankrupt. No deduction is available if the qualifying amount is less than $3,000. In somewhat simplified terms, this means that an individual can remove the types of payments described as qualifying amounts from the current year's income, to the extent that they relate to prior years.

14-12.   ITA 120.31 describes an alternative tax that will be payable on the amounts that are deducted under ITA 110.2(2). This tax is the total of the additional taxes that would have been triggered for each relevant preceding year, if the portion of the qualifying amount that relates to that preceding year was added to the individual's Taxable Income for that year. In addition to the tax for those years, a notional amount of interest is added to reflect the fact that the tax was not paid in the relevant years. This interest is accrued from May 1 of the year following the relevant preceding year, through the end of the year prior to the receipt of the lump-sum payment.

14-13.   The goal of these procedures is to spread the lump-sum payment over earlier years, thereby eliminating the influence of progressive rates on the total tax bill. For example, if a 2007 court settlement reflected a wage adjustment for the years 2002 through 2006, the recipient would pay the amount of taxes that would have been due if he had received the amounts in those earlier years. In many cases this will provide significant tax relief. However, if the individual is in the maximum tax bracket for all years under consideration, using this approach could result in higher taxes because of the addition of the notional amount of interest. In such cases, the taxpayer would not make the deduction under ITA 110.2(2).

Treatment Of Losses

Carry Over Provisions

General Rules

14-14. In earlier Chapters there have been references to a taxpayer's ability to carry back or carry forward losses. Before covering the carry over rules related to specific types of losses, we will consider the general procedures associated with these carry overs.

14-15. If a taxpayer experiences a loss in the current year with respect to a particular type of income, it must be used, to the extent possible, to offset other types of income in the current year. The taxpayer does not have any real discretion in this matter. If he is in a position to apply a loss to other types of income that are available in the loss year and he chooses not to do so, the loss cannot be carried over to either earlier or later years.

14-16. There are two basic reasons why it may not be possible to use a loss in the year in which it is incurred:

- The taxpayer may not have sufficient other sources of income to absorb the loss (e.g., a business loss that is greater than all other sources of income).
- The taxpayer may not have sufficient income of the right type to absorb the loss (e.g., an allowable capital loss that is greater than taxable capital gains).

14-17. If either of these situations arise in the current year, the taxpayer can either carry the loss back to apply against Taxable Income in previous years or, alternatively, carry the loss forward to apply against Taxable Income in future years. Unlike the situation with current year losses, provided that the use is within the specified carry back and carry forward periods, the decision as to when a loss carry over should be used is at the discretion of the taxpayer.

Carry Backs

14-18. With one exception, all types of current year losses can be applied against income in the three preceding taxation years. The one exception is limited partnership losses which cannot be carried back (see Chapter 20). When the loss is applied, the carry back will result in a refund of some or all of the taxes that were paid in the carry back year.

14-19. Note that, with several types of losses, the carry back amount can only be applied against income of the same type. More specifically:

- Net capital losses can only be applied against net taxable capital gains realized in the carry back year.
- Listed personal property losses can only be applied against listed personal property gains realized in the carry back year.
- Restricted farm losses (see Chapter 8) can only be applied against farm income realized in the carry back year.

Carry Forwards

14-20. Because a refund is available, most taxpayers will carry back losses to the extent possible. However, if there is not sufficient income of the appropriate type in any of the three preceding years, any unused portion of the loss becomes part of a loss carry forward balance.

14-21. Unlike the situation with carry backs, there is some variation in the carry forward period for different types of losses. In addition, recent budgets have extended the carry forward period for both non-capital losses and farm losses. The current rules are as follows:

Non-Capital Losses And Farm Losses For non-capital and farm losses in taxation years that end after 2005, the carry forward period is 20 years. Non-capital and regular farm losses can be applied against any type of income in the carry forward year. If the farm loss is restricted, it can only be applied against farm income in the carry forward year.

Net Capital Losses Net capital losses can be carried forward indefinitely, limited only by the life of the taxpayer. However, they can only be applied against taxable capital gains that arise in the carry forward year. As noted in Chapter 12, there is an exception for deceased taxpayers who can generally deduct any unused net capital losses remaining in year immediately preceding death and in the year of death.

Listed Personal Property Losses Listed personal property losses can be carried forward for 7 years. As noted previously, they can only be deducted against listed personal property gains that arise in the carry forward year.

Segregation By Type

14-22. We have noted that, with both loss carry back and loss carry forwards, some types of losses can only be applied against income of the same type. Because of this requirement, loss carry forward balances must be segregated by type. More specifically, the separate balances that must be tracked are:

- Non-Capital Losses (employment, business, and property losses)
- Net Capital Losses
- Allowable Business Investment Losses (defined in Paragraph 14-53)
- Regular Farm Losses
- Restricted Farm Losses

Applying The Deduction

14-23. With the exception of listed personal property losses (see coverage beginning in Paragraph 14-31), loss carry overs are deducted from total Net Income For Tax Purposes, thereby reducing Taxable Income in the carry over year.

14-24. In the case of a carry back, there is a reduction of Tax Payable in the carry back year. Provided the taxes for that year have been paid, the result will be a refund. As you would expect, the refund will be based on the tax rates applicable to the carry back year.

14-25. With respect to carry forwards, they serve to reduce Tax Payable in the carry forward year. As was the case with carry backs, the loss carry forward benefit will accrue at the tax rates applicable to the carry forward year.

Loss Carry Overs And Tax Credits

14-26. You will recall from Chapter 6 that most of the credits against Tax Payable that are available to individuals are not refundable. Further, most of them cannot be carried over to be used in subsequent taxation years. This means that, in the absence of sufficient Tax Payable to absorb these credits, they will be permanently lost.

14-27. These facts relate to loss carry overs in that, given the inability to use most tax credits in the absence of Tax Payable or to carry them over to subsequent periods, it is generally not advisable to use loss carry overs to reduce Taxable Income to nil.

> **Example** In 2006, Jan Teason's only income was a net rental loss of $30,000. She had no reported income in the three preceding years. However, in 2007, she has employment income of $25,000.
>
> **Analysis** If she wished to do so, Ms. Teason could reduce her 2007 Taxable Income to nil by applying $25,000 of the 2006 non-capital loss carry forward. However, if she used this approach she would lose at least her basic personal tax credit of $1,384, as well as any other available credits that could not be carried over. Given this, it would appear that the amount of the loss carry forward deducted should be limited to an amount that would leave sufficient Taxable Income and Tax Payable to absorb her 2007 tax credits.

14-28. What this example illustrates is that, in practical situations, loss carry overs should not be used to reduce Taxable Income to nil. In fact, most tax preparation software will automatically limit loss carry overs to prevent this from happening. However, trying to build this consideration into the examples and problems included in the text can have the effect of significantly complicating material that is already very difficult to understand. As a result, unless specified otherwise, we will generally ignore this issue in our text examples and problems.

14-29.   For example, when a problem asks you to minimize loss carry overs at the end of a particular year, you will not be expected to give consideration to whether this is an optimal solution in terms of using tax credits. While this approach is not consistent with real world tax planning considerations, we feel that it can be justified in terms of aiding your understanding of this difficult material on loss carry overs.

Personal Use Property Losses

14-30.   As covered in the discussion of personal use property in Chapter 10, taxable capital gains on personal use property, determined on the assumption that both the proceeds of disposition and the adjusted cost base are at least $1,000, are included in the calculation of Net Income For Tax Purposes. However, losses on such property, unless the property qualifies as "listed personal property" as described in the following material, are never deductible.

Listed Personal Property Losses

General Rules

14-31.   As defined in ITA 54, listed personal property includes:

- a print, etching, drawing, painting, sculpture, or other similar work of art;
- jewelry;
- a rare folio, rare manuscript, or rare book;
- a stamp; or
- a coin.

14-32.   As was the case with personal use property, taxable capital gains on listed personal property are included in Net Income For Tax Purposes, and are also calculated on the assumption that both the proceeds of disposition and the adjusted cost base are at least $1,000 (as noted in Chapter 10, this rule may not be applicable when a charitable donation is involved).

14-33.   The difference here is that allowable capital losses on listed personal property can be deducted. However, they can only be deducted against taxable capital gains on listed personal property. They cannot be used to reduce taxes on any other type of income, including taxable capital gains on other types of property.

Carry Over Provisions

14-34.   If a loss on listed personal property cannot be used in the current year, it can be carried back three years or forward for seven years. (Unlike other losses, the carry forward period of listed personal property losses has not been extended.) It can only be used in the carry over year to the extent that there are gains on listed personal property in that year.

14-35.   Unlike other loss carry overs, listed personal losses are not deducted from Net Income For Tax Purposes under ITA 111. Under ITA 41(2), the net gain on listed personal property is defined as the gains for the current year, reduced by the carry over amounts from the seven preceding years, or the three subsequent years. If this amount is positive, it is added in the calculation of Net Income For Tax Purposes under ITA 3(b). While the process is somewhat different, the result is the same reduction in Taxable Income that would result from the carry over of some other type of loss.

Exercise Fourteen-1

Subject: Listed Personal Property Losses

During 2006, Mr. Ronald Smothers was unemployed and had no income of any kind. In order to survive, he sold a painting on December 1, 2006 for $89,000. This painting had been left to Mr. Smothers by his mother and, at the time of her death, it had a fair market value of $100,000. During 2007, Mr. Smothers finds a job and has employment income of $62,000. In addition, during June he sells a second painting for $5,000. He had purchased this painting several years ago for $1,000. Determine Mr. Smothers' Net Income For Tax Purposes and Taxable Income for 2007. Indicate the amount and type of any losses available for carry forward at the end of the year. Assume the December 1, 2006 sale had been of publicly traded shares instead of a painting. How would this change your solution?

End of Exercise.   Solution available in Study Guide.

Non-Capital Losses

General Rules

14-36.   In terms of a simple dictionary meaning, the term non-capital would mean any loss other than a loss on the disposition of a capital asset. In fact, in many situations, this non-technical approach would provide the correct result. However, ITA 111(8) contains a very technical definition that must be used in more complex situations in order to ensure that we arrive at the appropriate answer. In simplified form, this definition is as follows:

ITA 111(8) The non-capital loss of a taxpayer for a taxation year means the amount determined by the formula:

$$A - D, \text{ where}$$

A   is the amount determined by the formula:

$$E - F, \text{ where}$$

E   is the total of all amounts each of which is the taxpayer's loss for the year from an office, employment, business or property, the taxpayer's allowable business investment loss for the year, and net capital loss carry overs deducted in the calculation of Taxable Income for the year (this amount cannot exceed the taxable capital gains for the year).

F   is the amount of income determined under ITA 3(c). [Sum of ITA 3(a) non-capital positive sources and ITA 3(b) net taxable capital gains, less Division B, Subdivision e deductions.]

D   is the taxpayer's farm loss for the year.

14-37.   Note that this definition excludes both current year capital losses and farm losses. These two types of losses are subject to different rules and, as a consequence, their balances must be tracked separately. The inclusion of net capital losses in this definition will be explained in our later discussion of net capital losses.

14-38.   As can be seen in the definition, non-capital losses can result from the calculation of income from employment, income from a business, or income from property. However, given the limited number of deductions from employment income, it is very unlikely that they will occur in that context. Normally, non-capital losses would result from the operation of a business or the ownership of property. For example, a non-capital loss on a rental property could occur when expenses associated with the property exceed the rental revenues.

Exercise Fourteen-2

Subject: Non-Capital Losses

During 2007, Janice McMann has net employment income of $35,000, as well as a taxable capital gain of $13,000. In addition, she has a business loss of $58,000 and a farm loss of $2,200. On January 1, 2007, her non-capital loss balance was nil. Determine her non-capital loss balance on December 31, 2007.

End of Exercise.   Solution available in Study Guide.

Carry Over Provisions

14-39.   Non-capital losses for the current year are deducted under ITA 3(d) in the calculation of Net Income For Tax Purposes and must be used to offset all other types of income, including net taxable capital gains. If current year non-capital losses remain after Net Income For Tax Purposes has been reduced to nil, these amounts can be carried over to other years.

14-40.   As we have noted, such losses may be carried back three years and applied against any type of income in those years. If there is not sufficient income in those years to absorb the full amount of these non-capital losses, any remaining balance can be carried forward for a period of 20 years. Whether the amounts are carried back or forward, they will be a deduction in the computation of Taxable Income under ITA 111(1)(a).

14-41.   Non-capital losses are defined in ITA 111(8) in such a fashion that a carry over is only available after the current year's income is reduced to nil. Stated alternatively, the current year's non-capital losses become available for carry over only after they have been applied to the maximum extent possible against the current year's income. If they are available for carry over, they can be applied, at the taxpayer's discretion, to any of the eligible carry over years. However, ITA 111(3) indicates that a non-capital loss carry over for a particular year cannot be used until the available non-capital loss carry overs from all preceding years have been exhausted.

Net Capital Losses

General Rules

14-42.   The term "net capital loss" is defined in ITA 111(8) as the excess of allowable capital losses over taxable capital gains for the current taxation year. Note carefully that, as the term is used in the *Act*, "net capital loss" refers to the deductible portion of capital losses, not to the 100 percent amounts. When these annual amounts are carried forward, the resulting balance is normally referred to as the "net capital loss balance".

Changing Inclusion Rates

14-43.   As covered in Chapter 10, the capital gains inclusion rate and the capital loss deduction rate for individuals has changed over the years as follows:

1972 to 1987	1/2
1988 and 1989	2/3
1990 to February 27, 2000	3/4
After February 27, 2000 and before October 18, 2000	2/3
After October 17, 2000	1/2

Carry Over Provisions

14-44.   While a net capital loss for the current year cannot be deducted in the calculation of the current year's Net Income For Tax Purposes, this amount is available for carry over to other years. Such losses may be carried back three years and forward to any subsequent year.

14-45.   When they are carried forward or back, they will be deducted under ITA 111(1)(b) in the calculation of Taxable Income. However, ITA 111(1.1) restricts the deduction of such carry over amounts to the amount included in Net Income For Tax Purposes under ITA 3(b) (net taxable capital gains). Expressed in less technical terms, you can only deduct a net capital loss carry over to the extent that you have net taxable capital gains in the carry over period.

14-46.   When net capital losses are carried over, in general they must be deducted at the rate that is applicable to the carry over year.

Example   If an individual experienced a $20,000 capital loss in 1990, it would be carried forward as a net capital loss of $15,000 [(3/4)($20,000)]. If this $15,000 net capital loss was carried forward to 2007, when the capital loss inclusion rate is one-half, it would have to be adjusted to $10,000 [(1/2)($20,000)] to reflect the applicable rate for the carry forward year.

Figure 14 - 1
Capital Gain And Loss Inclusion Rates

Example One An individual has a capital loss in 1990 of $60 (allowable amount $45) and a capital gain in 2007 of $120 (taxable amount $60). The 1990 net capital loss is carried forward and deducted in 2007. The deduction for 2007 is calculated as follows:

$$[\$45]\left[\frac{\frac{1}{2}}{\frac{3}{4}}\right] = \$30$$

Example Two An individual has a capital loss in 1989 of $90 (allowable amount $60) and a capital gain in 2007 of $120 (taxable amount $60). The 1989 net capital loss is carried forward and deducted in 2007. The deduction for 2007 is calculated as follows:

$$[\$60]\left[\frac{\frac{1}{2}}{\frac{2}{3}}\right] = \$45$$

Required Adjustment The required adjustment will multiply the net capital loss that is being claimed by the current inclusion rate of one-half, divided by the inclusion rate in the year in which the loss was realized. The two examples in Figure 14-1 illustrate this process.

14-47. The year 2000 presents a problem with capital loss carry overs in that, as documented in Paragraph 14-43, three different capital gains inclusion rates were used in that year. This is no longer a problem with carry backs because, as of 2004, it is no longer possible to carry back a capital loss to the year 2000. However, because capital losses have an unlimited carry forward period, the multiple rates applicable to the year 2000 will continue to be a problem for the foreseeable future.

Conversion Of A Net Capital Loss Carry Over To A Non-Capital Loss Carry Over

14-48. A problem can arise when a taxpayer has a net capital loss carry over, taxable capital gains in the current year, and a non-capital loss that is large enough to reduce his Net Income For Tax Purposes to nil. As allowable capital losses can only be deducted against taxable capital gains, the taxpayer usually prefers to use such carry overs whenever taxable capital gains are available. A simple example will illustrate this problem.

Example For 2007, Mr. Waring has property income of $25,000, taxable capital gains of $45,000 [(1/2)($90,000)], and a business loss of $150,000. He also has a net capital loss carry forward from 2006 of $60,000 [(1/2)($120,000)]. He does not anticipate having any further taxable capital gains in the foreseeable future.

14-49. The usual ITA 3 calculation of Net Income For Tax Purposes would be as follows:

ITA 3(a) Non-Capital Positive Sources	$ 25,000
ITA 3(b) Net Taxable Capital Gains	45,000
ITA 3(c) Sum Of ITA 3(a) And 3(b)	$ 70,000
ITA 3(d) Non-Capital Losses	(150,000)
Net Income For Tax Purposes	$ Nil

14-50. The business loss reduced Net Income For Tax Purposes to nil and this is a problem for Mr. Waring in that he does not anticipate having further taxable capital gains in the near future. Given this, it would appear that he has lost the ability to use this year's net taxable capital gains to absorb the net capital loss carry forward.

14-51. Fortunately, this is not the case. You will recall that, in the definition of non-capital loss in Paragraph 14-36, the taxpayer can add to the E component of the definition, any net capital loss carry overs deducted in the current year. This means that, if we assume that Mr. Waring chooses to deduct the maximum amount of his net capital loss carry forward in 2007, the non-capital loss carry over for 2007 would be as follows:

Business Loss For Year	$150,000
Net Capital Loss Carry Forward Deducted	
(Limited To Taxable Capital Gains)	45,000
Total For E	$195,000
F = Income Under ITA 3(c) ($25,000 + $45,000)	(70,000)
Non-Capital Loss Available For Carry Over	$125,000

14-52.   There are three points that should be made with respect to this analysis:

- The amount of the net capital loss carry forward deducted is limited to the $45,000 in net taxable capital gains that were realized during the year. As a result, he has utilized $45,000 of the $60,000 net capital loss carry forward from 2006.

- The deduction of the net capital loss carry over is discretionary. That is, the taxpayer can deduct any amount between nil and the maximum value of $45,000. In the solution presented, he has deducted the maximum amount, which results in a non-capital loss carry over of $125,000 and leaves a net capital loss carry forward of $15,000 ($60,000 - $45,000). An alternative would have been to deduct nothing. This would have left a non-capital loss of $80,000 ($150,000 - $70,000) available for carry over and a net capital loss carry forward of $60,000. A taxpayer might choose this latter alternative if he was more concerned about the 20 year time limit on the non-capital loss balance, and less concerned about having sufficient future taxable capital gains to absorb the net capital loss carry forward.

- With the confusion arising from the different inclusion rates, we have found it useful to verify calculations using the 100 percent figures. For example, the $15,000 net capital loss can be verified as [(1/2)($120,000 - $90,000)], or one-half of the difference between 100 percent of the 2005 capital loss carry forward and 100 percent of the 2006 capital gain.

Exercise Fourteen-3

Subject: Net Capital Loss Carry Overs

During 2006, Ms. Laura Macky had an allowable capital loss of $15,000. Prior to 2007, she has had no taxable capital gains and, as a consequence, she has not been able to deduct this loss. In 2007, her income consists of a taxable capital gain of $40,000 [(1/2)($80,000)] and a net rental loss of $30,000. She does not anticipate any future capital gains. Determine Ms. Macky's minimum 2007 Net Income For Tax Purposes, as well as the amount and type of any losses available for carry over at the end of the year.

End of Exercise. Solution available in Study Guide.

Allowable Business Investment Losses
Defined

14-53.   A Business Investment Loss (BIL), as defined in ITA 39(1)(c), is a special type of capital loss resulting from the disposition of shares or debt of a "small business corporation". In addition to losses on arm's length sales, business investment losses can be incurred when there is a deemed disposition for nil proceeds. This could occur for shares of a small business corporation due to bankruptcy or insolvency, or if the debt is considered uncollectible.

14-54.   A small business corporation is defined in ITA 248(1) as a Canadian controlled private corporation (CCPC) of which "all or substantially all", of the fair market value of its assets are used in an active business carried on "primarily" in Canada. In tax work, the term "substantially all" generally means 90 percent or more, while "primarily" is generally interpreted to mean more than 50 percent.

14-55.   In making this determination, shares or debt of a connected small business corporation would count towards the required 90 percent. A corporation is connected if the potential small business corporation either controls it, or owns more than 10 percent of its voting shares and shares that represent more than 10 percent of the fair market value of all of the corporation's outstanding shares. As you would expect, an Allowable Business Investment Loss (ABIL) is the deductible one-half of a BIL.

Special Treatment
14-56.   In general, allowable capital losses can only be deducted against taxable capital gains. However, ABILs are given special treatment in that the taxpayer is permitted to deduct these amounts from any source of income.

> **Example**   An individual with net employment income of $50,000 has an ABIL of $10,500 [(1/2)($21,000)].

> **Analysis**   This individual would be able to deduct the $10,500 ABIL against the employment income, resulting in a Net Income For Tax Purposes of $39,500. If this had been an ordinary allowable capital loss, the taxpayer's Net Income For Tax Purposes would be $50,000 and the unapplied allowable capital loss would become a net capital loss for the year which would be available for carry over to other years.

14-57.   If there is sufficient income, the ABIL must be deducted in the year in which it is realized. However, if other sources of income are not sufficient for deducting all or part of an ABIL under ITA 3(d) in the current year, it becomes a part of the non-capital loss carry over balance. This permits this special type of allowable capital loss to be deducted against any type of income in either the three year carry back, or the 20 year carry forward period. Note that, because they are being carried over as part of the non-capital loss balance, ABILs are not adjusted if the capital gains inclusion rate is different in the carry over year.

14-58.   If the ABIL has not been used by the end of the normal 20 year carry forward period, it reverts to its original status as an allowable capital loss and becomes a component of the net capital loss carry forward balance. While this restricts the types of income that the loss can be applied against, it gives the loss an unlimited carry forward period.

Effect Of The ITA 110.6 Lifetime Capital Gains Deduction
14-59.   As we shall see in our discussion of the ITA 110.6 lifetime capital gains deduction, beginning in Paragraph 14-66, the realization of a Business Investment Loss reduces the taxpayer's ability to take advantage of this deduction. Of note here, however, is the fact that under ITA 39(9), Business Investment Losses are disallowed by the use of the ITA 110.6 lifetime capital gains deduction. What this means is, to the extent that the individual has made a deduction under ITA 110.6, an equivalent portion of the Business Investment Loss will be disallowed (i.e., converted to an ordinary capital loss).

14-60.   The ITA 110.6 deduction is a fractional figure, with the fraction being dependent on the capital gains inclusion rate applicable to the year in which the deduction is made. In applying the ITA 39(9) rule, there is a need to convert the ITA 110.6 deduction to a 100 percent figure in order to determine the amount of the Business Investment Loss that will be disallowed. This will require multiplying the ITA 110.6 figure by a fraction, the fraction being 2/1 for deductions at the one-half inclusion rate, 3/2 for deductions at the two-thirds inclusion rate, and 4/3 for deductions at the three-quarters inclusion rate.

> **Example**   Mr. Mercer had a taxable capital gain in 1990 of $12,000 [(3/4)($16,000)] and deducted this amount under the provisions of the ITA 110.6 lifetime capital gains deduction. In July, 2007, he has a $60,000 loss on the sale of shares of a small business corporation. Mr. Mercer has no capital gains or losses in any other year.

> **Analysis**   If Mr. Mercer had made no use of ITA 110.6, he would have an allowable business investment loss of $30,000 [(1/2)($60,000)] in 2007. However, since he has

made a deduction under ITA 110.6, the business investment loss would be reduced as follows:

Actual Loss On Disposition	$60,000
Reduction For Capital Gains Deduction [(4/3)($12,000)]	(16,000)
Business Investment Loss	$44,000
Inclusion Rate	1/2
Allowable Business Investment Loss (ABIL)	$22,000

14-61.   As we have noted, the disallowed $16,000 does not disappear. It becomes an ordinary capital loss, subject to the usual restriction that it can only be deducted against capital gains. The remaining $22,000 ABIL can be deducted in 2007 against any source of income. If it is not deducted in that year or carried back, it becomes part of the non-capital loss carry forward for 20 years. If it is still not used after 20 years, it becomes part of the net capital loss carry forward.

Exercise Fourteen-4

Subject: Business Investment Losses

During 2005, Mr. Lawrence Latvik used his lifetime capital gains deduction to eliminate a taxable capital gain of $13,000 [(1/2)($26,000)]. During 2007, he has capital gains on publicly traded securities of $18,000, and a loss of $50,000 on the disposition of shares of a small business corporation. His employment income for 2007 is over $200,000. Determine the amount of the Allowable Business Investment Loss that can be deducted in 2007, as well as the amount and type of any losses available for carry over at the end of the year.

End of Exercise. Solution available in Study Guide.

Farm Losses

Regular Farm Losses

14-62.   For full time farmers, farm losses are not restricted. They are treated in the same manner as non-capital losses in that they can be carried back three years and forward for 20 years. Unlike restricted farm losses (see the following Paragraph), when they are deducted on a carry over basis, regular farm losses can be applied against any type of income.

Restricted Farm Losses

14-63.   As covered in Chapter 8, restricted farm losses arise when there is a reasonable expectation of a profit, but a taxpayer's chief source of income is neither farming nor a combination of farming and something else. The deduction of such farm losses from any source of income in a year is restricted to all of the first $2,500, plus one-half of the next $12,500, to a maximum of $8,750 [$2,500 + (1/2)($12,500)] on an actual loss of $15,000 ($2,500 + $12,500). The loss in excess of the deductible limit is the restricted farm loss. For example, the restricted amount of a total loss of $15,000 would be $6,250 ($15,000 - $8,750).

14-64.   Restricted farm losses can be carried over to other years. Such losses can be carried back three years and forward for a maximum of 20 years. In carry over periods, restricted farm losses can only be deducted to the extent that income from farming has been included in Net Income For Tax Purposes. For example, if a restricted farm loss carry forward of $15,000 was available at the beginning of 2007 and 2007 farming income totaled $12,000, only $12,000 of the carry forward could be deducted in calculating 2007 Taxable Income. The remaining $3,000 of the restricted loss could not be deducted, even if the taxpayer had large amounts of other types of income available.

14-65.   If land used in a farming business is disposed of before the taxpayer has an opportunity to fully utilize restricted farm losses carried forward, a part of the undeducted losses can be used to increase the adjusted cost base of the property. This would have the effect of reducing any capital gains arising on the disposition of the property. This treatment is only possible to the extent that the loss was created by property taxes or interest payments on the farm property.

Exercise Fourteen-5

Subject: Farm Losses

Ms. Elena Bodkin has a full time appointment as a professor at a Canadian university. As she has considerable free time, she is developing an organic vegetable farm. In 2006, the first year of operation, she had a loss of $16,000 and deducted the maximum allowable amount. In 2007, in addition to her employment income of $85,000, her farming operation showed a profit of $3,500. Determine Ms. Bodkin's minimum 2007 Net Income For Tax Purposes and Taxable Income, as well as the amount and type of any losses available for carry forward at the end of the year.

End of Exercise. Solution available in Study Guide.

Lifetime Capital Gains Deduction

Background
The Original Legislation
14-66.   The lifetime capital gains legislation was first introduced in 1985 and, in its original form, it allowed every individual resident in Canada to enjoy up to $500,000 in tax free capital gains during the course of their lifetime. This privilege was available without regard to the type of property on which the gain accrued. A resident Canadian could acquire a major tax benefit through the process of owning and disposing of a Florida condominium.

Limiting Its Scope
14-67.   Because of the magnitude of the possible benefits and the potential for abuse, the relevant legislation was extremely complex. Further, this new tax privilege created serious distortions in the allocation of economic resources. The provision appeared to have little economic justification other than providing a near outright gift to wealthy Canadians. Given this effect, it is not surprising that actions were taken to limit the scope of this very generous tax provision.

14-68.   The limiting process took place in two steps:

- In 1992, the deduction was eliminated for gains resulting from the disposition of most real property (a.k.a., non-qualifying real estate).
- In 1994, the deduction was eliminated with respect to all dispositions other than those involving qualified farm property and shares of qualified small business corporations.

14-69.   The 1994 change was accompanied by an election that allowed holders of capital assets with accrued gains to have a deemed disposition in order to make use of any remaining general lifetime capital gains deduction that was available to them. The election created a new adjusted cost base that would be used to calculate the capital gain or loss on the future disposition of the asset.

14-70.   These changes left a very complex legacy with respect to the determination of the adjusted cost base of either non-qualifying real estate held at the time of the 1992 change, or other assets on which the 1994 election was made. Although tax practitioners will have to deal with this problem for many years to come, these complicated rules are of little interest to most readers of this text.

May, 2006 And March, 2007 Budget Changes

14-71.   Subsequent to the changes introduced in 1992 and 1994, the $500,000 deduction was only available against gains resulting from the disposition of qualified small business corporation shares or qualified farm properties. Both the May, 2006 and March, 2007 budgets introduced changes:

Qualified Fishing Properties   The May, 2006 budget extended the availability of the $500,000 deduction to dispositions of qualified fishing properties that took place after May 1, 2006.

Increase To $750,000   The March, 2007 budget increased the deduction limit from $500,000 to $750,000. This is applicable to dispositions of qualifying property that take place after March 18, 2007.

Qualified Property

Types Of Property

14-72.   As noted in the preceding paragraph, the $750,000 lifetime capital gains deduction will be available on a disposition of shares of a qualified small business corporation, an interest in qualified farm property, or an interest in qualified fishing property. Note that the $750,000 limit is not available on each type of asset. Rather, it is a total amount that must be shared on dispositions of all three types.

14-73.   As it is the most common application of this provision, we will focus our attention on shares of qualified small business corporations. With respect to the other two types of qualified property, they can be generally described as follows:

Qualified Farm or Fishing Property Qualified farm property and qualified fishing property are defined in ITA 110.6(1). They include real property and eligible capital property used in Canada for farming or fishing by a taxpayer, the taxpayer's spouse, or their children. The definition also includes a share of a family farm or fishing corporation and an interest in a family farm or fishing partnership. To qualify for this deduction, the property must be owned for at least 24 months prior to its disposition.

Small Business Corporations

14-74.   As noted in our discussion of Business Investment Losses in Paragraph 14-53, ITA 248(1) defines a small business corporation as a Canadian controlled private corporation (CCPC) of which all, or substantially all (90 percent or more), of the fair market value of its assets are used in an active business carried on primarily (more than 50 percent) in Canada. In order to be a qualified small business corporation for the purposes of the lifetime capital gains deduction, the corporation is only required to satisfy this definition of a small business corporation at the point in time at which the shares are sold.

14-75.   In many cases this is not a difficult criterion to satisfy. If, at a particular point in time, less than 90 percent of the fair market value of the corporation's assets are involved in producing active business income, it is often a simple matter to sell some of the non-qualifying assets and distribute the proceeds to the shareholders. This process, commonly referred to as "the purification of a small business corporation", can normally be carried out in a short period of time, thereby satisfying the small business corporation criteria prior to the disposition of the shares.

Qualified Small Business Corporations

14-76.   Not all small business corporations are qualified small business corporations. To achieve this stature, ITA 110.6(1) requires that two other conditions be met. In somewhat simplified terms, they are:

- the shares must not be owned by anyone other than the taxpayer or a related person for at least 24 months preceding the disposition; and
- throughout this 24 month period, more than 50 percent of the fair market value of the corporation's assets must be used in an active business carried on primarily in Canada.

14-77.   There are additional rules that are applicable when intercorporate investments are involved in the preceding determinations. More specifically, additional requirements apply when the condition that 50 percent of the assets must be used in active business for a 24 month period can only be met by adding in the shares of another small business corporation. These special rules go beyond the scope of this text and, as a result, will not be covered here.

14-78.   As compared to meeting the small business corporation criteria, a failure to meet these additional qualifying criteria is more difficult to correct. As they involve measurements made over a period of time, a failure to satisfy them can only be corrected by the passage of time.

Determining The Deductible Amount

General Rules

14-79.   The determination of the amount of the lifetime capital gains deduction that can be deducted in a year involves some reasonably complex calculations. In general terms, the available deduction is the least of the following three items:

- Capital Gains Deduction Available
- Annual Gains Limit
- Cumulative Gains Limit

14-80.   These items will be explained in detail in the following material.

Capital Gains Deduction Available

14-81.   The "capital gains deduction available" is the lifetime maximum for the capital gains deduction, less any amounts that have been used up in preceding years. The lifetime maximum for all types of qualified assets is $375,000 [(1/2)($750,000)], provided the disposition is made after March 18, 2007.

14-82.   A problem arises in determining the amounts used up in previous years. Clearly, it would not be appropriate to subtract a $12,000 deduction made in 1990 when it represented the taxable portion of a $16,000 capital gain, from the 2007 limit of $375,000, which is based on one-half of the gain. Amounts used up in earlier years have to be adjusted to the current inclusion rate of one-half. Specifically, gains deducted at a one-half inclusion rate require no adjustment, gains deducted at a two-thirds inclusion rate have to be multiplied by 3/4 [(1/2) ÷ (2/3)], and gains deducted at a three-quarters inclusion rate have to be multiplied by 2/3 [(1/2) ÷ (3/4)].

> **Example**   Mr. Little realizes capital gains on sales of qualified small business corporation shares of $24,000 in each of 1987, 1998, and June, 2007. He has not claimed a capital gains deduction prior to 1987 and he has no other capital gains or losses in the period 1987 through 2007. He used his lifetime capital gains deduction to eliminate the 1987 and 1998 gains, and will use the deduction to eliminate the 2007 gain. Determine the amount of lifetime capital gains deduction that is available for use given that the disposition is after March 18, 2007.
>
> **Analysis**   As the $12,000 that was deducted in 1987 was at the one-half inclusion rate, no adjustment is required for the purpose of determining the available deduction for 2007. He would have deducted $18,000 [(3/4)($24,000)] in 1998. To determine how much of his $375,000 balance is left, this amount will have to be converted to $12,000 {[$18,000][(1/2) ÷ (3/4)]}. A further reduction of $12,000 will be used to eliminate the 2007 gain. This will leave an available amount of $339,000 ($375,000 - $12,000 - $12,000 - $12,000).

14-83.   This result can be verified using the full capital gain figures, usually the simpler approach. The $750,000 limit is reduced by $72,000 [(3)($24,000)] and, when the remaining $678,000 is multiplied by the current inclusion rate of one-half, it gives the balance of $339,000 as previously calculated.

Annual Gains Limit

14-84. The annual gains limit is defined in ITA 110.6(1) as follows:

Annual Gains Limit of an individual for a taxation year means the amount determined by the formula

$$A - B, \text{ where}$$

A is equal to the lesser of:

- net taxable capital gains for the current year on all capital asset dispositions [ITA 3(b)]; and
- net taxable capital gains for the current year on dispositions of qualified farm property, qualified fishing property, and qualified small business corporation shares.

B is equal to the total of:

- The amount, if any, by which net capital loss carry overs deducted for the year under ITA 111(1)(b), exceeds the excess of net taxable capital gains for the year [ITA 3(b)] over the amount determined in Part A of this formula; and
- Allowable Business Investment Losses realized during the current year.

14-85. The annual gains limit formula is made complex by the possibility of having capital gains on assets that are not eligible for the deduction in the same year that there is a capital gain on a qualified property. In a year in which there is a capital gain on a qualified property and no other capital gains, the formula can be stated more simply as follows:

Annual Gains Limit is equal to the taxable capital gains on qualified property, less:

- Allowable capital losses realized.
- Net capital loss carry overs deducted.
- Allowable Business Investment Losses realized.

14-86. We will make use of this abbreviated formula when there are no other capital gains in the years where there are capital gains on qualified property.

14-87. Additional points here are as follows:

- If the net capital loss is a carry forward from a year where the inclusion rate was not one-half, it will have to be converted to a one-half rate before it can be deducted.

- With respect to the Allowable Business Investment Losses realized, the full amount is subtracted in the preceding formula, without regard to whether they have been deducted in the calculation of Net Income For Tax Purposes. Also keep in mind that the amount of Allowable Business Investment Losses realized is based only on those amounts that have not been disallowed by the previous use of the lifetime capital gains deduction.

- As a further point here, the deduction of net capital loss carry forwards is discretionary. This means that, in cases where there is the possibility of using either the lifetime capital gains deduction or a net capital loss carry forward, the individual must choose between the two alternatives. This is inherent in the annual gains limit formula which, in many situations, will reduce the limit on a dollar for dollar basis for net capital loss carry overs deducted. While this choice between the two alternatives may have no influence on the current year's Taxable Income, we would suggest a preference for making maximum use of the lifetime capital gains deduction. There is no time limit on using the net capital loss carry forward and, more importantly, it can be used when any type of taxable capital gain is realized. In contrast, the lifetime capital gains deduction can only be used for particular types of capital gains. There was, for some time, the possibility that this deduction would be eliminated. However, with the addition of fishing properties as qualified property and the increase in the overall limit from $500,000 to $750,000, this possibility appears to be unlikely and would not be a factor in the decision.

Exercise Fourteen-6

Subject: Annual Gains Limit

On January 1, 2007, your client, Miss Jana Slovena, has a net capital loss carry forward from 2005 of $45,000. During 2007, Miss Slovena has taxable capital gains on sales of real estate in the amount of $114,000. Also during this year, she has allowable capital losses of $82,000. In addition, she sells shares in a qualified small business corporation realizing a taxable capital gain of $42,000. Finally, as the result of selling shares of a small business corporation that does not qualify for the lifetime capital gains deduction, she has an Allowable Business Investment Loss of $3,000. As she does not expect to have additional capital gains in the near future, Miss Slovena has asked you to deduct the full $45,000 of the 2005 net capital loss during 2007. Determine her annual gains limit for 2007 using this approach. What advice would you give Ms. Slovena regarding her net capital loss?

End of Exercise. Solution available in Study Guide

Cumulative Net Investment Loss (CNIL)

14-88. Cumulative Net Investment Loss (CNIL) is a restriction introduced in the 1988 tax reform legislation. The problem, as perceived by the government, was that it was inequitable for individuals to simultaneously deduct investment losses while sheltering investment income through the use of the lifetime capital gains deduction. As a consequence, legislation was introduced that, in simple terms, restricts the use of the lifetime capital gains deduction in a given year by the cumulative amount of post-1987 investment losses.

14-89. CNIL is defined as the amount by which the aggregate of investment expenses for the current year and prior years ending after 1987, exceeds the aggregate of investment income for that period. That is, the CNIL consists of post-1987 investment expenses minus investment income. You should note that, in this context, both investment income and investment expense are defined in the *Income Tax Act*. As a consequence, they have a meaning that can be different than the meaning associated with the everyday use of these terms.

14-90. As will be explained in the following material, individuals who have a CNIL will have their ability to use the lifetime capital gains deduction reduced. As a result, if qualified capital gains are anticipated, it is important to minimize the CNIL. Some examples of ways in which the impact of the CNIL can be reduced are as follows:

- Realizing capital gains on qualified assets early, if Cumulative Net Investment Losses are anticipated in future years.

- Delaying the disposition of qualified assets with accrued capital gains until the CNIL has been eliminated or reduced as much as possible.

- For owner/managers, having the business pay dividends or interest on shareholder loan accounts, rather than salaries, to increase investment income.

Cumulative Gains Limit

14-91. In somewhat simplified form, the cumulative gains limit can be defined as follows:

The sum of all annual gains limits for the current and previous years, unadjusted for changes in the capital gains inclusion rate. This total is reduced by:

- The sum of all amounts deducted under the lifetime capital gains deduction provision in computing the individual's taxable incomes for preceding taxation years (unadjusted for changes in the capital gains inclusion rate); and

- the individual's CNIL at the end of the year.

14-92.   In the absence of a CNIL balance, this formula would simply be the sum of all annual gains limits, reduced by all of the lifetime capital gains deductions made in previous years. As individuals will normally deduct the full amount of their annual gains limit, this balance will usually be equal to the annual gains limit for the current year. This result can be altered by an individual's failure to deduct the full amount of the annual gains limit in some previous year, either as a tax planning choice or as the result of a CNIL balance.

14-93.   All of the listed items are included in this definition without adjustment for different capital gains inclusion rates. This means that, depending on the year in which the gain, loss, or deduction occurred, there may be a mix of items included on the basis of one-half, two-thirds, or three-quarters of their full amounts.

Example   In 2007, Ms. Nolan has $5,600 of deductible interest on loans for investment purposes and $2,600 of net rental income. She has had no investment income or losses in years prior to 2007, so her Cumulative Net Investment Loss (CNIL) is $3,000 ($5,600 - $2,600). During August, 2007, she has a $60,000 taxable capital gain on the sale of qualified small business shares. Ms Nolan has no other capital gains or losses in 2007.

Analysis   As she has made no previous use of her lifetime capital gains deduction, her unused lifetime limit is $375,000. While her annual gains limit would be $60,000, the amount of the taxable capital gain, her ability to use the lifetime capital gains deduction would be limited by her CNIL to her cumulative gains limit of $57,000 ($60,000 - $3,000).

Example

14-94.   The example that follows illustrates the basic rules involved in the application of the lifetime capital gains deduction.

Example   Dwight Treadway's 2007 Net Income For Tax Purposes is as follows:

Employment Income	$ 60,000
Taxable Capital Gain On Sale Of Qualified Farm Property	200,000
Net Income For Tax Purposes	$260,000

In 1987, Mr. Treadway realized a $20,000 taxable capital gain [(1/2)($40,000)] from the sale of publicly traded shares and used his lifetime capital gains deduction to claim a deduction for this amount. In 1990, he realized an allowable capital loss of $13,500 [(3/4)($18,000)]. He was not able to use the loss in that year, or any other year, and he intends to deduct it as a net capital loss carry forward in 2007. Other than the 1987 taxable capital gain of $20,000 and the 1990 allowable capital loss of $13,500, Dwight Treadway had no capital gains, capital losses, loss carry overs, or Business Investment Losses from 1985 through 2006. He has no CNIL balance in 2007.

Analysis   For 2007, the maximum deduction under ITA 110.6 would be the least of the following amounts:

- **Capital Gains Deduction Available** This would be $355,000 ($375,000 - $20,000).

- **Annual Gains Limit** As Mr. Treadway has had no capital gains on non-qualified property in 2007, we can use the simplified version of this calculation. (See Paragraph 14-85.) This would result in an annual gains limit of $191,000, the $200,000 taxable capital gain for the year, less the $9,000 [(1/2)($18,000)] net capital loss carry forward deducted under ITA 111(1)(b).

- **Cumulative Gains Limit**   As the annual gains limit for 1987 would be equal to the $20,000 taxable capital gain on qualifying property, the sum of the annual gains limits would be $211,000 ($20,000 + $191,000). Subtracting from this the $20,000 lifetime capital gains deduction for 1987 leaves the cumulative gains limit of $191,000.

14-95.   Given these calculations, the maximum deduction for 2007 would be $191,000, the amount of both the annual gains limit and the cumulative gains limit. The full gain on the farm could have been deducted if Mr. Treadway had not chosen to deduct the net capital loss carry forward. The deduction of this amount reduced both the annual gains limit and the cumulative gains limit by $9,000.

Exercise Fourteen-7

Subject: Lifetime Capital Gains Deduction

Mr. Edwin Loussier had a 1986 taxable capital gain on qualifying property of $5,000 [(1/2)($10,000)] and a 1989 taxable capital gain on qualifying property of $17,333 [(2/3)($26,000)]. He used his lifetime capital gains deduction to eliminate both of these gains. He has no other capital gains, capital losses, or Business Investment Losses in the period 1985 through 2005. In December, 2006, he has a $63,000 capital loss which, because he has no capital gains in that year, he cannot deduct. In July, 2007, he has a $510,000 capital gain on the sale of a qualified farm property. In addition, he deducts the $63,000 net capital loss from 2006. Mr. Loussier does not have a CNIL balance. Determine Mr. Loussier's maximum lifetime capital gains deduction for 2007.

End of Exercise. Solution available in Study Guide.

Ordering Of Deductions And Losses

Significance Of Ordering

14-96.   If an individual has sufficient income to absorb all of the losses and deductions that are available in the calculation of Taxable Income, the question of ordering is not important. The real significance of provisions covering the ordering of losses and other deductions is in the determination of the amounts and types of items that can be carried over to previous or subsequent years.

14-97.   For example, assume that a taxpayer has taxable capital gains of $25,000, a business loss of $25,000, and allowable capital losses of $25,000. No matter how these items are ordered, the Net Income For Tax Purposes will be nil. However, it does make a difference whether the loss carry over is for the business loss, or for the net capital losses. A net capital loss carry forward can only be deducted to the extent of taxable capital gains in the carry forward period. On the other hand, the non-capital losses can only be used for a limited period of time (20 years) while, by contrast, the net capital losses can be carried forward indefinitely.

Ordering In Computing Net Income For Tax Purposes

14-98.   The basic rules for the computation of Net Income For Tax Purposes under Division B are found in ITA 3. In computing Net Income For Tax Purposes, ITA 3 indicates that we begin by adding together positive amounts of income from non-capital sources, plus net taxable capital gains. Net taxable capital gains are defined as the amount, if any, by which the current year's taxable capital gains exceed the current year's allowable capital losses. This, in effect, requires that capital losses be deducted prior to the deduction of non-capital losses.

14-99.   The various deductions available under Subdivision e (RRSP deductions, spousal support paid, child care costs, moving expenses, etc.) are subtracted from this total. If a positive balance remains, the final step in computing Net Income For Tax Purposes is to subtract any employment, business, or property losses, as well as Allowable Business Investment Losses.

Ordering In Computing Taxable Income

14-100.   With respect to the computation of Taxable Income for individuals, the *Act* is much more specific. Under ITA 111.1, the order in which individuals must deduct Division C items is as follows:

- Various deductions provided by ITA 110 (stock options, home relocation loans)
- Retroactive lump-sum payments under ITA 110.2
- Loss carry overs under ITA 111
- Lifetime capital gains deduction under ITA 110.6
- Northern residents deductions under ITA 110.7

14-101.   Within ITA 111, available loss carry overs can be deducted in any order the taxpayer wishes. The only constraint is the ITA 111(3) requirement that, within a particular type of loss (e.g., non-capital losses), the oldest losses have to be deducted first.

14-102.   When several different types of loss carry overs are available, decisions in this area can be difficult. On the one hand, certain types of carry overs have a limited period of availability (i.e., non-capital losses and farm losses can be carried forward for 20 years). In contrast, net capital losses have no time limit, but can only be deducted to the extent of taxable capital gains that have been realized in the year. Restricted farm loss carry overs and carry overs of losses on listed personal property have more onerous limitations. These losses are restricted with respect to both time and type of income (e.g., restricted farm loss carry forwards are available for 20 years and can only be deducted to the extent of farm income earned in the year).

14-103.   Decisions in this area will involve a careful weighing of which type of loss carry over is most likely to have continued usefulness in future years. For example, if a non-capital loss carry forward is 19 years old and the business is expecting no Taxable Income in the following year, then use of this carry forward would appear to be a prudent course of action. An additional consideration is that any credits against Tax Payable should be fully utilized before applying loss carry overs (see Paragraphs 14-26 through 14-29). The amount of loss carry over that is claimed should not be more than is needed to reduce Tax Payable to nil.

Example

14-104.   The following is an example of the ordering rules used in computing Taxable Income for individuals:

Example At the beginning of 2007, Miss Farnum had the following loss carry forwards:

Non-Capital Losses From 2005	$40,000
Net Capital Losses From 2001 [(1/2)($20,000)]	10,000
Restricted Farm Losses From 1999	5,000

For 2007, she can claim only the basic personal amount of $8,929. Also during 2007, she has no available subdivision e deductions. For this year, she had the following income amounts as calculated under Division B rules:

Employment Income	$15,000
Property Income (Interest)	4,000
Farm Income	2,000
Income From Sole Proprietorship	15,000
Capital Gains	12,000

Analysis Miss Farnum's Net Income For Tax Purposes would be calculated as follows:

Income Under ITA 3(a):		
Employment Income	$15,000	
Property Income	4,000	
Farming Income	2,000	
Business Income (Proprietorship)	15,000	$36,000
Income Under ITA 3(b):		
Taxable Capital Gains [(1/2)($12,000)]		6,000
Net Income For Tax Purposes		**$42,000**

Miss Farnum's Taxable Income would be calculated as follows:

Net Income For Tax Purposes	$42,000
Restricted Farm Loss Carry Forward (Limited to farming income)	(2,000)
Net Capital Loss Carry Forward (Limited to taxable capital gains)	(6,000)
Subtotal	$34,000
Non-Capital Loss Carry Forward ($34,000 - $8,929)	(25,071)
Taxable Income	**$ 8,929**

14-105. The remaining loss carry forwards consist of an unused restricted farm loss of $3,000 ($5,000 - $2,000), a 2001 net capital loss of $4,000 [(1/2)($20,000 - $12,000)], and an unused non-capital loss of $14,929 ($40,000 - $25,071). Note that, in this example, the amount of net capital and restricted farm losses deducted was limited by the amount of the taxable capital gains and farm income. The non-capital loss deducted was limited to the amount that would reduce her Taxable Income to her basic personal amount of $8,929. Since her Tax Payable will be nil at this point, there is no reason to deduct any further amount of the non-capital loss available.

Exercise Fourteen-8

Subject: Ordering Of Losses

At the beginning of 2007, Alan Barter had the following loss carry forwards available:

Restricted Farm Losses	$ 8,000
Non-Capital Losses	36,000
Net Capital Losses From 2001 [(1/2)($40,000)]	20,000

During 2007, he had the following amounts of income:

Taxable Capital Gains [(1/2)($18,000)]	$ 9,000
Business Income	12,000
Employment Income	56,000
Farm Income	3,500

Determine Alan's Net Income For Tax Purposes, as well as his minimum Taxable Income for 2007. He has no subdivision e deductions for the year and his only credit against Tax Payable is the basic personal amount of $8,929. Indicate the amount and type of any losses available for carry forward at the end of the year.

End of Exercise. Solution available in Study Guide.

Tax Payable Overview

General

14-106.   Chapter 6 provided detailed coverage of the application of federal tax rates to Taxable Income in order to provide an initial figure for an individual's Tax Payable. In addition, coverage of most of the tax credits available to individuals was also provided. The coverage of tax credits was extended in Chapter 9 with coverage of the dividend tax credit, as well as the credit for taxes withheld on foreign source income.

14-107.   None of this material will be repeated in this Chapter. However, as many of the Self Study and Assignment Problems that accompany this Chapter are comprehensive in nature and will require you to apply tax calculations and credits, you will probably wish to review the material in Chapter 6 before attempting to deal with the problems in this Chapter.

14-108.   As was the case with the material on Taxable Income, there are issues involved with the determination of individual Tax Payable that, because of the need for additional understanding of the income concepts presented in subsequent chapters, could not be dealt with in Chapter 6. Because of this, additional coverage of Tax Payable is included in this Chapter. Specifically, the following concepts and procedures are discussed in this material:

Tax On Split Income   This special tax was designed to limit the use of income splitting with minor children. It can be better understood now that we have covered the material on income attribution in Chapter 12.

Transfer Of Dividends To A Spouse Or Common-Law Partner   The calculations related to this tax credit require an understanding of the dividend gross up and tax credit procedures which were not introduced until Chapter 9.

Charitable Donations   The basic calculation of this tax credit was presented in Chapter 6. However, it was not possible to deal with gifts of capital property until the material in Chapters 7 through 10 on business income, property income and capital gains had been covered.

Foreign Tax Credits   These credits were introduced in Chapter 9. However, the full determination of the eligible amounts require the additional material on Taxable Income that is included in this Chapter.

14-109.   Now that we have covered the material in Chapters 7 to 12, we are in a position to complete our coverage of the determination of Tax Payable for individuals.

Basic Federal Tax Payable

14-110.   Basic federal Tax Payable is a figure from which some, but not all tax credits have been deducted. Prior to 2000, this was an important figure in that it was the base that the provinces and territories used in calculating their respective Tax Payable. With the 2001 adoption of the Tax On Income (TONI) system by the provinces, the basic federal tax figure is not of general importance.

14-111.   This concept does, however, have some limited use in specialized situations and, because of this, you will see references to this figure in the T1 tax return. The most important of these is that it is used to calculate the additional federal Tax Payable that must be paid by individuals who are deemed Canadian residents but do not reside in a province (e.g., members of the Canadian Armed Forces stationed outside of Canada). However, other than indicating that this concept exists, we will give basic federal tax no further consideration.

Tax On Split Income

14-112.   A number of arrangements have been used to channel property income into the hands of related individuals with little or no income. If, for example, the owner of a corporation can arrange his affairs so that corporate income is paid out as non-eligible dividends to his children, each child can receive over $35,000 per year of such income on a tax free basis.

14-113. This amount would be even larger if the dividends were eligible for the new 45 percent gross up. However, as will be discussed in more detail in our chapters on corporate taxation, dividends paid by private companies will generally be paid out of income that has benefited from the small business deduction. Such dividends are non-eligible and, as a consequence, the gross up will be limited to 25 percent.

14-114. The federal government had little success in attacking these income splitting arrangements through the courts and decided to solve the problem through legislation. Beginning in 2000, ITA 120.4 imposes a new tax on the "split income" of specified individuals (referred to by many writers as the "kiddie tax").

14-115. This tax is assessed at the maximum federal rate of 29 percent. It is applied to all such income, beginning with the first dollar received. Further, the only tax credits that can be applied against this income are the dividend tax credit and the credits for taxes withheld on foreign source income.

14-116. For the purposes of this Section, a specified individual is anyone who has not attained the age of 17 years before the year (i.e., it is applicable to a child who turns 17 in the year), is a resident of Canada throughout the year, and has a parent who is a resident of Canada at any time in the year.

14-117. The "split income" that is defined in ITA 120.4 includes the following:

(a) taxable dividends from private companies received directly, or through a trust or partnership;

(b) shareholder benefits or loans received from a private corporation; and

(c) income from a partnership or trust if the income is derived from the provision of property or services to a business:
- carried on by a person related to the individual,
- carried on by a corporation of which a person related to the individual is a specified shareholder (i.e., owns 10 percent or more of the shares), or
- carried on by a professional corporation of which a person related to the individual is a shareholder.

14-118. To avoid double taxation of this block of income subject to the high 29 percent rate, it is deductible under ITA 20(1)(ww) in calculating the individual's Taxable Income subject to regular taxation. In keeping with the tax policy to discourage the use of split income, under ITA 120.4(3), personal tax credits cannot be applied against the split income. This effectively restricts any personal credits to the non-split income only. Any excess personal credits are lost.

Example Helen, who is 15 years old, receives non-eligible dividends of $20,000 from a private company controlled by her father. In addition, she has interest income of $5,500 from an inheritance. Her only tax credits are the basic personal credit and the dividend tax credit.

Analysis Helen's Taxable Income equals $5,500 [(125%)($20,000) + $5,500 - $25,000]. The ITA 20(1)(ww) deduction removes the split income (i.e., the grossed up dividends) of $25,000 from her Taxable Income. Her federal Tax Payable of $3,917 would be calculated as the greater of the following two amounts:

	Tax Otherwise Determined	Tax Per ITA 120.4(3)
Tax On Split Income [(125%)($20,000)(29%)]	$7,250	$7,250
Tax On Taxable Income [($5,500)(15.5%)]	853	N/A
Dividend Tax Credit [(2/3)(25%)($20,000)]	(3,333)	(3,333)
Basic Personal Credit [($8,929)(15.5%)]	(1,384)	N/A
Federal Tax Payable	$3,386	$ 3,917

14-119.   Two other aspects of the tax on split income should be noted:

• To ensure that this tax is paid, the parents of the child are held jointly and severally liable for its remittance.
• The tax is not applicable to a child with no parent who is resident in Canada, to income from property inherited by a child from a parent, nor to income from property inherited from individuals other than a parent, if the child is either in full time attendance at a post-secondary educational institution, or eligible for the disability tax credit.

14-120.   While this legislation was met with howls of outrage from many in the tax community, in our view it was an appropriate modification of the existing system. There has been widespread use of vehicles such as family trusts to shelter income from taxes. In effect, it was possible to pay for a large portion of the expenses of raising children on a tax advantaged basis. This type of benefit is clearly not available to the majority of Canadians and it would be difficult to describe our tax system as fair and equitable if such arrangements were allowed to continue.

Exercise Fourteen-9

Subject: Tax On Split Income

During 2007, Norton James, who is 16 years old, receives non-eligible dividends of $15,000 from a private corporation controlled by his mother. In addition, he has income of $12,200 from contracts to create computer games. Assume his only tax credits are the basic personal credit and the dividend tax credit. Determine Norton's federal Tax Payable for 2007.

End of Exercise. Solution available in Study Guide.

Tax Credits Revisited

Transfer Of Dividends To A Spouse Or Common-Law Partner

14-121.   There may be situations in which a taxpayer's spousal credit has been reduced or eliminated by dividends received by that spouse. The ITA 82(3) election permits a transfer of all of the dividends from the spouse or common-law partner's income to that of the taxpayer, if it creates or increases the spousal credit. Consider the following example:

Example   Mrs. Albert's total income consisted of $10,000 in eligible dividends received from taxable Canadian corporations. Mrs. Albert's basic personal tax credit, along with part of the dividend tax credit, eliminate all taxation on the grossed up amount of $14,500 [(145%)($10,000)]. However, because she has this income receipt, Mr. Albert is not able to claim a spousal tax credit.

Analysis   In this situation, the transfer of dividends under ITA 82(3) would eliminate all of Mrs. Albert's income, and Mr. Albert would be able to claim the full spousal credit of $1,384. Mr. Albert would then be taxed on the 14,500 [(145%)($10,000)] of grossed up dividends. He would, however, be eligible for the dividend tax credit associated with these dividends. Whether this is a good alternative or not depends on Mr. Albert's marginal tax rate, as can be seen in the following calculations:

	15.5%	29%
Increase In Taxable Income [(145%)($10,000)]	$14,500	$14,500
Tax On $14,500	$ 2,248	$ 4,205
Increase In Spousal Credit	(1,384)	(1,384)
Dividend Tax Credit [(11/18)($4,500)]	(2,750)	(2,750)
Increase (Decrease) In Tax Payable	($ 1,886)	$ 71

As can be seen in the table, if Mr. Albert is in the 15.5 percent tax bracket, his federal tax would be reduced by $1,886. Alternatively, if he is in the 29 percent bracket, the transfer would not be desirable as his federal tax would be increased by $71.

Exercise Fourteen-10

Subject: Transfer Of Dividends To A Spouse

Mr. Albert Ho is 38 years old and has over $200,000 in 2007 Taxable Income. His wife's only 2007 source of income is $6,200 in eligible dividends received from taxable Canadian corporations. In terms of federal Tax Payable, would Mr. Ho benefit from the use of the ITA 82(3) election to include the eligible dividends received by his spouse in his Net Income For Tax Purposes? Justify your conclusion.

End of Exercise.   Solution available in Study Guide.

Charitable Donations Credit Revisited
Introduction
14-122.   A basic treatment of this credit was provided in Chapter 6. In that Chapter, we noted that the credit was calculated as 15.5 percent of the first $200 of donations, plus 29 percent of any additional amounts. In general, the base for calculating this credit was limited to 75 percent of the taxpayer's Net Income For Tax Purposes.

14-123.   In Chapter 6, we only dealt with simple cases involving gifts of cash, deferring coverage of gifts involving various types of capital property. Coverage of these more complex issues is included here.

14-124.   As many of you are aware, in recent years, a number of gift giving programs have been developed that appear to provide the taxpayer with benefits that exceed his cost and, in some cases, the value of the gift to the recipient charity.

14-125.   A classic example of this was the so-called art flips. Such arrangements might involve a taxpayer buying a large block of paintings directly from the inventories of the artist. The cost of the block was essentially a wholesale value and was significantly lower than the sum of the retail prices of the individual paintings. The paintings would then be appraised on the basis of individual retail values, followed by a gift of the art works to a registered charity. The taxpayer would then claim a tax credit based on the significantly higher appraised value, often resulting in a tax credit that was worth more than the original cost of the paintings.

14-126.   At this point in time (June, 2007) there are legislative proposals which would restrict the ability of taxpayers to use such schemes. Coverage of these provisions, located in proposed ITA 248(30) through ITA 248(41), will be found in the material which follows.

Donations Classified
14-127.   ITA 118.1 defines four types of charitable donations:

1. **Total Charitable Gifts** is defined to include all eligible amounts donated by an individual to a registered charity, a registered Canadian amateur athletic association, a Canadian municipality, the United Nations or an agency thereof, a university outside of Canada which normally enrolls Canadian students, and a charitable organization outside of Canada to which Her Majesty in right of Canada has made a gift in the year or in the immediately preceding year.

2. **Total Crown Gifts** is defined as the aggregate of eligible amounts donated to Her Majesty in right of Canada or a province.

3. **Total Cultural Gifts** is defined as the aggregate of all eligible gifts of objects that the Canadian Cultural Property Export Review Board has determined meet the criteria of the *Cultural Property And Import Act*.

4. **Total Ecological Gifts** is defined as all eligible gifts of land certified by the Minister of the Environment to be ecologically sensitive land, the conservation and protection of which is important to the preservation of Canada's environmental heritage. The beneficiary of the gift must be a Canadian municipality or a registered charity, the primary purpose of which is the conservation and protection of Canada's environmental heritage.

14-128.   In addition to the items specified in the *Act*, under the U.S./Canada tax treaty, Canadians can claim gifts to any qualifying U.S. charity in amounts up to 75 percent of their net U.S. income (75 percent of their net world income if the Canadian resident lives near the U.S. border and commutes to a U.S. place of business or employment).

Eligible Amounts

14-129.   In the preceding material on the classification of donations, each of the definitions contains the term "eligible amounts". The use of this term reflects the proposed anti-avoidance legislation. These proposals define this term as follows:

Proposed ITA 248(31) The eligible amount of a gift or monetary contribution is the amount by which the fair market value of the property that is the subject of the gift exceeds the amount of the advantage, if any, in respect of the gift.

14-130.   The proposed ITA 248(32) defines "advantage" very broadly to include a benefit to the taxpayer that is in any way related to the gift, including benefits that are contingent on future events.

Example The example provided for this proposal is the gift of real property with a fair market value of $300,000, with the registered charity assuming the $100,000 mortgage on the property. In this case, the eligible amount of the donation is $200,000 ($300,000 - $100,000).

14-131.   In addition to this eligibility requirement, a proposed ITA 248(30) introduces the concept of "intention to give". The basic idea here is that, if the advantage to the taxpayer resulting from making the gift exceeds 80 percent of the value of the gift, the gift will be disallowed unless the taxpayer can convince the Minister that the transfer was made with the intention to make a gift.

Deemed Fair Market Value

14-132.   In order to eliminate arrangements such as the art flip that was described in Paragraph 14-125, ITA 248(35) introduces the concept of "deemed fair market value". This proposed Subsection indicates that, if a taxpayer acquires a property less than three years prior to its donation as a gift or, if a taxpayer acquires a gift less than 10 years before the gift is made and it is reasonable to conclude that the taxpayer acquired the property with an intent to make a gift, the value of the gift will be based on the lesser of the cost to the taxpayer and the actual fair market value at the time of the gift. There is an exception to this rule for gifts made as a consequence of a taxpayer's death.

Limits On Amount Claimed And Carry Forward Provisions

14-133.   As noted in Chapter 6, it is the policy of the government to limit charitable donations that are eligible for the tax credit to a portion of a taxpayer's Net Income For Tax Purposes. Note that, while corporations deduct their donations as opposed to receiving a credit against Tax Payable, the limits on the amount of eligible donations are the same for corporations as they are for individuals.

14-134.   The limit on eligible amounts of charitable gifts is 75 percent of Net Income For Tax Purposes. For individuals, this limit is increased to 100 percent of Net Income For Tax Purposes in the year of death and the preceding year. In those situations where a gift of capital property resulted in a capital gain, the overall limit is increased by 25 percent of the taxable capital gain. In the case of gifts of depreciable capital property, 25 percent of any recaptured CCA resulting from such gifts is also added to the limit. The reasons for these additions to the limit are explained beginning in Paragraph 14-139. There is no income limit on the amount of

Crown gifts, cultural gifts, or ecological gifts. Credits can be claimed for these gifts up to their eligible amounts.

14-135. The *Income Tax Act* does not require that charitable donations be claimed in the year that they are made. Unused charitable donations can be carried forward and claimed in the subsequent five year period. In the carry forward period, the same income based limits will apply in determining eligible amounts.

Gifts Of Capital Property

14-136.   When an individual makes a charitable, Crown, or ecological (but not cultural) gift of capital property, an election is available under ITA 118.1(6). On such properties, there will usually be a difference between the tax cost of the property (i.e., adjusted cost base for non-depreciable properties or UCC for depreciable properties) and its fair market value. If the fair market value is the higher value, the taxpayer can elect to transfer the property at any value between the tax cost of the property and its fair market value.

14-137.   In the case of non-depreciable assets, if the fair market value exceeds the adjusted cost base of the asset, it is advisable to elect the fair market value. Any amount of elected value in excess of $200 will be eligible for a tax credit at the maximum federal tax rate of 29 percent. In contrast, only one-half of any capital gain that results from the disposition will be subject to tax.

Example Mr. Vignesh Menan has a non-depreciable capital asset with an adjusted cost base of $100,000 and a fair market value of $150,000. In July, 2007, he intends to gift this asset to a registered Canadian charity and would like to know whether he should elect to make the donation at $100,000 or alternatively, at $150,000. He has other income that puts him in the 29 percent federal tax bracket, without including any gain resulting from this disposition.

Analysis The tax consequences of the two alternatives are as follows:

Elected Value	$100,000	$150,000
Tax Credit [(15.5%)($200) + (29%)($99,800)]	$ 28,973	
Tax Credit [(15.5%)($200) + (29%)($149,800)]		$ 43,473
Tax On Gain	N/A	
Tax On Gain [(1/2)($150,000 - $100,000)(29%)]		(7,250)
Credit Net Of Tax	$ 28,973	$ 36,223

14-138.   It should be noted that a proposed ITA 118.1(6) places a floor on this election. This amendment indicates that the election cannot be below the amount of any advantage received by the taxpayer as a consequence of the gift.

Example Extended Mr. Vignesh Menan has a non-depreciable capital asset with an adjusted cost base of $100,000 and a fair market value of $150,000. In return for making this gift, he receives a cash payment from the registered charity of $110,000.

Analysis Mr. Menan cannot elect a value below $110,000. Assuming he elects to transfer the asset at the maximum value of $150,000, the eligible amount of his gift will be $40,000 ($150,000 - $110,000).

14-139.   A potential problem with electing a value that creates income is that, if an individual's eligible donations are restricted to 75 percent of Net Income For Tax Purposes for the year, making a gift and electing to use the fair market value may result in income that cannot be eliminated with the related tax credit. In other words, making a gift could result in the payment of taxes. To avoid this problem, two other components are added to the base for charitable donations, resulting in a total base equal to:

• 75 percent of Net Income For Tax Purposes for the year; plus
• 25 percent of any taxable capital gain resulting from a gift; plus
• 25 percent of any recaptured CCA resulting from a gift.

14-140.   An example will serve to illustrate the importance of these additions to the overall limit:

Example   In July, 2007, Jonas Anderson gifts a customized bus that was used in his proprietorship to a registered Canadian charity. The bus has a fair market value of $130,000, a capital cost of $100,000, and a UCC of $65,000. He elects to make the gift at the fair market value of $130,000. He has no other source of income, other than amounts arising as a result of the gift.

Analysis   The election to make the gift at the fair market value of $130,000 will result in a total increase in Net Income For Tax Purposes of $50,000. This is comprised of a taxable capital gain of $15,000 [(1/2)($130,000 - $100,000)] and recaptured CCA of $35,000 ($100,000 - $65,000).

As Mr. Anderson has no other source of income, his basic limit for charitable donations would be $37,500 [(75%)($50,000)]. If his limit was $37,500, he would be faced with paying tax on $12,500 ($50,000 - $37,500) less his personal tax credits, as a result of his generosity in making the gift. However, with the additions to the limit, his overall limit is as follows:

75 Percent Of Net Income For Tax Purposes [(75%)($50,000)]	$37,500
25 Percent Of Taxable Capital Gain [(25%)($15,000)]	3,750
25 Percent Of Recaptured CCA [(25%)($35,000)]	8,750
Total Limit (Equals Net Income For Tax Purposes)	$50,000

14-141.   As you can see, the additions to the limit serve the purpose of creating a base for charitable donations that includes 100 percent of any income resulting from gifts of capital property. Note, however, Mr. Anderson will not want to use the full $50,000 in 2007. As amounts over $200 will generate a credit at a rate of 29 percent and all of Mr. Anderson's income will be taxed at a lower rate, use of the full $50,000 would produce a credit that is larger than his Tax Payable. In addition, he will want to make use of any non-refundable tax credits that are available for 2007. The following Exercise illustrates the determination of the amount of an available tax credit that should be taken in order to reduce Tax Payable to nil.

Exercise Fourteen-11

Subject: Donation Of Depreciable Property

Ms. Sally Felder donates some food preparation equipment to the local food bank, a registered Canadian charity. The assets have a fair market value of $85,000, a capital cost of $62,000, and a UCC of $28,000. She elects to make the donation at the fair market value of $85,000. She has no other source of income during the year and her only tax credit other than the charitable donations tax credit is her basic personal credit of $1,384. Determine her maximum charitable donations tax credit for 2007 and the amount of the donation she should claim in 2007 in order to reduce her Tax Payable to nil. Calculate any carry forward of unused amounts that will be available in future years.

End of Exercise. Solution available in Study Guide.

Canadian Cultural Property

14-142.   We have noted that, when an individual makes a charitable, Crown or ecological gift of capital property, they can elect to have the proceeds of disposition be any value between the tax cost of the property and the fair market value. In the case of cultural gifts of capital property, ITA 118.1(10.1) deems the proceeds of disposition to be the fair market value of the property in all cases. Note, however, that this same Subsection indicates that the value established by the Canadian Cultural Property Export Review Board or the Minister of the Environment is deemed to be the fair market value of the donated asset.

14-143.   This fair market value rule must be considered in conjunction with the fact that a provision in ITA 39(1)(a)(i.1) indicates that, with respect to gifts of Canadian cultural property, the difference between the fair market value and the adjusted cost base of the asset does not fall within the meaning of capital gain. As a consequence, any gain on a gift of Canadian cultural property is not subject to tax. Losses, however, would be treated as normal capital losses. Given this, it is not unreasonable to require that the proceeds of disposition on cultural gifts of capital property be equal to the fair market value of the property.

Publicly Traded Securities And Ecologically Sensitive Land

14-144.   Prior to the May 2, 2006 budget, a special rule applied to donations of both publicly traded securities and ecologically sensitive land. When these assets were donated, only one-half of the usual capital gain rate applied. As a result only 25 percent of any capital gain arising from such gifts was included in Net Income For Tax Purposes.

14-145.   The 2006 budget made these types of gifts even more attractive to taxpayers. For donations after May 1, 2006, the capital gain on charitable donations of publicly traded securities and ecologically sensitive land is deemed to be zero.

Exercise Fourteen-12

Subject: Donation Of Listed Shares

Mr. Saheed Radeem has employment income of $90,000. He owns shares that are listed on the Toronto Stock Exchange. These shares have a fair market value of $110,000 and an adjusted cost base of $30,000. During 2007, these shares are given to a registered Canadian charity. He has no deductions in the calculation of Taxable Income (i.e., his Taxable Income is equal to his Net Income For Tax Purposes). His tax credits, other than the charitable donations credit, total $4,000. Determine Mr. Radeem's maximum federal charitable donations tax credit for 2007 and the amount of the donation he should claim in 2007 in order to reduce his Tax Payable to nil. Calculate any carry forward of unused amounts that will be available in future years.

End of Exercise. Solution available in Study Guide.

Gifts Of Publicly Traded Securities Acquired Through Stock Options

14-146.   Without special rules, there is a potential problem for donations of publicly traded shares purchased through stock options. You will recall from Chapter 5 that, in the case of these shares, any accrued gain that is present at the time the options are exercised is treated as an employment income inclusion. In order to give such gains effective capital gains treatment, a deduction of one-half is provided in the determination of Taxable Income.

Example Roberto Cerutti is provided with options to buy 1,000 of his employer's shares at an option price of $20 per share, the fair market value of the shares at the time the options are granted. Roberto exercises these options when the shares are trading at $32 per share. He gifts the shares immediately to a registered charity.

Analysis Roberto will have an increase in Taxable Income calculated as follows:

Employment Income [(1,000)($32 - $20)]	$12,000
Deduction Under ITA 110(1)(d) [(1/2)($12,000)]	(6,000)
Increase In Taxable Income	$ 6,000

14-147.   As this example makes clear, in the absence of a special rule, gifts of publicly traded securities acquired through stock options would not be given the same treatment as gifts of such shares that were acquired without the use of options. That is, when there is a gift of publicly traded shares that have been acquired through options, the employment income inclusion that arises when the shares are acquired would remain in income.

14-148.   Fortunately, ITA 110(1)(d.01) provides such a special rule. If the option acquired shares are donated in the year acquired and not more than 30 days after their acquisition date, this paragraph provides for an additional deduction from the employment income inclusion that was created when the shares were acquired.

14-149.   Prior to the May, 2006 budget, this addition deduction was equal to 25 percent of the employment income inclusion. When this was combined with the usual 50 percent deduction from employment, 75 percent of the income arising from the exercise of the options was eliminated.

14-150.   As you have probably anticipated, the 2006 budget increased the ITA 110(1)(d.01) deduction to 50 percent of the employment income inclusion. When this deduction is combined with the usual 50 percent deduction, the result is the elimination of 100 percent of the employment income arising from the exercise of the options to acquire the gifted shares.

Foreign Tax Credits Revisited

Rules For Corporations

14-151.   Corporations are allowed to use foreign non-business income and foreign business income tax paid as a basis for a credit against Canadian Tax Payable. The rules for corporations are somewhat different from those for individuals and, in addition, require an understanding of some concepts that have not been introduced at this stage in the material. As a result, the foreign tax credit rules applicable to corporations are discussed in Chapter 15.

Foreign Non-Business (Property) Income Tax Credit For Individuals

14-152.   ITA 126(1) provides for a tax credit in situations where a Canadian resident has paid foreign taxes on non-business income. We introduced coverage of foreign tax credits in Chapter 9, but could not fully discuss the calculations as we had not yet covered loss carry overs and the lifetime capital gains deduction.

14-153.   As was noted in Chapter 9, the full amount of foreign non-business income earned, including amounts withheld for taxes in the foreign jurisdiction, must be added to the taxpayer's Net Income For Tax Purposes. This 100 percent amount is then subject to Canadian taxes, with the amount withheld in the foreign jurisdiction being allowed as a credit against Canadian Tax Payable. The objective of this procedure is to tax non-business income earned in a foreign jurisdiction at the same overall rate as would apply to non-business income earned in Canada.

14-154.   There are a number of complications with this procedure. The first of these is that, for individuals, amounts withheld that exceed 15 percent of the total foreign non-business income must be deducted under ITA 20(11). If, for example, an individual earned $1,000 in a jurisdiction that withheld $200, $150 of this amount would serve as a credit against Tax Payable, with the remaining $50 being deducted under ITA 20(11).

14-155.   A further problem is that the federal government wants to ensure that taxpayers do not receive a credit that is greater than the Canadian taxes that would have been paid on the foreign non-business income. This is accomplished by limiting the foreign non-business tax credit to the lesser of the amount withheld, and the amount determined by multiplying the ratio of foreign non-business income to total income by Canadian Tax Payable. This approach is reflected in the following formula:

The **Foreign Non-Business Income Tax Credit** is the lesser of:

- The tax paid to the foreign government. For individuals, this is limited to 15 percent of foreign non-business income, and

- An amount determined by the following formula:

$$\left[\frac{\text{Foreign Non} - \text{Business Income}}{\text{Adjusted Division B Income}}\right][\text{Tax Otherwise Payable}]$$

14-156.   The "Adjusted Division B Income" in this formula is defined as follows:

Division B Income (i.e., Net Income For Tax Purposes), less:
- net capital loss carry overs deducted under ITA 111(1)(b);
- any lifetime capital gains deduction taken;
- any amounts deductible for stock options under ITA 110(1)(d) and (d.1);
- any amounts deductible under ITA 110(1)(f) for workers' compensation, social assistance or exempt foreign income; and
- any amounts deductible under ITA 110(1)(j) for a home relocation loan.

14-157.   "Tax Otherwise Payable" in this calculation consists of:

Part I Tax Payable before the deduction of:
- dividend tax credits;
- employment outside of Canada tax credits;
- political contributions tax credits;
- investment tax credits; and
- labour sponsored funds tax credits.

14-158.   You should note that the preceding definition of Adjusted Division B Income is unique to the calculation of foreign tax credits. It starts with Net Income For Tax Purposes (Division B Income), and proceeds to deduct some, but not all, of an individual's available Division C deductions. For example, if the individual has non-capital loss carry overs, they are not deducted in this calculation. As a result, "Adjusted Division B Income" is a figure that is neither Net Income For Tax Purposes nor Taxable Income.

14-159.   The preceding rules would have to be applied on a country by country basis if non-business income was received from more than one foreign source. If the amount of foreign non-business taxes withheld exceeds the amount determined by the formula, there is no carry over of the unused amount as a tax credit. However, ITA 20(12) allows a taxpayer to deduct such amounts in the determination of Net Income For Tax Purposes.

Foreign Business Income Tax Credit For Individuals
14-160.   If a Canadian resident has income from an unincorporated business in a foreign country, ITA 126(2) provides for a credit for foreign taxes paid that is similar to that for non-business income. As is the case with foreign non-business income tax credits, individuals must include 100 percent of the foreign business income in their Net Income For Tax Purposes, with foreign taxes withheld being allowed as a credit against Tax Payable.

14-161.   While the amount of the credit that can be used does not have the 15 percent limit that is applicable to foreign non-business income tax credits, it is limited by a formula that is similar to the formula applicable to the foreign non-business income tax credit. One of the main differences between these two formulas is that, with respect to the foreign business income tax credit, there is an additional limit based on the tax otherwise payable for the year, reduced by any foreign non-business income tax credit deducted. The calculation of the foreign business income tax credit is as follows:

The **Foreign Business Income Tax Credit** is the least of:

- The tax paid to the foreign government (no 15 percent limit).

- An amount determined by the following formula:

$$\left[\frac{\text{Foreign Business Income}}{\text{Adjusted Division B Income}}\right][\text{Tax Otherwise Payable}]$$

- Tax Otherwise Payable for the year, less any foreign tax credit taken on non-business income under ITA 126(1).

14-162.   A further important difference between the two foreign tax credits is that, when foreign business income taxes paid exceed the amount that can be used as a credit during the current year, there is a three year carry back and ten year carry forward available. That is, if a taxpayer does not have sufficient Tax Payable to use all of the foreign business income tax credits during the current year, the excess can be treated as a credit against Tax Payable in any of the three preceding years, or in any of the ten subsequent years. Note, however, that it can only be used in those years within the constraints provided by the formula in Paragraph 14-161.

Exercise Fourteen-13

Subject: Foreign Tax Credits

During 2007, Sarah Cheung has Net Income For Tax Purposes of $50,000, a figure that includes $3,500 of foreign non-business income. The foreign jurisdiction withheld 12 percent of this amount, resulting in a net receipt of $3,080. In calculating Taxable Income, she deducts a $4,000 non-capital loss carry forward and a $2,500 net capital loss carry forward, resulting in a figure of $43,500. Her only tax credits are the basic personal credit and the credit for foreign tax paid. What is the amount of her foreign non-business income tax credit for 2007?

End of Exercise. Solution available in Study Guide.

Alternative Minimum Tax

General Concept

14-163.   There is a strong public feeling that allowing wealthy individuals with high levels of economic income to pay little or no tax is not an equitable situation. While such cases usually involve no more than taking full advantage of the various provisions in the *Act* that allow individuals to reduce their Tax Payable, the government felt that it was necessary to have legislation in place to deal with this potential problem. As a result, an alternative minimum tax (AMT) was introduced in 1986.

14-164.   This tax is directed at individuals who take advantage of tax shelters and other "tax preference" items. The basic idea is that individuals who have certain types of income, deductions, or credits, must calculate an adjusted taxable income by adding back all of the "tax preferences" that have been used in the calculation of regular taxable income.

14-165.   After deducting a basic $40,000 exemption, a flat rate of 15.5 percent is applied to the remaining net adjusted taxable income. The resulting Tax Payable is reduced by some, but not all, of the individual's regular tax credits to arrive at a minimum tax. The taxpayer must pay the greater of the regular Tax Payable and the minimum tax.

Minimum Tax Calculation

Definition

14-166.   The minimum tax is specified in ITA 127.51 as follows:

An individual's minimum amount for a taxation year is the amount determined by the formula

$$A (B - C) - D, \text{ where}$$

A   is the appropriate percentage for the year (15.5 percent for 2007);
B   is his adjusted taxable income for the year determined under section 127.52;
C   is his basic exemption for the year determined under section 127.53 (currently $40,000); and
D   is his basic minimum tax credit for the year determined under section 127.531.

14-167.   The calculation of adjusted taxable income that is described in ITA 127.52 is illustrated in a somewhat more comprehensible fashion in Form T691. The basic idea behind this adjusted taxable income is to put back into regular taxable income those items that are felt to be "tax preferences". Examples of such preference items would be losses on tax shelters and the non-taxable portion of capital gains.

Adjusted Taxable Income

14-168.   The required calculation of adjusted taxable income is as follows:

Regular Taxable Income

Plus Additions:

- 30 percent of the excess of capital gains over capital losses (see Paragraph 14-169).
- 3/5 of the employee stock option deductions under ITA 110(1)(d) and (d.1).
- The home relocation loan deduction.
- Losses arising through the deduction of CCA on Certified Canadian Films.
- The excess of CCA and interest charges claimed on rental and leasing property, over the net income reported for such property.
- Losses arising as a result of Canadian Exploration Expense (CEE), Canadian Development Expense (CDE), or depletion, net of certain resource related income.
- Losses deducted by limited partners, and members of a partnership who have been specified members at all times since becoming partners, in respect of their partnership interests, net of certain gains allocated from the same partnership.
- Losses deducted in respect of investments identified or required to be identified under the tax shelter identification rules.

Less Deductions:

- The gross up of Canadian dividends.
- 60 percent of ABILs deducted (see Paragraph 14-170).

Equals: Adjusted Taxable Income For Minimum Tax Purposes

14-169.   Rather than require that all of the non-taxable component of capital gains be added back, which could result in an excessive number of taxpayers being exposed to alternative minimum tax, only 30 percent of the total capital gain is added in the Adjusted Taxable Income calculation. This brings the total inclusion of the excess of capital gains over capital losses to 80 percent (50 percent is already included in regular income, plus the additional 30 percent).

14-170. The government also decided that this 80 percent treatment was appropriate for ABILs. The Adjusted Taxable Income calculation requires an additional deduction of 60 percent of any ABILs deducted in the year. Since 60 percent of an ABIL is equal to 30 percent of the total Business Investment Loss and 50 percent is already deducted from regular income, this effectively provides for a total deduction equal to 80 percent of the Business Investment Loss.

Tax Payable Before Credits

14-171.   A basic exemption is subtracted from the adjusted taxable income figure. This basic exemption is specified in ITA 127.53. Since the introduction of the AMT, this amount has been $40,000.

14-172.   After subtraction of the basic exemption, a flat rate is applied to the resulting balance. This rate is referred to in the ITA 127.51 formula as the "appropriate percentage". Appropriate percentage is defined in ITA 248 as the lowest percentage applicable in calculating federal Tax Payable. For 2007, this rate will be 15.5 percent. The resulting figure could be described as the alternative minimum tax before the deduction of tax credits.

Tax Credits For AMT

14-173.   ITA 127.531 specifies the tax credits, as calculated for the determination of regular Tax Payable, which can be applied against the alternative minimum tax. The credits specified are as follows:

- Personal credits under ITA 118(1).
- Age credit under ITA 118(2), but not the transfer from a spouse.
- Canada Employment Credit under ITA 118(10).
- Adoption expense credit under ITA 118.01(2).
- Transit Pass Credit under ITA 118.02.
- Child Fitness Credit under ITA 118.03.
- Charitable donations credit under ITA 118.1.
- Medical expense credit under ITA 118.2.
- Disability credit under ITA 118.3, but not the transfer from a spouse or other dependant.
- Education, textbook, tuition, and interest on student loans credits under ITA 118.5, 118.6 and 118.62, but not the transfer from a spouse or other dependant.
- CPP and EI credits under ITA 118.7.

14-174.   While ITA 127.531 is written in terms of credits that can be claimed, an easier approach to the calculation of available credits is taken in Form T691. This form, which is used for the calculation of minimum tax, starts with the sum of all of the non-refundable credits from the regular tax calculation and removes those that cannot be used for minimum tax purposes. These include:

- the dividend tax credit;
- the pension income credit;
- all transfers from a spouse or other dependant (pension, age, disability, or education related credits);
- investment tax credits;
- the political contributions tax credit; and
- the labour sponsored funds tax credit.

14-175.   The deduction of these credits will produce the alternative minimum tax payable. If this amount exceeds the regular taxes that are payable on the regular taxable income, the amount of alternative tax must be paid.

AMT Carry Forward

14-176.   There will be individuals who become subject to this alternative minimum tax in only some taxation years. The most common example of this situation is the realization of a large capital gain that can be eliminated by the use of the lifetime capital gains deduction.

14-177.   To provide for this, an excess of alternative minimum tax over regular Tax Payable can be carried forward for up to seven years to be applied against any future excess of regular Tax Payable over the alternative minimum tax. Unlike non-capital loss carry forwards, the carry forward period for the alternative minimum tax remains at seven years and has not been changed to 20 years.

Exercise Fourteen-14

Subject: Alternative Minimum Tax

Mr. Norton Blouson has Taxable Income for 2007 of $85,000. This includes taxable capital gains of $22,500 and eligible dividends of $29,000 [(145%)($20,000)]. In addition, he received a $50,000 retiring allowance that was contributed to his RRSP. The full contribution was deductible. His only tax credits are the basic personal credit and the dividend tax credit. Determine Mr. Blouson's federal liability for alternative minimum tax.

End of Exercise.   Solution available in Study Guide.

Sample Comprehensive Personal Tax Return

14-178.   In the separate paper Study Guide, there is a comprehensive example containing a completed personal tax return included in the material for Chapter 14.

Key Terms Used In This Chapter

14-179.   The following is a list of the key terms used in this Chapter. These terms, and their meanings, are compiled in the Glossary Of Key Terms located at the back of the separate paper Study Guide and on the Student CD-ROM.

Active Business	Listed Personal Property
Active Business Income	Loss Carry Back
Adjusted Taxable Income	Loss Carry Forward
Allowable Business Investment Loss	Lump-Sum Payments
Alternative Minimum Tax (AMT)	Net Capital Loss
Annual Gains Limit	Net Income For Tax Purposes
Business Investment Loss	Ordering Rule
Carry Over	Personal Use Property
Charitable Donations Tax Credit	Purification Of A
Charitable Gifts	Small Business Corporation
Crown Gifts	Qualified Farm Property
Cultural Gifts	Qualified Fishing Property
Cumulative Gains Limit	Qualified Small Business Corporation
Cumulative Net Investment Loss	Restricted Farm Loss
Ecological Gifts	Small Business Corporation
Farm Property	Specified Individual
Fishing Property	Split Income
Foreign Taxes Paid Credit	Stock Option
Lifetime Capital Gains Deduction	Taxable Income

References

14-180.   For more detailed study of the material in this Chapter, we would refer you to the following:

ITA 82(3)	Dividends Received By Spouse Of Common-Law Partner
ITA 110	Deductions Permitted
ITA 110.6	Lifetime Capital Gains Deduction
ITA 111	Losses Deductible
ITA 111.1	Order Of Applying Provisions
ITA 118.1	Charitable Gifts
ITA 127.5	
To 127.55	Obligation To Pay Minimum Tax
IC 75-23	Tuition Fees And Charitable Donations Paid To Privately Supported Secular and Religious Schools
IC 84-3R5	Gifts To Certain Organizations Outside Canada
IT-110R3	Gifts And Official Donation Receipts
IT-113R4	Benefits To Employees — Stock Options
IT-226R	Gift To A Charity Of A Residual Interest In Real Property Or An Equitable Interest In A Trust
IT-232R3	Losses - Their Deductibility In The Loss Years Or In Other Years
IT-244R3	Gifts By Individuals Of Life Insurance Policies As Charitable Donations
IT-270R3	Foreign Tax Credit
IT-288R2	Gifts Of Capital Properties To A Charity And Others
IT-295R4	Taxable Dividends Received After 1987 By A Spouse
IT-322R	Farm Losses
IT-520	Unused Foreign Tax Credits - Carry Forward And Carry Back
IT-523	Order Of Provisions Applicable In Computing An Individual's Taxable Income And Tax Payable

Appendix: Revoked Stock Option Election

14A-1.   You will recall from Chapter 5 that, for employees of publicly traded companies, the employment income benefit from stock options is measured and recognized at the time the options are exercised. Also discussed in that Chapter was a provision which allows this benefit to be deferred until the shares are actually sold. This deferral is subject to an annual limit of $100,000 in specified value of securities acquired. Specified value is based on the fair market value of the securities acquired, measured at the time the options were granted.

14A-2.   The problem here is that there may be situations where, after using the full amount of the available deferral in a given year, the individual may find that an election on a different group of securities may involve a larger deferral. To deal with this problem, ITA 7(13) provides for the revocation of an election that was made at an earlier point in time. An example will serve to clarify this procedure.

Example On April 30, 2007, Francine's employer grants her options to acquire 10,000 of the publicly traded shares of the company. The exercise price is $10 per share, which is the fair market value of the shares at that time. The options vest immediately, are exercisable immediately, and expire on April 30, 2011. On September 30, 2007, Francine's employer grants her options to acquire another 5,000 of its publicly traded shares. The exercise price is $15 per share, which is the fair market value of the shares at that time. The options vest immediately and expire on September 30, 2011.

Francine exercises all of the $10 options on April 30, 2011, when the fair market value is $100 per share. She files an election at that time to defer, under ITA 7(8), recognition of the employment benefit of $900,000 [(10,000)($100 - $10)]. Since the total specified value of the shares in respect of which the election is made is $100,000 [(10,000)($10)], the election fully utilizes the deferral limit for 2011.

Francine exercises the remaining options on September 30, 2011, when the fair market value is $295 per share. She wishes to defer recognition of as much of the employment benefit of $1,400,000 [(5,000)($295 - $15)] as possible. However, because of the previous election on the $10 options, she has no deferral room available. Since she needs $75,000 [(5,000)($15)] of deferral room she immediately files with the employer a written request to revoke the election previously made on 7,500 of the $10 options. This provides her with sufficient room to make an election to defer the employment benefit on all of the $15 options.

On Francine's T4 slip for 2011, the employment benefit of $675,000 [(7,500)($100 - $10)] associated with the revoked election will be included as income for the year. The remaining benefit of $1,625,000 [(2,500)($100 - $10) + (5,000)($295 - $15)] will be reported as a deferred amount that will be taxed in the year in which Francine disposes of the shares.

14A-3. The revocation must be filed in writing with the employer with whom the election was originally filed. This must take place no later than January 15 of the year following the year in which the securities on which the election was made were acquired.

Exercise Fourteen-15

Subject: Revoked Election On Stock Options

Ms. Andrea Flux is an executive with a publicly traded company. In February, 2006, she is granted options to acquire 4,000 of her employer's common shares at a price of $20 per share. In October, 2006, she is granted options to acquire a further 8,000 shares at $25 per share. Both groups of options vest at the time of granting, and are issued with the option price equal to the fair market value at the time of granting. In February, 2007, Ms. Flux exercises the $20 options. The fair market value of the shares at this time is $50 per share and she files an election under ITA 7(8) to defer the employment income inclusion. In December, 2007, when the fair market value of the shares is $140 per share, she exercises the $25 options. Indicate the elections she should make in order to maximize her 2007 deferral of employment income.

End of Exercise. Solution available in Study Guide.

Problems For Self Study

(The solutions for these problems can be found in the separate Study Guide.)

Self Study Problem Fourteen - 1

Over a four year period ending on December 31, 2007, Mr. Edward Fox experienced the following income and losses:

	2004	2005	2006	2007
Employment Income	$18,000	$16,000	$19,000	$12,000
Business Income (Loss)	14,500	(39,000)	34,000	(52,000)
Farming Income (Loss)	(6,000)	Nil	8,000	(2,000)
Taxable Dividends	6,250	8,156	10,000	12,656
Capital Gains	Nil	7,400	6,300	Nil
Capital Losses	(3,600)	Nil	Nil	(6,000)

Both the business operation and the farming operation began in 2004. With respect to the farming operation, Mr. Fox expects to make some profit on this operation even though it is not a full time occupation for him. The dividend income is from taxable Canadian corporations and the amount includes the gross up.

When he has a choice, he would like to deduct the maximum amount of his net capital loss carry overs and carry back any losses to the earliest possible year. None of Mr. Fox's losses can be carried back to years prior to 2004.

Assume that Mr. Fox requires $10,000 in Taxable Income in each year to fully utilize his personal tax credits.

Required: For each of the four years, calculate the minimum Net Income For Tax Purposes and Taxable Income for Mr. Fox. Indicate the amended figures for any years to which losses are carried back. Also indicate the amount and types of loss carry overs that would be available to Mr. Fox at the end of each year.

Self Study Problem Fourteen - 2

At the beginning of 2007, Harold Borgen had a $9,900 net capital loss carry forward from 2006. His net employment income amounted to $36,000 in 2007.

During 2007, Mr. Borgen realized a taxable capital gain of $37,500 on the sale of shares of a qualified small business corporation, and an allowable capital loss of $9,000 on the sale of a video business.

Mr. Borgen paid interest of $17,000 in 2007 on a loan for the investment in the shares of a Canadian controlled private corporation. These shares paid no dividends in 2007. His investment expenses and investment income prior to 2007 were nil.

As of the beginning of 2007, Mr. Borgen had made no deduction under ITA 110.6 (lifetime capital gains deduction) in any previous year. His only prior sale of capital assets created the net capital loss carry forward.

Required: Calculate Mr. Borgen's minimum Taxable Income for 2007. Provide all of the calculations required to determine the maximum ITA 110.6 deduction. In addition, briefly explain why Mr. Borgen would prefer using his lifetime capital gains deduction rather than his net capital loss carry.

Self Study Problem Fourteen - 3

Mr. and Mrs. Bahry have been retired for several years. They are both in their early seventies, residents of Canada, and rely on pension income to provide for most of their needs. More specifically, the components of their income for the year ending December 31, 2007 are as follows:

	Mr. Bahry	Mrs. Bahry
Old Age Security Benefits	$ 5,900	$5,900
Receipts From Registered Pension Plan	12,340	820
Receipts From Registered Retirement Income Fund	N/A	1,000
Canada Pension Plan Receipts	3,690	830
Eligible Dividends Received From Canadian		
Public Corporations (100%)	1,600	336
Interest On Savings Accounts	1,239	443
Charitable Donations	1,210	300
Capital Gain On Sale Of Painting	N/A	500
Capital Loss On Sale Of Public Company Shares	3,975	820

Assume that Mr. and Mrs. Bahry do not elect to use the pension income splitting provisions.

Required: Determine the optimum Taxable Income for both Mr. and Mrs. Bahry and the maximum federal tax credits that will be available to Mr. Bahry for the 2007 taxation year. Also indicate the amount and types of any loss carry overs that would be available to Mr. and Mrs. Bahry at the end of 2007.

Self Study Problem Fourteen - 4

Ms. Linda Worthmore is employed by Intra Graphics Inc. and, for the year ending December 31, 2007, she has a gross salary of $73,532. The following amounts were withheld by her employer during the year:

Canada Pension Plan Contributions	$1,990
Employment Insurance Premiums	720
Registered Pension Plan Contributions	1,233
Donations To Registered Charities	342

During 2007, Intra Graphics Inc. paid the following amounts on behalf of Ms. Worthmore:

Premium For Private Drug Plan	$ 415
Premium For Private Extended Health Care	235

Ms. Worthmore is married and lives with her husband, Mr. John Dalton. During 2007, Mr. Dalton received $750 in interest on a five year term deposit and had earnings from part time employment of $2,475. No CPP or EI payments were deducted from this income.

Mr. Dalton was a full time student at a designated educational institution during four months of the year. His tuition fees, which were paid by Ms. Worthmore, were $2,300. His fees for dental work totalled $1,056 for 2007 and were paid by Ms. Worthmore.

Ms. Worthmore and her husband have three children, all of whom live at home. Relevant information on these children is as follows:

Joyce   Joyce is seven years of age and has no income of her own. During 2007, Ms. Worthmore was required to pay $2,200 in medical expenses for Joyce.

Jayne   Jayne is fourteen years of age and had earnings from part time employment of $1,225. On March 15, 2007, Ms. Worthmore gave her daughter 27 shares of a publicly traded Canadian company. The shares had cost Ms. Worthmore $18 per share and, at the time of the gift, they were trading at $27 per share. The shares paid no dividends during 2007 and are still held by Jayne on December 31, 2007.

June   June is seventeen years of age and, during 2007, had income of $5,000. In July, 2007, June was involved in a serious accident. As a result of the accident, Ms. Worthmore was required to pay $9,850 of medical expenses on June's behalf.

Other Information:

1. In 2006, Ms. Worthmore gave her husband 52 shares of a publicly traded Canadian company. Ms. Worthmore had acquired the shares at $12 per share and, at the time of the gift, the shares were trading at $32 per share. On June 15, 2007, the shares paid an eligible dividend of $3.50 per share. On August 31, 2007, Mr. Dalton sold these shares for $56 per share.

2. Ms. Worthmore is the sole shareholder of Lindworth Inc. This Canadian controlled private corporation has a December 31 year end and, during 2007, paid non-eligible dividends in the total amount of $4,325 to Ms. Worthmore. As an employee of this Company, she received a salary of $2,500 for the year. No CPP or EI payments were deducted from the salary.

3. On January 1, 2007, Lindworth Inc. loaned Ms. Worthmore an amount of $5,000 to help finance an extended vacation for her husband. The loan is interest free and must be repaid in 2012. Ms. Worthmore has no intention of repaying it before that time.

4. Under the provisions of a court decree, Ms. Worthmore pays spousal support to her former husband in the amount of $225 per month.

5. During 2007, Ms. Worthmore made contributions to a Registered Retirement Savings Plan in the amount of $7,500. A Pension Adjustment of $6,161 was reported on her 2006 T4. Assume that her 2006 Earned Income equals her 2007 Earned Income. At the end of 2006, she has no Unused RRSP Deduction Room or undeducted RRSP contributions.

6. During 2007, Ms. Worthmore sold 122 shares of Lackmere Ltd. at a price of $86 per share. Ms. Worthmore owned a total of 300 shares of this Company, having acquired 122 at a price of $92 in 2005, and the other 178 at a price of $71 per share in 2006. Lackmere is not a qualified small business corporation.

7. During 2007, Ms. Worthmore sold land to her older brother for $10,000. The land had a fair market value of $28,000 and had been acquired by Ms. Worthmore on January 1, 2002 for $10,000. The land had been rented out to local farmers for agricultural use. The land is not a qualified farm property.

8. During 2007, Ms. Worthmore makes contributions to the Federal Liberal Party in the amount of $100.

Required: Calculate, for the 2007 taxation year, Ms. Worthmore's minimum Taxable Income and federal Tax Payable. Assume that the prescribed rate through all of 2007 is 5 percent (not including the extra 2 or 4 percent applicable to payments that are due from or owing to the CRA). Ignore GST and PST considerations, as well as payments that were made by Ms. Worthmore through instalments or withholding.

Self Study Problem Fourteen - 5

The following information relates to Mr. Michael Slater for the year ending December 31, 2007:

Receipts

Revenue From Farming		$ 36,000
Drawings From Proprietorship		9,000
Interest On Savings Account		4,600
Gross Salary From Employer		35,000
Gambling Income		1,600
Canada Pension Plan Benefits		5,100
Loans To Friends:		
Interest Received	$12,000	
Principal Repaid	21,000	33,000
Cash Inheritance From Deceased Aunt		25,000
Eligible Dividends From Canadian Public Corporations (100%)		44,000
Dividends From U.S. Corporations -		
Net Of 15 Percent Withholding (Canadian dollars)		8,500
Proceeds From Sale Of Land		111,500
Total Receipts		**$313,300**

Disbursements

Contributions To Federal Conservative Party	$ 500
Interest On Bank Loan	2,300
Farm Expenses	45,000
Life Insurance Premiums	11,000
Mortgage Payments On Personal Residence	15,000
Personal Funds Invested In Proprietorship	42,000
Charitable Donations	2,700
Safety Deposit Rental (For Securities)	150
Total Disbursements	**$118,650**

Other Information:

1. Mr. Slater's farm is operated on a part time basis. While the operating results are highly variable, the overall profit picture has been favourable.

2. The proprietorship began operations on May 1, 2007 and has a fiscal year end of December 31. The proprietorship had income of $28,300 for the period May 1 to December 31, 2007. The bank loan on which interest was paid was used to finance the establishment of the proprietorship.

3. Mr. Slater owns 45 percent of the shares of the corporation that employs him. As a result, no EI premiums were withheld. Since Mr. Slater is over 70 years old, he does not have deductions from salary for CPP. His employer has withheld a total of $9,000 in income tax from his gross salary of $35,000 during 2007. In addition, Mr. Slater has made instalment payments totalling $2,500. This is sufficient to bring his total tax payments up to the level of his 2006 Tax Payable.

4. The land that was sold during 2007 was purchased at a cost of $23,000 three years ago. Mr. Slater had intended to build a cottage on it.

5. As Mr. Slater has had consistently high levels of income, the full $5,900 of Old Age Security benefits has been withheld.

6. Mr. Slater is 71 years old. His wife is 61 and has no income of her own. She has been blind for several years.

7. Mr. Slater files his 2007 return on July 15, 2008.

Required: Calculate Mr. Slater's minimum federal Tax Payable for the year ending December 31, 2007. Ignore any alternative minimum tax that might be payable. Include in your solution any penalties, interest, or other amounts that are payable on federal balances, as well as any carry overs that are available at the end of the year. Assume that the prescribed rate, including the extra 4 percent on amounts owing to the Minister, for all relevant periods is 9 percent compounded on an annual basis.

Self Study Problem Fourteen - 6

Cheryl Delancey, a tax consultant, has provided tax assistance on a regular basis to her two aunts, Alma and Irene Delancey. For the 2007 taxation year, Cheryl and her aunts are concerned about the impact of the alternative minimum tax on the amount of tax they will have to pay. In order to estimate the tax that will be payable, they each have estimated the amounts and types of income they expect to earn, and deductions to claim, for 2007. These estimates are as follows:

	Cheryl	Alma	Irene
Employment And Business Income	$60,800	$42,000	$ 22,900
Non-Eligible Dividends Received From Canadian Corporations	26,300	Nil	29,400
Taxable Capital Gains	9,100	Nil	450,000
Lifetime Capital Gains Deduction Claimed	9,100	Nil	375,000
Retiring Allowance	Nil	58,000	Nil
RRSP Contributions	3,500	58,000	Nil

On Cheryl's 2006 T4, a Pension Adjustment of $8,600 was reported. Assume that her 2006 Earned Income equals her 2007 Earned Income. She has no Unused RRSP Deduction Room or undeducted RRSP contributions at the end of 2006.

As Alma had worked for her present employer for over 40 years, she is eligible for a tax free rollover of the entire retiring allowance to an RRSP.

All taxable capital gains relate to the sale of shares of qualified small business corporations. All of these dispositions occurred in July, 2007.

None of the Delancey women have ever married and they have no dependants. All three women are under 65 years of age and in good health.

Required: Calculate the minimum regular 2007 federal Tax Payable for each of the three women, as well as the alternative minimum tax amount. Ignore all tax credits other than the basic personal tax credit and any dividend tax credits.

Self Study Problem Fourteen - 7

> **This is an extension of Self Study Case Fourteen -1 (tax return preparation case). It has been updated for 2007 rates.**

Ms. Eleanor Trubey's husband died two years ago. After her husband died, she moved from her house in Prince George, B.C., to a rented house in Victoria, B.C.

Ms. Trubey's widowed mother, Marjorie Takarabe, had extremely bad luck the last time she was in Las Vegas. She lost all of her life savings and her house. As a result, she has moved in with Ms. Trubey and takes care of the house, Ms. Trubey's younger daughter, Amy, and all of the household cooking. Marjorie has never filed a tax return and has no Social Insurance Number.

Diane Trubey, Eleanor's older daughter, is studying psychology at McGill University in Montreal. Her field is addiction research with a special emphasis on gambling. She does volunteer work at a gambling addiction treatment centre in Montreal in the summers. As Eleanor has paid for her tuition and living costs, Diane has agreed that any credits available should be transferred to her mother.

Diane has decided not to file a tax return this year as she is too busy with her studies and volunteer work. Her income was earned driving for a client of the addiction treatment centre who had lost his licence after being charged with driving under the influence.

Other information concerning Ms. Trubey for 2007 is as follows:

1. Eleanor was born on May 15, 1959. She lives in Victoria, B.C.

2. She paid instalments of $2,528 for 2007.

3. The birth dates and income for the year of her dependants are as follows:

	Birth Date (Y/M/D)	Annual Income
Diane	1987-05-14	$2,300
Amy	1995-10-11	Nil
Marjorie	1926-05-21	$5,900 (OAS)

4. Eleanor's T4 for 2007 showed the following:

Employment Income	$60,202
Employee's EI Premiums	720
Employee's CPP Contributions	1,990
RPP Contributions	2,406
Pension Adjustment	7,829
Income Tax Deducted	19,408
Union Dues	749
Charitable Donations	175

5. Eleanor and her family had the following medical expenses for 2007:

Patient	Medical Expenses	Description	Amount
Eleanor	Grace Hospital	Ambulance Charge	$ 392
Eleanor	Paramed Home Health	Nursing Care	1,350
Marjorie	Dr. Zhang	Acupuncture	50
Marjorie	Pharmacy	Prescription	75
Diane	Dr. Glassman	Physiotherapist	100
Amy	Walk Right Foot Clinic	Orthotics	450
Amy	Dr. Tamo	Dental	1,120
Total			$3,537

6. In addition to the $175 in charitable contributions withheld by Eleanor's employer, Eleanor and Diane had the following charitable donations for 2007:

Donor	Charitable Donation Receipts	Amount
Eleanor	Heart And Stroke	$ 375
Eleanor	Terry Fox Foundation	50
Diane	Addiction Research Council Of Canada	100

7. Diane's T2202A showed tuition fees of $7,000, full-time attendance for 8 months, and part-time attendance for 2 months.

8. Eleanor's T3 showed capital gains of $982 and foreign non-business income of $311. No foreign taxes were withheld.

9. The pension from Eleanor's previous employer totalled $22,249 and income tax of $3,511 was withheld.

10. Eleanor's CPP survivor benefits totalled $4,823 and no income tax was withheld.

11. Eleanor received two T5s. The Scotia Bank T5 had interest from Canadian sources of $509. The Bank of Montreal T5 had a taxable amount of eligible dividends of $2,324 (dividends received of $1,603, plus a gross up of $721).

12. Eleanor made an RRSP contribution of $2,620 on February 10, 2008. She had undeducted RRSP contributions of $1,665 from 2006. She had no unused deduction room on January 1, 2007. Her Earned Income for 2006 was $38,873 and her Pension Adjustment for 2006 was $4,376.

13. Eleanor sent Amy to the Croft Computer Camp for 2 weeks. The cost was $1,000. In addition, Amy attended the Y Day Camp for 3 weeks during July, 2007. The cost was $400.

14. Eleanor did not sell her house in Prince George when she moved to Victoria as it was her intention to move back into it within three years. It has been rented on a month-to-month lease since November, 2006. The revenues, costs, and expenditures related to her Prince George rented house for 2007 are as follows:

Gross Rents	$15,600
Property Taxes	2,190
Insurance	1,093
Interest On Mortgage	5,378
Payment On Principal	3,689
Plumbing Repairs	291
Snow Plow Annual Contract	300
Lawyer's Fees For New Lease	173
Hydro (During Vacancy)	288
Cost Of Building And UCC - Beginning Of Year	168,900
UCC Of Appliances - Beginning Of Year	921
Purchase Of Stove And Refrigerator During Year (Old Appliances Were Traded-In)	1,500

15. Assume that Eleanor's provincial Tax Payable has been calculated correctly as $5,831.

Required:

A. Calculate Ms. Trubey's minimum balance owing to (refund from) the CRA for 2007. List any assumptions you have made, and any notes and tax planning issues you feel should be placed in the file.

B. Calculate the maximum deductible contribution Ms. Trubey can make to her RRSP for the 2008 taxation year. What advice would you give Ms. Trubey concerning her RRSP contributions?

Self Study Case

Self Study Case Fourteen - 1 (Using ProFile T1 Software For 2006 Tax Returns)

This Case is extended in Self Study Problem Fourteen-7 to use 2007 rates. This Case is a continuation of the Chapter 6 version of the Self Study Case.

Ms. Eleanor Trubey's husband died two years ago. After her husband died, she moved from her house in Prince George, B.C., to a rented house in Victoria, B.C.

Ms. Trubey's widowed mother, Marjorie Takarabe, had extremely bad luck the last time she was in Las Vegas. She lost all of her life savings and her house. As a result, she has moved in with Ms. Trubey and takes care of the house, Ms. Trubey's younger daughter, Amy, and all of the household cooking. Marjorie has never filed a tax return and has no Social Insurance Number.

Diane Trubey, Eleanor's older daughter, is studying psychology at McGill University in Montreal. Her field is addiction research with a special emphasis on gambling. She does volunteer work at a gambling addiction treatment centre in Montreal in the summers. As Eleanor has paid for her tuition and living costs, Diane has agreed that any credits available should be transferred to her mother.

Diane has decided not to file a tax return this year as she is too busy with her studies and volunteer work. Her income was earned driving for a client of the addiction treatment centre who had lost his licence after being charged with impaired driving.

Information concerning Ms. Trubey for 2006 is given on the following pages.

Required:

A. Prepare the 2006 income tax return of Eleanor Trubey using the ProFile tax software program. List any assumptions you have made, and any notes and tax planning issues you feel should be placed in the file.

B. Calculate the maximum deductible contribution Ms. Trubey can make to her RRSP for the 2007 taxation year. What advice would you give Ms. Trubey concerning her RRSP contributions?

Personal Information	
Title	Ms.
First Name	Eleanor
Last Name	Trubey
SIN	527-000-087
Date of birth (Y/M/D)	1958-05-15
Marital Status	Widowed
Provide information to Elections Canada?	Yes
Own foreign property of more than $100,000 Canadian?	No
Instalments paid on March 15 and June 15 of $1,264	$2,528 total for 2006

Taxpayer's Address
1415 Vancouver Street, Victoria, B.C. V8V 3W4
Phone number (250) 363-0120

Dependants	Child 1	Child 2	Mother
First Name	Diane	Amy	Marjorie
Last Name	Trubey	Trubey	Takarabe
SIN	527-000-293	None	None
Date of birth (Y/M/D)	1986-05-14	1994-10-11	1925-05-21
Net income	$2,300	Nil	$5,800

T2202A - (Diane)	Box	Amount
Tuition fees - for Diane Trubey (daughter)	A	7,000
Number of months in school - part-time	B	2
Number of months in school - full-time	C	8

T4	Box	Amount
Issuer - 1750 Canada Inc.		
Employment income	14	60,201.80
Employee's CPP contributions	16	1,910.70
Employee's EI premiums	18	729.30
RPP contributions	20	2,406.16
Pension adjustment	52	7,829.00
Income tax deducted	22	19,408.00
Union dues	44	748.59
Charitable donations	46	175.00

Patient	(Y/M/D)	Medical Expenses	Description	Am't
Eleanor	2006-08-15	Grace Hospital	Ambulance charge	392
Eleanor	2006-08-18	Paramed Home Health	Nursing care	1,350
Marjorie	2006-05-20	Dr. Zhang	Acupuncture	50
Marjorie	2006-07-06	Pharmacy	Prescription	75
Diane	2006-09-01	Dr. Glassman	Physiotherapist	100
Amy	2006-05-11	Walk Right Foot Clinic	Orthotics	450
Amy	2006-01-23	Dr. Tamo	Dental	1,120

Donor	Charitable Donation Receipts	Am't
Eleanor	Heart and Stroke	375
Eleanor	Terry Fox Foundation	50
Diane	Addiction Research Council of Canada	100

T3	Box	Amount
Issuer - Global Strategy Financial		
Foreign country - United States		
Capital gains	21	982.22
Foreign non-business income	25	310.94

T4A	Box	Amount
Issuer - 3601 Canada Inc.		
Pension	16	22,249.44
Income tax deducted	22	3,510.78

T4A(P)	Box	Amount
Survivor benefit	15	4,823.28
Income tax deducted	22	Nil

T5	Box	Slip 1	Slip 2
Issuer		Scotia Bank	Bank of Montreal
Actual amount of eligible dividends	24		1,603.00
Taxable amount of eligible dividends	25		2,324.35
Interest from Canadian sources	13	509.45	

RRSP information	(Y/M/D)	Amount
Issuer of receipt - Scotia Bank	2007-02-10	2,620.00
Contributions made prior to 2006/03/02 and not deducted	2006-01-25	1,664.51
Unused deduction room at the end of 2005		Nil
Earned income for 2005		38,873.00
Pension adjustment for 2005		4,376.00

Child	Child Care Expenses (Organization or Name and SIN)	No. of weeks	Amount
Amy	Croft Computer Camp (14 days overnight)	2	1,000
Amy	Y Day Camp (July)	3	400

Eleanor did not sell her house in Prince George when she moved to Victoria as it was her intention to move back into it within three years. It has been rented on a month-to-month lease since November, 2005.

Real Estate Rental	Amount
Address - 280 Victoria Street, Prince George, B.C. V2L 4X3	
Gross rents (12 months for 2006)	15,600.00
Property taxes	2,190.73
Insurance	1,093.27
Interest on mortgage	5,377.58
Payment on principal	3,688.95
Plumbing repairs	290.94
Snow plow annual contract	300.00
Lawyer's fees for new lease	172.54
Hydro (during vacancy)	288.34
Building purchased October 1, 1998 for $168,900 - UCC beginning of year	168,900.00
Appliances purchased February 9, 2004 for $1,100 - UCC beginning of year	921.00
Purchase of stove and refrigerator on May 17, 2006 (old appliances traded-in)	1,500.00

Assignment Problems

(The solutions for these problems are only available in
the solutions manual that has been provided to your instructor.)

Assignment Problem Fourteen - 1

During 2003, Miss Lynn Atwater invested $170,000 to acquire 100 percent of the common shares of a corporation specializing in pet food products. The company was a Canadian controlled private corporation with a fiscal year ending on January 31. All of its assets were used to produce active business income.

In 2004 and 2005, the company operated successfully, but did not pay any dividends. In 2006, it began to experience serious financial difficulties. On July 15, 2007, the company was forced into bankruptcy by its creditors and it is clear to Miss Atwater that, after the claims of the creditors have been dealt with, her investment will be worthless.

Other financial data for Miss Atwater for the years ending December 31, 2006 and December 31, 2007, is as follows:

	2006	2007
Net rental income	$34,200	$35,200
Interest income	4,000	4,200
Basic personal amount	8,839	8,929

The only tax credit available to Miss Atwater in either year is the basic personal credit. Miss Atwater had no Taxable Income for 2004 and 2005. At the beginning of 2005, she did not have any loss carry overs from previous years.

Required: Determine Miss Atwater's optimum Taxable Income for the years ending December 31, 2006 and December 31, 2007. In your solution, consider the effect of the basic personal credit. Indicate any loss carry over that is present at the end of either year, and the rules applicable to claiming the loss carry over.

Assignment Problem Fourteen - 2

During the four year period 2004 through 2007, Ms. Brenda Breau had the following financial data:

	2004	**2005**	**2006**	**2007**
Business Income (Loss)	$18,000	($14,000)	$30,000	($19,000)
Farming Income (Loss)	(10,000)	2,000	3,150	(2,000)
Taxable Dividends	2,360	2,950	3,963	6,450
Capital Gains	1,200	2,000	4,000	4,500
Capital Losses	(4,200)	Nil	Nil	(14,500)

Because of the nature of her farming activities, Ms. Breau's farm losses are restricted. The dividend income is from taxable Canadian corporations and the amount includes the gross up.

When she has a choice, she would like to deduct the maximum amount of her net capital loss carry overs and carry back any losses to the earliest possible year. None of Ms. Breau's losses can be carried back before 2004.

Assume that Ms. Breau requires $12,000 in Taxable Income in each year to fully utilize her personal tax credits.

Required: Calculate Ms. Breau's minimum Net Income For Tax Purposes and Taxable Income for each of the four years. In applying carry over amounts, do not reduce Ms. Breau's Taxable Income below $12,000, the amount required to fully utilize her personal tax credits. Indicate the amended figures for any years to which losses are carried back. Also indicate the amount and types of loss carry overs that would be available at the end of each year.

Assignment Problem Fourteen - 3

At the beginning of 2007, Mr. Lindon had a $10,250 [(1/2)($20,500)] net capital loss from 2005. His net employment income amounted to $21,300 in 2007.

On July 1, 2007, Mr. Lindon realized a taxable capital gain of $18,300 on the sale of shares in a qualified small business corporation and an allowable capital loss of $4,800 on the sale of shares of a public company.

In 1994, Mr. Lindon used the lifetime capital gains deduction election to deduct $75,000 [(3/4)($100,000)] of capital gains. He has made no other deduction under ITA 110.6 (lifetime capital gains deduction). As of the end of 2007, he has no Cumulative Net Investment Loss.

Mr. Lindon would prefer to make maximum use of his lifetime capital gains deduction prior to applying any of the net capital loss carry forward from 2005.

Required: Calculate Mr. Lindon's minimum Taxable Income for 2007. Provide all of the calculations required to determine the maximum ITA 110.6 deduction. In addition, briefly explain why Mr. Lindon would prefer using his lifetime capital gains deduction rather than his 2005 net capital loss carry.

Assignment Problem Fourteen - 4

Mr. and Mrs. Hanson have been retired for several years. They are both in their early seventies, residents of Canada, and rely on pension income to provide for most of their needs. More specifically, the components of their income for the year ending December 31, 2007 are as follows:

Assignment Problems

	Mr. Hanson	Mrs. Hanson
Old Age Security Benefits	$ 5,900	$5,900
RRIF Income	50,000	Nil
Receipts From Registered Pension Plan	15,380	1,680
Eligible Dividends Received From Canadian		
Public Corporations (100%)	800	180
Interest On Government Bonds	500	2,359
Charitable Donations	600	200
Capital Gain On Sale Of Shares	N/A	375
Capital Loss On Sale Of Shares	N/A	725

Assume that Mr. and Mrs. Hanson do not elect to use the pension income splitting provisions.

Required: Determine the optimum Taxable Income for both Mr. and Mrs. Hanson, and the maximum federal tax credits that will be available to Mr. Hanson for the 2007 taxation year. Also indicate the amount and types of any loss carry overs that would be available to Mr. and Mrs. Hanson at the end of 2007.

Assignment Problem Fourteen - 5

Wanda Lanson, an established tax professional, has provided tax assistance on a regular basis to her two brothers, Wally and Wesley Lanson. For 2007, they are both concerned about the impact of the alternative minimum tax on the amount of tax they will have to pay. In order to help them prepare for any additional tax payments that they may encounter, she has asked them to estimate the amount of various types of income and deductions they expect to record for 2007. These estimates, along with the similar figures for herself, are as follows:

	Wanda	Wally	Wesley
Employment And Business Income	$39,500	$32,800	$ 18,250
Non-Eligible Dividends Received			
From Taxable Canadian Corporations	60,500	Nil	62,000
Taxable Capital Gains	24,500	Nil	267,750
Lifetime Capital Gains Deduction Claimed	24,500	Nil	267,750
Retiring Allowance	Nil	50,000	Nil
RRSP Contributions	Nil	50,000	Nil

As Wally had worked for his present employer for over 41 years, he was eligible for a tax free rollover of the entire retiring allowance to an RRSP.

All dispositions resulting in taxable capital gains were of shares of qualified small business corporations and occurred in September and October, 2007.

None of the Lansons have ever married, they have no dependants, they are all under 65 years of age, and they are not disabled.

Required: Calculate the minimum regular 2007 federal Tax Payable for each of the three Lansons, as well as the alternative minimum tax amount. Ignore all tax credits other than the basic personal tax credit and any dividend tax credits.

Assignment Problem Fourteen - 6

On June 3, 2007, Mrs. Steele unexpectedly died of complications associated with minor surgery. Her husband, a man with little experience in financial matters, has asked you to assist him with the administration of Mrs. Steele's estate. After working with her records for several days, you have accumulated the following information:

1. Mrs. Steele's tax return for the year ending December 31, 2006 was filed on April 10, 2007. It indicated a net capital loss carry forward of $76,500 from a disposition that occurred in 2005.

2. During 2007, but prior to the date of her death, Mrs. Steele's investments paid eligible dividends of $1,090. In addition, she had Canadian source interest income of $2,025 during this period.

3. Mrs. Steele's office desk contained uncashed matured bond coupons totalling $3,270 that were dated for payment in 2007. The bonds were issued October 1, 2006.

4. Mrs. Steele was the proprietor of a successful boutique that had been in operation for eight years. The fiscal year of this unincorporated business ends on December 31. From January 1, 2007, until the date of Mrs. Steele's death, this business had net business income for tax purposes of $55,200. The fair market value of the assets of the boutique at the time of Mrs. Steele's death was $4,800 greater than their UCC. None of the individual assets had a fair market value that exceed its capital cost.

5. In connection with the boutique, Mrs. Steele paid Mr. Steele wages of $425 during the period January 1, 2007 through June 3, 2007. This money was paid for assistance in handling the inventories of the operation. Mr. Steele's only other income for the year was $2,100 in interest on a group of mortgages, which had been given to him as a gift by Mrs. Steele three years ago.

6. Mrs. Steele had a rental property that she had owned for a number of years. Rents received in 2007, prior to her death, amounted to $41,200, while cash expenses totalled $24,650. The UCC of the building was $144,800 on January 1, 2007. The building had been purchased for $183,000. At the time of her death, an appraisal indicated that the fair market value of the building was $235,000. The land on which the building is situated has a cost of $92,000, and a fair market value at the time of her death that is estimated to be $164,000.

7. Other assets that were owned by Mrs. Steele at the time of her death are as follows:

    Shares In AGF Industries AGF Industries is a Canadian public company and Mrs. Steele purchased common shares at a cost of $10,600. Their value at the time of Mrs. Steele's death was $7,900.

    Shares In Rolston Inc. Rolston Inc. is also a Canadian public company and Mrs. Steele purchased shares at a cost of $36,800. Their value at the time of Mrs. Steele's death was $169,400.

    Painting A painting Mrs. Steele had purchased for $8,000 had a fair market value of $37,000 at the time of her death.

    Residence Mrs. Steele owned the family home. It had been purchased at a cost of $209,400. At the time of her death, the appraised value of the property was $344,000.

8. The terms of Mrs. Steele's will provide that the shares in AGF Industries and Rolston Inc., the painting, and the assets of the boutique be left to Mr. Steele. The family home and the rental property are to be left to Mrs. Steele's 27 year old daughter.

Required: Calculate Mrs. Steele's minimum 2007 federal Tax Payable. Provide the due date for her 2007 tax return(s).

Assignment Problem Fourteen - 7

On January 10, 2007, Ms. Marcia Klaus formally separated from her husband and retained custody of her 15 year old son, Martin. Martin has no income during 2007. Ms. Klaus is also responsible for her 20 year old daughter, Louise, who has a severe and prolonged disability (a medical doctor has certified her disability on Form T2201). Louise has 2007 income of $6,000, resulting from income on investments that were left to her by her grandmother.

Assignment Problems

In order to get a fresh start in life, Ms. Klaus found a new job. She resigned from her position in Ottawa and moved to a similar position in Toronto. The move took place on October 31, 2007. She has asked for your assistance in preparing an estimate of her 2007 personal tax liability and, in order to assist you with your calculations, she has prepared the following list of transactions that occurred during 2007:

1. Her gross salary from her Ottawa employer, a large public company, for the first 10 months of the year was $62,000. Her employer withheld from this amount CPP contributions of $1,990, EI premiums of $720, RPP contributions of $2,500, and income tax of $18,000. The employer also contributed $2,500 to the RPP on her behalf. She was a member of her employer's money purchase RPP during all of her years of employment.

    In appreciation of her 31 years of excellent service, the Ottawa employer paid her a retiring allowance of $30,000.

    Before leaving her Ottawa employer, she exercised stock options to acquire 2,000 of the company's shares at a price of $15 per share. The options were issued in 2005, when the market price of the shares was $12 per share. On August 12, 2007, the day that she exercised the options, the shares were trading at $20 per share. Ms. Klaus sells the shares as soon as she acquires them. Brokerage fees totalled $350 on the sale.

2. During November and December, her gross wages with her Toronto employer amounted to $13,000. Her new employer withheld CPP contributions of $500, EI premiums of $390, $650 in RPP contributions, and $4,000 in income tax. Her Toronto employer also contributed $650 to the company's money purchase RPP on her behalf.

    Ms. Klaus found a new home in Toronto during her September house hunting trip there. The legal arrangements for the house purchase were finalized on October 10. In Ottawa, she and her husband had lived in a home that they rented. Her agreement with her new employer requires that they pay her moving costs. In order to simplify the record keeping, the employer paid her an allowance of $7,500 and did not require a detailed accounting of expenses. Her actual expenses were as follows:

Moving company charges	$3,800
Airfare for September Toronto trip to acquire new home	350
Meals and lodging on September Toronto trip	275
Gas for October 31 move to Toronto	65
Lodging in Ottawa on October 30	110
Meals on October 30 and October 31	250
Charges for cancellation of lease on Ottawa home	935
Legal and other fees on acquisition of Toronto home	1,500
Total	$7,285

3. In 2004, Ms. Klaus' mother died, leaving her 5,000 shares of Lintz Industries, a private company. These shares had cost her mother $50,000, and had a fair market value at the time of her death of $95,000. Ms. Klaus received non-eligible dividends of $7,500 on these shares in May and, in December, she sells the shares for $105,000. Selling costs were $1,050.

4. Ms. Klaus made $1,500 in donations to a registered Canadian charity and $900 in contributions to the Libcon Rebloc Party, a registered federal political party.

5. Ms. Klaus incurred the following child care costs:

Payments To Individuals For Martin And Louise	$7,160
Fees For Martin To Attend Camp (4 Weeks At $200 Per Week)	800
Food And Clothing For The Children	6,400
Total	$14,360

6. Ms. Klaus paid the following medical expenses:

For Herself	$ 9,700
Martin	900
Louise	7,250
Total	$17,850

7. In previous years, Ms. Klaus' husband took care of her financial affairs. She has no under-standing of either RPPs or RRSPs, but will make the maximum deductible RRSP contribution for 2007 as soon as you have calculated it. Her RRSP Deduction Limit State-ment from the CRA states that her 2006 Earned Income was $61,100 and that, at the end of 2006, she had no Unused RRSP Deduction Room. Her 2006 T4 from her employer indicates a Pension Adjustment of $4,500. There are no undeducted contributions in her RRSP.

8. During the year, Ms. Klaus paid legal fees of $2,500 in connection with her separation agreement. This settlement requires her husband to make a lump sum payment of $25,000 on March 1, 2007, as well as child support payments of $4,000 at the end of each month beginning on January 31, 2007. All required payments were received for the year.

9. In addition to her employment income, Ms. Klaus operates an unincorporated mail order business with a December 31 year end. Her net business income for 2007 totaled $22,500. Included in this amount is interest of $950 that she paid on a demand loan taken out to finance inventory purchases. During the year ending December 31, 2007, Ms. Klaus withdraws $27,000 from the bank account maintained by the business.

10. Assume her provincial Tax Payable for 2007 has been correctly calculated as $6,900 and she does not use the simplified method to calculate moving costs.

Required:

A. Determine Ms. Klaus' minimum Net Income For Tax Purposes and her minimum Taxable Income for 2007. Ignore any GST or PST considerations. In the Net Income For Tax Purposes calculation, provide separate disclosure of:

- Net Employment Income,
- Net Business And Property Income,
- Taxable Capital Gains Less Allowable Capital Losses,
- Other Sources Of Income, And
- Other Deductions From Income.

B. Based on your answer to Part A, calculate Ms. Klaus' amount owing to (refund from) the CRA for 2007. Explain why you omitted any amounts from your calculations.

Assignment Problem Fourteen - 8

This is an extension of Assignment Case 14-2 (tax return preparation case). It has been updated for 2007 rates.

George Hall is a pharmaceutical salesman who has been very successful at his job in the last few years. Unfortunately, his family life has not been very happy. Three years ago, his only child, Anna, was driving a car that was hit by a drunk driver. She and her husband were killed and their 13 year old son, Kevin, was blinded in the accident. He also suffered extensive inju-ries to his jaw that have required major and prolonged dental work.

George and his wife, Valerie, adopted Kevin. Valerie quit her part-time job to care for him. She also cares for her mother, Joan Parker. Joan suffers from diabetes and severe depression and lives with George and Valerie. Valerie's parents separated two years ago in Scotland after her father, David Parker, suffered enormous losses in the stock market. They were forced to sell their home and David moved to South America. David phones periodically to request that money be deposited in his on-line bank account. Valerie does not meet the residency requirements necessary to qualify for Canadian Old Age Security payments.

George's brother, Martin, completed an alcohol rehabilitation program after being fired for drinking on the job. He is also living with George and Valerie while he is enrolled as a full-time student at the Northern Alberta Institute of Technology. George is paying his tuition and Martin has agreed to transfer the maximum education related credits to George. Although Martin plans to file his 2007 tax return, he has not done so yet.

In addition to George's salary, he also earns commissions. His employer requires him to have an office in his home and has signed Form T2200 each year to this effect.

Other information concerning George for 2007 is as follows:

1. George was born on July 2, 1943 and lives in Edmonton, Alberta.

2. The birthdates and income for the year of his family members are as follows:

	Birth Date (Y/M/D)	Annual Income
Valerie (income from CPP)	1942-12-30	$5,800
Kevin	1991-10-17	Nil
Joan Parker	1922-02-24	500
David Parker	1923-01-12	Nil
Martin	1960-06-02	8,300

3. George's T4 showed employment income of $378,000, which includes commissions of $82,000. His withholdings consisted of income tax of $125,000, CPP contributions of $1,990, EI premiums of $720, and charitable donations of $400.

4. Martin's T2202A showed tuition fees of $6,000 and full-time attendance for 8 months.

5. During the year, Valerie donated $1,000 to Mothers Against Drunk Drivers (MADD). George donated $3,000 to the Canadian National Institute For The Blind (CNIB).

6. George and his family had the following medical expenses for 2007:

Patient	Medical Expenses	Description	Amount
George	Johnson Inc.	Out Of Canada Insurance	$ 731
George	Dr. Smith	Dental Fees	155
George	Optician	Prescription Glasses	109
Valerie	Pharmacy	Prescription	67
Joan	Dr. Wong	Psychiatric Counseling	2,050
David	Tropical Disease Centre	Prescription	390
Martin	Dr. Walker	Group Therapy	6,000
Kevin	Dr. Takarabe	Orthodontics and Dental	30,000
Total			$39,502

7. George paid $800 for the care and feeding of Kevin's seeing eye dog, Isis, during 2007.

8. George's home has a total area of 5,000 square feet. The area of the home used as a home office is 650 square feet. Other costs for the home are as follows:

Telephone Line (including high speed internet connection)	$ 620
Hydro	3,200
Insurance - House	4,000
Maintenance And Repairs	3,800
Mortgage Interest	6,200
Mortgage Life Insurance Premiums	400
Property Taxes	6,700
Total	$24,920

9. George purchased a new computer and software that will be used solely in his home office for employment related uses. The computer cost $3,600 and the various software programs cost $1,250.

10. At the beginning of 2007, George had a net capital loss carry forward of $10,500 from the sale of shares in 2006. He had not disposed of any capital assets prior to 2006. During 2007, he had the following dispositions:

	Asset 1	Asset 2	Asset 3
Description	Molson Inc. Shares	Imperial Oil Shares	Sailboat
Proceeds of disposition	$37,000	$ 9,600	$74,000
Adjusted cost base	27,600	12,100	72,000
Outlays and expenses	35	29	N/A

	Asset 4	Asset 5	Asset 6
Description	Motorcycle	Painting	Coin Collection
Proceeds of disposition	$14,000	$1,100	$ 700
Adjusted cost base	21,000	450	1,800
Outlays and expenses	N/A	N/A	N/A

11. Mr. Hall owns a commercial property in Calgary that he purchased in 2003. Information related to the property is as follows:

Gross rents	$ 16,000
Property taxes	5,128
Insurance	1,890
Interest on mortgage	3,175
Payment on principal	2,200
Furnace repairs	550
Maintenance contract	3,469
UCC of building - beginning of year	107,441
UCC of fixtures - beginning of year	4,651

Required: Calculate Mr. Hall's minimum federal Tax Payable for 2007, without consideration of any income tax withheld. List any assumptions you have made, and any notes and tax planning issues you feel should be placed in the file. Include the amount and type of any loss carry overs available at the end of the year. Assume that George does not qualify for the GST rebate.

Assignment Cases

Assignment Case Fourteen - 1 (Using ProFile T1 Software For 2006 Tax Returns)

This Case is a continuation of the Chapter 6 version.

Mr. Buddy Cole (SIN 527-000-061) was born on August 28, 1939. He has spent most of his working life as a pianist and song writer. He and his family live at 1166 West Pender Street, Vancouver, B.C. V6E 3H8, phone (604) 669-7815.

Mr. Cole's wife, Natasha (SIN 527-000-129), was born on June 6, 1981. She and Mr. Cole have four children. Each child was born on April 1 of the following years, Linda; 2001, Larry; 2002, Donna; 2003, and Donald; 2004. Natasha had Net Income For Tax Purposes of $4,800 for 2006. This consisted of $2,400 [(4)($100)(6)] in universal child care benefits and $2,400 in interest income.

Buddy and Natasha Cole have two adopted children. Richard (SIN 527-000-285) was born on March 15, 1989 and has income of $2,800 for the year. Due to his accelerated schooling, he started full time attendance at university in September of 2006 at the age of 17. His first semester tuition fee is $3,000 and he requires books with a total cost of $375. These amounts are paid by Mr. Cole.

The other adopted child, Sarah, was born on September 2, 1986, and is in full time attendance at university for all of 2006 (including a four month summer session). Her tuition is $9,600 and she requires textbooks which cost $750. These amounts are also paid by Mr. Cole. Sarah has no income during the year.

Neither Richard nor Sarah will have any income in the next three years. Any unused credits of either child are available to be transferred to their father.

Mr. Cole's mother, Eunice, was born on April 10, 1919 and his father, Earl, was born on November 16, 1917. They both live with Mr. Cole and his wife. While his father is still physically active, his mother is blind. Eunice Cole had income of $9,500 for the year, while Earl Cole had income of $7,500.

Other information concerning Mr. Cole and his family for 2006 is as follows:

1. Mr. Cole earned $16,500 for work as the house pianist at the Loose Moose Pub. His T4 showed that his employer withheld $4,200 for income taxes and $349 for EI. Due to an error on the part of the payroll accountant, he overpaid his EI by $40. No CPP was withheld.

2. During the year, Mr. Cole made $3,000 in donations to Planned Parenthood Of Canada, a registered Canadian charity.

3. Mr. Cole has been married before to Lori Cole (SIN 527-000-319). Lori is 52 years old and lives in Fort Erie, Ontario.

4. Mr. Cole has two additional children who live with their mother, Ms. Dolly Holt (SIN 527-000-582), in Burnaby, British Columbia. The children are Megan Holt, aged 15 and Andrew Holt, aged 16. Neither child has any income during 2006. While Ms. Holt and Mr. Cole were never married, Mr. Cole acknowledges that he is the father of both children. Although Buddy has provided limited financial aid, the children are not dependent on Buddy for support.

5. Mr. Cole wishes to claim all his medical expenses on a calendar year basis. On December 2, 2006, Mr. Cole paid dental expenses to Canada Wide Dental Clinics for the following individuals:

Himself	$1,200
Natasha (wife)	700
Richard (adopted son)	800
Sarah (adopted daughter)	300
Linda (daughter)	100
Earl (father)	1,050
Lori (ex-wife)	300
Dolly Holt (mother of two of his children)	675
Megan Holt (daughter of Dolly Holt)	550
Total	$5,675

6. Mr. Cole receives $5,800 in Old Age Security payments and $5,500 in Canada Pension Plan payments over 12 months. There was no tax shown as withheld on his T4A(OAS) or his T4A(P).

7. Mr. Cole received $52,000 in payments from a life annuity purchased with funds accumulated in his RRSP. His T4RSP showed that total tax of $28,000 was deducted from these payments.

8. Several of Mr. Cole's songs, including his outstanding hit, "Drop Kick Me Jesus Through The Goal Posts Of Life", have provided him with substantial royalty payments over the years. Because he has never learned how to read music, he sings his newly composed songs at the Never Say Die Record Company to be transcribed. In 2006, the record company paid him $78,000 in royalty payments.

9. Mr. Cole is required by a court order to pay spousal support of $400 per month to his former spouse, Lori Cole. Mr. Cole made spousal support payments of $4,800 during 2006.

10. Mr. Cole is required by a 1994 court order to make child support payments of $350 per month for his two children, Megan and Andrew Holt. A total of $4,200 was paid during the year.

11. Mr. Cole made contributions to the Federal Liberal Party in the amount of $610 during the year.

12. Mr. Cole paid four quarterly instalments of $1,000 each (total of $4,000) for 2006, as requested on his Instalment Reminders from the CRA.

Required: With the objective of minimizing Mr. Cole's Tax Payable, prepare his 2006 income tax return using the ProFile tax software program. List any assumptions you have made, and any notes and tax planning issues you feel should be placed in the file. Ignore GST implications in your solution.

Assignment Case Fourteen - 2 (Using ProFile T1 Software For 2006 Tax Returns)
This is extended in Assignment Problem Fourteen-8 to use 2007 rates. This Case is a continuation of the Chapter 6 version.

George Hall is a pharmaceutical salesman who has been very successful at his job in the last few years. Unfortunately, his family life has not been very happy. Three years ago, his only child, Anna, was driving a car that was hit by a drunk driver. She and her husband were killed and their 13 year old son, Kevin, was blinded in the accident. He also suffered extensive injuries to his jaw that have required major and prolonged dental work.

George and his wife, Valerie, adopted Kevin. Valerie quit her part-time job to care for him. She also cares for her mother, Joan Parker. Joan suffers from diabetes and severe depression and lives with George and Valerie. Valerie's parents separated two years ago in Scotland after her father, David Parker, suffered enormous losses in the stock market. They were forced to sell their home and David moved to South America. David phones periodically to request that money be deposited in his on-line bank account. Valerie does not meet the residency requirements necessary to qualify for Canadian Old Age Security payments.

George's brother, Martin, completed an alcohol rehabilitation program after being fired for drinking on the job. He is also living with George and Valerie while he is enrolled as a full time student at the Northern Alberta Institute of Technology. George is paying his tuition and Martin has agreed to transfer the maximum tuition and education amounts to George. Although Martin plans to file his 2006 tax return, he has not done so yet.

In addition to George's salary, he also earns commissions. His employer requires him to have an office in his home and has signed the form T2200 each year to this effect.

Other information concerning George for 2006 is given on the following pages.

Required: Prepare the 2006 income tax return of George Hall using the ProFile tax software program. List any assumptions you have made, and any notes and tax planning issues you feel should be placed in the file. Assume that George does not qualify for the GST rebate.

Personal Information	Taxpayer
Title	Mr.
First Name	George
Last Name	Hall
SIN	527-000-509
Date of birth (Y/M/D)	1942-07-02
Marital Status	Married
Provide information to Elections Canada?	Yes
Own foreign property of more than $100,000 Cdn?	No

Taxpayer's Address
97 Jasper Avenue, Apt 10, Edmonton, Alberta   T5J 4C8
Phone number (780) 495-3500

Family Members	Spouse	Child	Mother-In-Law
First Name	Valerie	Kevin	Joan
Last Name	Hall	Hall	Parker
SIN	527-000-483	527-000-517	None
Date of birth (Y/M/D)	1941-12-30	1990-10-17	1921-02-24
Net income	$5,800 in CPP	Nil	$500

Family Members	Father-In-Law	Brother
First Name	David	Martin
Last Name	Parker	Hall
SIN	None	527-000-533
Date of birth (Y/M/D)	1922-01-12	1959-06-02
Net income	Nil	$8,300

T2202A - (Martin)	Box	Amount
Tuition fees - for Martin Hall (brother)	A	6,000
Number of months in school - part-time	B	0
Number of months in school - full-time	C	8

T4	Box	Amount
Issuer - Mega Pharma Inc.		
Employment income	14	378,000.00
Employee's CPP contributions	16	1,910.70
Employee's EI premiums	18	729.30
Income tax deducted	22	125,000.00
Employment commissions	42	82,000.00
Charitable donations	46	400.00

Donor	Charitable Donation Receipts	Am't
Valerie	Mothers Against Drunk Drivers (MADD)	1,000
George	Canadian Institute For The Blind (CNIB)	3,000

(Y/M/D)	Patient	Medical Expenses	Description	Am't
2006-12-31	George	Johnson Inc.	Out of Canada insurance	731.30
2006-08-31	George	Dr. Smith	Dental fees	155.40
2006-09-19	George	Optician	Prescription glasses	109.00
2006-11-07	Valerie	Pharmacy	Prescription	66.84
2006-06-07	Joan	Dr. Wong	Psychiatric counseling	2,050.00
2006-03-22	David	Tropical Disease Centre	Prescription	390.00
2006-12-20	Martin	Dr. Walker	Group therapy	6,000.00
2006-10-01	Kevin	Dr. Takarabe	Orthodontics and Dental	30,000.00

George paid $800 for the care and feeding of Kevin's seeing eye dog, Isis, during 2006.

Assignment Cases

House Costs	
Area of home used for home office (square feet)	650
Total area of home (square feet)	5,000
Telephone line including high speed internet connection	620
Hydro	3,200
Insurance - House	4,000
Maintenance and repairs	3,800
Mortgage interest	6,200
Mortgage life insurance premiums	400
Property taxes	6,700

George purchased a new computer and software that will be used solely in his home office for employment related uses. The computer cost $3,600 and the various software programs cost $1,250.

At the beginning of 2006, George had a net capital loss carry forward of $10,500 from the sale of shares in 2005. He had not disposed of any capital assets prior to 2005.

Asset Dispositions	Asset 1	Asset 2	Asset 3
Description	Molson Inc. shares	Imperial Oil shares	Sailboat
Number of units	150	387	N/A
Year of acquisition	2003	2004	2004
Date of disposition	February 14	June 6	October 1
Proceeds of disposition	37,000	9,600	74,000
Adjusted cost base	27,600	12,100	72,000
Outlays and expenses	35	29	N/A

Asset Dispositions	Asset 4	Asset 5	Asset 6
Description	Motorcycle	Painting	Coin collection
Year of acquisition	2006	2000	2003
Date of disposition	November 17	August 28	March 24
Proceeds of disposition	14,000	1,100	700
Adjusted cost base	21,000	450	1,800
Outlays and expenses	N/A	N/A	N/A

Real Estate Rental - Commercial Property	Amount
Address - 220 - 4th Avenue, South East, Calgary Alberta T2G 0L1	
Year of purchase	2002
Gross rents	16,000
Property taxes	5,128
Insurance	1,890
Interest on mortgage	3,175
Payment on principal	2,200
Furnace repairs	550
Maintenance contract	3,469
Building purchased August 28, 2002 for $120,100 - UCC beginning of year	107,441
Fixtures purchased August 28, 2002 for $8,500 - UCC beginning of year	4,651

Assignment Case Fourteen - 3 (Progressive Running Case - Chapter 14 Version Using ProFile T1 Software For 2006 Tax Returns)

This Progressive Running Case requires the use of the ProFile tax software program. It was introduced in Chapter 6 and is continued in Chapters 8 through 14. Each version must be completed in sequence. While it is not repeated in this version of the Case, all of the information in each of the previous versions (e.g., Mary's T4 content) is applicable to this version of the Case.

If you have not prepared a tax file incorporating the previous versions, please do so before continuing with this version.

On February 14, 2007, you receive a call from Mary Walford. She has just received an amended T4. The original T4 had not included information on the stock options in her employer, MoreCorp, that she had exercised.

Mary had options to purchase 500 shares of MoreCorp at $42 per share. When she received the options, the shares were trading at $40 per share. On December 20, 2006, when the shares were trading at $125 per share, she exercised her options for 200 shares. She left verbal instructions for MoreCorp to immediately donate all of the shares to Tax Behind Bars, a Canadian registered charity whose volunteers provide extensive tax education to prisoners in jails across Canada. As a result, she did not elect to have the stock option benefit deferral apply.

Unfortunately for Mary, the donation was not done and she did not receive a 2006 charitable donation receipt.

Amended T4 - Mary	Box	Original Am't	Amended Am't
Issuer - MoreCorp			
Employment income	14	152,866.08	169,466.08
Employee's CPP contributions	16	1,910.70	1,910.70
Employee's EI premiums	18	729.30	729.30
RPP contributions	20	Nil	Nil
Income tax deducted	22	48,665.11	48,665.11
Stock option deduction 110(1)(d)	39	Nil	8,300.00
Charitable donations	46	1,000.00	1,000.00

Mary informs you that she received more than $1 million in life insurance benefits and has made all of the RRSP contributions for 2006 and 2007 that you advised (see Chapter 13 version), but has not yet received the receipt from TD Asset Management.

Required:

A. If the shares from her stock options had been donated immediately, what effect would this have had on her Taxable Income?

B. Open the file that you created for the Chapter 13 version of the Case and save a copy under a different name. This will enable you to check the changes between different versions of the Case.

C. Revise Mary's tax return for the amended T4 and new RRSP contributions.

D. With the objective of minimizing the tax liability for the family, prepare Ms. Walford's 2006 income tax return and make any revisions necessary to Seymour's final 2006 return. Print both returns. List any assumptions you have made and provide any explanatory notes and tax planning issues you feel should be placed in the files.

E. Access and print Mary's summary (Summary on the Form Explorer, not the T1Summary). This form is a two column summary of the couple's tax information. By opening this form from Mary's return, the order of the columns is the same as the one in the previous chapter. For both returns, list the changes on this Summary form from the previous version of this Case. Exclude totals calculated by the program, but include the final Balance Owing (Refund) amount.

CHAPTER 15

Taxable Income And Tax Payable For Corporations

Computation Of Net Income

15-1. The day-to-day records of most corporations are kept in terms of accounting procedures and policies that are normally referred to as Generally Accepted Accounting Principles (GAAP). As noted in Chapter 8, Business Income, many of the rules for computing business income under the *Income Tax Act* are identical to those used under GAAP. However, there are a number of differences that are specifically provided for and, as a result, the first step in the computation of Taxable Income for a corporation is to convert accounting Net Income as determined under GAAP into Net Income For Tax Purposes. Only then can we move from Division B's Net Income For Tax Purposes to Division C's Taxable Income.

15-2. In making this conversion, there are many adjustments that could be required in particular circumstances. Some adjustments are necessary because of different allocation patterns that result in timing differences between accounting and tax income. Examples of this would be differences between accounting amortization and CCA, as well as alternative approaches to the determination of pension cost deductions. Other adjustments involve permanent differences between accounting and tax amounts. An example of this type of difference would be the non-taxable one-half of capital gains.

15-3. As is noted in Chapter 8, a reconciliation between accounting Net Income and Net Income For Tax Purposes is a required part of the corporate tax return. The form that the CRA provides for this reconciliation is designated Schedule 1. The most common adjustments from this Schedule are listed in Figure 8-1 in Chapter 8 and that list has been duplicated as Figure 15-1 (following page) for your convenience.

15-4. Chapter 8 on business income provided a detailed discussion of the conversion of Net Income for accounting purposes into Net Income For Tax Purposes. As that discussion is equally applicable to corporations and unincorporated businesses, it will not be repeated here. However, if you are not familiar with the material in Chapter 8, we suggest that you review it before proceeding with these Chapters on corporate taxation.

Figure 15 - 1
Conversion Of Accounting Net Income To Net Income For Tax Purposes

Additions To Accounting Income:
- Amortization, depreciation, and depletion of tangible and intangible assets (Accounting amounts)
- Recapture of CCA
- Tax reserves deducted in the prior year
- Losses on the disposition of capital assets (Accounting amounts)
- Scientific research expenditures (Accounting amounts)
- Warranty expense (Accounting amounts)
- Amortization of discount on long-term debt issued (see discussion in Chapter 9)
- Foreign tax paid (Accounting amounts)
- Excess of taxable capital gains over allowable capital losses
- Income tax expense
- Interest and penalties on income tax assessments
- Non-deductible automobile costs
- Fifty percent of business meals and entertainment expenses
- Club dues and cost of recreational facilities
- Non-deductible reserves in current year (Accounting amounts)
- Political contributions
- Charitable donations
- Asset write-downs including impairment losses on intangibles

Deductions From Accounting Income:
- Capital cost allowances (CCA)
- Amortization of cumulative eligible capital (CEC)
- Terminal losses
- Tax reserves claimed for the current year
- Gains on the disposition of capital assets (Accounting amounts)
- Deductible scientific research expenditures
- Deductible warranty expenditures
- Amortization of premium on long-term debt issued
- Foreign non-business tax deduction [ITA 20(12)]
- Allowable business investment losses

Exercise Fifteen-1

Subject: Schedule 1 Reconciliation

Available information for the S1 Company for the year includes the following:

1. A capital asset was sold for $48,300. It had a cost of $120,700 and a net book value of $53,900. It was the last asset in its CCA class and the UCC balance in this class was $34,600 before the disposition. There were no other additions or dispositions during the year.
2. During the year, the Company acquired goodwill at a cost of $180,000. Since there was no impairment of the goodwill during the year, no write-down was required for accounting purposes.
3. During the year, the Company expensed charitable donations of $15,000.
4. Premium amortization on the Company's bonds payable was $4,500 for the year.

You have been asked to prepare a Schedule 1 reconciliation of accounting Net Income and Net Income For Tax Purposes. Determine the addition and/or deduction that would be made in Schedule 1 for each of the preceding items.

End of Exercise. Solution available in Study Guide.

Computation Of Taxable Income

Deductions Available To Corporations

15-5. The reconciliation schedule illustrated in Figure 15-1 is used to establish a corporation's Net Income For Tax Purposes. When this task is completed, certain specified items are deducted from the resulting Net Income For Tax Purposes figure in order to arrive at Taxable Income. These deductions are specified in Division C of the *Income Tax Act* and the relevant items for individuals were given detailed coverage in Chapters 6 and 14. However, there are significant differences in the Division C deductions available to individuals and those available to corporations.

15-6. With respect to the Division C items that are available to individuals, the following are not available to corporations:

- lifetime capital gains deduction
- employee stock option deduction
- home relocation loan deduction
- northern residents deductions
- social assistance and workers' compensation benefits deduction

15-7. A further significant difference relates to two items that, with respect to individuals, serve as a base for credits against Tax Payable. While these items are not available as a base for credits against corporate Tax Payable, they are available as deductions in the calculation of corporate Taxable Income. These items are:

Charitable Donations Unlike the situation for individuals where charitable donations are the basis for a tax credit, corporations deduct charitable donations from Net Income For Tax Purposes in the determination of Taxable Income. While corporations have a deduction rather than a tax credit, the rules for determining which donations can be deducted by a corporation are essentially the same as the rules for determining which donations qualify for the tax credit for individuals. Further, corporations are subject to the same 75 percent of Net Income For Tax Purposes limit that applies to individuals. The five year carry forward provision is also applicable to corporations. These matters are given detailed consideration in Chapters 6 and 14 and will not be repeated here.

Dividends As noted in previous Chapters, individuals must gross up dividends received from taxable Canadian corporations by 25 percent for non-eligible dividends or 45 percent for eligible dividends. This is accompanied by a dividend tax credit equal to either two-thirds of the gross up or 11/18 of the gross up. There is no corresponding gross up or tax credit with respect to dividends received by a corporation. However, a corporation is permitted to deduct the full amount of such dividends in the calculation of Taxable Income. Note that, while this deduction removes dividends from Taxable Income and the Tax Payable calculation, they must be included in Net Income For Tax Purposes.

15-8. In addition to the two preceding deductions, corporations are allowed to deduct loss carry overs from previous or subsequent years in the calculation of Taxable Income. Other than in situations where a corporation has been the subject of an acquisition of control, the rules related to the deduction of corporate loss carry overs are basically the same as those applicable to individuals. These general rules are covered in Chapter 14 and will not be repeated here. Note, however, that this Chapter will contain detailed coverage of the special rules that apply to loss carry overs subsequent to an acquisition of control.

15-9. The calculation of corporate Taxable Income is outlined in Figure 15-2 (following page).

Figure 15 - 2

Conversion Of Corporate Net Income For Tax Purposes To Taxable Income

---

Net Income (Loss) For Tax Purposes

Less:
- Charitable donations (Limited to 75 percent of Net Income For Tax Purposes with a five year carry forward of unused amounts)
- Dividends received from taxable Canadian corporations
- Loss carry overs from subsequent or prior taxation years

Equals Taxable Income (Loss)

Dividends From Other Corporations

Deduction From Taxable Income

15-10.   In the calculation of Taxable Income, ITA 112(1) permits a corporation to deduct dividends that are received from taxable Canadian corporations in the determination of Taxable Income.

15-11.   The reason for this deduction is fairly obvious. If taxes were levied on transfers of dividends between companies, it could result in taxes being repeatedly assessed on the same diminishing stream of income. That is, the paying corporation would be taxed on the income that provided the dividend and if, in addition, the receiving corporation had to include the amount received in its Taxable Income, double taxation of the same income would result. In more complex, multi-level corporate structures, this could extend to triple, quadruple, or even greater applications of tax to a single stream of income.

Example   Mr. X owns 100 percent of the common shares of Company X, and Company X owns 100 percent of the common shares of Company Y. Both Companies pay out all of their after tax income as dividends. Company Y has income of $1,000 for the year and Company X has no income other than dividends from Company Y. Assume both Company X and Company Y are subject to a combined federal/provincial tax rate of 35 percent and Mr. X is subject to a combined federal/provincial tax rate on non-eligible dividends received of 30 percent.

Analysis   A comparison of the after tax flow through, with and without the intercompany dividend deduction, would be as follows:

	No Deduction	Deduction
Company Y Income	$1,000	$1,000
Corporate Taxes At 35 Percent	(350)	(350)
Dividends To Company X	$ 650	$ 650
Corporate Taxes At 35 Percent	(228)	Nil
Dividends To Mr. X	$ 422	$ 650
Personal Taxes At 30 Percent	(127)	(195)
After Tax Retention	$ 295	$ 455

15-12.   Without the deduction, the after tax retention is only $295. This means that the total tax rate on the $1,000 of income earned by Company Y is an almost confiscatory 70.5 percent. While the application of the dividend deduction provides a more reasonable level of taxation, you should note that the combined corporate and personal tax on the $1,000 income stream is $545 ($350 + $195). This heavy level of taxation reflects the fact that, with a corporate tax rate of 35 percent, flowing income through a corporation can result in the payment of higher taxes than would be the case with the direct receipt of income. This point is discussed more fully in Chapter 16, which provides coverage of the concept of integration.

Exercise Fifteen-2

Subject: Corporate Taxable Income

The Chapman Company had Net Income For Tax Purposes for the year ending December 31, 2007 of $263,000. This amount included $14,250 in taxable capital gains. During the year, the Company received dividends from taxable Canadian corporations in the amount of $14,200 and made donations to registered charities of $8,600. At the beginning of the year, the Company had a non-capital loss carry forward from 2003 of $82,000, as well as a net capital loss carry forward from 2004 of $18,000 [(1/2)($36,000)]. Determine the Company's minimum Taxable Income for the year ending December 31, 2007 and the type and amount of any carry forwards available at the end of the year.

End of Exercise. Solution available in Study Guide.

Dividends From Untaxed Income

15-13. While the preceding justifications for not taxing intercorporate dividends make sense in the majority of situations, problems can arise. One problem involves situations in which the corporation paying the dividend was not taxed on the funds prior to their distribution. Given the fact that, for most companies, accounting income is higher than Taxable Income, it would not be surprising to find cases where there is sufficient accounting income to warrant a dividend payment, combined with a tax loss for the period.

15-14. In this case, there will be no taxation of the original income at the corporate level. This means that only personal taxes will be paid on the income stream and, as a consequence, the use of a corporation will result in a significantly lower level of taxation than would be the case if the income were received directly by the individual. In addition, because no tax will be assessed until the income is paid out in dividends, this situation may result in a significant deferral of the taxation that is applicable to the income stream.

Term And Other Preferred Shares

15-15. A further problem arises when corporations attempt to achieve what is sometimes referred to as "after tax financing". Because of the favourable tax treatment given to both individual and corporate recipients of dividend income, rates that corporations will have to pay on preferred shares will generally be somewhat lower than rates paid on debt securities.

15-16. For most corporations, debt securities will continue to remain attractive because the tax deductibility of interest payments provides a lower after tax cost of funds than would be the case with the use of preferred shares. However, this is not the case when the corporation is in a loss position and, as a consequence, such companies have often issued preferred shares.

15-17. To make these preferred shares more attractive to investors, issuers add features such as redemption provisions. These features produce a preferred share that has most of the characteristics of debt. In fact, Section 3861 of the *CICA Handbook*, "Financial Instruments — Disclosure And Presentation" may require that such preferred shares be treated as debt for accounting purposes.

15-18. Despite many debt-like features, the payments made on such preferred shares are, for tax purposes, dividend income. As previously discussed, this type of income is taxed very favourably in the hands of individual investors and is not taxed at all in the hands of corporate investors.

15-19. The loss of tax revenues on this type of security could be very high. To prevent this loss, the ITA either imposes special taxes under Part IV.1 and Part VI.1, or denies the dividend deduction to alter the treatment of dividends on these preferred shares. However, these provisions go beyond the scope of this material.

Dividends On Shares Sold For Loss (Stop Loss Rules)

15-20.   As the declaration and payment of dividends by a corporation reduces the corporation's net assets, it would be expected that the value of the shares would fall by approximately the amount of any dividend declared and paid. Given this, it would be possible for one corporation to acquire shares in another corporation at a time when it was anticipated that a dividend would be paid on the acquired shares. The dividends on these shares could be received tax free and, if the value of the shares declined when they went ex-dividend, they could be sold to create a capital loss. The following example illustrates the problem that is created by this situation:

> **Example**   On June 30, 2007, Brian Company acquires 1,000 shares of Leader Company, a public company, at a cost of $20 per share. On July 1, 2007, the Leader Company declares and pays its regular $3 per share dividend. Because this dividend had been anticipated by the market, the price of the Leader Company stock falls $3 per share to $17 per share. On July 15, 2007, Brian Company sells all of its Leader Company shares at a price of $17 per share.

> **Analysis**   In the absence of a special rule, the preceding situation would provide very favourable results for Brian Company. They would have received $3,000 in dividends which, because of the deduction for intercorporate dividends, would not be included in their Taxable Income. In addition, they would have a potentially deductible capital loss of $3,000 on the disposition of the shares.

15-21.   To prevent this from happening, ITA 112(3) and (3.01) contain "stop loss" rules applicable to shares held as capital property, and ITA 112(4) and (4.01) contain similar rules for shares held as inventory. Under these rules, any loss resulting from a disposition of shares by a corporation must be reduced by the amount of dividends received that are eligible for deduction under ITA 112(1). Note, however, the rules do not apply if:

- the corporation owned the shares for more than 365 days prior to the disposition date, and

- the corporation and persons with whom the corporation was not dealing at arm's length own more than 5 percent of the outstanding shares of any class of stock of the corporation paying the dividend, at the time the dividend was received.

15-22   In the preceding example, Brian Company had owned the Leader Company shares for less than 365 days prior to the disposition and it would appear that 1,000 shares would be less than 5 percent of the shares outstanding. As a consequence, the $3,000 capital loss would be eliminated by the $3,000 dividend received.

Exercise Fifteen-3

Subject: Stop Loss Rules

On June 16, 2007, Loren Ltd. acquires 1,000 shares of Manon Inc., a widely held public company, at a cost of $25.30 per share. On July 1, 2007, these shares pay a dividend of $2.16 per share. Loren sells the shares on July 29, 2007 for $21.15 per share. Loren Ltd. has taxable capital gains of $50,000 in the year. What is the amount of the allowable capital loss, if any, that Loren Ltd. will include in its tax return for the taxation year ending December 31, 2007?

End of Exercise. Solution available in Study Guide.

Foreign Source Dividends Received

15-23.   The situation for dividends received from non-resident corporations is more complex. The general rules are discussed in Chapter 9, which notes that foreign source dividends are included in income on a gross basis, before the deduction of any foreign taxes withheld. However, in Chapter 14 we introduced the foreign non-business tax credit provisions. These credits against federal Canadian Tax Payable are designed to compensate the recipient of foreign source non-business income for foreign taxes withheld at source, provided the income has been subject to a reasonable amount of Canadian taxation. You will recall that, in most situations, the credit against Canadian Tax Payable will be equal to the amount of foreign taxes withheld at source. This topic is given further coverage in Chapter 22, International Taxation.

Acquisition Of Control Rules

Economic Background

15-24. Over a period of years, some corporations may experience sufficiently large losses that they have no hope of recovering their economic health. While they may have accumulated large amounts of net capital or non-capital loss carry forwards, they have no real prospect of being able to use these amounts. Such companies become attractive takeover targets for profitable corporations that are in a position to structure their affairs in a manner that will make use of the tax benefits associated with these losses.

15-25. This situation is of concern to the government in that there are billions of dollars of such benefits available in the economy at any point in time. If access to these benefits was relatively trouble-free, the cost to the government could be enormous. As a consequence, the government has enacted increasingly restrictive legislation with respect to the use of loss carry overs in situations where there has been an acquisition of control.

Acquisition Of Control Legislation

15-26. ITA 111(4) through 111(5.5) contains rules that are applicable when there has been an acquisition of control by a person or group of persons. IT-302R3, which deals with restrictions on loss carry overs, indicates that control requires ownership of shares that carry with them the right to elect a majority of the board of directors. In addition, ITA 110.1(1.2), prevents the use of charitable donation carry forwards subsequent to an acquisition of control.

15-27. An acquisition of control most commonly occurs when a majority shareholder sells his shares to an arm's length person. However, it can also occur through the redemption of shares. For example, if Ms. A owns 75 percent of AB Ltd. and Ms. B owns the other 25 percent, there would be an acquisition of control by Ms. B if AB Ltd. were to redeem all of Ms. A's shares.

Deemed Year End

15-28. To prevent losses from being used prior to the end of the taxation year in which the acquisition of control took place, ITA 249(4) requires that the corporation have a deemed year end on the day preceding an acquisition of control.

15-29. If the acquisition of control occurs prior to the corporation's normal year end, a short fiscal period will be created. For example, if the corporation's normal year end was December 31, and the acquisition of control took place on February 1, 2007, the deemed year end would create a fiscal year with only one month (January 1, 2007 through January 31, 2007). Further, if the corporation retains its old year end after the acquisition of control, there will be a second short fiscal year that runs from February 1, 2007 through December 31, 2007.

15-30. Note, however, ITA 249(4) allows the corporation to change its year end when there is an acquisition of control. This means that the corporation could have extended its first year after the acquisition of control to January 31, 2007.

15-31. The extra year end is of importance in that the non-capital losses that may be available after the acquisition of control are time limited. In our example, the deemed year end creates, in effect, an extra year end that shortens the period during which available losses can be used.

15-32.   Other implications of such short fiscal periods include the need to base CCA calculations on a fraction of the year, as well as a need to prorate the annual business limit for the small business deduction. (The annual business limit is discussed beginning in Paragraph 15-121.)

Restrictions On The Use Of Charitable Donations

15-33.   ITA 110.1(1.2) which places two restrictions on the deduction of these donations:

- Undeducted amounts that are present at the time of the acquisition of control cannot be carried forward to periods subsequent to that date.
- No deduction is available on a gift made subsequent to the acquisition of control if the gifted property was acquired prior to the acquisition date in anticipation of the acquisition of control.

15-34.   An example of the latter restriction would be a situation where an individual, who does not have sufficient tax payable to use a credit on the donation of a particular property, transfers that property to a corporation he controls, with the expectation that he will sell the shares in the corporation and the corporation will make the donation and take the deduction.

Restrictions On The Use Of Losses

General Rules

15-35.   The acquisition of control rules apply to any losses that have not been deducted at the deemed year end. This would include losses that have been carried forward from prior years, as well as any additional losses that accrue in the taxation year which is created by the deemed year end.

15-36.   As will be explained later, the losses in this deemed taxation year may be increased by provisions that require the recognition of unrealized losses on capital assets. They can also be reduced by an election to have one or more deemed dispositions.

Capital Losses

15-37.   The acquisition of control rules are particularly harsh in their treatment of capital losses. ITA 111(4)(a) indicates that any unused capital losses that are present at the deemed year end are simply lost. They cannot be carried forward to future years and, as a consequence, they will be of no benefit to the corporation subsequent to the acquisition of control. Note that this would include any unused Allowable Business Investment Losses that are present at the deemed year end.

15-38.   In addition, if there are capital gains in the three years before the deemed year end, ITA 111(4)(b) prevents capital losses from years subsequent to the deemed year end from being carried back to those years.

Non-Capital Losses

15-39.   While non-capital losses can be carried forward, they too are subject to restrictions. These restrictions, found in ITA 111(5), are that:

- after the acquisition of control has taken place, the corporation must carry on the business in which the loss occurred;
- there must be a reasonable expectation of profit in that business; and
- the losses can only be applied against future income generated by the same, or a similar business.

15-40.   A brief example can be used to illustrate these provisions:

Example   Bostox Ltd. has two separate businesses, manufacturing cameras and the sale of specialty food products. During the year ending December 31, 2007, the camera business experienced a loss for tax purposes of $5 million, while the food specialty products business had nil Taxable Income. The $5 million loss could not be carried back and, as a result, it became a loss carry forward. On January 1, 2008,

Bostox Ltd. is acquired by another company. During the year ending December 31, 2008, the camera business lost an additional $1 million, while the food products business earned $7 million.

Analysis If there was no acquisition of control, both the current 2008 loss of $1 million and the $5 million loss carry forward resulting from the camera business could be deducted against the income of the specialty food products business. This would have resulted in a 2008 Taxable Income of $1 million ($7 million profit on food products, offset by a current loss of $1 million on cameras and a non-capital loss carry forward of $5 million).

However, with the acquisition of control at the beginning of 2008, the loss carry forward can only be used against profits produced by the camera business. This means that none of the loss carry forward can be deducted in 2008, but the $1 million 2008 camera business loss can be netted against the $7 million food products income, resulting in a 2008 Taxable Income of $6 million. The $5 million loss carry forward will still be available, but can only be applied against future camera business income.

Exercise Fifteen-4

Subject: Acquisition Of Control

India Inc. has two separate businesses, one of which sells fountain pens, while the other provides professional accounting services. In its first year of operations ending on December 31, 2006, the pen business had a Net Loss For Tax Purposes of $192,000, and the accounting business had Net Income For Tax Purposes of $57,000. For the taxation year ending December 31, 2007, the pen business had Net Income For Tax Purposes of $42,000, and the accounting business had Net Income For Tax Purposes of $247,000. Determine Taxable Income for each of the two years assuming (1) that there was no acquisition of control in either year and (2) that there was an acquisition of control on January 1, 2007.

End of Exercise. Solution available in Study Guide.

Unrecognized Losses At Deemed Year End

The Problem

15-41.   As previously indicated, the acquisition of control restrictions apply to losses that accrue in the taxation year that has been created by the deemed year end. As there has been a deemed year end, there may be a loss from normal operations for the fiscal period that has ended. In addition, there may be losses resulting from actual dispositions of capital assets during the period.

15-42.   However, the acquisition of control rules are also concerned with accrued losses that have not been recognized at the deemed year end. The problem is that, if such accrued losses are realized after that time, they will not be subject to the acquisition of control restrictions.

> **Example** A corporation owned a parcel of land with an adjusted cost base of $200,000 and a fair market value of $150,000. If the land was to be disposed of subsequent to the acquisition of control, the result would be a deductible capital loss. This could be viewed as a way of avoiding the restrictions imposed by the acquisition of control rules.

Special Rules

15-43.   In recognition of this problem, the acquisition of control rules require a number of special procedures at the deemed year end. They are as follows:

Non-Depreciable Capital Property   ITA 111(4)(c) requires that non-depreciable capital property be written down to its fair market value, if that value is below its adjusted cost base. ITA 111(4)(d) requires that the amount of the write-down be treated as a capital loss. The new lower value becomes the adjusted cost base of the property. The resulting allowable capital loss can be applied against available taxable capital gains, or carried back. However, if it is not used at the deemed year end, it is lost forever.

Depreciable Capital Property   ITA 111(5.1) requires that depreciable capital property be written down to its fair market value, if that value is below the UCC. The write-down amount is treated as CCA to be deducted in the deemed taxation year. This will reduce the income for that period and, in some cases, create or increase the loss for that year. For capital gains purposes, the property will retain the original capital cost.

Eligible Capital Property   ITA 111(5.2) requires that eligible capital property be written down to three-quarters of its fair market value, if that value is below the Cumulative Eligible Capital balance. The write-down is a deduction under ITA 20(1)(b) and, as was the case with the write-down of depreciable capital property, this deduction can reduce income, increase a loss, or create a loss in the deemed taxation year.

Accounts Receivable   ITA 111(5.3) does not permit the deduction of a reserve for doubtful accounts under ITA 20(1)(l). Rather, amounts must be written off as specific bad debts on the basis of the largest possible amount. If a doubtful account is not written off at the time an acquisition of control occurs, no deduction is available if the account subsequently becomes uncollectible. This procedure will generally result in a larger deduction and will reduce income, increase a loss, or create a loss in the deemed taxation year.

Deemed Disposition Election

The Problem

15-44.   The requirement that non-depreciable capital property be written down to fair market value at the deemed year end is particularly onerous in that the resulting capital losses may simply disappear. To offset the harshness of this requirement, ITA 111(4)(e) allows the corporation to elect, at the time of the deemed year end, to have a deemed disposition/reacquisition of any depreciable or non-depreciable capital property on which there is an accrued gain or recapture of CCA. This election can be used to trigger capital gains that will offset either unused losses of the current period or unused loss carry forwards from earlier periods.

15-45.   The election can also be used to trigger recapture which can absorb non-capital losses from the current or previous years. This is a less important application in most situations as non-capital losses do not disappear at the deemed year end. However, as noted in Paragraph 15-39, there are restrictions on the use of such losses after the deemed year end. Given this, it may be desirable to minimize non-capital losses when an acquisition of control occurs.

Procedures

15-46.   The elected value, which will serve as the deemed proceeds of disposition, cannot exceed the fair market value of the asset at the time of the deemed disposition. Provided it is less than fair market value, the minimum value for the election is the adjusted cost base of the property. The elected value can be any amount between this minimum and maximum. This means that, in the case of property on which CCA has been taken, any election that will create a capital gain will also create recapture of CCA.

15-47. If the corporation has net capital losses and there are non-depreciable properties with accrued gains, this election is clearly desirable in that it will generate capital gains, which can be used to offset the net capital losses that would disappear as a result of the acquisition of control.

15-48. The situation is less clear cut when the gains are on depreciable capital property. While the deemed disposition will create the needed capital gains, in many situations it will also result in recapture of CCA. This may or may not be a desirable situation.

Example

15-49. The following example will illustrate the procedures associated with the ITA 111(4)(e) deemed disposition election:

Example Burkey Ltd. has a December 31 year end. On June 1, 2007, a new investor acquires control of the Company. While its basic operations have been profitable for many years, it has a net capital loss carry forward from 2003 of $200,000 [(1/2)($400,000)]. On May 31, 2007, the Company has non-depreciable capital assets with a fair market value of $800,000 and an adjusted cost base of $500,000. Its depreciable capital assets have a fair market value of $1,200,000, a capital cost of $1,100,000, and a UCC of $600,000.

Analysis The ITA 111(4)(e) election is clearly desirable with respect to the non-depreciable capital property. It generates a taxable capital gain of $150,000 [(1/2)($800,000 - $500,000)]. Deducting a $150,000 carry forward against this 2007 gain will use up $150,000 of the 2003 net capital loss. This will leave an unused amount of $50,000 ($200,000 - $150,000).

Using the ITA 111(4)(e) election on the depreciable capital property will create a $50,000 [(1/2)($1,200,000 - $1,100,000)] taxable capital gain. Deducting a $50,000 loss carry forward against this amount will use up the remaining $50,000 of the net capital loss balance. However, the election will also create recaptured CCA of $500,000 ($1,100,000 - $600,000), an amount on which it appears that tax would have to be currently paid. Given that, in the absence of this election, taxation on the recapture could be deferred indefinitely, the election may not be desirable with respect to the depreciable capital property.

Adjusted Cost Base After Election

15-50. In addition to serving as the deemed proceeds of disposition, the elected value also becomes the adjusted cost base or capital cost of the asset on which the election was made. If the elections were made at fair market value on both properties in the preceding example, the new adjusted cost base of the non-depreciable assets would be $800,000, while the capital cost of the depreciable assets would be $1,200,000.

15-51. However, if the $1,200,000 value was allowed to be used for CCA purposes, the Company would be able to deduct 100 percent of the $100,000 difference between the $1,200,000 elected value and the old capital cost of $1,100,000, despite the fact that they have, in effect, paid tax on only one-half of this amount.

15-52. To prevent this from happening, ITA 13(7)(f) specifies that, when an election is made under ITA 111(4)(e), the new capital cost of the property for CCA purposes only, is equal to the original capital cost of the asset, plus one-half of the excess of the elected value over the asset's original capital cost. In the example in Paragraph 15-49, this value would be $1,150,000 [$1,100,000 + (1/2)($1,200,000 - $1,100,000)].

15-53. Future CCA would be based on this $1,150,000 figure and, in addition, if the assets were sold for more than $1,150,000, the new capital cost would be subtracted from the UCC to determine any recapture. However, any future capital gain would be based on the new adjusted cost base of $1,200,000.

Exercise Fifteen-5

Subject: Election On Acquisition Of Control

Means Ltd. has a December 31 year end. On May 1, 2007, all of the Company's shares are acquired by a new owner. At this time, the Company has a net capital loss carry forward from 2006 of $110,000 [(1/2)($220,000)], non-depreciable assets with an adjusted cost base of $500,000 and a fair market value of $650,000, and depreciable assets with a capital cost of $400,000, a UCC of $350,000, and a fair market value of $500,000. For the period January 1, 2007 through April 30, 2007, the Company has an operating loss of $45,000. Advise the Company with respect to the most appropriate elections to be made prior to the acquisition of control.

End of Exercise. Solution available in Study Guide.

Other Taxable Income Considerations

Non-Capital Loss Carry Over For A Corporation
Additional Issues

15-54.   As the general rules for loss carry overs are the same for all taxpayers, most of the relevant material on this subject is dealt with in Chapter 14 when we discuss the determination of Taxable Income for individuals. There is, however, an additional problem in calculating the amount of the current year non-capital loss carry over for a corporation. This problem relates to the fact that dividends received from taxable Canadian corporations can be deducted by a corporation in the determination of its Taxable Income. To illustrate this problem, consider the following:

> **Example** During 2007, Marco Inc. has net taxable capital gains of $30,000 [(1/2)($60,000)], dividends of $25,000 received from taxable Canadian corporations, and an operating loss of $60,000. The Company also has a net capital loss carry forward from 2005 of $50,000 [(1/2)($100,000)].
>
> **Analysis** Using the ITA 3 rules for calculating Net Income For Tax Purposes, the result would be as follows:

ITA 3(a)	Dividends Received	$25,000
ITA 3(b)	Net Taxable Capital Gains	30,000
ITA 3(c)	Subtotal	$55,000
ITA 3(d)	Operating Loss	(60,000)
Net Income For Tax Purposes And Taxable Income		Nil

15-55.   From an intuitive point of view, it would appear that the non-capital loss for the year is $5,000, the ITA 3(c) subtotal less the operating loss. Further, as Net Income is nil, it appears that none of the net capital loss carry forward can be deducted, despite the $30,000 taxable capital gain. In addition, it does not appear that the Company will get any benefit from the potential deduction of the $25,000 in dividends that were received during the year. Fortunately, the ITA 111(8) definition of non-capital loss solves both of these problems.

An Expanded Definition

15-56.   You may recall that this definition was discussed previously in Chapter 14 (see the material starting at Paragraph 14-36). In that material, we explained how the definition permitted a net capital loss carry over to be deducted even in cases where current year losses had resulted in a nil Net Income For Tax Purposes. In effect, the definition allowed a net capital loss carry over to be converted to a non-capital loss carry over.

15-57.   In the Chapter 14 discussion, we were dealing only with the Taxable Income of individuals. Given this, we did not consider the additional problem that arises with the fact that dividends received by a corporation can be deducted in the calculation of corporate Taxable Income. While this was not apparent from the simplified version of the non-capital loss definition that was presented in Chapter 14, a more complete version of the ITA 111(8) definition deals with this problem. The expanded definition is as follows:

ITA 111(8) The non-capital loss of a taxpayer for a taxation year means the amount determined by the formula:

$$A - D, \text{ where}$$

A   is the amount determined by the formula:

$$E - F, \text{ where}$$

E   is the total of all amounts each of which is the taxpayer's loss for the year from an office, employment, business or property, the taxpayer's allowable business investment loss for the year, net capital loss carry overs deducted in the calculation of Taxable Income for the year (this amount cannot exceed the taxable capital gains for the year), and **dividends received from taxable Canadian corporations**.

F   is the amount of income determined under ITA 3(c). [Sum of ITA 3(a) non-capital positive sources and ITA 3(b) net taxable capital gains, less Division B, Subdivision e deductions.]

D   is the taxpayer's farm loss for the year.

15-58.   The only difference in this definition from the one that was presented in Paragraph 14-36 is the addition of "dividends received from taxable Canadian corporations" in the E component. However, it is an important change in that it allows dividends that cannot be deducted because of inadequate Net Income For Tax Purposes to be added to the non-capital loss carry over balance.

Example

15-59.   All of these points can be illustrated by returning to the example presented in Paragraph 15-54. If we assume that Marco Inc. wishes to deduct the maximum amount of the 2005 net capital loss carry forward in 2007, the non-capital loss for the year would be calculated as follows:

Amount E ($60,000 + $30,000* + $25,000)	$115,000
Amount F - ITA 3(c) Balance	(55,000)
Non-Capital Loss For The Year	$ 60,000

*The net capital loss carry forward deduction is limited to $30,000, the amount of taxable capital gains realized during the year. This leaves a net capital loss carry forward of $20,000 ($50,000 - $30,000).

15-60.   Note the results of applying the non-capital loss definition. In effect, if there is not sufficient Net Income to allow their deduction in the calculation of Taxable Income, both dividends and net capital loss amounts deducted can be added to the non-capital loss carry over balance. Although subject to a three year carry back, 20 year carry forward limit, the loss carry over can be deducted against any type of income.

Exercise Fifteen-6

Subject: Non-Capital Loss Carry Forward

The following information is for Loser Ltd., a Canadian public company, for the taxation year ending December 31, 2007:

Capital Gains	$111,000
Capital Losses	(84,000)
Allowable Business Investment Loss	(5,250)
Dividends Received	48,000
Canadian Source Interest Income	27,200
Business Loss	(273,000)

The Company also has a net capital loss carry forward from 2002 of $19,000 [(1/2)($38,000)]. It would like to deduct this loss during 2007. Determine the non-capital loss balance [ITA 111(8)] and net capital loss carry forward for Loser Ltd. at the end of the 2007 taxation year.

Exercise Fifteen-7

Subject: Net Income For Tax Purposes With Losses

For the taxation year ending December 31, 2007, Hacker Inc. has business and property income of $63,500. Also during this year, capital asset dispositions result in capital gains of $23,100 and capital losses of $38,400. The Company experiences a further loss on the arm's length sale of shares of a small business corporation in the amount of $151,500. Determine Hacker Inc.'s Net Income For Tax Purposes for 2007. Indicate the amount and type of any loss carry overs available at the end of the year.

End of Exercises.   Solutions available in Study Guide.

Ordering Of Taxable Income Deductions

15-61.   Chapter 14 covered the specific ordering rules in ITA 111.1 for claiming deductions in the calculation of Taxable Income. However, these rules are directed at individuals and do not apply to corporations. The *Act* does not contain an equivalent provision for corporations and, as a consequence, there is a question as to how deductions should be ordered for a corporation.

15-62.   Charitable donations in excess of 75 percent of Net Income For Tax Purposes are not deductible in the current year, but can be carried forward for five years, subject to the same 75 percent limitation in those years. As this is shorter than the carry forward period for any other type of loss, this would suggest using these amounts prior to claiming loss carry forwards. However, in reaching this conclusion, it should be noted that these donations can be deducted against any type of income.

15-63.   Turning to the deduction of loss carry overs, ITA 111(3) requires that losses within any single category must be deducted in chronological order. That is, if a corporation chooses to deduct a portion of its non-capital loss balance during the current year, the oldest losses of this type must be deducted first. However, there are no rules with respect to the order in which the individual types of loss carry forwards must be deducted.

15-64.   Farm loss carry forwards and non-capital loss carry forwards have restrictions on the time for which they are available. This would suggest that they be deducted first. However, while there is no restriction on the period of availability for capital loss carry forwards, these amounts can only be used to the extent that there are net taxable capital gains during the period.

15-65. For a corporation that experiences only limited capital gains, these restrictions may be a more important consideration than the period of time during which the loss will be available. This is particularly the case now that the carry forward period for non-capital losses has been extended to 20 years.

15-66. An additional factor in making decisions on whether to deduct non-capital or farm losses is the period left to their expiry. Clearly, items that expire in the current year should be deducted immediately, with additional consideration given to items near the end of their carry forward period.

Geographical Allocation Of Income

Permanent Establishments

15-67. After Taxable Income is calculated, in order to determine the amount of provincial taxes that are payable and the province(s) to which they are due, it is necessary to allocate the income of the corporation to the various provinces. Given the variations in provincial tax rates on corporations, this can be a matter of considerable significance.

15-68. The key concept here is the idea of a "permanent establishment". This concept is defined as follows:

> **ITR 400(2)** Permanent establishment means a fixed place of business of the corporation, including an office, a branch, a mine, an oil well, a farm, a timberland, a factory, a workshop or a warehouse.

15-69. This meaning has been extended to include having an agent or employee in a province, if that agent or employee has the general authority to contract for a corporation, or carries a stock of merchandise from which orders are regularly filled. The mere presence of a commission salesperson or an independent agent is not considered evidence of a permanent establishment. In addition, the presence of a controlled subsidiary in a province is not necessarily indicative of a permanent establishment.

15-70. However, ITR 400(2)(d) indicates that where a corporation that has a permanent establishment anywhere in Canada owns land in a province, such land will be deemed to be a permanent establishment. In addition, ITR 400(2)(e) indicates that where a corporation uses substantial machinery or equipment in a particular place, that corporation shall be deemed to have a permanent establishment in that place.

Activity At Permanent Establishments

15-71. Once the location of permanent establishments has been determined, income will be allocated on the basis of two variables. These are gross revenues from the permanent establishment, and salaries and wages paid by the establishment.

15-72. Once these values are established, ITR 402(3) provides a formula for using these variables to allocate Taxable Income to provinces. It requires calculating, for each province, that province's gross revenues as a percentage of total corporate gross revenues, and that province's salaries and wages as a percentage of total corporate salaries and wages. A simple average of these two percentages, without regard to the relative dollar values associated with the corporate totals, is then applied to corporate Taxable Income to determine the amount of Taxable Income that will be allocated to that province.

Example - Permanent Establishments

15-73. The following example illustrates the process of allocating Taxable Income on a geographic basis:

> **Example** The Linford Company has permanent establishments in Alberta, Manitoba, and Ontario. The Company's Taxable Income for the current year totaled $100,000, with gross revenues of $1,000,000 and salaries and wages of $500,000.

15-74.   The following allocation of the gross revenues and the salaries and wages among the provinces occurred during the current year:

| Province | Gross Revenues | | Salaries And Wages | |
	Amount	Percent	Amount	Percent
Alberta	$ 250,000	25.0	$100,000	20.0
Manitoba	400,000	40.0	200,000	40.0
Ontario	350,000	35.0	200,000	40.0
Totals	$1,000,000	100.0	$500,000	100.0

15-75.   Using the average of the two percentages for each province, the Linford Company's Taxable Income would be allocated to the three provinces as follows:

Province	Average Percent	Taxable Income	Amount Allocated
Alberta	22.5	$100,000	$ 22,500
Manitoba	40.0	100,000	40,000
Ontario	37.5	100,000	37,500
Totals	100.0	N/A	$100,000

15-76.   If the corporation has operations outside of Canada, the total allocated to the provinces will be less than 100 percent. This will be taken into consideration when the federal tax abatement is calculated (see Paragraph 15-83).

Federal Tax Payable

Federal Corporate Rates

Basic Rate

15-77.   All corporations are initially subject to the same basic tax rate. This rate is specified in ITA 123 and, for many years, has been set at 38 percent. However, as explained beginning in Paragraph 15-83, this rate is reduced by 10 percentage points for income earned in a province. This, in effect, leaves the basic rate at 28 percent.

General Rate Reduction

15-78.   Over the period 2001 through 2004, the government provided a phased in reduction of this basic rate. In order to provide flexibility with respect to future rate changes, they chose to do this in a less than straightforward manner. Rather than simply reducing the rate specified in ITA 123, they introduced a new ITA 123.4(2) that provides for a deduction based on multiplying the corporation's "general rate reduction percentage" by its "full rate taxable income" for the year.

15-79.   The reduction percentage reached 7 percent in 2004 and has remained at that level through 2007. However, further increases in this rate reduction percentage are scheduled for 2008 through 2011. These new percentages are as follows:

2008	7.5%
2009	8.0%
2010	9.0%
2011 And Subsequent	9.5%

15-80.   When these changes are fully implemented in 2011, the reduced basic rate will be 18.5 percent (38% - 10% - 9.5%).

Full Rate Taxable Income

15-81.   As noted, the "general rate reduction percentage" must be applied to "full rate taxable income". In fairly simple terms, full rate taxable income is income that does not benefit from certain other tax privileges. The most common of these privileges are the small business deduction, the manufacturing and processing profits deduction (M&P deduction), and the refundability of certain types of taxes on the investment income of private companies.

15-82.   Both the small business deduction and the M&P deduction are discussed later in this Chapter. Full Rate Taxable Income will also be considered in this Chapter, with detailed coverage beginning at Paragraph 15-209. The coverage of refundable taxes on the investment income of private companies will not be dealt with until Chapter 16.

Federal Tax Abatement

15-83.   ITA 124(1) provides a reduction of 10 percentage points in the federal tax rate. This is normally referred to as the federal tax abatement and it is designed to leave room for the provinces to apply their respective tax rates. This reduces the basic federal tax rate from 38 percent to 28 percent, before the application of the corporate surtax.

15-84.   Note that this 10 percentage point reduction in the federal tax rate is only applicable to income earned in a Canadian jurisdiction. When a corporation has foreign operations, less than 100 percent of its income will be allocated to the various provinces. When this is the case, the amount of abatement to be deducted is reduced by multiplying the 10 percent abatement by the total percentage of Taxable Income that was allocated to the provinces. For example, if only 80 percent of a corporation's Taxable Income was allocated to one or more provinces, the abatement would be reduced to 8 percent [(10%)(80%)].

Corporate Surtax

Current Legislation

15-85.   Since 1995, the corporate surtax rate has been 4 percent of "tax otherwise payable". The tax otherwise payable is defined as being the Tax Payable after the federal tax abatement, but before the additional refundable tax on investment income, the small business deduction, foreign tax credits, investment tax credits, political contributions tax credits, as well as any deduction under ITA 123.4 (general rate reduction).

15-86.   Another way of describing this calculation is to indicate that the rate is applied to Tax Payable after the deduction of the federal tax abatement. However, even this is complicated by the fact that, for purposes of this calculation only, the abatement is calculated without regard to the percentage of Taxable Income earned in a province.

15-87.   This means that, in cases where the abatement has been reduced to reflect income earned outside Canada, a different abatement calculation is required in order to determine the surtax. This would suggest that a more straightforward way to calculate the corporate surtax is to take 4 percent of 28 percent of Taxable Income. We will generally use this approach in our examples and problems.

> **Example**   Borders Inc. has full rate Taxable Income of $146,000 for the year ended December 31, 2007. Based on the ITR 402 formula, 83 percent of this income has been earned in a Canadian province. Federal corporate Tax Payable, including the applicable surtax, is calculated as follows:
>
> | | |
> |---|---:|
> | Base Amount Of Part I Tax [(38%)($146,000)] | $55,480 |
> | Corporate Surtax [(4%)(38% - 10%)($146,000)] | 1,635 |
> | Federal Tax Abatement [(10%)(83%)($146,000)] | (12,118) |
> | General Rate Reduction [(7%)($146,000)] | (10,220) |
> | Federal Tax Payable | $34,777 |

Repeal Of Surtax

15-88.   The 2006 budget proposed the repeal of the surtax for 2008 and subsequent years. The proposal has been implemented and this additional tax will not be assessed after 2007.

Exercise Fifteen-8

Subject: Geographical Allocation And Federal Tax Payable

Sundown Ltd., a Canadian public company, has Taxable Income for the taxation year ending December 31, 2007 in the amount of $226,000. It has Canadian permanent establishments in Ontario and Manitoba. The Company's gross revenues for the 2007 taxation year are $2,923,000, with $1,303,000 of this accruing at the permanent establishment in Ontario, and $896,000 accruing at the permanent establishment in Manitoba. Wages and salaries total $165,000 for the year. Of this total, $52,000 is at the permanent establishment in Ontario and $94,000 is at the permanent establishment in Manitoba. Sundown has sales to the U.S. through a U.S. permanent establishment. Calculate federal Tax Payable for the taxation year ending December 31, 2007. Ignore any foreign tax implications.

End of Exercise.   Solution available in Study Guide.

Provincial Tax Payable

General Rules

15-89.   In calculating Tax Payable for individuals, a graduated rate structure is involved at both the federal and provincial levels. While limits on the brackets may differ from those used at the federal level, all of the provinces except Alberta assess taxes on individuals using graduated rates applied to Taxable Income.

15-90.   In contrast, provincial corporate taxes are based on a flat rate applied to a Taxable Income figure. With the exception of Alberta, Ontario, and Quebec, the federal Taxable Income figure is used. While these three provinces collect their own corporate taxes, the Taxable Income figure that they use is normally similar to that used at the federal level.

General Rate

15-91.   As shown in Figure 15-3 (facing page), the general rate for corporations is 22.1 percent. This is calculated as follows:

Basic Corporate Rate	38.0%
Less: Abatement	(10.0%)
Balance	28.0%
Surtax [(4.0%)(28.0%)]	1.1%
Balance	29.1%
Less: General Rate Reduction	(7.0%)
General Corporate Rate	22.1%

15-92.   When the varying provincial rates are added to this, the general corporate tax rate ranges from a low of 32.1 percent in Alberta, to a high of 38.1 percent in Prince Edward Island.

Manufacturing And Processing Rate

15-93.   At one point in time, manufacturing and processing income (M&P) benefitted from a special deduction at the federal level. As will be discussed later in this Chapter, the deduction is still in place. However, with the completed phase in of the 7 percentage point general rate reduction, it is no longer of any benefit to corporations at the federal level. As shown in Figure 15-3, at the federal level, the M&P rate is identical to the general rate.

15-94.   This is also the situation with a majority of the provinces. However, Newfoundland, Ontario, Saskatchewan, and the Yukon Territories apply reduced rates to this type of income. Because of this, it is still relevant to provide coverage of this subject.

	General Rate	M&P Rate	Small Business Rate
Figure 15 - 3			
Combined Federal/Provincial Corporate Rates - January 1, 2007			
Federal Tax Only	22.1%	22.1%	13.1%
Combined Federal/Provincial			
Alberta	32.1%	32.1%	16.1%
British Columbia	34.1%	34.1%	17.6%
Manitoba	36.1%	36.1%	17.6%
New Brunswick	35.1%	35.1%	15.1%
Newfoundland	36.1%	27.1%	18.1%
Northwest Territories	33.6%	33.6%	17.1%
Nova Scotia	38.1%	38.1%	18.1%
Nunavut	34.1%	34.1%	17.1%
Ontario	36.1%	34.1%	18.6%
Prince Edward Island	38.1%	38.1%	19.6%
Quebec	32.0%	32.0%	21.6%
Saskatchewan	36.1%	32.1%	18.1%
Yukon Territories	37.1%	24.6%	17.1%

Small Business Rate

15-95.   The lowest rates in Figure 15-3 are referred to as the small business rates. As will be discussed later in this Chapter, Canadian controlled private corporations are eligible for a small business deduction that lowers their federal rate to 13.1 percent. For 2007 and subsequent years, this special rate is available on the first $400,000 of active business income (as opposed to property income).

15-96.   In general, the provinces provide reduced rates on the same $400,000 amount of active business income. Alberta and Saskatchewan have higher limits. However, the other provinces all use the federal figure of $400,000.

15-97. When the reduced federal and provincial rates are combined, the resulting rates range from a low of 15.1 percent in New Brunswick to a high of 21.6 percent in Quebec.

Investment Income Rates

15-98.   While this is not illustrated in Figure 15-3, different rates are applicable to certain types of investment income. We will provide coverage of these rates in Chapter 16.

Other Provincial Taxes

15-99.   In addition to their basic corporate income tax, most provinces also levy capital and payroll taxes on corporations. Unlike provincial income tax on corporations, these taxes are treated as deductions in the calculation of Taxable Income, a situation that lowers the amount of federal tax that can be collected on that corporation's income. This, in effect, reduces the cost of these capital and payroll taxes to the paying corporation.

15-100.   However, the use of such taxes at the provincial level also reduces federal tax revenues and, as a consequence, the federal government has threatened for some time to eliminate the deductibility of capital and payroll taxes. At present, there is an interim measure that has denied deductibility to any increases in these taxes after March, 1993. This "interim" measure is still in place at the time of writing (June, 2007).

Other Goals Of The Corporate Tax System

15-101.   If raising revenues was the only goal of the corporate taxation system, there would be nothing much to discuss with respect to this matter, and there would be little need for the Chapters on corporate taxation that follow.   However, in addition to raising revenues, the Canadian corporate taxation system has been structured to accomplish a number of other objectives.   These can be briefly described as follows:

- **Incentives For Small Business**   While there are several features of the tax system directed at encouraging small businesses, the major tax incentive for these organizations is the small business deduction.

- **Incentives For Certain Business Activities**   The Canadian tax system encourages scientific research through a generous system of tax credits and a liberal policy towards deductible amounts. Support is also provided to the natural resource industries through a variety of programs. While support is no longer available at the federal level for manufacturing and processing, generous incentives are available for undertaking scientific research and experimental development activities.

- **Incentives For Certain Regions**   While less common than in the past, certain regions of Canada are given assistance through investment tax credits and other programs.

- **Integration**   One of the goals of the Canadian tax system is to keep the level of taxes paid on a given stream of income the same, regardless of whether or not a private corporation is placed between the original source of the income and the ultimate recipient.

15-102.   The small business deduction, the manufacturing and processing profits deduction and incentive for scientific research and experimental development will be examined in this Chapter. Integration will be dealt with in detail in Chapter 16.

Small Business Deduction

Introduction

Rules For 2007

15-103.   It has been a longstanding goal of the Canadian taxation system to provide incentives to small business. The underlying assumption is that, particularly during their formative years, these businesses need some degree of tax relief in order to allow them to accumulate the capital required for expansion. In order to provide this relief, the small business deduction was introduced in 1972. In somewhat simplified terms, it provides a deduction against the Tax Payable of a Canadian controlled private corporation. For the year 2007, this deduction is equal to 16 percent of the first $400,000 of active business income earned in Canada.

Example   A Canadian controlled private corporation has Taxable Income of $100,000 for the year ending December 31, 2007. All of this income is earned in Canada and eligible for the small business deduction. The provincial tax rate applicable to income eligible for the small business deduction is 5 percent.

Analysis   The corporation's Tax Payable would be calculated as follows:

Base Amount Of Part I Tax [(38%)($100,000)]	$38,000
Federal Surtax [(4%)(28%)($100,000)]	1,120
Federal Tax Abatement [(10%)($100,000)]	(10,000)
Small Business Deduction [(16%)($100,000)]	(16,000)
General Rate Reduction (Note)	Nil
Federal Tax Payable	$13,120
Provincial Tax Payable [(5%)($100,000)]	5,000
Total Tax Payable	$18,120

Note   The general rate reduction is not available on income that is eligible for the small business deduction.

15-104.   As can be seen in the example, when the small business deduction is available, it reduces the federal rate to 13.12 percent ($13,120 ÷ $100,000). We have also applied a provincial rate of 5 percent which is roughly the average provincial rate on income that is eligible for this deduction.   This produces a combined federal/provincial rate of 18.12 percent ($18,120 ÷ $100,000).

15-105.   With the overall rate below 20 percent, the small business deduction should provide a significant incentive to businesses that qualify.   Only certain types of corporations qualify for this deduction and, in addition, it is only available on certain amounts and types of income.   The criteria for qualification can be described in non-technical terms as follows:

Type Of Corporation   The availability of the small business deduction is restricted to Canadian controlled private corporations (CCPCs).

Type Of Income   The deduction is only available on income earned in Canada that qualifies as "active business income".   This would include the income of professional corporations and management companies, provided they are private and Canadian controlled.   However, the income of specified investment businesses and personal services corporations (see definitions later in this Chapter) does not qualify.

Limit On Amount   For 2007 and subsequent years, the deduction is available on the first $400,000 of active business income earned in a year.   This amount is referred to as the annual business limit and, in some circumstances, it is subject to a reduction formula.

Associated Corporations   The $400,000 annual business limit must be shared among associated corporations.

15-106.   The issues associated with these criteria are discussed in the material that follows.

Scheduled Changes

15-107.   While the small business deduction rate for 2007 is the same 16 percent that has applied for many years, current legislation has scheduled changes for 2008 and 2009.   More specifically, the rate will go to 16.5 percent for 2008 and 17.0 percent for 2009 and subsequent years.   This will provide overall rates in 2007 and subsequent years as follows:

	2007	2008	2009 And Subsequent
ITA 123 Rate	38.00%	38.0%	38.0%
Surtax	1.12%	Nil	Nil
Abatement	(10.00%)	(10.0%)	(10.0%)
Rate Before Small Business Deduction	29.12%	28.0%	28.0%
Small Business Deduction	(16.00%)	(16.5%)	(17.0%)
Federal Small Business Rate	13.12%	11.5%	11.0%

Canadian Controlled Private Corporation (CCPC)

15-108.   CCPCs are defined in ITA 125(7) as private corporations that are not controlled, directly or indirectly, by one or more non-resident persons, by one or more public corporations, or a combination of non-resident persons and public corporations.   In addition, corporations that have shares listed on a designated stock exchange, in or outside of Canada, do not qualify as CCPCs. As an additional point here, in order to qualify for the small business deduction, the corporation must be a CCPC throughout the taxation year.

Active Business Income

The General Idea

15-109.   ITA 125(7) contains the following definition of active business:

"active business carried on by a corporation" means any business carried on by the corporation other than a specified investment business or a personal services business and includes an adventure or concern in the nature of trade.

15-110.   While the preceding defines active business, a further definition in ITA 125(7) defines income from an active business as:

"Income of the corporation for the year from an active business" means the total of

(i)   the income of the corporation for the year from an active business carried on by it including any income for the year pertaining to or incident to that business, other than income for the year from a source in Canada that is a property, and

(ii)   the amount, if any, included under subsection 12(10.2) in computing the income of the corporation for the year. [The reference to ITA 12(10.2) involves an income stabilization account for agricultural products and is of no interest in a text such as this.]

15-111.   While these definitions are not models of clarity, they express the basic idea that active business income involves "doing something" to produce income. The concept excludes what we usually refer to as property income. Property income is distinguished by the fact that it generally becomes available with little or no effort on the part of the recipient (e.g., interest earned on long-term bonds).

The Problem With Defining Property Income

15-112.   As noted, the preceding definitions of active business and active business income are largely directed towards excluding property income such as interest, dividends, and rents from eligibility for the small business deduction. The federal government does not wish to allow individuals to have access to the small business deduction by simply placing their passive investments in the shelter of a Canadian controlled private corporation. However, a blanket exclusion of property income is inappropriate since there are corporations that are "actively" involved in earning such income.

15-113.   The difficulty is in finding a way to distinguish between corporations that are simply being used as tax shelters for property or passive income, and corporations that engage in active property management. For example, if a corporation has a single residential rental property, the rents from this property would undoubtedly be viewed as passive income. Alternatively, a corporation that owns a chain of hotels with more than 10,000 rooms would certainly be entitled to view the rentals of these properties as an active business. The question is, at what point does the corporation cross the line between earning passive income and active business income?

15-114.   Similar, but less obvious problems arise with interest income. If a corporation has no activity other than collecting interest on term deposits, the amounts that it earns would almost certainly be viewed as passive income. Alternatively, interest earned by a company actively involved in providing mortgage financing to corporate clients could be viewed as business income. Again, a problem exists in finding the point at which a crossover is made between the two situations.

The Solution - Specified Investment Business

15-115.   The concept of a "specified investment business" provides a somewhat arbitrary solution to this problem. ITA 125(7) defines a specified investment business as follows:

Specified Investment Business specified investment business", carried on by a corporation in a taxation year, means a business (other than a business carried on by a credit union or a business of leasing property other than real or immovable property) the principal purpose of which is to derive income (including interest, dividends, rents and royalties) from property but, except where the corporation was a prescribed labour-sponsored venture capital corporation at any time in the year, does not include a business carried on by the corporation in the year where

(i) the corporation employs in the business throughout the year more than five full time employees, or

(ii) in the course of carrying on an active business, any other corporation associated with it provides managerial, administrative, financial, maintenance or other similar services to the corporation in the year and the corporation could reasonably be expected to require more than five full time employees if those services had not been provided.

15-116. As the activities of these specified investment businesses are excluded from the definition of active business, it means that income from property generated by such businesses is not eligible for the small business deduction. Stated alternatively, for corporations that are primarily engaged in earning income from property, the *Act* specifies that only those with more than five full time employees involved in earning such income are considered to be earning active business income and eligible for the small business deduction.

15-117. While this is an arbitrary solution to the problem of distinguishing between active and passive income from a business, it does serve to resolve most of the uncertainty in this area. With respect to interpreting this rule, IT-73R6 points out that, from the point of view of the CRA, the phrase "the corporation employs in the business throughout the year more than five full-time employees" means that at least six employees are working full business days on each working day of the year, subject to normal absences due to illness or vacation time. This clarifies the point that a group of part time employees performing the equivalent of full time work will not qualify as the required sixth employee.

Incidental Property Income

15-118. The definition of active business income includes incidental property income that is earned by a corporation engaged in an active business. In this regard, many corporations experience temporary excess cash balances, and these balances will usually be invested in interest bearing assets. Within reasonable limits, such interest can be included as a component of active business income. In similar fashion, revenues resulting from temporary rentals of excess space may be included in active business income.

Non-Qualifying Income From Property

15-119. Property income, income from a specified investment business, and non-incidental property income earned by an active business do not qualify for the small business deduction. However, when a corporation derives income from holding property, and the income is received from an associated company that deducted the amounts in computing active business income, ITA 129(6)(b) deems the income to be active business income to the recipient.

15-120. The logic behind this is that, while the amounts received by one of the associated companies must be considered property income, because of its legal form, the deduction by the payer corporation reduces the total active business income within the associated group.

> **Example** Lardin Inc. is associated with Dwarm Ltd. Lardin lends $100,000 to Dwarm to use in active business activities. During the current year, Dwarm pays $6,000 of interest to Lardin.

> **Analysis** Normally, Lardin could not classify the interest received as active business income. However, if Dwarm is earning active business income, the payment to Lardin reduced the amount of this income, as well as the total active business income of the associated group. In order to prevent this reduction, the recipient corporation is allowed to treat such interest as active business income.

Annual Business Limit

15-121.   For over 20 years, the annual business limit for the small business deduction was stuck at $200,000. Starting in 2002, the limit has been gradually increased. As of 2007, the limit is $400,000, with no further changes scheduled in subsequent years.

15-122.   A further important feature of this limit is described in the following Paragraph. This is the fact that a single annual business limit must be shared by associated corporations. As indicated in ITA 125(3), if the associated corporations choose to file Schedule 23 with their corporate tax return, they can allocate the annual business limit to members of the associated group in any manner they wish. However, if they fail to file the prescribed form, ITA 125(4) allows the CRA to make an allocation to one or more corporations on any basis.

Associated Companies

The Problem

15-123.   In the absence of special rules, it would be very easy to avoid the annual limit that applies to the small business deduction. This could be accomplished by dividing a single corporation's activities between two separate corporations, thereby doubling up on the annual business limit of $400,000. However, the *Act* prevents this by requiring that associated companies share their annual business limit.

15-124.   For example, assume that Mr. Robards owns all of the outstanding voting shares of both the Mark Company and the Grand Company. These two Companies would be considered to be associated and, as a consequence, would have to share the $400,000 annual business limit.

15-125.   As indicated previously, they can elect to allocate the annual limit in any proportion they wish, provided the total does not exceed $400,000. If the Mark Company has active business income and the Grand Company does not, it would be most advantageous to allocate the entire annual limit to the Mark Company, so that it could claim the maximum small business deduction.

15-126.   The preceding example is very clear cut and results in an allocation of the small business deduction that reflects the goals of the relevant legislation. However, with a deduction that can be worth over $80,000 per year in federal and provincial taxes, there is a significant incentive to develop arrangements that will avoid the intent of the legislation. Correspondingly, there is a need to have legislation that is sophisticated enough to frustrate these arrangements. As a consequence, the identification of associated companies can be very complex.

Definitions

15-127.   Associated corporations are defined in ITA 256(1). However, there are a number of definitions and rules that are used in the provisions related to identifying associated corporations. The most important of these are as follows:

> **ITA 251(2)(a) - Related Persons**   With respect to individuals, Paragraph (a) notes that individuals are related if they are connected by blood relationship, marriage, common-law partnership, or adoption. Various other Subsections in ITA 251 and 252 elaborate on this statement to point out that all of the following individuals would be "related" to the taxpayer:
>
> - Parents and grandparents, as well as parents and grandparents of the taxpayer's spouse or common-law partner.
> - The taxpayer's spouse or common-law partner, as well as the spouse or common-law partner's siblings and their spouses and common-law partners.
> - Siblings of the taxpayer, as well as spouses or common-law partners of the taxpayer's siblings.
> - Children, including those that are adopted, or born outside of marriage. Also included here would be spouses and common-law partners of children and

children of the taxpayer's spouse or common-law partner.

ITA 251(2)(b) indicates that a corporation is related to:
- a person who controls it, if it is controlled by one person;
- a person who is a member of a related group that controls it; or
- any person related to a person who controls it or who is related to a member of a related group that controls it.

ITA 251(2)(c) indicates that two corporations are related if:
- they are controlled by the same person or group of persons;
- each of the corporations is controlled by one person and the person who controls one of the corporations is related to the person who controls the other corporation;
- one of the corporations is controlled by one person and that person is related to any member of a related group that controls the other corporation;
- one of the corporations is controlled by one person and that person is related to each member of an unrelated group that controls the other corporation;
- any member of a related group that controls one of the corporations is related to each member of an unrelated group that controls the other corporation; or
- each member of an unrelated group that controls one of the corporations is related to at least one member of an unrelated group that controls the other corporation.

ITA 256(1.2)(c) - Control   The definition of associated corporations also involves the concept of control. While there may be complications in the application of this concept, where corporations are concerned, one corporation is deemed to control another if it owns either:

- shares (common and/or preferred) of capital stock with a fair market value of more than 50 percent of all issued and outstanding shares of capital stock; or
- common shares with a fair market value of more than 50 percent of all issued and outstanding common shares.

ITA 256(1.2)(a) - Definition Of Group   For purposes of defining associated companies, a group is two or more persons, each of whom owns shares in the corporation in question. A related group involves a group of persons, each member of which is related to every other member. An unrelated group is any group, other than a related group.

ITA 256(1.1) - Specified Class, Shares Of   In simplified terms, this definition refers to non-voting shares that have a fixed dividend rate and redemption amount. Such shares are normally referred to as preferred shares.

Deeming Rules   The most relevant deeming rules can be described as follows:

- **ITA 256(1.2)(d) - Holding Companies**   This provision indicates that where shares of a corporation are held by another corporation, a shareholder of the holding corporation is deemed to own the shares of the held corporation in proportion to his interest in the holding corporation. Similar provisions apply to shares held by partnerships and trusts.

- **ITA 256(1.3) - Children Under 18**   This provision requires that, in most circumstances, shares owned at any time during the year by a child under 18 are deemed to be shares owned by each parent for purposes of determining associated companies.

- **ITA 256(1.4) - Rights And Options**   This provision requires that rights to acquire shares be treated as though they were exercised for purposes of determining associated companies. This Subsection also indicates that, where a person has a right to require a shareholder to redeem, cancel, or acquire its own shares, for purposes of determining association, the corporation is deemed to have carried out the redemption, cancellation, or acquisition.

ITA 256(2) - Association Through A Third Corporation This provision indicates that two corporations, both of which are associated with a third corporation, are deemed to be associated with each other. This Subsection also includes an election that can mitigate this rule. The third corporation can elect on Schedule 28 not to be associated with the other two corporations. A consequence of this is that the third corporation's annual business limit will be set at nil. However, the election will allow the other two corporations to be exempt from the association rules under ITA 256(2).

15-128. Given these definitions and rules, we are now in a position to look at the definition of associated companies as it is found in ITA 256(1).

Examples - Associated Corporation Rules

15-129. The preceding definitions are essential to the understanding of the associated corporation rules found in ITA 256(1). This Subsection contains five Paragraphs designated (a) through (e), with each Paragraph describing a relationship involving association. These five Paragraphs will be given individual attention in the material that follows.

15-130. The first of the Paragraphs that define association states the following:

ITA 256(1)(a) One of the corporations controlled, directly or indirectly in any manner whatever, the other.

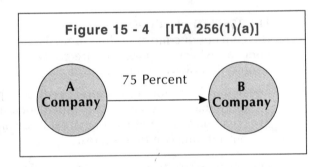

Figure 15 - 4 [ITA 256(1)(a)]

15-131. This type of association can be illustrated by the situation shown in Figure 15-4 in which A Company owns 75 percent of the outstanding voting shares of B Company. In this situation, Company A and Company B are associated by virtue of ITA 256(1)(a).

15-132. The second Paragraph in the ITA 256 definition of associated companies is as follows:

ITA 256(1)(b) Both of the corporations were controlled, directly or indirectly in any manner whatever, by the same person or group of persons.

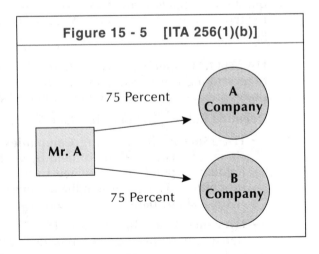

Figure 15 - 5 [ITA 256(1)(b)]

15-133. This type of association can be illustrated by the situation shown in Figure 15-5. In this situation, Mr. A owns 75 percent of the shares of both A Company and B Company. As a consequence, these two Companies are associated by virtue of ITA 256(1)(b), in that they are both controlled by the same person.

15-134. The third Paragraph in the ITA 256 definition of associated companies is as follows:

ITA 256(1)(c) Each of the corporations was controlled, directly or indirectly in any manner whatever, by a person and the person who so controlled one of the corporations was related to the person who so controlled the other and either of those persons owned, in respect of each corporation, not less than 25 percent of the issued shares of any class, other than a specified class, of the capital stock thereof.

15-135. This type of association can be illustrated by the situation shown in Figure 15-6. In this situation, Mr. A owns 70 percent of the shares of A Company and his spouse, Mrs. A, owns 70 percent of B Company. In addition, Mr. A owns not less than 25 percent of the shares of B Company. Provided that the B Company shares owned by Mr. A are not of a specified class, Companies A and B are associated under ITA 256(1)(c). As the required cross ownership can be in either direction, the two Companies would also be associated if the cross ownership was by Mrs. A in A Company.

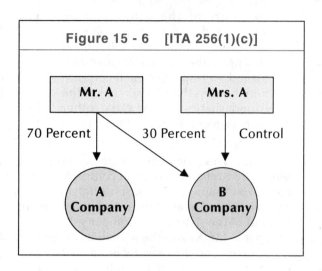

15-136. A fourth Paragraph in ITA 256(1) defining association is as follows:

> **ITA 256(1)(d)** One of the corporations was controlled, directly or indirectly in any manner whatever, by a person and that person was related to each member of a group of persons that so controlled the other corporation, and that person owned, in respect of the other corporation, not less than 25 percent of the issued shares of any class, other than a specified class, of the capital stock thereof.

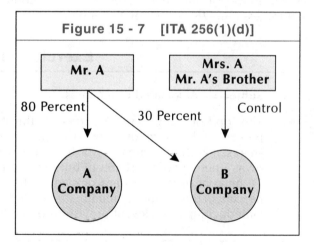

15-137. This type of association can be illustrated by the situation in Figure 15-7. In this situation, Mr. A owns 80 percent of the shares of A Company, while Mrs. A and Mr. A's brother each own 35 percent of the shares of B Company. This means that Mr. A is related to each member of a group that controls B Company. Mr. A also has the required cross ownership, in that he owns 30 percent of the shares of B Company. Provided that the shares of B Company owned by Mr. A are not of a specified class, A Company and B Company are associated by virtue of ITA 256(1)(d). Note that, under ITA 256(1)(d), the cross ownership has to be by Mr. A in B Company. If the cross ownership was in the other direction (e.g., Mrs. A owns 30 percent of A Company), the two Companies would not be associated under ITA 256(1)(d).

15-138. The final Paragraph in ITA 256(1) describing associated companies is as follows:

ITA 256(1)(e)   Each of the corporations was controlled, directly or indirectly in any manner whatever, by a related group and each of the members of one of the related groups was related to all of the members of the other related group, and one or more persons who were members of both related groups, either alone or together, owned, in respect of each corporation, not less than 25 percent of the issued shares of any class, other than a specified class, of the capital stock thereof.

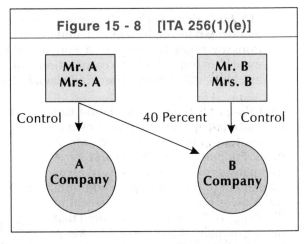

Figure 15 - 8   [ITA 256(1)(e)]

15-139.   This type of association can be illustrated by the situation in Figure 15-8. Mr. and Mrs. A are a related group that control A Company, and Mr. and Mrs. B are a related group that control B Company. If we assume that Mrs. B is Mr. A's sister, then each member of one related group is related to all of the members of the other related group. Mr. and Mrs. A each own 50 percent of the shares of A Company, Mr. and Mrs. B each own 30 percent of the shares of B Company. Mr. A owns the remaining 40 percent of the shares of B Company. In this situation, A Company and B Company are associated under ITA 256(1)(e). Once again, Mr. A's cross ownership has to be shares other than those of a specified class. However, if A Company shares were available, the cross ownership could be in the other direction (e.g., Mrs. B owns not less than 25 percent of A Company).

Exercise Fifteen-9

Subject: Associated Companies

The Top Company owns 65 percent of the shares of Middle Company, as well as 10 percent of the shares of Bottom Company. Middle Company owns 22 percent of the shares of Bottom Company. Mr. Top, who owns all of the shares of Top Company, also owns 5 percent of the shares of Bottom Company and has options to acquire another 10 percent of the Bottom Company's shares. Mr. Top's 12 year old son owns 15 percent of the Bottom Company shares. Indicate which of these Companies are associated, citing the relevant provisions of the *Income Tax Act*.

End of Exercise.   Solution available in Study Guide.

Calculating The Small Business Deduction

The General Formula

15-140.   After noting that to qualify for this deduction, a corporation must be a CCPC throughout the year, ITA 125(1) specifies that the deduction from federal Tax Payable is equal to 16 percent of the least of three figures:

A.   Net Canadian active business income.

B.   Taxable Income, less:

1.   10/3 times the ITA 126(1) credit for taxes paid on foreign non-business income, calculated without consideration of the additional refundable tax under ITA 123.3 (See Chapter 16) or the general rate reduction under ITA 123.4; and

2. 3 times the ITA 126(2) credit for taxes paid on foreign business income, calculated without consideration of the general rate reduction under ITA 123.4.

C. The annual business limit of $400,000, less any portion allocated to associated corporations, less the reduction for large corporations (see Paragraph 15-151).

Note For item B(2) in the preceding formula, current legislation specifies a multiplier of 10/4. However, draft legislation indicates that this will be changed to 3. As shown in the preceding formula, we intend to use the multiplier indicated in the draft legislation.

Constraints - Type Of Income And Annual Business Limit

15-141. We have already noted that the deduction is only available on active business income earned in Canada, the item A constraint. We have also discussed possible problems with allocating the annual business limit of $400,000, the item C constraint. These largely involve identification of associated companies and the allocation of this amount to the associated companies.

Constraints - Taxable Income

15-142. With respect to limiting the deduction to amounts of Taxable Income, we would note that active business income earned during the taxation year is included in Net Income For Tax Purposes. In many cases, this amount will also be included in full in Taxable Income. However, it is possible that large Division C deductions could eliminate all or part of this income from the Taxable Income total. Examples of Division C deductions that could remove all or part of active business income from the Taxable Income total would be as follows:

- charitable donations
- non-capital loss carry overs
- farm loss carry overs

15-143. You will notice that neither dividends nor net capital losses are included in this list. This reflects the fact that these amounts can only be deducted to the extent that either dividends or taxable capital gains are included in Net Income. Given this, they cannot serve to offset amounts of active business income that are included in Net Income For Tax Purposes.

15-144. A simple example will illustrate the need for this Taxable Income constraint on the small business deduction:

Example During the current year, Allard Ltd. has active business income of $123,000, taxable capital gains of $15,000, and dividends received from taxable Canadian corporations of $50,000. At the beginning of the year, Allard Ltd. has a net capital loss carry forward of $35,000 and a non-capital loss carry forward of $105,000. The Company will use the loss carry overs to the extent possible during the current year. The calculation of Allard's Net Income For Tax Purposes and Taxable Income would be as follows:

Net Income For Tax Purposes		
($123,000 + $15,000 + $50,000)		$188,000
Dividends	($ 50,000)	
Net Capital Loss Carry Forward		
(Restricted To Taxable Capital Gains)	(15,000)	
Non-Capital Loss Carry Forward	(105,000)	(170,000)
Taxable Income		$ 18,000

15-145. Note that if only the net capital loss carry forward and dividends were deducted, Taxable Income would have been equal to the $123,000 in active business income. The problem is the non-capital loss carry forward. It has further reduced Taxable Income to $18,000, an amount well below the active business income.

15-146. If, in this case, the small business deduction was based on active business income, the amount would be $19,680 [(16%)($123,000)]. As this deduction is far in excess of the Tax Payable on $18,000 of Taxable Income, this is not a reasonable outcome. The example clearly illustrates the need for the Taxable Income constraint on the small business deduction.

Constraints - Foreign Tax Credits

15-147. Another concern of the federal government is to ensure that the small business deduction is not provided on income that has not been taxed in Canada. To prevent this from happening, the B component of the ITA 125(1) formula reduces Taxable Income by:

- 10/3 times the ITA 126(1) credit for taxes paid on foreign non-business income, calculated without consideration of the additional refundable tax under ITA 123.3 or the general rate reduction under ITA 123.4; and

- 3 times the ITA 126(2) credit for taxes paid on foreign business income, calculated without consideration of the general rate reduction under ITA 123.4.

15-148. The 10/3 figure is based on the notional assumption that foreign non-business income will be subject to a federal tax rate of 30 percent (i.e., if the credit is equal to the taxes paid at 30 percent, 10/3 times the credit will equal the notional amount of income received).

15-149. In similar fashion, the proposed 3 times figure that is applicable to foreign business income is based on the notional assumption that this income will be subject to a federal tax rate of 33-1/3 percent. A higher rate is appropriate here as foreign business income is not "earned in a province" and, as a consequence, is not eligible for the ITA 124(1) federal tax abatement.

15-150. Based on the preceding analysis, subtracting these amounts from Taxable Income has the effect of removing from this figure the amounts of foreign income on which the foreign tax credit has eliminated the Canadian taxation at the assumed rates of 30 and 33-1/3 percent. A simple example can be used to clarify this point:

Example A corporation earns $100,000 in foreign non-business income, with $18,000 being withheld by the foreign government.

If this income had been earned in Canada, the tax would be $30,000 (using the notional rate on this type of income of 30 percent). Being received from a foreign source, the $30,000 in Canadian Tax Payable will be offset by the $18,000 foreign tax credit, leaving a net Canadian Tax Payable of $12,000.

The formula removes $60,000 [(10/3)($18,000)] from Taxable Income, and we are left with $40,000 ($100,000 - $60,000). Taxes at 30 percent on this amount would be $12,000, thereby demonstrating that the formula has served to remove the portion of Taxable Income on which the foreign tax credit has eliminated Canadian taxation.

Exercise Fifteen-10

Subject: Amount Eligible For The Small Business Deduction

Kartoom Ltd. is a CCPC throughout the year and is not associated with any other corporation. For the year ending December 31, 2007, Kartoom has Net Income For Tax Purposes of $570,000. This amount is made up of dividends from taxable Canadian corporations of $85,000, active business income of $425,000, and foreign non-business income of $60,000. The foreign income was subject to withholding in the foreign jurisdiction at a rate of 15 percent. Kartoom receives a foreign tax credit against federal Tax Payable that is equal to the amount withheld. Kartoom has a non-capital loss carry forward of $160,000 which it intends to deduct during 2007. Determine the amount eligible for the small business deduction for the year ending December 31, 2007.

End of Exercise. Solution available in Study Guide.

Elimination Of Small Business Deduction For Large CCPCs

The Problem

15-151.   As the name implies, the small business deduction was designed to provide assistance to small corporations.   For a variety of reasons, including the belief that such corporations have a positive impact on employment growth, and the fact that small corporations often experience financing difficulties in their formative years, the generous tax advantages provided by this deduction were thought to be appropriate.

15-152.   However, in designing the small business deduction provisions, eligibility was based on the type of income earned (active business income) and the type of corporation (CCPCs). No consideration was given to the size of the corporation's income or assets. As a consequence, at one time, some very large private corporations received the benefit of the small business deduction on amounts of active business income that were below the annual business limit. This was clearly not in keeping with the intent of this legislation.

The Solution

15-153.   To deal with this problem, the government introduced a formula that reduces the annual business limit on the basis of the size of the CCPC's Taxable Capital Employed In Canada. As found in ITA 125(5.1), the formula is as follows:

$$\textbf{Annual Business Limit Reduction} = A \times \frac{B}{\$11,250} \text{ where,}$$

A   is the amount of the corporation's annual business limit for the year ($400,000 or less if shared with associated corporations).

B   is .225 percent (.00225) of the excess of the corporation's Taxable Capital Employed In Canada for the previous year, over $10 million.

15-154.   Taxable Capital Employed in Canada is defined in ITA 181.2. In somewhat simplified terms, it has the following meaning:

Taxable Capital Employed In Canada (TCEC)   GAAP determined debt and equity capital of the corporation, less debt and equity investments in other corporations. When not all of the corporation's Taxable Income is allocated to a province, the resulting amount is multiplied by the same percentage that is applied to the abatement in order to determine the portion of the total capital that is employed in Canada.

15-155.   The mechanics of this formula are easily understood. Note that this formula calculates the **reduction** in the annual business limit, **not** the limit after the reduction. If a corporation has $10 million or less TCEC, B will equal nil ($10 million or less, minus the $10 million specified deduction). This means the formula amount will be nil and there will be no reduction in the corporation's annual business limit.

15-156.   When the amount of TCEC reached $15 million, B in the formula will be equal to $11,250 [(.00225)($15,000,000 - $10,000,000)]. The annual business limit will then be multiplied by one ($11,250 ÷ $11,250) and the reduction in the annual business limit will be 100 percent of the available amount.

15-157.   Not surprisingly, a CCPC that is associated with one or more other corporations in a taxation year ending in a given calendar year will be required to take into account the TCEC of all of these firms.

Example

15-158.   The following example illustrates the reduction of the small business deduction for a large CCPC:

Example Largess Inc. is a CCPC with a December 31 year end. All of its income is earned in Canada, and it is not associated with any other corporation. On December 31, 2007, the following information is available:

2007 Active Business Income	$ 423,000
2007 Taxable Income	550,000
Taxable Capital Employed In Canada During 2006	13,700,000

15-159. For the preceding year, 2006, B in the reduction formula would be equal to $8,325 [(.00225)($13,700,000 - $10,000,000)]. Using this in the ITA 125(5.1) formula would produce the following reduction in the 2007 annual business limit:

$$\$400,000 \times \frac{\$8,325}{\$11,250} = \$296,000 \text{ Reduction}$$

15-160. Given this, the reduced annual business limit would be $104,000 ($400,000 - $296,000) and the small business deduction for 2007 would be 16 percent of the least of:

Active Business Income	$423,000
Taxable Income	550,000
Reduced Annual Business Limit ($400,000 - $296,000)	104,000

15-161. The reduced annual business limit is the least of the three figures and the 2007 small business deduction would be $16,640 [(16%)($104,000)], a significant reduction from the $64,000 [(16%)($400,000)] that would have been available in the absence of the ITA 125(5.1) requirement for reducing the annual business limit for large CCPCs.

Exercise Fifteen-11

Subject: Small Business Deduction Reduction

Largely Small Inc. is a Canadian controlled private corporation. For the year ending December 31, 2007, its Net Income For Tax Purposes is $1,233,000, all of which is active business income, except for $36,000 in foreign source non-business income. Fifteen percent of this amount was withheld in the foreign jurisdiction and the corporation receives a foreign tax credit against federal Tax Payable that is equal to the amount withheld. The corporation's only deduction in the calculation of Taxable Income is for a non-capital loss carry forward of $914,000. The corporation had Taxable Capital Employed In Canada of $11,300,000 for the year ending December 31, 2006, and $11,600,000 for the year ending December 31, 2007. It is not associated with any other corporation. Determine the amount of Largely Small Inc.'s small business deduction for the year ending December 31, 2007.

End of Exercise. Solution available in Study Guide.

Personal Services Corporations

15-162. The small business deduction represents a very significant reduction in corporate taxes and, as a consequence, taxpayers have a strong incentive to channel income into a corporation qualifying for this benefit. At one point in time, this could be accomplished by having an executive of a corporation resign, establish a company, and immediately have this company sign a contract with his former employer to provide the same services as the individual was previously performing as an employee. Since this new corporation could then qualify for the small business deduction, the use of such personal services corporations provided significant tax deferral and, in some cases, significant tax avoidance, for individuals such as executives, professional athletes, and entertainers.

15-163. Under the current rules, such blatant tax avoidance schemes are no longer possible. To begin, ITA 125(7) defines a personal services business as follows:

... a business of providing services where

(a) an individual who performs services on behalf of the corporation (referred to as an incorporated employee), or

(b) any person related to the incorporated employee

is a specified shareholder of the corporation and the incorporated employee would reasonably be regarded as an officer or employee of the person or partnership to whom or to which the services were provided but for the existence of the corporation, unless

(c) the corporation employs in the business throughout the year more than five full time employees, or

(d) the amount paid or payable to the corporation in the year for the services is received or receivable by it from a corporation with which it was associated in the year.

15-164.   In somewhat less technical language, a business corporation will be classified as a personal services business when a specified shareholder of the corporation is providing services to another business and the individual who is performing the services can reasonably be regarded as an officer or employee of the entity for which the services are performed. As the term is used in this definition (ITA 248), specified shareholder refers to situations in which an individual owns, directly or indirectly, not less than a 10 percent interest in the company under consideration.

15-165.   If a corporation falls within the preceding definition, it is not eligible for the small business deduction on any of its income from the personal services business and, as a consequence, it is subject to tax at full corporate rates. In addition, no deduction is permitted to the corporation for any expenses other than:

- salaries, wages, other remuneration, and benefits paid in the year to the individual who performed the services on behalf of the corporation; and

- other expenses that would normally be deductible against employment income, for example, travel expenses incurred to earn employment income.

15-166.   These rules are designed to remove the availability of the small business deduction in certain situations where a corporation is being used as a device to channel an individual's income from performing services into a more favourably taxed classification.

15-167.   With respect to personal services corporations established to replace an executive's personal employment arrangements, these rules have served to eliminate most of the tax incentives for such arrangements. However, athletes, entertainers and consultants may still find it attractive to incorporate. In many cases, they will qualify for the small business deduction either because they have sufficient diversity of income or more than five full time employees.

Professional Corporations And Management Companies

15-168.   In general terms, these two types of corporations can be described as follows:

Professional Corporations   This term is used where a corporation is established to carry on the practice of a specified profession. These situations include the professional practice of an accountant, dentist, lawyer, medical doctor, veterinarian, or chiropractor. At one time, very few provinces permitted the incorporation of a professional practice. However, this is changing, as several provinces, including Alberta and Ontario, now permit this practice.

Management Companies   This is a term that refers to corporations established to provide various management services, primarily to an unincorporated business. The unincorporated business is usually a professional practice, such as that of a doctor or dentist, which is not permitted to incorporate because of provincial legislation.

The services provided by this type of company include various personnel functions, such as payroll and accounting services, purchasing all supplies and equipment necessary to carry on the business, and providing the necessary office space required by the professional practice.

The unincorporated business pays fees to the company to cover the cost of providing management services and to provide for some income. A 15 percent markup for profit is usually allowed. The fees paid are deductible from the revenues of the professional practice. These companies are often used to transfer a portion of a professional's income to a lower income spouse or other related parties.

15-169.   Both types of companies are eligible for the small business deduction. However, the fact that medical services are exempt goods under the GST legislation has made management companies less attractive for doctors and dentists. While GST must be paid on services billed by the management company, these amounts cannot be recovered by medical professionals because their services are GST exempt. Given this situation, and the fact that professionals can incorporate in some provinces, management companies for medical professionals delivering GST exempt services are not as common as they once were.

Manufacturing And Processing Profits Deduction

Introduction

15-170.   The manufacturing and processing sector of the Canadian economy accounts for almost 20 percent of both Gross Domestic Product and employment. Given this importance, it is not surprising that the government has provided tax assistance to enterprises that are involved in manufacturing and processing. As an example of this, in Chapter 7 (CCA) we noted that the 2007 budget is proposing an extra CCA allowance for buildings used in manufacturing and processing, as well as a temporary incentive rate for CCA on manufacturing and processing machinery and equipment.

15-171.   A more general incentive is the manufacturing and processing profits (M&P) deduction available to some corporations for their manufacturing and processing profits. However, as was explained previously, the general rate reduction is currently equal to 7 percentage points, the same amount as the M&P deduction. This, in effect, means that at the federal level, income that is eligible for the M&P deduction will be taxed at the same rate as other full rate taxable income.

15-172.   Given this situation, it would seem logical for the government to eliminate the legislation related to the M&P deduction. However, this does not appear to be happening. At this point in time, the only legislative proposal is removing the reference to 7 percent in the basic M&P formula, and replacing it with a reference to the corporation's general rate reduction percentage (which is currently equal to 7 percent).

15-173.   The probable explanation for this is that some provinces (Newfoundland, Ontario, Saskatchewan, and the Yukon) still provide special treatment for income that qualifies for the federal M&P deduction. Because of this, we will continue to provide coverage of the M&P rules.

Calculating The Deduction

General Formula

15-174.   ITA 125.1 provides for a deduction from Tax Payable equal to the general rate reduction (7 percent for 2007) times the company's M&P profits. Given that this amount is deducted from Tax Payable, it would be more consistent to refer to this "deduction" as a tax credit. However, ITA 125.1 uses the term deduction and, as a consequence, we will also use this terminology.

15-175.   While the basic idea is that the deduction is currently equal to the general rate reduction percentage applied to M&P profits, there are a number of other constraints on the amount that is eligible for this deduction. ITA 125.1(1) specifies that the deduction will be equal to the corporation's general rate reduction percentage multiplied by the lesser of:

A. manufacturing and processing profits, less amounts eligible for the small business deduction; and

B. taxable income, less the sum of:

1. the amount eligible for the small business deduction;

2. 3 times (see Paragraph 15-177) the foreign tax credit for business income (for this purpose only, the foreign tax credit is calculated without consideration of the ITA 123.4 general rate reduction); and

3. where the corporation is a Canadian controlled private corporation throughout the year, aggregate investment income as defined in ITA 129(4).

15-176.   Part A of this formula provides the basic limit based on the amount of M&P profits earned during the year. As will be explained subsequently, M&P profits is a technical term and must be calculated by a formula established in ITR 5200. In many cases, particularly for large public companies, this will be the factor that limits the amount of the M&P deduction.

15-177.   With respect to the multiplier of the foreign tax credit for business income, the current legislation states 10/4 of this amount. Draft legislation proposes to change the foreign business income tax credit multiplier from 10/4 to 3. Consistent with our approach to the equivalent change in the small business deduction formula, we will use the proposed multiplier of 3 in our text and problem material.

Constraints - Small Business Deduction

15-178.   As was previously discussed, the small business deduction provides certain corporations with a deduction equal to 16 percent of the first $400,000 of their active business income. It appears that the government believes that granting both the 7 percent M&P deduction, and the 16 percent small business deduction on the same income stream would be too generous. As a consequence, any amounts of income that are eligible for the small business deduction are not eligible for the M&P deduction. In the preceding ITA 125.1(1) formula, this is accomplished by removing amounts eligible for the small business deduction from both the A and B components.

Constraints - Taxable Income

15-179.   As was explained in our discussion of constraints on the availability of the small business deduction, the government wants to ensure that credits are not given on amounts that are not included in Taxable Income. As was the case with the active business income that is eligible for the small business deduction, M&P profits that are included in Net Income For Tax Purposes may not find their way into Taxable Income.

15-180.   This can occur when the corporation has deductions for such items as charitable donations, non-capital loss carry overs, or farm loss carry overs. For reasons that were discussed and illustrated in the discussion of the small business deduction, amounts eligible for the M&P deduction are limited by the amount of Taxable Income for the year.

Constraints - Foreign Tax Credit

15-181.   As was the case with the Taxable Income constraint, the nature of the constraint created by deducting a multiple of foreign tax credits was explained in our discussion of the small business deduction. There is, however, one significant difference.

15-182.   In the ITA 125.1(1) formula for the M&P deduction, Taxable Income is reduced by a multiple of the foreign business income credit only. It is not adjusted for the foreign non-business income credit as was the case with the ITA 125(1) formula for the small business deduction. This probably reflects the fact that the M&P formula contains an extra deduction from Taxable Income for aggregate investment income, an amount that includes foreign non-business income.

Constraints - Aggregate Investment Income

15-183.   This constraint is more difficult to explain at this stage. It is based on the fact that a part of federal tax paid on the "aggregate investment income" of a Canadian controlled private corporation can be refunded to the corporation. (This procedure is discussed in detail in Chapter 16.) As it would not appear to be appropriate to provide a tax credit against taxes that may eventually be refunded, these amounts are removed from the Taxable Income that is eligible for the M&P deduction.

15-184.   Note the reference to "aggregate investment income as defined in ITA 129(4)" in the formula in Paragraph 15-175. This somewhat unusual concept of investment income includes net taxable capital gains, interest, rents, and royalties, but does not include dividends that a corporation can deduct in the calculation of Taxable Income. It includes both foreign and Canadian amounts for these items, and is reduced by net capital losses deducted under the ITA 111(1)(b) provision for net capital loss carry overs.

Exercise Fifteen-12

Subject: Amounts Eligible For Small Business and M&P Deductions

Marion Manufacturing is a Canadian controlled private corporation throughout 2007. It has Net Income For Tax Purposes of $462,000, a figure that includes $411,000 in manufacturing and processing profits (as per ITR 5200). The $462,000 also includes foreign source business income of $21,000 and taxable capital gains of $30,000. Because of withholding on the foreign source business income, the Company is entitled to a foreign tax credit of $3,150 [(15%)($21,000)]. The Company's only deduction in the calculation of Taxable Income is donations to registered Canadian charities in the amount of $310,000. Marion anticipates large increases in Taxable Income in the next few years. It is not associated with any other company. Determine the amount of Marion's small business deduction and M&P deduction for the year ending December 31, 2007. Include in your answer any alternatives that could be used to save taxes.

End of Exercise.   Solution available in Study Guide.

Eligibility

15-185.   On the surface, eligibility for the M&P deduction appears to be easily determinable. Any corporation that derives 10 percent or more of its Canadian active business gross revenues from Canadian manufacturing or processing is eligible. The problem with this rule, however, is the determination of what constitutes M&P activity.

15-186.   The *Income Tax Act* does not define the terms manufacturing or processing. However, ITA 125.1(3) specifically excludes several types of activity from the designation of manufacturing or processing. These include logging, farming and fishing, construction, producing industrial minerals, and processing mineral resources.

15-187.   More guidance on the nature of manufacturing and processing is available in IT-145R. This IT Bulletin notes that manufacturing generally involves the creation of something or the shaping, stamping, or forming of an object from something. Correspondingly, processing is described as techniques of preparation, handling, or other activity designed to effect a physical or chemical change in an article or substance.

15-188.   Needless to say, these descriptions have not settled the issue and, as a consequence, the distinction between qualified and non-qualified activity has been the subject of numerous court cases. In fact, there is often a very fine line between qualified and non-qualified activities. For example, for the owner of a pub, IT-145R advises that the mixing of a drink is a qualified processing activity, whereas serving that same drink is a non-qualifying service activity.

M&P Profits Defined
Basic Formula
15-189.   We have previously noted that the amount of the M & P deduction is usually calculated as 7 percent of a company's Canadian M&P profits for the year. Since many businesses will have other types of income in addition to M&P profits, it is necessary to have a method for determining what portion of total income can be classified as M&P profits. This is accomplished through the use of the following formula, which is described in ITR 5200:

$$\begin{bmatrix} \text{Adjusted} \\ \text{Active} \\ \text{Business} \\ \text{Income} \end{bmatrix} \left[\dfrac{\left([^{100}\!/_{75}] \text{ of Canadian M\&P Labour Costs} \right) + \left([^{100}\!/_{85}] \text{ of Canadian M\&P Capital Costs} \right)}{\left(\text{Total Canadian Labour Costs} \right) + \left(\text{Total Canadian Active Business Income Capital Costs} \right)} \right]$$

15-190.   The application of this formula requires an understanding of the meaning of each of the components of the formula. These components are defined in ITR 5202 and discussed in the material that follows.

Adjusted Active Business Income
15-191.   As defined in ITR 5202, "adjusted active business income" simply means the corporation's income for the year from active business carried on in Canada, less the corporation's losses for the year from active business carried on in Canada. As is clear from the formula in Paragraph 15-189, M&P profits are a subset of active business income. Stated alternatively, all M&P profits are active business income, but not all types of active business income are derived from M&P activities.

Qualified Activities
15-192.   The ITR 5202 definitions provide guidance with respect to what activities qualify for the deduction. Specifically listed as qualifying activities are the following:

- engineering design of products and production facilities;
- receiving and storing of raw materials;
- producing, assembling, and handling of goods in process;
- inspecting and packaging of finished goods;
- line supervision;
- production support activities including security, cleaning, heating, and factory maintenance;
- quality and production control;
- repair of production facilities; and
- pollution control.

15-193.   Also included are all other activities that are performed in Canada directly in connection with non-excluded manufacturing or processing, as well as scientific research and experimental development.

15-194.   Specifically excluded by the definition of qualified activities are the following:

- storing, shipping, selling, and leasing of finished goods;
- purchasing of raw materials;
- administration, including clerical and personnel activities;
- purchase and resale operations;
- data processing; and
- providing facilities for employees, including cafeterias, clinics, and recreational facilities.

Cost Of Labour
15-195.   As defined in ITR 5202, the "cost of labour" includes salaries, wages, and commissions paid to employees of the company. In general, fringe benefits are excluded. In addition

to salaries and wages paid to employees of the corporation, the cost of labour includes amounts paid to non-employees for management and administration, scientific research, and other services that would normally be performed by an employee. This brings into the calculation employee services that have, in effect, been contracted out.

15-196.   Excluded from this total would be labour costs that have been added to the cost of capital assets (e.g., labour costs added to the cost of a self-constructed asset) and any labour costs related to foreign active business income. Note, however, that no attempt is made to segregate and remove labour costs associated with property or investment income.

Cost Of Manufacturing And Processing Labour

15-197.   ITR 5202 defines "manufacturing and processing labour" as 100/75 of that portion of the "cost of labour" that was engaged in "qualified activities" (see preceding definitions). The 100/75 gross up factor reflects the fact that even a company that is completely engaged in qualified activities will require some non-qualifying labour to administer M&P activities. The gross up provides for such administrative labour without eroding the availability of the M&P deduction.

15-198.   You should also note that the definition restricts the cost of manufacturing and processing labour to a maximum value equal to the total cost of labour. For example, if the "cost of labour" was $1,200,000 and the amount of this labour involved in qualifying activities was $1,000,000, the "cost of manufacturing and processing labour" in the definition would be $1,333,333 [($1,000,000)(100/75)].   However, the amount used in the M&P formula would be limited to $1,200,000, the "cost of labour".

Cost Of Capital

15-199.   A basic problem here is the need to deal with both assets owned by the corporation and assets leased (rented) by the corporation. The solution is a fairly arbitrary one. For depreciable assets owned by the corporation, the included amount is 10 percent of the gross cost of the asset.

15-200.   To be included, the property must be owned by the corporation at the end of the year and used by the corporation at any time during the year. "Gross cost" in this situation would be the cost before any deduction for government grants and investment tax credits that relate to the capital assets. As these amounts are usually deducted for accounting and tax purposes, they will have to be added back to asset values used for other purposes. The cost of land is not included in the cost of capital.

15-201.   In addition to 10 percent of the gross cost of depreciable assets owned, the cost of capital includes payments made to lease or rent assets during the year. This allocation equates 10 percent of the cost of the asset with the value of leasing that asset. While this is an arbitrary rule, it is certainly preferable to ignoring the fact that leased assets constitute a major part of the physical plant of many Canadian businesses.

15-202.   Where the rent is for property that is comprised of land and a building, only the rent that can be reasonably allocated to the building is included. This is consistent with the exclusion of land from the cost of capital.

15-203.   As was the case with the cost of labour, the cost of capital excludes assets used to produce foreign active business income. Unlike the determination of the cost of labour, the cost of capital excludes assets that are used to produce investment income as defined in ITA 129(4).

Cost Of Manufacturing And Processing Capital

15-204.   As defined in ITR 5202, "manufacturing and processing capital" is equal to 100/85 of the portion of the total cost of capital that is devoted to qualified activities (see previous definition). As was the case with the cost of M&P labour, this amount is grossed up to reflect the fact that, even if a company is completely engaged in M&P activity, some non-manufacturing assets will be required for administrative purposes.

15-205.   Similar to the limit placed on manufacturing and processing labour, manufacturing and processing capital cannot exceed the total cost of capital. As before, this means that if the application of the gross up factor to the capital cost of assets related to qualifying activities produces a number that is larger than the total cost of capital, the cost of manufacturing and processing capital is limited to the total cost of capital.

Applying The Formula

Example

15-206.   The following simple example illustrates the application of the preceding formula.

Example   For its current taxation year the Narder Company, a Canadian public company, had the following information:

Adjusted Active Business Income	$2,500,000
Manufacturing And Processing Labour Costs	3,700,000
Manufacturing And Processing Capital Costs	6,500,000
Total Labour Costs	5,200,000
Total Capital Costs	8,000,000

Based on this information, the calculation of M&P profits for the current year is as follows:

$$[\$2,500,000]\left[\frac{(^{100}\!/_{75})(\$3,700,000) + (^{100}\!/_{85})(\$6,500,000)}{(\$5,200,000 + \$8,000,000)}\right]$$

$$= [(\$2,500,000)(.95306)] = \underline{\$2,382,650}$$

This calculation indicates that Narder Company's M&P profits, as determined by the ITR 5200 formula, amount to $2,382,650. Provided Taxable Income, as adjusted by the requirements of the ITA 125.1(1) formula, exceeds this amount, the Company will be eligible for a deduction from federal Tax Payable of $166,786 [($2,382,650)(7%)].

Exercise Fifteen-13

Subject: Amount Of M&P Profits

Glass Formers Ltd., a corporation involved in the manufacture of various glass products, has active business income for the current year that totals $333,000. It owns $1,432,000 in depreciable capital assets, and leases additional capital assets at an annual cost of $26,000. All of the leased capital assets are used in producing glass products. With respect to the assets owned, they are used as follows:

Production And Handling	45%
Storing Finished Goods	12%
Storing Raw Materials	15%
Purchasing Operations	10%
Quality And Pollution Control	8%
Employee Cafeteria And Recreational Facilities	10%

The Company's total salaries and wages for the current year are $987,000. All of this labour is directed at qualified M&P activities. In addition, $45,000 is spent on contract workers involved in the administration of the corporation. Determine the Company's manufacturing and processing profits for the current year.

End of Exercise. Solution available in Study Guide.

General Rate Reduction - ITA 123.4(2)

Approach To Rate Reductions

15-207.   In our discussion of the basic federal tax rate for corporations, we noted that, in implementing reductions in corporate tax rates, the government has left the basic rate of 38 percent unchanged (see Paragraph 15-77). Instead of reducing the basic rate, they have created a deduction from this rate. This deduction is referred to as the "general rate reduction" percentage and, for 2007, the rate is 7 percent. As discussed in Paragraph 15-79, the rate will increase in subsequent years, reaching a level of 9.5 percent in 2011.

15-208.   While the government wished to reduce corporate tax rates through the use of this general rate reduction, they did not want it to be available on income that was already benefitting from some other tax privilege (e.g., the small business deduction). To deal with this potential problem, the government introduced the concept of Full Rate Taxable Income.

Full Rate Taxable Income

15-209.   As indicated in the preceding Paragraphs, in defining Full Rate Taxable Income, the goal was to develop a measure of income that did not benefit in a significant way from other types of benefits. In particular, the government did not want the general rate reduction to be applied to income that was eligible for:

- The M&P deduction. This deduction is available to CCPCs, public companies, and private companies that are not Canadian controlled.

- The small business deduction. This deduction is only available to CCPCs.

- Refundable Taxes. Refundable taxes are applicable to the investment income of CCPCs and, in some applications to the investment income of private companies that are not Canadian controlled. They are not applicable to public companies. While we need to consider the impact of refundable taxes on full rate taxable income at this point, the detailed procedures related to refundable taxes are discussed in Chapter 16.

15-210.   Since the availability of the relevant benefits depends on the type of company, we will have to give separate attention to the calculation of the Full Rate Taxable Income of CCPCs, and to the Full Rate Taxable Income of companies that are not CCPCs (public companies and private companies that are not Canadian controlled).

Application To Companies Other Than CCPCs

15-211.   For these companies, the only adjustment to Taxable Income that is required to determine Full Rate Taxable Income is the removal of income eligible for the M&P deduction. Given this, for companies other than CCPCs, Full Rate Taxable Income is defined as follows:

Regular Taxable Income	$x,xxx
100/7 Of The M&P Deduction*	(xxx)
Full Rate Taxable Income	**$x,xxx**

*100/7 of the deduction will equal the amount of income eligible for the deduction.

15-212.   A simple example will serve to illustrate the relevant calculations:

Example   For the year ending December 31, 2007, Daren Ltd., a Canadian public company, has Taxable Income equal to $100,000, with $40,000 of this amount eligible for the M&P deduction.

Analysis   Full Rate Taxable Income is equal to $60,000 ($100,000 - $40,000). Given this, total federal Tax Payable for Daren Ltd. would be calculated as follows:

Base Amount Of Part I Tax [(38%)($100,000)]	$38,000
Corporate Surtax [(4%)(28%)($100,000)]	1,120
Federal Tax Abatement [(10%)($100,000)]	(10,000)
M&P Deduction [(7%)($40,000)]	(2,800)
General Rate Reduction [(7%)($100,000 - $40,000)]	(4,200)
Federal Tax Payable	$22,120

15-213. For a corporation with income consisting entirely of M&P profits, there is no general rate reduction as there is no Full Rate Taxable Income. This is illustrated by revising the example in Paragraph 15-212:

Revised Example Assume that the $100,000 in Taxable Income of Daren Ltd. was generated solely by M&P activities.

Analysis Total federal Tax Payable for Daren Ltd. would be calculated as follows:

Base Amount Of Part I Tax [(38%)($100,000)]	$38,000
Corporate Surtax [(4%)(28%)($100,000)]	1,120
Federal Tax Abatement [(10%)($100,000)]	(10,000)
M&P Deduction [(7%)($100,000)]	(7,000)
General Rate Reduction [(7%)($100,000 - $100,000)]	Nil
Federal Tax Payable	$22,120

15-214. This calculation illustrates the fact that the overall federal rate on income that is eligible for the M&P deduction is 22.12 percent. (This is also the overall federal rate on income that is eligible for the general rate reduction.)

Exercise Fifteen-14

Subject: Federal Tax Payable For A Public Company

For the year ending December 31, 2007, Marchand Inc., a Canadian public company, has Taxable Income of $320,000. Of this total, $180,000 qualifies for the M&P deduction. Calculate Marchand's federal Tax Payable for the year ending December 31, 2007.

End of Exercise. Solution available in Study Guide.

Application To CCPCs

15-215. Not surprisingly, the calculation of Full Rate Taxable Income for a CCPC is somewhat more complex than it is for a public company. As we have noted, in addition to the M&P deduction, these companies may benefit from the small business deduction and the refundable tax provisions on investment income.

15-216. Given the potential presence of these additional tax privileges, Full Rate Taxable Income for a CCPC is defined as follows:

Taxable Income, reduced by:

1. Income eligible for the M&P deduction (the *Income Tax Act* refers to this amount as 100/7 of the M&P deduction).

2. Income eligible for the small business deduction (the *Income Tax Act* refers to this amount as 100/16 of the small business deduction).

3. The corporation's aggregate investment income for the year as defined in ITA 129(4) (To remove income that will benefit from refundable taxes when it is distributed by the corporation. These taxes are explained in Chapter 16).

Note We find it is easier to understand this material if we use the descriptions "income eligible for the M&P deduction" and "income eligible for the small business deduction", rather than the formulas used in the *Income Tax Act*. We will use this approach throughout the text and problem material which follows.

15-217.   The definition of aggregate investment income in ITA 129(4) includes net taxable capital gains, interest, rents, and royalties, but not dividends (see Paragraph 15-184). It includes both domestic and foreign amounts of such income, and the balance is reduced by net capital loss carry overs deducted during the year.

15-218.   As is covered in Chapter 16, a portion of the Part I tax paid by CCPCs on their aggregate investment income is refunded when dividends are paid. Since this type of income is already taxed advantageously when it is flowed through a CCPC, it does not receive the benefit of the general rate reduction.

15-219.   The following example illustrates the application of the general rate reduction rules to a CCPC.

Example For the year ending December 31, 2007, Zaptek Ltd., a CCPC, has $200,000 in Taxable Income. This amount is made up entirely of active business income earned in Canada, none of which relates to M&P activity. It is associated with another company and, as per the agreement with that company, it is entitled to $100,000 of the annual business limit.

Analysis The federal Tax Payable for Zaptek Ltd. would be calculated as follows:

Base Amount Of Part I Tax [(38%)($200,000)]	$76,000
Corporate Surtax [(4%)(28%)($200,000)]	2,240
Federal Tax Abatement [(10%)($200,000)]	(20,000)
Small Business Deduction [(16%)($100,000)]	(16,000)
General Rate Reduction [(7%)($200,000 - $100,000)]	(7,000)
Federal Tax Payable	$35,240

15-220.   The overall rate of federal tax in this example is 17.6 percent. This reflects a combination of a rate of 13.1% [(38% - 10%)(104%) - 16%] on the $100,000 of income that was eligible for the small business deduction, and a rate of 22.1% [(38% - 10%)(104%) - 7%] on income that is not eligible for this deduction.

Exercise Fifteen-15

Subject: Federal Tax Payable For A CCPC

Redux Ltd. is a Canadian controlled private corporation. For the year ending December 31, 2007, the Company has Taxable Income of $200,000, all of which is active business income. Of this amount, $145,000 results from M&P activity. As it is associated with two other corporations, its share of the annual business limit is $140,000 [(35%)($400,000)]. Determine the Company's federal Tax Payable for the year ending December 31, 2007.

End of Exercise. Solution available in Study Guide.

Foreign Tax Credits For Corporations

Introduction

15-221.   The foreign tax credits that are available to individuals earning foreign business or non-business income are discussed in detail in Chapter 14. Under rules that are very similar to those applicable to individuals, corporations are also allowed to use foreign taxes paid on business and non-business income as credits against Canadian Tax Payable. While the rules are similar to those for individuals, there are differences that will be discussed here.

Foreign Non-Business (Property) Income Tax Credit

15-222.   The formula that limits the Canadian tax credit for foreign taxes paid on foreign source non-business income appears to be the same as that applicable to individuals. It is as follows:

The **Foreign Non-Business Income Tax Credit** is the lesser of:

- The tax paid to the foreign government (for corporations, there is no 15 percent limit on the foreign non-business taxes paid); and

- An amount determined by the following formula:

$$\left[\frac{\text{Foreign Non}-\text{Business Income}}{\text{Adjusted Division B Income}}\right][\text{Tax Otherwise Payable}]$$

15-223.   While the general descriptions in the formula (e.g., Adjusted Division B Income and Tax Otherwise Payable) are the same as those applicable to individuals, their meaning is somewhat different. More specifically, for a corporation, "Adjusted Division B Income" is determined as follows:

Division B Income	$x,xxx
Net Capital Loss Carry Overs Deducted Under ITA 111(1)(b)	(xxx)
Taxable Dividends Deducted Under ITA 112	(xxx)
Dividends From A Foreign Affiliate Deductible Under ITA 113	(xxx)
Adjusted Division B Income	$x,xxx

15-224.   "Tax Otherwise Payable" is a particularly confusing term as its calculation is different for individuals and corporations. Adding to the confusion is the fact that its components differ depending on whether it is being used to calculate foreign non-business tax credits or foreign business tax credits for corporations. As a result, we have included here the following table that compares the components included in the calculation of foreign non-business tax credits with those used to calculate foreign business tax credits. More detailed coverage of foreign business tax credits will be found in the following section.

Tax Otherwise Payable Components	Non-Business	Business
Base Amount Of Part I Tax (38%)	Yes	Yes
Plus: Corporate Surtax	Yes	Yes
Plus: Additional Refundable Tax (ART) On		
Investment Income Of CCPC (See Chapter 16)	Yes	No
Minus: Federal Tax Abatement	Yes	No
Minus: General Rate Reduction	Yes	Yes

15-225.   You will recall that the purpose of the 10 percent federal tax abatement is to leave room for the provinces to tax corporations. It is deducted in the formula for determining foreign non-business tax credits because non-business income will, in general, be taxed in a province. As a consequence, it is appropriate to deduct this abatement in determining the limit on the foreign non-business tax credit.

15-226.   You will note in the following discussion of the foreign business income tax credit, that the federal tax abatement is not deducted from "Tax Otherwise Payable" in the formula which limits that credit. This reflects the fact that, in general, foreign business income will not be taxed in a province, and no abatement will be available on such amounts.

15-227.   Unlike the situation with individuals, where the amount of foreign taxes that can be used as a credit is limited to 15 percent of the foreign source non-business income, the only limit for a corporation is the limit that is found in the second component of the formula. If the actual amount of foreign taxes paid is greater than this limit, there is no carry over of the excess as a tax credit. However, as was noted in Chapter 14, unclaimed amounts can be deducted under ITA 20(12) in the determination of Net Income For Tax Purposes.

Foreign Business Income Tax Credit

15-228.   The formula that limits the amount of foreign business income taxes paid that can be used as a foreign tax credit is as follows:

The **Foreign Business Income Tax Credit** is the least of:

- The tax paid to the foreign government

- An amount determined by the following formula:

$$\left[\frac{\text{Foreign Business Income}}{\text{Adjusted Division B Income}} \right] [\text{Tax Otherwise Payable}]$$

- Tax Otherwise Payable for the year, less any foreign tax credit taken on non-business income under ITA 126(1).

15-229.   As was the case with individuals, there is an additional factor to consider in the case of foreign business income tax credits. This is the "Tax Otherwise Payable", reduced by any foreign non-business income tax credit deducted under ITA 126(1).

15-230.   The other difference in the calculation of the foreign non-business and foreign business income tax credit is the composition of the "Tax Otherwise Payable". As was noted previously, this figure is not reduced by the 10 percent federal tax abatement, reflecting the fact that foreign business income will not be taxed in a province. Also different is the fact that this calculation of "Tax Otherwise Payable" does not include the additional refundable tax on investment income under ITA 123.3. (See Chapter 16.)

15-231.   Unlike the case with foreign non-business income taxes paid in excess of amounts used as tax credits, unused foreign business taxes paid can be carried over as a tax credit to the three preceding taxation years or the ten subsequent taxation years. In calculating the allowable tax credit for such carry overs, these unused amounts will be added to the foreign tax paid factor in the calculation of the foreign business income tax credit.

Exercise Fifteen-16

Subject: Foreign Tax Credits

Internat Inc. is a Canadian public company. For the year ending December 31, 2007, it has Net Income For Tax Purposes of $146,000, including foreign business income of $20,000. The foreign government withheld $3,000 in taxes on this income, resulting in a net remittance of $17,000. None of the Company's income involves manufacturing and processing and, based on the ITR 402(3) formula, 85 percent of the Company's income was allocated to a province. In calculating Taxable Income, the Company deducts $30,000 in dividends received from taxable Canadian companies, a non-capital loss carry forward of $75,000, and a net capital loss carry forward of $25,000. Determine the Company's Part I Tax Payable for the year ending December 31, 2007.

End of Exercise. Solution available in Study Guide.

Investment Tax Credits

Background

15-232.   In terms of directing economic incentives to specific regions or types of activities, investment tax credits are a very effective tax policy tool. They can be used to provide tax reductions that are very specifically targeted (e.g., scientific research expenditures). In addition, by making some of them refundable, they can even provide benefits for enterprises with no Tax Payable.

15-233.   Despite their advantages in terms of targeting benefits, the use of investment tax credits has declined over the last 10 to 20 years. Prior to the 2006 budget, they were only available on expenditures made for scientific research and experimental development, or on qualifying expenditures made in the four Atlantic provinces and the Gaspe Peninsula.

15-234.   This decline appears to be ending in that both the 2006 and 2007 budgets expanded the use of investment tax credits:

Apprenticeship Job Creation Tax Credit   The 2006 budget added a credit for eligible salaries and wages paid to employed apprentices.

Child Care Spaces Tax Credit   The 2007 budget added a credit for eligible expenditures directed at creating child care spaces.

Procedures

15-235.   Investment tax credits are tax incentives that are available to Canadian taxpayers who are earning business income or undertaking scientific research and experimental development. They are available, on basically the same terms, to both individuals and corporations.

15-236.   In general terms, the procedures for investment tax credits, which are contained in ITA 127(5) through ITA 127.1(3), allow the taxpayer to deduct a specified percentage of the cost of certain types of current and capital expenditures from federal Tax Payable. The credits provide for a direct reduction in the amount of tax that is payable.

15-237.   When capital expenditures are involved, the amount of the investment tax credit must be removed from the capital cost of the asset, so that only the net capital cost is deductible through capital cost allowances (CCA). The deduction from undepreciated capital cost (UCC) will occur in the year after the claim is made. The capital cost must also be reduced by any government or non-government assistance received or receivable for the property, such as grants or subsidies. However, the reduction for these other types of assistance is made in the year in which the assistance is received or receivable.

15-238.   When the investment tax credits are earned by making deductible current expenditures, the deductible amount of the expenditures is reduced by the amount of the investment tax credits. Like investment tax credits related to capital expenditures, investment tax credits related to current scientific research and experimental development expenditures are deducted in the year following their incurrence.

15-239.   In effect, the tax mechanism that is involved with investment tax credits is that the enterprise gives up $1 of current or future tax deductions, in return for a $1 reduction in the amount of Tax Payable. This is clearly beneficial in that the cost of losing a $1 deduction is only $1 multiplied by the company's tax rate, a figure that could be below $0.20. By contrast, $1 of reduced tax payable is a cash flow savings of $1.

Eligible Expenditures

15-240.   To provide a general picture of the types of assets that are eligible for investment tax credits, brief descriptions are provided of expenditures that qualify for these credits:

Qualified Property is defined in ITA 127(9) with further elaboration provided in ITR 4600 and 4601. As presented in this material, qualified property must be newly acquired primarily for use in Canada, and it must be available for use in specified activities. These activities include manufacturing and processing, operating an oil or gas well, extracting minerals, logging, farming or fishing, storing grain, and producing industrial minerals.

Qualified Scientific Research And Experimental Development (SR&ED) Expenditures include amounts spent for basic or applied research, and for the development of new products and processes. Expenditures may be current, if they relate to administration or maintenance of related facilities or equipment, or they may be capital in nature. The formal definitions related to SR&ED are very technical. For those of you with an interest in this subject, additional information is found in the Appendix to this Chapter. If, however, you are involved in making actual claims for SR&ED, we would strongly urge you to seek the advice of a specialist in this area.

Salaries And Wages Of An Eligible Apprentice will qualify, provided the employee is working in the first two years of a provincially registered apprenticeship contract. The amount of the credit is the lesser of $2,000 and 10 percent of the salary and wages paid to each eligible apprentice.

Costs Of Creating Child Care Spaces   Eligible expenditures include amounts incurred for the sole purpose of creating a new child care space in a licensed child care facility operated for the benefit of children of the employees of the taxpayer and other children. The amount of the credit is the lesser of $10,000 and 25 percent of the cost of each child care space created.

Rates

15-241.   The rates for various types of expenditures are generally found under the definition of "specified percentage" in ITA 127(9). While there have been a number of changes over the years, the current rates are as follows:

Type Of Expenditure	Rate
Salaries And Wages Of Eligible Apprentices	
(Limited To $2,000 Per Apprentice)	10%
Costs Of Creating Child Care Spaces	
(Limited To $10,000 Per Space)	25%
Qualified Property	
In Atlantic Provinces And Gaspe Peninsula	10%
Prescribed Offshore Regions (East Coast)	10%
Rest Of Canada	Nil
Scientific Research And Experimental Development	
Incurred By Any Taxpayer	20%
Incurred By Some CCPCs (See Paragraph 15-242)	35%

15-242.   Note that there is an additional 15 percent credit on the SR&ED expenditures of some CCPCs. This 35 percent rate, which is provided for in ITA 127(10.1), is only available on the first $2 million of qualified SR&ED expenditures, a limit that must be shared by associated corporations.

15-243.   To qualify for this special rate on the full $2 million, the corporation must be a CCPC throughout the year, with Taxable Income in the immediately preceding year that is no more than $400,000 before loss carry backs. If the corporation's Taxable Income in the preceding year exceeds the $400,000 limit, the eligible amount is reduced.

15-244.   More specifically, under ITA 127(10.2) the $2 million limit for eligibility must be reduced by $10 for each $1 of the corporation's Taxable Income in excess of $400,000. This means that when the corporation's Taxable Income in the previous year reaches $600,000, the eligible limit is reduced by the full $2,000,000 [($10)($600,000 - $400,000)] to nil. In applying this limit, associated corporations have to be considered.

Refundable Investment Tax Credits

General Rules - 40 Percent Refund

15-245. A problem with tax credits is that, in general, they have value only when the taxpayer has a tax liability. To deal with this problem, some tax credits are "refundable". What this means is that, when a taxpayer has earned a tax credit and does not have sufficient Tax Payable to use it in full, the government will pay ("refund") all or part of the unused amount to the taxpayer. We have encountered this type of situation previously for individuals with respect to the refundable medical expense supplement tax credit (see Chapter 6).

15-246. A refund can be made for up to 40 percent of the refundable investment tax credits earned by a taxpayer, provided the taxpayer is:

- an individual;
- a "qualifying corporation", which is a Canadian controlled private corporation throughout the year with Taxable Income in the previous year of $400,000 or less before loss carry backs; or
- a trust where each beneficiary is an individual or a qualifying corporation.

15-247. This means that if, for example, an individual had $1,000,000 in SR&ED current expenditures, he would be eligible for a $200,000 [(20%)($1,000,000)] investment tax credit. If the individual did not have sufficient Tax Payable to use this credit, the government would provide a refund (payment) of up to $80,000 [(40%)($200,000)].

Additional Refund - 100 Percent Refund

15-248. In the case of a qualifying corporation (a CCPC with Taxable Income of $400,000 or less for the previous year), additional amounts are refundable. To the extent that current SR&ED expenditures are eligible for the additional 15 percent investment tax credit (total credit of 35 percent), the resulting credit is eligible for a 100 percent refund. This means that a qualifying corporation that spends $2,000,000 on current SR&ED expenditures is eligible for a refund payment of up to $700,000 [(35%)($2,000,000)] from the government. This is, of course, an extremely rich tax benefit for corporations that qualify.

15-249. The 100 percent refund is only available on the first $2,000,000 of current expenditures that qualify for the additional 15 percent investment tax credit. Capital expenditures that qualify for this additional 15 percent are refundable at a lower rate of 40 percent. An example will clarify this point:

Example   Research Inc., a Canadian controlled private corporation, has current SR&ED expenditures of $750,000 and capital SR&ED expenditures of $600,000. The Company has no Taxable Income in the current or the preceding year.

Analysis   The Company's total investment tax credit will be $472,500 [(35%)($750,000 + $600,000)]. The refundable portion will be $346,500 [(100%)(35%)($750,000) + (40%)(35%)($600,000)].

15-250. When the CCPC's Taxable Income before loss carry backs for the preceding year is more than $400,000, the amount eligible for the 15 percent additional credit is reduced in the manner described in Paragraph 15-244. As the 100 percent refund is only available on amounts that qualify for this additional credit, there is a corresponding reduction in the ability of the corporation to claim such a refund.

Carry Overs Of Investment Tax Credits

15-251. Under the definition of investment tax credit in ITA 127(9), unused investment tax credits may be carried back for up to three years and forward for 20 years. A taxpayer is required to claim all other available tax credits before calculating and claiming the investment tax credit for the year. Also, a taxpayer must reduce, to the fullest extent possible, federal Tax Payable for the current year before using investment tax credits to reduce previous years' federal Tax Payable.

Exercise Fifteen-17

Subject: Refundable Investment Tax Credits

Sci-Tech Inc. has made a number of expenditures that qualify for investment tax credits. They have invested $123,000 in Qualified Property in Nova Scotia. In addition, they have $1,200,000 in current expenditures for Scientific Research And Experimental Development, as well as $1,500,000 in capital expenditures for Scientific Research And Experimental Development. The Company is a Canadian controlled private corporation and has Taxable Income for the previous year of $176,000. As the Company has no Taxable Income for the current year, its Tax Payable is nil. Determine the amount of the refund that Sci-Tech will receive as a result of earning these investment tax credits and any available carry overs. Include in your answer any other tax consequences of these investment tax credits.

End of Exercise.   Solution available in Study Guide.

Acquisition Of Control

15-252.   As was the case with companies having accumulated loss carry forwards, the government is concerned about the large amount of unused investment tax credits that are being carried forward in the tax records of Canadian corporations. The carry forwards reflect the fact that these corporations have experienced losses and, as a consequence, have not had a tax liability to which the credits could be applied.

15-253.   While the government does not object to these credits being used against Tax Payable resulting from improved profitability for the corporations that have experienced losses, there is concern that these loss corporations will be acquired by profitable corporations in order to make use of these credits. As a consequence, there are acquisition of control rules that apply to the carry forward of investment tax credits in a manner similar to the acquisition of control rules that apply to the carry forward of non-capital losses.

15-254.   These rules are found in ITA 127(9.1) and (9.2). Their effect is described in IT-151R5 as follows:

> **Paragraph 84**   If control of a corporation has been acquired by a person or group of persons, subsections 127(9.1) and (9.2) and paragraphs (j) and (k) of the definition of "investment tax credit" in subsection 127(9) may apply to restrict the availability of the corporation's investment tax credits. In general, these provisions limit the application of investment tax credits to the tax on the income from a particular business carried on by the corporation before the acquisition of control or any other business substantially all the income of which is from the sale, leasing, rental, or development of properties or the rendering of services similar to those of the particular business carried on by the corporation before the acquisition of control.

15-255.   The effect of these provisions is to treat investment tax credits in a manner similar to the treatment of non-capital loss carry forwards when there is an acquisition of control.

Key Terms Used In This Chapter

15-256.   The following is a list of the key terms used in this Chapter. These terms, and their meanings, are compiled in the Glossary Of Key Terms located at the back of the separate paper Study Guide and on the Student CD-ROM.

Acquisition Of Control
Active Business
Active Business Income
Adjusted Active Business Income
Allowable Business Investment Loss
Allowable Capital Loss
Annual Business Limit
Apprenticeship Job Creation Tax Credit
Associated Corporations
Business Income
Business Investment Loss
Canadian Controlled Private Corporation
Carry Over
CCPC
Child Care Spaces Tax Credit
Common Shares
Control
Corporation
Cost Of Capital (M&P)
Cost Of Labour (M&P)
Deemed Disposition
Deemed Year End
Designated Stock Exchange
Disposition
Federal Tax Abatement
Foreign Taxes Paid Credit
Full Rate Taxable Income
GAAP
General Rate Reduction
Gross Cost
Group Of Persons
Investment Tax Credit
Loss Carry Back
Loss Carry Forward
M&P

M&P Capital
M&P Labour
M&P Profits
Manufacturing And Processing Profits
   Deduction (M&P Deduction)
Net Business Income
Net Capital Loss
Net Income
Net Income For Tax Purposes
Non-Capital Loss
Ordering Rule
Permanent Establishment
Personal Services Business
Preferred Shares
Prescribed Stock Exchange
Private Corporation
Property Income
Public Corporation
Qualified Activities
Qualified Property
Qualifying Corporation
Refundable Investment Tax Credit
Related Persons
Scientific Research And
   Experimental Development (SR&ED)
Small Business Deduction
Specified Class ITA 256(1.1)
Specified Investment Business
Specified Shareholder ITA 248(1)
Stop Loss Rules
Surtax
Taxable Capital Employed In Canada
Taxable Income
Term Preferred Shares

References

15-257. For more detailed study of the material in this Chapter, we refer you to the following:

ITA 37(1)	Scientific Research And Experimental Development
ITA 89(1)	Definitions (Private Corporation And Public Corporation)
ITA 110	Deductions Permitted
ITA 111	Losses Deductible
ITA 112	Deduction Of Taxable Dividends Received By Corporations Resident In Canada
ITA 113	Deduction In Respect Of Dividend Received From Foreign Affiliate
ITA 121	Deduction For Taxable Dividends
ITA 123	Rate For Corporations
ITA 123.1	Corporation Surtax
ITA 123.3	Refundable Tax On CCPC's Investment Income
ITA 123.4(2)	General Deduction From Tax
ITA 124	Deduction From Corporation Tax
ITA 125	Small Business Deduction
ITA 125.1(1)	Manufacturing And Processing Profits Deductions
ITA 127(5) to 127.1(3)	Investment Tax Credits
ITA 249(4)	Year End On Change In Control
ITA 251	Arm's Length
ITA 256	Associated Corporations
ITR 400	Taxable Income Earned In The Year In A Province
ITR 4600	Investment Tax Credit - Qualified Property
ITR 4601	Investment Tax Credit - Qualified Transportation Equipment
ITR 4602	Certified Property
ITR 5200	Canadian Manufacturing And Processing Profits - Basic Formula
ITR 5202	Canadian Manufacturing And Processing Profits - Interpretation
IC 78-4R3	Investment Tax Credit Rates
IC 86-4R3	Scientific Research And Experimental Development
IT-64R4	Corporations: Association And Control
IT-67R3	Taxable Dividends From Corporations Resident In Canada
IT-73R6	The Small Business Deduction
IT-145R	Canadian Manufacturing And Processing Profits — Reduced Rate Of Corporate Tax
IT-151R5	Scientific Research And Experimental Development Expenditures
IT-177R2	Permanent Establishment Of A Corporation In A Province And Of A Foreign Enterprise In Canada
IT-189R2	Corporations Used By Practising Members Of Professions
IT-206R	Separate Businesses
IT-232R3	Losses — Their Deductibility In The Loss Year Or In Other Years
IT-270R3	Foreign Tax Credit
IT-302R3	Losses Of A Corporation — The Effect That Acquisition Of Control, Amalgamations, And Wind Ups Have On Their Deductibility — After January 15, 1987
IT-391R	Status Of Corporations
IT-458R2	Canadian Controlled Private Corporation

Appendix: SR&ED Expenditures

General Rules

15A-1. There is a well established belief that Scientific Research And Experimental Development (SR&ED) expenditures are vital to the continued growth and prosperity of the Canadian economy. As a consequence, a generous system of tax incentives is available to businesses that make such expenditures. For example, under these programs, it is possible for a corporation to receive a cash payment (refundable investment tax credit) of up to $700,000 for a single year. It is recognized that Canada's system for encouraging SR&ED expenditures is one of the most generous in the world.

15A-2. Given the magnitude of the potential benefits associated with SR&ED expenditures, it is not surprising that the rules and regulations incorporated into these programs are very complex. While it would not be difficult to devote an entire chapter to this subject, that would not be in keeping with the objectives of this text. What follows is a broad overview of the provisions associated with SR&ED expenditures.

15A-3. The rules for the deduction of SR&ED expenditures are found in ITA 37 and in Part XXIX of the *Income Tax Regulations*. As specified in these sources, the treatment of SR&ED has the following special features:

- All qualifying SR&ED costs are allocated to a special SR&ED pool. Amounts included in this pool can be deducted in the current or any subsequent year. There is no time limit on their deductibility as would be the case if they simply contributed to a non-capital loss carry forward balance.

- In general, capital expenditures other than real property can be deducted, in full, in the year that the assets become available for use. There are exceptions to this that will be described in the subsequent material.

- The amounts added to the SR&ED cost pool are eligible for investment tax credits ranging from 20 percent to 35 percent, depending on the type of taxpayer making the expenditures and the amount of the expenditures.

15A-4. To be eligible for this treatment, expenditures must qualify as SR&ED expenditures, and they must be related to a business carried on by the taxpayer making the expenditures. Further, the expenditures are only deductible from income of a business carried on in Canada.

Qualifying Expenditures

Basic Definition

15A-5. Scientific research and experimental development is defined in ITA 248(1) as follows:

"scientific research and experimental development" means systematic investigation or search that is carried out in a field of science or technology by means of experiment or analysis and that is

(a) basic research, namely, work undertaken for the advancement of scientific knowledge without a specific practical application in view,
(b) applied research, namely, work undertaken for the advancement of scientific knowledge with a specific practical application in view, or
(c) experimental development, namely, work undertaken for the purpose of achieving technological advancement for the purpose of creating new, or improving existing, materials, devices, products or processes, including incremental improvements thereto,

and, in applying this definition in respect of a taxpayer, includes

(d) work undertaken by or on behalf of the taxpayer with respect to engineering, design, operations research, mathematical analysis, computer programming, data collection, testing or psychological research, where the work is commensurate with the needs, and directly in support, of work described in paragraph (a), (b), or (c) that is undertaken in Canada by or on behalf of the taxpayer,

but does not include work with respect to

(e) market research or sales promotion,
(f) quality control or routine testing of materials, devices, products or processes,
(g) research in the social sciences or the humanities,
(h) prospecting, exploring or drilling for, or producing, minerals, petroleum or natural gas,
(i) the commercial production of a new or improved material, device or product or the commercial use of a new or improved process,
(j) style changes, or
(k) routine data collection;

Rules For Current Expenditures

15A-6.   To qualify for SR&ED treatment, the current expenditure must be incurred for this purpose and must relate to the business of the taxpayer. This would include expenditures made for SR&ED outside of Canada on behalf of the taxpayer.

15A-7.   As described in IT-151R5, one category of current expenditures includes:

... expenditures of a current (or capital) nature incurred for and **all or substantially all** of which were attributable to the prosecution, or to the provision of premises, facilities, or equipment for the prosecution, of SR&ED in Canada.

15A-8.   The IT Bulletin points out that, in this context, all or substantially all means 90 percent or more. If this test is met, 100 percent of the expenditure goes into the SR&ED pool. If the usage is less than 90 percent for SR&ED, the expenditure will still be deductible, but not as an SR&ED expenditure.

15A-9.   A second category of current SR&ED expenditures is described in the Bulletin as follows:

... expenditures of a current nature that were directly attributable to the prosecution of SR&ED in Canada, or expenditures of a current nature that were directly attributable to the provision of premises, facilities or equipment for the prosecution of SR&ED in Canada.

15A-10.   In somewhat simplified terms, this is a reference to SR&ED related overhead. Such costs could include labour, general and administrative costs, the cost of heat and light, and long distance telephone charges. Note that, for these overhead type expenditures, there is no 90 percent test. These expenditures will be allocated on a pro rata basis, without the application of any minimum threshold.

15A-11.   For the costs of material and labour, qualification for inclusion in the SR&ED pool as an overhead cost requires only that they be directly attributable to the prosecution of SR&ED. With respect to other types of overhead costs, the taxpayer must be able to demonstrate that they would not have been incurred if the SR&ED activities were not being carried out.

Rules For Capital Expenditures

15A-12.   As previously noted, capital expenditures can be allocated to the SR&ED pool and written off in the year of acquisition, subject to the available for use rules. Assets excluded from this treatment are land and most buildings acquired after 1987. However, a building that has a special SR&ED purpose (e.g., a wind tunnel) does qualify. This same approach applies to rents for buildings. That is, the rents qualify for SR&ED treatment only if a special purpose building is involved.

15A-13.   Unlike current expenditures, capital expenditures must be for SR&ED carried on in Canada in order to qualify for inclusion in the pool. In addition, capital expenditures must meet the 90 percent (all or substantially all) threshold in order to be included in the SR&ED pool. If they do not meet this test, they will be allocated to the appropriate CCA class.

15A-14.   Capital assets that are allocated to the SR&ED pool cannot be allocated to a CCA class. Further, within the SR&ED pool, each asset must be in a separate class. The deduction of its cost will be considered deemed CCA, and its disposition may result in recapture or capital gains.

Shared Use Capital Equipment

15A-15.   We noted previously that there is no provision for pro rating the cost of capital expenditures where the use for SR&ED purposes is less than 90 percent. The costs of such assets are not eligible for inclusion in the SR&ED pool or, in general, for the special SR&ED investment tax credit rate.

15A-16.   While this 90 percent rule continues in place, with respect to adding the cost of shared use capital assets to the SR&ED pool, a different investment tax credit rule applies to capital equipment acquired after 1992 that does not meet the 90 percent test, but is used primarily (more than 50 percent) for SR&ED purposes. One-half of the cost of such shared use equipment is eligible for a special investment tax credit that becomes available over a two year period. In general terms, the credit is based on one-half the cost of the equipment and becomes available over the first two years of the asset's use.

15A-17.   More specifically, after the shared use equipment has been used for 12 months, an investment tax credit becomes available. It is calculated at one of the usual rates for SR&ED credits (20 percent or 35 percent) on one-quarter of the cost of the equipment. After 24 months of usage, a second investment tax credit becomes available with respect to this equipment. It is also calculated on one-quarter of the cost of the equipment.

15A-18.   Note, however, that none of the cost of such assets are allocated to the SR&ED pool. Rather, the full cost is allocated to the appropriate CCA class. It would appear to follow that the investment tax credits on these assets reduces the capital cost (and therefore the UCC of the class) in the following year.

Prescribed Proxy Amount

15A-19.   We have previously noted that current expenditures of an overhead nature could be allocated to the SR&ED pool, provided they are directly attributable to SR&ED activities. This allocation process can be difficult and time consuming in that the taxpayer has to be able to demonstrate that the costs are directly attributable to SR&ED activities, that they are pro rated to SR&ED and other activities on a reasonable basis, and, except in the case of materials or labour, that they would not have been incurred in the absence of SR&ED activity. To simplify this situation, an alternative approach can be elected.

15A-20.   This election would not change the treatment of current or capital SR&ED expenditures that meet the all or substantially all test. These costs, which meet the test of being at least 90 percent attributable to SR&ED, will continue to be allocated to the SR&ED pool and will be eligible for the usual SR&ED tax credits.

15A-21.   However, all other current expenditures, including those that are directly attributable to SR&ED and could be allocated to the pool as overhead costs, must be deducted as ordinary expenditures. The only effect of this change is that those expenditures that could have been included in the SR&ED pool lose their right to an unlimited carry forward period. In the absence of Taxable Income, they will contribute to the non-capital loss carry forward balance that is subject to a 20 year limitation.

15A-22.   In exchange for giving up SR&ED treatment of these SR&ED overhead amounts, the taxpayer would be allowed to establish what is referred to as a "prescribed proxy amount". This amount would be calculated as 65 percent of salaries and wages of employees that are directly engaged in SR&ED carried on in Canada.

15A-23.   The resulting prescribed proxy amount would not be added to the SR&ED pool, nor would it be deductible as an ordinary business expense. However, it would be eligible for investment tax credits at the usual SR&ED rates. In addition, the value of any investment tax credits earned on the prescribed proxy amount must be deducted from the SR&ED pool in the year following their use.

15A-24.   Whether or not this election is desirable will depend on whether actual SR&ED overhead costs are more or less than 65 percent of SR&ED labour costs. However, since the use of the election is much simpler than going through the detailed overhead allocation process, it is likely that many taxpayers will use the election and not make any effort to answer this question.

Problems For Self Study

(The solutions for these problems can be found in the separate Study Guide.)

Self Study Problem Fifteen - 1

One of your assistants has been calculating Net Income For Tax Purposes for the Sanklee Company. For both accounting and tax purposes, the Company uses a December 31 year end. Your assistant has been able to complete most of the required Schedule 1. However, there are a number of items that he would like you to review. The items are as follows:

1. The Company has recorded amortization expense in its accounting records of $254,000. The maximum deductible CCA for the taxation year is $223,000.

2. The Company has recorded interest expense of $57,000. The accounting Balance Sheet indicates that the bonds payable premium account declined by $2,000 during the year.

3. On August 12 of the current year, the Company sold an asset with an original cost of $80,000 for $120,000. In the accounting records, the asset had a net book value of $53,000. It was a Class 43 asset and, at the end of the year, there is a positive balance in this class. The Company still owns other Class 43 assets. Only one-half of the $120,000 proceeds is received in cash, with the remainder to be paid at the end of the following taxation year.

4. During the year, the Company paid $8,000 for two memberships in the Ottawa Ritz Golf And Country Club. The two Company executives that hold the memberships billed the Company $12,000 for entertainment of clients at this Club. Both of these amounts were deducted in the Company's accounting records.

5. During the year, the Company made charitable donations of $11,000. This amount was deducted in their accounting records.

6. During the year, the Company sold a Class 10 asset for $23,000. The original cost of the asset was $50,000 and its net book value at the time of sale was $39,000. This was the last asset in Class 10 and, at the beginning of the year, the balance in Class 10 was nil. No Class 10 assets were acquired during the current year.

Required: For each of the items listed, indicate the addition to and/or deduction from accounting Net Income that would be required in the calculation of the minimum Net Income For Tax Purposes.

Self Study Problem Fifteen - 2

Information related to Margo Ltd. for the year ending December 31, 2007, is as follows:

1. The calculation of Cost Of Goods Sold was based on an opening inventory of $225,000 and a closing inventory of $198,600. In addition, the closing inventory was reduced by $15,000 for a reserve for future declines in value. This is the first year the Company has used an inventory reserve.

2. Property Taxes include $1,200 for tax paid on vacant land. The company has held this land since 2003, in anticipation of relocating its head office.

3. As the result of a business combination on January 15, 2007, Margo Ltd. recorded $34,000 in goodwill. As of December 31, 2007, this goodwill was found to be impaired and a goodwill impairment loss of $1,700 was recorded. The goodwill qualifies as an eligible capital expenditure for tax purposes. At the beginning of the year, there is no balance in the cumulative eligible capital account.

4. The legal fees are made up of $1,200 paid to appeal an income tax assessment and $1,020 paid for general corporate matters.

5. The gain on the sale of investments involved marketable securities with a cost of $21,000. The securities were sold for $30,500.

6. The gross foreign interest income of $1,800 was received net of $270 in foreign tax withholdings.

7. The maximum CCA for the current year is $78,000.

The Income Statement that has been prepared by Margo Ltd.'s accountant for the year ending December 31, 2007, is as follows:

Sales Revenue		$925,000
Cost Of Goods Sold (Note 1)		(717,000)
Gross Profit		$208,000
Operating Expenses:		
Salaries And Wages	$40,200	
Rents	22,200	
Property Taxes (Note 2)	8,800	
Amortization Expense	35,600	
Write-Down Of Goodwill (Note 3)	1,700	
Charitable Donations	19,800	
Legal Fees (Note 4)	2,220	
Bad Debt Expense	7,100	
Warranty Provision	5,500	
Social Club Membership Fees	7,210	
Other Operating Expenses	39,870	(190,200)
Operating Income		$ 17,800
Other Revenues (Expenses):		
Gain On Sale Of Investments (Note 5)	$9,500	
Interest Revenue	2,110	
Interest On Late Income Tax Instalments	(1,020)	
Investment Counsellor Fees	(500)	
Foreign Interest Income (Note 6)	1,530	
Dividends From Taxable Canadian Corporations	3,000	
Premium On Redemption Of Preferred Shares	(480)	14,140
Income Before Taxes		$ 31,940

Required: Determine the minimum Net Income For Tax Purposes and Taxable Income of Margo Ltd., for the year ending December 31, 2007.

Self Study Problem Fifteen - 3

On May 1, 2007, Ontario Lawn Care Ltd. (OLC), which provides gardening and lawn services for the southern Ontario market, purchased, from an arm's length party, all of the shares of Lawn Fertilizer Inc. (LF), a company in the business of manufacturing lawn fertilizers. LF has a December 31 year end.

A highly competitive fertilizer market has resulted in the following losses for LF:

	Non-Capital Loss	Net Capital Loss
2005	180,000	$75,000
2006	140,000	Nil

It is estimated that business losses of $125,000 for the 2007 year will be experienced. This is made up of an actual loss of $55,000 up to April 30, 2007, and an estimated loss of $70,000 for the remainder of the year.

Relevant values for LF's assets at May 1, 2007 were as follows:

	Cost	UCC	FMV
Inventory	$100,000	N/A	$105,000
Land	450,000	N/A	925,000
Class 3 - Building	675,000	$515,000	650,000
Class 8 - Furniture	25,000	10,000	15,000
Class 43 - Manufacturing Equipment	415,000	375,000	285,000

Required: Describe the tax implications to LF of OLC acquiring its shares. Your answer should include a description of the elections that are available to LF and a recommendation as to which elections should be made. If any assumptions are made in arriving at your answer, specifically indicate what they are.

Self Study Problem Fifteen - 4

Linden Industries Inc. began operations in 2004 and has a December 31 fiscal year end. While it was fairly successful in its first year of operation, excessive production of an unmarketable product resulted in a large operating loss for 2005. Profits have come back in 2006 and 2007.

The relevant Division B income and loss figures, along with charitable donations made during the years under consideration are as follows:

	2004	2005	2006	2007
Business Income (Loss)	$95,000	($205,000)	$69,500	$90,000
Capital Gains	Nil	Nil	9,000	10,000
Capital Losses	(10,000)	(14,000)	Nil	Nil
Dividends Received	12,000	42,000	28,000	32,000
Charitable Donations	21,400	4,600	8,000	22,000

All of the dividends have been received from taxable Canadian corporations.

Required: Calculate the minimum Net Income For Tax Purposes and Taxable Income that would be reported for Linden Industries in each of the four years under consideration. Also indicate the amended figures for any years to which losses are carried back. Provide an analysis of the amount and type of carry overs that would be available at the end of each of the four years.

Self Study Problem Fifteen - 5

The Sundean Company has its national headquarters in Toronto, and all of its senior management people have their offices at this location. The Company also has operations in Vancouver, Calgary, Saskatoon, and Halifax. In each of these cities, warehouse space is maintained and orders are filled. In addition, a sales staff operates out of office space in each warehouse, taking orders throughout the province in which the warehouse is located.

For the current taxation year, the Company's Taxable Income totalled $1,546,000, on gross revenues of $10,483,000. Also during the current year, the Company had salaries and wages totalling $1,247,000. These gross revenues and expenses were distributed among the provinces where the Company has operations in the following manner:

	Gross Revenues	Wages And Salaries Accrued
Alberta	$ 1,886,940	$ 261,870
British Columbia	2,306,260	274,340
Nova Scotia	1,362,790	174,580
Saskatchewan	1,257,960	99,760
Ontario	3,669,050	436,450
Total	$10,483,000	$1,247,000

Required: Calculate the amount of the Sundean Company's Taxable Income for the current year that would be allocated to each of the five provinces. Any percentages used in your calculations should be rounded to one decimal place.

Self Study Problem Fifteen - 6

The following situations are **independent** of each other. All of the corporations involved are Canadian controlled private corporations.

A. John Fleming and Eric Flame are married to women who are sisters. John Fleming owns 100 percent of the outstanding common shares of Fleming Ltd. and 32 percent of the outstanding common shares of Lartch Inc. Eric Flame owns 100 percent of the outstanding common shares of Flame Ltd. and 28 percent of the outstanding common shares of Lartch Inc. The remaining common shares of Lartch Inc. are owned by an unrelated party.

B. Mr. Cuso owns 80 percent of the outstanding common shares of Male Ltd. The remaining 20 percent of the Male Ltd. shares are owned by his spouse, Mrs. Cuso. Mrs. Cuso owns 82 percent of the outstanding common shares of Female Inc. Her spouse owns the remaining 18 percent of the shares in this Company.

C. Ms. Jones, Mrs. Kelly, and Miss Lange are unrelated individuals. Ms. Jones owns 50 percent of the outstanding common shares of Alliance Ltd. and 25 percent of the outstanding voting shares of Breaker Inc. Mrs. Kelly does not own any of the Alliance Ltd. shares, but owns 50 percent of Breaker Inc.'s outstanding voting shares. Miss Lange owns 50 percent of the outstanding common shares of Alliance Ltd. and 25 percent of the outstanding voting shares of Breaker Inc.

D. Mr. Martin owns 60 percent of the outstanding voting shares of Martin Inc. and 50 percent of the outstanding voting shares of Oakley Ltd. Mr. Oakley, who is not related to Mr. Martin, owns 50 percent of the outstanding voting shares of Oakley Ltd. and 40 percent of the outstanding voting shares of Martin Inc.

Required: For each of these situations, indicate which of the involved corporations would be associated under the rules established in ITA 256(1) and related Sections of the *Act*. You should provide complete support for your conclusion, including references to appropriate provisions in the *Act*.

Self Study Problem Fifteen - 7

Mason Industries is a Canadian controlled public company involved in the manufacture of component parts used in the production of automobiles. The Company's only operation is in Regina, and it has a fiscal year ending on December 31. The building that houses its operations is rented under a long-term arrangement, at an annual rent of $375,000. Of this amount, $50,000 is applicable to the land. Because of the size of the facility, Mason Industries normally sublets 25 percent of the available space to an unrelated wholesaler. The annual net rental income from this arrangement is $106,000. In addition to the rental operation, approximately 20 percent of the floor space in the building is used as administrative offices.

Other Information:

1. Mason Industries' Taxable Income for 2007 is $1,556,000. With the exception of the net rental income, this entire amount would be considered active business income.

2. During 2007, the Company's total labour costs amounted to $1,940,000. Of this total, $30,000 was required as the result of responsibilities associated with the rental of the excess space in the warehouse, and the remainder of $1,910,000 was related to the production of active business income. Of the $1,910,000 related to active business income, $1,270,000 was direct manufacturing labour.

3. During 2007, the Company owned depreciable assets that cost $6,850,000. Of this total, assets with a cost of $5,560,000 were used directly in the manufacturing operations of the business. Other than the building, Mason Industries did not use any leased assets.

Required: Calculate federal Tax Payable for Mason Industries Ltd. for the year ending December 31, 2007.

Self Study Problem Fifteen - 8

The Serendipity Shop Corp. sells art works on consignment in Winnipeg. The shares of Serendipity Shop Corp. are all owned by Elizabeth Montgomery, a Canadian, resident in Winnipeg.

The Serendipity Shop Corp. has Net Income For Tax Purposes of $240,000 for the year ending December 31, 2007. The Net Income For Tax Purposes is comprised of $220,000 from business activity and $20,000 in dividends from various investments in public companies. In May, 2007, the Serendipity Shop Corp. donated $48,000 to the Canadian Indigenous Art Foundation, a registered Canadian charity. There are no carry forwards of donations or losses, and the corporation paid no dividends in the year.

Because Serendipity is associated with another corporation, its 2007 annual business limit is reduced to $135,000.

Required: Determine Taxable Income and Part I federal Tax Payable for the Serendipity Shop Corp. for the year ending December 31, 2007.

Self Study Problem Fifteen - 9

During the taxation year ending December 31, 2007, the condensed Income Statement of Borscan Inc. was prepared in accordance with generally accepted accounting principles. In condensed form it is as follows:

Borscan Inc.
Income Statement
Year Ending December 31, 2007

Revenues	$2,800,000
Expenses (Excluding Taxes)	(1,550,000)
Income Before Extraordinary Items And Taxes	$1,250,000
Extraordinary Gain (Before Income Tax Effects)	125,000
Income Before Taxes	$1,375,000

Other Information:

1. The Extraordinary Gain resulted from the expropriation of a building for proceeds of $525,000. The building had a capital cost of $500,000 and was acquired in 1984. As the Company leases all of its other assets, the building was the only asset in Class 3. The UCC balance of this class, prior to the disposition of the building was $350,000. The land on which the building is situated was leased, and the government entity expropriating the building has assumed Borscan's responsibilities under the lease.

2. Amortization included in the accounting expenses amounts to $255,000. Maximum available deductions for CCA amount to $287,000, without consideration of the building that was expropriated.

3. Expenses include interest and penalties of $500 resulting from a failure to pay the previous year's taxes on time.

4. Revenues include dividends from taxable Canadian corporations in the amount of $25,000.

5. Expenses include a deduction for charitable donations in the amount of $13,500.

6. Prior to the deduction of any 2007 amortization, the December 31 balance in the Company's cumulative eligible capital account is $85,000. The items reflected in this balance have been charged to expense in previous years for accounting purposes.

7. The Company has available non-capital loss carry overs from previous years that total $35,000. There is a net capital loss carry over from 2004 of $30,000 [(1/2)($60,000)].

8. The Company's shares are publicly traded, and none of its income is from manufacturing or processing.

Required:

A. Calculate the minimum Net Income For Tax Purposes for Borscan Inc. for 2007.

B. Calculate the minimum Taxable Income for Borscan Inc. for 2007. Indicate the amount, and type, of any carry overs that are available at the end of the year.

C. Calculate the minimum federal Tax Payable for Borscan Inc. for 2007.

Self Study Problem Fifteen - 10

The Mercury Manufacturing Company is a private corporation with two shareholders. Jennifer Mercury owns 47 percent of the voting shares and lives in Hamilton, Ontario. She is in charge of the Canadian operations, which are located in Hamilton. John Mason owns 53 percent of the voting shares and lives in Rochester, New York. He is in charge of the U.S. operations, which are located in Rochester. The Company's fiscal year ends on December 31.

All money amounts are expressed in Canadian dollars.

For the year ending December 31, 2007, the Company had accounting income, before any provision for income taxes, of $530,400. This amount included the following:

Dividends From Taxable Canadian Corporations	$ 9,400
Gain On Sale Of A Long-Term Investment In Shares	22,900
Interest Income From Canadian Sources	7,800
Donations To Registered Canadian Charity	18,700
Dividends From U.S. Portfolio Investments	
(Before $4,845 Of Taxes Withheld In U.S.)	32,300
U.S. Business Income (Before $20,700 Of Taxes Withheld In U.S.)	64,200

The Company has a non-capital loss of $21,950 available for carry forward to 2007. In addition, there is a net capital loss carry forward from 2006 of $13,500 [(1/2)($27,000)].

The Company's Canadian sales occur in Ontario and Manitoba. U.S. sales are all in the state of New York. Its head office and manufacturing operations are in Ontario. However, the Company has warehouses and sales people in Ontario and New York. Manitoba customers are serviced through Ontario warehouses and sales people. Sales, manufacturing salaries and wages, and non-manufacturing salaries and wages for these locations are as follows:

	Ontario	Manitoba	New York	Total
Sales	$3,850,000	$1,875,000	$565,000	$6,290,000
Salaries And Wages:				
Manufacturing	$3,250,000	Nil	$380,000	$3,630,000
Non-Manufacturing	290,000	Nil	58,000	348,000
Total Salaries And Wages	$3,540,000	Nil	$438,000	$3,978,000

With respect to the Company's property, gross costs are as follows:

Canadian Investment Property (This Property Had No Income Or Loss During 2007)	$ 472,000
Business Property In Canada (75% Used For Manufacturing)	2,680,000
Business Property In U.S. (85% Used For Manufacturing)	487,000
Total	$3,639,000

In addition to the preceding property, the Company's manufacturing operations use space in Canada that was rented at a cost of $67,200 for the year ending December 31, 2007.

All property costs and rent amounts given are only for the portions related to the buildings.

Required: Calculate the federal Part I Tax Payable for the taxation year ending December 31, 2007. Show all calculations, whether or not they are necessary to the final solution.

Assignment Problems

(The solutions for these problems are only available in
the solutions manual that has been provided to your instructor.)

Assignment Problem Fifteen - 1

It has been determined that, for the current year, the accounting Net Income, determined in accordance with generally accepted accounting principles, of Heather's Inc. is $456,000. Additional information was available for preparing the corporation's Schedule 1. For each of the following pieces of information, indicate the adjustment(s) that would be required to convert the Company's $456,000 accounting Net Income to minimum Net Income For Tax Purposes. Explanations are not required.

A.   Accounting amortization expense for the year was $28,000. Maximum CCA for the year is $22,500.

B.   For accounting purposes, the Company deducted $4,800 in estimated warranty costs during the year. Actual expenditures for providing warranties during the year totalled $5,100.

C.   During the year, the Company's bonds payable premium account declined by $2,400. Cash payment for interest on the relevant bonds amounted to $34,000.

D.   During the year, the Company sold depreciable assets with a net book value of $87,000 for cash proceeds of $56,000. These assets were the last assets in their CCA class, and there were no additions to the class during the year. At the beginning of the current year, the UCC balance in the CCA class was $62,000.

E.   Accounting Net Income for the year was reduced by the deduction of $3,700 in charitable donations.

F.   During the year, the Company sold temporary investments for proceeds of $14,000. The cost and adjusted cost base of these investments was $16,000. The Company did not have any taxable capital gains during the current year.

Assignment Problem Fifteen - 2

The following information relates to the operations of Notem Inc. for the taxation year ended December 31, 2007:

Dividends From Taxable Canadian Corporations	$ 33,500
Taxable Capital Gains	9,600
Allowable Capital Losses	(4,425)
Charitable Donations	5,400
Business Loss	(141,800)

At the beginning of the taxation year, the Company had a carry forward of unused charitable donations of $1,350 from the previous year, and a net capital loss carry forward from 2005 of $10,500 [(1/2)($21,000)].

Notem Inc. does not anticipate the sale of any capital assets in the near future.

Required: Compute the corporation's Net Income For Tax Purposes and Taxable Income for its 2007 taxation year. Indicate any balances available for carry forward to 2008 and subsequent years.

Assignment Problem Fifteen - 3

The following information on Dunway Ltd., a Canadian public company, is applicable to the year ending June 30, 2007:

Sales Of Merchandise	725,000
Operating Expenses	533,000
Dividends From Controlled Subsidiary	37,500
Dividends From Non-Controlled Public Companies	15,000
Capital Gain On Investment Sale	222,000
Dividends Paid	182,000
Donation To Canadian Government	26,000
Donations To Registered Canadian Charities	141,000

At the beginning of this fiscal year, the Company has a net capital loss carry forward from 2004 of $222,000 [(1/2)($444,000)] and a non-capital loss carry forward from 2006 of $137,000. Dunway Ltd. does not anticipate having any capital gains in the foreseeable future.

Required: Calculate the minimum Net Income For Tax Purposes and Taxable Income for Dunway Ltd. for the year ending June 30, 2007. Indicate the amount of any carry overs that will be available for use in future years.

Assignment Problem Fifteen - 4

Fortan Ltd. has normally had a fiscal year that ended on April 30. However, for 2007 and subsequent taxation years, the Company has requested and received permission from the CRA to switch its year end to December 31. Its Income Statement, before consideration of income taxes, for the period May 1, 2007 to December 31, 2007 is as follows:

Sales (All Within Canada)		$465,000
Cost Of Sales		(267,000)
Gross Margin		$198,000
Operating Expenses (Excluding Taxes):		
Wages And Salaries	$73,600	
Office Rent	17,600	
Bad Debt Expense	1,800	
Promotion Expense	3,405	
Warranty Reserve	4,440	
Amortization Expense	12,384	
Charitable Donations	2,160	
Foreign Exchange Loss	4,080	
Reserve For Self-Insurance	2,322	
Interest Expense	1,974	
Other Operating Expenses	14,400	(138,165)
Income Before Taxes		$ 59,835

Other Information:

1. As of May 1, 2007, the undepreciated capital cost of the Company's office furniture was $32,500. During the eight month period ending December 31, 2007, a new conference table and chairs were acquired at a cost of $2,000. There were no dispositions during this period.

2. On May 1, 2007, the Company has a non-capital loss carry forward of $10,800.

3. The Interest Expense relates to a bank loan that was incurred to acquire shares of a Canadian corporation. This investee corporation did not declare any dividends during the year.

4. On September 1, 2007, Fortan Ltd. declared common stock dividends of $7,200.

5. The Foreign Exchange Loss resulted from the purchase of merchandise in Germany.

6. Other than setting up reserves for self-insurance, the Company makes no provision for insuring its fixed assets.

7. The Bad Debt Expense includes a loss of $1,000 resulting from the bankruptcy of a major customer.

8. On September 1, 2007, the Company purchased a delivery van for $18,000. All other vehicles used by the Company are leased.

9. Promotion Expense includes a golf club membership fee of $1,080 and $1,505 in airfare and accommodation that was incurred by the sales manager in attending a sales convention in Denver. The golf club is used exclusively for entertaining clients. The remaining balance in the Promotion Expense account of $820 is the total reimbursement paid to the president of the Company for amounts spent on meals and refreshments while entertaining clients at the club.

10. Charitable donations include $1,680 for the United Way Appeal and $480 that was paid to the United States Organ Transplant Association. The Canadian government has never made a gift to this Association.

11. This is the first year that the Company has established a warranty reserve.

Required: Calculate the minimum Net Income For Tax Purposes and Taxable Income for Fortan Ltd. for the taxation year ending December 31, 2007.

Assignment Problem Fifteen - 5

Tasty Bread Inc. opened a large bakery operation on January 1, 2005. At this time, the Company's year end was established as December 31. In addition to baking bread, the Company was in charge of the wholesale distribution of its products, and operated a large retail outlet on the bakery premises.

The owners of the corporation had little experience in any aspect of baking or selling bread and, as a consequence, during the first two years they experienced the following losses:

	2005	**2006**
Non-Capital Losses	$63,500	$78,500
Capital Losses (100%)	68,000	85,000

At the beginning of 2007, the owners did not see any real hope for improved results under their own management and they began looking for new investors with more experience in the bakery industry. Their efforts met with success when, on April 1, 2007, Dough Products Ltd. acquired 72 percent of the outstanding shares of Tasty Bread Inc. Dough Products is a large Canadian public company with a December 31 year end, and many years of successful operation in the industry. It is the intent of the new owners to inject additional capital and management expertise with a view to making Tasty's operations profitable within two years.

As this acquisition of control will result in a deemed year end, Tasty prepared an Income Statement for the period January 1, 2007 through March 31, 2007. This three month Income Statement showed an additional business loss of $23,000 for the period, but no further capital losses.

On March 31, 2007, the values of the Company's assets were as follows:

	Cost	UCC	Fair Market Value
Temporary Investments	$ 53,000	N/A	$ 23,000
Accounts Receivable	45,000	N/A	33,000
Land	275,000	N/A	420,000
Building	285,000	$270,000	320,000
Fixtures And Equipment	120,000	95,000	90,000
Vehicles	110,000	80,000	87,000

Shortly after taking over Tasty Bread Inc., Dough Products Ltd. decided that some of the extra space in Tasty's facilities could be used for manufacturing illuminated glass figurines. Tasty's income (loss) from the two separate businesses for the period April 1, 2007 through December 31, 2007, was as follows:

Business	Income (Loss)
Figurines	$123,000
Bread Operations	(45,000)

For 2008, the income (loss) figures for the two separate businesses were as follows:

Business	Income (Loss)
Figurines	($ 40,000)
Bread Operations	211,000

Required:

A. If Tasty Bread Inc. makes all possible elections to minimize the net capital and non-capital loss balances, determine the amount of the non-capital loss balance that will be carried forward after the acquisition of control by Dough Products Ltd., and the amount of the net capital loss carry forward that will be lost as a result of this change in ownership.

B. Indicate the maximum amount of the non-capital loss carry forward that can be used during the period April 1 through December 31, 2007, and the amount remaining at December 31, 2007.

C. Indicate the maximum amount of the non-capital loss carry forward that can be used during 2008, and the amount remaining at December 31, 2008.

Assignment Problem Fifteen - 6

Fortunato Ltd. was incorporated in 1993 in Calgary. All of the shares were issued to Mr. Salvatore Fortunato. The corporation operated a bakery and, for several years, it enjoyed satisfactory profits. The Company has a December 31 year end.

In 2003, Mr. Fortunato retired and turned the management of the business over to his daughter, Angela Fortunato. Mr. Fortunato retained ownership of all of the Company's shares.

Unfortunately, Angela demonstrated considerably more interest in fast cars and handsome men than she did in running the business. As a consequence, Fortunato Ltd. has experienced losses in every year since 2003. As of December 31, 2006, it has a non-capital loss carry forward of $225,000, as well as a net capital loss carry forward of $26,000 [(1/2)($52,000)] from 2004.

On April 1, 2007, after a lengthy and heated discussion on the merits of various life styles, Mr. Fortunato fires his daughter and sells all of the shares in Fortunato Ltd. to Foodland Inc., a large public company involved in the production and distribution of a variety of food products.

For the period January 1, 2007 through March 31, 2007, Fortunato Ltd. experienced a business loss of $26,000. This figure includes a write-down of inventories to their fair market values on March 31, 2007, and a deduction for uncollectible receivables, calculated as per the provisions of ITA 111(5.3). It does not include any taxable capital gains, allowable capital losses, Allowable Business Investment Losses, or property losses.

On March 31, 2007, Fortunato Ltd.'s assets had the following values:

	Cost	UCC	Fair Market Value
Long-Term Investments*	$ 32,000	N/A	$ 90,000
Land	140,000	N/A	225,000
Building	426,000	$320,000	426,000
Equipment	250,000	120,000	100,000

*Foodland Inc. intends to sell these Investments as soon as possible.

Required:

A. Indicate the amount of any non-capital and net capital loss carry forwards that would remain after the April 1, 2007 acquisition of control, using the assumption that Foodland Inc. makes all elections required to minimize these amounts. Indicate the March 31, 2007 adjusted cost base and, where appropriate, UCC, for each of the assets listed.

B. If Foodland Inc. decides to only use the election(s) required to eliminate those losses that would expire at the acquisition of control, indicate the assets on which the elections should be made, and the amounts that should be elected.

C. Advise Foodland Inc. as to which course of action (Part A or B) they should take.

Assignment Problem Fifteen - 7

Rodem Inc. is a Canadian controlled private corporation. The Company began operations on January 1, 2004, and uses a taxation year that ends on December 31. Its income (loss) before taxes, calculated using generally accepted accounting principles, and amounts included in the GAAP income figures, for the four years 2004 through 2007 are as follows:

	2004	2005	2006	2007
Income (Loss) Before Taxes (GAAP)	$110,000	($180,000)	$85,000	($42,000)
Charitable Donations	3,200	5,800	4,100	2,900
Capital Gains (Losses)*	18,000	(9,000)	12,000	2,000
Dividends From Taxable				
Canadian Corporations	11,000	19,000	18,000	12,000

*All gains and losses are on the disposition of land. As a consequence, the capital gains and losses for tax purposes are equal to the accounting gains and losses.

It is the policy of the Company to deduct charitable donations prior to any loss carry overs. They also have a policy of minimizing non-capital loss carry overs, as opposed to net capital loss carry overs.

Required: Calculate the minimum Net Income For Tax Purposes and Taxable Income for each of the four years and indicate the amount and type of carry overs that are available at the end of each year.

Assignment Problem Fifteen - 8

Lockwood Industries is a Canadian controlled private corporation that qualifies for the small business deduction on its active business income. It began operations in 2004 and, during that year, experienced a modest loss. During 2005 and 2006, its basic operations moved into the black. However, in 2007, strong competition from offshore companies severely eroded the Company's competitive position and, as a consequence, a large loss was experienced. The loss has encouraged the owners to make significant changes in their operations, and they anticipate profits will be restored in 2008. The fiscal year end of Lockwood Industries is December 31.

The various components of Division B Income, along with the charitable donations made by the Company during the period January 1, 2004 through December 31, 2007 are as follows:

	2004	2005	2006	2007
Business Income (Loss)	($22,000)	$78,000	$95,000	($176,000)
Capital Gains	Nil	Nil	24,000	22,000
Capital Losses	(66,000)	Nil	Nil	Nil
Dividends Received	4,000	6,000	6,000	5,000
Charitable Donations	Nil	12,000	23,800	1,200

All of the dividends have been received from taxable Canadian corporations. It is the policy of the Company to minimize its net capital loss carry forward balance.

Required: Compute the minimum Net Income For Tax Purposes and Taxable Income for Lockwood Industries in each of the four years under consideration. Also indicate the amended figures for any years to which losses are carried back. Provide an analysis of the amount and type of carry overs that would be available at the end of each of the four years.

Assignment Problem Fifteen - 9

Borodin Ltd. has its national headquarters in Halifax, and all of its senior management people have their offices at this location. The Company also has operations in Victoria, Edmonton, Regina, and Toronto. In each of these cities, office and warehouse space is maintained, and orders are filled. In addition, a sales staff operates out of each office, taking orders throughout the province in which the office is located.

During the current year, the Company had salaries and wages totalling $5,800,000. The Company's gross revenues for the current year were $20,865,000. These were distributed among the provinces where the Company has operations in the following manner:

Province	Wages And Salaries Accrued	Gross Revenues
Alberta	$ 928,000	$ 3,338,400
British Columbia	1,160,000	4,798,950
Nova Scotia	754,000	2,921,100
Saskatchewan	464,000	2,503,800
Ontario	2,494,000	7,302,750
Total	$5,800,000	$20,865,000

For the current taxation year, the Company's Taxable Income totalled $2,983,000.

Required: Calculate the amount of the Borodin Ltd.'s Taxable Income for the current year that would be allocated to each of the five provinces. Any percentages used in your calculations should be rounded to one decimal place.

Assignment Problem Fifteen - 10

Each of the following is an **independent** Case involving the ownership of voting shares of Canadian controlled private corporations. All of the corporations have taxation years that end on December 31.

1. Mr. Jones owns 35 percent of the shares of Jones Ltd. and 20 percent of the shares of Twitty Inc. Mr. Twitty owns 20 percent of the shares of Jones Ltd. and 40 percent of the shares of Twitty Inc. Mr. Jones and Mr. Twitty are not related.

2. Ms. Wynette owns 60 percent of the shares of Wynette Enterprises Ltd. and 30 percent of the shares of Lynn Inc. The remaining 70 percent of the shares of Lynn Inc. are held by Ms. Wynette's sister and her spouse.

3. Mr. Travis, Mr. Jennings, and Mr. Cash, three unrelated individuals, each hold one third of the shares of Cowboys Ltd. In addition, Mr. Travis and Mr. Cash each hold 50 percent of the shares of Horses Inc.

4. Mr. Nelson owns 100 percent of the shares of Willie's Hits Ltd. and 30 percent of the shares of Randy's Boots Inc. The remaining 70 percent of the shares of Randy's Boots Inc. is owned by Mr. Nelson's brother.

5. Ms. Parton owns 90 percent of the shares of Alpha Company and her spouse owns 100 percent of the shares of Centra Company. Ms. Parton and her spouse each own 40 percent of the shares of Beta Company.

6. Ms. Gale owns 90 percent of the shares of Kristal Enterprises Ltd. and 10 percent of the shares of Norton Music Inc. Her 12 year old son owns 30 percent of the shares of Norton Music Inc., and Ms. Gale holds an option to buy 20 percent of the shares of Norton Music Inc. from an unrelated shareholder.

Required: For each of the preceding Cases, determine whether the corporations are associated. Support your conclusions with references to specific provisions of ITA 256.

Assignment Problem Fifteen - 11

The following situations are **independent** of each other. All of the corporations involved are Canadian controlled private corporations.

A. Barton Ltd. owns 51 percent of the shares of Norton Inc.

B. Thomas Boulding owns 60 percent of the shares of Boulding Ltd. and 70 percent of the shares of Boulding Inc.

C. Mary Cunningham and Brenda Parton each own 50 percent of the shares of Elm Ltd. In addition, they each own 50 percent of the shares of Maple Inc. Mary and Brenda are not related.

D. Alice Fielding owns 100 percent of the shares of Fielding Inc. and 40 percent of the shares of Lawson Ltd. Betty Falcon owns 100 percent of the shares of Falcon Inc. and 40 percent of the shares of Lawson Ltd. Alice is the sister of Betty's husband. The remaining 20 percent of the shares of Lawson Ltd. are owned by unrelated parties.

E. Michael Forbes owns 70 percent of the shares of Forbes Ltd. and 30 percent of the shares of Malcom Inc. Forbes Ltd. also owns 30 percent of the shares of Malcom Inc.

F. Richard Barnes, Susan Firth, and Terry Anson each own one-third of the shares of Rastau Ltd. In addition, Richard and Susan each own 50 percent of the shares of Sucrol Inc.

Required: For each of these situations, indicate which of the involved corporations would be associated under the rules established in ITA 256(1) and related Sections of the *Act*. You should provide complete support for your conclusion, including references to appropriate provisions in the *Act*.

Assignment Problem Fifteen - 12

Kannon Inc. is a Canadian controlled private corporation that retails photographic equipment. During its taxation year ending December 31, 2007, its Taxable Income was correctly determined to be $473,000, including $440,000 in Canadian active business income. The remainder of this income was foreign business income and, because of favourable treaty provisions, no foreign taxes were withheld on this income. The provincial and international distribution of its gross revenue and wages and salaries is as follows:

	Wages And Salaries	Gross Revenues
Saskatchewan	$ 560,000	$1,200,000
Manitoba	642,000	1,232,000
Foreign	96,000	447,000
Total	$1,298,000	$2,879,000

Kannon had Taxable Capital Employed In Canada of $12,488,890 for the year ending December 31, 2006, and $11,200,000 for the year ending December 31, 2007. It is not associated with any other corporation.

Required: Calculate Kannon's Part I federal Tax Payable for the year ending December 31, 2007.

Assignment Problem Fifteen - 13

Facturing Ltd. is a Canadian controlled public company. In order to assist you in calculating their manufacturing and processing profits deduction for the current taxation year, they have provided you with the following information:

1.   Taxable Income, all of which is earned in Canada, is made up of:

Investment Income	$ 93,500
Manufacturing Income	523,000
Net Income For Tax Purposes	$616,500
Donations To Registered Charities	(20,700)
Taxable Income	$595,800

2.   Facturing Ltd. owns the following assets:

Manufacturing Equipment	$1,275,000
Data Processing Equipment	69,300
Office Furniture And Equipment	141,400
Equipment For Employee Cafeteria	13,800
Total	$1,499,500

3.   Wage and salary costs are as follows:

Plant Employees	$1,132,000
Accounting Employees	277,300
Quality Control Employees	211,200
Plant Supervision And Maintenance Employees	127,300
Distribution Employees (Finished Goods)	91,700
Receiving Employees (Receiving And Storing Raw Materials)	62,800
Purchasing Employees (Raw Materials)	49,600
Total	$1,951,900

Required: Calculate Facturing Ltd.'s manufacturing and processing profits deduction for the current year.

Assignment Problem Fifteen - 14

During its taxation year ending December 31, 2007, the condensed Income Statement of Industrial Tools Ltd. was prepared in accordance with generally accepted accounting principles. In condensed form it is as follows:

Industrial Tools Ltd.
Condensed Income Statement
For The Year Ending December 31, 2007

Revenues	$6,585,000
Expenses (Excluding Taxes)	(4,280,000)
Net Income Before Taxes	$2,305,000

Other Information:

1.   The Company's shares are publicly traded and none of its income is from manufacturing or processing.

2. The January 1, 2007 balance in the Company's cumulative eligible capital account is $115,000.

3. Revenues include an accounting gain of $225,000, resulting from the sale of a building for $950,000 in cash. The building had a capital cost of $875,000 and was acquired in 2000. It is the only asset in Class 1, and the UCC balance in this class prior to the sale was $625,000. The land on which the building is situated was leased, and the purchaser of the building has assumed Industrial Tool's obligations under the lease.

4. There is a net capital loss carry over from 2004 of $90,000 [(1/2)($180,000)].

5. Expenses included a deduction for charitable donations in the amount of $28,000.

6. The Expenses include interest and penalties of $2,500, resulting from a failure to file last year's tax return within the prescribed time period.

7. Expenses include a warranty reserve of $20,000. This is the first year that the Company has deducted such a reserve.

8. Revenues include dividends from taxable Canadian corporations of $42,000.

9. Amortization included in the accounting Expenses amounts to $478,000. Maximum available deductions for CCA amount to $523,000.

Required:

A. Calculate the minimum Net Income For Tax Purposes for Industrial Tools Ltd. for the year ending December 31, 2007.

B. Calculate the minimum Taxable Income for Industrial Tools Ltd. for the year ending December 31, 2007. Indicate the amount and type of any loss carry overs that are still available for use in subsequent years.

C. Calculate the minimum federal Tax Payable for Industrial Tools Ltd. for the year ending December 31, 2007.

Assignment Problem Fifteen - 15

Worldwide Enterprises was established in 1992 and has been, since its incorporation under the Canada Business Corporations Act, a Canadian controlled private corporation. Its head office is located in Vancouver and it has branches in both Seattle, Washington and Portland, Oregon. Its taxation year ends on December 31. All income of the Company is derived from the sale of seafood in local markets.

During the 2007 taxation year, the Company's Net Income For Tax Purposes and Taxable Income amount to $219,000. This amount includes $32,000 (Canadian) that was earned by the two branches operating in the United States. The $32,000 earned by these branches is before the deduction of any U.S. or Canadian income taxes. As a result of earning this amount in the United States, the Company was required to pay $6,200 (Canadian) in U.S. federal income tax and $3,400 (Canadian) in state income taxes.

Required: Calculate Worldwide Enterprises' federal Part I Tax Payable for the 2007 taxation year.

CHAPTER 16

Integration, Refundable Taxes, And Corporate Surplus Distributions

Integration

The Basic Concept

16-1. In designing a system for assessing taxes on business income, there are two theories or perspectives as to the appropriate treatment of corporations. These two perspectives are referred to as the entity view and the integration view. They can be described as follows:

Entity View The entity view holds that corporations have a perpetual life of their own, that they are independent of their shareholders, and that they are legal entities. As such, they should pay tax separately on their earnings.

Integration View Under the integration approach to the taxation of business income, corporations are viewed as simply the legal form through which one or more individuals (shareholders) carry on business. Therefore, business income that flows through a corporation to an individual should not be taxed differently, in total, from business income earned directly by that individual as a proprietor or partner.

16-2. In practice, we find a variety of relationships between corporations and their shareholders. Given this situation, it would not be reasonable to apply either of these views to all Canadian corporations. For large corporations, where the shares are widely held and publicly traded, the entity view seems appropriate. Management of the corporation is separate from its ownership, with income allocation and distribution decisions being made without directly consulting the shareholders. Not all corporate profits are paid out to the shareholders. In addition, some of these amounts are paid to foreign shareholders, subject only to the non-resident withholding tax. In this type of situation, the entity view's treatment of the corporation as a separate taxable unit appears to be an equitable way to tax business income.

16-3. This would not be the case for small corporations where the shares are privately held, either by a single individual or a small group of related individuals. With these owner managed businesses, the affairs of the shareholders and the business are closely related. Tax planning decisions involving salaries, dividends, or capital gains affect both personal and corporate taxes and the line between the corporation and its owners is often faint. This would lead to the conclusion that the taxation of business income in these situations should not be influenced by the presence of the corporation. This conclusion is consistent with the integration view of business income taxation.

16-4.   In a strict legal sense, the *Income Tax Act* reflects the entity view in that corporations are considered to be taxable units that are separate from their owners. Both the corporation and the owners are subject to taxation and this, in effect, involves double taxation of the income earned initially by the corporation. In the absence of special provisions, there would be a significantly higher level of taxation on income earned by a corporation and paid out as dividends, than there would be on income earned directly, either through a proprietorship or partnership.

16-5.   Fortunately, there are special provisions that mitigate the effects of both the corporation and its shareholders being treated as taxable entities. The most important of these provisions is the dividend tax credit that is available to individuals who have received dividends from taxable Canadian corporations.

> **AN IMPORTANT NOTE** An understanding of dividend gross up and tax credit procedures is essential to the material which follows in this Chapter and Chapters 17, 18, and 19. If you do not fully understand these procedures, you should review Paragraphs 9-80 through 9-111 in Chapter 9 of this text.

Dividend Gross Up And Tax Credit

Eligible Dividends

16-6.   You may recall from Chapter 9 that ITA 89(1) defines eligible dividends as any taxable dividend that is designated as such by the company paying the dividend. Dividends that are designated as eligible qualify for the enhanced 45 percent gross up and tax credit procedures.

16-7.   With the exception of capital dividends, all types of dividends may be designated as eligible dividends. This includes the cash and stock dividends that were discussed in Chapter 9, as well as the various types of deemed dividends that will be introduced later in this Chapter (e.g., ITA 84(3) dividend on redemption of shares).

Non-Eligible Dividends

16-8.   We will refer to dividends that have not been designated as eligible as non-eligible dividends. These non-eligible distributions will be dealt with by continuing to apply the 25 percent gross up that has been in effect for many years. Recipients of these dividends will benefit from a federal dividend tax credit equal to two-thirds of the 25 percent gross up.

16-9.   Any dividend that has not been designated as eligible will be considered to be non-eligible. This includes cash dividends, stock dividends, dividends in kind, and the various types of deemed dividends that are discussed in this Chapter. Note, however, as capital dividends are not taxable dividends, they do not qualify for either dividend gross up and tax credit procedure.

Who Can Declare Eligible Dividends?

16-10.   Again referring to the discussion of dividends in Chapter 9, the reason for introducing the enhanced dividend gross up and tax credit procedures for eligible dividends was to provide better integration for corporate income that was subject to the general corporate tax rate. As demonstrated in that Chapter, the combined federal/provincial tax on income flowing through a large public company was far greater than the taxes that would be paid had the shareholders received the income directly. Given this, we will find that most of the dividends paid by large public companies can be designated as eligible.

16-11.   In contrast, the income of a CCPC may benefit from the small business deduction that was discussed in Chapter 15, or refundable taxes that will be discussed at a later point in this Chapter. For companies with this type of income, the 25 percent dividend gross up and tax credit procedures provided a reasonable level of integration. This would suggest that the dividends declared by this type of company should be non-eligible.

16-12.   It would be very convenient to have a rule that says that taxable dividends paid by non-CCPCs are eligible dividends, while dividends paid by CCPCs are non-eligible. Unfortunately, this simple dichotomy does not work because:

- some CCPCs have some portion of their income taxed at full rates (e.g., active business income in excess of the annual business limit of $400,000), and

- some non-CCPCs have some portion of their income taxed at favourable rates (e.g., a CCPC that goes public with a retained earnings balance that contains amounts that benefited from the small business deduction).

16-13.   Because of these complications, new legislation has been created to specify the conditions necessary for a corporation to designate a dividend payment as being eligible for the enhanced gross up and tax credit procedure. While we could discuss this legislation at this point, it will be much easier to understand after you have covered this Chapter's material on the taxation of corporate investment income. Given this, we will defer our coverage of this material until the end of this Chapter.

Integration And Business Income
Required Rates And Credits

16-14.   In Chapter 9 we noted that the goal of integration is to ensure that, if an individual chooses to channel an income stream through a corporation, he will retain the same after tax amount of funds that he would have retained if he had received the income directly. Stated alternatively, integration procedures are directed at equating the amount of taxes paid by an individual on the direct receipt of income, with the combined corporate/individual taxes that would be paid if that same stream of income was channeled through a corporation.

16-15.   In Chapter 9, we also demonstrated that, for integration to work, certain assumptions were required with respect to both the combined federal/provincial tax rate on corporations and the combined federal/provincial dividend tax credit. As noted in that chapter, those assumptions are as follows:

Federal/Provincial Tax Rate On Corporations The combined corporate tax rate that will make integration effective depends on the type of dividends:

- With respect to eligible dividends where the 45 percent gross up is applicable, the required rate is 31.03 percent.
- With respect to non-eligible dividends where the 25 percent gross up is applicable, the required rate is 20 percent.

If the applicable rate exceeds these benchmarks, the use of a corporation will result in additional taxation.

Federal/Provincial Dividend Tax Credit For integration to be effective, the combined federal/provincial dividend tax credit must be equal to the gross up. The required provincial dividend tax credit that will produce the combined credit depends on the type of dividends:

- With respect to eligible dividends where the 45 percent gross up is applicable, the federal dividend tax credit is equal to 11/18 of the gross up. This means that, for the combined credit to equal the gross up, the provincial credit must be equal to 7/18 of the gross up.
- With respect to non-eligible dividends where the 25 percent gross up is applicable, the federal dividend tax credit is equal to two-thirds of the gross up. This means that, for the combined credit to equal the gross up, the provincial credit must be equal to one-third of the gross up.

If the combined credit is less than one, the use of a corporation will result in additional taxation.

Actual Corporate Tax Rates

16-16.   With respect to eligible dividends, integration requires a federal/provincial tax on corporations of 31.03 percent. Actual rates for the public companies that pay such dividends are generally above this. For 2007, the rates range from a low of 32.0 percent in Quebec to 38.1 percent in Nova Scotia and Prince Edward Island (see Chapter 15, Paragraph 15-94). While the proposed reduction in federal rates will improve this situation, it is clear that the dividend gross up and tax credit procedures for eligible dividends do not currently achieve the goal of integration.

16-17.   The situation improves for CCPCs earning income eligible for the small business deduction. For 2007, the combined federal/provincial rates range from a low of 16.1 percent in Alberta to a high of 21.1 percent in Quebec (see Chapter 15, Paragraph 15-94). As the integration assumed rate for non-eligible dividends is 20 percent, it appears that, with the single exception of Quebec, channeling income through a CCPC can result in a lower lever of taxation.

Actual Dividend Tax Credits

16-18.   We have noted that, for integration to work, the provincial dividend tax credit has to be equal to 7/18 (38.9%) of the gross up for eligible dividends and one-third (33.3%) of the gross up for non-eligible dividends. At present, actual rates range from a low of 21 percent of the gross up, to a high of 39 percent of the gross up. This means that, depending on the province, the combined federal/provincial dividend tax credit may be higher or lower than one. As we have pointed out, if it is less than one, the use of a corporation will result in increased taxes. In contrast, if it exceeds one, channeling income through a corporation can result in a lower level of taxation.

Alternative Calculations

16-19.   We would also note that, while federal legislation calculates the dividend tax credit as a fraction of the gross up, other jurisdictions may base this credit on a percentage of dividends received, or on the grossed up amount of the dividends. In addition, on the T1 (personal) tax return, the federal dividend tax credit calculation is 13.3333% of the taxable (grossed up) amount of non-eligible dividends from taxable Canadian corporations.

16-20.   There is, however, no problem in converting these different approaches to a uniform base. For example, if a non-eligible dividend of $120 is paid, the federal dividend tax credit of $20 is equal to two-thirds of the $30 [(25%)($120)] gross up. This is the mathematical equivalent of 16-2/3 percent of dividends received [(16-2/3%)($120)], or 13-1/3 percent of the grossed up amount of dividends [(13-1/3%)($120)(125%)]. Because our focus is largely on federal legislation, we will generally present dividend tax credits as a fraction of the gross up.

Exercise Sixteen-1

Subject: Integration (Non-Eligible Dividends)

Jan Teason has a business that she estimates will produce income of $100,000 per year. If she incorporates this business, all of the income would be eligible for the small business deduction and any dividends paid will be non-eligible. In the province where she lives, such corporate income is taxed at a combined federal/provincial rate of 19 percent. Ms. Teason has other income sources that place her in a combined federal/provincial tax bracket of 45 percent. In her province, the provincial dividend tax credit is equal to 25 percent of the gross up. Would Ms. Teason save taxes if she was to channel this source of income through a corporation? Justify your conclusion.

End of Exercise.   Solution available in Study Guide.

Exercise Sixteen-2

Subject: Integration (Eligible Dividends)

John Horst has a business that he estimates will produce income of $100,000 per year. Because he controls another corporation that fully utilizes $400,000 of its small business deduction, if he incorporates this business, none of this income will be eligible for the small business deduction and any dividends paid would be designated eligible. In the province where he lives, such corporate income is taxed at a combined federal/provincial rate of 34 percent. Mr. Horst has other income sources that place him in a combined federal/provincial tax bracket of 42 percent. In his province, the provincial dividend tax credit is equal to 39 percent of the gross up. Would Mr. Horst save taxes if he was to channel this source of income through a corporation? Justify your conclusion.

End of Exercises. Solutions available in Study Guide.

Tax Basis Shareholders' Equity

Shareholders' Equity Under GAAP

16-21.   In this Chapter, we will be considering various distributions to shareholders and the fact that, in some circumstances, such distributions will trigger refunds of taxes that have been previously paid by the corporation. In order to comprehend this material, some understanding of the tax basis components of shareholders' equity is required.

16-22.   You are all familiar with the components of Shareholders' Equity as they appear in a Balance Sheet prepared using generally accepted accounting principles (GAAP). The two basic components of the total balance disclosed are:

- **Contributed Capital**   This is the amount that has been paid by investors in return for shares issued. In jurisdictions where par value shares can still be used, this balance may be divided into par value amounts and an excess over par amount, commonly designated contributed surplus.

- **Earned Capital (Retained Earnings)**   This component reflects amounts that have been earned by the corporation and retained in the business. While this balance is sometimes referred to as earned surplus, the more common designation is retained earnings. In some situations, part of this balance may be presented as separate reserves.

16-23.   This segregation is based on the general legal requirement that dividends cannot be paid out of contributed capital. By using this disclosure, investors are informed as to the legal basis for payment of dividends by the corporation. However, this legal basis may not be supported by the cash resources that would be needed to, in fact, pay cash dividends.

Paid Up Capital (Tax Basis Contributed Capital)

16-24.   ITA 89(1) defines paid up capital, normally referred to as "PUC". This Subsection indicates that the amount should be calculated without reference to the *Income Tax Act*, telling us that PUC should be based on legal stated capital as determined under the legislation governing the particular corporation (*Canada Business Corporations Act* or relevant provincial legislation). As contributed capital under GAAP is also based on legal stated capital, the initial PUC for shares issued will be equal to contributed capital under GAAP. However, as will be discussed in this and subsequent Chapters, there will be adjustments to PUC that have no equivalent adjustment under GAAP.

16-25.   PUC is applied on an average per share basis to each class of shares. This means, for example, that if a corporation issues 100,000 shares to one individual at $10 per share and, at a later point in time, issues an additional 100,000 shares of the same class to a different individual at $15 per share, the per share PUC will be $12.50 for all of the shares of that class. Stated alternatively, all shares of a particular class will have the same per share PUC value.

16-26.   Note the difference between the PUC value per share and the adjusted cost base (ACB) of a share. The ACB of a share is the average cost of the shares held by a particular shareholder. In the example in Paragraph 16-25, the taxpayer acquiring the first issue has an adjusted cost base of $10 per share, while the purchaser of the second issue has an adjusted cost base of $15 per share.

16-27.   The importance of PUC lies in the fact that it is a capital contribution and does not reflect accumulated earnings of the corporation. Because of this, it can be distributed to shareholders as a return of capital (subject to any restrictions imposed by corporate law), without tax consequences for either the corporation, or the shareholder. This may not be the case, however, when capital distributions are made to shareholders of public corporations.

Exercise Sixteen-3

Subject: Determination Of PUC And Adjusted Cost Base

Halide Ltd. has one class of shares. The Company issued its first 100,000 shares at a price of $1.10 each. Two years later, an additional 50,000 shares were issued for $1.35 per share. During the current year, a further 30,000 shares were issued for $1.82 per share. One of the investors in the Company acquired 2,400 shares of the first group of shares issued, and an additional 3,850 shares from the most recent issue. Determine the adjusted cost base per share, as well as the total PUC of this investor's shares.

End of Exercise.   Solution available in Study Guide.

Tax Basis Retained Earnings

Amount

16-28.   The situation with respect to Retained Earnings is much more complex. To begin, we will be dealing with a different total for tax purposes. As you are likely aware, there are significant differences between accounting Net Income and Net Income For Tax Purposes.

16-29.   While the accounting literature now defines accounting/tax differences as temporary differences with reference to Balance Sheet accounts (e.g., the difference between the Net Book Value and the UCC of a depreciable asset), most of these Balance Sheet differences are created by Income Statement differences (e.g., the difference between Amortization Expense and CCA). As a result, total Retained Earnings as determined under GAAP will, in most cases, be a significantly different number than the corresponding tax figure.

16-30.   A further point here relates to terminology. In general, the term Retained Earnings has replaced Earned Surplus in accounting literature and in published financial statements. However, the term surplus is still alive and well in tax work. As evidence, we would note that the *Income Tax Act* contains only 15 references to Retained Earnings, in contrast to 190 references to Surplus.

Basic Components

16-31.   Moving beyond the differences in the total amount, we encounter further problems in relating tax and GAAP figures. Under GAAP, Retained Earnings is generally a single homogenous balance, all of which has the same significance for financial statement users. This is not the case with the corresponding tax figure. It is made up of four different categories that can be described as follows:

- Pre-1972 Undistributed Surplus
- Post-1971 Undistributed Surplus

- Pre-1972 Capital Surplus On Hand (CSOH)
- Capital Dividend Account (private companies only)

16-32. "Pre-1972 Undistributed Surplus", sometimes referred to as Surplus Nothings, is simply earnings that accrued prior to 1972 and were retained in the corporation. Correspondingly, "Post-1971 Undistributed Surplus" is used for earnings retained after 1971 that do not have any special tax status. The distinction between these two balances is sometimes of importance. For an example of this, see the material on capital gains stripping in Chapter 18. When there is a distribution to shareholders related to the disposition of shares in another corporation, its treatment will depend on whether the distribution is made from the Pre-1972 Undistributed Surplus or, alternatively, from the Post-1971 Undistributed Surplus.

Pre-1972 Capital Surplus On Hand (CSOH)

16-33. In Chapter 10 we noted that, prior to 1972, capital gains were not subject to tax in Canada. The 1972 introduction of capital gains taxation resulted in the need to have a complex set of transitional rules to avoid taxation of gains accrued prior to that date. At one time these rules were very important and required significant coverage in Canadian tax texts.

16-34. With the passage of time this is no longer the case. In Chapter 10 we relegated our coverage of the median rule (a rule that deals with dispositions of assets acquired before 1972) to an Appendix to that Chapter.

16-35. The CSOH balance involves a similar situation. We cannot avoid mentioning it as it is still a legislatively based component of tax surplus. However, because it relates to assets acquired prior to 1972, it no longer warrants detailed coverage in a general tax text such as this. Given this we will provide only the following brief description of this balance:

Pre-1972 Capital Surplus On Hand (CSOH) This balance reflects capital gains and capital losses that accrued prior to 1972, but were realized subsequent to that date. For example, if shares were acquired in 1968 for $100,000, had a fair market value on December 31, 1971 of $120,000, and were sold in 2007 for $150,000, there would be an addition to the CSOH of $20,000 ($120,000 - $100,000).

Capital Dividend Account

Objective

16-36. The objective of the capital dividend account is to track items that can be distributed on a tax free basis to the shareholders of the corporation. While a number of different items can be included in this account, the reason for its use can best be understood in the context of capital gains.

Example During 2002, Uval Ltd. acquires land at a cost of $150,000. During 2007, the land is sold for $190,000, resulting in a capital gain of $40,000 ($190,000 - $150,000).

Analysis It is the intent of current capital gains legislation to assess tax on only one-half of capital gains. This means that Uval will have a taxable capital gain of $20,000 [(1/2)($40,000)]. However, the remaining $20,000 is still being held by the corporation. While the goal of current legislation is not to have taxes assessed on this balance, in the absence of some special provision, its distribution would be subject to tax in the hands of the recipient shareholders.

16-37. The capital dividend account provides the required relief in this situation. The untaxed balance of $20,000 will be added to the capital dividend account. This balance can then be used to pay a capital dividend, a special type of dividend that can be distributed tax free to the shareholders of the corporation. Such dividends will be discussed in more detail at a later point in this chapter.

16-38. While this analysis would appear to be relevant to all types of corporation, only private corporations can have a capital dividend account. Note, however, the use of this account is available to all private corporations, without regard to whether they are Canadian controlled.

16-39.   While this is no longer of great importance, we would remind you that gains that accrued prior to 1972 are allocated to the Pre-1972 Capital Surplus On Hand balance. Only gains on assets that are acquired after 1971 are allocated to the Capital Dividend Account.

Procedures

16-40.   As indicated in the preceding section, there are a number of different items that can be allocated to the capital dividend account. The complete definition of these items is found in ITA 89(1) and is very complex. Without becoming involved in some of the more complex issues found in that Subsection, the basic items that can be included in the Capital Dividend Account are as follows:

1.   The non-taxable portion of net capital gains realized during the year are added to the account (the non-taxable portion of capital gains, less the non-deductible portion of capital losses and Business Investment Losses). Note that the amounts are added at the fraction (one-half, one-third, or one-quarter) that is appropriate for the year in which the gains are realized. The amounts are not subsequently adjusted for changes in this fraction.

2.   Capital dividends received from other corporations are added. This preserves the tax free status of non-taxable amounts that pass through more than one corporation.

3.   The non-taxable portion of gains on the sale of eligible capital property is added to the account.

Note   You will not be able to understand this example unless you are familiar with the cumulative eligible capital procedures that were presented in Chapter 7. If you have not covered this material recently, we suggest that you review it prior to dealing with this example.

Example   A corporation acquires goodwill for $100,000 during 2005. Three-quarters of this amount, or $75,000, is added to the cumulative eligible capital (CEC) balance. This would be amortized at a 7 percent rate for two years, leaving a balance of $64,868 [($75,000)(93%)(93%)]. The goodwill is sold during 2007 for $150,000.

Analysis   The relevant calculations here are as follows:

2005 Addition To CEC	$ 75,000
2005 And 2006 Amortization ($75,000 - $64,868)	(10,132)
Balance - January 1, 2007	$ 64,868
Proceeds Deducted [(75%)($150,000)]	(112,500)
Subtotal	($ 47,632)
Income Inclusion For Amortization Taken	10,132
Negative Balance	($ 37,500)
Conversion Factor (3/4 To 1/2)	2/3
Additional Income Inclusion	$ 25,000

In economic terms, there has been a gain on the disposition of $50,000 ($150,000 - $100,000). As discussed in Chapter 7, ITA 14(1) acts to treat this gain in the same manner as a capital gain. That is, only one-half of the total is subject to tax. That one-half is the $25,000 that has been calculated in the preceding table (it was converted from a three-quarters inclusion rate to a one-half inclusion rate because the CEC rules were not changed in 2000 when the capital gains inclusion rate went from three-quarter to one-half). An equivalent amount of $25,000 will be added to the capital dividend account.

4. Life insurance proceeds received by the corporation are added to the account, net of the adjusted cost base of the policy. This can be an important addition when the company insures the life of one or more of its shareholders. This is a common procedure in owner-managed businesses, where life insurance proceeds are sometimes used to finance the buy out of the estate of a deceased shareholder.

5. The account is reduced by capital dividends paid [ITA 83(2) election required].

Exercise Sixteen-4

Subject: Capital Dividend Account

The following transactions involve the Knerd Corporation's capital dividend account:

- In 1987, they sold a capital asset with an adjusted cost base of $98,000, for cash of $123,000, resulting in a $12,500 taxable capital gain [(1/2)($25,000)].

- In 1996, they sold a capital asset with an adjusted cost base of $86,000, for cash of $98,000, resulting in a taxable capital gain of $9,000 [(3/4)($12,000)].

- During the year ending December 31, 2006, the Company received a capital dividend of $8,200.

- On July 1, 2007, they sold goodwill for proceeds of $42,000. They had paid $37,000 for this goodwill in the previous year. It is the Company's policy to make maximum CCA and CEC deductions.

- On October 31, 2007, the Company paid an ITA 83(2) capital dividend of $16,000. The appropriate election was made.

Determine the balance in the capital dividend account at December 31, 2007.

End of Exercise. Solution available in Study Guide.

Distributions Of Corporate Surplus

Introduction

16-41. Corporate surplus, generally referred to by accountants as Retained Earnings, is periodically distributed to shareholders of the corporation. This happens most commonly through the regular cash dividends that are paid by most Canadian companies. Less commonly, we encounter stock dividends and dividends in kind (distributions of corporate assets other than cash).

16-42. These fairly routine types of dividends were given coverage in Chapter 9 in our material on property income. However, they will be reviewed at this point as an introduction to the various types of deemed dividends that are under consideration here. We will also give further attention to ITA 83(2) capital dividends.

16-43. With the exception of capital dividends, all of these types of dividends may be either eligible or non-eligible. As we have noted, however, we will defer our discussion of the conditions necessary for a dividend to be designated as eligible until the end of this Chapter, subsequent to our discussion of refundable taxes on the investment income of private companies and CCPCs.

16-44. The types of deemed dividends that will be covered in this section are as follows:

- ITA 84(1) Deemed Dividend on Increase of PUC
- ITA 84(2) Deemed Dividend on Winding Up or Reorganization of a Business
- ITA 84(3) Deemed Dividend on Redemption, Acquisition, or Cancellation of Shares
- ITA 84(4) and (4.1) Deemed Dividend on Reduction of PUC

16-45.   You should note that, when such deemed dividends are received by an individual, they are treated in the same manner as cash dividends. They are subject to either a 45 percent gross up or a 25 percent gross up, depending on whether they have been designated as eligible dividends by the payor corporation. When such dividends are received by another corporation, they are generally deductible under ITA 112(1).

Regular Cash Dividends

16-46.   Regular cash dividends are paid out of a corporation's unrestricted surplus balances. The payment of cash dividends serves to reduce these balances. Unlike the payment of interest on debt, the payment of cash dividends does not create a tax deduction for the corporation.

16-47.   If cash dividends are received by an individual or a trust, they are subject to the usual gross up and tax credit procedures. In contrast, if they are paid to another corporation, they are generally received on a tax free basis.

16-48.   A further point here relates to dividends on certain types of preferred shares. Section 3861 of the *CICA Handbook*, "Financial Instruments - Disclosure And Presentation", recommends that shares which require mandatory redemption by the issuer be classified as liabilities. Consistent with this, the dividend payments on these shares must be disclosed as interest, resulting in the amount of the distribution being deducted in the determination of accounting net income.

16-49.   To date, this treatment has not been recognized by the CRA. From a tax point of view, the dividends paid on preferred shares with mandatory redemption provisions will be given the same treatment as any other dividend. This means that, even if the GAAP based financial statements of the enterprise present preferred dividends as interest expense, they will not be deductible to the paying corporation.

Stock Dividends

16-50.   A stock dividend is a pro rata distribution of new shares to the existing shareholder group of the corporation, accompanied by a capitalization of Retained Earnings.

Example On December 31, 2007, Jessica Rabin owns 100 shares of Fergis Ltd. She acquired these shares several years ago for $2,500 ($25 per share).

On January 1, 2007, the Shareholders' Equity of Fergis Ltd. is as follows:

No Par Common Stock (1,000,000 Shares)	$ 7,500,000
Retained Earnings	12,500,000
Total Shareholders' Equity	$20,000,000

On December 31, 2007, the shares of Fergis have a fair market value of $30 per share. On this date, the Company declares a 10 percent stock dividend and designates it as eligible.

Analysis - Fergis Ltd. At the time of the stock dividend, Fergis would transfer an amount equal to the $3,000,000 [($30)(10%)(1,000,000)] market value of these shares from Retained Earnings to the contributed capital account. Subsequent to this transfer, the Shareholders' Equity of Fergis would be as follows:

No Par Common Stock (1,100,000 Shares)	$10,500,000
Retained Earnings ($12,500,000 - $3,000,000)	9,500,000
Total Shareholders' Equity	$20,000,000

From a tax point of view, the $3,000,000 increase in contributed capital would be an increase in PUC, reflecting an increase in the amount that could be distributed to the shareholders of the company on a tax free basis.

Analysis - Jessica Rabin As a result of the stock dividend, she will receive 10 shares ([(10%)($100)] of stock worth $300 [(10)($30)]. This $300 would be a fully taxable dividend, subject to a 45 percent gross up. As the $300 is subject to tax, ITA 52(3) deems her to have acquired 10 additional shares at a cost and PUC of $300. With this addition, the average per share adjusted cost base would be $25.45 [($2,500 + $300) ÷ 110].

16-51.   These rules create an unfortunate situation for the taxpayer. An individual receiving stock dividends will require a cash outflow (taxes on the dividend received) with no corresponding cash inflows (the dividends are not received in cash). This approach to the taxation of stock dividends serves to significantly discourage their use in Canada, particularly in the case of large publicly traded companies.

16-52.   It should be noted however, that it is possible for a company to issue shares with a PUC that is less than fair market value. When this is the case, the negative tax effect that was described in the preceding paragraph can be minimized.

Dividends In Kind

16-53.   While somewhat unusual, corporations do sometimes declare dividends that are payable in assets other than cash, or the corporation's own shares. An example of this might be a situation in which a corporation has a major holding of another corporation's shares and wishes to dispose of them. If the block is large, sale on the open market could significantly depress the proceeds received. A possible alternative is to distribute the shares on a pro rata basis to the corporation's existing shareholders.

16-54.   From the point of view of the corporation, the dividend is treated as a disposition of the distributed property. Under ITA 52(2), the proceeds of disposition will be deemed to be the fair market value of the property distributed. Depending on the type of property, this could result in a capital gain, capital loss, recapture or terminal loss for the corporation.

16-55.   Also under ITA 52(2), the shareholders are deemed to have acquired the assets at their fair market value. This amount is considered to be a taxable dividend subject to the usual gross up and tax credit procedures for eligible and non-eligible dividends.

> **Example**   Hold Ltd. owns shares in Bold Inc. These shares have an adjusted cost base of $800,000 and a fair market value of $3,500,000. Hold Ltd. decides to distribute the Bold Inc. shares as a dividend in kind to its shareholders. The dividend is declared in June, 2007 and will be paid to the existing shareholders of Hold Ltd. in July, 2007.
>
> **Analysis**   The tax consequences of this dividend are as follows:
>
> - Based on deemed proceeds of $3,500,000, Hold Ltd. will have a taxable capital gain of $1,350,000 [(1/2)($3,500,000 - $800,000)].
>
> - Hold Ltd. will have declared a dividend of $3,500,000, resulting in a decrease in its undistributed surplus of this amount.
>
> - The shareholders will be deemed to have received a taxable dividend of $3,500,000, subject to either a 45 percent or 25 percent gross up.
>
> - The adjusted cost base of the Bold Inc. shares to the Hold Ltd. shareholders will be $3,500,000.

Capital Dividends Under ITA 83(2)

16-56.   As we have previously indicated, the balance in the capital dividend account reflects amounts that can be distributed on a tax free basis to the shareholders of the private corporation. However, this tax free status does not happen automatically. When a corporation makes a distribution, an amount not in excess of the balance in the capital dividend account can be designated as a capital dividend. This is accomplished through an election under ITA 83(2), using Form T2054.

16-57.   Distributing a capital dividend reduces the balance in the capital dividend account. It will be received by the taxpayer, whether the taxpayer is a corporation, a trust or an individual, on a tax free basis with no reduction in the adjusted cost base of their shares. You will recall that, if the recipient of the capital dividend is a private corporation, the amount of the dividend will be added to the recipient corporation's capital dividend account.

16-58.   If an election is made to pay a capital dividend in excess of the balance in the capital dividend account, a tax equal to 60 percent of the excess will be assessed under ITA 184(2) of the *Income Tax Act*. This will not affect the tax free nature of the dividend to the recipient.

16-59.   In some circumstances, an excess election can occur inadvertently. For example, the non-taxable portion of a capital gain may be added to the capital dividend account and, at a subsequent point in time, a reassessment will cause the gain to be reclassified as business, rather than capital. This in turn means that the capital dividend account will be reduced through the reassessment process. If this happens, ITA 184(3) and 184(4) contain provisions that allow for a revision of the election in order to avoid the 60 percent penalty.

16-60.   As a final point, the fact that capital dividends are not taxable dividends means that they are not subject to the dividend gross up and tax credit procedures. In turn, this means that they cannot be classified as eligible dividends under any circumstances.

Deemed Dividends Under ITA 84(1) - Increase In PUC
General Rules
16-61.   ITA 84(1) dividends involve a situation where there has been an increase in the corporation's PUC, accompanied by a smaller increase in the net assets of the corporation.

16-62.   The most common example of this type of deemed dividend would involve situations where a corporation issues shares to settle a debt obligation that has a carrying value that is smaller than the fair market value of the shares. For example, a corporation might issue shares with a PUC of $500,000 to a creditor, in settlement of debt with a carrying value of $450,000 (this type of transaction would occur when there has been a decline in interest rates, resulting in an increase in the fair market value of the debt). This transaction would result in an ITA 84(1) deemed dividend of $50,000 ($500,000 - $450,000).

16-63.   The reason for treating this $50,000 as a form of income to the shareholders is that it represents an increase in the amount that can be distributed to them on a tax free basis. Their economic position has clearly been improved as a result of this transaction.

16-64.   It is important to note that, because the extra $50,000 in PUC will be allocated to all of the shareholders of the particular class, a corresponding treatment will be given to the deemed dividend. That is, the $50,000 dividend will be allocated on a pro rata basis to all of the shareholders of the class, not just the new shareholder who acquired his shares by giving up $450,000 in debt securities.

16-65.   In order to provide equity in this situation, the amount assessed as a dividend will be added to the adjusted cost base of the shares. For the new shareholder, his share of the $50,000 ITA 84(1) deemed dividend is added to the adjusted cost base of the shares that were issued to him, resulting in an adjusted cost base for these shares of $450,000 plus his share of the deemed dividend. Note that this will not be the PUC of these shares, since PUC is calculated as an average value for all of the outstanding shares on a class by class basis.

Excluded Transactions
16-66.   There are a number of transactions involving increases in PUC that are specifically excluded from this deemed dividend treatment under ITA 84(1). The most important of these are:

- **Stock Dividends**   While there will be an increase in PUC in excess of the increase in net assets when a stock dividend is declared, such dividends are not considered to be an ITA 84(1) deemed dividend. Rather, they are taxed under ITA 82(1) as regular dividends. From the point of view of the recipient of the dividend, this distinction is of no consequence.

- **Shifts Between Classes**   When the PUC of one class of shares is decreased and, at the same time, the PUC of a different class is increased by a corresponding amount, there is no ITA 84(1) deemed dividend.

- **Conversion Of Contributed Surplus**   In situations where the consideration received for shares issued is in excess of the amount added to PUC, for tax purposes a contributed surplus balance is created. This contributed surplus balance can be converted to PUC, without the increase in PUC being treated as a deemed dividend under ITA 84(1).

Exercise Sixteen-5

Subject: ITA 84(1) Deemed Dividends

At the beginning of the current year, Unilev Inc. has 126,000 shares of common stock outstanding. The shares were originally issued at $10.50 per share for total proceeds of $1,323,000, with this amount constituting the PUC. During the current year, a creditor holding $450,000 of the Company's debt agrees to accept 40,000 newly issued common shares of the Company in exchange for settlement of the debt obligation. At the time of this exchange, the shares are trading at $12.70 per share. Subsequent to the exchange, Mr. Uni, who had purchased 5,000 Unilev Inc. shares at the time of their original issue, sells the shares for $13.42 per share.

Describe the tax consequence(s) to all of the shareholders of Unilev Inc. as a result of the exchange of debt for common shares. In addition, describe the tax consequences to Mr. Uni resulting from the sale of his Unilev Inc. shares.

End of Exercise. Solution available in Study Guide.

Deemed Dividends Under ITA 84(2) - On Winding-Up

16-67.   When there is a winding-up of a Canadian corporation under the provisions of ITA 88(2), the corporate assets will be sold and the liabilities, including taxes on the various types of income created by the sale of the assets, will be paid. The remaining cash will then be distributed to the shareholders of the corporation. Subsequent to this distribution, the shares of the corporation will be canceled. This process is covered in more detail in Chapter 19.

16-68.   In this Chapter, we would note that ITA 84(2) indicates that the excess of the amount distributed over the PUC of the shares that are canceled is considered to be a deemed dividend. While ITA 84(2) defines this entire amount as a deemed dividend, some components of this total are, in effect, redefined under ITA 88(2)(b). Specifically, ITA 88(2)(b) indicates that the ITA 84(2) dividend will be dealt with as follows:

Distribution Of Pre-1972 CSOH   To the extent that the corporation has a pre-1972 CSOH balance, the distribution of this amount will be deemed not to be a dividend. Mere mortals may have trouble grasping the awkward manner in which this balance has been dealt with. It was deemed to be a dividend by ITA 84(2). Now we find that ITA 88(2)(b) has deemed this deemed dividend not to be a deemed dividend.

Capital Dividend   To the extent that the corporation has a balance in its capital dividend account, ITA 88(2)(b) indicates that this amount of the distribution will be considered a separate dividend, which will be received on a tax free basis under ITA 83(2). As was noted in our discussion of capital dividends, this treatment will only apply if an appropriate election is made.

Taxable Dividend   Any remaining distribution will be treated as a taxable dividend under ITA 84(2), subject to either the 45 percent or the 25 percent gross up and tax credit procedures.

16-69.   To illustrate these provisions, consider the following:

Example   After selling its assets and paying all of its liabilities, a corporation has cash of $1,200,000 available for distribution to its only shareholder. The PUC of the company's shares is $100,000 and this is also their adjusted cost base. The balance in the capital dividend account is $175,000. The company makes the appropriate election to have the distribution of the $175,000 treated as a capital dividend under ITA 83(2). There is no pre-1972 CSOH balance.

Analysis   The analysis of the $1,200,000 distribution would be as follows:

Cash Distributed	$1,200,000
PUC Of Shares	(100,000)
ITA 84(2) Deemed Dividend	$1,100,000
ITA 83(2) Capital Dividend	(175,000)
ITA 88(2)(b) Wind-Up Dividend	$ 925,000

Depending on whether the $925,000 wind-up dividend is designated as eligible or non-eligible, it would be subject to either the 45 percent or the 25 percent gross up and tax credit procedures.

16-70.   From the point of view of the shareholder, there has been a disposition of his shares. This creates a problem in that the amount received as proceeds of disposition for the shares includes taxable dividends as indicated in the preceding example.

16-71.   However, this problem is resolved by the ITA 54 definition of "proceeds of disposition". This definition indicates that, to the extent that an amount received is considered to be a deemed dividend under ITA 84(2), it is excluded from the proceeds of disposition. This means that the capital gain on the disposition of the shares in the example would be calculated as follows:

Proceeds Of Disposition	$1,200,000
ITA 84(2) Deemed Dividend	(1,100,000)
ITA 54 Proceeds Of Disposition	$ 100,000
Adjusted Cost Base	(100,000)
Capital Gain	$ Nil

Exercise Sixteen-6

Subject: ITA 84(2) Deemed Dividends

After selling its assets and paying all of its liabilities, a corporation has cash of $2,350,000 available for distribution to its only shareholder. The corporation was established 20 years ago with an investment of $250,000. This figure is both the PUC and the adjusted cost base of the shares. The balance in the capital dividend account is $340,000 and the company makes the appropriate election to have the distribution of this amount be treated as a capital dividend under ITA 83(2).   What are the tax consequences of distributing the $2,350,000 to the corporation's only shareholder?

End of Exercise. Solution available in Study Guide.

Deemed Dividends Under ITA 84(3) -
On Redemption, Acquisition, Or Cancellation Of Shares

16-72.   An ITA 84(3) deemed dividend occurs most commonly when a corporation redeems some of its outstanding shares. Such dividends can also occur when the corporation acquires or cancels some of its outstanding shares. To the extent that the redemption amount paid by the corporation exceeds the PUC of the shares redeemed, a deemed dividend is assessed under ITA 84(3). For the corporation, this is a distribution of their unrestricted surplus balance.

16-73. From the point of view of the person receiving the redemption proceeds, the deemed dividend component of the proceeds will be treated as an ordinary taxable dividend, subject to either the 45 percent or the 25 percent gross up and tax credit procedures. However, the transaction also involves a disposition of the shares being redeemed, with the redemption proceeds being the amount received from the corporation.

16-74. The problem with this is that, unlike the proceeds of disposition in an ordinary capital asset disposition, a portion of the amount received here is subject to tax as a deemed dividend. As was the case with ITA 84(2) dividends, this problem is resolved by the ITA 54 definition of proceeds of disposition. This definition excludes any amounts received that are deemed to be ITA 84(3) dividends.

Example   Mr. Jonas owns all of the preferred shares of Jonas Ltd. They were issued with a PUC of $75,000. However, their adjusted cost base to Mr. Jonas is $25,000. They are redeemed by the corporation for $200,000.

Analysis   The analysis of this transaction is as follows:

Cash Distributed	$200,000
PUC Of Shares Redeemed	(75,000)
ITA 84(3) Deemed Dividend	$125,000

The deemed dividend would be subject to either the 45 percent or the 25 percent gross up and tax credit procedures. The capital gain would be calculated as follows:

Proceeds Of Redemption	$200,000
Less: ITA 84(3) Deemed Dividend	(125,000)
ITA 54 Proceeds Of Disposition	$ 75,000
Adjusted Cost Base	(25,000)
Capital Gain (PUC - ACB)	$ 50,000
Inclusion Rate	1/2
Taxable Capital Gain	$ 25,000

Exercise Sixteen-7

Subject: ITA 84(3) Deemed Dividends

When first incorporated, Tandy Ltd. issued 233,000 common shares in return for $1,922,250 in cash ($8.25 per share). All of the shares were issued to Ms. Jessy Tandy, the founder of the Company. Except for 15,000 shares, she is still holding all of the originally issued shares. The 15,000 shares were sold to Ms. Tandy's brother, Jesuiah, for $10.57 per share, the estimated market value of the shares at that time. Because of ongoing difficulties between the two siblings, Ms. Tandy has arranged for Tandy Ltd. to redeem all of her brother's shares at a price of $11.75 per share during the current year. Determine the tax consequences of this redemption to Ms. Tandy and Ms. Tandy's brother, Jesuiah.

End of Exercise.   Solution available in Study Guide.

Deemed Dividends Under ITA 84(4) And ITA 84(4.1)

16-75. This type of dividend is not as common as the other deemed dividends we have discussed. It arises when a corporation resident in Canada distributes a part of its invested capital to its shareholders, without redeeming or canceling any of its shares. It might occur, for example, if a corporation divested itself of a major division and did not wish to reinvest the proceeds from the sale in other corporate assets. In this type of situation, the proceeds may be distributed to shareholders. Such distributions are commonly referred to as liquidating dividends.

16-76.   In order to make all, or part, of the distribution tax free, it is usually accompanied by a reduction in PUC. If the reduction in PUC is equal to the amount distributed, no dividend arises. However, if the distribution exceeds the PUC reduction, an ITA 84(4) deemed dividend is created. The rules for determining this dividend depend on whether or not the shares of the company are publicly traded.

> **Example** Jong Ltd., a CCPC, has shares with a PUC of $5,000,000. As it has disposed of a major division for cash, it will distribute $1,000,000 to its shareholders. In order to limit the tax effects of this distribution, the PUC of the shares will be reduced by $700,000.

> **Analysis** Under ITA 84(4), $700,000 of the total distribution will be a tax free distribution of PUC. The remaining $300,000 is treated as a deemed dividend, subject to the usual gross up and tax credit procedures. The adjusted cost base of the shares would be reduced by $700,000, the amount of the tax free distribution to shareholders. However, there would be no reduction in the adjusted cost base for the $300,000 distribution as it would be subject to tax as a deemed dividend.

16-77.   ITA 84(4.1) provides a different rule that overrides ITA 84(4) in the case of public companies. For these companies, if a payment is made to shareholders in conjunction with a reduction of PUC that is not part of a reorganization of the corporation's business or its capital, and there is no redemption, acquisition, or cancellation of shares, the entire distribution is generally treated as a deemed dividend. (ITA 84(3) would be applicable if there was a redemption, acquisition, or cancellation of shares.)

16-78.   With respect to our example, this means that, if Jong Ltd. is a public company, the entire $1,000,000 distribution will be considered to be a deemed dividend under ITA 84(4.1). As the $1,000,000 amount will be subject to tax, the adjusted cost base of the shares will not be reduced by this distribution.

16-79.   There is an exception to this general rule for public corporations. If the payment can reasonably be considered to be derived from a transaction that is outside the ordinary course of business for the corporation, it can be considered a tax free return of capital to the extent that it is accompanied by a PUC reduction.

16-80.   An example of this would be where the company disposes of a business unit of the corporation and does not wish to reinvest the proceeds in some other line of business activity. The distribution would have to be made within 24 months of the occurrence of the non-ordinary transaction and the exception would only apply to the first such payment made. If there is more than one payment, the second and any subsequent payments would come under the general ITA 84(4.1) deemed dividend rule.

Exercise Sixteen-8

Subject: ITA 84(4) Deemed Dividends

Mr. Jondo owns all of the outstanding shares of Jondo Ltd., a CCPC. The shares have a PUC of $450,000 and an adjusted cost base of $625,000. Because it has recently consolidated its operations, Jondo Ltd. pays a liquidating dividend of $330,000, accompanied by a PUC reduction of $225,000. What are the tax consequences of this distribution to Mr. Jondo?

End of Exercise. Solution available in Study Guide.

Refundable Taxes On Investment Income

Meaning Of Aggregate Investment Income

16-81.   In the following material on refundable taxes, we will be using the term "investment income". For purposes of determining the amount of refundable taxes available, this term has a very specific meaning. Further, it is not the usual meaning that we associate with this term. Under ITA 129(4), the relevant "aggregate investment income" is defined as follows:

- Net taxable capital gains for the year, reduced by any net capital loss carry overs deducted during the year.

- Income from property including interest, rents, and royalties, but excluding dividends that are deductible in computing Taxable Income. Since foreign dividends are generally not deductible, they would be included in aggregate investment income.

16-82.   Note carefully the differences between this "aggregate investment income" and what we normally think of as property or investment income. Unlike the normal definition of property or investment income, this concept includes net taxable capital gains for the current year, reduced by net capital loss carry overs deducted during the year.

16-83.   The other difference between aggregate investment income and the usual definition of investment income is that it excludes most dividends from other Canadian corporations. This reflects the fact that dividends from Canadian corporations generally flow through a corporation without being subject to corporate taxes. You should also note that aggregate investment income includes income from both Canadian and foreign sources.

Basic Concepts

The Problem

16-84.   As shown in Figure 16-1, when income is flowed through a corporation, it is subject to two levels of taxation. It is taxed first at the corporate level and, if the after tax corporate amount is distributed to the individual shareholder, it will be taxed again in the hands of that individual. If we assume that the corporate tax rate on the investment income of a CCPC is 45 percent and that the individual shareholder is taxed at a rate of 30 percent on non-eligible dividends received, the overall rate of taxation on investment income flowed through a corporation would be 61.5 percent [45% + (1 - 45%)(30%)].

16-85.   If the same individual had received the investment income directly, without it having been flowed through a corporation, the individual's tax rate on investment income would have been about 45 percent. This difference is clearly not consistent with the concept of integration, which attempts to neutralize the influence of using a corporation on the after tax amount of income received by an individual.

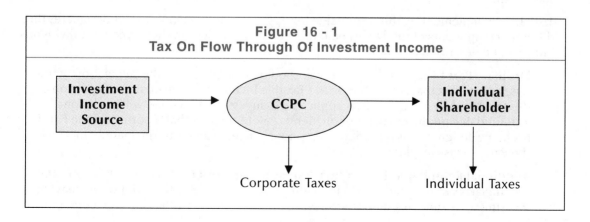

Figure 16 - 1
Tax On Flow Through Of Investment Income

The Solution

16-86.   The most obvious solution to this problem would be to lower the rate of corporate taxation on the investment income of a CCPC. For example, if the corporate rate was lowered to 21 percent, the overall rate on the flow through of income would be taxed at 45 percent [21% + (1 - 21%)(30%)]. This is within the range of rates that are applied to individuals that receive business or property income directly.

16-87.   The problem with this solution is that it would provide for a significant deferral of taxes on investment income. If an individual received the investment income directly, the full amount of taxes must be paid when the income is earned. In contrast, when a corporation is used, only the first, or corporate level, of taxation is assessed when the income is earned. If the after tax amount is left in the corporation, the assessment of the individual level of tax can be deferred indefinitely.

16-88.   For higher income individuals who do not require their investment income for current expenditures, this would present an outstanding opportunity for tax deferral. This would be the case whenever the corporate tax rate on investment income was below the rate applicable to the individual on the direct receipt of income.

16-89.   Given the opportunity for tax deferral that would result from the use of lower corporate tax rates, it is not surprising that a different solution to the problem of excessive tax rates on the flow through of a CCPC's investment income has been adopted. This solution involves leaving the corporate tax rate at a high level, but having a portion of the tax being designated as refundable. The refund of this portion of the corporate tax occurs when the income is distributed in the form of dividends that will be subject to the second level of taxation in the hands of the shareholders.

16-90.   We would remind you that, in keeping with this concept of keeping the basic rate high, aggregate investment income of a CCPC is excluded from the definition of Full Rate Taxable Income and, as a consequence, is not eligible for the general rate reduction.

Refundable Tax Procedures

16-91.   While the detailed procedures related to these refundable taxes are complex, the basic concept is not. Some part of the tax paid on investment income at the corporate level is refunded when the income is distributed to investors in the form of dividends. This keeps the corporate tax rate in line with the rate that would be applicable to an individual on the direct receipt of income. This rate of corporate tax discourages tax deferral, while at the same time, the refund procedures avoid the excessive rate of taxation that would occur if a high corporate tax rate was combined with individual taxes on the same income stream.

16-92.   Stated simply, the use of a refundable tax allows the government to charge a corporate tax rate that is high enough to remove much of the incentive for accumulating investment income in a corporation and, at the same time, provides a reasonable overall rate of taxation when the income is flowed through the corporation and taxed in the hands of the individual shareholder.

16-93.   In implementing this refundable tax approach, the *Income Tax Act* designates three different components of total taxes paid that can be refunded on the payment of dividends. They can be described as follows:

Ordinary Part I Tax   At this point, you should be familiar with the calculation of the regular Part I tax that is assessed on the Taxable Income of a corporation. A portion of this tax, basically the part that is applicable to investment income, will be designated as refundable on the payment of dividends. Note the fact that a portion of the Part I tax being designated as refundable does not change, in any way, the manner in which the Part I tax is calculated.

Additional Refundable Tax On Investment Income (ART)   In the early 1990s, the provincial tax rates applicable to individuals had increased to the point where leaving investment income in a corporation was attractive, despite the fairly high combined rate of federal/provincial taxes on this type of income earned by a corporation. In order to discourage the use of corporations to defer tax on investment income, it was felt that a higher rate of corporate taxation was required. To implement this view, an additional Part I tax was added under ITA 123.3, applicable only to the aggregate investment income of CCPCs.

This additional refundable tax, often referred to by the acronym ART, is assessed at a rate of 6-2/3 percent on the investment income of CCPCs, and is refundable when the corporation pays dividends. This tax will be given detailed consideration in this Chapter. It might be noted that this tax has been left in place, despite the fact that, in more recent years, provincial tax rates on individuals have fallen, in some cases fairly dramatically (e.g., Ontario and Alberta).

Part IV Tax   Even with the Part I refundable tax and ART in place, there is still the possibility of using a related group of corporations to defer taxation on investment income. The Part IV refundable tax is a 33-1/3 percent tax on certain intercorporate dividends that is designed to prevent this from happening. This Part IV tax will also be given detailed consideration in this Chapter.

16-94.   In dealing with this material, we will first consider the issues involved with a single corporation. In these single corporation situations, only the refundable Part I tax and the additional refundable tax on investment income will be considered.

Refundable Part I Tax On Investment Income

Additional Refundable Tax On Investment Income (ART)

Basic Calculations

16-95.   As was noted previously, tax legislation contains a refundable tax on the investment income of a Canadian controlled private corporation (CCPC). This additional refundable tax (ART) is assessed under ITA 123.3, with the amount payable equal to 6-2/3 percent of the lesser of:

- the corporation's "aggregate investment income" for the year [as defined in ITA 129(4)]; and

- the amount, if any, by which the corporation's Taxable Income for the year exceeds the amount that is eligible for the small business deduction.

16-96.   The basic objective of this tax is to make it less attractive to shelter investment income within a corporate structure in order to defer full taxation of the amounts earned. When this additional 6-2/3 percent is added to the usual rates applicable to a CCPC's investment income, the combined rate is in the 46 to 52 percent range. This is made up of 36 percent at the federal level [(38% - 10%)(104%) + 6-2/3%], plus 10 percent to 16 percent at the provincial level. As noted in Chapter 6, the combined federal/provincial maximum rates on individuals range from 39 to 48.6 percent.

16-97.   This means that, with the addition of the ART, rates on the investment income of a CCPC will generally be higher than the rates applicable to an individual receiving the same income. Given this, there is little or no incentive to use a corporation to defer taxation on this type of income.

16-98.   As described in Paragraph 16-95, the ART is based on the lesser of aggregate investment income and the amount of Taxable Income that is not eligible for the small business deduction. The reason for the latter limit is to ensure that such deductions as charitable donations or non-capital loss carry overs have not totally or partially eliminated the investment income from the amount flowing through to Taxable Income. The goal is to prevent the ART from being inappropriately applied to active business income.

Exercise Sixteen-9

Subject: Additional Refundable Tax On Investment Income

Zircon Inc. is a CCPC with a December 31 year end. Zircon is not associated with any other company. For the 2007 taxation year, its Net Income For Tax Purposes is equal to $281,000. This is made up of active business income of $198,000, dividends from taxable Canadian corporations of $22,000, taxable capital gains of $46,000 and interest income of $15,000. The Company also has a net capital loss carry forward from 2005 of $26,000 and a non-capital loss carry forward of $23,000. The Company intends to deduct both of these carry forwards in the 2007 taxation year. For the 2007 taxation year, determine Zircon's Taxable Income and its additional refundable tax on investment income.

End of Exercise. Solution available in Study Guide.

ART And Foreign Tax Credit Calculations

16-99.   As discussed in Chapter 15, the use of foreign taxes paid as credits against Canadian Tax Payable is limited by a formula that includes the "tax otherwise payable". In the case of foreign taxes paid on non-business income, the "tax otherwise payable" in the formula includes the ART that is assessed under ITA 123.3.

16-100.   This creates a potential problem in that the calculation of the ART includes the amount eligible for the small business deduction [ITA 123.3(b)]. Since one of the factors limiting the small business deduction [ITA 125(1)(b)] is Taxable Income reduced by 10/3 of the foreign non-business income tax credit and 3 times the foreign business income tax credit, this could have created an insolvable circular calculation.

16-101.   To avoid this problem, ITA 125(1)(b)(i) was modified in a manner that, for the purpose of calculating the small business deduction, permits the foreign tax credit for taxes paid on foreign non-business income to be calculated using a "tax otherwise payable" figure that does not include the ART under ITA 123.3.

16-102.   A further potential problem arises from the fact that the "tax otherwise payable" in the foreign tax credit calculation also includes the effects of the general rate reduction under ITA 123.4. As the calculation of this amount also requires knowing the amount of income that is eligible for the small business deduction, a second circularity issue arises. It is dealt with in a similar fashion by indicating that, for the purpose of determining the small business deduction, both of the foreign tax credit amounts will be calculated using a "tax otherwise payable" figure that excludes any reduction under ITA 123.4.

16-103. This means that in situations where the small business deduction, foreign tax credits, and the ART are involved, the following procedures should be used:

1. Calculate the foreign non-business tax credit using a "tax otherwise payable" figure that excludes both ITA 123.3 (ART) and ITA 123.4 (general rate reduction). This initial version of the foreign non-business tax credit will be used only for the purpose of determining the small business deduction, with the actual credit available calculated after the ITA 123.3 and 123.4 amounts have been determined.

2. Calculate the foreign business tax credit using a "tax otherwise payable" figure that excludes ITA 123.4 (as business income is involved, ITA 123.3 is excluded by definition). However, this credit is limited by the amount of tax otherwise payable, reduced by the foreign non-business tax credit. As a consequence, it will be necessary to calculate an initial version of this foreign business tax credit, using the initial version of the foreign non-business tax credit. This initial version will be used only for the purpose of determining the small business deduction.

3. Calculate the amount eligible for the small business deduction using the numbers determined in steps 1 and 2.

4. Using the amount eligible for the small business deduction determined in step 3, calculate the ART and the general rate reduction.

5. Calculate the actual foreign non-business tax credit using a "tax otherwise payable" figure that includes the ART and the general rate reduction determined in step 4.

6. Calculate the actual foreign business tax credit using the actual foreign non-business tax credit determined in step 5 and the general rate reduction from step 4.

Problem One: Excessive Tax Rates On The Flow Through Of A CCPC's Investment Income

16-104.   With the addition of the 6-2/3 percent ART on the investment income of a Canadian controlled private corporation, this investment income will be taxed at an overall federal rate of 36 percent [(38% - 10%)(104%) + 6-2/3%]. With the addition of provincial taxes at corporate rates ranging from 10 percent to 16 percent, the combined federal/provincial rate on this income will range from 46 percent to 52 percent.

16-105.   All of these combined rates are more than double the 20 percent rate required for perfect integration (the 20 percent rate is used as the investment income of a CCPC cannot be used as a basis for paying eligible dividends). In the absence of some type of relieving mechanism, the objective of integrating corporate and individual tax rates would not be met.

16-106.   The problem of excessive rates of tax on investment income flowed through a corporation was discussed previously in Paragraph 16-84. A more complete example will be presented here.

Example   Mr. Monroe has investments that generate interest income of $100,000 per year. He is subject to a combined federal/provincial tax rate of 43.5 percent. The dividend tax credit in his province of residence is equal to one-third of the gross up. Calculate the amount of cash Mr. Monroe will retain from this investment income under the following alternative assumptions:

Case A   He receives the $100,000 in interest income directly.

Case B   Mr. Monroe is the sole shareholder of a Canadian controlled private corporation that earns the $100,000 of investment income. The corporation is subject to a combined federal/provincial tax rate, including the ITA 123.3 tax on investment income, of 50 percent. The corporation pays out all of its after tax earnings as non-eligible dividends, resulting in a dividend to Mr. Monroe of $50,000. Ignore any refund of Part I tax paid.

16-107.   The calculations comparing the investment income if it was received directly (Case A) and if it was earned through a corporation (Case B), are as follows:

Case A - Investment Income Received Directly

Investment Income - Direct Receipt	$100,000
Personal Tax At 43.5 Percent	(43,500)
After Tax Cash Retained Without Corporation	$ 56,500

Case B - Investment Income Flowed Through Corporation

Corporate Investment Income	$100,000
Corporate Tax At 50 Percent (Includes The ART)	(50,000)
Non-Eligible Dividends Paid To Mr. Monroe	$ 50,000

Non-Eligible Dividends Received	$ 50,000
Gross Up Of 25 Percent	12,500
Personal Taxable Income	$ 62,500
Personal Tax Rate	43.5%
Tax Payable Before Dividend Tax Credit	$ 27,188
Dividend Tax Credit [(2/3 + 1/3)(Gross Up)]	(12,500)
Personal Tax Payable With Corporation	**$ 14,688**
Non-Eligible Dividends Received	$ 50,000
Personal Tax Payable	(14,688)
After Tax Cash Retained With Corporation	**$ 35,312**

Savings - Direct Receipt

Income Received Directly	$ 56,500
Income Flowed Through Corporation	35,312
Net Savings On Direct Receipt	**$ 21,188**

16-108.   The results show that, in the absence of the refundable component of Part I tax, interest income flowed through a corporation is subject to an effective tax rate of nearly 65 percent [($100,000 - $35,312) ÷ $100,000]. This is significantly higher than the 43.5 percent rate that is applicable to the direct receipt of the investment income, an outcome that would represent a major failure in the government's attempt to achieve integration.

16-109.   Before leaving this example you should note that, with the inclusion of the ART on investment income, there is no deferral advantage associated with using a corporation. Prior to the introduction of this tax, in some situations, the amount of tax paid at the corporate level on investment income was less than the amount that would be paid by an individual receiving the income directly. This is no longer the case. In our example, corporate taxes alone are $50,000, well in excess of the $43,500 that would be paid if Mr. Monroe had received the income directly.

16-110.   Even if we use the highest provincial rates on individuals in effect in Canada (48.64% combined rate), taxes at the corporate level in our example would still be higher than taxes on the direct receipt of the income. As was the intent of the government, the ART has eliminated any significant tax advantage associated with using a corporation to defer taxes on investment income. In fact, in view of the current provincial rates on individuals, the 6-2/3 percent ART may constitute overkill.

Solution To Problem One: Refundable Portion Of Part I Tax

Basic Concepts

16-111.   The preceding example makes it clear that taxes on investment income earned by a corporation and flowed through to its shareholders are potentially much higher than would be the case if the shareholders received the income directly. This major imperfection in the system of integration results from a federal/provincial tax rate on the investment income of CCPCs that is generally around 50 percent.

16-112.   In those cases where the income is retained in the corporation, this is an equitable arrangement in that this high rate discourages the use of a CCPC to temporarily shelter passive income from a portion of the taxes that would be assessed on the direct receipt of the income by the individual. However, when the investment income is flowed through a CCPC and paid as dividends, the result is not consistent with the government's desire to tax CCPCs under the integration view of corporate taxation.

16-113.   As noted previously, the government could have dealt with this problem by reducing the corporate tax rate on the investment income of CCPCs. However, this would have allowed the owners of CCPCs to defer personal taxes on this income by leaving the investment income in the corporation. To avoid this, the refundable tax approach is used.

16-114.   Under this approach, the investment income of Canadian controlled private corporations is taxed at the usual high rates, including the ART on investment income. However, when the corporation distributes its after tax income in the form of dividends, a part of this tax is refunded. The refund is based on the amount of dividends paid by the corporation, with the refund being equal to $1 for each $3 of dividends paid.

Concepts Illustrated

16-115.   In order to give you a better understanding of how the concepts associated with the refund of Part I tax work, we will use an example based on the corporate tax rates that are inherent in the integration procedures contained in the *Income Tax Act*. You will recall that, for non-eligible dividends, the dividend gross up and tax credit procedures are based on an assumed rate of corporate tax of 20 percent. In our example, we will assume that this is the combined federal/provincial rate applicable to income eligible for the small business deduction.

16-116.   For income that is not eligible for the small business deduction, we will assume a combined federal/provincial rate of 40 percent. This is before the addition of the ART and without the benefit of the general rate reduction (not available on the aggregate investment income of a CCPC). While this is somewhat lower than most of the combined rates, the use of these notional rates will permit us to illustrate how integration is supposed to work in this situation. We will subsequently present a second example that uses more realistic rates.

16-117.   The basic idea here is that the investment income of a Canadian controlled private corporation will be taxed at a rate of 46-2/3 percent (the 40 percent described in the preceding Paragraph, plus the ART of 6-2/3 percent). When the residual after tax income is paid out in dividends, a refund of the tax in excess of 20 percent will be provided. This can be accomplished by providing a dividend refund equal to $1 for each $3 of dividends paid. These ideas can be illustrated with the following example:

Example   Ms. Banardi has investments that generate interest income of $100,000 per year. You have been asked to advise her as to whether there would be any benefits associated with transferring these investments to her wholly owned Canadian controlled private corporation. Ms. Banardi is subject to a combined federal/provincial tax rate of 43.5 percent on her individual Taxable Income and the non-eligible dividend tax credit in her province is equal to one-third of the gross up. Her corporation would be taxed on this income at a combined federal/provincial rate of 46-2/3 percent, including the ART on investment income.

16-118.   The calculations comparing the after tax investment income if it was earned in a corporation and if it was received directly, are as follows:

Corporate Investment Income	$100,000
Corporate Tax At 46-2/3 Percent (Includes The ART)	(46,667)
After Tax Income	$ 53,333
Dividend Refund (See Note)	26,667
Non-Eligible Dividends Paid To Ms. Banardi	$ 80,000

Note In these somewhat academic examples of the dividend refund mechanism, it is assumed that all of the after tax income of the corporation will be paid out as dividends. As this will trigger a $1 for $3 refund ($26,667 ÷ $80,000), the after tax balance represents two-thirds of the dividend ($53,333 ÷ $80,000). This means that the amount of the refund will be calculated as one-half (1/3 ÷ 2/3) of the after tax balance of corporate income. This approach is not consistent with the real world approach in which the amount of the dividend is determined by a variety of factors (e.g., availability of cash or alternative investment opportunities) and the refund is calculated as one-third of the amount paid.

Non-Eligible Dividends Received	$ 80,000
Gross Up Of 25 Percent	20,000
Personal Taxable Income	$100,000
Personal Tax Rate	43.5%
Tax Payable Before Dividend Tax Credit	$ 43,500
Dividend Tax Credit [(2/3 + 1/3)(Gross Up)]	(20,000)
Personal Tax Payable With Corporation	**$ 23,500**

Non-Eligible Dividends Received	$ 80,000
Personal Tax Payable	(23,500)
After Tax Cash Retained With Corporation	**$ 56,500**

Investment Income - Direct Receipt	$100,000
Personal Tax At 43.5 Percent	(43,500)
After Tax Cash Retained Without Corporation	**$ 56,500**

16-119.   The same amount of after tax cash is retained under both scenarios, demonstrating that this refundable tax restores integration to the system with respect to total taxes paid. Also of importance is the fact that the use of a corporation has not provided any tax deferral. Corporate taxes prior to the refund total $46,667, an amount that is in excess of the $43,500 in taxes that would be paid by Ms. Banardi on direct receipt of the income.

Use Of Other Rates In Refundable Part I Tax Example

16-120.   The preceding example is useful in that it illustrates how perfectly integration can work if the appropriate rates are used. As has been discussed in Chapters 6 and 15, there is considerable variance in provincial rates for both corporations and individuals. Not surprisingly, these variations will influence how well the integration measures succeed. In order to illustrate this effect, we will present the following second example using different rates.

Example   Mr. Leoni has investments that generate interest income of $100,000 per year. He has over $200,000 in other income and is subject to a combined federal/provincial tax rate of 47 percent. The provincial dividend tax credit is equal to 25 percent of the gross up. Mr. Leoni is the sole shareholder of a Canadian controlled private corporation and is considering the transfer of these investments to his corporation. His corporation would be taxed on this income at a combined federal/provincial rate of 51.8 percent, including the ART on investment income [(38% - 10%)(104%) + 6-2/3% + 16%].

16-121.   The calculations comparing the after tax investment income if it was earned through a corporation and if it was received directly, are as follows:

Corporate Investment Income	$100,000
Corporate Tax At 51.8 Percent (Includes The ART)	(51,800)
After Tax Income	$ 48,200
Dividend Refund ($1 For Each $3 Of Dividends Paid)	24,100
Non-Eligible Dividends Paid To Mr. Leoni	**$ 72,300**

Non-Eligible Dividends Received	$ 72,300
Gross Up Of 25 Percent	18,075
Personal Taxable Income	$ 90,375
Personal Tax Rate	47%
Tax Payable Before Dividend Tax Credit	$ 42,476
Dividend Tax Credit [(2/3 + 25%)($18,075)]	(16,569)
Personal Tax Payable With Corporation	**$ 25,907**

Non-Eligible Dividends Received	$ 72,300
Personal Tax Payable	(25,907)
After Tax Cash Retained With Corporation	**$ 46,393**

Investment Income - Direct Receipt	$100,000
Personal Tax At 47 Percent	(47,000)
After Tax Cash Retained Without Corporation	**$ 53,000**

16-122.   While the numbers are quite different, the conclusion on deferral is the same as the one for the example presented in Paragraph 16-117. Corporate taxes before the refund are $51,800, significantly higher than the $47,000 that would have been paid if Mr. Leoni had received the income directly. As was the case in the previous example, the use of a corporation does not provide tax deferral. In fact, the opposite is true in that, when a corporation is used, there is actually a prepayment of a larger amount of tax.

16-123.   With respect to the after tax flow through of income, in our previous example the use of a corporation was neutral. After tax income was the same, without regard to whether a corporation was used. This is not the case here. After the income is flowed through the corporation, Mr. Leoni retains only $46,393, significantly less than the $53,000 he would have retained on the direct receipt of income. With the use of these fairly realistic numbers, there is clearly a tax disadvantage in flowing investment income through a CCPC. In this example, both the high provincial tax rate on the corporation and the low provincial dividend tax credit rate are unfavourable to the use of a corporation.

Exercise Sixteen-10

Subject: Flow Through Of Investment Income

Ms. Shelly Nicastro has investments that generate interest income of $100,000 per year. Due to her employment income, she is in the top tax bracket, with a combined federal/provincial rate of 49 percent. She is considering the transfer of these investments to her CCPC which would be subject to a tax rate on investment income of 48 percent. The dividend tax credit in her province is equal to 40 percent of the gross up. Any dividends paid by the CCPC out of investment income will be non-eligible. Advise her as to whether there would be any tax benefits associated with this transfer.

End of Exercise.   Solution available in Study Guide.

Refundable Part IV Tax On Dividends Received

Problem Two: Use Of Multi-Level Affiliations To Defer Taxes On Investment Income

16-124.   In the preceding section, we demonstrated how refund procedures applicable to Part I tax payable are used to lower the overall rate of taxation on the investment income of a CCPC, while at the same time preventing the use of a corporation to defer a portion of the overall taxation on such income. While varying provincial tax rates on corporations and individuals prevent these procedures from providing perfect results, they appear to produce results that come close to achieving the goal of integration of personal and corporate taxes.

16-125.   The situation becomes more complex when a group of related companies is involved. The refundable tax procedures that were previously described are not effective in preventing tax deferral in this case. As a result, there is a need for additional procedures.

Refundable Part IV Tax On Dividends Received

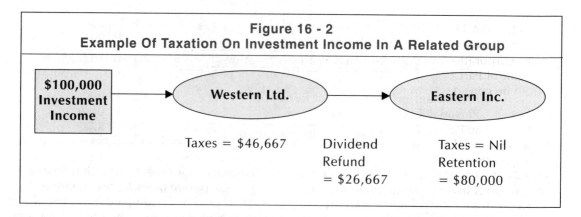

Figure 16 - 2
Example Of Taxation On Investment Income In A Related Group

16-126.   As an example of this type of situation, Eastern Inc. has a 100 percent owned subsidiary, Western Ltd. Both Companies are Canadian controlled private corporations and have a December 31 year end. During the year ending December 31, 2007, Western has income of $100,000, made up entirely of interest and taxable capital gains. Assume that the combined federal/provincial tax rate for both Companies is 40 percent (including the corporate surtax, but before the ART). Western pays out all of its after tax income in dividends to Eastern Inc. This situation is illustrated in Figure 16-2.

16-127.   On receipt of the $100,000 of investment income, Western would pay taxes of $46,667, including the ART. However, when the remaining $53,333 is paid out in dividends, a refund of $26,667 (one-third of the $80,000 total dividend) becomes available, resulting in a total dividend of $80,000 as shown in the following calculation:

Investment Income		$100,000
Basic Corporate Tax At 40 Percent	($40,000)	
ART At 6-2/3 Percent	(6,667)	(46,667)
Income Before Dividends		$ 53,333
Dividend Refund ($1 For Each $3 Of Dividends Paid)		26,667
Dividends Paid To Eastern		$ 80,000

16-128.   As the dividends from Western will be received tax free by Eastern, they will have after tax retention of $80,000. Until such time as Eastern pays out taxable dividends to its shareholders, no additional Part I tax will be assessed. This means that, in the absence of additional procedures for dealing with this type of situation, there would be a significant deferral of taxes on investment income resulting from the use of two related corporations.

Solution To Problem Two: Refundable Part IV Tax
Corporations Subject To Part IV Tax

16-129.   To eliminate this potential flaw in integration, a Part IV tax is assessed on dividends received by a private corporation from certain other types of corporations. Note that this tax is assessed without regard to whether or not the private corporation is Canadian controlled.

16-130.   In general, only private corporations are liable for Part IV tax. However, there remains the possibility that a company that is controlled largely for the benefit of an individual, or a related group of individuals, might use a small issue of shares to the public in order to avoid this tax. Such corporations are referred to as subject corporations and they are defined in ITA 186(3) as follows:

> **Subject Corporation**   means a corporation (other than a private corporation) resident in Canada and controlled, whether because of a beneficial interest in one or more trusts or otherwise, by or for the benefit of an individual (other than a trust) or a related group of individuals (other than trusts).

16-131.   ITA 186(1) indicates that, for purposes of Part IV tax, subject corporations will be treated as private corporations. This means that both private corporations, as well as those public corporations that fall within the definition of subject corporations, will be liable for the payment of Part IV tax. In this Chapter, any subsequent references to private corporations should be considered to include subject corporations.

Rates
16-132.   The Part IV tax is assessed at a rate of 33-1/3 percent. It is applicable to portfolio dividends as well as some dividends from connected corporations (both of these terms will be subsequently explained). The rate at which this tax is refunded is the same as the rate for refunds of Part I tax. Refunds of Part IV tax are equal to $1 for each $3 of dividends paid. Corporate tax instalment calculations do not take into consideration the Part IV tax liability.

Applicable Dividends
16-133.   The Part IV tax is not applicable to all of the dividends received by a private corporation. Specifically, Part IV tax is payable on dividends received by private corporations in the following circumstances:

- A dividend is received from an unconnected company that is deductible in the calculation of the recipient's Taxable Income. While the *Income Tax Act* refers to such dividends as "assessable dividends", it is a common practice to refer to such dividends as "portfolio dividends", a practice we will follow in the remainder of this text.

- The dividend is received from a connected company, and the company paying the dividend received a refund as a consequence of making the dividend payment.

16-134.   Each of these types of dividends will be given attention in the material which follows.

Part IV Tax On Portfolio Dividends Received
Portfolio Dividends And Connected Corporations Defined
16-135.   A portfolio dividend is defined as a dividend received by a private corporation from a corporation to which it is not connected, and that is deductible in the determination of the private corporation's Taxable Income. As with many *Income Tax Act* terms, the definition of a portfolio dividend includes another term which requires definition. This term is "connected corporation" and the definition is found in ITA 186(4). Under this definition, a connected corporation is either:

- a controlled corporation, where control represents ownership of more than 50 percent of the voting shares by any combination of the other corporation and persons with whom it does not deal at arm's length, or

- a corporation in which the other corporation owns more than 10 percent of the voting shares, and more than 10 percent of the fair market value of all of the issued shares of the corporation.

16-136.   Given the definition of connected corporation, a 10 percent shareholding test is generally used to determine whether the dividends received are portfolio dividends or dividends from a connected corporation.

> **Example**   An example of a portfolio dividend would be a dividend received on an investment made by a private company in 500 shares of a large publicly traded company. The 500 shares would be significantly less than 10 percent of the total shares outstanding and would not constitute control of the company. As a consequence, the dividends would be considered portfolio dividends and the Part IV tax would be applicable.

Portfolio Dividends And Integration
16-137.   The tax policy issue with respect to portfolio dividends relates to integration. If such dividends are received by an individual, they are normally subject to taxation. For

example, assume that an individual receives $100,000 in eligible dividends from a large publicly traded company. If this individual is subject to a combined federal/provincial marginal rate of 44 percent and lives in a province with a dividend tax credit equal to 7/18 of the gross up, the resulting Tax Payable would be calculated as follows:

Eligible Dividends Received	$100,000
Gross Up Of 45 Percent	45,000
Taxable Income	$145,000
Personal Tax Rate	44%
Tax Payable Before Dividend Tax Credit	$ 63,800
Dividend Tax Credit [(11/18 + 7/18)(Gross Up)]	(45,000)
Personal Tax Payable	$ 18,800

16-138.   As an alternative, consider what would happen if the same $100,000 in dividends had been received by a corporation. Under the general rules for intercorporate dividends, the $100,000 would be deductible in the calculation of the corporation's Taxable Income, resulting in no Part I tax at the corporate level. While tax will ultimately be paid when the corporation distributes this income to its shareholders, there is a potential for significant deferral of taxes on this income stream.

16-139.   In order to correct this flaw in the corporate tax integration system, Part IV tax is applied as follows:

Part IV Tax - Portfolio Dividends   When a private corporation receives a dividend on shares that are being held as a portfolio investment, the recipient company is liable for a Part IV tax of 33-1/3 percent of the dividends received. This Part IV tax is refundable, on the basis of $1 for each $3 of dividends paid, when such dividends are passed on to the shareholders of the recipient corporation.

16-140.   We can see the reasoning behind the rate of this tax by referring back to the preceding example in Paragraph 16-137. You will notice that the effective tax rate on the dividends received by the individual is 18.8 percent ($18,800 ÷ $100,000). By charging a Part IV tax of 33-1/3 percent at the corporate level, the tax paid by the corporation is in excess of the 18.8 percent effective tax rate that would apply to dividends received by an individual with a tax rate of 44 percent. This makes it unattractive to use a private corporation as a shelter to defer the payment of taxes on dividend income. Again, however, by making the tax refundable, it allows the dividends to flow through the recipient corporation without a permanent increase in taxes.

Eligible Vs. Non-Eligible Dividends

16-141.   We would also note that with the introduction of the 45 percent gross up and tax credit procedures, the maximum rate that individuals will pay on dividends has been significantly reduced (if you apply the old 25 percent gross up and tax credit procedures to the example in Paragraph 16-137, the tax rate is 30 percent). Given this, a lower Part IV rate could have been introduced for eligible dividends.

16-142.   For example, reducing the rate from 33-1/3 percent to 20 percent could have been effective in preventing deferral at the corporate level when the maximum rate on dividends is 18.8 percent. The reason for not reducing the Part IV tax probably reflects the fact that some of the dividends that will generate a Part IV refund will be non-eligible dividends as they are paid out of a connected corporation's investment income. (See following text.)

Dividends From A Connected Corporation

The Investment Income Problem

16-143.   It is the intent of the government to allow a Canadian controlled private corporation to be used to defer taxes on active business income. Earning such income entitles the corporation to the use of the small business deduction and this, in most situations, provides a rate of corporate taxation that will effectively defer taxes on income left in the corporation. To the extent that a connected corporation is paying dividends out of such income, there will be no dividend refund and no Part IV tax to be paid by the recipient corporation. This maintains the tax deferral on active business income as it moves between corporations.

16-144.   However, when the connected corporation is a private company (whether or not it is Canadian controlled) and the dividends are paid out of investment income, a problem arises. This problem was illustrated by the example presented in Paragraph 16-126.

16-145.   In that example, Western paid an $80,000 dividend to Eastern, a payment that included a $26,667 refund of taxes previously paid by Western. Under the general rules for dividends, the $80,000 dividend paid by Western would be included in the calculation of Eastern's Net Income For Tax Purposes and deducted in the determination of its Taxable Income, with the net result that no Part I taxes would be paid on the $80,000. This would, in effect, allow retention of 80 percent of the investment income within the corporate group, a result that is contrary to the general concept of integration.

The Solution

16-146.   In order to correct this situation, a second application of Part IV tax is as follows:

> **Part IV Tax - Connected Companies**   When a private corporation receives dividends from a connected private corporation that has received a dividend refund under ITA 129(1) as a result of paying the dividends, the recipient company is liable for a Part IV tax equal to its share of the refund received by the paying corporation. If the dividend paid is eligible for a full $1 refund on each $3 paid, the Part IV tax can also be expressed as 33-1/3 percent of the dividends received.

> However, the payor corporation may be earning both active business income and investment income. In such situations, if dividends reflect a distribution of both types of income, the dividend refund will not be at the full $1 for $3 rate. (See the Paragraph 16-154 example.) This is why the Part IV tax on dividends received from a connected corporation is expressed in terms of the recipient's share of the refund received by the paying corporation, not in terms of a specific rate.

> As was the case with the Part IV tax on portfolio dividends, this Part IV tax is refundable on the basis of $1 for each $3 of dividends paid by the assessed corporation.

Example

16-147.   Returning to the example presented in Paragraph 16-126, you will recall that Western has $100,000 in investment income and pays maximum dividends of $80,000 to Eastern. When the Part IV tax is taken into consideration, the tax consequences for the two companies are as follows:

Investment Income Received By Western		$100,000
Basic Corporate Tax At 40 Percent	($40,000)	
ART At 6-2/3 Percent	(6,667)	(46,667)
Income Before Dividends		$ 53,333
Dividend Refund ($1 For Each $3 Of Dividends Paid)		26,667
Dividends Paid To Eastern		$ 80,000
Investment Income (Dividends Received From Western)		$80,000
Part IV Tax Payable (100% Of Western's Refund*)		(26,667)
Income Retained By Eastern		$53,333

*Because all of Western's income was from investments, the dividend refund to Western is the full $1 for each $3 of dividends. This means that Eastern's Part IV tax can also be calculated as 33-1/3% of the $80,000 in dividends received from Western.

16-148.   As this simple example shows, after the application of the Part IV tax, the amount retained in Eastern is the same $53,333 that was retained in Western. This retention reflects a tax rate on the amount retained within the corporate group of 46.7 percent [($100,000 - $53,333) ÷ $100,000], about the same rate that would be paid by an individual taxpayer on the direct receipt of the $100,000 in investment income. Clearly, the application of Part IV tax has served to maintain integration in situations involving connected companies.

16-149.   If Eastern decides to distribute the retained income to its shareholders, the results would be as follows:

Income Retained By Eastern	$53,333
Dividend Refund ($1 For Each $3 Of Dividends Paid)	26,667
Dividend To Shareholders	$80,000

16-150.   In effect, the $100,000 of investment income has passed through two corporations and into the hands of individual shareholders, subject to corporate taxes of only 20 percent. This has been accomplished, despite the fact that the initial level of corporate taxation was sufficiently high to discourage allocating investment income to a multi-level corporate structure.

16-151.   Note, however, because the overall level of corporate taxation is only 20 percent, the dividends paid out by Eastern will not be eligible dividends. The applicable gross up will only be 25 percent and the federal dividend tax credit will be two-thirds of the gross up.

Applicability

16-152.   We would remind you again that the Part IV tax on dividends from a connected company is only applicable when the paying corporation has received a dividend refund. This means that only those dividends that are paid out of the corporation's investment income will be subject to Part IV tax. If the paying corporation was earning only active business income, no refund would be available when this after tax income was paid out as dividends. As a consequence, no Part IV tax would be assessed on the corporation receiving the dividend.

16-153.   This result is consistent with the goals of integration in that, when a corporation is earning active business income that is taxed at the low small business rate, tax deferral is permitted on income that is retained in the corporation, and not paid out as dividends.

Dividends Paid Out Of Mixed Income Of A Connected Corporation

16-154.   In many cases, a corporation will be earning both investment income and active business income. This will result in a situation, unlike the example previously presented, where some part of the dividends paid by the corporation will be eligible for a refund, and the remainder will not. In this type of situation, the Part IV tax will not be equal to 33-1/3 percent of the dividends received. An example will make this point clear:

Example   On December 1, 2007, Lower Ltd. declares and pays a dividend of $45,000. As a result of paying this dividend, the Company receives a dividend refund of $8,000. Upper Inc. owns 60 percent of the outstanding shares of Lower Ltd. and receives dividends of $27,000.

Analysis   In this case, the dividend refund is clearly less than one-third of the dividends paid, indicating that Lower's income is made up of a combination of investment income and other income. In this more realistic situation, the Part IV Tax Payable by Upper will be based on Upper's 60 percent share of the $8,000 dividend refund of Lower that resulted from paying the dividend. Upper's Part IV tax would be $4,800 [(60%)($8,000)].

Exercise Sixteen-11

Subject: Part IV Tax

Opal Ltd., a Canadian controlled private corporation, received the following amounts of dividends during the current year:

Dividends On Various Portfolio Investments	$14,000
Dividends From Wholly Owned Subsidiary (No Dividend Refund Received)	41,500
Dividends From Ruby Inc. [(30%)($60,000)]	18,000

Opal Ltd. owns 30 percent of Ruby Inc. As a result of paying this dividend, Ruby Inc. received a dividend refund of $15,000.

Determine the amount of Part IV Tax Payable by Opal Ltd. as a result of receiving these dividends.

End of Exercise. Solution available in Study Guide.

Other Part IV Tax Considerations

16-155.   The preceding material has dealt with the basic features of the Part IV tax on dividends received by private corporations. There are a few additional points to be made. First, you should note what kinds of dividends are not subject to Part IV tax. For a private company, or a subject company, the only dividends that will not be subject to Part IV tax are those received from a connected corporation that does not get a dividend refund as a result of paying the dividend.

16-156.   A second point is that ITA 186(1) allows a corporation to use unabsorbed non-capital losses to reduce any Part IV tax. One-third of any non-capital or farm losses claimed for this purpose is deducted from the Part IV tax otherwise payable. However, if this option is chosen, the corporation has effectively used a possible permanent reduction in future taxes to acquire a reduction of Tax Payable that could otherwise ultimately be refunded. This would only make sense in situations where the non-capital loss carry forward was about to expire, or where the company did not expect to have Taxable Income in the carry forward period.

Refundable Dividend Tax On Hand (RDTOH)

Basic Concepts

A Tracking Mechanism

16-157.   In the simple examples we used to illustrate refundable taxes, it was easy to see the direct connection between the amounts of investment income and the amount of the refund that could be made on the payment of dividends. In the real world, such direct relationships do not exist.

16-158.   Corporations usually earn a combination of investment and business income, they seldom pay out all of their earnings in the form of dividends, and there are usually lags between the period in which income is earned and the period in which dividends are paid. As a consequence, some mechanism is needed to keep track of amounts of taxes that have been paid that are eligible for the refund treatment. This mechanism is the Refundable Dividend Tax On Hand account (RDTOH).

General Overview

16-159.   The RDTOH will normally start with an opening balance, reflecting amounts carried over from the previous year. This balance will be increased by the payment of the various types of refundable taxes. In somewhat simplified terms, these additions will be:

- The refundable portion of Part I tax paid, calculated as 26-2/3 percent of aggregate investment income.

- Part IV tax on dividends received, calculated at a rate of 33-1/3 percent of portfolio dividends, plus an amount equal to the recipient's share of the dividend refund received by a connected corporation paying dividends.

16-160.   After these amounts are added, the total is then reduced by the dividend refund received by the corporation for the preceding year. One common point of confusion is that the RDTOH balance at the end of the taxation year is calculated without deducting the dividend refund for that year. As a result, any dividend refund for the preceding year must be deducted from the RDTOH carried forward from the preceding year in order to calculate the opening RDTOH.

16-161.   The dividend refund for the current year will be limited by the balance in this account. That is, the dividend refund for the current year will be equal to the lesser of the balance in the RDTOH at the end of the year, and one-third of the dividends paid for the year. These concepts will be presented in a more technical form in the following material.

RDTOH - General Definition

16-162.   ITA 129(3) defines the RDTOH at the end of a taxation year as the aggregate of four items. The first three are additions and can be described as follows:

ITA 129(3)(a)   Refundable Part I tax for the year.

ITA 129(3)(b)   The total of the taxes under Part IV for the year.

ITA 129(3)(c)   The corporation's RDTOH at the end of the preceding year.

16-163.   The fourth item, the corporation's dividend refund for its preceding taxation year, is subtracted from the total of the first three under **ITA 129(3)(d)**.

16-164.   The only one of these four items that requires further elaboration is ITA 129(3)(a), the refundable portion of Part I tax for the year.

Refundable Portion Of Part I Tax Payable

The Problem

16-165.   The situation here is made complex by the fact that in calculating a corporation's Part I tax payable, there is no segregation of taxes on investment income from taxes on other types of income. This means that there is no direct measure of what portion of the regular Part I tax payable should be refunded. To deal with this situation, the RDTOH definition limits this addition to the least of three amounts. These are specified under ITA 129(3)(a)(i), (ii), and (iii).

Investment Income Limit

16-166.   The first of these limiting amounts is determined as follows:

ITA 129(3)(a)(i)   the amount determined by the formula

$$A - B\text{, where}$$

A   is 26-2/3 percent of the corporation's aggregate investment income for the year, and

B   is the amount, if any, by which the foreign non-business income tax credit exceeds 9-1/3 percent of its foreign investment income for the year.

16-167.   Aggregate investment income is as defined in ITA 129(4). As indicated previously, the components of aggregate investment income are:

- Net taxable capital gains for the year, reduced by any net capital loss carry overs deducted during the year.

- Income from property, excluding dividends that are deductible in computing the corporation's Taxable Income.

16-168. These amounts do not include interest or rents that are incidental to the corporation's efforts to produce active business income. As noted in Chapter 15, these amounts would be considered active business income. Note, however, the definition does include both Canadian and foreign sources of the types of income listed.

16-169. If the corporation has no foreign source investment income, the ITA 129(3)(a)(i) amount is simply 26-2/3 percent of aggregate investment income. From a conceptual point of view, this 26-2/3 percent is the difference between a notional 46-2/3 percent combined federal/provincial rate on investment income, and the 20 percent rate that is assumed in the integration procedures. The idea here is, that if 26-2/3 percent of the Part I tax paid is refunded, it will restore the overall corporate rate to the 20 percent that is assumed in the dividend gross up and tax credit procedures that are applicable to non-eligible dividends.

16-170. The RDTOH legislation is based on the assumption that the Canadian tax rate on foreign non-business income is 36 percent. Reflecting this assumption, the B component in the ITA 129(3)(a)(i) formula subtracts any amount of foreign tax credit that is in excess of 9-1/3 percent of foreign investment income for the year.

16-171. The basic idea here is that a foreign tax credit of 9-1/3 percent will reduce the Canadian taxes paid to 26-2/3 percent (36 percent, less 9-1/3 percent, equals 26-2/3 percent, the rate applicable to the refund). If the foreign tax credit exceeds 9-1/3 percent of the foreign investment income, the Canadian taxes paid would be less than the potential refund of 26-2/3 percent. In other words, without the 9-1/3 percent subtraction, the Canadian government would be providing a refund that is larger than the amount of Canadian tax paid on the foreign investment income.

16-172. In the comprehensive example that follows, we will find that the corporation earns $20,000 in foreign investment income and receives a foreign non-business tax credit of $3,000 or 15 percent. At an assumed 36 percent rate, Canadian tax on this income would be $7,200, with the foreign tax credit of $3,000 reducing the Canadian tax to $4,200 or 21 percent ($4,200 ÷ $20,000).

16-173. The problem here is that, in the absence of some adjustment, the refundable taxes on the $20,000 of foreign non-business income would be $5,333 [(26-2/3%)($20,000)]. This means that the refund would be $1,133 ($5,333 - $4,200) larger than the $4,200 in Canadian taxes paid on the foreign income. This $1,133 can also be calculated as 5-2/3 percent (26-2/3% - 21%) of the $20,000 in foreign source non-business income.

16-174. This problem is dealt with by subtracting from the amount eligible for the 26-2/3 percent refund, any excess of the actual foreign non-business income tax credit over 9-1/3 percent of the foreign investment income. For the example described in the preceding Paragraph, this would be the appropriate $1,133 [$3,000 - (9-1/3%)($20,000)]. Note that if the foreign non-business tax credit was 9-1/3 percent or less of the foreign investment income, the B component of the ITA 129(3)(a)(i) formula would be nil.

16-175. An additional way of thinking of this adjustment is that 9-1/3 percent is the difference between the 36 percent notional rate on foreign source business income and the refund rate of 26-2/3 percent. This means that, if the tax credit on the foreign income exceeds 9-1/3 percent, it reduces the Canadian taxes below 26-2/3 percent. When this is the case, it would not be appropriate to provide the full 26-2/3 percent refund.

Taxable Income Limit

16-176. A further problem with respect to determining the refundable portion of Part I tax payable is that the corporation's Taxable Income may include amounts that are not taxed at full corporate rates (e.g., amounts eligible for the small business deduction). Further, Taxable Income may be reduced by such items as non-capital loss carry overs to a level that is less than the amount of investment income on which ITA 129(3)(a)(i) would provide a refund. To deal with this, the refundable portion of the Part I tax is limited as follows:

ITA 129(3)(a)(ii)   26-2/3 percent of the amount, if any, by which the corporation's taxable income for the year exceeds the total of:

A   the amount eligible for the small business deduction;

B   25/9 of the tax credit for foreign non-business income; and

C   3 times the tax credit for foreign business income.

16-177.   Component B is designed to remove foreign investment income that is not taxed because of the foreign non-business tax credit. The elimination is based on the assumption that it is taxed at a notional rate of 36 percent (9/25). In similar fashion, Component C is designed to remove foreign business income that is not taxed because of the foreign business income tax credit. The elimination here is based on the assumption that this type of income is taxed at a notional rate of 33-1/3 percent.

Tax Payable Limitation

16-178.   A final problem here relates to the fact that the dividend refund could exceed the corporation's actual Tax Payable for the year. This could happen if, for example, the company had large amounts of tax credits for scientific research and experimental development. To deal with this problem, the refundable portion of Part I tax paid is limited as follows:

ITA 129(3)(a)(iii)   the corporation's tax for the year payable under this Part [Part I] determined without reference to Section 123.2 [the 4 percent corporate surtax].

Summary

16-179.   Taking all of these items into consideration, the addition to the RDTOH for Part I tax is the least of:

ITA 129(3)(a)(i)   26-2/3 percent of aggregate investment income, reduced by the excess of foreign non-business income tax credits over 9-1/3 percent of foreign investment income.

ITA 129(3)(a)(ii)   26-2/3 percent of the amount, if any, by which Taxable Income exceeds the sum of the amount eligible for the small business deduction, 25/9 of the foreign non-business tax credit, and 3 times the foreign business tax credit.

ITA 129(3)(a)(iii)   Part I tax payable, calculated without the inclusion of the surtax.

The Dividend Refund

16-180.   While in theory, dividend refunds should only be available when dividends are paid out of investment income, corporate tax legislation does not provide a basis for tracking the income source of a particular dividend payment. As a consequence, a dividend refund is available on any dividend that is paid by the corporation as long as there is a balance in the RDTOH. Given this, the dividend refund will be equal to the lesser of:

- the balance in the RDTOH account at the end of the year; and
- 1/3 of all taxable dividends paid during the year.

Example

16-181.   The following example illustrates the refundable tax calculations.   In Chapter 16 of the separate paper Study Guide which accompanies this text, there is an example containing a completed corporate tax return.   This includes coverage of this material on the RDTOH account.

Example   Fortune Ltd. is a Canadian controlled private corporation. Based on the formula in ITR 402, 90 percent of the Company's income is earned in a province. The following information is available for the year ending December 31, 2007:

Canadian Source Investment Income	
(Includes $25,000 In Taxable Capital Gains)	$100,000
Gross Foreign Non-Business Income (15 Percent Withheld)	20,000
Gross Foreign Business Income (15 Percent Withheld)	10,000
Active Business Income (No Associated Companies)	150,000
Portfolio Dividends Received	30,000
Net Income For Tax Purposes	$310,000
Portfolio Dividends	(30,000)
Net Capital Loss Carry Forward Deducted	(15,000)
Taxable Income	$265,000

RDTOH - December 31, 2006	$110,000
Dividend Refund For 2006	20,000
Taxable Dividends Paid During 2007	40,000

Aggregate investment income for Fortune Ltd. is equal to $105,000 ($100,000 + $20,000 - $15,000).

The Part I Tax Payable would be calculated as follows:

Base Amount Of Part I Tax [(38%)($265,000)]	$100,700
Surtax [(4%)(28%)($265,000)]	2,968
Federal Tax Abatement [(10%)(90%)($265,000)]	(23,850)
Foreign Non-Business Tax Credit (Note 1)	(3,000)
Foreign Business Tax Credit (Note 1)	(1,500)
Small Business Deduction (Note 2)	(24,000)
ART: Equal To The Lesser Of:	
• [(6-2/3%)($100,000 + $20,000 - $15,000)] = $7,000	
• [(6-2/3%)($265,000 - $150,000)] = $7,667	7,000
General Rate Reduction (Note 3)	(700)
Part I Tax Payable	$ 57,618

Note 1 The foreign tax credits are assumed to be equal to the amounts withheld (15 percent). Additional calculations would be required to support this conclusion.

Note 2 The small business deduction would be equal to 16 percent of the least of:

1. Active Business Income	$150,000
2. Taxable Income	$265,000
Deduct:	
[(10/3)($3,000 Foreign Non-Business Tax Credit)]	(10,000)
[(3)($1,500 Foreign Business Tax Credit)]	(4,500)
Total	$250,500
3. Annual Business Limit	$400,000

The small business deduction is $24,000 [(16%)($150,000)].

Note 3 The ITA 123.4(2) general rate reduction would be calculated as follows:

Taxable Income	$265,000
Amount Eligible For Small Business Deduction (Note 2)	(150,000)
Aggregate Investment Income	
($100,000 + $20,000 - $15,000)	(105,000)
Full Rate Taxable Income (= Foreign Business Income)	$ 10,000
Rate	7%
General Rate Reduction	$ 700

Refundable Dividend Tax On Hand (RDTOH)

16-182.   Based on the preceding information, the refundable portion of Part I tax would be the least of the following three amounts:

26-2/3% Of Aggregate Investment Income		
[(26-2/3%)($105,000)]		$ 28,000
Deduct Excess Of:		
Foreign Non-Business Tax Credit	$3,000	
Over 9-1/3% Of Foreign Investment Income		
[(9-1/3%)($20,000)]	(1,867)	(1,133)
ITA 129(3)(a)(i)		**$ 26,867**

Taxable Income		$265,000
Deduct:		
Amount Eligible For Small Business Deduction	($150,000)	
[(25/9)($3,000 Foreign Non-Business Tax Credit)]	(8,333)	
[(3)($1,500 Foreign Business Tax Credit)]	(4,500)	(162,833)
Total		$102,167
Rate		26-2/3%
ITA 129(3)(a)(ii)		**$ 27,245**

ITA 129(3)(a)(iii) Adjusted Part I Tax Payable ($57,618 - $2,968)	**$ 54,650**

The refundable portion of Part I tax is equal to $26,867, which is the least of the preceding three amounts.

16-183.   The Part IV tax would be $10,000, one-third of the $30,000 in portfolio dividends received. Given this, the balance in the RDTOH account at the end of the year is as follows:

RDTOH - End Of Preceding Year	$110,000	
Deduct: Dividend Refund For The Preceding Year	(20,000)	$ 90,000
Refundable Portion Of Part I Tax	$ 26,867	
Part IV Tax Payable [(33-1/3%)($30,000)]	10,000	36,867
RDTOH - December 31, 2007		**$126,867**

16-184.   The dividend refund for the year would be $13,333, the lesser of:

- One-Third Of Taxable Dividends Paid ($40,000 ÷ 3) = $13,333
- RDTOH Balance - December 31, 2007 = $126,867

16-185.   Using the preceding information, the total federal Tax Payable for Fortune Ltd. is calculated as follows:

Part I Tax Payable	$57,618
Part IV Tax Payable	10,000
Dividend Refund	(13,333)
Federal Tax Payable	**$54,285**

Exercise Sixteen-12

Subject: Refundable Part I Tax

During the current year, Debut Inc. has the following amounts of property income:

Dividends From Portfolio Investments	$22,000
Foreign Non-Business Income (Net Of 5 Percent Withholding)	14,250

Capital Gains	38,250
Net Rental Income	6,500
Interest Income On Ten Year Bond	9,200

The Company's Net Income For Tax Purposes is $121,825. The only deductions in the calculation of Taxable Income are the dividends on portfolio investments and a net capital loss from 2002 of $9,000 [(1/2)($18,000)]. Debut Inc. is a Canadian controlled private corporation. An $8,000 small business deduction and a foreign tax credit of $750 served to reduce Tax Payable. Assume that the Company's Part I Tax Payable has been correctly determined to be $20,420, including $1,017 in corporate surtax. Determine the refundable amount of Part I tax for the current year.

Exercise Sixteen-13

Subject: Dividend Refund

Quan Imports Ltd. is a Canadian controlled private corporation. At the end of the previous year, it had an RDTOH balance of $12,500. It paid dividends during that year of $6,000, resulting in a dividend refund of $1,000. During the current year, Quan Imports' only income is $24,000 in taxable capital gains and $6,000 in dividends received from an investment in Royal Bank shares. During the year, the Company declares and pays a $15,000 dividend on its common shares. Determine the Company's dividend refund for the year.

End of Exercises. Solutions available in Study Guide.

Designation Of Eligible Dividends

Basic Concepts

The Problem

16-186.   In Chapter 9, we first introduced the concept of eligible dividends, a new category of dividends introduced by the May, 2006 budget. A particular dividend becomes eligible by having the paying corporation designate it as such. From the point of view of the recipient, if it is designated as eligible by the paying corporation, it will be subject to the eligible dividend procedures, even if the paying corporation did not qualify for making such a designation.

16-187.   This new category of dividends was introduced to deal with the fact that integration did not work for corporations that were taxed at full general rates. In particular, the combined federal/provincial rates that were paid by large public companies ranged from just over 30 percent to nearly 40 percent. This was combined with maximum rates paid by individuals on dividend income which could be as high as 37 percent. The result was that income which flowed through these corporations could be assessed at a rate in excess of 60 percent, far higher than the rate applicable to direct receipt of the same income stream.

The Solution

16-188.   While other approaches could have been used, the government chose to alleviate this problem through the dividend gross up and tax credit procedures. As discussed previously, the dividend gross up for eligible dividends was increased from 25 percent to 45 percent. Accompanying this change, the dividend tax credit rate has been reduced from 66-2/3 percent of the gross up to 11/18 (61.1 percent) of the gross up.

16-189.   While the amount of the change will vary from province to province, this enhanced gross up and tax credit procedure significantly reduces tax rates on eligible dividends. In Chapter 9 we provided a table which compared tax rates on interest income, capital gains, non-eligible dividends and eligible dividends. It is reproduced here for your convenience.

	Interest Income	Capital Gains	Non-Eligible Dividends	Eligible Dividends
Tax Rate (In Maximum Bracket)	43.0%	21.5%	28.8%	23.6%

Note The rates in this table are for an individual with sufficient other income to place him in the 29 percent federal bracket for any additional income. In his province, the applicable tax rate is 14 percent, the dividend tax credit on non-eligible dividends is one-third of the gross up, and the dividend tax credit on eligible dividends is 25 percent of the gross up.

16-190.   While the use of different provincial rates and credits will produce variations in these results, interest income will always be subject to the highest rates, while eligible dividends will always have a lower rate than non-eligible dividends. However, different provincial dividend tax credits could change the relative position of eligible dividend rates as compared to capital gains rates.

Implementing The Solution

16-191.   The eligible dividend rules were introduced to deal with maintaining integration in situations where a corporation is taxed at rates that do not benefit from the small business deduction or tax refunds on dividend distributions. In order to keep the combined corporate and individual tax rate on income that is flowed through a corporation at roughly the same level that would be paid by an individual on direct receipt of income, these procedures serve to reduce the individual tax rate applicable to dividends.

16-192.   A simple solution to this problem would be to simply state that dividends paid by public corporations would be eligible dividends (these corporations are generally subject to full corporate rates) and dividends paid by CCPCs would be non-eligible dividends (these corporations get either the small business deduction or a partial refund of taxes paid). However, public corporations may have income that has been taxed at low rates and, somewhat more commonly, CCPCs may have income that has been taxed at full corporate rates.

16-193.   Given this situation, a system has been developed which gives separate treatment to CCPCs and non-CCPCs:

CCPCs It will be assumed that, in general, dividends paid by CCPCs are non-eligible. However, to track components of their income that have been taxed at full corporate rates, CCPCs will have a notional account referred to as a General Rate Income Pool (GRIP). The balance in this account will be available to pay eligible dividends.

Non-CCPCs In general, non-CCPCs are comprised of public companies and private companies that are not Canadian controlled. For these companies, it will be assumed that, in general, dividends paid are eligible. However, to track components of their income that have been taxed at low rates, they will have to use a notional account referred to as a Low Rate Income Pool (LRIP). The balance in this account must be reduced to nil by the payment of non-eligible dividends prior to the payment of eligible dividends.

16-194.   We will provide a separate discussion of the procedures applicable to both CCPCs and non-CCPCs. However, prior to considering these procedures, attention must be given to the new Part III.1 tax on excessive designation of eligible dividends.

Part III.1 Tax On Excessive Eligible Dividend Designations

16-195.   The enhanced dividend gross up and tax credit is available on any dividend that the paying corporation has designated as eligible. This raises the possibility that a corporation might designate a dividend as eligible under circumstances where such a designation is not appropriate (e.g., a CCPC designating a dividend as eligible when it has no balance in its GRIP). To discourage this, the government has introduced a new Part III.1 tax on what is referred to as an Excessive Eligible Dividend Designation (EEDD).

16-196.   ITA 89(1) defines EEDD separately for CCPCs and non-CCPCs. These definitions will be considered when we look at the designation rules for these types of corporations.

16-197.   If the EEDD is inadvertent, the Part III.1 tax is equal to 20 percent of the excess amount. In these circumstances, Part III.1 provides for an election that will allow the taxpayer to effectively undo the designation.

16-198.   If the CRA concludes that the EEDD reflects an attempt to artificially manipulate either a GRIP or an LRIP, the Part III.1 tax rate goes to 30 percent. In addition, there are two other consequences:

• The tax applies to the entire dividend, not just the EEDD.
• No election is available to undo the excessive election.

16-199.   In order to appropriately track all dividend payments, any resident Canadian corporation that pays a taxable dividend is required to file a return for the year under Part III.1.

CCPCs And Their GRIP
Default Treatment
16-200.   Provided no associated corporations are involved, a CCPC qualifies for a small business deduction equal to 16 percent of up to $400,000 per year of active business income. This currently has the effect of reducing the federal rate on this income to 13.12 percent and the combined federal/provincial rate to an average of around 20 percent.

16-201.   In addition, the investment income of these corporations has an available refund of tax that, in a manner similar to the small business deduction, reduces the effective federal/provincial tax rate on such income to the same 20 percent level, provided the after tax amounts have been distributed to shareholders.

16-202.   For many, perhaps the majority of CCPCs, all of their income benefits from one of these two provisions. With a 20 percent applicable corporate tax rate, the enhanced 45 percent dividend gross up and tax credit procedures are not required to achieve the objectives of integration. Given this situation, the government has concluded that dividends paid by CCPCs will, in general, be non-eligible dividends. Stated alternatively, these dividends cannot, in general, be designated as eligible without creating an EEDD.

General Rate Income Pool (GRIP)
16-203.   The legislation recognizes, however, that some types of CCPC income should provide a basis for designating eligible dividends. In order to provide for this, ITA 89(1) defines a notional account to track the amounts that qualify. This account is referred to as the General Rate Income Pool (GRIP) and, to the extent there is a balance in this account, a CCPC can declare dividends that can be designated as eligible.

16-204.   In ITA 89(1), the definition is based on an amount A, reduced by an amount B, with this latter amount defined in a way that adjusts for future events such as non-capital loss carry backs. As dealing with the B component goes beyond the scope of this text, we will focus on the content of A. The component A is defined as follows:

$$A = C + [(68\%)(D - E - F)] + G + H - I$$

Where:

C   is the CCPC's GRIP at the end of the preceding taxation year.
D   is the CCPC's taxable income for the year.
E   is the amount eligible for the small business deduction for the year.
F   is the CCPC's aggregate investment income for the year.
G   is the amount of eligible dividends received by the CCPC during the year.
H   involves a group of technical additions related to amalgamations, wind-ups and corporate earnings generated prior to 2006.
I   is the amount of eligible dividends paid during the preceding year.

16-205. Several comments on this formula are relevant at this point:

- The (D - E - F) component calculates a Taxable Income that is adjusted to eliminate the types of income for which CCPCs receive favourable tax treatment. As dividends are paid out of after tax funds, the residual income is multiplied by 68 percent, reflecting a notional federal/provincial tax rate of 32 percent.

- If a CCPC receives dividends that are eligible for the enhanced 45 percent dividend gross up and tax credit, the addition in G allows these dividends to retain that status on their flow through to the shareholders of the CCPC.

- The components of H will be given some attention in subsequent Chapters.

- Note that the balance is reduced, not by eligible dividends paid in the current year, but by eligible dividends paid in the preceding year.

16-206. A simple example will illustrate these provisions:

Example At the end of 2006, Norgrave Ltd., a CCPC, has a GRIP of $81,600. During 2006, the company designated $25,000 of dividends as eligible.

For 2007, Norgrave has Taxable Income of $225,000. This amount includes aggregate investment income of $55,000. In addition, the Company receives eligible dividends during the year of $50,000. In determining 2007 Tax Payable, the Company has a small business deduction of $24,000 [(16%)($150,000)]. During 2007, Norgrave Ltd. pays dividends of $40,000, with $20,000 of this amount being designated as eligible.

Analysis For 2006, there will be no opening balance in the GRIP and no eligible dividends paid in the preceding year. The 2006 addition to GRIP will be as follows:

Balance At End Of 2006		$ 81,600
Taxable Income	$225,000	
Income Eligible For SBD	(150,000)	
Aggregate Investment Income	(55,000)	
Adjusted Taxable Income	$ 20,000	
Rate	68%	13,600
Eligible Dividends Received		50,000
Eligible Dividends Designated in 2006		(25,000)
GRIP At End Of 2007		$120,200

The eligible dividends paid during 2007 will be deducted from the GRIP in 2008.

EEDD For A CCPC

16-207. If a CCPC designates an amount of eligible dividends during a given year that is in excess of its GRIP at the end of the year, it will be considered an EEDD and be subject to Part III.1 tax.

Example At its December 31, 2006 year end, Sandem Inc., a CCPC, has a GRIP of $45,000. During 2007, the Company pays dividends of $100,000, of which $60,000 are designated as eligible. There are no additions to the Company's GRIP during 2007.

Analysis The Company has an EEDD of $15,000 ($60,000 - $45,000). Provided the CRA believes that this was an inadvertent result, this amount will be subject to a Part III.1 tax of 20 percent on the excess of $15,000. There is also the possibility of electing to have the EEDD treated as a non-eligible dividend.

If the CRA concludes that the EEDD was a deliberate attempt to manipulate the Company's GRIP, an additional 10 percent is added to the Part III.1 tax. In addition, the applicable 30 percent tax is assessed on the entire eligible amount of $60,000, not just the EEDD amount and no election is available to undo the excessive election.

Non-CCPCs And Their LRIP

Default Treatment

16-208.   For non-CCPCs, their income will generally be taxed at full corporate rates. Given this situation, the government has concluded that the default treatment of dividends paid by non-CCPCs is to classify them as eligible. In the absence of a LRIP, any dividend paid by these companies can be designated as eligible.

Low Rate Income Pool (LRIP)

16-209.   While less common than a CCPC having income that is taxed at general rates, there is the possibility that a non-CCPC will have income that is taxed at low rates. This could include amounts of income retained by a CCPC before it became a public company, as well as non-eligible dividends received from a CCPC. Once again, ITA 89(1) defines a notional account that is designed to track amounts that cannot be used to pay eligible dividends.

16-210.   Note, however, the difference in application of this account. In the case of a CCPC, eligible dividends can only be paid to the extent that there is a balance in the company's GRIP. However, the presence of a positive GRIP balance does not require that all dividends be designated as eligible until the balance is eliminated.

16-211.   In contrast, if a non-CCPC has a positive balance in its LRIP, all dividends must be treated as non-eligible until that balance is eliminated.

16-212.   The LRIP is defined in ITA 89(1) as follows:

$$(A + B + C + D + F) - (G + H)$$

Where:

A   is the non-CCPCs LRIP at the end of the preceding year.

B   is the amount of non-eligible dividends received by the non-CCPC from a CCPC.

C   is a group of technical additions related to corporate reorganizations.

D   is an adjustment for a non-CCPC that was a CCPC in some preceding year.

E   is an adjustment for a non-CCPC that was a credit union in some preceding year.

F   is an adjustment for a non-CCPC that was an investment company in some preceding year.

G   is the amount of taxable dividends, other than eligible dividends, paid by the non-CCPC during the year.

H   is the amount of any EEDD made by the non-CCPC during the year.

EEDD For A Non-CCPC

16-213.   In somewhat simplified terms, an EEDD for a non-CCPC is equal to the lesser of its eligible dividends paid and its LRIP at the time the dividend is paid. For example, if a non-CCPC paid an eligible dividend of $50,000 at a point in time that its LRIP was equal to $40,000, the EEDD would be $40,000. Note that, unlike the situation with EEDDs for CCPCs, where the amount is based on the end of year balance of the GRIP, the EEDD for a non-CCPC is based on the balance of the LRIP at the point in time when the eligible dividend becomes payable.

16-214.   A simple example will illustrate these provisions:

Example Victor Ltd., a Canadian public company, receives $42,000 in non-eligible dividends from a CCPC on June 15, 2007. Its LRIP has a balance of nil prior to this. On September 23, 2007, Victor pays dividends of $100,000, with $30,000 of this amount being designated as eligible.

Analysis   At September 23, 2007, the balance in the LRIP would be $42,000. The lesser of this amount and the eligible dividend would be $30,000 and this would be the amount of the EEDD. Provided there were no further dividend transactions, the LRIP balance at the end of the year would be a negative $58,000 ($42,000 - $70,000 - $30,000).

With respect to the Part III.1 tax, a tax of 20 percent would normally be assessed on the EEDD of $30,000. However, if the CRA concludes that a deliberate attempt to manipulate the LRIP was involved, the tax rate will be increased to 30 percent.

This result seems somewhat counter-intuitive in that a non-eligible dividend was paid in an amount sufficient to eliminate the LRIP. However, the legislation is clear that the LRIP is measured at a particular point in time and, if an eligible dividend is paid when there is a positive balance in this account, it creates an EEDD. We would note that this situation could have been avoided had the non-eligible dividend been paid before, even by one day, the payment of the eligible dividend.

A Final Word On Eligible Dividends

16-215.   You should be aware that the preceding is a fairly simplified version of the provisions related to eligible dividends and their designation. The complete legislation is far more complex, dealing with a number of transitional situations, changes in a corporation's classification, as well as problems associated with corporate reorganizations. However, we feel that this version of the material is appropriate for an introductory text in taxation.

Key Terms Used In This Chapter

16-216.   The following is a list of the key terms used in this Chapter. These terms, and their meanings, are compiled in the Glossary Of Key Terms located at the back of the separate paper Study Guide and on the Student CD-ROM.

Additional Refundable Tax On Investment Income (ART)	Liquidating Dividend
	Low Rate Income Pool (LRIP)
Aggregate Investment Income	Net Assets
ART	Paid Up Capital
Canadian Controlled Private Corporation	Part IV Tax
Capital Dividend	Portfolio Dividend
Capital Dividend Account	Post-1971 Undistributed Surplus
CCPC	Pre-1972 Capital Surplus On Hand
Connected Corporation	Pre-1972 Undistributed Surplus
Contributed Capital	Private Corporation
Deemed Dividends	Public Corporation
Dividend Gross Up	PUC
Dividend Tax Credit	RDTOH
Dividends	Redemption Of Shares
Dividends In Kind	Refundable Dividend Tax On Hand
Earned Capital	Refundable Part I Tax
Earned Surplus	Retained Earnings
Eligible Dividends	Shareholders' Equity
Excessive Eligible Dividend Designation (EEDD)	Stock Dividend
	Subject Corporation
General Rate Income Pool (GRIP)	Winding-Up Of A Canadian Corporation
Integration	

References

16-217. For more detailed study of the material in this Chapter, we refer you to the following:

ITA 52(2)	Cost Of Property Received As Dividend In Kind
ITA 52(3)	Stock Dividends
ITA 82(1)	Taxable Dividends Received
ITA 83(2)	Capital Dividend
ITA 84	Deemed Dividend
ITA 88(2)	Winding Up Of A Canadian Corporation
ITA 89(1)	Definitions (Canadian Corporations, GRIP and LRIP)
ITA 123.3	Refundable Tax On CCPC's Investment Income
ITA 123.4	Definitions (General Rate Reduction)
ITA 129(1)	Dividend Refund To Private Corporation
ITA 129(3)	Definition Of Refundable Dividend Tax On Hand
ITA 129(4)	Definitions (Aggregate Investment Income)
ITA 184(2)	Tax On Excessive Elections
ITA 186	Part IV Tax
IT-66R6	Capital Dividends
IT-67R3	Taxable Dividends From Corporations Resident In Canada
IT-149R4	Winding Up Dividend
IT-243R4	Dividend Refund To Private Corporations
IT-269R4	Part IV Tax On Taxable Dividends Received By a Private Corporation Or A Subject Corporation
IT-328R3	Losses On Shares On Which Dividends Have Been Received
IT-391R	Status Of Corporations
IT-419R2	Meaning Of Arm's Length
IT-426R	Shares Sold Subject to an Earnout Agreement
IT-432R2	Benefits Conferred On Shareholders
IT-458R2	Canadian Controlled Private Corporation
IT-463R2	Paid-Up Capital

Problems For Self Study

(The solutions for these problems can be found in the separate Study Guide.)

Self Study Problem Sixteen - 1

Groman Ltd. is a Canadian controlled private corporation. On December 31 of the current year, the Company's condensed Balance Sheet is as follows:

Total Assets		$62,000
Liabilities		$22,000
Shareholders' Equity:		
500 Preferred Shares (Paid Up Capital)	$11,000	
600 Common Shares (Paid Up Capital)	15,600	
Retained Earnings	13,400	40,000
Total Equities		$62,000

Any dividends paid or deemed to be paid by Groman Ltd. would be non-eligible.

Required: Discuss the tax consequences of each of the following **independent** transactions. Tax consequences would include both the increase or decrease in the individual shareholder's Taxable Income, as well as any change in the adjusted cost base of any shares that are still in the hands of the individual shareholder after the described transaction(s).

A. (i) A long-term debtholder has agreed to convert $10,000 of his debt to 500 Preferred Shares, with a Paid Up Capital (PUC) of $11,000. This conversion does not qualify for the ITA 51 rollover that is described in Chapter 19 of the text.

    (ii) After the conversion described in A(i), a different shareholder, with 250 Preferred Shares, sold them for $11,000 in an arm's length transaction. His shares cost $4,100 a number of years ago.

B. The Company declared and distributed a 5 percent stock dividend on the Common Shares. An addition of $780 was made to Paid Up Capital, with Retained Earnings reduced accordingly.

C. In return for assets with a fair market value of $17,500, the Company issued a demand note for $7,500 and 250 fully paid Preferred Shares having a per share Paid Up Capital equal to those currently outstanding.

D. An investor owns 100 of the Common Shares. They were purchased at a price of $15 per share. The Company redeems these shares at a price of $32 per share.

Self Study Problem Sixteen - 2

Mr. Stevens, a Canadian resident, owns 100 percent of the shares of Stevens Holdings Inc. (SHI), which owns 100 percent of Fancy Operating Ltd. (FOL). Both SHI and FOL have a December 31 year end. Neither Company paid any dividends in 2006.

The following information pertains to the year ending December 31, 2007:

Stevens Holdings Inc.

- The balance in the Refundable Dividend Tax On Hand account at December 31, 2006 was $8,000.
- The Company received a taxable dividend from FOL of $75,000.
- The Company received a taxable dividend from Petro-Canada of $8,000.
- The Company earned Canadian interest income of $12,000.

- The Company realized a capital gain of $47,250.
- The Company paid a capital dividend of $10,500 and a taxable dividend of $50,000 to Mr. Stevens.

Fancy Operating Ltd.

- The balance in the Refundable Dividend Tax On Hand account at December 31, 2006 was $2,000.
- The Company earned active business income of $80,000 and Canadian interest income of $7,000.
- The Company paid taxable dividends to SHI of $75,000.

Required:

A. Calculate the dividend refund for FOL for 2007.
B. Calculate the Part IV Tax Payable for SHI for 2007.
C. Calculate the dividend refund for SHI for 2007.

Self Study Problem Sixteen - 3

Burton Investments Ltd. is a Canadian controlled private corporation that sells office supplies. It owns 52 percent of the outstanding shares of Puligny Inc. On December 15, 2007, Puligny Inc. declared and paid a dividend of $122,000, of which Burton Investments Ltd. received $63,440 (52 percent). As a result of paying the $122,000 dividend, Puligny Inc. received a dividend refund in the amount of $12,500.

Other 2007 income that was reported by Burton Investments consisted of the following amounts:

Capital Gain	$18,000
Dividends From Bank Of Montreal	13,480
Interest	1,150

The capital gain was on the sale of land that had been used as an auxiliary parking lot, but was no longer needed.

Burton's office supply business is seasonal and, as a consequence, temporary cash balances must be set aside for the purchase of inventories during the busy parts of the year. All of the $1,150 in interest was earned on such temporary cash balances.

At the end of 2006, the Company's Refundable Dividend Tax On Hand balance was $22,346. The 2006 dividend refund was $7,920.

The Company's Taxable Income for the year ending December 31, 2007 was $62,800. No foreign income was included in this total. Assume the Part I Tax Payable for the year ending December 31, 2007 was correctly calculated as $12,560, including surtax of $483. Because of its association with Puligny Inc., its share of the annual business limit on income eligible for the small business deduction is $40,000. Burton's active business income is equal to its share of the annual business limit.

Burton Investments paid taxable dividends of $22,500.

Required: For the taxation year ending December 31, 2007, determine the Part IV and refundable Part I taxes that will be payable by Burton Investments Ltd. In addition, determine the balance in the Refundable Dividend Tax On Hand account at December 31, 2007, and any dividend refund available.

Self Study Problem Sixteen - 4

Sinzer Ltd. is a Canadian controlled private corporation. Its business operations consist of sales and consulting with respect to interior design and decoration, and its head office is in

Windsor, Ontario. For the taxation year ending December 31, 2007, Taxable Income for Sinzer Ltd. was calculated as follows:

Interest Income From Canadian Sources (Note 1)	$ 48,300
Dividends From Taxable Canadian Corporations (Note 2)	88,100
Foreign Investment Income (Note 3)	55,000
Taxable Capital Gains On Sale Of Shares	24,500
Income From Design Consulting (Note 4)	103,000
Income From Sales (Note 4)	386,000
Net Income For Tax Purposes	$704,900
Dividends From Taxable Canadian Corporations	(88,100)
Donations To A Registered Charity	(24,600)
Non-Capital Loss Carry Forward Deducted	(76,400)
Net Capital Loss Carry Forward Deducted	(12,300)
Taxable Income	$503,500

Note 1   The Canadian interest is from the following sources:

Interest On Loan To A Majority Owned Subsidiary (The Subsidiary Has No Active Business Income)	$43,250
Term Deposit And Bank Interest Arising From Seasonal Investment Of Excess Cash From Operations	5,050
Total	$48,300

Note 2   The dividends from taxable Canadian corporations consisted of the following:

Portfolio Dividends From Non-Connected Corporations	$19,600
Dividends From 75 Percent Owned Subsidiary (Total Dividend Refund Of $12,750 To The Subsidiary)	68,500
Total	$88,100

Note 3   The $55,000 is before withholding of $8,250 in foreign taxes. Assume that the foreign non-business income tax credit in the calculation of Part I Tax Payable is equal to $8,250.

Note 4   The Income From Design Consulting includes $38,200 in income from operations in the U.S. The $386,000 in Income From Sales includes $98,000 in sales made in the U.S. A total of $34,000 was paid in U.S. taxes on this income. Assume that the foreign business income tax credit in the calculation of Part I Tax Payable is equal to $34,000.

Other Information:

1. Sinzer was allocated $200,000 of the annual business limit. Assume that this is the amount that is eligible for the small business deduction.

2. During 2007, Sinzer declared four quarterly taxable dividends in the amount of $28,000 each. The first of these dividends was paid in March, 2007, the second in June, 2007, the third in October, 2007, and the fourth was paid in January, 2008. A $25,000 taxable dividend, declared in December, 2006, was paid in January, 2007.

3. The balance in the Refundable Dividend Tax On Hand account on December 31, 2006 was $23,500, and the dividend refund for 2006 was $9,600.

Required:

A. Calculate Sinzer's Part I Tax Payable for the 2007 taxation year.

B. Determine the December 31, 2007 balance in Sinzer's Refundable Dividend Tax On

Hand account.

C. Determine the amount of Sinzer's dividend refund for 2007.

Show all of the calculations used to provide the required information, including those for which the result is nil.

Self Study Problem Sixteen - 5

Acme Imports Ltd. is a Canadian controlled private corporation. Its basic business activity is importing a variety of consumer products for distribution to wholesalers in Canada. The before income taxes Balance Sheet and Income Statement of Acme Imports Ltd. for the year ending December 31, 2007 are as follows:

Acme Imports Ltd.
Income Statement Before Income Taxes
Year Ending December 31, 2007

Sales	$7,387,700
Dividend Income	24,000
Interest Revenue	10,000
Gain On Sale Of Equipment	57,000
Total Revenues	$7,478,700
Cost Of Goods Sold	$6,071,400
Rent	118,000
Selling Expenses	283,000
Wages And Salaries	276,000
Employee Benefits	32,000
Office Expenses	158,000
Fees For Professional Services	43,000
Interest	47,000
Promotional Expenses	99,000
Amortization Expense	20,000
Charitable Donations	25,000
Vehicle Costs	74,000
Total Expenses Not Including Income Taxes	$7,246,400
Income Before Taxes	$ 232,300

Acme Imports Ltd.
Balance Sheet Before Income Taxes
As At December 31, 2007

Assets

Accounts Receivable		$1,080,000
Inventories		940,000
Loan To Shareholder		97,000
Federal Income Tax Instalments Paid		28,000
Investment In Sarco Ltd.		695,000
Land		385,000
Equipment - Cost	$840,000	
Accumulated Amortization	(414,000)	426,000
Intangible Assets		183,000
Total Assets		$3,834,000

Equities

Bank Overdraft	$ 87,000
Note Payable To Bank	306,000
Accounts Payable	682,000
Mortgage On Land	244,000
Future Income Tax Liability	53,000
Common Stock - No Par	32,000
Retained Earnings	2,430,000
Total Equities	**$3,834,000**

Other Information: The following additional information is available with respect to the 2007 operations of Acme Imports Ltd.:

1. The Intangible Assets consist of an amount paid for a list of potential customers. This list was acquired during December, 2007 from a competitor who had ceased doing business. The intangible asset has been tested for impairment, but none was found. As a consequence, no write-down is included in Total Expenses.

2. On January 1, 2007, the Equipment, which is all in Class 8, had a UCC of $256,000.

3. The gain on the sale of Equipment resulted from selling display fixtures and equipment with an original cost of $62,000 and a net book value of $27,500, for cash proceeds of $84,500.

4. A small group of new shares were issued during the year. The cost of printing these shares was $950 and was included in Office Expenses. In addition, $7,000 of the professional fees paid were for legal and other costs associated with obtaining the supplementary letters patent required to issue these shares.

5. The loan outstanding to the shareholder was made in January of 2005. It is a non-interest bearing loan.

6. Included in Promotional Expenses is a $2,800 membership fee to a local golf and country club. In addition, there were charges at this club for business meals and entertainment totalling $6,720.

7. The Company provides cars for the principal shareholder and the manager of the Company. Both of these individuals are considered to be employees of the Company. Included in vehicle costs are lease payments of $500 per month, for 12 months, for each car, and a total of $11,000 in operating costs associated with providing these cars. While these individuals use the cars for some business purposes, it is estimated that over 80 percent of their usage is personal.

8. Acme Imports Ltd. did not declare or pay any dividends during the year. On December 31, 2006, Acme Imports Ltd. had a nil balance in its Refundable Dividend Tax On Hand account.

9. The dividend income of $24,000 was Acme's share of a dividend declared by Sarco Ltd., a 60 percent owned subsidiary company. As a result of declaring the dividend, Sarco received a total dividend refund of $5,000. None of the annual limit for the small business deduction was allocated to Sarco.

10. The interest income came from corporate bonds that had been held for four years and sold during the year.

11. During the year, the Company decided that it had grown to the point where additional space was needed and, rather than continue to rent space, it has decided to acquire its own premises. It paid a fee of $3,500 (included in Fees For Professional Services) to a site consultant and, on the basis of his recommendation, acquired land at a cost of $385,000. The site was purchased on April 1, 2007, and construction of the new facility is to begin early in 2008. The Company's Other Expenses included $12,300 in interest on the mortgage used to finance this land.

Required:

A. Determine Acme Imports Ltd.'s minimum Taxable Income for the year ending December 31, 2007.

B. Determine Acme Imports Ltd.'s active business income for the year ending December 31, 2007.

C. Determine Acme Imports Ltd.'s minimum federal Tax Payable for the year ending December 31, 2007.

D. Determine the December 31, 2007 balance in Acme Imports Ltd.'s Refundable Dividend Tax On Hand account.

Show all of the calculations used to provide the required information, including those for which the result is nil.

Self Study Problem Sixteen - 6

Brasco Distributors is a Canadian controlled private corporation. Its primary business is the distribution of a variety of consumer products to retailers throughout Canada. Its fiscal year ends on December 31.

While its current operations are providing a reasonable rate of return on invested capital, losses have been experienced in previous years. As a result, at the beginning of the year ending December 31, 2007, it has available a non-capital loss carry forward of $25,800 and a net capital loss carry forward of $64,500 [(1/2)($129,000)] from 2006.

Other Information:

1. During the year ending December 31, 2007, the Company made donations of $11,900 to registered Canadian charities.

2. Its net taxable capital gains for 2007 amounted to $36,000 [(1/2)($72,000)].

3. The Company's 2007 active business income, computed in accordance with the requirements of the *Income Tax Act*, amounted to $171,000.

4. Total dividends paid to shareholders of the Company amounted to $69,500. This total was made up of $39,000 in taxable dividends and $30,500 paid out of the capital dividend account.

5. During 2007, the Company received $2,200 in interest from long-term Canadian bonds. In addition, on common shares that represent portfolio investments in taxable Canadian companies, the Company received dividends of $15,800. The Company received foreign source investment income of $3,825. This was the net amount, after the withholding of $675 in taxes by the taxation authorities in the foreign jurisdiction.

6. Brasco owns 60 percent of the outstanding voting shares of Masco, a Canadian subsidiary. During the year, Brasco received $37,800 in dividends from Masco. The total 2007 dividends paid by the subsidiary amounted to $63,000 and, as a result of paying these

dividends, Masco claimed a dividend refund of $21,000. Because it is an associated Company, Brasco must share the annual limit on its small business deduction with Masco. Brasco has been allocated $125,000 of the annual business limit.

7. The balance in the Company's Refundable Dividend Tax On Hand account was $7,000 on December 31, 2006. Brasco paid no dividends in 2006.

Required:

A. Calculate Brasco's Net Income For Tax Purposes and Taxable Income for the year ending December 31, 2007.

B. Calculate Brasco's minimum Tax Payable for the year ending December 31, 2007. This should include both Part I and Part IV Tax Payable, net of any dividend refund. For purposes of this calculation, assume that the foreign non-business income tax credit is equal to the amount withheld.

C. Do the complete calculation required to determine the foreign non-business income tax credit that will be used in determining the small business deduction, as well as the complete calculation that will be used to determine the foreign non-business income tax credit that will be deducted.

Show all of the calculations used to provide the required information, including those for which the result is nil.

Assignment Problems

(The solutions for these problems are only available in
the solutions manual that has been provided to your instructor.)

Assignment Problem Sixteen - 1

Using the following assumptions, provide an example of how integration works:

- The corporation's business income for the year is $50,000.
- Any dividends paid are designated non-eligible dividends.
- The individual's marginal federal tax rate is 29 percent and his marginal provincial tax rate is 14.5 percent.
- The provincial dividend tax credit is equal to one-third of the gross up.
- The combined federal and provincial corporate tax rate is 20 percent.

Assignment Problem Sixteen - 2

During the current year, Hemingway Industries Ltd. sold a number of its capital properties. None of the properties disposed of were depreciable capital properties. The relevant facts are as follows:

Property	Proceeds Of Disposition	Adjusted Cost Base	Selling Expenses
1	$8,100	$4,200	$200
2	7,900	3,950	375
3	2,200	4,300	700
4	1,900	3,450	260

Required: Compute the effects of the dispositions on the capital dividend account assuming Hemingway Industries is:

A. a Canadian controlled private corporation.
B. a private corporation that is not a CCPC.

Assignment Problem Sixteen - 3

Deemit Inc. is a Canadian controlled private corporation. However, it is not a qualified small business corporation. All of the shares of the Company are held by individuals resident in Canada. On December 31 of the current year, its condensed Balance Sheet is as follows:

Total Assets		$790,000
Total Liabilities		$110,000
Shareholders' Equity:		
Preferred Shares (Paid Up Capital)	$150,000	
Common Shares (Paid Up Capital)	370,000	
Retained Earnings	160,000	680,000
Total Equities		$790,000

There are 20,000 Preferred Shares outstanding and they were issued at a price of $7.50 per share. The Paid Up Capital (PUC) of these shares is equal to their carrying value of $150,000.

There are 185,000 Common Shares outstanding and they have been issued at various prices. The PUC of these shares is equal to their carrying value of $370,000.

Any dividends paid or deemed to be paid by Deemit Inc. would be non-eligible.

Required: Indicate the tax consequences to the relevant shareholders of the transaction(s) described in each of the following **independent** Cases. Tax consequences would include both the increase or decrease in the individual shareholder's Taxable Income, as well as any change in the adjusted cost base of any shares that are still in the hands of the individual shareholder after the described transaction(s).

Case A An individual owns 10,000 of the outstanding Preferred Shares. His adjusted cost base for the shares is $72,000. The Company redeems these shares, providing the individual with a payment of $78,000.

Case B The Company declares a dividend of $.50 per share on the outstanding Common Shares. The total amount of the dividend is less than the balance in the capital dividend account, and the Company makes the appropriate election under ITA 83(2).

Case C In order to partially liquidate the Company, a dividend of $2.10 per share is declared on the Common Shares. This dividend is accompanied by a $370,000 reduction in the PUC of the Common Shares.

Case D A $50,000 loan, from an individual who is not a shareholder of the Company, is settled by the issuance of 8,000 Preferred Shares with a PUC of $60,000. The Preferred Shares received by this individual are immediately sold at their fair market value of $60,000.

Assignment Problem Sixteen - 4

Conrod Holdings Ltd. is a Canadian controlled private corporation that sells farm supplies. It owns 70 percent of the outstanding shares of Morsal Inc. On November 1, 2007, Morsal Inc. declared and paid a dividend of $21,000, of which Conrod Holdings Ltd. received $14,700 (70 percent). As a result of paying the $21,000 dividend, Morsal Inc. received a dividend refund in the amount of $7,000.

Other income that was reported by Conrod Holdings consisted of the following amounts:

Capital Gain	$9,200
Dividends From Imperial Oil	500
Interest	450

The capital gain was on the sale of land that was formerly used as a storage area for inventories. Improved inventory control procedures have eliminated the need for this land.

The interest is on deposits of temporary cash balances set aside for the purchase of inventories.

At the end of 2006, the Company's Refundable Dividend Tax On Hand balance was $8,950. The 2006 dividend refund was $4,000.

The Company's Taxable Income for the year ending December 31, 2007 was $44,000. No foreign income was included in this total. Assume the Part I Tax Payable for the year ending December 31, 2007 was correctly calculated as $9,250, including surtax of $501. Because of its association with Morsal Inc., its share of the annual business limit on income eligible for the small business deduction is $10,000. Conrod's active business income is equal to its share of the annual business limit.

Conrod Holdings paid taxable dividends of $10,000 during the year.

Required   For the taxation year ending December 31, 2007, determine the Part IV and refundable Part I taxes that will be payable by Conrod Holdings. In addition, determine the balance in the Refundable Dividend Tax On Hand account at December 31, 2007, and any dividend refund available.

Assignment Problem Sixteen - 5

Vader Ltd. is a Canadian controlled private corporation involved in the distribution of domestically produced laser products. It had the following Net Income For Tax Purposes for the year ending December 31, 2007:

Active Business Income	$216,300
Dividends From Canadian Corporations:	
Wholly-Owned Subsidiary	108,000
Portfolio Investments	56,000
Interest On Government Bonds	36,300
Taxable Capital Gains [(1/2)($114,600)]	57,300
Net Income For Tax Purposes	$473,900

During 2006, Vader Ltd. paid no dividends. On October 1, 2007, Vader Ltd. paid taxable dividends to its shareholders in the amount of $32,400. The dividends paid to Vader Ltd. by the wholly-owned subsidiary did not entitle the subsidiary to any dividend refund.

The balance in the Refundable Dividend Tax On Hand account was nil on December 31, 2006. The wholly-owned subsidiary is allocated $100,000 of the annual small business deduction. The remainder is allocated to Vader Ltd. This is the first year that Vader Ltd. has reported any capital gains.

Required: For Vader Ltd.'s 2007 taxation year, calculate the following items:

A. Federal Part I Tax Payable.
B. Part IV Tax Payable.
C. The balance in the Refundable Dividend Tax On Hand account on December 31, 2007.
D. The dividend refund, if any.
E. The balance in the capital dividend account.
F. Federal Tax Payable (net of any dividend refund).

Assignment Problem Sixteen - 6

The following data is for Masterson Ltd., a Canadian controlled private corporation. The data is for the taxation year ending December 31, 2007:

Canadian Source Active Business Income (Includes $99,000 Of Manufacturing And Processing Profits)	$133,000
Foreign Investment Income (Net Of $1,200 In Withheld Foreign Taxes)	6,800
Net Income For Tax Purposes (Division B Income)	141,000
Taxable Income	95,000

No net capital loss carry forwards were deducted during 2007.

Assume that the tax credit on foreign investment income is equal to the $1,200 in taxes withheld.

Required: Calculate the federal Part I Tax Payable for the taxation year ending December 31, 2007.

Assignment Problem Sixteen - 7

Gardner Distributing Company, a Canadian controlled private corporation, was established ten years ago by Mr. Hugh Gardner. Its only business activity is the distribution of specialty gardening products to retailers across Canada. Mr. Gardner is a Canadian resident and is the sole shareholder of the Company. The Company has a fiscal year ending on December 31, and, for 2007, the Company's accountant produced the following Income Statement:

Sales Revenue		$1,900,000
Cost Of Goods Sold		940,000
Gross Profit		**$ 960,000**
Operating Expenses:		
Selling And Administration	$ 315,000	
Amortization Expense	47,000	
Charitable Donations	15,000	
Total Operating Expenses		**$ 377,000**
Operating Income		**$ 583,000**
Other Income And Losses:		
Dividends From Taxable Canadian Companies	27,000	
Loss On Sale Of Truck	(19,000)	
Gain On Sale Of Investments	7,000	
Pre-Tax Accounting Income		**$ 598,000**

Other Information:

1. The Company had depreciable assets with the following undepreciated capital cost (UCC) balances at the beginning of its 2007 taxation year:

	UCC
Class 3 (5%)	$726,000
Class 8 (20%)	472,000
Class 10 (30%)	22,000

The balance in Class 10 reflects a single truck that was used for deliveries. It had an original cost in 2005 of $38,000 and a net book value for accounting purposes of $29,000. It was sold in 2007 for $10,000, and replaced with a leased truck.

The only other transaction involving depreciable assets during the year was the acquisition of $82,000 in Class 8 assets.

2. On December 31, 2006, the Company had a balance in its Refundable Dividend Tax On Hand account of $19,000. The Company claimed a dividend refund of $5,000 in its 2006 corporate tax return.

3. The balance in the capital dividend account was $27,200 on December 31, 2006.

4. The investments that were sold during the year had been purchased for $93,000. They were sold for $100,000.

5. The Gardner Distributing Company paid $17,000 in taxable dividends to Mr. Gardner. In addition, the Company elected to pay a capital dividend of $10,000 to Mr. Gardner during the year.

Required:

A. Determine Gardner Distributing Company's minimum Taxable Income for the year ending December 31, 2007.

B. Determine Gardner Distributing Company's Part I Tax Payable for the year ending December 31, 2007.

C. Determine the December 31, 2007 balance in the Gardner Distributing Company's Refundable Dividend Tax On Hand account.

D. Determine Gardner Distributing Company's minimum federal Tax Payable for the year ending December 31, 2007.

E. Determine the December 31, 2007 balance in the Gardner Distributing Company's capital dividend account.

Show all of the calculations used to provide the required information, including those for which the result is nil.

Assignment Problem Sixteen - 8

B & C Limited is a Canadian controlled private corporation throughout its taxation year ending December 31, 2007. For that year, its Net Income For Tax Purposes and Taxable Income can be calculated as follows:

Canadian Manufacturing And Processing Profits As Per ITR 5200 Formula	$123,000
Other Canadian Active Business Income	78,000
Canadian Source Interest Income	10,000
Canadian Source Taxable Capital Gains	24,000
Foreign Non-Business Income (Before $3,000 Withholding)	20,000
Foreign Business Income (Before $6,000 Withholding)	40,000
Portfolio Dividends From Taxable Canadian Corporations	26,000
Net Income For Tax Purposes	$321,000
Portfolio Dividends From Taxable Canadian Corporations	(26,000)
Charitable Donations	(32,000)
Net Capital Loss Carry Forward From 2006	(18,000)
Taxable Income	$245,000

Other Information:

1. B & C Limited paid taxable dividends of $124,000 during the year.

2. It has been determined that 91 percent of B & C Limited's Taxable Income was earned in Canada.

3. The December 31, 2006 balance in the Refundable Dividend Tax On Hand account was $132,000. The dividend refund for the year ending December 31, 2006 was $28,000.

4. B & C Limited is associated with another Canadian controlled private corporation. B & C Limited has been allocated $100,000 of the annual business limit.

5. Assume that the foreign tax credits for the foreign business and non-business income are equal to the amounts withheld.

Required:

A. Determine B & C Limited's federal Part I Tax Payable for the year ending December 31, 2007.

B. Determine the December 31, 2007 balance in the Refundable Dividend Tax On Hand account.

C. Determine the dividend refund for the year ending December 31, 2007.

Show all of the calculations used to provide the required information, including those for which the result is nil.

Assignment Problem Sixteen - 9

Startop Ltd. is a Canadian controlled private corporation that was established in Manitoba in 2002. For the year ending December 31, 2007, its accounting Net Income Before Taxes, as determined under generally accepted accounting principles, was $462,000. Other information for the 2007 fiscal year follows.

Other Information:

1. Startop sold depreciable assets for $450,000. These assets had an original cost of $390,000 and a net book value of $330,000. They were Class 8 assets and, at the beginning of 2007, the balance in this class was $350,000. The Company has other assets left in this class at the end of the year.

2. The Company's amortization expense was $546,000. Maximum deductible CCA for the year was $730,000.

3. The Company spent $50,000 on business meals and entertainment.

4. During the year, the Company begins selling a product on which they provide a five year warranty. At the end of the year, they established a warranty reserve of $20,000 to reflect the expected costs of providing warranty services.

5. It has been determined that Startop has active business income of $190,000 for the year. Included in this amount were manufacturing and processing profits, as determined by the *Income Tax Regulations*, of $150,000.

6. The Company's revenues included foreign source non-business income of $17,000 (Canadian dollars). This was the amount that was received after the withholding of $3,000 (15 percent of the gross amount) by the foreign tax authorities.

7. During the year, the Company had the following amounts of Canadian source investment income:

Interest On Long-Term Investments	$25,000
Taxable Capital Gains	30,000
Dividends On Bank of Nova Scotia Shares	11,000

8. At December 31, 2006, the Company had a non-capital loss carry forward of $205,000 and a net capital loss carry forward of $19,000 [(1/2)($38,000)] from 2005.

9. Because of losses in previous years, no instalment payments were made for the year.

10. As of December 31, 2006, the balance in Startop's capital dividend account was $20,000.

11. As of December 31, 2006, the balance in Startop's RDTOH account was $17,000. No dividends were paid during 2006. During the year ending December 31, 2007, the Company used its existing cash resources to pay taxable dividends of $210,000.

Required:

A. Calculate Startop's minimum Taxable Income for the year ending December 31, 2007.

B. Calculate Startop's Part IV Tax Payable for the year ending December 31, 2007.

C. Assume the foreign non-business tax credit is equal to the foreign tax withheld. Calculate Startop's Part I Tax Payable for the year ending December 31, 2007.

D. Assume the foreign non-business tax credit is equal to the foreign tax withheld. Calculate Startop's dividend refund for the year ending December 31, 2007.

E. Do not assume the foreign non-business tax credit is equal to the foreign tax withheld. Using the amounts calculated in Part C, compare your results under this new scenario with the Part C calculation of Part I Tax Payable. As part of your solution, provide a detailed calculation of the small business deduction, the ITA 123.3 refundable tax (ART) and the foreign tax credit available to Startop for the year ending December 31, 2007. Any excess of foreign tax withheld over the federal foreign tax credit will be applied against the provincial tax liability.

F. Comment on any tax planning issues that should be reviewed.

Show all of the calculations used to provide the required information, including those for which the result is nil.

Assignment Case

Case Sixteen - 1 *(Using ProFile T2 Software For Corporate Returns)*

Radion Industries Ltd. (RIL) is a Canadian controlled private corporation, located at 333 Laurier Avenue West in Ottawa, Ontario K1A 0L9. It was incorporated on February 24, 1990. Its Business Number is 111111118RC 0001, its Ontario Corporation tax account number is 1234567, and its telephone number is (613) 598-2290. The Company has 1,000 shares of common stock issued and outstanding, all of which are held by Margaret Reid (SIN 527-000-301). Ms. Reid, the president of the Company, is the person who should be contacted with respect to matters concerning the Company's books and records.

RIL is a retailer of patio furniture. All of its sales occur within Canada. RIL also holds some of the investments that Ms. Reid inherited from a substantial estate two years earlier.

It owns all of the 500 common shares of Reid Inc., which holds most of Ms. Reid's inherited investments. Reid Inc. is also involved in earning active business income through the marketing and distribution of RIL's products. Reid Inc. has a December 31 fiscal year end and has not registered for a Business Number. (Enter NR in ProFile in the field for Business Number.)

For the taxation year ending December 31, 2006, RIL's GAAP based Income Statement, before any deduction for income taxes, was as follows:

Sales Revenues	$580,000
Interest On Long-Term Debt	27,500
Interest Received On Foreign Bank Account (Note 1)	18,000
Dividends On Royal Bank Shares	17,500
Dividends From Reid Inc. (Note 2)	42,000
Gain On Sale Of Shares (Note 3)	27,000
Total Revenues	$712,000
Cost Of Goods Sold	$208,000
Amortization Expense	122,000
Other Operating Expenses	147,000
Total Expenses (Excluding Taxes)	$477,000
Net Income (Before Taxes)	$235,000
Dividends Declared And Paid	(92,000)
Increase In Retained Earnings	$143,000

Note 1 This interest is net of $2,000 in taxes withheld in Ireland.

Note 2 As a result of paying this $42,000 in dividends to RIL, Reid Inc. received a dividend refund of $14,000.

Note 3 On March 23, 2006, RIL sold 2,700 shares of Canadian Imperial Bank of Commerce. The common shares had cost $118,800 on June 6, 2003 and were sold for net proceeds of $145,800.

Other Information:

1. Expenses include a deduction for charitable donations to the Ottawa Civic Hospital in the amount of $5,000.

2. RIL's Expenses include penalties of $3,500 resulting from a judgment in the Tax Court Of Canada.

Assignment Case

3. RIL reimbursed Ms. Reid $34,000 for business meals and entertainment for clients and suppliers during the year.

4. During the year, RIL incurred $20,000 in landscaping costs. For accounting purposes these are being treated as a capital asset, to be amortized using the straight-line method over 10 years. The related amortization is included in the Amortization Expense shown on the Income Statement.

5. The opening UCC balances were $246,000 for Class 1, $135,000 for Class 8 and $90,000 for Class 10. The only fixed asset disposition during the year was the sale of a delivery truck. The truck had cost $35,000 and was sold for its net book value of $12,000. The only fixed asset acquisition was $52,000 in office furniture.

6. At December 31, 2005, the balance in RIL's RDTOH account was $5,200. No dividends were paid in 2005.

7. RIL allocates $60,000 of the annual business limit to Reid Inc. This is $5,000 more than Reid Inc. can utilize in 2006.

8. RIL has total assets of $3,236,000, including cash of $235,000 as at December 31, 2006.

9. As RIL had no Taxable Income in the previous year, no tax instalments were paid during the year.

Required: Prepare the federal corporate tax return for RIL for the 2006 taxation year using the ProFile T2 corporate software program. Ignore the GIFI requirements.

Hint: It is possible to eliminate the warning messages generated by ProFile related to the GIFI without completing all of the GIFI requirements. This will not affect the calculations in the tax return.

On GIFI Schedule 125:
  • Input the total revenues on the line "Total Sales Of Goods And Services" (Code 8000).
  • Choose "Amortization of tangible assets" (Code 8670) from the drop down menu under Operating Expenses and input the amortization expense.
  • Choose "Other expenses" (Code 9270) from the drop down menu under Operating Expenses and input the Total Expenses less Amortization Expense.

On GIFI Schedule 100:
  • Input the Net Income figure as "Cash and deposits" (Code 1000) in order to make the total assets equal to the total liabilities and equity.

Although this will not properly complete the GIFI statements, this will give the correct Net Income figure that will carry forward to the Schedule 1 and eliminate the warning messages that would otherwise be generated.

CHAPTER 17

Corporate Taxation And Management Decisions

The Decision To Incorporate

Basic Tax Considerations

Deferral And Reduction

17-1.   One of the more important decisions facing the owner of a business is deciding whether or not the business should be incorporated.   There are, of course, a number of non-tax considerations involved in this decision and these factors will be reviewed in this Chapter. At this point, however, we are concerned with the influence of corporate taxation on this decision.

17-2.   The decision to incorporate, both from a legal and a tax point of view, has the effect of separating the business from its owners. This means that, in order for incorporated business income to be made available to the owner, it must go through two levels of taxation. First, the amount of Tax Payable applicable to the corporation will be determined. Then, when any after tax amounts are distributed to the owner, either as salary or as dividends, additional personal taxes will be payable on the amounts received.

17-3.   This dual system of taxation may or may not be advantageous to the owner of the business. In terms of the direct tax advantages resulting from a single individual incorporating business income, there are two possibilities:

Tax Reduction   In some situations, the total taxes that would be paid at the combined corporate and personal level will be less when the business is incorporated than would be the case if the individual had earned the business income directly as an individual proprietor.

Tax Deferral   As was noted in Paragraph 17-2, getting income from its source through a corporation and into the hands of a shareholder involves two levels of taxation. If the shareholder does not require all available income for his personal needs, after tax funds can be left in the corporation, resulting in a postponement of the second level of taxation. If the rate at which the corporation is taxed is lower than the rate at which the individual would be taxed on the direct receipt of the income, the use of a corporation provides tax deferral.

17-4.   As you probably discerned while proceeding through the previous corporate taxation chapters, whether the presence of a corporation will provide a deferral or reduction of taxes depends on both the type of corporation and the type of income that is being earned by that business entity.

17-5.   This means that there is no one answer to the question of whether incorporation will provide tax reduction and/or tax deferral. Given this, we will devote a major section of this Chapter to examining the various possible combinations of income types and corporate classifications in order to provide you with a general understanding of the availability of these two tax features. This material begins in Paragraph 17-12.

Using Imperfections In The Integration System

17-6.   We have previously noted that the integration provisions that are contained in Canadian tax legislation are based on the assumption that certain corporate and personal tax rates prevail. Even at the federal level, actual corporate tax rates vary from the notional rates required for effective integration.

17-7.   In addition, there are significant variations in the corporate tax rates used by the provinces. This means that it is unlikely that the combined federal/provincial rate in any given province will be equal to the notional combined rates assumed in the integration model. As it may be possible to use incorporation to take advantage of these imperfections in the integration system, it is important for you to understand how the imperfections can influence the decision to incorporate. We will provide a section which deals with this issue, beginning in Paragraph 17-61.

Income Splitting

17-8.   Even in situations where the use of a corporation neither reduces, nor defers significant amounts of taxes, incorporation may be attractive to a family or other related group of individuals. In a typical family situation, it is fairly common to find some individuals earning amounts far in excess of the amount required to put them in the maximum personal tax bracket while, at the same time, other members of the group have incomes that leave them in a lower bracket or free of taxes altogether.

17-9.   As was discussed in Chapter 3, if some method can be found to redistribute the aggregate family or group income from high income to low income individuals, the tax savings can be significant. We will provide a section which deals with this possibility, commonly referred to as income splitting, beginning in Paragraph 17-90 of this Chapter.

Other Advantages And Disadvantages

Advantages

17-10.   Other advantages that are normally associated with the use of a corporation are as follows:

> **Limited Liability**   Because a corporation is a separate legal entity, the shareholders' liability to creditors is limited to the amount that they have invested. That is, creditors of the corporation can look only to the assets of the corporation for satisfaction of their claims. However, for smaller corporations, obtaining significant amounts of financing will almost always require the owners to provide personal guarantees on any loans, making this advantage somewhat illusory for this type of company. Note, however, limited liability may still be important for a business that is exposed to significant product or environmental claims.

> **Lifetime Capital Gains Deduction**   Individuals who dispose of the shares of a qualified small business corporation are eligible to claim the $750,000 lifetime capital gains deduction. To qualify, a business must be a Canadian controlled private corporation with substantially all of the fair market value of its assets (at least 90 percent) used in an active business carried on primarily in Canada (at least 50 percent) at the time of disposition. In addition, no one other than the seller, or related persons, can

own the shares during the 24 months preceding the sale. During this 24 month period, more than 50 percent of the fair market value of the assets must have been used in active business carried on primarily in Canada. For a more complete discussion of this provision, see Chapter 14.

Foreign Taxes   Foreign estate taxes can often be avoided by placing foreign property in a Canadian corporation.

Estate Planning   A corporation can be used in estate planning, particularly with respect to freezing the asset values of an estate (see Chapter 21).

Disadvantages

17-11.   Disadvantages that are normally associated with incorporation include the following:

Loss Deductions   An individual can deduct business and unrestricted farm losses against any other source of income, including employment and property income. If the business or farm is incorporated, such losses can only be deducted against past or future corporate income. The corporation's losses cannot be used to offset a shareholder's other sources of income. This is of particular importance to operations that are just getting started as they will frequently experience significant losses in their formative years.

Tax Credits   A corporation is not eligible for personal tax credits, such as the basic personal, tuition fee, education, age, pension, and disability tax credits.

Charitable Donations   Charitable donations provide the basis for a tax credit for individuals, largely at the maximum 29 percent federal rate. In contrast, they are a deduction in calculating Taxable Income for a corporation. If the corporate tax rate is low, they will be of less value to a corporation than they would be to an individual.

Additional Maintenance Costs   The legal, accounting, and other costs associated with maintaining a business operation will be significantly higher in the case of a corporation (e.g., the cost of filing a corporate tax return on an annual basis).

Winding Up Procedures   The complications associated with the termination of an incorporated business will be greater than would usually be the case with a proprietorship or partnership. In addition, there may be adverse tax effects on winding up.

Tax Reduction And Deferral

Approach

17-12.   As we have noted, whether the use of a corporation will result in a reduction or deferral of taxes will depend on the type of income being earned, as well as the type of corporation. In this section, we will examine this issue by using a basic example to consider this issue in the following situations:

- A public corporation earning both income eligible for the M&P deduction and income that is not eligible for this deduction.

- A CCPC earning active business income that is eligible for the small business deduction and income that is not eligible for the small business deduction.

- A CCPC earning investment income (net taxable capital gains and other property income, excluding dividends).

- A CCPC earning both eligible and non-eligible dividend income.

17-13.   These cases should serve to provide you with a good understanding of the ability of incorporation to provide either tax avoidance or tax deferral for an individual taxpayer.

Basic Example

The Taxpayer

17-14.   In order to consider the various results that can be achieved by incorporating a source of income, we will use a simple example in which an individual, Mr. Renaud, has access to $100,000 in income that he can either receive directly or channel through a corporation. We will assume that, before any consideration of this additional $100,000, Mr. Renaud has sufficient Taxable Income to place him in the maximum federal tax bracket of 29 percent ($120,887 for 2007). The Tax Payable on his other income is sufficient to absorb all of his personal and other tax credits.

17-15.   To illustrate the effects of incorporating different types of income, several cases will be presented with varying assumptions as to the source of this income and the type of corporation that will be established.   However, before turning to these cases, we will give consideration to the various personal and corporate tax rates that will be used.

Personal Tax Rates And Tax Payable

17-16.   In these examples, we will assume that Mr. Renaud lives in a province where the maximum provincial tax rate on individuals is 16 percent. As all of Mr. Renaud's additional income will be subject to this maximum rate, his combined federal/provincial marginal rate will be 45 (29 + 16) percent. Referring to the listing of combined rates on ordinary income in Paragraph 6-25 of the text, this rate is roughly the average provincial rate.

17-17.   This 45 percent rate is applicable to the direct receipt of income. This means that, if Mr. Renaud receives the $100,000 in income without channeling it through a corporation, taxes of $45,000 will be paid and $55,000 will be retained.

17-18.   If the income is received in the form of dividends from a taxable Canadian corporation, the situation is more complex. The amount of the dividends received must be grossed up, with this amount providing the basis for a credit against taxes payable. The amounts involved will depend on whether the dividends are eligible (e.g. paid by a non-CCPC out of fully taxed income) or non-eligible (e.g., paid by a CCPC out of income that has benefited from the small business deduction):

Non-Eligible Dividends These dividends will be grossed up by 25 percent and will benefit from a federal dividend tax credit of 2/3 of the gross up. We will assume that Mr. Renaud lives in a province where the dividend tax credit on non-eligible dividends is 28 percent of the dividend gross up (roughly the average for all provinces).

Eligible Dividends These dividends will be grossed up by 45 percent and will benefit from a federal dividend tax credit of 11/18 of the gross up. We will assume that Mr. Renaud lives in a province where the dividend tax credit on eligible dividends is 30 percent of the dividend gross up (roughly the average for all provinces).

17-19.   Using these gross up and tax credit amounts, the rates applicable to Mr. Renaud on eligible and non-eligible dividends can be calculated as follows:

	Non-Eligible Dividends	Eligible Dividends
Dividends Received	100.0%	100.0%
Add: Gross Up	25.0%	45.0%
Equals: Personal Taxable Income	125.0%	145.0%
Times The Combined Federal/Provincial Tax Rate	45.0%	45.0%
Equals: Combined Federal/Provincial Tax Rate On Dividends Received	56.3%	65.3%
Less: Dividend Tax Credit:		
[(2/3 + 28%)(25%)]	(23.7%)	N/A
[(11/18 + 30%)(45%)]	N/A	(41.0%)
Effective Personal Tax Rate On Dividends Received	32.6%	24.3%

17-20.   In the examples that follow, we will round the rate on non-eligible dividends to 33 percent of dividends received. For eligible dividends, we will round the rate to 24 percent of dividends received.

Corporate Tax Rates

17-21.   In making the required calculations, we will use the corporate federal tax rates that apply for the 2007 calendar year. With respect to provincial rates, we will use 5 percent for income eligible for the small business deduction and 14 percent for other income. These rates are approximately the average of the rates used in the various provinces. Other rates to be used are as follows:

General Part I Tax Rate	38.0%
Corporate Surtax	4.0%
Federal Tax Abatement	10.0%
General Rate Reduction	7.0%
Refundable Tax On Investment Income Of A CCPC (ART)	6-2/3%
Federal Manufacturing And Processing Profits Deduction	7.0%
Federal Small Business Deduction	16.0%
Provincial Tax Rates	
Income Eligible For Federal Small Business Deduction	5.0%
Income Not Eligible For Federal Small Business Deduction	14.0%
Refundable Portion Of Part I Tax On Investment Income	26-2/3%
Refundable Part IV Tax	33-1/3%

17-22.   Note that the general rate reduction is not applicable to income that benefits from either the small business deduction or the M&P deduction. In addition, in the case of a CCPC, it is not applicable to aggregate investment income (net taxable capital gains and property income).

17-23.   To assist you in understanding this material (which is covered in detail in Chapter 16), we remind you that eligible dividends include:

- Designated dividends paid by non-CCPCs that do not have a positive Low Rate Income Pool (LRIP) balance.
- Designated dividends paid by CCPCs with a positive General Rate Income Pool (GRIP).

17-24.   We will apply this basic information, in a number of different situations, in order to examine the question of whether the incorporation of $100,000 in income will serve to either reduce or defer taxes for an individual taxpayer.

Public Corporation

General Results

17-25.   With only $100,000 of income, it is not likely that Mr. Renaud would be in a position to establish a public company. However, this case does serve to illustrate a simple calculation of corporate taxes. In addition, this same tax calculation would apply to a CCPC on amounts of active business income in excess of $400,000, or active business income in excess of a CCPC's allocated annual business limit.

17-26.   With the M&P rate reduction equal to the general rate reduction, the federal taxes that would be paid on $100,000 in Taxable Income would be the same on both M&P income and on income that does not qualify for the M&P deduction. While the calculation is somewhat different, the results are the same for both types of income. We would remind you that we continue to illustrate this calculation as a reflection of the fact that the M&P legislation is still in place and is of some significance in provinces that have special rates for this type of income. For example, in Ontario, the general rate for public corporations is reduced by 2 percentage points on M&P income (from 14 percent to 12 percent).

17-27.   As discussed in Chapter 16, dividends paid by non-CCPCs, a category that includes public companies, will generally be designated as eligible. There will be situations, however, where a public corporation has an LRIP. While this raises the possibility that at least some of the dividends paid by such a company would be non-eligible, we do not feel that this situation is of sufficient importance that an illustration of the tax reduction and deferral results is warranted. It should be fairly obvious to you that for non-eligible dividends, the tax reduction results would be significantly worse than those illustrated in the following calculations.

Public Corporation	M&P Deduction	No M&P
Federal Tax [(38%)($100,000)]	$38,000	$38,000
Corporate Surtax [(4%)(28%)($100,000)]]	1,120	1,120
Federal Tax Abatement [(10%)($100,000)]	(10,000)	(10,000)
M&P Deduction [(7%)($100,000)]	(7,000)	N/A
General Rate Reduction [(7%)($100,000)]	N/A	(7,000)
Federal Tax Payable	$22,120	$22,120
Provincial Tax Payable [(14%)($100,000)]	14,000	14,000
Corporate Tax Payable	$36,120	$36,120
Corporate Business Income	$100,000	$100,000
Corporate Tax Payable	(36,120)	(36,120)
Maximum Eligible Dividend Payable	$ 63,880	$ 63,880
Personal Tax On Eligible Dividends [(24%)($63,880)]	(15,331)	(15,331)
Income Retained By The Individual	$ 48,549	$ 48,549
After Tax Retention - With Corporation	$ 48,549	$ 48,549
After Tax Retention - Without Corporation	(55,000)	(55,000)
Advantage (Disadvantage) With Corporation	($ 6,451)	($ 6,451)

Analysis

17-28.   If the $100,000 had been received directly, $55,000 [($100,000)(1 - .45)] would be retained, an amount significantly greater than the $48,549 that is retained when the $100,000 is flowed through either corporation. Clearly, in terms of total taxes paid, Mr. Renaud has not done as well with the use of a corporation.

17-29.   However, there is a deferral of tax on income that is left within the corporation. The corporate taxes in both calculations are $36,120, compared with $45,000 in personal taxes that would be paid if the income was received directly. There is some question as to whether this amount of deferral would justify the payment of an additional $6,451 in taxes.

17-30.   More to the point is that, in real world terms, deferral is not an issue for shareholders of publicly traded companies. In the case of private corporations with a single shareholder or a small shareholder group, these individuals can control the extent to which their corporation distributes resources. If they do not have an immediate need for funds, tax deferral can be achieved by leaving resources in their corporation.

17-31.   This is not the case with large publicly traded companies. Their dividend decisions are based on a large number of factors, including cash flow needs and the maximization of share values. The financial needs of individual shareholders would rarely be at the top of this list.

Integration And Eligible Dividends

17-32.   The preceding examples are based on the public corporation paying eligible dividends. The government's stated goal in bringing in the eligible dividends legislation was to improve integration by lowering the total corporate and personal taxes paid on income flowed through a public company. The calculations in Paragraph 17-27 make it clear that, at current corporate tax rates, this stated goal has not been achieved.

17-33. With a federal tax rate of 22.12 percent [(38% - 10%)(1.04) - 7%] and a provincial tax rate of 14 percent, there is still a significant tax disadvantage, $6,451 on $100,000 of income, for income that is flowed through a public corporation.

17-34. As discussed in Chapter 9, the enhanced gross up and tax credit procedures are based on a notional corporate tax rate of about 31 percent, well below 36.12 percent that is applicable in this example. In order to have integration work for public corporations, the combined federal/provincial tax rate will have to fall to the 31 percent level that is assumed in the eligible dividend procedures.

Corporate Rate Reductions

17-35. As discussed in Chapter 15, the federal tax rate on corporations will be reduced to 18.5 percent by the year 2011. This will serve to improve integration for publicly traded corporations. However, in order to achieve the required federal/provincial rate of 31 percent, the provincial rate will have to be 12.5 percent (31.0% - 18.5%). While such rates are available in some provinces (e.g., Quebec is at 9.9 percent), the majority of provinces have rates in excess of 12.5 percent (e.g., Nova Scotia is at 16.0 percent).

CCPC - Active Business Income

General Results

17-36. A CCPC can be subject to two different tax rates on its active business income. A low rate is available on up to $400,000 of income that is eligible for the small business deduction, with a higher tax rate assessed on income that is not eligible for this valuable deduction. With respect to the provinces, there is a similar dual rate system. In addition, we will have to take into consideration that dividends that have been paid out of income that has benefited from the small business deduction cannot be designated as eligible dividends.

17-37. We will continue to use the Mr. Renaud example from Paragraph 17-14 to illustrate the tax consequences of applying these two rates. While continuing to use the basic data from this example, we will consider two different cases:

Case One   In this Case One, we will assume that the corporate income is eligible for the small business deduction. This means that dividends that are paid to Mr. Renaud will be non-eligible and subject to tax at a rate of 33 percent.

Case Two   In this Case Two, we will assume that none of the corporate income is eligible for the small business deduction (the full amount has been allocated to an associated corporation). This means that the dividends that are paid to Mr. Renaud will be eligible and subject to tax at a rate of 24 percent. You will note that the results in this case are identical to those for a public corporation (see Paragraph 7-27).

Active Business Income Of CCPC	Case One SBD Deduction	Case Two No SBD
Federal Tax [(38%)($100,000)]	$ 38,000	$ 38,000
Corporate Surtax [(4%)(28%)($100,000)]	1,120	1,120
Federal Tax Abatement [(10%)($100,000)]	(10,000)	(10,000)
Small Business Deduction [(16%)($100,000)]	(16,000)	N/A
General Rate Reduction [(7%)($100,000)]	N/A	(7,000)
Federal Tax Payable	$ 13,120	$ 22,120
Provincial Tax Payable:		
At 5 Percent	5,000	N/A
At 14 Percent	N/A	14,000
Corporate Tax Payable	$ 18,120	$ 36,120

Active Business Income Of CCPC	Case One SBD Deduction	Case Two No SBD
Corporate Business Income	$100,000	$100,000
Corporate Tax Payable	(18,120)	(36,120)
Maximum Dividend Payable	$ 81,880	$ 63,880
Personal Tax At 33 Percent	(27,020)	N/A
Personal Tax At 24 Percent	N/A	(15,331)
Income Retained By The Individual	$ 54,860	$ 48,549
After Tax Retention - With Corporation	$ 54,860	$ 48,549
After Tax Retention - Without Corporation	(55,000)	(55,000)
Advantage (Disadvantage) With Corporation	($ 140)	($ 6,451)

Analysis

17-38. As can be seen in the preceding table, even in situations where the corporate income benefits from the small business deduction, there is small tax cost associated with the use of a corporation. After tax retention of $100,000 flowed through a corporation is $54,860, $140 less than the amount that would be retained without the use of a corporation.

17-39. However, in this situation the use of a corporation can provide substantial tax deferral, whether or not the income benefits from the small business deduction. On income that benefits from this deduction, the tax that is assessed at the corporate level is $18,120, well below the $45,000 that would be applicable if Mr. Renaud had received the income directly. Even on the more heavily taxed ineligible income, the corporate taxes of $36,120 are still below the $45,000 that would be applicable on the direct receipt of the $100,000.

17-40. While this situation does offer excellent opportunities for tax deferral, one point is sometimes overlooked. Any income that is left in the corporation should not be left idle. If it is not needed in the principal activities, it is likely that it will be invested in assets that will produce investment income. If this income is not eligible for the small business deduction, the amount of deferral at the corporate level is significantly smaller. This will be illustrated in a later example when we look at the taxation of investment income received by a Canadian controlled private corporation.

"Bonusing Down" Active Business Income

17-41. A traditional tax planning technique for owners of CCPCs that have active business income in excess of their annual business limit, is to "bonus down". As our example has shown, income that is eligible for the small business deduction benefits from significant tax deferral, as well as a modest tax savings. In contrast, if a CCPC's Taxable Income does not benefit from the small business deduction, the total taxes that will be paid on the flow through of this excess income will be significantly higher. As shown in Paragraph 17-37, the total corporate and individual taxes on $100,000 of income that is not eligible for the small business deduction are $51,451 ($36,120 + $15,331).

17-42. When it is likely that a CCPC will have Taxable Income in excess of the $400,000 annual business limit, the simple solution is for the owner of the CCPC to pay himself sufficient additional salary that the corporation's Taxable Income will be reduced to $400,000.

> **Example** In our example, if Mr. Renaud had a CCPC with active business income of $500,000, paying additional salary of $100,000 would result in his paying additional taxes of $45,000 on receipt of this salary. This, of course, is much lower than the $51,451 that would be paid if the $100,000 ($500,000 - $400,000) that is not eligible for the small business deduction was taxed at the corporate level, with the residual amount being paid to Mr. Renaud as dividends.

17-43. Prior to the introduction of the enhanced 45 percent gross up and tax credit procedures, the case for bonusing down was stronger. On $100,000 of income not benefiting from the small business deduction, the tax cost to Mr Renaud of not paying this amount out in salary would have been over $12,000. The introduction of the enhanced gross up and credit procedures has reduced this to $6,451. At this reduced level, it is likely that some individuals will conclude that enjoying the tax deferral associated with leaving the income in the corporation is more beneficial that this reduced amount of tax savings. This view is more likely to prevail in situations where the shareholder can afford to leave the income in the corporation for a long period of time.

17-44.   At one point in time, there was concern as to whether such arrangements would be attacked by the CRA using the General Anti-Avoidance legislation. Fortunately, this is not the case. In Income Tax Technical News #30 (May 21, 2004), the CRA explained their policy of not challenging the reasonableness of remuneration to a shareholder who is active in the business' operations.

> The general purpose of the policy is to provide flexibility to a CCPC and its active shareholder/managers to take advantage of marginal tax rates by reducing the corporation's taxable income to, or below, the small business deduction limit through the payment of salaries and bonuses from income derived from normal business operations, and to provide certainty as to the taxable status of the transactions.

17-45.   Given this statement, it seems clear that bonusing down to a level that will eliminate all corporate Taxable Income that is not eligible for the small business deduction will generally not be questioned by the CRA.

17-46.   As a final point here, many owner-managers may not be convinced that bonusing down is a good idea. The problem is that bonusing down involves paying taxes out of the owner-manager's personal funds. It is not uncommon to encounter individuals who, even in situations where there is a clear cut tax advantage to using this procedure, will simply refuse to make the required salary payments. While this is usually not a rational decision, it appears to reflect a greater level of comfort for an owner-manager when he does not have to pay the taxes directly out of his personal assets.

Electing Out Of The Small Business Deduction

17-47.   ITA 89(11) allows a CCPC to make an election not to be a CCPC. The good news is that making this election will allow the corporation to designate its dividends as eligible. The bad news is that it will lose the small business deduction.

17-48.   If this election is made, the tax reduction and deferral results would be the same as those shown in Paragraph 17-37 for the no small business deduction case. While there may be some situations where this election may be useful, the fact that it appears to have a significant tax cost would suggest that its application would not be common.

Exercise Seventeen-1

Subject: Incorporation Of Active Business Income

Keith Slater has an unincorporated business that he anticipates will have active business income of $126,000 during the coming year. He has employment income in excess of $200,000, with additional amounts subject to a provincial tax rate of 14 percent. The provincial dividend tax credit is equal to one-third of the dividend gross up for all dividends. Also in his province of residence, the corporate tax rate is 5 percent on income eligible for the small business deduction and 15.4 percent on other income. Mr. Slater has asked your advice as to whether he should incorporate this business. Advise him with respect to any tax deferral that could be available on income left in the corporation and on any tax savings that could be available if all of the income is paid out as dividends.

End of Exercise.   Solution available in Study Guide.

CCPC - Investment Income Other Than Dividends

17-49. The aggregate investment income of a CCPC is taxed at full corporate rates. Neither the small business deduction nor the general rate reduction is available to offset these rates. In addition, there is an additional refundable tax under ITA 123.3 (the ART) equal to 6-2/3 percent of investment income.

17-50. To offset this high level of taxation, a dividend refund is available on dividends paid at a rate of $1 for each $3 of dividends paid. Note, however, these dividends cannot be designated as eligible for the enhanced 45 percent dividend gross up and tax credit procedures.

17-51. Continuing our Mr. Renaud example from Paragraph 17-14, after tax retention on $100,000 of investment income received by a CCPC, compared to the direct receipt of investment income, would be as follows:

Investment Income Of CCPC

Federal Tax [(38%)($100,000)]	$ 38,000
Corporate Surtax [(4%)(28%)($100,000)]	1,120
Additional Refundable Tax [(6-2/3%)($100,000)]	6,667
Federal Tax Abatement [(10%)($100,000)]	(10,000)
Federal Tax Payable	$ 35,787
Provincial Tax Payable [(14%)($100,000)]	14,000
Corporate Tax Payable	$ 49,787
Corporate Investment Income	$100,000
Corporate Tax Payable	(49,787)
Net Corporate Income Before Dividend Refund	$ 50,213
Maximum Dividend Refund (See Note)	25,107
Maximum Dividend Payable	$ 75,320
Personal Tax On Non-Eligible Dividends At 33 Percent	(24,856)
Income Retained By The Individual	$ 50,464
After Tax Flow Through With Corporation	$ 50,464
After Tax Flow Through Without Corporation	(55,000)
Advantage (Disadvantage) With Corporation	($ 4,536)

Note There was a $26,667 [($100,000)(26-2/3%)] addition to the RDTOH during the year. However, the amount of the refund is the lesser of this balance and one-third of dividends paid. As only $50,213 in after tax income was available for the payment of dividends, the refund is limited to $25,107 [(1/3)($75,320)]. Note that the $25,107 can also be calculated as one-half of $50,213, the funds available prior to the refund. An additional amount of $1,560 ($26,667 - $25,107) remains refundable on future dividends.

17-52. In terms of either tax deferral or tax savings, there does not appear to be any advantage associated with using a CCPC to receive investment income. Not only is there no deferral, there is a fairly large prepayment of taxes when a corporation is used ($49,787 vs. $45,000). In addition, the total tax bill on the flow through of the income is $4,536 higher using this approach.

Exercise Seventeen-2

Subject: Incorporation Of Interest Income

David Slater has investments that he anticipates will earn interest income of $126,000 during the coming year. He has employment income in excess of $200,000, with additional amounts subject to a provincial tax rate of 14 percent. The provincial dividend tax credit is equal to one-third of the dividend gross up for all dividends. Also in his province of residence, the corporate tax rate is 5 percent on income eligible for the small business deduction and 15.4 percent on other income. Mr. Slater has asked your advice as to whether he should transfer these investments to a corporation in which he would own all of the shares. Advise him with respect to any tax deferral that could be available on income left in the corporation and on any tax savings that could be available if all of the income is paid out as dividends.

End of Exercise. Solution available in Study Guide.

CCPC - Dividend Income

Possible Sources Of Dividend Income

17-53. Depending on its nature and source, the dividend income of a CCPC is subject to a variety of possible tax treatments. The various possibilities are as follows:

Eligible Portfolio Dividends These dividends will be subject to Part IV tax. However, because they are eligible dividends, they will be added to the CCPC's GRIP. This means that they can be designated as eligible dividends to the CCPC's shareholders.

Non-Eligible Portfolio Dividends These dividends will be subject to Part IV tax. They will not be added to the CCPC's GRIP and cannot be distributed to the CCPC's shareholders as eligible dividends.

Connected Company Dividends - Dividend Refund These dividends will be subject to Part IV tax. As these dividends were paid out of the investment income of a CCPC, they will not be added to the CCPC's GRIP and cannot be distributed to the CCPC's shareholders as eligible dividends.

Connected Company Dividends - No Dividend Refund These dividends will not be subject to Part IV tax. The fact that there is no refund generally means that the connected company paid these amounts out of income that benefited from the small business deduction. This means they will not be added to the CCPC's GRIP and cannot be distributed to the CCPC's shareholders as eligible dividends.

Analysis

17-54. Recalling (see Paragraph 17-20) that Mr. Renaud would pay taxes on eligible dividends received at a rate of 24 percent, his after tax retention on the direct receipt of $100,000 of these dividends would be $76,000 [($100,000)(1 - .24)]. His rate on non-eligible dividends is 33 percent (see Paragraph 17-20) and this would result in after tax retention of $67,000 [($100,000)(1 - .33)]. A comparison of this retention with the after tax results from using a corporation would be as follows:

Dividend Income Of CCPC	Eligible Portfolio Dividends	Non-Eligible Portfolio Dividends	Connected With Refund	Connected No Refund
Corporate Dividend Income	$100,000	$100,000	$100,000	$100,000
Part IV Tax Payable At 33-1/3%	(33,333)	(33,333)	(33,333)	N/A
Net Corporate Income				
Before Dividend Refund	$ 66,667	$ 66,667	$ 66,667	$100,000
Dividend Refund ($1/$3)	33,333	33,333	33,333	N/A
Maximum Dividend Payable	$100,000	$100,000	$100,000	$100,000
Personal Tax On:				
Eligible Dividends At 24%	(24,000)			
Non-Eligible Dividends At 33%	N/A	(33,000)	(33,000)	(33,000)
Income Retained By Individual	$ 76,000	$ 67,000	$ 67,000	$ 67,000
After Tax Flow Through:				
With Corporation	$ 76,000	$ 67,000	$ 67,000	$ 67,000
Without Corporation	(76,000)	(67,000)	(67,000)	(67,000)
Advantage (Disadvantage)	Nil	Nil	Nil	Nil

17-55.   In all cases, the dividends that can flow through to the investor total the full $100,000 that was received by the corporation. As a result, the total Tax Payable on dividends is the same whether the investment is held personally or in a corporation.

17-56.   The Part IV tax does, however, influence the conclusions on tax deferral. If the dividends are subject to Part IV tax, this 33-1/3 percent tax is slightly higher than either the 24 percent tax rate on eligible dividends received by an individual, or the 33 percent tax rate applicable to non-eligible dividends. As a result, there is no deferral available through incorporating to receive dividend income that is subject to Part IV tax.

17-57.   The situation is different in the absence of a Part IV tax in that no taxes will be assessed on dividends received at the corporate level. This, of course, provides for a significant deferral of Tax Payable on dividends not subject to Part IV tax.

Conclusions On Tax Reductions And Deferrals

17-58.   The results the we have calculated in the preceding cases can be summarized as follows:

	Corporate Taxes Before Dividend Refund	After Tax Retention On Flow Through
Public Corporation ($100,000 Of Income):		
Eligible For M&P (Paragraph 17-27)	$36,120	$48,549
Not Eligible For M&P (Paragraph 17-27)	36,120	48,549
CCPC ($100,000 Of Active Business Income):		
Eligible For SBD (Paragraph 17-37)	$18,120	$54,860
Not Eligible For SBD (Paragraph 17-37)	36,120	48,549
CCPC ($100,000 Of Interest Income):		
Investment Income (Paragraph 17-51)	$49,787	$50,464
CCPC ($100,000 Of Dividend Income):		
Eligible Portfolio Dividends (Paragraph 17-54)	$33,333	$76,000
Non-Eligible Portfolio Dividends (Paragraph 17-54)	33,333	67,000
Connected With Refund (Paragraph 17-54)	33,333	67,000
Connected No Refund (Paragraph 17-54)	Nil	67,000

17-59.   The conclusions reached can be summarized as follows:

Tax Reduction Available   As illustrated previously, Mr. Renaud is subject to taxes on the direct receipt of income, other than dividends, at a rate of 45 percent, while his rate on the direct receipt of dividends is 24 percent (eligible) or 33 percent (non-eligible). This means that his after tax retention on the direct receipt of income would be:

- $55,000 On $100,000 Of Business Or Interest Income
- $76,000 On $100,000 Of Eligible Dividend Income
- $67,000 On $100,000 Of Non-Eligible Dividend Income

Comparing these amounts to those in the preceding table, we find that none of the case involve tax reduction. When a public company is involved, the use of a corporation results in the payment of significantly more taxes, without regard to whether the income is eligible for the M&P deduction. The same is true for CCPCs with respect to any of their income that is not eligible for the small business deduction. Even when a CCPC has income that is eligible for the small business deduction, there is a small tax cost associated with using a corporation. In the case of dividend income received by a CCPC, the after tax results are the same whether the income is received directly or flowed through a corporation.

Tax Deferral Available   Tax deferral occurs when income is not distributed to shareholders and taxes paid at the corporate level are less than those that would be paid if the income was received directly by the shareholder. On direct receipt of relevant amounts, Mr. Renaud would pay the following amounts in income tax:

- $45,000 On $100,000 Of Business Or Interest Income
- $24,000 On $100,000 Of Eligible Dividend Income
- $33,000 On $100,000 Of Non-Eligible Dividend Income

Comparing these amounts to the corporate tax amounts in the preceding table, we find that there is tax deferral in all cases except those involving interest or dividend income earned by a CCPC. The corporate taxes on $100,000 of interest income earned by a CCPC total $49,787, significantly more than the $45,000 that would be paid on the direct receipt of the interest income. In the cases where Part IV tax is applicable, the $33,333 that would be required when that tax is assessed, is larger than either the $24,000 that would be paid on the direct receipt of eligible dividends or the $33,000 that would be paid on the direct receipt of non-eligible dividends.

The most significant amounts of deferral are available to a CCPC earning active business income eligible for the small business deduction, or dividend income that is not subject to Part IV tax. In the case of income eligible for the small business deduction, taxes at the corporate level are $18,120, nearly $27,000 less than would have been paid on the direct receipt of this income. Even if a CCPC has active business income that is not eligible for the small business deduction, taxes on $100,000 of this additional income would only be $36,120, still below the $45,000 payable on the direct receipt of this amount of income.

There is also deferral in the case of dividend income when it is not subject to Part IV tax. However, for dividends to not be subject to Part IV tax, they must be received from a connected corporation that did not receive a dividend refund on their payment. This would generally involve payment from a CCPC earning business income. This means that deferral would have been available at the level of the paying corporation, without the use of an additional corporation to receive the dividends.

Even in the case of public companies, some deferral is available. Taxes on $100,000 of income would be $36,120, nearly $9,000 less than the amount payable on direct receipt of this amount of income.

17-60.   These conclusions are based on assumed provincial personal and corporate tax rates as outlined previously. These assumptions have a great deal of general applicability as the tax rates used are close to the average rates that apply in the various provinces. However, exceptions to these conclusions can be important, and some attention will be given to other possibilities in the material in the next section of this Chapter.

Exercise Seventeen-3

Subject: Incorporation Of Interest And Dividend Income

One of your clients has asked your advice on whether he should transfer a group of investments to a new Canadian controlled private corporation that can be established to hold them. He anticipates that the transferred investments will have the following amounts of income during the current year:

Eligible Dividends On Portfolio Investments	$46,000
Dividends From 100 Percent Owned Subsidiary (A Dividend Refund Of $29,000 Will Be Received by The Payor)	87,000
Interest Income	32,000

Despite having employment income of over $200,000, your client needs all of the income that is produced by these investments. On additional amounts of income, your client is subject to a provincial tax rate of 15 percent. The provincial dividend tax credit is equal to one-third of the dividend gross up for eligible and non-eligible dividends. The corporation will be subject to a provincial tax rate of 5 percent on income eligible for the small business deduction and 15 percent on other income. The corporation will make the maximum eligible dividend designation. Provide the advice requested and justify your conclusion.

Exercise Seventeen-4

Subject: Incorporation Of Capital Gains

One of your clients has asked your advice on whether she should transfer a group of investments to a new corporation that can be established to hold them. The corporation will be a Canadian controlled private corporation and she anticipates that, during the coming year, the market value of these investments will increase by $92,000, creating taxable capital gains of $46,000 [(1/2)($92,000)]. No other income will be generated by the investments. Despite having employment income in excess of $200,000, your client will sell these investments by the end of the year to realize the capital gains. The corporation will be subject to a provincial tax rate of 5 percent on income eligible for the small business deduction and 14 percent on other income. On additional income, your client is subject to a provincial tax rate of 16 percent. The provincial dividend tax credit is equal to one-third of the dividend gross up for all dividends. Provide the advice requested and justify your conclusion.

End of Exercises. Solutions available in Study Guide.

Provincial Taxes And Integration

Introduction

17-61. We have presented a number of different cases dealing with the question of whether it is better, both in terms of tax reduction and tax deferral, for an individual to receive income directly or, alternatively, channel that income through a corporation. In doing so, we have given consideration to both the type of income being earned, and whether the corporation would be a public company or, alternatively, a CCPC.

17-62. The conclusions that we reached were presented in Paragraph 17-59. We found that, while in many of the cases the use of a corporation provided some degree of tax deferral, there were no scenarios in which the use of a corporation reduced taxes.

17-63. It is important to note, however, that all of our conclusions were based on calculations that used an average for the:

- provincial tax rate on individuals;
- provincial tax rates on corporations;
- provincial dividend tax credits on eligible and non-eligible dividends.

17-64. As discussed in other Chapters of this text, there are wide variations in all of these provincial amounts. Further, these variations can provide results that are different than those summarized in Paragraph 17-58 and 17-59. For example, if a province legislates a tax free period of time for corporations that move within its jurisdiction, this will make the use of a corporation more attractive in that province.

17-65. This section will be concerned with how provincial variations in the variables listed in Paragraph 17-63 can influence the decision to incorporate. In doing so, we will not attempt to delineate every possible combination of rates, types of income, and corporate classification. With 13 provinces and territories, several different types of income, three different rates to consider, as well as two different classifications of corporations, there are literally hundreds of possible combinations. Given this, our goal will be to help you understand how changes in each of the provincial rates will act to influence conclusions on the use of a corporation for tax deferral or tax reduction purposes.

Tax Deferral

17-66. The analysis of using a corporation to provide tax deferral is very straightforward. If the combined federal/provincial tax rate on corporations is less than the combined federal/provincial tax rate on individuals, the use of a corporation provides for deferral. Some examples of this analysis are as follows:

Alberta CCPC Earning Active Business Income The combined federal/provincial tax rate on the corporation would be 16.1 percent. For an Alberta resident individual in the maximum tax bracket, the combined federal/provincial rate would be 39.0 percent. In this case, the use of a corporation would clearly provide deferral.

Manitoba CCPC Earning Investment Income The combined federal/provincial tax rate on the corporation would be 50.3 percent. For a Manitoba resident individual in the maximum tax bracket, the combined federal/provincial rate would be 46.4 percent. In this case, the use of a corporation would not provide deferral.

British Columbia Public Corporation The combined federal/provincial tax rate on the corporation would be 34.1 percent. For a British Columbia resident individual in the maximum tax bracket, the combined federal/provincial rate would be 43.7 percent. In this case, the use of a corporation would provide deferral.

17-67. We would remind you not to look at the deferral issue in isolation from other considerations. For example, in the case of the British Columbia public corporation, the available deferral is not without cost. In this case, the use of the corporation would result in significant additional taxes once the income is distributed out of the corporation. This would not be the case with the Alberta CCPC. When there is a possibility that the income will be distributed out of the corporation in the near future, both tax deferral and tax cost must be taken into consideration.

Tax Reduction
Provincial Rates On Individuals

17-68. Maximum provincial tax rates on individuals range from a low of 39 percent in Alberta to a high of 48 percent in Newfoundland. However, variations in these rates influence both the direct receipt of income and the amounts that are flowed through a corporation. This means that, while the level of provincial rates on individuals will affect the analysis of tax deferral, this factor will not significantly alter conclusions about tax reduction. A simple example will illustrate this point.

Example   A CCPC has $100,000 of active business income that will be taxed at a combined federal/provincial rate of 18 percent. The provincial dividend tax credit on non-eligible dividends is equal to one-third of the gross up. We will consider two cases, the first based on the assumption that the shareholders are taxed at a combined federal/provincial rate of 39 percent (29% federal, plus 10% provincial), the second based on the assumption that the shareholders are taxed at a combined federal/provincial rate of 48 percent (29% federal, plus 19% provincial).

Analysis   If the individuals received the $100,000 directly, their after tax retention would be $61,000 [($100,000)(1 - .39)] and $52,000 [($100,000)(1 - .48)], respectively. The after retention if the income is flowed through a corporation would be as follows:

	39% Rate	48% Rate
Corporate Income	$100,000	$100,000
Corporate Taxes At 18 Percent	(18,000)	(18,000)
Available For Dividends	$ 82,000	$ 82,000
Non-Eligible Dividends Received	$ 82,000	$ 82,000
Gross Up (25%)	20,500	20,500
Taxable Dividends	$102,500	$102,500
Individual Tax Rate	39%	48%
Taxes Before Dividend Tax Credit	$ 39,975	$ 49,200
Dividend Tax Credit (Equal Gross Up)	(20,500)	(20,500)
Individual Taxes	$ 19,475	$ 28,700
Dividends Received	$ 82,000	$ 82,000
Individual Taxes	(19,475)	(28,700)
After Tax Retention	$ 62,525	$ 53,300
After Tax Retention With Corporation	$ 62,525	$ 53,300
Direct Receipt Retention	(61,000)	52,000
Advantage With Corporation	$ 1,525	$ 1,300

17-69.   What this example illustrates is that, while the provincial tax rate on individuals has an impact on the amounts of income retained, the impact is roughly the same, whether the income is received directly or, alternatively, flowed through a corporation. For an individual in the 39 percent bracket, the advantage with using a corporation is $1,525, little different than the $1,300 advantage for the individual in the 48 percent bracket.

Provincial Dividend Tax Credit Rates

17-70.   The example in the preceding section illustrates that, with respect to tax savings through the use of a corporation, the rate applicable to individuals does not have a significant impact. This is not the case, however, with the provincial rate for dividend tax credits.

17-71.   For eligible dividends, the provincial dividend tax credit rates range from 21.5 percent of the gross up to 38.5 percent of the gross up. The corresponding rates for non-eligible dividends are 18.5 percent to 38.5 percent. These differences will have an impact on the desirability of using a corporation for tax savings purposes.

17-72. In general, higher dividend tax credit rates enhance the value of dividend income. All other things being equal, a high provincial dividend tax credit will make flowing income through a corporation more attractive. A simple example will serve to illustrate this point.

Example A CCPC has $100,000 of active business income that will be taxed at a combined federal/provincial rate of 18 percent. The shareholders are taxed at a federal/provincial rate of 45 percent (29% federal, plus 16% provincial). We will consider two cases, the first based on the assumption that the provincial dividend tax credit on non-eligible dividends is equal to 18.5 percent of the gross up, the second based on the assumption that the provincial dividend tax credit is equal to 38.5 percent of the gross up.

Analysis If the $100,000 of income is received directly by the individuals, they will retain $55,000 [($100,000)(1 - .45)]. If the income is flowed through a corporation, the after tax retention would be calculated as follows:

	18.5% Credit	**38.5% Credit**
Corporate Income	$100,000	$100,000
Corporate Taxes At 18 Percent	(18,000)	(18,000)
Available For Dividends	$ 82,000	$ 82,000
Non-Eligible Dividends Received	$ 82,000	$ 82,000
Gross Up (25%)	20,500	20,500
Taxable Dividends	$102,500	$102,500
Individual Tax Rate	45%	45%
Taxes Before Dividend Tax Credit	$ 46,125	$ 46,125
Dividend Tax Credit:		
[($20,500)(2/3 + 18.5%)]	(17,459)	N/A
[($20,500)(2/3 + 38.5%)]	N/A	(21,559)
Individual Taxes	$ 28,666	$ 24,566
Dividends Received	$ 82,000	$ 82,000
Individual Taxes	(28,666)	(24,566)
After Tax Retention	$ 53,334	$ 57,434
After Tax Retention With Corporation	$ 53,334	$ 57,434
Direct Receipt Retention	(55,000)	(55,000)
Advantage (Disadvantage)	($ 1,666)	$ 2,434

17-73. This example clearly illustrates the impact of the provincial dividend tax credit rate on the use of a corporation to achieve tax savings. When the low dividend tax credit rate of 18.5 percent is used, the use of a corporation results in total taxation that is $1,666 higher than that applicable to the direct receipt of the $100,000 of income. In contrast, with the high rate of 38.5 percent, the use of a corporation results in a tax savings of $2,434.

Provincial Corporate Tax Rates

17-74. The example in the preceding section illustrates that the provincial dividend tax credit rates influence the amount of tax savings available through the use of a corporation. A similar situation exists with respect to provincial tax rates on corporations. As presented in Paragraph 15-94, the combined federal/provincial rate for CCPCs earning active business income ranges from 15.1 percent in New Brunswick to 21.6 percent in Quebec. For public companies, the general rate ranges from 32.0 percent in Quebec to 38.1 percent in Nova Scotia and P.E.I.

17-75.   In general, higher corporate tax rates make the use of a corporation less attractive. A simple example will serve to illustrate this point.

Example   A CCPC has $100,000 of active business income. The shareholders are taxed at a federal/provincial rate of 45 percent (29% federal, plus 16% provincial) and the provincial dividend tax credit on non-eligible dividends is equal 1/3 of the gross up. We will consider two cases, the first based on the assumption that the corporation is taxed at a combined federal/provincial rate of 15 percent, the second based on the assumption that the corporation is taxed at a combined federal/provincial rate of 22 percent.

Analysis   If the $100,000 of income is received directly by the individuals, they will retain $55,000 [($100,000)(1 - .45)]. If the income is flowed through a corporation, the after tax retention would be as follows:

	Combined Corporate Tax Rate	
	15% Rate	**22% Rate**
Corporate Income	$100,000	$100,000
Corporate Taxes	(15,000)	(22,000)
Available For Dividends	$ 85,000	$ 78,000
Non-Eligible Dividends Received	$ 85,000	$ 78,000
Gross Up (25%)	21,250	19,500
Taxable Dividends	$106,250	$97,500
Individual Tax Rates	45%	45%
Taxes Before Dividend Tax Credit	$ 47,813	$ 43,875
Dividend Tax Credit (Equal To Gross Up)	(21,250)	(19,500)
Individual Taxes	$ 26,563	$ 24,375
Dividends Received	$ 85,000	$ 78,000
Individual Taxes	(26,563)	(24,375)
After Tax Retention	$ 58,437	$ 53,625
After Tax Retention With Corporation	$ 58,437	$ 53,625
Direct Receipt Retention	(55,000)	55,000
Advantage (Disadvantage)	$ 3,437	($ 1,375)

17-76.   This example clearly illustrates the impact of provincial corporate tax rate on the use of a corporation to achieve tax savings. When the rate is at 15 percent, the savings is a fairly substantial $3,437. In contrast, when the corporate rate is 22 percent, there is a tax cost of $1,375.

Summary: Tax Reduction And Provincial Tax Rates

17-77.   The preceding examples provide the basis for making the following general statements about the impact of varying provincial rates on the use of a corporation to achieve tax savings:

Provincial Rates On Individuals   High provincial rates on individuals will reduce after tax retention of income, whether the income is received directly or, alternatively flowed through a corporation. However, differences in the rates on individuals do not have a significant impact on the choice of receiving the income directly or flowing it through a corporation.

Provincial Dividend Tax Credit Rates   In general, high provincial dividend tax credits will enhance the use of a corporation to achieve tax savings, while low rates will make the use of a corporation less desirable.

Provincial Corporate Tax Rates In general, high provincial tax rates on corporations will make the use of a corporation to achieve tax savings less attractive, while lower rates will encourage flowing income through a corporation.

Tax Free Dividends

Tax Rates On Dividends

17-78. In this Chapter we are concerned with owner-managed businesses and these will typically be CCPCs. In most cases, the bulk of their income will either be active business income that benefits from the small business deduction or, alternatively, investment income that qualifies the corporation for a refund of taxes paid. While such corporations may have a positive GRIP account that will allow them to pay eligible dividends, most of their dividends will be non-eligible. Given this, our analysis will focus on non-eligible dividends that are subject to the limited gross up of 25 percent.

17-79. For an individual in the 29 percent federal tax bracket, subject to a 16 percent provincial tax rate on Taxable Income, and living in a province where the dividend tax credit is equal to one-third of the gross up, the combined federal/provincial rate on non-eligible dividends received is 31.25 percent [(29% + 16%)(125%) - (2/3 + 1/3)(25%)]. This rate is well above the 22.5 percent rate [(29% + 16%)(1/2)] that is applicable to capital gains and the 20.25 rate that would apply to eligible dividends. However, it is well below the maximum 45 percent rate (29% + 16%) that would be applicable to most other types of income.

17-80. In addition to the fact that dividends are taxed at favourable rates, the structure of the dividend tax credit system is such that a substantial amount of dividends can be received without incurring any taxation. This very desirable result will be explained and illustrated in this section on tax free dividends.

Use Of Tax Credits

Credits In General

17-81. For 2007, every individual has a personal credit against federal Tax Payable based on $8,929. As the actual basic personal tax credit is based on $8,929 multiplied by the 15.5 percent rate applicable to the lowest federal tax bracket, it means that the first $8,929 of an individual's income can be received tax free.

17-82. Extending this analysis, it can be said that, for most types of income, the amount that can be received tax free is limited to the total tax credit amounts available to the individual. That is, for every dollar of tax credit amount, one dollar of income can be received on a tax free basis. There are two exceptions to this:

Charitable Donations The tax credit on amounts of charitable donations over $200 is based on 29 percent, rather than the 15.5 percent applicable to other credit amounts. This means that a dollar of charitable donations in excess of $200 will allow an individual in the lowest tax bracket to receive $1.87 in tax free income. More specifically, a $1 contribution in excess of $200 is eligible for a tax credit of $0.29. This $0.29 would eliminate $0.29 of tax payable, the amount of tax that an individual in the lowest bracket would pay on $1.87 of income [(15.5%)($1.87) = $0.29]. This is unlikely to be an important exception in that it would be unusual for someone in the 15.5 percent federal tax bracket to be making significant charitable donations.

Dividends An individual with only the basic personal credit of $1,384 [(15.5%)($8,929)] can receive tax free dividends of over four times the $8,929 base for this credit. More specifically, such an individual can receive $35,083 in dividends without incurring any liability for federal tax. (See the calculations in Paragraph 17-87). Note that, depending on the amount of the provincial dividend tax credit, this amount may or may not be totally free of provincial tax.

Special Rules For Dividends

17-83. How can an individual receive such a large amount of dividends without paying federal tax? The answer lies in the dividend gross up and tax credit mechanism. For an individual in the lowest tax bracket, the increase in tax associated with one dollar of non-eligible dividends received compared to one dollar of interest income can be calculated as follows:

	Dividend	Interest
Cash Received	$1.0000	$1.0000
Gross Up At 25 Percent	.2500	N/A
Taxable Income	$1.2500	$1.0000
Federal Tax Payable At 15.5 Percent	$0.1938	$0.1550
Federal Dividend Tax Credit [(2/3)($0.25))	(0.1667)	N/A
Increase In Federal Tax Payable	$0.0271	$0.1550

17-84. For each dollar of non-eligible dividends received, an individual must add a taxable dividend of $1.25 ($1 + $0.25 gross up) to Taxable Income. For individuals in the lowest federal tax bracket, the federal tax on this amount will be $0.1938 [($1.25)(15.5%)]. However, there will be a federal credit against this tax payable equal to two-thirds of the gross up, or $0.1667 [(2/3)($0.25)]. This means that there is only a $0.0271 increase in federal tax for each one dollar increase in non-eligible dividends compared to an increase in federal tax of $0.155 for each one dollar increase in non-dividend income. This means that dividend income uses up an individual's available tax credits at a much lower rate than other types of income.

17-85. For example, one dollar of interest income will use up one dollar [($1.00)($.155 ÷ $.155)] of an individual's personal tax credit base of $8,929. In contrast, one dollar of dividends received will use up only $0.1748 of this base [($1.00)($.0271 ÷ $.155)]. This means that, in comparison with other types of income, a much larger amount of dividends can be received before an individual's tax credits are absorbed and taxes will have to be paid.

17-86. The amount of tax free dividends that can be received by an individual with no other source of income is a function of the total amount of personal tax credits available and can, in fact, become a fairly large amount. You should note however, that even for an individual with no other income, the amount of tax free dividends is such that the grossed up amount is more than $37,178, the top of the lowest tax bracket. As the amount of dividends received moves into the 22 percent tax bracket, the relationship described in Paragraph 17-84 becomes less favourable and the amount of tax free dividends available for each dollar of tax credits declines.

Tax Free Amounts For 2007

17-87. For 2007, ignoring possible tax credits other than the basic personal and spousal, the amount of dividends that can be received free of federal tax by a single individual, and by an individual with a dependent spouse (or eligible dependant) with no other source of income, is as follows:

	Single Individual	Dependent Spouse
Non-Eligible Dividends Received	$35,083	$47,859
Gross Up Of 25 Percent	8,771	11,965
Taxable Income	$43,854	$59,824
Taxed At 15.5%	(37,178)	(37,178)
Taxed At 22%	$ 6,676	$22,646

	Single Individual	Dependent Spouse
Federal Tax At 15.5%	$5,763	$5,763
Federal Tax At 22%	1,468	4,982
Dividend Tax Credit - 2/3 Of Gross Up	(5,847)	(7,977)
Basic Personal Credit [(15.5%)($8,929)]	(1,384)	(1,384)
Spousal Credit [(15.5%)($8,929)]	N/A	(1,384)
Federal Tax Payable	**$ Nil**	**$ Nil**

Note While this is not relevant to our analysis in this section, you might wish to note that, with respect to eligible dividends, the tax free amount for a single individual would be $66,420, and $79,988 for an individual with a dependent spouse.

17-88. There may or may not be provincial tax payable on the amounts in the preceding table. A number of provincial factors would have to be considered. These include the provincial tax rates, the provincial tax brackets, the provincial tax credit amounts and the provincial dividend tax credit rates.

17-89. The alternative minimum tax is not a factor in determining the amount of dividends that can be received on a tax free basis. As the dividend tax credit is not available in the calculation of the alternative minimum tax payable, the receipt of dividends can create problems in this area for high income individuals. However, the $40,000 basic exemption that is provided by the alternative minimum tax legislation, combined with the personal tax credits, would serve to eliminate the alternative minimum tax on the tax free dividends calculated in Paragraph 17-87.

Income Splitting

Basic Concept

17-90. In Chapter 3 we provided a very simple example of income splitting. As illustrated in that example, if an individual can find a way to share a large block of income with related parties in lower tax brackets, the result can be a significant reduction in taxes, not just in the current year, but on an ongoing basis.

17-91. While the examples presented earlier in this Chapter suggested that there are limits on an individual's ability to reduce or defer taxes through the use of a corporation, these examples did not take into consideration that a corporation could be used to effectively implement income splitting. This possibility is further enhanced by the fact that, as discussed in the preceding section, individuals without other sources of income can receive substantial amounts of dividends without paying any taxes at the federal level. If any family members are under 18 years of age, the tax on split income (see Chapter 14) may have to be considered.

17-92. This section will provide a fairly simple example of how a corporate structure can be used to significantly reduce taxes within a large family group.

Example

17-93. While there are a variety of ways a corporation could be used to accomplish income splitting, at this stage we will use a simple illustration involving the establishment of a holding company. The data for this example is as follows:

Example Mrs. Breck has an investment portfolio with a fair market value of $1,000,000. Because of Mrs. Breck's great skill in assessing stock market trends, her annual return on this portfolio has averaged 25 percent per year before taxes. All of this return has been in the form of capital gains. In addition to her investment income, Mrs. Breck has employment income sufficient to place her in a combined federal/provincial tax bracket of 45 percent. Mrs. Breck has five children over 17 years of age, none of whom have any income of their own. Although she wishes all of her children to have an equal share of the income from her investments, Mrs. Breck wants to retain control over the management of these funds. As he is already in the maximum tax bracket, she does not wish to share any of the income with her husband.

17-94.   Mrs. Breck's wishes can be accomplished through the use of an investment company, established with two classes of shares. The preferred shares will have the right to vote and 10 of these shares will be issued to Mrs. Breck at a price of $1 per share. The common shares will not have voting rights and 20 of these shares will be issued to, and will be paid for by, each of her five children at a price of $10 per share. The initial capital structure of the company would be as follows:

10 Voting Preferred Shares	$ 10
100 Non-Voting Common Shares	1,000
Total Equities	**$1,010**

17-95.   At this point, Mrs. Breck's $1,000,000 in investments would be transferred to the corporation in return for long-term debt that pays interest at a rate of 4 percent. Assuming this is the prescribed rate at the time of the transfer, there will be no corporate income attributed back to Mrs. Breck. If there are accrued, but unrealized gains on any of Mrs. Breck's investments, they can be transferred to the corporation on a tax free basis using the provisions of ITA 85(1). This procedure is discussed in Chapter 18.

17-96.   The resulting initial Balance Sheet of this Canadian controlled private corporation would be as follows:

Assets

Cash	$ 1,010
Investments	1,000,000
Total Assets	**$1,001,010**

Equities

Long-Term Debt	$1,000,000
Preferred Stock	10
Common Stock	1,000
Total Equities	**$1,001,010**

17-97.   All of the income of this CCPC will be investment income and, as a result, a dividend refund will be available when dividends are paid. Continuing to use the corporate rates that were presented in Paragraph 17-21, we will base our analysis of the situation on a combined federal/provincial corporate rate of 49.8 percent [(38% - 10%)(104%) + 6-2/3% + 14%]. Assuming Mrs. Breck's investments earn $250,000 in capital gains (a 25 percent rate of return on the $1,000,000 of investments) during the corporation's first year, corporate taxes and the maximum dividend payable are calculated as follows:

Taxable Capital Gains [(1/2)($250,000)]	$125,000
Interest On Debt [(4%)($1,000,000)]	(40,000)
Taxable Income	$ 85,000
Corporate Tax Payable At 49.8%	(42,330)
Income Before Dividends	$ 42,670
Dividend Refund ($1/$3)*	21,335
Maximum Non-Eligible Dividend	$ 64,005
Capital Dividend [(1/2)($250,000)]	125,000
Total Dividends	**$189,005**

*Before the refund, the balance in the RDTOH was $22,667 [(26-2/3%)($85,000)].

The remaining balance of $1,332 ($22,667 - $21,335) is refundable on the payment of future dividends.

17-98.   Based on the preceding calculations, each of the five children would receive a total of $37,801, $25,000 ($125,000 ÷ 5) in the form of a tax free capital dividend and $12,801 ($64,005 ÷ 5) in the form of a taxable dividend. However, as these children have no other source of income, they could receive the $12,801 in taxable dividends without any payment of taxes. The amount of dividends that can be received on a tax free basis by low income individuals was discussed starting in Paragraph 17-78.

17-99.   As a consequence, the only taxes that would be paid on the $250,000 of investment income would be at the corporate level, plus the personal taxes that Mrs. Breck would pay on the interest received from the corporation. A comparison of taxes payable with, and without, the investment company would show the following:

Tax If Income Directly Received By Mrs. Breck [(45%)(1/2)($250,000)]	$56,250
Net Taxes Paid By The Company ($42,330 - $21,335)	(20,995)
Taxes Paid By Mrs. Breck On Interest [(45%)($40,000)]	(18,000)
Tax Savings	$17,255

17-100.   This example makes a basic point clear — incorporation can significantly reduce taxes payable when it is used to split income among family members in lower tax brackets, particularly when those family members have little or no other source of income and can receive dividends on a tax free basis. Of importance is the fact that the tax savings are not a one time improvement in Mrs. Breck's tax position. These savings will continue to be available in subsequent years, as long as the conditions that produced them remain unchanged.

Management Compensation

General Principles

Salary As The Bench Mark

17-101.   The most obvious and straightforward way to compensate managers is to pay salaries. Provided they are reasonable, the amounts are a deductible expense to the corporation. At the same time, they are fully taxable to the recipient, rendering such payments neutral in terms of tax planning. For large publicly traded corporations, where the managers are not the principal owners of the business, salary is the usual starting point in negotiating management compensation. However, for some high income executives, stock based compensation may be of greater importance than salary.

17-102.   Even with a public corporation, however, the tax effects of various methods of compensation should not be ignored. By paying salaries, a corporation receives a deduction from Taxable Income in the year of accrual, while the recipient employee receives an equal addition to Taxable Income in the year of payment.

17-103.   Any form of compensation that creates an excess of the corporation's deductions over the employee's inclusions creates an aggregate tax savings. In addition, any form of compensation that is deductible to the corporation prior to inclusion in the income of the employee involves tax deferral. These considerations can allow for improved after tax benefits to the employee or, alternatively, a lower after tax cost to the corporation. In large corporations, these trade-offs provide the basis for management compensation policies.

Tax Effective Alternatives

17-104.   Some simple examples of compensation features that can be used to defer or reduce the payment of taxes are as follows:

- **Registered Pension Plans** Within prescribed limits, a corporation can deduct contributions to Registered Pension Plans in the year of contribution. These contributions will not become taxable to the employee until they are received as a pension benefit, resulting in an effective tax deferral arrangement.

- **Deferred Profit Sharing Plans**   In a fashion similar to Registered Pension Plans, amounts that are currently deductible to the corporation are deferred with respect to inclusion in the employee's Taxable Income.

- **Provision Of Private Health Care Plans**   The premiums paid by the corporation for such benefits as dental plans can be deducted in full by the corporation and will not be considered a taxable benefit to the employee.

- **Stock Options**   Stock options provide employees with an incentive to improve the performance of the enterprise. In addition, taxation of any benefits resulting from the options is deferred until they are exercised or sold (for a full discussion of the deferral of stock option benefits, see Chapter 5). Further, the value of the employment benefit received is enhanced by the fact that, in general, one-half of the amount can be deducted in the calculation of Taxable Income.

From the point of view of the corporation, evaluation of stock option compensation is more complex. Discouraging the use of options is the fact that no tax deduction is available for the granting of options. Until recently, this negative feature was offset by the fact that the granting of options did not create an accounting expense. However, Section 3870 of the *CICA Handbook* now requires that the estimated value of options be charged to expense when they are granted. It would appear that this change, when combined with the inability to deduct the cost of granting options, has significantly reduced the use of this form of compensation.

17-105.   Changes in tax legislation over the years have served to restrict the tax benefits associated with employee compensation. Perhaps most importantly, the current rules related to taxable benefits on employer provided automobiles can be quite unfavourable, in some cases resulting in a taxable benefit that exceeds the value derived from having use of the vehicle. The rules related to employee and shareholder benefits have been covered in Chapter 5 (employee fringe benefits and stock options), Chapter 9 (shareholder loans), and Chapter 13 (deferred compensation).

17-106.   With respect to the rules related to shareholder loans, these are an important consideration in the compensation of owner-managers. For that reason, you may wish to review the material on this subject that is covered in Chapter 9.

Salary Vs. Dividends

17-107.   For large public corporations, there is little point in considering the tax benefits related to salary/dividend trade-offs. The dividend policy of public corporations is normally based on considerations that extend well beyond the compensation that is provided to the management group of the company.

17-108.   In situations where the manager of the business is also an owner, such an individual is in a position to receive compensation in the form of either salary or dividends. If there are no other owners involved in the decision, the choice is completely at the discretion of the owner-manager and tax factors will generally be an important consideration in making this decision. The choice between compensation in the form of salary or in the form of dividends — the salary vs. dividend decision, is the subject of the remainder of this Chapter.

Salary Vs. Dividends For The Owner - Manager

The Basic Trade-Off

Example

17-109.   To illustrate the basic trade-off that is involved in salary vs. dividend decisions, assume that Ms. Olney owns all of the shares of a corporation that has $100,000 in Taxable Income, and that she has sufficient property income from other sources to place her in the 45 percent federal/provincial tax bracket (29% federal rate plus 16% provincial rate).

17-110. If the full $100,000 of corporate income is paid to Ms. Olney in the form of salary, it can be deducted by the corporation and will reduce the corporation's Taxable Income to nil. This means that no taxes will be paid at the corporate level. However, the $100,000 will be taxed at Ms. Olney's marginal rate of 45 percent. This means that she will pay tax of $45,000 and be left with after tax funds of $55,000.

17-111. If no salary is paid to Ms. Olney, corporate taxes will be assessed and any remaining amount, after adjustments for any refundable taxes, will be paid in dividends. This amount will be subject to personal tax and the resulting after tax cash flow to her can be determined. These amounts, which are dependent on the type of corporation and the type of income earned, were calculated earlier in this Chapter. The results of those calculations were summarized in Paragraph 17-58. You may wish to refer to this summary as you work through the remainder of this Chapter.

Analysis Of The Example

17-112. In looking at the question of whether or not to incorporate an income source, we looked at the possibilities for both tax deferral and tax reduction through the use of a corporation. In salary vs. dividend decisions, we are not concerned with deferral. The question here is — "What is the most tax effective way to have a corporation provide its owner-manager with a required amount of after tax income?" There is, of course, no deferral available on amounts that are to be removed from the corporation.

17-113. In comparing Ms. Olney's $55,000 retained with the various results listed in Paragraph 17-58, it is very clear that in all cases, the use of dividends as opposed to tax deductible salary results in the same or higher levels of taxation. Even in the case of a Canadian controlled private corporation earning active business income, payment of dividends results in after tax retention that is lower by $104 ($54,860 vs. $55,000).

17-114. This would suggest that, in general, salary should be used. However, the preceding analysis is based on a number of assumptions with respect to provincial tax rates on personal and corporate income. In addition, other factors such as RRSP contributions, CPP contributions and payroll tax costs have been ignored. These factors will be considered in the following material.

Other Considerations

Provincial Tax Rates And Credits

17-115. The results that were presented in Paragraph 17-58 assumed a provincial tax rate on individuals of 16 percent, a provincial dividend tax credit on non-eligible dividends equal to 28 percent of the gross up, and provincial rates on corporations for income eligible for the small business deduction and other types of income of 5 and 14 percent, respectively. While these numbers are fairly representative, they are not the only possible rates.

17-116. In assessing the importance of these differences, you should recognize that the payment of salaries is analogous to the direct receipt of income. That is, if a corporation has $100,000 in income and pays this entire amount in salaries, there will be no corporate Tax Payable. Further, the taxes paid by the individual on the salary will, in most cases, be the same as would be paid if he had received the income directly. This means that the comparison of salary payments with dividends involves the same analysis as the comparison of the after tax retention from the direct receipt of income with the after tax retention resulting from channeling income through a corporation.

17-117. Given this, we can discuss the effect of varying provincial tax rates on the salary vs. dividend decision by using the conclusions reached in the comparison of the direct receipt vs. flow through decisions. Direct receipt vs. flow through decisions were considered in Paragraphs 17-61 through 17-77. Applying that analysis to salary vs. dividend decisions, the following statements can be made:

> **Tax Rates For Individuals** In the analysis contained in Paragraphs 17-61 through 17-77, we noted that higher tax rates on individuals made the use of a corporation

more attractive from the point of view of deferring taxes on income retained within the corporation. Here, however, we are concerned only with amounts that will be distributed, either in the form of dividends or in the form of salary and, as a consequence, tax deferral is not an issue. This means that the level of individual tax rates is not an issue in this type of decision. This point is illustrated with the example found in Paragraph 17-68.

Dividend Tax Credit Rates   As discussed in Paragraphs 17-70 through 17-73, the basic integration model is based on the assumption that the combined federal/provincial dividend tax credit is equal to the gross up. While our basic examples assumed a provincial dividend tax credit on non-eligible dividends of 28 percent, the example in Paragraph 17-72 considers rates of 18.5 percent and 38.5 percent. As this example illustrates, all other things being equal, higher provincial dividend tax credits increase the after tax retention of income. This would encourage the payment of dividends as opposed to salary.

Corporate Tax Rates   As discussed in Paragraphs 17-74 through 17-77, all other things being equal, higher corporate tax rates make the deductibility of salaries more desirable. Alternatively, lower corporate rates make this deductibility less valuable, making the use of dividends more attractive. The example in Paragraph 17-75 illustrates this point using alternative combined rates of 15 percent and 22 percent.

Income Splitting

17-118.   When a corporation is used for income splitting purposes, amounts may be distributed to individuals with little or no other source of income. As was noted in Paragraph 17-87, over $35,000 in dividends can be paid to such an individual without any federal tax liability being incurred. The fact that this is a much larger amount than can be distributed tax free in any other form clearly favours the use of dividends for distributions of corporate assets in these circumstances.

Earned Income For RRSP And CPP

17-119.   One of the most attractive features of the Canadian income tax system is the fact that individuals can make deductible contributions to RRSPs. Not only are the contributions deductible at the time that they are made, once inside the plan they enjoy the tremendous benefits associated with tax free compounding over, what may be, a period of many years. Most individuals will want to take advantage of these provisions.

17-120.   Dividends do not constitute Earned Income for the purposes of determining the maximum RRSP contributions, nor do they count as pensionable earnings on which CPP contributions can be based. As a consequence, if the owner-manager has no other source of Earned Income (e.g., employment income from a source other than his corporation), it will be necessary for the corporation to pay salary if the individual wishes to make RRSP and CPP contributions.

17-121.   For 2008, the maximum annual RRSP contribution is equal to the lesser of $20,000 and 18 percent of the individual's Earned Income for the previous year. This means that, if the owner-manager has no other source of Earned Income, a 2007 salary of $111,111 will be required to make the maximum annual RRSP contribution of $20,000 in 2008. The maximum for CPP pensionable earnings in a year is considerably less than $111,111 ($43,700 for 2007). In order to be eligible for the maximum CPP payments at retirement, salary of at least the maximum pensionable earnings for the year should be paid.

Cumulative Net Investment Loss

17-122.   An individual's Cumulative Net Investment Loss (CNIL) is the cumulative amount by which investment expenses exceed investment income since 1987 (see Chapter 14 for an explanation of this amount, as well as the general provisions of the lifetime capital gains deduction). An individual's ability to make a deduction under the provisions of the lifetime capital gains deduction is reduced, on a dollar-for-dollar basis, by the balance in the CNIL account. This means that, if an individual contemplates selling shares of a qualified small business corporation, or an interest in a qualified farm or fishing property, sensible tax planning would suggest the elimination of any CNIL balance.

17-123.   For an individual whose income is provided by his owner-managed corporation, dividends can assist with this problem. The receipt of dividends reduces the CNIL by $1.25 for each $1.00 of non-eligible dividends received. In contrast, salary payments leave this balance unchanged. Another possibility, if the corporation has an amount owing to the shareholder, is to pay interest to the shareholder on the balance outstanding. This interest would also decrease any CNIL.

Tax Payable

17-124.   In a particular year, an owner-manager may wish to withdraw amounts in excess of the earnings of the corporation. If this happens, there will be no current tax savings associated with the payment of salaries, a fact that would tend to make the payment of such amounts less attractive.

17-125.   However, payment of salaries in this situation would serve to create a loss carry over and, if we assume that the loss carry over can be used in some past or future year, the corporate tax savings associated with the payment of salaries would not be lost. The savings, however, will be deferred in the case of a carry forward and this means that, to properly evaluate the payment of salaries in this situation, consideration would have to be given to the time value of money.

Added Costs Of Salary - CPP And EI

17-126.   In our example from Paragraph 17-109, we ignored the fact that salaries cannot be paid without contributions being made to the CPP. In addition, some provinces levy a payroll tax on salaries and wages. These costs can constitute a significant reduction in the after tax cash flow associated with the payment of salaries.

17-127.   We have not mentioned Employment Insurance (EI) premiums in this context because, if the owner-manager owns more than 40 percent of the voting shares of the corporation, he cannot participate in this program.

17-128.   With respect to CPP contributions, 2007 employee contributions are based on 4.95 percent of $43,700 (maximum pensionable earnings), less a basic exemption of $3,500. This results in a maximum employee contribution for 2007 of $1,990. The employer is required to withhold this contribution and, in addition, is required to make a further contribution in an amount that is equal to the contribution made by the employee. This brings the total CPP cost of paying salaries of $43,700 or more to $3,980.

17-129.   While generally not relevant here, an employee's maximum EI premium for 2007 is 1.8 percent of $40,000 (maximum insurable earnings), with no basic exemption. This gives a maximum employee premium of $720. In addition, the employer must contribute 1.4 times the employee's premium, an amount of $1,008. This results in a total cost of $1,728 for an employee with maximum insurable earnings in excess of $40,000.

Added Costs Of Salary - Provincial Payroll Taxes

17-130.   With respect to provincial payroll taxes, six provinces assess such taxes. In three of these, there is a fairly high threshold that must be reached before the tax kicks in. In Ontario, the annual payroll threshold is $400,000. The corresponding figures for Manitoba and Newfoundland are $1,000,000 and $600,000. For smaller owner-managed corporations, these high threshold levels will not serve as a constraint on the payment of salaries.

17-131.   In the Northwest Territories, Nunavut, and Quebec, the relevant payroll tax is assessed beginning with the first dollar of payroll. The payroll tax liability, which is 1 percent in Nunavut, 2 percent in the Northwest Territories and 2.7 percent in Quebec on the first $1 million of salaries, is likely to discourage the use of salaries.

Added Benefits Of Salary - CPP And Canada Employment Tax Credits

17-132.   While CPP is an added cost of choosing the salary alternative, the payment of these costs adds a benefit in the form of the CPP tax credit. You will recall from Chapter 6 that this credit is equal to 15.5 percent of amounts paid. This provides a maximum credit of $308 on the payment of the 2007 maximum CPP of $1,990. Note that this would not be a consideration if the individual has other sources of income which required the payment of maximum CPP.

17-133.   A further benefit of paying salary is the Canadian employment credit of $155 [(15.5%)($1,000)]. Unless the individual has other sources of employment in excess of $1,000, this credit is only available on the payment of salary by the corporation.

Added Costs And Benefits Of Salary - Example

17-134.   Returning to our example of Ms. Olney from Paragraph 17-109, as the owner of 100 percent of the shares of the corporation, she is not eligible to participate in the EI program. In addition, assume the province in which she lives assesses a 2.7 percent payroll tax to finance its health care program and provides a provincial credit for CPP contributions at a 6 percent rate. Her corporation is a Canadian controlled private corporation and all of its $100,000 in income is eligible for the small business deduction. Given this income and the costs associated with paying salary, the maximum salary that could be paid to Ms. Olney would be $95,433, a figure that would result in no corporate Tax Payable.

Pre-Tax Corporate Income	$100,000
Employer's CPP Contribution	(1,990)
Gross Salary [($100,000 - $1,990) ÷ 1.027]	(95,433)
Payroll Tax [(2.7%)($95,433)]	(2,577)
Corporate Taxable Income	Nil

17-135.   If $95,433 is paid to Ms. Olney as salary, her personal taxes are as follows:

Federal Tax Before Credit [(29% + 16%)($95,433)]	$42,945
CPP Credit [(15.5% + 6%)($1,990)]*	(428)
Canada Employment Credit [(15.5%)($1,000)]	(155)
Personal Tax Payable	$42,362

*We have assumed that Ms. Olney has sufficient property income to place her in the maximum federal tax bracket. This income would absorb other tax credits and, as a consequence, only the CPP and Canada employment credits that result from the payment of salary is included in this analysis.

17-136.   With this amount of taxes payable, Ms. Olney's after tax retention would be calculated as follows:

Salary Received	$95,433
Employee's CPP Contribution	(1,990)
Personal Tax Payable	(42,362)
After Tax Cash Retained	$51,080

17-137.   This more realistic result compares with the after tax retention of salary when CPP, payroll taxes and the Canada Employment credit are ignored of $55,000 (see Paragraph 17-109). This makes payment of salary less desirable than dividends paid out of income eligible for the small business deduction (retention was $54,860), but more desirable than dividends paid out business income not eligible for the small business deduction (retention was $48,549) or investment income (retention was $50,464). See Paragraph 17-58 for the retention figures.

Exercise Seventeen-5

Subject: Salary Compensation

Broadmoor Inc. is a Canadian controlled private corporation with Net Income For Tax Purposes and Taxable Income of $450,000 for the year ending December 31, 2007. All of this income is from active business activities. The cash balance of the Company, prior to any payments on the current year's taxes, is also equal to this amount. It is subject to a provincial tax rate of 5 percent on income eligible for the small business deduction and 14 percent on other income. There is no payroll tax in this province. Its only shareholder, Ms. Sarah Broad, has no income other than dividends or salary paid by the corporation and has combined federal/provincial personal tax credits of $3,800. She lives in a province that has a flat personal tax rate equal to 10 percent. The provincial dividend tax credit is equal to 30 percent of the dividend gross up for all dividends. Determine the amount of after tax cash that Ms. Broad will retain if the maximum salary is paid by the corporation out of the available cash of $450,000. Ignore the required CPP contributions and the Canada employment tax credit.

Exercise Seventeen-6

Subject: Dividend Compensation

Broadmoor Inc. is a Canadian controlled private corporation with Net Income For Tax Purposes and Taxable Income of $450,000 for the year ending December 31, 2007. All of this income is from active business activities. The cash balance of the Company, prior to any payments on the current year's taxes, is also equal to this amount. It is subject to a provincial tax rate of 5 percent on income eligible for the small business deduction and 14 percent on other income. Its only shareholder, Ms. Sarah Broad, has no income other than dividends or salary paid by the corporation and has combined federal/provincial personal tax credits of $3,800. She lives in a province that has a flat personal tax rate equal to 10 percent. The provincial dividend tax credit is equal to 30 percent of the gross up for all dividends. Ms. Broad would like to make the maximum eligible dividend designation. Determine the amount of after tax cash that Ms. Broad will retain if the maximum amount of eligible and non-eligible dividends are paid by the corporation.

End of Exercise. Solution available in Study Guide.

Use Of Tax Credits

17-138.   Our example in this section has involved an individual with other sources of income that placed her in the maximum federal tax bracket. This amount of income would generally be sufficient to absorb any tax credits available to the individual. However, there may be situations where a salary vs. dividend decision is being made with respect to an individual with no other source of income. This would be a fairly common situation when a corporation is being used for income splitting purposes, or for a corporation with only a limited amount of income to distribute.

17-139.   If the individual has no other source of income and provincial tax rates favour the use of dividends, there may be a problem with the full use of available tax credits. We noted earlier in this Chapter that dividend payments use up tax credits at a much lower rate than other types of income, such as salary. If only limited amounts of income are being distributed, the use of dividends may leave a portion of the individual's tax credits unused. When this is the case, some combination of salary and dividends may provide the optimum solution.

17-140.   A further potential complication stems from the fact that provincial tax credits can only be deducted against the provincial tax liability and federal tax credits can only be deducted against the federal tax liability. In our examples and problems we have not taken this into consideration and have given a single figure for combined federal/provincial tax credits.

17-141.   In the real world, it would be possible to have a situation where an individual would have to pay some federal tax in order to use up all of their provincial tax credits, or alternatively, a situation where an individual would have to pay some provincial tax in order to use up all of their federal tax credits, for example the federal Canada employment tax credit. Given this text's focus on federal income taxes, no further attention will be given to this issue.

17-142.   The following example illustrates the salary vs. dividend issue when the full utilization of tax credits is a consideration.

> **Example**   Mr. Eric Swenson is the sole shareholder of Swenson Sweets, a Canadian controlled private corporation. The Company has a December 31 year end and, at December 31, 2007, it has Taxable Income for the year of $29,500, all of which results from active business activities. This amount is available in cash, prior to the payment of any salary or dividends. Mr. Swenson has combined federal/provincial personal tax credits of $3,920.
>
> The corporation operates in a province with a corporate tax rate on active business income of a CCPC of 5 percent and no payroll taxes. The provincial tax rate on personal income is 10 percent of the first $37,178 of Taxable Income, with a provincial dividend tax credit on non-eligible dividends that is equal to one-third of the gross up. In solving this problem, we will ignore CPP contributions and the Canada employment tax credit.

17-143.   If the full $29,500 is paid out in salary, there would be no corporate tax and Mr. Swenson's after tax cash retention would be as follows:

Salary Received		$29,500
Taxes At 25.5% (15.5% + 10%)	$7,523	
Personal Tax Credits (Given)	(3,920)	(3,603)
After Tax Cash Retained (Salary)		$25,897

17-144.   As dividends are not tax deductible, corporate tax must be paid prior to any dividend distribution. The combined federal/provincial tax rate would be 18.12 percent [(38% - 10%)(104%) - 16% + 5%] resulting in corporate taxes of $5,345. This means that the maximum dividend that can be paid will be $24,155 ($29,500 - $5,345). The after tax retention in this case is as follows:

Non-Eligible Dividends Received	$24,155
Gross Up Of 25%	6,039
Taxable Dividends	$30,194
Personal Tax At 25.5%	$7,699
Personal Tax Credits (Given)	(3,920)
Dividend Tax Credit [(2/3 + 1/3)($6,039)]	(6,039)
Tax Payable ($2,260 In Unused Credits)	Nil
Dividends Received	$24,155
Personal Tax Payable	Nil
After Tax Cash Retained (Dividends)	$24,155

17-145.   While the low provincial tax rate on corporations suggests that dividends should be the best alternative, the preceding results do not confirm this view. The problem is that dividend income absorbs available tax credits at a much lower rate than other types of income. The fact that the all dividend solution leaves $2,260 of unused tax credits suggests that a better solution might be to pay a lesser amount of dividends, plus sufficient salary to absorb these unused credits.

17-146.   To investigate this possibility, we need to determine the salary/dividend mix that will fully utilize all of Mr. Swenson's credits. To begin, consider what would happen when we add a $1,000 salary payment to the all dividends case. As the salary will be fully deductible, the after tax cost of making this payment is $818.80 [($1,000)(1.0000 - 0.1812)]. As a consequence, in this type of problem, where the goal is to distribute all of the available corporate income, dividends will only have to be reduced by this $818.80 per $1,000 of salary increase.

17-147.   The resulting decrease in taxes payable can be calculated as follows:

Increase In Salary	$1,000.00
Decrease In Dividends	(818.80)
Decrease In Dividend Gross Up [(25%)($818.80)]	(204.70)
Decrease In Taxable Income	($ 23.50)
Decrease In Tax At 25.5%	($ 5.99)
Decrease In Dividend Tax Credit [(2/3 + 1/3)($204.70)]	204.70
Increase In Personal Tax Payable	$198.71

17-148.   This analysis demonstrates that each $1,000 increase in salary results in an increase in personal Tax Payable of $198.71. Alternatively, this can be stated as an increase in personal Tax Payable of $0.19871 for every dollar of increase in salary. This means that to utilize Mr. Swenson's $2,260 in unused tax credits, he will have to receive salary of $11,373 ($2,260 ÷ $0.19871). This results in the following amount being available for dividends:

Pre-Salary Taxable Income	$29,500
Salary	(11,373)
Corporate Taxable Income	$18,127
Corporate Tax At 18.12%	(3,285)
Available For Dividends	$14,842

17-149.   When this dividend is paid out to Mr. Swenson, his after tax retention is as follows:

Non-Eligible Dividends Received	$14,842
Gross Up Of 25%	3,711
Taxable Dividends	$18,553
Salary	11,373
Taxable Income	$29,926
Personal Tax At 25.5%	$7,631
Personal Tax Credits (Given)	(3,920)
Dividend Tax Credit [(2/3 + 1/3)($3,711)]	(3,711)
Personal Tax Payable	Nil
Dividends Received	$14,842
Salary Received	11,373
Personal Tax Payable	Nil
After Tax Cash Retained (Dividends And Salary)	$26,215

17-150.   As shown in the preceding calculations, this mix of salary and dividends is such that it utilizes all of Mr. Swenson's tax credits and leaves Tax Payable of nil. This results in a solution that not only improves on the $24,155 that was retained in the all dividend scenario, it also improves on the $25,897 that was retained in the all salary case. It would appear to be the optimum solution for this example. Although not considered in this example, the first $1,000 in salary would be tax free for federal purposes due to the Canada employment tax credit. As it is under $3,500, there would be no CPP payable. As a result, as a general rule, it would be advantageous to a pay a minimum of $1,000 in salary if the owner has no other employment income.

Optimizing A Limited Payment Of Cash

17-151.   A similar analysis could be done if the corporation had limited cash. Assume that, while the corporation in the example (Paragraph 17-142) had Taxable Income of $29,500, it had only $16,000 in cash. To determine the maximum salary that can be paid of $12,890, it is necessary to solve the following equation:

$$x = \text{maximum salary} = \$16,000 - [(\$29,500 - x)(18.12\%)]$$

17-152.   The full $12,890 in salary would be retained as the applicable tax of $3,287 [(25.5%)($12,890)] is less than the $3,920 in credits available.   Corporate taxes of $3,110 [(18.12%)($29,500 - $12,890)] would have to be paid.

17-153.   As dividends are not deductible, in the dividend approach, corporate taxes of $5,345 [(18.12%)($29,500)] would have to be paid. This leaves cash available for dividends of $10,655 ($16,000 - $5,345). As no individual taxes would be payable on this amount of dividends (see Paragraph 17-87), the full $10,655 would be retained.

17-154.   It is clear that the salary approach results in a considerably larger after tax retention than the dividend approach. This result would be expected given that the corporate cash was insufficient to utilize the personal tax credits in either approach.

Exercise Seventeen-7

Subject: Salary vs. Dividends

Fargo Ltd. has Net Income For Tax Purposes and Taxable Income for the year ending December 31, 2007 of $21,500. The Company's cash balance, prior to the payment of any taxes for the year is $18,500. The Company's Taxable Income is subject to a combined federal/provincial tax rate of 17.3 percent. There is no payroll tax in this province. Mr. Fargo, the Company's president and sole shareholder, is 71 years of age and has no other source of income (he has not applied for OAS). He has combined federal/provincial personal tax credits of $3,950 and lives in a province that has a personal tax rate on the first $37,178 of Taxable Income equal to 10 percent. The provincial dividend tax credit is one-third of the gross up for all dividends. Mr. Fargo would like to remove all of the cash from the corporation and has asked your advice as to whether it would be better to take it out in the form of dividends or salary. As Mr. Fargo is over 70 years old, no CPP contributions are required. Ignore the Canada employment tax credit. Provide the requested advice.

Exercise Seventeen-8

Subject: Salary vs. Dividends

Mortell Inc. has Net Income For Tax Purposes and Taxable Income for the year ending December 31, 2007 of $198,000. The Company's cash balance is over $200,000. It is subject to a combined federal/provincial tax rate of 16.5 percent. Ms. Mortell, the Company's only shareholder, has employment income of over $150,000 and, under normal circumstances, does not make withdrawals from the corporation. However, because of an increasing fondness for certain types of mood enhancing chemicals, she needs an additional $30,000 in cash. Ms. Mortell lives in a province where the provincial tax rate in her bracket is equal to 16 percent and the provincial dividend tax credit is equal to 25 percent of the dividend gross up for all dividends. She has asked your advice as to the best way to obtain the required funds from the corporation. Provide the requested advice.

End of Exercises. Solutions available in Study Guide.

Conclusion

17-155. As the preceding discussion makes clear, the salary vs. dividend decision is complex. Determination of the total tax consequences of the two alternatives does not necessarily resolve the issue. Among other factors that are specific to individual taxpayers, consideration should be given to:

- other sources of income,
- the need to provide for retirement income,
- the ability to split the corporation's income among various members of a family unit,
- the personal level of expenditures desired, and
- the need to reduce corporate income to the annual limit for the small business deduction.

17-156. The preceding material does not give you a comprehensive approach to solving these problems on a quantitative basis. In actual fact, there are problems here that are probably not subject to quantitative solutions. For example, whether or not an individual feels a need for retirement income involves many subjective considerations. With an issue such as this, a tax advisor can only outline the various possible outcomes.

Key Terms Used In This Chapter

17-157. The following is a list of the key terms used in this Chapter. These terms, and their meanings, are compiled in the Glossary Of Key Terms located at the back of the separate paper Study Guide and on the Student CD-ROM.

Active Business Income	Integration
Aggregate Investment Income	Interest Income
Annual Business Limit	Lifetime Capital Gains Deduction
Bonusing Down	Limited Liability
Canadian Controlled Private Corporation	Low Rate Income Pool (LRIP)
Charitable Donations Tax Credit	Manufacturing And Processing
Dividend Gross Up	Profits (M&P) Deduction
Dividend Tax Credit	Private Corporation
Dividends	Public Corporation
Eligible Dividends	Tax Avoidance
Estate Planning	Tax Deferral
General Rate Income Pool (GRIP)	Tax Planning
Income Splitting	Taxable Benefit

References

17-158.   For more detailed study of the material in this Chapter, we refer you to the following:

ITA 6(1)	Amounts To Be Included As Income From Office Or Employment
ITA 15(1)	Benefit Conferred On Shareholder
ITA 15(2)	Shareholder Debt
ITA 18(1)	General Limitations (On Deductions)
ITA 20(1)(j)	Repayment Of Loan By Shareholder
ITA 67	General Limitation Re Expenses
ITA 80.4(2)	Idem (Loans To Shareholders)
ITA 82(1)	Taxable Dividends Received
ITA 121	Deduction For Taxable Dividends
ITA 123 To 125.4	Rules Applicable To Corporations
ITA 146	Registered Retirement Savings Plans
ITA 147	Deferred Profit Sharing Plans
IT-67R3	Taxable Dividends From Corporations Resident In Canada
IT-119R4	Debts Of Shareholders And Certain Persons Connected With Shareholders
IT-124R6	Contributions To Registered Retirement Savings Plans
IT-307R4	Spouse Or Common-Law Partner Registered Retirement Savings Plans
IT-421R2	Benefits To Individuals, Corporations And Shareholders From Loans Or Debt
IT-432R2	Benefits Conferred On Shareholders
IT-470R	Employee's Fringe Benefits
IT-487	General Limitation On Deduction Of Outlays Or Expenses
IT-533	Interest Deductibility And Related Issues

Problems For Self Study

(The solutions for these problems can be found in the separate Study Guide.)

Self Study Problem Seventeen - 1

Dr. Ashley is a successful dentist with an established practice in a major Canadian city. On January 1, 2007, she established a new CCPC, Ashley Management Services, to manage her professional practice and to hold some of her investments. The Company's year end is December 31.

Dr. Ashley's husband became unemployed in 2006. She hired him to manage this Company and he is paid a salary of $18,400 per year. This salary is reasonable in view of the services that he performs for Ashley Management Services.

During its first year of operation, the Company had the following revenues:

Interest Income	$ 21,600
Eligible Dividends From Canadian Public Companies	13,900
Management Fees	82,900
Rental Revenues	34,600
Total Revenues	$153,000

In the process of earning these revenues, Ashley Management Services incurred the following expenses, including the salary paid to Dr. Ashley's husband:

Expenses On Rental Property (Including CCA)	$27,800
Mr. Ashley's Salary	18,400
Office Salaries	25,400
Office Rent	8,180
CCA On Office And Dental Equipment	5,700
Other Business Expenses	2,170
Total Expenses	$87,650

The corporation's active business income will be taxed at a combined federal/provincial rate of 20 percent, and its investment income will be taxed at a combined federal/provincial rate of 51 percent (including the ITA 123.3 refundable tax on the investment income of Canadian controlled private corporations). It is the intended policy of the Company to pay out all of the after tax corporate income as dividends.

Mr. Ashley owns 60 percent of the voting shares in the Company. The shares were purchased with funds that he earned in his previous job.

Dr. Ashley's professional income, without inclusion of any income from Ashley Management Services, is sufficient to give her a combined federal/provincial tax rate of 47 percent. Mr. Ashley's only income is his salary and dividends from Ashley Management Services. In order to simplify calculations, assume that Mr. Ashley's combined federal/provincial rate is 30 percent. They live in a province where the dividend tax credit on both eligible and non-eligible dividends is equal to 25 percent of the gross up.

Required: (Ignore personal tax credits, the Canada employment tax credit and CPP contributions in your solution.)

A. Calculate the minimum Tax Payable by Ashley Management Services and its shareholders for 2007 and the total after tax retention.

B. Assume Dr. Ashley had not established a corporation and had received all of the income personally, with no salary being paid to Mr. Ashley. Calculate the minimum Tax Payable by Dr. Ashley for 2007 and her after tax retention.

Self Study Problem Seventeen - 2

Ms. Lusk is divorced and has no dependants. She is the sole shareholder and only employee of Lusk Esthetics, a private Canadian corporation. All of the income of this Corporation is derived from active business activity. Lusk Esthetics qualifies for the small business deduction on all of its 2007 income and, as a consequence, is subject to a combined federal and provincial tax rate, including the corporate surtax, of 18 percent on its Taxable Income. During 2007, the Corporation has not paid any salaries or dividends to Ms. Lusk. Any dividends paid would be non-eligible.

Ms. Lusk estimates her 2007 Taxable Income will be $44,385 before consideration of any salary or dividend payments from Shields Inc. This includes $50,000 of employment income from a lucrative part-time job.

The provincial tax rate applicable to Ms. Lusk's personal income is a flat rate of 10 percent. The provincial dividend tax credit is equal to one-third of the dividend gross up for both eligible and non-eligible dividends.

In reviewing her budget, it is clear to Ms. Lusk that by the end of 2007, she will need an additional $10,000 of after tax funds to meet all of her personal expenditures. She expects Lusk Esthetics to be the source of this additional amount, as her Company has had a successful year. She would like to acquire the funds in a manner that will minimize the combined tax cost to both herself and her corporation.

Required: Determine whether the payment of salary by Lusk Esthetics or, alternatively, the payment of dividends by the Company, would provide the required $10,000 in after tax funds at the lowest combined tax cost to Ms. Lusk and Lusk Esthetics.

Self Study Problem Seventeen - 3

Mr. Bedford is the only shareholder of Bedford Inc., a Canadian controlled private corporation. The Company has a December 31 year end and, at December 31, 2007, Mr. Bedford determines that the Taxable Income of the Company for the year will be $27,500. The Company has this amount available in cash, prior to the payment of taxes, dividends, or salary. All of the Company's income qualifies as active business income.

The Company's activities are confined to a province in which the applicable corporate rate of taxation is 6 percent on income that is eligible for the small business deduction. The province does not levy a payroll tax for health care or post-secondary education. Any dividends paid by Bedford Inc. would be non-eligible.

Mr. Bedford has no other source of income. In his tax bracket, the combined federal/provincial tax rate is 25 percent. For both eligible and non-eligible dividends, the provincial dividend tax credit is equal to 30 percent of the dividend gross up. Mr. Bedford has combined federal/provincial personal tax credits for the 2007 taxation year in the amount of $3,750.

Required:

A. Determine the after tax amount of cash that Mr. Bedford will retain if all of the Company's income is paid to him in the form of salary. Ignore CPP contributions and the Canada employment tax credit.

B. Determine the after tax amount of cash that Mr. Bedford will retain if the Company pays the maximum possible dividend.

C. Can Mr. Bedford improve his after tax cash retention by using a combination of salary and dividends? Explain your conclusion.

D. Determine the combination of salary and dividends that will produce the maximum after tax cash balance for Mr. Bedford. Calculate the amount of this after tax cash retention.

E. Briefly describe any other factors that Mr. Bedford should consider in deciding whether to pay himself dividends or, alternatively, salary.

Assignment Problems

(The solutions for these problems are only available in
the solutions manual that has been provided to your instructor.)

Assignment Problem Seventeen - 1

Mrs. Martin is considering investing $200,000 in interest bearing securities at a rate of 7 percent. The pre-tax interest income on this investment would be $14,000 and Mrs. Martin has no other investment income. The combined federal and provincial corporate tax rate on investment income is 50 percent, including the ITA 123.3 refundable tax on the investment income of a Canadian controlled private corporation. Mrs. Martin is subject to a federal marginal tax rate of 29 percent and a provincial marginal tax rate of 19 percent. The provincial dividend tax credit is equal to one-third of the dividend gross up for all dividends.

Required: Prepare calculations that will compare the after tax retention of income that will accrue to Mrs. Martin if:

A. The investment in the interest bearing securities is owned by her as an individual.

B. The investment is owned by a corporation in which she is the sole shareholder, and which pays out all available income in dividends.

Assignment Problem Seventeen - 2

Mr. Martin is considering investing $200,000 in the preferred shares of a Canadian public company. These shares pay eligible dividends at a rate of 7 percent, resulting in annual pre-tax dividend income of $14,000. Mr. Martin has no other investment income.

The combined federal and provincial corporate tax rate on investment income is 50 percent, including the ITA 123.3 refundable tax on the investment income of a Canadian controlled private corporation. Mr. Martin is subject to a federal marginal tax rate of 29 percent and a provincial marginal tax rate of 17 percent. The provincial dividend tax credit on eligible dividends is equal to 7/18 of the dividend gross up.

Required: Prepare calculations that will compare the after tax retention of income that will accrue to Mr. Martin if:

A. The investment in the dividend paying securities is owned by him as an individual.

B. The investment is owned by a corporation in which he is the sole shareholder, and which pays out all available income in dividends.

Assignment Problem Seventeen - 3

Mr. Jerome Farr owns all of the outstanding shares of Farr Flung Ltd. (FFL), a Canadian controlled private corporation with an October 31 year end. The Company has been extremely successful and, as a consequence, it has accumulated over $1,500,000 in cash that is not needed in the operations of the business. Given this situation, Mr. Farr has decided to give himself loans for a variety of purposes. Because of the abundance of cash in the corporation, Mr. Farr has indicated that, with respect to loans that will be used to acquire a dwelling or an automobile to be used in the business, loans will be extended to other employees of the Company on the same basis that they are extended to himself. Mr. Farr spends at least 40 hours per week working in the business and, in most years, receives a significant amount of salary from the Company.

He has been advised by his accountant that he should keep detailed records with respect to the date on which each loan was made and the purpose of the loan. During the calendar year ending December 31, 2007, his records indicate the following:

Personal Expenditures   Because of his increasing appreciation of the finer things in life, Mr. Farr experienced a need for larger amounts of cash to be used for personal expenditures. During 2007, his Company loans him three separate amounts, with the details of the loans as follows:

- June 30, 2007   The Company loans him $20,000 on an interest free basis. The loan is to be repaid on June 30, 2008.

- October 31, 2007   The Company loans him $40,000 with an interest rate of 2 percent per annum. The loan is to be repaid on November 1, 2008.

- December 1, 2007   The company loans him $60,000 with an interest rate of 4 percent per annum. The loan is to be repaid on January 1, 2009.

Dwelling   On January 1, 2007, Mr. Farr gives himself a $100,000 loan to acquire a dwelling. The rate on the loan is 2 percent per annum and the loan agreement calls for five annual payments of $20,000, plus accrued interest, commencing January 1, 2008. The loan does not qualify as a home relocation loan.

Automobile   On June 30, 2007, Mr. Farr gives himself an interest free $50,000 loan to acquire an automobile to be used in the business . Because of his commitment to repay the other loans, Mr. Farr is not sure when he will be able to repay this loan.

All repayments are made as scheduled. In all of the years under consideration, assume the prescribed rate is 6 percent (not including the extra 2 or 4 percent on amounts owing to or from the CRA).

Required   Indicate the tax consequences, in each of the years 2007, 2008, and 2009, that will accrue to Mr. Farr as a result of receiving these loans. Briefly explain your conclusions. Base your interest calculations on the number of months the loans are outstanding.

Assignment Problem Seventeen - 4

Morcan Inc. is a Canadian controlled private corporation with a single shareholder, Mrs. Nadia Litvak. Since its inception, all of the Corporation's income has been active business income.

For the taxation year ending December 31, 2007, after the deduction of a $300,000 salary to Mrs. Litvak, the Company expects to have Taxable Income of $650,000. This is the first year during which the Corporation's Taxable Income has exceeded the annual business limit for the small business deduction.

The Company is subject to a combined federal/provincial tax rate of 37 percent on active business income in excess of $400,000. As Mrs. Litvak's tax consultant, you have advised her that she should consider taking out additional salary of $250,000 in order to reduce her Company's Taxable Income to the annual business limit of $400,000. She is resisting this suggestion because she feels her present salary is more than adequate to meet her current living needs.

In Mrs. Litvak's province of residence, the maximum combined federal and provincial tax bracket is 45 percent. The combined federal/provincial dividend tax credit is equal to the dividend gross up for all dividends.

Required: Explain to Mrs. Litvak the tax advantages that would be associated with withdrawing the additional salary and the tax consequences of retaining the $250,000 in the corporation and paying it out in dividends at a later date. Include in your explanation any other factors that should be considered in choosing whether to bonus down or not.

Assignment Problem Seventeen - 5

Miss Morgan established and has operated an extremely successful retail operation. The business is incorporated and Miss Morgan is the sole shareholder. All of the income of this Corporation qualifies for the small business deduction and, as a consequence, is subject to a combined federal and provincial tax rate, including the corporate surtax, of 19 percent on its Taxable Income.

Due to the excellent returns on her portfolio investments, Miss Morgan is in the 29 percent federal tax bracket and the 12 percent provincial tax bracket. In her province, the dividend tax credit is equal to 25 percent of the dividend gross up for all dividends.

During the 2007 fiscal year, Miss Morgan expects the business to have Net Income For Tax Purposes of about $170,000. This figure includes a deduction for the payment of her own salary of $84,000.

As Miss Morgan wishes to take an extended holiday during January and February of next year, she is in need of an extra $20,000 in cash in December of 2007. Her company has sufficient excess cash to allow her to either pay additional salary or to declare a dividend. Any dividends paid would be non-eligible.

Required: Determine the amount that would be required in the way of salary and in the way of dividends, in order to provide Miss Morgan with the required after tax funds of $20,000. What would you advise her to do?

Assignment Problem Seventeen - 6

Ms. Barbra Stickle is the only shareholder of Stickle Ltd., a Canadian controlled private corporation. The Company has a December 31 year end and, at December 31, 2007, Ms. Stickle determines that the Taxable Income of the Company for the year will be $24,200. The Company has this amount available in cash, prior to the payment of taxes, dividends, or salary.

All of the Company's income qualifies as active business income and any dividends that it pays will be non-eligible. The Company's activities are confined to a province in which the applicable corporate rate of taxation is 5 percent on income eligible for the small business deduction. The province does not levy a payroll tax.

Ms. Stickle has no other source of income. In her tax bracket, the combined federal/provincial tax rate for individuals is 25 percent. For both eligible and non-eligible dividends, the provincial dividend tax credit has been set at 30 percent of the dividend gross up. Ms. Stickle has combined personal tax credits for the 2007 taxation year in the amount of $3,423.

Required:

A. Determine the after tax amount of cash that Ms. Stickle will retain if all of the Company's income is paid to her in the form of salary. Ignore CPP contributions and the Canada employment tax credit.

B. Determine the after tax amount of cash that Ms. Stickle will retain if the Company pays the maximum possible dividend.

C. Can Ms. Stickle improve her after tax cash retention by using a combination of salary and dividends? Explain your conclusion.

D. Determine the combination of salary and/or dividends that will produce the maximum after tax cash retention for Ms. Stickle. Calculate the amount of this after tax cash retention.

E. Briefly describe any other factors that Ms. Stickle should consider in deciding whether to pay herself dividends or, alternatively, salary.

Assignment Problem Seventeen - 7

Your client, Keith Slater, is contemplating the creation of Slater Ltd. He would be the sole shareholder and he plans to transfer his accounting business and investment portfolio to the Company. All of the after tax corporate income would be paid out to him in dividends, to finance his passion for art collecting. He has annual pension and RRIF income of over $200,000, placing him in the maximum federal tax bracket of 29 percent. This income is sufficient to absorb all of his currently available tax credits.

Having taken tax courses in the distant past, he vaguely remembers that something called integration plays a role in whether a corporation is tax advantageous or not. After some discussion and research, you compile the following estimated income amounts and tax rates:

Taxable income of accounting business	
(Active Business Income)	$80,000
Eligible portfolio dividends	96,000
Federal corporate tax rate after federal abatement	28%
Federal small business deduction	16%
Federal corporate surtax	4%
General rate reduction	7%
Provincial corporate tax rate - CCPC rate	5%
Marginal federal personal tax rate	29%
Marginal provincial personal tax rate	13%
Provincial dividend tax credits on:	
Eligible dividends	7/18 of dividend gross up
Non-eligible dividends	1/3 of dividend gross up

Required:

A. Briefly summarize the concept of integration.

B. Assume no corporation is used and the income is received directly. Calculate Mr. Slater's personal Tax Payable, showing separately the Tax Payable on the active business income and the dividends.

C. Assume the income and dividends are received by Slater Ltd. Calculate corporate Tax Payable, after tax income available for distribution, and personal taxes that would be payable on the distribution. Your calculations should show separately the Tax Payable on the active business income and any eligible or non-eligible dividends.

D. Compare the Tax Payable with and without the use of Slater Ltd. and explain why the Tax Payable amounts are different.

Assignment Problem Seventeen - 8

Cora Yates is a contract engineer who is joining the real estate firm Glenora Developers as the firm's tenth partner. Cora can join the partnership as an individual or she can form a corporation to join the partnership. Cora knows that a corporation will not provide the benefit of limited liability for her professional actions, but she would like to know if it would be advantageous in maximizing her after tax income from the partnership.

Cora estimates that for the partnership's fiscal year ended December 31, 2007, her share of the partnership income will be $70,000 (one-tenth of $700,000 net partnership income), all of which will be active business income. Cora needs all of her after tax partnership income for personal living expenses as she has no other source of income.

After researching this issue, you find that:

- Contract engineers are allowed to form corporations that can carry on a professional practice and join partnerships.

• The corporation would be eligible for the small business deduction. It would not be deemed a personal services business as the work is independent and the duties can be subcontracted. The annual business limit must be allocated on a pro rata basis among all incorporated and unincorporated partners. (This requirement is not discussed in the text material.)

Ms. Yates is subject to graduated provincial tax rates of 8 percent on the first $37,178 of Taxable Income and 12 percent on the next $37,179. She has combined federal/provincial personal tax credits of $3,342. The combined federal/provincial dividend tax credit is equal to the gross up on both eligible and non-eligible dividends.

The corporation would be subject to combined federal/provincial taxes on income eligible for the small business deduction at a rate of 19 percent and on other active business income at a rate of 36 percent.

You are reviewing three different scenarios as follows:

Scenario 1   Cora joins the partnership as an individual, and she does not form a corporation. All partnership income is received directly.

Scenario 2   Cora forms a corporation that joins the partnership. The corporation pays corporate tax on all of the partnership income, and pays the after tax partnership income to Cora as dividends. Cora's share of the annual business limit for the small business deduction of the partnership is established at $40,000.

Scenario 3   Cora forms a corporation that joins the partnership. The corporation pays corporate tax on the portion of partnership income that qualifies for the small business deduction and distributes the after tax amount to Cora as dividends. The balance of the partnership income in the corporation is paid to Cora as salary. Cora's share of the annual business limit for the small business deduction of the partnership is established at $40,000.

Required: Calculate the after tax personal retention of Cora's share of the partnership income for each of the three Scenarios. Which Scenario would you recommend? Briefly explain why this Scenario is the best.

Assignment Problem Seventeen - 9

Judith Hughes owns an investment portfolio that will generate the following Canadian source income for the current year:

Interest	$12,000
Capital Gains	30,000
Eligible Portfolio Dividends	40,000

She estimates that her Taxable Income for this year from other sources will be over $200,000. Her combined federal/provincial rate on additional interest income or taxable capital gains is 47 percent. Her combined rate on eligible dividends received is 23 percent. On non-eligible dividends received, her combined rate is 33 percent.

You are a tax consultant and Judith is meeting with you to find out how she can minimize her next year's Tax Payable. Should she form a holding company and transfer some or all of the investments into the company? Alternatively, should Judith continue to hold any, or all, investments personally?

The federal/provincial corporate tax rate applicable to the investment income of a CCPC is 50 percent. This includes the corporate surtax, as well as the ITA 123.3 refundable tax on aggregate investment income.

Required:

A. Assume that Judith does not form a holding company and continues to hold all the investments personally. For each investment, calculate the amount of after tax cash she would retain for the current year.

B. For each investment, describe how the investment income earned would be taxed if her investments were transferred to a CCPC. Based on this information, indicate whether she should transfer any of these investments to a CCPC or, alternatively, continue to hold them personally.

CHAPTER 18

Rollovers Under Section 85

Rollovers Under Section 85

Introduction

18-1. Chapter 17 gave detailed consideration to the question of whether it would be advantageous to establish a corporation in order to reduce, defer, or redistribute the amount of Tax Payable. If the results of this analysis favour the use of a corporation, Section 85 of the *Act* provides an attractive basis for the transfer of property to the new corporation.

18-2. The problem that is involved with such a transfer is that the assets may have been owned by the transferor for some period of time. In these circumstances, it is possible that their fair market values may be well in excess of their adjusted cost base and/or their undepreciated capital cost. As a transfer by a taxpayer to a corporation would be considered a disposition by that taxpayer, the incorporation of an existing business could result in a need to include both capital gains and recapture in the transferor's Taxable Income. In a typical situation, where the owner of an operating business decides to transfer all of its assets to a newly formed corporation, the resulting tax liability could be significant.

18-3. Section 85 of the *Income Tax Act* is designed to provide relief in this type of situation. In somewhat simplified terms, it permits property to be transferred to a corporation on either a tax free basis, or with a level of taxation that is determined at the discretion of the transferor. Such transactions are referred to in tax work as rollovers. Of the rollovers that are available, the provisions in Section 85 provide for one of the most important and widely used.

General Rules For The Transfer

Transferor And Transferee

18-4. As indicated in the introduction, we are concerned here with transfers of property to a corporation at a value that can be elected by the transferor and the corporation. With respect to the identity of the transferor, ITA 85(1) refers to taxpayers, and this could be an individual, a trust, or a corporation. As partnerships are not "taxpayers" for income tax purposes, a separate ITA 85(2) provides for the transfer of assets to a corporation by a partnership.

18-5. With respect to transferees, Section 85 requires that they be taxable Canadian corporations. A "Canadian corporation" is defined in ITA 89(1) as a corporation that is currently resident in Canada and that was either incorporated in Canada, or has been a resident continuously since June 18, 1971. ITA 89(1) also defines a "taxable Canadian corporation" as a

Canadian corporation that was not, by virtue of a statutory provision, exempt from taxation under Part I of the *Income Tax Act*.

Eligible Property

18-6.   Only "eligible property", the components of which are defined in ITA 85(1.1), can be transferred under Section 85. Items listed in the Subsection are as follows:

- both depreciable and non-depreciable capital property, not including real property owned by non-residents;
- eligible capital property;
- Canadian resource properties;
- foreign resource properties;
- inventories, other than inventories of real property; and
- real property owned by a non-resident person and used in the year in a business carried on by that person in Canada.

18-7.   The general exclusion of real property owned by non-residents reflects the fact that this type of property is Taxable Canadian Property and gains on its disposition are subject to Canadian taxes, without regard to the residency of the seller. The exclusion is designed to prevent a non-resident who owns Canadian real estate from being able to transfer the property on a tax free basis to a corporation, and subsequently selling the shares in the corporation on a tax free basis.

18-8.   The second exclusion from assets eligible for the Section 85 rollover would be Canadian resident owned real property that constitutes an inventory. That is, if a group of real property assets is being actively traded, rather than being held for their income producing ability, they are not eligible for a tax free rollover under ITA 85.

18-9.   This latter exclusion of inventories of real property can be a particularly troublesome provision due to the fact that, in practice, some taxpayers may not be certain as to the status of their real estate holdings. If a taxpayer was to go through the Section 85 rollover procedures and then, after the fact, find that the transferred real estate holdings were considered inventory by the CRA, the tax consequences would be very severe. In this type of situation, it would be advisable that any real properties transferred be held by the corporation for some period of time before they are sold.

Consideration To Transferor

18-10.   In return for the property transferred to the corporation, the corporation may provide various types of consideration to the transferor. The one requirement that is specified in ITA 85(1) is that some part of this consideration must consist of shares of the transferee corporation.

18-11.   The shares issued may be either preferred, common, or some combination of the two types. Further, the requirement for share consideration to be used can be satisfied by the issuance of as little as one share to the transferor. For reasons that will become evident later in this Chapter, the usual Section 85 transaction involves the use of a combination of shares and non-share consideration. In this context, the non-share consideration is usually referred to as the "boot".

Making The Election

18-12.   Both the transferor and the transferee corporation must elect to have the Section 85 provisions apply. This joint election is accomplished by filing Form T2057 (transfers from individuals, trusts, and corporations) or T2058 (transfers from partnerships), on or before the earliest of the dates on which the normal tax returns are due for the two taxpayers.

18-13.   A late election may be filed for up to three years after this date and, with the permission of the CRA, a late election will be accepted after the end of this three year period. Whenever there is a late election, a penalty of one-quarter of 1 percent of any deferred gain will be assessed for each month beyond the normal filing date. The maximum penalty is $100 per month to a maximum of $8,000.

18-14.   In making the election, it is crucial that the taxpayer list all of the properties that are to be covered. If a property is omitted from the forms, the normal rules associated with dispositions will apply. This could result in the need to recognize capital gains, recapture, or business income on the transfer, an outcome that might require needless payment of taxes.

Establishing The Transfer Price
Importance
18-15.   One of the most significant features of ITA 85 is that it provides for the transfer of various properties to a corporation at values that are jointly elected by the transferor and transferee. Careful consideration must be given to the election of an appropriate transfer price in that, in general, this transfer price establishes three important values. These are:

Transferor   The deemed proceeds of disposition for the property given up.

Transferor   The adjusted cost base of the property received from the corporation.

Transferee   The adjusted cost base of the property received by the corporation.

General Rules
18-16.   While there are a number of complications associated with establishing transfer prices, the basic rules are very straightforward. The elected values cannot exceed fair market values and cannot be less than the adjusted cost base of non-depreciable assets, or the UCC of depreciable assets (as we will see in the next section, the floor elected value is also limited by the boot, or non-share consideration, received).

18-17.   For example, assume Mr. Thompson owns non-depreciable assets with a fair market value of $750,000 and an adjusted cost base of $500,000. On the transfer of these assets to a corporation, he will receive consideration with a fair market value of $750,000. However, under the provisions of ITA 85, the elected value can be any value between a floor of $500,000 and a ceiling of $750,000.

18-18.   In most situations, the transferor wishes to avoid recognizing income on the transfer and, in order to do this, the elected value will be the floor of $500,000. The election of this value will have the following tax consequences for the transferor and the transferee:

• The $500,000 will be the proceeds of disposition to the transferor. As this is equal to his adjusted cost base for the asset, there will be no capital gain on the transfer.

• The adjusted cost base to the corporation will be $500,000. This means that, if the corporation were to sell the asset immediately for its fair market value of $750,000, a capital gain of $250,000 ($750,000 - $500,000) would have to be recognized. This reflects the fact that the gain on the asset at the time of transfer was only deferred, not eliminated, by the use of the ITA 85 rollover.

• While we have not specified the type of consideration that will be received by the transferor, the election of $500,000 as the transfer price means that the adjusted cost base of the consideration will be this amount. This will be less than the $750,000 fair market value of the consideration.

18-19.   You should note that this scenario raises the possibility of double taxation on the $250,000 gain. The adjusted cost base of the property transferred and the consideration received by the transferor is $500,000. If the corporation sells the asset for its fair market value of $750,000, there will be a $250,000 gain at the corporate level. If the consideration received by the transferor is in the form of shares, a sale of these shares at their fair market value of $750,000 would result in the $250,000 gain being taxed a second time at the individual level. This would suggest that, if either the assets transferred, or the consideration received by the transferor are to be sold, the election should be made at the fair market value of $750,000.

Non-Share Consideration (Boot)

18-20. The term, "boot", is commonly used to refer to non-share consideration given to the transferor in an ITA 85 rollover. It would include cash paid to the transferor and new debt of the transferee corporation issued to the transferor. In those cases where an existing business is being transferred under these provisions, boot would include the assumption by the transferee corporation of any debt of the existing business that is being transferred.

18-21. Other types of non-share consideration (e.g., capital assets) could be used in an ITA 85 rollover and, if this was the case, the term boot would still be appropriate. However, in most situations, boot is restricted to cash, new debt issued by the transferee corporation, or existing debt of the transferor assumed by the transferee corporation.

18-22. Boot is of considerable significance in that, if the rollover is properly structured, it constitutes an amount of cash or cash equivalent that will be received by the transferor on a tax free basis. Because of this, the other basic rule on establishing a transfer price is that the elected amount cannot be less than the value of the non-share consideration provided to the transferor.

18-23. Revising the basic example that was presented in Paragraph 18-17, assume that Mr. Thompson receives the following from the transferee corporation:

Cash	$600,000
Shares Of Transferee Corporation	150,000
Total (Equals Fair Market Value Of Assets Transferred)	$750,000

18-24. Because the elected value cannot be below the value of the non-share consideration, the minimum elected value would be $600,000. If $600,000 was the elected value, it would result in the following tax consequences:

- The proceeds of disposition to the transferor would be $600,000, resulting in a taxable capital gain of $50,000 [(1/2)($600,000 - $500,000)].

- The adjusted cost base of the assets for the corporation would be the transfer price of $600,000. This means that if the corporation sells the assets for their fair market value of $750,000, the capital gain would be $150,000.

- The adjusted cost base of the consideration received by the transferor would be $600,000. As will be discussed at a later point, all of this amount must be allocated to the non-share consideration, leaving the share consideration with an adjusted cost base of nil.

The Usual Scenario

18-25. As illustrated in the preceding example, if the boot exceeds the tax values (adjusted cost base or UCC) of the assets transferred, the result is income for tax purposes. As one of the usual goals in using ITA 85 is to avoid a tax liability on the transfer of assets, the normal procedure is to set the transfer price at an amount equal to the tax values of the assets and to restrict the use of boot to this value. In the example presented, this would mean using $500,000 as the elected value and paying or issuing non-share consideration in this same amount.

18-26. In addition, as the fair market value of the consideration received by the transferor must be equal to the fair market value of the assets transferred to the corporation, share consideration with a fair market value of $250,000 would be issued to the transferor. Expanding on the consequences of the original example discussed in Paragraph 18-18, there would be the following tax consequences:

- As the proceeds of disposition would be $500,000, no capital gain would arise on the transfer to the corporation.

- The adjusted cost base to the corporation of the assets acquired will be $500,000.

- The adjusted cost base of the non-share consideration to the transferor would be $500,000. This means that the adjusted cost base of the share consideration would be nil.

• The adjusted cost base of the shares received by the transferor would be nil.

18-27.   There are a number of complications associated with rollovers under ITA 85 and they will be the subject of much of the remainder of this Chapter. However, the great majority of these transactions will follow the pattern illustrated in the preceding simple example.

Transfer Prices - Detailed Rules

Rules Applicable To All Assets

18-28.   There are a number of rules in ITA 85 that apply to all types of property. To begin, ITA 85(1)(a) establishes that the amount elected by the taxpayer and corporation shall be deemed to be the taxpayer's proceeds of disposition, as well as the cost of the property to the corporation.

18-29.   A further general rule is as follows:

ITA 85(1)(b)   ...where the amount that the taxpayer and corporation have agreed on in their election in respect of the property is less than the fair market value, at the time of the disposition, of the consideration therefor (other than any shares of the capital stock of the corporation or a right to receive any such shares) received by the taxpayer, the amount so agreed on shall, irrespective of the amount actually so agreed on by them, be deemed to be an amount equal to that fair market value;

18-30.   This establishes that the elected value cannot be less than the boot ("consideration other than shares of stock of the corporation").

18-31.   Finally, a further provision limits the elected value to the fair market value of the property transferred:

ITA 85(1)(c)   ... where the amount that the taxpayer and the corporation have agreed on in their election in respect of the property is greater than the fair market value, at the time of the disposition, of the property so disposed of, the amount so agreed on shall, irrespective of the amount actually so agreed on, be deemed to be an amount equal to that fair market value;

18-32.   These general rules apply to all assets transferred, thereby establishing a range for the election. This range can be outlined as follows:

Ceiling Value   Fair market value of the assets transferred to the corporation.

Floor Value   The floor value will be equal to the greater of:

• the fair market value of the non-share consideration (boot) given to the transferor in return for the assets transferred; and
• the tax values (adjusted cost base or UCC) of the assets transferred.

18-33.   The application of the term," tax values", in the preceding outline of the rules will vary with the type of asset involved. Attention will be given to these differences in the material which follows.

Accounts Receivable

18-34.   As was discussed in Chapter 8, when accounts receivable are transferred in conjunction with all of the other assets of a business, the disposition will be treated as a capital transaction, with any resulting loss being only one-half deductible. Further, as the transferee has not included these amounts in income, no deduction can be made for bad debts. If less than the transfer amount of the accounts receivable is collected, the difference must be treated as a capital loss, only one-half of which will be deductible.

18-35.   To avoid these results, the usual procedure is to use a joint election under ITA 22. This election allows any loss to be treated as a fully deductible business loss and permits the transferee to deduct bad debts after the transfer. You may recall that this election was discussed in Chapter 8, starting at Paragraph 8-154.

18-36.   While accounts receivable can be transferred under ITA 85, taxpayers are not permitted to elect under both ITA 85 and ITA 22. In general, it will be to the advantage of the taxpayer to make the ITA 22 election and, as a result, accounts receivable will usually not be one of the assets listed in the ITA 85 election.

18-37.   Note, however, this does not prevent these assets from being transferred. Using the ITA 22 joint election, they can be transferred at fair market value, with any resulting loss being fully deductible to the transferor. The corporation will have to include the difference between the face value and the price paid in income, but any difference between the face value and the amounts collected will be fully deductible.

Inventories And Non-Depreciable Capital Property

18-38.   Unlike the situation with accounts receivable, when inventories are disposed of in conjunction with the sale of substantially all of the assets of a business, any difference between fair market value and cost is automatically treated as business income or loss, not as a capital gain or loss. This is specifically provided for in ITA 23, with no election being required to bring this provision into effect.

18-39.   Non-depreciable capital property of a business would include land, temporary investments, and long-term investments. As capital property is involved, any gain or loss on their disposition would be treated as a capital gain or loss.

18-40.   In making the election here, the highest value will be the fair market value of the assets transferred to the corporation. The minimum election cannot be below the amount of the boot received by the transferor. However, a further floor limit is specified for the inventories and non-depreciable capital property in ITA 85(1)(c.1) to ensure that artificial losses cannot be created. This limit is the lesser of the fair market value of the property and its tax cost. For non-depreciable capital assets, the tax cost would be the adjusted cost base of the property. For inventory, tax cost would be either cost or market, depending on how the inventory balance is carried for tax purposes.

18-41.   Putting these limits together means that the minimum elected value for the floor, as specified in ITA 85(1)(e.3), will be the greater of:

A.   The fair market value of the boot (the general floor for all assets); and

B.   The lesser of:
   • the fair market value of the property; and
   • the tax cost of the property.

18-42.   These rules can be illustrated using the three examples that follow:

	Example One	Example Two	Example Three
Fair Market Value Of Asset	$15,000	$10,000	$20,000
Adjusted Cost Base	12,000	12,000	14,000
Fair Market Value Of The Boot	5,000	5,000	17,000

18-43.   In Example One, the maximum transfer value is the fair market value of $15,000 and the minimum value is the cost of $12,000. The normal election value would be $12,000. Also note that up to $12,000 of boot could have been taken out without changing the minimum election, or creating tax consequences.

18-44.   In Example Two, the $10,000 fair market value is both the floor and the ceiling. If the property is inventories, this required election will result in a fully deductible business loss of $2,000 ($12,000 - $10,000). Alternatively, if the election was made on non-depreciable capital property, the result would be an allowable capital loss of $1,000 [(1/2)($12,000 - $10,000)]. As explained beginning in Paragraph 18-47, this capital loss would be disallowed.

18-45.   In Example Three, the maximum value is again the fair market value. While the $14,000 cost is lower than the $20,000 fair market value, it is also lower than the boot. This means that, in this example, the minimum value that can be elected is the boot of $17,000. If this property is inventory, this election will result in fully taxable business income of $3,000 ($17,000 - $14,000). If the election was made on non-depreciable capital property, the result will be taxable capital gain of $1,500 [(1/2)($17,000 - $14,000)].

18-46.   If the goal is to structure the rollover to avoid any gain on the transfer of assets, Example Three will not accomplish this objective. In order to avoid a gain, the usual procedure is to limit the non-share consideration to the minimum elected value as otherwise determined, or $14,000 in Example Three.

Exercise Eighteen-1

Subject: Elected Value For Non-Depreciable Property

Jean Doan's unincorporated business has inventories with a fair market value of $125,000 and a tax cost of $140,000. In addition, he owns land with a fair market value of $350,000 and a tax cost of $125,000. He intends to transfer these assets to a new corporation, taking back $125,000 in cash for the inventories and $150,000 in cash for the land. If he uses ITA 85 for the transfer, what is the possible range of values that can be elected for the two properties? Assume he elects the lowest possible value in each case. What are the tax consequences for Mr. Doan?

End of Exercise.   Solution available in Study Guide.

Non-Depreciable Capital Property - Disallowed Capital Losses
General Rules
18-47.   The special rules described in the following material apply only to non-depreciable capital assets. They do not apply to either inventories or depreciable capital assets as it is not possible to have capital losses on these types of assets.

18-48.   While we are discussing these rules in the material related to Section 85 rollovers, you should note that they are applicable to transfers to affiliated persons, without regard to whether Section 85 is being used. The discussion is located here because, when a non-depreciable capital asset is transferred under ITA 85, the recognition of a loss may be unavoidable because of the rules limiting the elected values. This was the case in Example Two in Paragraph 18-42.

18-49.   The basic rule applicable to these situations is found in ITA 40(2)(g), which indicates that a taxpayer's loss, to the extent that it is a "superficial loss", is deemed to be nil. As with many other concepts related to capital assets, the definition of "superficial loss" is found in ITA 54:

> **"superficial loss"** of a taxpayer means the taxpayer's loss from the disposition of a particular property where
>
> (a) during the period that begins 30 days before and ends 30 days after the disposition, the taxpayer or a person affiliated with the taxpayer acquires a property (in this definition referred to as the "substituted property") that is, or is identical to, the particular property, and
>
> (b) at the end of that period, the taxpayer or a person affiliated with the taxpayer owns or had a right to acquire the substituted property.

18-50.   Read together, these provisions deem to be nil any capital loss arising on a transfer to an affiliated person. While the allocation of the loss will depend on whether the taxpayer is an individual, a trust or a corporation, the denial of the loss is applicable to all taxpayers. The actual allocation of the denied loss will be dealt with after our discussion of affiliated persons.

Affiliated Persons

18-51.   The term "affiliated person" is defined in ITA 251.1(1) as follows:

A. An individual is affiliated to another individual only if that individual is his spouse or common-law partner.

B. A corporation is affiliated with:
1. a person who controls the corporation;
2. each member of an affiliated group of persons who controls the corporation; and
3. the spouse or common-law partner of a person listed in (1) or (2).

C. Two corporations are affiliated if:
1. each corporation is controlled by a person, and the person by whom one corporation is controlled is affiliated with the person by whom the other corporation is controlled;
2. one corporation is controlled by a person, the other corporation is controlled by a group of persons, and each member of that group is affiliated with that person; or
3. each corporation is controlled by a group of persons, and each member of each group is affiliated with at least one member of the other group.

18-52.   ITA 251.1(3) contains definitions that are required in the application of these rules. The two that are of importance here are:

Affiliated group of persons means a group of persons each member of which is affiliated with every other member.

Controlled means controlled, directly or indirectly, in any manner whatever. [The reference here is to de facto control, which does not necessarily require majority ownership of shares.]

18-53.   As was previously noted, if a capital loss arises on a transfer to an affiliated person, it is deemed to be nil. This rule applies to all taxpayers, including both individuals and corporations.

Allocation Of Disallowed Capital Loss

18-54.   When the transferor is an individual, the disallowed loss is allocated to the adjusted cost base of the transferred property. This requirement is dictated by ITA 53(1)(f), which describes adjustments to the cost base of a transferred property.

Example   Ms. Hannah Howard, the sole shareholder of HH Ltd., transfers land with an adjusted cost base of $50,000 and a fair market value of $40,000, to HH Ltd. The transfer is made under Section 85 at an elected value of $40,000.

Analysis   The $10,000 loss ($40,000 - $50,000) on the transfer is disallowed. As the transferor is an individual, it will be allocated to the adjusted cost base of the land in the tax records of HH Ltd. This means that the adjusted cost base to HH Ltd. will be the same $50,000 ($40,000, plus the $10,000 loss) that was the adjusted cost base to Ms. Howard.

18-55.   When the transferor is a corporation, trust, or partnership, the allocation of the disallowed loss is covered under ITA 40(3.4). In effect, this provision keeps the loss in the tax records of the transferor, to be recognized when one of the following events occurs:

• the transferee disposes of the property to a non-affiliated person (includes deemed dispositions);
• if the transferor is a corporation,
    • it is subject to an acquisition of control; or
    • it is subject to an ITA 88(2) winding up.

Example   HC Ltd. transfers land with an adjusted cost base of $50,000 and a fair market value of $40,000 to HCSub, a corporation controlled by HC Ltd., i.e., an affiliated person. Two years later, HCSub sells the land for $35,000 to a non-affiliated person.

Analysis   The $10,000 ($40,000 - $50,000) loss on the transfer to HCSub will be disallowed at the time of the transfer. However, when the land is sold by HCSub for $35,000, the $10,000 loss that was disallowed at the time of the transfer will be recognized by HC Ltd. HCSub will recognize a $5,000 ($40,000 - $35,000) loss at the time of sale.

Tax Planning

18-56.   To the extent that the asset with the unrealized loss is necessary to the continued operations of the business, for example land on which the enterprise's factory is located, it makes no difference whether it is transferred under the provisions of ITA 85 or outside the election. In either case, the loss will be disallowed at the time of the transfer.

18-57.   If an asset is not essential to the operations of the corporation, a preferable course of action may be to sell it to an arm's length party. This will permit the immediate recognition of any loss on its disposition. However, if the asset is an integral part of the operations of the transferor this is not a viable alternative.

18-58.   The other basic point here is, that if the asset in question has an unrealized loss, there is no reason to elect to transfer it under Section 85. The objective that the taxpayer is attempting to achieve in using Section 85 is to defer the taxation of income. When losses are involved on particular assets, including those assets in the Section 85 rollover complicates the election without contributing to the taxpayer's desired goals.

Depreciable Property

General Rules

18-59.   As with other assets, the ceiling for the election is the fair market value of the asset and the general floor is the fair market value of the non-share consideration received by the transferor. However, as was the case with inventories and non-depreciable capital property, a further lower limit is specified in the *Income Tax Act*.

18-60.   ITA 85(1)(e) indicates that for depreciable property, the lower limit is the least of the UCC for the class, the fair market value of each individual property, and the cost of each individual property. This means that the overall lower limit for the election, as specified in ITA 85(1)(e.3), is the greater of:

A.   The fair market value of the boot (general floor for all assets), and

B.   The least of:

- the balance of the UCC for the class;
- the cost to the taxpayer of each individual property; and
- the fair market value of each individual property.

Examples - Elected Values

18-61.   These rules can be illustrated by the following two examples, each involving the transfer of the only asset in a CCA class:

	Example One	Example Two
Fair Market Value Of The Property	$50,000	$18,000
UCC Of Class (Last Asset In Class)	20,000	20,000
Cost Of The Property	27,000	30,000
Fair Market Value Of The Boot	15,000	15,000

Example One Analysis   In Example One, the range of the election would extend from the UCC of $20,000 as the floor to the fair market value of $50,000. Note that any election in between the UCC of $20,000 and the cost of $27,000 would result in recapture of CCA. The normal election here would be the UCC of $20,000, which results in the transferor not recognizing a capital gain or recapture of CCA. In addition, the transferor would usually take out $20,000 in boot. In Example One, $5,000 more boot could be taken out without creating tax consequences.

Example Two Analysis   In Example Two, the ceiling value and the floor value would be the $18,000 fair market value of the property. With the ceiling and floor at the same value, the general rules would indicate that only this $18,000 value could be elected. In Example Two, $3,000 more boot could be taken out without creating tax consequences. Since the transfer of the property removes the last asset in this CCA class, the fact that the elected value is below the UCC suggests a terminal loss. As will be discussed beginning in Paragraph 18-67, this terminal loss will be disallowed.

Example - Order Of Disposition

18-62.   An additional problem arises in the case of depreciable assets in situations where a number of different assets that belong to the same CCA class are being transferred. This problem can be illustrated by the following example:

> **Example**   An individual owns two assets in a particular CCA class and the UCC for that class is $28,000. Data on the two assets is as follows:
>
> | | Asset One | Asset Two |
> |---|---|---|
> | Cost Of Asset | $15,000 | $30,000 |
> | Fair Market Value | 20,000 | 25,000 |

18-63.   The problem here is that the wording of the transfer price rules for depreciable assets requires the floor to be based on the least of the cost of each individual asset, fair market value of each individual asset, but UCC for the class as a whole. This determination has to be made with respect to each asset in the class, with the resulting figures summed for purposes of the election floor.

18-64.   This means that, if the general rules were applied, the floor values would be $15,000 for Asset One, plus $25,000 for Asset Two. This reflects the fact that both of these individual values are less than the $28,000 UCC for the class. However, if these values are elected, a total of $40,000 would be subtracted from the class. Since the UCC balance for the class is only $28,000, this would result in recapture of $12,000.

18-65.   To alleviate this problem, ITA 85(1)(e.1) allows an assumption that the properties are transferred one at a time. This means that for the transfer of Asset One, if the floor value of $15,000 was elected (this assumes that the non-share consideration provided to the transferor does not exceed this amount), this $15,000 would be subtracted from the UCC of $28,000.

18-66.   The resulting UCC balance would be $13,000, and when the depreciable asset rules are applied to Asset Two, this UCC balance of $13,000 would become the floor. If the taxpayer again elected to use the floor value, the $13,000 would be deducted from the UCC and this would reduce the UCC balance to nil without triggering recaptured CCA.

Exercise Eighteen-2

Subject: Elected Value For Depreciable Property

Eric Li has two depreciable assets - a Class 1 building and a Class 10 vehicle. The assets are to be transferred to a corporation using ITA 85. Relevant information on the assets is as follows:

	Class 1	Class 10
Fair Market Value Of The Property	$475,000	$12,000
UCC Of Class (Last Asset In Class)	150,000	8,000
Cost Of The Property	220,000	28,000
Fair Market Value Of The Boot	250,000	10,000

What is the possible range of values that can be elected for the two properties? Assume he elects the lowest possible value in each case. What are the tax consequences for Mr. Li?

End of Exercise. Solution available in Study Guide.

Depreciable Property - Terminal Losses Disallowed

General Rules

18-67.   In Paragraph 18-61, we noted that the terminal loss resulting from the required election on the asset in Example Two will be disallowed. More specifically, if a depreciable property with a fair market value that is less than its UCC is transferred by a person (individual, trust, or corporation) or a partnership to an affiliated person (see Paragraph 18-51), ITA 13(21.2) indicates that:

- ITA 85 does not apply;

- the proceeds of the disposition are deemed to be the UCC amount, thereby disallowing the terminal loss; and

- the transferee's capital cost for the property is deemed to be the transferor's capital cost, with the excess of that amount over the fair market value of the asset deemed to be CCA deducted in previous periods.

18-68.   In Example Two from Paragraph 18-61, the property had a fair market value of $18,000. As this was less than the UCC of $20,000, the fair market value would be both the floor and the ceiling for the elected value, resulting in a situation where the property would have to be transferred at $18,000. While this would create a potential terminal loss of $2,000 ($20,000 - $18,000), ITA 13(21.2) would disallow this loss on the transfer. As you would expect, however, the loss does not disappear.

18-69.   For the transferee corporation, the property will have a deemed capital cost of $30,000 and a UCC value of $18,000. The $2,000 disallowed loss will be deemed to be a depreciable property that is owned by the transferor. It will be allocated to the same class as the transferred property for CCA purposes and will be subject to the usual CCA procedures. However, it will be kept in a separate class so that any unamortized amount can be recognized when one of the following events occurs:

- the transferee disposes of the property to a non-affiliated person (includes deemed dispositions);
- the use of the property is changed from income earning to non-income earning;
- if the transferor is a corporation,
  - it is subject to an acquisition of control; or
  - it is subject to an ITA 88(2) winding up.

Tax Planning

18-70.   As was noted in our discussion of capital losses on transfers of non-depreciable capital property, Section 85 is normally used in order to defer the taxation of various types of income. If there is a terminal loss present on a depreciable property, to the extent that the asset is necessary to the continued operations of the business, it makes no difference whether it is transferred under the provisions of ITA 85 or outside the election. In either case, the terminal loss will be disallowed at the time of the transfer. Electing to transfer the asset under Section 85 can complicate the transaction, without improving the situation of the taxpayer.

Eligible Capital Property

General Rules

18-71.   As is the case for all other assets, the general ceiling and floor for making an election under ITA 85(1) is the fair market value of the assets transferred and the fair market value of the non-share consideration received, respectively.   As was the case with inventories, non-depreciable property, and depreciable property, a further lower limit is specified in the *Act* for eligible capital property.

18-72.   ITA 85(1)(d) limits the floor to the least of 4/3 of the taxpayer's cumulative eligible capital in respect of the business immediately before the disposition, the cost to the taxpayer of the property, and the fair market value of the property at the time of the disposition. This means that the overall lower limit for the election, as specified in ITA 85(1)(e.3), is the greater of:

A.   The fair market value of the boot (general floor for all assets), and

B.   The least of:

- 4/3 of the cumulative eligible capital balance;
- the cost of the individual property; and
- the fair market value of the individual property.

Examples - Transfers Of Eligible Capital Property

18-73.   Assuming that the corporation has only one eligible capital property, these provisions can be illustrated using the following examples:

	Example One	Example Two
Fair Market Value Of The Property	$60,000	$60,000
Cumulative Eligible Capital Balance	37,500	52,500
4/3 Cumulative Eligible Capital Balance	50,000	70,000
Cost Of The Property	55,000	80,000
Fair Market Value Of The Boot	40,000	40,000

18-74.   In Example One, the range of election values would extend from a floor of $50,000 to a ceiling of $60,000. The floor value would normally be elected because its use would have no immediate tax implications. Note that additional non-share consideration of $10,000 could be taken out in this example without creating tax consequences.

18-75.   In Example Two, $60,000 is both the floor and the ceiling and if this amount is elected, it would result in the reduction of the transferor's cumulative eligible capital account by $45,000 (three-quarters of $60,000). This disposition would normally produce a loss of $7,500 ($52,500 - $45,000). However, such losses may be disallowed. This point will be covered beginning in Paragraph 18-78.

Transfers Of Goodwill

18-76.   As discussed in Chapter 7, the most important component of cumulative eligible capital is usually goodwill. An individual transferring a business to a corporation would generally not have a balance in the cumulative eligible capital account, reflecting the fact that only purchased goodwill is given recognition for either accounting or tax purposes. This means that under the general rules for transfer price elections, the goodwill could be transferred at a value of zero.

18-77.   The danger in doing this is that giving no consideration to goodwill could result in this asset being inadvertently omitted from the election. This would make the transfer a non-arm's length gift and, under ITA 69, the proceeds would be deemed to be fair market value. To avoid this possibility, a value of at least $1 should be assigned to goodwill when assets that constitute a business entity are being transferred to a corporation.

Exercise Eighteen-3

Subject: Elected Value For CEC

During 2006, Joan's Enterprises acquires an unlimited life franchise at a cost of $135,000. Maximum CEC is deducted for that year. At the beginning of 2007, all of the assets of Joan's Enterprises are transferred to a new corporation. At this time, the fair market value of the franchise is estimated to be $175,000. Joan's consideration for this asset is made up of $135,000 in cash, plus shares in the new corporation with a fair market value of $40,000. What is the possible range of values that can be elected for the franchise? If the minimum value is elected, what would be the tax consequences for Joan's Enterprises?

End of Exercise. Solution available in Study Guide.

Eligible Capital Property - Disallowed Deductions
General Rules
18-78.   When a taxpayer ceases to carry on business, three-quarters of any disposition proceeds allocated to cumulative eligible capital items will be subtracted from the balance in this account. If the result is a negative balance in the cumulative eligible capital account, the result will be an income inclusion under ITA 14(1). Alternatively, if a positive balance remains, it can generally be deducted under ITA 24(1).

18-79.   Note that these amounts are very much like recaptured CCA and terminal losses on depreciable assets. However, these latter items are included or deducted under other Sections of the *Act* and, as a consequence, those terms are not used when the analogous events occur with respect to cumulative eligible capital.

18-80.   With respect to the deduction under ITA 24(1), ITA 14(12) disallows this deduction when the transfer is to an affiliated person (see Paragraph 18-51 for a definition of affiliated person). This is analogous to the disallowance under ITA 13(21.1) of terminal losses on transfers of depreciable assets to affiliated persons (see Paragraph 18-67).

18-81.   There is, however, an important difference. ITA 13(21.2) disallows terminal losses when the transferor is an individual, corporation, trust, or partnership. In contrast ITA 14(12) disallows the ITA 24(1) deduction when the transferor is a corporation, trust, or partnership. In other words, if the transfer is from an individual to an affiliated person, the deduction is allowed.

18-82.   When ITA 14(12) disallows the deduction, the transferor is deemed to continue to own the cumulative eligible capital. The positive balance in this account will continue to be subject to the usual rules related to writing off cumulative eligible capital until such time as:

• the transferee disposes of the property to an arm's length person (includes deemed dispositions);
• the use of the property is changed from income earning to non-income earning;
• if the transferee is a corporation,
    • it is subject to an acquisition of control; or
    • it is subject to an ITA 88(2) winding up.

18-83.   On the occurrence of one of these events, any remaining unamortized balance can be deducted under ITA 24(1).

18-84.   With respect to Example Two from Paragraph 18-73, if the transferor was an individual, the $7,500 [(3/4)($70,000 - $60,000)] loss could be deducted. However, if the transferor was a corporation, trust, or partnership, the $7,500 would be left as a cumulative eligible capital balance in its books. The transferor would continue to write off the balance (he is deemed not to have ceased carrying on business). This would continue until one of the events specified in Paragraph 18-82 occurs. At the occurrence of one of these events, the transferor can deduct the remaining balance in the cumulative eligible capital account under ITA 24(1).

Tax Planning

18-85. We have previously noted with respect to capital losses on non-depreciable capital assets and terminal losses on depreciable capital assets that, in most circumstances, there is no reason to list the relevant assets under the ITA 85 election. Identical results can be obtained by simply selling the assets at their fair market value.

18-86. Implementation of this advice with respect to cumulative eligible capital may be more difficult. While some balances included in cumulative eligible capital can be sold independently of the related business (e.g., an unlimited life government licence), other components (e.g., goodwill) may have no meaningful value when measured independently of the business. This may require their inclusion in the ITA 85 election, even if it creates a disallowed deduction.

Allocation Of The Elected Value

Consideration Received By The Transferor (Shareholder)

18-87. As noted previously, the elected value for the assets transferred is used to establish the adjusted cost base of all consideration received by the transferor. The rules for allocating this total to the various types of consideration that may be used are found in ITA 85(1)(f), (g), and (h). They involve a sequential process that can be outlined as follows:

Elected Value (Total Adjusted Cost Base Of All Consideration)	$xxx
Less: Adjusted Cost Base Of Non-Share Consideration (Fair Market Value)	(xxx)
Adjusted Cost Base Of All Shares Issued (Usually Nil)	$xxx
Less: Adjusted Cost Base Of Preferred Stock Issued (Usually Nil, But Limited To Fair Market Value)	(xxx)
Adjusted Cost Base Of Common Stock Issued (A Residual - Usually Nil)	$xxx

18-88. As noted in our description of the usual ITA 85 scenario, minimum asset values will normally be elected in order to avoid the recognition of income on the transfer. Boot will then be taken out in an amount equal to these minimum values. This means that in the usual situation, non-share consideration will be equal to the elected value and, in terms of the preceding allocation process, both preferred and common shares will have an adjusted cost base of nil.

Exercise Eighteen-4

Subject: Transfers Under Section 85 - ACB Of Consideration

Using ITA 85, Mrs. Jennifer Lee transfers non-depreciable property to a corporation at an elected value of $62,000. The property has an adjusted cost base of $62,000 and a fair market value of $176,000. As consideration, she receives a note for $51,000, preferred shares with a fair market value of $53,000, and common shares with a fair market value of $72,000. Indicate the adjusted cost base of the individual items of consideration received by Mrs. Lee.

End of Exercise. Solution available in Study Guide.

Assets Acquired By The Corporation

General Rules

18-89. With respect to the assets acquired by the transferee corporation, the basic rules are as follows:

Non-Depreciable Property   The elected transfer price becomes the tax cost of these assets to the corporation.

Depreciable Property   Where the transferor's capital cost exceeds the elected value for the property, ITA 85(5) requires that the capital cost to the transferee be equal to the amount that was the capital cost to the transferor. In most cases, the elected value will be equal to the transferor's UCC. ITA 85(5) requires that the difference between these two values be treated as deemed CCA. To illustrate this, consider the following asset:

Cost	$100,000
UCC	67,000
Fair Market Value	105,000
Non-Share Consideration	67,000
Elected Value	67,000

The capital cost of the asset to the transferee will be $100,000, there will be deemed CCA taken of $33,000, and future CCA will be based on the elected value of $67,000. The reason for requiring the transferee to retain the transferor's capital cost is to avoid having the transferor convert potential recaptured CCA into a capital gain, only one-half of which would be taxed.

You should also note that, in the usual situation where the transferor is not dealing at arm's length with the transferee corporation, the first year rules do not apply to the calculation of CCA by the transferee. This is the case as long as the transferor has owned the asset for at least 364 days before the end of the taxation year of the transferor in which the property was acquired, and used it as a capital property to earn business or property income.

18-90.   What these rules mean is that, in cases where the election has been made at an amount equal to the transferor's tax cost, the transferee corporation essentially assumes the tax position of the transferor.

Capital Gains On Transfers Of Depreciable Property

18-91.   The objective of using ITA 85(1) is usually to avoid tax consequences when assets are transferred to a corporation. This means that, in general, the elected values will be equal to the transferor's tax values (adjusted cost base or UCC).

18-92.   There are, however, circumstances in which the transferor may wish to generate a capital gain through the transfer of assets to a corporation. An example of this might be an individual who has large losses in the current year, or who has unused capital or non-capital loss carry forwards that he wishes to claim.

18-93.   This creates a problem with respect to depreciable assets in that, under the general ITA 85 rules, the elected value becomes the basis for calculating future CCA amounts. An election on a depreciable asset at a value in excess of the capital cost would result in a capital gain, only one-half of which would be taxable. Under the usual disposition rules, this same excess would become part of the UCC, the basis for calculating fully deductible amounts of CCA. The following example will serve to clarify this point.

Cost	$ 80,000
Fair Market Value	120,000
UCC	75,000
Elected Value	120,000

18-94.   The election at $120,000 would create the following amounts of income:

Recaptured CCA ($80,000 - $75,000)	$ 5,000
Taxable Capital Gain [(1/2)($120,000 - $80,000)]	20,000
Total Income	$25,000

18-95.   In the absence of a special rule, the cost and UCC of this asset to the corporation would be $120,000. This value would create $45,000 more CCA for the corporation than would have been available to the transferor ($120,000 - $75,000). This has been accomplished through an increase in the transferor's Taxable Income of only $25,000, clearly not an equitable situation from the point of view of the government.

18-96.   ITA 13(7)(e) acts to correct this situation. Note that this provision applies to all non-arm's length transfers of depreciable property which result in a capital gain for the transferor, not just those involving Section 85.

18-97.   When such transfers occur, ITA 13(7)(e) limits the capital cost of the asset for CCA purposes to the transferor's cost, plus one-half of any capital gain that results from the transfer. As applied to the example in Paragraph 18-93, the capital cost to the transferor, for CCA, recapture and terminal loss purposes only, under ITA 13(7)(e) would be as follows:

Transferor's Cost		$ 80,000
Elected Transfer Price	$120,000	
Transferor's Cost	(80,000)	
Capital Gain	$ 40,000	
Taxable Portion	1/2	20,000
Capital Cost To The Transferee For CCA Purposes		$100,000

18-98.   Based on this capital cost, the increased CCA base to the corporation is only $25,000 ($100,000 - $75,000), the same amount the transferor recognized as income as a result of the transfer. Note, however, that for future capital gains calculations, the adjusted cost base of the asset to the transferee is the elected value of $120,000.

Paid Up Capital Of Shares Issued

General Rules

18-99.   Establishing the Paid Up Capital (PUC) of the shares received is important as it represents an amount that can be distributed to the shareholders as a tax free return of capital. In general, the amount of PUC for tax purposes is equal to the amount attributed to the shares under the appropriate corporate laws (legal stated capital).

18-100.   While there are some complications in those provinces that still permit the issuance of par value shares, the legal stated capital of a corporation is generally based on the fair market value of the consideration received in return for issued shares. In the case of shares issued in an ITA 85 rollover, this amount would be the fair market value of the assets transferred.

18-101.   From the point of view of the taxpayer receiving the new shares, their adjusted cost base will be determined by the values elected for the transfer of assets. In the normal scenario, the taxpayer will elect minimum values for the assets transferred and these will usually be less than fair market values. With the PUC of the shares initially based on fair market values and adjusted cost base determined using elected values, the initial PUC of the shares will usually be larger than the adjusted cost base of the shares.

Paid Up Capital Reduction

18-102.   As you are now aware, ITA 85 permits assets to be transferred without the recognition of the income that would normally be associated with their disposition. As the transferor's old tax values are generally flowed through to the transferee corporation, the potential income is deferred until the assets are used or disposed of by that corporation. Consider the following example:

Example   Assets with a fair market value of $200,000, a capital cost of $180,000, and a UCC of $120,000 are transferred under ITA 85 using an elected value of $120,000. The consideration given consists of cash of $120,000 and shares with a fair market value and legal stated capital of $80,000 (total consideration equals $200,000).

18-103.   If these assets had been sold to an arm's length party, the vendor would have had to pay taxes on a total of $70,000, $60,000 ($180,000 - $120,000) in recapture and $10,000 [(1/2)($200,000 - $180,000)] in taxable capital gains. As is the intent of the legislation, these amounts of income are deferred when Section 85 is used properly. The problem is that, if the $80,000 legal stated capital of the shares issued is used as their PUC, this amount can be withdrawn from the corporation on a tax free basis. This would mean the potential recapture and taxable capital gain would permanently escape taxation.

18-104.   Given this problem, ITA 85(2.1) requires that the PUC of issued shares be reduced by an amount equal to the total increase in legal stated capital, less any excess of the elected value over non-share consideration given.   Continuing with our example, the reduction would be as follows:

Increase In Legal Stated Capital		$80,000
Less Excess, If Any, Of:		
Total Elected Value	($120,000)	
Over The Non-Share Consideration	120,000	Nil
Reduction In Paid Up Capital		**$80,000**
Balance Of Paid Up Capital ($80,000 - $80,000)		**Nil**

18-105.   It is easy to see the conceptual basis for this reduction.   Unless the non-share consideration is less than the elected value, the PUC reduction will be equal to the full fair market value of the shares, and the resulting PUC will be nil. This process also sets the PUC equal to the adjusted cost base that is allocated to the shares.

More Than One Class Of Shares

18-106.   In the majority of Section 85 rollovers, the ITA 85(2.1) formula will reduce the PUC of all shares issued to nil. This reflects the fact that the non-share consideration taken will equal the elected value, resulting in the PUC reduction being equal to the increase in legal stated capital. This was the case in the calculation in Paragraph 18-104. If this is the case, having more than one class of shares does not create any difficulties.

18-107.   If, however, the non-share consideration is less than the elected value, the PUC reduction must be allocated to the various classes of shares. You will recall that, when we allocated the adjusted cost base, it was a sequential process (see Paragraph 18-87).   The total adjusted cost base (i.e, the elected value) was allocated first to non-share consideration, then to preferred shares to the extent of their fair market value, and finally to the common shares.

18-108.   This is not the case with the PUC reduction. The formula in ITA 85(2.1) is such that the reduction is allocated to different classes of shares on the basis of their relative fair market values.

> **Example**   Joan Creek transfers non-depreciable assets with a fair market value of $1,600,000 to a corporation under the provisions of ITA 85(1). The elected value is equal to the $900,000 cost of the assets and, as consideration, she receives cash of $600,000, redeemable preferred shares with a fair market value of $250,000, and common shares with a fair market value of $750,000.

> **Analysis**   The total adjusted cost base for the consideration would be allocated as follows:

Section 85 Rollovers — Comprehensive Example

Elected Value (Total Adjusted Cost Base Of All Consideration)	$900,000
Non-Share Consideration (Fair Market Value)	(600,000)
Adjusted Cost Base Of All Shares Issued	$300,000
Less: Adjusted Cost Base Of Preferred Stock Issued	
(Limited To Fair Market Value)	(250,000)
Adjusted Cost Base Of Common Stock Issued (Residual)	$ 50,000

The PUC reduction would be calculated as follows:

Increase In Legal Stated Capital		
($250,000 + $750,000)		$1,000,000
Less Excess, If Any, Of:		
Total Elected Value	($900,000)	
Over The Non-Share Consideration	600,000	(300,000)
Reduction In Paid Up Capital		$ 700,000

The PUC of the two classes of shares, reduced by a pro rata allocation of the $700,000 PUC reduction on the basis of relative fair market value, would be as follows:

$$\text{PUC Of Preferred Stock} \left[\$250,000 - \left(\frac{\$250,000}{\$1,000,000} \right)(\$700,000) \right] = \$75,000$$

$$\text{PUC Of Common Stock} \left[\$750,000 - \left(\frac{\$750,000}{\$1,000,000} \right)(\$700,000) \right] = \$225,000$$

18-109.   Note that the total PUC of the two classes is equal to $300,000 ($75,000 + $225,000). As you would expect, this is equal to the total adjusted cost base of the two classes ($250,000 + $50,000) as well as the difference between the elected value of $900,000 and the non-share consideration of $600,000. The fact that the amounts are different reflects the difference between the sequential allocation process for the adjusted cost base amount and the pro rata allocation of the PUC reduction.

Exercise Eighteen-5

Subject: Transfers Under Section 85 - PUC Reduction

Using ITA 85, Mr. Rob McCleen transfers non-depreciable property to a corporation at an elected value of $114,000. The property has an adjusted cost base of $114,000 and a fair market value of $234,000. As consideration he receives a note for $83,000, preferred shares with a fair market value and legal stated capital of $97,000, and common shares with a fair market value and legal stated capital of $54,000. Indicate the adjusted cost base and the PUC of the preferred and common shares that were issued to Mr. McCleen.

End of Exercise. Solution available in Study Guide.

Section 85 Rollovers — Comprehensive Example

Basic Information

18-110.   John Martin has been operating an unincorporated business. The tax costs (UCC or adjusted cost base) and fair market values for its assets and liabilities are as follows:

	Tax Value	Fair Market Value
Cash	$ 20,000	$ 20,000
Accounts Receivable	50,000	49,000
Inventories	100,000	100,000
Prepaid Expenses	10,000	10,000
Land	50,000	70,000
Building (Capital Cost = $150,000)	110,000	140,000
Equipment (Capital Cost = $70,000)	40,000	35,000
Goodwill	Nil	50,000
Total Assets	$380,000	$474,000
Liabilities	$100,000	$100,000

Excluded Assets

18-111.   The rollover would involve a new corporation, the Martin Company, assuming all of Mr. Martin's liabilities and acquiring all of his business assets except the following:

Excluded Asset	Tax Value	Fair Market Value
Cash	$ 20,000	$ 20,000
Accounts Receivable	50,000	49,000
Prepaid Expenses	10,000	10,000
Equipment	40,000	35,000
Total Values For Excluded Assets	$120,000	$114,000

18-112.   With respect to the Cash and Prepaid Expenses, they have fair market values that are equal to their tax values and, as a result, there is no advantage to including them in the ITA 85 election.

18-113.   The Accounts Receivable could be transferred under ITA 85. However, the $1,000 ($50,000 - $49,000) loss would have to be treated as a capital loss, which would be disallowed as a superficial loss by ITA 40(2)(g). Further, any additional bad debts incurred by the corporation would also have to be treated as capital losses.

18-114.   The alternative is a joint election under ITA 22. This allows the $1,000 current loss to be treated as a fully deductible business loss. In addition, the corporation will then be able to deduct the full amount of any additional bad debts. Taxpayers are not permitted to use both the ITA 22 and the ITA 85 elections for their accounts receivable and, as a consequence, we have excluded it from the ITA 85 election.

18-115.   The equipment is excluded because there is a terminal loss of $5,000 present. While the property could be transferred under ITA 85(1), it makes no sense to use ITA 85(1) for this asset. The usual reason for using ITA 85(1) is to defer the taxation of gains. As a loss is involved with respect to the equipment, there is no tax advantage in using this election. The equipment can simply be sold to the corporation at its fair market value, thereby avoiding the additional complications associated with listing it under the ITA 85(1) election. The terminal loss would be denied regardless of whether it was sold or transferred using ITA 85(1).

Implementing The Election

18-116.   Mr. Martin is interested in deferring all of the capital gains that are present on his assets and, as a consequence, he elects tax values for most of the assets that are to be transferred under ITA 85. The one exception to this is goodwill, which is transferred at a value of $1 to ensure that it is listed in the election. There would be a $.75 income inclusion under ITA 14(1) with respect to the $1.00 elected value for goodwill.

18-117.   Mr. Martin's total elected value of $260,001 is calculated as follows:

Section 85 Rollovers — Comprehensive Example

Tax Values Of Total Assets	$380,000
Tax Value Of Excluded Assets (Paragraph 18-111)	(120,000)
Nominal Value To Goodwill	1
Total Elected Value	**$260,001**

18-118.   With respect to the consideration to be given to Mr. Martin, it must equal the fair market value of the assets transferred. This amount would be $360,000 ($474,000 total, less the $114,000 fair market value of the excluded assets listed in Paragraph 18-111).

18-119.   The normal procedure would be to take back non-share consideration, in this example debt, with a fair market value equal to the elected value of $260,001, along with shares with a fair market value equal to the $99,999 excess of the fair market values of the assets transferred over their elected values. Assuming that the non-share consideration is all in the form of debt, the analysis of the rollover would be as follows:

	Elected Value	Consideration At Fair Market Value	
		Non-Share	Share
Inventories	$100,000	$100,000	Nil
Land	50,000	50,000	$20,000
Building (Capital Cost = $150,000)	110,000	110,000	30,000
Goodwill	1	1	49,999
Total Assets	**$260,001**	**$260,001**	**$99,999**

Note   This schedule relates each asset to a particular type of consideration and allocates non-share consideration to each asset only up to the value elected for that particular asset. This allocation has no basis in tax legislation. However, it does provide an analysis that ensures that each asset transferred is supported by an appropriate amount of consideration when measured at fair market value. The widespread use of this type of analysis in textbooks probably reflects the fact that it is in a form similar to that used in the T2057 form on which the ITA 85 election is made.

18-120.   The $260,001 in debt consideration is made up of $100,000 in debt of the existing business that has been assumed by the corporation, plus $160,001 in new debt issued by the corporation.

18-121.   From the point of view of the corporation, the elected values would become the tax values to be used in subsequent periods of operation. The adjusted cost base of the shares that were issued to Mr. Martin would be determined as follows:

Total Elected Value	$260,001
Non-Share Consideration	(260,001)
Adjusted Cost Base Of Shares	**Nil**

18-122.   The PUC of these shares would initially be their legal stated capital, an amount equal to their fair market value of $99,999. However, there would be an ITA 85(2.1) reduction in this balance as follows:

Increase In Legal Stated Capital		$99,999
Less Excess, If Any, Of:		
Total Elected Value	($260,001)	
Over The Non-Share Consideration	260,001	Nil
Reduction In Paid Up Capital		**$99,999**

18-123.   At this point, both the adjusted cost base and the PUC of the shares are nil. If they were redeemed at their $99,999 fair market value, Mr. Martin would have to recognize an ITA 84(3) deemed dividend of $99,999. This deemed dividend would reduce the proceeds of disposition for capital gains purposes to nil, resulting in no capital gain on the redemption.

18-124.   Alternatively, if he were to sell the shares at their fair market value, the result would be a capital gain of $99,999. In either case, the gain that was deferred by the use of ITA 85 would have to be recognized in order for Mr. Martin to remove his remaining investment in the Martin Company.

Exercise Eighteen-6

Subject: Transfers Under Section 85 - Tax Consequences

John Savage owns a depreciable property with a capital cost of $120,000 and a fair market value of $180,000. It is the only asset in its CCA class and the UCC balance for the class is $98,000. He uses ITA 85 to transfer this property to a corporation at an elected value of $160,000. In return for the property, he receives a note for $160,000, in addition to common shares with a fair market value of $20,000. What are the tax implications of this transaction for both John Savage and the transferee corporation?

End of Exercises. Solutions available in Study Guide.

Gift To Related Person - Section 85

General Rules

18-125.   If the transferor of the assets is the only shareholder of the transferee corporation, the indirect gift rules in ITA 85(1)(e.2) are not applicable. However, Section 85 rollovers are often used for income splitting purposes, and this usually means that other members of the transferor's family will be involved as shareholders in the transferee corporation. The indirect gift rules are designed to ensure that, while other family members will be permitted to share in the future growth and income of the corporation, they are not permitted to receive a portion of the current values of the transferred assets in the form of a gift.

18-126.   The general rule is as follows:

If the fair market value of the transferred property exceeds the greater of:

1. the fair market value of all consideration received from the corporation; and
2. the amount elected for the transfer;

and it is reasonable to regard that excess as a gift made by the taxpayer for the benefit of any related shareholder, the elected transfer price is increased by the excess, without any increase in the adjusted cost base of the shares received.

Example

18-127.   The following example will serve to illustrate these indirect gift rules.

Example   Mr. Pohl owns a non-depreciable property with the following values:

Adjusted cost base of property	$ 30,000
Fair market value of property	180,000

A new corporation is formed with all of the common shares being issued to Mr. Pohl's son for $1,000. Using the provisions of ITA 85(1), Mr. Pohl then transfers his non-depreciable property to the corporation at an elected value of $30,000. As consideration for this property, the corporation issues a $30,000 note payable and preferred shares with a fair market value of $100,000. The total consideration received by Mr. Pohl is $130,000 ($30,000 + $100,000). The adjusted cost base of the preferred shares would be nil.

18-128.   The gift can be calculated as follows:

Fair Market Value Of Property Transferred	$180,000
Less - Greater Of:	
• Fair Market Value Of Consideration Received = $130,000	
• Elected Amount = $30,000	(130,000)
Gift	$ 50,000

18-129.   Under ITA 85(1)(e.2), the $50,000 gift must be added to the $30,000 elected amount to determine the adjusted cost base of the assets to the corporation and the proceeds of the disposition to Mr. Pohl. The resulting value would be $80,000 and, as a consequence, Mr. Pohl would have a taxable capital gain on the transfer of $25,000 [(1/2)($80,000 - $30,000)]. However, the adjusted cost base of the preferred shares issued to Mr. Pohl remains at nil.

18-130.   This means that, if these shares were sold, there would be a $100,000 capital gain. In addition, the fair market value of his son's common shares would be increased to $51,000 ($1,000 + $50,000) by the gift, while their adjusted cost base would remain at $1,000. This creates a potential capital gain of $50,000.

18-131.   When the $150,000 ($100,000 + $50,000) in potential capital gains on the preferred and common shares is added to the $50,000 capital gain arising on the transfer, the total amount of $200,000 exceeds the $150,000 ($180,000 - $30,000) that would have resulted from simply selling the non-depreciable property. In effect, the $50,000 amount of the gift will be subject to double taxation.

18-132.   The way to avoid this problem is fairly obvious. In situations where the rollover is being used for income splitting purposes and other members of the transferor's family will be holding shares, the transferor should always take back an amount of consideration that is equal to the fair market value of the property transferred.

18-133.   This will usually involve the transferor taking back a non-growth security such as preferred shares for the difference between the fair market value of the property and its cost base for tax purposes. Common shares can then be issued to the other family members at a nominal value. While the initial value of these shares will be nominal, it will be these shares that will have growth in value in the future.

Exercise Eighteen-7

Subject: Section 85 - Gift To Transferee

Janice Bellows establishes a new CCPC, arranging to have all of its common shares issued to her daughter for cash of $1,000. Ms. Bellows then transfers, using ITA 85, non-depreciable capital property with an adjusted cost base of $50,000 and a fair market value of $110,000. The transfer is made at an elected value of $50,000. As consideration for this property, the corporation gives Ms. Bellows a note for $50,000 and preferred stock with a fair market value and a legal stated capital of $15,000. Describe the tax consequences of these transactions for both Ms. Bellows and her daughter.

End of Exercise. Solution available in Study Guide.

Section 85 - Excess Consideration

Introduction

18-134.   In the previous section we considered the tax consequences of the transferor receiving consideration that is less than the fair market value of the property transferred. In situations when parties related to the transferor were also shareholders of the transferee corporation, the difference in value could be viewed as a gift to that related party. We also pointed out that the *Income Tax Act* contained provisions which, in effect, penalized the transferor for his behaviour.

18-135.   In this section we are concerned with the opposite case — situations in which the transferor receives consideration with a value in excess of the fair market value of the property being transferred. Such situations may result in the shareholder being assessed a benefit under ITA 15 (see Paragraph 9-155 for a discussion of these benefits). A further possibility is that there may be an ITA 84(1) deemed dividend (see Paragraph 16-61 for a description of these dividends).

ITA 15(1) Shareholder Benefit

18-136.   The following example will illustrate a situation in which the use of ITA 85(1) results in a taxable benefit to the transferor.

Example   Ms. Sally Swit transfers property with an adjusted cost base of $90,000 and a fair market value of $150,000, to a new CCPC in which she is the sole shareholder. She takes back debt with a fair market value of $120,000 and redeemable preferred shares with a fair market value and legal stated capital of $80,000. She elects to make the transfer at $150,000 (she cannot elect above the ceiling of fair market value) and, as a result, must recognize a capital gain of $60,000 ($150,000 - $90,000).

Analysis   To begin, there would be a PUC reduction on the preferred shares calculated as follows:

Increase In Legal Stated Capital		$80,000
Less Excess, If Any, Of:		
Total Elected Value	($150,000)	
Over The Non-Share Consideration	120,000	(30,000)
ITA 85(2.1) PUC Reduction		**$50,000**

The $200,000 value of the consideration exceeds the $150,000 fair market value of the property transferred by $50,000. This is clearly a benefit to Ms. Swit and would result in an ITA 15(1) taxable benefit calculated as follows:

Fair Market Value Of Consideration ($120,000 + $80,000)		$200,000
Less The Sum Of The:		
Fair Market Value Of Transferred Property	($150,000)	
ITA 84(1) Deemed Dividend	Nil	(150,000)
ITA 15(1) Shareholder Benefit		**$ 50,000**

18-137.   It would appear that Ms. Swit was attempting to provide herself with a benefit that would not be subject to tax. As is indicated in the preceding analysis, she was not successful. The $50,000 ITA 15(1) benefit will be included in her income in full, a result that would be identical to having the CCPC pay her salary of $50,000.

18-138.   In fact, this result is even less desirable in that, while she will be taxed on the full $50,000, there will be no corresponding deduction for the corporation. You should also note that the ITA 15(1) benefit would be added to the original $30,000 ($150,000 - $120,000) adjusted cost base of the preferred shares. This means that if the shares were sold for their fair market value of $80,000, there would be no capital gain [$80,000 - ($30,000 + $50,000) = nil] on the disposition.

ITA 84(1) Deemed Dividend

18-139.   We have examined the situation were the fair value of the total consideration given to the transferor exceeds the value of the property transferred. However, in the example presented in Paragraph 18-136, the value of the shares given to the transferor ($80,000) did not exceed the value of the property transferred ($150,000). As a result, there is no ITA 84(1) deemed dividend as shown in the following calculation:

PUC Of New Preferred Shares ($80,000 - $50,000)	$30,000
Less: Increase In Net Assets ($150,000 - $120,000)	(30,000)
ITA 84(1) Deemed Dividend	Nil

18-140.   There remains the further possibility that the value of the share consideration can exceed the value of the property transferred. In this case, there is likely to be an increase in PUC that exceeds the value of the corresponding increase in net assets. When this happens, the transferor will be assessed an ITA 84(1) deemed dividend.

Exercise Eighteen-8

Subject: Section 85 - Benefit To Transferor

Mr. Larry Custer uses ITA 85 to transfer non-depreciable property to a new CCPC. The adjusted cost base of the property is $123,000 and he elects the fair market value of $217,000 as the transfer price. In consideration for this property, Mr. Custer receives a note for $195,000 and preferred stock with a fair market value and a legal stated capital of $75,000. Any dividends will be non-eligible. What are the tax consequences of this transaction to Mr. Custer?

Exercise Eighteen-9

Subject: Section 85 - Benefit To Transferor

Goodwill with a cost of $42,000 and a fair market value of $86,000 is reflected in a cumulative eligible capital balance of $25,337. Using ITA 85, an individual transfers the goodwill to a new corporation in return for preferred shares with a fair market value and a legal stated capital of $93,000. Indicate the minimum and maximum transfer values that can be elected. Assume he elects the minimum value. Calculate the amount of any taxable capital gain, the amount of any benefit that will have to be included in the transferor's income under ITA 15(1) or ITA 84(1), and the adjusted cost base of the preferred shares issued. Any dividends will be non-eligible.

End of Exercises. Solutions available in Study Guide.

GST And Section 85 Rollovers

18-141.   When property used in a commercial activity is rolled into a corporation under Section 85 of the *Income Tax Act*, the rollover is a taxable transaction for GST purposes. For example, if a sole proprietorship or partnership transfers property when a business is incorporated, the rollover of property will be deemed to be a taxable supply for consideration equal to the fair market value of the property. This amount will then be subject to GST.

18-142.   A joint election may be available to avoid any related GST liability, providing the vendor sells or transfers all, or substantially all (i.e., 90 percent or more) of the assets that can reasonably be regarded as being necessary for the purchaser to carry on the business. A further requirement is that, if the vendor is a GST registrant, the purchaser must also be a GST registrant.

18-143.   If the transfer of property is a taxable supply, GST will be payable on the total fair market value of the share and non-share consideration exchanged for the property, with the elected amount under Section 85 of the *Income Tax Act* being irrelevant. If the transferred property is subsequently used in commercial activities, an input tax credit may be claimed by the transferee for any GST paid on the transfer of the property.

18-144.   The GST implications in this area will be covered at the end of Chapter 19, after we have discussed the sale of an incorporated business.

Dividend Stripping — ITA 84.1

Background

The General Concept

18-145.   The term dividend stripping is applied to two types of situations, depending on when the relevant shares were issued by the corporation. In simple terms, both scenarios involve an individual who is attempting to remove assets from a corporation on a tax free basis.

18-146.   Accomplishing this goal would not be a problem if the individual was willing to give up control by selling his shares to an arm's length party. However, when this is not the case and the individual retains control, the dividend stripping rules will often prevent the tax free removal of assets.

18-147.   One approach to removing assets from a corporation while still retaining control would be to pay dividends. However, dividends will be taxed in the hands of the recipient and, being a rational individual, the owner of the corporation would prefer to receive the assets on a tax free basis.

18-148.   The usual approach to accomplishing the goal of removing funds from a controlled corporation on a tax free basis is to convert what is, in effect, a dividend payment into a capital gain. This is the origin of the term "dividend stripping". ITA 84.1 will generally act to thwart such efforts.

Pre-1972 Shares

18-149.   At an earlier point in time, the most important application of ITA 84.1 was to prevent the conversion of pre-1972 earnings into a pre-1972 capital gain. As we noted in Chapter 10, prior to 1972, capital gains were not subject to tax in Canada. Given this, such a conversion could have resulted in the tax free receipt of a considerable amount of assets. While such situations still arise, they are not of sufficient importance to cover in a general text such as this. As a consequence, the application of ITA 84.1 in this type of situation will not receive further attention.

Qualified Small Business Corporation Shares

18-150.   The most important current application of the dividend stripping rules from ITA 84.1 involves shares of a qualified small business corporation. The capital gains on dispositions of such shares are eligible for the $750,000 lifetime capital gain deduction. This means that, if an individual can convert the retained earnings of such a corporation into a capital gain, a very large amount of income can be received on a tax free basis. In general, ITA 84.1 serves to make such conversions difficult. The text and problems in this section will focus on this application of the dividend stripping rules.

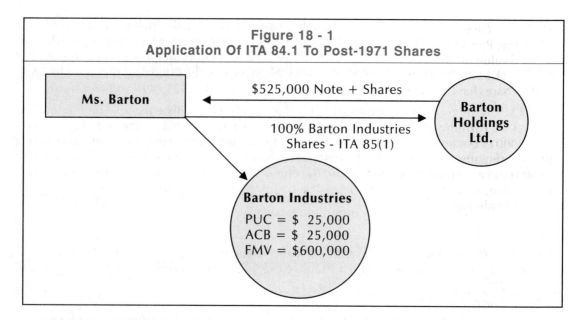

Figure 18 - 1
Application Of ITA 84.1 To Post-1971 Shares

Applicability Of ITA 84.1

18-151.   Without regard to whether pre-1972 or post-1971 shares are involved, ITA 84.1(1) specifies the conditions under which the dividend stripping rules become applicable. These conditions are as follows:

- there is a disposition by a resident Canadian taxpayer (other than a corporation) of shares of a resident Canadian corporation (the subject corporation);

- the taxpayer held the shares as capital property (i.e., were held to produce income, not for resale at a profit);

- the disposition is made to a corporation with which the taxpayer does not deal at arm's length; and

- the subject corporation must be connected with the purchaser corporation after the disposition of shares (i.e., the purchaser corporation must control the subject corporation or own more than 10 percent of the voting shares and 10 percent of the fair market value of all shares).

18-152.   When these conditions are present, the provisions of ITA 84.1 will generally serve to eliminate the individual's ability to achieve their dividend stripping goals.

Dividend Stripping Example - Post-1971 Shares
Basic Example

18-153.   A simple example will serve to illustrate the application of ITA 84.1 to post-1971 shares. As shown in Figure 18-1, Ms. Barton is the only shareholder of Barton Industries (BI), a Canadian controlled private corporation. The Company was established in 1986 with an investment of $25,000 on the part of Ms. Barton. There has been no additional investment in the Company and, as a consequence, this is the adjusted cost base of her shares as well as their PUC. The shares have a fair market value of $600,000 and Ms. Barton has available $500,000 of her lifetime capital gains deduction. BI is a qualified small business corporation and it has no balance in its GRIP account.

18-154.   Ms. Barton could, of course, make use of her lifetime capital gains deduction by selling the BI shares to an arm's length party and realizing a capital gain of $575,000 ($600,000 - $25,000). However, this approach would result in tax payable as the capital gain exceeds the amount of her available lifetime capital gains deduction. In addition, Ms. Barton would lose control of the Company.

18-155.   Given these considerations, she chooses to transfer the BI shares to a new company, Barton Holdings Ltd. (BHL), using the provisions of ITA 85(1). Ms. Barton uses an elected value for the transfer of $525,000, in order to limit her capital gain to $500,000. She takes back $525,000 in new debt of BHL, along with the common shares of the new Company. These shares have a fair market value of $75,000 ($600,000 - $525,000) and an adjusted cost base of nil.

18-156.   Through this procedure, Ms. Barton appears to have realized the required $500,000 of the accrued capital gain on the BI shares and, at the same time, retained control of the Company. However, Ms. Barton is a resident Canadian who has made a disposition of shares held as capital property to a corporation with which she does not deal at arm's length. In addition, BI is connected with BHL subsequent to the transaction. As a consequence, ITA 84.1 is applicable.

ITA 84.1 Procedures

18-157.   The ITA 84.1 procedures begin with a reduction in the PUC of any shares received by Ms. Barton. The required ITA 84.1(1)(a) PUC reduction would be calculated as follows:

Increase In Legal Stated Capital Of BHL Shares		$75,000
Less Excess, If Any, Of:		
PUC Of Barton Industries Shares (Note One)	($ 25,000)	
Over The Non-Share Consideration	525,000	Nil
ITA 84.1(1)(a) PUC Reduction (Note Two)		$75,000

Note One   This amount is technically the greater of the PUC of the subject shares and their adjusted cost base. In this example, the two amounts are equal.

Note Two   In those cases where the boot exceeds the greater of the PUC and the adjusted cost base of the subject corporation shares, the PUC reduction will be 100 percent of the PUC of the new shares.

18-158.   This would leave the PUC of the new shares at nil ($75,000 - $75,000). Given this, the ITA 84.1(1)(b) deemed dividend would be calculated as follows:

Increase In Legal Stated Capital Of BHL Shares		$ 75,000
Non-Share Consideration		525,000
Total		$600,000
Less The Sum Of:		
PUC Of Barton Industries Shares	($25,000)	
PUC Reduction Under ITA 84.1(1)(a)	(75,000)	(100,000)
ITA 84.1(1)(b) Deemed Dividend (Non-Eligible)		$500,000

18-159.   The results from Ms. Barton's disposition of her BI shares would be as follows:

Elected Proceeds Of Disposition	$525,000
ITA 84.1(1)(b) Deemed Dividend (See Note)	(500,000)
ITA 54 Deemed Proceeds Of Disposition	$ 25,000
Adjusted Cost Base (Barton Industries)	(25,000)
Capital Gain	$ Nil

Note The definition of proceeds of disposition in ITA 54 indicates that it does not include any amount that is deemed by ITA 84.1(1) to be a dividend. In the absence of this exclusion, the deemed dividend could be taxed a second time as part of a taxable capital gain.

18-160.   As the preceding example makes clear, the effect of ITA 84.1 in this situation is to convert the $500,000 capital gain on the BI shares into an ITA 84.1 deemed dividend. This means that Ms. Barton will not be able to make use of her lifetime capital gains deduction and that she will be subject to taxation on the deemed dividend. ITA 84.1 has clearly served to make this type of transaction unattractive.

18-161.   As a final point, you should note that Ms. Barton could have achieved her goal of triggering a capital gain for purposes of the lifetime capital gains deduction. Her problem was that she also wanted to remove the gain in the form of non-share consideration. If, as an alternative, she had elected a transfer price of $525,000, but limited the non-share consideration to the $25,000 PUC amount, she would have had her $500,000 capital gain without creating an ITA 84.1 deemed dividend.

Exercise Eighteen-10

Subject: Dividend Strips

Miss Sarah Cole owns 100 percent of the outstanding shares of Cole Inc., a qualified small business corporation. The shares have a PUC and an adjusted cost base of $125,000 and a fair market value of $767,000. The Company has no balance in its GRIP account. In order to make full use of her lifetime capital gains deduction, Miss Cole uses ITA 85(1) to transfer these shares to Sarah's Holdings Ltd., at an elected value of $625,000. As consideration, she receives a note for $450,000 and preferred shares with a fair market value and a legal stated capital of $317,000. Miss Cole owns all of the shares of Sarah's Holdings Ltd. What are the tax consequences of this transaction to Miss Cole?

End of Exercise. Solution available in Study Guide.

Capital Gains Stripping — ITA 55(2)

The Problem

18-162.   A problem similar to that involved in dividend stripping arises when a corporation owns shares in a different corporation. If there is an accrued capital gain on these shares, a disposition of the shares will result in the recognition of that income. Further, corporations are not eligible to use the lifetime capital gains deduction. This means that a disposition of the shares will increase both the Taxable Income and Tax Payable of the corporation.

18-163   While capital gains are subject to corporate income taxes, intercorporate dividends can escape corporate taxes. This means that, if the investor corporation can devise some method of disposing of its investment so that the proceeds of disposition are received in the form of dividends, payment of corporate taxes could be avoided.

18-164.   In the absence of an anti-avoidance provision, this could be accomplished in a variety of ways. If we assume that Investee Company is a wholly owned subsidiary of Investor Company, two ways in which Investor could dispose of Investee are as follows:

- Investee could borrow sufficient funds to pay Investor dividends equal to the accrued capital gain. This could serve to reduce the fair market value of its shares to Investor's adjusted cost base and the disposition could be made with no capital gain being recognized.

- ITA 85(1) could be used to roll the Investee shares into a purchaser corporation in return for redeemable preferred shares. Redemption of the shares would result in an ITA 84(3) deemed dividend as opposed to a capital gain.

18-165.   Such procedures are referred to as capital gains stripping, reflecting the fact that it is an attempt to "strip" out a capital gain in the form of a non-taxable, intercorporate dividend. ITA 55(2) is an anti-avoidance provision designed to prevent such conversions of capital gains to dividends by a corporation disposing of an investment in shares.

Application Of ITA 55(2)

18-166. The provisions of ITA 55(2) are applicable when:

- A corporation has received dividends that are deductible under ITA 112(1) as part of a transaction, or series of transactions, involving a disposition of shares.
- One of the purposes of the dividend was to effect a significant reduction in any capital gain which, in the absence of the dividend, would have been realized on the disposition of shares.
- The disposition was to an arm's length party, or there has been a significant increase in the interest of an arm's length party, in either corporation.

18-167. If these conditions are present, the following rules apply to the dividend:

ITA 55(2)(a) The dividend shall be deemed not to be a dividend received by the corporation.

ITA 55(2)(b) Where a corporation has disposed of the share, the dividend shall be deemed to be proceeds of disposition of the share except to the extent that it is otherwise included in computing such proceeds.

ITA 55(2)(c) Where a corporation has not disposed of the share, the dividend shall be deemed to be a gain of the corporation for the year in which the dividend was received from the disposition of a capital property.

18-168. These rules do not apply if the dividend represents a distribution of what is commonly referred to as "safe income". This "safe income" is income that has accrued after 1971 or, if the acquisition of the shares was after that date, after the date on which the shares were acquired.

Capital Gains Stripping - Example One

18-169. The first example is diagramed in Figure 18-2 (following page). In this example, Lor Inc. owns 100 percent of the shares of Lee Ltd. The shares have a fair market value of $800,000, an adjusted cost base of $200,000, and a potential capital gain of $600,000. Lee Ltd. has safe income of $250,000. An arm's length purchaser is willing to pay $800,000 for these shares. In order to implement this sale, Lor Inc. arranges the following:

- Lee Ltd. borrows $600,000 from a financial institution.
- The borrowed funds are used to pay a $600,000 tax free dividend to Lor Inc. This reduces the fair market value of Lee Ltd. to $200,000.
- Lor Inc. sells the shares to the arm's length purchaser for $200,000 in cash. As this is the adjusted cost base of the shares, there will be no capital gain.
- The arm's length purchaser invests $600,000 in Lee Ltd., with the funds being used to retire the $600,000 loan.

18-170. In the absence of ITA 55(2), Lor Inc. would have managed to dispose of its interest in Lee Ltd. in a series of transactions for $800,000 ($200,000 received directly from the purchaser and $600,000 of tax-free dividends financed indirectly by the purchaser), without the recognition of a capital gain. However, ITA 55(2) will prevent this from happening.

18-171. Under ITA 55(2)(a), the $600,000 dividend will be deemed not to be a dividend. Under ITA 55(2)(b), the dividend will be treated as proceeds of disposition. This results in the following capital gain calculation:

Dividends Received (Tax Free)	$600,000
Dividend Attributable To Safe Income	(250,000)
Deemed Proceeds Of Disposition	$350,000
Actual Proceeds Of Disposition	200,000
Total Proceeds Of Disposition	$550,000
Adjusted Cost Base	(200,000)
Capital Gain	$350,000

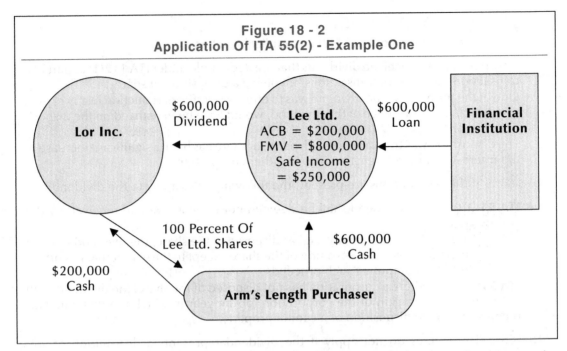

Figure 18 - 2
Application Of ITA 55(2) - Example One

18-172.   As can be seen in the preceding calculation, ITA 55(2) has served to convert the portion of the dividend not paid from safe income into a capital gain, which will be taxed. The $250,000 dividend attributable to safe income will be deducted in calculating Taxable Income resulting in no tax cost.

Capital Gains Stripping - Example Two

18-173.   This example is diagramed in Figure 18-3 and involves the same two Companies that were used in Example One. The only difference is in the approach that they use in attempting to convert the taxable capital gain into a tax free dividend.

18-174.   In this case, ITA 85(1) is used to roll the Lee Ltd. shares into the purchaser corporation at an elected value equal to the $200,000 adjusted cost base of the shares. As consideration for the shares, Lor Inc. takes back $800,000 in redeemable preferred shares. These shares have a PUC and an adjusted cost base of $200,000.

18-175.   As the elected value was equal to the adjusted cost base of the shares, there will be no capital gain on the transaction. Further, in the absence of ITA 55(2), the redemption of the shares would have the following results:

Redemption Proceeds	$800,000
PUC Of Shares	(200,000)
ITA 84(3) Deemed Dividend [Absence Of ITA 55(2)]	$600,000

Redemption Proceeds	$800,000
ITA 84(3) Deemed Dividend	(600,000)
ITA 54 Deemed Proceeds Of Disposition	$200,000
Adjusted Cost Base	(200,000)
Capital Gain [Absence Of ITA 55(2)]	Nil

18-176.   In this example, ITA 55(2)(a) would deem the portion of the dividend that is not from safe income to not be a dividend. This would reduce the ITA 84(3) dividend as follows:

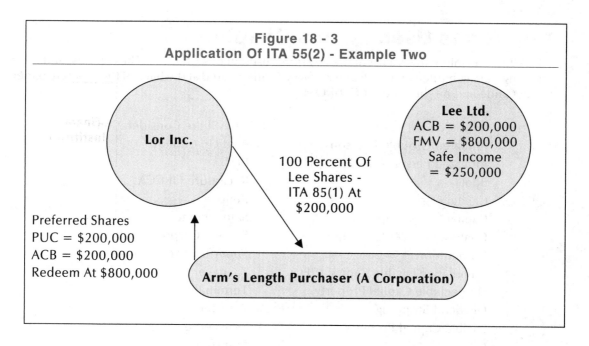

Figure 18 - 3
Application Of ITA 55(2) - Example Two

Lor Inc.

Lee Ltd.
ACB = $200,000
FMV = $800,000
Safe Income
= $250,000

100 Percent Of
Lee Shares -
ITA 85(1) At
$200,000

Preferred Shares
PUC = $200,000
ACB = $200,000
Redeem At $800,000

Arm's Length Purchaser (A Corporation)

ITA 84(3) Deemed Dividend	$600,000
Amount Deemed Not To Be A Dividend	
($600,000 - $250,000)	(350,000)
Remaining ITA 84(3) Deemed Dividend	$250,000

18-177.   Given this reduction in the ITA 84(3) dividend, the capital gain calculation is as follows:

Redemption Proceeds	$800,000
ITA 84(3) Deemed Dividend	(250,000)
ITA 54 Deemed Proceeds Of Disposition	$550,000
Adjusted Cost Base	(200,000)
Capital Gain	$350,000

18-178.   In this example, ITA 55(2) has served to convert the ITA 84(3) dividend that was not paid from safe income into a capital gain which will be taxed.

Exercise Eighteen-11

Subject: Capital Gains Strips

Markem Ltd. owns 100 percent of the outstanding common shares of Larkin Ltd. The shares of Larkin have an adjusted cost base of $75,000 and a fair market value of $840,000. Included in its Retained Earnings balance is $225,000 of income that has been earned since its acquisition by Markem Ltd. Markem Ltd. would like to sell its shares in Larkin Ltd. In order to implement this sale, Markem Ltd. has instructed Larkin Ltd. to borrow $750,000 from its bank, and use all of these funds to pay a dividend on the shares held by Markem Ltd. The shares are then sold to Mr. J. Leaner for $90,000. Mr. Leaner is not related to Markem Ltd. or Larkin Ltd. What are the tax consequences to Markem Ltd. of these transactions?

End of Exercise. Solution available in Study Guide.

Key Terms Used In This Chapter

18-179.   The following is a list of the key terms used in this Chapter. These terms, and their meanings, are compiled in the Glossary Of Key Terms located at the back of the separate paper Study Guide and on the Student CD-ROM.

Adjusted Cost Base	Non-Share Consideration
Affiliated Group Of Persons	Paid Up Capital
Affiliated Person - ITA 251.1(1)	PUC
Boot	Recapture Of CCA
Capital Cost	Rollover
Capital Gains Stripping	Safe Income
Controlled - ITA 251.1(3)	Subject Corporation
Corporation	Superficial Loss - ITA 54
Cumulative Eligible Capital (CEC)	Taxpayer
Depreciable Capital Property	Terminal Loss
Dividend Stripping	Transfer
Eligible Capital Property	Transferee
Gift	Transferor
Individual	Undepreciated Capital Cost (UCC)
Non-Depreciable Capital Property	

References

18-180.   For more detailed study of the material in this Chapter, we would refer you to the following:

ITA 15(1)	Benefits Conferred On A Shareholder
ITA 54	Definitions (Proceeds Of Disposition And Superficial Loss)
ITA 55(2)	Deemed Proceeds Or Capital Gain
ITA 84.1(1)	Non-Arm's Length Sale Of Shares
ITA 85(1)	Transfer Of Property To Corporation By Shareholders
ITA 251.1	Affiliated Persons
IC 76-19R3	Transfer Of Property To A Corporation Under Section 85
IT-188R	Sale of Accounts Receivable
IT-291R3	Transfer Of Property To A Corporation Under Subsection 85(1)
IT-489R	Non-Arm's Length Sale Of Shares To A Corporation

Problems For Self Study

(The solutions for these problems can be found in the separate Study Guide.)

Self Study Problem Eighteen - 1

Ms. Audrey Flack has operated a gift shop for 15 years as a sole proprietorship. After considerable analysis, she has decided that she would experience a number of advantages if she were to incorporate. On December 1, 2007, the assets that she proposes to transfer to the new corporation are as follows:

	Tax Cost	Fair Market Value
Cash	$ 27,000	$ 27,000
Accounts Receivable	51,000	45,000
Inventories	73,000	88,000
Furniture And Fixtures	62,000	45,000
Goodwill	Nil	150,000
Totals	$213,000	$355,000

The UCC of the Furniture And Fixtures is $38,000 at this point in time.

Ms. Flack will receive no consideration other than shares and, as she has no immediate family, she will be the only shareholder in the new company. She has used all of her lifetime capital gains deduction on other dispositions of capital assets.

Required:

A. If no elections are made by Ms. Flack, and the assets are transferred at fair market values on December 31, 2007, calculate the Taxable Income resulting from the transfer that Ms. Flack would have to report.

B. Indicate the elections that could be used by Ms. Flack to reduce the amount of Taxable Income on the transfer of these assets to the new corporation. Calculate the amount of Taxable Income that would result from the transfer being made using these elections.

Self Study Problem Eighteen - 2

For nearly 20 years, Ms. Monica Speaks has operated a very successful manufacturing business. During much of this period you have constantly reminded her that there would be many advantages associated with incorporation, including the availability of the small business deduction. In the past, she has indicated that she has all of the money that she requires and simply cannot be bothered with the complications associated with incorporation. However, in late 2007, you have finally convinced her that incorporation may be the wisest course of action.

She indicates that she is still concerned with respect to taxes that might arise on the transfer of her business assets to a corporation. In response, you have indicated that Section 85 of the *Income Tax Act* provides a method of transfer that will result in little or no taxation at the time of the transfer. As a consequence, she decides to proceed with incorporation, indicating that all of the shares in the new company (Speaks Inc.) will be issued to her.

On October 1, 2007, the transfer date, the business assets of Ms. Speaks have tax values and fair market values as follows:

	Tax Value	Fair Market Value
Cash	$ 36,300	$ 36,300
Accounts Receivable	78,500	78,500
Inventories	261,000	311,000
Land	196,000	282,000
Building (Cost = $155,500)	103,600	253,000
Equipment (Cost = $222,000)	67,000	32,500
Goodwill	Nil	339,000
Total	$742,400	$1,332,300

Ms. Speaks will only use the ITA 85 provisions to transfer a specific asset if there is a tax advantage in doing so.

Required:

A. Indicate which assets should be transferred under the provisions of ITA 85(1).

B. Given that Ms. Speaks wishes to minimize the tax consequences of the incorporation transaction, calculate the minimum transfer price for each asset.

C. Describe the tax consequences for both Ms. Speaks and Speaks Inc. if she transfers the assets at the values calculated in Part B.

Self Study Problem Eighteen - 3

During 2006, Mr. Richard Dix acquired a business location consisting of land with a brick store building located on it. The total price was $1,260,000, with $315,000 of this amount allocated to the land and $945,000 allocated to the building.

After operating the grocery store during 2006 and the first six months of 2007 as a proprietorship, Mr. Dix decides to incorporate. In this process, he uses the provisions of ITA 85 to transfer the land and building to the corporation on a tax free basis. He elects a transfer price of $1,241,100. The details of the transfer are as follows:

	Land	Building
Capital Cost Or UCC	$315,000	$ 926,100
Appraised Value	787,500	1,102,500
Elected Amount	315,000	926,100
Consideration:		
Debt*	315,000	926,100
Shares	472,500	176,400

*The debt related to the Land and Building includes the corporation's assumption of an existing mortgage of $519,750. This means that the total new debt issued by the corporation is as follows:

Debt On Land	$ 315,000
Debt On Building	926,100
Total Debt	$1,241,100
Mortgage Assumed	(519,750)
Net Debt Issued	$ 721,350

On December 1, 2007, the corporation pays off the $721,350 of new debt issued at its face value. On December 28, 2007, Mr. Dix sells his shares in the corporation for $894,000.

The corporation is a qualified small business corporation. Mr. Dix has never utilized his life-time capital gains deduction and he has no Cumulative Net Investment Loss.

Required:

A. Describe the tax consequences of the transfer and compute the adjusted cost base of the consideration received by Mr. Dix.

B. Describe the tax consequences of the debt being paid off and the share sale for Mr. Dix.

Self Study Problem Eighteen - 4

Mr. Lardner is the owner of an unincorporated business that is involved in the distribution of various types of paper products. It is his wish that all of the assets of this business be trans-ferred to a new corporation, Lardner Distribution Ltd. Mr. Lardner will be the only shareholder of this new corporation.

The assets of the business have "tax values" (adjusted cost base or UCC, as appropriate) that total $492,000. The liabilities of the business total $122,000. The total fair market value of all of the assets of the business is $746,000. Except in the case of accounts receivable, the fair market values of the individual assets exceed their respective tax values. The accounts receiv-able have a carrying value of $25,000 and a fair market value of $20,000. A joint election will be made under ITA 22 to transfer them to the corporation and, as a consequence, they will be excluded from the ITA 85 election.

The assets other than the accounts receivable will be transferred under the provisions of Section 85 using a total elected value of $467,000 ($492,000 - $25,000). The new corpora-tion will assume the $122,000 of liabilities owed by the unincorporated business. As consideration for the net assets of the business, Mr. Lardner will receive from the corporation $128,000 in new debt securities, preferred shares with a fair market value of $150,000, and common shares with a fair market value of $326,000. The total value of the consideration, including both the old and the new debt, is equal to the $726,000 fair market value of the assets transferred under ITA 85 ($746,000 - $20,000).

Immediately after the transfer of the assets to Lardner Distribution Ltd., the Company redeems both the preferred shares and the common shares at their respective fair market values. The Company borrows the funds required to make the redemption. Lardner Distribu-tion Ltd. does not have a balance in its GRIP account in any of the years under consideration.

Required:

A. Determine the adjusted cost base for both the preferred and common stock issued to Mr. Lardner.

B. Determine the Paid Up Capital for both the preferred and common stock issued to Mr. Lardner.

C. Indicate the tax consequences to Mr. Lardner that would result from the corporation redeeming the preferred and common shares.

Self Study Problem Eighteen - 5

Miss Doreen Brock owns an unincorporated business that operates out of leased premises. Her accounting records are based on the same information that has been used for tax purposes. On December 31, 2007, the business has the following assets and liabilities:

	Tax Value	Fair Market Value
Accounts Receivable	$ 88,000	$ 85,000
Inventory	174,000	208,000
Equipment (Cost = $420,000)	234,000	317,000
Goodwill	Nil	350,000
Total Assets	$496,000	$960,000
Liabilities	(95,000)	(95,000)
Net Assets	$401,000	$865,000

All of the assets of the unincorporated business will be transferred to the new corporation. The Accounts Receivable will be transferred in return for cash of $85,000. These will be transferred using ITA 22, rather than the provisions of ITA 85(1).

The remaining assets will be transferred under the provisions of ITA 85(1). The total consideration received by Ms. Brock will be $875,000 ($960,000 - $85,000), the fair market value of the assets other than Accounts Receivable. The consideration is made up of new debt of $75,000, assumption of the old debt of $95,000, preferred stock with a fair market value of $225,000, and common stock with a fair market value of $480,000. The new corporation does not have a balance in its GRIP account in any of the years under consideration.

Miss Brock wishes to incorporate her business in a manner that minimizes or eliminates any tax effects resulting from the transaction. She has totally utilized her lifetime capital gains deduction.

Required:

A. Do you agree with the decision to transfer the accounts receivable using ITA 22? Explain your conclusion.

B. Given that Miss Brock wishes to minimize or eliminate current taxes, indicate the values that should be elected for each of the assets to be transferred.

C. Determine the adjusted cost base of the debt, preferred shares, and common shares that would be received by Miss Brock on the rollover.

D. Determine the Paid Up Capital of the common stock and preferred stock that were issued by the new corporation to Miss Brock.

E. Determine the tax consequences to Miss Brock if the preferred and common shares that she received in the rollover were immediately redeemed by the new corporation at fair market values.

Self Study Problem Eighteen - 6

Mr. Martin Fleck is the sole owner of an unincorporated retail business. Because he has not been asked to present audited financial statements to any of his creditors, his accounting records are based on the same information as his tax records. The December 31, 2007 Balance Sheet of the business, including additional information on current fair market values, is as follows:

	Tax Values	Fair Market Values
Cash	$ 20,000	$ 20,000
Accounts Receivable	42,000	38,500
Equipment (Cost = $120,000)	62,000	66,000
Land	106,000	185,000
Building (Cost = $246,000)	178,000	323,000
Goodwill	Nil	95,000
Total Assets	$408,000	$727,500
Liabilities	$123,000	$123,000
Owners' Equity	285,000	604,500
Total Equities	$408,000	$727,500

Mr. Fleck has established a new corporation, Fleck Ltd. Unless there is some tax reason not to do so, he would like to transfer all of the assets of the unincorporated business to the new corporation. He is aware that by using the provisions of ITA 85(1) he could avoid any additional taxes at the time of transfer. However, he has a net capital loss carry forward of $20,000 [(1/2)($40,000)]. As he has no other assets with accrued capital gains, he would like to elect under ITA 85(1) in a manner that will create a $20,000 taxable capital gain. He would like to avoid having any other tax consequences resulting from the transfer.

The corporation will assume all of the liabilities of the unincorporated business. In addition, it will issue new debt to Mr. Fleck in the amount of $77,000 and new common shares with a fair market value equal to the difference between the fair market value of the assets transferred and the fair market value of the non-share consideration received by Mr. Fleck. Fleck Ltd. does not have a balance in its GRIP account in any of the years under consideration.

Required:

A. Indicate which assets should be transferred to Fleck Ltd. under the provisions of ITA 85(1). In addition, indicate the values that should be elected for each asset, taking into consideration Mr. Fleck's desire to record a taxable capital gain of $20,000. Explain your conclusions.

B. Determine the fair market value of the common shares issued to Mr. Fleck, as well as their adjusted cost base and their Paid Up Capital.

C. Determine the tax consequences to Mr. Fleck if one-half of the common shares that he received on the rollover were immediately redeemed for their fair market value.

Self Study Problem Eighteen - 7

Ms. Doreen Chisholm owns 75 percent of the outstanding shares of Dor Manufacturing Ltd. (DML). The remaining 25 percent of this Canadian controlled private corporation are held by her daughter, Elaine Lee.

When the Company was founded ten years ago, all of the shares were issued to Ms. Chisholm in return for $100,000 in cash. This $100,000 amount is the Paid Up Capital of the DML shares, as well as Ms. Chisholm's adjusted cost base.

In 2002, Ms. Chisholm sold 25 percent of the DML shares to her daughter for cash of $25,000, the fair market value of the shares at that time. There have been no other transactions in the shares since DML was founded. Her daughter continues to hold the remaining 25 percent of the DML shares.

On December 31, 2007, the fair market value of Ms. Chisholm's holding of DML shares is $900,000. At her direction, Ms. Chisholm's lawyer establishes a new company, Dorlaine Inc. Using the provisions of ITA 85(1), Ms. Chisholm's DML shares are transferred to this new Company at an elected value of $575,000. In return for the DML shares, Ms. Chisholm receives debt securities of the new Company with a fair market value of $500,000, along with newly issued Dorlaine Inc. common shares with a fair market value of $400,000.

Ms. Chisholm transfers a substantial portfolio of investments she is holding personally into Dorlaine Inc. in return for debt securities equal to the investments' fair market values.

Ms. Chisholm has made no use of her lifetime capital gains deduction. Neither of the Companies have a balance in their GRIP account in any of the years under consideration.

Required

A. What are the tax consequences to Ms. Chisholm of transferring the DML shares to Dorlaine Inc.?

B. Ms. Chisholm dies on January 1, 2008. The terms of her will leave all of the Dorlaine Inc. shares to her daughter. What are the tax consequences arising as a result of Ms. Chisholm's death?

Your answer to both Part A and Part B should be expressed in terms of the type (e.g., dividends, taxable capital gains, or allowable capital losses) and amount of Net Income For Tax Purposes resulting from the transaction or event.

Assignment Problems

(The solutions for these problems are only available in
the solutions manual that has been provided to your instructor.)

Assignment Problem Eighteen - 1

Several years ago, Ms. Fox acquired a small apartment building for total consideration of $950,000. This total was allocated on the basis of $225,000 for the land and $725,000 for the building.

At present, the property has a fair market value of $1,200,000, with $300,000 of this total attributable to the land. Ms. Fox would like to transfer the property to a corporation using a Section 85 rollover. At the beginning of the current year, the building had a UCC of $582,000. The value elected for the transfer is $807,000 ($225,000 + $582,000). The consideration given to Ms. Fox for the property is 12,000 common shares.

Shortly after the Section 85 rollover is completed, Ms. Fox sells all of the common shares she received as a result of the transfer to Mr. Hound, an arm's length party, for proceeds of $1,200,000.

Required:

A. Describe the tax consequences for Ms. Fox of using Section 85 and selling the common shares.

B. How do these results compare with the tax consequences of simply selling the building directly to Mr. Hound for $1,200,000?

Assignment Problem Eighteen - 2

The following four **independent** Cases involve transfers of assets under ITA 85. For each of the four Cases indicate:

A. the minimum and maximum transfer prices that could be elected under the provisions of ITA 85;

B. the minimum amount to be included in the income of the transferor, assuming ITA 85 is used advantageously;

C. the adjusted cost base of the preferred and common stock consideration, assuming ITA 85 is used advantageously; and

D. any benefits that will have to be included in the income of the shareholder as a shareholder appropriation [ITA 15(1)] or a deemed dividend [ITA 84(1)], assuming ITA 85 is used advantageously.

Case One   Inventories with a fair market value of $15,000 and a cost of $10,000 are transferred in exchange for $12,000 in non-share consideration and $3,000 in preferred stock (fair market value and legal stated capital).

Case Two   Land with a cost of $120,000 and a fair market value of $150,000, is transferred in exchange for non-share consideration of $120,000, and preferred stock of $30,000 (fair market value and legal stated capital).

Case Three   Equipment with a cost of $50,000, a fair market value of $35,000, and a UCC of $20,000, is transferred in exchange for non-share consideration of $25,000, preferred stock of $5,000 (fair market value and legal stated capital) and common stock of $5,000 (fair market value and legal stated capital).

Case Four   Goodwill with a cost of $20,000, a fair market value of $40,000, and a Cumulative Eligible Capital account balance of $10,950, is transferred in exchange for preferred stock of $44,000 (fair market value and legal stated capital).

Assignment Problem Eighteen - 3

Miss Suzanne Blake intends to transfer a parcel of land to a new corporation using the provisions of Section 85. The land has an adjusted cost base of $400,000 and a fair market value of $800,000. Miss Blake will transfer the land at an elected value of $400,000.

Miss Blake is considering the following alternative consideration packages:

	Alternative		
	One	Two	Three
Debt Of The New Corporation	$300,000	$200,000	$320,000
Preferred Shares	50,000	600,000	Nil
Common Shares	450,000	Nil	480,000
Total	$800,000	$800,000	$800,000

All of the amounts in the preceding table are fair market values.

Required:

A. For each of the three alternatives, determine the adjusted cost base of the individual items of consideration received by Miss Blake.

B. For each of the three alternatives, determine the legal stated capital and the Paid Up Capital for the preferred and/or common shares issued.

Assignment Problem Eighteen - 4

During December, 2007, Mr. Norris Notion transferred a depreciable capital property to a new corporation. The property is the only asset in its CCA class, and Mr. Notion will own all of the shares of the new corporation. The CCA class had a UCC of $52,000. The property had an original cost of $58,000 and a fair market value of $92,000. As Mr. Notion had a capital loss of $20,000 during 2007, he elected to transfer the property, under the provisions of ITA 85(1), at a value of $78,000. As consideration for the property, Mr. Notion takes back a note for $68,000, preferred shares with a fair market value of $20,000, and common shares with a fair market value of $4,000.

Required: Describe the income tax implications resulting from this transaction. Your answer should include both current tax implications, and the determination of values that will have future tax implications.

Assignment Problem Eighteen - 5

Several years ago, Ms. Katrina Bond acquired a business location that included land and a building for a total of $950,000. At the time, it was estimated that the value of the land was $220,000 and the value of the building was $730,000.

Ms. Bond operated the business for several years as a sole proprietorship and, during this period, she took CCA on the building. As there were years in which she experienced losses, she did not always take the maximum amount of CCA.

Ms. Bond has finally agreed to take your advice and incorporate the business. She will use ITA 85(1) to transfer the land and building to the new corporation. At the time of the transfer, the building had a UCC of $625,000. Other relevant values were as follows:

Asset	Tax Cost	Appraised Value	Elected Amount
Land	$220,000	$ 510,000	$220,000
Building	625,000	980,000	730,000
Total	$845,000	$1,490,000	$950,000

There is a $400,000 mortgage on the land and building that will be assumed by the new corporation. In addition, the new corporation will issue $500,000 in new debt to Ms. Bond. The remaining consideration will be in the form of common shares with a fair market value of $590,000. The new corporation does not have a balance in its GRIP account in any of the years under consideration.

Required:

A. What are the tax consequences of making this transfer at the elected value of $950,000? Your answer should include amounts to be included in Ms. Bond's income as a result of the transfer, as well as the corporation's tax values for the assets.

B. Compute the adjusted cost base of each component of the consideration that Ms. Bond has received from the corporation.

C. Compute the PUC of the corporation's newly issued common shares.

D. What amounts would be included in Ms. Bond's Net Income For Tax Purposes if, at a later point in time, she sells her common shares for $650,000?

E. What amounts would be included in Ms. Bond's Net Income For Tax Purposes if, at a later point in time, the corporation redeems her common shares for $650,000?

Assignment Problem Eighteen - 6

Mike Danforth has, for a number of years, operated a successful proprietorship involved in retail sales of home improvement products. Mr. Danforth has decided to incorporate his business operations under the name of Danforth Inc. For tax purposes, this decision will be implemented using ITA 85(1).

At the end of 2007, the tax values (adjusted cost base or UCC) and fair market values of the assets and liabilities on his Balance Sheet are as follows:

	Tax Value	Fair Market Value
Cash	$ 2,500	$ 2,500
Temporary Investments	27,500	37,500
Accounts Receivable	13,750	12,500
Inventories	17,500	17,500
Prepayments	7,500	7,500
Land	105,000	77,500
Buildings (Cost = $113,000)	70,000	125,000
Equipment (Cost = $48,000)	20,000	7,500
Goodwill	Nil	117,500
Total Assets	$263,750	$405,000
Liabilities	(20,000)	(20,000)
Net Assets (Owner's Equity)	$243,750	$385,000

Other Information:

1. The Temporary Investments contain securities that have been purchased in order to absorb a seasonal excess of cash.

2. With respect to the Accounts Receivable, the $1,250 difference between their tax value and their fair market value reflects Mr. Danforth's estimate of potential bad debts.

3. The new corporation will assume the outstanding liabilities of the proprietorship.

4. In implementing this rollover, Mr. Danforth will be issued new debt. Additional consideration, in excess of the maximum amount of non-share consideration that can be taken without incurring a tax liability, will be taken in the form of common shares.

5. Mr. Danforth will only use the ITA 85 provisions to transfer a specific asset if there is a tax advantage in doing so.

6. In 2008, Mr. Danforth sells the shares that he received in this rollover for $208,000. Danforth Inc. is a qualified small business corporation. Mr. Danforth has never utilized his lifetime capital gains deduction and he has no Cumulative Net Investment Loss.

Required:

A. Advise Mr. Danforth with respect to which assets should be transferred under the provisions of ITA 85(1), and the values that should be elected in order to minimize his current Tax Payable. Indicate the appropriate alternative treatment for any assets that you do not recommend transferring with the use of ITA 85(1).

B. Indicate the maximum amount of non-share consideration that Mr. Danforth can receive without being subject to additional taxation.

C. Calculate Mr. Danforth's taxable capital gain on the sale of the shares and indicate the effect of the 2008 sale of shares on his Taxable Income.

Assignment Problem Eighteen - 7

For the last six years, Ms. Sarah Delmor has operated Delmor Industries as a sole proprietorship. The business has been very successful and, as a consequence, has experienced rapid growth. Given this situation, Ms. Delmor has concluded that in order to enhance her ability to raise additional capital, the assets and liabilities of Delmor Industries should be transferred to a new corporation, Delmor Inc.

On July 1, 2007, the tax values (adjusted cost base or UCC) and fair market values of the assets and liabilities of Delmor Industries are as follows:

	Tax Value	Fair Market Value
Accounts Receivable	$ 120,000	$ 112,000
Temporary Investments	42,000	37,000
Inventories	220,000	231,000
Depreciable Assets - CCA Class 8 (Note One)	53,000	61,500
Machinery (Note Two)	197,000	273,000
Land	150,000	311,000
Building (Note Three)	416,000	523,500
Total Assets	$1,198,000	$1,549,000
Liabilities	(72,000)	(72,000)
Net Assets (Owner's Equity)	$1,126,000	$1,477,000

Note One   There are two assets in Class 8. Asset A has a cost of $27,000 and a fair market value of $32,500. Asset B has a cost of $33,000 and a fair market value of $29,000.

Note Two   The cost of the Machinery was $212,500.

Note Three   The cost of the Building was $472,000.

The transfer of the Delmor Industries assets to Delmor Inc. will take place on July 1, 2007, and an election will be made under ITA 85. Delmor Inc. will assume the liabilities of Delmor Industries and, in addition, will issue $800,000 in new debt to Ms. Delmor. With respect to share consideration, the new Company will issue preferred stock with a fair market value of $200,000 and common stock with a fair market value of $477,000.

Any shares issued by Delmor Inc. as part of this rollover will be issued to Ms. Delmor. Delmor Inc. does not have a balance in its GRIP account in any of the years under consideration.

Required:

A. Determine whether the Accounts Receivable and Temporary Investments should be transferred under the provisions of ITA 85. Explain your conclusion and, if you recommend that ITA 85 should not be used, indicate the appropriate alternative treatment.

B. Without regard to your conclusions in Part A, assume that all of the assets are transferred to the new corporation under the provisions of ITA 85. Indicate the minimum values that can be elected for each of the assets. Include a detailed explanation of how the election would apply to Asset A and Asset B in Class 8.

C. Assume the transfer of the assets of Delmor Industries to Delmor Inc. is going to be made using the provisions of ITA 85. Ms. Delmor will elect the values that you have determined in Part B, and transfer all of the assets of Delmor Industries (whether or not appropriate) under this rollover provision. Determine the adjusted cost base of the non-share consideration, preferred stock and common stock received by Ms. Delmor. In addition, determine the Paid Up Capital amounts for the preferred stock and the common stock.

D. Indicate the tax consequences to Ms. Delmor if the preferred stock and common stock that she received in the rollover were immediately redeemed by the new corporation at fair market values.

Assignment Problem Eighteen - 8

Norton Ltd. is a Canadian controlled private corporation, established six years ago, with an initial investment by Ms. Nora Chadwick of $225,000. In return for her investment, Ms. Chadwick received 22,500 common shares with a paid up capital of $225,000. The corporation has a December 31 year end.

The Company has been very successful and, as a consequence, it is estimated that the current fair market value of the common shares is $2,465,000. Ms. Chadwick has a serious heart condition that has significantly reduced her life expectancy. As a consequence, she would like to transfer any future increase in value of the Norton Ltd. shares to her companion of the last 25 years, Mr. Bobby Borque. Mr. Borque cohabits with Ms. Chadwick in a conjugal relationship.

In order to accomplish this goal, she intends to have Bobby establish a new Company, Borque Inc. All 100 of the common shares of Borque Inc. will be issued to Bobby, in return for a cash investment of $1,000.

Once the new company is established, Ms. Chadwick will transfer all of her common shares in Norton Ltd. to Borque Inc. She will make the transfer under the provisions of ITA 85(1), electing a value of $725,000. It is her intention to take back consideration consisting of a $725,000 interest bearing note (fair market value = $725,000) along with retractable preferred shares with a fair market value and a Paid Up Capital of $1,740,000.

Neither of the Companies have a balance in their GRIP account in any of the years under consideration.

Norton Ltd. is a qualified small business corporation and Ms. Chadwick has made no use of her lifetime capital gains deduction. She believes that this rollover transaction has been structured in a manner that will allow her to utilize $500,000 of this deduction.

Required:

A. Explain the tax consequences of the proposed ITA 85(1) transfer of the Norton Ltd. shares to Borque Inc.

B. Describe how you would change the transaction to improve Ms. Chadwick's tax position, and determine the tax implications that would result from this new approach.

C. As an alternative approach to using her lifetime capital gains deduction, Ms. Chadwick proposes selling 5,022 shares of Norton Ltd. to Borque Inc. for cash. The shares would be sold for their current fair market value. Explain the tax consequences of this proposed transaction.

Show all calculations to support your answers.

Assignment Problem Eighteen - 9

Gaynor Ltd., a Canadian controlled private company has owned 100 percent of the outstanding shares of Northcote Inc. for five years. The Northcote shares have a PUC and an adjusted cost base of $250,000 and a fair market value of $1,300,000. Northcote Inc. has safe income of $450,000 and has a nil balance in its Refundable Dividend Tax On Hand account. Neither Gaynor Ltd. nor Northcote Inc. has a GRIP balance.

Required: Indicate the amount, and type, of income that would accrue to Gaynor Ltd. in both of the following **independent** situations:

A. Northcote Inc. obtains a bank loan in the amount of $1,050,000 and uses all of the acquired funds to pay a dividend to Gaynor Ltd. Subsequent to the receipt of this dividend, Gaynor Ltd. sells the Northcote shares to Mr. Jones, an arm's length party, for $250,000.

B. Using ITA 85, Gaynor transfers the Northcote shares to Jones Ltd., an unrelated corporation. The elected value is $250,000. In return for the Northcote shares, Gaynor receives Jones Ltd. preferred stock with a PUC of $250,000 and a redemption value of $1,300,000. Immediately after the transfer, Jones Ltd. redeems the preferred stock for $1,300,000.

CHAPTER 19

Other Rollovers, Business Valuation, Sale Of An Incorporated Business And Tax Shelters

Introduction

19-1.   The preceding Chapter gave detailed consideration to the Section 85 rollover provisions, which provide for a tax deferred transfer of property to a corporation. In addition, Chapter 12 dealt with rollovers involving transfers to a spouse and transfers of farm property to children. There are a number of other rollover provisions in the *Act* that will be discussed in this Chapter.

19-2.   These additional rollover provisions cover share for share exchanges among corporations, share exchanges in the process of the reorganization of a corporation, amalgamations of existing corporations, the winding-up of a 90 percent or more owned subsidiary, and conversions of debt to shares. The winding-up of a Canadian corporation that is not a 90 percent owned subsidiary is also covered. This latter transaction does not involve a rollover, but is dealt with in the same Section of the *Income Tax Act* as the winding-up of a 90 percent or more owned subsidiary.

19-3.   In the process of arranging a rollover, a valuation of business assets is often required. As a result, we will briefly cover alternative methods of valuation in this Chapter. Valuations are also integral to decisions involving a sale of a business. Issues associated with selling the assets and shares of a business are addressed, along with the substantially different income tax consequences of each. Finally, the concept of tax shelters is introduced, followed by a summary of methods to evaluate such investments.

Share For Share Exchanges

19-4.   ITA 85.1 provides for a rollover in which a shareholder exchanges his shares for shares of an acquiring corporation. When there are many diverse shareholders, a share for share exchange is easier to accomplish than a Section 85 rollover, because there is no need for each shareholder to file an election. Further, the provisions of ITA 85.1 apply automatically, unless the vendor includes any gain or loss on the transaction in his income tax return. Given these features, an ITA 85.1 exchange is an important arrangement in business combination transactions.

19-5.   A brief example will serve to illustrate the basic provisions of ITA 85.1:

Example   Ms. Cowper is the sole shareholder of Cowper Inc., owning a total of 1,000 shares with a Paid Up Capital (PUC) and an adjusted cost base of $10,000. Mega Holdings Ltd. acquires these shares in return for 5,000 of its common shares. The Mega Holdings shares are currently trading at $25 per share, resulting in a total value for the 5,000 shares of $125,000.

19-6.   In the absence of the share for share exchange provisions in ITA 85.1, Ms. Cowper would have a capital gain of $115,000 ($125,000 - $10,000). However, under the rollover provisions of ITA 85.1, Ms. Cowper is deemed to have disposed of her shares for an amount equal to their adjusted cost base and to have acquired the shares in Mega Holdings for the same amount. Also, the PUC of the Mega shares is limited to $10,000, which is the PUC of the Cowper shares.

19-7.   There are a number of restrictions on this rollover, as follows:

- Ms. Cowper must hold the shares of Cowper Inc. as capital property. That is, they must be held to earn investment income or capital appreciation, and cannot be held as a temporary investment or as inventory.
- Mega Holdings Ltd. must be a Canadian corporation.
- Ms. Cowper must deal at arm's length with Mega Holdings Ltd.
- Ms. Cowper, or persons with whom she does not deal at arm's length, cannot control Mega Holdings Ltd. (the purchasing corporation) immediately after the exchange. Likewise, they cannot own shares having a fair market value in excess of 50 percent of the total fair market value of the corporation's outstanding shares.
- Mega Holdings Ltd. must issue its own shares in the exchange, and it can issue only one class of shares to Ms. Cowper.
- No election can be made under ITA 85(1) or (2) with respect to the exchanged shares.

19-8.   The adjusted cost base of the Cowper shares to Mega Holdings Ltd. will be the lesser of their fair market value and PUC. In this case, PUC is the lower figure, establishing the adjusted cost base of the Cowper shares at $10,000.

19-9.   In most circumstances, the PUC of the shares will equal the legal stated capital of the shares. In general, legal stated capital is the amount paid for the shares. In contrast, paid up capital (PUC) is an income tax term, and while the calculation starts with the legal stated capital amount, certain adjustments may be required in rollover situations.

19-10.   ITA 85.1(2.1) applies to limit the addition to the PUC of the purchaser corporation (Mega Holdings Ltd.) to the amount of the PUC of the shares acquired (Cowper Inc. shares). In this example, it is likely that the legal stated capital of the Mega Holdings Ltd. shares issued would be their fair market value of $125,000, well in excess of the PUC of the Cowper Inc. shares. If this is the case, there would be a PUC reduction (or grind) mechanism applied to limit the PUC to $10,000.

Exercise Nineteen-1

Subject: Share For Share Exchange

Ms. Aly Alee is the sole shareholder of Aayee Ltd., a Canadian controlled private corporation. The corporation was established several years ago by Ms. Alee with an investment of $450,000. It has identifiable net assets with a fair market value of $2,200,000. The shares of her company are acquired by a large publicly traded company, Global Outreach Inc., through the issuance of 50,000 new shares. At the time of this business combination, the Global Outreach Inc. shares are trading at $49 per share. Ms. Alee has fully utilized her lifetime capital gains deduction in the past. Indicate the tax consequences of this transaction to both Ms. Alee and Global Outreach Inc.

End of Exercise. Solution available in Study Guide.

Exchange Of Shares In A Reorganization

Application Of Section 86

Basic Procedure

19-11.   Under Section 86, a reorganization involves an exchange of shares within a single corporation. The Section applies to situations where a shareholder of a corporation exchanges shares held in at least one class of existing shares, for authorized shares in the same company, or for authorized shares in the same company combined with non-share consideration. In effect, there is a redemption of the taxpayer's current shareholding, combined with an acquisition of a new shareholding. Section 86 allows this transaction to take place without tax consequences to the taxpayer whose shares are being redeemed.

Use In Estate Freeze

19-12.   One of the most common applications of ITA 86 is in an estate freeze, where an owner of a business wishes to pass on the future growth of the business to other family members, or to arrange an orderly succession to another individual or group.

Example   A father holds all of the outstanding common shares of a corporation. These shares have a fair market value in excess of their adjusted cost base and, as a consequence, their sale or redemption would normally result in a capital gain. Further, if the father continues to hold the shares, future growth in the corporation will accrue to him.

Analysis   To avoid this situation, the father will exchange the common, or growth, shares of the corporation for newly issued preferred shares of the corporation. The preferred shares will have a fixed redemption value equal to the fair market value of the common shares and the fact that their value is fixed will serve to freeze the value of the father's interest in the corporation.

19-13.   Common shares will then be issued to a spouse, a child, or some other related person. As the preferred shares held by the father reflect the full fair market value of the company, the new common shares can be issued to the related person at a fairly nominal value. However, any future growth in the value of the company will accrue to these common shares. Section 86 provides for the father's exchange of shares to take place on a rollover or tax free basis (see Chapter 21 for a more detailed discussion of estate freezes).

Conditions For The Reorganization

General Conditions

19-14.   For the provisions of Section 86 to apply, several conditions must be met.

Shares Must Be Capital Property   First, the original owner's shares must be capital property to the owner. They cannot be part of an inventory of securities that is being held for trading purposes.

All Shares Of The Class Held By Transferor   A second condition is that the transaction must result in an exchange of all of the outstanding shares of a particular class that are owned by the transferor. For example, all Class A common shares that are owned by the transferor must be exchanged for some other type of share. Note that there is no requirement that Class A common shares that are held by other shareholders be exchanged as part of the transaction. Further, it is not necessary that other classes of shares owned by the transferor be exchanged for new shares.

Reorganization Of Capital   A third condition is that the share exchange must be integral to a reorganization of the capital of the corporation. This will often require that the articles of incorporation be amended to authorize any new class of shares.

Transferor Must Receive Shares   A final condition is that the transferor must receive shares of the capital stock of the corporation. While this does not preclude the transferor from receiving non-share consideration, such non-share consideration should not exceed the adjusted cost base or the PUC of the shares transferred. If it does, the excess will have to be taken into income, either as a taxable capital gain, a deemed dividend, or some combination of the two income inclusions.

Establishing Market Value For Preferred Shares

19-15.   In the more common applications of Section 86, the new shares received by the transferor will usually be preferred shares. These shares must be designed in such a fashion as to clearly establish their fair market value. If this is not the case, a subsequent dispute with the CRA could result in some of the benefits of using Section 86 being lost. Adding the following characteristics to the preferred shares will serve to establish a defensible fair market value:

- The preferred shares must be redeemable at the option of the shareholder. The CRA rigorously enforces this requirement to protect the fair market value of the preferred shares.

- The preferred shares should be entitled to a dividend at a reasonable rate. Without a reasonable dividend entitlement to the original shareholder, the incoming shareholders could benefit by receiving a disproportionate share of the corporation's future profits. However, there is no requirement for the entitlement to be cumulative.

- The corporation must guarantee that dividends will not be paid on any other class of shares, if the payment would result in the corporation having insufficient net assets to redeem the preferred shares at their specified redemption price.

- The preferred shares must become cumulative if the fair market value of the net assets of the corporation falls below the redemption value of the preferred shares, or if the corporation is unable to redeem the shares on a call for redemption.

- The preferred shares may or may not have normal voting rights. However, they should carry votes on any matter regarding the rights attached to the preferred shares.

- The preferred shares should have preference on liquidation of the corporation. While the very nature of preferred shares tends to guarantee preference, the CRA requires additional assurance that the normal provisions for such shares will not be avoided.

Procedures

General Rules

19-16.   As noted previously, an ITA 86 reorganization involves a redemption of a given shareholder's holding of a particular class of shares (old shares, hereafter). In return, the shareholder receives shares of a different class (new shares, hereafter) and, in some reorganizations, non-share consideration. ITA 86(1) specifies a number of rules that apply in such a reorganization of capital. These are as follows:

Non-Share Consideration   ITA 86(1)(a) indicates that the cost to the shareholder of this consideration is deemed to be its fair market value.

Cost Of New Shares   ITA 86(1)(b) indicates that the cost of the new shares to the shareholder is equal to the cost of the old shares, less the cost of any non-share consideration received.

Proceeds Of Redemption For Old Shares   Because there is a redemption of shares, there is the possibility of an ITA 84(3) deemed dividend. ITA 84(3)(a) defines such dividends as the excess of the "amount paid" over the PUC of the shares being redeemed. This amount clearly includes any non-share consideration and, when shares are included in the redemption payment, ITA 84(5)(d) indicates that their value is based on any increase in PUC resulting from the issuance of these shares. Putting this together leads to the conclusion that the total proceeds for the redemption will be equal to the non-share consideration plus the PUC of any new shares issued. Note that, in the usual ITA 86 scenario, the PUC of the new shares will often be reduced by a PUC reduction under ITA 86(2.1)(a). (See Paragraph 19-17.)

Proceeds Of Disposition For Old Shares   As the redemption of the old shares is a type of disposition, there is also the possibility of a capital gain or loss. For the purposes of determining the capital gain or loss on this disposition, ITA 86(1)(c) defines the proceeds of disposition for the old shares as being equal to the cost of the new shares (the cost of the old shares, less non-share consideration), plus any non-share consideration received by the taxpayer.

In our general discussion of ITA 84(3) redemptions in Chapter 16, we discuss the possibility that the combination of redemption procedures and disposition proce- dures could result in the double counting of all or part of any gain on the transaction. As we noted there, this possibility is eliminated by the fact that the ITA 54 definition of proceeds of disposition excludes ITA 84(3) dividends.

PUC Reduction

19-17.   As noted in the preceding rules, a PUC reduction may be required on the new shares. This is specified in ITA 86(2.1)(a). This reduction is calculated as follows:

Increase In Legal Stated Capital Of New Shares		$xx,xxx
Less The Excess, If Any, Of:		
PUC Of Old Shares	($x,xxx)	
Over The Non-Share Consideration	x,xxx	(x,xxx)
ITA 86(2.1)(a) PUC Reduction		$xx,xxx

19-18.   In reviewing this PUC reduction formula, note that where the non-share consider- ation is equal to, or greater than the PUC of the old shares, the amount subtracted from the increase in the legal stated capital of the new shares will be nil. This means that the PUC reduction will be equal to the increase in legal stated capital for the new shares. In common sense terms, if the shareholder takes back the full amount of the old PUC in the form of non-share consideration, the PUC of the new shares will be nil.

19-19.   As was the case with rollovers to a corporation under Section 85, if the PUC reduc- tion applies to more than one class of shares, it will be allocated to the individual classes on the basis of the relative fair market value of each class.

Example Using ITA 86 In An Estate Freeze
Basic Data
19-20.   An example will serve to illustrate the ITA 86 procedures. You might note that the example illustrates the manner in which an ITA 86 reorganization of capital can be used to freeze the value of an individual's estate.

Example   Mr. David Jones owns all of the outstanding shares of Jones Inc. These common shares have an adjusted cost base of $50,000 and a paid up capital of $75,000. Because of the successful operations of the Company, the current fair market value of these common shares is $500,000.

Mr. Jones would like to have future growth in the value of the corporation accrue to his daughter, Ms. Veronica Jones. To accomplish this, Mr. Jones exchanges his common shares for a $150,000 note payable from the corporation and preferred shares with a fair market value and a legal stated capital of $350,000. Common shares are purchased by Veronica Jones for $1,000. These are the only Jones Inc. common shares outstanding subsequent to these transactions.

PUC Reduction
19-21.   The first step in applying the ITA 86 rules in this situation would be to calculate the required PUC reduction and the resulting PUC value for the new shares. As the non-share consideration of $150,000 exceeds the $75,000 PUC of the old shares, we would expect the PUC reduction formula to reduce the PUC of the new shares to nil. The following calculations support this expected result:

Exchange Of Shares In A Reorganization

Cost Of Non-Share Consideration (Note Payable)		$150,000

Increase In Legal Stated Capital Of New Shares		$350,000
Less The Excess, If Any, Of:		
PUC Of Old Shares	($ 75,000)	
Over The Non-Share Consideration	150,000	Nil
ITA 86(2.1)(a) PUC Reduction		$350,000

Increase In Legal Stated Capital Of New Shares	$350,000
ITA 86(2.1)(a) PUC Reduction	(350,000)
PUC Of New Shares	Nil

Other Required Values

19-22.   Other required values can be calculated as follows:

Adjusted Cost Base Of Old Shares	$ 50,000
Non-Share Consideration	(150,000)
Adjusted Cost Base Of New Shares	Nil

PUC Of New Shares	Nil
Plus Non-Share Consideration	$150,000
Proceeds Of Redemption Under ITA 84(5)(d)	$150,000
PUC Of Old Shares	(75,000)
ITA 84(3) Deemed Dividend	$ 75,000

Adjusted Cost Base Of New Shares	Nil
Plus Non-Share Consideration	$150,000
Proceeds Of Disposition Under ITA 86(1)(c)	$150,000
ITA 84(3) Deemed Dividend	(75,000)
Adjusted Proceeds	$ 75,000
Adjusted Cost Base Of Old Shares	(50,000)
Capital Gain	$ 25,000

Economic Analysis

19-23.   The shares held by his daughter, Veronica, will have an adjusted cost base of $1,000 and this will also be their current fair market value. However, if the corporation prospers, all future increases in its value will accrue to her. In other words, by exchanging his common shares for non-growth preferred shares, Mr. Jones has frozen the value of his interest in Jones Inc.

19-24.   In reviewing this example, you should note that Mr. Jones' potential gain has not disappeared. If he had simply sold his shares without the reorganization, he would have realized a gain of $450,000 ($500,000 - $50,000). As a result of the reorganization, he has recognized $100,000 ($75,000 dividend + $25,000 capital gain) of this amount, leaving a deferred gain of $350,000. After the reorganization, his holding of preferred shares has an adjusted cost base and PUC of nil. As the fair market value of the shares is $350,000, any redemption or sale of these shares will result in Mr. Jones having to take the deferred $350,000 into income.

19-25.   A final point here is that this example does not represent a typical ITA 86 estate freeze. While it does accomplish the goal of transferring future growth in the corporation to a related party, the approach used has resulted in current Tax Payable for Mr. Jones. This occurred because the non-share consideration received was greater than both the PUC and the adjusted cost base of the old shares. Had he limited the non-share consideration to $50,000, the estate freeze objective could have been accomplished without current taxation.

Exercise Nineteen-2

Subject: Exchange Of Shares In Reorganization (ACB = PUC = Boot)

Mr. Sam Samson is the sole shareholder of Samdoo Ltd. It is a Canadian controlled private corporation and its common shares have a fair market value of $2,300,000, an adjusted cost base (ACB) of $1,000,000, and a paid up capital (PUC) of $1,000,000. At this time, Samdoo Ltd. has no balance in its GRIP account. Mr. Samson exchanges all of his Samdoo Ltd. shares for cash of $1,000,000 and preferred shares that are redeemable for $1,300,000. Determine the ACB and the PUC of the redeemable preferred shares. Indicate the amount, and type, of any income that will result from this transaction.

Exercise Nineteen-3

Subject: Exchange Of Shares In Reorganization (ACB > PUC, PUC = Boot)

Mr. Sam Samson is the sole shareholder of Samdoo Ltd. It is a Canadian controlled private corporation and its common shares have a fair market value of $2,300,000, an adjusted cost base (ACB) of $1,250,000, and a paid up capital (PUC) of $1,000,000. At this time, Samdoo Ltd. has no balance in its GRIP account. Mr. Samson exchanges all of his Samdoo Ltd. shares for cash of $1,000,000 and preferred shares that are redeemable for $1,300,000. Determine the ACB and the PUC of the redeemable preferred shares. Indicate the amount, and type, of any income that will result from this transaction.

Exercise Nineteen-4

Subject: Exchange Of Shares In Reorganization (ACB > Boot > PUC)

Mr. Sam Samson is the sole shareholder of Samdoo Ltd. It is a Canadian controlled private corporation and its common shares have a fair market value of $2,300,000, an adjusted cost base (ACB) of $1,250,000, and a paid up capital (PUC) of $1,000,000. At this time, Samdoo Ltd. has no balance in its GRIP account. Mr. Samson exchanges all of his Samdoo Ltd. shares for cash of $1,200,000 and preferred shares that are redeemable for $1,100,000. Determine the ACB and the PUC of the redeemable preferred shares. Indicate the amount, and type, of any income that will result from this transaction.

End of Exercises. Solutions available in Study Guide.

Gift To Related Person (Benefit Rule)

19-26. ITA 86(2) contains a rule designed to prevent a taxpayer from using this rollover provision to confer a benefit on a related person. This rule is applicable whenever the fair market value of the old shares exceeds the sum of the fair market value of the new shares and the fair market value of the non-share consideration received, and it is reasonable to regard all, or part, of this excess as a gift to a related person.

19-27. This type of situation can be illustrated by returning to our Jones Inc. example from Paragraph 19-21. In that example, Mr. David Jones owned shares with an adjusted cost base of $50,000, a paid up capital of $75,000, and a current fair market value of $500,000.

Exchange Of Shares In A Reorganization

19-28.   If, instead of taking back the $150,000 note and preferred shares with a fair market value of $350,000, Mr. Jones exchanged his common shares for a $150,000 note and preferred shares with a fair market value of $250,000, the $100,000 difference between the $500,000 fair market value of the old shares he gave up and the $400,000 fair market value of the consideration he received would accrue to the common shareholders of Jones Inc. As his daughter is the only holder of common shares, this $100,000 gift would accrue to her. As she is clearly a related person, ITA 86(2) would be applicable.

19-29.   In situations where ITA 86(2) applies, the rules for the reorganization of share capital are as follows:

Proceeds Of Disposition   Under ITA 86(2)(c), the proceeds of the disposition for capital gains purposes on the old shares will be equal to the lesser of:

- the fair market value of the non-share consideration, plus the gift; and
- the fair market value of the old shares.

This compares to the proceeds of disposition under ITA 86(1), which is equal to the cost of the new shares, plus the fair market value of the non-share consideration.

Capital Losses   Under ITA 86(2)(d), any capital loss resulting from the disposition of the old shares will be deemed to be nil.

Cost Of New Shares   Under ITA 86(2)(e), the cost to the taxpayer of the new shares will be equal to:

- the cost of the old shares; less
- the sum of the non-share consideration, plus the gift.

This compares to a cost for the new shares under ITA 86(1) equal to the cost of the old shares, less the non-share consideration.

19-30   To illustrate these procedures, we will use the example presented in Paragraph 19-20, as modified in Paragraph 19-28.

Example   Mr. David Jones owns all of the outstanding shares of Jones Inc. These common shares have an adjusted cost base of $50,000 and a paid up capital of $75,000. Because of the successful operations of the Company, the current fair market value of these common shares is $500,000.

Mr. Jones would like to have future growth in the value of the corporation accrue to his daughter, Ms. Veronica Jones. To accomplish this, Mr. Jones exchanges his common shares for a $150,000 note payable from the corporation and preferred shares with a fair market value and a legal stated capital of $250,000. Common shares are purchased by Veronica Jones for $1,000. These are the only Jones Inc. common shares outstanding subsequent to these transactions.

PUC Reduction

19-31.   The PUC reduction and PUC of the new shares is calculated as follows:

Cost Of Non-Share Consideration (Note Payable)		$150,000
Increase In Legal Stated Capital Of New Shares		$250,000
Less The Excess, If Any, Of:		
PUC Of Old Shares	($ 75,000)	
Over The Non-Share Consideration	150,000	Nil
ITA 86(2.1)(a) PUC Reduction		$250,000
Increase In Legal Stated Capital Of New Shares		$250,000
ITA 86(2.1)(a) PUC Reduction		(250,000)
PUC Of New Shares		Nil

Other Calculations

19-32.   The remaining calculations that would be required under ITA 86(2) are as follows:

Adjusted Cost Base Of Old Shares	$ 50,000
Non-Share Consideration	(150,000)
Gift ($500,000 - $150,000 - $250,000)	(100,000)
Adjusted Cost Base Of New Shares	**Nil**
PUC Of New Shares	Nil
Plus Non-Share Consideration	$150,000
Proceeds Of Redemption Under ITA 84(5)(d)	**$150,000**
PUC Of Old Shares	(75,000)
ITA 84(3) Deemed Dividend	**$ 75,000**
Non-Share Consideration	$150,000
Plus Gift	100,000
Total Proceeds Of Disposition Under ITA 86(2)(c)	**$250,000**
(Less Than $500,000 FMV Of Old Shares)	
ITA 84(3) Deemed Dividend	(75,000)
Adjusted Proceeds	**$175,000**
Adjusted Cost Base Of Old Shares	(50,000)
Capital Gain	**$125,000**

19-33.   The final capital gain figure of $125,000 is $100,000 in excess of the gain recorded in the original version of this example in Paragraph 19-22. In effect, the amount of the gift has been added to the capital gain that must be included in the income of Mr. Jones.

19-34.   While there is less deferral of income, the total amount of the gain that will be taxed in Mr. Jones' hands is unchanged. Mr. Jones has preferred shares with a fair market value of $250,000 and a cost of nil, reflecting the initial $450,000 gain that was present, less the $200,000 ($75,000 + $125,000) in income recognized as a result of the reorganization.

19-35.   ITA 86 does, however, involve a penalty to the taxpayer and his daughter as a group. The new common shares issued to his daughter will have a fair market value equal to $101,000, the $1,000 she paid plus the $100,000 gift. The $100,000 additional value will not be reflected in the adjusted cost base of her shares and, as a consequence, this amount will be taxed when she disposes of the shares.

19-36.   In effect, the granting of the benefit has increased the amount that will be subject to taxation in the hands of his daughter by the $100,000 amount of the gift, without reducing Mr. Jones' total current and deferred income on the shares. This makes it clear that Section 86 reorganizations should be structured in a manner that avoids such benefits being granted.

Exercise Nineteen-5

Subject: Gift To A Related Party

Ms. Jan Reviser owns 80 percent of the shares of Janrev Inc. The remaining shares are held by her 19 year old daughter. The corporation is a Canadian controlled private corporation and its shares have a fair market value of $1,600,000, an adjusted cost base (ACB) of $250,000, and a paid up capital (PUC) of $250,000. At this time, Janrev has no balance in its GRIP account. Ms. Reviser exchanges all of her Janrev Inc. shares for cash of $300,000 and preferred shares that are redeemable for $800,000. Indicate the amount, and type, of any income that will result from this transaction.

End of Exercise. Solution available in Study Guide.

Practical Considerations

19-37.   Some of the practical considerations in a reorganization of capital can be described as follows:

- The first step requires a valuation of the existing common shares. The valuation should be carefully documented and the assistance of professional valuators may be required.

- As a second step, it is often necessary to amend the articles of incorporation to introduce one or more new classes of shares. Depending on the wishes of the original owner, the new shares may be voting or non-voting.

- The third step is the exchange of the existing shares for the new shares. As previously discussed, the preferred shares should be redeemable at their fair market value on the date of the share exchange. This requirement exists so that the past success of the corporation accrues to the existing shareholder, and no benefit is bestowed on the incoming shareholders.

- The fourth step involves issuing new common shares to the incoming shareholders. Note that the incoming shareholders should provide the capital required from their own sources to avoid potential attribution problems. The required amounts are often nominal.

- An agreement should be drawn up to document the share reorganization. To ensure future flexibility, a price adjustment clause should be included to provide for a change in the redemption amount or the number of issued shares in certain circumstances. The price adjustment clause is particularly useful if the CRA assesses the original shares as having a higher fair market value. The price adjustment clause protects the incoming shareholders from a potential tax liability related to the reorganization.

Using Section 86 - Advantages and Disadvantages
General Usage

19-38.   The major advantages of using Section 86 can be described as follows:

- A Section 86 share reorganization is simpler to implement than a Section 85 rollover as it does not require setting up of a new corporation.
- The corporate law steps are easier, only requiring shares to be exchanged, and possibly new share classes to be formed.
- The use of Section 86 does not require an election to be filed with the CRA.

19-39.   The disadvantages associated with using Section 86 are as follows:

- When only a single corporation is used, it is difficult to segregate investment income from active business income.
- A single corporation exposes all of the assets to any operating risk, and limited liability protection is reduced.
- In a Section 86 reorganization, all of the taxpayer's shares of a particular class have to be exchanged. This can be a problem if the original shareholder wishes to retain some of the common or growth shares.

19-40.   It usually possible to get around this last disadvantage. This can be accomplished by re-issuing common shares to the original shareholder after the reorganization is completed.

Use In Key Employee Successions

19-41.   In addition to its use in estate freezes, an exchange of shares can be very effective when arranging for gradual succession to a key employee. For example, consider a situation where an employee has little personal equity, but has a good work record with the company and excellent owner-manager potential.

19-42.   A Section 86 reorganization could be used to convert common shares owned by the existing shareholder into preferred shares. The employee could then purchase the common shares over some agreed upon succession period. The annual investments in common shares would likely be modest, as most of the company's value would be reflected in the preferred shares, making the investments feasible for the incoming shareholder. The original owner could continue to be involved in the business throughout the succession years.

19-43.   Eventually, when the original owner is ready to sell the preferred shares, the incoming shareholder will have the benefit of several years of management experience, and should be able to obtain funding to acquire the preferred shares from the original owner.

Amalgamations

The Nature Of An Amalgamation

19-44.   ITA 87 provides for a tax deferred rollover in situations where there is an amalgamation of corporations. This may involve two independent corporations wishing to merge and continue their business affairs on a combined basis. Alternatively, associated or related corporations may amalgamate to pursue common corporate goals.

19-45.   If the two corporations want to transfer their assets to a new corporation on a tax free basis, the rollover provisions of ITA 87 would apply. The following simple example will illustrate this kind of situation:

> **Example**   The shareholders of Company Alpha have shares with an adjusted cost base of $1,000,000 and a fair market value of $5,000,000, while the shareholders of Company Beta have shares with an adjusted cost base of $1,700,000 and a fair market value of $5,000,000. All of the assets and liabilities (except intercompany balances) of Company Alpha and Company Beta are transferred to a new Company, Alpha-Beta Ltd. The shareholders of Company Alpha and Company Beta exchange their shares for shares in Alpha-Beta Ltd.

19-46.   If the assets of Alpha and Beta had simply been sold to a new company, the sales would be viewed as dispositions for proceeds equal to the fair market value of the assets. This would normally result in the realization of significant capital gains and recapture. However, under corporate amalgamation legislation, the combined company is not viewed as a new company and, as a consequence, there is no disposition of assets. The provisions of ITA 87 support this view of the transaction.

19-47.   To facilitate amalgamations of corporations, ITA 87 contains rollover provisions for both the transfer of assets to the amalgamated corporation and for the exchange of shares. For the ITA 87 provisions to be applicable, the following conditions must be met:

- Both of the predecessor corporations must be taxable Canadian corporations.

- All shareholders of the predecessor corporations must receive shares of the amalgamated corporation due to the amalgamation.

- All of the assets and liabilities of the predecessor corporations, other than intercompany balances, must be transferred to the amalgamated corporation in the amalgamation.

- The transfer cannot simply be a normal purchase of property, or involve the distribution of assets on the winding-up of a corporation.

Position Of The Amalgamated Company

19-48.   The tax values for the amalgamated corporation's assets will simply be the sum of the tax values of the assets that were present in the records of the predecessor corporations. In addition, all types of loss carry forwards (capital, non-capital, and farm) of the predecessor corporations flow through and become available to the amalgamated corporation.

19-49.   The predecessor corporations will be deemed to have a taxation year that ends immediately before the amalgamation and, in most situations, this will result in an extra taxation year that will count towards the expiration of losses with a limited carry forward period.

The amalgamated corporation is deemed to have been formed on the date of the amalgamation and may choose any year end it wishes.

19-50.   With respect to assets, reserves, loss carry forwards, and other tax accounts of the old companies, ITA 87 provides rollover provisions as follows:

Rollover Provisions In ITA 87 Amalgamations

Item	Rollover Effect
Inventories	At Cost
Depreciable Capital Property	At UCC
Non-Depreciable Capital Property	At ACB
Eligible Capital Property	4/3 Of CEC
Reserves	Flowed Through
Non-Capital Losses	Flowed Through
Net Capital Losses	Flowed Through
Restricted Farm Losses	Flowed Through
General Rate Income Pool (GRIP) (See Note 1)	Flowed Through
Low Rate Income Pool (LRIP) (See Note 2)	Flowed Through
Capital Dividend Account (See Note 3)	Flowed Through
Refundable Dividend Tax On Hand (See Note 3)	Flowed Through

Note 1 If a CCPC is formed as the result of an amalgamation, ITA 89(5) may be applicable. In situations where a predecessor corporation was a CCPC, this subsection provides for the flow through of its GRIP account to the amalgamated company.

Note 2 If a non-CCPC is formed as the result of an amalgamation, ITA 89(9) may be applicable. In situations where a predecessor corporation was a non-CCPC, this subsection provides for the flow through of its LRIP account to the amalgamated company.

Note 3   The capital dividend account and the Refundable Dividend Tax On Hand account are only available to private companies. If either of the predecessor companies is a public company, these accounts would be lost.

19-51.   As can be seen in the preceding table, ITA 87 basically provides for a summing of the relevant tax values of the assets of the two companies that are amalgamating. The amalgamated corporation will be liable for recapture and capital gains on the same basis as the predecessor corporations.

19-52.   With respect to loss carry forwards, the limitations that were discussed in Chapter 15 are applicable if there is an acquisition of control. As noted, the deemed year end of the predecessor corporations will count as one year in any carry forward period. However, losses carried forward may qualify for deduction in the first taxation year of the amalgamated company.

Position Of The Shareholders

19-53.   The shareholders of the predecessor corporations are deemed to dispose of their shares for proceeds equal to the adjusted cost base of the shares, and they are deemed to acquire the shares of the amalgamated company at the same value. For these general provisions to apply, the following conditions must be met:

- The shareholders must not receive any consideration other than shares in the amalgamated company, or its Canadian parent.

- The original shares must be capital property of the shareholders.

- The amalgamation must not result in a deemed gift to a person related to the shareholders.

Vertical Amalgamations (Parent And Subsidiary)

19-54.   In situations where there is a desire to combine a parent and its subsidiary, a choice of rollovers may be available. The alternative to ITA 87, "Amalgamations", is the use of ITA 88(1), "Winding-Up". However, ITA 88(1) is only applicable to situations where the parent company owns 90 percent or more of the shares of each class of capital stock of a subsidiary. In contrast, ITA 87 can be used without regard to the percentage of ownership.

19-55. You may recall from an advanced financial accounting course that the cost of acquiring a subsidiary will usually exceed both the carrying values and the sum of the fair values of the acquired identifiable assets.

> **Example** Placor Inc. acquires 100 percent of the outstanding voting shares of Lacee Ltd. at a cost of $1,000,000. At this time the net identifiable assets of Lacee had carrying values of $700,000 and tax values of $650,000. The fair value of these assets totaled $900,000.

19-56. The excess of the $1,000,000 investment cost over the tax values total of $650,000 creates a problem, without regard to whether ITA 87 or ITA 88(1) is used to amalgamate the subsidiary with the parent. Both of these rollover provisions transfer the subsidiary's assets and liabilities at tax values. This means that, in the absence of a special legislative provision, the $350,000 excess of the investment cost over tax values will be lost.

19-57. Fortunately, there are provisions that provide a limited amount of relief from this adverse tax consequence. Both ITA 87 and ITA 88(1) provide for a "bump-up" in asset values to reflect the parent company's excess of investment cost over tax values. This bump-up provision is only available on certain assets.

19-58. Further, it is only available under ITA 87 if the parent owns 100 percent of the subsidiary's issued shares, or under ITA 88(1) in situations where the parent owns 90 percent or more of the issued shares. No bump-up is available when the parent owns less than 90 percent of the subsidiary's issued shares.

19-59. The ITA 87 legislation provides for the bump-up by referring to the ITA 88(1) provision. Given this, we will defer our coverage of this until we have completed our discussion of ITA 88(1).

Non-Tax Considerations

19-60. While a statutory amalgamation does not involve a new company, there are likely to be significant legal complications. Each of the predecessor companies will have contracts with employees, suppliers, and customers. While they are still legally in force, modifications may be required to make the terms more compatible throughout the organization. There may also be problems with creditors. In fact, it is not uncommon for debt covenants to have a provision requiring the approval of debt holders before an amalgamation can take place. These factors may add considerable complexity to the amalgamation process.

Tax Planning Considerations

19-61. A Section 87 amalgamation offers a number of opportunities for tax planning. Some of the possibilities include:

- The utilization of loss carry forward amounts that the predecessor corporation(s) might not be able to absorb. Note, however, that if there is an acquisition of control, the usual restrictions on the use of loss carry forwards apply.

- Current year losses of one predecessor corporation can effectively be utilized against Taxable Income of the other.

- Bringing together a profitable and an unprofitable corporation may allow for a faster write-off of capital assets (through CCA) than would otherwise be possible by the unprofitable predecessor corporation.

- The amalgamation may provide for an increase in the amount of the manufacturing and processing profits tax deduction.

19-62.   The timing of an amalgamation can be an important tax planning issue. As the amalgamation transaction results in a deemed year end, the company may have a short fiscal year for purposes of calculating CCA. In addition, outstanding reserves may have to be brought into income sooner, and the short fiscal period will count as a full year in the eligible loss carry forward years.

19-63.   For income tax instalments there is a look through provision. While the amalgamated company does not have a previous tax year on which to base instalment payments of income tax, prepayments continue to be required based on the instalment history of the predecessor corporations.

Exercise Nineteen-6

Subject: ITA 87 Amalgamations

During its taxation year ending December 31, 2006, Downer Ltd. incurs a non-capital loss of $93,000 and a net capital loss of $150,000. Neither loss can be carried back. On January 1, 2007, using the provisions of ITA 87, the Company is amalgamated with Upton Inc., a company that also has a December 31 year end. The combined company is named Amalgo Inc. and it elects to use a December 31 year end. The terms of the amalgamation give 20,000 Amalgo Inc. shares to the Downer Ltd. shareholders and 150,000 Amalgo Inc. shares to the Upton Inc. shareholders. During the year ending December 31, 2007, Amalgo Inc. has Net Income For Tax Purposes of $1,200,000, including over $300,000 in taxable capital gains. During its 2007 taxation year, will Amalgo Inc. be able to deduct the losses incurred by Downer Ltd. prior to the amalgamation? Explain your conclusion.

End of Exercise. Solution available in Study Guide.

Winding-Up Of A 90 Percent Owned Subsidiary

The Nature Of A Winding-Up

Winding-Up Of Corporations In General

19-64.   IT-126R2 states that a corporation is considered to have been "wound up" where:

(a) it has followed the procedures for winding-up and dissolution provided by the appropriate federal or provincial companies *Act* or winding-up *Act*, or

(b) it has carried out a winding-up, other than by means of the statutory procedures contemplated in (a) above, and has been dissolved under the provisions of its incorporating statute.

19-65.   In general, a winding-up operation requires that all outstanding creditor claims be satisfied and that all corporate property be distributed to the shareholders before the winding-up is undertaken. IT-126R2 also notes that, where there is substantial evidence that dissolution procedures will be completed within a short period of time, Section 88(1) can be used prior to the completion of the wind-up.

19-66.   A winding-up may be undertaken for several reasons. As with amalgamations, a winding-up allows for the losses of a subsidiary to be carried over to the parent corporation. Winding-ups are also undertaken to simplify an organizational structure, or when a subsidiary is ceasing its business operations.

90 Percent Owned Subsidiary

19-67.   The two major Subsections of ITA 88 can be described as follows:

ITA 88(1)   This Subsection is a rollover provision, providing for the tax free combination of the assets of a 90 percent or more owned subsidiary with those of its parent.

ITA 88(2)   This Subsection deals with the general winding-up of corporations, other than those to which ITA 88(1) is applicable. It is not a rollover provision.

19-68.   At this point we are concerned only with the provisions contained in ITA 88(1). The content of ITA 88(2) will be considered beginning in Paragraph 19-92.

19-69.   To use the ITA 88(1) rollover, the parent corporation must own at least 90 percent of each class of the subsidiary's shares. Therefore, not all winding-ups of subsidiaries qualify for the treatment described in ITA 88(1). A winding-up involving a subsidiary where a parent corporation has control, but owns less than 90 percent of the issued shares, would be implemented under the provisions of ITA 88(2).

19-70.   If the parent has the required 90 percent or more ownership, it is permitted to exchange the subsidiary's shares for the assets of the subsidiary on a tax deferred basis. This transaction is very similar to an amalgamation, as it allows the assets of the two companies to be combined without recognizing any accrued capital gains or recaptured CCA on the transfers required to effect the combination.

19-71.   As with other rollovers, there are two components to a winding-up transaction. The first is the acquisition of the subsidiary's assets by the parent, and the second is the deemed disposition of the subsidiary's shares by the parent. We will now turn our attention to these components.

Acquisition Of Assets
General Rules
19-72.   In an ITA 88(1) winding-up, the subsidiary is deemed to have disposed of its assets and the parent is deemed to have acquired the assets on the following basis:

- A cost of nil in the case of Canadian or foreign resource property.

- Four-thirds of the balance in the subsidiary's cumulative eligible capital account immediately before the winding-up.

- The "cost amount" to the subsidiary in the case of other property. Cost amount is defined in ITA 248(1) as UCC for depreciable property and adjusted cost base for non-depreciable capital property.

GRIP Balances
19-73.   ITA 89(6) applies to situations in which a CCPC has wound up a subsidiary under ITA 88(1). If the subsidiary was also a CCPC, this provision provides for a flow through of the subsidiary's GRIP balance to the GRIP balance of the parent company.

19-74.   A second, much more complex provision in ITA 89(6), applies when the subsidiary is a non-CCPC. This provision attempts to measure what the subsidiary's GRIP would have been at the end of its last taxation year had it been a CCPC at that time. This amount will also be included in the parent company's GRIP.

LRIP Balances
19-75.   ITA 89(10) applies when a non-CCPC has wound up a subsidiary under ITA 88(1). If the subsidiary was also a non-CCPC, this provision provides for a flow through of the subsidiary's LRIP balance to the LRIP balance of the parent company.

19-76.   Once again, a second and much more complex provision applies when the subsidiary is a CCPC. This provision attempts to measure what the subsidiary's LRIP would have been at the end of its last taxation year had it been a non-CCPC at that time. This amount will also be transferred to the parent company's LRIP.

Deferral Of Loss Carry Forwards

19-77.   As indicated previously, an ITA 88(1) winding up is very similar to an amalgamation. There is, however, one important difference between an amalgamation under ITA 87 and the winding-up of a subsidiary under ITA 88(1) and this involves loss carry forwards.

19-78.   As is generally the case under ITA 87, non-capital losses and net capital losses of the subsidiary will be available to the parent company when ITA 88(1) is used. However, under ITA 88(1), they will not become available until the first taxation year of the parent that begins after the date that the winding-up period commences.

> **Example** If a parent's fiscal year begins on February 1 and the winding-up occurs on February 15, 2007, the losses of the subsidiary will not be available to the parent until its fiscal year beginning February 1, 2008.

19-79.   In those situations where the subsidiary has a different year end than the parent, subsidiary losses are deemed to have occurred in the parent's fiscal year that includes the subsidiary's year end.

> **Example** A parent has a June 30 year end, while its subsidiary has a September 30 year end. There is a winding-up on August 31, 2007. The subsidiary has a non-capital loss for the period that is terminated on August 31, 2007 by the winding-up.

> **Analysis** The loss will be deemed to have occurred in the parent's year ending June 30, 2008. This would suggest that the loss would not expire until the parent's year ending June 30, 2028. However, ITA 88(1.1)(b) limits the carry forward period to the period that would have been available to the subsidiary if it had not been wound up. This means that, in actual fact, the loss expires on June 30, 2027.

Exercise Nineteen-7

Subject: Losses In A Winding-Up

Park Inc. has a September 15 year end, while its 100 percent owned subsidiary, Side Ltd., has an October 31 year end. Side Ltd. has a non-capital loss carry forward of $50,000 from its year ending October 31, 2006. On June 30, 2007, there is a winding-up of Side Ltd., using the rollover provision found in ITA 88(1). What is the earliest taxation year in which the $50,000 loss can be deducted? If it is not deducted then, in what taxation year will it expire?

End of Exercise. Solution available in Study Guide.

Asset Bump-Up

19-80.   As we pointed out in our discussion of vertical amalgamations, ITA 88(1) provides for a transfer of all or part of the excess of the purchase price of a subsidiary's shares over the tax values of the subsidiary's assets. As noted, this bump-up is also available under ITA 87 when the parent owns 100 percent of the subsidiary. Under either of these provisions, the amount of this bump-up in tax values is limited by two amounts:

1. The basic amount of the bump-up is found in ITA 88(1)(d)(i) and (i.1). This amount is the excess of the adjusted cost base of the subsidiary shares held by the parent, over the sum of:

    * the tax values of the subsidiary's net assets at the time of the winding-up; and
    * dividends paid by the subsidiary to the parent since the time of the acquisition (including capital dividends).

2. ITA 88(1)(d)(ii) further limits the amount that can be recognized to the excess of the fair market value of the subsidiary's non-depreciable capital property over their tax values at the time the parent acquired control of the subsidiary.

19-81.   The following example will illustrate these procedures:

Example   On December 31, 1997, ParentCo acquires 100 percent of the outstanding shares of SubCo for $5,000,000. At that time, the only non-depreciable capital property owned by SubCo was land with a fair market value of $2,000,000 and a cost of $1,000,000. Between December 31, 1997 and December 31, 2007, SubCo pays dividends of $150,000 to ParentCo. On December 31, 2007, when the tax values of SubCo's assets total $4,200,000, SubCo is absorbed in a Section 88(1) winding-up.

Analysis   The amount of the available asset bump-up will be the lesser of the two amounts described in Paragraph 19-80:

Adjusted Cost Base Of SubCo Shares		$5,000,000
Tax Values Of SubCo Assets At Winding-Up	($4,200,000)	
Dividends Paid By SubCo Since Its Acquisition	(150,000)	(4,350,000)
Excess		$ 650,000

Fair Market Value Of Land At Acquisition	$2,000,000
Cost Of Land At Acquisition	(1,000,000)
Excess	$1,000,000

19-82.   In this situation, the write-up of the land is restricted to the lower figure of $650,000. Fortunately, ParentCo is able to use the entire excess of the purchase premium over the tax values of the assets at the winding-up date, but only because the pre-acquisition appreciation on the land was greater than $650,000.

Exercise Nineteen-8

Subject: Winding-Up Of A 90 Percent Owned Subsidiary

On January 1, 2003, Procul Ltd. acquired 100 percent of the outstanding shares of Lorne Inc. at a cost of $1,200,000. At this point in time, the fair market value of Lorne's identifiable net assets was $850,000, including $270,000 for the Land. The tax value for the net assets at that time was $410,000.

On December 31, 2007, the condensed Balance Sheet of Lorne Inc. was as follows:

Cash	$120,000
Land - At Cost (Purchased In 1999)	140,000
Depreciable Assets - At UCC (Purchased In 1999)	240,000
Total Assets	$500,000

Liabilities	$ 75,000
Shareholders' Equity	425,000
Total Equities	$500,000

On December 31, 2007, there is a winding-up of Lorne Inc. under the provisions of ITA 88(1). Lorne Inc. has paid no dividends since its acquisition by Procul Ltd. Determine the tax values that will be recorded for Lorne Inc.'s assets after they have been incorporated into the records of Procul Ltd.

End of Exercise. Solution available in Study Guide.

Disposition Of Shares

19-83.   The disposition of shares component of the winding-up is straightforward. In general, the parent is deemed to have disposed of its shares of the subsidiary for proceeds equal to the adjusted cost base of the shares. As an example, assume the parent had paid $4,000,000 for the subsidiary's shares. This amount would also be the deemed proceeds of the disposition and there would be no capital gain.

19-84.   An exception to this general rule will arise if the tax values of the subsidiary's assets transferred and the paid up capital of the subsidiary's shares is more than the amount paid for the shares by the parent. In this case, the deemed proceeds of disposition will be the lesser of the paid up capital and the tax values of the assets transferred. As a result, a capital gain can arise in these situations.

Example Prawn Ltd. owns 100 percent of the outstanding shares of Shrimp Inc. The cost of these shares was $4,000,000. This subsidiary is being wound up under the provisions of ITA 88(1). At the time of the winding-up, the tax values of the subsidiary's assets total $4,800,000 and the PUC of the subsidiary's shares is $4,500,000.

Analysis Given these facts, the exception applies and the deemed proceeds of disposition would be the greater of the $4,000,000 cost of the shares and $4,500,000. This latter figure is the lesser of the $4,800,000 tax value of the subsidiary's assets and the $4,500,000 PUC of the subsidiary's shares. This gives proceeds of disposition of $4,500,000 and a capital gain of $500,000 ($4,500,000 - $4,000,000). It is expected that such gains situations would be fairly rare and, because the proceeds are defined using cost except when it is less than the alternative values, there is no possibility of a capital loss.

Tax Planning Considerations - Amalgamation Vs. Winding-Up

19-85.   Figure 19-1 contains a comparison of the features of an amalgamation under ITA 87 and the winding-up of a subsidiary that is at least 90 percent owned under ITA 88(1). A discussion of several of the items follows.

Figure 19 - 1 Comparison Of Amalgamation Under ITA 87 And Winding-Up Under ITA 88(1)		
Factor	**Amalgamation - ITA 87**	**Winding-Up Of 90% Owned Subsidiary - ITA 88(1)**
Valuation of assets	Tax values of assets of predecessor corporations carried forward to amalgamated company.	Tax values of subsidiary's assets carried forward to parent.
Recognition of the excess of investment cost over tax values	Recognition only if 100 percent owned subsidiary. If 100 percent owned, same treatment as ITA 88(1).	Write-up allowed if excess is associated with values of non-depreciable capital property.
Capital cost allowances	Claim in last year of predecessor and first year of amalgamated corporation.	No claim by subsidiary in year of winding-up, but available to parent in year of winding-up.
Loss carry forwards	Carried forward, but acquisition of control rules apply.	Carried forward, but only available to parent beginning in taxation year after winding-up.
Year end	Deemed year end before amalgamation, counts one year for loss carry forwards.	Year end of parent corporation continued. Subsidiary has a terminal year end that counts as one taxation year.

19-86.   A significant consideration in deciding between an amalgamation under ITA 87 and a winding-up under ITA 88(1) is the ability to recognize all or part of the excess of investment cost over tax values. In the case of an ITA 87 amalgamation, recognition is possible only in cases involving a parent and a 100 percent owned subsidiary. Under ITA 88(1), recognition can occur as long as the parent owns 90 percent or more of each class of the subsidiary's issued shares.

19-87.   Under either provision, it is possible that substantial tax values will disappear in the transaction. This would suggest that, when the adjusted cost base of the parent's investment is significantly greater than the tax values of the subsidiary's assets, it may be better to continue to operate the subsidiary as a separate legal entity.

19-88.   Under the amalgamation procedures, the predecessor corporations will have a deemed year end, which will count towards the expiry of time limited non-capital loss carry forwards. However, the amalgamated company will be able to use the losses immediately.

19-89.   In contrast, the parent company that is using ITA 88(1) to absorb a 90 percent owned subsidiary will have its usual year end. However, it will not be able to use subsidiary loss carry forwards until the first taxation year beginning subsequent to the winding-up. In addition, the wind-up will count as an additional year in the expiry of time limited loss carry forwards. The analysis of this situation may be complicated by differing year ends for the two corporations.

19-90.   In considering CCA claims, ITA 87 creates a deemed year end for both predecessor corporations, requiring them to take pro rata CCA claims for what will normally be a short fiscal period. Under the ITA 88(1) procedures, the subsidiary disposes of its assets prior to its year end and, as a consequence, there will be no claim for CCA in the subsidiary's final year. However, CCA may be claimed on these assets by the parent company, subsequent to their being acquired under the winding-up procedures.

19-91.   If the subsidiary is not 100 percent owned, a Section 88(1) winding-up will have implications for the minority shareholders. A winding-up will require reporting of capital gains and recaptured CCA on property distributed by the subsidiary to the minority share-holders in the course of the wind-up and in satisfaction of their interests in the subsidiary. Further, any liquidating dividend paid to the minority shareholders will be a taxable dividend.

Winding-Up Of A Canadian Corporation

The Nature Of The Transaction

Wind-Up Vs. Rollover

19-92.   The winding-up procedures for a Canadian corporation, as described in ITA 88(2), are applicable where a corporation is being liquidated. If, for example, owners of a corporation decide that the business is no longer viable, winding-up procedures can be used in the disposition of the corporation's assets and the distribution of the resulting proceeds to the shareholders.

19-93.   In distinguishing the winding-up of a 90 percent or more owned subsidiary from a liquidating winding-up, you should note that the liquidation of a business has quite different objectives. In the case of the winding-up of a 90 percent or more owned subsidiary, we are usually not disposing of the business but, rather, are transferring its assets to a different legal entity that is controlled by the same investor or group of investors that previously had indirect control of its operations. This explains why a rollover is available on the winding-up of a 90 percent or more owned subsidiary, and no equivalent provision is available for the winding-up when a liquidation is under way.

Distributions To Shareholders

19-94.   While a winding-up can be implemented by distributing corporate assets directly to the shareholders, it is generally simpler for the corporation to liquidate its assets, pay off its creditors, pay any taxes that are applicable at the corporate level, and distribute the after tax proceeds to the shareholders.

19-95. The distribution to shareholders becomes a fairly complex issue when a corporation is liquidated, as the proceeds available for distribution will consist of a combination of capital being returned, earnings that can be distributed on a tax free basis, and earnings that can only be distributed in the form of taxable dividends. A further complication is that there may be a combination of eligible and non-eligible dividends.

Disposition Of An Incorporated Business

19-96. Later in this Chapter we will discuss the transfer of an incorporated business to a different group of owners. This can be accomplished through a sale of shares or, alternatively, through a sale of the corporation's assets. If the sale of assets is the more advantageous approach, the provisions of ITA 88(2) apply. That is, the sale of assets will be followed by a winding-up, with the after tax proceeds of the winding-up being distributed to the shareholders. While the business itself will continue to operate, the assets will now be on the books of a different legal entity.

Example

Basic Data

19-97. The ITA 88(2) procedures will be illustrated in the following example.

Example The Marker Company, a Canadian controlled private corporation, has been in operation since 1989. On June 1, 2007, the following Balance Sheet, based on tax values, has been prepared in contemplation of liquidating the Company:

The Marker Company
Balance Sheet - As At June 1, 2007

Accounts Receivable (Net Realizable Value)	$ 12,000
Refundable Dividend Tax On Hand	8,000
Land - At Cost (Note One)	250,000
Building - At UCC (Note Two)	195,000
Total Assets	$465,000
Liabilities	Nil
Common Stock - No Par (Note Three)	$ 10,000
Retained Earnings (Note Three)	455,000
Total Equities	$465,000

Note One The current fair market value of the Land is $300,000.

Note Two The cost of the Building was $320,000. Its current fair market value is $350,000.

Note Three The paid up capital and adjusted cost base of the common shares is $10,000. The Retained Earnings includes $75,000 in the capital dividend account. The Company's GRIP balance is nil.

The assets of the Company are sold for their fair market values which total $662,000 ($12,000 + $300,000 + $350,000). The Company has no other income for the taxation year. The corporation pays tax at a combined federal and provincial rate of 18 percent on income eligible for the small business deduction and 50 percent on investment income. This includes the ITA 123.3 tax on investment income.

Cash Available For Distribution

19-98. At the corporate level, the proceeds from the disposition of the individual assets and the related tax effects are as follows:

Asset	Proceeds	Taxable Capital Gain	Business Income
Accounts Receivable	$ 12,000	Nil	Nil
Land	300,000	$25,000	Nil
Building	350,000	15,000	$125,000
Totals	$662,000	$40,000	$125,000

19-99.   The balance in the Refundable Dividend Tax On Hand account, subsequent to the preceding dispositions, is calculated as follows:

Balance Before Dispositions (From Balance Sheet)	$ 8,000
Additions [(26-2/3%*)($40,000)]	10,667
Balance Available	$18,667

*Given the absence of foreign non-business income tax credits and the absence of large deductions from Taxable Income or credits against Tax Payable, we have omitted the full ITA 129(3) calculation of this amount.

19-100.   The after tax amount of cash that is available for distribution to shareholders is calculated as follows:

Gross Proceeds	$662,000
Tax On Investment Income [(50%)($40,000)]	(20,000)
Tax On Recapture [(18%)($125,000)]	(22,500)
Refundable Dividend Tax On Hand*	18,667
Available For Distribution	$638,167

*Given the size of the gross proceeds, the balance in the RDTOH is clearly going to be less that one-third of the dividends that will be declared.

Distribution To Shareholders

19-101.   The balance in the capital dividend account can be distributed to the shareholders as a tax free capital dividend. This balance is calculated as follows:

Balance Before Dispositions (Balance Sheet Note Three)	$ 75,000
Disposition Of Land	25,000
Disposition Of Building	15,000
Capital Dividend Account - Ending Balance	$115,000

19-102.   Prior to the sale of assets, the Company's GRIP balance was nil. As all of the income resulting from the sale of assets was either investment income or eligible for the small business deduction, there would be no addition to the GRIP account resulting from the sale of assets. This means that all dividends paid that are subject to tax would be non-eligible. The non-eligible taxable dividend component of the total distribution to the shareholders is calculated as follows:

Total Distribution	$638,167
Paid Up Capital	(10,000)
ITA 84(2) Deemed Dividend On Winding-Up	$628,167
Capital Dividend Account	(115,000)
Non-Eligible Dividend Subject To Tax	$513,167

19-103.   Treatment of the $115,000 as a capital dividend is conditional on the appropriate election being made under ITA 83(2). The remaining taxable non-eligible dividend will be grossed up to $641,459 [(125%)($513,167)]. The shares will have a federal dividend tax credit of $85,528 [(2/3)(25%)($513,167)].

19-104. In the ITA 54 definition of "proceeds of disposition", Paragraph j indicates that amounts that are deemed to be a dividend under ITA 84(2) are not included in this amount. As a consequence, in determining the capital gain resulting from the distribution to the shareholders, the ITA 84(2) dividend will be subtracted as follows:

Total Distribution to Shareholders	$638,167
ITA 84(2) Deemed Dividend	(628,167)
Deemed Proceeds Of Disposition	$ 10,000
Adjusted Cost Base Of Shares	(10,000)
Capital Gain	Nil

Exercise Nineteen-9

Subject: Winding-Up Of A Canadian Corporation

Windown Inc. is a Canadian controlled private company. After disposing of all of its assets and paying all of its liabilities, including Tax Payable resulting from the asset dispositions, the Company is left with cash of $865,000. The PUC of the Company's shares is equal to their adjusted cost base, an amount of $88,000. After the sale of assets, the Company has an RDTOH account balance of $47,000, a capital dividend account balance of $26,000, and a GRIP of nil. Determine the tax consequences to the shareholders associated with making the maximum distribution of cash to shareholders on the winding-up of Windown Inc. Assume that appropriate elections will be made to minimize the taxes that will be paid by the shareholders.

End of Exercise. Solution available in Study Guide.

Convertible Properties

Application

19-105. There is one more rollover that you should be familiar with. ITA 51 contains a provision that permits a holder of shares or debt of a corporation to exchange those securities for shares of that corporation on a tax free basis. For this rollover provision to apply, the following two conditions must be met:

- The exchange must not involve any consideration other than the securities that are being exchanged.

- The exchange must not be part of a reorganization of capital or a rollover of property by shareholders to a corporation.

19-106. In practical terms, this provision is designed to accommodate a tax deferred conversion of debt or preferred shares of a corporation into preferred or common shares of the same corporation.

Example An investor acquires convertible bonds with a par value of $10,000 at a price equal to par value. The bonds are convertible into 50 shares of the issuing company's common stock and, at the time of purchase, this common stock is trading at $180 per share (the conversion value of the bonds is $9,000). The bonds are converted when the common shares are trading at $220 per share.

Analysis The conversion of the bonds is a disposition and, in the absence of a special provision, the tax consequences would be as follows:

Proceeds Of Disposition [(50)($220)]	$11,000
Adjusted Cost Base	(10,000)
Capital Gain	**$1,000**

19-107.   ITA 51 avoids the recognition of this gain by deeming the exchange to not be a disposition. While no gain is recognized, the adjusted cost base of the common stock received is deemed to be equal to the $10,000 adjusted cost base of the bonds that were converted.

Other Considerations

19-108.   A conversion provision can assist corporations seeking to add an equity kicker to enhance the marketability of their debt or preferred shares. In addition, conversion arrangements can be used to facilitate income splitting within a corporation. Different classes of shares can be used to allow the redistribution of income and, with the ability to convert different classes of shares on a tax deferred basis, an additional element of flexibility is introduced into such arrangements.

19-109.   ITA 51.1 contains a similar provision to cover situations under which bondholders of a particular company are allowed to convert their holdings into a different debt security of that company. Here again, there is a tax deferred rollover with the adjusted cost base of the old bond holding becoming the creditor's adjusted cost base for the new debt security.

19-110.   We would call your attention to the fact that the accounting rules on debt that is convertible into common or preferred shares require that the proceeds from its issuance be divided between the amount paid by investors for the liability component of the financial instrument and the amount paid for the equity option (see Section 3861 of the *CICA Handbook*). This important issue has not, at this point in time, been given recognition in tax legislation. For tax purposes, the full amount received for convertible debt must be allocated to the debt component of the security.

The Valuation Of A Business

Coverage Of Subject

19-111.   In our discussion of the various rollovers that are available to corporations, we frequently referred to the fair market value of the common shares of a corporation. In contrast to the valuation of preferred shares or non-share consideration such as debt, the valuation of common shares requires that a value be placed on the business as an operating entity. This, in turn, requires a knowledge of business valuation techniques. Knowledge of this subject will also be required at a later point in this Chapter when we deal with the procedures involved in the sale of an incorporated business.

19-112.   Business valuations is far too broad a subject to be dealt with in a text on taxation. In actual fact, it is not a subject that is normally given any consideration in such texts. Rather, it is usually dealt with in separate or specialized books giving exclusive coverage to the topic, or as a component of a finance text. However, because some understanding of this subject is required in considering the procedures used in the sale of a corporation, we will provide very brief coverage of business valuations.

Alternative Methods Of Valuation

19-113.   Essentially, there are two approaches to the valuation of a business. In limited circumstances, it may be possible to arrive at an appropriate value for a business by determining the current fair values of its identifiable assets and liabilities. However, this approach does not take into consideration how successfully the assets have been combined into an operating company.

19-114.   As any accountant will know, businesses that use their assets in an effective manner, as measured by higher than normal rates of return, will tend to have a worth that exceeds the sum of their net asset values. This excess is commonly referred to as goodwill. Correspondingly, a business with earnings that provide less than normal rates of return on the assets invested will tend to be worth less than the sum of its net asset values and this is referred to as negative goodwill.

19-115.   In the great majority of situations, the value of a business will be determined on the basis of its expected future earnings stream, rather than on the basis of its identifiable net asset values. While there are many pitfalls in this approach, expected future earnings are generally based on the past earnings trend.

Asset Based Methods
General Principles
19-116.   One approach to the valuation of a business is to simply determine the current fair values of the identifiable assets and liabilities of the enterprise. Using various appraisal and estimation techniques, a value can be arrived at for each asset and liability and these values can be totaled to arrive at a value for the business. No attention will be given to estimating any goodwill values and, in most cases, other intangibles will also be ignored.

19-117.   As in any other appraisal process, attention should be given to the tax status of the various assets. For example, in determining the current fair value of a depreciable asset, the amount of the UCC of the asset is clearly a relevant component of the valuation process.

19-118.   As indicated in the introduction to this section, this asset by asset approach to the valuation of a business is of limited usefulness. Businesses are seldom worth the sum of their asset values, being worth more if the business generates high levels of income, and less if the income returns on the assets are not adequate. Since an asset based approach to business valuations would not give any consideration to the earning power that has been generated by the particular combination of assets in a business, the results of using such a method could be seriously misleading.

Applicability Of The Approach
19-119.   There are, however, two special situations in which an asset based approach to business valuations would be appropriate. First, in situations where the business is simply a holding company for a variety of investments, the company's earning power is limited to the earnings produced by the various investments and it would be difficult to justify a price for the business that would be significantly different from the sum of the values of the individual investments.

19-120.   Note, however, that if the investments included holdings of equity shares that were not publicly traded, we would still be confronted with a business valuation problem requiring income based valuation techniques.

19-121.   The second situation in which asset based valuation methods could be appropriate would be for a business liquidation. Since there will be no continued operation of the business, the only relevant values here are the liquidation values of the individual assets. The value of the business would coincide with the estimated proceeds resulting from the sale of individual assets, less the funds required to extinguish any liabilities.

Income Based Methods
General Principles
19-122.   It is a well established principle in management accounting and finance that the value of an asset is determined by the present value of discounted cash flows that will be produced by that asset. This means that to place a value on a business as a going concern, an estimate is required of cash flows that the business is expected to provide. Note that these cash flows are not equal to the income of the business. Rather, in the case of an incorporated business, they would be the anticipated dividend payments and, in the case of an unincorporated business, the cash withdrawals available to the owner.

19-123.   There are of course, a number of problems in the use of discounted cash flows. First, the estimation of the undiscounted cash flows is a difficult undertaking that often produces unreliable results. There are also questions related to the choice of an appropriate risk adjusted discount rate, how to distinguish between normal and abnormal levels of earnings, and the question of what time horizon to use as the estimation period. Despite these problems, the discounted cash flow techniques provide important valuation information. As a reflection of this, they are widely used in business valuations.

19-124.   However, the predominate approach to business valuations still relies on the use of earnings (Net Income) or gross revenue figures, rather than cash flows. In addition, relatively primitive techniques such as earnings multipliers are often used in place of the more complex and sophisticated present value techniques.

19-125.   In practical terms, the reliability of the estimates used in business valuations is very weak. Further, the establishment of a price for a business is normally the result of complex negotiations in which many financial and non-financial considerations enter the picture. To attempt to make this process appear more scientific by using present value factors that are accurate to five decimal places may, in fact, mislead the users of the information with respect to the accuracy that can be attached to the results.

19-126.   In view of these problems, there is some justification for the use of less sophisticated valuation techniques that are based on income streams and simple multipliers of those streams. These techniques will be described in the sections that follow.

Valuation Based On Gross Revenues

19-127.   It is possible to value a business on the basis of some multiplier of its gross revenues. However, in view of the tremendous variations in the percentage of gross revenues that reach the bottom line profit figures, this approach is of only limited use.

19-128.   The one situation in which it may be applicable would be when the purchaser of the business is in a position to service the revenues of the acquired business within the existing cost structure. For example, a practicing professional, such as a lawyer, accountant, or insurance agent, might be able to absorb another professional practice without any significant increase in either their fixed or variable costs. However, when additional costs would be incurred, the basis for valuation of the business should shift to an income oriented approach.

19-129.   In situations where the valuation based on gross revenues approach is practical, the purchase multiple will tend to be lower than would be the case with earnings multiples. For example, a purchaser might pay 1.5 to 2 times the annualized gross revenues for a small professional practice that could be absorbed into an existing practice, without a significant increase in costs.

Valuation Based On Earnings

19-130.   The usual process of business valuation is based on an examination of past net earnings and the application of an appropriate multiple to an average of these earnings to provide a capitalized value for the business. In general terms, the process can be described as follows:

Establish Normalized Earnings   This will involve an examination of the earnings of the business over some period of time. The most usual period that is used for this purpose is the preceding five years. These earnings will be adjusted for any factors that do not have a bearing on the future earning power of the business. For example, all non-recurring items, whether their effect was favourable or unfavourable, would be removed. In addition, the financial effects of any operations that are no longer a part of the business would also have to be eliminated. The earnings would be calculated on an after tax basis and, for the purposes of applying a multiplier, an average earnings figure for the period chosen would be used.

Establish An Appropriate Multiplier   The choice of an appropriate multiplier will be based on a number of different considerations. The most important of these would be the risk associated with the earnings stream and the potential for income growth. Risk would generally be measured by the variability of past earnings. If past earnings were highly variable, a smaller multiple would be required than would be the case with a relatively smooth stream of earnings.

With respect to growth potential, in establishing normalized earnings, attention would be given to the trend of these earnings. If a pattern of growth was present, the investor would pay a higher multiplier than would be the case with flat or declining earnings.

In practical terms, these multipliers tend to range between a value of 5 (this would provide an earnings return of 20 percent on the established value) and an upper limit of 10 (this would provide an earnings return of 10 percent on the established value). Multiples in excess of 10 would require either extremely low risk, or the expectation that there will be significant income growth in future years.

Other Factors   The preceding techniques will provide a rough value for the business. At this point, many other tangible and intangible factors will have to be considered. For example, the business may have redundant assets that can be sold. If this is the case, the anticipated sales price of such assets should be added to the rough initial value.

Other factors would include the company's prospective competitive position, the anticipated continuity of management, specific developments related to particular products or markets, trends in the cost structure of the business, and the question of whether any abnormally high profits can be maintained. Only when all of these factors have been given some kind of a quantitative weight can we arrive at a final figure for consideration as a value for the business.

19-131.   In general terms, the preceding describes a common approach to business valuations. It is a relatively unsophisticated approach, but is representative of a common solution to this problem that is found in practice. The method's lack of sophistication is simply a reflection of the subjective nature of the decision that is under consideration. However, the presentation of this approach to the problem does provide a basis for the following discussion, which deals with the sale of an incorporated business.

Sale Of An Incorporated Business

Alternatives

19-132.   Assume that you are the sole owner of an incorporated business and that you have decided to dispose of your company. If the business has a value that extends beyond your personal services, it should be possible to arrange a sale of the business. In approaching the problem of selling an incorporated business, you are usually confronted with the following three alternatives:

- Sale of the individual assets of the business, on a piecemeal basis.
- Sale of the shares of the business.
- Sale of the total net assets of the business, including any unrecorded intangibles such as goodwill.

19-133.   In the next section, consideration will be given to the advantages and disadvantages, as well as to the tax effects that are associated with each of these alternatives. However, before turning our attention to these alternatives, some attention must given to the tax treatment of restrictive covenants.

Restrictive Covenants (a.k.a. Non-Competition Agreements)
General Rules

19-134.   Restrictive covenants are arrangements under which a taxpayer agrees to have his ability to provide goods or services restricted in one or more ways. Such agreements may relate to particular products or services (e.g., the taxpayer will not provide audit services) and may refer to specific geographic areas (e.g., the taxpayer will not provide audit services in the greater Calgary area). They may or may not be limited in terms of time. It is not uncommon, particularly in the case of owner-managed businesses, for the purchaser to require the seller to sign a restrictive covenant.

19-135.   Until recently, the *Income Tax Act* did not contain specific guidance on amounts paid to taxpayers for agreeing to restrictive covenants. In the past, the CRA made repeated efforts to force recipient taxpayers to include such amounts in income. However, the courts foiled such attempts with great regularity, indicating that such receipts could be received by a taxpayer without tax consequences.

19-136.   Ever the sore loser, the CRA concluded that the best way to achieve the desired result would be through new legislation. A proposed ITA 56.4(2) would require that, in general, payments made to a taxpayer for agreeing to a restrictive covenant be included in income as an "other source" under Subdivision d. Under this general treatment, 100 percent of the amount paid would have to be included in the recipient's income when received or receivable.

Exceptions

19-137.   Fortunately for taxpayers, ITA 56.4(3) creates three exceptions to this general rule:

ITA 56.4(3)(a) - Employment Income   In cases where the payment relates to past employment with the payor, the receipt will be treated by the recipient as employment income. While 100 percent of the amount would still be subject to tax, classification as employment income would mean that it does not have to be included in the recipient's income until it is received (employment income is on a cash basis). When this exception is applicable, ITA 56.4(4)(a) allows the payor to treat the payment as wages paid or payable.

ITA 56.4(3)(b) - Cumulative Eligible Capital   When intangible capital property is being sold and the payor and the recipient jointly elect in prescribed form, the payment can be treated by the recipient as a deduction from cumulative eligible capital (CEC). In this case, ITA 56.4(4)(b) requires the purchaser to treat the payment as an eligible capital expenditure.

Without going through the fairly complex details, this treatment can result in none of the payment being currently taxed, three-quarters of the payment being taxed, one-half of the payment being taxed, or some combination of three-quarters and one-half of the payment being taxed.

ITA 56.4(3)(c) - Sale Of An Eligible Interest   An eligible interest is an interest in shares in a corporation that carries on business, or in a partnership that carries on business. In a situation where a restrictive covenant is sold in conjunction with an eligible interest, the amount received can be added to the proceeds of disposition. As was the case with the ITA 56.4(3)(b) exception, the payor and the recipient must file a joint election for this exception to apply. When this exception is applicable, ITA 56.4(4)(c) requires the purchaser to treat the payment as a cost of the purchase.

If this addition creates or increases a capital gain, only one-half of this amount will be subject to tax. Note that the application of this provision is more complex when there is more than one restrictive covenant involved in the sale of a single eligible interest.

19-138.   The first of these exceptions, treatment of the restrictive covenant payment as employment income, is not relevant to the material in this Chapter. However, the other two exceptions are very significant when a business is being sold and will be given further attention in our discussion of the alternative ways in which a business can be sold.

Sale Of Individual Assets

General Procedures

19-139.   Disposing of a business via a piece-by-piece sale of individual assets would only occur in certain situations. These could be described as follows:

- The business has not been successful in producing an adequate rate of return on the assets invested. In such situations, the most reasonable course of action may be the sale of individual assets.

- Some owner-managed businesses have income producing activities that are so closely tied to the skills of the owner/manager that the sale of the business independent of those skills would not be feasible.

19-140.   This type of disposition would only be appropriate in limited circumstances. Given that the circumstances associated with the particular business will dictate whether this approach will be used, there is no need to devote any attention to the advantages or disadvantages of this alternative.

Restrictive Covenants

19-141.   In the situations that are involved here, it is unlikely that a restrictive covenant will be used. However, if this was to occur, treatment of the amount involved as cumulative eligible capital would be possible. This treatment will be discussed in the next section dealing with the sale of total assets as a going concern, beginning in Paragraph 19-147.

Sale Of Assets As A Going Concern

General Procedures

19-142.   In contrast to a liquidation, where the assets are sold on an individual basis, the purchaser in this situation would acquire the corporation's assets as a going concern and, in so doing, would acquire any goodwill or other intangible assets that might be associated with the enterprise.

19-143.   The disposition of an incorporated business by selling all of the assets is considerably more complex than a disposition of shares. As was the case with the piece by piece sale of individual assets, the sale of all assets as a going concern may result in a combination of business income, capital gains, recapture, and terminal losses.

19-144.   In both types of asset sales, you should note that there are really two transactions involved. The first transaction involves the sale of assets and the payment of liabilities at the corporate level. Included in this process will be the determination of any tax liability resulting from the sale of the assets. At this point, the corporate assets would consist entirely of the after tax proceeds resulting from the disposition of the tangible and other assets of the corporation. In most situations, the owner will choose to distribute these assets and wind up the corporation.

19-145.   This distribution of the after tax proceeds of the sale of corporate assets is the second transaction and, in general, it will involve income tax effects for the recipient shareholders. Given this two transaction process, a complete analysis of the alternatives of selling the assets of the business versus disposing of the shares will require dealing with both taxation on the corporation as a result of disposing of the assets, and personal taxation as a result of distributing the after tax proceeds of this sale.

19-146.   In dealing with the sale of corporate assets, an understanding of the tax effects associated with such dispositions is required. These effects can be outlined as follows:

Cash   In most circumstances, the cash of the business will be retained in the business. If it is "sold", there will be no tax consequences associated with its disposition.

Accounts Receivable   In the absence of any special election, the sale of accounts receivable as a component of the sale of a business will be treated as a capital transaction. This means that any difference between the face value and the consideration received will be treated as a capital loss, only one-half of which will be deductible. However, ITA 22 provides for a joint election to treat the sale of receivables as an income transaction. This allows the purchaser to treat any difference between the amount paid for the receivables and the amount actually collected as a bad debt expense. A more detailed description of this election is presented in Chapter 8.

Inventories   Even when inventories are sold as part of the sale of a business, any difference between the sales price and the vendor's cost will be treated as ordinary business income. This is provided for in ITA 23 and, unlike the situation with the ITA 22 treatment of receivables, no election is required. From the point of view of the purchaser, the transfer price becomes the tax cost that will eventually be allocated to cost of goods sold.

Prepayments   There is no specific provision in the *Act* dealing with prepayments. However, in practice, their sale will be treated as an income transaction using the same general procedures that are applied to inventories. However, in most cases, prepayments will have a fair market value equal to their tax value. This means that they can be sold at fair market value without any tax consequences.

Non-Depreciable Capital Assets   The most common non-depreciable capital assets of a business are land and investments. Depending on the amount of consideration received for these assets, the transferor will have a capital gain or loss. With respect to capital losses, they can only be deducted from capital gains. If some of the consideration being paid for these assets is deferred, the corporation can use capital gains reserves to defer part of the applicable taxation. For the purchaser, the adjusted cost base of non-depreciable capital assets will be the purchase price, which presumably is the fair market value.

Depreciable Assets   The disposition of a depreciable asset can result in recapture, a terminal loss, or some combination of recapture and a capital gain. Unlike capital gains, recapture and terminal losses will be subject to 100 percent inclusion in, or deduction from, active business income and will be included in income eligible for the small business deduction. As was the case with non-depreciable capital assets, if some of the consideration for these assets is not received immediately, reserves can be used to defer the taxation of capital gains. The capital cost of depreciable assets to the purchaser will be the purchase price, which presumably is the fair market value.

Goodwill   If goodwill is present, in many cases it will not have a tax value in the records of the transferor. When the goodwill is sold, three-quarters of the consideration received will be subtracted from the cumulative eligible capital (CEC) account. If the existing CEC balance was nil, this will create a negative balance equal to three-quarters of the payment. After being adjusted to reflect the 50 percent capital gains inclusion rate, this negative balance will be included in the corporation's income. However, unlike a taxable capital gain, this inclusion will be included under ITA 14(1) as business income.

If the corporation has a positive CEC balance, the subtraction of three-quarters of the payment may leave a positive balance or, alternatively, a negative balance that is less than the amount that is subtracted. In the former case, the positive amount will be deductible in a manner similar to terminal losses on depreciable assets. In the latter case, the negative balance will have to be added to income to the extent that the corporation has made previous CEC deductions. If the negative balance exceeds the previous deductions, the remainder will be adjusted to the 50 percent capital gains inclusion rate and then added to income.

The purchaser will add three-quarters of the amount paid to his CEC balance.

Restrictive Covenants

19-147.   Restrictive covenants may take one of two different forms when there is a sale of the total assets of the corporation. If it is anticipated that the corporation will continue in business, the agreement can be between the purchaser of the assets and the corporation. In contrast, if the corporation is to be liquidated, the agreement will likely be between the purchaser and the former owner(s) of the shares. It is also possible that the purchaser will require both the corporation and the shareholders to sign a restrictive covenant.

19-148.   Whether the agreement is between the purchaser and the corporation or, alternatively, the purchaser and the shareholder(s) of the corporation, treatment of the amount as CEC would be possible (see Paragraph 19-137). If both parties are prepared to sign a joint election requiring the purchaser to add three-quarters of the payment to his CEC balance and the vendor to deduct three-quarters of the payment from his CEC balance, this treatment can be used. You should note that this election is only available when intangible capital property is involved in the sale.

19-149.   From the point of view of the vendor, the result will vary depending on whether there was an existing CEC balance at the time of the deduction. The various alternatives here were covered in our Paragraph 19-146 discussion of the sale of goodwill.

19-150.   If the payment is eligible for the joint election and the election is made, the purchaser will have to treat the payment for the restrictive covenant as an eligible capital expenditure. However, if the payment is not eligible or, if no joint election is filed, ITA 56.4 provides no specific guidance for the purchaser.

19-151.   This means that the purchaser will have to apply basic principles from other Sections of the *Income Tax Act*. Without regard to the fact that the vendor will be taxed on the full amount of the payment under ITA 56.4(2), the purchaser's treatment may involve a deduction of the full amount of the payment, an addition of the payment to one or more assets, or an addition of three-quarters of the payment to his CEC balance. The specific treatment by the purchaser will depend on the nature of the payment as determined under general tax principles.

Sale Of Shares

General Procedures

19-152.   In terms of accounting, legal, and tax considerations, this is the simplest way to sell a business. The calculation of the gain on the sale only requires the adjusted cost base of the shares to be subtracted from the proceeds received from their disposition. Any resulting difference will be a capital gain or loss, and will be subject to the usual treatment accorded to share dispositions.

19-153.   In preparing for the sale of shares, a shareholder will generally pay out any dividends that are reflected in the capital dividend account and/or that will generate a dividend refund. In addition, outstanding shareholder loans, either to or from the corporation, should be settled prior to the sale.

Lifetime Capital Gains Deduction

19-154.   If the corporation is a "qualified small business corporation" as defined in ITA 110.6(1), the disposition of shares may qualify for the lifetime capital gains deduction of $750,000. The conditions associated with the designation "qualified small business corporation" are discussed in Chapter 14. Note here, however, that this deduction is only available on the sale of shares by an individual. If the corporate assets are sold, either separately or as a group, this valuable deduction is not available.

Restrictive Covenants

19-155.   In cases where a business disposition involves a sale of shares, any restrictive covenant that is required will involve an agreement between the purchaser of the shares and the vendor of the shares.   In this situation the exception under ITA 56.4(3)(c) (see Paragraph 19-137) becomes important. The sale of shares would be a disposition of an eligible interest and this would allow the taxpayer receiving payment for the restrictive covenant to include it as part of the proceeds of disposition. As such, it would serve to create or increase a capital gain on the sale, only one-half of which would be taxable.

19-156.   Note that this treatment requires the vendor and purchaser to file a joint election and, if they fail to do so, the vendor will have to include the full amount of the payment in income when it is received or becomes receivable. If the election is filed, the purchaser will include the payment in the cost of his purchase. If the election is not filed, the treatment by the purchaser will require the application of general tax principles.

Evaluation Of Alternatives

Advantages Of Selling Shares

19-157.   Generally speaking, the vendor of a business will favour selling shares over selling assets. Factors favouring this alternative are as follows:

- The sale of shares offers the simplicity of a single transaction. In contrast, in a sale of assets, the vendor must deal with the legal and tax consequences arising at the corporate level. In addition, the vendor must steer the corporation through a winding-up procedure and deal with the personal tax consequences of these procedures. The greater complexity will require additional personal efforts on the part of the vendor. Also, the legal and accounting fees associated with these transactions are likely to be significant.

- Any income produced by the sale of shares will usually be reported as capital gains. At worst, only one-half of such gains are taxable. At best, the taxable gains may be reduced or eliminated through the use of the $750,000 lifetime capital gains deduction. If assets are sold by the corporation, some of the resulting income could be recaptured CCA, which must be included in income in full. In addition, if capital gains arise on the sale of assets, they will be treated as investment income to the corporation and will not be eligible for the small business deduction.

- If the enterprise has an unused non-capital loss carry forward, it will still be available to the enterprise if shares are sold. Any non-capital loss carry forwards are, of course, subject to the acquisition of control rules, requiring that they be applied against income earned in the same line of business in which the losses were incurred. However, if the sale of assets alternative is chosen, such loss carry forward balances will be completely unavailable to the purchaser.

- When a payment for a restrictive covenant is a component of the sale of shares, the vendor may be able to treat the amount received as an addition to his proceeds of disposition, rather than an amount that has to be fully included in income. This treatment is conditional on the vendor and purchaser filing a joint election, in which case the purchaser will add the amount paid to his acquisition cost.

- A sale of assets could result in the payment of land transfer taxes that would not be applicable if shares are sold.

Advantages Of Purchasing Assets

19-158.   As just described, there are a number of advantages that can be associated with selling shares, most of them benefitting the vendor. From the point of view of the purchaser, a purchase of assets is generally more desirable than a purchase of shares. Some of the advantages of purchasing assets are as follows:

- In acquiring assets, the purchaser acquires a completely new, and usually higher, set of tax values for the assets transferred. For example, consider a depreciable asset with a capital cost of $100,000, a UCC of $40,000, and a fair market value of $400,000. If shares are acquired, the CCA deductions available to the corporation will continue to be based on $40,000 and, if the assets are subsequently disposed of, capital gains will be determined from the original capital cost of $100,000. In contrast, if the asset was purchased in an arm's length transaction for its fair market value of $400,000, this amount would be the capital cost and UCC to the purchaser. This bump-up in asset values and the availability of higher CCA claims will significantly reduce the tax liabilities of the purchaser from the level that would have prevailed had the shares been purchased.

- Goodwill (cumulative eligible capital) can be recognized when assets are acquired. The CEC deductions related to these amounts are not available if shares are acquired.

- If shares are acquired, all of the assets must be acquired. If redundant assets are present, they can be left out of an acquisition of assets.

- If shares are acquired, the purchaser becomes responsible for any future tax reassessments. This exposure results because the corporation continues to operate and the new owner inherits any difficulties that may be lurking in past returns. If assets are purchased, the new owner starts with a clean slate and, in general, has no responsibility for any tax problems that may exist from previous corporate tax returns. The same may also apply to potential non-tax liabilities such as those related to polluting the environment.

- Most of the preceding discussion has implicitly assumed that the corporation's assets have fair market values in excess of their related tax values. If this is not the case and unrealized losses are present, selling assets may be advantageous to the vendor as well as the purchaser. This is based on the fact that the vendor would prefer to have fully deductible terminal or business losses, rather than capital losses that are only one-half deductible against taxable capital gains.

Conclusion

19-159. While each situation needs to be evaluated on the basis of the specific assets and values involved, in general, a vendor will wish to sell shares while a purchaser will wish to acquire assets. As a result, negotiations will usually involve higher prices being offered for the assets of the business than are offered for the shares of the incorporated business. The following very simplified example illustrates the type of analysis that is required in comparing a sale of assets and a sale of shares.

Example

19-160. To illustrate the sale of an incorporated business, we will use the following example.

> **Example**   Mr. O'Leary owns all of the outstanding shares of O'Leary Ltd., a Canadian controlled private corporation established in 1989. Mr. O'Leary has reached retirement age and wishes to dispose of the business. He has received an offer to buy the shares for $180,000 or, alternatively, the assets of the business for $200,000. All of the liabilities of the business have been settled in preparation for the sale.
>
> The cost of Mr. O'Leary's original investment was $50,000. As no additional investment has been made, this is also his adjusted cost base and paid up capital for the outstanding shares. The corporation is taxed at a combined federal/provincial rate of 18 percent on business income and 50 percent on investment income (this includes the ITA 123.3 tax on investment income). The corporation has no balance in its RDTOH account, its capital dividend account or its GRIP account. Mr. O'Leary is subject to a combined federal/provincial rate of 46 percent on non-dividend income and 31 percent on non-eligible dividends received.
>
> Relevant information on the assets of the business is as follows:

Asset	Cost	Fair Market Value
Cash	$ 5,000	$ 5,000
Receivables	10,000	10,000
Inventories	55,000	60,000·
Land	20,000	40,000
Plant And Equipment (UCC = $45,000)	95,000	60,000
Goodwill	Nil	25,000
Total	$185,000	$200,000

Sale Of Shares For $180,000

19-161.   With respect to the sale of shares, the tax consequences are as follows:

Proceeds Of Disposition	$180,000
Adjusted Cost Base	(50,000)
Capital Gain	$130,000
Inclusion Rate	1/2
Taxable Capital Gain (For Mr. O'Leary)	$ 65,000

19-162.   At a 46 percent rate, the normal Tax Payable on this gain would be $29,900, leaving Mr. O'Leary with after tax funds of $150,100 ($180,000 - $29,900). However, it is likely that O'Leary Ltd. is a qualified small business corporation. If this is the case, the $750,000 lifetime capital gains deduction could be used to eliminate all of the taxes on this disposition of shares, resulting in Mr. O'Leary retaining the entire $180,000 proceeds. Alternative minimum tax might be applicable if the capital gain is sheltered through the lifetime capital gains deduction.

Sale Of Assets For $200,000

19-163.   The tax consequences resulting from selling the assets are calculated as follows:

Account	Taxable Income
Inventories ($60,000 - $55,000)	$ 5,000
Plant And Equipment - Recaptured CCA ($60,000 - $45,000)	15,000
Goodwill [($25,000)(3/4)(1/2 ÷ 3/4)]	12,500
Active Business Income	$32,500
Taxable Capital Gain On Land [($40,000 - $20,000)(1/2)]	10,000
Corporate Taxable Income	$42,500

19-164.   Except for the $10,000 taxable capital gain on the disposition of Land, all of this income is active business income. The resulting Tax Payable would be calculated as follows:

Business Income [(18%)($32,500)]	$ 5,850
Aggregate Investment Income [(50%)($10,000)]	5,000
Corporate Tax Payable	$10,850

19-165.   The taxable capital gain would result in a $2,667 [(26-2/3%)($10,000)] addition to the RDTOH. The allocation to the capital dividend account would be as follows:

Non-Taxable Portion Of Capital Gain On Land [(1/2)($20,000)]	$10,000
Non-Taxable Portion Of Goodwill [($25,000)(1/4)(1/2 ÷ 1/4)]	12,500
Capital Dividend Account	$22,500

19-166.   Given the preceding analysis of the liquidation of the corporate assets, the net cash retained by Mr. O'Leary after the distribution of corporate assets can be calculated as follows:

Proceeds Of Disposition - Sale Of Assets	$200,000
Corporate Tax Payable (Before Dividend Refund)	(10,850)
Dividend Refund (RDTOH balance)	2,667
Available for Distribution	$191,817
Paid Up Capital	(50,000)
ITA 84(2) Deemed Dividend	$141,817
Capital Dividend (Balance In Account - Election Required)	(22,500)
Deemed Taxable Dividend	$119,317
Tax Rate (On Non-Eligible Dividends Received)	31%
Personal Tax Payable On Non-Eligible Dividend	$ 36,988

19-167.   There would be no capital gain on the distribution as shown in the following:

Total Distribution	$191,817
ITA 84(2) Deemed Dividend	(141,817)
Deemed Proceeds Of Disposition	$ 50,000
Adjusted Cost Base Of The Shares	(50,000)
Capital Gain	Nil

19-168.   Based on the preceding calculations, Mr. O'Leary's after tax retention from the sale of assets would be calculated as follows:

Amount Distributed	$191,817
Tax On Deemed Dividend	(36,988)
Cash Retained	$154,829

19-169.   This amount is larger than the $150,100 that would be retained from a sale of shares if the resulting capital gain was subject to tax. However, it is significantly smaller than the $180,000 that would be retained from a sale of shares if the lifetime capital gains deduction could be used to eliminate the entire gain on the sale.

GST Implications

Sale Of Assets Or Shares

19-170.   The sale of the taxable assets of a business is a taxable supply under the GST. This applies regardless of the legal form in which the business is carried on. However, where "all or substantially all" of the assets that the purchaser needs to carry on a business are being acquired by the purchaser, the GST legislation allows the vendor and purchaser to elect to treat the supply as if it were zero-rated.

19-171.   This applies to businesses that provide exempt supplies, as well as to businesses that provide fully taxable or zero-rated supplies. The use of the election is not permitted when the vendor is a registrant and the purchaser is a non-registrant. However, the election can be used when both the vendor and the purchaser are not GST registrants.

19-172.   If the election is made, the vendor does not collect GST on the sale of taxable supplies, and the purchaser cannot claim an input tax credit. As a result, a transfer of the assets of a business can be made without payment of GST. When this occurs, the vendor and purchaser are required to file a joint election with the CRA by the due date of the GST return covering the reporting period in which the sale took place. The purpose of this election is to provide cash flow relief to the purchaser of a business, who would normally have to wait for a refund from the CRA of the GST paid on the purchase of the assets of a business.

19-173.   If the election is not made, and the assets being sold were last used by the vendor primarily in commercial activities, GST will be collected on the sale. Offsetting input tax credits may be available to the purchaser through the normal input tax credit procedures. Whether or not the election is used, if the transferred business is a commercial activity, the vendor and purchaser will be able to claim input tax credits on any costs incurred to carry out the transaction.

19-174. In determining whether "all or substantially all" of the assets necessary to carry on the business are transferred, the CRA relies on a 90 percent or more test. The CRA has several policy papers on this election in order to provide registrants with guidance in determining compliance with the 90 percent or more test.

19-175. As a general rule, the sale of shares in a corporation is not a taxable supply because, under the GST legislation, the sale of a financial instrument such as a share is an exempt supply. As a result, share for share exchanges are not taxable for GST purposes. Any related costs, such as legal and accounting fees that are subject to GST will generally be refundable, provided the business is involved in a commercial activity.

Other Situations

Amalgamations, Mergers, Winding-Up Of A Business

19-176. Where two corporations are merged or amalgamated into a single corporation, or the activities of one corporation are wound up through a merger with another corporation, the new corporation is generally treated for GST purposes as a person separate from each of the predecessor corporations.

19-177. If the transfer of assets involves an amalgamation under ITA 87 or a winding-up under ITA 88(1), the transfer of assets is deemed not to be a taxable supply for GST purposes and no election is required. The asset or property transferred on the merger or amalgamation is not a taxable supply under the legislation. As a result, there are no GST consequences.

19-178. For GST reporting and remittance purposes, the new corporation's threshold amounts are calculated with reference to supplies made by the predecessor corporations. The summation of the threshold amounts to become the new corporation's threshold amount may necessitate more frequent GST reporting and remitting.

Transfers Within Corporate Groups

19-179. Transfers of goods and services between members of corporate groups will normally attract GST. However, an election can be made to have such transfers deemed to be made for nil consideration (only for GST purposes), resulting in no required payment of GST.

19-180. The conditions for this election are quite strict and require either the ownership of at least 90 percent of the voting shares of one corporation by the other, or that the companies be sister corporations owned by a parent corporation. In addition, the electing corporations must be Canadian residents and the supplies involved must be used exclusively (more than 90 percent) in a commercial activity.

Holding Companies

19-181. Although many holding companies only hold shares or debt and do not carry on a "commercial activity" in the usual sense, GST legislation allows holding companies to register for the GST and claim input tax credits if they hold shares or debt in another company that owns property that is used at least 90 percent for commercial activities. These provisions allow holding companies to obtain refunds of GST paid on the purchase of property or services solely related to the holding of the shares or debt.

Ceasing To Carry On Business

19-182. When a person ceases to carry on a commercial activity, or becomes a small supplier and, as a result, ceases to be a registrant, the person is deemed to have sold all assets at fair market value upon deregistration. Similar rules, discussed in Chapter 10, apply to changes in the use of capital property used or acquired for use in a commercial activity and the cessation of use of capital property in a commercial activity. If the assets are used for commercial purposes, GST will be payable on the deemed dispositions.

Tax Shelters

A Cautionary Note

19-183.   As with any area where large sums of money are involved, tax shelters are an extremely complex area of tax practice. As a reflection of this fact, we hesitated to include material on this subject in a general text on Canadian income tax such as this one.

19-184.   However, it is our experience that all sorts of taxpayers become involved in these schemes. It is difficult to advise a couple with moderate income, who are eager to invest in a limited partnership that is supposed to ensure the future financial well-being of their family, when they have no idea of the nature of their investment and, in many cases, do not realize that the cost of having to deal with its tax aspects exceeds the potential real return on the investment. Given this problem, we have included a brief discussion of tax shelters in this material.

19-185.   Our goal in including this review is not to make you an expert in this area. Rather, our hope is that we can provide enough information to give you some familiarity with the types of tax shelters that exist and to show that these investments should not be made without sound and, most importantly, independent advice.

Introduction

19-186.   The term tax shelter is used in a variety of ways, most commonly to describe various types of investments that either defer the taxation of income to a later point in time or, alternatively, generate an absolute reduction in Tax Payable. This distinction is not always a clear one in that, if a deferral results in Taxable Income being recognized in a period in which the taxpayer is in a lower tax bracket, the deferral process may also generate an absolute reduction in Tax Payable.

19-187.   In a practical context, the term tax shelter has two different meanings. In some cases, an investment will have a negative or nil cash flow, but will produce tax deductions that can be applied against other sources of income. For example, an investment in a limited partnership might produce no cash flows during the first year after acquisition. However, the partnership losses may be applied against the investor's employment or other income. In this situation, other sources of income are being sheltered.

19-188.   In other circumstances, the tax shelter investment may produce nil Taxable Income, despite the fact that it is generating a positive cash flow. Ordinary real estate investments, where positive operating cash flows are offset by CCA deductions, often exhibit this characteristic. In this case, the positive cash flow, rather than another source of income, is being sheltered.

19-189.   ITA 237.1 provides a definition of tax shelters. In general terms, this definition indicates that tax shelters involve the acquisition of a property, including property acquired under a gifting arrangement, in respect of which it is represented that the acquisition of the property, or the donation or contribution of the property under a gifting arrangement, would generate any combination of tax credits or deductions that in total would equal or exceed the cost of acquiring the property.

19-190.   Tax changes during recent years have severely limited publicly available investments for sheltering income. There are not many tax shelters available and those that exist have had their tax benefits restricted. The major type of tax shelter remaining is resource investments.

Marketing Of Tax Shelters

19-191.   It is important to stress at the outset that losing money is not a desirable tax shelter. Millions of dollars have been lost by investors attempting to reduce taxes without looking at the underlying investment characteristics that were present. It is unlikely that a bad investment can be converted into a desirable one because of its tax features.

19-192. Investors must use great caution in evaluating the claims made by promoters of tax shelters, with decisions being based on all of the tax and non-tax features that the investment provides. At the end of this section, there is a list of some important factors to consider in the evaluation of tax shelter investments.

Legal Forms

Direct Investment

19-193. The most straightforward tax shelter investment involves an individual investor making a direct investment in the relevant property. This approach is very common in real estate investments, particularly in situations involving relatively small amounts of funds. However, when films, resource properties, or significant parcels of real estate are involved, the need to accumulate larger amounts of funds will generally require that the amounts be raised from a number of investors.

Limited Partnerships

19-194. When more than one investor is needed to support a project, a common legal form is the limited partnership. The general partner in a limited partnership has unlimited liability and has control of the business. Limited partners cannot play an active role in the control of the business operations of the partnership. While the limited partners have limited liability similar to that of shareholders in a corporation, they can also take advantage of tax benefits resulting from being a partner.

19-195. This approach allows the funds of several investors to be combined and, at the same time, any possibility that the limited partners' other assets are at risk is avoided. This form has been widely used for investments in real estate, Canadian films, and resource properties.

At-Risk Rules

19-196. At one point in time the limited partnership form could be used to create an investment in which the potential tax deductions exceeded the amount that the investor could lose on the investment. To correct this situation, the "at-risk" rules were created. These rules limit the amount that a partner can deduct for tax purposes to the "at-risk amount" at the end of the year.

19-197. The following simple example will serve to give you a basic understanding of how ITA 96(2.2) requires the "at-risk" amount to be calculated. If you have further interest in these rules, there is a more extensive discussion of their application in Chapter 20. This Chapter also provides general coverage of partnerships.

Example Mr. Hilary has purchased a limited partnership interest that has a cost of $100,000 with only $5,000 paid in cash. The remaining $95,000 of the cost is owed to the partnership. If Mr. Hilary's share of the limited partnership loss for the first year is $12,000, he can only deduct his $5,000 at-risk amount on his current year's tax return. This is calculated as follows:

The partner's adjusted cost base		$100,000
Deduct:		
Amounts owing to the partnership by the partner	($95,000)	
Amounts or benefits that the partner has been promised to protect him from loss on the investment	Nil	(95,000)
At-Risk Amount (before allocation of current loss)		$ 5,000
Deduct - The partner's share of the current year's undistributed loss		(12,000)
Limited Partnership Loss Carry Forward		($ 7,000)

Flow Through Shares

19-198.   Flow through shares are issued by corporations, usually in the resource industries, so that certain claims for tax deductions or credits can be transferred to the purchaser. Through such arrangements, the investor is entitled to claim the company's deductions for such items as Canadian Exploration Expense and, in the case of mining exploration, Earned Depletion Allowances. After using the available deductions, the investor is left with shares that constitute capital property.

19-199.   In most cases, the write-offs are sufficiently generous that the adjusted cost base of the shares will be nil, and all of the proceeds from any subsequent sale will be treated as capital gains. The liquidity of the shares will depend on whether they are publicly traded, which in turn will influence the entire disposition process and the ultimate return that is made on the investment.

19-200.   Prior to 1986, it was possible for the issuer to ensure the liquidity of the investment by agreeing to buy back the shares at a price specified at the time of issue. Current legislation requires that any future repurchase of shares be based on the fair market value at the time of repurchase, an arrangement that can result in financial losses.

Resource Investments

19-201.   Tax shelter investments in the oil and gas, and mining industries are usually in the form of flow through shares or limited partnership interests. The basic types of tax deductions available through these investment vehicles are briefly described as follows:

Canadian Exploration Expenses   Provided these costs are incurred within the appropriate time period, they are 100 percent deductible on a flow through basis.

Canadian Development Expenses   These costs are fully deductible, but only on the basis of 30 percent per year, with the 30 percent applied to the declining balance amount.

19-202.   The losses that can be deducted through resource limited partnerships are limited by the previously mentioned "at-risk" rules. For individuals subject to maximum rates of personal taxation, these deductions can generate tax savings in excess of the cash flows required to carry the investment. This, of course, is dependent on financing a significant portion of the investment. It hardly needs to be pointed out, however, that there are significant risks associated with investments of this type.

Rental Properties

General Rules

19-203.   The general rules with respect to the taxation of rental properties were presented in Chapter 9 and will not be repeated here. As previously mentioned, three factors limit the tax advantages related to owning rental properties. These are as follows:

- Capital cost allowances cannot be used to produce or increase a rental loss to be deducted against other income.

- Each rental property, with a building cost in excess of $50,000, must be allocated to a separate CCA class.

- At the owner's death there is a deemed disposition at fair market value, unless the property is bequeathed to a spouse or a spousal trust.

19-204.   Prior to 1972, it was possible to generate non-cash flow losses on rental properties for indefinite periods of time. Older properties could be replaced as their UCC decreased. Further, in the absence of the separate class requirement, the replacement process did not engender recapture. In fact, this could go on until the taxpayer died, at which point the property could be transferred to a spouse, again without creating recapture. In those "good old days", rental properties represented an almost perfect tax shelter. Unfortunately, the "good old days" are gone for investments in rental properties.

19-205. The inability to deduct CCA to produce a rental loss has reduced the tax advantages associated with real estate investments. However, CCA can still be used to shelter a positive cash flow from real estate investments. For example, a $200,000 building might produce a net cash flow (gross rents, less interest, property taxes, and other out of pocket costs) of $7,000 per year. As the CCA rate on such a building is 4 percent, the $8,000 (ignoring the half-year rules) of CCA would produce a nil Net Income For Tax Purposes, despite the presence of a positive cash flow.

19-206. In many cases, the major motivation for holding real estate is its appreciation in value, particularly in view of the fact that such increases in value are taxed at favourable capital gains rates. Very large gains have been realized during certain periods of time in particular markets. However, this is not always the case. During some periods of time and in some markets, gains may be modest or non-existent. Another potential problem in some areas of Canada is that real estate can be a very illiquid investment.

Evaluation Of Tax Shelter Investments

19-207. As noted previously, the evaluation of a tax shelter investment should take into consideration all of the tax and non-tax factors that are associated with the investment. This, of course, requires a complex evaluation process that must be applied on an investment by investment basis. However, there are a number of general points that can be relevant in this evaluation:

Alternative Minimum Tax   Promoters of tax shelter investments rarely include the alternative minimum tax in their projections. As tax shelters can create an alternative minimum tax liability, it should be considered in the evaluation process. An investor who uses tax shelters to an extent that minimum tax is incurred will often find that the actual rates of return, after accounting for the alternative minimum tax cost, are not attractive.

Capital Gains Treatment   As the projected return on tax shelters often includes a capital gains component, it is important to examine the particular characteristics of the investment to ascertain whether the expected capital gains treatment will be available.

CNIL   Many tax shelter investments will cause additions to the Cumulative Net Investment Loss (CNIL) balance. When this happens, the availability of the $500,000 lifetime capital gains deduction on qualified property is reduced.

Interest Deductibility   As noted in Chapter 9, care has to be exercised to ensure that interest related to investments is deductible. To be deductible, the interest must be incurred to earn property or business income. However, interest expense incurred to make investments for capital appreciation, only, does not qualify. For example, if a tax shelter involves vacant land to be held for capital appreciation, interest costs on financing associated with this land will not be deductible as they are incurred. Special rules also limit the deduction of interest related to vacant land being held for business purposes. The lack of interest deductibility can significantly change the expected rate of return on a tax shelter investment.

Guarantees   Tax shelter investments can provide cash flow or repurchase guarantees and, in many cases, these appear to significantly reduce the risk associated with the investment. However, such guarantees are only as good as the financial ability of the guarantor to make good on promised payments. Guarantees can also affect the calculation of an investor's at-risk amount.

The Promoter   To a certain extent, the success of virtually all tax shelters requires a promoter with the ability and integrity to protect the interest of investors in the arrangement. Care should be taken to ascertain the reputation of the vendor of the tax shelter, both in the business community at large and in the more specific area of the tax shelter investment.

Filing Requirements The tax shelter promoter must provide the CRA with an annual information return and investors with a supplementary information form T5003 each year. The investors' form contains an identification number for the tax shelter and must be filed in order to claim any shelter benefits on a tax return. The investor should ensure that the tax shelter promoter has an identification number before investing. Since many of the tax shelters require more complex tax reporting, the investor should be assured that the information form will be issued by the promoter in a timely fashion and will contain accurate and appropriate tax information. If there is a dispute over the validity of the tax shelter, the CRA can readily identify the investors involved by using the identification number.

19-208. An additional consideration is that investments in tax shelters can significantly complicate filing the investor's personal tax return. Such investments can easily convert the filing of a simple T1 tax return into a process in which professional assistance is essential. It would also be prudent for an investor to discuss the tax shelter with a tax professional before investing. The costs of such assistance can significantly reduce the effective rate of return on tax shelter investments.

Key Terms Used In This Chapter

19-209. The following is a list of the key terms used in this Chapter. These terms, and their meanings, are compiled in the Glossary Of Key Terms located at the back of the separate paper Study Guide and on the Student CD-ROM.

Adjusted Cost Base	Proceeds Of Disposition
Amalgamation	PUC
Business Combination	Qualified Small Business Corporation
Canadian Corporation	Recapture Of CCA
Capital Gain	Redemption Of Shares
Control (CICA Handbook)	Reorganization Of Capital (ITA 86)
Convertible Property	Rollover
Corporation	Share For Share Exchange (ITA 85.1)
Disposition	Small Business Corporation
Exchange Of Shares In A	Subsidiary
Reorganization (ITA 86)	Tax Shelter (ITA 237.1)
Gift	Tax Shelter (Other Meaning 1)
Goodwill	Tax Shelter (Other Meaning 2)
Legal Stated Capital	Taxable Canadian Corporation
Lifetime Capital Gains Deduction	Terminal Loss
Merger	Vertical Amalgamation
Non-Share Consideration	Winding-Up Of A 90 Percent Owned
Paid Up Capital	Subsidiary
Parent Company	Winding-Up Of A Canadian Corporation

References

19-210. For more detailed study of the material in this Chapter, we refer you to the following:

ITA 22	Sale Of Accounts Receivable
ITA 23	Sale Of Inventory
ITA 39(4)	Election Concerning Disposition Of Canadian Securities
ITA 51	Convertible Property
ITA 51.1	Conversion Of Debt Obligation
ITA 54	Definitions (Proceeds Of Disposition)
ITA 84(2)	Distribution on Winding-Up, Etc.
ITA 84(3)	Redemption Of shares
ITA 84(5)	Amount Distributed Or Paid Where A Share ...
ITA 85	Transfer Of Property To Corporation By Shareholders
ITA 85.1	Share For Share Exchange
ITA 86	Exchange Of Shares By A Shareholder In Course Of Reorganization Of Capital
ITA 87	Amalgamations
ITA 88(1)	Winding-Up (Of A 90 Percent Owned Subsidiary)
ITA 88(2)	Winding-Up Of A Canadian Corporation
ITA 96(2.2)	At-Risk Amount
ITA 110.6	Capital Gains Exemption
ITA 237.1	Definitions (Tax Shelters)
IC 89-3	Policy Statement On Business Equity Valuations
IC 89-4	Tax Shelter Reporting
IT-115R2	Fractional Interest In Shares
IT-126R2	Meaning Of "Winding-Up"
IT-140R3	Buy-Sell Agreements
IT-142R3	Settlement Of Debts On The Winding-up Of A Corporation
IT-146R4	Shares Entitling Shareholders To Choose Taxable Or Capital Dividends
IT-149R4	Winding-Up Dividend
IT-169	Price Adjustment Clauses
IT-188R	Sale Of Accounts Receivable
IT-195R4	Rental Property - Capital Cost Allowance Restrictions
IT-243R4	Dividend Refund To Private Corporations
IT-287R2	Sale Of Inventory
IT-302R3	Losses Of A Corporation - The Effect That Acquisitions Of Control, Amalgamations, And Windings-Up Have On Their Deductibility - After January 15, 1987
IT-444R	Corporations — Involuntary Dissolutions
IT-450R	Share For Share Exchange
IT-474R	Amalgamations Of Canadian Corporations
IT-533	Interest Deductibility and Related Issues

Problems For Self Study

(The solutions for these problems can be found in the separate Study Guide.)

Self Study Problem Nineteen - 1

John Farnsworth owns 75 percent of the outstanding common shares of Farnsworth Inc. His original investment was $99,000 on December 31, 2004. On this same date, his only daughter acquires the remaining 25 percent of the common shares of Farnsworth Inc. for $33,000.

Mr. Farnsworth's original investment of $99,000 is also the paid up capital and the adjusted cost base of his shares. On December 31, 2007, the fair market value of Mr. Farnworth's shares is $450,000.

As Mr. Farnsworth is nearing retirement, he would like to freeze the value of his estate. To this end, he exchanges his common shares in Farnsworth Inc. for cash of $69,000 and preferred shares that are redeemable at his discretion for $381,000 in cash. The new shares have a legal stated capital of $99,000 and a fair market value of $381,000. The Company has a nil balance in its General Rate Income Pool (GRIP) account.

The exchange takes place on December 31, 2007.

Required: Determine the following:

A. The paid up capital of the newly issued redeemable preferred shares.

B. The adjusted cost base of the newly issued redeemable preferred shares.

C. The proceeds of disposition that Mr. Farnsworth would use to calculate any capital gain arising from the disposition of his old common shares of Farnsworth Inc.

D. The tax consequences for Mr. Farnsworth of this reorganization of the capital of Farnsworth Inc.

E. The tax consequences for Mr. Farnsworth if the new Farnsworth Inc. preferred shares are redeemed for $381,000.

Self Study Problem Nineteen - 2

Mr. Jerry Long owns 90 percent of the outstanding common shares of Long Industries Ltd., while his 35 year old daughter, Ms. Gerri Long, owns the remaining 10 percent. The Company was established in 1994 by Mr. Ian Seto, an unrelated party, with an initial investment of $100,000. No further investment was made by Mr. Seto and, during 1997, Mr. Long purchased 100 percent of the shares for their fair market value of $360,000.

During 2001, he gave 10 percent of the shares to his daughter. The fair market value of 100 percent of the shares at that time was $450,000.

It is now December 1, 2007, and the fair market value of 100 percent of the Long Industries Ltd. shares is $900,000. In order to freeze his estate, Mr. Long would like to use the provisions of ITA 86 to reorganize the capital of the corporation. He is considering two alternative approaches to structuring this reorganization as follows:

> **Approach One**   Mr. Long would exchange all of his common shares in return for a note with a fair market value of $90,000, and retractable preferred shares with a legal stated capital of $234,000 and a fair market value of $720,000.

> **Approach Two**   Mr. Long would exchange all of his common shares in return for a note with a fair market value of $50,000, and retractable preferred shares with a legal stated capital of $40,000 and a fair market value of $660,000.

The Company has a nil balance in its General Rate Income Pool (GRIP) account.

Required: For each of the two suggested approaches determine:

- the amount of any gift that Mr. Long has made to his daughter;
- the PUC of the new preferred shares;
- his adjusted cost base for the new preferred shares;
- the amount of any deemed dividends arising on the exchange;
- any capital gain or loss resulting from the exchange of the common shares, and
- a brief description of the net economic effect of the reorganization transaction that includes whether or not he has succeeded in freezing his estate.

Self Study Problem Nineteen - 3

Ricon Ltd. owns 90 percent of the outstanding shares of Lynn Inc. Ricon acquired the Lynn shares in 2005 at a cost of $380,000. Their current fair market value is $490,000. The only asset owned by Lynn Inc. is a parcel of land. Lynn had paid $175,000 for this land in 2000 and, at the time Ricon Ltd. acquired the shares of Lynn Inc., the fair market value of the land was $390,000. The land now has a fair market value of $425,000. Lynn has paid no dividends since its shares were acquired by Ricon.

Required: The two Companies wish to combine using either ITA 87 or ITA 88(1). Which provision should be used in this situation? Explain your conclusion.

Self Study Problem Nineteen - 4

Intertel Inc., a Canadian controlled private corporation, has been in operation for a number of years, and in the beginning was a profitable enterprise. However, in recent years it has become apparent that its competitive position has been badly eroded and it is not likely to earn a satisfactory return on its invested capital. As a consequence, the shareholders have agreed to a liquidation of the Company. The Company's year end is December 31.

In contemplation of the liquidation, a Balance Sheet has been prepared based on the tax values of its assets and liabilities as at December 31, 2007. This Balance Sheet, after all closing entries, is as follows:

Intertel Inc.
Balance Sheet
As At December 31, 2007

Inventories (Net Realizable Value And Tax Cost)	$ 43,750
Refundable Dividend Tax On Hand	33,750
Land - Capital Cost	778,750
Building - Undepreciated Capital Cost	732,500
Total Assets	**$1,588,750**
Liabilities	Nil
Paid Up Capital	$ 68,750
Retained Earnings	1,520,000
Total Equities	**$1,588,750**

Other Information:

1. The Land has a current fair market value of $1,553,750. The Building had an original cost of $1,093,750. The building's fair market value on December 31, 2007 is $1,591,250.

2. On December 31, 2007, the Company has a balance in its Capital Dividend account of $268,750. It has a nil balance in its General Rate Income Pool (GRIP) account.

3. The adjusted cost base of the shares is equal to $68,750, the original capital investment by the shareholders.

4. The corporation pays tax at a combined federal and provincial rate of 18 percent on income eligible for the small business deduction, 37 percent on other active business income, and 50-2/3 percent on investment income. This latter rate includes the ITA 123.3 refundable tax on the investment income of Canadian controlled private corporations.

5. No dividends were paid in the previous year ending December 31, 2006.

6. All of the assets are disposed of at their fair market values on January 1, 2008.

Required:

A. Calculate the amount that will be available for distribution to the shareholders after the liquidation.

B. Determine the components of the distribution to the shareholders, and the amount of taxable capital gains that will accrue to them once the proceeds of the liquidation are distributed. Assume that appropriate elections or designations will be made to minimize the taxes that will be paid by the shareholders.

Self Study Problem Nineteen - 5

Mr. Donald Brock is the sole shareholder of Brock Enterprises, a Canadian controlled private corporation. While the business has, for the most part, operated successfully, Mr. Brock wishes to devote his attention to other matters and is considering selling the enterprise. The corporation has a December 31 year end.

To date, he has received two different offers for the business. An individual has offered to pay $455,000 for all of the shares of Brock Enterprises. Alternatively, a company has offered to pay $491,000 for the assets of the business and assume all current liabilities.

In order to be in a better position to analyze the offers that he has received for the business, Mr. Brock has had a statement of assets prepared as at December 31, 2007. This statement provides the values included in his accounting records, values that are relevant for tax purposes and the estimated fair market values. This statement, after all closing entries, is as follows:

	Accounting Book Value	Tax Value	Fair Market Value
Cash	$ 14,000	$ 14,000	$ 14,000
Accounts Receivable	24,500	24,500	24,500
Inventories	105,000	105,000	109,500
Land	35,000	35,000	70,000
Building (Note)	122,500	35,000	136,500
Equipment (Note)	87,500	63,000	42,000
Goodwill	Nil	Nil	164,500
Totals	$388,500	$276,500	$561,000

Note   The accounting value in the assets schedule equals its capital cost (the accumulated depreciation is shown with the equities).

The related accounting and tax figures on the equity side of the Balance Sheet, on this same date, were as follows:

	Accounting Book Value	Tax Value
Current Liabilities	$ 70,000	$ 70,000
Future Income Tax Liability	10,500	N/A
Accumulated Depreciation On Buildings And Equipment	77,000	N/A
Common Stock - No Par	52,500	52,500
Capital Dividend Account	N/A	70,000
Other Income Retained	N/A	84,000
Retained Earnings	178,500	N/A
Totals	$388,500	$276,500

On December 31, 2007, Brock Enterprises has no balance in its RDTOH account or its General Rate Income Pool (GRIP) account.

The adjusted cost base of the shares of Brock Enterprises is equal to the invested capital of $52,500. The corporation is subject to a combined federal and provincial tax rate of 18 percent on income eligible for the small business deduction and 47 percent (including the ITA 123.3 refundable tax on the investment income of Canadian controlled private corporations) on other income.

The sale of the business will take place early in January, 2008.

Mr. Brock will be in the maximum tax bracket and will taxed at an overall combined rate of 47 percent on regular income and 31 percent on any non-eligible dividend income that he receives. He has realized other capital gains sufficient to absorb the maximum limit for the lifetime capital gains deduction.

Required: Determine which of the two offers Mr. Brock should accept. Assume that appropriate elections or designations will be made to minimize the taxes that will be paid by Mr. Brock.

Assignment Problems

(The solutions for these problems are only available in the solutions manual that has been provided to your instructor.)

Assignment Problem Nineteen - 1

Limbo Company currently has the following assets:

Asset	Capital Cost	Tax Value	FMV
Equipment	$ 1,000	$ 300	$ 700
Land	14,000	14,000	16,500
Goodwill	Nil	Nil	2,000

There are no liabilities and no tax loss carry forwards. Limbo is 90 percent owned by Dunbar Holdings Ltd., who purchased the shares of Limbo Company for $18,000 five years ago. At that time, the Equipment was valued at its capital cost, the Land was valued at $19,000, a total of $20,000. There was no Goodwill. Limbo has paid dividends of $2,000 since its acquisition.

Required: Dunbar does not wish to have Limbo continue as a separate legal entity. As a consequence, it will use either ITA 87 or ITA 88(1) to absorb Limbo into its operations. For each asset owned by Limbo, outline what the tax consequences would be if:

A. Limbo was amalgamated into Dunbar Holdings using Section 87.
B. Limbo was rolled into Dunbar Holdings using a Section 88(1) winding-up.

Assignment Problem Nineteen - 2

In 2003, Acme Ltd. purchased all of the outstanding voting shares of Cross Industries for cash of $1,400,000. The assets of Cross Industries at the time of the acquisition had tax values of $1,250,000, and included a piece of land that was being held as a location for a possible second manufacturing facility. This land had been acquired in 1999 for $640,000 and, at the time Acme acquired the Cross shares, it had a fair market value of $705,000.

Acme believes that the operations of Cross Industries have become so integrated with its own, that it no longer makes sense to operate Cross as a separate entity. As a consequence, they are considering the possibility of absorbing Cross using an ITA 88(1) winding-up. At this time, the tax values of the assets of Cross Industries total $1,270,000. The Company is still holding the land for the additional manufacturing facility and it now has a fair market value of $790,000. Cross Industries has paid Acme Ltd. dividends totaling $20,000 since its acquisition.

Required: Explain the tax implications of the proposed winding-up from the point of view of both Acme Ltd. and Cross Industries.

Assignment Problem Nineteen - 3

Mr. Mark and his son, Jack, own, respectively, 80 percent and 20 percent of the 1,000 common shares of Markit Ltd. They acquired their shares four years ago, when the Company was incorporated, for $8,000 and $2,000, respectively. The current fair market value of the Markit shares is $2,400,000. Markit Ltd. is not a qualified small business corporation.

The Company has a nil balance in its General Rate Income Pool (GRIP) account.

Mr. Mark wishes to freeze the value of his shares at their current value. To accomplish this goal, he will exchange these shares for preferred shares of Markit Ltd. with legal stated capital of $8,000 and a fair market value of $1,600,000. Subsequent to this reorganization of capital, his son, Jack, will own all of the outstanding common shares.

Required:

A. Describe the immediate tax consequences of this transaction to Mr. Mark, including the following:

- the amount of any gift that Mr. Mark has made to Jack;
- the PUC of the new preferred shares;
- the adjusted cost base for the new preferred shares;
- the amount of any deemed dividends arising on the exchange; and
- any capital gain or loss resulting from the exchange of the common shares.

B. Describe the tax consequences of this transaction to Jack.

C. Describe the tax consequences of this transaction to Mr. Mark, if the new preferred shares in Markit Ltd. were redeemed at their fair market value of $1,600,000.

Assignment Problem Nineteen - 4

Lyle Hunter started an automobile dealership, Hunter Motors Inc., in 1986. As the business is running smoothly, he is planning to turn most of the administration over to his 27 year old daughter, Pat, and his 24 year old son, Alan. This will allow Lyle to concentrate on improving his golf game in preparation for retirement.

He is eventually planning to gift his shares of Hunter Motors Inc. to his children, but the immediate tax cost of the disposition might be prohibitive. Instead, Lyle would like to know how a share for share exchange can be used to transfer the business, and pass on any future growth to the children. Each child has $5,000 of their own funds available to invest in the Company.

On November 30, 2007, the condensed Balance Sheet of the business is as follows:

Hunter Motors Inc.
Balance Sheet
As At November 30, 2007

Assets (Book Value)	$10,000,000
Bank Loan	$1,490,000
Common Stock (No Par - 100 Shares)	10,000
Retained Earnings	8,500,000
Total Debt And Shareholders' Equity	$10,000,000

An independent appraiser has indicated that the fair market value of the tangible assets is equal to their book values. However, he estimates the goodwill of the corporation to be worth $1,000,000.

Required: Advise Mr. Hunter. Include in your solution the Shareholders' Equity section of the Balance Sheet after your proposed share transactions.

Assignment Problem Nineteen - 5

Ms. Suzanne Platt founded the corporation Platt Industries Ltd. (PIL) with an initial investment of $120,000 in cash. At that time, she was issued common shares with a fair market value and paid up capital equal to her investment of $120,000.

Thanks to Ms. Platt's expertise in managing the enterprise, after 10 years, the fair market value of her common shares increased from their original value of $120,000, to a fair market value of $960,000 on December 31, 2003. On this date, she sells 25 percent of the common shares of PIL to her 22 year old son for $240,000. The son uses funds that he won in a lottery to pay for the shares.

In December, 2007, Ms. Platt decides to retire. She would like to transfer control of PIL to her son and, if possible, freeze the value of her interest in the Company. As at December 31, 2007, her holding of PIL common shares has a fair market value of $1,350,000. It is her understanding that she can exchange her common shares in PIL for a combination of non-voting preferred shares and non-share consideration without incurring any immediate tax consequences. With this in mind, she has proposed two alternative approaches to transferring control of PIL to her son:

Approach One   She exchanges her common shares in PIL for cash of $50,000 and preferred shares that are redeemable at her discretion for $1,300,000. The preferred shares have a legal stated capital of $90,000 and a fair market value of $1,300,000.

Approach Two   She exchanges her common shares in PIL for cash of $50,000 and preferred shares that are redeemable at her discretion for $1,270,000. The preferred shares have a legal stated capital of $1,270,000 and a fair market value of $1,270,000.

PIL is not a qualified small business corporation. The Company has a nil balance in its General Rate Income Pool (GRIP) account for all years under consideration.

Required: For each of the two suggested approaches determine:

A. The amount of the gift to a related party, if any, resulting from the exchange of shares.

B. The paid up capital of the newly issued preferred shares.

C. The adjusted cost base of the newly issued preferred shares.

D. The proceeds of redemption/disposition that Ms. Platt received for the old common shares of PIL.

E. The immediate tax consequences for Ms. Platt of the reorganization of the capital of PIL.

F. The tax consequences for Ms. Platt if the new PIL preferred shares are immediately redeemed for their fair market value.

Assignment Problem Nineteen - 6

For a number of years, Ms. Conrad has operated a very successful gourmet chocolate store in London, Ontario. As she is approaching retirement age, she is considering selling her unincorporated business and has sought your advice in establishing a reasonable asking price.

The business is operated in leased premises that, until recently, required payments of $2,000 per month. However, under the terms of a new long-term lease, the rent has been increased to $4,500 per month.

The current fair market values of the identifiable assets of the business are as follows:

Inventories	$206,000
Furniture And Fixtures (Class 8)	$ 56,000

The fair market value of the Furniture And Fixtures is equal to the UCC balance in Class 8.

While Ms. Conrad currently manages the business herself, she has two full-time sales clerks and part-time help during the Christmas season. Ms. Conrad does not draw a salary from the business, and she estimates that it would require a salary of about $50,000 per year to find someone to adequately replace her. The most recent Income Statement for the store, which is very representative of the last several years of operation, is as follows:

Sales	$982,000
Cost Of Goods Sold	747,600
Gross Margin	$234,400
Salaries And Wages	$ 31,000
Rent	24,000
Amortization Expense	11,000
Advertising	10,500
Other Operating Costs	9,700
Operating Expenses	$ 86,200
Operating Income Before Taxes	$148,200

Required: Given that investors in this type of business are looking for a 25 percent pre-tax rate of return on the total investment in the business, calculate the price you would recommend that Ms. Conrad ask for her business. Based on your suggested price, determine the amount of goodwill that can be associated with this business.

Assignment Problem Nineteen - 7

Kruger Ltd. is a Canadian controlled private corporation that has been in operation for over ten years. Due to increased competition and an inability to adapt to the rapidly changing technological advancements in the industry, it appears unlikely that Kruger Ltd. will be able to earn a satisfactory return on its invested capital in the future. As a consequence, the shareholders have agreed to a liquidation of the Company.

In contemplation of this liquidation, a Balance Sheet has been prepared based on the tax values of its assets and liabilities as at December 31, 2007, the end of the Company's taxation year. This Balance Sheet, after all closing entries, is as follows:

Kruger Ltd.
Balance Sheet
As At December 31, 2007

Inventories (Net Realizable Value And Tax Cost)	$ 35,000
Refundable Dividend Tax On Hand	27,000
Land - Capital Cost	623,000
Building - Undepreciated Capital Cost	586,000
Total Assets	**$1,271,000**
Liabilities	Nil
Paid Up Capital	$ 447,000
Capital Dividend Account	215,000
Other Income Retained	609,000
Total Equities	**$1,271,000**

Other Information:

1. The current fair market value of the Land is $1,243,000.

2. The Building had an original cost of $775,000. Its fair market value on December 31, 2007 is $1,173,000.

3. The adjusted cost base of the common shares is equal to $447,000, their paid up capital.

4. On December 31, 2007, the Company has a nil balance in its General Rate Income Pool (GRIP) account.

5. All of the assets are disposed of on January 1, 2008 at their fair market values.

6. The corporation pays tax at a combined federal and provincial rate of 18 percent on income eligible for the small business deduction, and 50 percent on investment income (including the ITA 123.3 refundable tax on the investment income of a Canadian controlled private corporation).

7. No dividends have been paid in the previous two years.

Required:

A. Calculate the amount that will be available for distribution to the shareholders after the liquidation.

B. Determine the components of the distribution to the shareholders, and the amount of taxable capital gains that will accrue to the shareholders as a result of the winding-up of Kruger Ltd. Assume that appropriate elections or designations will be made to minimize the taxes that will be paid by the shareholders.

Assignment Problem Nineteen - 8

Mr. Cecil Tyrone owns 100 percent of the shares of CT Industries, a Canadian controlled private corporation. The Company was incorporated in 1986, with an investment of $84,000 for common share capital. The Company has a December 31 year end.

Mr. Tyrone is 73 years old and has never cared for women, children, or small animals. As a consequence, he has no heirs with an interest in taking over the operation of the business. At this point in time, he would like to sell the business and devote his attention to the study of astronomy.

He has received two offers for the corporation. The first, made by Ms. Heather Greenwand, is an offer to buy all of the shares for $1,250,000. The second offer has been made by Mr. Barkley Charms, and is an offer to acquire the assets of the business. The specific assets that he would buy, and the prices that he is offering, are as follows:

Accounts Receivable	$ 58,000
Inventories	185,000
Land	411,000
Building	406,000
Goodwill	251,000
Total	$1,311,000

Both offers would require the purchase to take place on January 1, 2008.

On December 31, 2007, the Balance Sheet of CT Industries, after all closing entries, is as follows:

Term Deposits	$158,000
Accounts Receivable (Face Amount = $62,000)	51,000
Marketable Securities At Cost (Equal To Fair Market Value)	173,000
Inventories At Cost	150,000
Land At Cost	102,000
Building At Net Book Value*	156,000
Total Assets	$790,000

Liabilities	$221,000
Paid Up Capital	84,000
Retained Earnings	485,000
Total Equities	$790,000

*The capital cost of the Building was $363,000, it is the only asset in its CCA class, and the UCC balance for the class is $112,000.

At December 31, 2007, there is no balance in the Company's Capital Dividend Account (CDA), Refundable Dividend Tax On Hand account (RDTOH), or General Rate Income Pool (GRIP) account.

The Term Deposits have been on the Company's books for over five years. They represent an investment of excess funds. Mr. Tyrone had no personal need for these funds and he wished to defer personal taxation on the earnings they were generating. All of the Company's non-current assets have been acquired in the last ten years.

CT Industries is taxed at a rate of 17 percent on income eligible for the small business deduction, 37 percent on additional active business income, and 50-2/3 percent on investment income (including the ITA 123.3 refundable tax on the investment income of a Canadian controlled private corporation).

Mr. Tyrone will have other sources of income in excess of $200,000 and, as a consequence, his tax rate on all additional income is 29 percent at the federal level, plus an additional 16 percent at the provincial level. He lives in a province where the provincial dividend tax credit on both eligible and non-eligible dividends is equal to one-third of the gross up. Mr. Tyrone has not used any of his lifetime capital gains deduction.

If Mr. Tyrone accepts Mr. Charms' offer to purchase the business' assets, Mr. Tyrone will sell the Term Deposits and Marketable Securities for their carrying values. The fair market values for these assets are equal to their carrying values. With respect to the sale of the Accounts Receivable, Mr. Charms and Mr. Tyrone will jointly elect to transfer them under the provisions of ITA 22. There would be a winding-up of the corporation subsequent to the sale of its assets.

Required: Determine which of the two offers will provide Mr. Tyrone with the largest amount of personal, after tax funds. Ignore the possibility that Mr. Tyrone might be subject to the alternative minimum tax. Assume that appropriate elections or designations will be made to minimize the taxes that will be paid by Mr. Tyrone.

Assignment Problem Nineteen - 9

Mr. David Carson is the president and only shareholder of Carson Enterprises Ltd., a Canadian controlled private corporation. The Company's fiscal year ends on December 31. Mr. Carson established the Company in 1983, by investing $265,000 in cash.

Mr. Carson is considering selling the corporation and, in order to better evaluate this possibility, he has prepared a special Statement Of Assets. In this special statement, comparative disclosure is provided for the values included in his accounting records, values that are relevant for tax purposes, and fair market values. This statement, after all closing entries, is as follows:

Carson Enterprises Ltd.
Statement Of Assets
As At January 1, 2007

	Accounting Net Book Value	Tax Value	Fair Market Value
Cash	$ 54,500	$ 54,500	$ 54,500
Accounts Receivable	406,000	406,000	372,250
Inventories	869,750	869,750	976,000
Land	201,500	201,500	405,000
Building (Note One)	538,000	469,250	2,061,000
Equipment (Note Two)	434,000	294,000	171,250
Goodwill	Nil	Nil	811,000
Totals	$2,503,750	$2,295,000	$4,851,000

Note One   Mr. Carson built this Building on the Land for a total cost of $1,281,000.

Note Two   The Equipment had a cost of $807,500.

At the same time that this Statement Of Assets was prepared, a similar Statement Of Equities was drawn up. This latter statement contained the following accounting and tax values:

	Accounting Book Value	Tax Value
Current Liabilities	$ 697,000	$ 697,000
Loan From Shareholder	137,500	137,500
Future Income Tax Liability	542,000	N/A
Common Stock - No Par	265,000	265,000
Capital Dividend Account	N/A	164,500
Other Income Retained	N/A	1,031,000
Retained Earnings	862,250	N/A
Totals	$2,503,750	$2,295,000

In addition to the information included in the preceding statements, the following other information about the Company is available:

- The Company has available non-capital loss carry forwards of $83,000.

- The Company has available a net capital loss carry forward of $129,650 [(1/2)($259,300)].

- Carson Enterprises Ltd. is subject to a provincial tax rate of 5 percent on income that qualifies for the federal small business deduction and 16 percent on income that does not qualify for this deduction.

- On December 31, 2006, the Company has no balance in either its RDTOH account or its GRIP account.

Mr. Carson has received two offers for his Company, and he plans to accept one of them on January 2, 2007. The first offer involves a cash payment of $3,508,000 in return for all of the shares of the Company. Alternatively, another investor has expressed a willingness to acquire all of the assets, including goodwill, at a price equal to their fair market values. This investor would assume all of the liabilities of the corporation and has agreed to file an ITA 22 election with respect to the Accounts Receivable. If the assets are sold, it is Mr. Carson's intention to wind up the corporation.

Mr. Carson will have over $300,000 in income from other sources and, as a consequence, any income that arises on the disposition of this business will be taxed at the maximum federal rate of 29 percent, combined with a provincial rate of 14 percent. He lives in a province where the provincial dividend tax credit on both eligible and non-eligible dividends is equal to one-third of the gross up. He has used all of his lifetime capital gains deduction in prior years.

Required: Determine which of the two offers Mr. Carson should accept. Ignore the possibility that Mr. Carson might be subject to the alternative minimum tax. Assume that appropriate elections or designations will be made to minimize the taxes that will be paid by Mr. Carson.

CHAPTER 20

Partnerships

Introduction

Taxable Entities In Canada

20-1.   As is noted in Chapter 1, the *Income Tax Act* (ITA) is applicable to individuals (human beings), corporations, and trusts. In the case of individuals and corporations, these taxable entities have a separate legal existence. In contrast, trusts are simply arrangements for trans-ferring property and, as such, are not separate legal entities. Partnerships are similar to trusts in that they do not have a legal existence separate from the participating partners. More to the point here is the fact that, under the provisions of the *Income Tax Act*, partnerships are not defined taxable entities.

20-2.   The *Income Tax Act* deals with this situation through the use of a deeming rule. A deeming rule is a statutory fiction that requires an item or event be given a treatment for tax purposes that is not consistent with the actual nature of the item or event. We have encoun-tered a number of such rules in previous chapters:

- A member of the Canadian armed forces is deemed to be a resident of Canada, even if he does not set foot in the country during the year.
- A change in use is deemed to be a disposition of an asset combined with its immediate re-acquisition.
- The death of an individual results in a deemed disposition of all of his capital property.

20-3.   The deeming rule that is applicable to partnerships is that, for purposes of deter-mining the income or loss of its members, such organizations are considered to be a person resident in Canada. Note that this rule applies only for the purpose of calculating the income or loss of members. It does not make a partnership a taxable entity and there is no require-ment that these organizations file a separate tax return.

20-4.   In general terms, a partnership is treated as a flow-through entity. The preceding deeming rule requires that an income figure be determined at the partnership level using the usual rules for various types of income (e.g., capital gains). Then, using the provisions of the partnership agreement, this "partnership" income is allocated to the taxable entities that are members of the partnership (i.e., individuals or corporations). Taxes are then paid by these partnership members. The partnership itself, is assessed taxes under Part I of the *Act*.

20-5.   We would remind you that, while partnerships are not taxable entities under the *Income Tax Act*, they are considered taxable entities for GST purposes (see Chapter 4).

Chapter Coverage

20-6.   In this Chapter we will examine the income taxation rules applicable to partnerships, as well as some of the GST implications associated with these organizations. We will begin by defining partnerships. This will be followed by an examination of the various types of partnerships, as well as other arrangements that resemble partnerships. These other arrangements include co-ownerships, joint ventures, and syndicates. Our focus will then shift to looking at the rules for calculating income for a partnership and the process of allocating this income and other amounts to partners.

20-7.   This Chapter will also cover some special rules related to the taxation of partnerships. These include:

- the determination of the adjusted cost base of a partnership interest;
- limited partnerships, limited partnership losses and the at-risk rules;
- the transfer of property between the partners and the partnership; and
- reorganizing a partnership as a new partnership, as a corporation, and as a sole proprietorship.

Partnerships Defined

The Importance Of Defining A Partnership

20-8.   The general rules for determining the income tax consequences for partnerships and their members are found in Subdivision j of Division B of Part I of the *Income Tax Act*, ITA 96 through 103. However, since these rules apply specifically to partnerships, we must first determine if we are, in fact, looking at a partnership. To do this requires a definition of a partnership.

20-9.   The importance of this definition is that it allows us to distinguish a partnership from other similar types of organizations such as syndicates, joint ventures, and co-ownership arrangements. This is necessary in that, unlike the situation for other similar types of organizations, there is a separate calculation of the income of a partnership.

20-10.   This calculation must be carried out using the assumption that the partnership is a separate person resident in Canada. Further, as the calculation must be used for allocating income to all of the members of the partnership, individual partners have no flexibility with respect to the amounts to be included in the calculation (e.g., the amount of CCA to be taken).

20-11.   In contrast, if the organization is considered to be a co-ownership, syndicate, or joint venture, there is no requirement for a separate calculation of income. This provides the participants with much greater flexibility in determining the tax procedures to be used (e.g., an individual participant with losses could choose not to deduct CCA).

Basic Partnership Elements

20-12.   Unfortunately, there is no specific definition of a "partnership" in the *Income Tax Act*. There are several definitions of certain types of partnerships. For example ITA 102(1) defines a "Canadian Partnership". However, all of these specialized definitions presume that a partnership already exists. This leaves the question of defining a partnership unanswered.

20-13.   While the *Income Tax Act* does not provide a definition of a partnership, IT-90, *What Is A Partnership*, provides the following guidance:

> **Paragraph 2**   Generally speaking, a partnership is the relation that subsists between persons carrying on business in common with a view to profit. However, co-ownership of one or more properties not associated with a business, (which under Common Law might be a joint tenancy or a tenancy in common), does not of itself create a partnership, and this is so regardless of an arrangement to share profits and losses. For guidance on whether a particular arrangement at a particular time constitutes a partnership, reference should be made to the relevant provincial law on the subject, and such law will be viewed as persuasive by the Department of National Revenue.

2-14. While additional guidance from provincial legislation may be required in particular situations, this Paragraph 2 establishes the three basic elements that are required for an organization to be considered a partnership:

1. There must be two or more persons (taxable entities) involved.
2. These persons must be carrying on a business.
3. The business must be carried on with a view to making a profit.

20-15. While it is not listed as a basic element of such arrangements, the presence of a valid partnership agreement would serve to support the view that a partnership exists. Such agreements will usually include provisions that deal with the following issues:

- the allocation of profits and losses;
- the filing of financial statements and income tax returns as a partnership;
- the mutual right of control for management of the enterprise;
- the location of partnership bank accounts;
- the rights and duties of the partners; and
- the registration of the partnership with the appropriate provincial jurisdiction.

20-16. As an indication of the difficulties that arise in this area, the Supreme Court of Canada has heard three cases relating to the taxation of partnerships. The main issue in each of these cases was whether a partnership existed. The relevant cases were *Continental Bank Leasing* (1998 DTC 6505), *Spire Freezers Limited* (2001 DTC 5158) and *Backman* (2001 DTC 5149). A good review of these cases can be found in Income Tax Technical News No. 25, October 30, 2002.

Types Of Partnerships

General Partnerships

20-17. A general partnership is composed of partners, called general partners, who manage the business and are equally liable for partnership debt and wrongful or negligent actions of other partners. Unless specified as a limited partnership or a limited liability partnership, the term partnership usually refers to a general partnership. Provincial partnership law lays down the ground rules with respect to the more important rights, duties and obligations of the general partners. These include:

- Each partner is considered to act on behalf of the partnership, which means that the actions of each partner are generally binding on the other partners.

- Partners are jointly and severally liable for partnership debt and wrongful acts of other partners. This means that a partner can be liable, together with all other partners, for unpaid partnership debt and wrongful acts of other partners.

- Property contributed to the partnership or acquired with partnership funds is considered partnership property and is to be held exclusively for partnership use.

- Partners are entitled to share equally in profits and losses, unless there is an agreement to the contrary.

- Partners are not entitled to remuneration or to interest on capital contributions. As is explained later in this Chapter, any remuneration or interest on capital is treated as an income allocation and is not deductible to the partnership.

Limited Partnerships

20-18. A limited partnership is a partnership with at least one general partner (i.e, a partner whose liability is unrestricted) and one or more limited partners. If a partnership has not registered with the provincial authorities to be legally considered as a limited partnership, it is considered to be a general partnership.

20-19. A limited partner has the same rights, duties, and obligations as a general partner with one important difference, a limited partner is only liable for partnership debt and wrongful or negligent actions of other partners to the extent of the partner's actual and promised contributions to the partnership.

Example   A limited partner contributes $1,000 and agrees to contribute a further $2,000 within a certain period of time. That partner will be potentially liable for up to $3,000 of claims against the partnership.

20-20.   It should be noted, however, that a limited partner will lose his limited liability protection, and therefore become a general partner, if he participates in the management of the partnership.

Limited Liability Partnerships (LLP)

20-21.   This form of partnership is only available to certain types of professionals as specified in provincial legislation. For example, in Ontario, only lawyers, chartered accountants, and certified general accountants are currently permitted to form such partnerships. In contrast, Alberta extends this legislation to include several other professional groups.

20-22.   Unlike members of limited partnerships, members of limited liability partnerships are personally liable for most types of partnership debt. There is, however, an important exception. Member of limited liability partnerships are not personally liable for obligations arising from the wrongful or negligent action of:

- their professional partners; or
- the employees, agents or representatives of the partnership who are conducting partnership business.

Co-Ownership, Joint Ventures And Syndicates

Introduction

20-23.   Our major concern in this Chapter is the taxation of partnerships. However, as we have noted, there are other types of organizations that have structures similar to partnership arrangements. Co-ownership, joint ventures, and syndicates are specific types of arrangements that contain features common to partnerships. For example, each of these organizational structures requires two or more persons. This common feature is but one of several that may make it difficult to determine whether a specific arrangement is, in fact, a partnership or, alternatively, a different type of arrangement.

20-24.   As was discussed in the preceding material, the ability to distinguish these arrangements from partnerships is a critical factor in determining how a given organization will be taxed. To facilitate this process, the following material will provide additional clarification as to the nature of these other types of organizations.

Co-Ownership

20-25.   Two or more persons co-own property when they share a right of ownership in the property. For income tax purposes, the most important consideration is that profits and losses are shared in partnerships, but are typically accounted for individually by joint or co-owners.

20-26.   Two common forms of co-ownership are joint tenancy and tenancy in common. A joint tenancy is a form of property ownership where two or more joint tenants have ownership and possession of the same property. Individual interests are identical and the property cannot be sold or mortgaged without the consent of the other joint tenant(s). Spouses commonly own their principal residence and other properties in joint tenancy.

20-27.   In a tenancy in common arrangement, tenants in common can sell or mortgage their interests without the consent of other tenants in common. An example of a situation where a tenancy in common might be used would be the ownership of a vacation property by three brothers.

Joint Ventures

Defined

20-28.   Those of you familiar with financial reporting will recognize that some corporations are referred to as joint ventures. They are distinguished by the fact that control of the corporation is shared by two or more of the shareholders. This type of joint venture does not present any special problems in terms of tax procedures. They are subject to the same rules that are applicable to other corporate taxpayers.

20-29.   Our concern here is with unincorporated joint ventures. Like partnerships, joint ventures are not defined taxable entities under the *Income Tax Act*. Further, such arrangements are not governed by provincial legislation. However, both the *Income Tax Act* and the *Excise Tax Act* refer to joint ventures, implicitly giving recognition to this form of organization.

20-30.   The similarity of partnerships and joint ventures has led the CRA to make the following statement in 1988:

> Unlike partnerships, the concept of joint venture is not recognized by statute (i.e. provincial legislation). Although the Canadian courts have, in certain cases, recognized joint venture as being a business relationship that is distinct from partnership, in our experience, many so-called joint ventures are in fact partnerships... The CRA would rely on provincial partnership law in making such a determination.

20-31.   This would suggest that, even if participants in a joint venture call the arrangement a joint venture, if it contains the three basic partnership elements, it will be considered a partnership and treated accordingly for tax purposes.

20-32.   Despite this lack of clarity, joint ventures do appear to exist for tax purposes. Factors that have been used to distinguish this type of organization include:

- co-venturers contractually do not have the power to bind other co-venturers;
- co-venturers retain ownership of property contributed to the undertaking;
- co-venturers are not jointly and severally liable for debt of the undertaking;
- co-venturers share gross revenues, not profits; and
- while partnerships may be formed for the same purpose as a joint venture, they are usually of longer duration and involve more than a single undertaking.

Tax Procedures

20-33.   If an arrangement is considered to be a joint venture rather than a partnership, there will be no separate calculation of income at the organization level. The individual participants will be subject to the usual rules applicable to individuals or corporations. As we have noted this will provide these taxable entities with greater flexibility on such issues as how much CCA to take for the current year.

Syndicates

20-34.   A syndicate is generally defined as a group of persons who have agreed to pool their money or assets for some common purpose. Because a syndicate is not a legal entity, a reference to an interest in a syndicate usually means an interest in the combined assets of the syndicate members. The Canadian courts have traditionally reserved the name "syndicate" for specialized projects that are financial in nature. An example of a syndicate would be an association of insurance companies who combine forces to underwrite substantial high-risk insurance policies.

20-35.   There are no specific income tax rules that apply to syndicates. This means that, if there are any activities of the syndicate that result in assessable amounts of income, the relevant amounts will have to be allocated to the members of the syndicate.

Partnership Income, Losses And Tax Credits

Introduction

20-36.   The goal of partnership taxation is to apply the income tax consequences of partnership income, losses, and tax credits to the persons who are its partners. There are three general steps in this process:

1. Determine that the arrangement is a partnership.
2. Determine income, losses, and tax credits at the partnership level.
3. Allocate the income, losses, and tax credits to the partners.

20-37.   As we have noted, the second step requires the assumption that the partnership is a person resident in Canada. The partnership's accounting Net Income figure is then converted to Net Income For Tax Purposes. To the extent that the accounting Net Income figure is made up of business income, this conversion will be made using the procedures that were discussed in Chapter 8. We will find, however, that there are certain items in this conversion process that are specific to partnerships. These will be given special attention in the following material.

Basic Concepts

Separate Person Assumption

20-38.   A partnership is considered a separate person only for the purpose of determining income or loss of the members of the partnership. This means that, in general, only the rules in the *Income Tax Act* that directly relate to the calculation of income or loss under Part I will apply to partnerships.

20-39.   For example, the rules that allow a deduction for CCA will apply to partnerships since these rules affect the determination of income or loss. On the other hand, a partnership is not considered a separate person for the rules that relate to the filing of income tax returns, since those rules do not directly affect the determination of income or loss.

Taxation Year

20-40.   If a partnership is to calculate income or loss as a separate person, it must also have a fiscal period in which to measure its income or loss. ITA 96(1), when read in conjunction with the ITA 249.1(1) definition of fiscal period, makes it clear that the fiscal period that will be used by a partnership in determining its income or loss for a period will be affected by the type of taxpayers that make up the partnership group.

20-41.   If all of the members of the partnership group are corporations, other than professional corporations, the partnership can select any period that does not exceed 12 months. However, if any member of the partnership is an individual or a professional corporation, the general rules require the use of the calendar year as its fiscal period.

20-42.   If all of the partners are individuals and the partnership is not involved in tax shelter arrangements, ITA 249.1(4) allows the partnership to use a non-calendar fiscal period. Coverage of this election can be found in Chapter 8, beginning at Paragraph 8-128.

> **Example**   ABC Partnership has five corporate partners, two of which are professional corporations, and one partner who is an individual. The partnership wants to choose a March 31 fiscal year end.
>
> **Analysis**   The partnership must use a December 31 fiscal year end. The presence of both an individual and professional corporations as partners prevents the use of a non-calendar fiscal period under ITA 249.1(1). Similarly, the presence of corporations prevents the election of a non-calendar fiscal period under ITA 249.1(4).

Partnership Property

20-43.   In general, partners legally own a percentage interest in partnership property in co-ownership. The partnership cannot own property since it is not a legal entity. This creates a problem for income tax purposes because the partnership income tax rules require that the partnership determine its income or loss as if it were a separate person.

20-44.   If the partnership does not own partnership property, then gains and losses from the disposition of such property would not be considered those of the partnership. In addition, the partnership would not be able to claim CCA or write off Cumulative Eligible Capital. The *Income Tax Act* resolves this problem with an assumption that the partnership, for income tax purposes, is considered to own partnership property.

Retention Of Income Characteristics

20-45.   Partnerships are treated as a conduit for transferring income from an originating source into the hands of the partners. Further, it is an unobstructed conduit in that the character of various types of income is not altered as it flows through to the partners. If a partnership earns dividend income, taxable capital gains, or realizes a business loss, these sources would be received as dividend income, taxable capital gains, or business losses in the hands of the partners.

> **Example** Partnership Deux has two equal general partners. It earns $50,000 of interest income and realizes a $20,000 capital gain. None of this amount is withdrawn by the two partners. Corporation Dos has two equal shareholders. It also earns $50,000 of interest income and realizes a $20,000 capital gain. The corporation does not pay out any of this amount as dividends.

> **Analysis** For Partnership Deux, each partner is considered to have received $25,000 of interest income and to have realized a $5,000 taxable capital gain [($20,000)(1/2)(1/2)]. Note that the income is subject to taxation, despite the fact that none of it has been withdrawn from the partnership (see next section on Accrual Basis).

> In the case of Corporation Dos, the shareholders will not be taxed until the income is withdrawn from the corporation. The income will, however, be taxed at the corporate level and, when it is distributed to the shareholders, it will not retain its characteristics as interest and capital gains. Rather, the entire amount will be taxed in the hands of the shareholders as dividends.

20-46.   In addition to retaining its basic character, the originating location of each source of income is retained. If, for example, a partnership earns dividends on shares of U.S. corporations, this income would be received by the partners as foreign source dividends. Not surprisingly, the related foreign tax credits would also be flowed through to the partners.

Accrual Basis

20-47.   The partnership must calculate its income on an accrual basis. On its determination, this income is then allocated to the partners. The partners include their share of this income at the time of allocation, without regard to when the funds are withdrawn from the partnership. It is the allocation, not the receipt of the funds, that creates income for the partners that is subject to tax.

20-48.   In effect, this places the partners on an accrual basis for the determination of their individual income amounts. As the income is taxed when it is accrued at the partnership level and allocated to the individual partners, it will not be taxed again when it is withdrawn from the partnership.

Calculating Partnership Income Or Loss

Introduction

20-49.   As we have noted, partnership income is calculated as if the partnership was a separate person resident in Canada. To the extent that property income or taxable capital gains are involved, the calculations are discussed in Chapters 9 and 10.

20-50.   As for business income, it would be the usual reconciliation calculation that was introduced in Chapter 8. Starting with the accounting figure for business income, adjustments would be made to arrive at a figure for net business income for income tax purposes. In applying this schedule to partnership situations, there are several individual items that need further attention.

Individual Items

20-51. The items that require separate attention in the context of determining the income or loss of a partnership are as follows:

Salaries Or Wages To Partners Partnership agreements often provide that partners be paid salaries or wages to recognize the time they devote to partnership business. The CRA's view is that such amounts cannot be deducted as expenses in the determination of partnership income. Any amounts deducted in the determination of accounting income will be added back to arrive at partnership Net Income For Tax Purposes.

The partners' entitlements to salaries and wages will be considered as either a return of capital or an allocation of a partnership income figure that has been determined without the deduction of these salaries and wages.

Interest On Partner Capital Contributions Partnership agreements may provide that partners receive interest on capital contributions. Here again, the CRA's view is that such amounts cannot be deducted as expenses in the determination of partnership income. Any amounts deducted in the determination of accounting income will be added back to arrive at partnership Net Income For Tax Purposes.

The partners' entitlements to interest on capital contributions will be considered as either a return of capital or an allocation of a partnership income figure that has been determined without the deduction of these interest amounts.

Business Transactions With Partners There are no legal restrictions on the ability of partners to enter into legitimate business transactions with their partnerships. Examples include loans made by partners to the partnership and the renting of a partner's property to the partnership. As long as the transactions are on regular commercial terms, relevant amounts will be inclusions or deductions in the determination of partnership income.

Capital Cost Allowance Any CCA that is deducted on partnership property must be deducted at the partnership level. Therefore, the half-year rule, the available for use rules, the rental property restrictions and other depreciable property rules are all applicable when determining the amount of CCA that a partnership may claim. In addition, any capital gains, recapture, or terminal loss that occur with respect to partnership property, must be added or deducted at the partnership level.

You should note that this requirement removes the possibility of individual partners taking different amounts of CCA. If maximum CCA is deducted at the partnership level, all partners must, in effect, deduct maximum CCA.

Dividend Income Partnerships include the full amount of dividends received from all sources in calculating income. There is no gross up of these amounts at the partnership level. Further, as the partnership does not pay taxes, the dividend tax credit on these dividends is not available at the partnership level. These amounts will be allocated to the partners as eligible or non-eligible dividend income and, at the partner level, the appropriate gross up and tax credit procedures will be applied.

Taxable Capital Gains And Allowable Capital Losses Taxable capital gains and allowable capital losses of the partnership are included in the determination of partnership income in the same manner as they would be for individuals. In addition, the partnership may claim capital gains reserves.

Political Contributions And Charitable Donations   For taxpayers who are persons, these amounts are eligible for either a deduction in determining Taxable Income or as a credit against Tax Payable. Since a partnership is only considered a person for purposes of determining income or loss of a partner, the deductions or credits are not available at the partnership level. However, the *Income Tax Act* contains rules that allow a flow through of these amounts to the partners where they can be used as deductions or credits.

Personal Expenditures   In some situations, a partnership may pay personal expenses of one or more partners. While these amounts may be deducted as an expense for accounting purposes, they are not deductible to the partnership in determining partnership income for tax purposes. Consistent with this treatment, they are generally not included in the income of the partners who benefit from the payments. Rather, these amounts are considered as partnership withdrawals.

Reserves   The use of reserves is discussed in both Chapter 8 (e.g., reserve for bad debts) and Chapter 10 (e.g., capital gains reserve). These reserves are claimed by the partnership in exactly the same manner as individuals, corporations, and trusts.

Special Elections   Many special elections are available to partnerships on the same basis that they are available to taxable entities. However, as the partnership is not a taxpayer, an authorized partner acting on behalf of the partnership must make the required election [see ITA 96(3)].

Once the election is made, it is considered applicable to the partnership and in effect for each partner. Examples include the ITA 34 election to account for revenue on a billed basis and the ITA 22 election used to deal with the sale of accounts receivable as part of the sale of a business. Both of these elections are discussed in Chapter 8.

Exercise Twenty-1

Subject: Partnership Salaries And Interest

The PM Partnership (PMP) determines that its net accounting income for the current year is $146,000. The spouses of both partners do some contract work for PMP. In arriving at that amount, the following deductions were made:

Interest On Partner Loan Used In PMP Business	$ 1,900
Interest On Partners' Capital Accounts	4,400
Salaries To Partners	37,000
Salaries To Partners' Spouses	28,000

Determine the amount of partnership income that would be allocated to the partners for tax purposes.

Exercise Twenty-2

Subject: Partnership Deductions

Determine whether the following are deductible in determining partnership income for tax purposes:

A. Office rent paid to one partner for a building owned outside the partnership.
B. Political contributions to a federal party.
C. Interest on a short-term loan from a partner.
D. Donations to a registered Canadian charity.

End of Exercises. Solutions available in Study Guide.

Exercise Twenty-3

Subject: Partnership Income

The AM Partnership (AMP) provides security guard services. AMP calculates a net accounting loss of $71,600 for the current year. In determining that loss, the following amounts were included:

- $1,000 of qualifying political contributions were deducted.
- $8,000 of personal expenditures for one of the partners were deducted.
- $12,000 of rental expenses were not deducted because they relate to a lease of business premises from one of the partners.

Determine the income or loss for AMP for income tax purposes for the current year.

End of Exercise. Solution available in Study Guide.

Allocations To Partners And Partner Expenses

Method Of Allocation

20-52.   Once the partnership accounting Net Income or loss has been converted to Net Income For Tax Purposes on a source-by-source basis, allocations are made to each partner based on the partner's share of each source. This allocation is usually determined by the partnership agreement. Partners will include the allocated amounts in their income for the taxation year in which the partnership's fiscal period ends.

20-53.   There are many ways in which the members of a partnership may agree to allocate income or loss. These allocations may be fixed, variable, or a combination of fixed and variable elements. Factors such as the value of services provided to the partnership (a salary component), capital contributions (an interest component), and amounts of risk assumed (personal assets at risk) may be taken into consideration. Alternatively, allocations may be based upon fixed ratios determined by the partners or, in the absence of some other agreement, the equal fixed ratios that automatically apply under partnership law.

20-54.   The *Income Tax Act* requires that allocations be made on a source-by-source basis. However, there is no requirement that the allocation for each source be the same. Business income could be shared on an equal basis, with taxable capital gains being allocated on a completely different basis.

20-55.   In general, the CRA will accept any income allocation agreement that is reasonable. It is possible, however, that the agreement could be constructed in a manner that would reduce or postpone taxes (e.g., an example of this would be the allocation of all partnership losses to partners with high levels of current income). In addition, an allocation could be used for income splitting purposes (e.g., allocation of large amounts of partnership income to a low-income spouse on a basis that is not consistent with his contribution of services or capital). In either of these circumstances, the CRA can challenge the allocation in the partnership agreement as being unreasonable. If the challenge is successful, the allocation will have to be altered.

Allocation Of Specific Items

Dividend Income

20-56.   Both eligible and non-eligible dividends from taxable Canadian corporations flow through to the partners. Their treatment subsequent to allocation will depend on the type of taxpayer involved or the type of dividend received:

- Partners who are individuals must gross up the dividends by either 45 percent or 25 percent. The dividends are then eligible for a dividend tax credit.

- Dividends allocated to corporate partners will not be grossed up. One hundred percent of the amount allocated will be included in Net Income For Tax Purposes, with this same amount deducted in the determination of Taxable Income.

- Capital dividends received by the partnership are allocated as capital dividends to the partners, generally retaining their tax-free nature.

- Foreign source dividends received by the partnership will not be grossed up by partners who are individuals or deducted by corporate partners. Such dividends will normally provide the partners with foreign tax credits.

Capital Gains And Losses

20-57.   Capital gains and losses flow through to the partners and are eligible for the same income tax treatment in the hands of the partners as would be the case if those partners had realized them directly. Only one-half of the amount received will be included in income. In addition, the lifetime capital gains deduction may be available, losses may qualify for Allowable Business Investment Loss treatment, and the capital dividend account will be increased or decreased for partners that are private corporations. As is the usual situation, allowable capital losses can be deducted by a partner only to the extent that the partner has taxable capital gains.

Restricted Farm Losses

20-58.   As discussed in Chapter 8, farm losses are restricted where farming is not the main or chief occupation of the taxpayer. The determination of whether farm losses are restricted is determined separately for each partner based on their individual circumstances.

> **Example**   FL Partnership has three equal individual partners and is involved in grain farming. One of the partners is a full time farmer with extensive grain operations of his own. The other two partners are lawyers whose only involvement with farming is through the partnership. During the current year, the partnership realizes significant farm losses.

> **Analysis**   One-third of the farm losses flow through to each of the partners. The loss allocated to the partner who is a full time farmer will likely remain unrestricted since his main occupation is farming. The deductibility of the farm losses allocated to the lawyers, however, would likely be limited by the restricted farm loss rules. We would also note that, if the grain farming operation did not have a reasonable expectation of profit, the losses would be disallowed rather than restricted.

Foreign Tax Credits

20-59.   Foreign taxes paid by the partnership on sources of foreign income are flowed through to the partners based on the proportion of the foreign source income each partner is required to include in income.

Charitable Donations

20-60.   Donations made by a partnership that otherwise qualify as charitable donations are flowed to the partners based on their partnership agreement. Corporations are entitled to a deduction in arriving at Taxable Income, whereas individuals are entitled to a credit against Tax Payable. Donations, and the related credit or deduction, are only allocated to those partners who are partners on the last day of the partnership's year end.

Political Contributions

20-61.   ITA 127(4.2) provides that qualifying political contributions are allocated to each partner as per the partnership agreement. The allocation of the contributions and the related credit is dependent on being a partner on the last day of the partnership's year in which the political contribution was made.

Partner Expenses

20-62.   Partnership agreements may provide that certain partnership expenditures are to be paid personally by the partners without reimbursement. These amounts are not deductible to the partnership, but are generally deductible to the partners, subject to any limitations within the *Income Tax Act*. These amounts may include partner payments for home office expenses, automobile expenses, advertising, conventions, professional dues and entertainment. If, however, the partnership reimburses the partners for such costs, the deduction will be made at the partnership level, rather than by the partners as individuals.

Exercise Twenty-4

Subject: Partnership Income Allocation

Emily Luft and Ruth Blakie are partners in the Emblem Partnership. Emily and Ruth share equally in the business income or loss. However, since Emily contributed much of the capital to buy the partnership's investments, any dividend income and capital gains are allocated 65 percent to Emily and 35 percent to Ruth. In the current year, the partnership has Net Income of $35,000 which is made up of a business loss of $10,000, eligible dividends received of $25,000 and net taxable capital gains of $20,000. Determine how the partnership income should be allocated between Emily and Ruth.

End of Exercise. Solution available in Study Guide.

The Partnership Interest

The Concept

20-63.   A person who is a member of a partnership has the right to participate in profits and losses of the partnership and the right to an interest in partnership property, usually on the dissolution of the partnership. Such rights, collectively referred to as a partnership interest, constitute property for income tax purposes much in the same manner as a share of capital stock of a corporation.

20-64.   A partnership interest is generally considered a non-depreciable capital property and, as a consequence, a disposition of a partnership interest will usually result in a capital gain or loss.

20-65.   The adjusted cost base (ACB) of a capital property is defined in ITA 54 as its cost, plus or minus the adjustments in ITA 53. In practice, the ACB of the current partnership interest is determined by starting with the ACB of the preceding year, then adjusting for the current year profit or loss, current year capital contributions, current year drawings, as well as a number of other adjustments. It is unlikely that the ACB of a partnership interest for tax purposes will be equal to the capital account of a partner as calculated for accounting purposes.

Acquiring A Partnership Interest

New Partnership

20-66.   For founding members of a new partnership, establishment of the ACB of the partnership interest is very straightforward. For each of the partners, the ACB of their interest will simply be the fair value of the assets contributed to the partnership. If the contributions involve non-monetary assets, appraisals may be required. This, however, represents only a minor complication.

Admission To Existing Partnership

20-67.   A somewhat more complex situation exists when a new partner is admitted to an existing partnership. This can be accomplished either by acquiring all or part of the interest of a current partner or, alternatively, by acquiring a new interest by contributing directly to the partnership assets.

20-68.   From a technical point of view, partnership law provides that a partnership terminates on a change in the composition of the members.   However, this problem can be overridden by the partnership agreement. In the discussion that follows, we assume that a partnership is not dissolved because of a change in its members.

20-69.   Cost is generally equal to the fair market value of the consideration given up. If a person becomes a partner by acquiring another partner's interest, then cost will equal the purchase price. For example, if Mr. Davis acquires the one-third interest of Mr. Allan for $90,000, then both the cost to Mr. Davis and the proceeds of disposition to Mr. Allan would be $90,000. If Mr. Allan's ACB of his partnership interest was $16,000, then Mr. Allan would have a capital gain of $74,000 ($90,000 – $16,000).

20-70.   As a variation on the previous example, assume that each of the three existing equal partners has an ACB of $16,000 and each partner agrees to sell one-quarter of their interest to Mr. Davis in return for a payment of $30,000 to each of the partners. Note that selling one-quarter of each of the interests of the three partners leaves each of them with 25 percent [(1/3)(75%)] of the partnership and an ACB of $12,000 [(75%)($16,000)]. The tax consequences are as follows:

ACB to Mr. Davis = $ 90,000 (same as preceding example)

Proceeds Of Disposition To Each Partner	$30,000
ACB of Part Interest [(25%)($16,000)]	(4,000)
Capital Gain For Each Partner	$26,000

20-71. The capital accounts in the accounting records of the partnership and the partners' ACB will be as follows:

	Partner 1	Partner 2	Partner 3	Mr. Davis
Capital Before Admitting Davis	$16,000	$16,000	$16,000	Nil
Adjustment For Admission Of Davis	(4,000)	(4,000)	(4,000)	$12,000
Ending Capital Accounts	$12,000	$12,000	$12,000	$12,000
ACB Of Partnership Interest	$12,000	$12,000	$12,000	$90,000

20-72.   Note that, while the accounting values for the interests of the original three partners are equal to their ACBs, this is not the case for Mr. Davis. In contrast to his accounting value of $12,000, his ACB would be his cost of $90,000 [(3)($30,000)].

Exercise Twenty-5

Subject: Admission Of Partner

Alan and Balan are equal partners in the Alban Partnership. On September 1, 2007, Alan and Balan's partnership capital account balances are $48,000 each. This is also equal to the adjusted cost base of their interests. As the result of paying $40,000 to each of Alan and Balan, Caitlan is admitted as an equal partner (1/3 interest) on September 1, 2007. Calculate the tax effects of the partner admission for Alan and Balan and determine the capital account balances and adjusted cost base for each partner after the admission of Caitlan.

End of Exercise. Solution available in Study Guide.

Adjustments To The ACB Of A Partnership Interest

Need For Adjustments

20-73.   The ITA provides for several types of adjustments to the ACB of a partnership interest. Common adjustments include capital contributions, drawings, and adjustments for business income, capital gains, and tax credits.

20-74.   When a partnership interest is sold, the proceeds of disposition will reflect such items as additional capital contributions and income retained in the partnership. If the ACB was not adjusted for these items, the additional amounts paid by a purchase would be treated as a gain on the disposition of the partnership interest. This inequitable result is prevented through adjustments to the ACB of the partnership interest.

Timing Of Adjustments

20-75.   Before proceeding to a discussion of the more common adjustments to the cost base of a partnership interest, some attention must be given to the timing of these adjustments. With respect to capital contributions and drawings, the timing is very straightforward. These adjustments are made at the time of the contribution or drawing.

20-76.   In contrast, those adjustments related to allocations of income or tax credits are not made during the period in which the income or tax credit arises. Rather, these adjustments to the ACB of a partnership interest are made on the first day of the following fiscal period. These procedures will be illustrated in the material that follows.

Capital Contributions And Drawings

20-77.   Contributions of capital made to the partnership increase the ACB of a partnership interest. For this purpose, loans from partners are not considered capital contributions and do not increase ACB.

20-78.   As you would expect, drawings or other withdrawals of partnership assets reduce the ACB of the partnership interest. Included as drawings would be amounts paid by the partnership that were personal expenses of a partner. However, loans to a partner would not be treated as drawings.

> **Example** The ACB of Mr. Allan's partnership interest is $20,450 at January 1, 2007. In March, 2007, he contributes $8,200 to the partnership as a capital contribution and makes withdrawals of $2,000 in each of May, August, and November, 2007.

> **Analysis** The ACB of Mr. Allan's partnership interest is calculated as follows:

> | | |
> |---|---:|
> | ACB – January 1, 2007 | $20,450 |
> | Capital Contributions – March 2007 | 8,200 |
> | Drawings – May, August And November 2007 [($2,000)(3)] | (6,000) |
> | ACB – December 31, 2007 | $22,650 |

Partnership Income Or Loss

20-79.   The accounting Net Income of the partnership is first converted to Net Income For Tax Purposes and then allocated to the partners based on their profit sharing ratios. In general, an income allocation increases the partner's ACB, while a loss allocation reduces the partner's ACB. The increase or decrease in the partnership interest is on a dollar-for-dollar basis with the income allocation, but does not occur until the first day of the next fiscal period.

> **Example** Tom and Theresa begin the Double T partnership in January, 2007 and select December 31 as their year end. They each contribute $1,000 to Double T. During 2007, the partnership earns $21,000 in gross service revenue. The only expenses incurred are $6,000 in business meals and entertainment.

> **Analysis** Accounting Net Income for the partnership would be $15,000 ($21,000 - $6,000). However, Net Income For Tax Purposes would be $18,000, the $15,000 of accounting Net Income, plus $3,000, the non-deductible one-half of the expenses for

business meals and entertainment. This means that the ACB of each partnership interest would be $10,000 [$1,000 + (1/2)($18,000)]. This is not the same as the accounting net book value of $8,500 [($1,000 + (1/2)($15,000)]. You should also note that the adjustment to the ACB of the partnership interest would not be made until January 1, 2008.

Charitable Donations and Political Contributions

20-80. Amounts donated or political contributions made by a partnership in a particular year are considered donated or contributed by each partner in proportion to that partner's profit sharing ratio. As it is the individual partners who enjoy the benefits of making the contributions (i.e., the deductions or tax credits), such amounts reduce the ACB of a partnership interest. Note, however, this adjustment does not occur until the first day of the following fiscal period.

Example During the taxation year ending December 31, 2007, a partnership with three partners, each with a one-third interest in profits, contributed $7,500 to charitable organizations. All contributions are eligible for the charitable donations tax credit.

Analysis Each of the three partners would be entitled to allocations of $2,500 towards the calculation of their individual charitable donations tax credit for 2007. As a consequence of this allocation, the ACB of each of their partnership interests would be reduced by $2,500. Note, however, that this reduction will not occur until January 1, 2008.

Dividends

20-81. Taxable dividends earned by a partnership would retain their character when they are allocated to the individual partners. This would include whether they were eligible or non-eligible dividends. In the year of allocation, the individual partners would include the grossed up amount in their Net Income For Tax Purposes and would be able to claim the associated dividend tax credit.

20-82. In those situations where a partnership has received capital dividends, these would be allocated to partners as capital dividends. As such, they would not be subject to tax at the partner level.

20-83. In calculating the ACB of a partnership interest, a partner's share of both capital and taxable dividends is added to the ACB of his partnership interest. For the purposes of ACB calculations, no gross up is added.

Example Fred and Barney are equal partners in Stone-works Partnership that began operations January 1, 2007. A December 31 year end was selected. Each partner initially contributed $5,000. The only income received by the partnership was $13,000 of eligible dividends that are subject to the enhanced gross up and tax credit procedures, and $4,200 of capital dividends. No amounts were withdrawn from the partnership in 2007.

Analysis Each partner is required to include one-half of the taxable dividends of $13,000, plus an additional 45 gross-up, in his 2007 Net Income For Tax Purposes. This amounts to income of $9,425 [(1/2)($13,000)(145%)]. The capital dividends are not included in each partner's income as they are tax free. The ACB of Fred and Barney's interest would be as follows:

Cost	$ 5,000
Taxable Dividends Allocated [(50%)($13,000)]	6,500
Capital Dividends Allocated [(50%)($4,200)]	2,100
ACB Of Partnership Interest - January 1, 2008	$13,600

20-84. Two things should be noted in this calculation. First, for purposes of calculating the

ACB of the partnership interests, no gross up is added to the taxable dividend. Second, the dividends are not added to the ACB until the first day of the year following their allocation to the partners.

Capital Gains And Losses

20-85.   As with other types of income, capital gains and losses retain their tax characteristics when they are allocated to partners. While only the taxable portion of the gain or loss is included in the Net Income For Tax Purposes of the partners, the adjustment to the ACB of the partnership interest is for the full amount of the capital gain or loss. This inclusion of the full amount provides for the non-taxable one-half of the gain to be recovered on a tax free basis if the partnership interest is sold.

Example   Monday, Tuesday, Wednesday, and Friday are four equal partners in the Weekday Partnership. Each partner contributed $1,950 when the partnership began May 1, 2007. The partnership selects December 31 as its year end. Weekday used the initial contributions of $7,800 to acquire two parcels of land that were both capital property. Both parcels were sold in December, 2007. The sale of parcel A resulted in a capital gain of $5,300 and the sale of parcel B resulted in a capital loss of $700. There were no other transactions during the year.

Analysis   The partnership income that would be allocated to each partner is equal to $575 [(1/4)(1/2)($5,300 – $700)]. The ACB of each partnership interest is calculated as follows:

ACB Of Partnership Interest - May 1, 2007	$1,950
Capital Gain Allocated [(1/4)($5,300)]	1,325
Capital Loss Allocated [(1/4)($700)]	(175)
ACB Of Partnership Interest – January 1, 2008	$3,100

Negative ACB

20-86.   In general, if negative adjustments to the ACB of a capital asset exceed its cost plus any positive adjustments to the ACB, the excess must be taken into income under ITA 40(3) as a capital gain. While technically an ACB can only be positive or nil, it is common to refer to assets that have experienced such adjustments as having a negative adjusted cost base.

20-87.   This creates a problem for partnership interests in that withdrawals are deducted from the ACB of the partnership interest in the year they occur, while income allocations are only recorded on the first day of the following year. As partners usually withdraw their anticipated income allocations during the year in which they accrue, negative ACBs for partnership interests would not be unusual.

20-88.   Because of this problem, the *Income Tax Act* allows general partners to carry forward a negative ACB, without taking the capital gain into income. This deferral is applicable until the partner disposes of his interest, either through a sale or as the result of a deemed disposition at death.

20-89.   When the disposition results from a deemed disposition at death, there are rollover provisions that allow a continued carry forward of the negative ACB when the partnership interest is bequeathed to a spouse or common-law partner, or a trust in favour of a spouse or common-law partner.

20-90.   Note that the preceding rules only apply to active general partners. In the case of limited partners or general partners who are not active in the partnership, the deferral of the gain that is implicit in carrying forward a negative ACB is not available. Such amounts must be taken into income in the year in which they occur.

Exercise Twenty-6

Subject: ACB Of Partnership Interest

On January 1, 2007 Raymond and Robert form the RR Partnership. The partnership has a December 31 year end. The partnership agreement provides Robert with a 40 percent share of profits and losses. Robert initially contributes $12,500 and makes a further contribution of $7,200 on June 10, 2007. He withdraws $4,000 on October 31, 2007. RR Partnership has the following sources of income for 2007:

Capital Gain On Corporate Shares	$11,600
Eligible Dividends Received From Canadian Corporations	3,100
Net Business Income	46,700

Determine the ACB of Robert's partnership interest on December 31, 2007, and at January 1, 2008. In addition, determine the amount that would be included in Robert's 2007 Net Income For Tax Purposes as a consequence of his interest in the RR Partnership.

End of Exercise. Solution available in Study Guide.

Limited Partnerships And Limited Partners

Definitions

Limited Partner

20-91.   A partner whose liability is limited under partnership law is considered a limited partner for income tax purposes. Members of a limited liability partnership, however, are generally excluded from the definition and are therefore not considered a limited partner since they remain personally liable for most partnership debt.

20-92.   The definition also includes general partners when their liability is limited by the presence of specific contractual arrangements. Examples of this type of situation include:

- guarantees that someone will acquire their partnership interest regardless of its value;
- provisions indicating that amounts a partner has agreed to contribute to the partnership may never have to be paid; and
- provisions that guarantee the partner that he will be reimbursed for any partnership losses, usually by the general partner.

Specified Member

20-93.   This definition is generally aimed at preventing limited partners and inactive general partners from enjoying the generous incentives that are available to partnerships that are carrying out scientific research and experimental development. A specified member of a partnership includes all limited partners. In addition, this broader definition also includes general partners who are not actively involved in the partnership business on a regular and continuous basis.

At-Risk Rules

Basic Concept

20-94.   Historically, limited partnership structures have been used to fund high-risk ventures that benefit from generous income tax incentives. These structures have been used with Canadian films, Canadian mining and exploration operations, scientific research and experimental development, real estate, and construction.

20-95.   General partners entice investors with limited liability protection, combined with the advantages of significant flow through of tax deductions. The general partners usually do not share in the deductions, receiving their compensation through fees that are charged to the limited partners for managing the partnership.

20-96.   The at-risk rules were introduced in order to restrict the ability of certain investors in partnerships, typically limited partners, to receive tax deductions or tax credits in excess of the amount that they stand to lose on their investment. In simple terms, the at-risk rules work to ensure that $30,000 of tax deductions are not available to a limited partner who has less than $30,000 at risk.

The At-Risk Amount

20-97.   The at-risk amount sets the annual limit on the amount of tax preferences and incentives that may flow through to limited partners. Specifically, the *Income Tax Act* provides restrictions on the allocation to limited partners of scientific research and experimental development credits, resource expenditures, investment tax credits, property losses, and non-farming business losses. Under ITA 96(2.2), the at-risk amount is calculated at the end of a partnership's fiscal period as follows:

ACB Of The Partnership Interest		$xxx
Share Of Partnership Income For The Current Period		
(Income For ACB Purposes - See Paragraph 20-98)		xxx
Subtotal		$xxx
Less:		
Amounts Owed To The Partnership	($xxx)	
Other Amounts Intended To Reduce The Investment Risk	(xxx)	(xxx)
At-Risk Amount		$xxx

20-98.   The addition of the share of partnership income (not losses) is intended to ensure that current year income allocations, which will not be added to the ACB of the partnership interest until the following fiscal year, are taken into consideration. The amount that is added here is the same amount that will be added to the ACB. That is, it does not include the dividend gross up, nor is it adjusted downwards for the non-taxable portion of capital gains.

20-99.   The at-risk amount is reduced by two amounts. The first represents the outstanding balance of any amount owing by the partner to the partnership for the acquisition of the partnership interest. This amount is subtracted as it is included in the partnership interest but, prior to its actual payment, it is not really at risk.

20-100.   The second amount relates to financial incentives designed to reduce the investment risk or exposure to the limited partner. An example of this would be a promise by the general partner to acquire the partnership interest at an amount in excess of the value of the partnership interest at the option of the limited partner.

Limited Partnership Losses

20-101.   The at-risk rules limit the ability of a limited partner to utilize certain types of losses. The rules do not directly affect farm losses and capital losses since these losses carry their own restrictions. Farm losses during the current year may be limited by the restricted farm loss rules and, in addition, any carry over of such restricted farm losses can only be applied against farming income. Similarly, current year allowable capital losses are only deductible to the extent of current year taxable capital gains.

20-102.   ITA 96(2.1)(c) indicates that a partner's share of losses, other than those associated with farming or the disposition of capital assets, can be deducted to the extent of the at-risk amount. The excess is referred to as the "limited partnership loss". It is a carry forward balance that can be carried forward indefinitely and can only be claimed to the extent of the at-risk amount from that same partnership. There is no carry back of limited partnership losses.

Example On January 1, 2007, Jenny Johnson acquires a 10 percent limited partnership interest in Tax-Time, a partnership that provides tax preparation services. This interest cost her $15,000, with $6,000 payable in cash and the balance of $9,000 payable in 36 months, without interest. At December 31, 2007, Tax-Time determines that it has a $22,000 capital gain and a $111,000 business loss. Jenny is allocated 10 percent of these amounts.

Analysis As a 10 percent limited partner, Jenny is allocated a portion of the business loss equal to $11,100. However, her at-risk amount restricts the business loss that Jenny may be able to use. The at-risk amount is calculated as follows:

ACB Of The Partnership Interest		$15,000
Share Of Partnership Income [(10%)($22,000 Capital Gain)]		2,200
Subtotal		$17,200
Less:		
Amounts Owed To The Partnership	($9,000)	
Other Amounts Intended To Reduce		
The Investment Risk	Nil	(9,000)
At-Risk Amount – December 31, 2007		$ 8,200

For 2007, Jenny will be able to deduct her share of the total partnership loss to the extent of her $8,200 at-risk amount. This will leave a non-deductible limited partnership loss for 2007 of $2,900 ($11,100 - $8,200). In general, Jenny will be able to use the limited partnership loss in 2008 or subsequent years if her at-risk amount increases. This may occur if she makes additional contributions, is allocated additional income from the partnership in 2008, or repays the loan to the partnership. It should also be noted that there are special adjustments to the ACB of a limited partner's partnership interest that are beyond the scope of this material.

Exercise Twenty-7

Subject: Limited Partnership Loss

During 2007, Stuart Jones acquires an interest in a mining limited partnership for $200,000. An initial $50,000 is paid immediately, with the $150,000 balance payable in eight years. The general partner has agreed to acquire Scott's interest at any subsequent date, returning his $50,000 payment and assuming responsibility for the $150,000 payable. For the current year, the limited partnership has allocated losses of $75,000 to Stuart. How much of this loss is Stuart entitled to claim as a deduction on his tax return? What is the amount of his limited partnership loss at the end of the year?

End of Exercise. Solution available in Study Guide.

Transfer Of Property To And From A Partnership

Introduction

20-103.   Since the ITA treats partners as distinct from the partnership, transferring property between the partners and the partnership may have income tax consequences. Such consequences are generally dependent on the purpose of the property transfer and whether the underlying partnership meets the ITA 102 definition of a "Canadian partnership":

ITA 102   In this subdivision, "Canadian partnership" means a partnership all of the members of which were, at any time in respect of which the expression is relevant, resident in Canada.

20-104.   Whether the partnership is a general, limited, or limited liability partnership is irrelevant to the determination of its status as a Canadian partnership. In addition, the definition does not require that the partnership be formed in Canada. For example, a U.S. based partnership with all Canadian resident members would qualify.

20-105.   If the required conditions are met, the *Income Tax Act* contains rollover provisions that provide for tax deferral on such transactions. However, where the rollover conditions are not met, the transfers will be taxed as a disposition/acquisition at fair market value.

20-106.   In covering this material, we will first look at the rules applicable to transfers of property to and from a partnership when a rollover provision is not used. This will be followed by a discussion of some of the more commonly used partnership rollover provisions.

Transfers With No Rollover Provision
Transfers From Partners To The Partnership
20-107.   If a person transfers property to a partnership of which he is member, or to a partnership of which he becomes a member as a result of the transfer, ITA 97(1) deems the person to have disposed of the property at fair market value and the partnership to have acquired the property at the same amount.

20-108.   In general, the fair market value of the transferred asset is added to the ACB of the person's partnership interest. However, this addition would be reduced by any consideration given to the contributor because of his contribution. This rule is applicable without regard to whether the partnership qualifies as a Canadian partnership.

> **Example**   Diane Jefferson is a member of CG Partnership and decides to make an additional 2007 capital contribution to the partnership by transferring investments to it that she had acquired in 2006 for $10,000. At the time of the transfer, they have a fair market value of $24,000.

> **Analysis**   Diane will be considered to have disposed of the investments for $24,000. This will result in a $7,000 [($24,000 - $10,000)(1/2)] taxable capital gain for 2007. Diane will also be considered to have made a $24,000 capital contribution that will increase the ACB of her partnership interest by the same amount. The partnership will be considered to have acquired the investments from Diane for $24,000.

Exercise Twenty-8

Subject: Transfers From Partner To Partnership

Charles Woodward is one of four equal partners in LIU Partnership (LIU). During the current year, Charles contributes a tract of land to the partnership. Charles acquired the land for $33,000 and, at the time of transfer, it is valued at $100,000. Describe the tax consequences to Charles and LIU in the following three situations:

A.   No consideration is received from LIU.
B.   Charles receives $25,000 in cash from LIU on the transfer.
C.   Charles receives $112,000 in cash from LIU on the transfer.

End of Exercise.   Solution available in Study Guide.

Transfers From The Partnership To Partners
20-109.   If a partnership transfers property to a partner, ITA 98(2) deems the partnership to have disposed of the property at fair market value and the partner to have acquired the property at the same amount. There is no requirement that the partner remain a partner after the transfer and the rule is applicable without regard to whether the partnership qualifies as a Canadian partnership. This provision is typically used when a partnership is dissolved, or when partial distributions of partnership property are made in an ongoing partnership.

Example Bill Davis is a 40 percent partner in the FV Partnership. The partnership owns a piece of land that has an ACB of $2,900 and transfers it to Bill in June, 2007 for no consideration. The land has a fair market value of $10,000 at this time.

Analysis The partnership is considered to have disposed of the land for its fair market value of $10,000, resulting in a capital gain of $7,100 ($10,000 - $2,900). Bill's share of this gain is $2,840 [(40%)($7,100)]. This amount will be allocated to Bill and, as a consequence, he will report a taxable capital gain of $1,420 [($2,840)(1/2)] in his 2007 tax return. Bill will also be considered to have acquired the land for $10,000 and to have made a withdrawal from the partnership of $10,000. The ACB of his partnership interest will be reduced by the $10,000 withdrawal and increased by the $2,840 allocation of the capital gain.

Exercise Twenty-9

Subject: Transfers From Partnership To Partners

Darlene is one of five equal partners in the DG Partnership. During the taxation year ending December 31, 2007, DG distributes some of its investments to each of the partners. The distributed investments have an adjusted cost base of $39,000 and, at the time of transfer, they have a fair market value of $94,000. Darlene receives one-fifth of these investments. At the time of this transfer, the adjusted cost base of Darlene's partnership interest is $30,000. What are the tax consequences to DG and Darlene with respect to this distribution? Your answer should include Darlene's adjusted cost base on December 31, 2007, and on January 1, 2008.

End of Exercise. Solution available in Study Guide.

Common Partnership Rollovers

Transfers From Partners To The Partnership

20-110.   If a person transfers property to a Canadian partnership and all members of that partnership jointly elect, then property transferred to the partnership may be transferred on a rollover basis. This means that the property can be transferred at elected values (usually tax values), rather than at the fair market values that must be used in the absence of a rollover provision. This rule applies both to persons who are existing partners, as well as to persons who become partners by contributing property to the partnership.

20-111.   ITA 97(2) indicates that, for this type of transfer, the ITA 85(1) rules apply. The ITA 85(1) rules are generally applicable to transfers of property to a corporation and are discussed in detail in Chapter 18. There are, however, some differences in the application of these rules when the transfer is to a partnership. The more notable of these differences are as follows:

- Real property inventory can be transferred to a partnership, but not to a corporation.

- When a transferor takes back consideration with a value less than that of the property transferred to a corporation, it may involve a gift to a related party. In the case of transfers to a partnership, the gift portion is added to the ACB of the partnership interest. As discussed in Chapter 18, if such a transfer was made to a corporation, it would usually result in double taxation of the gifted amount.

- When a transferor receives consideration in excess of the value of the property transferred to a corporation, the excess is subject to taxation. When this happens in conjunction with a transfer of property to a partnership, the excess is viewed as a drawing and is not subject to taxation.

20-112.   Differences between the elected amounts and consideration other than a partnership interest affect the ACB of the partnership interest.

Example   Janice Donovan will join the On-Off Partnership that provides interior lighting products. During 2007, she plans to make a capital contribution of a parcel of land with an ACB of $100,000 and a fair market value of $250,000. She wishes to transfer the land at an elected value of $160,000. The existing members agree and file a joint election authorizing the transaction for $160,000.   Janice has a choice between three different packages of consideration:

A. No cash.
B. Cash of $100,000.
C. Cash of $160,000.

Analysis   ITA 97(2) uses the transfer limits described within ITA 85. The basic acceptable transfer range is from the land's ACB of $100,000 to its fair market value of $250,000. While not applicable in this case, the elected value is also limited to the amount of non-partnership interest consideration received. The relevant values for the three Cases are as follows:

Case	ACB Of Partnership Interest	Capital Gain
A	$160,000 Increase	$60,000
B	$ 60,000 Increase	60,000
C	No Effect	60,000

Partnership Property Transferred To A New Partnership

20-113.   A partnership may be dissolved in a number of situations. Included would be the addition or retirement of partners in cases where the partnership agreement does not provide for the continuation of the partnership. The dissolution of a partnership is considered to be a disposition of partnership property and, in the absence of a rollover provision, would result in tax consequences to the partners. However, this treatment can be avoided if the partnership property is transferred to a new partnership.

20-114.   ITA 98(6) provides automatic (i.e., no election is required) rollover treatment where all of the property of a Canadian partnership that has ceased to exist is transferred to a new Canadian partnership. A further condition is that all of the members of the new partnership must have been members of the old partnership.

20-115.   While many rollover provisions provide tax free treatment by providing for a deemed disposition at the tax cost of the property, ITA 98(6) takes a different approach. This Subsection deems the old and new partnerships to be the same entity, with the result being that there is no disposition of the property and no tax consequences to the transferor. This means that the ITA 98(6) rollover involves fewer complications than would be found in most rollover applications.

20-116.   It is important to note that, while all of the members of the new partnership have to have been members of the old partnership, not all of the members of the old partnership have to become members of the new partnership. This rollover is typically used when there is no continuity provision in place, and an existing partner retires.

20-117.   The retirement of a partner usually involves distributing some of the partnership property to the retiring partner. This makes it impossible to fully comply with the requirement of ITA 98(6) that all of the property of the old partnership be transferred. This problem was resolved by IT-338R2, "Partnership Interests - Effects On Adjusted Cost Base Resulting From The Admission Or Retirement Of A Partner", which states that all of the property of the old partnership is considered to mean all the property after the settlement of a retired partner's interest. While IT-338R2 has been archived, it would appear that this guidance is still applicable.

Partnership Property Transferred To A Sole Proprietorship

20-118.   This rollover applies automatically where a Canadian partnership ceases to exist and, within three months of the cessation date, one of the partners continues to carry on the partnership business as a sole proprietor. This rollover treatment is provided for partnership property distributed to the proprietor and, in general, ensures that there are no tax consequences associated with the disposition of that proprietor's partnership interest.

20-119. There is an exception in situations where the tax cost of partnership property received by the proprietor exceeds the ACB of his or her partnership interest. In this case, there will be a capital gain. Alternatively, if the ACB of the proprietor's partnership interest exceeds the tax cost of partnership property received by the proprietor, the rules allow the cost of partnership property to be increased to reflect this difference.

20-120. This rollover typically applies where one of the partners in a two-person partnership retires or dies, leaving the remaining person to continue the business. As a partnership must have at least two partners, there is no possibility of the partnership continuing. Note, however, that the rollover only applies to the partner who continues the business. A retiring partner will have a disposition at fair market value with the usual tax consequences associated with such a disposition.

Partnership Property Transferred To A Corporation

20-121. The decision to convert a partnership to a corporation, or to incorporate a partnership, generally arises when a partnership that has realized losses in its initial years becomes profitable. Corporate status may be preferred because of the availability of the small business deduction, the possibility of deferring taxes on income retained within the corporation, or the desire to split income with other related persons.

20-122. The process of incorporating a partnership on a tax deferred basis generally requires two rollovers, ITA 85(2) and ITA 85(3). Under ITA 85(2), eligible partnership property is transferred to a taxable Canadian corporation for either shares or a combination of shares and other consideration. The transfer takes place at elected values which can include the tax cost of the property, thereby avoiding tax consequences to the partnership. This rollover treatment is only available if the corporation and all the partners jointly elect rollover treatment.

20-123. At this point, the partnership is holding shares in the corporation and the partners are continuing to hold their partnership interests. ITA 85(3) then provides for a transfer at tax values of the partnership's holding of the corporation's shares to the partners in return for their partnership interests. This is accompanied by a wind-up of the partnership.

20-124. If the following conditions are met, the ITA 85(3) rollover treatment is automatic, with no election required:

- The partnership must have disposed of property to a taxable Canadian corporation under ITA 85(2).
- The partnership must be wound up within 60 days of the disposition of its property to the corporation.
- Immediately before the partnership is wound up, the only property it holds is money or property received from the corporation as a result of the application of ITA 85(2).

20-125. The winding-up of a partnership usually requires the distribution of all partnership property, the settlement of partnership obligations, as well as certain provincial formalities such as de-registration.

20-126. These rules are designed to provide a tax free means of incorporating a partnership. However, tax consequences may arise in two particular instances. First, ITA 85(2) only applies to "eligible property" as defined in ITA 85(1.1). The major item that would not be included in this definition would be an inventory of real property (i.e., real property held for sale rather than use). If such non-eligible property is transferred from a partnership to a corporation, the transfer will be at fair market value, resulting in the usual tax consequences.

20-127. A second situation in which the incorporation of a partnership may result in tax consequences would arise when a partner receives consideration in excess of the ACB of his partnership interest. While this may result in a capital gain, it can be avoided with the proper use of the ITA 85(3) rollover provision.

Example   Danielle and Christine are equal partners in the Flag Partnership. The recent success of the business has led to a decision to incorporate. The only asset Flag owns is an inventory of flags that cost $50,000, but is currently worth $200,000. The ACB of each partner's partnership interest is $34,000. The corporation will issue only common shares as consideration for the acquisition of the flag inventory.

Analysis   Danielle, Christine, and the corporation will jointly elect to transfer the inventory from the Flag Partnership at its tax cost of $50,000. Flag will be deemed to have disposed of the inventory for $50,000 and the corporation will be considered to have acquired the inventory for $50,000. No tax consequences will arise on the disposition. Flag Partnership will receive common shares of the corporation that will have an ACB and PUC of $50,000. At this point, Flag Partnership owns shares of the corporation and the corporation owns the inventory.

When the Flag Partnership distributes the shares to Danielle and Christine, the following tax consequences will arise:

- Flag will be considered to have disposed of the shares for their tax cost of $50,000, resulting in no tax consequences.
- Each partner will be considered to have acquired the shares for an amount equal to the ACB of her partnership interest ($34,000).
- Each partner will be considered to have disposed of her partnership interest for the cost of the shares acquired from the partnership ($34,000). As a result, there is no capital gain or loss.

Partnerships And GST

General Rules

20-128.   The ITA treats a partnership as a person only for the purpose of computing income or loss to its partners. The *Excise Tax Act* considers partnerships to be persons that are generally required to register for the GST with respect to commercial activities. In addition, anything a partner does with respect to partnership activities is considered done by the partnership and not by the partners themselves.

20-129.   The result is that it is the partnership, and not the partners, who is required to register for the GST with respect to partnership business. Given this, partnerships are required to collect and remit GST on taxable supplies and are eligible for input tax credits. Partners are jointly and severally liable however with respect to GST that relates to the partnership business.

Partner Expenses

20-130.   Non-reimbursed expenditures for property or services incurred personally by individual partners, which relate to the partnership business and that are deductible for income tax purposes by the partners, are generally eligible for a rebate. Such property and services include office expenses, travel expenses, meals and entertainment, parking, lodging and CCA on certain capital assets such as motor vehicles. This rebate is similar to the rebate available to employees, as discussed in Chapter 5.

20-131.   A partner can only claim a rebate to the extent that the partnership could have otherwise claimed an ITC if it had incurred the expense directly. This means that, if a partnership provides only exempt goods or services, the partners would not be eligible to claim a GST partner rebate for the expenses that they can deduct from their share of partnership income.

Disposition Of A Partnership Interest

20-132.   A partnership interest may be disposed of or acquired in many situations. These include the admission of a new partner or retirement of an existing partner. A partnership interest is considered a "financial instrument" and is exempt from the GST. In addition, any legal and accounting fees related to the acquisition or disposition of a partnership interest are not eligible for an input tax credit since they relate to a financial instrument and not to the partnership's business. Finally, drawings and capital contributions that specifically relate to a partnership interest are considered "financial services" and are also exempt from the GST.

Transfers Between Partners And Partnerships

20-133. In general, there is no GST counterpart to the rollover rule that allows property to be transferred by a partner to a partnership on a tax deferred basis. An exception to this is the case where a business is being transferred and 90 percent or more of the property that is necessary to carry on that business is also transferred. In such cases, the transfer is not subject to GST as long as both transferor and transferee are registrants.

20-134. Transfers of property between partnerships and partners may be subject to GST, generally depending on the status of the transferor and transferee as registrants and whether they are engaged in commercial activities. GST is not applicable to transfers of cash, accounts receivable, or debt however, since these are either not considered property for GST purposes or are considered exempt financial services.

Reorganization Of The Partnership

20-135. The admission of new partners or retirement of existing partners that terminate the old partnership and result in the creation of a new partnership will not cause the new partnership to register for GST as a new person. As a result, there are no GST implications on the transfer of the old partnership property to the new partnership.

20-136. There are no GST implications to the new partnership where a partnership has ceased to exist, more than half of its members form a new partnership, and transfer 90 percent or more of the property they receive on the cessation of the old partnership to the new partnership. The new partnership is considered to be a continuation of the old partnership for GST purposes.

Key Terms Used In This Chapter

20-137. The following is a list of the key terms used in this Chapter. These terms, and their meanings, are compiled in the Glossary Of Key Terms located at the back of the separate paper Study Guide and on the Student CD-ROM.

Adjusted Cost Base	Limited Liability
At-Risk Amount	Limited Liability Partnerships
At-Risk Rules	Limited Partner
Canadian Partnership	Limited Partnership
Capital Gain	Limited Partnership Loss
Co-Ownership	"Negative" Adjusted Cost Base
Deeming Rule	Partner
Dividend Gross Up	Partnership
Dividend Tax Credit	Partnership Interest
General Partner	Specified Member
General Partnership	Syndicates
Joint Tenancy	Tenancy In Common
Joint Venture	

References

20-138.   For more detailed study of the material in this Chapter, we refer you to the following:

ITA 40(3)	Negative ACB
ITA 53(1)(e)	Addition To Cost Base Of An Interest In A Partnership
ITA 53(2)(c)	Deduction From Cost Base Of An Interest In A Partnership
ITA 85(2)	Transfer Of Property To Corporation From Partnership
ITA 85(3)	Where Partnership Wound Up
ITA 96	General Rules (Partnerships And Their Members)
ITA 97	Contribution Of Property To Partnership
ITA 98	Disposition Of Partnership Property
ITA 99	Fiscal Period Of Terminated Partnership
ITA 100	Disposition Of An Interest in a Partnership
ITA 102	Definition Of "Canadian Partnership"
ITA 103	Agreement To Share Income
IC-89-5R	Partnership Information Return
IT-81R	Partnerships - Income Of Non-Resident Partners
IT-90	What Is A Partnership?
IT-231R2	Partnerships - Partners Not Dealing At Arm's Length
IT-242R	Retired Partners
IT-278R2	Death Of A Partner Or Of A Retired Partner
IT-378R	Winding Up Of A Partnership
IT-413R	Election By Members Of A Partnership Under Subsection 97(2)
IT-457R	Election By Professionals To Exclude Work In Progress From Income
IT-471R	Merger Of Partnerships
P-171R	GST/HST Policy Statement, "Distinguishing Between a Joint Venture and a Partnership for the Purposes of the Section 273 Joint Venture Election", February 24, 1999.
T4068	Guide for the Partnership Information Return

Problems For Self Study

(The solutions for these problems can be found in the separate Study Guide.)

Self Study Problem Twenty - 1

Wayout Ltd. is a company that has operated a vinyl record business for years. Wayout owns three buildings in Toronto and operates a store in each building . The management always believed that records would make a comeback and refused to introduce CD's. As a result, Wayout Ltd. is expected to declare bankruptcy within the next few months. If Wayout Ltd. sold all of its property, significant tax losses would result. As Wayout has had no profits for years, the losses cannot be used as a carry back. Wayout's accountant recommends the following plan to stave off bankruptcy:

1. A general partnership will be formed and a partnership agreement written up with Wayout Ltd. as the managing partner.

2. The partnership agreement will provide the following:

    - the required capital contributions by each partner;
    - the profit/loss sharing ratios (1 percent to Wayout and 99 percent split equally among the other investors);
    - the appointing of accountants to file necessary partnership tax returns;
    - that each partner will have a say in the management;
    - that the property contributed by Wayout Ltd. is partnership property; and
    - that the partnership will be dissolved upon the final sale of partnership property.

3. Wayout Ltd. will contribute all of the property from two of its locations, including the land and buildings. The property will be transferred on a rollover basis.

4. Ninety-nine individual Canadian investors will each contribute $10,000 to the partnership.

If this plan is put into place, Wayout Ltd. will have access to almost $1 million of new capital to deal with creditors and invest in the remaining store. In addition, it is anticipated that each investor will be allocated $50,000 in losses. The estimated tax savings, assuming a marginal tax rate of 50 percent, will be $25,000.

Required: Has a valid partnership been created? Analyze the facts using the three elements of a partnership. Ignore other income tax implications.

Self Study Problem Twenty - 2

Mr. Baker and Mr. Caldwell are members of a partnership that provides accounting services. Information concerning the partnership for the current taxation year ending December 31 is as follows:

1. The partnership agreement calls for Net Income to be allocated equally to the two partners. In addition, the Salaries And Wages in the preceding Income Statement include a payment of $44,000 to each of the two partners.

2. The convention costs were for the two partners to attend the annual conference of the Canadian Institute Of Certified General Management Accountants.

3. Both partners use their personal vehicles for business purposes and pay their own operating expenses. Mr. Caldwell's car cost $24,000 and, at the beginning of the current year, it had a UCC of $13,500. His operating expenses for the year were $4,000, for a total of 48,000 kilometers driven. Only 25 percent of these kilometers were for personal use.

4. At the beginning of the current fiscal year, the partnership had fees receivable from clients of $27,000. At the end of the year, the corresponding balance was $56,000.

5. At the beginning of the year, the UCC of the office furniture was $26,000 and the UCC of the computer equipment (Class 45) was $14,000. During the year, a computer was purchased for $8,500.

The Income Statement of the partnership, for the current taxation year ending December 31, is as follows:

Baker And Caldwell
Partnership Income Statement
Current Year Ending December 31

Fees Received In Cash		$403,000
Capital Gains On Temporary Holdings Of Canadian Securities		14,000
Eligible Dividends Received From Canadian Corporations		48,000
Total Revenues		$465,000
Less Expenses:		
Salaries And Wages	($197,000)	
Rent On Office Space	(19,200)	
Interest On Bank Loans	(5,800)	
Depreciation - Office Furniture And Equipment	(12,500)	
General Office Expenses	(28,400)	
Charitable Donations	(7,200)	
Costs Of Attending Convention	(2,800)	(272,900)
Net Income (Accounting Values)		$192,100

Required: Calculate the minimum Net Income For Tax Purposes for Mr. Caldwell for the current year. Include in the calculation Mr. Caldwell's share of Net Business Income from the partnership. Also indicate other amounts that would be allocated to Mr. Caldwell by the partnership, as well as any credits against Tax Payable that would result from these allocations. Ignore GST and PST considerations.

Self Study Problem Twenty - 3

On March 1, 2004, John Olson, his son Fred Olson, and Eric Beam form a partnership to provide accounting and tax services. The partners each contribute $225,000 and agree that all income and losses are to be shared equally. The fiscal year for the partnership is established to end on December 31.

For the period March 1, 2004 to December 31, 2006, the following information is available:

1. The partnership earned net business income of $195,000.

2. The partnership realized a capital gain of $66,000 (this amount is not included in the net business income figure).

3. The partnership made a number of charitable donations during the period. The total amount involved was $12,000, and this total was allocated equally to each of the three partners (this amount is not included in the net business income figure).

4. During this period, Eric Beam made withdrawals from the partnership totaling $43,000.

5. Additional capital was required to expand the operations of the office and, as a consequence, each partner contributed an additional $54,000 in cash.

Eric Beam decided to withdraw from the partnership effective January 1, 2007. After some negotiations, the other partners agreed to pay him $355,000 in cash for his interest in the partnership. The payment is made on February 1, 2007. Eric Beam incurred legal and accounting fees in conjunction with this transaction totalling $1,800.

Required: Calculate Eric Beam's gain or loss on the disposition of his partnership interest. Explain how this amount, and any other amounts related to the partnership, will be taxed in his hands.

Self Study Problem Twenty - 4

Mark and Matt Doan are brothers and professional engineers. In early 2006 they formed a partnership in order to provide professional engineering services. When the partnership was formed each of the brothers made a capital contribution of $280,000 in cash. They have agreed to share all profits and losses equally.

During the partnership taxation ending December 31, 2006, the partnership had Net Income For Tax Purposes of $180,000, all of which was business income. During 2006, Mark withdrew $75,000 in partnership funds, while Matt's drawings were only $23,000.

The partnership's 2007 Income Statement, prepared in accordance with generally accepted accounting principles, is as follows:

Income Statement
Mark And Matt Doan Partnership
Year Ending December 31, 2007

Revenues		$708,000
Operating Expenses:		
Rent	($48,000)	
Amortization Expense (Note 1)	(12,000)	
Office Salaries	(41,000)	
General Office Costs	(18,000)	
Meals And Entertainment	(23,000)	
Charitable Donations	(17,000)	(159,000)
Operating Income		$549,000
Other Income:		
Gain On Sale Of Investments (Note 2)	$14,000	
Eligible Dividends Received From Canadian Corporations	8,000	22,000
Net Income		$571,000

Note 1 Maximum 2007 CCA, which the partners intend to deduct, is $19,000.

Note 2 The gain resulted from the sale of temporary investments. The investments had an adjusted cost base of $60,000 and were sold for $74,000.

During 2007, Mark had drawings of $190,000 while Matt had drawings of $290,000.

Other information with respect to Matt's 2007 taxation year is as follows:

- Other than amounts related to owning and selling the partnership, Matt's only other income was eligible dividends received from Canadian companies of $34,000.

- Other than credits related to his ownership of the partnership and dividend paying shares, Matt's only tax credit was his basic personal credit.

On January 1, 2008, Matt sells his interest in the partnership to an arm's length individual for $435,000.

Required:

A. Calculate Matt's federal Tax Payable for the year ending December 31, 2007.

B. Determine the taxable capital gain or allowable capital loss that would result from Matt's sale of his partnership interest.

Self Study Problem Twenty - 5

On January 1, 2007, Melanie Millionaire acquired a 4 percent limited partnership interest in the Cross Your Fingers Partnership, which provides internet based dating services to professionals. The agreement Melanie signed required her to pay $20,000 for her interest in the Partnership. $3,200 is paid in cash and an interest free promissory note of $16,800 is signed for the balance. The promissory note is payable in eight equal annual instalments of $2,100, due on December 31 of each year, beginning in 2007. In addition, the agreement states that the general partner will acquire Melanie's partnership interest on December 31, 2007, for $1,500 more than its fair market value.

Melanie's share of all income and losses of the Cross Your Fingers Partnership is 4 percent. For the year ending December 31, 2007, the Partnership had the following sources of income and loss:

Eligible Dividends Received From Canadian Corporations	$ 12,000
Capital Gains	17,500
Interest Income	20,000
Business Loss	(180,000)

Required: Calculate the following amounts for Melanie's investment in the Cross Your Fingers Partnership for 2007:

- The at-risk amount on December 31, 2007.
- The limited partnership income (loss) for the year.
- The deductible income (loss) for the year.
- The limited partnership loss carry forward at the end of the year.
- The adjusted cost base on December 31, 2007 and January 1, 2008.
- The at-risk amount on January 1, 2008.

Self Study Problem Twenty - 6

A number of years ago, Jack Porter, Cid Quinn, and Norman Roberts established the Porter, Quinn, and Roberts partnership. At the time the partnership was formed, each of the partners invested $350,000 in cash. The partnership agreement calls for all income and losses to be shared equally. The fiscal year of the partnership ends on December 31.

On January 1 of the current year, the adjusted cost base of the interests of the three partners is as follows:

Jack Porter	$ 382,000
Cid Quinn	526,000
Norman Roberts	726,000
Total	$1,634,000

On January 2 of the current year, the property of the partnership is transferred to a corporation under the provisions of ITA 85(2) in return for the following consideration:

Cash	$ 722,000
Preferred Shares (At Fair Market Value)	540,000
Common Shares (At Fair Market Value)	1,080,000
Total Consideration	$2,342,000

On February 20 of the current year, the partners decide to wind up the partnership. Reflecting this decision, the consideration provided by the corporation is transferred to the individual partners. Under the terms of the partnership agreement, they receive the following amounts:

	Porter	Quinn	Roberts	Total
Cash	$ 78,000	$222,000	$422,000	$ 722,000
Preferred Shares	180,000	180,000	180,000	540,000
Common Shares	360,000	360,000	360,000	1,080,000
Total	$618,000	$762,000	$962,000	$2,342,000

Required: Determine the adjusted cost base of the assets received by the partners as a result of this transfer of partnership assets to the corporation. Calculate the capital gain or loss for each partner resulting from the transfer under the provisions of ITA 85(3).

Assignment Problems

(The solutions for these problems are only available in the solutions manual that has been provided to your instructor.)

Assignment Problem Twenty - 1

John and Janet Bovi have been married for 12 years. John is a professional recording artist earning substantial income. Janet stays home and raises their 4 children. Three years ago, John began a stereo speaker repair business. John acquired a building, tools, office furniture and hired repair technicians. He also registered the business and opened up a bank account under his own name. John spends a few hours each day managing the business. John and Janet report profits as a partnership on a 50-50 basis when filing their annual income tax returns. There is no partnership agreement.

Required: In the following two **independent** Cases, determine whether a partnership exists.

A. Assume that Janet's involvement with the business consists of helping John pick out some office furniture and occasionally taking messages when John is out of town. The business has been profitable each year.

B. Assume that Janet does all the accounting, payroll and invoicing for the repair business from home. She also does most of the parts ordering on-line and is responsible for paying the suppliers and all other expenses. The business has not been profitable in any year.

Assignment Problem Twenty - 2

Mr. Poliacik joined Mr. Ewing's practice by entering into a business association with Mr. Ewing. They operated under the name " Ewing/Poliacik". Mr. Poliacik made no capital contribution on joining.

Both individuals were lawyers. Mr. Poliacik's specialty was litigation. Mr. Ewing was involved in non-litigation matters.

An agreement was signed, but it never referred to the individuals as partners or the association as a partnership. When asked why they did not refer to themselves as partners, Mr. Poliacik stated that they did not know each other well enough to accept the risks of partnership. The agreement stated that all fees billed by each individual belonged to that individual.

Both parties agreed to open a combined general and trust bank account. Both parties had signing authority on the general account, although Mr. Poliacik's authority was limited to client disbursements only. Mr. Ewing had sole signing authority on the trust account. The accounts did not indicate that they were registered to a partnership.

Mr. Poliacik's fees were to be split based on a graduated scale. The first $100,000 was to be split 50-50, then 60-40 on the next $25,000, 80-20 on the next $25,000 and 90-10 thereafter. The larger percentage went to Mr. Poliacik. In addition, Mr. Poliacik was entitled to 10 percent of fees billed by Mr. Ewing to clients introduced by Mr. Poliacik.

Mr. Ewing agreed to be 100 percent liable for office expenses and bookkeeping services. Mr. Poliacik's share of the office operating expenses was $62,500 in the first year. This amount would be adjusted in the future as the expenses increased. Mr. Poliacik was not entitled to the 10 percent finder's fee from Mr. Ewing until his share of the annual expenses had been paid.

Mr. Poliacik was required to pay his own income taxes, CPP, employer health tax and professional insurance.

There were no income tax filings as partners. The combined business was not registered for GST purposes. There were no filings with the law society indicating that Mr. Poliacik and Mr. Ewing were partners.

Required: Determine whether the business association is a partnership.

Adapted from Poliacik (TCC) 1999 DTC 3482

Assignment Problem Twenty - 3

Mr. Marrazzo owns an undeveloped parcel of land in Suburbia. He purchased the land four years ago with the intention of developing residential lots. The land cost $400,000 and has a fair market value of $1,300,000 on December 1, 2007.

Banks are reluctant to lend for real estate development, so Mr. Marrazzo has been unsuccessful in obtaining the $1,200,000 financing that is required for site servicing costs. Digger Inc., a heavy equipment supplier, agrees to provide interest-free financing in return for ownership of 50 percent of the property and 50 percent of the profits from the sale of the lots.

Mr. Marrazzo proceeds with his plan in 2007. Site servicing costs during 2008 total $1,200,000. All the lots are sold before December 31, 2008 for proceeds of $4,400,000.

Assume that he is developing his land under the following two scenarios:

Case A A partnership is created with Digger Inc. on December 1, 2007. Mr. Marrazzo uses the rollover provision to defer reporting the accrued gain on the land. The partnership agreement specifies that Mr. Marrazzo is entitled to 100 percent of the gain that has accrued on the property up to December 1, 2007 and 50 percent of any subsequent gains.

Case B He enters into a joint venture agreement with Digger Inc. on December 1, 2007. He transfers ownership of 50 percent of the property to Digger Inc. on December 1, 2007.

Required:

A. For Case A, calculate the Taxable Income inclusions for Mr. Marrazzo in 2007 and 2008. Also calculate the ACB of his partnership interest on December 31, 2008 and January 1, 2009.

B. For Case B, calculate the Taxable Income inclusions for Mr. Marrazzo in 2007 and 2008.

C. Compare the results for Case A and Case B.

Assignment Problem Twenty - 4

Jennifer, Christine, and Danny recently graduated from college and began a business called the Canadian Coffee Club ("CCC") that they operate as a partnership. They share profits and losses equally.

Based on the accounting rules applicable to partnerships, the income statement of CCC for the 2007 year is as follows:

Canadian Coffee Club
Partnership Income Statement
Year Ending December 31, 2007

Gross Business Revenues		$86,000
Operating Expenses	($31,500)	
Administrative Expenses	(17,300)	(48,800)
Net Business Income		$ 37,200
Eligible Dividends Received		
From Canadian Corporations		3,440
Gain On Sale Of Shares		6,000
Total Income		$ 46,640

Other Information:

1. Included in operating and administrative expenses are the following:

   • $2,400 of salaries to each of the three partners.

   • $3,300 of interest to Christine ($1,300 relates to a bona fide loan she made to CCC and the remaining $2,000 relates to her capital contribution).

   • $1,100 paid to Danny for personal expenses.

   • $1,700 to Jennifer as a reimbursement of CCC expenses.

   • $1,000 of charitable donations

   • $1,450 of accounting depreciation.

2. The partnership is entitled to maximum CCA of $2,000.

3. The shares that were sold during 2007 had an adjusted cost base of $11,000. They were sold for $17,000.

Required: Calculate the minimum amount of Net Business Income from the partnership to be recorded in the tax returns of each of the partners for 2007. Also indicate other amounts that would be allocated to the partners by the partnership, as well as any credits against Tax Payable that would result from these allocations.

Assignment Problem Twenty - 5

Burt and Sam Jones are brothers and professional accountants. They operate a partnership that specializes in doing accounting and tax work for small to medium sized manufacturing companies. The partnership agreement calls for them to share the partnership profits equally. The partnership has a fiscal year that ends on December 31.

For the current year, they have prepared the following Income Statement for the partnership:

Burt And Sam Jones
Partnership Income Statement
Current Year Ending December 31

Revenues		$707,000
Eligible Dividends Received From Canadian Corporations		32,000
Gain On Sale Of Shares Of Canadian Public Corporations		52,000
Total Revenues		$791,000
Expenses:		
Salaries To Staff	($286,000)	
Office Rent	(64,000)	
Office Supplies	(26,000)	
CCA On Office Equipment	(29,000)	
Charitable Donations	(63,000)	
Drawings By Burt	(145,000)	
Drawings By Sam	(153,000)	(766,000)
Net Income (Accounting Values)		$ 25,000

The Revenues include the December 31 balance of work in process of $232,000. The corresponding balance as at the previous December 31 year end was $98,000, and this amount was included in the accounting revenues for that year. While the Jones brothers have chosen to include work in process as a revenue in their accounting statements, they have elected under ITA 34 to exclude these amounts from their tax calculations.

Required: Calculate the minimum amount of Net Business Income from the partnership to be recorded in the tax returns of each of the brothers for the current year ending December 31. Also indicate other amounts that would be allocated to the brothers by the partnership, as well as any credits against Tax Payable that would result from these allocations.

Assignment Problem Twenty - 6

Two of your university friends, who became lawyers, left the firms where they were employed, and set up their own practice on January 1, 2007. They started the practice by contributing $10,000 working capital each and decided to split the profits equally. They pay themselves equal salaries that they withdraw throughout the year. Their bookkeeper has prepared the following financial statements:

Friends Forever Law Practice
Balance Sheet
As At December 31, 2007

Cash	$ 2,000
Accounts Receivable	30,000
Work In Progress	25,000
Computer Hardware (At Cost)	10,000
Computer Applications Software (At Cost)	8,000
Total Assets	$75,000
Accounts Payable	$15,000
Initial Partner Capital	20,000
Income For The Period	40,000
Total Equities	$75,000

Friends Forever Law Practice
Income Statement
For The Year Ending December 31, 2007

Revenues	$230,000
Meals And Entertainment	$ 6,000
Office Supplies	4,000
Partners' Salaries	130,000
Rent	24,000
Secretary's Salary	26,000
Total Expenses	$190,000
Income For The Period (Accounting Values)	$ 40,000

The work in progress represents work done by the lawyers at their standard charge rate that has not been billed to clients at the year end.

Required:

A. Your friends have come to you to determine the minimum amount that they must include in their 2007 tax returns as business income from the partnership.

B. They would also like to know if there are any partnership related expenses that they may have incurred personally that they can deduct on their 2007 tax return.

C. Compute the ACB of each partner's partnership interest at December 31, 2007 and January 1, 2008.

Your answers should ignore GST and PST considerations.

Assignment Problem Twenty - 7

On May 1, 2004, Susan Field, Christine Black, and John Henderson form a partnership to provide management consulting services. The partners each contribute $350,000 and agree that all income and losses are to be shared equally. The fiscal year for the partnership is established to end on December 31.

For the period May 1, 2004 to December 31, 2006, the following information is available:

• The partnership earned net business income of $273,000.

• The partnership realized a $42,000 capital gain (this amount is not included in the net business income figure).

• During 2006, the partnership made a number of charitable donations. The total amount involved was $9,000, and this total was allocated equally to each of the three partners (this amount is not included in the net business income figure).

• During this period, John Henderson made withdrawals from the partnership totaling $81,000.

• Additional capital was required to expand the operations of the office and, as a consequence, each partner contributed an additional $100,000 in cash.

John Henderson decided to withdraw from the partnership effective January 1, 2007. After some negotiations, the other partners agreed to pay him $550,000 in cash for his interest in the partnership. The payment is made on January 31, 2007. John incurred legal and accounting fees in conjunction with this transaction totaling $2,500.

Required: Calculate John Henderson's gain or loss on the disposition of his partnership interest. Explain how this amount, and any other amounts related to the partnership, will be taxed in his hands.

Assignment Problem Twenty - 8

Yoho Airways became a limited partner in the new Frontier Holidays Partnership in 2007. The partnership agreement required a payment of $50,000 for a 10 percent interest in the Partnership. Of this amount, $30,000 was paid in cash in 2007, with the remainder paid in January, 2008. Yoho's share of all income and losses of the Frontier Holidays Partnership is 10 percent.

Frontier experienced a $400,000 loss in 2007, a $70,000 loss in 2008, followed by no income or loss in 2009. In each of the years under consideration, Yoho has income of over $100,000 from other sources.

Required: For each of 2007, 2008 and 2009, calculate the following for Yoho Airways:

- The adjusted cost base at the end of the year.
- The at-risk amount.
- The limited partnership income (loss) for the year.
- The deductible income (loss) for the year.
- The limited partnership loss carry forward at the end of the year.

Assignment Problem Twenty - 9

A number of years ago, Jack Howard, Bud Jones, and Dwight Delaney established the Howard, Jones, and Delaney Partnership. At the time the partnership was formed, each of the partners invested $600,000 in cash. The partnership agreement calls for all income and losses to be shared equally. The fiscal year of the partnership ends on December 31.

On January 1 of the current year, the adjusted cost base of the partnership interests that are applicable to the three partners are as follows:

Jack Howard	$1,173,000
Bud Jones	930,000
Dwight Delaney	756,000
Total	$2,859,000

Early in the current year, the property of the partnership was transferred to a corporation in return for the following consideration:

Cash	$1,200,000
Preferred Shares (At Fair Market Value)	900,000
Common Shares (At Fair Market Value)	1,800,000
Total Consideration	$3,900,000

The partners elect to use the rollover provisions of ITA 85(2) and ITA 85(3). As a result, the partnership will be liquidated within 60 days of the ITA 85(2) rollover and property received from the corporation by the partnership will be transferred to the three partners in accordance with ITA 85(3). Under the terms of the partnership agreement, they receive the following amounts:

	Howard	Jones	Delaney	Total
Cash	$ 620,000	$ 377,000	$ 203,000	$1,200,000
Preferred Shares	300,000	300,000	300,000	900,000
Common Shares	600,000	600,000	600,000	1,800,000
Total	$1,520,000	$1,277,000	$1,103,000	$3,900,000

Required: Determine the adjusted cost base for the assets received by the partners as a result of this rollover of partnership assets to the corporation. Calculate the capital gain or loss for each partner resulting from the transfer under the provisions of ITA 85(3).

Assignment Problem Twenty - 10

Note This problem involves knowledge of "additional business income" when the election of a non-calendar fiscal period is made. This material is covered in Chapter 8 of the text.

On April 1, 2004, Craig Cardinal and Don Kvill formed a partnership to teach small craft flying lessons. They elected to use a March 31 fiscal year end, to coincide with the end of the winter aircraft maintenance program and the beginning of the summer training schedule. The two partners share equally in the profits of the partnership.

During the year ending March 31, 2006, the partnership earned Taxable Income of $64,000, of which $42,200 was deemed earned before December 31, 2005 for the alternative income reserve purposes. Also, the partners withdrew $56,000.

From April 1, 2006 to March 31, 2007, the partnership earned $58,000 and the partners withdrew $74,000.

Required: Determine the minimum amount of partnership income that Craig Cardinal and Don Kvill will have to include in their personal tax returns for the years 2006 and 2007.

CHAPTER 21

Trusts And Estate Planning

Introduction

21-1.   As is noted in Chapter 3, the *Income Tax Act* recognizes three groups of taxpayers: individuals, corporations, and trusts. In previous Chapters we have given detailed consideration to the determination of Taxable Income and Tax Payable for both individuals and corporations. In this Chapter, we will turn our attention to how this process works in the case of trusts.

21-2.   Also in Chapter 3, we provide a brief introduction to tax planning, providing general descriptions of tax avoidance, tax deferral, and income splitting. In this Chapter we will find that trusts are one of the most powerful weapons in the tax planner's arsenal. They can provide a convenient and cost effective mechanism for splitting large amounts of property income among family members. Trusts can also be used to access the deferral and income splitting opportunities that are present in estate freeze transactions. In addition, they can play a significant role in many other tax and business planning arrangements.

21-3.   While trusts remain a very powerful tax planning tool, you should note that the Government has, over the last decade, introduced legislative changes which have made trusts more difficult to use. This includes the introduction of the tax on split income (a.k.a. kiddie tax), the elimination of the general preferred beneficiary election, trust migration rules, and proposals that affect offshore trusts.

21-4.   A further problem is that many tax professionals do not have a very complete understanding of how to use trusts. This probably reflects the fact that, in order to deal effectively with the implementation of effective trust structures requires both legal and accounting training. In some cases, particularly those involving estates, some degree of knowledge of sociology, philosophy, and religion could also be helpful.

21-5.   We have previously encountered trusts in this text. In Chapter 9, which deals with property income, we indicated that most mutual funds are organized as trusts. Also in that Chapter, we noted that, for a variety of reasons, investments in income trusts have become very popular with both individual and institutional investors. In Chapter 13, when we considered various types of retirement savings arrangements, we noted that most of these arrangements involve the use of trusts. Registered Pension Plans, Registered Retirement Savings Plans, Registered Retirement Income Funds, and Deferred Profit Sharing Plans, all involve assets being contributed to a trust.

21-6.   In this Chapter, we will not revisit the types of trusts that were considered in earlier Chapters. Rather, our focus in this Chapter will be on personal trusts that have been established by individuals as a part of a tax or estate planning scenario. This will include both trusts established during the lifetime of an individual, as well as trusts that arise as a consequence of the death of an individual. While trusts can be very important in tax planning arrangements that involve private corporations, we will not deal with this subject. In our view, the complexities involved in such arrangements go beyond the scope of this text.

21-7.   In the course of this Chapter we will give specific attention to the use of trusts in estate planning. Because of the importance of this subject and the fact that we have not provided coverage elsewhere in this text, we will expand our coverage of estate planning to issues that go beyond the use of trusts. Particular attention will be given to general coverage of estate freeze transactions.

Basic Concepts

What Is A Personal Trust?

Legal Perspective

21-8.   From a legal perspective, a personal trust is a relationship that arises when a settlor transfers property to a trustee to hold and administer for the exclusive benefit of the beneficiaries. This relationship is depicted Figure 21-1.

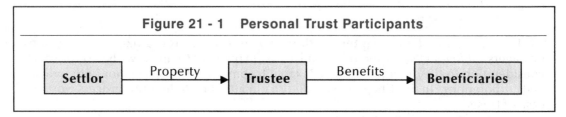

Figure 21 - 1   Personal Trust Participants

Settlor → Property → Trustee → Benefits → Beneficiaries

21-9.   The settlor is the person who sets up the trust and makes the initial transfer of property to the trustee. The trustee is the individual or institution that holds formal legal title to that property, while the beneficiaries are persons who will benefit from the property that is held by the trustee. The beneficiaries can have an interest in the income from the property, the capital value of the property, or both.

21-10.   While each of these roles is separate in terms of its function in the trust arrangement, it is possible for more than one of the roles to be played by a single individual. A common example of this would be a father who is the settlor of a trust in favour of his children, but also serves as the trustee who holds the trust assets.

21-11.   A basic feature of trust arrangements is the separation of the legal and beneficial ownership of the transferred property. Outside of trust arrangements, the legal owner of a property is normally entitled to any benefits associated with owning the property. This is not the case here. While the trustee holds legal title to the property, all of the benefits will accrue to the persons who are specified as the beneficiaries of the trust.

21-12.   Note that the trust is not a separate entity, from a legal perspective. A trust cannot own property, cannot enter into contracts, and cannot be a defendant or plaintiff in a legal action. With respect to the transferred property, these rights and obligations belong to the trustee(s).

21-13.   Trusts are subject to provincial legislation and, as a consequence, the detailed rules will vary from province to province. One point to note, however, is that it is generally difficult to vary or revoke a trust. This is of particular importance in the case of deceased individuals. While the content of a will can be challenged by a disgruntled beneficiary and its intentions altered by a surviving spouse, this is a much more difficult process when assets are placed in a trust.

Tax Perspective

21-14. While a trust is not a separate entity from a legal perspective, the *Income Tax Act* takes a different view. With respect to this issue, the *Act* states the following:

> **ITA 104(2)** A trust shall, for the purposes of this Act, and without affecting the liability of the trustee or legal representative for that person's own income tax, be deemed to be in respect of the trust property an individual, ...

21-15. By indicating that, with respect to trust property, a trust is deemed to be an individual, the *Act* gives trusts separate entity tax status. This means that there must be a determination of Taxable Income and Tax Payable for a trust, and that a trust will have to file a separate tax return.

Trusts And Estates

21-16. The dictionary contains several definitions of the term estate, the most general of which indicates that an estate consists of the property and possessions of any individual. However, as the term is used in the *Income Tax Act*, the meaning is more restrictive. In this context, the term estate refers to the property of a deceased person. Further, the *Act* uses the terms trust and estate as having the same meaning. This approach is indicated as follows:

> **ITA 104(1)** In this Act, a reference to a trust or estate (in this subdivision referred to as a "trust") shall, ...

21-17. This is a somewhat peculiar approach to terminology in that a trust is not the same as an estate, from a legal perspective. When an individual dies and bequeaths his property through a will, his estate will be administered by an executor. This executor will have responsibilities similar to those of a trustee. However, the beneficiary of a trust holds an equitable title to the trust property, while the trustee holds legal title. In contrast, the beneficiary of an estate does not have any interest in the estate assets while they are under the administration of an executor.

21-18. Given these differences, why does the *Act* treat the terms trust and estate in an identical manner? The answer is procedural in nature. When an individual dies and bequeaths his property through a will, immediate distribution of all of his property may not be possible. For example, if there is real estate that must be sold, this process may require a significant period of time.

21-19. During the period between an individual's death and the time that all of his property is distributed to his beneficiaries, it is possible that some income will accrue on the estate property held by the executor. The deceased person's income to the date of death will be included in his final tax return. However, the income earned by the estate during the period that it is administered by the executor cannot be allocated to either the deceased person or to his beneficiaries. To solve this problem, the *Act* requires that the income of the estate be included in a trust return (T3). As the rules for filing a return for this "estate" are the same as those applicable to a trust, the *Act* treats these two terms as synonyms.

Establishing A Trust

Three Certainties

21-20. The trusts that we are dealing with in this Chapter are established by words that are set out in a trust agreement. While some provinces allow, under limited circumstances, the use of oral trust agreements, this is rarely a wise course of action. Even if such agreements are accepted for legal purposes, the CRA tends to be skeptical of such agreements and may take the position that no trust exists.

21-21. In deciding whether or not a trust has, in fact, been created, it is important to look at what the courts have referred to as the three certainties. These can be described as follows:

> **Certainty Of Intention** The person creating the trust must intend to create the trust and that intention must be clear to outside observers. This is usually accomplished by preparing a written document establishing the trust.

Certainty Of Property The property that is to be held in the trust must be known with certainty at the time the trust is created. This is usually accomplished by specifying the property in the trust document.

Certainty Of Beneficiaries The persons who will benefit from the trust property must be known with certainty at the time the trust is created. This is usually accomplished by specifying these persons in the trust document. Note that these persons must either be named (e.g., Ms. Sally Phar) or be part of an identifiable class (e.g., my children).

21-22. In addition to establishing the facts required by the three certainties criteria, there must be an actual transfer of the trust property to the trustee. Until this transfer is completed, the trust does not exist.

Importance Of Proper Documentation

21-23. Care must be taken to ensure that all of the necessary actions to create a trust have been carried out effectively. If one or more of the required elements is missing, the tax consequences can be significant. For example, if an individual attempted to establish a trust to split income with his adult children, a failure to complete all of the requirements necessary to that process could result in his being taxed on the property income, rather than having it taxed in the hands of his adult children. This could result in the payment of significant additional taxes.

Exercise Twenty-One - 1

Subject: Establishing A Trust

In each of the following Cases, an individual is attempting to establish a trust. For each of these Cases, indicate whether the attempt has been successful. Explain your conclusion.

Case A Jack Black sends a cheque to his sister to be used for the education of her two children.

Case B Jane Folsem transfers property to a trustee, specifying that the income from the property should be distributed to her friends.

Case C Robert Jones transfers property to a trustee, specifying that the income from the property should be distributed to his children.

Case D Suzanne Bush has signed an agreement that specifies that she will transfer her securities portfolio to a trustee, with the income to be distributed to her spouse.

End of Exercise. Solution available in Study Guide.

Non-Tax Reasons For Using Trusts

21-24. In this Chapter we are largely concerned with the tax planning uses of trusts. However, it is important to note that trusts have non-tax uses which, in some situations, may be more important than the tax features of the particular arrangement. Some of these non-tax uses are as follows:

Administration Of Assets A trust can be used to separate the administration of assets from the receipt of benefits. For example, an individual with extensive investment knowledge might have assets transferred to a trust for his spouse at the time of his death. The goal here could be to provide professional management of the assets for the benefit of a spouse with only limited knowledge of investments.

Protection From Creditors An individual proprietor of a business might place some of his personal assets in a trust in order to protect them from claims by the creditors of the business. However, if this transfer is made when the individual is experiencing financial difficulties with his business, there are provisions in bankruptcy legislation which may undo the transfer.

Privacy If assets are bequeathed in a will, they will be subject to probate, the results of which are available to the public. This is not the case with assets that are in a trust when an individual dies.

Avoiding Changes In Beneficiaries If a father places assets in a trust for the benefit of his minor children, it ensures that these children will be the ultimate beneficiaries of the property. In contrast, if, as is common, his will bequeaths his assets to his wife with the intention that his children will be the ultimate beneficiaries of his property, his wife has no legal obligation to carry out this intention. This can be a particularly important issue if the surviving spouse remarries and other children become part of the family.

21-25.   While there are additional examples of non-tax uses of trusts, the preceding should serve to give you some idea of the versatility of trust arrangements.

Classification Of Trusts

Introduction

21-26.   The CRA's *Trust Guide* lists 17 different types of trusts, largely based on definitions that are included in the *Income Tax Act*. Understanding the meaning of the terms on this CRA list is complicated by the fact that some of the listed items are, in fact, a sub-classification of other items included on the list (e.g., an alter ego trust is a type of personal trust). A further road block to understanding the classification of trusts is that trusts are also classified in popular usage in terms of their goals or objectives. Such terms as "family trusts" and "spendthrift trusts" are commonly used, despite the fact that they have no real meaning in terms of tax legislation.

21-27.   In this material, we will not provide a comprehensive classification of trusts, nor will we attempt to provide definitions for all of the terms that are applied to trusts in tax legislation and general practice. As indicated in the introduction to this Chapter, our coverage is limited to trusts that have been established by individuals as part of a tax or estate planning scenario. As all of these trusts fall within the classification of personal trusts, we will begin by considering this category.

Personal Trusts

General Definition

21-28.   The *Income Tax Act* contains the following definition of a personal trust:

ITA 248(1)   Personal Trust means
(a) a testamentary trust, or
(b) an inter vivos trust, no beneficial interest in which was acquired for consideration payable directly or indirectly to
(i) the trust, or
(ii) any person who has made a contribution to the trust by way of transfer, assignment or other disposition of property (does not include unit trusts).

Testamentary Trust

21-29.   As is often the case in tax legislation, an understanding of the preceding definition requires definitions of some of the included terms. The first of these definitions is as follows:

ITA 108(1)   Testamentary Trust in a taxation year means a trust that arose on and as a consequence of the death of an individual.

21-30.   You will recall that, as used in the *Income Tax Act*, the term trust means trust or estate. This means that a testamentary trust can either be specifically established through an individual's will or, alternatively, if no trust is explicitly established in the will, the deceased individual's estate becomes a trust for tax purposes.

21-31.   If a testamentary trust is established for an individual's spouse or common-law partner, it is referred to as a spousal or common-law partner trust and special tax rules apply. There is no special designation for testamentary trusts with beneficiaries other than a spouse.

Inter Vivos Trust

21-32.   The *Income Tax Act* also contains a definition of inter vivos trust:

> **ITA 108(1)   Inter Vivos Trust** means a trust other than a testamentary trust.

21-33.   As a testamentary trust is one that is established by the death of an individual, for our purposes, an alternative way of defining an inter vivos trust is that it is a trust that is established by a living individual.

21-34.   In this material, we will give consideration to four categories of inter vivos trusts. Two of these categories, alter ego trusts and joint spousal or common-law partner trusts, are defined in the *Income Tax Act*. The remaining two, family trusts and spousal or common-law partner trusts are defined only through common usage in practice.

Testamentary Vs. Inter Vivos Trusts

Types Of Testamentary And Inter Vivos Trusts

21-35.   As defined in the previous section, the basic classification of personal trusts is between testamentary and inter vivos trusts. In this Chapter, we will deal with two types of testamentary trusts and four types of inter vivos trusts. This sub-classification is outlined in Figure 21-2:

Figure 21 - 2 Classification Of Personal Trusts	
Testamentary	**Inter Vivos**
Spousal Or Common-Law Partner	Spousal Or Common-Law Partner
Other Beneficiaries	Alter Ego
	Joint Spousal Or Common-Law Partner
	Family

21-36.   The individual types of trusts identified in Figure 21-2 can be described as follows:

Spousal Or Common-Law Partner Trust This category of trust is not defined in the *Income Tax Act*. Rather, it is a term that is used when a trust is established for a spouse or common-law partner. Such trusts can either be an inter vivos trust established by a living person or, alternatively, a testamentary trust that is established when an individual dies.

As will be discussed when we present material on the taxation of trusts, if such trusts meet certain conditions, the *Income Tax Act* contains rollover provisions (ITA 73(1.01) for inter vivos trusts and ITA 70(6) for testamentary trusts) which allow property to be transferred to the trustee on a tax free basis. When these conditions are met, the trust is usually referred to as a qualifying spousal or common-law partner trust.

Alter Ego Trust An alter ego trust is an inter vivos trust created by an individual who is 65 years of age or older with himself as the sole beneficiary during his lifetime. As was the case with spousal or common-law partner trusts, if certain conditions are met, the *Income Tax Act* contains a rollover provision that allows property to be transferred into or out of the trust on a tax free basis.

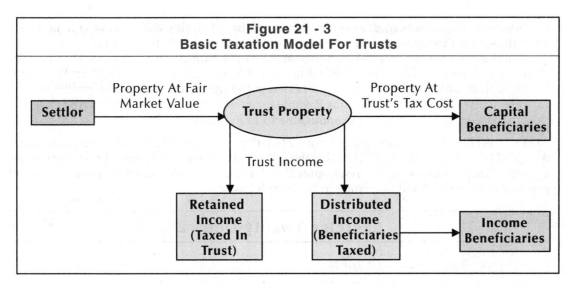

Figure 21 - 3
Basic Taxation Model For Trusts

Joint Spousal Or Common-Law Partner Trust A joint spousal or common-law partner trust is an inter vivos trust created by an individual who is 65 years of age or older. Similar to the alter ego trust, this type of trust is created with the individual and his spouse or common-law partner as the sole beneficiaries during their lifetimes. Also similar to the alter ego trust scenario, if certain conditions are met, there is a roll-over provision in the *Income Tax Act* that allows property to be transferred into the trust on a tax free basis.

Family Trust While the term family trust is not always used in a consistent manner, it generally refers to a trust that has been established by an individual for the benefit of family members. While a family trust could be a testamentary trust, the term is usually used in reference to an inter vivos trust. The most common goal of this type of trust is income splitting.

Taxation Of Trusts

The Basic Model

21-37.   While there are many variations that depend on the particular type of trust we are dealing with, as well as complications associated with the measurement of trust Taxable Income and Tax Payable, the basic model for the taxation of trusts is as shown in Figure 21-3. There are three features of this basic model that should be noted:

Settlor's Transfer Of Property To The Trust   When property is transferred to a trust by a settlor, it generally results in a disposition for tax purposes. In the usual situation, these dispositions are deemed to occur at fair market value, triggering various tax consequences (e.g., capital gains, recapture, or terminal losses). There are, however, some important rollover provisions for property transferred into a trust. These are discussed beginning in Paragraph 21-39.

Transfers Of Trust Property To Beneficiaries   If trust property is transferred to a capital beneficiary, ITA 107(2) provides a rollover provision that allows the property to be transferred at the tax cost to the trust. The proceeds of disposition to the trust and the cost to the beneficiary will be equal to the tax cost that is recorded in the trust. For exceptions to this general provision, see Rollovers To Beneficiaries beginning in Paragraph 21-52.

Income From The Trust Property   Once property has been transferred to the trust, income will begin to accrue to the trust. It is fundamental to most of the tax planning uses of trusts that income earned in the trust can be deducted by the trust from Taxable Income to the extent that it is either distributed to beneficiaries or they are entitled to enforce payment. We will find that in many situations, trusts will distribute all of their income, resulting in no Tax Payable at the trust level.

Any income that a trust does not distribute to beneficiaries will be taxed in the trust. Subsequent distribution of this income is on a tax free basis. At this point you should note that there is a very important difference in the calculation of Tax Payable for an inter vivos trust and the calculation of Tax Payable for a testamentary trust. In the case of an inter vivos trust, all of the income that is retained in the trust is taxed at the maximum federal rate of 29 percent. In contrast, Tax Payable for a testamentary trust is calculated using the graduated rate schedule that is applicable to individuals.

21-38.   While it is not illustrated in Figure 21-3, there is a special anti-avoidance rule that is designed to prevent extended deferral of the potential tax on capital gains. This rule requires a deemed disposition of capital assets after they have been held in the trust for 21 years and will be discussed in detail beginning in Paragraph 21-58.

Exercise Twenty-One - 2

Subject: Basic Taxation Of Trusts

On January 1, 2007, Joanne March transfers debt securities with a fair market value of $220,000 to a newly established inter vivos trust for which her 28 year old daughter, Jocelyn, is the only beneficiary. The cost of these securities to Joanne March was $200,000. During 2007, the securities earn and receive interest of $15,000, all of which is distributed to Jocelyn.

On January 1, 2008, the securities are transferred to Jocelyn in satisfaction of her capital interest in the trust. At this time, the fair market value of the securities has increased to $230,000.

Indicate the tax consequences for Joanne, Jocelyn, and the trust, in each of the years 2007 and 2008.

End of Exercise.   Solution available in Study Guide.

Rollovers To A Trust

Introduction

21-39.   The general taxation model for trusts requires that contributions to the trust be recorded at fair market value, often resulting in a significant tax cost for the contributor. However, as we noted in our material on the classification of trusts, spousal or common-law partner trusts, alter ego trusts, and joint spousal or common-law partner trusts can make such transfers on a rollover basis, provided certain specific conditions are met.

21-40.   In this section we are concerned with the conditions that qualify these three special types of trusts for the tax free rollover of contributions. When the trust qualifies, the rollover is accomplished by deeming the property to have been disposed of by the settlor at either its adjusted cost base (non-depreciable property) or its UCC (depreciable property), resulting in no tax consequences for the settlor at the time of transfer. The trust is deemed to have acquired the property at a value equal to the proceeds of disposition to the settlor. In the case of depreciable property, the trust retains the settlor's original capital cost for purposes of determining recapture of CCA.

21-41.   We will revisit these three types of trusts in our later section on tax planning. At that point we will discuss how these trusts can be used to reduce or defer taxes.

Qualifying Spousal Or Common-Law Partner Trust

21-42.   You may recall from Chapter 12 that ITA 73(1.01) contains a rollover provision that allows a living individual to transfer capital property to a spouse or common-law partner without tax consequences. ITA 70(6) provides for a similar rollover for the capital property of a deceased individual.

21-43.   While we did not discuss this in Chapter 12, these rollovers apply whether the transfer is directly to the spouse or common-law partner or, alternatively, to a trust in favour of a spouse or common-law partner. However, in the case of a transfer to a trust, the trust arrangement must meet certain conditions in order to qualify for the rollover. When it meets these conditions, it is commonly referred to as a qualifying spousal or common-law partner trust.

21-44.   With respect to inter vivos spousal or common-law partner trusts, the conditions for qualifying for the rollover are as follows:

ITA 73(1.01)(c)(i)   The individual's spouse or common-law partner is entitled to receive all of the income of the trust that arises before the spouse's or common-law partner's death and no person except the spouse or common-law partner may, before the spouse's or common-law partner's death, receive or otherwise obtain the use of any of the income or capital of the trust.

21-45.   A similar provision provides the rollover conditions for testamentary spousal or common-law partner trusts:

ITA 70(6)(b)   A trust, created by the taxpayer's will, that was resident in Canada immediately after the time the property vested indefeasibly in the trust and under which

(i)   the taxpayer's spouse or common-law partner is entitled to receive all of the income of the trust that arises before the spouse's or common-law partner's death, and

(ii)   no person except the spouse or common-law partner may, before the spouse's or common-law partner's death, receive or otherwise obtain the use of any of the income or capital of the trust.

21-46.   When these conditions are met, any property that is contributed to the trust, either by a living person or as the result of the individual's death, will be transferred at the individual's tax cost. For non-depreciable property, this value is the transferor's adjusted cost base. For depreciable property, the transfer is at the transferor's UCC amount. However, for purposes of determining recaptured CCA, the transferor's original capital cost is deemed to be the transferee's capital cost.

21-47.   While these rollover provisions are, in general, a desirable way to avoid paying taxes on transfers to a spousal or common-law partner trust, there may be circumstances where the taxpayer would prefer a transfer at fair market value. For example, if the settlor of the trust has unused capital loss carry forwards or property that is eligible for the lifetime capital gains deduction, he might wish to trigger capital gains in order to absorb these amounts. Fortunately, the settlor has the choice of electing out of the rollover provisions. For inter vivos transfers, the election is under ITA 73(1). For testamentary transfers the election is made by the settlor's legal representative is under ITA 70(6.2).

Exercise Twenty-One - 3

Subject: Transfers To Spousal Trusts

Louise died late this year, and bequeathed a parcel of land to a qualifying spousal trust created in her will. Louise is survived by her husband. The land has an adjusted cost base of $60,000 and was valued at $90,000 on the date of her death. Determine the tax consequences of the transfer, including the adjusted cost base for the land in the trust.

End of Exercise. Solution available in Study Guide.

Alter Ego Trust

21-48.   An alter ego trust is an inter vivos trust established by a settlor who is 65 years of age or older at the time the trust is settled. To qualify for a tax free rollover of assets to the trust, the *Income Tax Act* specifies the following conditions:

ITA 73(1.01)(c)(ii)   The individual is entitled to receive all of the income of the trust that arises before the individual's death and no person except the individual may, before the individual's death, receive or otherwise obtain the use of any of the income or capital of the trust.

21-49.   As was the case with the spousal or common-law partner trust, an individual can elect out of this rollover, choosing to have the transfer to the trust take place at fair market value.

Joint Spousal Or Common-Law Partner Trust

21-50.   Like an alter ego trust, a joint spousal or common-law partner trust is an inter vivos trust established by a settlor who is 65 years of age or older at the time the trust is settled. The difference in this case is that both the settlor and his spouse or common-law partner are beneficiaries of the trust. More specifically, to qualify for the tax free rollover of assets to the trust, the *Income Tax Act* specifies the following conditions:

ITA 73(1.01)(c)(iii) either

(A) the individual or the individual's spouse is, in combination with the other, entitled to receive all of the income of the trust that arises before the later of the death of the individual and the death of the spouse and no other person may, before the later of those deaths, receive or otherwise obtain the use of any of the income or capital of the trust, or

(B) the individual or the individual's common-law partner is, in combination with the other, entitled to receive all of the income of the trust that arises before the later of the death of the individual and the death of the common-law partner and no other person may, before the later of those deaths, receive or otherwise obtain the use of any of the income or capital of the trust.

21-51.   As was the case with the alter ego trust, an individual can elect out of this rollover, choosing to have the transfer to the trust take place at fair market value.

Exercise Twenty-One - 4

Subject: Transfers To Trusts

An individual has common shares with a cost of $1,000 and a current fair market value of $1,600. Seven Scenarios are presented for the transfer of these shares to a trust. For each Scenario, indicate the tax consequences to the settlor at the time of transfer, as well as the adjusted cost base of the property within the trust.

Scenario 1:	Transfer by settlor to inter vivos trust for adult child.
Scenario 2:	Transfer by settlor to inter vivos trust for minor child.
Scenario 3:	Transfer to testamentary trust for friend.
Scenario 4:	Transfer to inter vivos qualifying spousal trust.
Scenario 5:	Transfer to testamentary qualifying spousal trust.
Scenario 6:	Transfer to joint spousal trust.
Scenario 7:	Transfer to alter ego trust.

End of Exercise. Solution available in Study Guide.

Rollovers To Capital Beneficiaries

General Rule

21-52.   As is the case with transfers by a settlor into a trust, the transfer of assets to a capital beneficiary is a disposition. However, for many trusts ITA 107(2) provides a tax free rollover for these transfers. The rollover is accomplished by deeming the property to have been disposed of by the trust at either its adjusted cost base (non-depreciable property) or its UCC (depreciable property).

21-53.   The beneficiary is deemed to have acquired the property at a value equal to the cost amount to the trust, resulting in no tax consequences at the time of transfer to the beneficiary. In the case of depreciable property, the beneficiary retains the capital cost of the property to the trust for purposes of determining subsequent recapture of CCA.

Exceptions

21-54.   The logic of the preceding rule is based on the fact that the transfer of assets into the trust was, in terms of the beneficial interest in the assets, a transfer of the assets to the beneficiaries. Provided that tax was assessed on the transfer into the trust, it would not be equitable to assess tax again when the asset is legally transferred to the beneficiaries.

21-55.   We have noted, however, that with certain types of trusts, the transfer from the settlor to the trust is not a taxable transaction. Specifically, qualifying spousal or common-law partner trusts, alter ego trusts, and joint spousal or common-law partner trusts can use a rollover provision to transfer assets into a trust. Since no tax was assessed on the transfer into these trusts, it would not seem equitable to allow the assets to be transferred to all beneficiaries on a rollover basis.

21-56.   Tax legislation agrees with this view. Instead of being transferred at the tax cost to the trust, the ITA 107(2) rollover does not apply in the following cases:

- if property is transferred out of an **alter ego** trust to anyone other than the settlor,

- if property is transferred out of a **joint spousal** or common-law partner trust to anyone other than the settlor or the spouse or common-law partner, and

- if property is transferred out of a **qualifying spousal** or common-law partner trust to anyone other than a spouse or common-law partner.

21-57.   When the ITA 107(2) rollover provision does not apply, the transfer of assets from the trust to a capital beneficiary will be recorded at the fair market value of the transferred assets. This will generally result in tax consequences for the trust.

21 Year Deemed Disposition Rule

21-58.   Trust arrangements ordinarily allow capital gains on trust assets to accumulate without tax consequences for extended periods of time. Unless the capital assets are sold or distributed by the trust, accrued gains will not attract any taxes and the assets can be left in a trust for periods that exceed the life of the individual establishing the trust.

21-59.   In order to place limits on this deferral process, ITA 104(4)(b) requires that there be a deemed disposition and reacquisition of trust capital property every 21 years. The disposition is deemed to be at fair market value, resulting in the recognition of any accrued gains on the assets. In the case of depreciable assets, if the deemed proceeds are less than the original capital cost, the original value is retained for purposes of determining recapture.

21-60.   This rule is generally applicable only to personal trusts and does not apply to trusts such as employee benefit plans or registered education savings plans. Further, the rules are modified in the case of qualifying spousal or common-law partner trusts, alter ego trusts, and joint spousal or common-law partner trusts.

21-61.   For qualifying spousal or common-law partner trusts, the deemed disposition occurs with the death of the spouse or common-law partner. In the case of alter ego trusts, the death of the settlor is the event that triggers the deemed disposition. Finally, with joint spousal or common-law partner trusts, the deemed disposition occurs only at the later of the death of the settlor or the death of the spouse or common-law partner.

Net Income For Tax Purposes Of A Trust

Basic Rules

21-62.   The overriding principle in determining the Net Income For Tax Purposes of a trust results from the statement in ITA 104(2) that a trust should be treated as an individual. This means that the general rules used by individuals, as modified by trust legislation, are applicable in computing a trust's Net Income For Tax Purposes.

21-63.   Capital gains and losses are realized on the disposition of capital assets. Also, in the calculation of Net Income For Tax Purposes, any taxable dividends that are not allocated to beneficiaries are grossed up as they would be for individuals. Finally, deductions are allowed for non-capital, net capital, and certain other types of loss carry overs.

21-64.   There are, however, additional items that must be added or deducted in calculating the Net Income For Tax Purposes of a trust. These items can be described as follows:

Amounts Paid Or Payable To Beneficiaries   As was noted in our description of the basic trust taxation model, a trust can deduct amounts that are paid or payable to one or more beneficiaries. This is usually the most important of the adjustments to the trust's income in that, in many cases, all of the trust's income will be allocated to beneficiaries. Because of the importance of this deduction, it will be the subject of a separate section of this Chapter beginning in Paragraph 21-74.

Trustee's Or Executor's Fees   Any amounts paid that are related to earning trust income, or that are paid to an executor or trustee whose principal business includes the provision of such services, are deductible to the trust.

Amounts Paid By The Trust And Allocated To The Income Of A Beneficiary   A trust can make payments to third parties to provide goods or services to beneficiaries. The CRA considers such amounts to be another way of paying income to beneficiaries and, as a consequence, such amounts are deductible to the trust and included in the income of the beneficiaries.

Income Allocated To A Preferred Beneficiary   As will be discussed beginning in Paragraph 21-66, trusts can allocate income to a preferred beneficiary while retaining the income in the trust. While such retained income would normally be taxed in the trust, because it is being taxed in the hands of a beneficiary, it can be deducted from the income of the trust.

Amounts Deemed Not Paid   A trust can designate amounts to be deemed not paid when they are, in fact, paid or payable to beneficiaries. This means that the trust will include these amounts in its own Net Income For Tax Purposes and the beneficiaries will be able to receive these amounts on a tax free basis. The reasons for doing this are discussed beginning in Paragraph 21-69.

Amounts Retained For Beneficiary Under 21 Years Of Age   Provided the eventual payment is not subject to any future condition, amounts that are held in trust for a beneficiary who is under 21 at the end of the year can be deducted by the trust and taxed in the hands of the beneficiary. (See Paragraph 21-71.)

21-65.   While positive amounts of all types of income can be allocated to beneficiaries, losses cannot be. If a trust has a capital or non-capital loss, it must be used by the trust, either as a carry back to a previous year, or as a carry forward to a subsequent year.

Preferred Beneficiary Election

21-66.   Normally a trust can only deduct amounts that are paid or payable to a beneficiary. An exception to this can arise if a joint election is made by a trust and a beneficiary. Under this preferred beneficiary election, the beneficiary will be taxed on amounts that remain in the trust [ITA 104(14)], and the trust can deduct these amounts [ITA 104(12)].

21-67. The preferred beneficiary election is only available for certain disabled beneficiaries. The beneficiary must either be eligible for the disability tax credit, or be eligible to be claimed by another individual as an infirm dependant 18 years or older.

21-68. This election is normally used in situations where it is desirable to have income taxed in the hands of a low income individual without actually giving that individual full access to the funds. An example of this would be a mentally disabled child with no other source of income, but lacking in the ability to deal responsibly with financial matters.

Amounts Deemed Not Paid

21-69. Amounts allocated to a beneficiary are normally deducted by the trust and included in the income of the beneficiary. However, ITA 104(13.1) permits a trust to designate all or part of its income as "not to have been paid" or "not to have become payable in the year". As we have noted, the amounts so designated are not included in the beneficiaries' Net Income and are not deductible in computing the Net Income of the trust. This designation is only available to trusts that are resident in Canada throughout the taxation year and are subject to Part I tax.

21-70. The reasons for using this designation include the following:

Lower Rates In the case of a testamentary trust that pays taxes at graduated rates, the trust may have a lower marginal tax rate than the beneficiary.

Instalment Avoidance Trusts are generally not required to make instalment payments. In contrast, if the income is taxed in the hands of a beneficiary, that individual may be required to make instalment payments on the trust income.

Use Of Trust Losses As noted in Paragraph 21-65, a trust cannot allocate losses to beneficiaries. This means that the only way that an unused current year trust loss can be used is through a carry over to another year. With many trusts, this cannot happen under normal circumstances because they are legally required to distribute all of their income to beneficiaries, resulting in a nil Net Income For Tax Purposes. A solution to this problem is to designate sufficient income as having not been paid to absorb the loss carry forward. This can satisfy the legal requirement to distribute the income, while simultaneously creating sufficient Net Income For Tax Purposes to absorb the loss carry forward.

Amounts Retained For A Beneficiary Under 21 Years Of Age

21-71. If benefits are actually paid to a minor beneficiary, the amounts can clearly be deducted by the trust. However, an adult settlor may decide that it would be better for the income to be held in trust until the beneficiary reaches some specified age. Provided the beneficiary has not reached 21 years of age prior to the end of the year, ITA 104(18) deems amounts that are retained to have become payable during the year. This means that the trust will be able to deduct the amount retained and the beneficiary will be subject to taxes on it.

21-72. To qualify for this treatment, the amounts must be vested with the beneficiary and there cannot be any future condition that would prevent payment. When these amounts are eventually distributed, they will be received by the beneficiary on a tax free basis.

Taxable Income Of A Trust

21-73. Once the Net Income For Tax Purposes of a trust is determined, calculation of Taxable Income involves the same deductions that would be available to individuals. Provided there is a positive Net Income For Tax Purposes, the trust can deduct non-capital losses of other years, net capital losses of other years, and farming and fishing losses of other years. The carry over periods for these losses that are applicable to individuals are equally applicable to trusts.

Exercise Twenty-One - 5

Subject: Trust Net And Taxable Income

During the current year, the Jordan family trust, an inter vivos trust, has business income of $220,000. Of this amount, $50,000 is retained in the trust, with a joint election being made to have this amount taxed in the hands of a disabled beneficiary with no other income. The remaining $170,000 is distributed to the other beneficiaries of the trust.

At the beginning of the current year, the trust had a business loss carry forward of $35,000. In order to make use of this loss, the trust designates an amount of $35,000 under ITA 104(13.1) as not having been paid during the year.

Determine the trust's Net Income For Tax Purposes and Taxable Income for the current year. Briefly explain why the trust would make the preferred beneficiary election and designate amounts not paid that were paid.

End of Exercise. Solution available in Study Guide.

Income Allocations To Beneficiaries

General Rules

21-74.   Since a trust is a separate taxable entity, any income that is earned by trust assets will initially accrue to the trust. As we have noted, however, any income that is allocated to a beneficiary can be deducted in the calculation of the trust's Net Income For Tax Purposes. Correspondingly, the amount deducted by the trust must be included in the Net Income For Tax Purposes of the relevant beneficiary. In effect, when trust income is allocated to a beneficiary, the obligation to pay taxes on that income is transferred from the trust to the beneficiary.

21-75.   We have also noted that a trust can make payments to third parties for goods or services that will be provided to a beneficiary. These can include such expenses as day care, tuition, and medical fees. These amounts are deductible by the trust as allocations to beneficiaries, but will be considered income paid or payable to the beneficiaries.

21-76.   For a trust to be able to deduct amounts that will be distributed to beneficiaries, the amounts must be paid or payable. While it is easy to determine whether an amount has been paid, questions often arise in determining whether or not an amount is payable to a beneficiary. ITA 104(24) provides that an amount is:

> ... deemed not to have become payable in a taxation year unless it was paid in the year to the beneficiary or the beneficiary was entitled in the year to enforce payment of the amount.

21-77.   Issuing a promissory note or a cheque payable to the beneficiary for the share of the trust income will usually fulfill the payable requirement. The CRA expands the definition of payable in IT-286R2 by stating that an amount is not considered to be payable in any of the following circumstances:

- A beneficiary can only enforce payment of an amount of income by forcing the trustee to wind up the trust.
- The beneficiary's right to income is subject to the approval of a third party.
- Payment of income is at the trustee's discretion.
- The beneficiary has the power to amend the trust deed and must do so to cause the income to be payable.

Discretionary And Non-Discretionary Distributions

21-78.   Both testamentary and inter vivos trusts can be set up as either discretionary or non-discretionary trusts. A discretionary trust is one in which the trustees are given the power to decide the amounts that will be allocated to each of the beneficiaries, usually on an annual basis.

21-79.   In many cases, this discretionary power will apply only to annual income distributions. However, the trust could be structured to provide discretion on both income and capital distributions, or to capital distributions only. The trustees may also be given the power to control the timing of distributions to beneficiaries.

21-80.   When discretionary trusts are used, it is important that only the amounts allocated to beneficiaries are considered to be paid or payable. If, for example, a trustee's exercise of discretion requires the approval of a third party, IT-286R2 would indicate that the amounts are not payable. This would result in the trust not being able to deduct the allocated amounts.

21-81.   A non-discretionary trust is one in which the amounts and timing of allocations to income and capital beneficiaries are specified in the trust agreement. In many cases, a given trust agreement may have a combination of discretionary and non-discretionary provisions.

Flow Through Provisions
General Applicability

21-82.   You may recall from Chapter 13 that income earned in registered retirement savings plan trusts and registered retirement income fund trusts does not retain its tax characteristics when paid out to the beneficiaries of such plans. Amounts received by the beneficiaries are fully taxed at the individual's regular rates, without regard to whether the source of the income was interest, dividends, or capital gains.

21-83.   Fortunately, this is not the case with personal trusts. Income paid out to beneficiaries retains the same tax characteristics as when it was earned in the personal trust. This is a very important feature of personal trusts in that dividends and capital gains are taxed much more favourably than other types of income. In the absence of such flow through provisions, in many instances the use of trusts would be much less attractive.

Dividends

21-84.   If either eligible or non-eligible dividends from taxable Canadian corporations are received by a trust and distributed to beneficiaries of the trust, the beneficiaries will use the same gross up and tax credit procedures that would be applicable had they received the dividends directly. At the trust level, these amounts will not be grossed up and the amount received and distributed will be deducted in the determination of the trust's Net Income For Tax Purposes.

21-85.   In contrast, if either eligible or non-eligible dividends from taxable Canadian corporations are retained in the trust, the grossed up amount of these dividends will be included in the trust's Net Income For Tax Purposes. Consistent with this, the trust will be able to deduct the appropriate dividend tax credit when it determines its Tax Payable for the year.

Capital Gains

21-86.   Under trust law, capital gains are considered to be an addition to capital and, in the absence of a special provision in the trust agreement, would not be payable to income beneficiaries. However, tax legislation views one-half of capital gains as a taxable amount. As a consequence, if this amount is not paid out to beneficiaries, it will be taxed in the hands of the trust. The remaining one-half of the capital gain will become part of the trust's capital and can be paid to beneficiaries on a tax free basis at any point in time.

21-87.   If the trust pays out the full amount of the capital gain, one-half of this amount will be included in the recipient's income as a taxable capital gain. The remaining one-half can be received as a tax free distribution of capital.

Tax On Split Income

21-88.   As discussed in Chapter 14, an individual who is under 17 years of age before the beginning of the year (i.e., who has not reached 18 years of age by the end of the year) is subject to a tax on split income (a.k.a., kiddie tax). This tax is applicable to specified types of income including dividends from private companies, benefits or loans received from private companies, and partnership income if the partnership is providing property or services to a business owned by a related individual. The tax is assessed at the maximum federal rate of 29 percent on all eligible amounts, with the only available tax credits being the dividend tax credit and credits for foreign taxes assessed on foreign source income.

21-89.   If any of the specified types of income are earned by a trust and allocated to a beneficiary who is under 17 years of age before the beginning of the year, they will retain their tax characteristics in the hands of the beneficiary. Because of this, the income will be subject to the tax on split income.

Exercise Twenty-One - 6

Subject: Flow Through To Beneficiaries

During the current year, the Ho family trust received eligible dividends from publicly traded Canadian corporations in the amount of $100,000. In addition, it received non-eligible dividends from the family owned Canadian controlled private corporation in the amount of $30,000. Its only other source of income was a capital gain of $20,000 on a disposition of investments in publicly traded equity securities.

The only beneficiary of the trust is the family's 19 year old son, Bryan Ho. During the current year, $60,000 of the eligible dividends from public companies, all of the non-eligible dividends from the family's private company, and all of the $20,000 capital gain were paid to Bryan.

Indicate the tax effects of these transactions on the current year's Net Income For Tax Purposes for both the trust and for Bryan.

End of Exercise.   Solution available in Study Guide.

Business Income, CCA, Recapture, And Terminal Losses

21-90.   Under trust law, the amount of income that may be distributed to beneficiaries should be determined after providing for amortization expense calculated using methods similar to those specified under generally accepted accounting principles. While this could create a difference between a trust's accounting Net Income and its Net Income For Tax Purposes, this problem is resolved by most trustees by setting accounting amortization expense equal to maximum CCA.

21-91.   As was the case with partnerships, business income must be calculated at the trust level, prior to allocation to the beneficiaries. This calculation would include the CCA deduction, as well as any recapture or terminal losses that might arise during the year.

Exercise Twenty-One-7

Subject: CCA And Recapture On Trust Assets

The Husak family trust has only one beneficiary, Martin Husak, the 32 year old son of the settlor, Dimitri Husak. It is an inter vivos trust and its only asset is a rental property. All available trust income is distributed to Martin. During the year ending December 31, 2007 the property will have net rental income, before the deduction of CCA, of $32,000. Maximum CCA for the year will be $26,000. Dimitri is considering having the trust sell the rental property at the end of 2007. If that is done, there will be recapture of CCA of $65,000. The trust is required to distribute all of its income to Martin. He has asked you to compare the tax consequences for both Martin and the trust if the sale takes place on December 31, 2007 and if the trust continues to hold the property.

End Of Exercise. Solution Available In Study Guide

Principal Residence Exemption

21-92.   This exemption is usually considered to be available only to individuals. However, personal trusts can also benefit from the principal residence capital gain exemption. A residence held in a trust will qualify for the exemption if the residence was ordinarily inhabited in the year by a beneficiary of the trust, or by a spouse or common-law partner, former spouse or common-law partner, or child of a beneficiary. As well, the full gain on a principal residence will qualify for the exemption where the trust has more than one beneficiary, but only one of the beneficiaries occupies the residence.

Tax Payable Of Personal Trusts

General Approach

21-93.   In keeping with the previously expressed idea that trusts are to be taxed in the same manner as individuals, the Tax Payable for a trust is calculated using the same rates that are applicable to individuals. However, how these rates will be applied differs, depending on whether the trust is an inter vivos trust or, alternatively, a testamentary trust. These differences will be discussed in the material that follows.

Taxation Of Testamentary Trusts

General Approach

21-94.   Testamentary trusts are taxed using the same schedule of progressive rates that apply to individuals. For 2007, the rates range from a low of 15.5 percent on the first $37,178 of Taxable Income to a maximum of 29 percent on taxable amounts in excess of $120,887. These rates are applied to Taxable Income, generally determined after the amounts allocated to beneficiaries have been deducted.

Multiple Testamentary Trusts

21-95.   The fact that the full range of progressive rates is available to each trust suggests that when an individual wishes to have several beneficiaries of his estate, a separate testamentary trust should be established for each one. In contrast to the use of a single trust for all beneficiaries, this arrangement would provide for multiple applications of the low rates in the progressive rate schedule that is applicable to individuals.

21-96.   While there is no general prohibition against an individual being a beneficiary of more than one testamentary trust, there is concern that this type of arrangement might be used for the purpose of creating multiple applications of the low tax brackets.

21-97.   To prevent multiple trusts from being created solely for this purpose, ITA 104(2) notes that where substantially all of the property of two or more trusts has been received from a single individual and the income from the trusts will ultimately accrue to the same beneficiary, group or class of beneficiaries, the CRA may designate the multiple trusts as a single trust. The CRA has indicated that members of one family could be viewed as a class of beneficiaries.

21-98.   To avoid this result, a will should include a clear direction as to whether distinct trusts are to be established for each beneficiary. Further, guidance should be provided stating that trust administrators can seek independent investment objectives suitable to the needs of the respective beneficiaries. Ideally, each trust should be created with separate terms and conditions.

Tainted Testamentary Trusts

21-99.   Contributions by living persons to an existing testamentary trust can cause that trust to become tainted and lose its testamentary status. If this happens, the trust will no longer benefit from the use of graduated rates and will be taxed as an inter vivos trust with all of its income taxed at the maximum federal rate of 29 percent.

Taxation Of Inter Vivos Trusts

21-100.   Under ITA 122(1), inter vivos trusts are generally subject to a flat federal tax rate of 29 percent on all trust income that is not distributed to beneficiaries, allocated to a preferred beneficiary, or held in trust for a beneficiary under 21 years of age. Since the top federal marginal rate for individuals is also 29 percent, the flat federal tax levy on trusts is equal to, or greater than, the tax that would be paid by a beneficiary receiving the income. Given this, there is little income tax incentive to allow income to accumulate in an inter vivos trust.

Tax Credits And The Alternative Minimum Tax

21-101.   While, in principle, trusts are to be taxed in the same manner as individuals, there are obvious differences between a legally constructed entity and a living, breathing human being. These differences are reflected in the fact that trusts are not eligible for many of the tax credits that are available to individuals.

21-102.   To begin, ITA 122(1.1) specifically prohibits a trust from making any of the deductions listed under ITA 118 (personal tax credits). Further, most of the other credits listed in ITA 118.1 through 118.9 are clearly directed at individuals (e.g., a trust is not likely to have medical expenses). However, some tax credits are available to trusts, generally on the same basis as they are available to individuals. These include:

  • donations and gifts (As is the case with individuals, there is a credit of 15.5 percent on the first $200 of donations and 29 percent on additional amounts.)
  • eligible and non-eligible dividend tax credits
  • foreign tax credits
  • investment tax credits
  • political contributions tax credits

21-103.   As is the case with individuals, trusts are subject to the alternative minimum tax legislation. However, there is one important difference. The exemption with respect to the first $40,000 of income is only available to testamentary trusts. For inter vivos trusts, the alternative minimum tax calculation is based on all income amounts.

Exercise Twenty-One - 8

Subject: Taxation Of Inter Vivos Trusts

The sole income receipt for 2007 of an inter vivos trust is $20,000 in eligible dividends received from a publicly traded Canadian corporation. The only beneficiary of the trust is the adult son of the settlor. The beneficiary was paid $15,000 from the dividend income, which also was his sole income for the year. He has no personal tax credits other than his basic personal tax credit. Calculate the Taxable Income and federal Tax Payable for 2007, for both the trust and the beneficiary.

End of Exercise. Solution available in Study Guide.

Trust Tax And Information Returns

21-104.   The procedural aspects related to trust tax returns are covered in Chapter 2. While we will not provide a detailed review of that material, we note the following for your convenience in using this Chapter:

- The T3 tax return must be filed within 90 days of the trust's year end. Any Tax Payable must be remitted at this time. While testamentary trusts can use a non-calendar fiscal year, inter vivos trusts must use a calendar year.

- Testamentary trusts are not required to pay instalments. While there is a legislative requirement that inter vivos trusts pay instalments, as an administrative practice, the CRA has not enforced this requirement.

- T3 Information Returns must be issued within 90 days of the trust's year end. This return is used to report allocations of the trust's income.

Income Attribution

General Rules

21-105.   We introduced the income attribution rules, as they apply to individuals, in Chapter 12. Briefly summarized, they are as follows:

Transfer To A Spouse Or Common-Law Partner   Under ITA 74.1(1), if property is transferred to a spouse or common-law partner for consideration that is less than fair market value, income earned by this property while it is held by that person, as well as any capital gain resulting from a disposition of the property by the transferee, will be attributed back to the transferor.

Transfer To A Related Minor   Under ITA 74.1(2), if property is transferred to a related individual under the age of 18 for consideration that is less than fair market value, income earned by this property while it is held by the minor will be attributed back to the transferor until the year the individual is 18 or older. Capital gains on a subsequent sale of the property will not be attributed back to the transferor.

21-106.   While we did not discuss this point in Chapter 12, these rules are equally applicable when there is a transfer to a trust where a spouse, common-law partner, or a related minor is a beneficiary. As was the case with individuals, these rules apply both to transfers below fair market value, as well as to loans that do not bear interest at the prescribed rate.

21-107.   You should note that attribution does not occur at the time the assets are transferred to a trust in which a spouse, common-law partner, or related minor is a beneficiary. Rather, attribution occurs when income from those assets is allocated to one of these individuals. If the trust chooses to be taxed on the income before allocation, or if the income is allocated to individuals other than a spouse, common-law partner, or related minor, income will generally not be attributed to the transferor.

Exercise Twenty-One - 9

Subject: Income Attribution

Last year, Trevor Carlisle transferred to a family trust, for no consideration, bonds that pay interest of $27,000 per annum. The beneficiaries of the trust are Trevor's spouse, Carmen, and their two children, Mitch (16 years old) and Rhonda (22 years old). The trust income and capital gains are allocated equally, and are payable to each beneficiary during the year. Total interest income earned by the trust during the year was $27,000. As well, a taxable capital gain of $3,000 was realized on the trust's disposition of one of the bonds that Trevor Carlisle transferred into the trust. The trust designated $1,000 of the taxable capital gain as payable to each beneficiary. Determine the Taxable Income allocations to each beneficiary and any effect these allocations have on the Taxable Income of Trevor.

End of Exercise. Solution available in Study Guide.

Attribution To Settlor (Reversionary Trust)

21-108.   There is a further form of income attribution that is unique to trust situations. Both income from holding the transferred property and capital gains from the disposition of the transferred property will be attributed back to the settlor if a trust meets the conditions specified in ITA 75(2).

21-109.   ITA 75(2) is applicable, without regard to the identity of the beneficiaries of the trust, if any one of the following conditions is satisfied:

1. The transferred property can revert to the settlor at a later point in time. In this situation, the trust is commonly referred to as a reversionary trust.

2. The transferred property will pass to persons to be determined by the settlor at a later point in time.

3. The transferred property cannot be disposed of except with the settlor's consent or in accordance with the settlor's direction.

21-110.   You should note that the second condition will limit the ability of the settlor of the trust from acting as a trustee. If the settlor is the only trustee or if unanimous agreement of the trustees is required, the settlor is in a position to determine who will ultimately receive the transferred property. To avoid the application of ITA 75(2) when the settlor acts as a trustee, there would have to be at least three trustees and decisions would have to be based on majority rule.

Purchase Or Sale Of An Interest In A Trust

Income Interest

21-111.   An income interest in a trust is the right of a beneficiary under the trust to receive all or part of the income from the trust. The purchaser of an income interest in a trust will have a cost equal to the fair market value of the consideration given for that interest. This cost can be deducted against amounts of trust income that would otherwise be included in the individual's Taxable Income. Any portion of the cost that is not deducted against income from the trust in the current year can be carried forward for deduction against allocated trust income in subsequent years. When income allocations have reduced the cost of the interest to nil, subsequent receipts of income will be fully taxable.

21-112.   From the point of view of the vendor of an income interest, the proceeds of disposition will be equal to the fair market value of the consideration received. If the cost of the income interest (often nil) is different than the proceeds received, there will be a gain or loss on the disposition. As an income interest is not a capital asset, the gain or loss on its disposition will be treated as a fully taxable or deductible property income or loss.

Capital Interest

21-113.   As defined in ITA 108(1), a capital interest is all of the rights of a beneficiary of a trust, other than an income interest. As the name implies, a capital interest is a capital asset and any gain or loss on its disposition will be treated as a capital gain or loss.

21-114.   When a capital interest in a trust is purchased, the adjusted cost base is equal to the fair market value of the consideration given. This amount will be reduced by future distributions of assets from the trust. As we have noted, ITA 107(2) generally provides for a tax free rollover of assets from a trust to a beneficiary.

21-115.   If a beneficiary sells a capital interest in a trust, the proceeds of disposition will equal the fair market value of the consideration received. Unless the taxpayer has purchased the capital interest, its adjusted cost base will be nil. This means that the entire proceeds of disposition could be a capital gain. However, to determine the gain on a disposition of a capital interest in a trust resident in Canada, ITA 107(1)(a) defines the adjusted cost base to be the greater of:

- the adjusted cost base as usually determined, and
- the "cost amount" to the beneficiary.

21-116.   ITA 108(1) defines this cost amount as the beneficiary's proportionate interest in the net assets of the trust at their carrying value to the trust. This prevents the beneficiary from being taxed on the cost amount of the trust's assets, an amount that could be received on a tax free basis as a distribution from the trust. Capital losses on the disposition of a capital interest in a trust are determined in the usual manner. Since ACB is usually nil, capital losses are uncommon.

Exercise Twenty-One - 10

Subject: Sale Of A Capital Interest

The Jardhu family trust was established when the father transferred publicly traded securities with a cost of $120,000 and a fair market value of $250,000 into the trust. The beneficiaries of the trust are the father's two sons, Sam, aged 25 and Mehrdad, aged 27. They have an equal interest in the income and capital of the trust.

At the beginning of the current year, Mehrdad sells his capital interest in the trust to Sam. There have been no capital distributions from the trust. At the time of the sale, the fair market value of the securities in the trust is $380,000. Based on this, the transfer price for the capital interest is $190,000 [(1/2)($380,000)]. Determine the tax consequences of this transaction to each of the two brothers.

End of Exercise. Solution available in Study Guide.

Tax Planning

Family Trusts
Defined
21-117.   As we have noted, the term family trust is not defined in the *Income Tax Act*. Rather, it is term that is used in practice to refer to a personal trust that has been established with members of the settlor's family as beneficiaries. These trusts can either be inter vivos trusts established during the settlor's lifetime or, alternatively, testamentary trusts created when the settlor dies. The provisions of these trusts often contain a fixed arrangement for the payments to beneficiaries. However, in some cases they are established with the payments to the beneficiaries left to the discretion of the trustees.

21-118.   While family trusts can be used for a variety of purposes, the common objective of these trusts is income splitting. This process was introduced in Chapter 3, with further elaboration on the role of corporate structures in income splitting discussed in Chapter 17. In this Chapter we will give further attention to income splitting in the context of family trusts.

Discretionary Trusts
21-119.   As we have noted, a family trust is usually established for income splitting purposes, typically by a wealthy individual with children or other family members who are in low tax brackets. Such individuals commonly have difficulty deciding which of their family members are, and will continue to be, the most deserving. A solution to this problem is the use of a discretionary trust.

21-120.   The provisions of discretionary trusts leave the amount and/or timing of payments to beneficiaries at the discretion of the trustees. This means that, if a particular beneficiary neglects his family duties on a regular basis, or appears to be profligate in his spending habits, his share of the income can be reduced, eliminated, or delayed to a later date. Tax planners like to point out that this provides the settlor with great flexibility. A less charitable view of the settlor's objectives is that this type of arrangement provides for continued control over the behaviour of family members (e.g., if a child fails to show up for family dinners, he can be reminded that his receipts from the family trust are discretionary).

21-121. It is important to note that the settlor of the trust cannot be in a position of unilateral control over the amount and timing of the discretionary distributions, particularly if he is also one of the beneficiaries. If the settlor is in a position of control, the provisions of ITA 75(2) (see Paragraph 21-108) may be applicable, resulting in all of the income being attributed back to him. The usual way to avoid this problem is to have at least three trustees, with the amount of the discretionary distributions determined by majority rule. The CRA has indicated that, for this approach to be effective, the settlor cannot a required part of the majority.

Income Splitting

21-122. If a family trust is set up properly, the potential tax savings from income splitting can be significant. For example, in 2007, a beneficiary with no other source of income can receive $66,420 of eligible Canadian dividends and pay no federal income tax (see Chapter 17). Alternatively, if the same amount of eligible dividends is received by a taxpayer subject to the maximum federal tax rate of 29 percent, the federal Tax Payable on the receipt of this amount of dividends can be calculated as follows.

Eligible Dividends Received	$66,420
Gross Up At 45 Percent	29,889
Taxable Dividends	$96,309
Federal Tax Rate	29%
Tax Payable Before Dividend Tax Credit	$27,930
Federal Dividend Tax Credit [(11/18)($29,889)]	(18,266)
Federal Tax Payable	$9,664

21-123. This calculation illustrates that if a high income individual transfers investments that pay eligible dividends to a trust and flows the income through to beneficiaries with no other source of income, there is a potential federal tax savings of $9,664 per beneficiary. Of equal importance is the fact that this is not a one-time event. These tax savings can be accomplished on an annual basis as long as the relevant beneficiary has no other source of income.

21-124. The preceding example illustrates the maximum potential benefit, involving a beneficiary who has no other source of income and who is not subject to the income attribution rules. However, as long as some adult family members are in a lower tax bracket than the settlor of the trust, some level of tax savings is available. Note, however, in situations where the beneficiary will be subject to the tax on split income at the maximum rate of 29 percent, the use of a family trust does not provide for a tax savings.

Exercise Twenty-One - 11

Subject: Family Trusts

Sarah Block is holding debt securities which produce interest income of $110,000 per year. She has other sources of income in excess of $200,000.

She has two children. Her daughter, Jerri, is 22 years old and currently has no income that is subject to tax. Jerri's only tax credit is the basic personal credit. Sarah's son, Mark, is 26 years old. He is married and his wife has no income of her own. Mark has annual business income of $45,000. Assume that Mark's only tax credits are the basic personal credit and the spousal credit.

Determine the savings in federal taxes that could be achieved by transferring the debt securities to a family trust with her two children as equal income beneficiaries. The trust will be required to distribute all of its income on an annual basis.

End of Exercise. Solution available in Study Guide.

Spousal Or Common-Law Partner Trusts

21-125. As is discussed in Chapter 12, a rollover of assets to a spouse can be accomplished without the use of a trust. In the case of a living individual, the rollover is provided for under ITA 73(1) and (1.01), while for a deceased individual, the enabling provision is ITA 70(6). This makes it clear that a trust is not required to implement a tax free transfer of property for the benefit of a spouse. Why then are we concerned with qualifying spouse or common-law partner trusts? There are essentially two important reasons:

1. A trust can provide for the appropriate management of the transferred assets, particularly when these assets include an active business. In many cases, the spouse or common-law partner of a settlor may have no experience in the management of assets and, in such situations, the trust document can ensure that professional management is used. If the assets were simply transferred to the spouse or common-law partner, the use of such management would be left to the discretion and control of the transferee.

2. Also of importance is that the use of a trust can ensure that the assets are distributed in the manner desired by the settlor. While qualification requires that the transferred assets must "vest indefeasibly" with the spouse or common-law partner, the trust document can specify who the assets should be distributed to after the spouse or common-law partner dies. This could ensure, for example, that the assets are ultimately distributed only to the settlor's children if the spouse or common-law partner was to remarry.

Alter Ego Trusts

21-126. The most commonly cited reason for using an alter ego trust is that the trust property will not be included in the settlor's estate and, as a consequence, will not be subject to probate procedures (probate is a court process that proves the authenticity and validity of a will). There are a number of advantages associated with avoiding probate:

- The probate fees can be high. In Ontario, for example, they are equal to 0.5 percent on the first $50,000 of the fair market value of the estate, plus 1.5 of the excess, with no upper limit. On a $10 million estate these fees would total almost $150,000, a payment that can be completely eliminated with the use of an alter ego trust.

- The probate process can be time consuming. This can create difficulties for the management of an active business, as well as liquidity problems for the estate.

- When assets such as real estate are held in more than one jurisdiction (e.g., Canada and the U.S.), the probate procedures must be undertaken in multiple jurisdictions.

- Once probated, a will is in the public domain. For a nominal fee, any interested individual can obtain a copy, with the possibility that this will invade the privacy of surviving family members.

21-127. While this point has not been widely discussed in the literature that we have seen on this subject, an additional tax feature involved in establishing an alter ego trust is the possibility of establishing the trust in a low tax rate province. When there is a deemed disposition at death or on emigration, the taxation will occur in the province where the trust is resident. Given that there is about a 10 percentage point difference between the maximum combined federal/provincial tax rate in Alberta (39.0%) and the corresponding maximum rate in Newfoundland (48.6%), this could result in a substantial tax savings.

21-128. We would also note that there is a significant non-tax reason for using an alter ego trust. From a legal point of view, it is much easier to challenge the validity of a will than it is to challenge the validity of a trust. Courts can be asked to consider moral obligations to family members in distributing the assets of an estate. With a trust, there is no will to challenge.

Joint Spousal Or Common-Law Partner Trusts

21-129. A joint spousal or common-law partner trust has the same tax characteristics as an alter ego trust. The basic difference is that these trusts are established to hold the combined assets of both an individual and his spouse or common-law partner. Given this, their tax planning features are largely the same as those discussed in the preceding Paragraph 21-126 through 21-128.

Estate Planning

Non-Tax Considerations

21-130. The subject of estate planning is complex and involves considerations that go well beyond the scope of this text. In fact, appropriate planning for a large estate will often involve lawyers, investment advisors, accountants, and tax advisors. Indeed, it may even be necessary to have religious advisors or psychological counselors participate in order to deal with some of the moral or emotional issues that are involved.

21-131. The following points are among the more important non-tax considerations in planning an estate:

Intent Of The Testator The foremost goal of estate planning is to ensure that the wishes of the testator (a person who has died and left a will) are carried out. This will involve ensuring that the assets left by the testator are distributed at the appropriate times and to the specified beneficiaries. The primary document for ensuring that the intent of the testator is fulfilled is, of course, the will.

Preparation Of A Final Will The major document in the estate planning process is the final will. It should be carefully prepared to provide detailed instructions for the disposition of assets, investment decisions to be made, and the extent to which trusts will be used. An executor should be named to administer the estate, and the will should be reviewed periodically to ensure that it reflects the testator's current wishes and family status.

Preparation Of A Living Will Equally important to the preparation of a final will, a living will provides detailed instructions regarding investments and other personal decisions in the event of physical or mental incapacity at any point in a person's lifetime. A power of attorney is similar, except that it requires an individual to be of sound mind when any action is taken on one's behalf.

Ensuring Liquidity A plan should be established to provide for liquidity at the time of death. Major expenses, often including funeral expenses and income taxes, will arise at this time. Funds needed for these payments should be available, or adequate life insurance should be arranged in advance, to avoid the need for emergency sales of capital assets to raise the necessary cash.

Simplicity While the disposition of a large estate will rarely be simple, effective estate planning should ensure that the plan can be understood by the testator and all beneficiaries of legal age. In addition, any actions that can reduce the cost and complexity of administering the estate should be considered. This might involve disposing of investments in non-public shares, or repatriating assets that are located in foreign countries that might become subject to foreign taxation.

Avoidance Of Family Disputes Unfortunately, disputes among beneficiaries are a common part of estate settlement procedures. If equitable treatment of beneficiaries is a goal of the testator, efforts should be made to ensure that all beneficiaries believe that they have been treated in an equitable manner. If the testator wants to distribute assets in a fashion that could be viewed as inequitable by any of the interested parties, care should be taken to make this intention unequivocal.

Expediting The Transition The procedures required in the settlement of an estate should be designed to expedite the process. A long settlement period can increase uncertainties related to the value of assets, add to the complications associated with the required distribution of the assets, and prolong the frustration of the beneficiaries.

Tax Considerations

21-132.   In addition to the preceding non-tax considerations, estate planning must also consider various tax factors. Fundamental tax planning goals for all taxpayers apply equally to estate planning. Briefly, these goals involve the legal and orderly arrangement of one's affairs, before the time of a transaction or event, to reduce and defer income taxes.

21-133.   In effective estate planning, the overriding income tax goals are to defer and minimize tax payments. Several important issues should be considered in dealing with this objective. These can be described as follows:

Prior To Death   Planning should attempt to minimize taxes for the individual in the years prior to death. If the individual earns income that is not required in these years, attempts should be made to defer the payment of tax and transfer the before-tax income to the ultimate beneficiaries. The use of a discretionary trust can assist in achieving this goal.

Year Of Death   Planning should attempt to minimize income taxes payable in the year of death. Deemed dispositions will occur at death and, in addition, amounts in certain types of deferred income plans usually must be included in the taxpayer's final return. Relief can be achieved through tax deferred rollovers to a spouse and transfers of certain types of property (e.g., farm property) to children or grandchildren. The will can also contain instructions to ensure that the maximum RRSP contribution is made to the spouse's RRSP within the deadline.

Income Splitting   Effective planning should allow income splitting among family members who are in lower tax brackets. This can be accomplished by the appropriate splitting of income (e.g., paying salaries and wages for services rendered) and distributing property among beneficiaries throughout a taxpayer's lifetime, recognizing the limitations imposed by the tax on split income.

Foreign Jurisdictions   Planning should normally attempt to minimize taxes that will be incurred in foreign jurisdictions. This is especially true for jurisdictions with significant estate taxes as such taxes are generally not eligible for foreign tax credits or deduction in Canada. To the extent that it is consistent with the individual's investment plans and the residence of intended beneficiaries, holdings of foreign assets at death, or distributions to beneficiaries in foreign locations, should usually be avoided by residents of Canada. Minimizing foreign investments will also simplify the administration of an estate.

Administration Period   Planning should minimize taxes payable while the estate is being administered. Discretion provided to trustees in distributing the income of an inter vivos trust may assist in achieving this goal.

21-134.   Most of the tax procedures related to these issues have already been introduced. We have discussed spouse and common-law partner rollovers in previous Chapters and the use of trusts was covered earlier in this Chapter. An important aspect of estate planning that requires additional consideration is the estate freeze. Procedures to be used in these arrangements are outlined in the material that follows.

Estate Freeze

Objectives Of An Estate Freeze

21-135.   The objective of an estate freeze is, as the name implies, to freeze the value of the estate for tax purposes at a particular point in time. Typically, arrangements are made for all future appreciation to accrue to related parties such as a spouse, children, or grandchildren.

Transfers of income generating private company shares to minor children may be deferred to avoid the tax on split income.

Example   Mr. Chisholm is a wealthy and successful entrepreneur who has a wife and two young children. He owns a variety of capital assets that are producing Taxable Income and appreciating in value. He has several objectives in creating his estate plan:

- During the remainder of his life, Mr. Chisholm would like to transfer all or part of his Taxable Income to a group of individuals and charities who will ultimately be the beneficiaries of his estate.

- Mr. Chisholm would like to freeze the tax values of his assets and allow future growth to accrue to the intended beneficiaries.

- Since the current fair market value of his assets exceeds their tax cost, Mr. Chisholm would like to avoid any immediate taxation resulting from a disposition of these assets with accrued gains.

- Mr. Chisholm would like the transfer of future growth in asset values to accrue so that his beneficiaries will not be subject to taxation in the year of the estate freeze, in any intervening years, or in the year of his death.

- Mr. Chisholm wants to retain the right to the current value of the property at the time of the estate freeze. In addition, he wishes to retain control of the use of the property until his death.

21-136.   This example will be used as a basis for discussing a variety of techniques that can be used to freeze an estate's value. Some of these techniques will achieve all of Mr. Chisholm's goals, while others will only succeed in achieving one or two of them.

Techniques Not Involving Rollovers

Gifts

21-137.   Mr. Chisholm can freeze the value of his estate without using rollover provisions. The most straightforward technique is to simply give property to his prospective beneficiaries. While this would accomplish the goal of transferring future growth in the estate to the beneficiaries, unless the transfer was to a spouse or common-law partner, this approach would have the serious drawback of attracting immediate capital gains taxation on any difference between the fair market value of the assets and Mr. Chisholm's adjusted cost base.

21-138.   In addition, if the person receiving the gift is a spouse or minor child, income attribution rules could apply after the gift is made. Further drawbacks are the fact that Mr. Chisholm would lose control over the assets and that certain income received by minor children may be subject to the tax on split income.

21-139.   While gifts result in a loss of control, Mr. Chisholm may want to accelerate his donations to registered charities. The value of the tax credit associated with such gifts can more than offset any income arising as the result of such distributions. In particular, if a gift is made of shares listed on a designated stock exchange, the capital gains inclusion rate is reduced to nil. (See Chapter 14, Paragraph 14-144.)

Instalment Sales

21-140.   Mr. Chisholm could freeze the value of the estate by selling the assets to the intended beneficiaries on an instalment basis. Capital gains could be deferred until payment is received, but the gains would need to be reported over the next five years based on the capital gains reserve calculations.

21-141.   To avoid income attribution and inadequate consideration problems, the sale should be made at fair market value. However, if the intended beneficiaries do not have sufficient assets to make the purchase, this may not be a feasible solution. A further problem is that Mr. Chisholm would lose control over the property.

Establishing A Trust

21-142.   An estate freeze can also be accomplished by setting up a trust in favour of one or more beneficiaries. Here again, this will transfer income and future growth from Mr. Chisholm's hands to the trust. The trust can be structured so that he retains some control over the assets in the trust.

21-143.   The problem with this arrangement is that, except in the case of a qualifying spouse or common-law partner trust, a joint spousal or common-law partner trust, or an alter ego trust, there is no rollover provision that provides for tax deferred transfers of assets to a trust. As a result, if the trust is set up for beneficiaries other than Mr. Chisholm or his spouse, Mr. Chisholm will incur taxation on any capital gains accrued at the time of the transfer. As well, any dividends received from a private corporation by minor beneficiaries will be subject to the tax on split income, whether the shares are held directly or through a trust.

Use Of A Holding Company

21-144.   Mr. Chisholm could transfer assets to a holding company in which intended beneficiaries have a substantial equity interest, without using a rollover provision. This will freeze the value of his estate and, if the assets transferred have fair market values that are equal to or less than their adjusted cost base, it can be an effective vehicle for realizing losses. However, without the use of a rollover provision, such as that found in ITA 85, any capital gains that have accrued to the time of the transfer will become subject to immediate taxation.

Section 86 Share Exchange

Nature Of The Exchange

21-145.   Chapter 19 provided an overview of ITA 86 which applies to the exchange of shares by a shareholder in the course of a reorganization of capital. In certain situations, a share exchange constitutes an ideal solution to the estate freeze problem. Specifically, this rollover is most appropriate in a situation that involves an individual who is the sole owner of a successful private corporation.

21-146.   By exchanging common shares for preferred shares that have equal value, the owner will, in effect, eliminate his participation in the future growth of the company. At the same time, common shares can be issued to intended beneficiaries at a nominal value, and these shareholders can participate in the company's future income and any growth in the value of its assets.

Example

21-147.   While detailed consideration was given to ITA 86 rollovers in Chapter 19, the following simple example will serve to review these procedures.

> **Example**   Over her lifetime, Mrs. Hadley has been the sole owner and driving force behind Hadley Inc., a manufacturing business located in Alberta. At the end of the current year, the condensed Balance Sheet of this Company was as follows:

Hadley Inc.
Balance Sheet

Net Identifiable Assets	$10,000,000
Common Stock (No Par - 1,000 Shares)	$ 2,000,000
Retained Earnings	8,000,000
Total Shareholders' Equity	$10,000,000

On the basis of an independent appraisal, the fair market value of this business was established at $15,000,000. Mrs. Hadley has a husband and three adult children and would like them to share equally in her estate.

21-148.   Under ITA 86, Mrs. Hadley can exchange, on a tax deferred basis, her common shares that have an adjusted cost base of $2 million (also the amount of contributed capital and PUC) for preferred shares with a redemption value of $15 million (the fair market value of the business). These preferred shares would have no participation in the future growth of the Company and, as a result, Mrs. Hadley has effectively frozen the value of her estate.

21-149.   If Mrs. Hadley wishes to retain control of the Company, the preferred shares can be established as the only outstanding voting shares. While this share exchange will be free of any capital gains taxation, Mrs. Hadley's adjusted cost base and PUC for the new preferred shares remains at the former common share value of $2 million. If the preferred shares are sold for their market value of $15 million, a $13 million capital gain will result ($15 million - $2 million). Alternatively, if the shares are redeemed for $15 million by the Company, there will be a $13 million taxable dividend under ITA 84(3).

21-150.   The tax cost basis for the identifiable assets owned by the Company has not been altered by the share exchange transaction.

21-151.   At this point, the redemption value of Mrs. Hadley's preferred shares represents the entire fair market value of the business and, as a consequence, the value of any common shares issued will not exceed the amount contributed by the investors. This means that such shares can be issued for a nominal value, without any appearance that the purchasers are indirectly receiving a gift from Mrs. Hadley. Thus, 1,000 common shares could be issued to Mrs. Hadley's intended beneficiaries at $10 per share as follows:

Spouse (250 Shares At $10)	$ 2,500
Child One (250 Shares At $10)	2,500
Child Two (250 Shares At $10)	2,500
Child Three (250 Shares At $10)	2,500
Total Common Stock Contributed	$10,000

21-152.   These common shares would benefit from the future income and growth in asset values that may be experienced by Hadley Inc.

21-153.   As illustrated in this example, a Section 86 rollover can provide an ideal solution to the estate freeze problem. It can be used to transfer all future growth in the estate into the hands of intended beneficiaries with no immediate tax effects on the individual making the transfer. The beneficiaries will be taxed on income earned subsequent to the estate freeze. (If any beneficiary had been a minor, they would have had to pay the tax on split income on any dividends received.) A Section 86 rollover is fairly straightforward to administer and does not require the formation of a separate holding corporation.

Rollover Provisions - Section 85 vs. Section 86

21-154.   A Section 85 tax deferred rollover of property to a holding corporation can also be used to implement an estate freeze. The rollover provisions of ITA 85 were given full consideration in Chapter 18, and will not be repeated here.

21-155.   In choosing between the use of ITA 85 and ITA 86, you should note that Section 85 can be used in a broader variety of circumstances than is the case with Section 86. More specifically, Section 86 deals only with exchanges of shares in the course of the reorganization of an existing corporation. This means that Section 86 can only be used in situations where the assets involved in the estate freeze are shares of a corporation. Section 85 would have to be used where the estate consists of other types of property.

21-156.   When Section 86 can be used, it is an easier procedure to implement. Unlike Section 85, which requires a formal election to be made and either an existing corporation or the formation of a new corporation, Section 86 applies automatically once the required conditions are met. By using a Section 86 reorganization, the savings in legal and accounting fees can be significant. However, the complexities involved In effecting an estate freeze using rollovers make it difficult to comment on the relative desirability of Sections 85 and 86.

GST And Trusts

21-157.   A trust is included in the definition of person under the *Excise Tax Act* and, as a consequence, a trust that is engaged in commercial activities is required to register and collect GST on taxable supplies. However, an interest in a trust is considered to be a financial instrument, so the sale of an interest in a trust is an exempt financial service and is not subject to GST.

21-158.   A distribution of trust property by a trustee to a beneficiary of a trust is treated as a supply by the trust. The consideration is the same as proceeds of disposition for purposes of the *Income Tax Act*. Distributions of non-commercial property by a trust in the process of the settlement of an estate are generally not considered to be in the course of commercial activities of the trust and are GST exempt. Similarly, a distribution of financial securities is GST exempt as a financial service. The GST only applies to properties acquired by the trust that are used in a commercial activity.

21-159.   Where property is settled through the use of an inter vivos trust, including an alter ego or joint spousal or common-law partner trust, the consideration for the property transferred is deemed to equal the amount determined under the *Income Tax Act*. The supply is considered to be made at fair market value and GST is payable on all taxable supplies. However, when an estate is settled, an election can be filed to distribute any property of a deceased registrant without the payment of GST. In this situation, the beneficiary of the deceased's estate must be a registrant, and the beneficiary is deemed to have acquired the property for use exclusively in a commercial activity.

Key Terms Used In This Chapter

21-160.   The following is a list of the key terms used in this Chapter. These terms, and their meanings, are compiled in the Glossary Of Key Terms located at the back of the separate paper Study Guide and on the Student CD-ROM.

Adjusted Cost Base	Preferred Beneficiary
Alter Ego Trust	Preferred Beneficiary Election
Beneficiary	Qualifying Spousal or
Capital Interest (In A Trust)	Common-Law Partner Trust
Discretionary Trust	Reorganization Of Capital (ITA 86)
Estate	Reversionary Trust
Estate Freeze	Rollover
Executor	Settlor
Family Trust	Split Income
Income Attribution	Spousal Or Common-Law Partner Trust
Income Interest (In A Trust)	Tax Planning
Income Splitting	Testamentary Trust
Inter Vivos Trust	Trust
Joint Spousal Or Common-Law	Trustee
Partner Trust	Twenty-One (21) Year
Non-Discretionary Trust	Deemed Disposition Rule
Personal Trust	Will

References

21-161.   For more detailed study of the material in this Chapter, we would refer you to the following:

ITA 70(6)	Transfers To Spousal Trusts On Death
ITA 73(1)	Inter-Vivos Transfers To Spousal Trusts
ITA 74.1 to 74.5	Attribution Rules
ITA 85(1)	Transfer Of Property To Corporation By Shareholders
ITA 86(1)	Exchange Of Shares By A Shareholder In Course Of Reorganization Of Capital
ITA 104 to 108	Trusts And Their Beneficiaries
ITA 122	Tax Payable By Inter Vivos Trust
IC-76-19R3	Transfer Of Property To A Corporation Under Section 85
IT-209R	Inter-Vivos Gifts Of Capital Property To Individuals Directly Or Through Trusts
IT-286R2	Trusts - Amount Payable
IT-291R3	Transfer Of Property To A Corporation Under Subsection 85(1)
IT-305R4	Testamentary Spouse Trusts
IT-342R	Trusts - Income Payable To Beneficiaries
IT-369R	Attribution Of Trust Income To Settlor
IT-381R3	Trusts - Capital Gains And Losses And The Flow-Through Of Taxable Capital Gains To Beneficiaries
IT-385R2	Disposition Of An Income Interest In A Trust
IT-394R2	Preferred Beneficiary Election
IT-406R2	Tax Payable By An Inter Vivos Trust
IT-447	Residence Of A Trust Or Estate
IT-465R	Non-Resident Beneficiaries Of Trusts
IT-510	Transfers and Loans of Property Made After May 22, 1985 to a Related Minor
IT-511R	Interspousal And Certain Other Transfers And Loans Of Property
IT-524	Trusts - Flow Through Of Taxable Dividends To A Beneficiary After 1987

Problems For Self Study

(The solutions for these problems can be found in the separate Study Guide.)

Self Study Problem Twenty-One - 1

A testamentary trust was created when Mr. Rowand died four years ago. The beneficiaries are his wife, Mrs. Roward and Roger Rowand, Mr. Rowand's adult son. For the year ended December 31, 2007, the following amounts are reported for the trust:

Business Income	$20,000
Interest	3,000
Eligible Dividends Received From Canadian Corporations	50,000
Rent Receipts	12,000
Rental Operating Expenses	6,000
CCA On Rental Property	2,000

Mrs. Rowand and Roger have no other sources of income. They have no personal tax credits under ITA 118 other than their basic personal credit.

Case A The trust provides for one-half of any dividend income to be retained in the trust. The remaining one-half of the dividend income, as well as all of the other net income is to be paid 60 percent to Mrs. Rowand and 40 percent to Roger Rowand.

Case B All of the trust's income will be allocated to Mrs. Rowand and Roger on a 60 percent and 40 percent basis.

Required:

A. For both Cases, calculate Taxable Income and federal Tax Payable for 2007 for each person, including the trust.

B. Compare the total federal Tax Payable by all persons in Case A with the total Tax Payable by all persons in Case B. Explain any difference.

Self Study Problem Twenty-One - 2

Ms. Robinson is a very successful business person. She wishes to have most of her property ultimately transferred to her son, Malcolm and daughter, Maisy. Both of Ms. Robinson's children are over 30 years old. To achieve her goal, she transferred a substantial amount of property to a trust in their favor ten years ago. The trust has a December 31 year end, and Ms. Robinson assists with its management. However, she has no beneficial interest in either its income or its capital.

The terms of the trust call for the son to receive 30 percent of the income, while the daughter receives 50 percent. The remaining income is to accumulate within the trust, to be paid to Ms. Robinson's two children at the time of her death. For the purpose of distributions to beneficiaries, trust income includes any capital gains earned in the trust. The current year's income figures for the trust are as follows:

Interest On Government Bonds	$ 65,000
Eligible Dividends From Canadian Corporations	250,000
Revenues From Rental Property	492,000
Cash Expenses On Rental Property	342,000

In previous years, CCA was deducted from the rental income in order to determine net rental income. However, late in the current year, the rental property was sold. The property consisted of an apartment building and the land on which it was located. It was transferred into the trust when the trust was first established. The relevant information related to the disposition is as follows:

	Building	Land
Proceeds Of Disposition	$4,560,000	$2,300,000
Undepreciated Capital Cost	3,380,000	N/A
Capital Cost/Adjusted Cost Base	3,840,000	1,430,000

Required:

A. Calculate the Taxable Income of the trust, Malcolm, and Maisy for the current year.

B. Calculate the federal Tax Payable for the trust, for the fiscal year ending on December 31 of this year.

C. Will the 21 year deemed disposition rule affect the trust or beneficiaries in the current year? What actions should be taken to mitigate the effect of the rule and when?

Self Study Problem Twenty-One - 3

On June 6, 2007, Mr. Masters died at his home in Corner Brook, Newfoundland. Under the terms of his will, all of his property was transferred to a testamentary trust. The trust document establishes December 31 as the year end for the trust and contains the following additional provisions:

1. Thirty percent of the income is to be paid to Mr. Masters' daughter, Mrs. Joan Nelson.

2. Fifty percent of the income is to be paid to Mr. Masters' son, Charles Masters.

3. The remaining income is to be retained by the trust, to be distributed at the discretion of the trustees. No distributions were made prior to December 31, 2007.

Between June 6 and December 31, 2007, the trust had the following income and expenses:

Eligible Dividends Received From Canadian Companies		$ 87,000
Interest On British Bonds		
(Net Of 15 Percent Withholding Tax)		93,500
Rental Income	$123,000	
Rental Expenses (Including CCA)	(107,000)	16,000
Total Income		$196,500

Required:

A. Determine the Taxable Income for the trust and each beneficiary for 2007.

B. Calculate the total federal Tax Payable for the trust for 2007.

Self Study Problem Twenty-One - 4

Mrs. Turner died on October 1, 2006. The capital cost and the fair market value of the assets she owned at the time of her death were as follows:

Asset	Capital Cost	Fair Market Value
Principal Residence	$100,000	$165,000
Cottage	62,000	72,000
Warehouse - Land	55,000	75,000
Warehouse - Building (UCC = $45,000)	85,000	85,000
Stock Market Portfolio	22,000	28,000

According to her will, the principal residence and the warehouse were transferred to a trust for the benefit of her daughter, Melanie. The trust is to pay for the maintenance of the principal residence.

The cottage and stock market portfolio were transferred into another trust for the exclusive benefit of Mr. West, Mrs. Turner's second husband.

Mr. West died of grief on January 10, 2007. The fair market values of all of the assets did not change between October 1, 2006 and January 10, 2007.

Required: Outline the income tax consequences for Mrs. Turner, her daughter Melanie, and Mr. West, resulting from:

A. the transfers of property to the two trusts; and

B. the death of Mr. West.

Assignment Problems

(The solutions for these problems are only available in
the solutions manual that has been provided to your instructor.)

Assignment Problem Twenty-One - 1

Each of the following independent Cases involve transfers of property to trusts by a settlor for no consideration. Two of the Cases also involve capital distributions from trusts to capital beneficiaries.

A. A gift of non-depreciable capital property is made to an inter vivos trust in favour of the settlor's adult children. The adjusted cost base of the property to the settlor was $1,000. Its fair market value on the date of the gift is $1,500.

B. A gift of depreciable capital property is made to an inter vivos trust in favour of the settlor's adult children. The capital cost of the depreciable property to the settlor was $1,000. On the date of the gift, the UCC was $750 and the fair market value was $1,100.

C. A gift of non-depreciable capital property is made to an inter vivos trust in favour of the settlor's adult children. At the time of this transfer, the property had a cost of $1,200 and a fair market value of $1,500. At a later time, when the value of the property has increased to $2,000, this property is distributed to a capital beneficiary of the trust.

D. A gift of depreciable capital property is made to an inter vivos trust in favour of the settlor's adult children. At the time of this transfer, the property had a capital cost of $1,300, a UCC of $800, and a fair market value of $1,100. At a later time, the property is distributed to a capital beneficiary. On the date of distribution, the property has a UCC of $900 and a fair market value of $1,200.

E. Capital property is transferred to an alter ego trust. The cost of the capital property to the settlor was $800 and the fair market value on the date of the gift is $2,200.

F. A transfer of non-depreciable capital property is made to a qualifying spousal testamentary trust. The cost of the capital property to the deceased spouse was $1,000, and the fair market value on the date of the transfer to the trust is $4,500. At the time of his death, the decedent had net capital loss carry forwards in excess of $5,000.

Required: For each Case indicate:

- the tax consequences to the settlor that result from the transfer of property to the trust assuming the transfer price is chosen to optimize the tax position of the settlor,
- the tax value(s) for the transferred property that will be recorded by the trust and,
- in those cases where property is transferred to a beneficiary, the tax value(s) that will be recorded by the beneficiary.

Assignment Problem Twenty-One - 2

In planning an estate freeze, Mrs. Dion plans to settle cash and portfolio investments in a trust. The terms of the trust will provide that:

- Sixty percent of the annual income will be paid to her husband, Mr. Dion.

- Forty percent of the annual income will be allocated to the Dion twins, who are 20 years old and in university. The income will be split equally, and the timing of payments is at the discretion of the trustee.

- The trust capital will be distributed on December 31, 2018, following the same allocation as for income.

The trust's income will consist of interest, dividends, and capital gains.

Required:

A. Identify the type of trust that is being used.

B. Indicate what the trust's year end date will be.

C. Indicate the persons that will have to include the trust's income in their Taxable Income.

D. Explain how your answer to Part C would change if Mrs. Dion formed the trust by the settlement of a nominal amount of cash. Mrs. Dion then lends money to the trust to purchase the portfolio investments.

E. Explain how the taxation of the trust income will change should Mr. and Mrs. Dion divorce before the trust capital is distributed.

Assignment Problem Twenty-One - 3

Genevieve Marcoux is a biochemist who annually earns a $125,000 salary. In addition, she has $40,000 in investment income from an $800,000 term deposit she inherited.

Genevieve is a single mother with two children. Her daughter, Lisa, is 21 years old and attends university in the U.S. Lisa plans to become a medical doctor and expects to attend university for another seven years. Lisa's tuition and books cost $30,000 (Canadian) each year. Genevieve's son, Philip, is one year old, and is cared for by a nanny who is paid $14,500 a year. When Philip is five years old, Genevieve intends to send him to a private school, and the fees will be comparable to the cost of a nanny. In addition, Genevieve incurs $500 each month in direct expenses for each child, totaling $12,000 a year. Genevieve does not expect either Lisa or Philip to earn any Taxable Income until they complete university.

Genevieve would like to transfer the term deposit to a trust for her children, so the family can benefit from income splitting currently, and in the future. While she supports her children fully, she does not want them to receive any cash directly from the trust until they are each 35 years old. Until then, she wants the trust to pay for their care, education, and other direct expenses.

Required: Outline how a trust might be used to split income among Genevieve's family members.

Assignment Problem Twenty-One - 4

Mr. Hyde died early in 2007, and a testamentary trust was established under his will. The trust will have a December 31 year end. The beneficiaries of the trust are Mrs. Hyde, an architect earning more than $150,000 per year, and her son, Ross, an unemployed actor with no reliable source of income in the foreseeable future.

Each year, payments of $25,000 and $15,000 will be made to Mrs. Hyde and Ross, respectively. While the payments to Mrs. Hyde are fixed, the trustee may pay Ross additional amounts from the trust as he considers appropriate for Ross's personal needs. The trustee can make discretionary capital distributions to either beneficiary in any year. After 10 years, the remaining capital and any retained income of the trust will be distributed to Ross.

For the years ended December 31, 2007 and 2008, the trustee projects the following trust income receipts:

Trust Income	2007	2008
Interest	$24,000	$24,000
Eligible Dividends Received From		
Canadian Corporations	22,000	24,000
Total Income	$46,000	$48,000

Payments to Mrs. Hyde and Ross are expected to be as follows:

Trust Payments	2007	2008
Mrs. Hyde	$25,000	$25,000
Ross Hyde	15,000	24,000

Required: With a view to minimizing total Tax Payable by the trust and the beneficiaries, identify any potential tax planning opportunities and potential tax savings. Include in your answer what type of income the distributions to each beneficiary should be comprised of.

Assignment Problem Twenty-One - 5

Mr. Samuel Rosen is a successful businessman who has two sons. He wishes to have most of his property ultimately pass into their hands. In a move designed to help achieve this goal, he transferred a substantial amount of property to a trust in their favour 15 years ago. The fiscal year of the trust ends on December 31, and Mr. Rosen has no beneficial interest in either the income or capital of the trust.

The terms of the trust provide for the older son, Jonathan, age 38, to receive 35 percent of the income of the trust, while the younger son, Robert, age 35, is to receive a 25 percent share. Trust income includes any capital gains earned in the trust. Both Jonathan and Robert Rosen are single and have no current sources of income other than the trust. The undistributed income is to accumulate within the trust, to be paid out to the two sons at the time of Mr. Samuel Rosen's death. The income figures for the current year, ending on December 31, are as follows:

Interest Income On Government Bonds	$ 55,000
Eligible Dividends Received From Canadian Corporations	245,000
Revenues From Rental Property	394,000
Cash Expenses On Rental Property	247,000

On September 1 of this year, the rental property was sold. The property consisted of an apartment building and the land on which it was located, all of which was transferred into the trust when it was established. The relevant information related to the disposition is as follows:

	Building	Land
Proceeds Of Disposition	$1,857,000	$1,100,000
Undepreciated Capital Cost	1,371,000	N/A
Capital Cost/Adjusted Cost Base	1,620,000	785,000

This is the first disposition of capital property by the trust since its establishment.

Required:

A. Calculate the Taxable Income of the trust, Jonathan Rosen, and Robert Rosen for the current year.

B. Calculate the federal Tax Payable for the trust, for the fiscal year ending on December 31 of this year.

C. Will the 21 year deemed disposition rule affect the trust or beneficiaries in the current year? What actions should be taken to mitigate the effect of the rule and when?

Assignment Problem Twenty-One - 6

On March 3, 2007, Ms. Denise Lord died at her home in Victoria. Under the terms of her will, all of her property is transferred to a testamentary trust. This trust will have a fiscal year that ends on December 31, and the trust agreement contains the following provisions:

- Twenty percent of the income is to be paid to her 43 year old son, Richard Lord.

- Forty percent of the income is to be paid to her 38 year old daughter, Joan Lord.

- The remaining income will be retained by the trust. While this income can be distributed at the discretion of the trustees, there were no distributions prior to December 31, 2007.

Neither of her children have any income other than income from the trust.

Between March 3 and December 31, 2007, the following income and expense amounts were recorded by the trust:

Eligible Dividends Received From Canadian Corporations		$ 58,000
U.S. Source Interest ($13,000, Net Of 10 Percent Withholding Tax)		11,700
Net Rental Income:		
Rental Revenues	$158,000	
Rental Expenses Other Than CCA	(31,000)	
CCA Claimed	(51,000)	76,000
Total Income		$145,700

Required:

A. Determine the Taxable Income for the trust and each beneficiary for 2007.

B. Calculate the total federal Tax Payable for the trust for 2007.

CHAPTER 22

International Taxation

Introduction

Background

22-1. International taxation procedures deal with transactions or other events that involve multiple jurisdictions. Unlike the situation in accounting where the world is clearly moving towards the use of a single set of internationally determined standards, there does not appear to be any possibility that the world will develop uniform tax legislation that will be applied on an international basis.

22-2. This means that, in determining the tax implications of international transactions, each country begins by applying its own domestic tax legislation. With respect to income taxes, such legislation is usually based on the right of each country to tax its residents on their worldwide income. This is commonly referred to as the residence approach to taxation and, as was noted in Chapter 3, the Canadian *Income Tax Act* applies Part I tax to the worldwide income of Canadian residents, without regard to its source.

22-3. Complicating matters is the fact that, in most venues, there is at least some taxation of income based on its source, without regard to the residence of the recipient. This approach is referred to as the source approach to taxation. Again referring to Chapter 3, the Canadian *Income Tax Act* assesses Part I tax on employment income that is earned in Canada, without regard to the residence of the recipient.

22-4. With the tax legislation of most countries using a combination of the residence approach and the source approach, there is an obvious potential for the same income stream to be taxed in two different jurisdictions. For example, in the absence of mitigating legislation, a U.S. resident earning employment income in Canada could have this income taxed under the residence approach in the U.S. and then have it taxed again under the source approach in Canada. Fortunately, international tax treaties generally provide relief from such double taxation situations.

Chapter Content

22-5. If Canada was self-sufficient, there was no cross-border investment with any other country, and every individual Canadian or Canadian business remained and earned income exclusively within our borders, then a discussion of international taxation would be unnecessary. The reality, however, is that the growing importance of international trade and investment have made an understanding of international taxation concepts and procedures an essential component of general tax knowledge. Reflecting this fact, we have included this Chapter dealing with the basics of international taxation.

22-6.   The focus of the material in this Chapter is on two major areas:

- The taxation of non-residents earning Canadian source income.
- The taxation of Canadian residents earning foreign source income. This includes foreign source employment income, business income, capital gains, and investment income.

22-7.   However, before we deal with these subjects, attention will be given to the coverage of a number of more general issues and concepts that are a pre-requisite to understanding these more specific areas. We will provide coverage of the concept of neutrality in international taxation, the role of international tax treaties, the determination of residence for tax purposes, and the problem of double taxation.

Neutrality In International Taxation

The Basic Concept

22-8.   One of the important qualitative characteristics of an effective tax system is neutrality. This characteristic is described in Chapter 1 as follows:

Neutrality   The concept of neutrality calls for a tax system that interferes as little as possible with decision making. An overriding economic assumption is that decisions are always made to maximize the use of resources. This may not be achieved when tax factors affect how taxpayers save, invest, or consume. Taxes, by influencing economic decisions, may cause a less than optimal allocation of resources.

22-9.   In the context of international taxation, neutrality contributes to cross-border trade and investment, thereby contributing to economic growth and job creation. From the point of view of using the tax system to promote neutrality in the global context, the two main types of neutrality are:

- capital export neutrality, and
- capital import neutrality.

22-10.   These two concepts will be discussed in the material that follows.

Capital Export Neutrality

22-11.   The goal of capital export neutrality is to reduce or eliminate any tax incentive for residents of Canada to export capital for investment in other countries. The basic approach to achieving this is to have all income earned by residents taxed at the same rates, without regard to where that income is earned. Presumably, if Canadians are subject to the same tax rates on income earned both at home and abroad, their inclination will be to invest capital within Canada, rather than in a foreign jurisdiction.

22-12.   While provisions related to capital export neutrality discourage investment outside of Canada by Canadian residents, the downside is that it can impede the ability of Canadians to compete abroad, particularly in countries where the effective tax rates are lower than in Canada. Canada's international taxation rules attempt to minimize these distortions. However, many developed countries tend to downplay capital export neutrality because the disadvantages of having their residents investing outside of the country are outweighed by the economic advantages to the country.

Capital Import Neutrality

22-13.   The purpose of capital import neutrality is to reduce or eliminate the tax impact of movements of capital to a particular country. The objective is to tax all sources of income earned by non-residents in a country at the same tax rates that apply to residents of that country. The overriding principle is to avoid tax discrimination between residents and non-residents earning income within a particular country.

22-14.   The advantage of capital import neutrality is the elimination of bias in favour of either residents or non-residents earning income in Canada. On the other hand, investment in Canada may be discouraged to the extent that Canadian tax rates are above those of investor countries. Recent trends to reduce the tax rate on corporations and withholdings (i.e., Part XIII tax), and the re-negotiation of many of Canada's tax treaties, have been motivated by capital import neutrality concerns that Canadian tax rates were higher than those of other countries, particularly the U.S.

Exercise Twenty-Two - 1

Subject: Tax Neutrality

In the following situations, identify whether capital export neutrality or capital import neutrality is demonstrated;

1.   ITA 2 requires all residents of Canada to include their worldwide income in determining Canadian Tax Payable.

2.   ITA 2(3) states that non-residents are liable for Canadian tax on income from employment and business earned in Canada.

3.   Part XIII of the *Income Tax Act* requires that a withholding tax apply to certain types of passive income earned by non-residents such as interest and dividends. For example, a U.S. resident earns $500 of interest on a term deposit held in Canada. The person making the payment is generally required to withhold a 10 percent tax of $50. The U.S. resident would be taxed in the U.S. on the full amount of the interest.

End of Exercise. Solution available in Study Guide.

The Role Of Tax Treaties

22-15.   Tax treaties are entered into between countries for the purpose of facilitating cross-border trade and investment by removing income tax obstacles. For example, a Canadian resident employed in the U.S. is potentially subject to Canadian tax under the residence approach. In the absence of a treaty, he could also be subject to U.S. tax on the same income under the source approach. This would, of course, create a significant impediment to cross-border employment.

22-16.   In addition to dealing with double taxation problems such as this, treaties also provide income tax certainty, prevent discrimination, ensure a proper division of cross-border revenues, and provide an information-sharing mechanism for the purposes of administration and enforcement of each country's tax laws.

22-17.   Canada's tax treaties are based on the *"Model Double Taxation Convention On Income And Capital",* or what is commonly referred to as the Organization Of Economic Cooperation And Development (OECD) model. The OECD model was developed to promote a variety of international goals, one of which was the promotion of multilateral agreements between its member countries, currently numbering thirty. Both Canada and the U.S. are members. The structure of this model, as applied in Canadian tax treaties, is summarized in Figure 22-1 (following page).

Part	Subject	Content
	Figure 22 - 1 **Tax Treaty Structure**	
1	Scope	Answers the question of who is eligible for treaty protection and which taxes are covered.
2	Definitions	Limited definitions such as "person", "Canadian tax", "United States tax", and the meaning of "residence" and "permanent establishment".
3	Income	Rules on which country has the right to tax different types of income, including income from business, rents, royalties, retirement, employment, interest, dividends, etc.
4	Capital	Rules on the right to apply a capital tax to certain property.
5	Double Taxation	Provides that when both countries reserve the right to tax the same income, relief from double taxation will be provided by the exemption or credit method. Limited use of the deduction method is also permitted.
6	Special Rules	Includes non-discrimination rules, as well as exchange of information and competent authority procedures designed to open discussion for the resolution of disputes.
7	Entry Into Force And Termination	Describes when the treaty becomes effective and under what circumstances and time frames it may be terminated.

22-18.   Although member countries are encouraged to follow the OECD model, few members follow the model to the letter. In Canada, for example, the small business deduction discussed in Chapter 15 is a tax incentive targeted at certain Canadian owned corporations. Such incentives are generally viewed as contrary to the discrimination provisions of the OECD model.

22-19.   In cases where there are conflicts, Canada's tax treaties generally override the *Income Tax Act*. This override occurs through legislation that implements the tax treaty, as well as specific provisions of the *Income Tax Act* that recognize the priority given to the tax treaty. For example, ITA 2(3) requires a U.S. resident to pay Canadian tax on employment income earned in Canada. The tax treaty, on the other hand, may, in specific circumstances, state that such income is only taxable in the U.S. In such cases, the inconsistency is resolved in favour of the tax treaty with the result that no Canadian tax is payable by the U.S. resident.

Exercise Twenty-Two - 2

Subject: Tax Treaties

Melissa, who is a resident and citizen of the U.S., received dividends paid to her by a Canadian corporation. Part XIII of the *Income Tax Act* requires that 25 percent of the dividends paid to her be withheld as Canadian tax. Article X(2) of the Canada/U.S. tax treaty allows Canada to withhold 15 percent. Which rate is applicable and why?

End of Exercise.   Solution available in Study Guide.

Residence

Importance

22-20.   Residence is the cornerstone of Canadian income taxation. If a person is considered a resident of Canada in a given year, that person will be subject to Canadian income tax for that year on all sources of income, regardless of where that income is earned. Alternatively if the person is a non-resident, Canadian Part I tax will only apply to Canadian employment income, Canadian business income, and gains on the disposition of taxable Canadian property.

22-21.   Residency status is determined by applying certain rules and guidelines that originate from jurisprudence, common law, the *Income Tax Act*, and tax treaties. These rules vary depending on whether the person is an individual, corporation, or trust.

22-22.   With respect to trusts, they are generally considered to reside where the trustees, executors, or other legal representatives who manage the trust assets reside. Given that trustees are either individuals or corporations, an understanding of the residence concepts applicable to these taxpayers will be used to determine the residence of trusts. This means that we do not have to give separate consideration to residence concepts for trusts.

Factual Vs. Deemed Residence

22-23.   An individual or a corporation is either a resident or non-resident of a particular country at a particular time. In some cases, residence is determined by factual considerations. For individuals, this would involve considerations such as where the person is physically located, where his spouse and children are located, and where his principal residence and other possessions are located. For a corporation, factual residence is determined by the location of the mind and management of the corporation. In general, this would be where the board of directors meet.

22-24.   With respect to deemed residence, for individuals, this involves a number of situations that are specified in ITA 250(1). For example, a member of the Canadian armed forces is considered a Canadian resident without regard to his physical location. Other provisions apply to corporations.

22-25.   The determination of factual residence and deemed residence for both individuals and corporations is covered in detail in Chapter 3. For individuals, this material can be found in Paragraphs 3-5 through 3-23. Similarly, the material on residence for corporations can be found in Paragraphs 3-24 through 3-30. This material will not be repeated here.

Dual Residence

Background

22-26.   A problem that was not dealt with in Chapter 3 was the possibility that an individual might simultaneously be considered a resident of two countries. For example, a given individual might be considered a resident in Canada because of the deeming rules in ITA 250(1) and at the same time be considered a resident of some other country on a factual basis. In many cases, this raises the possibility of double taxation of all or part of the individual's income.

22-27.   In such situations, the presence of an international tax treaty becomes crucial. These bilateral treaties contain provisions, generally referred to as tie-breaker rules, that are designed to provide relief from the potential double taxation that is inherent in dual residence situations.

22-28.   While there is a general presumption that the provisions of international treaties override domestic tax legislation, these tie-breaker rules are of such importance that they are formally acknowledged in Canada's *Income Tax Act*. Specifically, ITA 250(5) indicates that a person is deemed not to be a resident of Canada if the terms of a particular tax treaty make them a resident of another country and not a resident of Canada.

22-29.   The application of the tie-breaker rules may result in an individual being deemed a non-resident in situations where he or she would otherwise be a factual or deemed resident. The tax implications of this may be quite onerous since the individual or corporation, on becoming a non-resident, will simultaneously be considered to have emigrated from Canada. In these circumstances, there could be a deemed disposition of many types of capital property, resulting in significant amounts of capital gains or recapture (see Chapter 12).

Individuals

2-30.   The Canada/U.S. tax treaty rules resolve the dual residency problem for individuals by examining a list of factors. These factors are applied in the following order:

Permanent Home   If the individual has a permanent home available in only one country, the individual will be considered a resident of that country. A permanent home means a dwelling, rented or purchased, that is continuously available at all times. For this purpose, a home that would only be used for a short duration would not be considered a permanent home. If the individual has permanent homes in both countries, or in neither, then the next factor, the centre of vital interests, must be examined.

Centre of Vital Interests   This test looks to the country in which the individual's personal and economic relations are greatest. Such relations are virtually identical to the ties that are examined when determining factual residence for individuals.

Habitual Abode   If the first two tests do not yield a determination, then the country where the individual spends more time will be considered the country of residence.

Citizenship   If the tie-breaker rules still fail to resolve the issue, then the individual will be considered resident of the country where the individual is a citizen.

Competent Authority   If none of the above tests answer the question of residency then, as a last resort, the competent authorities will decide the issue by mutual agreement.

Corporations

22-31.   Corporations may be considered factually resident in Canada if the central management and control is exercised in Canada. Alternatively, they will be a deemed resident of Canada if the company was incorporated in Canada after April 26, 1965. As was the case with individuals, this may create situations of dual residency. For example, a corporation that was incorporated in Canada after April 26, 1965, might have its mind and management located in the U.S. This would make this company a deemed resident of Canada and a factual resident of the U.S. Article IV(3) of the Canada/U.S. tax treaty resolves this type of problem by indicating that, in such situations, the corporation will be considered to be a resident of the country in which it is incorporated.

Exercise Twenty-Two - 3

Subject: Dual Residency - Individuals

Using the tie breaker rules, determine the resident status of Dizzy and Donna for 2007 in the following two Cases:

Case 1   Dizzy Jones is an unmarried saxophone player from Los Angeles who has always lived in the U.S. He decides to spend some time in Canada and arrives in Vancouver on May 5, 2007, looking for work in various nightclubs. A friend watches his home in Los Angeles while he is gone. He lives in boarding rooms and hotels throughout his time in Canada and returns to Los Angeles on February 14, 2008.

Case 2   Donna, a U.S. citizen, lives in the state of New York. In the fall of 2006, while attending a business convention in Toronto, she met Donald. They decided to get married the following year and live permanently in the U.S. as soon as Donald could arrange his business affairs in Canada. In December, 2006, Donna took an eight month leave of absence from her job and gave notice to her landlord. On January 1, 2007, they moved in together, sharing an apartment in Toronto which was leased on a monthly basis while Donald finalized his business affairs. In August, 2007, they terminated the lease and returned to New York where they were married and purchased a house.

Exercise Twenty-Two - 4

Subject: Dual Residency - Corporations

Using the tie breaker rules, determine the resident status of the corporations in the following two Cases:

Case 1   Taxco is a company incorporated in Nova Scotia in February of 2004 to hold investments in other Canadian companies. Taxco never carried on business in Canada. All the shareholders and members of the board of directors are residents of the U.S. All board of directors meetings are held in the U.S.

Case 2   Junkco is a company incorporated in Delaware in 2005. The majority of the members of the board of directors, however, reside in Montreal, where all board of directors meetings take place. Junkco does not carry on any business in Canada.

End of Exercises. Solutions available in Study Guide.

The Problem Of Double Taxation

Sources Of The Problem

22-32.   We previously noted that Canada uses both the residence approach and the source approach. The same situation prevails in the tax legislation of most of Canada's important trading partners, including the United States. Further problems arise from the fact that different countries may have different concepts of both residence and source. Given the pervasive use of both jurisdictional approaches, double taxation can result from the following types of conflicts:

Dual Residence   There are situations in which a person may be considered to be a resident of more than one country. If the residence approach is applied in both countries, the result is potential double taxation.

Dual Source   In this second type of conflict, a given stream of income may be considered to be sourced in more than one country. If the source approach is applied in both countries, there is again a potential for double taxation.

Residence Vs. Source   The most common type of problem arises when one country claims the right to tax its residents on their worldwide income and some of this income is earned in another country which taxes all of the income that is earned within its borders. Without some form of relief, there is potential for double taxation.

22-33.   When the potential double taxation is caused by either dual residence or dual source, relief is usually found in international tax treaties. In contrast, residence vs. source problems are usually resolved through legislation.

Dual Source/Dual Residence

Individuals

22-34.   As discussed in Paragraph 22-30, international tax treaties usually resolve dual residency problems through the use of tie-breaker rules. These rules can be used to identify which of the two countries will have primary taxing authority in those cases where the usual rules would result in taxes being assessed in both countries.

22-35.   Dual source conflicts are also addressed by treaty with a set of rules, generally found in Part 3 of Canada's tax treaties. These rules identify which country has the primary right to tax a particular source of income while recognizing the right of the source country to share in the tax revenues, in many cases through a withholding tax.

22-36.   When the specific treaty rules fail to resolve a dual residence or dual source conflict, the fallback is to the so-called "competent authority procedures" that are contained within Part 6 of Canada's tax treaties. Without describing them in detail, these procedures are aimed at opening a dialogue between the two countries for the purpose of resolving the conflict.

Corporations

22-37.   As noted in Paragraph 22-31, for corporations, dual residency situations are usually resolved by giving taxing authority to the country of incorporation. Without some mechanism for relief, application of this rule would mean that the residency of a corporation could not be changed for tax treaty purposes.

22-38.   Under corporate law, corporations are permitted to change their corporate jurisdiction using a concept called continuation. Given the availability of this provision in corporate legislation, Canada has re-negotiated many tax treaties to expressly provide that corporations continued into another jurisdiction or country would be considered incorporated in that country from the date of continuation. ITA 250(5.1) recognizes this notion.

Residence Vs. Source - Legislative Solutions

Alternative Methods

22-39.   As we have noted, when there are residence vs. source problems, double taxation is usually avoided through some type of domestic legislation. In various countries, three different approaches are used:

- The deduction method.
- The exemption method.
- The tax credit method.

22-40.   While we will give brief consideration to each of these methods, you should note that, in general, Canada uses the tax credit method. This method was previously discussed in Chapters 14 (individuals) and 15 (corporations).

22-41.   In order to illustrate these alternatives, the following example will be used.

Example   Ms. Johnson, a Canadian resident, is subject to a Canadian marginal tax rate of 45 percent on all of her worldwide income. During the current year, she earns foreign source income of $1,000, from which the source country assesses and withholds taxes at a rate of 30 percent.

Deduction Method

22-42.   This method treats foreign taxes paid as a deduction from income. If this method is applied to our example, Ms. Johnson's after tax retention and overall tax rate would be calculated as follows:

Gross Foreign Interest Income	$1,000
Foreign Tax Withheld	(300)
Taxable Income Addition	$ 700
Canadian Tax Payable [(45%)($700)]	$ 315
Foreign Tax Withheld	300
Total Taxes Payable	$ 615

After Tax Retention ($1,000 - $615)	$ 385

Overall Tax Rate ($615 ÷ $1,000)	61.5%

22-43.   The basic problem with this method is that, by deducting the foreign taxes paid against Canadian Taxable Income instead of against Canadian Tax Payable, Ms. Johnson only gets $135 [($300)(45%)] of Canadian tax relief, despite the payment of $300 in foreign taxes. This is clearly not an equitable solution to the problem of double taxation. Because of this, the Organization Of Economic Cooperation And Development (OECD) does not approve of this method. In Canada, there is very limited use of this method. However, it is applied under ITA 20(11) when an individual has amounts withheld that exceed 15 percent of the total foreign non-business income.

Exemption Method

22-44.   Under the exemption method, income derived from foreign sources is exempt from tax in the country of residence and is subject to tax only in the foreign source country. Using our basic example, the only tax Ms. Johnson would pay is the foreign tax of $300, resulting in an overall effective tax rate of 30 percent. No Canadian tax would be payable since the interest would be exempt in Canada. The advantage of this approach is that it is relatively easy to administer and, in addition, avoids many of the complexities of other methods. The main disadvantage is that such an approach encourages Canadians to move sources of income offshore to low tax jurisdictions. While the OECD approves of the use of this method, it is not widely used in Canada.

22-45.   The one significant use of the exemption method in Canada is in situations where dividends are received by Canadian corporations from certain non-resident subsidiaries ("foreign affiliates"). As discussed later in this Chapter, such dividends are exempt from Canadian tax, provided the underlying income was earned in a country with which Canada has a tax treaty, the income is sourced in that country, and the income is from an active business.

Credit Method

22-46.   Under this method, the pretax amount of foreign income would be included in Taxable Income, with the foreign taxes paid by a Canadian resident generating a credit against Canadian Tax Payable. Unlike the deduction method, where the foreign taxes paid reduce Canadian Tax Payable only by the amount paid multiplied by the relevant Canadian tax rate, this method provides a dollar for dollar reduction in Canadian Tax Payable for the full amount of foreign taxes paid. This appears to be a very equitable result and, as a consequence, this method is endorsed by the OECD.

22-47.   As we have noted, this is the method that is generally used in Canada. Returning to our Paragraph 22-41 example, the results for Ms. Johnson would be as follows:

Foreign Interest Income Received	$ 700
Foreign Tax Withheld	300

Taxable Income Addition	$1,000

Canadian Tax Payable [(45%)($1,000)]	$ 450
Foreign Tax Credit = Foreign Tax Withheld	(300)

Net Canadian Tax Payable	$ 150
Foreign Tax Withheld	300

Total Taxes Payable	$ 450

After Tax Retention ($1,000 - $450)	$ 550

Overall Tax Rate ($450 ÷ $1,000)	45.0%

22-48.   This simple example makes it clear why this method is widely considered to be the most equitable remedy for the double taxation that could arise when an income stream is subject to tax on the basis of both residence and source. The combined foreign and Canadian taxes total $450, exactly the same amount that would have been paid if Ms. Johnson had received the $1,000 in interest income from a Canadian source.

Exercise Twenty-Two - 5

Subject: Relieving Double Taxation

Jason Abernathy is a Canadian resident living in Kitchener, Ontario. In 2007, he earns $18,000 of U.S. source interest income. Income taxes of $1,800 were assessed and withheld at the source on that income. All amounts are in Canadian dollars. Jason's marginal combined federal/provincial tax rate is 44 percent. Determine his after tax retention and overall tax rate using the deduction method, the exemption method, and the credit method.

End of Exercise. Solution available in Study Guide.

Non-Residents Earning Canadian Source Income

Basic Approaches - Part I Or Part XIII Tax

Employment Income, Business Income, And Gains On Taxable Canadian Property

22-49.   The approach that will be used in taxing the Canadian source income of non-residents will depend on the type of income that is being taxed. As we have noted, ITA 2(3) explicitly refers to non-residents being taxed on employment income earned in Canada, business income earned in Canada, and capital gains arising on the disposition of Taxable Canadian Property. This means that, with respect to these types of income, Part I Canadian tax will be assessed on non-residents using the same rules that are applicable to Canadian residents.

22-50.   Also of importance is the fact that, in general, the Canada/U.S. tax treaty does not override ITA 2(3). Subject to some limitations, the treaty supports Canada's ability to assess Part I tax on non-residents earning the types of income specified in that Subsection.

Other Types Of Income

22-51.   This leaves the question of whether non-residents will be subject to Canadian taxes on other types of income that are sourced from Canada. These other types of income include property income such as interest, rents, royalties, and dividends, as well as pension income, management fees, and capital gains on the disposition of property other than taxable Canadian property.

22-52.   With respect to Part I tax, the answer is generally no. Part I of the *Income Tax Act* does not assess taxes on these types of income when they are earned or received by non-residents. This is supported by the Canada/U.S. tax treaty which, in general, does not allow Part I Canadian tax to be assessed on U.S. residents other than the types of income described in Paragraph 22-49 (e.g., U.S. residents generally do not pay Part I Canadian tax on interest income).

22-53.   This, however, is not the end of the story. In general, when a non-resident receives these other types of income, they are subject to Canadian taxes under Part XIII of the *Income Tax Act*. This is a very different type of tax than that which is assessed under Part I. Under Part I, the relevant tax rate is applied to Taxable Income, a figure that is made up of components which are calculated on a net basis. For example, interest revenues are only included after any related expenses are deducted. In contrast, the Part XIII tax is assessed on the gross amount of income received.

> **Example** Ms. Johnson borrows $100,000 to invest in high yield bonds. During the current year, they produce interest income of $9,000, while the interest costs for the borrowing amount to $4,000.

> **Analysis** If Ms. Johnson was a Canadian resident being taxed under Part I of the *Income Tax Act*, the applicable tax rate would be applied to $5,000 ($9,000 - $4,000). In contrast, if Ms. Johnson was a non-resident being taxed under Part XIII, the Part XIII withholding rate would be applied to the $9,000 in interest received.

22-54. The Part XIII rate that is specified in ITA 212(1) is 25 percent. However, when the non-resident is from a country with which Canada has a tax treaty, the rate is usually reduced.

22-55. While the Canada/U.S. tax treaty does not allow Canada to assess Part I tax on these other types of income, it generally permits the assessment of Part XIII tax on U.S. residents. However, as we have noted, the treaty alters the rate to be used. In many cases, the Canada/U.S. tax treaty reduces the Part XIII tax rate from the statutory 25 percent, down to 10 percent. There are other variations, depending on the type of income that is involved.

Employment Income
General Rules

22-56. Under ITA 2(3), non-resident individuals are taxable in Canada on Canadian source employment income. The rules for calculating employment income discussed in Chapter 5 are equally applicable to non-residents and will not be repeated here.

22-57. In addition to this general provision, ITA 115(2) deems certain non-resident individuals to be employed in Canada, even when the work is not carried on in this country. Such individuals include:

- Teachers who have taken up residence in another country to continue teaching at the post-secondary level.

- Individuals who have become residents of another country and continue to receive remuneration from a resident Canadian source, provided a tax treaty exempts that salary from taxation in the foreign country.

- Non-resident individuals who have received signing bonuses and other similar amounts that relate to services to be performed in Canada, in situations where the resident Canadian employer is entitled to deduct the amounts in computing Canadian Taxable Income.

22-58. These deeming rules are designed to ensure that some types of payment from Canada continue to be taxable in Canada. Note, however, that employee remuneration is specifically exempted from Canadian taxation if it is subject to tax by the foreign country.

Exercise Twenty-Two - 6

Subject: Non-Resident Employment In Canada

Dawn Johnson is employed by Alberta Oil Ltd. as an oil well technician in Edmonton. She has accepted a transfer to the Egyptian offices of the Company for three years beginning January 1, 2007. Dawn severs her residential ties to Canada on December 31, 2006 and takes up residence in Egypt. Alberta Oil continues to pay her salary. Although the government of Egypt would normally tax such salary, the tax treaty between Canada and Egypt exempts the salary from tax in Egypt. Is Dawn required to pay Canadian tax on the salary paid to her by Alberta Oil? Justify your conclusion.

End of Exercise. Solution available in Study Guide.

Canada/U.S. Tax Treaty On Employment Income

22-59.   In general, a source country has the right to tax the employment income of non-residents when it is earned within its borders. For example, Canada will assess taxes under ITA 2(3) on employment income earned in Canada by a U.S. resident. However, article XV of the Canada/U.S. tax treaty contains two special rules which are exceptions to this general approach.

$10,000 Rule   Under this rule if, during a calendar year, a U.S. resident earns employment income in Canada that is $10,000 or less in Canadian dollars, then the income is taxable only in the U.S.

183 Day Rule   This rule exempts Canadian source employment income from Canadian taxation, provided it is earned by a U.S. resident who was physically present in Canada for no more than 183 days in the calendar year. This exemption is conditional on employment income not being paid by an employer with a permanent establishment in Canada who would be able to deduct the amount paid from their Canadian Taxable Income. Stated alternatively, if the employment income exceeds $10,000 and is deductible in Canada, it will be taxed in Canada, even if the employee is present in Canada for less than 183 days.

22-60.   It is important not to confuse the 183 day period in the treaty with the 183 day sojourner rule for determining residence. While the treaty rule applies to any physical presence in Canada, the sojourner rule applies to temporary visits or stays. Daily commutes to Canada from the U.S. for employment purposes would count towards the 183 days in the treaty rule, but not towards the 183 days in the sojourner rule.

Exercise Twenty-Two - 7

Subject: Non-Resident Employment In Canada

In each of the following Cases, determine whether the employment income is taxable in Canada:

Case 1   David resides in the state of Washington. He accepted temporary employment as a technician with a Canadian company in Vancouver beginning September 1, 2007. The Canadian employer agreed to pay him $2,800 Canadian per month. David remained a non-resident of Canada throughout his Canadian employment.

Case 2   Assume the same facts as in Case 1, except the employer was resident in Washington and did not have a fixed base or permanent establishment in Canada.

Case 3   Sandra resides in Detroit, Michigan and commutes daily to a full-time job in Windsor, Ontario. In 2007, she spent 238 days at her job in Canada. She works for the municipality of Windsor and earned $50,000 Canadian in employment income. Sandra is a U.S. resident throughout the year.

End of Exercise. Solution available in Study Guide.

Carrying on Business in Canada

General Rules

22-61.   As we have noted, non-residents are subject to Part I tax in Canada on income from businesses carried on in Canada. The rules for calculating business income discussed in Chapter 8 are generally applicable to non-residents. However, for non-residents, ITA 253 expands the concept of a business by deeming non-residents to be carrying on a business with respect to certain activities such as:

- Producing, growing, mining, creating, manufacturing, fabricating, improving, packing, preserving, or constructing, in whole or in part, anything in Canada.

- Soliciting orders or offering anything for sale in Canada through an agent or servant, whether the contract or transaction is to be completed inside or outside Canada.

- Disposing of certain property, such as real property inventory situated in Canada, including an interest in, or option on, such real property.

22-62.   These rules are intended to ensure that certain Canadian activities that are connected to the non-resident's foreign business, are potentially taxable in Canada as business income. Without these rules, it could be questionable whether the non-resident person would be considered to be carrying on a business in Canada.

> **Example**   A U.S. business sends sales representatives to Canada to solicit orders. If the sales contracts can only be finalized in the U.S., under the general rules applicable to business income, it could be argued that no business was carried on in Canada. However, ITA 253 makes it clear that the soliciting of orders in Canada is carrying on business in Canada, without regard to where the contracts are finalized.

Canada/U.S. Tax Treaty On Business Income

22-63.   There are two general rules in the Canada/U.S. tax treaty that deal with the right to tax business income. The first, article VII, provides rules for determining which country can tax business profits and how those profits are to be determined. The second, article XIV, applies to self-employed individuals providing services.

22-64.   The treaty allows Canada to tax the business income of U.S. residents, provided that business is operated in Canada through what is referred to as a permanent establishment or, alternatively, a fixed base of operations. While the treaty only provides a definition for permanent establishment, the terms permanent establishment and fixed base of operations are generally viewed as interchangeable.

22-65.   Article V of the Canada/U.S. tax treaty defines a "permanent establishment" as a fixed place of business through which the business of a non-resident is wholly or partly carried on. The treaty provides additional clarification by adding that fixed places of business include a place of management, a branch, an office, a factory, a workshop, a mine, an oil or gas well, a quarry or other place of extraction of natural resources. Additional rules provide permanent establishment status only if certain conditions are met (e.g., most construction projects are only considered permanent establishments if they last for more than twelve months).

22-66.   The treaty specifically excludes facilities from being considered a fixed place of business if they are used exclusively for certain activities. These activities include:

- use of facilities solely for storage, display, or delivery of goods;
- maintenance of a stock of goods or merchandise for storage, display, or delivery;
- maintenance of a fixed place of business solely for purchasing goods or merchandise, or for collecting information; or
- maintenance of a fixed place of business solely for the purpose of carrying on any other activity of a preparatory or auxiliary character.

22-67.   The tax treaty also deems certain persons to be permanent establishments of a non-resident. Specifically, an agent who acts on behalf of a non-resident enterprise and who is authorized to conclude contracts in the name of that enterprise, is considered a permanent establishment. The treaty excludes independent agents (e.g. brokers, commission agents) who provide services to the non-resident enterprise, but do so as an independent contractor.

Exercise Twenty-Two - 8

Subject: Carrying On Business In Canada

In each of the following Cases, determine whether Jazzco, a U.S. corporation, is taxable in Canada:

Case 1   Jazzco, a U.S. corporation, is the parent company of Bluesco, a company incorporated in Ontario. Jazzco produces and sells Jazz CDs, while Bluesco produces and sells Blues CDs. Jazzco sells CDs to Bluesco, who in turn sells them in Canada.

Case 2   Jazzco sets up a factory in Toronto where they produce CDs for the Canadian market. The CDs are sold exclusively to an independent Canadian franchise retail outlet at a 50 percent mark-up.

Case 3   Jazzco manufactures Jazz CDs in the U.S. Jazzco ships CDs to a warehouse located in Calgary that they have rented on a five year lease. Jazzco has employed an individual in Calgary to sell the CDs throughout western Canada. The employee, however, is not allowed to conclude contracts without approval by the U.S. office.

Case 4   Assume the same facts as in Case 3, except that the employee has the authority to conclude contracts on behalf of the employer.

Case 5   Assume the same facts as in Case 3 except that the employee has an office in the warehouse premises where they solicit orders.

End of Exercise. Solution available in Study Guide.

Dispositions of Taxable Canadian Property

General Rules

22-68.   As we have previously noted, under ITA 2(3), non-residents are taxable on gains resulting from dispositions of taxable Canadian property. The general rules for dealing with capital gains and losses were covered in detail in Chapter 10. While we only considered their application to Canadian residents in that Chapter, they are equally applicable to non-residents.

22-69.   As discussed in Chapter 12, the main categories of Taxable Canadian Property are as follows:

- Real property situated in Canada.

- Shares of unlisted corporations resident in Canada (e.g. private companies).

- Shares of listed corporations resident in Canada (e.g. public companies) if at any time during the preceding 60 month period the person owned more than 25 percent of the issued shares of any class of its stock.

- Shares of an unlisted non-resident corporation if at any time in the 60 month preceding period more than 50 percent of the value of the corporation's properties and its shares derive their value from taxable Canadian property.

- Shares of a listed non-resident corporation if at any time in the 60 month preceding period more than 50 percent of the value of the corporation's properties and its shares derive their value from taxable Canadian property and the person owned more than 25 percent of the issued shares of any class of its stock.

- Certain investments in partnerships and trusts where the value of the investment is generally attributable to taxable Canadian property.

Canada/U.S. Tax Treaty On Taxable Canadian Property Dispositions

22-70.   While the general rule in ITA 2(3) indicates that non-residents are taxable on gains resulting from dispositions of taxable Canadian property, it is necessary to examine the Canada/U.S. tax treaty to see if any of its provisions override this general rule. The treaty acts to limit Canadian taxation on U.S. residents to gains arising from only the following specific types of Taxable Canadian Property:

- real property situated in Canada;

- property forming part of a permanent establishment or fixed base of operations of the non-resident in Canada; and

- investments such as shares of resident corporations and interests in partnerships and trusts where the value of those investments is primarily attributable to real property situated in Canada.

22-71.   Without some mechanism for tracking such dispositions, it would be very difficult to collect Canadian taxes from non-residents on their sales of taxable Canadian property. Because of this need, non-residents are required to file tax returns reporting such dispositions, without regard to whether they may, in fact, be treaty exempt.

22-72.   In addition, a clearance certificate procedure is in place under ITA 116. This procedure requires a withholding tax of 25 percent to be paid on the disposition of most types of taxable Canadian property (the notable exception is shares of public corporations). The liability for the withholding tax passes to the Canadian purchaser in the event that a non-resident seller fails to pay the required amount.

Exercise Twenty-Two - 9

Subject: Dispositions Of Taxable Canadian Property

In each of the following Cases the individual is a U.S. resident who is disposing of a property. Determine whether any gain on the disposition is taxable in Canada.

Case 1   In 2007, Nancy Gordon disposed of shares of a widely held Canadian public company that she acquired in 2004. Nancy never owned more than one-quarter of one percent of the outstanding shares of this company. The company's assets consist entirely of real estate situated in Canada.

Case 2   In 2002, Joe Nesbitt acquired a condo in Whistler that he rented to Canadian residents. He sold the condo in 2007 at a considerable gain. Joe never occupied the condo.

Case 3   Assume the same facts as in Case 2, except that Joe incorporates a private corporation under British Columbia legislation solely to acquire the condo. At a later point in time, Joe sells the shares at a considerable gain.

Case 4   Assume the same facts as in Case 3, except the corporation is created under Washington state legislation.

End of Exercise. Solution available in Study Guide.

Income From Property And Other (Passive) Sources

Part XIII Tax

22-73.   As was discussed in Paragraphs 22-51 through 22-55, when a non-resident has Canadian source income other than employment income, business income, and gains on the disposition of taxable Canadian property, Part I of the *Income Tax Act* is not applicable. Rather, these other types of income are subject to tax under Part XIII of the *Act*.

22-74.   The Part XIII tax applies to a long list of income types. However, in the following material, we will limit our coverage to interest, royalties, rents, dividends, and pension benefits earned or accruing to non-residents.

Interest Income

22-75.   ITA 212(1)(b) provides that interest paid or credited to non-residents by a person resident in Canada is generally subject to a 25 percent Part XIII withholding tax. However, this general rule contains numerous specific exceptions, some of which completely exempt such income from Canadian taxation. These exceptions are generally designed to encourage investment by non-residents in the debt of the Canadian government, and to avoid discouraging debt issuances by Canadian companies in foreign capital markets. Examples of situations where interest income received by non-residents is tax exempt under the provisions of Part XIII are as follows:

- Interest payable on both federal and provincial government bonds (e.g. Canada Savings Bonds).

- Interest payable in a foreign currency to an arm's length non-resident lender on borrowings related to a business carried on outside of Canada if the interest is deductible by the borrower under Part I of the *Income Tax Act*.

- Interest payable by a corporation resident in Canada to an arm's length non-resident lender where the corporation is not obligated to repay more than 25 percent of the principal within 5 years of the borrowing.

- Interest payable on a mortgage secured by real property situated outside of Canada, as long as the funds are not used in a Canadian business or used to earn any property income except property income from the foreign real property.

22-76.   When it is established that Part XIII tax is applicable, it is then necessary to consult the relevant international tax treaty to determine whether Canada has the right to tax such amounts. For example, the Canada/U.S. tax treaty allows for the application of Part XIII tax to interest payments made to non-residents. It also provides for a reduced rate of 10 percent.

2007 Budget Proposals

22-77.   The 2007 budget proposes the elimination of the Part XIII withholding tax on all interest payments to non-residents that are at arm's length with the payor. The tax will also be eliminated on non-arm's length interest payments. However, in this case, the elimination will be phased in over three years.

Exercise Twenty-Two - 10

Subject: Interest Payments To Non-Residents

In each of the following Cases, determine whether the interest payments made to non-residents are subject to Part XIII withholding tax, and if so, at what rate.

Case 1   Jason, a resident of Virginia, earns $3,000 in interest from a term deposit in a Canadian bank.

Case 2   Janice, a resident of Texas, earned interest of $1,800 on Canada Savings Bonds.

Case 3   Julian, a resident of Ottawa, acquired a vacation property in Florida for personal purposes. The property is mortgaged with a U.S. bank. Julian paid $12,000 in interest to the U.S. bank in 2007.

Case 4   Assume the same facts as in Case 3, except that Julian had acquired the Florida condo in 2001 for cash. In 2007, he mortgages the property with a U.S. bank and uses the money to support a business he carries on in Ottawa.

End of Exercise. Solution available in Study Guide.

Royalties

22-78.   Royalties paid or credited to non-residents by a person resident in Canada are generally subject to a 25 percent Part XIII withholding tax under ITA 212(1)(d). Specifically excluded under Canadian legislation are payments for copyright use, payments made under cost-sharing arrangements where the costs are shared with non-residents, and payments made that are deductible under Part I against income earned outside Canada.

22-79.   The Canada/U.S. tax treaty, in general, allows the imposition of Part XIII tax. Once again, however, it is at the reduced rate of 10 percent. The treaty further provides that copyright and computer software royalties are not taxable by the source country.

Rent

22-80.   The tax consequences of Canadians paying rent to non-residents are also within the parameters of Part XIII tax, although an additional analysis is required. Firstly, the *Income Tax Act* is designed to give priority to Part I tax over Part XIII tax. If the non-resident can be said to be in a rental business, then Part I of the *Income Tax Act* will apply rather than Part XIII, since the non-resident will be considered to be carrying on a business in Canada.

22-81.   If the non-resident is not involved in carrying on a rental business, the 25 percent Part XIII tax will apply. However, a further examination of the nature of the property rented is required to determine the tax consequences. For example, if the rental property is something other than real property in Canada (e.g. equipment or machinery), the Canada/U.S. tax treaty reduces the Part XIII withholding rate from 25 to 10 percent. If the rental property is real property situated in Canada, the tax consequences are a little less clear.

22-82.   When the rental property is real property, the 25 percent Part XIII tax is applicable. This creates a particular problem in that the Part XIII tax would be applied to the gross amount of rents received, without consideration of the related expenses. This can create significant inequities in that, in many cases, the expenses related to real property rentals can approach or even exceed the amounts of rent received. Unlike the application of Part XIII tax to the rental of property other than real property, the Canada/U.S. tax treaty does not serve to reduce the rate from the statutory 25 percent.

22-83.   To deal with this problem, ITA 216 allows, in the case of rentals of real property, the non-resident to elect to pay taxes under Part I, instead of under Part XIII. The following example illustrates the importance of this election.

> **Example**   Doris, a U.S. resident, owns a ski lodge just outside of Banff, Alberta. In 2007, she received gross rental payments of $24,000 and had related expenses of $20,000.
>
> **Analysis Using Part XIII**   If Doris does not elect to be taxed under Part I, taxes would be assessed at a rate of 25 percent on the $24,000 in gross rental payments. This would result in the payment of Part XIII tax of $6,000 [(25%)($24,000)].
>
> **Analysis Using Part I**   If Doris elects to be taxed under Part I, she will be taxed using Part I rates on only her net rental income of $4,000 ($24,000 - $20,000). Note that the failure to make this election would result in an effective tax rate of 150 percent ($6,000 ÷ $4,000) on her real economic income.
>
> If Doris elects under ITA 216, the non-refundable tax credits discussed in Chapter 6 are available to Doris without limitation, provided 90 percent or more of her worldwide income is subject to Canadian tax in 2007. If her income subject to Canadian

income tax is below the 90 percent limit, her access to these credits will be significantly restricted and, with respect to some credits, completely eliminated.

Exercise Twenty-Two - 11

Subject: Rental Payments To Non-Residents

In each of the following Cases, determine how the rental payments made to non-residents will be taxed by Canada.

Case 1   Rentco is a U.S. corporation with worldwide rental facilities dedicated to various equipment rentals. Rentco has offices in Saskatchewan, where it rents out farming equipment.

Case 2   In 2004, Jack Foster, a U.S. resident, acquired a hunting and fishing lodge in northern Ontario that he rents out. In 2007, he rented the lodge to Canadian residents exclusively. Jack received $42,000 in gross rents and estimates that expenses, including CCA, totaled $14,000.

Case 3   Assume the same facts as in Case 2, with one additional consideration. Jack acquired three motor boats in 2005, which he rented to guests of the lodge. In 2007, he received $8,000 in gross boat rents and estimates boat related expenses of $7,000.

End of Exercise. Solution available in Study Guide.

Dividends

22-84.   Most types of dividends are subject to the 25 percent Part XIII tax, including capital dividends that are generally not subject to tax in Canada. While there is nothing in the Canada/U.S. tax treaty to prevent the application of this tax to U.S. residents, the treaty once again serves to reduce the applicable rate. In this case, there are two different reduced rates, depending on the percentage of the dividend paying corporation that is owned by the non-resident recipient.

5 Percent Rate   If the U.S. resident recipient owns 10 percent or more of the voting shares of the resident Canadian company that is paying the dividend, the applicable rate is only 5 percent. This 5 percent rate for inter-corporate dividends reflects a view of the OECD, adopted by both Canada and the U.S., that dividend payments between parent companies and their subsidiaries should be less heavily taxed to encourage international trade and investment.

15 Percent Rate   Other dividends paid by resident Canadian companies to U.S. residents are subject to the Part XIII withholding tax at a rate of 15 percent.

Pension Benefits And Other Retirement Related Benefits

22-85.   Amounts received by non-residents as pension or other retirement related benefits are generally subject to tax under Part XIII. This would include OAS payments, CPP payments, death benefits, certain retiring allowances, as well as payments from RRSPs, RRIFs, and DPSPs.

22-86.   There are some exceptions under Canadian legislation that are designed to ensure that a non-resident will only be taxed on amounts that would have been taxable had the non-resident been resident in Canada at the time the benefits were earned. For example, a non-resident may receive a pension from a former Canadian employer, most of which relates to years in which the person was non-resident and worked outside Canada. Part XIII may exempt the part of the pension that relates to employment outside Canada.

22-87.   In a manner similar to the ITA 216 election available for rental income paid to non-residents, ITA 217 allows the non-resident recipient of pension income to be taxed under Part I of the *Income Tax Act*, rather than under Part XIII. For a low income individual, this may provide a significant advantage in that it can allow such an individual to make use of the tax credits that are available under Part I. However, for high income individuals, the Part XIII rate is likely to be lower than the rate that would be applicable under Part I of the *Act*.

22-88. The Canada/U.S. tax treaty permits the application of Part XIII tax to pension or other related benefits paid to non-residents. As usual, the treaty acts to reduce the applicable Part XIII rate, in this case to 15 percent. However, this rate is only available on benefits that are periodic payments. If the benefit is a lump-sum payment (e.g., a retiring allowance), the statutory Part XIII rate of 25 percent must be used.

22-89. Payments from OAS, CPP and QPP are generally subject to Part XIII tax and eligible for the optional Part I treatment discussed in Paragraph 22-87. However, in the Canada/U.S. tax treaty, Canada and the U.S. agree that special treatment is provided for social benefit payments received from one country by residents of the other country. In general OAS, CPP and QPP payments made to a resident of the U.S. will only be taxable in the U.S. There will be no withholding or filing requirements with respect to such amounts.

Foreign Source Employment Income

22-90. Individuals who are resident in Canada are taxable on employment income regardless of where the employment duties are performed. This creates a potential problem in that an individual earning employment income in a foreign country could be subject to Canadian taxes because they have retained their status as a Canadian resident and, at the same time, be subject to taxes in the foreign country because it is the source of the employment income. Tax treaties would normally be used to resolve this potential conflict.

22-91. This, of course, is the mirror image of the issue that arises when a U.S. resident is earning employment income while working in Canada. You may recall in our discussion of that situation that the Canada/U.S. tax treaty generally allows the source country to tax the employment income that arises in these situations. As we noted then, when a U.S. resident earns employment income in Canada, it will be subject to Canadian taxes. In an analogous manner, a Canadian resident earning employment income in the U.S. will be taxed in the U.S.

22-92. In Paragraph 22-58, we noted that there were two exceptions to the general rule that Canadian employment income of U.S. residents would be taxed in Canada. These exceptions are also applicable when the situation is reversed:

$10,000 Rule Under this rule if, during a calendar year, a Canadian resident earns employment income in the U.S. that is $10,000 or less in U.S. dollars, then the income is taxable only in Canada.

183 Day Rule This rule exempts U.S. source employment income from U.S. taxes, provided it is earned by a Canadian resident who was physically present in the U.S. for no more than 183 days in the calendar year. This exemption is conditional on employment income not being paid by an employer with a permanent establishment in the U.S. who would be able to deduct the amount paid from their U.S. Taxable Income. Stated alternatively, if the employment income exceeds $10,000 and is deductible in the U.S., it will be taxed in the U.S., even if the employee is present in the U.S. for less than 183 days during the year.

Foreign Source Business Income

22-93. The general rule that Canadian residents are taxable on their worldwide income would suggest that Canadian residents are taxable on foreign source business income. As was the case with foreign source employment income, this creates a potential problem in that a person earning business income in a foreign country could be subject to Canadian taxes because they have retained their status as a Canadian resident and, at the same time, be subject to taxes in the foreign country because it is the source of the business income. As mentioned previously, tax treaties are normally used to resolve these potential conflicts.

22-94.   As was discussed when we considered the Canadian business income of non-residents, the Canada/U.S. tax treaty indicates that business income will be taxed in the source country in those situations where the business is operated through a permanent establishment or fixed place of business. Applying this here would mean that if a Canadian resident earns business income in the U.S. without having a permanent establishment in that country, it will be taxed in Canada, rather than in the U.S. Alternatively, if the business income is earned through a permanent establishment in the U.S., it will be taxed in that country. Any taxes withheld by a foreign country would be eligible for treatment as a foreign business tax credit. See Chapters 14 and 15 for coverage of this credit.

Foreign Source Capital Gains

22-95.   Residents of Canada are taxable on dispositions of property regardless of the location of that property. The rules of the *Income Tax Act* relating to the calculation of capital gains and losses are generally applicable in determining the taxable or allowable portion of a capital gain or loss. As was the case with foreign source employment and business income, dispositions of foreign property may result in potential taxation in both Canada and the foreign country. Again, the tax treaties would normally offer a way to resolve any conflicts.

22-96.   The Canada/U.S. tax treaty gives priority to tax to the vendor's country of residence. However, the treaty allows the U.S. to tax gains from the disposition of real property interests situated in the U.S., as well as gains on most types of property that are used in a permanent establishment through which a Canadian resident has carried on business in the U.S. Real property interests are defined to include interests in U.S. real property held through trusts, partnerships, and U.S. corporations, but the definition does not include shares of corporations that are not resident in the U.S.

Foreign Source Investment Income

Basic Concepts

General Approach

22-97.   As is explained in Chapter 3, Canadian income taxes are assessed on the basis of residency. This means that Canadian residents are liable for taxes on all of their income, without regard to the country in which it is earned. In general terms, foreign source income is taxed in much the same manner as would have been the case had it been earned in Canada.

22-98.   A small technical problem arises where some amount of such income is withheld by taxing authorities in the foreign jurisdiction. However, as is explained in Chapter 9, this is dealt with by including 100 percent of the foreign source income in Taxable Income and providing a credit against Tax Payable for the foreign taxes that were withheld.

The Problem With Dividends

22-99.   Subject to the need to calculate the appropriate foreign tax credits, most foreign source investment income is taxed under the rules that are applicable to similar sources of income earned in Canada. An exception to this is dividends received from non-resident corporations. Because Canadian corporations generally pay dividends out of income that has been subject to Canadian taxation at the corporate level, dividends received by Canadian residents from taxable Canadian corporations receive favourable tax treatment.

22-100.   When such dividends are received by individuals, they are subject to the gross up and tax credit procedures, a process that significantly reduces the effective tax rate on this type of income. When the recipient shareholder is a corporation, the dividends generally escape all taxation in that they can be deducted under ITA 112(1) in the calculation of Taxable Income. Both of these provisions are designed to make up for the fact that Canadian taxes have been paid at the corporate level.

22-101.   The problem with dividends received from a non-resident corporation is that the corporation that paid the dividends has not paid taxes in Canada. In fact, in some jurisdictions (e.g., tax havens), the corporation may not have paid any taxes whatsoever. This means that the usual reason for providing favourable treatment of dividend income is not present when dividends are received from a non-resident corporation.

22-102.　As a reflection of this situation, foreign source dividends received by individuals do not get the benefit of the gross up and tax credit procedures, and foreign dividends received by corporations are not generally deductible under ITA 112(1). However, as we will see in the material that follows, there are exceptions to this general conclusion.

Other Issues

22-103.　A further point here is that the reporting of foreign investment income is an area where there are significant compliance problems. Individuals "forget" that they have foreign assets or, in some cases, do not understand that the income from these assets is subject to Canadian taxation. To deal with this situation, the government has stringent requirements for individuals to report holdings of foreign assets. These requirements are covered in Chapter 2 and will be reviewed briefly in the following material.

22-104.　Other problems arise because of the complexity associated with the use of non-resident entities (i.e., corporations, trusts, and others). These problems have been dealt with by introducing such concepts as foreign affiliates, foreign accrual property income, and foreign investment entities. These concepts will also be discussed in this Chapter.

Foreign Investment Reporting Requirements

22-105.　As noted in Chapter 2, "Procedures and Administration", reporting requirements apply to foreign investments totaling more than $100,000 held by Canadian residents. These reporting obligations are intended to discourage Canadians from concealing assets offshore in foreign trusts, corporations, or other investments.

22-106.　Canadian taxpayers and partnerships are required to file an information return to report specified assets situated outside Canada if the total cost exceeds $100,000 at any time in the year. A "check-the-box" reporting format requires taxpayers to indicate the range and location of different categories of foreign property investments, and the total income earned in the year from the investments.

22-107.　Most foreign assets, including passive investments such as bank accounts, real property, and shares must be disclosed. Related debt cannot be deducted from the cost of the assets in determining the total cost. However, several types of property need not be disclosed, including property that is used primarily for the enjoyment of the taxpayer or the taxpayer's family, certain pension arrangements, and assets used in an active business.

22-108.　The information return titled "Foreign Income Verification Statement" (T1135) must be completed to comply with the foreign reporting rules. The information provided in this information return is intended to be used to ensure compliance with Canadian tax laws, to remind resident taxpayers of their tax obligations on their worldwide income, to discourage tax evasion and aggressive tax avoidance, and to alleviate public concern that there is a bias in favour of foreign based income.

22-109.　Information on the total cost of most foreign asset holdings and any related income must be provided on the T1135. These include funds held outside of Canada, shares of non-resident corporations other than foreign affiliates (see Paragraph 22-121 for coverage of foreign affiliates), debts owed to the taxpayer by non-residents, real estate other than properties held for personal use or use in an active business, and interests in non-resident trusts. Information on non-controlled foreign affiliates must be provided on Form T1134A, "Information Return Relating to Foreign Affiliates That Are Not Controlled Foreign Affiliates".

22-110.　Substantial penalties will result from failure to comply with these reporting requirements. There are generally two types of penalties. The first is for failure to file the prescribed form on time. This penalty is $500 for each month late if the return is filed within 24 months of the filing date. If the late filing exceeds 24 months, additional penalties may be charged, generally based on the value of the foreign investment. The second penalty is for purposefully making false statements on a filed return. Such penalties are generally equal to a minimum of $24,000 and can be as much as 5 percent of the value of the investment property.

Exercise Twenty-Two - 12

Subject: Foreign Investment Reporting

During 2007, Simon Taylor, a Canadian resident, has a U.K. bank account with a balance of £30,000. In 2006, he made a two year interest free loan of £35,000 to his brother-in-law in Scotland. No formal loan agreement was involved. Assume 1£ = $2.40 for 2007. Describe any foreign investment reporting obligations that Simon has for 2007.

End of Exercise. Solution available in Study Guide.

Non-Resident Entities

Defined

22-111. A non-resident entity is defined as a corporation, trust, or any other type of entity that was formed, organized, last continued under, or governed under the laws of a country, or a political subdivision of a country, other than Canada. This is a very broadly based definition that is designed to pick up every form of organization that could be used for investment purposes, including some that may not even exist in the Canadian legal environment.

22-112. The tax rules related to investments made by Canadian residents in these non-resident entities are extremely complex, and their application varies with the particular type of entity. In this Chapter, we will restrict our discussion to the rules as they apply to non-resident corporations. As you read this material, you should be aware that similar rules apply to other types of entities, in particular to trusts. However, coverage of these other types of non-resident entities is beyond the scope of this text.

Classification

22-113. The *Income Tax Act* identifies three types of non-resident entities:

- Foreign Affiliates
- Controlled Foreign Affiliates
- Foreign Investment Entities (Including Non-Resident Trusts)

22-114. These three types of non-resident entities will be defined and described in detail in the material that follows.

Basic Issues

22-115. Canadian resident corporations are taxable on all sources of income, without regard to whether such amounts are earned within Canada's borders. In contrast, non-resident corporations are not subject to Canadian taxation at the corporate level, and may not be subject to significant taxation at their local level.

22-116. As was discussed in Paragraph 22-101, the general solution to this problem is not to allow foreign source dividends to have the favourable tax treatment that is provided to dividends received from Canadian corporations. Dividends received by Canadian individuals from non-resident corporations are not eligible for the dividend gross up and tax credit procedures. This means that they will be taxed at the individual's full marginal tax rate, rather than the significantly more favourable rate that is created by the gross up and tax credit procedures when applied to dividends from Canadian corporations.

22-117. With respect to corporate receipt of dividends from resident corporations, they are generally deductible under ITA 112(1) in the calculation of the corporation's Taxable Income. This means that they are, in effect, received on a tax free basis. In contrast, dividends received by Canadian corporations from non-resident corporations are not eligible for the ITA 112(1) deduction. As a consequence, they are included in Taxable Income and taxed at the appropriate corporate rate.

22-118.   While the elimination of favourable tax treatment for dividends from a foreign source provides a partial solution to the problem of dividends being paid out of corporate income that has not been taxed in Canada, two significant problems remain:

1. While the elimination of favourable treatment for dividends received from non-resident corporations makes up for the fact that such dividends are paid from income that has not been taxed in Canada, this procedure can result in double taxation. For example, income earned by a foreign subsidiary of a Canadian corporation could be fully taxed in the foreign jurisdiction and, in the absence of the ITA 112(1) dividend deduction, it would be taxed again in Canada.

2. Under the general rules applicable to corporations, income from a non-resident corporation will not be taxed in Canada until such time as it is distributed to Canadian residents. This means that a Canadian resident can achieve significant tax deferral by placing investments in a foreign corporation, in situations where the income from the investments is not currently needed. This is particularly attractive when the non-resident corporation is located in a jurisdiction where there is little or no taxation of investment income.

22-119.   The first of these problems has been dealt with by introducing the concept of a Foreign Affiliate. As will be discussed in the next section, dividends received from this type of non-resident corporation will generally be deductible to a recipient Canadian corporation.

22-120.   Finding a solution to the second problem has proved to be more complex. Since 1976, the general approach has been to require, under certain circumstances, some accrual of the undistributed property income of non-resident corporations (the Foreign Accrual Property Income, or FAPI, rules). This appears not to have been a totally satisfactory solution and, as a consequence, additional rules related to foreign investment entities have been introduced. These concepts and procedures will be discussed in the material that follows.

Foreign Affiliates
Defined

22-121.   A foreign affiliate of a Canadian taxpayer is defined in ITA 95(1) as a non-resident corporation in which that taxpayer has an equity percentage of at least 1 percent. As well, the aggregate equity percentages of the taxpayer and each person related to the taxpayer must be at least 10 percent. The ownership percentage can be established on either a direct or indirect basis, and is defined as the greatest percentage holding in any class of the non-resident corporation's capital stock.

22-122.   As an example of both the direct and indirect application of this rule, consider the following example:

Example Candoo, a resident Canadian corporation, owns 70 percent of the only class of shares of Forco One, a non-resident corporation. In turn, Forco One owns 20 percent of the only class of shares of Forco Two, a second non-resident corporation.

Analysis Forco One is a foreign affiliate of Candoo because of Candoo's 70 percent direct ownership. Forco Two is also a foreign affiliate of Candoo because the indirect ownership percentage is 14 percent [(70%)(20%)].

22-123.   We would also note that the ownership thresholds are applied on a shareholder by shareholder basis. A non-resident company will be a foreign affiliate of a Canadian resident, only if that resident owns directly or indirectly at least 1 percent of the shares of that non-resident company and, in addition, that resident, together with related persons, owns at least 10 percent of the shares of that non-resident company.

Example   Carson Ltd. and Dawson Inc., two resident Canadian companies, each own 8 percent of Belgique, a non-resident corporation. While Carson Ltd. is part of a related group that controls Belgique, Dawson Inc. is not related to any of the other shareholders of Belgique.

Analysis   Belgique would be a foreign affiliate of Carson Ltd. as Carson Ltd. owns more than 1 percent of the shares and, in addition, is part of a related group that owns more than 10 percent of the shares. Belgique would not be a foreign affiliate of Dawson Inc.

Dividends Received From Foreign Affiliates

22-124.   We have previously noted that, in general, only dividends received from a taxable Canadian corporation can be deducted under ITA 112(1) in the determination of the Taxable Income of a resident Canadian corporation. However, ITA 113(1) provides an equivalent deduction for dividends received by a resident corporate shareholder from a foreign affiliate.

22-125.   This ITA 113(1) deduction is allowed in order to ensure that earnings are not subject to a double application of corporate tax. If a Canadian firm is burdened with a Canadian tax liability over and above any applicable foreign tax liability, the Canadian firm may not be competitive and may be unable to take advantage of potential international business opportunities.

22-126.   A full explanation of which dividends are eligible for this deduction cannot be provided until we have discussed controlled foreign affiliates and foreign accrual property income. As a consequence, we will defer our discussion of this issue until we have covered that material.

22-127.   However, two additional points can be made prior to this additional coverage:

Individuals   There is no equivalent relief for individuals. Even if the income from which the foreign affiliate dividends has been paid is already subject to tax in the foreign country, it is still not eligible for the gross up and tax credit procedures that provide tax relief for recipients of dividends from Canadian companies.

Tax Credits   In those cases where dividends from a foreign affiliate have been subject to foreign withholding taxes, they may generate a foreign non-business income tax credit for individuals.

Controlled Foreign Affiliates

22-128.   While establishing the concept of a foreign affiliate alleviated the problem of excessive taxation on dividends received by Canadian corporations from non-resident corporations, it did not deal with the problem of using a non-resident corporation to defer Canadian taxation on property income. In order to deal with this issue, the government developed the concept of a controlled foreign affiliate.

22-129.   Under ITA 95(1), a controlled foreign affiliate is defined as follows:

Controlled Foreign Affiliate, at any time, of a taxpayer resident in Canada means a foreign affiliate of the taxpayer that was, at that time, controlled by

(a) the taxpayer,
(b) the taxpayer and not more than four other persons resident in Canada,
(c) not more than four persons resident in Canada, other than the taxpayer,
(d) a person or persons with whom the taxpayer does not deal at arm's length, or
(e) the taxpayer and a person or persons with whom the taxpayer does not deal at arm's length.

22-130.   The significance of this concept is that, if an investment in a non-resident corporation falls within this definition, the Canadian shareholder must recognize its foreign accrual property income (FAPI, hereafter) prior to its actual distribution. That is, the FAPI of controlled foreign affiliates must be recorded as it is earned, rather than when it is distributed in the form of dividends. A detailed discussion of FAPI begins in Paragraph 22-132.

22-131.   This provision is somewhat mitigated by the fact that Canadian residents are not required to report the FAPI of controlled foreign affiliates unless it exceeds $5,000. The $5,000 exemption figure recognizes that the calculation of FAPI is quite complex and should not be required when the amount of income is small. As FAPI income is taxed as it accrues, dividends subsequently paid out of such income are not taxable.

Foreign Accrual Property Income (FAPI)
General Rules
22-132.   In simplified terms, FAPI is the passive income of a controlled foreign affiliate. FAPI includes income from property (e.g. interest, portfolio dividends), income from non-active businesses (e.g. rental income), as well as capital gains resulting from the disposition of properties that are not used in an active business. An important distinguishing feature of this type of income is that, with the exception of rental income, its source can be easily moved from one tax jurisdiction to another.

22-133.   The property income definition for FAPI also includes income from a foreign investment business. This type of business is analogous to the specified investment business that is used in determining income eligible for the small business deduction (see Chapter 15).

22-134.   As is the case with the specified investment business rules, a foreign affiliate would be considered to be earning active business income if it either employs more than five full time employees or the equivalent of more than five full time employees, to earn income that would normally be considered property income. This "five-employee" exception is especially important in deciding whether foreign rental income is active (exempt from the FAPI rules) or passive (subject to the FAPI rules).

Taxation Of FAPI
22-135.   As noted in Paragraph 22-130, if a taxpayer has an investment in a controlled foreign affiliate, FAPI must be accrued as it is earned by that affiliate. Note that this is a separate issue from the taxation of dividends from either controlled or other foreign affiliates. We will deal with this latter issue in the next section. Not surprisingly, we will find that if dividends are paid out of FAPI income that has been accrued by a taxpayer, the dividends will not be taxed a second time when received by that investor.

> **Example**   Paul Peterson, a Canadian resident, owns 80 percent of the shares of Tabasco Ltd., a company that is incorporated in Trinidad. During 2007, the Company has income of $100,000, all of which is earned by passive investments. No income taxes are paid on this income in Trinidad, and no dividends are paid out of this income to Mr. Peterson.

> **Analysis**   Tabasco Ltd. is clearly a controlled foreign affiliate (it is a foreign affiliate that is controlled by the taxpayer). Further, all of its income is from passive sources. Given this, under ITA 91(1), Mr. Peterson will have to include $80,000 [(80%)($100,000)] in his Net Income For Tax Purposes for the current year.

22-136.   The preceding example was simplified by the fact that Tabasco Ltd. was not subject to taxes in the foreign country. If it had been, the income of this controlled foreign affiliate would have been subject to double taxation. Fortunately, the *Income Tax Act* provides relief in the form of a deduction under ITA 91(4) that is designed to compensate for foreign taxes that have been paid on FAPI.

22-137.   Note that this is a deduction against income, rather than a tax credit. As you will recall from discussions in other Chapters (e.g., the value of investment tax credits), a deduction against income will only reduce Tax Payable by the amount of the deduction multiplied by the tax rate. This means that its value to the taxpayer is less than the amount of foreign taxes paid and, given this, it would not be equitable to set the deduction equal to those taxes.

22-138.   The ITA 91(4) deduction recognizes this difference by multiplying the foreign taxes paid on FAPI by what is referred to as a relevant tax factor (RTF, hereafter). As defined in ITA 95(1), the RTF for individuals is different than it is for corporations.

Canadian Resident Individual   If the investor in the controlled foreign affiliate is an individual, the RTF is 2.2. This is based on the notional assumption that the Canadian tax rate on this income would have been about 45.45 percent if the individual had received it from a Canadian source (1 ÷ 45.45% = 2.2).

Canadian Resident Corporation   If the investor in the controlled foreign affiliate is a corporation, the RTF for 2002 and subsequent years is 3.2258. This is based on the notional assumption that the Canadian tax rate on this income would have been 31 percent if the corporation had received it from a Canadian source (1 ÷ 31% = 3.2258).

22-139.   If the controlled foreign affiliate's income is taxed in the foreign jurisdiction at the notional rate applicable to the investor, the ITA 91(4) deduction will completely eliminate the FAPI. In most cases, the foreign tax rate will be below the notional rates, resulting in some FAPI being included in income. Note, however, that the ITA 91(4) deduction cannot exceed the FAPI.

Example Continued   Paul Peterson, a Canadian resident, owns 80 percent of the shares of Tabasco Ltd., a company that is incorporated in Trinidad. During 2007, the Company has income of $100,000, all of which is earned by passive investments. The Company pays Trinidadian taxes at a rate of 20 percent. No dividends are paid out of this income to Mr. Peterson.

Analysis   The tax consequences to Mr. Peterson would be as follows:

FAPI [(80%)($100,000)]	$80,000
Deduct Lesser Of:	
• FAPI = $80,000	
• ITA 91(4) Deduction [(2.2)(80%)(20%)($100,000)] = $35,200	(35,200)
Addition To Net Income For Tax Purposes - FAPI	$44,800

Exercise Twenty-Two - 13

Subject: FAPI

Forco is a wholly owned foreign subsidiary of Canco, a resident Canadian company. Forco earns $100,000 of investment income in 2007 and pays 18 percent in tax in the foreign jurisdiction. None of the after tax income is paid out as dividends. What are the tax consequences for Canco?

End of Exercise. Solution available in Study Guide.

Dividends From FAPI

22-140.   A final problem remains when the controlled foreign affiliate subsequently distributes the FAPI to the Canadian resident shareholders as a dividend. While these dividends must be included in income, the *Income Tax Act* provides a deduction to reflect the fact that all or a part of the dividend may have already been taxed in an earlier year as FAPI.

22-141.   The deduction is provided solely through ITA 91(5) in the case of individuals and a combination of ITA 91(5) and ITA 113(1)(b) in the case of corporations. The deductions are designed to eliminate taxation on previously taxed FAPI. It is equal to the lesser of the dividends received and the FAPI previously taxed to that shareholder after the ITA 91(4) deduction. Any withholding taxes on dividends paid to corporate shareholders of foreign affiliates are not eligible for a foreign tax credit.

Example Continued   Paul Peterson, a Canadian resident, owns 80 percent of the shares of Tabasco Ltd., a company that is incorporated in Trinidad. During 2007, the Company has income of $100,000, all of which is earned by passive investments. The Company pays Trinidadian taxes at a rate of 20 percent. Tabasco Ltd. declares and pays dividends of $40,000 in January, 2008.

Analysis   As shown in Paragraph 22-139, Mr. Peterson's addition to Net Income For Tax Purposes in 2007 was $44,800. The consequences of receiving the dividend in 2008 would be nil as shown in the following calculation.

Foreign Source Dividend [(80%)($40,000)]	$32,000
Deduct Lesser Of:	
• Previous FAPI = $80,000	
• Dividend Received = $32,000	(32,000)
Addition To Net Income For Tax Purposes - Dividends	Nil

Exercise Twenty-Two - 14

Subject: Dividends From FAPI (An Extension Of Exercise Twenty-Two - 13)

Forco is a wholly owned foreign subsidiary of Canco, a resident Canadian company. Forco earns $100,000 of investment income in 2007 and pays 18 percent in tax in the foreign jurisdiction. In 2008, Forco distributes its net after-tax FAPI of $82,000 to Canco as a dividend. Assume that there are no withholding taxes on the dividend payment. What are the tax consequences for Canco in 2008?

End of Exercise. Solution available in Study Guide.

Foreign Affiliate Dividends
Objective Of Legislation
22-142.   The purpose of the foreign affiliate rules is to provide relief from double taxation of active business income earned by Canadian corporations through foreign affiliates. The rules are designed to allow certain types of dividend distributions to be received on a tax free basis by Canadian corporations who are shareholders in foreign affiliates. There is no provision that provides similar relief for shareholders in foreign affiliates who are individuals.

22-143.   In somewhat simplified terms, the tax relief for corporate shareholders is limited to those dividends that are paid out of active business income. At present, the general rules that are presented here apply only to foreign affiliates located in countries with which Canada has a tax treaty. However, the 2007 budget has proposed the extension of this exemption to non-treaty countries that enter into Tax Exchange Information Agreements (TEIAs). The exemption will apply for a period of 5 years, after which, if no TEIA has been negotiated, the FAPI rules will again apply to active business income from that country.

Surplus Tracking
22-144.   It would be unusual for a foreign affiliate to accumulate earnings that consist entirely of a single type of income. This means that, in the usual situations, achieving the objective of the foreign affiliate rules requires a set of rules that relate a specific dividend payment to a particular type of income. This is accomplished by allocating various types of income to one of three surplus categories. These surplus categories and their basic content are as follows:

Exempt Surplus   This surplus balance includes the following:

- Active business income of a foreign affiliate earned in a country with which Canada has negotiated a tax treaty or a TEIA.
- The non-taxable portion of capital gains from dispositions of property that were included in FAPI.
- The non-taxable portion of capital gains from dispositions of property used in an active business carried on in non-treaty or non-TEIA countries.
- All of the capital gains from dispositions of property used in an active business carried on in treaty or TEIA countries.

This total is reduced by foreign taxes paid on the included items, as well as dividends paid out of exempt surplus.

Taxable Surplus   The principal components of this account include:

- FAPI
- Active business income earned in non-treaty or non-TEIA countries.
- The taxable portion of capital gains from the disposition of certain investment assets and assets used in an inactive business that are a component of FAPI.
- The taxable portion of capital gains from the disposition of property used in an active business carried on in a non-treaty or non-TEIA country.

This total is reduced by foreign taxes paid on the included items, as well as dividends paid out of taxable surplus.

Pre-Acquisition Surplus   The major items included here are as follows:

- Passive or active income, net of foreign taxes, earned by the corporation before it became a foreign affiliate of a Canadian resident.
- Amounts contributed to the foreign affiliate.

This total is reduced by dividends paid out of pre-acquisition surplus.

Ordering Rule

22-145.   At any given point in time, a foreign affiliate may have a balance in more than one of these surplus accounts. Because of this, an ordering rule is required in order to specify which balance a particular dividend is being paid out of. The general rule that is found in the *Income Tax Regulations* is that dividends are deemed to be paid first out of exempt surplus. If that balance is exhausted, dividends are then deemed to be paid out of taxable surplus. Finally, if there is no balance in either exempt surplus or taxable surplus, dividends are deemed to be paid out of pre-acquisition surplus.

Deductible Dividends

22-146.   As you are aware, ITA 112(1) allows dividends received by resident Canadian corporations from taxable Canadian corporations to be deducted in the determination of Taxable Income. This procedure, in a relatively simple manner, prevents double taxation of income that flows through multi-level corporate structures where all of the corporations are resident in Canada.

22-147.   ITA 113(1) is an analogous provision that deals with dividends received by Canadian resident corporations from their foreign affiliates. However, this provision is considerably more complex in its application. The ITA 113 system is designed to provide relief for double taxation and acts as a substitute for the foreign tax credit system. As a result, withholding taxes on dividends paid to corporate shareholders of foreign affiliates are not eligible for a foreign tax credit. Specifically, the following amounts are deductible under the various Paragraphs of ITA 113(1):

ITA 113(1)(a)   Allows a 100 percent deduction for dividends that are paid out of exempt surplus.

ITA 113(1)(b)   Allows a deduction for foreign income taxes paid on amounts that have been included in taxable surplus and from which dividends are currently being paid. For corporations, the deduction is equal to the lesser of the foreign income taxes multiplied by the RTF less one [(3.2258 - 1) = 2.2258] and the amount of the dividend. This deduction is designed to result in a combined domestic and foreign Tax Payable that is equal to the amount that would have be paid if the Canadian corporation earned the income in Canada.

ITA 113(1)(c)   Allows a deduction for any foreign withholding taxes imposed on a dividend paid from taxable surplus equal to the withheld tax multiplied by the RTF of 3.2258. The total of the ITA 113(1)(b) and (c) amounts is limited to the amount of the dividend.

ITA 113(1)(d)   Allows a 100 percent deduction for any dividends paid from the pre-acquisition surplus account. Note, however, that such dividends reduce the adjusted cost base of the shares under ITA 92(2).

22-148.   A brief example will serve to illustrate the calculations associated with these procedures.

Example   NR Ltd. is a 100 percent owned foreign affiliate of Zedco, a Canadian resident corporation. NR Ltd. carries on an active business in a non-treaty country. In 2007, NR Ltd. earns $100,000 of active business income and pays foreign income taxes of $20,000. NR Ltd. writes a cheque of $72,000 to Zedco as payment of a dividend of $80,000 after paying a 10 percent withholding tax of $8,000. The Net Income of $80,000 is added to the taxable surplus account of NR Ltd.

Analysis   The receipt of the dividend has the following tax consequences:

Gross Foreign Dividend – ITA 90(1)	$80,000
Less:	
ITA 113(1)(a) - Exempt Surplus Dividend	Nil
ITA 113(1)(b) - Lesser Of:	
• (i) [(2.2258)($20,000)] = $44,516	
• (ii) Dividend = $80,000	(44,516)
ITA 113(1)(c) - Lesser Of:	
• (i) [(3.2258)($8,000)] = $25,806	
• (ii) Dividend Less The ITA 113(1)(b) Amount	
($80,000 - $44,516) = $35,484	(25,806)
ITA 113(1)(d) - Pre-acquisition Surplus Dividend	Nil
Addition To Net Income For Tax Purposes	$ 9,678

22-149.   You may recall that the notional Canadian tax rate that is implicit in the RTF for corporations is 31 percent. The procedures that we have will, in this example, produce a combined Canadian and foreign tax rate that is the same as that notional rate. This is illustrated in the following calculation:

Canadian Tax On Net Income For Tax Purposes [(31%)($9,678)]	$ 3,000
Foreign Income Tax Paid On Business Income	20,000
Foreign Withholding Tax On Dividends Paid	8,000
Total Tax Paid [(31%)($100,000)]	$31,000

Foreign Investment Entities

Background

22-150.   By the early 1980s, it was clear that the FAPI rules were not completely effective in preventing offshore entities from being used to defer taxation on investment income. The reason for this was that it was fairly easy to structure a non-resident corporation in a manner that prevented it from being classified as a foreign affiliate.

22-151.   As a consequence, the government introduced the concept of a foreign investment entity. Under this concept, ITA 94.1 could apply to require an amount to be included in income on an annual accrual basis in a manner considerably different from that of FAPI. The accrual amount was based on the cost of the investment, rather than the income earned by the foreign investment entity. This meant that Canadian investors would have been taxed on amounts regardless of actual distributions and whether or not the foreign investment entity was, in fact, earning any income.

22-152.   However, there was a further problem with this legislation. In order to require the income inclusion, the CRA had to demonstrate a tax avoidance motive on the part of the Canadian taxpayer. As this was often difficult to do, the 1984 legislation was not fully successful in achieving its policy objective.

22-153.   Never an organization to give up easily, the government, in 1999, announced the introduction of a new ITA 94.1 to ITA 94.4 designed to replace the existing ITA 94.1. This extensive legislation was introduced in draft form for the first time on June 22, 2000. Extensive refinements and modifications have been made annually since, with the latest on November 9, 2006 (over 500 pages of legislative amendments and explanations). These proposals will be reflected in the material which follows. The implementation date of this legislation is taxation years beginning after 2006.

Foreign Investment Entities Defined

22-154.   As previously discussed in Paragraph 22-111, the broadly based definition of a non-resident entity was designed to pick up every form of non-resident organization that could be used for investment purposes, including a corporation, trust, or any other type of entity.

22-155.   A foreign investment entity is defined in the proposed ITA 94.1(1) as a subset of these non-resident entities. In somewhat simplified terms, a foreign investment entity is any non-resident entity, unless at the end of its taxation year:

- it is a partnership (unless the taxpayer elects otherwise);
- it is an exempt non-resident trust (largely those organized for non-profit objectives);
- the carrying value of its investment property does not exceed one-half of the carrying value of all of its property; or
- its principal business is not an investment business.

22-156.   These are the exceptions listed under the definition of a foreign investment entity. Other than the more specialized exceptions related to partnerships and trusts, it appears that it would be appropriate to generally describe a foreign investment entity as a non-resident entity that is largely devoting its activities to the production of investment or property income.

Exempt Interests In Foreign Investment Entities

22-157.   Some of the investment interests that are considered to be foreign investment entities are classified as exempt interests. This means that, while they are still considered to be foreign investment entities, they are not subject to the income inclusion rules that are applicable to foreign investment entities in general (see following Paragraph). The two most important of these exempt interests are:

- Interests in a foreign investment entity that is a controlled foreign affiliate. This means that a corporation that is accruing income under the FAPI rules will not have an additional income inclusion because of the foreign investment entity rules.

- Interests in a foreign investment entity that is resident in a country where there is a designated foreign stock exchange, provided there are identical interests in the foreign investment entity that are widely held and actively traded and there is no avoidance motive.

Taxation Of Foreign Investment Entities

22-158. If a non-resident entity is considered to be a foreign investment entity and it is not an exempt interest, the taxpayer holding this interest will have to include an arbitrarily determined amount in income each year. While there is an alternative method available, the default method for determining the income inclusion involves an application of the prescribed interest rates in ITR 4301.

22-159. The prescribed rate plus 2 percent, the same rate that is applicable to amounts owed to taxpayers by the CRA, is applied to the designated cost of the taxpayer's investment in the foreign investment entity. For existing foreign investment entities, the designated cost is, in general, the fair market value of the investment in the foreign investment entity on January 1, 2007.

> **Example** The fair market value of an investment in a non-exempt foreign investment entity on January 1, 2007 is $500,000. Assume the average prescribed rate for 2007 is 5 percent.
>
> **Analysis** Under the proposed ITA 94.1(4), the investor would have to include in his Net Income For Tax Purposes $35,000 [(5% + 2%)($500,000)]. This amount would have to be included in income without regard to whether the foreign investment entity earned income of $1,000,000, had a loss of $1,000,000, or broke even.

22-160. Subsequent dividend distributions from the foreign investment entity are generally deductible under ITA 94.4(2) to the extent the amount was previously included in income. If the dividend from the foreign investment entity is subject to withholding tax, there is limited relief. While there is no tax credit available under ITA 126(1), ITA 94.4(3) allows a deduction based on a simulated foreign tax credit to a maximum of 15 percent of the distribution. There is no relief provided for any withholding tax in excess of 15 percent to any taxpayer, nor is there any relief provided for any income taxes paid by the foreign investment entity as a result of earning that income.

> **Example** A resident Canadian corporation with a 31 percent marginal tax rate holds an interest in a foreign investment entity throughout 2006. Imputed income of $100,000 is allocated to the Canadian corporation in 2006. In 2007, the foreign investment entity declares and pays a dividend to the Canadian corporation of $100,000. The foreign government withholds taxes of $20,000, providing for a net payment to the Canadian corporation of $80,000.
>
> **Analysis** In 2006, the Canadian corporation will pay Canadian taxes of $31,000 [(31%)($100,000)]. In 2007, there will be a net deduction calculated as follows:

Gross Foreign Dividends – ITA 90(1)	$100,000
Previously Taxed Income – ITA 94.3(2)	(100,000)
Deduction For Withholding Tax – ITA 94.4(3)	
15 Percent Of Dividends At RTF of 3.2258	(48,387)
Net Income For Tax Purposes Addition (Deduction)	**($ 48,387)**
Tax Paid On Imputed Income In 2006	$ 31,000
Foreign Withholding Tax In 2007	20,000
2007 Tax Savings [(31%)($48,387)]	(15,000)
Net Tax	**$ 36,000**

22-161. Alternative methods of calculating this income are available under ITA 94.2(4) and ITA 94.3(4). One method employs a mark-to-market approach where the income inclusion would be based on changing the fair market value of the investment in the foreign investment entity. The use of this method is conditional on having the required fair market value information, a condition that is unlikely to be met in many situations. If this information is available, the foreign investment entity is likely to be an exempt interest because it is traded on a designated foreign stock exchange.

Dividends From Foreign Non-Affiliated Companies

22-162.   The FAPI and foreign affiliate rules, as previously discussed, each have specific tax policy objectives, but these rules are designed for investments in non-resident corporations where the intention of the investor is something other than simply an investment in the true sense of that word.

22-163.   Many countries, including Canada, have historically drawn a distinction between what are commonly referred to as portfolio type dividends (i.e., dividends from non-affiliated companies) and an investment where an element of control or influence may exist. The *Income Tax Act* generally sets a 10 percent interest as the dividing line between portfolio dividends and something more significant.

22-164.   In general, when dividends are received from a foreign non-affiliated company, they will be subject to the same foreign tax credit treatment that was covered in Chapters 14 and 15. That material will not be repeated here.

Transfer Pricing

Definition

22-165.   Transfer pricing is a term used to describe the price at which services, tangible property, and intangible property are traded across international borders between related or non-arm's length parties. A transfer price is generally distinguished from a market price which is a price determined in the marketplace for goods and services between arm's length or unrelated parties. Multinational corporations typically use transfer prices for the transfer of goods and services between members of the corporate group within or across jurisdictional boundaries.

The Problem

22-166.   Transfer prices, unlike market prices, present an opportunity to manipulate profits. Transfer pricing concerns are not necessarily restricted to cross-border transactions. For example, the manipulation of profits between provinces and territories within Canada will alter the inter-provincial income allocations and will affect provincial or territorial tax revenues.

22-167.   When transfers cross international boundaries, the concerns are multiplied because of the significance of cross border trade. Statistics Canada reported exports of Canadian goods in 2006 of $440 billion, of which $359 billion were to the U.S. Imports of foreign goods in 2006 totaled $396 billion, of which $217 billion was from the U.S. A further indication of the importance of transfer pricing is that it is estimated that two-thirds of international trade transactions occur between related parties.

22-168.   Consider Canco, a Canadian corporation that manufactures an automotive component for its parent corporation. The direct cost of manufacturing this component is $75. The parent company of Canco is a resident of a low tax jurisdiction relative to Canada and sells the product in that jurisdiction for $200. Ignoring other associated costs, the profit on this component is $125 ($200 - $75). Consider the tax consequences of two alternative transfer prices:

> **Transfer At $100**   If the component is transferred at $100, $25 of the profit will be taxed in Canada, while the remaining $100 will be taxed in the low tax jurisdiction.

> **Transfer At $160**   If the component is transferred at $160, $85 of the profit will be taxed in Canada, while the remaining $40 will be taxed in the low tax jurisdiction.

22-169.   As this simple example makes clear, the parent company has a significant incentive to use a low transfer price. However, if it chooses the low transfer price of $100, Canada could impose a higher price, resulting in the possibility of double taxation. Given this situation, it is not surprising that Canada's international tax treaties provide guidance in this area.

The Solution

22-170.   Canada follows the OECD guidelines that provide a consensus among its member nations on acceptable approaches for dealing with transfer pricing issues. These guidelines are embodied in transfer pricing legislation introduced in 1997 through ITA 247, as well as in Canada's tax treaties. ITA 247(2) for instance codified the "arm's length principle" adopted by the OECD. This principle requires that the transfer price reflect prices that would have been negotiated between arm's length parties (i.e. parties acting independently of each other).

22-171.   In addition, article IX of the Canada/U.S. tax treaty lends further support by requiring one country to make corresponding transfer pricing adjustments made by the other country to avoid double taxation. The competent authority is required to address any disagreements between countries on acceptable transfer price adjustments.

22-172.   In an attempt to discourage profit manipulation, the transfer pricing rules in ITA 247 include penalties of 10 percent of the transfer pricing adjustments. These penalties can be avoided if the taxpayers can establish that reasonable efforts were made to determine arm's length prices. ITA 247(4) imposes documentation requirements to successfully prove that reasonable efforts were made.

22-173.   In 1993, prior to the introduction of the current transfer pricing legislation, the CRA introduced an advanced transfer pricing service called Advance Pricing Arrangements. These types of arrangements are encouraged by the OECD and are formalized pricing arrangements between the CRA and resident taxpayers. The goals of these Advance Pricing Arrangements are to help avoid double taxation, resolve potential transfer pricing disputes, achieve a level of certainty, and avoid global risk to corporate or other groups.

Transfer Pricing Methods

22-174.   There are two types of methods used to establish a basis for arm's length transfer pricing. The first group of methods are transaction based, looking to individual transactions to establish the required values. The second group of methods is profit based, attempting to allocate an appropriate share of aggregate profits to individual transactions. The application of each method is based on the particular facts and the availability of certain information. In general, the OECD favours transaction based methods. The methods used under these two approaches can be described as follows:

Comparable Uncontrolled Price   Under this transaction based method, the transfer price is determined by reference to comparable transactions between arm's length buyers and sellers operating in the same market under the same terms and conditions. The use of this method is generally restricted to commodities that have an active market such as gas, wheat, corn etc. This method is generally unworkable however for unfinished or intermediate goods where value is added at each stage or special know-how is employed. The comparable uncontrolled price method is favoured by the CRA.

Resale Price Method   This transaction based method is generally used where fair market value comparables are unavailable because of the uniqueness of the products. It also applies to situations where the purchaser adds little or no value and effectively acts as a distributor or sales agent. The method is applied by determining the appropriate mark-up that a distributor would generally make on similar transactions with arm's length parties. Assume Canco, a Canadian company, manufactures specialty leather sofas that cost $400. The sofas are distributed to its U.S. subsidiary that in turn sells them for $1,000 Canadian. If specialty sofa distributors generally earn 20 percent on the selling price, then the U.S. subsidiary's profit should be $200. The transfer price would then be set at $800.

Cost Plus Method   This last transaction based method is also used when fair market comparables are unavailable. Under this method, a mark-up is determined for the seller instead of the purchaser. This usually occurs where the purchaser adds value to the product, perhaps by affixing a brand name. Returning to the sofa example, assume that the subsidiary affixes a reputable brand name to the sofa and that it is determined that manufacturers generally receive a 25 percent mark-up on cost. In that case, the Canadian company should earn a profit of $100 [(25%)($400)]. The result is a transfer price of $500.

Profit-Split Method   This profit based method requires a determination of the combined profit of the non-arm's length parties on all related party transactions. The profit is then allocated among the parties in proportion to the contribution made in the income earning process. This method is only used when transfer prices cannot be determined under any of the transaction based methods.

Transactional Net Margin Method   This profit based method is one that is recognized by the U.S., although generally considered a method of last resort in Canada. The transactional net margin method is generally applied in a one-sided manner as opposed to the profit-split method that examines the combined profit of non-arm's length parties. This method uses the financial information of corporations within the same industry to determine an industry comparable for one of the parties. It usually focuses on the least complex party. In the preceding sofa example, an industry comparable may be that sofa manufacturers generally earn an average return of 9 percent on invested capital. If the invested capital were, say, $1,000 then a $90 return would be expected. That would produce a $490 transfer price.

Key Terms Used In This Chapter

22-175.   The following is a list of the key terms used in this Chapter. These terms, and their meanings, are compiled in the Glossary Of Key Terms located at the back of the separate paper Study Guide and on the Student CD-ROM.

Business Income
Capital Export Neutrality
Capital Gain
Capital Import Neutrality
Comparable Uncontrolled Price
Competent Authority
Controlled Foreign Affiliate
Credit Method
Deduction Method
Deemed Resident
Dividends
Double Taxation
Dual Resident
Employment Income
Exempt Surplus
Exemption Method
Foreign Accrual Property Income (FAPI)
Foreign Affiliate

Foreign Investment Entity
Interest Income
International Tax Treaty
    (a.k.a., International Tax Convention)
International Taxation
Non-Resident
Permanent Establishment
Person
Pre-Acquisition Surplus
Resale Price Method
Resident
Revenue Jurisdiction Approach
Source Jurisdiction Approach
Tax Haven
Tax Neutrality
Taxable Surplus
Tie-Breaker Rules
Transfer Pricing

References

22-175. For more detailed study of the material in this Chapter, we refer you to the following:

ITA 2	Tax Payable By Persons Resident In Canada
ITA 20(11)	Foreign Taxes On Income From Property Exceeding 15 Percent
ITA 90	Dividends Received From Non-Resident Corporation
ITA 91	Amounts To Be Included In Respect Of Share Of Foreign Affiliate
ITA 94	Application Of Certain Provisions To Trusts Not Resident In Canada
ITA 94.1	Offshore Investment Fund Property
ITA 94.1 To 94.4	Foreign Investment Entity Rules (Proposed)
ITA 95	Definitions [Foreign Accrual Property Income]
ITA 113	Deduction In Respect Of Dividend Received From Foreign Affiliate
ITA 115	Non-Resident's Taxable Income In Canada
ITA 116	Disposition By Non-Resident Person Of Certain Property
ITA 118.94	Tax Payable By Non-Resident (Tax Credits)
ITA 126	Foreign Tax Credits
ITA 212	Tax On Income From Canada Of Non-Resident Persons (This is the principal section in ITA Part XIII which deals with Canadian income of non-resident persons.)
ITA 216	Alternatives Re Rents And Timber Royalties
ITA 217	Alternative Re Canadian Benefits
ITA 247	Transfer Pricing
ITA 250	Person Deemed Resident
ITA 253	Extended Meaning Of Carrying On Business
IC 72-17R5	Procedures Concerning The Disposition Of Taxable Canadian Property By Non-Residents Of Canada - Section 116
IC 75-6R2	Required Withholding from Amounts Paid to Non-Resident Persons Performing Services in Canada
IC 76-12R5	Applicable Rate Of Part XIII Tax On Amounts Paid Or Credited To Persons In Countries With Which Canada Has A Tax Convention
IC 77-16R4	Non-Resident Income Tax
IC 87-2R	International Transfer Pricing
IC 94-4R	International Transfer Pricing: Advance Pricing Agreements (APA)
IC 06-1	Income Tax Transfer Pricing And Customs Valuation
IT-137R3	Additional Tax On Certain Corporations Carrying On Business In Canada
IT-173R2	Capital Gains Derived In Canada By Residents Of The United States
IT-176R2	Taxable Canadian Property - Interests In And Options On Real Property And Shares
IT-221R3	Determination Of An Individual's Residence Status
IT-262R2	Losses Of Non-Residents And Part-Year Residents
IT-270R3	Foreign Tax Credit
IT-303	Know-How And Similar Payments To Non-Residents
IT-360R2	Interest Payable In A Foreign Currency
IT-361R3	Exemption From Part XIII Tax On Interest Payments To Non-Residents
IT-395R2	Foreign Tax Credit - Foreign-Source Capital Gains And Losses
IT-420R3	Non-Residents - Income Earned In Canada
IT-468R	Management Or Administration Fees Paid To Non-Residents

Problems For Self Study

(The solutions for these problems can be found in the separate Study Guide.)

Self Study Problem Twenty-Two - 1

Paul Brossard accepts an offer to move to the U.S. from Canada to become a manager for a revitalized Black Hills Gold Savings and Loan branch in South Dakota. Paul has resigned from his Canadian federal government position, and severed his professional association ties. Further, he purchased a home in South Dakota. However, his daughter is nearing completion of an elite French immersion secondary school program in Ottawa, so Paul's wife and daughter intend to remain in Canada for two years. They continue to live in the family home in Ottawa.

After six months in South Dakota, the Savings and Loan branch closed. Paul then sold the U.S. home and moved back to Canada.

Required: Assess whether or not Paul became a non-resident of Canada, and if Paul will be taxed in Canada for the period during which he was living and working in the U.S.

Self Study Problem Twenty-Two - 2

Malcolm and Melissa are twins, both of whom were born in the U.S. In 2005, Malcolm moved to Canada with his wife and children, severing all residential ties to the U.S. and establishing residence in Canada. Melissa continues to live in the U.S., where she is employed and lives with her husband and children. For 2007, they have the following amounts and types of income:

	Malcolm	
Employment In Canada		$60,000
Dividends From U.S. Companies		$ 4,200
Interest On Canadian Term Deposit		$ 2,500
Interest On U.S. Bank Account		$ 3,700
	Melissa	
Employment In The U.S.		$58,000
Dividends From Canadian Company		$ 1,900
Capital Gain From Sale Of Land In Toronto		$41,500

Required: Indicate whether the residence or source jurisdiction approach applies to Melissa and Malcolm and identify the sources of their 2007 income that are subject to Canadian tax.

Self Study Problem Twenty-Two - 3

Note Completion of this problem will require a review of several other Chapters in the text.

Debbie Maari is the vice-president of communications for an international advertising agency. Having risen to the pinnacle of success in Canada, she is en route to Hong Kong to rebuild the firm's base in the Pacific Rim. The transfer will be for an indefinite duration, and Debbie has already obtained approval for immigration that does not restrict the length of her family's stay in Hong Kong. Debbie's family includes her husband and the family pets.

Debbie's husband is a sales representative for a pharmaceuticals firm, and he plans to develop a client base in Asia over the next six months. Meanwhile, he plans to service his North American clients from Toronto, and will commute monthly to Hong Kong.

On November 1, 2007, Debbie owned the following assets:

Description	Date Acquired	Original Cost	Fair Market Value
Interest in CCPC (10 percent)	1999	$ 90,000	$ 140,000
House (Note)	1998	150,000	225,000
Whistler ski chalet (Note)	2005	125,000	185,000
Sports car	2002	18,000	15,000
Paintings	1993	50,000	175,000
RRSP	1997-2006	66,000	86,000
10 percent interest in Sorrento Co., a Canadian public company	1997	180,000	110,000

Note   The reported amounts for the house reflect Debbie's 50 percent ownership share. The other 50 percent is owned by her husband. Debbie owns 100 percent of the ski chalet.

Debbie plans to sell all of the assets except for the house and ski chalet, which she plans to rent out. She has used all of her lifetime capital gains deduction in previous years.

Debbie's firm is prepared to pay her a $50,000 allowance to cover moving costs, with no requirement that Debbie provide supporting receipts.

Debbie has enquired about the Hong Kong tax system and has been informed that the personal tax rates are lower than the rates in Canada. Further, the Hong Kong tax system is expected to continue as a "source" system rather than a "residence" system, meaning that only income arising in, or derived from, Hong Kong will be taxable there. Any additional income that Debbie earns in 2007 while a resident of Canada will be taxed in Canada at a combined federal/provincial rate of 45 percent.

Required: Debbie would like to know the Canadian tax implications of moving to Hong Kong, and whether there are any tax planning opportunities to minimize her Canadian Tax Payable for the current and future years.

Self Study Problem Twenty-Two - 4

A. A Canadian resident hockey player is recruited during the off-season to lead one hockey school in Florida and another in Ontario. The hockey schools are run by a Florida promoter, and the hockey player is paid US$1,000 per day. Each of the schools lasts for seven days, resulting in total earnings of US$14,000 for 14 days. He has no other U.S. source income.

B. A Montreal theater production firm employs a Winnipeg computer wizard to prepare special three-dimensional animation effects. During the current year, the computer wizard works in California for three periods, each of which is for two months (60 days). In California, the work involves using special animation equipment that is unavailable in Canada.

Required: For each of the above situations, evaluate whether or not the individual will be taxed in the U.S.

Self Study Problem Twenty-Two - 5

Note   Completing this problem may require some review of the material on this subject in Chapter 2.

The following assets are owned by different Canadian taxpayers who hold no other foreign investments at any time during the year.

A. An individual owns term deposits totaling $23,000, located in a bank in Missoula, Montana.

B. An individual owns a Florida condominium. It was purchased for $127,000 in August, 1998.

C. An individual owns an Arizona condominium. It was purchased in 1998 for a $25,000 cash down payment and the assumption of a $77,000 mortgage.

D. A Canadian public corporation owns a small manufacturing plant and related machinery. The plant is located in Boise, Idaho.

Required: For each investment, evaluate whether or not the foreign investment reporting rules apply, and explain why.

Self Study Problem Twenty-Two - 6

Tritec Enterprises is a Canadian controlled private corporation with its only offices in Vancouver. It is involved in providing consulting and real estate management services to a wide variety of clients. As it has been very successful in its operations in British Columbia, it is considering opening operations in various cities on the west coast of the United States. While it would expect to initially lose money on these operations, there is little doubt in management's mind that such operations will eventually be profitable. Management intends to invest the eventual U.S. profits in various real estate developments in Southern California. In considering this possible foreign venture, the Company has sought your advice as to whether they should carry out their operations as a branch, or as a wholly-owned subsidiary incorporated in the United States.

Required: Prepare a memorandum contrasting the tax treatment of a branch operation with that of a subsidiary incorporated in the United States.

Assignment Problems

(The solutions for these problems are only available in
the solutions manual that has been provided to your instructor.)

Assignment Problem Twenty-Two - 1

Note   Completion of this problem will require reviewing the material on residency in Chapter 3 and the material on emigration in Chapter 12 of your text.

Holly Rancher, a Canadian resident, has been asked by the Brazilian government to start a strip farming operation in the Brazilian rain forest. Holly and her husband own equal shares in the following assets:

	Fair Market Value	Capital Cost Or Adjusted Cost Base
Home in Cochrane, Alberta	$500,000	$200,000
Land Rover 4x4 truck	15,000	20,000
Cash	10,000	

In addition, Holly owns the following assets personally:

	Fair Market Value	Capital Cost Or Adjusted Cost Base
Cottage on Lake Manitou	$ 65,000	$ 45,000
RRSP	55,000	
Shares in IOU Ranch Ltd, CCPC	40,000	25,000
Shares in public companies	40,000	30,000

Holly is seriously considering the Brazilian government's offer, and would like to know what the tax effect of a move would be. Holly has fully utilized her $500,000 lifetime capital gains deduction.

Required:

A. Analyze the Canadian income tax effect if Holly becomes a non-resident of Canada.

B. Identify important factors that could influence Holly's residence status.

C. If Holly decides to move to Brazil, and in so doing becomes a non-resident of Canada, identify effective tax planning opportunities to be considered.

Assignment Problem Twenty-Two - 2

Note   Completion of this problem will require a review of the foreign investment reporting material in Chapter 2.

The following assets are owned by different Canadian taxpayers who hold no other foreign investments at any time during the year.

A. A warehouse in Miami with a cost of $568,000, owned by a Canadian corporation, and used to store its products for distribution.

B. Units in a U.S. special growth mutual fund purchased in a self-directed RRSP, where the cost of the units is $113,000.

C. A Hawaiian cottage, purchased for $56,000 cash down, and assumption of a $200,000 mortgage.

D. Shares of a U.S. operating company, costing $10,000 and representing 100% of the voting shares and value of the company.

E. An individual owns a 5 percent share of a U.S. company with a cost of $32,000, and a bank account in Vermont with $95,000 on deposit. No related person owns any of the shares of the U.S. company directly or indirectly.

F. An individual owns a 10 percent share of a U.S. company with a cost of $32,000, and a bank account in Vermont with $95,000 on deposit.

Required: For each investment, evaluate whether or not the foreign investment reporting rules apply, and explain why.

Assignment Problem Twenty-Two - 3

Amy Borody works and resides in Winnipeg, Manitoba. Amy has been discreetly saving for her retirement by investing in the U.S. In the current year, she earned the following investment income. The dividends and interest are net of any U.S. withholding taxes. The withholding rate on the interest was 10 percent and the withholding rate on the dividends was 15 percent.

Dividends U.S. Corporation (Amount Received)	US$ 5,100
Interest on U.S. Term Deposits (Amount Received)	US$19,800
Net rental income from Palm Beach apartment	US$18,000

Required: Describe how the investment income should be reported in Canada, and discuss any related foreign investment reporting requirements.

Assignment Problem Twenty-Two - 4

A Canadian gun cabinet manufacturer is considering entering the buoyant U.S. market by following a gradual business expansion strategy. The enterprise will use one of the following market expansion approaches:

A. Advertising in gun magazines.

B. Selling cabinets to U.S. distributors. The distributors pay the shipping costs on the cabinets from the Canadian port or border crossing closest to them.

C. Direct sales to wholesalers by non-exclusive agents. The agents will represent other suppliers.

D. Direct sales to wholesalers by full-time salespeople in each of three regions of the U.S. No sales offices will be opened, and the cabinets will be shipped from a warehouse in Canada. Shipment will be made only after a customer's credit and contract are approved by the Canadian head office.

E. The salespeople will report to a sales office in each region. The sales offices will coordinate marketing and shipping of products from warehouses located in the U.S. However, formal approval of contracts will be administered in the Canadian head office.

F. The sales offices become independent profit centres, with regional credit managers, and warehouses will be stocked nearby, from which orders are filled.

Required: For each market expansion approach, assess whether or not the Canadian manufacturer will be deemed to have a permanent establishment in the U.S. Support your assessment, and identify any other information required to back up your position.

Assignment Problem Twenty-Two - 5

A California company, Generation Inc., distributes a Seventh Generation software package in Canada through a Canadian subsidiary. Generation Inc. also distributes Millennium Nexus software directly through a sales representative who works in Canada and is an employee of Generation Inc. To ensure the sales of the Millennium Nexus software are administered efficiently, the Canadian subsidiary provides the Millennium Nexus sales representative with an office, pays the salary, and withholds appropriate source deductions. The related expenses are reimbursed by Generation Inc.

Required: Determine if Generation Inc. is subject to tax in Canada on profits from its direct sales of the Millennium Nexus software and its indirect sales of the Seventh Generation software.

Assignment Problem Twenty-Two - 6

Case A The Maple Company, a public company resident in Canada, has 2,400,000 shares of its no par common stock outstanding. Sixty percent of these shares are owned by its American parent, the Condor Company. The remaining shares are owned by Canadian residents. In addition to the common shares, the Condor Company holds all of an outstanding issue of Maple Company debenture bonds. Two of the five directors of the Maple Company are

Canadian residents, while the remaining three are residents of the United States. During the current year, the Maple Company paid a dividend of $1 per share on its common stock and interest of $900,000 on its outstanding debenture bonds.

> **Required:**   Calculate the amount of Part XIII taxes to be withheld by the Maple Company with respect to the interest and dividend payments to its American parent.

Case B   Mr. John McQueen was for many years a resident of Ontario. On his retirement in 1982, he returned to his native Scotland and has not since returned to Canada. However, he has retained considerable investments in Canada, as follows:

- **Common Stocks**   He has a large portfolio of common stocks that are registered in the name of his Toronto broker. The broker receives all dividends and periodically sends a cheque to Mr. McQueen in Scotland.

- **Mortgage Portfolio**   He has a large portfolio of second mortgages. All collections on these mortgages are made by a Toronto law firm and are deposited into a Toronto bank account in the name of Mr. McQueen.

> **Required:**   Who is responsible for tax withholdings under Part XIII of the *Income Tax Act,* and on which amounts must withholdings be made?

Case C   Hotels International is a U.S. corporation with hotel properties throughout the world. It has recently developed a property in Nova Scotia that will open during the current year. A long-term management lease has been signed with Hotel Operators Ltd., a Canadian company specializing in the management of hotels. Under the terms of the lease, Hotel Operators Ltd. will pay all of the operating expenses of the hotel and, in addition, make an annual lease payment of $1,250,000 to the American owners of the new hotel.

> **Required:**   Will the U.S. corporation, Hotels International, be subject to Canadian income taxes on the annual lease payment, and, if so, to what extent?

Case D   Mr. Jack Holt is an employee of Stillwell Industries, an American manufacturing Company. During the period June 15 through December 6 of the current year, Mr. Holt worked in Canada providing technical assistance to a Canadian subsidiary of Stillwell Industries. His salary was U.S. $5,500 per month. During the period that Mr. Holt was in Canada, Stillwell Industries continued to deposit his salary into his normal U.S. bank account. Both his salary for this period and all of his related travelling expenses were billed to the Canadian subsidiary.

> **Required:**   Explain Mr. Holt's tax position, including the question of whether any withholdings should have been made with respect to Canadian taxes owing.

Assignment Problem Twenty-Two - 7

Each of the following independent Cases describes an investment by a resident Canadian taxpayer in a foreign corporation.

> **Case 1**   Janice Pearson acquired a small number of shares in a publicly listed foreign company that is a world leader in computer software.

> **Case 2**   Dan Bedard owns all of the shares of a company he created in the Cayman Islands. The company's only activity is the earning of returns on investments, some of which were transferred by him to the company.

> **Case 3**   Eleven unrelated individuals decide to incorporate a company in Bermuda, then transfer their investments to that company. The company's only activity will be investments. Each individual will own approximately 9.1 percent of the only class of shares issued.

Case 4   Corporation A, a resident of Canada, owns an 82 percent interest in the outstanding shares of Cayman Ltd., a foreign manufacturing corporation. Corporations B and C, which are related to Corporation A and are resident in Canada, each own a 9 percent interest in the outstanding shares of Cayman Ltd.

Required: For each of the preceding Cases, determine whether the corporation is a foreign investment entity, a foreign affiliate, or a controlled foreign affiliate.

Assignment Problem Twenty-Two - 8

CTP is a Canadian corporation that has acquired 15 percent of the shares of FTP, a corporation that is established in a foreign country. During the year ending December 31, 2006, FTP earns $20,000 in investment income, $70,000 from an active business and $20,000 of capital gains from the sale of investment assets.

In early 2007, FTP distributes all of its 2006 after tax income as a dividend to its shareholders. FTP has no additional income in 2007. In both 2006 and 2007, CTP is subject to Canadian taxes at a combined federal/provincial rate of 31 percent.

The following Cases make use of the preceding information. However, the individual Cases make various additional or alternative assumptions.

Case 1   Assume that FTP is located in a country that does not have a tax treaty or a TEIA with Canada, that this country does not assess income taxes on corporations, does not assess withholding taxes on dividend payments to non-residents, and that FTP is a non-controlled foreign affiliate of CTP. What are the tax consequences for CTP resulting from its investment in FTP during 2006 and 2007?

Case 2   Assume the same facts as in Case 1, except that FTP is a controlled foreign affiliate of CTP. How would the tax consequences for CTP differ from the tax consequences described in Case 1, for 2006 and 2007?

Case 3   Assume the same facts as in Case 1, except that FTP is not a foreign affiliate of CTP. How would the tax consequences for CTP differ from the tax consequences described in Case 1, for 2006 and 2007?

Case 4   Assume the same facts as in Case 1, except that FTP is located in a country that has a tax treaty or a TEIA with Canada. How would the tax consequences for CTP differ from the tax consequences described in Case 1, for 2006 and 2007?

Case 5   Assume that FTP is located in a country that has a tax treaty or a TEIA with Canada, that this country assesses income taxes on active business income at a rate of 10 percent, does not assess withholding taxes on dividend payments to non-residents, and that FTP is a non-controlled foreign affiliate of CTP. The income taxes paid by FTP in the foreign country total $7,000 [(10%)($70,000)]. What are the tax consequences for CTP resulting from its investment in FTP during 2006 and 2007?

Case 6   Assume the same facts as in Case 5, except that the foreign country levies the 10 percent income tax on all of FTP's 2006 income. This income tax would total $11,000 [(10%)($110,000)]. In addition, a further 8 percent withholding tax of $7,920 [(8%)($110,000 - $11,000)] was assessed on the dividend paid in 2007. The resulting dividend payment was $91,080 ($110,000 - $11,000 - $7,920). What are the tax consequences for CTP resulting from its investment in FTP during 2006 and 2007?

Case 7   Assume the same facts as in Case 5, except that there is a $10,000 balance in the pre-acquisition surplus of FTP. Based on this amount, CTP receives an additional $1,500 of 2007 dividends. What tax consequences would be associated with this additional dividend payment?

Required: Provide the information that is requested in each of the preceding Cases.

INDEX

"AS IS" LICENSE AGREEMENT AND LIMITED WARRANTY

READ THIS LICENSE CAREFULLY BEFORE OPENING THE BOTH CD PACKAGES. BY OPENING THE PACKAGES, YOU ARE AGREEING TO THE TERMS AND CONDITIONS OF THIS LICENSE. IF YOU DO NOT AGREE, DO NOT OPEN THE PACKAGES. PROMPTLY RETURN THE UNOPENED PACKAGES AND ALL ACCOMPANYING ITEMS TO THE PLACE YOU OBTAINED THEM. THESE TERMS APPLY TO ALL LICENSED SOFTWARE ON THE DISKS EXCEPT THAT THE TERMS FOR USE OF ANY SHAREWARE OR FREEWARE ON THE DISKETTES ARE AS SET FORTH IN THE ELECTRONIC LICENSES LOCATED ON THE DISKS:

1. GRANT OF LICENSE and OWNERSHIP: The enclosed computer programs and any data ("Software") are licensed, not sold, to you by Pearson Education Canada Inc. ("We" or the "Company") in consideration of your adoption of the accompanying Company textbooks and/or other materials, and your agreement to these terms. You own only the disk(s) but we and/or our licensors own the Software itself. This license allows instructors and students enrolled in the course using the Company textbook that accompanies this Software (the "Course") to use and display the enclosed copies of the Software for academic use only, so long as you comply with the terms of this Agreement. You may make one copy for back up only. We reserve any rights not granted to you.

2. USE RESTRICTIONS: You may not sell or license copies of the Software or the Documentation to others. You may not transfer, distribute or make available the Software or the Documentation, except to instructors and students in your school who are users of the adopted Company textbook that accompanies this Software in connection with the course for which the textbook was adopted. You may not reverse engineer, disassemble, decompile, modify, adapt, translate or create derivative works based on the Software or the Documentation. You may be held legally responsible for any copying or copyright infringement that is caused by your failure to abide by the terms of these restrictions.

3. TERMINATION: This license is effective until terminated. This license will terminate automatically without notice from the Company if you fail to comply with any provisions or limitations of this license. Upon termination, you shall destroy the Documentation and all copies of the Software. All provisions of this Agreement as to limitation and disclaimer of warranties, limitation of liability, remedies or damages, and our ownership rights shall survive termination.

4. DISCLAIMER OF WARRANTY: THE COMPANY AND ITS LICENSORS MAKE NO WARRANTIES ABOUT THE SOFTWARE, WHICH IS PROVIDED "AS-IS." IF THE DISKS ARE DEFECTIVE IN MATERIALS OR WORKMANSHIP, YOUR ONLY REMEDY IS TO RETURN THEM TO THE COMPANY WITHIN 30 DAYS FOR REPLACEMENT UNLESS THE COMPANY DETERMINES IN GOOD FAITH THAT THE DISKS HAVE BEEN MISUSED OR IMPROPERLY INSTALLED, REPAIRED, ALTERED OR DAMAGED. THE COMPANY DISCLAIMS ALL WARRANTIES, EXPRESS OR IMPLIED, INCLUDING WITHOUT LIMITATION, THE IMPLIED WARRANTIES OF MERCHANTABILITY AND FITNESS FOR A PARTICULAR PURPOSE. THE COMPANY DOES NOT WARRANT, GUARANTEE OR MAKE ANY REPRESENTATION REGARDING THE ACCURACY, RELIABILITY, CURRENTNESS, USE, OR RESULTS OF USE, OF THE SOFTWARE.

5. LIMITATION OF REMEDIES AND DAMAGES: IN NO EVENT SHALL THE COMPANY OR ITS EMPLOYEES, AGENTS, LICENSORS OR CONTRACTORS BE LIABLE FOR ANY INCIDENTAL, INDIRECT, SPECIAL OR CONSEQUENTIAL DAMAGES ARISING OUT OF OR IN CONNECTION WITH THIS LICENSE OR THE SOFTWARE, INCLUDING, WITHOUT LIMITATION, LOSS OF USE, LOSS OF DATA, LOSS OF INCOME OR PROFIT, OR OTHER LOSSES SUSTAINED AS A RESULT OF INJURY TO ANY PERSON, OR LOSS OF OR DAMAGE TO PROPERTY, OR CLAIMS OF THIRD PARTIES, EVEN IF THE COMPANY OR AN AUTHORIZED REPRESENTATIVE OF THE COMPANY HAS BEEN ADVISED OF THE POSSIBILITY OF SUCH DAMAGES. SOME JURISDICTIONS DO NOT ALLOW THE LIMITATION OF DAMAGES IN CERTAIN CIRCUMSTANCES, SO THE ABOVE LIMITATIONS MAY NOT ALWAYS APPLY.

6. GENERAL: THIS AGREEMENT SHALL BE CONSTRUED AND INTERPRETED ACCORDING TO THE LAWS OF THE PROVINCE OF ONTARIO. This Agreement is the complete and exclusive statement of the agreement between you and the Company and supersedes all proposals, prior agreements, oral or written, and any other communications between you and the company or any of its representatives relating to the subject matter.

Should you have any questions concerning this agreement or if you wish to contact the Company for any reason, please contact in writing: Editorial Manager, Pearson Education Canada, 26 Prince Andrew Place, Don Mills, Ontario M3C 2T8.

INSTALLATION INSTRUCTIONS FOR THE ENCLOSED CD-ROMS

1. Canadian Tax Principles Student CD-ROM

The Student CD-ROM, created by the Canadian Institute of Chartered Accountants (CICA), includes the following items:

- The CICA's Federal Income Tax Collection (FITAC) infobase that cross references the following:
  - o the text of *Canadian Tax Principles*, 2007–2008 Edition
  - o the complete *Income Tax Act*
  - o Interpretation Bulletins, Information Circulars, and other primary and secondary information
- A "Guide to Using Your Student CD-ROM" for students who require more help to install the programs
- And much more!

How do I install the FITAC infobase?

- Insert the Student CD-ROM into your CD drive
- Click "FITAC Folio Views/CTP Infobase" in the menu
- Click on the "Install FITAC Folio Views/CTP Infobase" button
- An install wizard will appear in a pop-up window. Click through the install procedure to automatically install the Folio software and FITAC/CTP Infobase on your hard drive
- The install wizard will place a shortcut icon on your desktop

How do I open and use the FITAC infobase?

- Double-click on the shortcut icon on your desktop to open the program
- For tips on how the infobase can help you maximize your use of *Canadian Tax Principles,* open and review the Getting Started file. You can find it by clicking on the Start menu, selecting "Programs," then "FITACCTP," and finally "Getting Started."

2. ProFile Professional Tax Suite CD-ROM

The ProFile Professional Tax Suite CD-ROM includes the following items:

- ProFile professional tax software for T1 (individual), T2 (corporate), and T3 (trust) returns, along with the FX module containing other forms and returns from the Canada Revenue Agency (CRA)
- The InTRA research tool, available in all three versions (personal, corporate, and GST/Excise)
- Quick Reference Cards for both the ProFile Professional Tax Software Suite and the InTRA Research Tool

How do I install ProFile and InTRA?

- Insert the ProFile Professional Tax Suite CD-ROM into your CD drive
- For ProFile, click "ProFile" in the menu, then click on "Install ProFile"
- For InTRA, click "InTRA" in the menu, then click on "Install InTRA"
- In each case, an install wizard will appear in a pop-up window. Click through the install procedure to automatically install the software on your hard drive

Note: To activate each of these components, enter the following information when prompted for the licensee name and access code:

ProFile

Licensee Name: Pearson Education
Access Code: 2DD44 7P5XM PGR

InTRA

Licensee Name: Pearson Education
Access Code: PTJG CKR0 XSD0

These access codes allow you to use the software until December 31, 2008. You can use all the capabilities of ProFile with one exception: you cannot file tax returns using this trial version. All of the forms will print with the word "TRIAL" across them, and tax returns and forms submitted with the word "TRIAL" across them will be rejected by federal and provincial authorities.

How do I open and use ProFile and InTRA?

In each case, once you have successfully completed installation of the program, an icon will appear on your computer's desktop. Double-click on the icon to open the program.

ProFile Tutorials

When you open the ProFile software, the **ProFile QuickStart** screen will launch (if it does not launch on startup, select "Help > QuickStart"). In the Resource Corner area, click on "2006 T1/TP1 Tutorials." This will launch the T1 Getting Started tutorial. Simply follow the instructions that display in the Welcome window at the top of the page to learn how to use the software. Once you've completed the Getting Started tutorial, select "Tutorials > T1/TP1" from the ProFile menu to access additional training.

To access the T2 tutorial from the ProFile QuickStart, click the T2 tab at the top of the QuickStart screen and select "T2 Tutorials" from the Resource Corner area. Follow the instructions in the Welcome window to learn about the T2 software.

© 1997–2006 Intuit Canada or one of its affiliates. Intuit, ProFile, InTRA, and the Intuit logo are registered trademarks or service marks of Intuit Inc., registered in Canada and/or the United States and other countries. Other parties' brands or product names are trade-marks or registered trade-marks of their respective holders.

Please see the preceding page for the Pearson Education Canada license agreement. Do not open either of the CD-ROM packages until you have read this license.